the **law** *of* tax-exempt organizations

Thirteenth Edition

the **law** *of*
tax-exempt
organizations

Thirteenth Edition

 + website

Shane T. Hamilton
Bruce R. Hopkins

WILEY

Published by John Wiley & Sons, Inc., Hoboken, New Jersey.
Published simultaneously in Canada.

For general information on our other products and services or for technical support, please contact our Customer Care Department within the United States at (800) 762-2974, outside the United States at (317) 572-3993 or fax (317) 572-4002.

Wiley also publishes its books in a variety of electronic formats. Some content that appears in print may not be available in electronic formats. For more information about Wiley products, visit our web site at www.wiley.com.

Library of Congress Cataloging-in-Publication Data is Available:

ISBN: 9781394258420 (cloth)
ISBN: 9781394258437 (ePub)
ISBN: 9781394258444 (ePDF)

Cover Design: Wiley
Cover Image: © Christina Krivonos/Shutterstock

SKY10099100_022825

Contents

CONTENTS

CONTENTS

CONTENTS

13 Social Welfare Organizations

CONTENTS

CONTENTS

CONTENTS

CONTENTS

CONTENTS

CONTENTS

CONTENTS

CONTENTS

A Letter to the Reader

It is with a heavy heart that we relay the news to you that Bruce Richard Hopkins, JD, LLM, SJD, passed away on October 31, 2021. Bruce's love for the law and for writing resulted in a wonderful relationship with Wiley that lasted for better than 30 years. Throughout that time, Bruce penned more than 50 books as well as writing *Bruce R. Hopkins' Nonprofit Counsel* (a newsletter published monthly for 40 years). Bruce's texts are practical guides about nonprofits written for both lawyers *and* laypeople, many of which are considered vital to law libraries across the country. The ideas just kept flowing.

Beloved by many, Bruce was often referred to as the "Dean of Nonprofit Law." His teaching muscle was built over a period of 19 years when he was a Professional Lecturer in Law at George Washington University National Law Center. Later, as Professor from Practice at the University of Kansas, School of Law, Bruce exercised his generative spirit teaching and mentoring younger colleagues. Always the legal scholar, he could brilliantly take complicated concepts and distill them down into easily understood principles for beginners, seasoned colleagues, and those unfamiliar with the subject matter. He was a presenter and featured speaker, both nationally and internationally, at numerous conferences throughout his career, among them Representing and Managing Tax-Exempt Organizations (Georgetown University Law Center, Washington, DC) and the Private Foundations Tax Seminar (El Pomar Foundation, Colorado Springs, Colorado). He practiced law in Washington, DC, and Kansas City, Missouri, for over 50 years, receiving numerous awards and forms of recognition for his efforts.

Bruce will be dearly missed, not solely for his contributions to the Wiley catalog, but because he was a wonderful person who was loved and respected both by all of us at Wiley and by all those he encountered.

About the Authors

SHANE T. HAMILTON is the managing member of Hamilton Law Group PLLC. He exclusively represents nonprofit, tax-exempt organizations, with a significant concentration in the area of company-sponsored and family-endowed private foundations. In addition to advising private foundations and other tax-exempt organizations on a wide variety of tax compliance and other legal matters, Mr. Hamilton also represents them before the IRS in the context of IRS examinations, protests to the IRS Independent Office of Appeals, and closing agreement and private letter ruling requests.

In addition to being the coauthor of *The Law of Tax-Exempt Organizations, Thirteenth Edition*, Mr. Hamilton is the coauthor, also with Bruce R. Hopkins, of *The Tax Law of Private Foundations, Sixth Edition*.

Mr. Hamilton earned his JD at the University of Virginia School of Law and also earned a BA in Economics and an MA in English Literature from the University of Virginia. He is a member of the bars of the District of Columbia, the State of Texas, and the Commonwealth of Virginia. While attending law school, he was an executive editor and the tax cite editor of the *Virginia Tax Review*.

BRUCE R. HOPKINS was the principal in the Bruce R. Hopkins Law Firm, LLC, Kansas City, Missouri. He concentrated his practice on the representation of tax-exempt organizations. His practice ranged over the entirety of law matters involving exempt organizations, with emphasis on the formation of nonprofit organizations, acquisition of recognition of tax-exempt status for them, the private inurement and private benefit doctrines, governance, the intermediate sanctions rules, legislative and political campaign activities issues, public charity and private foundation rules, unrelated business planning, use of exempt and for-profit subsidiaries, joint venture planning, tax shelter involvement, review of annual information returns, the law of charitable giving, and fundraising law issues.

Mr. Hopkins served as chair of the Committee on Exempt Organizations, Tax Section, American Bar Association; chair, Section of Taxation, National Association of College and University Attorneys; and president, Planned Giving Study Group of Greater Washington DC.

Mr. Hopkins was the series editor of Wiley's Nonprofit Law, Finance, and Management Series. In addition to being the author of *The Law of Tax-Exempt Organizations, Twelfth Edition*, he was the author of *The Tax Law of Charitable Giving, Sixth Edition*; *The Tax Law of Private Foundations, Fifth Edition*; *The Planning Guide for the Law of Tax-Exempt Organizations: Strategies and Commentaries*; *Bruce R. Hopkins' Nonprofit Law Library* (e-book); *Tax-Exempt Organizations and Constitutional Law: Nonprofit Law as Shaped by the U.S. Supreme Court*; *Bruce R. Hopkins' Nonprofit Law Dictionary*; *IRS Audits of Tax-Exempt Organizations: Policies, Practices, and Procedures*; *The Tax Law of Associations*; *The Tax Law of Unrelated Business for Nonprofit Organizations; The Nonprofits' Guide to Internet Communications Law; The Law of Intermediate Sanctions: A Guide for Nonprofits; Starting and Managing a Nonprofit Organization: A Legal Guide, Seventh Edition; Nonprofit Law Made Easy; Charitable Giving Law Made Easy; Private Foundation Law Made Easy; 650 Essential Nonprofit Law Questions Answered; The First Legal Answer Book for Fund-Raisers; The Second Legal Answer Book for Fund-Raisers; The Legal Answer Book for Nonprofit Organizations;* and *The Second Legal Answer Book for Nonprofit Organizations.* He was the coauthor, with Thomas K. Hyatt, of *The Law of Tax-Exempt Healthcare Organizations, Fourth Edition;* with Alicia M. Beck, of *The Law of Fundraising, Fifth Edition;* with Douglas K. Anning, Virginia C. Gross, and Thomas J. Schenkelberg, of *The New Form 990: Law, Policy, and Preparation;* also with Ms. Gross, of *Nonprofit Governance: Law, Practices & Trends;* and with Ms. Gross and Mr. Schenkelberg, of *Nonprofit Law for Colleges and Universities: Essential Questions and Answers for Officers, Directors, and Advisors.* He also wrote *Bruce R. Hopkins' Nonprofit Counsel,* a monthly newsletter, published by John Wiley & Sons.

A legacy website providing information about the law of tax-exempt organizations is available at www.brucerhopkinsbooks.com. Materials posted on this site include discussions of his books and various indexes that accompany his monthly newsletter.

Mr. Hopkins received the 2007 Outstanding Nonprofit Lawyer Award (Vanguard Lifetime Achievement Award) from the American Bar Association, Section of Business Law, Committee on Nonprofit Corporations. He was listed in *The Best Lawyers in America,* Nonprofit Organizations/Charities Law, 2007–2021.

Mr. Hopkins was the Professor from Practice at the University of Kansas School of Law, where he taught courses on the law of tax-exempt organizations.

Mr. Hopkins earned his JD and LLM degrees at George Washington University, his SJD at the University of Kansas, and his BA at the University of Michigan. He was a member of the bars of the District of Columbia and the state of Missouri.

Preface

Longtime readers, users, and aficionados of *The Law of Tax-Exempt Organizations* will no doubt notice that this thirteenth edition of the book bears the name of a second author for the first time in the book's nearly 50 years of existence. But make no mistake, this is and will always be Bruce R. Hopkins's book. As your new coauthor, I view my role as primarily that of a steward. My great hope is that my ongoing contributions to the book will ensure Bruce's literary legacy is kept alive in a way that stays true to Bruce's style, grace, and learned poise.

One of the major highlights of Bruce's life was writing books about the tax law applicable to nonprofit organizations. He began doing this in the early 1970s and did not stop until he passed away at the end of 2021. He authored or coauthored more than 50 books during his lifetime, but *The Law of Tax-Exempt Organizations* has always been regarded as his flagship text. Many a young nonprofit lawyer, including myself, would never have succeeded without it. More than 25 years after I first sought nonprofit law enlightenment in its pages, I continue to be an avid user of the book in addition to being its new coauthor.

Most of the law reflected in the book did not exist when Bruce penned the first edition. Tax exemption was introduced, constitutionally, in 1913, and the unrelated business income rules arrived in 1950. A considerable portion of the statutory law of exempt organizations is the product of enactment of the Tax Reform Act of 1969. This body of statutory law has been significantly expanded by many major and minor tax acts. In recent years, the field has been enlarged by the Pension Protection Act of 2006, the Patient Protection and Affordable Care Act, the Tax Increase Prevention Act of 2014, the Protecting Americans from Tax Hikes (PATH) Act of 2015, the Tax Cuts and Jobs Act (TCJA), and the Taxpayer First Act.

This thirteenth edition covers developments in the federal law of tax-exempt organizations through the period ending in the fall of 2024. The TCJA has dominated the exempt organizations current developments scene in recent years. The Treasury Department and the IRS have been issuing guidance, primarily final regulations, in the aftermath of the TCJA, such as in the context of the bucketing (or silo) rule for computation of unrelated business taxable income, taxation of certain private colleges' and universities' endowment income, and taxation of the excess compensation paid by exempt organizations to certain of their executives.

The Taxpayer First Act brought more statutory law to the tax-exempt organizations setting. This statute instituted mandatory electronic filing of exempt organizations' returns, provided some relief for organizations that may otherwise have their exemptions revoked for failure to file returns, and established a statutory Independent Office of Appeals in the IRS.

PREFACE

In October 2023, the IRS finalized the regulations originally proposed in 2016 that affect certain Type I and Type III supporting organizations and their supported organizations. The requirements for qualifying as a functionally integrated Type III supporting organization as either a governmental supporting organization or a parent of a supporting organization have been finalized.

The IRS continues to invigorate the law of tax-exempt organizations with private letter rulings in areas such as the commerciality doctrine, the organizational and operational tests, the private inurement and private benefit doctrines, non-qualification of organizations as exempt business leagues, and the unrelated business rules.

***

Thanks go to the wonderful team of editors and assistants at Wiley—Brian T. Neill, Sangeetha Suresh, and Gabriela S. Mancuso—for their assistance and support in connection with the creation of this thirteenth edition. I am especially appreciative of Brian for reaching out to me and trusting me to pick up and carry the torch with this thirteenth edition and the annual supplements to come.

Shane T. Hamilton
2025

About the Online Resources

The Law of Tax-Exempt Organizations, Thirteenth Edition is complemented by a number of online resources.

Please visit www.wiley.com/go/hopkins/lawoftaxexempt13e-2025 to download various appendixes and tables in PDF format to use alongside this edition.

The appendixes are:

- Appendix A - Sources of Tax-Exempt Organizations Law
- Appendix B - Internal Revenue Code Sections
- Appendix C - 76 Categories of Tax-Exempt Organizations

The tables are:

- Table of Cases
- Table of IRS Revenue Rulings
- Table of IRS Revenue Procedures
- Table of IRS Determinations Cited in Text
- Table of Other IRS Determinations
- Table of Cases Discussed in *Bruce R. Hopkins' Nonprofit Counsel*
- Table of IRS Determinations Discussed in *Bruce R. Hopkins' Nonprofit Counsel*

Book Citations

Throughout this book, five other books by Bruce R. Hopkins (in some instances as coauthor), all published by John Wiley & Sons, are referenced as follows:

Book	Cited As
The Law of Fundraising, Sixth Edition (2022), with Alicia Beck	*Fundraising*
The Law of Tax-Exempt Healthcare Organizations, Fourth Edition (2013), with Thomas K. Hyatt	*Healthcare Organizations*
Tax-Exempt Organizations and Constitutional Law: Nonprofit Law as Shaped by the U.S. Supreme Court (2012)	*Constitutional Law*
The Tax Law of Charitable Giving, Sixth Edition (2021)	*Charitable Giving*
The Tax Law of Private Foundations, Sixth Edition (2024), with Shane T. Hamilton	*Private Foundations*

CHAPTER ONE

Definition of and Rationales for Tax-Exempt Organizations

Nearly all federal and state law pertains, directly or indirectly, to tax-exempt organizations; there are few areas of law that have no bearing whatsoever on these entities. The fields of federal law that directly apply to exempt organizations include tax exemption and charitable giving requirements, and the laws concerning antitrust, contracts, education, employee benefits, the environment, estate planning, health care, housing, labor, political campaigns, the postal system, securities, and fundraising for charitable and political purposes. The aspects of state law concerning exempt organizations are much the same as the federal ones, along with laws pertaining to the formation and operation of corporations and trusts, insurance, real estate, and charitable solicitation acts. Both levels of government have much constitutional and administrative law directly applicable to exempt organizations. A vast array of other civil and criminal laws likewise applies. The principal focus of this book is the federal tax law as it applies to nonprofit organizations.

§ 1.1 DEFINITION OF *NONPROFIT ORGANIZATION*

A tax-exempt organization is a unique entity; among its features is the fact that it is (with few exceptions) a nonprofit organization. Most of the laws that pertain to the concept and creation of a nonprofit organization originate at the state level, while most laws concerning tax exemption are generated at the federal level. Although almost every nonprofit entity is incorporated or otherwise formed under state law, a few nonprofit organizations are chartered by federal statute. The nonprofit organizations that are the chief focus from a federal tax law standpoint are corporations, trusts, and unincorporated associations. There may also, however, be the use of limited liability companies in this regard.

A nonprofit organization is not necessarily a tax-exempt organization. To be exempt, a nonprofit organization must meet certain criteria. As noted, most of these criteria are established under federal law. State law, however, may embody additional criteria; those rules can differ in relation to the tax from which exemption is sought (such as taxes on income, sales of goods or services, use of property, tangible personal property, intangible personal property, or real property).[1] Thus, nonprofit organizations can be taxable entities, under both federal and state law.[2]

(a) *Nonprofit Organization* **Defined**

The term *nonprofit organization* does not refer to an organization that is prohibited by law from earning a *profit* (that is, an excess of earnings over expenses). In fact, it is quite common for nonprofit organizations to generate profits. Rather, the definition of nonprofit organization essentially relates to requirements as to what must be done with the profits earned or otherwise received.

The legal concept of a nonprofit organization is best understood through a comparison with a *for-profit* organization. The essential difference between nonprofit and for-profit organizations is reflected in the private inurement doctrine.[3] Nonetheless, the characteristics of the two categories of organizations are often identical, in that both mandate a legal form,[4] one or more directors or trustees, and usually officers; both of these types of entities can have employees (and thus pay compensation), face essentially the same expenses, make investments, enter into contracts, sue and be sued, produce goods and/or services, and, as noted, generate profits.[5]

A fundamental distinction between the two entities is that the for-profit organization has owners who hold the equity in the enterprise, such as stockholders of a corporation. The for-profit organization is operated for the benefit of its owners; the profits of the business undertaking are passed through to them, such as by the payment of dividends on shares of stock. That is what is meant by the term *for-profit* organization: It is one that is designed to generate a profit for its owners. The transfer of the profits from the organization to its owners is the inurement of net earnings to them in their private capacity.

---

[1] In establishing its criteria for tax exemption, however, a state may not develop rules that are discriminatory to the extent that they unconstitutionally burden interstate commerce (Camps Newfound/ Owatonna, Inc. v. Town of Harrison, 520 U.S. 564 (1997)). See *Constitutional Law*, Chapter 3.

[2] An illustration of the use of a taxable nonprofit corporation is in IRS Private Letter Ruling (Priv. Ltr. Rul.) 201722004.

[3] See Chapter 20.

[4] See § 4.1.

[5] The word *nonprofit* should not be confused with the term *not-for-profit* (although it often is). The former describes a type of organization; the latter describes a type of activity. For example, in the federal income tax setting, expenses associated with a not-for-profit activity (namely, one conducted without the requisite profit motive) are not deductible as business expenses (IRC § 183).

By contrast, a nonprofit organization generally is not permitted to distribute its profits (net earnings) to those who control it (such as directors and officers).[6] (A nonprofit organization rarely has owners.)[7] Simply stated, a nonprofit organization is an entity that cannot lawfully engage in private inurement. Consequently, the private inurement doctrine is the substantive defining characteristic that distinguishes nonprofit organizations from for-profit organizations for purposes of the federal tax law.

In addition to the prohibition on private inurement, several state nonprofit corporation acts require the nonprofit entity to devote its profits to ends that are beneficial to society or the public, such as purposes that are classified as agricultural, arts promotion, athletic, beneficial, benevolent, cemetery, charitable, civic, cultural, debt management, educational, eleemosynary, fire control, fraternal, health promotion, horticultural, literary, musical, mutual improvement, natural resources protection, patriotic, political, professional, religious, research, scientific, and/or social.[8]

(b)   Nonprofit Sector

Essential to an understanding of the nonprofit organization is appreciation of the concept of the *nonprofit sector* of society. This sector of society has been termed, among other titles, the *independent sector*, the *third sector*, the *voluntary sector*, and the *philanthropic sector*.

---

[6] The U.S. Supreme Court wrote that a "nonprofit entity is ordinarily understood to differ from a for-profit corporation principally because it 'is barred from distributing its net earnings, if any, to individuals who exercise control over it, such as members, officers, directors, or trustees'" (Camps Newfound/Owatonna, Inc. v. Town of Harrison, 520 U.S. 564, 585 (1997)). Other discussions by the Court concerning nonprofit organizations are in Burwell v. Hobby Lobby Stores, Inc., 134 S. Ct. 2751, 2768–72 (2014), and Corporation of the Presiding Bishop of the Church of Jesus Christ of Latter-Day Saints v. Amos, 483 U.S. 327, 344–46 (1987) (concurring opinion).

[7] As one state's supreme court put it, "[n]on-profit corporations do not have owners" or "shareholders or any other way for third parties (whether individuals or entities) to assert a similar 'ownership' role" (Farrow v. Saint Francis Medical Center, 407 S.W.3d 579, 593 (Sup. Ct. Mo. 2013)). However, a few states allow nonprofit organizations to issue stock. This is done as an ownership (and control) mechanism only; this type of stock does not carry with it any rights to earnings (such as dividends). Ownership of this type of stock does not preclude federal tax exemption, although the IRS occasionally rules to the contrary (e.g., Priv. Ltr. Rul. 201835009).

An individual, desiring to engage in certain activities appropriate for a nonprofit entity, formed a nonprofit corporation. Matters did not go well with this entity, programmatically or financially, and losses were generated. This individual, who was the corporation's incorporator and president, and a director, filed a retroactive election for S corporation status for the entity as of the date of incorporation. This was done to try to report pass-through operating losses on his personal income tax returns. To this end, he claimed that he held an ownership interest in the organization equivalent to that of a shareholder. The IRS disagreed, disallowing the passthrough losses. The U.S. Tax Court upheld the IRS's position, rejecting the argument that this individual held "exclusive beneficial ownership" of the corporation and writing that "there is no interest in a nonprofit corporation equivalent to that of a stockholder in a for-profit corporation who stands to profit from the success of the enterprise" (Deckard v. Comm'r, 155 T.C. 118 (2020)).

[8] Use of the word *corporation* in the law context usually means both nonprofit and for-profit corporations (e.g., Charleston Area Med. Center, Inc. v. United States, 940 F.3d 1362 (Fed. Cir. 2019); Wichita Center for Graduate Medical Education v. United States, 917 F.3d 1221 (10th Cir. 2019); Medical College of Wisconsin Affiliated Hosps., Inc. v. United States, 854 F.3d 930 (7th Cir. 2017); United States v. Detroit Medical Center, 833 F.3d 671 (6th Cir. 2016); and Maimonides Medical Center v. United States, 809 F.3d 85 (2d Cir. 2015)).

A tenet of political philosophy is that a democratic state—or, as it is sometimes termed, civil society—has three sectors. These sectors contain institutions and organizations that are governmental, for-profit, and nonprofit in nature. Thus, in the United States, the governmental sector includes the branches, departments, agencies, and bureaus of the federal, state, and local governments; the class of for-profit entities comprises the business, trade, professional, and commercial segment of society; and nonprofit entities constitute the balance of this society. The nonprofit sector is seen as being essential to the maintenance of freedom for individuals and a bulwark against the excesses of the other two sectors, particularly the governmental sector.

There are subsets within the nonprofit sector. Tax-exempt organizations represent a subset of nonprofit organizations. Organizations that are eligible to attract deductible charitable gifts, charitable organizations (using the broad definition),[9] and other types of exempt organizations are subsets of exempt organizations. Charitable organizations (in the narrow, technical sense of that term) are subsets of charitable organizations (as defined in the broader sense).[10]

§ 1.2 DEFINITION OF *TAX-EXEMPT* ORGANIZATION

The term *tax-exempt organization* is somewhat of a fabrication, in that nonprofit organizations are rarely excused from being subject to all taxes, including the federal income tax. There are, of course, other applicable federal taxes, such as excise and employment taxes; there are categories of exemptions from them. At the state level, there are exemptions associated with income, sales, use, excise, and property taxes.

The income tax that is potentially applicable to nearly all tax-exempt organizations is the tax on income derived from an unrelated trade or business.[11] Exempt entities can be taxed for engaging in political activities;[12] public charities are subject to tax in the case of substantial efforts to influence legislation[13] or participation in political campaign activities;[14] business leagues may elect to pay a proxy tax;[15] donor-advised funds are subject to taxes;[16] and some exempt organizations, such as social clubs and political organizations, are taxable on

---

[9] This broad definition carries with it the connotation of *philanthropy*. The term *philanthropic* was added to the federal tax law when the concept of the *philanthropic business* was enacted (see § 12.4(c), text accompanied by note 299).

[10] The complexity of the federal tax law is such that the charitable sector (using the term in its broadest sense) is also divided into two segments: charitable organizations that are considered *private* (private foundations) and charitable organizations that are considered *public* (all charitable organizations other than those that are considered private); these nonprivate charities are frequently referred to as *public charities*. See Chapter 12.

[11] See Chapters 24, 25.

[12] See §§ 17.5, 17.6, 23.4.

[13] See §§ 22.3(d)(iii), 22.4.

[14] See § 23.3.

[15] See § 22.6(c).

[16] See § 12.5.

their investment income.[17] Private foundations are caught up in a variety of excise taxes.[18]

This anomaly of a tax-exempt organization being an entity that is subject to various taxes is addressed in the Internal Revenue Code. There it is written that an organization that is exempt from tax[19] shall nonetheless be subject to certain taxes but, notwithstanding that tax exposure, "shall be considered an organization exempt from income taxes for the purpose of any law which refers to organizations exempt from income taxes."[20] The Internal Revenue Service (IRS) advanced the argument that an organization, having paid tax on unrelated business income for some of its years, should not be considered a tax-exempt organization for a federal tax law purpose,[21] but that argument was rejected by a court as being inconsistent with the purpose of the quoted statute.[22]

There is no entitlement in a nonprofit organization to tax exemption; there is no entity that has some inherent right to exempt status. The existence of tax exemption and the determination of entities that have it are essentially at the whim of the legislature involved. Thus, the IRS wrote that "[e]xemption from federal income taxation is not a right; it is a matter of legislative grace that is strictly construed."[23] There is no constitutional law principle mandating tax exemption.[24]

There are several illustrations of this point. Congress granted tax-exempt status to certain mutual organizations—albeit with the stricture that to qualify for the exemption, an organization must have been organized before September 1, 1957.[25] A challenge to this law by an otherwise qualified organization formed in 1962 failed, with the U.S. Supreme Court holding that Congress did not act in an arbitrary and unconstitutional manner in declining to extend the exemption beyond the particular year.[26]

---

[17] See §§ 15.4, 17.5.

[18] See § 12.4.

[19] By reason of IRC § 501(a).

[20] IRC § 501(b). Also, IRC § 527(a), second sentence; IRC § 528(a), second sentence; IRC § 529A(a), second sentence.

[21] IRC § 4980(c)(1)(A).

[22] Research Corp. v. Comm'r, 138 T.C. 192 (2012). This argument would cause an otherwise tax-exempt organization to cease being an exempt organization once it had to pay some income tax, even if the tax exposure was due to transferee liability (e.g., Salus Mundi Found., Transferee v. Comm'r, 103 T.C.M. 1289 (2012), *vacated and remanded sub nom.* Diebold Found., Inc. v. Comm'r, 736 F.3d 172 (2d Cir. 2013), *rev'd and remanded*, 776 F.3d 1010 (9th Cir. 2014), 112 T.C.M. 227 (2016) (two private foundations held liable for income taxes as transferees of a transferee)).

A court held that the Federal National Mortgage Association and the Federal Home Loan Mortgage Corporation are exempt, by broad construction of a statute, from all state and local taxes, other than real estate taxes (Montgomery Cnty., Maryland v. Federal Nat'l Mortgage Ass'n, 740 F.3d 914. (4th Cir. 2014)). Likewise, Delaware Cnty., Pennsylvania v. Federal Housing Finance Agency, 2013 WL 1234221 (E.D. Pa. 2013), *aff'd*, 747 F.3d 215 (3d Cir. 2014).

[23] Priv. Ltr. Rul. 200830028. Nor can an organization premise its right to an exemption by showing that the IRS has treated similarly situated organizations more generously, leniently, or erroneously (Easter House v. United States, 12 Cl. Ct. 476, 490 (1987)).

[24] See *Constitutional Law*, Chapter 1.

[25] IRC § 501(c)(14)(B).

[26] Maryland Sav.-Share Ins. Corp. v. United States, 400 U.S. 4 (1970).

For years, organizations like Blue Cross and Blue Shield entities were tax-exempt;[27] Congress, however, determined that these organizations had evolved to be essentially no different from commercial health insurance providers and thus generally legislated this exemption out of existence.[28] (Later Congress realized that it had gone too far in this regard and restored exemption for some providers of insurance that function as charitable risk pools.)[29] Congress allowed the exempt status for group legal services organizations[30] to expire without ceremony in 1992; it also created a category of exemption for state-sponsored workers' compensation reinsurance organizations, with the stipulation that they be established before June 1, 1996.[31] Indeed, in 1982, Congress established exemption for a certain type of veterans' organization, with one of the criteria being that the entity was established before 1880.[32]

There is a main statutory list of tax-exempt organizations[33] to or from which Congress periodically adds or deletes categories of organizations. Occasionally, Congress extends the list of organizations that are exempt as charitable entities.[34] Otherwise, it may create a new provision describing the particular exemption criteria.[35]

§ 1.3 TAX-EXEMPT ORGANIZATIONS LAW PHILOSOPHY

The definition in the law of the term *nonprofit organization* and the concept of the nonprofit sector as critical to the creation and functioning of a civil society do not distinguish nonprofit organizations that are tax-exempt from those that are not. This is because the tax aspect of nonprofit organizations is not relevant to either subject. Indeed, rather than defining either the term *nonprofit organization* or its societal role, the federal tax law principles respecting tax exemption of these entities reflect and flow out of the essence of these subjects.

This is somewhat unusual; many provisions of the federal tax laws are based on some form of rationale that is inherent in tax policy. The law of tax-exempt organizations, however, has little to do with any underlying tax policy. Rather, this aspect of the tax law is grounded in a body of thought rather distant from tax policy: political philosophy as to the proper construct of a democratic society.

---

[27] By reason of IRC § 501(c)(4). See Chapter 13.

[28] See § 28.13(b).

[29] See § 11.6.

[30] See former IRC § 501(c)(20).

[31] See § 19.16.

[32] See § 19.11(b).

[33] IRC § 501(c).

[34] E.g., IRC §§ 501(e), 501(f), 501(k), 501(n), concerning cooperative hospital service organizations (see § 11.4), cooperative service organizations of educational organizations (see § 11.5), childcare organizations (see § 8.8), and charitable risk pools (see § 11.6), respectively.

[35] E.g., IRC §§ 521, 526–529A, concerning tax exemptions for farmers' cooperatives (see § 19.12), ship owners' protection and indemnity associations (see § 19.13), political organizations (see Chapter 17), homeowners' associations (see § 19.14), qualified tuition programs (see § 19.19), and qualified ABLE programs (see § 19.20), respectively.

This raises, then, the matter of the rationale for the eligibility of nonprofit organizations for tax-exempt status. That is, what is the fundamental characteristic that enables a nonprofit organization to qualify as an exempt organization? In fact, there is no single qualifying feature; the most common one is, as noted, the doctrine of private inurement. This circumstance mirrors the fact that the present-day statutory exemption rules are not the product of a carefully formulated plan. Rather, they are a hodgepodge of statutory law that has evolved over more than 100 years, as various Congresses have deleted from (infrequently) and added to (frequently) the roster of exempt entities, causing it to grow substantially over the decades.

There are six basic rationales underlying qualification for tax-exempt status for nonprofit organizations. On a simplistic plane, a nonprofit entity is exempt because Congress wrote a provision in the Internal Revenue Code according exemption to it. Thus, some organizations are exempt for no more engaging reason than that Congress said so. Certainly, there is no grand philosophical construct buttressing this type of exemption.

Some of the federal income tax exemptions were enacted in the spirit of being merely declaratory of, or furthering, then-existing law. The House Committee on Ways and Means, in legislating a forerunner to the provision that exempts certain voluntary employees' beneficiary associations,[36] commented that "these associations are common today [1928] and it appears desirable to provide specifically for their exemption from ordinary corporation tax."[37] The exemption for nonprofit cemetery companies[38] was enacted to parallel then-existing state and local property tax exemptions. The exemption for farmers' cooperatives[39] is an element of the federal government's policy of supporting agriculture. The provision exempting certain U.S. corporate instrumentalities from tax[40] was deemed declaratory of the exemption simultaneously provided by the particular enabling statute.[41] The provision according exemption to multiparent title-holding corporations was derived from the IRS's refusal to recognize exempt status for title-holding corporations serving more than one unrelated parent entity.[42] The exemptions for certain workers' compensation reinsurance organizations[43] and for state-sponsored qualified tuition plans[44] were created to avoid having their exemption rested on the view that these entities are instrumentalities of states.[45]

Tax exemption for categories of nonprofit organizations can arise as a by-product of enactment of other legislation. In these instances, exemption is granted to facilitate accomplishment of the purpose of another legislative end. Thus, exempt status was approved for funds underlying employee benefit programs.[46]

---

[36] See § 18.3.
[37] H.R. Rep. No. 78-72, at 17 (1928).
[38] See § 19.6.
[39] See § 19.12.
[40] See § 19.1.
[41] H.R. Rep. No. 73-704, at 21–25 (1934). This policy has changed, however (see § 19.1).
[42] See § 19.2(b).
[43] See § 19.16(b).
[44] See § 19.19(a).
[45] See § 19.22.
[46] See Chapter 18.

Other examples include exemption for professional football leagues (and thus other sports leagues) that emanated out of the merger of the National Football League and the American Football League,[47] and for state-sponsored providers of health care to the needy and for certain insurance issuers, which were required to accommodate the goals of Congress in creating health care delivery legislation.[48]

There is a pure tax rationale for a few tax-exempt organizations. The exemption for social clubs, homeowners' associations, and political organizations is reflective of this rationale.[49]

The fourth rationale for tax-exempt status is a policy one—not tax policy, but policy with regard to less essential elements of the structure of a civil society. This is why, for example, exempt status has been granted to fraternal organizations,[50] title-holding companies,[51] and qualified tuition plans.[52]

The fifth rationale for tax-exempt status is one that rests solidly on a philosophical principle. Yet there are degrees of scale here; some principles are less grandiose than others. Thus, there are nonprofit organizations that are exempt because their objectives are of direct importance to a significant segment of society and indirectly of consequence to all society. Within this frame lies the rationale for exemption for entities such as labor organizations,[53] trade and business associations,[54] and veterans' organizations.[55]

The sixth rationale for tax-exempt status for nonprofit organizations is predicated on the view that exemption is required to facilitate achievement of an end of significance to the entirety of society. Most organizations that are generally thought of as *charitable* in nature[56] are entities that are meaningful to the structure and functioning of society in the United States. At least to some degree, this rationale embraces social welfare organizations.[57] This rationale may be termed the *political philosophy* rationale.

§ 1.4 POLITICAL PHILOSOPHY RATIONALE

The policy rationale for tax exemption, particularly for charitable organizations, is, as noted, one involving political philosophy rather than tax policy. The key concept underlying this philosophy is the pluralism of institutions, which is a function of competition and tension between various institutions within the

---

[47] See § 19.21.
[48] See §§ 19.15, 19.18.
[49] See § 1.5.
[50] See § 19.4.
[51] See § 19.2.
[52] See § 19.19.
[53] See § 16.1.
[54] See Chapter 14.
[55] See § 19.11.
[56] These are the charitable, educational, religious, scientific, and like organizations referenced in IRC § 501(c)(3).
[57] See Chapter 13. Tax exemption for social welfare organizations originated in 1913; the promotion of social welfare is one of the definitions of the term *charitable* for federal tax purposes (see § 7.11).

three sectors of society. In this context, the competition is between the nonprofit and the governmental sectors. This element is particularly critical in the United States, the history of which originates in distrust of government. (Where the issue is unrelated business income taxation, the matter is one of competition between the nonprofit and for-profit sectors.) Here, the nonprofit sector serves as an alternative to the governmental sector as a means for addressing society's problems.

One of the greatest proponents of pluralism is John Stuart Mill. He wrote in *On Liberty*, published in 1859:

> In many cases, though individuals may not do the particular thing so well, on the average, as officers of government, it is nevertheless desirable that it should be done by them, rather than by the government, as a means to their own mental education—a mode of strengthening their active faculties, exercising their judgment, and giving them a familiar knowledge of the subjects with which they are thus left to deal. This is a principal, though not the sole, recommendation of. . .the conduct of industrial and philanthropic enterprises by voluntary associations.

Following a discussion of the importance of "individuality of development, and diversity of modes of action," Mill continued:

> Government operations tend to be everywhere alike. With individuals and voluntary associations, on the contrary, there are varied experiments, and endless diversity of experience. What the State can usefully do is to make itself a central depository, and active circulator and diffuser, of the experience resulting from many trials. Its business is to enable each experimentalist to benefit by the experiments of others, instead of tolerating no experiments but its own.

This conflict among the sectors—a sorting out of the appropriate role of governments and nonprofit organizations—is, in a healthy society, a never-ending process, ebbing and flowing with the politics of the day.

Probably the greatest commentator on the impulse and tendency in the United States to utilize nonprofit organizations is Alexis de Tocqueville. Writing in 1835, he observed in *Democracy in America*:

> Feelings and opinions are recruited, the heart is enlarged, and the human mind is developed only by the reciprocal influence of men upon one another. I have shown that these influences are almost null in democratic countries; they must therefore be artificially created, and this can only be accomplished by associations.

Tocqueville's classic formulation on this subject came in his portrayal of the use by Americans of "public associations" as a critical element of societal structure:

> Americans of all ages, all conditions, and all dispositions constantly form associations. They have not only commercial and manufacturing companies, in which all take part, but associations of a thousand other kinds, religious, moral,

serious, futile, general or restricted, enormous or diminutive. The Americans make associations to give entertainments, to found seminaries, to build inns, to construct churches, to diffuse books, to send missionaries to the antipodes; in this manner they found hospitals, prisons, and schools. If it is proposed to inculcate some truth or to foster some feeling by the encouragement of a great example, they form a society. Wherever at the head of some new undertaking you see the government in France, or a man of rank in England, in the United States you will be sure to find an association.

This was the political philosophical climate concerning nonprofit organizations in place when Congress, toward the close of the nineteenth century, began considering enactment of an income tax. Although courts would subsequently articulate policy rationales for tax exemption, one of the failures of American jurisprudence is that the Supreme Court and the lower courts have never fully articulated this political philosophical doctrine.[58]

Contemporary Congresses legislate by writing far more intricate statutes than their forebears and in doing so usually leave in their wake rich deposits in the form of extensive legislative histories. Thus, it is far easier to ascertain what a recent Congress meant when creating law than is the case with respect to an enactment well over 100 years ago.

At the time a constitutional income tax was coming into existence (the first enacted in 1913),[59] Congress legislated in spare language and rarely embellished on its statutory handiwork with legislative histories. Therefore, there is no contemporary record in the form of legislative history of what members of Congress had in mind when they first started creating categories of tax-exempt organizations. Congress, it is generally assumed, saw itself doing what other legislative bodies have done over the centuries. That is, the political philosophical policy considerations pertaining to nonprofit organizations at that time were such that taxation of these entities—considering their contributions to the well-being and functioning of society—was unthinkable.

Thus, in the process of writing the Revenue Act of 1913, Congress viewed tax exemption for charitable organizations as the only way to consistently correlate tax policy with political theory on the point, and saw exemption of charities in the federal tax statutes as an extension of comparable practice throughout the whole of history. No legislative history expands on the point. Presumably, Congress believed that these organizations ought not be taxed and found the proposition sufficiently obvious so that extensive explanation of its actions was not necessary.

---

[58] See *Constitutional Law* §§ 1.5–1.7.

[59] In 1894, Congress imposed a tax on corporate income. This was the first time Congress was required to define the appropriate subjects of tax exemption (inasmuch as prior tax schemes specified the entities subject to taxation). The Tariff Act of 1894 provided exemption for nonprofit charitable, religious, and educational organizations; fraternal beneficiary societies; certain mutual savings banks; and certain mutual insurance companies. The 1894 legislation succumbed to a constitutional law challenge (Pollock v. Farmers' Loan & Trust Co., 157 U.S. 429 (1895), overruled on other grounds, South Carolina v. Baker, 485 U.S. 505 (1988)), the Sixteenth Amendment was subsequently ratified, and the Revenue Act of 1913 was enacted.

Some clues in this regard are found in the definition of *charitable activities* in the income tax regulations,[60] which are considered to be reflective of congressional intent. The regulations refer to purposes such as relief of the poor, advancement of education and science, erection and maintenance of public buildings, and lessening the burdens of government. These definitions of charitable undertakings have an obvious derivation in the Preamble to the Statute of Charitable Uses,[61] written in England in 1601. Reference is there made to certain charitable purposes:

> . . .some for relief of aged, impotent and poor people, some for maintenance of sick and maimed soldiers and mariners, schools of learning, free schools, and scholars in universities, some for repair of bridges, ports, havens, causeways, churches, sea banks and highways, some for education and preferment of orphans, some for or towards relief, stock or maintenance for houses of correction, some for marriages of poor maids, some for supportation, aid and help of young tradesmen, handicraftsmen and persons decayed, and others for relief of redemption of prisoners or captives. . .

As this indicates, a subset of this political philosophical doctrine implies that tax exemption for charitable organizations derives from the concept that they perform functions that, in the absence of these organizations, government would have to perform. This view leads to the conclusion that government is willing to forgo the tax revenues it would otherwise receive in return for the public interest services rendered by charitable organizations. This rationale is, of course, inapplicable in the case of many religious organizations.[62]

Since the founding of the United States and during the colonial period, tax exemption—particularly with respect to religious organizations—was common. Churches were uniformly spared taxation. This practice has been sustained throughout the history of the nation—not only at the federal level but also at the state and local levels of government, which grant property tax exemptions, as an example.

The U.S. Supreme Court concluded, soon after enactment of the income tax, that the foregoing rationalization was the basis for the federal tax exemption for charitable entities (although in doing so it reflected a degree of uncertainty in the strength of its reasoning, undoubtedly based on the paucity of legislative history). In 1924, the Court stated that "[e]vidently the exemption is made in recognition of the benefit which the public derives from corporate activities of the class named, and is intended to aid them when [they are] not conducted for private gain."[63] Nearly 50 years later, in upholding the constitutionality of the federal income tax exemption for religious organizations, the Court observed that the "State has an affirmative policy that considers these groups as beneficial and stabilizing

---

[60] Income Tax Regulations (Reg.) § 1.501(c)(3)-1(d)(2).
[61] Stat. 43 Eliz. i, ch. 4.
[62] See Chapter 10.
[63] Trinidad v. Sagrada Orden de Predicadores, 263 U.S. 578, 581 (1924).

influences in community life and finds this classification [tax exemption] useful, desirable, and in the public interest."[64] Subsequently, the Court wrote that, for most categories of nonprofit organizations, "exemption from federal income tax is intended to encourage the provision of services that are deemed socially beneficial."[65]

Other courts have taken up this theme. A federal court of appeals wrote that the "reason underlying the [tax] exemption granted" to charitable organizations "is that the exempted taxpayer performs a public service."[66] This court continued:

> The common element of charitable purposes within the meaning of the. . . [federal tax law] is the relief of the public of a burden which otherwise belongs to it. Charitable purposes are those which benefit the community by relieving it pro tanto from an obligation which it owes to the objects of the charity as members of the community.[67]

This federal appellate court subsequently observed, as respects tax exemption for charitable organizations, that one "stated reason for a deduction or exemption of this kind is that the favored entity performs a public service and benefits the public or relieves it of a burden which otherwise belongs to it."[68] Another federal court opined that the justification of the charitable contribution deduction was "historically. . .that by doing so, the Government relieves itself of the burden of meeting public needs which in the absence of charitable activity would fall on the shoulders of the Government."[69]

Only one federal court has fully articulated this political philosophical doctrine, noting that the "very purpose" of the charitable contribution deduction is "rooted in helping institutions because they serve the public good."[70] The doctrine was explained as follows:

> [A]s to private philanthropy, the promotion of a healthy pluralism is often viewed as a prime social benefit of general significance. In other words, society can be seen as benefiting not only from the application of private wealth to specific purposes in the public interest but also from the variety of choices made by individual philanthropists as to which activities to subsidize. This decentralized choice-making is arguably more efficient and responsive to public needs than the cumbersome and less flexible allocation process of government administration.[71]

---

[64] Walz v. Tax Comm'n of City of New York, 397 U.S. 664, 673 (1970).

[65] Portland Golf Club v. Comm'r, 497 U.S. 154, 161 (1990).

[66] Duffy v. Birmingham, 190 F.2d 738, 740 (8th Cir. 1951).

[67] Id.

[68] St. Louis Union Trust Co. v. United States, 374 F.2d 427, 432 (8th Cir. 1967).

[69] McGlotten v. Connally, 338 F. Supp. 448, 456 (D.D.C. 1972).

[70] Green v. Connally, 330 F. Supp. 1150, 1162 (D.D.C. 1971), aff'd sub nom. Coit v. Green, 404 U.S. 997 (1971).

[71] Id., 330 F. Supp. at 1162.

Occasionally, Congress issues a pronouncement on this subject. One of these rare instances occurred in 1939, when the report of the House Committee on Ways and Means, part of the legislative history of the Revenue Act of 1938, stated:

> The exemption from taxation of money or property devoted to charitable and other purposes is based upon the theory that the government is compensated for the loss of revenue by its relief from financial burden which would otherwise have to be met by appropriations from public funds, and by the benefits resulting from the promotion of the general welfare.[72]

The doctrine is also referenced from time to time in testimony before a congressional committee. For example, the Secretary of the Treasury testified before the House Committee on Ways and Means in 1973, observing:

> These organizations [which he termed "voluntary charities, which depend heavily on gifts and bequests"] are an important influence for diversity and a bulwark against over-reliance on big government. The tax privileges extended to these institutions were purged of abuse in 1969 and we believe the existing deductions of charitable gifts and bequests are an appropriate way to encourage those institutions. We believe the public accepts them as fair.[73]

The literature on this subject is extensive. The contemporary versions of it are traceable to 1975, when the public policy rationale was reexamined and reaffirmed by the Commission on Private Philanthropy and Public Needs.[74] Here, the concept of *philanthropy* enters, with the view that charitable organizations, maintained by tax exemption and nurtured by the ability to attract deductible contributions, reflect the American philosophy that not all policy making and problem solving should be reposed in the governmental sector.

Consequently, it is error to regard tax exemption (and, where appropriate, the charitable contribution deduction) as anything other than a reflection of this larger political philosophical construct. Congress is not merely "giving" eligible nonprofit organizations "benefits"; the exemption from income taxation (or charitable deduction) is not a "loophole," a "preference," or a "subsidy"—it is not really an "indirect appropriation."[75] Rather, the various provisions of the federal

---

[72] H.R. Rep. No. 75-1860, at 19 (1939).

[73] Department of the Treasury, "Proposals for Tax Change," Apr. 30, 1973.

[74] *Giving in America: Toward a Stronger Voluntary Sector*, Report of the Commission on Private Philanthropy and Public Needs 9–10 (1975).

[75] The staff of the Joint Committee on Taxation and the Department of the Treasury measure the economic value (revenue "losses") of various tax preferences, such as tax deductions, credits, and exclusions (termed tax expenditures). The income tax charitable contribution deduction has traditionally been among the largest tax expenditures. The Department of the Treasury, on March 11, 2024, issued its report on tax expenditures for fiscal years 2023–2033; the estimated tax expenditure associated with the income tax charitable contribution deduction (excluding contributions to health and educational institutions) in this report is the fifth largest (at $846.7 billion). Tax expenditures attributable to health- and

and state tax exemption system exist as a reflection of the affirmative policy of American government to refrain from inhibiting by taxation the beneficial activities of qualified tax-exempt organizations acting in community and other public interests.

Regrettably, however, the tax law is not evolving in conformity with this political philosophical framework; long-term political philosophical principles are being sacrificed to short-term views as to practical economical realities. This is reflected in the U.S. Supreme Court's confusion in thinking; the Court has been correct on some occasions as to the rationale for tax exemption for nonprofit organizations,[76] yet in its fear of misuse of exemptions, such as to promote racial discrimination,[77] or in furtherance of unconstitutional ends, such as government promotion of religion,[78] it has on other occasions trimmed the political philosophical construction. Thus, for example, in striking down a state sales tax exemption solely for the sale of religious publications, the Court wrote that it is "difficult to view" this "narrow exemption as anything but state sponsorship of religious belief."[79]

From a constitutional law perspective, it may have been appropriate for the Court to use the word *sponsorship* in that setting. Certainly it would have been preferable, not to mention more accurate, for the Court to have confined this characterization to that word. Unfortunately, the Court found it necessary to amplify this point by observing that "[e]very tax exemption constitutes a subsidy that affects

---

education-related charitable contribution deductions are estimated at an additional $141.7 billion and $104.6 billion, respectively. Tax expenditures that are larger than the income tax charitable contribution deduction are the exclusion from gross income of employer contributions for health insurance premiums and health care, exclusion of net imputed rental income, the reduced rates of tax on long-term capital gains, and defined contribution employer plans.

Tax exemption for qualified nonprofit organizations is not considered a tax expenditure. There are two rationales for this approach. One is that exempt status is not a tax expenditure because the nonbusiness activities of these organizations, such as charities, generally must predominate and their unrelated business activities are subject to tax. The exemption of certain nonprofit cooperative business organizations, including trade and business associations, is not treated as a tax expenditure because the tax benefits are available to any entity that chooses to organize itself and operate in the required manner to avoid the entity-level tax.

Under the current approach taken by the staff of Congress's Joint Committee on Taxation, however, "tax exemption for noncharitable organizations that have a direct business analogue or compete with for-profit organizations organized for similar purposes is a tax expenditure" (Staff of Joint Comm. on Tax'n, Estimates of Federal Tax Expenditures for Fiscal Years 2023–2027 9 (Comm. Print JCX-59-23)). These organizations include state and federal credit unions (see § 19.7), small insurance companies (see § 19.9), and mutual or cooperative electric companies (see § 19.5(b)) (JCX-59-23, *supra*, at 9 n.21). Also, exceptions that allow otherwise taxable unrelated business income to escape taxation (see Chapter 25) are considered tax expenditures (JCX-59-23, *supra*, at 9 n.23).

In a report published by the Urban-Brookings Tax Policy Center, the value of tax-exempt status was estimated to $21.2 billion in 2018, with charitable organizations receiving 83 percent of the benefit ($17.7 billion), social welfare organizations (see Chapter 13) receiving $1.2 billion, business leagues (see Chapter 14) receiving $600 million, and social clubs (see Chapter 15) receiving $1.2 billion (Born and Looney, "How Much Do Tax-Exempt Organizations Benefit from Tax Exemption?" (July 2022)).

[76] See text accompanied by *supra* notes 63–65.

[77] E.g., Bob Jones Univ. v. United States, 461 U.S. 574 (1983).

[78] Texas Monthly, Inc. v. Bullock, 489 U.S. 1 (1989).

[79] *Id*. at 15.

nonqualifying taxpayers."[80] While this "subsidy" is accurate terminology from the standpoint of the pure economics of the matter,[81] it misconstrues and distorts the larger (and far more important) political philosophical rationalization for tax exemption for nonprofit organizations. The policy underlying this tax exemption simply reflects the nature of the way U.S. society is structured. Inasmuch as it is not the government's money to begin with, the governmental sector and those who fund it should not be seen as "subsidizing" the nonprofit sector.[82]

§ 1.5   INHERENT TAX RATIONALE

Aside from considerations of public policy, an inherent tax theory for tax exemption exists. The essence of this rationale is that the receipt of what otherwise might be deemed income by an exempt organization is not a *taxable event*, in that the organization is merely a convenience or means to an end, a vehicle by which each of those participating in the enterprise may receive and expend money in much the same way as they would if the money was expended by them individually.

---

[80] *Id.* at 14. Also, Regan v. Taxation With Representation of Washington, 461 U.S. 540, 544 (1983), observing that tax exemption is "a form of subsidy that is administered through the tax system" but is not "in all respects identical." But see Walz v. Tax Comm'n of New York, 397 U.S. 664, 690 (1970) (Brennan, J., concurring), distinguishing an exemption from a subsidy because an exemption (unlike a subsidy) does not involve "the direct transfer of public monies to the subsidized enterprise and uses resources exacted from taxpayers as a whole."

The lower courts, not surprisingly, follow the Supreme Court's occasional view that tax exemption is a government-provided subsidy (e.g., American Civil Liberties Union Found. of Louisiana v. Crawford, 2002 WL 461649 (E.D. La. 2002)) (where the court enjoined application of three state statutes providing tax exemptions only for religious organizations) *rev'd* (on another issue), American Civil Liberties Union Found. of Louisiana v. Bridges, 334 F.3d 416 (5th Cir. 2003).

Actually, the matter is somewhat worse. The Supreme Court, in addition to asserting that these tax exemptions are subsidies, also regarded nonexempted taxpayers as "indirect and vicarious donors" (Bob Jones Univ. v. United States, 461 U.S. 574, 591 (1983), quoted in Texas Monthly, Inc. v. Bullock, 489 U.S. 1, 14 (1989)). Persons who are required to pay a tax because they do not qualify for an exemption, however, are hardly "donors," indirect or otherwise; characterization of such persons as "donors" is wholly inconsistent with the Court's jurisprudence on that subject (e.g., Comm'r v. Duberstein, 363 U.S. 278, 285 (1960), where the Court stated that a *gift* is a transfer of money or property motivated by "detached or disinterested generosity"). In general, *Charitable Giving* § 3.1.

Lower courts that have considered the issue generally have held that a tax exemption is not a form of federal financial assistance for purposes of Title IX of the Education Amendments Act of 1972 (20 U.S.C. § 1681, et seq.) and other civil rights legislation (Buettner-Hartsoe v. Baltimore Lutheran High Sch. Ass'n, __ F.4th __ (4th Cir. 2024), *rev'g* 2022 WL 2869041 (D. Md. 2022); Johnny's Icehouse v. Amateur Hockey Ass'n of Illinois, 134 F. Supp. 2d 965, 972 (N.D. Ill. 2001); Stewart v. New York Univ. 430 F. Supp. 1305, 1314 (S.D.N.Y. 1976)). But see McGlotten v. Connally, 338 F. Supp. 448 (D.D.C. 1972), holding charitable contribution deductions to be akin to government matching grants and therefore federal financial assistance.

[81] Usually, every tax exemption, deduction, credit, or other preference accorded to certain persons causes other persons to pay more tax; that almost always is an inevitable outcome when a tax base is narrowed (see *supra* note 75).

[82] E.g., Arizona Christian School Tuition Org. v. Winn, 563 U.S. 125, 142 (2011). See *Constitutional Law* § 1.12.

This rationale chiefly underlies the tax exemption for certain social clubs, which enable individuals to pool their resources for the purpose of provision of recreation and pleasure more effectively than can be done on an individual basis.[83] This tax rationale was summarized by a federal court as follows:

> Congress has determined that in a situation where individuals have banded together to provide recreational facilities on a mutual basis, it would be conceptually erroneous to impose a tax on the organization as a separate entity. The funds exempted are received only from the members and any "profit" which results from overcharging for the use of the facilities still belongs to the same members. No income of the sort usually taxed has been generated; the money has simply been shifted from one pocket to another, both within the same pair of pants.[84]

This rationale is likewise reflected in congressional committee reports.[85] It was invoked by Congress when enacting the tax exemption for homeowners' associations.[86] Thus, the Senate Finance Committee observed that, "[s]ince homeowners' associations generally allow individual homeowners to act together in order to maintain and improve the area in which they live, the committee believes it is not appropriate to tax the revenues of an association of homeowners who act together if an individual homeowner acting alone would not be taxed on the same activity."[87] This rationale, however, operates only where "public" money is not unduly utilized for private gain.[88]

The inherent tax theory also serves as the rationale for the tax exemption for political organizations.[89] Thus, the legislative history underlying this exemption stated that these organizations should be treated as exempt organizations, inasmuch as "political activity (including the financing of political activity) as such is not a trade or a business which is appropriately subject to tax."[90]

§ 1.6 OTHER RATIONALES AND REASONS FOR EXEMPT ORGANIZATIONS

There are, as noted,[91] rationales for exempting organizations from federal income tax other than the political philosophy rationale[92] and the inherent tax rationale.[93]

---

[83] See Chapter 15.
[84] McGlotten v. Connally, 338 F. Supp. 448, 458 (D.D.C. 1972).
[85] H.R. Rep. No. 91-413, at 48 (1969); S. Rep. No. 91-552, at 71 (1969).
[86] See § 19.14.
[87] S. Rep. No. 94-938, at 394 (1976).
[88] West Side Tennis Club v. Comm'r, 111 F.2d 6 (2d Cir. 1940), cert. denied, 311 U.S. 674 (1940).
[89] See Chapter 17.
[90] S. Rep. No. 93-1357, at 26 (1974).
[91] See § 1.3.
[92] See § 1.4.
[93] See § 1.5.

One of these rationales, less lofty than that accorded charitable and social welfare organizations, is extended as justification for the exemption of trade associations and other forms of business leagues.[94] These entities function to promote the welfare of a segment of society: the business, industrial, and professional community. An element of the philosophy supporting this type of exemption is that a healthy business climate advances the public welfare. The exemption for labor unions and other labor organizations rests on a comparable rationale.

The tax exemption for fraternal beneficiary organizations also depends, at least in part, on this concept. A study of the insurance practices of large fraternal societies by the U.S. Department of the Treasury[95] concluded that this rationale is inapplicable with respect to the insurance programs of these entities because the "provision of life insurance and other benefits is generally not considered a good or service with significant external benefits" to society generally. This report added, however, that "tax exemption for these goods and services [insurance and like benefits] may be justified in order to encourage" the charitable activities conducted by these organizations. The inherent tax rationale[96] "may" provide a basis for exemption for "certain" of these societies' services, according to the report. Further, the report observed that "[i]nsurance is not a type of product for which consumers may lack access to information on the appropriate quantity or quality that they need."

Other federal tax exemption provisions may be traced to an effort to achieve a particular objective. These provisions tend to be of more recent vintage, testimony to the fact of a more complex Internal Revenue Code. For example, exemption for veterans' organizations[97] was enacted to create a category of organizations entitled to use a particular exemption from the unrelated business income tax,[98] and exemption for homeowners' associations[99] came about because of a shift in the policy of the IRS regarding the scope of exemption provided for social welfare organizations. The exemption for college and university investment vehicles was the result of Congress's effort to salvage the exempt status of a common investment fund in the face of a determination by the IRS to the contrary.[100] As is so often the case with respect to the tax law generally, a particular exemption provision can arise as the result of case law, or to clarify it; this was the origin of statutes granting exemption to cooperative hospital service organizations,[101] charitable risk pools,[102] child care organizations,[103] public safety testing organizations,[104] and prepaid tuition programs.[105]

---

[94] See Chapter 14.
[95] Report to the "Congress on Fraternal Benefit Societies," U.S. Department of the Treasury, January 15, 1993.
[96] See § 1.5.
[97] See § 19.11(a).
[98] See § 25.4(b).
[99] See § 19.14.
[100] See § 11.5.
[101] See § 11.4.
[102] See § 11.6.
[103] See § 8.8.
[104] See § 11.3.
[105] See § 19.19.

§ 1.7 FREEDOM OF ASSOCIATION DOCTRINE

Tax exemption for nonprofit membership organizations may be viewed as a manifestation of the constitutionally protected right of association accorded the members of these organizations. There are two types of *freedoms of association*. One type—termed the *freedom of intimate association*—is the traditional type of protected association derived from the right of personal liberty. The other type—the *freedom of expressive association*—is a function of the right of free speech protected by the First Amendment to the U.S. Constitution.

By application of the doctrine of freedom of intimate association, the formation and preservation of certain types of highly personal relationships are afforded a substantial measure of sanctuary from interference by government.[106] These personal bonds are considered to foster diversity and advance personal liberty.[107] In assessing the extent of constraints on the authority of government to interfere with this freedom, a court must make a determination of where the objective characteristics of the relationship, which is created where an individual enters into a particular association, are located on a spectrum from the most intimate to the most attenuated of personal relationships.[108] Relevant factors include size, purpose, policies, selectivity, and congeniality.[109]

The freedom to engage in group effort is guaranteed under the doctrine of freedom of expressive association[110] and is viewed as a way of advancing political, social, economic, educational, religious, and cultural ends.[111] Government, however, has the ability to infringe on this right where compelling state interests, unrelated to the suppression of ideas and not achievable through means significantly less restrictive of associational freedoms, are served.[112]

These two associational freedoms were the subject of a U.S. Supreme Court analysis concerning the scope of a nonprofit organization's right to exclude women from its voting membership.[113] The Court concluded that the governmental interest in eradicating gender-based discrimination is superior to the associational rights of the organization's male members.[114]

---

[106] Pierce v. Society of Sisters, 268 U.S. 510 (1925); Meyer v. Nebraska, 262 U.S. 390 (1923).

[107] Zablocki v. Redhail, 434 U.S. 374 (1978); Quilloin v. Walcott, 434 U.S. 246 (1978); Smith v. Org. of Foster Families, 431 U.S. 494 (1977); Carey v. Population Servs. Int'l, 431 U.S. 678 (1977); Moore v. East Cleveland, 431 U.S. 494 (1977); Cleveland Bd. of Educ. v. LaFleur, 414 U.S. 632 (1974); Wisconsin v. Yoder, 406 U.S. 205 (1973); Stanley v. Illinois, 405 U.S. 645 (1972); Stanley v. Georgia, 394 U.S. 557 (1969); Griswold v. Connecticut, 381 U.S. 479 (1965); Olmstead v. United States, 277 U.S. 438 (1928).

[108] Runyon v. McCrary, 427 U.S. 160 (1976).

[109] Roberts v. United States Jaycees, 468 U.S. 609 (1984).

[110] Rent Control Coalition for Fair Hous. v. Berkeley, 454 U.S. 290 (1981).

[111] NAACP v. Claiborne Hardware Co., 458 U.S. 886 (1982); Larson v. Valente, 456 U.S. 228 (1982); In re Primus, 436 U.S. 412 (1978).

[112] Brown v. Socialist Workers '74 Campaign Comm., 459 U.S. 87 (1982); Democratic Party v. Wisconsin, 450 U.S. 107 (1981); Buckley v. Valeo, 424 U.S. 1 (1976); Cousins v. Wigoda, 419 U.S. 477 (1975); American Party v. White, 415 U.S. 767 (1974); NAACP v. Button, 371 U.S. 415 (1963); Shelton v. Tucker, 364 U.S. 486 (1960); NAACP v. Alabama, 347 U.S. 449 (1958).

[113] Roberts v. United States Jaycees, 468 U.S. 609 (1984).

[114] *Id.* at 622–29.

The Court held that an organization had a constitutional right, under the First Amendment, to exclude gay individuals from leadership positions because of their sexual orientation, overruled this opinion.[115] Application of the state's antidiscrimination law was found to be a "severe intrusion" on the organization's rights to freedom of expressive association.[116] The Court's review of the record resulted in a finding that there was a sufficient basis to conclude that the organization does "not want to promote homosexual conduct as a legitimate form of behavior."[117] The Court wrote: "The forced inclusion of an unwanted person in a group infringes the group's freedom of expressive association if the presence of that person affects in a significant way the group's ability to advocate public or private viewpoints."[118]

---

[115] Boy Scouts of Amer. v. Dale, 530 U.S. 640 (2000).

[116] *Id.* at 659.

[117] *Id.* at 651.

[118] *Id.* at 648. In general, *Constitutional Law* § 1.9.

CHAPTER TWO

Overview of Nonprofit Sector and Tax-Exempt Organizations

The nonprofit sector in the United States and the federal tax law with respect to it have a common feature: enormous and incessant growth. As to the sector, this expansion is reflected in all the principal indicators, such as the number of organizations, the sector's asset base, the amount of charitable giving and granting, its annual expenditures, its share of the gross domestic product, and the size of its workforce. There is, however, this direct correlation: As the nonprofit sector expands, so too does the body of federal and state law regulating it. No end to either of these expansions is in sight.[1]

Over the years, there have been many efforts to analyze and portray the nonprofit sector. One of the first of these significant undertakings, utilizing statistics, conducted jointly by the Survey Research Center at the University of Michigan and the U.S. Census Bureau, was published in 1975 as part of the findings of the Commission on Private Philanthropy and Public Needs, informally known as the Filer Commission.[2] The data compiled for the Commission's use were for 1973. Contemporary charitable giving statistics are explored below, but one striking basis of comparison cannot be resisted at this point: Charitable giving in the United States in the year the first edition of this book was published—1975—was $28.56 billion, whereas for 2022 the amount of charitable giving was an estimated $499.33 billion.[3]

Research of the nature developed for the Filer Commission spawned recurring statistical portraits of the sector. One of the most comprehensive of these analyses is that provided in a periodic almanac published by the Urban Institute.[4]

---

[1] The "rapid growth of the nonprofit sector in the last half century has led to greatly increased attention from the media, scholars, the government, and the public" (O'Neill, *Nonprofit Nation: A New Look at the Third America* 34 (Jossey-Bass, 2002) (*Nonprofit Nation*)).

[2] *Giving in America: Toward a Stronger Voluntary Sector*, Report of the Commission on Private Philanthropy and Public Needs (1975).

[3] See text accompanied by *infra* note 46.

[4] The most recent version of this almanac is McKeever, Dietz, and Fyffe, *The Nonprofit Almanac, Ninth Edition* (Roman & Littlefield/Urban Institute 2016).

Others include a fascinating portrait of the "third America"[5] and the annual survey of charitable giving published by the Giving USA Foundation.[6] The IRS's Statistics of Income Division collects data on tax-exempt organizations.[7] Further, various subsets of the nonprofit sector are the subject of specific portrayals.[8]

The nonprofit sector in the United States is not uniformly labeled; it goes by many names. In addition to *nonprofit*,[9] adjectives used include *tax-exempt, nongovernmental, independent,* and *voluntary.* In its most expansive definition, the nonprofit sector comprises all tax-exempt organizations and some entities that cannot qualify for exemption. The Independent Sector coalition defined the *independent sector* as all charitable[10] and social welfare organizations.[11]

As Independent Sector defined the sector, it comprises "many, varied" organizations, such as "religious organizations, private colleges and schools, foundations, hospitals, day-care centers, environmental organizations, museums, symphony orchestras, youth organizations, advocacy groups, and neighborhood organizations, to name a few." This analysis continued: "What is common among them all is their mission to serve a public purpose, their voluntary and self-governing nature, and their exclusion from being able to distribute profits to stockholders."[12]

§ 2.1 PROFILE OF NONPROFIT SECTOR

Any assessment of any consequence of the contours of the nonprofit sector includes a discussion of the number and types of organizations in the sector. Yet it is "surprisingly difficult to answer the seemingly simple question, How many nonprofit organizations are there in the United States?"[13] The simple answer is: There are "several million" nonprofit organizations, although "no one really knows how many."[14]

---

[5] *Nonprofit Nation.*

[6] These annual publications are titled *Giving USA.*

[7] The IRS publishes various editions of the *Statistics of Income Bulletins.*

[8] E.g., *Yearbook of American and Canadian Churches* (Nat'l Council of the Churches of Christ in the United States of America, various editions); *Foundation Giving: Yearbook of Facts and Figures on Private, Corporate and Community Foundations* (The Foundation Center, various editions); *Foundation Management Report* (Council on Foundations, various editions). The American Hospital Association publishes statistics concerning hospitals; the National Center for Education Statistics publishes data on independent colleges and universities; and the American Society of Association Executives publishes information concerning the nation's trade, business, and professional associations. There are several other analyses of this nature.

[9] Indeed, there is no uniformity as to this term (see § 1.1).

[10] That is, organizations that are tax-exempt pursuant to IRC § 501(a) because they are described in IRC § 501(c)(3) (see Part Three).

[11] That is, organizations that are tax-exempt pursuant to IRC § 501(a) because they are described in IRC § 501(c)(4) (see Chapter 13).

[12] Roeger, Blackwood, and Pettijohn, *The Nonprofit Almanac 2012* (Washington, DC: Urban Institute Press, 2012) (*Nonprofit Almanac*) at 3.

[13] *Nonprofit Nation* at 8.

[14] *Id.* at 1.

In an understatement, the observation was made that "[m]easuring the number of organizations in the independent sector is a complex activity, largely because of the diversity of its components."[15] There are several reasons for this. One reason is that churches (of which there are an estimated 350,000)[16] are not required to file annual information returns with the IRS,[17] so that data concerning them is difficult to amass. Also, hundreds of organizations are under a group exemption[18] and thus not separately identified. Further, smaller nonprofit organizations need not seek recognition of tax exemption from the IRS.[19] Small organizations are not required to file annual information returns with the IRS but are required to electronically submit an annual notice as to their existence.[20]

According to data provided by the IRS, as of the close of the federal government's 2023 fiscal year, there were 1,847,501 recognized tax-exempt organizations.[21] Within this group of organizations are 1,514,558 charitable (including educational, scientific, and religious) entities,[22] 73,467 social welfare organizations,[23] 59,764 business leagues,[24] 47,327 social clubs,[25] 44,478 labor and agricultural organizations,[26] 37,755 fraternal beneficiary organizations,[27] 26,913 veterans' organizations,[28] 15,033 domestic fraternal beneficiary societies,[29] 9,535 cemetery companies,[30] 5,597 voluntary employees' beneficiary associations,[31] 5,378 benevolent life insurance associations,[32] 4,181 title-holding corporations,[33] 1,497 state-chartered credit unions,[34] 548 holding companies for pensions and other entities,

---

[15] *Id.* at 8. The point was articulated more forcefully (albeit less elegantly) in the fifth edition of the *Nonprofit Almanac,* where it was stated that "[c]ounting the number of institutions in the independent sector is a challenge" (Hodgkinson & Weitzman, *Nonprofit Almanac: Dimensions of the Independent Sector* 25 (Jossey-Bass, 1996)).

[16] *Nonprofit Almanac* at 139. The term *church* includes analogous religious congregations, such as temples and mosques. See § 10.3.

[17] See § 28.2(c)(i).

[18] See § 26.11.

[19] These are organizations that normally do not generate more than $5,000 in revenue. See § 26.2(b).

[20] See §§ 28.2(c)(ii), 28.3.

[21] Pub. 55-B, *IRS Data Book, 2023* (Apr. 2024) at 30 (Table 14). This reference to tax-exempt organizations is to entities that are exempt from federal income tax pursuant to IRC § 501(a) by reason of description in IRC § 501(c) (see Parts Three and Four). The concept of *recognition* of tax exemption is the subject of § 3.2.

[22] That is, organizations described in IRC § 501(c)(3). See Part Three.

[23] That is, organizations described in IRC § 501(c)(4). See Chapter 13.

[24] That is, organizations described in IRC § 501(c)(6). See Chapter 14.

[25] That is, organizations described in IRC § 501(c)(7). See Chapter 15.

[26] That is, organizations described in IRC § 501(c)(5). See Chapter 16.

[27] That is, organizations described in IRC § 501(c)(8). See § 19.4(a).

[28] That is, organizations described in IRC § 501(c)(19). See § 19.11(a).

[29] That is, organizations described in IRC § 501(c)(10). See § 19.4(b).

[30] That is, organizations described in IRC § 501(c)(13). See 19.6.

[31] That is, organizations described in IRC § 501(c)(9). See § 18.3.

[32] That is, organizations described in IRC § 501(c)(12). See § 19.5.

[33] That is, organizations described in IRC § 501(c)(2), (c)(25). See § 19.2.

[34] That is, organizations described in IRC § 501(c)(14). See § 19.7.

705 instrumentalities of the federal government,[35] 622 mutual insurance companies,[36] 88 supplemental unemployment compensation trusts,[37] and 55 other types of exempt entities.[38] In addition, according to the IRS, there are 46,951 political organizations[39] and 222 religious and apostolic associations.[40] Not surprisingly, a court had occasion to observe that "[t]rying to understand the various exempt organization provisions of the Internal Revenue Code is as difficult as capturing a drop of mercury under your thumb."[41]

During the government's 2023 fiscal year, there were 119,491 closures of applications for recognition of tax-exempt status, with 103,073 applicants (86.3 percent) approved and 88 disapproved. Entities receiving recognition of exemption included charitable organizations (98,417), social welfare organizations (1,202), labor and agricultural organizations (341), business leagues (998), and social clubs (1,064).[42] The IRS received 3,025 notices of intent to operate as social welfare organizations,[43] of which 587 were rejected.[44] The agency examined 7,666 returns of tax-exempt organizations, retirement plans, government entities, and tax-exempt bonds during this period, including those in the Form 990 series (1,029), other annual returns (e.g., Form 990-PF) (81), employment tax returns (1,645), Forms 990-T (268), and Forms 4720 (231).[45]

Charitable giving in the United States in 2022 is estimated to have totaled $499.33 billion.[46] Religious organizations received 27 percent of these 2022 charitable dollars, human services 14 percent, educational organizations 13 percent, grantmaking foundations 11 percent, and health-related organizations 10 percent. Giving by individuals in 2022 constituted 64 percent of total giving; by private

---

[35] That is, organizations described in IRC § 501(c)(1). See § 19.1.

[36] That is, organizations described in IRC § 501(c)(15). See § 19.9.

[37] That is, organizations described in IRC § 501(c)(17). See § 18.4.

[38] These other types of exempt entities include teachers' retirement funds (IRC § 501(c)(11); see § 18.7); corporations organized to finance crop operations (IRC § 501(c)(16); see § 19.10); employee-funded pension trusts (IRC § 501(c)(18); see § 18.7); black lung benefit trusts (IRC § 501(c)(21); see § 18.5); veterans' associations founded prior to 1880 (IRC § 501(c)(23); see § 19.11(b)); trusts described in section 4049 of the Employee Retirement Income Security Act of 1974 (IRC § 501(c)(24); see § 18.7); state-sponsored high-risk health insurance organizations (IRC § 501(c)(26); see § 19.15); state-sponsored workers' compensation reinsurance organizations (IRC § 501(c)(27); see § 19.16(a)); and qualified nonprofit health insurance issuers (IRC § 501(c)(29); see § 19.18).

[39] That is, organizations described in IRC § 527. See Chapter 17.

[40] That is, organizations described in IRC § 501(d). See § 10.8. The federal tax law recognizes about 80 categories of tax-exempt organizations (see Appendix B (available online)).

[41] Weingarden v. Comm'r, 86 T.C. 669, 675 (1986), rev'd (on other grounds), 825 F.2d 1027 (6th Cir. 1987).

[42] Pub. 55-B, IRS Data Book, 2023 (Apr. 2023) at 28 (Table 12). The Treasury Inspector General for Tax Administration reported that the average number of days to process determination requests fluctuates from year to year but dropped 12 percent from 192 days to 169 days from fiscal year 2015 to fiscal year 2019 (TIGTA, "Fiscal Year 2019 Statistical Trends Review of the Tax Exempt and Government Entities Division," Rep. No. 2021-10-031 (May 3, 2021)).

[43] See § 26.13.

[44] Pub. 55-B, IRS Data Book, 2023 (Apr. 2023) at 29 (Table 13).

[45] Id. at 53 (Table 21).

[46] These data are from the National Philanthropic Trust, which curates statistics from recent studies and reports on charitable giving in the United States (https://www.nptrust.org/philanthropic-resources/charitable-giving-statistics/).

foundations 21 percent of total giving; by charitable bequests 9 percent of total giving; and by corporations 4 percent of total giving.

In 2015, there were 1,088,447 registered public charities, of which 314,744 were sufficiently large to file Form 990.[47] In 2016, these organizations reported $4.0 trillion in total assets ($2.5 trillion in net assets) and total revenue of $2.1 trillion (approximately 11 percent of gross domestic product). Most of the Form 990 filers were relatively small (assets of less than $500,000) or medium-sized (assets of $500,000 up to $10 million) charities (40.2 percent and 47.7 percent, respectively). The larger organizations, those with at least $10 million in assets, were 12 percent of Form 990 filers; 93.3 percent of assets were held by, 88.5 percent of revenues were received by, and 72.6 percent of contributions were made to, these entities. The primary source of revenue for these organizations was program service revenue (72.2 percent), with charitable contributions accounting for a much smaller amount (13.3 percent).[48]

For some other perspectives on the nonprofit sector, it:

- Accounts for 5 to 10 percent of the nation's economy.

- Accounts for 8 percent of the nation's noninstitutional civilian employees.

- Has more civilian employees than the federal government and the 50 state governments combined.

- Employs more people than any of these industries: agriculture, mining, construction, transportation, communications, and other public utilities; and finance, insurance, and real estate.

- Generates revenue that exceeds the gross domestic product of all but six foreign countries: China, France, Germany, Italy, Japan, and the United Kingdom.[49]

§ 2.2   ORGANIZATION OF IRS

Among the departments of the U.S. government is the Department of the Treasury (the Treasury Department), which is headed by the Secretary of the Treasury. One of the functions of the Treasury Department is assessment and collection of federal income and other taxes.[50] The Secretary is authorized to conduct examinations,[51] issue and serve summonses,[52] and undertake what is necessary for "detecting and

---

[47] See § 28.2(a)(i).

[48] The data in this paragraph are derived from Congressional Research Service, "Tax Issues Relating to Charitable Contributions and Organizations," Rep. No. R45922 (Aug. 4, 2020).

[49] *Nonprofit Nation* at 12.

[50] IRC § 7601(a), which provides that the Secretary of the Treasury "shall, to the extent he deems it practicable, cause officers or employees of the Treasury Department to proceed, from time to time, through each internal revenue district [authorized by IRC § 7621] and inquire after and concerning all persons therein who may be liable to pay any internal revenue tax, and all persons owning or having the care and management of any objects with respect to which any tax is imposed."

[51] IRC § 7602. See § 27.6.

[52] IRC §§ 7602, 7603.

bringing to trial and punishment persons guilty of violating the internal revenue laws or conniving at the same."[53] This tax assessment and collection function has largely been assigned to the IRS, which is an agency (or bureau) of the Treasury Department.[54]

The Treasury Department formulates the nation's tax policies, including those pertaining to tax-exempt organizations. This policy formulation is the direct responsibility of the Assistant Treasury Secretary for Tax Policy.

(a) IRS in General

The mission of the IRS is to "provide America's taxpayers with top quality service by helping them understand and meet their tax responsibilities and by applying the tax law with integrity and fairness to all."[55] One of the functions of this agency is to administer and enforce the law of tax-exempt organizations.

The IRS is headquartered in Washington, D.C.; its operations there are housed in its National Office. An Internal Revenue Service Oversight Board is responsible for overseeing the agency in its administration, conduct, direction, and supervision of the execution and application of the nation's internal revenue laws.[56] A function of this board is to recommend to the President candidates for the position of Commissioner of Internal Revenue.[57] The Commissioner, who need not be a tax lawyer or accountant but must have a "demonstrated ability in management," serves one or more five-year terms.[58] The Commissioner is charged with administering, managing, conducting, directing, and supervising the execution and application of the internal revenue laws.[59]

Congress in 1998 directed the Commissioner of Internal Revenue to reorganize the IRS in a way that substantially altered the then-existing structure (which was based on regional divisions) by restructuring the agency into units serving groups of taxpayers[60] with similar needs.[61] Consequently, the IRS is organized into four operating divisions; this structure is reflected in the IRS's regional offices. These divisions are the Large Business and International, the Small Business/Self-Employed, the Tax Exempt and Government Entities, and the Wage and Investment Divisions.

This reorganization of the IRS, in the form of a four-division structure, resulted in delegation to each division of the responsibility for developing procedures and establishing priorities for servicing its customers. In the words of a Treasury Inspector General for Tax Administration report, this organizational

---

[53] IRC § 7623.

[54] Reg. § 601.101(a).

[55] https://www.irs.gov/about-irs/the-agency-its-mission-and-statutory-authority.

[56] IRC §§ 7802(a), (c)(1)(A).

[57] IRC § 7802(d)(3)(A).

[58] IRC § 7803(a)(1).

[59] IRC § 7803(a)(2)(A). Also, Reg. § 601.101(a) (providing that the Commissioner has "general superintendence of the assessment and collection of all taxes imposed by any law providing national revenue").

[60] A *taxpayer* is any person subject to any internal revenue tax (IRC § 7701(a)(14)); this term includes a tax-exempt organization.

[61] Internal Revenue Service Restructuring and Reform Act of 1998, Pub. L. No. 105-206, § 1001(a)(3), 112 Stat. 685.

methodology "enabled each division to establish end-to-end accountability for its respective customer base."[62]

Within the Treasury Department there is an IRS Chief Counsel who is appointed by the President and serves as the chief legal advisor to the IRS Commissioner on all matters pertaining to the interpretation, administration, and enforcement of the Internal Revenue Code, as well as all other legal matters. The IRS Chief Counsel reports to both the IRS Commissioner and the Treasury Department General Counsel. Among the associate chief counsels in the IRS Office of Chief Counsel is the Associate Chief Counsel (Employee Benefits, Exempt Organizations, and Employment Taxes). The responsibilities of this Associate Chief Counsel's office include issues pertaining to the uniform interpretation and application of federal tax laws involving tax-exempt organizations. The Associate Chief Counsel (EEE) provides legal and technical advice with respect to legislation, issues, regulations, and other guidance, letter rulings, and advisory opinions, and provides litigation support within its jurisdiction.

(b)   Tax Exempt and Government Entities Division

The first of these four divisions—the Tax Exempt and Government Entities (TE/GE) Division—was established on December 5, 1999.[63] Within the TE/GE Division is the Exempt Organizations (EO) Division, which develops policy concerning and administers the law of tax-exempt organizations. The director of the Exempt Organizations Division, who reports to the Commissioner of the TE/GE Division, is responsible for planning, managing, and executing nationwide IRS activities in the realm of exempt organizations. This director also supervises and is responsible for the programs of the offices of Customer Education and Outreach, Rulings and Agreements, Examinations, and Exempt Organizations Electronic Initiatives.

The Rulings and Agreements office is the function that is primarily responsible for up-front, customer-initiated activities such as determination letter requests, taxpayer assistance, and assistance to other Division offices.[64] This office includes EO Technical and EO Determinations, the latter being the function that is primarily responsible for processing initial applications for recognition of tax-exempt status. It includes the main Determinations office located in Cincinnati, Ohio, and other field offices. Applications are generally processed in the centralized Determinations office in Cincinnati.[65] The IRS's lawyers in the field are part of the Office of Division Counsel (TE/GE); those in the Office of Associate Chief Counsel (EEE) are part of EO Technical and report to the IRS Deputy Chief Counsel (Technical).[66]

The Examinations office focuses on tax-exempt organizations examination programs and compliance checks. Its support functions include Examination Planning and Programs, Classification, Mandatory Review, Special Review,

---

[62] TIGTA, "A Corporate Approach Is Needed to Provide for a More Effective Tax-Exempt Fraud Program," Rep. No. 2009-10-096 (July 6, 2009), at 2.

[63] IRS News Release (IR) 1999-101.

[64] IRS Revenue Procedure (Rev. Proc.) Rev. Proc. 2024-5, 2024-1 I.R.B. 262 § 1.01(2).

[65] *Id.* § 1.01(3).

[66] Internal Revenue Manual §§ 1.1.6.6, 1.1.6.19. The IRS Deputy Chief Counsel (Technical) serves as the principal deputy to the Chief Counsel and has jurisdiction over legal issues arising in published guidance, letter rulings, technical advice, and other processes (*id.* §§ 1.1.6.1.1(1), 1.1.6.2).

and Examinations Special Support. An Exempt Organizations Compliance Unit addresses instances of exempt organizations' compliance with the tax law by conducting compliance checks.

Also within the TE/GE Division are the Employee Plans and Government Entities functions. Within the latter are the Federal, State, and Local Governments; Indian Tribal Governments; and Tax Exempt Bonds offices.

(c) Restructuring of IRS

The IRS is in the process of a complete restructuring, as directed by Congress in 2019 in the form of directives to the Treasury Department and the IRS through the Taxpayer First Act.[67]

As part of this restructuring, Congress established within the IRS an Independent Office of Appeals. This office is under the supervision of a Chief of Appeals, who reports directly to the Commissioner of the Internal Revenue. The Chief of Appeals is required to have experience and expertise in the administration of, and compliance with, the federal tax laws, a broad range of compliance cases, and management of large service organizations. The function of this office is to resolve federal tax controversies without litigation on a basis that is fair and impartial both to the government and to the taxpayer, promotes a consistent application and interpretation and voluntary compliance with the federal tax laws, and enhances public confidence in and efficiency of the IRS.[68]

Congress also created the position in the IRS of a Chief Information Officer (CIO), appointed by the Commissioner of Internal Revenue. This CIO is to develop, implement, and maintain information technology for the IRS. The CIO is also required to develop and implement a multiyear strategic plan for the information technology needs of the IRS.[69]

The overall framework of the new structure and functioning of the IRS is the subject of a comprehensive report, as directed by the legislation,[70] submitted to Congress in early 2021.[71] The agency billed this report as a "comprehensive set of recommendations that will reimagine the taxpayer experience, enhance employee training and restructure the organization to increase collaboration and innovation."[72]

The essence of this report is a description of a way to "transform the IRS into a modern, efficient, and taxpayer-centric centered agency." The strategies outlined in the report are intended to "re-shape the IRS into a nimbler enterprise, readily capable of taking advantage of emerging technology." As is emphasized

---

[67] Pub. L. No. 116-25, 133 Stat. 981 (2019) (for purposes of this section, TFA).

[68] IRC § 7803(e). The Treasury Department and the IRS have issued regulations relating to the Independent Office of Appeals' resolution of federal tax controversies without litigation (see § 27.1) and referrals to that office following the issuance of a notice of deficiency to a taxpayer (Reg. §§ 301.7803-2, -3, 90 Fed. Reg. 3645 (2025)). These proposed regulations reflect amendments to the law made by the Taxpayer First Act.

[69] IRC § 7803(f).

[70] TFA § 1302.

[71] Pub. 5426, *Taxpayer First Act Report to Congress* (Jan. 2021).

[72] IR-2021-07.

throughout, the report observes that "delivering the type of experience American taxpayers expect and deserve will require funding."

The strategies focus on customer service, training of employees, and modernization of the IRS's organizational structure. As to organizational redesign, the IRS states that "changing times call for new ways of doing business." The IRS expects that the coming restructuring "will increase agency-wide collaboration and deconstruct operational silos, thereby improving [the IRS's] ability to provide seamless service to [its] employees and taxpayers."

There is to be an Enterprise Change and Innovation Division, to "coordinate annual strategic planning and prioritization activities to streamline decision making and enable the agency to set and meet its short and long-term strategic goals." A Chief Taxpayer Experience Officer "will seek to drive strategic direction for improving the taxpayer experience across the IRS—including both service and compliance interactions." The current senior executive team will be replaced by a "smaller, taxpayer-focused" senior leadership team. Expected is a Relationships and Services Division, a Data Office and an Enterprise Digitalization and Case Management Office, and consolidation of examination operations into a new Compliance Division. An Operations Management Division is to be a "revitalized support structure that will help the agency address many of the challenges [the IRS faces] in today's current tax administration environment." In addition to the Commissioner of Internal Revenue, there will be a deputy commissioner, five assistant commissioners, and 32 chiefs (plus chief counsel).

In 2023, following the enactment of the Inflation Reduction Act,[73] the Treasury Department and the IRS developed a Strategic Operating Plan outlining how the IRS plans to use funding from this legislation to better serve taxpayers, tax professionals, and the "broader tax ecosystem." The planning process leveraged prior IRS planning efforts, including the Taxpayer First Act Report, new thinking around best practices and available technology capabilities, and current and past input from a wide range of stakeholders in tax administration.[74]

The Taxpayer First Act report says little, and the Strategic Operating Plan says nothing, about how existing operations are to be integrated into this new structure. The existing four "business units," including Tax Exempt/Government Entities, will be folded into the Compliance Division. This is to be done to ensure "more efficient operations and provid[e] consistent outcomes for resolving taxpayer compliance issues." The roles of Chief Counsel and the National Taxpayer Advocate will remain essentially unchanged.[75]

---

[73] Pub. L. No. 117-169, 136 Stat. 1818 (2022).

[74] Pub. 3744, *IRS Inflation Reduction Act Strategic Operating Plan FY2023–2031* (Apr. 2023).

[75] Pub. 5426, *Taxpayer First Act Report to Congress* (Jan. 2021).

Tax Exemption: Source and Recognition

As subsequent chapters indicate, there are many categories of tax-exempt organizations. Accordingly, the advantages and disadvantages of tax exemption will differ, depending on the particular category.

§ 3.1   SOURCE OF TAX EXEMPTION

Section 61(a) of the Internal Revenue Code provides that "[e]xcept as otherwise provided in this subtitle [Subtitle A—income taxes], gross income means all income from whatever source derived," including items such as interest, dividends, compensation for services, and receipts derived from business. The Code provides for a variety of deductions, exclusions, and exemptions in computing taxable income. Many of these are contained in Internal Revenue Code Subtitle A, Subchapter B, entitled "Computation of taxable income." Of pertinence in the tax-exempt organizations context, however, is the body of exemption provisions contained in Subtitle A, Subchapter F, captioned "Exempt organizations."

Exemption from federal income taxation is derived from a specific provision to that end in the Internal Revenue Code. A federal tax exemption is a privilege (a matter of legislative grace), not an entitlement,[1] and—being an exception to the norm of taxation—is often strictly construed.[2] (The same principle applies with

---

[1] As discussed, however, the federal tax exemption for many nonprofit organizations (such as charitable ones) reflects the heritage and societal structure of the United States (see § 1.3).

[2] E.g., Knights of Columbus Bldg. Ass'n of Stamford, Conn., Inc. v. United States, 88-1 U.S.T.C. ¶ 9336 (D. Conn. 1988) ("A tax exemption is a benefit conferred by the legislature in its discretion. Because there is no entitlement to an exemption absent allowance by the legislature, the exemption provisions are strictly construed"); Mercantile Bank & Trust Co. v. United States, 441 F.2d 364 (8th Cir. 1971) ("Special benefits to taxpayers, such as tax exemption status, do not turn upon general equitable considerations but are matters of legislative grace" (*id.* at 366)). Also, Conference of Major Religious Superiors of Women, Inc. v. District of Columbia, 348 F.2d 783 (D.C. Cir. 1965); American Automobile Ass'n v. Comm'r, 19 T.C. 1146 (1953); Associated Indus. of Cleveland v. Comm'r, 7 T.C. 1449 (1946); Bingler v. Johnson, 394 U.S. 741 (1969), and authorities cited therein.

respect to tax deductions and tax exclusions.)[3,4] This type of exemption must be by enactment of Congress and will not be granted by implication.[5] Two related tax precepts are that a person requesting exemption must demonstrate compliance with the requirements set forth in the statute that grants the exemption,[6] and the party claiming the exemption bears the burden of proof of eligibility for the exemption.[7] Thus, a court wrote that the federal tax statutory law "generally consists of narrowly defined categories of exemption" and is "replete with rigid requirements which a putatively exempt organization must demonstrate it meets."[8] The IRS and the courts are alert for efforts to gain a tax exemption where the underlying motive is the purpose of "confounding tax collection."[9]

Nonetheless, provisions according tax exemption for charitable organizations are usually liberally construed. Thus, a court wrote that the "judiciary will liberally construe, and rightfully so, provisions giving exemptions for charitable, religious, and educational purposes."[10] Another court said that "in view of the fact that bequests for public purposes operate in aid of good government and perform by private means what ultimately would fall upon the public, exemption from taxation is not so much a matter of grace or favor as rather an act of justice."[11] Similarly, the exemption of income devoted to charity by means of the charitable contribution deductions has been held to not be narrowly construed.[12] These provisions respecting income destined for charity are accorded favorable construction, since they are "begotten from motives of public policy"[13] and any ambiguity therein has been traditionally resolved against taxation.[14]

The provision in the Internal Revenue Code that is the general source of the federal income tax exemption is IRC § 501(a), which states that an "organization

---

[3] Deputy v. Du Pont, 308 U.S. 488 (1940); White v. United States, 305 U.S. 281 (1938). In a case involving tax deductions claimed by a trust, the court wrote that the deductions "must fit into a statutory category of deductibility, else the trustees must carry out their fiduciary duty at the expense of the trust, rather than the public fisc" (Alfred I. duPont Testamentary Trust v. Comm'r, 514 F.2d 917, 922 (5th Cir. 1975)).

[4] E.g., Estate of Levine v. Comm'r, 526 F.2d 717 (2d Cir. 1975) (where the court was prompted to observe that "[o]ne suspects that because the Internal Revenue Code. . .piles exceptions upon exclusions, it invites efforts to outwit the tax collector" (id. at 718)).

[5] E.g., Mescalero Apache Tribe v. Jones, 411 U.S. 145 (1973).

[6] E.g., Christian Echoes Nat'l Ministry v. United States, 470 F.2d 849 (10th Cir. 1972), cert. denied, 414 U.S. 864 (1973); Parker v. Comm'r, 365 F.2d 792 (8th Cir. 1966), cert. denied, 385 U.S. 1026 (1967).

[7] E.g., Bubbling Well Church of Universal Love v. Comm'r, 670 F.2d 104 (9th Cir. 1981); Senior Citizens Stores, Inc. v. United States, 602 F.2d 711 (5th Cir. 1979); Harding Hospital, Inc. v. United States, 505 F.2d 1068 (6th Cir. 1974); Kenner v. Comm'r, 318 F.2d 632 (7th Cir. 1963).

[8] Knights of Columbus Bldg. Ass'n of Stamford, Conn., Inc. v. United States, 88-1 U.S.T.C. ¶ 9336 (D. Conn. 1988).

[9] Granzow v. Comm'r, 739 F.2d 265, 268–69 (7th Cir. 1984).

[10] American Inst. for Economic Research, Inc. v. United States, 302 F.2d 934, 937 (Ct. Cl. 1962), cert. denied, 372 U.S. 976 (1963), reh'g denied, 373 U.S. 954 (1963).

[11] Harrison v. Barker Annuity Fund, 90 F.2d 286, 288 (7th Cir. 1937). The court also said that the "courts quite generally have extended liberal construction to statutes furthering the encouragement of bequests for purposes which tend toward the public good, without reference to personal or selfish motives" (id.).

[12] SICO Found. v. United States, 295 F.2d 924, 930, n.19 (Ct. Cl. 1962), and cases cited therein.

[13] Helvering v. Bliss, 293 U.S. 144, 151 (1934).

[14] C. F. Mueller Co. v. Comm'r, 190 F.2d 210 (3d Cir. 1951).

described in subsection (c) or (d) or section 401(a) shall be exempt from taxation under this subtitle [Subtitle A—income taxes] unless such exemption is denied under section 501 or 503."

The U.S. Supreme Court characterized IRC § 501(a) as the "linchpin of the statutory benefit [exemption] system."[15] The Court summarized the exemption provided by IRC § 501(a) as extending "advantageous treatment to several types of nonprofit corporations [and trusts and unincorporated associations], including exemption of their income from taxation and [for those that are also eligible charitable donees] deductibility by benefactors of the amounts of their donations."[16]

Most categories of tax exemption are manifested in the list of them that comprises IRC § 501(c). Yet, references to exemption are found elsewhere in the Internal Revenue Code, namely, IRC §§ 501(d), 521, 526–529A, and 664.[17]

An organization that seeks to obtain tax-exempt status, therefore, bears the burden of proving that it satisfies all the requirements of the exemption statute involved.[18]

§ 3.2 *RECOGNITION* OF TAX EXEMPTION

An organization's tax-exempt status may be *recognized* by the IRS; indeed, the law may mandate this recognition. Recognition of tax exemption is a function of the IRS, which it accomplishes, where the organization qualifies for exemption, by making a written determination[19] that the entity constitutes an exempt organization. (The role of the IRS in recognizing the exempt status of organizations is part of its general function of evaluating the tax status of organizations.)[20] Recognition of exempt status, however, must be contrasted with *eligibility* for exempt status. Congress, not the IRS, is responsible for *granting* exempt status.[21] Thus, if an organization qualifies for exemption pursuant to the federal tax law, it is exempt—although the law may require a procedural step, such as filing for recognition of exemption by or providing a notice to the IRS.

---

[15] Simon v. Eastern Ky. Welfare Rights Org., 426 U.S. 26, 29 n.1 (1976).

[16] *Id.*, at 28.

[17] Indeed, the list is even longer, in that individual retirement accounts (IRC §§ 408, 408A), domestic international sales corporations (IRC § 991), employee stock ownership plans and related employee stock ownership trusts (e.g., Val Lanes Recreation Center Corp. v. Comm'r, T.C. Memo. 2018-92), and Coverdell education savings accounts (IRC § 530) are tax-exempt organizations. For an interplay between some of these provisions, see Benenson v. Comm'r, 887 F.3d 511 (1st Cir. 2018).

[18] E.g., Harding Hosp., Inc. v. United States, 505 F.2d 1068, 1071 (6th Cir. 1974); Haswell v. United States, 500 F.2d 1133, 1140 (Ct. Cl. 1974).

[19] See § 26.1(a).

[20] Reg. §§ 601.201(a)(1), 601.201(d)(1).

[21] As a court stated, a "tax exemption is a benefit conferred by the legislature at its discretion" (Knights of Columbus Building Ass'n of Stamford, Connecticut v. United States, 88-1 U.S.T.C. ¶ 9338 (D. Conn. 1988)). This court added that the federal statutory law "generally consists of narrowly defined categories of exemption" and is "replete with rigid requirements which a putatively exempt organization must demonstrate it meets" (*id.*).

(a) General Rules

As a general rule, recognition of tax exemption by the IRS is not required in connection with most categories of exempt organizations. (The IRS informally refers to these types of entities as *self-declarers*.)[22] Frequently there is confusion on this point because there is no rule of statutory law that affirmatively so provides. Rather, this conclusion has to be reached by implication, as a matter of statutory construction, in that the federal tax law requires certain types of organizations to secure recognition of exemption to be exempt; thus, the other types of entities need not make the filing.[23] That is, for an organization to be exempt as a charitable entity (with exceptions), a credit counseling organization that desires exemption as a social welfare entity, a nonprofit health insurance issuer, or an employee benefit entity, it must file an application for recognition of exemption with the IRS and receive a favorable determination.[24] Nonetheless, an organization that is not obligated to seek recognition of exemption may voluntarily do so.[25]

There is little formal evidence of this distinction in the law between organizations that are required to file for recognition of tax exemption and those that do not have to file. The distinction is somewhat reflected in an IRS revenue ruling,[26] which is predicated on the rule that an organization that desires tax exemption as a charitable entity from the outset of its existence must file for recognition of exemption within a threshold period; if it does so, the recognition of exemption is effective as of the date the entity was formed (that is, the recognition is retroactive).[27] The point of this ruling is that an organization that qualifies for exemption both as a charitable entity and as a social welfare entity,[28] and that filed for recognition of exemption after expiration of this threshold period and thus cannot qualify as a charitable entity from its beginning, can qualify as an exempt social welfare entity during the period starting with the date of its formation and ending on the date the exempt charitable entity status commences—the underlying concept being that social welfare organizations are not required to file for recognition of exemption to be exempt. This ruling is somewhat confusing and misleading, however, in that it states that an organization in this circumstance "may" file an application for recognition of exemption as a social welfare organization during the initial period, implying to some that it *must* file an application. In fact, an organization of this nature (that is, an entity that is not a charity credit counseling/social welfare organization,

---

[22] E.g., Priv. Ltr. Rul. 202233017.

[23] The IRS's procedures state that an organization seeking recognition of tax-exempt status must file the appropriate application (Rev. Proc. 2024-5, 2024-1 I.R.B. 262 § 4.02) but are silent on the point that recognition of exemption is not always required.

[24] IRC §§ 508(a), 501(q)(3), 501(c)(29)(B)(i), 505(c), respectively. See §§ 26.2, 26.5, 26.8, 26.6, respectively.

[25] This is done, for example, to obtain government confirmation of tax-exempt status. By contrast, for an organization to be regarded as an exempt political organization, it must give notice to the IRS (IRC § 527(i); see Chapter 17 and § 26.14). Similarly, an organization wanting to operate as a tax-exempt social welfare entity (IRC § 501(c)(4); see Chapter 13) is required to notify the IRS of its intent to do so (IRC § 506), although the sanction for not so doing in this case is a penalty, not disqualification of exempt status (see § 26.13).

[26] IRS Revenue Ruling (Rev. Rul.) 80-108, 1980-1 C.B. 119.

[27] See § 26.2(a).

[28] See Chapter 13.

nonprofit health insurance issuer, or employee benefit fund) can achieve the same result without filing for recognition of social welfare organization status merely by operating as such an organization.

This dichotomy is also reflected in the application for recognition of exemption filed by organizations seeking tax exemption as charitable entities.[29] If the applicant organization is submitting the application more than 27 months after the end of the month in which it was formed,[30] it may be eligible for exemption only from the date the application was sent to the IRS.[31] Nonetheless, the IRS observes that the organization may be eligible for exemption as a social welfare organization from the date of its formation to the postmark date of the application. A box on the application is to be checked if the organization wants the IRS to regard the submission as a request for exemption as a social welfare organization during this initial period. Then the IRS requires the organization to attach page 1 of the application that is filed by social welfare organizations.[32] Once again, this is somewhat misleading, because the applicant organization could qualify as an exempt social welfare organization during the interim period without making any submission to the IRS—because social welfare organizations (like most other categories of exempt entities) do not have to file for recognition of exemption with the IRS to be exempt.

Subject only to the authority of the IRS to revoke a determination letter or ruling for good cause (a material change in the facts or a revision of law), an organization, the tax exemption of which has been recognized by the IRS, can rely on that determination as long as there are no substantial changes in the entity's character, purposes, or methods of operation.[33] Should one of these changes occur, the organization is expected to notify the IRS to accord the agency the opportunity to reevaluate the entity's exempt status.

(b)   Concept of *Recognition*

Thus, rather than *grant* tax-exempt status, the IRS's function is to *recognize* exempt status (assuming the organization so qualifies). The concept of *recognition* is based on the fact that the tax exemption exists before the IRS commences its review of the applicant organization. The IRS thereafter recognized the fact of exemption, by agreeing with the applicant that it is an exempt entity, as manifested by the issuance of a favorable determination letter.[34]

This distinction is reflected in the IRS's instructions that accompany Form 1023. It is there stated that, organizations organized and operated exclusively for religious, charitable, scientific, testing for public safety, literary, or educational purposes, or to foster national or international amateur sports competition, or

---

[29] See § 26.2(a).

[30] Form 1023 (Jan. 2020), Part VIII.

[31] Form 1023 (Jan. 2020), Schedule E, line 2.

[32] Form 1024-A.

[33] Reg. § 1.501(a)-1(a)(2).

[34] The Treasury Department and the IRS occasionally use the word *establish* as a synonym for *recognize* (e.g., Reg. § 1.501(a)-1(a)(2)). Sometimes the two words are used interchangeably in the same document (e.g., Rev. Proc. 2018-15, 2018-9 I.R.B. 379).

for the prevention of cruelty to children or animals "must file Form 1023 . . . to obtain *recognition* of exemption from federal income tax under section 501(c)(3)."[35] In explaining that certain organizations are not required to file this application to be tax-exempt (such as churches),[36] the IRS stated that "these organizations may choose to file Form 1023 . . . in order to receive a determination letter that *recognizes* their section 501(c)(3) status."[37]

This distinction is also reflected in a publication the IRS prepared on tax-exempt status. This document, the IRS stated, "explains the procedures [an applicant organization] must follow to obtain an appropriate determination letter *recognizing* [the] organization's exemption."[38] The IRS added: "To *qualify* for exemption under the Code, [the] organization must be organized for one or more of the purposes specifically designated in the Code."[39] In other words, if an organization satisfies the requirements of the federal tax law for exemption, it qualifies for exemption, but it may have to have that qualification recognized by the IRS to actually achieve exemption.

§ 3.3 RECOGNITION OF PUBLIC CHARITY, PRIVATE FOUNDATION STATUS

The IRS expanded this concept of *recognition* to include recognition of changes in public charity status;[40] although an organization is not required to obtain a determination letter[41] to qualify for a new public charity classification, in order for the IRS's records to recognize a change in public charity status[42] an organization must obtain a new determination of this status.[43] Likewise, a private foundation[44] may qualify as a private operating foundation[45] without an IRS determination letter, but the IRS will not recognize the status in its records without a determination.[46] An organization claiming to be an exempt operating foundation[47] must obtain an IRS determination letter recognizing that status to be exempt from the tax on its net investment income.[48]

---

[35] IRS Instructions for Form 1023 (Jan. 2020) 1 (emphasis added).
[36] See § 26.2(b).
[37] Instructions for Form 1023 (Jan. 2020) 2 (emphasis added).
[38] Pub. 557, *Tax-Exempt Status for Your Organization* (Jan. 2024) 3 (emphasis added).
[39] *Id.* (emphasis added).
[40] See § 12.3.
[41] See § 26.1(a).
[42] The possible changes are summarized in Rev. Proc. 2024-5, 2024-1 I.R.B. 262 § 7.
[43] *Id.* § 7.04(1). See § 28.1(c).
[44] See § 12.1(a).
[45] See § 12.1(b).
[46] Rev. Proc. 2024-5, 2024-1 I.R.B. 262 § 7.04(4). See § 28.1(c).
[47] See § 12.1(c).
[48] Rev. Proc. 2024-5, 2024-1 IRB 262 § 7.04(4). These determinations of change of status may be requested by the filing of Form 8940. *Id.* §§ 4.02(6), 7.02. See § 28.1(c).

§ 3.4   ALTERNATIVES TO TAX-EXEMPT STATUS

An organization may elect or be required to operate without formal recognition as a tax-exempt entity and yet achieve the same basic objective: the nonpayment of income tax. The legitimate alternatives to this type of exempt status are, however, few.

Alternatives to conventional tax-exempt organizations include a variety of trusts, partnerships,[49] and limited liability companies.[50] For the most part, these entities do not pay tax.

Perhaps the simplest illustration of this principle is the organization (nonprofit or not) that is operated so that its deductible expenses equal or exceed income in any tax year. In essence, this is the basis on which cooperatives function without having to pay tax.

The rules as to nonexempt cooperatives[51] apply to any "corporation operating on a cooperative basis" (with exceptions) and to certain farmers' cooperatives.[52] Basically, a qualified cooperative escapes taxation because, in computing taxable income, a deduction is available for patronage dividends and qualified and nonqualified "per-unit retain allocations."[53] Moreover, a farmers' cooperative is entitled to certain deductions for nonpatronage dividends.[54] Generally, amounts received as patronage dividends and qualified per-unit retain certificates are includable in the patrons' gross income.

An organization that loses its tax-exempt status may continue to operate without taxation by conversion to operation as a cooperative.[55] Similarly, an organization that cannot qualify as an exempt entity may choose to function as a cooperative.[56]

If a nonexempt organization that does not operate on a cooperative basis seeks to avoid taxation by matching deductions and income, federal tax law may foil the scheme if the organization is a social club or other membership organization operated to furnish goods or services to its members.[57] In this situation, the expenses of furnishing services, goods, or other items of value (such as insurance) to members are deductible only to the extent of income from members (including income from institutes or trade shows primarily for members' education). This means that any expenses attributable to membership activities in excess of membership income may not be deducted against membership income (although the increment may be carried forward). Prior to the enactment of these rules, the courts had upheld contrary treatment.[58]

---

[49] See § 31.1.

[50] See §§ 4.1(b), 4.3(e), 32.3–32.4.

[51] IRC §§ 1381–1383.

[52] See § 19.12.

[53] IRC §§ 1382(b), 1388.

[54] IRC § 1382(c).

[55] E.g., A. Duda & Sons Coop. Ass'n v. United States, 495 F.2d 193 (5th Cir. 1974), *superseded by* 504 F.2d 970 (5th Cir. 1975).

[56] E.g., Rev. Rul. 69-633, 1969-2 C.B. 121.

[57] IRC § 277.

[58] E.g., Anaheim Union Water Co. v. Comm'r, 321 F.2d 253 (9th Cir. 1963). Applications of IRC § 277 are the subject of Texas Med. Ass'n Ins. Trust v. United States, 391 F. Supp. 2d 529 (W.D. Tex. 2005); Boating Trade Ass'n of Metro. Houston v. United States, 75-1 U.S.T.C. ¶ 9398 (S.D. Tex. 1975).

A line of law permits nontaxability of an organization where it is merely a *conduit* for the expenditure of a fund established for a specific purpose. Thus, a soft drink manufacturer that received funds from bottlers for a national advertising fund was held to not be taxable on these funds, inasmuch as they were earmarked for advertising purposes; the manufacturer was considered merely an administrator of a trust fund.[59] Initially, the IRS took the position that this precept would be followed only where the recipient of the funds received them with the obligation to expend them solely for a particular purpose.[60] This position was superseded, however, by a ruling that taxes to the recipient organization the amounts received and that permits related deductions, subject to the previously discussed expense allocation rules.[61] Also, the IRS distinguished the previously described factual setting involving a soft drink manufacturer from one in which the participants (dealers, bottlers, and the like) formed an unincorporated organization to conduct a national advertising program; the IRS ruled that the organization is separately taxable as a corporation.[62]

If tax-exempt status is unavailable, lost, or not desired, and if deductions do not or cannot equal income, and if cooperative status is either unavailable or unwanted, and if the organization is not formally incorporated, perhaps the entity can escape taxation by contending it is nonexistent for tax purposes. This is generally nonviable, however, in view of the authority of the IRS to treat an unincorporated entity as a taxable corporation.[63]

Thus, to be exempt from federal income taxation, an organization generally must formally qualify as a tax-exempt organization (by means of recognition or otherwise), operate as a cooperative, legally marshal deductions against income, or seek a change in the law. Otherwise, it is nearly certain that the entity will be liable for tax as a taxable corporation, even if it is organized as a nonprofit organization. That is, it is possible that an entity will be a taxable nonprofit organization.[64]

---

[59] The Seven-Up Co. v. Comm'r, 14 T.C. 965 (1950). Also, Rev. Rul. 69-96, 1969-1 C.B. 32; Ford Dealers Advertising Fund, Inc. v. Comm'r, 55 T.C. 761 (1971), *aff'd*, 456 F.2d 255 (5th Cir. 1972); Park Place, Inc. v. Comm'r, 57 T.C. 767 (1972); Greater Pittsburgh Chrysler Dealers Ass'n of W. Pa. v. United States, 77-1 U.S.T.C. ¶ 9293 (W.D. Pa. 1977); Insty-Prints, Inc. Nat'l Advertising Fund Trust v. Comm'r, 44 T.C.M. 556 (1982); Broadcast Measurement Bur., Inc. v. Comm'r, 16 T.C. 988 (1951).

[60] Rev. Rul. 58-209, 1958-1 C.B. 19.

[61] Rev. Rul. 74-318, 1974-2 C.B. 14.

[62] Rev. Rul. 74-319, 1974-2 C.B. 15. Also, Michigan Retailers Ass'n v. United States, 676 F. Supp. 151 (W.D. Mich. 1988); Dri-Power Distribrs. Ass'n Trust v. Comm'r, 54 T.C. 460 (1970); New York State Ass'n Real Est. Bd. Group Ins. Fund v. Comm'r, 54 T.C. 1325 (1970); Angelus Funeral Home v. Comm'r, 47 T.C. 391 (1967), *aff'd*, 407 F.2d 210 (9th Cir. 1969), *cert. denied*, 396 U.S. 824 (1969).

[63] E.g., Rev. Rul. 75-258, 1972-2 C.B. 503 (where the IRS ruled that the "Family Estate" trust is an association taxable as a corporation under IRC § 7701) and Rev. Rul. 77-214, 1977-1 C.B. 408 (where the IRS determined that a type of German unincorporated business organization—the "Gesellschaft mit beschränkter Haftung" or "GmbH"—was taxable as a corporation). Also, a court concluded that real estate syndicates organized under the California limited partnership act are associations taxable as corporations with the meaning of IRC § 7701(a)(3) (Larson v. Comm'r, 65 T.C. 10 (1975) (withdrawn), 66 T.C. 159 (1976)). In general, Morrissey v. Comm'r, 296 U.S. 344 (1935); Reg. § 301.7701-1(a).

[64] See § 1.1.

Organizational, Operational, and Related Tests and Doctrines

The federal tax law mandates adherence to certain general organizational and operational requirements as a condition of tax exemption. These requirements are the most pronounced with respect to charitable organizations.[1]

---

[1] That is, organizations described in IRC § 501(c)(3) and tax-exempt by reason of IRC § 501(a).

§ 4.1 FORMS OF TAX-EXEMPT ORGANIZATIONS

Generally, the Internal Revenue Code does not prescribe a specific organizational form for entities to qualify for tax exemption.

(a) General Rules

Basically, a tax-exempt organization will be a nonprofit corporation, trust (*inter vivos* or testamentary), or unincorporated association.[2] Exempt charitable and social welfare organizations may be formed as limited liability companies,[3] although the IRS has suggested that this form of entity may be inappropriate for exempt social clubs.[4] Some provisions of the Code, however, mandate, in whole or in part, the corporate form,[5] and other Code provisions (particularly in the employee plan context) mandate the trust form for exempt organizations.[6] Throughout the categories of exempt organizations are additional terms such as *clubs, associations, societies, foundations, leagues, companies, boards, orders, posts,* and *units,* which are not terms referencing legal forms. For tax purposes, an organization may be deemed a corporation even though it is not formally incorporated.[7]

The federal tax provision that describes charitable organizations provides that an organization described in that provision must be a corporation, community chest, fund, or foundation; only the first of these terms has any efficacy in law. An unincorporated association or trust can qualify under this provision, presumably as a fund or foundation or perhaps, as noted, as a corporation.[8] A partnership cannot, however, be tax-exempt as a charitable organization.[9]

---

[2] In the context of religious organizations (see Chapter 10), state law may recognize the *corporation sole,* which is an entity "composed of a series of natural persons who, one after another, hold the office of the religious leader of the particular religious organization" (In re Catholic Bishop of Spokane, 329 B.R. 304 (U.S. Bankr. Ct. E.D. Wash. 2005), *rev'd, in part on other grounds,* 364 B.R. 81 (E.D. Wash. 2006)). Also in this context, entities can be established in dubious forms, such as *ministerial trusts* (e.g., United States v. Hovind, 2009-1 U.S.T.C. ¶ 50,143 (11th Cir. 2008)), which can be or edge close to being fraudulent tax schemes (e.g., United States v. Stoll, 2005 WL 1763617 (W.D. Wash. June 27, 2005)) or *personal ministries* (see § 10.2(c)).

[3] See § 4.3(e).

[4] Priv. Ltr. Rul. 200450041.

[5] IRC §§ 501(c)(1), 501(c)(2), 501(c)(3), 501(c)(14), 501(c)(16). Thus, for example, in determining that an organization did not qualify for tax exemption by reason of IRC § 501(c)(16), one reason given by the IRS was that the state involved had suspended the organization's corporate status (Priv. Ltr. Rul. 201333014).

[6] IRC §§ 501(c)(17), 501(c)(18), 501(c)(19), 501(c)(20), 401(a).

[7] IRC § 7701(a)(3). See § 4.1(b). The IRS ruled that a tax-exempt organization that had its corporate status irrevocably terminated by a state because of failure to file state annual reports, yet continued to operate, was deemed to have elected to be classified as an association taxable as a corporation pursuant to the check-the-box rules (Priv. Ltr. Rul. 200607027).

[8] Fifth-Third Union Trust Co. v. Comm'r, 56 F.2d 767 (6th Cir. 1932).

[9] Emerson Inst. v. United States, 356 F.2d 824 (D.C. Cir. 1966), *cert. denied,* 385 U.S. 822 (1966). In one opinion, a court, in deciding that an organization could not qualify for tax-exempt status because of its role as a general partner in a limited partnership (see § 31.2), placed emphasis on the fact that the partnerships involved "are admittedly for-profit entities" and that none of these partnerships is "intended to be nonprofit" (Housing Pioneers, Inc. v. Comm'r, 65 T.C.M. 2191, 2195 (1993)); however, the law does not provide for an entity such as a nonprofit partnership.

§ 4.1 FORMS OF TAX-EXEMPT ORGANIZATIONS

An organization already exempt from federal taxation may establish a separate fund or like entity that is itself an exempt organization.[10] The attributes of this type of fund include a separate category of exemption (e.g., an educational research and scholarship fund established by a bar association),[11] a separate governing body, and separate books and accounts.[12] A mere bank deposit cannot, however, amount to a requisite fund.[13]

For purposes of the rules concerning charitable organizations, an organization tax-exempt by reason of those rules may be a unit of government[14] or a foreign organization,[15] or may conduct all or part of its activities in foreign countries.[16]

The formalities of organization of an entity may have a bearing on the tax exemption. This is the case not only in connection with the sufficiency of the governing instruments,[17] but also, and more fundamentally, with regard to whether there is a separate organization in the first instance. An individual may perform worthwhile activities, such as providing financial assistance to needy students, but will receive no tax benefits from their beneficence unless they establish and fund a qualified organization that in turn renders the charitable works, such as scholarship grants. One court observed, in the process of denying a charitable contribution deduction, that the federal tax law makes no provision for a charitable deduction in the context of personal ventures, however praiseworthy in character. The court noted that "[t]here is no evidence of such enterprise being a corporation, community chest, fund, or foundation and little information, if any, as to its organization or activities."[18] Assuming the organization is not operated to benefit private interests, its tax exemption will not be endangered because its creator serves as the sole trustee and exercises complete control,[19] although state law may limit or preclude close control.

A formless aggregation of individuals cannot be tax-exempt as a charitable entity. At a minimum, the entity—to be exempt—must have an organizing instrument, some governing rules, and regularly chosen officers.[20] These rules have been amply illustrated in the cases concerning so-called personal churches.[21]

---

[10] See Chapter 29.

[11] American Bar Ass'n v. United States, 84-1 U.S.T.C. ¶ 9179 (N.D. Ill. 1984); Rev. Rul. 58-293, 1958-1 C.B. 146.

[12] Rev. Rul. 54-243, 1954-1 C.B. 92.

[13] E.g., Pusch v. Comm'r, 39 T.C.M. 838 (1980).

[14] Rev. Rul. 60-384, 1960-2 C.B. 172.

[15] Rev. Rul. 66-177, 1966-1 C.B. 132.

[16] Rev. Rul. 71-460, 1971-2 C.B. 231.

[17] Cone v. McGinnes, 63-2 U.S.T.C. ¶ 9551 (E.D. Pa. 1963). See § 4.2.

[18] Hewitt v. Comm'r, 16 T.C.M. 468, 471 (1957). Also, Doty, Jr. v. Comm'r, 6 T.C. 587 (1974); Walker v. Comm'r, 37 T.C.M. 1851 (1978).

[19] Rev. Rul. 66-219, 1966-2 C.B. 208.

[20] E.g., George v. Comm'r, 110 T.C.M. 190 (2015); Kessler v. Comm'r, 87 T.C. 1285 (1986); Trippe v. Comm'r, 9 T.C.M. 622 (1950). Cf. Morey v. Riddell, 205 F. Supp. 918 (S.D. Cal. 1962). A claim that it is unconstitutional not to permit individuals to be tax-exempt was dismissed (Fields v. United States, Civ. No. 96-317 (D.D.C. 1998)). An example, however, of a nonentity qualifying as a tax-exempt organization (a custodial individual retirement account) is in Lakeview Devel. Corp. v. UBS Fin. Servs., Inc., 614 B.R. 603 (Bank. Ct. for D. Col. 2020).

[21] E.g., United States v. Jeffries, 88-2 U.S.T.C. ¶ 9459 (7th Cir. 1988). In general, see § 10.2(c).

Among the nontax factors to be considered in selecting an organizational form are legal liabilities in relation to the individuals involved (the corporate form can limit certain personal liabilities), local law requirements, necessities of governing instruments, local annual reporting requirements, organizational expenses, and any membership requirements.[22] Federal law other than the tax laws may also have a bearing on the choice, such as the organization's comparable status under the postal laws.[23]

(b) Check-the-Box Regulations

In general, the classification of an entity as a particular type of organization can have significant federal tax consequences. Although this is an issue principally for for-profit entities, there are some ramifications in this area for tax-exempt organizations.

(i) Basic Rules. Under rules known as the *check-the-box* regulations,[24] an organization is either a trust[25] or a *business entity*.[26] A business entity with two or more members is classified for federal tax purposes as a corporation or a partnership. A business entity with only one owner either is classified as a corporation or is disregarded. When an entity is disregarded, its activities are treated as those of the owner, in the manner of a sole proprietorship.[27] A *corporation* includes a business entity organized under a federal or state statute, an *association*, or a business entity owned by a state or political subdivision of a state.[28]

A business entity that is not classified as a corporation is an *eligible entity*. An eligible entity with at least two members can elect to be classified as either an association (and thus a corporation)[29] or a partnership. An eligible entity with a single

---

[22] A separate form (even the corporate form), however, is not always respected. For example, courts can find charitable organizations to be the "alter ego" of their founders or others in close control and operating proximity, so that IRS levies against the organizations for their income and assets to satisfy the individuals' tax obligations are upheld (e.g., Towe Antique Ford Found. v. Internal Revenue Serv., 999 F.2d 1387 (9th Cir. 1993); United States v. Kitsos, 770 F. Supp. 1230 (N.D. Ill. 1991), aff'd, 968 F.2d 1219 (7th Cir. 1992); Zahra Spiritual Trust v. United States, 910 F.2d 240 (5th Cir. 1990); Loving Savior Church v. United States, 556 F. Supp. 688 (D.S.D. 1983), aff'd, 728 F.2d 1085 (8th Cir. 1984); United States v. Hovind, 2009 WL 2369340 (N.D. Fl., July 29, 2009); Faith Missionary Baptist Church v. Internal Revenue Serv., 174 B.R. 454 (U.S. Bankr. Ct. E.D. Tex. 1994); Church of Hakeem v. United States, 79-2 U.S.T.C. ¶ 9651 (N.D. Cal. 1979)).

[23] 39 C.F.R. Part 132 (second class), Part 134 (third class).

[24] This name is derived from the simple way in which entity classification is made: by checking the appropriate box on Form 8832 (Reg. § 301.7701-3(c)(1)). A federal district court held that these regulations are lawful as a valid exercise of a government agency's rulemaking authority (Littriello v. United States, 2005-1 U.S.T.C. ¶ 50,385 (W.D. Ky. 2005), aff'd, 484 F.3d 372 (6th Cir. 2007), cert. denied, 552 U.S. 1186 (2008)).

[25] A *trust* essentially is a nonbusiness entity; it is an arrangement created by a will or lifetime instrument by which trustees take title to property for the purpose of protecting or conserving it for designated beneficiaries (Reg. § 301.7701-4(a)).

[26] Reg. § 301.7701-2(a).

[27] Id. Also, Reg. § 301.7701-2(c).

[28] Reg. § 301.7701-2(b). An organization wholly owned by a state is not recognized as a separate entity for these purposes if it is an integral part of a state (Reg. § 301.7701-1(a)(3)). See § 19.22(c).

[29] Reg. § 301.7701-2(b)(2).

owner can elect to be classified as an association or to be disregarded as an entity separate from its owner.[30] If there is no election, an eligible entity with two or more members is a partnership, and an eligible entity with a single member is disregarded as an entity separate from its owner.[31] Thus, an eligible entity is required to act affirmatively only when it desires classification as a corporation.

(ii) Exempt Organization Rules.   There is a *deemed election* in the tax-exempt organization's context. That is, an eligible entity that has been determined to be, or claims to be, exempt from federal income taxation[32] is treated as having made the election to be classified as an association.[33] As noted, this in turn causes the exempt entity to be regarded as a corporation.[34]

Some organizations are tax-exempt because of a relationship to a state or a political subdivision of a state.[35] When a state or political subdivision conducts an enterprise through a separate entity, the entity may be exempt from federal income tax,[36] or its income may be excluded from federal income tax.[37] Generally, if income is earned by an enterprise that is an integral part of a state or political subdivision of a state, that income is not taxable. In determining whether an enterprise is an integral part of a state, it is necessary to consider all the facts and circumstances, including the state's degree of control over the enterprise and the state's financial commitment to the enterprise.

These distinctions are reflected in the check-the-box regulations. A business entity can be recognized as a distinct entity when it is wholly owned by a state or a political subdivision of a state; it then is classified as a corporation.[38] Yet an entity formed under local law is not always recognized as a separate entity for federal tax purposes. The regulations specify that an "organization" wholly owned by a state is not recognized as a separate entity for federal tax purposes if it is an "integral part of the State."[39]

Another instance of an interrelationship between the law of tax-exempt organizations and the check-the-box regulations is the matter of formation by exempt charitable organizations of single-member limited liability companies (LLCs) for various purposes. Under a default rule,[40] these LLCs are disregarded for federal income tax purposes; these entities are known as *disregarded LLCs*.[41]

---

[30] Reg. § 301.7701-3(a).

[31] Reg. § 301.7701-3(b)(1).

[32] That is, exempt from tax by reason of IRC § 501(a).

[33] Reg. § 301.7701-3(c)(1)(v)(A).

[34] See text accompanied by *supra* note 30.

[35] See, e.g., §§ 7.15, 19.22.

[36] That is, exempt from tax by reason of IRC § 501(a).

[37] IRC § 115. See § 19.22(b).

[38] Reg. § 301.7701-2(b)(6).

[39] Reg. § 301.7701-1(a)(3).

[40] See text accompanied by *supra* note 31.

[41] In one illustration of the use of disregarded LLCs by charitable organizations, the IRS ruled that a charitable organization may transfer parcels of contributed real property to separate LLCs—for the purpose of sheltering other properties from legal liability that may be caused by the gifted property—yet report the gift properties on its annual information return as if it owned them directly (Priv. Ltr. Rul. 200134025). See § 32.4.

The IRS contemplated whether a single-member LLC can qualify for tax-exempt status.[42] In the case of an LLC owned wholly by a charitable organization, the issue was whether the LLC, like its owner,[43] is obligated to file an application for recognition of tax-exempt status. The IRS decided that a disregarded LLC is regarded as a branch or division of its member owner.[44] Thus, separate recognition of tax exemption for these LLCs is not required (or available).[45] The IRS subsequently addressed the matter of the tax-exempt status of LLCs that have more than one tax-exempt member.[46]

§ 4.2 GOVERNING INSTRUMENTS

An organization must have governing instruments to qualify for tax exemption, if only to satisfy the appropriate organizational test. This is particularly the case for charitable organizations, for which the federal tax law imposes specific organizational requirements.[47] These rules are more stringent if the charitable organization is a private foundation[48] or a supporting organization.[49]

If the corporate form is used, the governing instruments will be articles of incorporation and bylaws.[50] An unincorporated organization will have articles of organization, perhaps in the form of a constitution, and, undoubtedly, also bylaws. If a trust, the basic document will be a declaration of trust or trust agreement. If an LLC, the organizing document will be an operating agreement.

The articles of organization should contain provisions stating the organization's purposes; whether there will be members and, if so, their qualifications and classes; the initial board of directors or trustee(s); the registered agent and incorporators (if a corporation); the dissolution or liquidation procedure; and the required language referencing the appropriate tax law (federal and state) requirements and prohibitions. If the organization is a corporation, particular attention should be given to the appropriate state nonprofit corporation statute, which will contain requirements that may supersede the provisions of the articles of incorporation and bylaws or may apply where the governing instruments are silent.

---

[42] An LLC is not taxable; that is, it is treated, for federal income tax purposes, as a partnership (IRC § 701). The issue, however, is whether an LLC can qualify for tax-exempt status under IRC § 501.

[43] See § 26.2.

[44] IRS Announcement (Ann.) 99-102, 1999-43 I.R.B. 545. Accordingly, a contribution to a disregarded LLC of a U.S. charitable organization is treated as being to a branch or a division of the charity and therefore is deductible if it otherwise meets the applicable charitable contribution deduction requirements in I.R.C. § 170 (Notice 2012-52, 2012-35 I.R.B. 317). Similarly, the IRS stated that a private foundation may make a grant for charitable purposes to a disregarded LLC of an unrelated public charity and treat the transfer as a qualifying distribution, without the need to exercise expenditure responsibility (see § 12.4(b), (e)) (INFO 2010-0052).

[45] E.g., Priv. Ltr. Rul. 200134025. Caution must be exercised in this context because of state law. Some states do not recognize the concept of the disregarded LLC. There can be issues as to the availability of income, sales, use, and/or property taxation where an LLC is involved.

[46] See § 4.3(e).

[47] See § 4.3.

[48] IRC § 508(e). See § 12.1(g).

[49] See § 12.3(c).

[50] Reg. § 1.501(c)(3)-1(b)(2).

The bylaws may also contain the provisions of the articles of organization and, in addition, should contain provisions amplifying or stating the purposes of the organization, the terms and conditions of membership (if any), the manner of selection and duties of the directors or trustees and the officers, the voting requirements, the procedure for forming committees, the accounting period, any indemnification provisions, the appropriate tax provisions, and the procedure for amendment of the bylaws.

§ 4.3 ORGANIZATIONAL TEST

An organization, to be tax-exempt as a charitable entity, must be both organized and operated exclusively for one or more of the permissible exempt purposes. This requirement has given rise to an *organizational test* and an *operational test*[51] for charitable organizations. If an organization fails to meet either the organizational test or the operational test, it cannot qualify for exemption from federal income taxation as a charitable entity.[52] The federal tax regulations barely provide for an organizational test for other categories of exempt organizations. Yet this test is inherent in each category of exemption. For example, the IRS referenced an organizational test for exempt social clubs.[53]

An organization is organized exclusively for one or more tax-exempt, charitable purposes only if its articles of organization limit its purposes to one or more exempt purposes[54] and do not expressly empower it to engage, other than as an insubstantial part of its activities, in activities that in themselves are not in furtherance of one or more exempt purposes.[55]

Some states' nonprofit corporation acts differentiate between public benefit corporations and mutual benefit corporations. An organization that is seeking recognition of exemption as a charitable entity[56] must, as to one of these jurisdictions, be structured as a public benefit corporation.[57] This is also the case for social welfare organizations.[58]

The fact that an organization's organizational documents are not properly executed can be viewed by the IRS as a violation of the organizational test.[59]

(a) Statement of Purposes

In meeting the organizational test, a charitable organization's purposes, as stated in its articles of organization, may be as broad as, or more specific than, the particular exempt purposes, such as religious, charitable, or educational ends. Therefore, an organization that, by the terms of its articles of organization, is formed

---

[51] See § 4.5.

[52] Reg. § 1.501(c)(3)-1(a); Levy Family Tribe Found. v. Comm'r, 69 T.C. 615, 618 (1978).

[53] Priv. Ltr. Rul. 200450041. See Chapter 15.

[54] See Reg. § 1.501(c)(3)-1(d).

[55] Reg. § 1.501(c)(3)-1(b)(1)(i).

[56] That is, an entity described in IRC § 501(c)(3). See Part Three.

[57] E.g., Priv. Ltr. Rul. 202114023.

[58] E.g., Priv. Ltr. Rul. 202226014. See Chapter 13.

[59] E.g., Priv. Ltr. Rul. 200508019.

for "literary and scientific purposes within the meaning of section 501(c)(3) of the Internal Revenue Code" shall, if it otherwise meets the requirements of the organizational test, be considered to have met the test. Similarly, articles of organization stating that the organization is created solely to "receive contributions and pay them over to organizations which are described in section 501(c)(3) and exempt from taxation under section 501(a) of the Internal Revenue Code" are sufficient for purposes of the organizational test. If the articles of organization state that the organization is formed for "charitable purposes," the articles ordinarily will be adequate for purposes of the organizational test.[60]

Articles of organization of charitable entities may not authorize the carrying on of nonexempt activities (unless they are insubstantial), even though the organization is, by the terms of its articles, created for a purpose that is no broader than the specified charitable purposes.[61] Thus, an organization that is empowered by its articles to "engage in a manufacturing business" or to "engage in the operation of a social club" does not meet the organizational test, regardless of the fact that its articles of organization may state that the organization is created for "charitable purposes within the meaning of section 501(c)(3) of the Internal Revenue Code."[62]

An organization will not be organized exclusively for one or more tax-exempt charitable purposes if, by the terms of its articles of organization, the purposes for which the organization is created are broader than the specified charitable purposes. The fact that the actual operations of the organization have been exclusively in furtherance of one or more exempt purposes is not sufficient to permit the organization to meet the organizational test. An organization wishing to qualify as a charitable entity should not provide in its articles of organization that it has all of the powers accorded under the particular state's nonprofit corporation act, since those powers are likely to be broader than those allowable under federal tax law.[63] Similarly, an organization will not meet the organizational test as a result of statements or other evidence that its members intend to operate only in furtherance of one or more exempt purposes.[64]

An organization is not considered organized exclusively for one or more exempt charitable purposes if its articles of organization expressly authorize it to (1) devote more than an insubstantial part of its activities to attempting to influence legislation by propaganda or otherwise;[65] (2) directly or indirectly participate in, or intervene in (including the publishing or distributing of statements), any political campaign on behalf of or in opposition to any candidate for public office;[66] or (3) have objectives and engage in activities that characterize it as an

---

[60] Reg. § 1.501(c)(3)-1(b)(1)(ii).

[61] Rev. Rul. 69-279, 1969-1 C.B. 152; Rev. Rul. 69-256, 1969-1 C.B. 151.

[62] Reg. § 1.501(c)(3)-1(b)(iii). Also, Interneighborhood Housing Corp. v. Comm'r, 45 T.C.M. 115 (1982); Santa Cruz Bldg. Ass'n v. United States, 411 F. Supp. 871 (E.D. Mo. 1976).

[63] E.g., IRS General Counsel Memorandum (Gen. Couns. Mem.) 39633.

[64] Reg. § 1.501(c)(3)-1(b)(1)(iv).

[65] An organization organized and operated to reform, repeal, and decriminalize laws meant to protect children from sexual abuse and sexual predators failed to achieve tax-exempt status as a charitable entity in part because its articles of incorporation mandated substantial legislative activity (Mysteryboy Incorporation v. Comm'r, 99 T.C.M. 1057 (2010)). See Chapter 22.

[66] See Chapter 23.

action organization.[67] The organizational test is not violated, however, where an organization's articles empower it to make the expenditure test election (relating to expenditures for legislative activities)[68] and, only if it so elects, to make direct lobbying or grassroots lobbying expenditures that are not in excess of the ceiling amounts prescribed by that test.[69] The organizational test, however, does not require that references be made in the organizational document to the prohibitions on private inurement, substantial private benefit, substantial lobbying, and political campaign activities.

The organizational test requires that the articles of organization limit the purposes of the entity to one or more exempt purposes. Exempt purposes are described in the statute,[70] and include purposes such as charitable, educational, religious, and scientific. These purposes are also enumerated in the tax regulations in explication of the term *charitable*,[71] and include purposes such as advancement of religion, lessening the burdens of government, and promotion of social welfare. There is no requirement in the law that the statement of purposes, when exempt purposes are referenced, expressly refer to IRC § 501(c)(3).

There are many other permissible functions of a charitable organization that are not formally recognized as exempt purposes in the Code or the regulations that nonetheless have been recognized as exempt functions (generically) in IRS revenue rulings and court decisions (and thus satisfy the operational test).[72] Purposes of this nature include promotion of health, promotion of the arts, operation of a school, and protection of the environment. Inasmuch as functions of this nature are not exempt functions (as technically defined), they cannot stand alone in a statement of purposes. That is, for the organizational test to be satisfied, one of two statements must be in the articles of organization: (1) If the document contains a purpose that is not an exempt purpose, it should expressly limit the organization's purposes to those described in IRC § 501(c)(3), or (2) if the document contains a purpose that is not an exempt purpose, but that purpose is not expressly contrary to exempt purposes, the document should include a "notwithstanding" clause to appropriately limit the organization's purposes.[73]

An overly broad statement of purposes cannot be cured by a provision stating that the organization's activities will be confined to those described in IRC § 501(c)(3). Again, this is because activities are considered in connection with the operational test, while the organizational test is concerned with purposes. Also, despite the rules of law governing charitable entities, there is nothing in the organizational test that requires reference to the private inurement doctrine,[74] limitation

---

[67] Reg. § 1.501(c)(3)-1(b)(3). See § 4.5(d).

[68] See § 22.3(d)(vi).

[69] Reg. § 1.501(c)(3)-1(b)(3).

[70] IRC § 501(c)(3).

[71] Reg. § 1.501(c)(3)-1(d)(2). See Chapter 7.

[72] See § 4.5.

[73] This provision may read as follows: "Notwithstanding other language (or provisions) in the creating document, the purposes will be limited exclusively to exempt purposes within the meaning of IRC [§] 501(c)(3)" ("Organizational Test—IRC 501(c)(3)," Topic D, IRS Exempt Organizations Continuing Professional Education Text for FY 2004).

[74] See Chapter 20.

on attempts to influence legislation,[75] or the prohibition on political campaign activities in the articles of organization.[76]

It is the view of one court, however, that the organizational test entails a "purely . . . factual inquiry" and that it is not required to "myopically consider *only*" articles of incorporation or another creating document; in the case, an organization was found to qualify as a charitable organization meeting the organizational test because of suitable language in its bylaws.[77]

The law of the state in which an organization is created is controlling in construing the terms of its articles of organization.[78] An organization that contends that the terms have, under state law, a different meaning from their generally accepted meaning must establish the special meaning by clear and convincing reference to relevant court decisions, opinions of the state attorney general, or other evidence of applicable state law.[79]

An organization that would be classified as a private foundation[80] if it were recognized as a charitable entity does not satisfy the organizational test by virtue of having complied with the special governing instrument provisions applicable only to private foundations.[81] In so ruling, the IRS considered a case where an organization's articles of incorporation lacked the requisite provision requiring the distribution of its assets for charitable purposes on dissolution. The state law under which the organization operates had not been construed to assure dedication of assets to charitable purposes,[82] although the state had a statute that mandates reference to the various private foundation rules in the foundation's articles of incorporation on all private foundations formed in the state.[83] The IRS reasoned that a private foundation is a charitable organization, yet an organization cannot be so classified where its governing instrument fails to include a dissolution clause, and the special governing instrument provisions apply only to private foundations. Also, the IRS reviewed the legislative history of the private foundation rules, which makes it clear that these rules comprise requirements that are in addition to the general tax exemption requirements.[84]

(b) Dissolution Requirements

An organization is not organized exclusively for one or more tax-exempt charitable purposes unless its assets are dedicated to an exempt purpose.[85] An organization's assets will be considered dedicated to an exempt purpose, for example, if, on dissolution, the assets would, by reason of a provision in the organization's

---

[75] See Chapter 22.

[76] See Chapter 23.

[77] Colorado State Chiropractic Soc'y v. Comm'r, 93 T.C. 487, 495 (1989).

[78] Estate of Sharf v. Comm'r, 38 T.C. 15 (1962), *aff'd*, 316 F.2d 625 (7th Cir. 1963); Holden Hosp. Corp. v. Southern Ill. Hosp. Corp., 174 N.E. 2d 793 (Ill. 1961).

[79] Reg. § 1.501(c)(3)-1(b)(5).

[80] See § 12.1(a).

[81] IRC § 508(e). See § 12.1(g).

[82] See text accompanied by *supra* note 78.

[83] See *Private Foundations* § 1.7.

[84] Rev. Rul. 85-160, 1985-2 C.B. 162.

[85] Reg. § 1.501(c)(3)-1(b)(4).

articles of organization or by operation of law, be distributed for one or more exempt purposes, or to the federal government, or to a state or local government, for a public purpose or would be distributed by a court to another organization to be used in a manner that in the judgment of the court will best accomplish the general purposes for which the dissolved organization was organized.[86] For these purposes, "articles of organization" include the trust instrument, the corporate charter, the articles of association, or any other written instrument by which an organization is created.[87]

A charitable organization does not meet the organizational test if its articles of organization or the law of the state in which it was created provide that its assets would, on dissolution, be distributed to its members or shareholders.[88] Consequently, exemption as a charitable organization will be denied where, on dissolution of the organization, its assets would revert to the individual founders rather than to one or more qualifying charities.[89] Organizations that are organized for both tax-exempt and nonexempt purposes fail to satisfy the organizational test.[90]

The IRS is of the view that a dissolution provision is defective if it would transfer the dissolving organization's assets to a specified charitable organization without a contingency clause should the transferee no longer exist, refuse to accept the transfer, or is no longer organized and operated for one or more exempt purposes at the time of the transfer.[91] Likewise, the IRS will likely revoke a charitable organization's exemption for removal of a dissolution clause, with the revocation retroactive to the date the clause was deleted.[92]

A charitable organization's assets may, on dissolution, be transferred for charitable purposes without necessarily being transferred to a charitable organization, provided the distributed assets are held in trust for such charitable purposes.[93] The dedication-of-assets requirement contemplates that, notwithstanding the dissolution of a charitable entity, the assets will continue to be devoted to a charitable purpose (albeit a substituted one). Under the *cy pres* rule, a state court, in the exercise of its equity power, may modify the purpose of a charitable trust or place the funds of a charitable corporation in a new entity.[94]

As noted, to satisfy the dissolution requirement, a charitable organization either must include an express dissolution clause in its articles of organization or

---

[86] *Id.*

[87] Treas. Reg. § 1.501(c)(3)-1(b)(2).

[88] Reg. § 1.501(c)(3)-1(b)(4). E.g., Chief Steward of the Ecumenical Temples & Worldwide Peace Movement & His Successors v. Comm'r, 49 T.C.M. 640 (1985). Cf. Bethel Conservative Mennonite Church v. Comm'r, 746 F.2d 388 (7th Cir. 1984).

[89] Church of Nature in Man v. Comm'r, 49 T.C.M. 1393 (1985); Stephenson v. Comm'r, 79 T.C. 995 (1982); Truth Tabernacle v. Comm'r, 41 T.C.M. 1405 (1981); Calvin K. of Oakknoll v. Comm'r, 69 T.C. 770 (1978), *aff'd*, 603 F.2d 211 (2d Cir. 1979); General Conference of the Free Church of Am. v. Comm'r, 71 T.C. 920 (1979).

[90] Rev. Rul. 69-256, 1969-1 C.B. 151.

[91] Program Manager Tech. Adv. Mem. 2024-02.

[92] E.g., Priv. Ltr. Rul. 200842047.

[93] Gen. Couns. Mem. 37126, *clarifying* Gen. Couns. Mem. 33207. In one instance, the absence of a dissolution clause was held not to be fatal to IRC § 501(c)(3) status for an organization that expected itself to be of "eternal life" (Universal Church of Scientific Truth, Inc. v. United States, 74-1 U.S.T.C. ¶ 9360 (N.D. Ala. 1973)).

[94] E.g., Davis v. United States, 201 F. Supp. 92 (S.D. Ohio 1961).

must be created in a state the laws of which satisfy the dissolution requirement. Prior IRS guidance that identified states and circumstances where an express dissolution clause for charitable organizations is not required has been obsoleted.[95] Consequently, a charitable organization is responsible for verifying whether the federal dissolution requirements are satisfied by state law if its articles of organization do not contain an appropriate dissolution clause.[96]

Most other categories of tax-exempt organizations are not subject to federal tax law dissolution requirements. Consequently, there is almost no law on the subject outside the charitable context. In one instance, however, an organization was denied recognition of exemption as a social welfare entity because it was not promoting the common good and general welfare of a community,[97] with the IRS citing the organization's dissolution clause, which left its assets to its members, as "further illustrat[ing]" that it was not serving a "wider community."[98] In another instance, the IRS approved dissolution of an exempt labor organization[99] by transfer of all or substantially all of its assets to another exempt labor organization having similar purposes, noting that relevant state laws were complied with, permission of a state attorney general was not required, and no compensation was paid to any director or officer of either organization in connection with the dissolution.[100] The dissolution rule in the exempt voluntary employees' beneficiary association[101] setting provides that prohibited inurement does not occur if amounts distributed to members are determined on the basis of objective and reasonable standards that do not result in unequal payments to officers, shareholders, or highly compensated employees.[102] The IRS applied this rule in connection with dissolution of an exempt teachers' retirement fund[103] where the fund's plan of dissolution, involving transfers to its members, appeared to be in accordance with the "plain and ordinary" meaning of the teachers' retirement fund rules and the VEBA regulation, so that private inurement did not occur in connection with the distribution, and the exemption of the fund would not be imperiled.[104]

---

[95] Rev. Proc. 82-2, 1982-1 C.B. 367, *obsoleted by* Rev. Proc. 2024-22, 2024-22 I.R.B. 1332. Many state laws identified in the prior guidance have materially changed since 1982, and a revenue procedure cannot be relied upon to the extent it is predicated on state law and that state law has materially changed (*id.*; Rev. Proc. 89-14, 1989-1 C.B. 814). The IRS has, however, provided nonbinding, internal guidance identifying states with laws that operate to ensure the dedication of assets to exempt purposes, with the caveat that subsequent changes to state law may affect the accuracy of this information (Program Manager Tech. Adv. Mem. 2024-02).

[96] Rev. Proc. 2024-22, 2024-22 I.R.B. 1332 § 2.08. The IRS will accept the following phraseology of a dissolution clause: "Upon the dissolution of [this organization], assets shall be distributed for one or more exempt purposes within the meaning of section 501(c)(3) of the Internal Revenue Code, or corresponding section of any future federal tax code, or shall be distributed to the federal government, or to a state or local government, for a public purpose" (Pub. 557, *Tax-Exempt Status for Your Organization* (Jan. 2024), at 71; Rev. Proc. 2024-22, 2024-22 I.R.B. 1332 § 2.08).

[97] See § 13.2.

[98] Priv. Ltr. Rul. 201736027.

[99] See § 16.1.

[100] Priv. Ltr. Rul. 201136027.

[101] See § 18.3.

[102] Reg. § 1.501(c)(9)-4(d).

[103] See § 18.7.

[104] Priv. Ltr. Rul. 201149032.

An organization that was tax-exempt[105] during any of its last five tax years preceding its liquidation, dissolution, termination, or substantial contraction is required to disclose the development to the IRS.[106] The disclosure is made on its annual information return or, if the organization is no longer exempt at the time, the annual information return it would have been required to file when it was exempt.[107] Churches, their integrated auxiliaries, conventions or associations of churches,[108] and any organization other than a private foundation with annual gross receipts that are normally not more than $5,000, are excepted by statute from this reporting requirement.[109] The IRS has exercised discretionary authority conferred on it by statute to relieve certain other organizations from this filing requirement.[110]

(c)   Mission Statements

Form 990[111] requests, in two instances, a description of the filing organization's *mission*.[112] An organization may thus have a mission statement in addition to a statement of purposes. A mission statement should not, of course, be inconsistent with the purposes statement.

(d)   Board Composition

The IRS has developed a policy, predicated on the private benefit doctrine,[113] that an organization, particularly one striving to qualify as a public charity, cannot qualify for tax-exempt status if it has a small board or a board wholly or principally composed of related individuals.[114] Traditionally, of course, this has been solely a matter of state law; most states require a governing board consisting of at least three persons.

The optimum size of a governing board of a nonprofit organization depends on many factors, including the type of organization involved, the nature and size of the organization's constituency, the manner in which the directors are selected, and the role and effectiveness of an executive committee (if any). In some instances, particularly in connection with trusts, an institutional trustee may be involved.

(e)   Rules for Limited Liability Companies

The IRS has issued guidance[115] on the standards an LLC with two or more members[116] must meet to qualify for tax exemption as a charitable organization.

---

[105] Under IRC § 501(a).

[106] IRC § 6043(b).

[107] Reg. § 1.6043-3(a)(1).

[108] See §§ 10.3, 10.4, 10.5.

[109] IRC § 6043(b)(1).

[110] IRC § 6043(b)(2); Reg. § 1.6043-3(b) (providing a list of other entities excepted from the filing requirement).

[111] See § 28.2(a)(i).

[112] Form 990, Part I, line 1 (with an option to report *most significant activities*), Part III, line 1 (if the mission statement has been approved by the board).

[113] See § 20.13.

[114] See § 5.7(c).

[115] Notice 2021-56, 2021-45 I.R.B. 716.

[116] A single-member LLC generally is a disregarded entity for tax purposes (see § 4.1(b)).

To qualify for exemption, both the LLC's articles of organization and its operating agreement must each include (1) provisions requiring that each member of the LLC be either an organization exempt from taxation as an organization described in IRC § 501(c)(3) or a governmental unit[117] or a wholly owned instrumentality thereof; (2) charitable purpose and charitable dissolution provisions;[118] (3) Chapter 42 compliance provisions if the LLC is a private foundation;[119] (4) an acceptable contingency plan (such as suspension of its membership rights until a member regains recognition of its exempt status) if one or more members cease to qualify as one of the permitted types of member organizations described previously.[120]

In a few states applicable law may not allow an LLC to be organized and operated exclusively for charitable purposes; therefore, the LLC must represent that all provisions in its articles of organization and operating agreement are consistent with applicable state law and are legally enforceable.[121]

Where applicable state law prohibits the addition of provisions to an LLC's articles of organization other than certain specific provisions required by the state law, these requirements will be deemed satisfied if the LLC's operating agreement includes these provisions and if its articles of organization and operating agreement do not include any inconsistent provisions.[122]

Previous IRS commentary indicates that an LLC may also qualify as a tax-exempt social welfare organization[123] if the LLC otherwise meets the requirements of that category of exemption and complies with certain other conditions.[124] The IRS has yet to establish its position as to whether an LLC can qualify as any other type of exempt organization. The IRS appears to be of the view that a social club,[125] to be exempt, cannot be structured as an LLC because the members, rather than the club itself, would directly control the entity's assets under an LLC structure.[126]

§ 4.4 PRIMARY PURPOSE TEST

A basic concept of the law of tax-exempt organizations is the *primary purpose rule*. The rule is one of the fundamental bases for determination of the appropriate category of tax exemption (if any) for an organization. The principle is formally explicated, by use of the word *exclusively*,[127] in the context

---

[117] As described in IRC § 170(c)(1).

[118] Reg. § 1.501(c)(3)-1(b)(1), (4). Exempt status was denied to an LLC that failed the first two requirements, in that it had individuals for members and did not have charitable purpose and dissolution provisions in its articles of organization and operating agreement (Priv. Ltr. Rul. 202323011).

[119] As described in IRC § 508(e)(1). See § 12.1(g).

[120] Notice 2021-56, *supra* note 115, § 3.02.

[121] *Id.* § 3.03.

[122] *Id.* § 3.04.

[123] See Chapter 13.

[124] "Limited Liability Companies as Exempt Organizations—Update," Topic B, IRS Exempt Organization Continuing Professional Education Text for FY 2001.

[125] See Chapter 15.

[126] Priv. Ltr. Rul. 200450041.

[127] See § 4.6.

of exempt charitable organizations,[128] exempt social welfare organizations,[129] exempt cemetery companies,[130] exempt health care coverage organizations,[131] and exempt workers' compensation coverage organizations,[132] and by use of the word *substantially* in the case of exempt social clubs.[133] The terms *exclusive* and *substantial* are generally subsumed, in this context, in the word *primary*.[134] This principle of the federal tax law is generally applicable to all categories of exempt organizations.[135]

Consequently, the definition of the word *exclusively*, in the law of tax-exempt organizations, is different from the meaning normally associated with the word. As one court nicely stated, the term *exclusively* "in this statutory context is a term of art and does not mean 'solely.'"[136] The law could not reasonably be interpreted in any other way. That is, if *exclusively* truly meant exclusively (as in solely), there would not be an opportunity for the conduct of unrelated business activity. Since that interpretation would render the entire law of unrelated business income taxation[137] meaningless, the interpretation would not be reasonable. Consequently, by treating the word *exclusively* as if it meant *primarily*, the law accommodates the coexistence of some unrelated activities with related ones.

The primary purpose test looks to an organization's purposes rather than its activities,[138] although the test is frequently misapplied. The focus should not be on an organization's primary activities as the test of tax exemption but on whether the activities accomplish one or more tax-exempt purposes.[139] This is why, for example, an organization may engage in nonexempt or profit-making activities and nonetheless qualify for exemption.[140]

The general rule, as stated by the U.S. Supreme Court in the context of charitable organizations, is that the "presence of a single . . . [nonexempt] purpose, if substantial in nature, will destroy the exemption regardless of the number or importance of truly . . . [exempt] purposes."[141] A federal court of appeals held that nonexempt activity will not result in loss or denial of exemption where it is

---

[128] See Chapter 7.

[129] See Chapter 13.

[130] See § 19.6.

[131] See § 19.15.

[132] See § 19.16.

[133] See Chapter 15.

[134] E.g., Reg. §§ 1.501(c)(3)-1(a)(1), 1.501(c)(3)-1(c)(1).

[135] E.g., Orange Cnty. Agric. Soc'y, Inc. v. Comm'r, 55 T.C.M. 1602 (1988), aff'd, 893 F.2d 647 (2d Cir. 1990).

[136] New Dynamics Found. v. United States, 2006-1 U.S.T.C. ¶ 50,286 (U.S. Ct. Fed. Cl. 2006). Also, Easter House v. United States, 12 Ct. Cl. 476, 483 (1987), aff'd, 846 F.2d 78 (Fed. Cir. 1988), cert. denied, 488 U.S. 907 (1988).

[137] See Chapters 24, 25.

[138] Reg. § 1.501(c)(3)-1(c)(1).

[139] Aid to Artisans, Inc. v. Comm'r, 71 T.C. 202 (1978).

[140] Nonetheless, the courts occasionally stretch this criterion, as illustrated by the decision denying tax-exempt status to a scholarship fund, for violation of the primary purpose test, because its fundraising activities were conducted in a cocktail lounge and attracted customers to the lounge (P.L.L. Scholarship Fund v. Comm'r, 82 T.C. 196 (1984); also, KJ's Fund Raisers, Inc. v. Comm'r, 74 T.C.M. 669 (1997), aff'd, 166 F.3d 1200 (2d Cir. 1998)). Cf. Hope Charitable Found. v. Ridell, 61-1 U.S.T.C. ¶ 9437 (S.D. Cal. 1961).

[141] Better Business Bureau of Washington, D.C. v. United States, 326 U.S. 279, 283 (1945). Also, Universal Church of Jesus Christ, Inc. v. Comm'r, 55 T.C.M. 143 (1988).

"only incidental and less than substantial" and that a "slight and comparatively unimportant deviation from the narrow furrow of tax approved activity is not fatal."[142] In the words of the IRS, the rules applicable to charitable organizations in general have been "construed as requiring all the resources of the organization [other than an insubstantial part] to be applied to the pursuit of one or more of the exempt purposes therein specified."[143] Consequently, the existence of one or more authentic exempt purposes of an organization will not be productive of tax exemption as a charitable (or other) entity if a substantial nonexempt purpose is present in its operations.[144]

Thus, for example, the IRS frequently denies tax-exempt status to an organization engaged in some exempt activities but also in substantial social and recreational activities.[145] In one instance, an organization that arranged wintertime ocean cruises was deemed ineligible for tax-exempt status notwithstanding that some lectures, discussions, workshops, and shore excursions furthered religious and educational purposes.[146] In another instance, a court held that even if an organization providing recreational flight time to Air National Guard members could be said to further a charitable purpose, its substantial recreational purposes prevented it from receiving tax-exempt status.[147] This court also denied tax-exempt status to an organization operating a mountain lodge as a religious retreat facility, where recreational and social activities at the lodge were substantial.[148] Likewise, the "predominantly social and recreational tone" of an organization's annual science fiction convention precluded it from being recognized as tax-exempt.[149]

There is no formal definition of the term *insubstantial* in this setting. Thus, application of the primary purpose test entails an issue of fact to be determined under the facts and circumstances of each case.[150] A court opinion suggested that, where a function represents less than 10 percent of total efforts, the primary purpose test will not be applied to prevent exemption.[151] Another court opinion stated

---

[142] St. Louis Union Trust Co. v. United States, 374 F.2d 427, 431–32 (8th Cir. 1967). Also, Seasongood v. Comm'r, 227 F.2d 907, 910 (6th Cir. 1955).

[143] Rev. Rul. 77-366, 1977-2 C.B. 192.

[144] Stevens Bros. Found. v. Comm'r, 324 F.2d 633 (8th Cir. 1963), *cert. denied*, 376 U.S. 969 (1964); Scripture Press Found. v. United States, 285 F.2d 800, 806 (Ct. Cl. 1961), *cert. denied*, 368 U.S. 985 (1962); Fides Publishers Ass'n v. United States, 263 F. Supp. 924, 935 (N.D. Ind. 1967); Edgar v. Comm'r, 56 T.C. 717, 755 (1971); Media Sports League, Inc. v. Comm'r, 52 T.C.M. 1093 (1986).

[145] E.g., Priv. Ltr. Rul. 202420031, in which tax-exempt status was denied to a matchmaking organization that promoted religion but also provided substantial social and recreational benefits to participants.

[146] Rev. Rul. 77-366, 1977-2 C.B. 192. See § 8.4. A garden club was similarly denied exempt status because a substantial part of its activities consisted of social functions for the benefit, pleasure, and recreation of its members (Rev. Rul. 66-179, 1966-1 C.B. 139).

[147] Syrang Aero Club, Inc. v Comm'r, 73 T.C. 717 (1980).

[148] Schoger Found. v. Comm'r, 76 T.C. 380 (1981). By contrast, an organization formed to construct and sell or lease housing at a religious retreat facility owned and operated by a church was held to be tax-exempt as a charitable entity because the predominant use of the housing units was inextricably tied to the religious activities of the church and recreational purposes were not substantial (Junaluska Assembly Housing, Inc. v. Comm'r, 86 T.C. 1114 (1986)). See § 10.10.

[149] St. Louis Science Fiction Ltd. v. Comm'r, 49 T.C.M. 1126, 1129 (1985). See § 8.4.

[150] E.g., Kentucky Bar Found. v. Comm'r, 78 T.C. 921 (1982); Spanish Am. Cultural Ass'n of Bergenfield v. Comm'r, 68 T.C.M. 931 (1994).

[151] World Family Corp. v. Comm'r, 81 T.C. 958 (1983).

that an organization that received approximately one-third of its revenue from an unrelated business could not qualify for tax-exempt status, in that the level of nonexempt activity "exceed[ed] the benchmark of insubstantiality."[152] Yet the IRS allowed a charitable organization to remain exempt where it derived two-thirds of its income from unrelated businesses, inasmuch as the net income from these businesses was used to further exempt purposes.[153]

In application of the primary purpose rule, a court concluded that a police benevolent association could not qualify for tax exemption as a charitable organization because the payment of retirement benefits to its members was a substantial nonexempt activity.[154] This approach was again followed by the court in a case holding that a religious organization was ineligible for exemption because a substantial portion of its receipts was expended for the nonexempt function of medical care of its members.[155] The second of these two holdings was reversed, however, with the appellate court holding that the medical aid plan was carried out in furtherance of the church's religious doctrines and therefore advanced an exempt purpose.[156]

The primary purpose test was invoked to deny tax exemption as a charitable entity to an organization formed to provide a service by means of which public and private libraries, commercial organizations, and other entities centrally pay license fees for the photocopying of certain copyrighted publications, with a court finding that the "potential for a substantial private profit was the driving force" behind the organization and its operations.[157] Thereafter, in application of this test, the same court found that a scholarship fund established pursuant to a collective bargaining agreement was not entitled to exemption, in part because the class of individuals served was "too restricted" to confer the requisite public benefit.[158] This test was applied by another court to preclude exempt status as charitable entities to two cemetery associations because their activities included the sale of burial plots and maintenance of the cemetery.[159]

As another example, the retail sale of goods and services normally is a nonexempt business activity. This is the case, for example, when a tax-exempt museum is selling souvenir items relating to the city in which the museum is located.[160] Yet an

[152] Orange Cnty. Agric. Soc'y, Inc. v. Comm'r, 55 T.C.M. 1602, 1604 (1988), aff'd, 893 F.2d 647 (2d Cir. 1990).
[153] IRS Technical Advice Memorandum (Tech. Adv. Mem.) 200021056.
[154] Policemen's Benevolent Ass'n of Westchester Cnty., Inc. v. Comm'r, 42 T.C.M. 1750 (1981). Also, Police Benevolent Ass'n of Richmond, Va. v. United States, 87-1 U.S.T.C. ¶ 9238 (E.D. Va. 1987).
[155] Bethel Conservative Mennonite Church v. Comm'r, 80 T.C. 352 (1983).
[156] Bethel Conservative Mennonite Church v. Comm'r, 746 F.2d 388 (7th Cir. 1984). This approach, however, is not always followed. For example, a grantmaking organization (that would not have been a private foundation) was denied exemption by application of the primary purpose test because it failed to provide grant criteria (Church in Boston v. Comm'r, 71 T.C. 102 (1978)). Cf. IRC § 4945(d) (see § 12.4(e)). The primary purpose test can intersect with the commerciality doctrine (see § 4.9) (e.g., Federation Pharmacy Servs., Inc. v. Comm'r, 72 T.C. 687 (1979), aff'd, 625 F.2d 804 (8th Cir. 1980)).
[157] Copyright Clearance Center, Inc. v. Comm'r, 79 T.C. 793, 807, 808 (1982).
[158] Local Union 712, I.B.E.W. Scholarship Trust Fund v. Comm'r, 45 T.C.M. 675, 678 (1983). See § 6.3(a).
[159] Smith v. United States, 84-2 U.S.T.C. ¶ 13,595 (W.D. Mo. 1984). The IRS also takes the position that the operation of a cemetery and the sale of burial plots to the public does not further a charitable purpose (e.g., Priv. Ltr. Rul. 202234007). Such an organization may, however, qualify for exemption as a cemetery company (see § 19.6).
[160] Rev. Rul. 73-105, 1973-1 C.B. 264.

organization with the primary purpose of providing assistance to needy women to enable them to earn income was held to be exempt as a charitable entity because it operated a market for the cooking and needlework of this category of women, who were not otherwise able to support themselves and their families.[161] Likewise, an organization that operated a consignment shop as a place where "industrious and meritorious" women could sell articles and foodstuffs prepared by them was held to be exempt.[162] By contrast, an organization was denied exempt status as a social club in part because the IRS concluded that its "purposes and operations are primarily of a business [nonexempt] nature."[163]

In addition to being applied to allow or deny tax-exempt status, the primary purpose test can be utilized to determine the appropriate category of exemption. For example, when an organization promotes and sponsors recreational and amateur sports, with an emphasis on training and education, the organization may qualify as an exempt charitable and/or educational entity.[164] By contrast, if the principal purpose of an organization is advancement of the social and recreational interests of the players, the organization cannot be an exempt charitable or educational entity;[165] it may, however, qualify as an exempt social club.[166] Likewise, the IRS ruled that an organization that conducts festivals to promote Mexican American culture, including *folklórico* dancers and a beauty contest, cannot qualify as an exempt charitable entity but can constitute an exempt social welfare organization.[167] Similarly, the IRS converted an organization's exempt status from that of a veterans' organization to that of a social club.[168] Also, the IRS denied recognition of exemption as a charitable organization in part because the entity was functioning essentially as a professional society.[169]

In addition, the IRS ruled that (1) an organization formed to promote soccer was ineligible for exemption as a charitable or educational organization because its primary purpose was the promotion of recreational sports for adults;[170] (2) an organization established to "spread the gospel of Jesus Christ through professionally run fishing tournaments" did not qualify as an exempt religious entity because its primary purpose was socializing;[171] (3) an organization could not be tax-exempt on the basis of operating a religious camp, because its primary activities were fishing and socializing;[172] (4) an organization formed as an "Italian culture club"

---

[161] Rev. Rul. 68-167, 1968-1 C.B. 255.

[162] Tech. Adv. Mem. 200021056.

[163] Priv. Ltr. Rul. 200450041. Similarly, an organization with the primary purpose of fostering networking between vendors and prospective clients within the legal profession was held to not qualify as an exempt social club (Priv. Ltr. Rul. 200906057).

[164] E.g., Hutchinson Baseball Enters., Inc. v. Comm'r, 73 T.C. 144 (1979), aff'd, 696 F.2d 757 (10th Cir. 1982). See §§ 7.16(c), 8.4.

[165] Media Sports League, Inc. v. Comm'r, 52 T.C.M. 1093 (1986); Wayne Baseball, Inc. v. Comm'r, 78 T.C.M. 437 (1999).

[166] See Chapter 15.

[167] Priv. Ltr. Rul. 200621023. See Chapter 13.

[168] Priv. Ltr. Rul. 201103062. See § 19.11(a), Chapter 13.

[169] Priv. Ltr. Rul. 201143020. See § 14.1(e).

[170] Priv. Ltr. Rul. 200849018.

[171] Priv. Ltr. Rul. 200851040.

[172] Priv. Ltr. Rul. 200905028.

did not constitute a charitable or educational entity, in that it was more akin to a fraternal organization;[173] (5) an organization whose primary purpose was enjoyment of the art of riding motorcycles with members could not qualify as an exempt social welfare entity, because social activities were its substantial function;[174] (6) an organization that sought exempt status as a charitable and educational organization could not qualify for the exemption because its activities were conducted exclusively for recreational and/or social purposes;[175] and (7) an organization operating a hunting club and providing its members with instruction and practice on the safe handling of weapons.[176]

The primary purpose of an organization is not taken into account only when determining whether it qualifies for tax-exempt status. This purpose can also be a critical factor in application of the unrelated business rules.[177]

§ 4.5 OPERATIONAL TEST

The operational test, as its name indicates, is concerned with how an organization functions in relation to the applicable requirements for tax-exempt status. Thus, in a generic sense, every type of exempt organization is subject to an operational test.

(a) Basic Rules

An organization, to qualify as a charitable entity, is regarded as operated exclusively for one or more tax-exempt purposes only if it engages primarily in activities that accomplish one or more of its exempt purposes.[178] The IRS observed that, to satisfy this *operational test*, the organization's "resources must be devoted to purposes that qualify as exclusively charitable within the meaning of section 501(c)(3) of the Code and the applicable regulations."[179] An organization will not be so regarded if more than an insubstantial part of its activities is not in furtherance of an exempt purpose.[180] An organization is not considered as operated exclusively for one or more exempt purposes if its net earnings inure in whole or in part to the benefit of private shareholders or individuals.[181] An organization can be substantially dominated by its founder without, for that

---

[173] Priv. Ltr. Rul. 200905029.

[174] Priv. Ltr. Rul. 200909072.

[175] Priv. Ltr. Rul. 200930049.

[176] Priv. Ltr. Rul. 202305017.

[177] See Chapters 24, 25.

[178] Reg. § 1.501(c)(3)-1(c)(1).

[179] Rev. Rul. 72-369, 1972-2 C.B. 245.

[180] Reg. § 1.501(c)(3)-1(c)(1). See § 4.4. In one instance, the operational test was found to be unmet because the organization involved, which was organized for the study and promotion of the philately of the Central American republics, operated a mail bid stamps sales service for its members as a substantial activity (Society of Costa Rica Collectors v. Comm'r, 49 T.C.M. 304 (1984)).

[181] Reg. §§ 1.501(c)(3)-1(c)(2), 1.501(a)-1(c). Also, Wildt's Motorsport Advancement Crusade, Bill v. Comm'r, 56 T.C.M. 1401 (1989); Athenagoras I Christian Union of the World, Inc. v. Comm'r, 55 T.C.M. 781 (1988); Levy Family Tribe Found. v. Comm'r, 69 T.C. 615 (1978). See Chapter 20.

reason alone, failing to satisfy the operational test.[182] A court concluded, however, that an organization cannot qualify for tax exemption where one individual controls all aspects of the organization's operations and "is not checked" by any governing body.[183]

An organization may meet the federal tax law requirements for charitable entities even though it operates a trade or business as a substantial part of its activities.[184] If the organization has as its primary purpose the carrying on of a trade or business, however, it may not be tax-exempt.[185] The core issue is whether the substantial business activity accomplishes or is in furtherance of an exempt purpose.[186] (The existence of an operating profit is not conclusive as to a business purpose.)[187] Even though the operation of a business does not deprive an organization of classification as a charitable entity, there may be unrelated trade or business tax consequences.[188]

The operational test focuses on the actual purposes the organization advances by means of its activities, rather than on the organization's statement of purposes or the nature of its activities, in recognition of the fact that an organization may conduct a business in furtherance of a tax-exempt purpose and qualify as a charitable entity:

> Under the operational test, the purpose towards which an organization's activities are directed, and not the nature of the activities themselves, is ultimately dispositive of the organization's right to be classified as a section 501(c)(3) organization exempt from tax under section 501(a) . . . [I]t is possible for . . . an activity to be carried on for more than one purpose . . . The fact that . . . [an] activity may constitute a trade or business does not, of course, disqualify it from classification under section 501(c)(3), provided the activity furthers or accomplishes an exempt purpose . . . Rather, the critical inquiry is whether . . . [an organization's] primary purpose for engaging in its . . . activity is an exempt purpose, or whether its primary purpose is the nonexempt one of operating a commercial business producing net profits for . . . [the organization].[189]

---

[182] E.g., Church of the Visible Intelligence That Governs the Universe v. United States, 83-2 U.S.T.C. ¶ 9726 (Cl. Ct. 1983).

[183] Chief Steward of the Ecumenical Temples & Worldwide Peace Movement & His Successors v. Comm'r, 49 T.C.M. 640, 643 (1985).

[184] E.g., Rev. Rul. 64-182, 1964-1 C.B. 186. See § 4.7.

[185] Reg. § 1.501(c)(3)-1(e)(1).

[186] Federation Pharmacy Servs., Inc. v. Comm'r, 72 T.C. 687 (1979), aff'd, 625 F.2d 804 (8th Cir. 1980); est of Hawaii v. Comm'r, 71 T.C. 1067 (1979), aff'd, 647 F.2d 170 (9th Cir. 1981).

[187] Rev. Rul. 68-26, 1968-1 C.B. 272; Elisian Guild, Inc. v. United States, 412 F.2d 121 (1st Cir. 1969). Cf. Fides Publishers Ass'n v. United States, 263 F. Supp. 924 (N.D. Ind. 1967).

[188] See Chapters 24, 25.

[189] B.S.W. Group, Inc. v. Comm'r, 70 T.C. 352, 356–57 (1978). Also, American Campaign Academy v. Comm'r, 92 T.C. 1053 (1989); Goldsboro Art League, Inc. v. Comm'r, 75 T.C. 337 (1980); Aid to Artisans, Inc. v. Comm'r, 71 T.C. 202 (1978); Ohio Teamsters Educ. & Safety Training Fund v. Comm'r, 77 T.C. 189 (1981), aff'd, 692 F.2d 432 (6th Cir. 1982). To determine whether the operational test has been satisfied, the Tax Court wrote that it looks beyond the "four corners of the organization's charter to discover the actual objects motivating the organization" (American Campaign Academy v. Comm'r, 92 T.C. at 1064).

This important distinction between activities and purpose is sometimes overlooked by the IRS and the courts. For example, in one case a court concluded that the operational test was not satisfied because the organization failed to describe its activities in sufficient detail in its application for recognition of exemption.[190]

Although an organization might be engaged in only a single activity, that activity may be directed toward multiple purposes, both exempt and nonexempt. If the nonexempt purpose is substantial in nature, the organization will not satisfy the operational test.[191]

Whether an organization has a substantial nonexempt purpose is a question of fact, to be resolved on the basis of all the appropriate evidence.[192] The U.S. Tax Court observed: "Factors such as the particular manner in which an organization's activities are conducted, the commercial hue of those activities, and the existence and amount of annual or accumulated profits are relevant evidence of a forbidden predominant purpose."[193]

An illustration of application of the operational test was provided by a case concerning the tax-exempt status of an organization granting scholarships to contestants in a beauty pageant. The court found that the payments were forms of compensation, not scholarships; because this was the organization's only activity, it was not engaged in any exempt purposes.[194] Another example of application of these rules is inherent in a court decision concluding that an organization that principally administered donor-advised funds[195] qualified as a charitable entity inasmuch as its "goal is to create an effective national network to respond to many worthy charitable needs at the local level which in many cases might go unmet" and its activities "promote public policy and represent the very essence of charitable benevolence."[196] Still another example of these rules involved a court opinion concerning an otherwise qualifying school that was held to confer private benefit on its graduates, who were pursuing careers as political campaign professionals serving only candidates of one political party.[197]

A court held that an organization could not qualify as a tax-exempt charitable entity, because of violation of the operational test, in that the organization's activities and those of its founder, sole director, and officer were essentially identical.[198] The court wrote that the affairs of the organization and of this

---

[190] General Conference of Free Church of Am. v. Comm'r, 71 T.C. 920 (1979). See § 26.1(b)(i).

[191] KJ's Fund Raisers, Inc. v. Comm'r, 74 T.C.M. 669 (1997), aff'd, 166 F.3d 1200 (2d Cir. 1998); Manning Ass'n v. Comm'r, 93 T.C. 596 (1989); Copyright Clearance Center, Inc. v. Comm'r, 79 T.C. 793 (1982).

[192] Church by Mail, Inc. v. Comm'r, 765 F.2d 1387 (9th Cir. 1985), aff'g 48 T.C.M. 471 (1984).

[193] B.S.W. Group, Inc. v. Comm'r, 70 T.C. 352, 358 (1978).

[194] Miss Georgia Scholarship Fund, Inc. v. Comm'r, 72 T.C. 267 (1979).

[195] See § 12.5.

[196] Nat'l Found., Inc. v. United States, 87-2 U.S.T.C. ¶ 9602 (Ct. Cl. 1987).

[197] American Campaign Academy v. Comm'r, 92 T.C. 1053 (1989). Other cases in which the operational test has been found to have been transgressed include Larry D. Bowen Family Found. v. Comm'r, 77 T.C.M. 1954 (1999); Tate Family Found. v. Comm'r, 77 T.C.M. 2016 (1999); Tamaki Found. v. Comm'r, 77 T.C.M. 2020 (1999); Share Network Found. v. Comm'r, 78 T.C.M. 6 (1999); Resource Management Found. v. Comm'r, 78 T.C.M. 44 (1999); Hart Found. v. Comm'r, 78 T.C.M. 57 (1999); Oliver Family Found. v. Comm'r, 78 T.C.M. 104 (1999).

[198] Salvation Navy, Inc. v. Comm'r, 84 T.C.M. 506 (2002).

individual are "irretrievably intertwined," so that the "benefits" of exemption would "inure" to him.[199]

The operational test is used to apply the tests of *commerciality* and *competition* to charitable and other categories of tax-exempt organizations. Previously, the test had been used in conjunction with the exclusivity requirement[200] and the rules defining business for unrelated income taxation purposes.[201] This application of the commerciality doctrine has largely been by the U.S. Tax Court, where, for example, it denied exempt status, as a charitable and religious entity, to an organization associated with the Seventh-Day Adventist Church that, in advancement of Church doctrine, operated vegetarian restaurants and health food stores; the court wrote that the organization's "activity was conducted as a business and was in direct competition with other restaurants and health food stores" and that "[c]ompetition with commercial firms is strong evidence of a substantial nonexempt commercial purpose."[202] Likewise, the Tax Court held that an organization that supported religious missionary work properly had its exemption revoked because it conducted a mail-order business in tape and electronic equipment as a substantial part of its activities and purposes,[203] and that an organization could not be exempt because it functioned the same as a purchasing, brokering, or consulting organization in the private sector.[204] The only prior opinion from the Tax Court that invoked the commerciality standard is one that looked at the issue from a somewhat different slant, in that the court wrote that the operational test is violated where the organization's "primary purpose is the nonexempt one of operating a commercial business producing net profits for" the organization.[205]

The IRS, from time to time, denies recognition of tax-exempt status to, or revokes the exempt status of, organizations that, in the view of the agency, fail the operational test.[206] In one instance, the IRS ruled that an organization failed to qualify for exemption because the agency was unable to determine whether the entity would ever meet the operational test because the "timeframe" for the organization to "become operational is extremely indeterminate."[207] By contrast, a charitable organization was allowed by the IRS to maintain its exempt status, even though it was a "dormant shell" (because it transferred all of its then assets for

---

[199] *Id.* at 508. It is not uncommon, however, for an exempt organization to engage in activities that its founder previously undertook (or would otherwise undertake). For example, the IRS ruled that a foreign farm, previously conducted as a for-profit operation by the creator of a private foundation, can be operated by the foundation after his death as an exempt demonstration project and thus be a program-related investment (see § 12.4(d)) and a functionally related business (see § 12.4(c)) (Priv. Ltr. Rul. 200343027).

[200] See § 4.6.

[201] See § 24.2(c), (d).

[202] Living Faith, Inc. v. Comm'r, 60 T.C.M. 710, 713 (1990), *aff'd*, 950 F.2d 365 (7th Cir. 1991). See § 4.9.

[203] United Missionary Aviation, Inc. v. Comm'r, 60 T.C.M. 1152 (1990), *rev'd and remanded*, 89-2 U.S.T.C. ¶ 9595 (8th Cir. 1989), *cert. denied*, 506 U.S. 816.

[204] Public Indus., Inc. v. Comm'r, 61 T.C.M. 1626 (1991). The operation of a commercial bank as one of an organization's substantial divisions was held to be a nonexempt function precluding tax exemption as a charitable entity (Amend16RobertWirengard v. Comm'r, 89 T.C.M. 785 (2005)).

[205] B.S.W. Group, Inc. v. Comm'r, 70 T.C. 352, 356 (1978).

[206] E.g., IRS Exemption Denial and Revocation Letter (Ex. Den. and Rev. Ltr.) 20044002E.

[207] Priv. Ltr. Rul. 200506024. See § 26.1(b)(i).

charitable purposes), inasmuch as additional funds were to be received by it and it had a plan to continue its charitable operations.[208]

On occasion, tax exemption of an organization will be revoked for inactivity (failure of an entity to operate at all).[209]

(b) Activities Tests

The IRS sometimes references, in private letter rulings, an *activities test*, which it applies in determining whether a nonprofit organization qualifies for tax exemption. For example, the IRS cited this test in differentiating between traditional and nontraditional activities of exempt social clubs.[210] On occasion, this activities test is applied in addition to an operational test. As an illustration, the IRS, in denying recognition of exemption to an entity seeking to qualify as a telephone cooperative,[211] ruled that the organization did not satisfy the operational test because it was not operated as a cooperative, and it failed an activities test because its operations did not facilitate communication between its members and others.[212]

(c) Quantification of Activities

The foregoing summary of the basic rules of the operational test have historically been applied on a facts-and-circumstances basis. This is because the federal tax law lacks a formal methodology for quantifying an organization's activities for the purposes of measuring the scope of each of them and ascertaining whether there is a sufficient combination of them to satisfy the requisite of primary activity.[213] To the extent that there has been much attention to this obvious omission in this analytic process, it has been in the area of legislative activities of public charities, where there is uncertainty as to how to measure the substantiality of legislative activities for the purpose of determining whether lobbying imperils an organization's tax exemption.[214]

The IRS occasionally considers this matter. For example, the IRS observed that a tax-exempt organization operated three contiguous shops, each of which was "approximately the same size," but did not explain the basis for that conclusion.[215] In another instance, the IRS accepted an organization's portrayal of its primary activities, expressed in terms of percentages of total activities, without discussion of the basis for the percentages.[216] An organization conducting formal education

---

[208] Priv. Ltr. Rul. 201448026.

[209] E.g., Priv. Ltr. Rul. 200646020. Likewise, Tikar, Inc. v. Comm'r, 121 T.C.M. 1408 (2021); Community Education Found. v. Comm'r, 112 T.C.M. 637 (2016), *appeal dismissed for lack of prosecution* (D.C. Cir., Aug. 3, 2018).

[210] Tech. Adv. Mem. 201430019. See § 15.1(b).

[211] See § 19.5(b).

[212] Priv. Ltr. Rul. 201431031.

[213] See § 4.5(a), text accompanied by *supra* note 192. In one instance, the IRS asked an organization to assign percentages of "time and money" to its various activities; the organization replied that it was unable to because "it is extremely difficult to separate these activities from each other and estimate timing [sic] and resource allocation" (Priv. Ltr. Rul. 201405022).

[214] See, e.g., § 22.3(c)(ii).

[215] Tech. Adv. Mem. 200021056.

[216] Priv. Ltr. Rul. 201349019.

that entailed 13 percent of its functional expenses, 7 percent of its contributions, and 6 percent of its revenue, and involved 20 percent of its employees, was ruled to not constitute a qualifying organization for unrelated debt-financed income purposes.[217]

In a certainly troublesome and seemingly incorrect ruling, the IRS concluded, as to an organization that had been operational for at least three years, that it did not qualify for tax-exempt status as a social welfare organization because 100 percent of its expenditures were for political campaign activities in one year, even though it expended 100 percent of its volunteer time on exempt functions in the ensuing two years, because this organization did not make any exempt function expenditures in those two years.[218]

This development has enormous implications for the law of tax-exempt organizations. If a methodology is (somehow) developed that measures the activities of exempt organizations and if there is a definitive answer as to appropriate and required "proportions" of activities, these two elements are bound to be applicable in all exempt organizations settings. This will dramatically impact the primary purpose test. The outcome will directly affect the quantification of legislative and unrelated business activities.[219] Overall, if the government issues proposals concerning the measurement and proportionality of exempt organizations' activities and they become law, much law and many practices in the exempt organizations area will be transformed.

(d) Action Organizations

An organization is not operated exclusively for one or more exempt charitable purposes if it is an action organization.[220]

An organization is an *action organization* if a substantial part of its activities is attempting to influence legislation.[221] For this purpose, an organization is regarded as attempting to influence legislation if the organization contacts, or urges the public to contact, members of a legislative body for the purpose of proposing, supporting, or opposing legislation or if it advocates the adoption or rejection of legislation. The term *legislation* includes action by the U.S. Congress, a state legislature, a local council or similar governing body, or the public in a referendum, initiative, constitutional amendment, or similar procedure. An organization will not fail to meet the operational test merely because it advocates, as an insubstantial part of its activities, the adoption or rejection of legislation.[222] Also, an organization for which the expenditure test election (relating to expenditures for legislative activities)[223] is in effect for a tax year is not considered an action organization for the year if it avoids loss of tax exemption by reason of that test.[224]

---

[217] Tech. Adv. Mem. 201407024. See § 24.10.

[218] Priv. Ltr. Rul. 201615014. Shortly thereafter, the IRS issued a private letter ruling analyzing an organization's total activities based solely on categories of time expended (Priv. Ltr. Rul. 201639016).

[219] As to the latter, see § 24.1, text accompanied by note 11.

[220] Reg. § 1.501(c)(3)-1(c)(3).

[221] Thus, an organization with the primary activity of influencing legislation was held to not qualify for exemption as a charitable entity (Priv. Ltr. Rul. 200952069).

[222] Reg. § 1.501(c)(3)-1(c)(3)(ii).

[223] See § 22.3(d)(vi).

[224] Reg. § 1.501(c)(3)-1(c)(3)(ii).

An organization is an action organization if it participates or intervenes, directly or indirectly, in any political campaign on behalf of or in opposition to any candidate for public office. The phrase *candidate for public office* means an individual who offers themself, or is proposed by others, as a contestant for an elective public office, whether the office is national, state, or local. Activities that constitute participation or intervention in a political campaign on behalf of or in opposition to a candidate include, but are not limited to, the publication or distribution of written or printed statements or the making of oral statements on behalf of or in opposition to the candidate.[225]

An organization is an action organization if it has the following two characteristics: (1) Its main or primary objective or objectives (as distinguished from its incidental or secondary objectives) may be attained only by legislation or a defeat of proposed legislation, and (2) it advocates or campaigns for the attainment of this main or primary objective or objectives as distinguished from engaging in nonpartisan analysis, study, or research, and making the results thereof available to the public. In determining whether an organization has these characteristics, all the surrounding facts and circumstances, including one or more provisions in the articles of organization and all activities of the organization, are considered.[226]

Application of the operational test is, therefore, intertwined with the proscriptions on private inurement and on legislative and political campaign activities.[227] In essence, however, to meet the operational test, an organization must be engaged in activities that further public rather than private purposes.[228]

The entwining of the operational test with the other requirements of the federal tax rules governing charitable organizations was recognized by a court in a decision refusing to reclassify a health and welfare fund, which was tax-exempt as an employee beneficiary association,[229] as a charitable organization.[230] The court ruled against the organization on the ground that it was not operated exclusively for charitable purposes[231] and that its activities were furthering private interests[232] but cloaked its opinion in the mantle of the operational test. (The organization's activities consisted of operating child day-care centers—which the court implied was not a charitable activity[233]—and providing services to members, and the organization charged the employees less tuition for the day-care services than it charged other parents.)

An organization deemed to be an action organization, other than because of more than merely incidental political campaign activities, though it cannot for that

---

[225] Reg. § 1.501(c)(3)-1(c)(3)(iii).

[226] Reg. § 1.501(c)(3)-1(c)(3)(iv).

[227] See Chapters 20, 22, 23, respectively.

[228] Reg. § 1.501(c)(3)-1(d)(1)(ii). E.g., American Campaign Academy v. Comm'r, 92 T.C. 1053 (1989).

[229] See § 18.3.

[230] Baltimore Regional Joint Bd. Health & Welfare Fund, Amalgamated Clothing & Textile Workers Union v. Comm'r, 69 T.C. 554 (1978).

[231] See § 4.6.

[232] See Chapter 20.

[233] Cf. Rev. Rul. 70-533, 1970-2 C.B. 112; San Francisco Infant School, Inc. v. Comm'r, 69 T.C. 957 (1978); Michigan Early Childhood Cent., Inc. v. Comm'r, 37 T.C.M. 808 (1978). See § 8.8.

reason qualify as a charitable organization, may nonetheless qualify as a social welfare organization.[234]

(e) Aggregate Principle

The activities of a partnership or other form of joint venture are often considered to be the activities of the partners; this is termed the *aggregate principle*.[235] This principle applies for purposes of the operational test, in that the operations of a joint venture that includes a tax-exempt organization are attributed to the exempt organization when it is being evaluated pursuant to the test.[236]

Thus, where a limited liability company that is taxable as a partnership had as its members a for-profit holding company wholly owned by a tax-exempt organization and a for-profit corporation, the IRS ruled that the holding company's activities are attributable to the exempt organization for purposes of assessing its ongoing qualification for exemption; since the holding company also is a limited liability company taxable as a partnership, the activities of the limited liability company are attributable to the holding company for purposes of determining whether the limited liability company's functions are substantially related to the accomplishment of the exempt organization's purposes.[237]

Some in the exempt organizations community are uncomfortable with the concept (or prospect) that all of the operations of a joint venture may be attributed to a tax-exempt organization in this setting, irrespective of the extent of the membership interest and/or the presence or absence of control. In this regard, some solace may be found in the IRS's observation, in the accountable care organization context,[238] that if there is attribution of nonexempt functions of an ACO to an exempt participant, the participant's exempt status will not be jeopardized if the ACO's nonexempt activities "represent no more than an insubstantial part of the participant's total activities."[239]

§ 4.6 EXCLUSIVELY STANDARD

To be tax-exempt as a charitable organization, an entity must be organized and operated *exclusively* for exempt purposes. As noted,[240] this rule is a term of art that is reflected in the primary purpose test. There is, however, additional law pertaining to the *exclusivity* rule.

A controversial opinion in this regard was issued by a federal court of appeals, which accorded tax exemption as a charitable organization to an entity

---

[234] Reg. § 1.501(c)(3)-1(c)(3)(v). See Chapter 13.

[235] Butler v. Comm'r, 36 T.C. 1097 (1961).

[236] Rev. Rul. 98-15, 1998-1 C.B. 718; Rev. Proc. 2004-51, 2004-1 C.B. 974. This principle was also stated by the IRS in its summary of tax-exempt organizations issues relating to exempt organizations' participation in accountable care organizations (see § 7.6(m)(ii), text accompanied by note 264).

[237] Priv. Ltr. Rul. 200528029.

[238] See *supra* note 236.

[239] See § 7.6(m)(ii), text accompanied by note 264.

[240] See § 4.4.

operating a public parking facility.[241] The IRS contended that this activity, replete with a validation stamp system for shoppers, was commercial in nature[242] and generated private benefit to the participating businesses.[243] Concluding that the city involved was the primary beneficiary of the organization's activities, the district court held that the "business activity itself is similar to that which others engage in for profit, but it is not carried on in the same manner; it is carried on only because it is necessary for the attainment of an undeniably public end."[244] On appeal, the appellate court observed that the lower court "made a quantitative comparison of the private versus the public benefits derived from the organization and operation of the plaintiff corporation" and determined that the requirements for exemption were "adequately fulfilled."[245]

The IRS does not subscribe to the principles of the public parking corporation case and announced that it does not follow the decision,[246] asserting that this type of a public parking corporation does not operate exclusively for charitable purposes and carries on a business with the public in a manner similar to organizations that are operated for profit. This position was made clear earlier when the IRS ruled that an organization formed to revive retail sales in an area suffering from continued economic decline by constructing a shopping center that would complement the area's existing retail facilities could not qualify for tax exemption as a charitable entity. The IRS, then taking no notice of the appellate court decision, said that the activities of the organization "result in major benefits accruing to the stores that will locate within the shopping center," thereby precluding the exemption.[247] (An organization that provided free parking to persons visiting a downtown area can, however, qualify as an exempt social welfare organization.)[248]

Application of the concept of *exclusively* may require even more flexibility than has been previously displayed. This may be particularly unavoidable with respect to organizations performing services that are considered necessary in today's society, even where the services are parallel with those rendered in commercial settings. For example, the provision of medical services can obviously be an enterprise for profit, yet the IRS was able to rule that an organization formed to attract a physician to a medically underserved rural area, by providing the doctor with a building and facilities at a reasonable rent, qualified as a charitable organization.[249] "In these circumstances," said the IRS, any "personal benefit derived by the physician (the use of the building in which to practice medicine) does not detract from the public purpose of the organization nor lessen the public benefit flowing from its activities."[250] Similarly, an organization formed to provide

---

[241] Monterey Public Parking Corp. v. United States, 481 F.2d 175 (9th Cir. 1973), aff'd, 321 F. Supp. 972 (N.D. Cal. 1970).

[242] See § 4.9.

[243] See § 20.13.

[244] Monterey Public Parking Corp. v. United States, 321 F. Supp. 972, 977 (N.D. Cal. 1970).

[245] Monterey Public Parking Corp. v. United States, 481 F.2d 175, 177 (9th Cir. 1973). Cf. Rev. Rul. 73-411, 1973-2 C.B. 180.

[246] Rev. Rul. 78-86, 1978-1 C.B. 151.

[247] Rev. Rul. 77-111, 1977-1 C.B. 144. Also, Rev. Rul. 64-108, 1964-1 C.B. 189.

[248] Rev. Rul. 81-116, 1981-1 C.B. 333. Social welfare organizations are the subject of Chapter 13.

[249] Rev. Rul. 73-313, 1973-2 C.B. 174.

[250] Id. at 176, citing In re Estate of Carlson, 358 P.2d 669 (Kan. 1961). Cf. Rev. Rul. 69-266, 1969-1 C.B. 151.

legal services for residents of economically depressed communities was ruled to be engaged in charitable activities.[251] Even though those providing the services were subsidized by the organization, the IRS minimized this personal gain by the rationale that they were merely the instruments by which the charitable purposes were accomplished.[252]

A court concluded that an organization, the primary purpose of which was to promote, improve, and expand the handicraft output of disadvantaged artisans in developing nations, was an exempt charitable entity[253] because it alleviated economic deficiencies in these societies, educated the U.S. public as to the cultural significance of these handicrafts, preserved the production of authentic handicrafts, and achieved economic stabilization in disadvantaged communities.[254]

By contrast, the same court refused to find a scholarship fund established pursuant to a collective bargaining agreement to be a charitable entity, holding it to be a voluntary employees' beneficiary association.[255] The court also found that an organization failed the exclusively test because its primary purpose was to operate bingo games for other tax-exempt organizations.[256]

The IRS revoked the tax-exempt status of a charitable organization that had as its purpose the promotion of understanding among the people of the world through learning of nations' sports activities, because of its extensive golf and tennis tours, which were found to be substantial nonexempt activities.[257] A nonprofit organization, created to provide "travel grants" to indigent and antisocial individuals, was denied exemption as a charitable entity because its purpose was to protect the commercial interests of its founders (restaurateurs on the East Coast) by ridding their community of disruptive homeless individuals by transporting them westward.[258] Exempt status was denied, pursuant to the exclusively doctrine, to an organization that was part of a hierarchy of churches and other entities because its essential purpose was to serve the financing interests of nonexempt organizations.[259]

The IRS, from time to time, issues rulings holding that organizations were not in compliance with this exclusivity standard.[260] For example, an organization formed by local businesses to offer discounts to encourage families to "shop local" was denied exemption because a substantial part of its activities supported and promoted its members' economic interests.[261] Likewise, an organization did not

---

[251] Rev. Rul. 72-559, 1972-2 C.B. 247. Also, Rev. Rul. 70-640, 1970-2 C.B. 117; Golf Life World Entertainment Golf Championship, Inc. v. United States, 65-1 U.S.T.C. ¶ 9174 (S.D. Cal. 1964). Cf. Rev. Rul. 72-369, 1972-2 C.B. 245.

[252] See § 6.3(b).

[253] The court held that the first of these activities relieved the poor and distressed or the underprivileged (see §§ 7.1, 7.2) and that the fourth of these activities promoted social welfare (see § 7.11).

[254] Aid to Artisans, Inc. v. Comm'r, 71 T.C. 202 (1978).

[255] Newspaper Guild of N.Y. v. Comm'r, 57 T.C.M. 812 (1989). See § 18.3.

[256] Make a Joyful Noise, Inc. v. Comm'r, 56 T.C.M. 1003 (1989).

[257] Tech. Adv. Mem. 9540002.

[258] Westward Ho v. Comm'r, 63 T.C.M. 2617 (1992).

[259] Church of Spiritual Technology v. United States, 92-1 U.S.T.C. ¶ 50,305 (Cl. Ct. 1992), aff'd, 991 F.2d 812 (Fed. Cir. 1993), cert. denied, 510 U.S. 870 (1993).

[260] E.g., Priv. Ltr. Rul. 201031033.

[261] Priv. Ltr. Rul. 202302017.

measure up to the exclusivity standard where it provided funding and education to "help any entrepreneur that demonstrates growth potential" and received "repayment fees" in return for this assistance—activities that neither benefited a charitable class nor were limited to purposes "that the law regards as charitable."[262]

§ 4.7 COMMENSURATE TEST

Somewhat related to the operational test is another test developed by the IRS, termed the *commensurate test*, which was first articulated in 1964.[263] Under this test, the IRS is empowered to assess whether an organization, to be tax-exempt as a charitable entity, is maintaining program activities that are commensurate in scope with its financial resources. In the facts underlying this initial ruling, the organization derived most of its income in the form of rent yet was successful in preserving its exempt status because it satisfied the test in that it was engaging in an adequate amount of charitable functions notwithstanding the extent of its rental activities.

In 1990, the IRS revoked the tax-exempt status of a charitable organization on a variety of rationales, including the ground that its fundraising costs were too high and thus violated the commensurate test. In a technical advice memorandum,[264] the IRS concluded that the test was transgressed because of its finding that the charity involved expended, during the two years examined, only about 1 percent of its revenue for charitable purposes; the rest was allegedly spent for fundraising and administration. (The matter of the organization's tax-exempt status was ultimately resolved in court, albeit without application of the commensurate test; the case turned out to be one involving private inurement.)[265]

The commensurate test and the primary purpose test have an awkward coexistence. For example, a charitable organization was allowed to retain its tax-exempt status while receiving 98 percent of its support in the form of unrelated business income since 41 percent of the organization's activities were charitable programs.[266] Likewise, an organization retained its exemption despite the fact that two-thirds of its operations were unrelated businesses.[267] Yet a public charity had its tax exemption revoked by application of the commensurate test, because, in the two years under examination, although its bingo gross income was 73 percent

---

[262] Priv. Ltr. Rul. 202305015.

[263] Rev. Rul. 64-182, 1964-1 C.B. 186. Shortly thereafter, the IRS recognized tax exemption for an organization that carried "on no operations other than to receive contributions and incidental investment income and to make distributions of income to such exempt organizations [charitable entities] at periodic intervals." Rev. Rul. 67-149, 1967-1 C.B. 133.

[264] This technical advice memorandum is reproduced at 4 *Exempt Org. Tax Rev.* (No. 5) 726 (July 1991) and is discussed in detail in *Fundraising* § 5.9.

[265] United Cancer Council, Inc. v. Comm'r, 109 T.C. 326 (1997), *rev'd and remanded*, 165 F.3d 1173 (7th Cir. 1999).

[266] Tech. Adv. Mem. 9711003. The IRS concluded, by application of the commensurate test, that the tax-exempt status of four charities should not be revoked because of the small amount of money they grant for charitable purposes (Field Serv. Adv. Mem. 199910007). Also, Help the Children v. Comm'r, 28 T.C. 1128 (1957); Rev. Rul. 68-489, 1968-2 C.B. 210.

[267] Tech. Adv. Mem. 200021056.

and 92 percent of total gross income, only a small amount of this money was distributed for charitable purposes.[268]

The commensurate test can be invoked in connection with organizations that seek to be tax-exempt charitable entities where their functions consist of fundraising and grantmaking for exempt purposes. On occasion, the IRS will rule that this type of organization cannot qualify for exemption.[269] Yet, in one instance, the IRS wrote that an organization that conducts bingo games may be exempt as a charitable entity "if it uses the proceeds from bingo to conduct a charitable program, commensurate in scope with its financial resources, of making grants to other charitable organizations."[270]

§ 4.8 STATE ACTION DOCTRINE

The *state action doctrine* can cause a tax-exempt organization to be subject to one or more constitutional law principles. The purpose of the doctrine is to treat otherwise private organizations as components or extensions of a state for the purpose of applying constitutional law standards in situations in which the state is responsible for the conduct at issue.

(a) Doctrine in General

Tax-exempt organizations are, nearly always, *private*—that is, nongovernmental—entities.[271] Thus, the operations of exempt organizations are usually not subject to constitutional law principles.[272] These principles, embedded in the U.S. Constitution and made applicable to the states by the Fourteenth Amendment to the Constitution, include free speech rights, due process, and equal protection. Consequently, whereas *state action* is subject to Fourteenth Amendment scrutiny, private conduct normally is not.

The distinction between state action and private operations sometimes is not clear; as the Supreme Court observed, it is called on from time to time to "plot a line" between the two,[273] noting that the fashioning and application of a precise formula for recognition of state responsibility is an "impossible task."[274] The courts' obligation in this setting is threefold: to "'preserv[e] an area of individual freedom by limiting the reach of federal law' and avoid[] the imposition of responsibility

---

[268] Priv. Ltr. Rul. 200825046. An organization making "minimal distributions" suffered the same outcome (Priv. Ltr. Rul. 201415003).

[269] See § 24.5(i).

[270] Priv. Ltr. Rul. 201103057. See §§ 24.1, 24.5(i)(i). The commensurate test may be applied to categories of exempt organizations other than public charities, such as fraternal entities (e.g., Priv. Ltr. Rul. 201332015).

[271] Cf. §§ 7.15, 19.22.

[272] See § 1.7.

[273] Brentwood Academy v. Tennessee Secondary School Athletic Ass'n, 531 U.S. 288, 295 (2001). Also, Nat'l Collegiate Athletic Ass'n v. Tarkanian, 488 U.S. 179, 191 (1988); Jackson v. Metropolitan Edison Co., 419 U.S. 345, 349 (1974).

[274] Kotch v. Bd. of River Port Pilot Comm'rs for the Port of New Orleans, 330 U.S. 552, 556 (1947).

on a State for conduct it could not control,"[275] as well as assure that constitutional law standards are invoked "when it can be said that the State is *responsible* for the specific conduct of which the plaintiff complains."[276]

The determination as to whether the state action doctrine is applicable to a tax-exempt organization, by attributing its activity to a government, is made pursuant to a facts-and-circumstances test; the "criteria lack rigid simplicity."[277] The Court held, for example, that a challenged activity may be state action when it results from a state's exercise of "coercive power";[278] when a state provides "significant encouragement, either overt or covert";[279] when a private organization operates as a "willful participant in joint activity with the State or its agents";[280] when the "private actor" is controlled by an "agency of the State";[281] when it has been delegated a public function by a state;[282] or when it is "entwined with governmental policies" or when government is "entwined in [its] management or control."[283]

One of the principal Supreme Court cases involving the state action doctrine concerned the operation of a private restaurant located within a state-owned automobile parking facility; the restaurant refused service to an individual because of his race. The Court held that this exclusion of the individual was discriminatory state action in violation of the Equal Protection Clause.[284] Another significant state action case had the Court considering the circumstances of an individual who, because of his race, was refused service as a guest in a dining room and bar by a fraternal lodge, which was a local branch of a national tax-exempt fraternal organization.[285] In this instance, the conclusion was that the discriminatory guest policies of the lodge did not trigger application of equal protection principles because the state involved was not sufficiently implicated.

This background led the Court to the conclusion that the "character of a legal entity is determined neither by its expressly private characterization in statutory law, nor by the failure of the law to acknowledge the entity's inseparability from recognized government officials or agencies."[286] In one instance, a privately

---

[275] Nat'l Collegiate Athletic Ass'n v. Tarkanian, 488 U.S. 179, 191 (1988), quoting Lugar v. Edmondson Oil Co., 457 U.S. 922, 936–37 (1982).

[276] Blum v. Yaretsky, 457 U.S. 991, 1004 (1982) (emphasis in the original).

[277] Brentwood Academy v. Tennessee Secondary School Athletic Ass'n, 531 U.S. 288, 295 (2001).

[278] Blum v. Yaretsky, 457 U.S. 991, 1004 (1982).

[279] *Id.*

[280] Lugar v. Edmondson Oil Co., 457 U.S. 922, 941 (1982) (internal quotation marks omitted). This type of joint activity may be cast as a conspiracy between a private party and a state official. The Supreme Court held, for example, that an individual could show a violation of their Fourteenth Amendment rights if the individual could prove that an employee of a private company and a city policeman "somehow reached an understanding to deny [her] service in the [company's] store, or cause her subsequent arrest because she was a white person in the company of Negroes" (Adickes v. Kress & Co., 398 U.S. 144, 152 (1970)).

[281] Pennsylvania v. Bd. of Directors of City Trusts of Philadelphia, 353 U.S. 230, 231 (1957).

[282] West v. Atkins, 487 U.S. 42 (1988).

[283] Evans v. Newton, 382 U.S. 296, 299, 301 (1966).

[284] Burton v. Wilmington Parking Authority, 365 U.S. 715 (1961).

[285] Moose Lodge No. 107 v. Irvis, 407 U.S. 163 (1972).

[286] Brentwood Academy v. Tennessee Secondary School Athletic Ass'n, 531 U.S. 288, 296 (2001).

endowed college was held to be a state actor and enforcement of its private found-er's limitation of admission to whites attributable to a state, because, consistent with the terms of the settlor's gift, the college's board of directors was a state agency established by state law.[287] In another case, private trustees to whom a city had transferred a park were nonetheless state actors barred from enforcing racial segregation, because the park served the public purpose of providing community recreation and the "municipality remain[ed] entwined in [its] management [and] control."[288] In still another instance, the doctrine was held inapplicable where a state university suspended one of its coaches in order to comply with the rules of a national association of colleges and universities.[289]

The law in this area significantly changed in 2001, when the Court, in another athletic association case, held that the nonprofit association was to be treated as part of a state's government and thus was bound by constitutional law princi-ples.[290] The association in this case was organized to regulate interscholastic sport among the public and private high schools in the state that were its members. The constitution, bylaws, and rules of this association set standards of school mem-bership and the eligibility of students to play in interscholastic games. The Court majority wrote: "The nominally private character of the Association is overborne by the pervasive entwinement of public institutions and public officials in its com-position and workings, and there is no substantial reason to claim unfairness in applying constitutional standards to it."[291]

Consequently, where there is "public entwinement" in the management and control of ostensibly separate nonprofit entities, the state action doctrine is likely to apply to these tax-exempt organizations.

(b) Doctrine as Applied to Social Clubs

The U.S. Constitution, in the Fifth and Fourteenth Amendments, prohibits racial discrimination by government and government-supported private institutions. In general, private organizations may lawfully discriminate, absent applicability of the *state action* doctrine (or a transgression of the public policy doctrine).[292]

The relationship between the state action doctrine and tax exemptions for social clubs[293] and other nonprofit organizations has been the focus of several cases. This relationship with regard to social clubs was the subject of a case in which a black individual, allegedly denied membership in a lodge of a frater-nal organization solely because of his race, brought a class action to enjoin the granting of tax benefits to nonprofit fraternal organizations that exclude non-white individuals from membership.[294] In this case, the court concluded that an

---

[287] Pennsylvania v. Bd. of Directors of City Trusts of Philadelphia, 353 U.S. 230 (1957).
[288] Evans v. Newton, 382 U.S. 296, 301 (1966).
[289] Nat'l Collegiate Athletic Ass'n v. Tarkanian, 488 U.S. 179 (1988).
[290] Brentwood Academy v. Tennessee Secondary School Athletic Ass'n, 531 U.S. 288 (2001).
[291] *Id.* at 298.
[292] See § 6.2.
[293] See Chapter 15.
[294] McGlotten v. Connally, 338 F. Supp. 448 (D.D.C. 1972).

exempt social club's policy of racial discrimination did not preclude exemption, although the exemption given to fraternal organizations[295] required the absence of discriminatory practices. The rationale underlying this distinction in treatment turned on the peculiar manner in which social clubs are taxed; because they are taxed on all receipts other than exempt-function income, there is no state action type "benefit" but only a matter of defining appropriate subjects of taxation, whereas fraternal organizations, being taxed only on unrelated business taxable income, do receive a government benefit in that investment income goes untaxed.

In another social club case, involving claims of religious and racial discrimination, the fact of a lease by a city to a private club, of land underlying club-constructed and club-maintained dock facilities, was held to be insufficient to supply the requisite Fourteenth Amendment significant state involvement in the membership policies of the club.[296] In another case a nonprofit swim club was held to not be a private club, enabling the court to explore whether it engaged in racial discrimination with respect to its guest policy.[297] Still another organization was held to be a private club and thus not subject to antidiscrimination laws.[298]

The Supreme Court held that a nonprofit, single-function (swimming) recreational club was not a private club and concluded that its racially discriminatory policies as to guests were violative of civil rights legislation.[299] Membership was largely keyed to a surrounding geographical area. The Court wrote: "When an organization links membership benefits to residency in a narrow geographical area, that decision infuses those benefits into the bundle of rights for which an individual pays when buying or leasing within the area."[300] The Court continued: "The mandate of [the civil rights law] then operates to guarantee a nonwhite resident who purchases, leases, or holds this property, the same rights as are enjoyed by a white resident."[301]

(c)   Doctrine and Other Exempt Organizations

The Supreme Court issued an opinion that looked like a state action case, in that a union, acting under authority of a federal statute as the exclusive bargaining representative of a craft or class of railway employees, having engaged in racial discrimination, was found liable for breach of the statutory duty to represent the interests of all of its members.[302] The Court did not resolve this case on constitutional law grounds, stating: "The economic discrimination against Negroes practiced by the

---

[295] IRC § 501(c)(8). See § 19.4(a).
[296] Golden v. Biscayne Bay Yacht Club, 530 F.2d 16 (5th Cir. 1976).
[297] Olzman v. Lake Hills Swim Club, Inc., 495 F.2d 1333 (2d Cir. 1974).
[298] Cornelius v. Benevolent Protective Order of Elks, 382 F. Supp. 1182 (D. Conn. 1974).
[299] Tillman v. Wheaton-Haven Recreational Ass'n, Inc., 410 U.S. 431 (1973).
[300] Id. at 437.
[301] Id. Also, Sullivan v. Little Hunting Park, 396 U.S. 229 (1969) (holding that a nonprofit corporation operating a community park for residents in a county was not a private social club but was a park operated on a racially discriminatory basis in violation of the Constitution).
[302] Steele v. Louisville & Nashville Railroad Co., 323 U.S. 192 (1944).

[union] and the railroad under color of Congressional authority raises a grave constitutional issue that should be squarely faced."[303]

A federal court of appeals held that a private university was not subject to the dictates of the First Amendment or the Fifth Amendment (procedural due process) in connection with the firing of a teacher; government chartering of the institution, federal and local tax exemptions, and federal funding for certain of its programs and capital expenditures were held to not represent substantial governmental involvement to trigger application of the state action doctrine.[304] Similarly, financial assistance to a private university by means of tax exemptions and student aid was held to be insufficient to render its actions as state action, in the face of a complaint that a suspended student had her First, Fifth, and Fourteenth Amendments rights violated.[305] Another appellate court held that procedures followed in the expulsion of students by a private university were not subject to the requirements of due process and equal protection, despite a state statute undertaking to set policy for coping with campus demonstrations.[306]

A test in some federal circuits is that there must be a nexus between the questioned activity (not just the entity) and the governmental funding.[307] Thus, a private hospital receiving Hill-Burton funds, having engaged in discriminatory conduct, was found to have violated the Fourth Amendment,[308] whereas a similarly funded hospital that denied a physician readmittance to the hospital staff was held to have not contravened the First, Fifth, Eighth, Ninth, and Fourteenth Amendments because the funding did not have a nexus with the employment and termination policies applied with regard to staff.[309] The receipt of Hill-Burton funds, plus financial and regulatory involvement by a state, by a private hospital was enough for a federal court of appeals to find state involvement in the hospital policy that was challenged.[310]

Another variation on the state action theme is that some courts recognize a double state action doctrine, which is a "less onerous test for cases involving racial discrimination, and a more rigorous standard for other claims."[311] In one of these cases, which proved unsuccessful, an individual brought suit against 13 charitable

---

[303] *Id.* The Court held that a privately owned and publicly regulated transit company's practice of broadcasting radio programs on its buses and trolleys was susceptible to challenge as state action (Public Utilities Comm'n of District of Columbia v. Pollak, 343 U.S. 451 (1952)) and that a political party required to perform certain significant duties by law and to conform its internal operation to statutory standards was not permitted to evade the Fourteenth Amendment's proscription of racial segregation to the conduct of primary elections (Smith v. Allwright, 321 U.S. 649 (1944)).

[304] Greenya v. George Washington Univ., 512 F.2d 556 (D.C. Cir. 1975).

[305] Berrios v. Inter American Univ., 409 F. Supp. 769 (D. P.R. 1975).

[306] Coleman v. Wagner College, 429 F.2d 1120 (2d Cir. 1970).

[307] E.g., Powe v. Miles, 407 F.2d 73 (2d Cir. 1968).

[308] Simkin v. Moses H. Cone Memorial Hosp., 323 F.2d 959 (4th Cir. 1963), *cert. denied*, 376 U.S. 938 (1964).

[309] Barrett v. United Hosp., 376 F. Supp. 791 (S.D.N.Y. 1974), *aff'd*, 506 F.2d 1395 (2d Cir. 1974). This court cited four cases where this requisite nexus was not found: Wahba v. New York Univ., 492 F.2d 96 (2d Cir. 1974); Grafton v. Brooklyn Law School, 478 F.2d 1137 (2d Cir. 1974); Mulvihill v. Julia Butterfield Memorial Hosp., 329 F. Supp. 1020 (S.D.N.Y. 1971); Grossner v. Trustees of Columbia Univ., 287 F. Supp. 535 (S.D.N.Y. 1968).

[310] Doe v. Charleston Area Med. Center, Inc., 529 F.2d 638 (4th Cir. 1975).

[311] Jackson v. Statler Found., 496 F.2d 623, 629 (2d Cir. 1974).

foundations alleging racial discrimination against himself, his children, and his foundation, inasmuch as these foundations refused to hire him as a director, to provide scholarships to his children, and to make grants to his foundation.[312]

Another factor that can lead to a finding of state action is the mandatory presence of government officials on the board of a nonprofit organization. The Supreme Court held that the position of a state agency as trustee of an organization was sufficient, without more, to constitute state action.[313] Noting that, in another case, the control by government officials was "less absolute and direct," a court wrote that "even indirect governmental participation in the management of an organization is persuasive evidence of the existence of 'state action' where that participation is both substantial and other than neutral."[314] (The states' traditional *parens patriae* role with respect to charitable organizations does not alone transform actions by charities into actions by the state.)[315]

(d)   Statutory Law

Congress concluded that it is "inappropriate" for a tax-exempt social club to have a "written policy" of discrimination on account of race, color, or religion. Accordingly, Congress, in 1976, enacted a rule that bars tax exemption for social clubs maintaining any of these types of discriminatory policies.[316] It is the position of the IRS that this proscription on discriminatory practices does not extend to exempt social clubs that limit membership on the basis of ethnic or national origin.[317]

In 1980, Congress refined this requirement to allow tax-exempt social clubs that are affiliated with fraternal beneficiary societies[318] to retain tax exemption even though membership in the clubs is limited to members of a particular religion. Also, this law change allows certain alumni clubs, which are limited to members of a particular religion in order to further the religion's teachings or principles, to retain their exemption as social clubs.[319]

§ 4.9   COMMERCIALITY DOCTRINE

Occasionally, as part of the law of tax-exempt organizations, the courts will create law or develop law that is in addition to the statutory criteria. This phenomenon is most obvious and extensive in connection with the evolution and application of the *commerciality doctrine*. These principles are impacting the law concerning

---

[312] *Id.* Also Lefcourt v. Legal Aid Society, 445 F.2d 1150 (2d Cir. 1971); Wolis v. Port Authority, 392 F.2d 83 (2d Cir. 1968), *cert. denied*, 393 U.S. 940 (1969).

[313] Pennsylvania v. Bd. of Directors of City Trusts of the City of Philadelphia, 353 U.S. 230 (1969).

[314] Jackson v. Statler Found., 496 F.2d 623, 635 (2d Cir. 1974). Minority involvement by representatives of government agencies on an advisory council of an organization providing consulting services to a nonprofit organization was held insufficient to entail state action (New York City Jaycees, Inc. v. United States Jaycees, Inc., 512 F.2d 856 (2d Cir. 1975)).

[315] E.g., Mayers v. Ridley, 465 F.2d 630 (D.C. Cir. 1972).

[316] IRC § 501(i).

[317] Tech. Adv. Mem. 8317004.

[318] See § 19.4(a).

[319] IRC § 501(i), last sentence.

qualification for exemption, principally for charitable organizations, and in the process helping shape the law of unrelated business activities.

(a) Summary of Doctrine

The commerciality doctrine essentially is this: A tax-exempt organization (most likely, a public charity) is engaged in a nonexempt activity when that activity is undertaken in a manner that is *commercial* in nature. An activity is a commercial one if it has a direct counterpart in, or is conducted in the same or similar manner as in, the realm of for-profit organizations. (Having stated the essence of the doctrine, it must also be said that it is unevenly applied.)

The usual sanction for violation of the commerciality doctrine is denial of recognition of, or revocation of, tax-exempt status.

(b) Assumption Underlying Doctrine

The commerciality doctrine is largely predicated on the assumption that a non-profit organization that is operating in the same manner as, and/or is directly competing with, a for-profit organization is thus a *commercial* entity and therefore is ineligible for federal tax exemption. The criteria for assessing operations *in the same manner* as for-profit companies principally are pricing formulas, hours of operation, marketing, officers' and employees' competence, use of employees, and lack of funding by charitable contributions and grants.

The biggest problem presented by this assumption is that it is inconsistent with reality. With the rise of for-profit companies' involvement in fields such as education and health, there are thousands of instances on an ongoing basis where nonprofit and for-profit entities are essentially operating in the same manner and/or are in competition (for example, hospitals, schools, theaters, and publishing entities).

(c) Origin of Doctrine

The doctrine was initiated long before Congress enacted the unrelated income rules in 1950. It was first mentioned, at the federal level, in 1924, by the U.S. Supreme Court.[320] The case concerned a tax-exempt religious order that was operated for religious purposes, but that engaged in other activities that the government alleged destroyed the basis for its exemption; the order had extensive investments in real estate and stock holdings that returned a profit, as well as some incidental sales of wine, chocolate, and other articles. The Supreme Court found that the order was exempt as a religious entity, justifying its investment and business efforts by writing that "[s]uch [religious] activities cannot be carried on without money."[321]

In this case, the Court did not articulate a commerciality doctrine. The Court characterized the government's argument as being that the order "is operated also for business and *commercial* purposes."[322] The Court rejected this characterization, writing that there is no "competition" and that while the "transactions yield some profit [it] is in the circumstances a negligible factor."[323] Thus, in this case,

---

[320] Trinidad v. Sagrada Orden de Predicadores, 263 U.S. 578 (1924).
[321] *Id.* at 581.
[322] *Id.* (emphasis added).
[323] *Id.* at 582.

the Supreme Court did not enunciate the commerciality doctrine; however, by using the word in describing the government's position, the commerciality doctrine was born.

(d)   Focus on Publishing

Courts' scrutiny of nonprofit publishing organizations provides telling applications of the doctrine. An entity that published religious literature in an effort to upgrade the quality of Bible teaching materials was held to be of a "nonexempt character" because of its commercial nature.[324] By contrast, without referencing commerciality, a court held that an organization publishing a system for indexing library collections was tax-exempt,[325] as was an organization that sold religious publications and charged admission fees to conclaves.[326] Yet, an organization disseminating publications containing investment advice to subscribers was denied exemption as an educational entity.[327]

Another court rejected the government's contention that the publication and sale of religious magazines, books, pamphlets, Bibles, records, tape recordings, and pictures amounted to commercial activity.[328] This court was faced with another case involving the operation of alleged commercial enterprises, this time concerning a religious organization that conducted training projects. The court rejected the commerciality doctrine, with the observation that "we regard consistent nonprofitability as evidence of the absence of commercial purposes."[329]

Still another case involving a religious publishing organization was considered by a federal district court, which refined the commerciality doctrine by distinguishing between organizations that have commercial activities as a part of their overall activities and those that have commercial activities as their sole activity.[330] Organizations that retained their tax exemption in the prior cases were grouped in the first category;[331] the other organizations were placed in the second category. The court thus relied on the other cases[332] in concluding that the publishing company was not exempt. The nonexempt purpose[333] was portrayed as the "publication and sale of religious literature at a profit."[334] The court said its conclusion could not be otherwise—"If it were, every publishing house would be entitled to an exemption on the ground that it furthers the education of the public."[335]

---

[324] Scripture Press Found. v. United States, 285 F.2d 800, 807 (Ct. Cl. 1961).

[325] Forest Press, Inc. v. Comm'r, 22 T.C. 265 (1954).

[326] Saint Germain Found. v. Comm'r, 26 T.C. 648 (1956).

[327] American Inst. for Economic Research v. United States, 302 F.2d 934 (Ct. Cl. 1962).

[328] A.A. Allen Revivals, Inc. v. Comm'r, 22 T.C. 1435 (1963).

[329] Golden Rule Church Ass'n v. Comm'r, 41 T.C. 719, 731 (1964).

[330] Fides Publishers Ass'n v. United States, 263 F. Supp. 924 (N.D. Ind. 1967).

[331] This includes decisions such as Saint Germain Found. v. Comm'r, 26 T.C. 648 (1956); Golden Rule Church Ass'n v. Comm'r, 41 T.C. 719 (1964); A.A. Allen Revivals, Inc. v. Comm'r, 22 T.C. 1435 (1963).

[332] Scripture Press Found. v. United States, 285 F.2d 800 (Ct. Cl. 1961); American Inst. for Economic Research v. United States, 302 F.2d 934 (Ct. Cl. 1962).

[333] Following the rationale in Better Business Bureau of Wash., D.C. v. United States, 326 U.S. 279 (1945).

[334] Fides Publishers Ass'n v. United States, 263 F. Supp. 924, 935 (N.D. Ind. 1967).

[335] Id.

Another federal district court came to the identical result. A publisher of religious materials was denied tax exemption because it was "clearly engaged primarily in a business activity, and it conducted its operations, although on a small scale, in the same way as any commercial publisher of religious books for profit would have done."[336] The fact that the organization's ultimate purpose was a religious one did not, for that court, confer exemption.

The next year, this opinion was reversed. The case was won before the appellate court on the ground that the organization did not have "operational profits."[337] The court concluded that the "deficit operation reflects not poor business planning nor ill fortune but rather the fact that profits were not the goal of the operation."[338] Although the nonprofit organization involved in the case prevailed, this opinion went a long way toward establishment of the point that the existence of profit is evidence of commerciality.

An organization that disseminated sermons to ministers to improve their religious teachings was held to be tax-exempt.[339] The same court concluded that an entity that published and sold books written by its founder was not exempt.[340] Another court decided that an organization publishing religious literature should be deprived of its exemption because it evolved into a "highly efficient business venture" with a "commercial hue,"[341] although its similar decision in a subsequent case was reversed.[342]

(e) Other Applications of Doctrine

An organization that purchased and sold products manufactured by blind individuals was ruled to be tax-exempt because it alleviated the hardships experienced by these individuals.[343] But an entity that benefited the poor by assisting in the operation of businesses that employ these individuals was denied exemption on the basis of the commerciality doctrine.[344] An ostensibly religious organization failed to achieve exemption because the information it provided was no different from that furnished by a commercial tax service.[345] An organization that assisted in the process of transfer of technology from universities and research institutions to industry was ruled to be operating in a commercial manner.[346] An entity operating a religious retreat center, as an integral part of a conference of the United Methodist Church, was found to be exempt and not commercial in nature because it did not compete

---

[336] Elisian Guild, Inc. v. United States, 292 F. Supp. 219, 221 (D. Mass. 1968).

[337] Elisian Guild, Inc. v. United States, 412 F.2d 121, 125 (1st Cir. 1969).

[338] *Id.* at 125.

[339] Pulpit Resource v. Comm'r, 70 T.C. 594 (1978).

[340] Christian Manner Int'l v. Comm'r, 71 T.C. 661 (1979).

[341] Incorporated Trustees of Gospel Worker Soc'y v. United States, 510 F. Supp. 374, 381 (D.D.C. 1981), *aff'd*, 672 F.2d 894 (D.C. Cir. 1981), *cert. denied*, 456 U.S. 944 (1981).

[342] Presbyterian & Reformed Publishing Co. v. Comm'r, 79 T.C. 1070 (1982), *rev'd*, 743 F.2d 148 (3d Cir. 1984).

[343] Industrial Aid for the Blind v. Comm'r, 73 T.C. 96 (1979).

[344] Greater United Navajo Dev. Enters., Inc. v. Comm'r, 74 T.C. 69 (1980).

[345] Ecclesiastical Order of the Ism of Am, Inc. v. Comm'r, 80 T.C. 833 (1983).

[346] Washington Research Found. v. Comm'r, 50 T.C.M. 1457 (1985). This opinion was "overturned" by Congress when it enacted § 1605 of the Tax Reform Act of 1986 (see H. R. Rep. 99-841, at II-827 (1986)). See § 9.5.

with for-profit businesses.[347] An organization that was ruled to be charitable because it produced plays in a theater had its exemption revoked because it ceased educating the public in the theater arts and began hosting tribute band concerts, which the IRS, not surprisingly, found to be a commercial undertaking.[348]

A major commerciality doctrine case concerned a nonprofit organization that operated an adoption agency.[349] It was held that this organization could not qualify as an exempt charitable or educational entity because adoption services are not inherently exempt functions; the organization was cast as operating in a manner not "distinguishable from a commercial adoption agency," because it generated substantial profits, accumulated capital, was funded entirely by fees, had no plans to solicit contributions, and had a paid staff.[350]

(f)   Elements of Commerciality

A court concluded that the commerciality doctrine was the basis for denial of tax-exempt status, as a charitable and religious entity, to an organization associated with the Seventh-Day Adventist Church that operated, in advancement of church doctrine, vegetarian restaurants and health food stores.[351] The court wrote that the organization's "activity was conducted as a business and was in direct competition with other restaurants and health food stores."[352] The court added: "Competition with commercial firms is strong evidence of a substantial nonexempt commercial purpose."[353]

When this case was considered on appeal, the appellate court affirmed the lower court decision.[354] The appellate court opinion detailed the factors that the court relied on in finding commerciality and thus offered the fundamental basis for contemporary explication of the commerciality doctrine. These factors were that (1) the organization sold goods and services to the public (this factor alone was said to make the operations "presumptively commercial"),[355] (2) the organization was in "direct competition" with for-profit restaurants and food stores, (3) the prices set by the organization were based on pricing formulas common in the retail food

---

[347] Junaluska Assembly Hous., Inc. v. Comm'r, 86 T.C. 1114 (1986).

[348] Priv. Ltr. Rul. 201846007.

[349] Easter House v. United States, 846 F.2d 78 (Fed. Cir. 1988), aff'g 12 Ct. Cl. 476 (87-1 U.S.T.C. ¶ 9359) (Ct. Cl. 1987), cert. denied, 488 U.S. 907 (1988).

[350] Id., 12 Ct. Cl. at 482.

[351] Living Faith, Inc. v. Comm'r, 60 T.C.M. 710 (1990).

[352] Id. at 713.

[353] Id.

[354] Living Faith, Inc. v. Comm'r, 950 F.2d 365 (7th Cir. 1991). In another case, a court concluded that an organization's principal activity was the "operation of a number of canteen-style lunch trucks," which is a commercial activity, and upheld revocation of the organization's tax exemption (New Faith, Inc. v. Comm'r, 64 T.C.M. 1050 (1992)). Likewise, a nonprofit organization, the activities of which were the same as a temporary service agency, was denied tax-exempt status because it was "essentially a commercial venture" (At Cost Services, Inc. v. Comm'r, 80 T.C.M. 573 (2000)).

[355] Interestingly, a report found that in 2016 charitable contributions accounted for only 13.3 percent of revenue received by charitable organizations that file Form 990, with 72.2 percent of their revenue coming from "program services, such as tuition paid by college and university students, payments for hospital stays, and entry fees" (Congressional Research Service, "Tax Issues Relating to Charitable Contributions and Organizations" Rep. No. R45922 (Aug. 4, 2020), at 14).

business (with the "profit-making price structure loom[ing] large" in the court's analysis and the court criticizing the organization for not having "below-cost pricing"), (4) the organization utilized promotional materials and "commercial catch phrases" to enhance sales, (5) the organization advertised its services and food ($15,500 expended for advertising over two years), (6) the organization's hours of operation were basically the same as for-profit enterprises, (7) the guidelines by which the organization operated required that its management have "business ability" and six months of training, (8) the organization did not utilize volunteers but paid salaries (totaling $63,000 in one year and more than $25,000 in another year), and (9) the organization did not receive charitable contributions.

Subsequently, a federal district court denied tax-exempt status to an organization whose principal purpose was operation of a conference center, on the ground that there was a distinctly commercial hue associated with its operations.[356] The commerciality doctrine as applied in this case was based on a close following of the foregoing appellate court decision.[357] The court stated that among the "major factors" courts have considered in "assessing commerciality" are competition with for-profit entities, the extent and degree of low-cost services provided, pricing policies, and the reasonableness of financial reserves.[358] Additional factors were said to include whether the organization uses "commercial promotional methods (e.g., advertising)" and the extent to which the organization receives charitable contributions.[359] The conference center was portrayed as operated in a commercial manner, in part because its patrons were not confined to tax-exempt organizations and because the facility was used for weddings and similar events.

(g) IRS Ruling Policy

The IRS enthusiastically embraces the commerciality doctrine, utilizing its precepts in a wide variety of settings. So have courts. A court applied the commerciality doctrine in the context of ascertaining whether a tax-exempt charitable organization should lose its exempt status because its fundraising costs are too "high."[360] Further, it was held that an organization selling religious tapes was a nonexempt commercial organization,[361] and that an organization operating prisoner rehabilitation programs was not eligible for tax exemption because of commercial activities.[362]

The IRS's policy of denying recognition of tax exemption to, or revoking the exempt status of, credit counseling and down payment assistance organizations entails frequent invocation of the doctrine.[363] Other instances of IRS utilization of the doctrine in its rulings include denial of exempt status to an organization

---

[356] Airlie Found. v. Internal Revenue Service, 283 F. Supp. 2d 58 (D.D.C. 2003).
[357] See *supra* note 354.
[358] Airlie Found. v. Internal Revenue Service, 283 F. Supp. 2d 58, 63 (D.D.C. 2003).
[359] *Id.*
[360] United Cancer Council, Inc. v. Comm'r, 109 T.C. 326 (1997), *rev'd and remanded*, 165 F.3d 1173 (7th Cir. 1999).
[361] United Missionary Aviation, Inc. v. Comm'r, 60 T.C.M. 1152 (1990), *rev'd and remanded*, 985 F.2d 564 (8th Cir. 1989), *cert. denied*, 506 U.S. 816 (1992).
[362] Public Indust., Inc. v. Comm'r, 61 T.C.M. 1626 (1991).
[363] See §§ 7.3, 7.5.

that facilitates the sale of health insurance for for-profit insurance companies;[364] an organization that facilitates charitable contributions of boats and other items of tangible personal property to charitable organizations;[365] an organization that established a center to provide rest and relaxation to caregivers of chronically and terminally ill individuals (because the services to be provided are akin to those provided by a commercial inn);[366] an organization that maintained a golf course open to the public on a fee-for-service basis;[367] an organization that sells books and other religious products as part of a network involving a church that is expanding the distribution of religious materials (because, according to the IRS, it is operating in a manner comparable to that of a for-profit publisher);[368] an organization providing free Internet access throughout a state, primarily through wireless networking, in part because it is enhancing the interests of for-profit companies that facilitate Internet access by enhancing their ability to attract customers;[369] an organization believing itself to be an incubator of small businesses and nonprofit organizations (which are often tax-exempt) but which the IRS held to be similar to for-profit consulting companies that charge fees for their services;[370] an organization operating a fee-based health care cooperative in a commercial manner;[371] an organization conducting raffles as a commercial business;[372] an organization that functioned as a licensing agency for products devised by children in contests, where it served to further children's education and establish a social network to further children's education funding;[373] an organization that was said by the IRS to be competing with for-profit companies (although that point was not explained) and had an insubstantial amount of charitable gifts;[374] and an organization that leases modified property to individuals with disabilities, for the purpose of advertising for businesses.[375]

A church attempted to create an exempt coffeehouse, to enable it to appear "truly concerned" about its community, but the IRS rejected the idea, taking the position that the enterprise was a commercial one, competing with for-profit coffee shops.[376] In an extraordinary application of the commerciality doctrine, a nonprofit organization formed to combat organized theft and fraud that supports opioid and heroin addiction, by utilizing innovative software in conjunction with retailers and law enforcement agencies, was denied recognition of exemption as a charitable entity, with the IRS invoking the doctrine by characterizing the organization as merely providing a "service for a fee to retail stores."[377] The better

[364] Priv. Ltr. Rul. 200512023.
[365] Priv. Ltr. Rul. 200512027.
[366] Priv. Ltr. Rul. 200525020.
[367] Priv. Ltr. Rul. 200815035.
[368] Priv. Ltr. Rul. 201205013.
[369] Priv. Ltr. Rul. 201231012.
[370] Priv. Ltr. Rul. 201403017.
[371] Priv. Ltr. Rul. 201409012.
[372] Priv. Ltr. Rul. 201410035.
[373] Priv. Ltr. Rul. 201545029.
[374] Priv. Ltr. Rul. 201548021.
[375] Priv. Ltr. Rul. 202039019.
[376] Priv. Ltr. Rul. 201150034.
[377] Priv. Ltr. Rul. 202021026.

analysis would have been to recognize exemption as an entity promoting health and lessening the burdens of government,[378] with services to retailers cast as a means to larger exempt ends.[379]

Additional private letter rulings are being issued on this subject.[380]

The commerciality doctrine is being applied in some of the cases involving the provision of *commercial-type insurance*.[381] For example, in one of these cases, the court wrote that the "various factors to consider in determining whether an organization promotes a forbidden nonexempt purpose" under the rules concerning charitable organizations include the "manner in which an organization conducts its activities; the commercial hue or nature of those activities; the competitive nature of the activities; the existence of accumulated profits; and the provision of free or below cost services."[382] The organization, the tax status of which was at issue in the case, was characterized by the court as existing "solely for the purpose of selling insurance to nonprofit exempt organizations at the lowest possible cost on a continued, stable basis"; the court continued with the observation that "[s]elling insurance undeniably is an inherently commercial activity ordinarily carried on by a commercial for-profit company."[383] The court added that, although the organization "may not possess every attribute characteristic of a mutual insurance company, it possesses a majority of the qualifying characteristics, which only further enhances the determination that . . . [it] is presumptively commercial in nature."[384] In another of these cases, a court concluded that a group of self-insurance pools had a "commercial hue."[385] For example, a court assumed that an activity labeled *recreational* was "inherently commercial" and decided on that basis that an organization providing recreational therapy could not qualify as a charitable entity.[386]

(h) Contemporary Perspective on Doctrine

The commerciality doctrine has become one of the IRS's most potent tools to invoke when denying recognition of, or revoking, tax exemption, particularly where the issue involved is status as a charitable organization. The IRS has pushed the doctrine beyond the boundaries of the elements of commerciality articulated by courts.[387] Meanwhile, these elements are increasingly appearing quaint and even nonsensical today.

---

[378] See §§ 7.6, 7.7, respectively.

[379] See § 6.3(b).

[380] E.g., Priv. Ltr. Rul. 202307007. In applying the commerciality doctrine, the IRS may compound its adverse (from the standpoint of the applicant or exempt organization) findings by borrowing a precept from the unrelated business rules (see § 24.4(b)) and hold that the commercial operation is being conducted on a scale larger than is reasonably necessary for the conduct of the activities as exempt functions (e.g., Priv. Ltr. Rul. 200815035).

[381] See § 24.9.

[382] Nonprofits' Ins. Alliance of Cal. v. United States, 94-2 U.S.T.C. ¶ 50,593 (Fed. Cl. 1994).

[383] Id.

[384] Id.

[385] Paratransit Ins. Corp. v. Comm'r, 102 T.C. 745, 754 (1994). Subsequently, Congress enacted a limited tax exemption for certain charitable risk pools (see § 11.6).

[386] GameHearts v. Comm'r, 110 T.C.M. 454, 457 (2015).

[387] See § 4.9(f).

The IRS's expansive view as to the factors "indicative of commercial operations" is that they include "regular and ongoing . . . sales [to the public], competition with other [organizations], common retail pricing structures, marketing and advertising, and the reliance on sales and fees versus contributions."[388]

The competition element is most troublesome, particularly when the lines of demarcation between nonprofit and for-profit organizations are, in some instances, blurring.[389] Nonprofit organizations are becoming increasingly reliant on revenue in the form of fees for services. For-profit organizations are more concerned than ever about their public image and the extent to which they can provide assistance to their communities. For-profit organizations are entering domains of producing and providing services that were once the sole province of nonprofit organizations. Laws are changed to promote greater parity between the sectors, such as the Office of Management and Budget regulations, which require tax-exempt organizations pursuing government contracts to calculate tax revenues forgone. Management of nonprofit organizations is becoming more sophisticated.[390]

The IRS provided a unique application of the commerciality doctrine, holding that a community foundation can, in furtherance of charitable purposes, sell grant-making services to charitable organizations in its community, although the sales of administrative and clerical services were held to be nonexempt functions.[391] The IRS suggested that the purchasing charitable entities constituted a charitable class,[392] a fact that trumped the "commercial nature of the service." The IRS dismissed the matter of the charging of fees,[393] stating that the fees would be reasonable.[394]

Two categories of charitable organizations continue to evolve: those that are supported largely by gifts (*donative* organizations)[395] and those that are supported

---

[388] Priv. Ltr. Rul. 201710033.

[389] An entity was held to not qualify for tax exemption as a charitable and educational organization, in part because it competed with for-profit companies and engaged in the same activities as its for-profit predecessor (Asmark Institute, Inc. v. Comm'r, 101 T.C.M. 1067 (2011), *aff'd*, 2102-2 U.S.T.C. ¶ 50,436 (6th Cir. 2012)).

[390] There are, to be sure, some obvious instances of commerciality in this context. The IRS applied the commerciality doctrine in denying recognition of tax exemption to an organization whose primary activity was being a landlord (Priv. Ltr. Rul. 200950047), an online publishing business (Priv. Ltr. Rul. 201029031), a "first of its kind" nonprofit restaurant that proposed to offer "quality fine dining" and "excellence in customer service" to its members and other patrons (Priv. Ltr. Rul. 201046016), a provider of investment and borrowing opportunities to its members (Priv. Ltr. Rul. 201051024), an operator of a grocery store and bait shop (Priv. Ltr. Rul. 201122022), an organization offering spa retreats (Priv. Ltr. Rul. 201122028), an operator of a residential construction business (Priv. Ltr. Rul. 201446028), an operator of a pharmacy for the public (Priv. Ltr. Rul. 201743018), an operator of a tavern (Priv. Ltr. Rul. 202016019), and an operator of a used car dealership (Priv. Ltr. Rul. 202031010). Likewise, an organization was denied exemption as a charitable entity because its function was selling flowers at market prices to the public online, as part of a network of florists (even though charitable organizations were to receive the profits arising from the sales transactions, at the designation of customers) (Zagfly, Inc. v. Comm'r, 105 T.C.M. 1214 (2013)).

[391] Priv. Ltr. Rul. 200832027.

[392] See § 6.3(a).

[393] See §§ 6.3(h), 24.2(e).

[394] Likewise, an organization derived income in the form of "service fees," with the IRS rationalizing the appropriateness of this revenue by explaining how the money will be used in support of related activities (Priv. Ltr. Rul. 201250025).

[395] See § 12.3(b)(i).

principally by exempt function revenue (*service provider* organizations).[396] As this trend continues, it will force new pressures on the concept of tax exemption. New rationales for exemption may emerge. The battles that are building over the ground rules for exemptions for hospitals[397] and credit unions[398] should be appreciated from this perspective. The growth of the social enterprise movement is likely to exacerbate this phenomenon.[399]

The IRS is not content with the existence of the courts' factors evidencing (ostensible) commerciality. In one ruling, the agency came up with these items "demonstrating" the presence of commercial operations: free WiFi, existence of a website, and the provision of power outlets for use by the entity's patrons.[400] In another instance, the IRS ruled that the fact that an organization collected testimonials on its website was evidence that the entity was being operated in a commercial manner.[401] An organization was ruled to have violated the doctrine by establishing chapters and charging them operational fees.[402] The IRS has stretched the doctrine to the point where it declares that tax-exempt organizations "should not duplicate services or facilities provided by commercial entities."[403]

The IRS issues, on a regular basis, rulings finding commerciality because a nonprofit organization was competing with a for-profit company,[404] engaging in sales activity (generation of fee-for-service revenue),[405] engaging in marketing efforts,[406] lacking in the use of volunteers,[407] using comparable hours of operation,[408] and failing to receive charitable contributions.[409] The IRS is beginning to utilize the commerciality doctrine in defining an unrelated business.[410]

Matters would be helped in this regard if the IRS based its adverse rulings on bodies of law other than the commerciality doctrine, such as the operational test,[411] the private inurement doctrine,[412] the private benefit doctrine,[413] and the

---

[396] See § 12.3(b)(iv).
[397] See § 7.6(a), (b).
[398] See § 24.5(g).
[399] See § 4.10.
[400] Priv. Ltr. Rul. 201645017.
[401] Priv. Ltr. Rul. 201540019.
[402] Priv. Ltr. Rul. 201712017.
[403] Priv. Ltr. Rul. 201801014.
[404] E.g., Priv. Ltr. Rul. 201548021.
[405] E.g., Priv. Ltr. Rul. 201548025.
[406] E.g., Priv. Ltr. Rul. 201710033.
[407] E.g., Priv. Ltr. Rul. 201428022.
[408] Priv. Ltr. Rul. 201645017.
[409] E.g., Priv. Ltr. Rul. 201428022.
[410] E.g., Priv. Ltr. Rul. 201814009.
[411] See § 4.5.
[412] See Chapter 20.
[413] See § 20.13.

unrelated business rules.[414] The IRS occasionally does this.[415] This also can happen with a court.[416]

§ 4.10   SOCIAL ENTERPRISE DEVELOPMENTS

Among the contemporary forces shaping the law of tax-exempt organizations is emergence of *entrepreneurialism*: the open and accepted conduct of businesses by exempt organizations, with a for-profit mentality to the end of supplementing or even supplanting charitable contributions and grants. The unabashed aim of organizations undertaking entrepreneurial activities is to generate funds for the mission, upgrade the quality of staff and other resources, and become self-sufficient (that is, not dependent for financial support on external funders). This element of entrepreneurialism is a component of what has become known as the *social enterprise* movement. Another aspect of this movement is the emergence of new forms of entities.

(a)   Concept of *Social Enterprise*

The nomenclature surrounding the social enterprise phenomenon is illuminating: *business ventures, corporate partnerships, strategic partnerships,* and *cause-related marketing.* This parlance is decorated with verbs such as *leverage, develop* (the mission), *license, capitalize,* and *invest.*

There is, of course, nothing new in the fact that tax-exempt organizations undertake related and unrelated businesses.[417] What is different in the social enterprise setting is the underlying spirit or philosophy of entrepreneurialism. Its proponents see heavy reliance on contributors and grantors as arcane and confining. They disregard concern about traditional federal tax law constraints; rarely in the literature of social enterprisers is much written about the actual or potential impact of these business ventures on organizations' tax-exempt status or susceptibility to unrelated business income taxation. Instead, the emphasis is on business

---

[414] See Chapters 24, 25. In one instance, the IRS applied the commerciality doctrine, then also held that much of an organization's activities constituted unrelated business (Priv. Ltr. Rul. 201918019).

[415] For example, the IRS denied recognition as an exempt charitable entity to an organization that operated a banquet center available for fees to the public, on the ground that it was operating an unrelated business (Priv. Ltr. Rul. 201803009), as was the case where the primary activity of an organization was the sale and rental of durable medical equipment (Priv. Ltr. Rul. 201925015), and where an organization provided business development and marketing and consulting services for a fee to various types of nonprofit organizations (Priv. Ltr. Rul. 201925017). In other cases, the IRS revoked exempt status because the organization was engaging in substantial nonexempt activities (Priv. Ltr. Ruls. 201929021, 201926016). In one instance, the IRS applied the commerciality doctrine, where use of the private benefit doctrine would have been more appropriate (Priv. Ltr. Rul. 201941029).

[416] E.g., Abovo Found., Inc. v. Comm'r, 115 T.C.M. 1277 (2018) (finding "consulting" services a violation of the operational test and private benefit doctrine).

[417] See Chapters 24, 25.

opportunities, asset base expansion, productivity incentives, employee training and advancement, and public relations. Terms heretofore uttered only in the for-profit sector now dominate the social enterprise lexicon: *profit margin, return on investment, risk tolerance, capacity building, self-sufficiency, diversified revenue strategy,* and the irrepressible *new paradigm.*

The thinking and actions of this form of entrepreneurialism dramatically clash with the commerciality doctrine.[418] As discussed, that doctrine holds that a charitable organization's tax-exempt status is endangered when elements such as focus on the wants and needs of the public, profits, and marketing are taken into account by it, not to mention trained employees and decreased reliance on gifts and grants.

Social enterprise philosophy tends to eschew the use of for-profit subsidiaries.[419] The attraction is to partnerships—not in the sense of discrete legal entities[420] but rather direct interrelationships with for-profit businesses, where the entities function in tandem (*partner* or form a *strategic alliance*) to advance charitable causes (*missions*), rely on in-kind gifts, engage in unique fundraising promotions, utilize technical assistance, and operate using other forms of *mission alignment.*

Public charities contemplating involvement in social enterprises may consider doing so other than by directly partnering with a for-profit business. Alternatives include use of a supporting organization,[421] a for-profit subsidiary, or a limited liability company or other form of joint venture vehicle.[422] Entrepreneurialism can have an adverse impact on tax-exempt and/or public charity status,[423] cause application of the unrelated business rules, and/or attract forms of legal liability.

To date, the federal tax law has not dampened the enthusiasm or curbed the innovativeness of the structures of the social enterprise movement. This is somewhat surprising, given the robust expansion of the private inurement and private benefit doctrines,[424] the potency of the intermediate sanctions rules,[425] and the unrelated business rules.

(b) Program-Related Investments

Historically, the blending of charitable activity and potentially nonexempt functions (investing) has appeared in the private foundation rules concerning *program-related investments*, which do not constitute jeopardizing investments.[426] This is because the primary purpose of a program-related investment is to accomplish one or more charitable purposes.[427] Also, no significant purpose of the investment

---

[418] See § 4.9.
[419] See Chapter 30.
[420] See § 31.1(a).
[421] See § 12.3(c).
[422] See Chapters 30–32.
[423] See § 12.3.
[424] See Chapter 20.
[425] See Chapter 21.
[426] See § 12.4(d).
[427] Reg. § 53.4944-3(a).

may be the production of income or the appreciation of property; no purpose of the investment may be for lobbying or intervention in political campaigns.[428]

Program-related investments constitute private foundation qualifying distributions[429] and are not subject to the excess business holdings restrictions.[430] Where the investment is in an entity that is not a public charity, expenditure responsibility must be exercised by the foundation.[431]

(c)   Low-Profit Limited Liability Companies

As noted, an aspect of the social enterprise movement is the emergence of new forms of entities. The most common of these organizations to date, spawned because of the program-related investments rules, is the *low-profit limited liability company* (L3C). These organizations are the subject of state statute. These L3Cs are likely to be for-profit, taxable entities, with one or more taxable members. An L3C has as its primary purpose the accomplishment of one or more charitable purposes. The production of income is a permitted secondary purpose of an L3C.

The principal federal tax law issue in this regard is whether an investment by a private foundation in an L3C qualifies as a program-related investment. The requirements for qualification as an L3C are essentially identical to the preexisting law for these investments. An investment in an L3C, however, does not automatically mean that the investment is a program-related investment.

(d)   B Corporations

B corporations are not a form of entity but are business corporations that are certified by the B Lab (a tax-exempt charitable entity) as companies working to solve social and environmental problems. To be certified, a corporation must meet performance and legal accountability standards and build constituencies.

(e)   Benefit Corporations

Another type of hybrid or blended corporation is the *benefit corporation*, which is an entity that has socially responsible and business purposes. These corporations are formed by state statute; they elect to be this type of corporation, pursuing ends such as environmental preservation, promotion of health, and promotion of the arts and sciences. In determining what is in the best interests of a benefit corporation, its directors are to consider the effects of any action or decision on a variety of stakeholders, including its shareholders, employees, and customers, as well as community and societal aspects.

(f)   Flexible Purpose Corporations

Efforts are under way in California to create a new type of corporation that has flexibility in combining profitability and social purposes—the *flexible purpose corporation*. This entity would have essentially the same characteristics as the benefit corporation.

---

[428] *Id.* See *Private Foundations* § 8.3.
[429] See § 12.4(b).
[430] See § 12.4(c).
[431] See *Private Foundations* § 9.7.

Nonprofit Governance

The law concerning the governance of tax-exempt organizations, including the composition and role of governing boards, has traditionally been the province of state law, principally nonprofit corporation and trust statutes, augmented by court opinions. In recent years, however, much attention has been given to these matters at the federal law level, including the law of exempt organizations, with emphasis on the practices of public charities. Indeed, questions on board composition and various governance policies and procedures are part of the basic federal annual information return.[1]

§ 5.1 BOARDS OF DIRECTORS BASICS

The fundamentals of the law concerning the boards of directors of tax-exempt organizations include the nomenclature assigned to the group, the number of directors, the origin(s) of the director positions, the control factor, the scope of the board's authority, and the relationship to the officer positions.

---

[1] See §§ 5.6(c), 28.2.

§ 5.2 BOARD COMPOSITION AND TAX LAW

Generally, the federal statutory tax law, the federal tax regulations, or the public revenue rulings from the IRS have nothing to say about the composition of the governing board of a tax-exempt organization; it is, as noted, essentially a state law matter. There are six exceptions: (1) exempt health care organizations are required to satisfy a community benefit test, which includes a requirement of a community board;[2] (2) organizations that qualify as publicly supported entities by reason of a facts-and-circumstances test are likely to be required to have a governing board that is representative of the community;[3] (3) the rules concerning supporting organizations often dictate the manner in which board members are selected;[4] (4) there are unique requirements for credit counseling organizations;[5] (5) the rules for public interest law firms require a board reflective of the public;[6] and (6) the tax regulations concerning community foundations contain slight references to the fiduciary responsibilities of their boards.[7] Basically, then, those forming and operating an exempt organization are free to structure and populate its board in any manner they determine, within the bounds of state law.

Nonetheless, the courts have constructed certain presumptions in this context. For example, the U.S. Tax Court has expressed the view that "where the creators [of an organization] control the affairs of the organization, there is an obvious opportunity for abuse, which necessitates an open and candid disclosure of all facts bearing upon the organization, operation, and finances so that the Court can be assured that by granting the claimed exemption it is not sanctioning an abuse of the revenue laws."[8]

In another case, where all of the directors and officers of an organization were related, the Tax Court could not find the "necessary delineation" between the organization and these individuals acting in their personal and private capacity.[9] Earlier a court of appeals concluded that the fact that a married couple made up two of three members of an organization's board of directors required a special justification of certain payments by the organization to them.[10] Before that, an appellate court decided that an individual who had "complete and unfettered control" over an organization has a special burden to explain certain withdrawals from the organization's bank account.[11] In still another setting, the small size of an organization (five individuals) was held to be "relevant," with the court

---

[2] See § 7.6(a).

[3] See § 12.3(b)(ii); *Private Foundations* § 15.4(d).

[4] See § 12.3(c); *Private Foundations* § 15.6(e), (f).

[5] See § 5.6(d).

[6] Rev. Proc. 92-59, 1992-2 C.B. 411. See § 7.16(d).

[7] Reg. § 1.170A-9(f)(11), (12). See § 12.3(b)(iii).

[8] United Libertarian Fellowship, Inc. v. Comm'r, 65 T.C.M. 2175, 2181 (1993). Identical phraseology was used by the court in a prior case (Bubbling Well Church of Universal Love, Inc. v. Comm'r, 74 T.C. 531, 535 (1980), aff'd, 670 F.2d 104 (9th Cir. 1981)).

[9] Levy Family Tribe Found., Inc. v. Comm'r, 69 T.C. 615, 619 (1978).

[10] Founding Church of Scientology v. United States, 412 F.2d 1197 (Ct. Cl. 1969), *cert. denied*, 397 U.S. 1009 (1970).

[11] Parker v. Comm'r, 365 F.2d 792, 799 (8th Cir. 1966), *cert. denied*, 385 U.S. 1026 (1967).

finding private inurement and private benefit because of the "amount of control" the founder exercised over the organization's operations and the "blurring of the lines of demarcation between the activities and interests" of the organization.[12] The court observed, nonetheless, that "[t]his is not to say that an organization of such small dimensions cannot qualify for tax-exempt status."[13]

Consequently, while there is nothing specific in the operational test[14] concerning the size or composition of the governing board of a charitable or other tax-exempt organization, the courts have grafted onto the test a greater burden of proof when the organization has a small board of directors and/or is dominated by an individual.[15]

§ 5.3   BOARD DUTIES AND RESPONSIBILITIES

Out of the common law of charitable trusts has evolved the concept that a director or trustee of a tax-exempt organization, particularly a charitable entity, is a fiduciary of the organization's resources and a facilitator of its mission. Consequently, the law imposes on directors of exempt organizations standards of conduct and management that comprise *fiduciary responsibility*. These standards mean that board members are expected to regard and treat the nonprofit organization's assets and other resources with the same care with which they treat their personal assets and resources.

The duties of the board of directors of a nonprofit, tax-exempt organization essentially are the duty of care, the duty of loyalty, and the duty of obedience.

---

[12] Western Catholic Church v. Comm'r, 73 T.C. 196, 213 (1979).

[13] *Id*. In Blake v. Comm'r, 29 T.C.M. 513 (1970), an organization of similar dimensions was ruled to be tax-exempt; private inurement and private benefit were not at issue in the case. In comparable circumstances, the IRS refused to grant recognition of exemption to an organization, although private inurement was not in evidence, because the agency suspected private inurement would occur in the future (Priv. Ltr. Rul. 200535029). The U.S. Tax Court denied an organization exempt status as a charitable entity, in part because it had only one director (permissible under state law) (Ohio Disability Ass'n v. Comm'r, 98 T.C.M. 462 (2009)) yet did not address the issue when denying exempt status to an entity that had only two directors (again, allowable under state law) (Free Fertility Found. v. Comm'r, 135 T.C. 21 (2010)). On another occasion, the Tax Court wrote, in connection with denial of tax exemption to an organization, that the entity "has not adopted an operating structure or procedures necessary to ensure that its activities are properly focused to further its alleged charitable purpose," adding that "prominent" among these "shortcomings" is the "lack of a formal business plan and an independent board of directors to provide operational guidance and oversight" (Council for Education v. Comm'r, 106 T.C.M. 669 (2013)).

[14] See § 4.5(a).

[15] The IRS, on occasion, adheres to this body of law. In one instance, the agency's lawyers wrote that when an organization is "totally controlled" by its founder and their immediate family, the entity "bears a very heavy burden to be forthcoming and explicit about its plans for the use of [its] assets" for charitable purposes, and warned that this structure lacks "institutional protections," that is, a board of directors consisting of "active, disinterested persons" (Tech. Adv. Mem. 200437040). Thus, this rule: "Small, closely controlled exempt organizations—and especially those that are closely controlled by members of one family— . . . require thorough examination to [e]nsure that the arrangements serve charitable purposes rather than private interests" (*id*.). It was written, nonetheless, that "[t]here is nothing that precludes an organization that is closely controlled . . . from qualifying, or continuing to qualify, for exemption" (*id*.).

Defined by case law and in certain jurisdictions state statutory law, these are the legal standards against which all actions taken or not taken by directors are measured. They are collective duties adhering to the entire board.

(a) Duty of Care

The duty of care generally requires that each of the directors of a tax-exempt organization be reasonably informed about the organization's activities, participate in decision-making, and act in good faith and with the care of an ordinarily prudent person in comparable circumstances.

This duty of care is satisfied by attendance at meetings of the board and appropriate committees; preparation for board meetings, such as reviewing reports and the agenda prior to meetings of the board; obtaining and reviewing appropriate information before voting, to make informed decisions; use of independent judgment; periodic examination of the credentials and performance of those who serve the organization; regular review of the organization's finances and financial policies; and exercising oversight over compliance with filing requirements, particularly annual information returns.

(b) Duty of Loyalty

The duty of loyalty requires board members to exercise their authority in the interest of the tax-exempt organization and not in their personal interest or the interests of another entity, particularly one with which they have a formal relationship. When acting on behalf of the exempt organization, board members are expected to place the interests of the organization before their own personal and professional interests. The duty of loyalty extends to a beneficiary of an exempt organization.[16]

The duty of loyalty generally is satisfied when board members disclose any conflicts of interest, otherwise adhere to the organization's conflict-of-interest policy, avoid the use of corporate opportunities for the individual's personal gain or other benefit, and do not disclose confidential information concerning the organization.

(c) Duty of Obedience

The duty of obedience requires that directors of a tax-exempt organization comply with applicable federal, state, and local laws; adhere to the organization's

---

[16] This aspect of fiduciary responsibility principles may come into play where the beneficiary is another tax-exempt organization. For example, a court held that a trustee of a charitable trust breached his duty as a trustee by refusing to execute documents required to effect distributions of funds to another charitable entity in its capacity as a beneficiary of the trust (Cook v. Marshall, 2019 WL 917598 (E.D. La. 2019)). Likewise, a court held that the trustees of a supporting organization (see § 12.3(c)) breached their duty of loyalty to the supported organization in a variety of ways (Cohen v. Minneapolis Jewish Federation, 286 F. Supp. 3d 949 (W.D. Wis. 2017)), with this court subsequently holding that the fees and costs owed to the supported organization must be paid by the trustees of the supporting organization personally and that these trustees must be removed and replaced (Cohen v. Minneapolis Jewish Federation, 346 F. Supp. 3d 1274 (W.D. Wis. 2018)). These opinions were affirmed (776 Fed. Appx. 912 (7th Cir. 2019)).

governing documents; and remain guardians of the organization's mission. This duty generally is complied with when the board takes appropriate measures to ensure the organization is complying with applicable regulatory requirements, complies with and periodically reviews all documents governing the organization's operations, and makes decisions in advancement of the organization's mission and within the scope of the entity's governing documents.[17]

§ 5.4 BOARD MEMBER LIABILITY

Actions by or on behalf of a tax-exempt organization can give rise to personal liability. The term *personal liability* means that one or more managers of an exempt organization (its trustees, directors, officers, and/or key employees) may be found personally liable for something done (commission) or not done (omission) while acting in the name of the organization. Some of this exposure can be limited by incorporation, indemnification, insurance, and/or immunity.[18]

§ 5.5 SARBANES-OXLEY ACT

For-profit corporate governance legislation—the Sarbanes-Oxley Act—was enacted in 2002.[19] The focus of this body of law is on publicly traded corporations and large accounting firms. The emergence of this legislation helped bring about intense attention to the subject of governance of tax-exempt organizations.

Although the provisions of the Act are generally inapplicable to tax-exempt organizations,[20] Sarbanes-Oxley standards as to corporate governance parallel in many ways the fiduciary principles applicable to public charities and to some extent other exempt organizations. In the immediate aftermath of enactment of the Act, the boards of various public charities began voluntarily adopting certain of its governance practices. Thereafter, the IRS began making much of nonprofit governance, including integration of corporate responsibility principles in the application for recognition of exemption[21] and the annual information return.[22] Assorted policies, practices, and procedures are now expected by the IRS, particularly in the case of public charities.[23]

---

[17] In general, Hopkins, *Legal Responsibilities of Nonprofit Boards, Third Ed.* (Washington, DC: Board-Source, 2019).

[18] *Id.*, Chapter 2. A liability exposure for board members that cannot be protected against in these manners is the personal liability for an organization's employment (trust fund) taxes (IRC § 6672).

[19] Pub. L. No. 107-204, 116 Stat. 745 (2002).

[20] The applicable portions of the Act are the extension of protection to whistle-blowers and the criminal law rule concerning the inappropriate destruction of documents and other evidence.

[21] Form 1023. See §§ 26.1–26.3.

[22] Form 990. See § 28.2(a)(i).

[23] See § 5.6(c).

§ 5.6 NONPROFIT GOVERNANCE PRINCIPLES

In recent years, regulators and lawmakers at the federal level have been focusing on the principles of governance of nonprofit, tax-exempt organizations. Among the manifestations of these analyses are the emergence and refinement of a variety of written policies.

A sampling of these emerging views follows.

(a) Governance Philosophy in General

In some quarters, the philosophy underlying the concept of governance of nonprofit organizations is changing. The traditional role of the nonprofit board is oversight and policy determination; implementation of policy and management is the responsibility of the officers and key employees. An emerging view, sometimes referred to as *best practices*, imposes on the nonprofit board greater responsibilities and functions, intended to immerse the board far more in management.

(b) Inventory of Sets of Principles

The Senate Committee on Finance, in 2004, held a hearing on a range of subjects pertaining to tax-exempt organizations.[24] In connection with that hearing, the staff of the committee prepared a paper as a discussion draft, containing a variety of proposals.[25]

The Treasury Department's Anti-Terrorist Financing Guidelines provide that a charitable organization's governing instruments should (1) delineate the organization's basic goal(s) and purpose(s); (2) define the structure of the charity, including the composition of the board, how the board is selected and replaced, and the authority and responsibilities of the board; (3) set forth requirements concerning financial reporting, accountability, and practices for the solicitation and distribution of funds; and (4) state that the charity shall comply with all applicable federal, state, and local law.[26]

The American National Red Cross Governance Modernization Act of 2007 was signed into law on May 11, 2007.[27] The essence of the legislation is unique to the National Red Cross entity, yet there are elements of the act with larger significance. For example, the legislation refers to the governing board as a "governance and strategic oversight board."[28] It outlines the board's responsibilities (a checklist for boards in general): (1) review and approve the organization's mission statement; (2) approve and oversee the organization's strategic plan and maintain strategic oversight of operational matters; (3) select, evaluate, and determine the level of compensation of the organization's chief executive officer; (4) evaluate

---

[24] "Charity Oversight and Reform: Keeping Bad Things from Happening to Good Charities," Hearing before the Committee on Finance, U.S. Senate, June 24, 2004 [Senate Hearing 108-603], 108th Cong., 2nd Sess. (2004).

[25] "Finance Committee Staff Paper Proposes Sweeping Reforms, Law Additions," 21 *Nonprofit Counsel* (No. 8) 1 (Aug. 2004).

[26] U.S. Department of the Treasury Anti-Terrorist Financing Guidelines: Voluntary Best Practices for U.S.-Based Charities (Nov. 2005).

[27] Pub. L. No. 110-26, 121 Stat. 103 (2007).

[28] *Id.* § 2(a)(5).

the performance and establish the compensation of the senior leadership team and provide for management succession; (5) oversee the financial reporting and audit process, internal controls, and legal compliance; (6) ensure that the chapters of the organization are geographically and regionally diverse; (7) hold management accountable for performance; (8) provide oversight of the financial stability of the organization; (9) ensure the inclusiveness and diversity of the organization; (10) provide oversight of the protection of the brand of the organization; and (11) assist with fundraising on behalf of the organization.

Independent Sector issued the 2015 edition of its principles for good governance for public and private charitable organizations.[29] The principles are predicated on the need for a "careful balance between the two essential forms of regulation—that is, between prudent legal mandates to ensure that organizations do not abuse the privilege of their exempt status, and, for all other aspects of sound operations, well-informed self-governance and mutual awareness among nonprofit organizations." These principles, organized under four categories, are as follows (slightly edited for brevity):

(i) Legal Compliance and Public Disclosure

- An organization must comply with applicable federal, state, and local laws. If the organization conducts programs outside the United States, it must abide by applicable international laws and conventions.

- An organization should have a formally adopted, written code of ethics with which all its trustees or directors, staff, and volunteers are familiar and to which they adhere.

- An organization should implement policies and procedures to ensure that all conflicts of interest, or appearance of them, within the organization and its board are appropriately managed through disclosure, recusal, or other means.

- An organization should implement policies and procedures that enable individuals to come forward with information on illegal practices or violations of organizational policies. This whistle-blower policy should specify that the organization will not retaliate against, and will protect the confidentiality of, individuals who make good-faith reports.

- An organization should implement policies and procedures to preserve the organization's important data, documents, and business records.

- An organization's board should ensure that the organization has adequate plans to protect its assets—its property, documents and data, financial and human resources, programmatic content and material, and integrity and reputation—against damage or loss. The board should regularly review the organization's need for general liability and directors' and officers' liability insurance, as well as take other actions to mitigate risk.

---

[29] Principles for Good Governance and Ethical Practice (Independent Sector (2015)).

- An organization should make information about its operations, including its governance, finances, programs, and other activities, widely available to the public. Charitable organizations should also consider making information available on the methods they use to evaluate the outcomes of their work and sharing the results of the evaluations.

(ii) Effective Governance

- An organization must have a governing body that is responsible for approving the organization's mission and strategic direction; its annual budget; and key financial transactions, compensation practices, and fiscal and governance policies.

- The board of an organization should meet regularly to conduct its business and fulfill its duties.

- The board of an organization should establish its size and structure, and periodically review these. The board should have enough members to allow for full deliberation and diversity of thinking on organizational matters. Except for very small organizations, this generally means there should be at least five members.

- The board of an organization should include members with the diverse background (including ethnic, racial, and gender perspectives), experience, and organizational and financial skills necessary to advance the organization's mission.

- A substantial majority of the board (usually at least two-thirds) of a public charity should be independent. Independent members should not be compensated by the organization or receive material financial benefits from the organization except as a member of a charitable class served by the organization, and they should not be related to or reside with any person who is compensated by the organization.

- The board should hire, oversee, and annually evaluate the performance of the chief executive of the organization, and should conduct such an evaluation prior to any change in that individual's compensation, unless a multiyear contract is in force or the change consists solely of routine adjustments for inflation or cost of living.

- The board of an organization that has paid staff should ensure that separate individuals hold the positions of chief staff officer, board chair, and board treasurer. Organizations without paid staff should ensure that the position of board chair and treasurer are separately held.

- The board should establish an effective, systematic process for educating and communicating with board members to ensure that they are aware of their legal and ethical responsibilities, are knowledgeable about the programs and other activities of the organization, and can effectively carry out their oversight functions.

- Board members should evaluate their performance as a group and as individuals no less than every three years and should have clear procedures for removing board members who are unable to fulfill their responsibilities.

- The board should establish clear policies and procedures, setting the length of terms and the number of consecutive terms a board member may serve.

- The board should review the organization's governing instruments at least every five years.

- The board should regularly review the organization's mission and goals, and evaluate at least every five years the organization's goals, programs, and other activities to be sure they advance its mission and make prudent use of its resources.

- Board members are generally expected to serve without compensation, other than reimbursement for expenses incurred to fulfill their board duties. An organization that provides compensation to its board members should use appropriate comparability data to determine the amount to be paid, document the decision, and provide full disclosure to anyone, on request, of the amount and rationale for the compensation.

(iii) Financial Oversight

- An organization must keep complete, current, and accurate financial records. Its board should review timely reports of the organization's financial activities and have a qualified, independent financial expert audit or review these statements annually in a manner appropriate to the organization's size and scale of operations.

- The board of an organization must institute policies and procedures to ensure that the organization (and, if applicable, its subsidiaries) manages and invests its funds responsibly, in accordance with requirements of law. The full board should approve the organization's annual budget and monitor performance against the budget.

- An organization should not provide loans (or the equivalent, such as loan guarantees, purchasing or transferring ownership of a residence or office, or relieving a debt or lease obligations) to its trustees, directors, or officers.

- An organization should spend a significant portion of its annual budget on programs that pursue its mission. The board should ensure that the organization has sufficient administrative and fundraising capacity.

- An organization should establish clear, written policies for paying or reimbursing expenses incurred by anyone conducting business or traveling on behalf of the organization, including the types of expenses that can be paid or reimbursed and the documentation required. These policies should require that travel on behalf of the organization be undertaken in a cost-effective manner.

- An organization should neither pay for nor reimburse travel expenditures for spouses, dependents, or others who are accompanying someone conducting business for the organization unless they are also conducting the business.

(iv) Responsible Fundraising

- Solicitation materials and other communications addressed to prospective donors and the public must clearly identify the organization and be accurate and truthful.

- Contributions must be used for purposes consistent with the donor's intent, whether as described in the solicitation materials or as directed by the donor.

- An organization must provide donors with acknowledgments of charitable contributions, in accordance with federal tax law requirements, including information to facilitate the donor's compliance with tax law requirements.

- An organization should adopt clear policies to determine whether acceptance of a gift would compromise its ethics, financial circumstances, program focus, or other interests.

- An organization should provide appropriate training and supervision of the individuals soliciting funds on its behalf to ensure that they understand their responsibilities and applicable law, and do not employ techniques that are coercive, intimidating, or intended to harass potential donors.

- An organization should not compensate internal or external fundraisers based on a commission or percentage of the amount raised.

- An organization should respect the privacy of individual donors and, except where disclosure is required by law, should not sell or otherwise make available the names and contact information of its donors without providing them an opportunity to at least annually opt out of use of their names.

(c) Form 990 Approach to Governance

The IRS, in 2007, issued a radically redesigned annual information return (Form 990),[30] for use beginning with the 2008 filing year, which dramatically reshaped the law of tax-exempt organizations. This extensively revamped return includes a series of questions that directly reflect the agency's views as to governance principles applicable to tax-exempt organizations. Indeed, this return, particularly in Part VI, is designed to influence and modify exempt organizations' behavior, by in essence forcing them to adopt certain policies and procedures so they can check "yes" rather than "no" boxes. Almost none of these policies and procedures is required by the federal tax law.

[30] See § 28.2(a)(i).

(d)   Boards of Credit Counseling Organizations

Tax-exempt credit counseling organizations[31] must have a governing body (1) that is controlled by persons who represent the broad interests of the public, such as public officials acting in their capacities as such, persons having special knowledge or expertise in credit or financial education, and community leaders; and (2) not more than 20 percent of the voting power of which is vested in individuals who are employed by the organization or who will benefit financially, directly or indirectly, from the organization's activities (other than through the receipt of reasonable directors' fees[32] or the repayment of consumer debt to creditors other than the credit counseling organization or its affiliates); and not more than 49 percent of the voting power of which is vested in individuals who are employed by the organization or who will benefit financially, directly or indirectly, from the organization's activities (other than through the receipt of reasonable directors' fees).[33]

§ 5.7   IRS AND GOVERNANCE

The IRS has become extremely active in the realm of governance of tax-exempt organizations, particularly public charities. This new interest of the agency is manifested in a variety of speeches and private letter rulings, the college and university compliance check questionnaire, its 2009 annual report, and the training materials and governance check sheet adopted by the IRS for its agents.

(a)   Matter of Agency Jurisdiction

Controversy abounds as to whether the IRS should be so heavily involved in the governance of public charities and other categories of tax-exempt organizations in terms of priorities, competence, and jurisdiction. As to the latter two elements, a Supreme Court justice wrote, in a concurring opinion, that the "business" of the IRS is to "administer laws designed to produce revenue for the Government, not to promote 'public policy.'"[34] Some would add: "and not to regulate nonprofit governance."[35]

This justice added: "This Court often has expressed concern that the scope of an agency's authorization be limited to those areas in which the agency fairly may be said to have expertise."[36] The Court wrote that "an agency's general duty to

---

[31] See § 7.3(b).

[32] See § 20.4(f).

[33] IRC § 501(q)(1)(D).

[34] Bob Jones Univ. v. United States, 461 U.S. 574, 611 (1983). The public policy doctrine is the subject of § 6.2. The mission of the IRS, as stated in each issue of the *Internal Revenue Bulletin*, is to "promote a uniform application of the *tax laws*" (emphasis added). The mission of the Tax Exempt and Government Entities Division is to provide top quality service to its customers by helping them "understand and comply with applicable *tax laws*" (emphasis added).

[35] This justice (in *Bob Jones Univ., supra* note 34, at 611) quoted a former Commissioner of Internal Revenue, who wrote that questions concerning religion and civil rights "are far afield from the more typical tasks of tax administrators—determining taxable income" (Kurtz, "Difficult Definitional Problems in Tax Administration: Religion and Race," 23 *Cath. Law.* 301 (1978)).

[36] Bob Jones Univ. v. United States, 461 U.S. 574, 611 (1983).

enforce the public interest does not require it to assume responsibility for enforcing legislation that is not directed at the agency."[37] It also wrote: "It is the business of the Civil Service Commission to adopt and enforce regulations which will best promote the efficiency of the federal civil service. That agency has no responsibility for foreign affairs, for treaty negotiations, for establishing immigration quotas or conditions of entry, or for naturalization policies."[38] Also: "The use of the words 'public interest' in the Gas and Power Acts is not a directive to the [Federal Power] Commission to seek to eradicate discrimination, but, rather, is a charge to promote the orderly production of supplies of electric energy and natural gas at just and reasonable rates."[39]

The U.S. Supreme Court stated that one of the tasks of courts is to determine "whether [a governmental] agency has stayed within the bounds of its statutory authority."[40] Courts have not been reticent in finding that the IRS has strayed outside the bounds of its jurisdiction. For example, it has been held that the IRS does not have the authority to regulate tax-return preparers[41] and that the IRS lacks the authority to regulate the preparation and filing of ordinary refund claims.[42]

In what appears to be the most direct court case on point, an appellate court held that the Federal Energy Regulatory Commission did not have the statutory authority to make or enforce its order endeavoring to dictate the composition of the board of a public benefit corporation over which it had some regulatory authority.[43] The FERC took the position that the nonprofit organization violated its rules concerning independent system operators; its order dictated replacement of the board. The court of appeals ruled that the FERC "has no authority to replace the selection method or membership of the governing board of an ISO."[44] The court, having found the FERC's position "breathtaking," wrote that the agency "commit[ed] . . . an absurdity."[45] The court added that the FERC was "overreaching," its attempt to order the nonprofit entity to change its board was an "extreme measure," and the agency was "stretching" in asserting its authority over this aspect of nonprofit governance.[46]

Courts, in assessing the validity of agency regulations and comparable pronouncements, follow a two-step process. The first step is to determine whether Congress has directly spoken to the precise question at issue; if it has, that is the end of the analysis.[47] In this context, Congress has hardly spoken to the matter at

[37] Community Television of Southern Cal. v. Gottfried, 459 U.S. 498, 510–11, n.17 (1983).

[38] Hampton v. Mow Sun Wong, 426 U.S. 88, 114 (1976).

[39] NAACP v. Federal Power Comm'n, 425 U.S. 662, 670 (1976).

[40] City of Arlington v. Federal Communications Comm'n, 569 U.S. 290, 297 (2013).

[41] Loving v. IRS, 742 F.3d 1013 (D.C. Cir. 2014).

[42] Ridgely v. Lew, 55 F. Supp. 3d 89 (D.D.C. 2014).

[43] California Indep. System Operator Corp. v. Federal Energy Regulatory Comm'n, 372 F.3d 395 (D.C. Cir. 2004).

[44] Id. at 398.

[45] Id. at 402.

[46] Id.

[47] Chevron U.S.A., Inc. v. Natural Resources Defense Council, Inc., 467 U.S. 837 (1984). The Supreme Court stated that the principles of Chevron apply in the federal tax law context (Mayo Found. for Medical Education & Research v. United States, 562 U.S. 44 (2011)) but Chevron has since been overruled (see infra note 49).

all, in that no statute defines the IRS's jurisdiction.[48] A court is then to move to a second step, which is to determine whether the agency's regulation or other interpretation is based on a permissible construction of the statute.[49]

To return to the analogy of the IRS's role in enforcing aspects of public policy, a dissenting justice wrote that, where the "philanthropic organization is concerned, there appears to be little to circumscribe the almost unfettered power of the Commissioner. This may be very well so long as one subscribes to the particular brand of social policy the Commissioner happens to be advocating at the time . . . but application of our tax laws should not operate in so fickle a fashion. Surely, social policy in the first instance is a matter for legislative concern."[50]

(b)   IRS Officials' Speeches

The policy of the IRS concerning tax-exempt (particularly public) charities and matters of governance has evolved over recent years. Perhaps the best evidence of the contours of this evolution is the content of three speeches delivered by the then TE/GE Commissioner during 2007 and 2008.

When the TE/GE Commissioner first began talking about the IRS's role in nonprofit governance, in an April 2007 speech, he conceded that for the IRS to propound and enforce good governance principles, the agency would have to go "beyond its traditional spheres of activity." The Commissioner on that occasion revealed that he was pondering the question of "whether it would benefit the public and the tax-exempt sector [for the IRS] to require organizations to adopt and follow recognized principles of good governance." He asserted that there is a "vacuum" that needs to be filled in the realm of education on "basic standards and practices of good governance and accountability."

The TE/GE Commissioner, that day, made the best case that can be asserted for the intertwining of the matter of governance and nonprofit, tax-exempt organizations' compliance with the federal tax law. He said that a "well-governed organization is more likely to be compliant, while poor governance can easily lead an exempt organization into trouble." He spoke, for example, of

---

[48] Congress has twice obliquely addressed this matter. The general duty of the Commissioner of Internal Revenue is to "administer, manage, conduct, direct, and supervise the execution and application of the internal revenue laws or related statutes" (IRC § 7803(a)(2)(A)). The general responsibility of the IRS Oversight Board is to oversee the IRS "in its administration, management, conduct, direction, and supervision of the execution and application of the internal revenue laws or related statutes" (IRC § 7802(c)(1)(A)). The mission of the IRS, as stated by the agency, appears in *supra* note 34.

[49] Under *Chevron*, an agency's interpretation of a statute is given controlling weight unless it is arbitrary, capricious in substance, or manifestly contrary to the statute (467 U.S. at 844). The IRS's policies as to nonprofit governance are solely articulated in private letter rulings, which are not entitled to *Chevron* deference. Even if they were entitled to that level of deference, the policies could not be validated by *Chevron* step two because there is no statute as to which they can be manifestly contrary and because the IRS's interpretation of the law in this area is arbitrary and capricious because (1) it generally is clearly erroneous and (2) the rulings are inconsistent. See § 5.7(c). Moreover, the Court has since overruled *Chevron*'s judicial deference framework in a pair of cases, Loper Bright Enter. v. Raimondo and Relentless, Inc. v. Dep't of Com., 144 S. Ct. 2244 (2024).

[50] Comm'r v. "Americans United" Inc., 416 U.S. 752, 774–75 (1974). In general, Hopkins, *Ultra Vires: Why the IRS Lacks the Jurisdiction and Authority to Regulate Nonprofit Governance* (Talbot Publishing, Clark, N.J.: 2017).

an "engaged, informed, and independent board of directors accountable to the community . . . [that the exempt organization] serves."

By the time the TE/GE Commissioner returned to this subject in a November 2007 speech, his attitude and tone had dramatically changed. No more pondering, musing, and speculating. Rather, the Commissioner stated that "[w]hile a few continue to argue that governance is outside our jurisdiction, most now support an active IRS that is engaged in this area." He expressed his view that the IRS "contributes to a compliant, healthy charitable sector by expecting the tax-exempt community to adhere to commonly accepted standards of good governance." He continued: "We are comfortable that we are well within our authority to act in these areas." And: "To more clearly put our weight behind good governance may represent a small step beyond our traditional sphere of influence, but we believe the subject is well within our core responsibilities."

When April 2008 rolled around, the TE/GE Commissioner had once again significantly evolved in his thinking on these points. In two speeches he made his view quite clear: (1) the IRS has a "robust role" to play in the realm of charitable governance; (2) the IRS does not even entertain the thought that involvement in governance matters is beyond the sphere of the agency's jurisdiction; and (3) he cannot be convinced that, "outside of very, very small organizations and perhaps family foundations, the gold standard should be to have an active, independent and engaged board of directors overseeing the organization." Thus, the "question is no longer whether the IRS has a role to play in this area, but rather, what that role will be." The governance section of the new annual information return, he said, will primarily dictate that role.

In the aftermath of these speeches, the then-director of the Exempt Organizations Division stated that the IRS is stepping back from recommending best practices as to governance and is focusing on education as to good governance. On that occasion, she conceded that "not all IRS agents have gotten the message." Apparently, this cadre of agents is not inconsequential in terms of size. The facts of a 2008 court opinion reflect the policy of some agents to demand changes in board composition, adoption of a conflict-of-interest policy, and adoption of other policies and procedures as a condition of recognition of tax exemption.[51]

The then-Commissioner of the IRS made his first public comments about nonprofit governance in November 2008. After expressing his admiration for the nonprofit sector, and its "diversity, its creativity, and its risk taking," he stated that the IRS "shouldn't supplant the business judgment of organizational leaders, and certainly shouldn't determine how a nonprofit fulfills its individual mission." He said that he "clearly see[s] our role as working with you and others to promote good governance, beginning with the proposition that an active, engaged, and independent board of directors helps assure that an organization is carrying out a tax-exempt purpose and acts as its best defense against abuse." The Commissioner concluded his remarks by saying: "We want to arm you with information and guidance you need to help you comply."

---

[51] Exploratory Research, Inc. v. Comm'r, 95 T.C.M. 1347 (2008). In another instance, as part of an IRS examination of a tax-exempt school, where the agent discovered that the school's two officers were married to each other, the agent was said to have concerns that the institution "lacked appropriate oversight, a lack which, in turn, created [unspecified] governance problems"; the couple agreed to a "series of internal control improvements" (Archer v. Comm'r, 112 T.C.M. 675, 676 (2016)).

The next TE/GE Commissioner took office in early 2009. In her first public address on nonprofit governance in June of that year, she said that the IRS "has a clear, unambiguous role to play in governance [of tax-exempt organizations]. Some have argued that we do not need to be involved, because we can count on the states to do their job and the sector to stay on the path of self-regulation. While both state regulation and sector self-regulation are important, and I welcome and respect them, they do not get the IRS off the hook. Congress gave us a job to do, and we cannot delegate to others our obligation to enforce the conditions of federal tax exemption. The federal tax law must be applied consistently across the country, and we will use both our education and outreach programs and a meaningful enforcement presence to accomplish this."

These IRS speeches on nonprofit governance are inconsistent and are sending mixed messages to the nonprofit community. There is the message of militancy, stating that the IRS will robustly impose and enforce rules as to the governance of tax-exempt organizations, particularly public charities, while simultaneously conceding that these rules are not conditions of exemption. There is the message of the IRS as adviser, not an imposer of nonprofit governance requirements, focusing on educational efforts and other forms of guidance to assist organizations in complying with the federal tax laws.

(c) IRS Ruling Policy

The IRS is actively issuing private letter rulings in the area of nonprofit governance, founded principally on an expansive interpretation of the private benefit doctrine.[52] One set of these rulings holds that an organization cannot qualify as an exempt charitable entity if it has a small board (even if the board size is permissible under state law). For example, the IRS ruled that an organization could not be exempt as a charitable entity, in part because it had only two board members.[53] The IRS privately ruled that an organization could not qualify as an exempt charitable entity, in part because two individuals exercised "absolute control" over the organization.[54] Indeed, the agency ruled that an organization cannot constitute an exempt charitable entity in part because its three directors had "unfettered control" over the organization and its assets.[55] Not surprisingly, then, the IRS is ruling that one-person boards are evidence of private benefit.[56]

The IRS began moving away from a focus on board size as such to an insistence that an organization, to be a tax-exempt charitable entity, must be under control by a "community" or the "public." The IRS issued a private letter ruling holding that an organization could not be an exempt, charitable entity, in part because it was "not operated by a community-based board of directors."[57] Likewise, the IRS ruled that an organization that refused to transform its board into an

---

[52] See § 20.13.
[53] Priv. Ltr. Ruls. 200736037, 200737044.
[54] Priv. Ltr. Rul. 200843032.
[55] Priv. Ltr. Rul. 200845053. It is not clear, in an organizational structure such as this, where the control is supposed to be, in the view of the IRS.
[56] E.g., Priv. Ltr. Ruls. 201016088, 201242016 (denial of recognition of exemption as a business league), 201252021, 201443021.
[57] Priv. Ltr. Rul. 200828029.

"independent" one could not qualify as a charitable entity.[58] The IRS has gone so far as to rule that an organization did not constitute an exempt synagogue, in part because there was no "public oversight" of the entity's board.[59]

Likewise, the IRS held that an organization with a board of five individuals was ineligible for exemption as a charitable entity in part because it is governed by a "small group of individuals" who have "exclusive control over the management of [the entity's] funds and operations."[60] Indeed, a health care organization was denied recognition of exemption as a charitable organization because its six-member board of directors did "not have a majority of directors representing the community,"[61] and another health care entity was similarly denied exemption inasmuch as no one on its 28-member board of directors "will represent the broad interest of the community."[62]

When a small board is presented to the IRS as part of the application-for-recognition-of-exemption process, the agency may attempt to persuade the entity to expand its board as a condition of receipt of the recognition. In some instances, the applicant refuses to change the board composition.[63] An organization may comply with this type of request, only to have the IRS deny recognition of exemption on other grounds.[64]

Another set of rulings has it that private benefit arises where an organization's board is composed of related individuals.[65] For example, the IRS ruled that an organization was not entitled to exemption as a charitable entity, in part because the entity is "governed by a board of directors that is controlled by members of the same family."[66] The IRS privately ruled that the existence of a board of a nonprofit organization, with a majority of related individuals, was *per se* evidence of violation of the private benefit doctrine.[67] The agency observed, in a private letter ruling, that an organization was controlled by members of a family, with the governing board consisting of the president's "family members or professional friends."[68] The IRS ruled that an organization was not entitled to exemption as a charitable entity, in part because it refused to expand its three-person board of directors, two of the members of which are related, to "place control in the hands

---

[58] Priv. Ltr. Rul. 200830028. Likewise, Priv. Ltr. Rul. 201252021.

[59] Priv. Ltr. Rul. 201242014. Likewise, Priv. Ltr. Ruls. 201325017, 201427018. Surely such a rule would not be upheld in the face of the First Amendment's Religion Clauses. See § 10.1(a); *Constitutional Law*, Chapter 2. Also, Priv. Ltr. Rul. 201429027.

[60] Priv. Ltr. Rul. 201421022.

[61] Priv. Ltr. Rul. 201436050.

[62] Priv. Ltr. Rul. 201440020. It appears, although the IRS did not so state, that the agency took this position in this ruling and the one referenced in *supra* note 61 in conformity with its practice referenced in the text accompanying *supra* note 2.

[63] E.g., Priv. Ltr. Rul. 201507026.

[64] E.g., Priv. Ltr. Rul. 201541013.

[65] Were this the law, there would not be any tax-exempt family private foundations (e.g., Priv. Ltr. Rul. 201244020, where the IRS tolerated a family foundation board consisting of four related individuals).

[66] Priv. Ltr. Rul. 200916035. Likewise, Priv. Ltr. Rul. 201016088. The president of an organization engaged in many forms of private inurement, all of which happened, the IRS concluded, because there was a "family-based governing board" (Priv. Ltr. Rul. 201113041).

[67] Priv. Ltr. Rul. 201203025.

[68] Priv. Ltr. Rul. 201209011.

of unrelated individuals."[69] An organization was denied recognition of exemption as a charitable entity in part because it had a "closely related" governing board.[70] An organization was denied recognition of exemption in part because it would not expand its two-person (related) board; the organization's board did not do so on the ground that "no one shares our vision."[71] An organization was denied recognition of exemption as a charitable entity in part because its governing board consisted of members of the same family.[72] Similarly, an entity was denied recognition of exemption in part because its governing board was composed of five related individuals.[73] The IRS ruled that a five-individual board consisting only of family members was a violation of the private benefit doctrine because the organization is governed "by a small group of individuals who have exclusive control over the management of [its] funds and operations."[74] Structures where a three-individual board includes two individuals married to each other were deemed by the IRS to entail private benefit, precluding exemption.[75] Most recently, the IRS wrote: "Generally, a governing board that consists primarily of family members or of members who share a domestic life, does not constitute an independent body, and has an inherent conflict of interest when placed in a position to approve financial transactions involving other members of the family unit."[76]

A third set of private letter rulings concerns situations where the IRS denied recognition of exemption in part because an entity did not adopt a particular policy. For example, the IRS has found private benefit in part where an entity did not have a conflict-of-interest policy.[77] An organization failed to gain exemption in part because it lacked an executive compensation policy.[78] The IRS, in connection with a private letter ruling, while not revoking exemption on this basis, went out of its way to highlight the fact that an organization did not have a conflict-of-interest policy or a document-retention-and-destruction policy, noting also that it lacked any internal control reports, annual reports, or audited financial statements (none of which are required by law).[79]

These applications of the private benefit doctrine are flatly erroneous. There is absolutely no authority for the positions taken by the IRS about board composition, independent boards, conflict-of-interest policies, and other policies. Indeed, in what obviously is an aberration, the IRS stated in a private letter ruling that the

[69] Priv. Ltr. Rul. 201218041.
[70] Priv. Ltr. Rul. 201221022.
[71] Priv. Ltr. Rul. 201236033.
[72] Priv. Ltr. Rul. 201302040 (in this instance, the IRS applied the doctrine of private inurement).
[73] Priv. Ltr. Rul. 201421022.
[74] Priv. Ltr. Rul. 201540019.
[75] E.g., Priv. Ltr. Rul. 201801014.
[76] Priv. Ltr. Rul. 202010025. Subsequently, the IRS issued a private letter ruling involving a nonprofit board consisting of eight related individuals; the agency did not address the governance issue (Priv. Ltr. Rul. 202109007).
[77] Priv. Ltr. Ruls. 200830028, 200843032, 201221022.
[78] Priv. Ltr. Rul. 200843032. Another issue is the matter of lifetime board positions (permissible under some states' laws). The IRS is of the view that this form of board composition is analogous to majority stockholders in a for-profit corporation, giving rise to private inurement (or at least the potential for it) (e.g., Priv. Ltr. Rul. 201233017) or private benefit (e.g., Priv. Ltr. Rul. 201236033).
[79] Priv. Ltr. Rul. 201543019.

fact that an organization had a board of three related individuals is a factor that "alone is not enough to deny exemption."[80] Aside from the issue of whether the IRS should be involved with nonprofit governance at all, it is certainly inappropriate to use the private benefit doctrine as a bolster for insertion of the agency into this realm. Moreover, these applications of the doctrine are based on speculation. The private benefit doctrine is to be applied where there has been unwarranted private benefit, not where there is some amorphous potential for private benefit. Indeed, in some of its rulings in the governance context, the agency has so stated. For example, in an instance where a small governing body controlled by an organization's founders was considered by the IRS, the agency did not find private benefit but instead observed that the facts created the need for the organization to be open and candid.[81] Likewise, the IRS, noting that an organization's board consists of three related individuals, wrote that this fact is "creating the potential for private control of" the entity.[82]

(d) IRS Training Materials

The IRS released materials for the training of its agents in the field of nonprofit governance, for their edification in reviewing applications for recognition of exemption and annual information returns, and during examinations. For the most part, these materials do not contain anything new in relation to what the IRS has been saying over the past several years about its position on governance issues pertaining to public charities. They reflect the inherent tension as to what the federal tax law requires, the IRS's lack of jurisdiction and competence in this area, and its positions on various governance matters.

Here (again) is the ultimate rationale the IRS uses to justify its involvement in nonprofit governance, particularly with respect to public charities: The agency "believes that a well-governed charity is more likely to obey the tax laws, safeguard charitable assets, and serve charitable interests than one with poor or lax governance."

These materials are replete with contradictory statements. For example, the IRS states that a charity that has "clearly articulated purposes that describe its mission, a knowledgeable and committed governing body and management team, and sound management practices is more likely to operate effectively and consistent with tax law requirements." Then, it writes that the tax law "generally does not mandate particular management structures, operational policies, or administrative practices."

The federal tax law "does not require charities to have governance and management policies." Then: The IRS "will review an organization's application for [recognition of] exemption and annual information returns to determine whether the organization has implemented policies relating to executive compensation, conflicts of interest, investments, fundraising, documenting governance decisions, document retention and destruction, and whistleblower claims." In other words, even

---

[80] Priv. Ltr. Rul. 201232034. Earlier, the IRS wrote that a small governing body controlled by an organization's founder did not preclude exemption but created a need for the entity to be "open and candid" (Priv. Ltr. Rul. 200846040).

[81] Priv. Ltr. Rul. 200846040.

[82] Priv. Ltr. Rul. 200926037.

though the law does not require these policies, the IRS is going to look for (and probably demand) them anyway.

There are many *should*s in these materials, even though there is no justification in law for any of them. For example, the IRS states that a governing board "should include independent members and should not be dominated by employees or others who are not, by their very nature, independent individuals because of family or business relationships." (Elsewhere the materials state that this is a suggestion and the IRS will not enforce the requirement.) The "nominating process" for members of the governing body "should reach out for candidates, actively recruiting individuals whose commitment, skills, life experience, background, perspective, and other characteristics will serve the public charity and its needs." "Attention should also be paid to the size of the board ensuring that it is the appropriate size." Governing boards "should be composed of persons who are informed and active in overseeing a charity's operations and finances." And: "Term limits for board members are an effective way to ensure board vitality."

(e) IRS Governance Check Sheet

In 2009, the IRS made public a Governance Check Sheet that its examination agents are using to gather data about the governance practices of public charities,[83] accompanied by a set of instructions.

Some of the areas explored in connection with governing bodies and management: (1) whether the organization has a written mission statement that articulates its current exempt purposes; (2) whether the organization's bylaws set forth information about its governing body, such as its composition, duties, qualifications, and voting rights; (3) the extent to which copies of the organization's articles and bylaws have been distributed; and (4) the frequency of meetings of voting board members with a quorum present.

As to compensation, (1) whether compensation arrangements for all trustees, directors, officers, and key employees are approved in advance by an authorized body of the organization composed of individuals with no conflict of interest with respect to the arrangement; (2) whether this body relies on comparability data in making compensation determinations; and (3) whether the basis for compensation determinations is contemporaneously documented.

As to organizational control, (1) whether none of the organization's voting board members have a family relationship and/or outside business relationship with any other voting or nonvoting trustee, director, officer, or key employee; and (2) whether effective control of the organization does not rest with a single or select few individuals.

As to conflicts of interest, (1) whether the organization has a written conflict-of-interest policy and, if so, whether it addresses recusals and requires annual written disclosures of conflicts; and (2) if any actual or potential conflicts of interest were disclosed, whether the organization's policy was adhered to.

As to financial oversight, (1) whether there are systems or procedures in place intended to ensure that assets are properly used, consistent with the organization's mission; (2) the frequency with which the organization provides its board

[83] Form 14114.

members with written reports on its financial activities; (3) whether, prior to filing, the organization's annual information return was reviewed by the entire board and/or a committee; (4) whether an independent accountant's report was prepared and, if so, whether it was considered by the board and/or a committee; and whether an independent accountant prepared a management letter and, if so, whether this letter was reviewed by the board and/or a committee and whether the organization adopted any of the recommendations in the letter.

As to document retention, (1) whether the organization has a written policy for document retention and destruction; (2) if so, whether the organization adheres to this policy; and (3) whether the board contemporaneously documents its meetings and retains this documentation.[84]

---

[84] In general, Hopkins, "IRS Regulation of Nonprofit Governance: A Critique," 29 *Tax. of Exempts* (No. 7) 4 (July/Aug. 2018).

CHAPTER SIX

Concept of *Charitable*

Organizations that are exempt from federal income tax by reason of IRC § 501(c)(3) are frequently simply referred to as *charitable* organizations. The pertinent portion of this provision is the basis of tax exemption for:

> Corporations, and any community chest, fund or foundation, organized and operated exclusively for religious, charitable, scientific, testing for public safety, literary, or educational purposes, or to foster national or international amateur sports competition (but only if no part of its activities involve the provision of athletic facilities or equipment), or for the prevention of cruelty to children or animals . . .

The term *charitable* is often used in this broader context notwithstanding the fact that *charitable* is only one of the eight descriptive words and phrases used in the federal tax law to describe the various organizations embraced by this provision.

That is, the term *charitable* is considered a generic term and, in its expansive sense, includes *religious, scientific, educational,* and the other entities.[1]

The use of the term *charitable* to describe all IRC § 501(c)(3) organizations has arisen in part because, with one exception, all of these organizations are also qualified charitable donees[2] and thus are eligible to attract charitable contributions that are deductible for federal tax purposes. (The exception is public safety testing organizations.)[3]

§ 6.1 FEDERAL TAX LAW DEFINITION OF *CHARITABLE*

The term *charitable*, from the standpoint of U.S. law, has three meanings: one that is sometimes referenced as the "popular and ordinary" use of the term, one derived from the common law, and one that is predicated on the federal tax law.

(a) Popular and Ordinary Definition

The concept of charity that is considered the "popular and ordinary" (or "vulgar") usage of the term sees charity as confined to forms of assistance to the poor, the indigent, the destitute. That is, there are some who believe that this is the only true form of charitable undertakings.

(b) Common Law Definition

The term *charitable* has been recognized in the law for centuries, inasmuch as the term emanates from the English common law of charitable trusts.[4] The general rule is that the word *charitable* at common law encompassed "trusts for the relief of poverty; trusts for the advancement of education; trusts for the advancement of religion; and trusts for other purposes beneficial to the community, not falling under any of the preceding heads."[5]

The term *charitable*, under the English common law, had a broadly inclusive scope, yet it remained a definable legal concept. The definition of the term *charitable* is traceable to the definition of *charitable purposes* in the Preamble to the

---

[1] E.g., United States v. Proprietors of Social Law Library, 102 F.2d 481 (1st Cir. 1939). Indeed, the U.S. Supreme Court, in Bob Jones Univ. v. United States, 461 U.S. 574 (1983), *aff'g* 639 F.2d 147 (4th Cir. 1980), *rev'g* 468 F. Supp. 890 (D.S.C. 1978), held that all organizations described in IRC § 501(c)(3) and tax-exempt under IRC § 501(a) are charitable entities for purposes of exempt organizations and charitable gift deductibility law analysis. Frequently, therefore, throughout this book, the term *charitable* is used to reference any category of organization described in IRC § 501(c)(3).
[2] IRC §§ 170(c)(2) (income tax deduction), 2055(a)(2) (estate tax deduction), 2522(b)(2) (gift tax deduction).
[3] See §§ 11.3, 12.3(d).
[4] Of course, the definition of the term *charitable* is independent of and predates modern tax regimes. Thus, for example, in the Bible, it is stated that "also we certify you, that, touching any of the priests and Levites, singers, porters, Nethinim, or Ministers of this House of God, it shall not be lawful to impose toll, tribute, or customs upon them" (Ezra 7:24).
[5] Comm'rs for Special Purposes of Income Tax v. Pemsel, A.C. 531, 583 (1891).

Statute of Charitable Uses of 1601.[6] The Statute is based on holdings of the English Court of Chancery before 1601 and on earlier experiences (such as the Codes of Justinian) of previous civilizations, including those of Rome and Greece and in early Judaism, as well as in many other early cultures and religions. The Statute enumerates certain charitable purposes:

> . . . some for relief of aged, impotent and poor people, some for maintenance of sick and maimed soldiers and mariners, schools of learning, free schools, and scholars in universities, some for repair of bridges, ports, havens, cause-ways, churches, seabanks and highways, some for education and preferment of orphans, some for or towards relief, stock or maintenance for houses of correction, some for marriages of poor maids, some for supportation, aid and help of young tradesmen, handicraftsmen and persons decayed, and others for relief or redemption of prisoners or captives, and for aid or ease of any poor inhabitants concerning payments of fifteens, setting out of soldiers and other taxes.

These and other classifications of the concept of charity were discussed by Lord Macnaghten in 1891, who said that, "[o]f all words in the English language bearing a popular as well as a legal significance I am not sure that there is one which more unmistakably has a technical meaning in the strictest sense of the term, [than the word *charity* . . . being] peculiar to the law as understood and administered in this country, and not depending upon or coterminous with the popular or vulgar use of the word."[7] Lord Macnaghten's discussion was cited with approval by the U.S. Supreme Court.[8]

The English common law concept of *philanthropy* is considerably broader than that of *charity*. The basic opinion on this point was authored in 1896, wherein L. J. Lindley wrote: "Philanthropy and benevolence both include charity; but they go further, and include more than mere charitable purposes. 'Philanthropic' is a very wide word, and includes many things which are only for the pleasure of the world, and cannot be called 'charitable.'"[9] In the case, J. Sterling wrote that the word *philanthropic*, in meaning "goodwill to mankind at large," is "wide enough to comprise purposes which are not charitable in the technical sense."[10] This approach is traceable into the common law of the United States.[11]

Consequently, the categories of organizations described in IRC § 501(c)(3) may be referred to on occasion as *philanthropic* or also as *benevolent* or *eleemosynary*.

---

[6] Stat. 43 Eliz., c. 4.

[7] Comm'rs for Special Purposes of Income Tax v. Pemsel, A.C. 531, 583 (1891).

[8] Evans v. Newton, 382 U.S. 296, 303 (1966).

[9] 2 Ch. 451, 459 (1896).

[10] *Id.* at 457.

[11] E.g., Drury v. Inhabitants of Natick, 10 Allen 169 (Mass. 1865). A minority view evident in English common law and reflected in U.S. cases was that the terms *philanthropic* and *charitable* are synonymous (e.g., Comm'rs for Special Purposes of Income Tax v. Pemsel, A.C. 531 (1891); Jackson v. Phillips, 14 Allen 539 (Mass. 1867); Rotch v. Emerson, 105 Mass. 431 (1870)).

These terms, however, are generally regarded, from a federal tax law standpoint, as overbroad in relation to IRC § 501(c)(3) organizations, as being less descriptive, or invoking peculiarities of local law.[12] The term *charitable*, then, has a legal meaning and is regarded as a term of art, while terms such as *philanthropy* generally remain popularized words lacking in legal significance.

(c) Federal Tax Law Definition

Congress, in enacting and perpetuating federal income tax exemption for non-profit organizations described in IRC § 501(c)(3), was influenced by the common law definition, rather than by the popular and ordinary definition, of the term *charitable*. At the same time, that does not mean that all organizations described in IRC § 501(c)(3) must meet the common law definition of the term. As an exercise in statutory construction, the search for congressional intent starts with the express words of the statute.[13]

The provision—IRC § 501(c)(3)—describes as organizations that are eligible for federal income tax exemption those that are "organized and operated exclusively for" eight enumerated purposes or functions. These purposes or functions include those that are considered *charitable, educational, religious,* and *scientific.* This enumeration of the exempt functions or purposes is framed in the disjunctive: The law describes "religious, charitable, scientific . . . or educational purposes . . . " This use of the disjunctive evidences congressional intent to accord tax exemption to any organization organized and operated for any *one* (or more) of the designated purposes or functions. As the U.S. Supreme Court noted: "Canons of construction ordinarily suggest that terms connected by a disjunctive be given separate meanings, unless the context dictates otherwise."[14] Thus, the distinct references in IRC § 501(c)(3) to charitable *or* educational *or* scientific *or* like organizations confirms "Congress' intent that [for example] not all educational institutions must also be charitable institutions (as that term was used in the common law) in order to receive tax-exempt status."[15]

Another applicable canon of statutory construction is that related statutory provisions should be interpreted together.[16] This has considerable relevance in this context, inasmuch as sister provisions of IRC § 501(c)(3) (both those in existence and those since repealed) reiterate the separate and disjunctive purposes or

---

[12] Westchester Cnty. Soc'y for Prevention of Cruelty to Animals v. Mengel, 54 N.E. 329, 330 (N.Y. 1944); Schall v. Comm'r, 174 F.2d 893, 894 (5th Cir. 1949); Allebach v. City of Friend, 226 N.W. 440, 441 (Neb. 1929); In re Downer's Estate, 142 A. 78 (Sup. Ct. Ver. 1938); Thorp v. Lund, 116 N.E. 946 (Mass. 1917). Several state charitable solicitation (charitable fundraising regulation) statutes, however, use terms such as *philanthropic* and *eleemosynary* to define charitable organizations (see *Fundraising* § 3.2(a)). The word *philanthropic* was added to the federal tax law in connection with an exception to the excess business holdings rules for holdings in a philanthropic business (see § 12.4(c)).

[13] E.g., Northwest Airlines, Inc. v. Transport Workers Union, 451 U.S. 77 (1981); United States v. Oregon, 366 U.S. 643 (1961).

[14] Reiter v. Sonotone Corp., 442 U.S. 330, 339 (1979).

[15] Prince Edward School Found. v. United States, 450 U.S. 944, 947 (1981) (dissent from denial of certiorari).

[16] E.g., Kokoska v. Belford, 417 U.S. 642 (1974); United States v. Cooper Corp., 312 U.S. 600 (1941).

functions described in IRC § 501(c)(3).[17] The principal one of these sister provisions is IRC § 170(c)(2)(B), which defines the term *charitable contribution* for purposes of the federal income tax charitable contribution deduction. This provision also recites the eight separate and independent categories of exempt functions, thereby providing further support for the proposition that Congress intended to recognize each category of purpose or function enumerated in IRC § 501(c)(3) as a distinct basis for tax exemption.[18]

Thus, it can be argued that, in IRC § 501(c)(3) and its sister provisions, Congress has "spoken in the plainest of words"[19] in intending to accord federal income tax exemption to any organization organized and operated exclusively for any one (or more) of the purposes or functions enumerated in IRC § 501(c)(3).

The scarce legislative history that exists reflects the influence of the common law view of charity. The chief component of this legislative history is a portion of a report of the House of Representatives issued in 1939, explaining the theory that inspired Congress to exempt organizations devoted to charitable and other purposes:

> The exemption from taxation of money or property devoted to charitable and other purposes is based upon the theory that the Government is compensated for the loss of revenue by its relief from financial burdens which would otherwise have to be met by appropriations from other public funds, and by the benefits resulting from the promotion of the general welfare.[20]

This phraseology, which includes words such as "public" and "general welfare," can thus be read as evidencing the need to follow the dictates of the common law meaning of *charitable*. Another element of legislative history that suggests a broader use of the term *charitable* is a statement by the sponsor of the 1909 tax exemption statute that the provision was designed to relieve from the income tax (then imposed only on corporations) those organizations "devoted exclusively to the relief of suffering, to the alleviation of our people, and to all things which commend themselves to every charitable and just impulse."[21]

The courts will occasionally look to contemporaneous administrative agency interpretation of a statute in an attempt to divine the statute's true meaning.[22] It is, therefore, instructive to note that, as early as 1923, in reviewing the law that is now

---

[17] For example, phraseology in the disjunctive similar to that in IRC § 501(c)(3) can be found in IRC §§ 170(c)(2) (income tax charitable contribution deduction), 513(a) (defining the phrase *unrelated trade or business*), 2055(a)(2) (estate tax charitable contribution deduction), and 2522(a)(2) (gift tax charitable contribution deduction).

[18] A contrasting argument (ultimately adopted by the U.S. Supreme Court) is stated in Bob Jones Univ. v. United States, 639 F.2d 147 (4th Cir. 1980), where, in part because contributions to all organizations described in IRC § 170(c)(2)(B) are referred to as *charitable contributions*, the court concluded that each of the separately enumerated purposes are to be considered as within a broad classification of *charitable*.

[19] TVA v. Hill, 437 U.S. 153, 194 (1978).

[20] H.R. Rep. No. 75-1860, at 19 (1938).

[21] 44 Cong. Rec. 4150 (1909).

[22] As the U.S. Supreme Court observed, "a consistent and contemporaneous construction of a statute by the agency charged with its enforcement is entitled to great deference" (NLRB v. Boeing Co., 412 U.S. 67, 75 (1973); Power Reactor Dev. Co. v. Electricians, 367 U.S. 396 (1961)).

IRC § 501(c)(3), the IRS interpreted the word *charitable* in its "popular and ordinary sense" and not in its common law sense.[23] As revenue acts were subsequently enacted, the accompanying regulations stated: "Corporations organized and operated exclusively for charitable purposes comprise, in general, organizations for the relief of the poor,"[24] which clearly reflected the contemporary "popular and ordinary" meaning of the term *charitable*. During the 15 years that the Internal Revenue Code of 1939[25] was in effect, three sets of regulations were issued, each of which defined the term *charitable* in its popular and ordinary sense.[26] When the Internal Revenue Code of 1954 was enacted, IRC § 501 was carried over from the 1939 Code.[27] As to IRC § 501, a report of the House Committee on Ways and Means stated that "[n]o change in substance has been made."[28] Consequently, it appears that, as of the adoption of the Internal Revenue Code of 1954, the "popular and ordinary" meaning of the term *charitable* governed the definition of that word for federal tax purposes.

In 1959, regulations were promulgated that vastly expanded the federal tax definition of the term *charitable*. This regulation (currently in effect) reads as follows:

> The term "charitable" is used in section 501(c)(3) in its generally accepted legal sense and is, therefore, not to be construed as limited by the separate enumeration in section 501(c)(3) of other tax-exempt purposes which may fall within the broad outlines of "charity" as developed by judicial decisions. Such term includes: Relief of the poor and distressed or of the underprivileged; advancement of religion; advancement of education or science; erection or maintenance of public buildings, monuments, or works; lessening of the burdens of Government; and promotion of social welfare by organizations designed to accomplish any of the above purposes, or (i) to lessen neighborhood tensions; (ii) to eliminate prejudice and discrimination; (iii) to defend human and civil rights secured by law; or (iv) to combat community deterioration and juvenile delinquency.[29]

This regulation has several striking features. One of these is its statement that the definition of the term *charitable* in IRC § 501(c)(3) is used in its "generally accepted legal sense," which is at least somewhat akin to its common law meaning. Another is that "[r]elief of the poor"[30] is only one of several ways in which an organization can qualify as a charitable entity.

---

[23] I.T. 1800, II-2 C.B. 152, 153 (1923), which discussed the intended meaning of the word *charitable* in section 231(6) of the Revenue Acts of 1918 and 1921.

[24] Reg. 65, Art. 517 (Revenue Act of 1924, 43 Stat. 282); Reg. 69, Art. 517 (Revenue Act of 1926, 44 Stat. 40); Reg. 74, Art. 527 (Revenue Act of 1928, 45 Stat. 813); Reg. 77, Art. 527 (Revenue Act of 1932, 47 Stat. 193); Reg. 86, Art. 101(6)-1 (Revenue Act of 1934, 48 Stat. 700); Reg. 94, Art. 101(6)-1 (Revenue Act of 1936, 49 Stat. 1674); Reg. 101, Art. 101(6)-1 (Revenue Act of 1938, 52 Stat. 481).

[25] 53 Stat. 1.

[26] Reg. 103, § 19.101(6)-1; Reg. 111, § 29.101(6)-1; Reg. 118, § 39.101(6)-1(b).

[27] Specifically, 1939 Code §§ 101, 421.

[28] H.R. Rep. No. 83-1337, at A165 (1954).

[29] Reg. § 1.501(c)(3)-1(d)(2).

[30] See § 7.1.

The Supreme Court seemingly emphasized the overarching application of the term *charitable* when it observed that "Congress, in order to encourage gifts to religious, educational *and other charitable objects,* granted the privilege of deducting such gifts from gross income."[31] Earlier, the Court wrote that "[e]vidently the exemption [was] made in recognition of the benefit which the public derives from corporate activities of the class named, and [was] intended to aid them when not conducted for private gain."[32]

This approach is also reflected in a variety of appellate court opinions. Thus, a federal court of appeals determined that the term *charitable* is a generic term and includes "literary, religious, scientific and educational institutions."[33] Likewise, another federal court of appeals stated: "That Congress had in mind these broader definitions is confirmed by the words used in the [District of Columbia Code] for by its terms it embraces religious, charitable, scientific, literary or educational corporations, thus including within the exemption clause every nonprofit organization designed and operating for the benefit and enlightenment of the community, the State, or the Nation."[34] Similarly, still another federal court of appeals (and later the U.S. Supreme Court) held that the structure of the statutory framework (IRC §§ 170 and 501(c)) demonstrates that an organization seeking tax exemption under IRC § 501(c)(3) must show that it is charitable, irrespective of the particular nature of its activities (e.g., religious, educational, or scientific).[35]

A federal court of appeals observed that "we must look to established [trust] law to determine the meaning of the word 'charitable.'"[36] Subsequently, the same appellate court stated that Congress intended to apply these tax rules to "those organizations commonly designated charitable in the law of trusts."[37]

This approach thus makes certain fundamental criteria applicable to all IRC §§ 501(c)(3) and 170(c)(2) organizations. As the Supreme Court observed well over 130 years ago, a "charitable use, where neither law nor public policy forbids, may be applied to almost any thing that tends to promote the well-doing and well-being of social man."[38] A federal district court later held, in application of the broader definitional approach to educational entities, that this "doctrine operates as a necessary exception to or qualifier of the precept that in general trusts for education are considered to be for the benefit of the community."[39]

All of the organizations described in IRC § 501(c)(3) share certain common characteristics of *charitable* organizations. This fact is reflected in the public policy doctrine.

---

[31] Helvering v. Bliss, 293 U.S. 144, 147 (1934) (emphasis added).

[32] Trinidad v. Sagrada Orden de Predicadores de la Provincia del Santisimo Rosario de Filipinas, 263 U.S. 578, 581 (1924). Likewise, St. Louis Union Trust Co. v. United States, 374 F.2d 427, 432 (8th Cir. 1967).

[33] United States v. Proprietors of Social Law Library, 102 F.2d 481, 483 (1st Cir. 1939).

[34] Int'l Reform Fed'n v. District Unemployment Comp. Bd., 131 F.2d 337, 339 (D.C. Cir. 1942).

[35] Bob Jones Univ. v. United States, 639 F.2d 147 (4th Cir. 1980).

[36] Pennsylvania Co. for Ins. on Lives v. Helvering, 66 F.2d 284, 285 (D.C. Cir. 1933).

[37] Int'l Reform Fed'n. v. District Unemployment Comp. Bd., 131 F.2d 337, 339 (D.C. Cir. 1942).

[38] Ould v. Washington Hosp. for Foundlings, 95 U.S. 303, 311 (1877).

[39] Green v. Connally, 330 F. Supp. 1150, 1160 (D.D.C. 1971), *aff'd sub nom.,* Coit v. Green, 404 U.S. 997 (1971).

§ 6.2 PUBLIC POLICY DOCTRINE

The U.S. Supreme Court ruled that tax exemption as a charitable organization is available only where the organization is operating in conformity with federal public policy.[40] This rule of law, a judicially imposed overlay of the statutory law, is known as the *public policy doctrine*.

(a) General Principles

Authority for this doctrine is traceable to a 1958 U.S. Supreme Court opinion, holding that tax benefits such as deductions and exclusions generally are subject to limitation on public policy grounds.[41] At issue in that case was the deductibility of fines as "ordinary and necessary" business expenses.[42] The Court held that an expense is not "necessary" to the operation of a business if allowance of a tax deduction would "frustrate sharply defined national or state policies proscribing particular types of conduct, evidenced by some governmental declaration thereof."[43]

The Court subsequently adopted the view that the purpose of a charitable entity "may not be illegal or violate established public policy."[44] It was written that "[h]istory buttresses logic to make clear that, to warrant [tax] exemption under § 501(c)(3), an institution must . . . demonstrably serve and be in harmony with the public interest" and not have a purpose that is "so at odds with the common community conscience as to undermine any public benefit that might otherwise be conferred."[45] The Court added that "determinations of public benefit and public policy are sensitive matters with serious implications for the institutions affected" and that a "declaration that a given institution is not 'charitable' should be made only where there can be no doubt that the activity involved is contrary to a fundamental public policy."[46]

In a concurring opinion, a justice stated that he was "troubled by the broader implications of the Court's opinion,"[47] "find[ing] it impossible to believe that all or even most of . . . [the IRC § 501(c)(3)] organizations could prove that they 'demonstrably serve and [are] in harmony with the public interest' or that they are 'beneficial and stabilizing influences in community life.'"[48] Quoting other passages of the majority's opinion that impart the "element of conformity that appears to inform the Court's analysis," this justice wrote that "these passages suggest that the primary function of a tax-exempt organization is to act on behalf of the Government

---

[40] Bob Jones Univ. v. United States, 461 U.S. 574 (1983).

[41] Tank Truck Rentals, Inc. v. Comm'r, 356 U.S. 30 (1958).

[42] The deduction at issue was available pursuant to the predecessor of IRC § 162(a).

[43] Tank Truck Rentals, Inc. v. Comm'r, 356 U.S. 30, 33 (1958).

[44] Bob Jones Univ. v. United States, 461 U.S. 574, 591 (1983).

[45] *Id*. at 591–92.

[46] *Id*. at 592. Earlier, the Court wrote that the federal income tax is a "tax on net income, not a sanction against wrongdoing" and that the "statute does not concern itself with the lawfulness of the income it taxes" (Comm'r v. Tellier, 383 U.S. 687, 691 (1966)).The Court, in articulating this public policy doctrine, rested its determination on the precept that all of the types of organizations referenced in IRC § 501(c)(3) must meet "certain common law standards of charity" (Bob Jones Univ. v. United States, 461 U.S. 574, 586 (1983)), in large part because of the overlap with the charitable deduction rules. Cf. § 6.1(c).

[47] *Id*. at 606.

[48] *Id*. at 609.

in carrying out governmentally approved policies."[49] Moreover, he disassociated himself from the majority by being "unwilling to join any suggestion that the Internal Revenue Service is invested with authority to decide which public policies are sufficiently 'fundamental' to require denial of tax exemptions."[50]

The public policy doctrine applicable to tax-exempt charitable organizations was articulated in the context of racial discrimination by exempt private schools.[51] The reach of the doctrine has not been extensive. In one case, the government contended that an organization was ineligible for exemption because it engaged in violent and illegal activities; although the case was dismissed, the court concluded that the doctrine could have been applied in the case had the court decided the matter on its merits.[52] On another occasion, a court revoked the exemption of an organization, finding a violation of the doctrine in its "conspir[acy] to impede the IRS in performing its duty to determine and collect taxes" from the organization, in contravention of federal criminal laws.[53]

The IRS occasionally applies the rule that an organization must satisfy the public policy test to qualify under IRC § 501(c)(3). For example, in determining whether activities such as demonstrations, economic boycotts, strikes, and picketing are permissible means for furthering charitable ends, the IRS adheres to the public policy doctrine.[54] The IRS applied the public policy doctrine to revoke the exemption of a charitable organization where a state court found the organization to have violated state fundraising laws.[55]

Likewise, an organization formed by a violent sexual predator to sexually exploit children by promoting repeal of child pornography and exploitation laws was found by the IRS to have a purpose that is "contrary to public policy to protect the sexual exploitation of children."[56] Knowing that illegal activity cannot be maintained in a conventional tax-exempt religious organization,[57] because the public policy doctrine will not tolerate it, a religious trust tried to sidestep this application of the law by placing its practice of polygamy in an exempt apostolic entity,[58] but that was not successful due to an implicit application of the common-law standards for charitable organizations to apostolic groups.[59]

(b) Race-Based Discrimination

Private schools may not racially discriminate and be tax-exempt and eligible for deductible charitable contributions.[60]

---

[49] *Id.*

[50] *Id.* at 611.

[51] See § 6.2(b).

[52] Synanon Church v. United States, 579 F. Supp. 967 (D.D.C. 1984), *aff'd*, 820 F.2d 421 (D.C. Cir. 1987).

[53] Church of Scientology of Cal. v. Comm'r, 83 T.C. 381 (1984), *aff'd*, 823 F.2d 1310 (9th Cir. 1987).

[54] Gen. Couns. Mem. 37858.

[55] Priv. Ltr. Rul. 202240020.

[56] Priv. Ltr. Rul. 200826043. This position of the IRS was upheld in court (Mysteryboy Incorporation v. Comm'r, 99 T.C.M. 1057 (2010)).

[57] See § 6.3(i).

[58] See § 10.8.

[59] Priv. Ltr. Rul. 201310047, citing Kleinsasser v. United States, 707 F.2d 1024 (9th Cir. 1983).

[60] Bob Jones Univ. v. United States, 461 U.S. 574 (1983). E.g., Priv. Ltr. Rul. 200447038.

(i) Supreme Court Pronouncement. This conclusion, as reached by the U.S. Supreme Court, was expressly made applicable to all nonprofit private schools, including those that engage in racial discrimination on the basis of religious beliefs. As to religious schools, the Court found that the "governmental interest at stake here is compelling" and that this interest substantially outweighs the burden that the denial of the tax benefits places on the schools' exercise of their religious beliefs.[61]

The Court majority unabashedly adopted a public policy argument. The Court found in the "Congressional purposes" underlying this tax exemption are "unmistakable evidence" of an "intent that entitlement to tax exemption depends on meeting certain common law standards of charity—namely, that an institution seeking tax-exempt status must serve a public purpose and not be contrary to established public policy."[62]

(ii) IRS Policy. Prior to the Supreme Court's forceful pronouncement, the law was not so clear. The IRS had taken the position since 1967 that, to be tax-exempt, private educational institutions may not have racially discriminatory policies. In a 1971 case,[63] the Secretary of the Treasury and the Commissioner of Internal Revenue were enjoined from approving any application for recognition of tax exemption, continuing any current exemption, or approving charitable contribution deductions for any private school in Mississippi that failed to show that it had a publicized policy of nondiscrimination. The court found a "Federal public policy against support for racial segregation of schools, public or private" and held that the law "does not contemplate the granting of special Federal tax benefits to trusts or organizations . . . whose organization or operation contravene[s] Federal public policy."[64]

The IRS in 1971 stated that it would deny recognition of tax-exempt status to any private school that otherwise meets the requirements for exemption and charitable donee status but that "does not have a racially nondiscriminatory policy as to students."[65] The IRS initially announced its position on the exempt status of private nonprofit schools in 1967, stating that exemption and deductibility of contributions would be denied if a school was operated on a segregated basis.[66] This position was basically reaffirmed early in 1970, and the IRS began announcing denials of exemption later that year. A clamor began for stricter guidelines, however, when the recognition of exemptions resumed to allegedly segregated schools.[67]

---

[61] *Id.* at 604.

[62] *Id.* at 586.

[63] Green v. Connally, 330 F. Supp. 1150 (D.D.C. 1971), *aff'd sub nom.* Coit v. Green, 404 U.S. 997 (1971).

[64] *Id.*, 330 F. Supp. at 1162, 1163.

[65] Rev. Rul. 71-447, 1971-2 C.B. 230. The federal public policy against racial discrimination in education, as reflected in this ruling and subsequent case law and IRS guidance, "pervades every aspect of the educational area"; therefore, the IRS applies the policy to all facets of the educational process, including privately administered scholarship trusts (e.g., Priv. Ltr. Rul. 7851096).

[66] Rev. Rul. 67-325, 1967- 2 C.B. 113.

[67] E.g., *Equal Educational Opportunity: Hearings Before the Senate Select Committee on Equal Educational Opportunity,* 91st Cong. 1991–2038 (1970).

In 1972, the IRS issued guidelines and record-keeping requirements for deter-mining whether private schools that have tax exemption rulings or are applying for recognition of tax exemption have racially nondiscriminatory policies as to stu-dents.[68] In 1975, the IRS promulgated new guidelines on the subject, which super-seded the 1972 rules.[69] Under the 1975 guidelines, the racially nondiscriminatory policy of every private school must be stated in its governing instruments or gov-erning body resolution, and in its brochures, catalogs, and similar publications. The school must also maintain the following specific records for a minimum of three years and furnish them to the IRS on request: records indicating the racial composi-tion of the student body, faculty, and administrative staff for each academic year; records sufficient to document that scholarship and other financial assistance is awarded on a racially nondiscriminatory basis; and copies of all brochures, catalogs, and advertising dealing with student admissions, programs, and scholarships; and copies of all materials used by or on behalf of the school to solicit contributions.

This policy must be publicized by the school to all segments of the gen-eral community served by the school, by notice in a newspaper, use of broadcast media, or (pursuant to guidelines issued in 2019)[70] display of a notice on its pri-mary publicly accessible Internet homepage in a manner reasonably expected to be noticed by visitors to the homepage. All programs and facilities must be oper-ated in a racially nondiscriminatory manner, and all scholarships or comparable benefits must be offered on this basis. Each school must annually certify its racial nondiscrimination policy.[71]

It is the position of the IRS that church-related schools that teach secular sub-jects and generally comply with state law requirements for public education for the grades for which instruction is provided may not rely on the First Amendment to avoid the bar on tax exemption to those educational institutions that practice racial discrimination.[72] It is therefore the view of the agency that a church-sponsored school (that is not an entity separate from the church) that has racially discrimina-tory policies (in violation of IRS guidelines)[73] causes the sponsoring church to fail to qualify for tax exemption.[74]

The Supreme Court held that private schools are barred by federal law from denying admission to children solely for the reason of race.[75] The Court held that a statute that grants equal rights to make and enforce contracts is contravened where a minority applicant is denied a contractual right that would have been

---

[68] Rev. Proc. 72-54, 1972-2 C.B. 834.

[69] Rev. Proc. 75-50, 1975-2 C.B. 587, *modified by* Rev. Proc. 2019-22, 2019-22 I.R.B. 1260. These guide-lines are applicable only to organizations that are classified as schools under IRC § 170(b)(1)(A)(ii) (see §§ 8.3, 12.3(a)), although the doctrine of the *Bob Jones University* opinion (see text accompanied by *supra* notes 60–62) may nonetheless be applicable (Gen. Couns. Mem. 39757).

[70] Rev. Proc. 2019-22, 2019-22 I.R.B. 1260, *modifying* Rev. Proc. 75-50, 1975-2 C.B. 587.

[71] TIR-1449 (Mar. 19, 1976); also, Ann. 76-57, 1976-16 I.R.B. 24. E.g., Priv. Ltr. Rul. 200703039.

[72] Rev. Rul. 75-231, 1975-1 C.B. 158. In general, Brown v. Dade Christian Schools, Inc., 556 F.2d 310 (5th Cir. 1977); Goldsboro Christian Schools, Inc. v. United States, 436 F. Supp. 1314 (E.D.N.C. 1977), *aff'd in unpublished opinion* (4th Cir. 1981).

[73] Rev. Proc. 75-50, 1975-2 C.B. 587, *modified by* Rev. Proc. 2019-22, 2019-22 I.R.B. 1260.

[74] Gen. Couns. Mem. 39574.

[75] This position is based on 42 U.S.C. § 1981.

granted if they were a member of the racial majority. This statute has been characterized as a limitation on private discrimination and, by virtue of the Court's decision, applies to private schools irrespective of state action or tax exemption.[76]

In an effort to further regulate in this field, the IRS proposed guidelines in 1978[77] and again in revised form in 1979[78] for ascertaining whether private schools have racially discriminatory policies toward students. These rules would have established certain presumptions as to discriminatory practices by a private school, such as the nature of its minority enrollment and the relationship between formation or expansion of the school and local public school desegregation.

While these guidelines were pending, Congress, in enacting the fiscal year 1980 appropriations act for the Treasury Department,[79] prohibited the IRS from using funds appropriated under that law to implement the guidelines. In addition to specifically precluding the use of these appropriations to carry out the proposed guidelines, the legislation stated that none of the appropriations "shall be used to formulate or carry out any rule, policy, procedure, guideline, regulation, standard, or measure which would cause the loss of tax-exempt status to private, religious, or church-operated schools under section 501(c)(3) of the Internal Revenue Code of 1954 unless in effect prior to August 22, 1978."[80]

The position of the IRS in this regard became particularly aggravated when, notwithstanding the prohibition on the use of appropriated funds, a court ordered the IRS to refrain from according or continuing tax-exempt status for racially discriminatory private schools in the state of Mississippi.[81]

A federal court subsequently gave considerable impetus to the philosophy underlying the proposed IRS guidelines, when it upheld the IRS's revocation of tax-exempt status of a private school on the ground that the institution maintained a racially discriminatory admissions policy.[82]

Thereafter, a federal court of appeals ordered the government not to grant recognition of tax exemption to any private schools with racially discriminatory practices.[83] The government asked the Supreme Court to consider the private school issue; the Court did so, responding with its historic decision in 1983.[84]

(iii) Broader Policy Impact. This application of the public policy doctrine is having an impact on the tax-exempt status of other racially discriminatory

---

[76] Runyon v. McCrary, 424 U.S. 941 (1976), as limited by Patterson v. McLean Credit Union, 491 U.S. 164 (1989).

[77] 43 Fed. Reg. 37296.

[78] 44 Fed. Reg. 9451.

[79] Pub. L. No. 96-74, 93 Stat. 559 (1979).

[80] Congress, in this legislation, also barred the IRS from carrying out any ruling to the effect "that a taxpayer is not entitled to a charitable deduction for general purpose contributions which are not used for educational purposes by [an exempt] religious organization," thereby prohibiting enforcement of Rev. Rul. 79-99, 1979-1 C.B. 108, during fiscal year 1980. Rev. Rul. 79-99 was revoked by Rev. Rul. 83-104, 1983-2 C.B. 46, which stated guidelines as to when payments to private schools are deductible charitable contributions or nondeductible tuition payments.

[81] Green v. Miller, 80-1 U.S.T.C. ¶ 9401 (D.D.C. 1980).

[82] Prince Edward School Found. v. United States, 80-1 U.S.T.C. ¶ 9295 (D.D.C. 1980), *aff'd in unpublished opinion* (D.C. Cir. 1981), *cert. denied*, 450 U.S. 944 (1981).

[83] Wright v. Regan, 49 A.F.T.R. 2d 82-757 (D.C. Cir. 1982).

[84] See § 6.2(b)(i).

organizations. An organization that published material advocating racial and ethnic discrimination was ruled to not qualify for exemption on the ground that it failed to meet the standard of what constitutes educational undertakings.[85] The U.S. Supreme Court ruled that parents of black schoolchildren lacked standing to challenge the process being utilized by the IRS in denying recognition of exemption to racially discriminatory private schools.[86] Another court ruled that an organization that made grants to private schools was not entitled to exemption, because substantial portions of its funds were granted to schools that have failed to adopt racially nondiscriminatory policies with respect to students.[87]

In application of its guidelines, the IRS adheres to a judicially recognized position that, under certain circumstances, rebuttable inferences of discriminatory policies as to students can arise.[88] Thus, for example, where a school has a history of racial discrimination, efforts by the school to attract minority group applicants will be regarded as ineffective in relation to the guidelines unless they are "reasonably calculated to succeed," such as active and vigorous recruitment of minority students and teachers, financial assistance to minority students, and effective communication of the nondiscriminatory policy to the minority population.[89] "[A]ctual enrollment of minority students," the IRS's lawyers observed, "while not determinative of the issue, is generally the most convincing evidence of the existence of a nondiscriminatory policy as to students."[90] Thus, the IRS ruled that a school could not be tax-exempt because of ineffective advertising, failure to reach out to the African American community, failure to have any African Americans on its scholarship committee or board of directors, and lack of full minority scholarships; the agency wrote that the school "failed to demonstrate that . . . [it has] taken sufficient steps to overcome the inference of discrimination."[91] These principles have been applied by a court that, holding that a private school seeking tax exemption must prove racial nondiscrimination by a preponderance of the evidence, concluded that a school failed to meet this burden of proof because it was founded at a time when courts were forcing desegregation in public schools, had never enrolled a black student, and did not adequately publicize a policy of racial nondiscrimination.[92]

The IRS applies the rule denying recognition of tax-exempt status as a charitable organization because of racially discriminatory policies to all entities seeking that classification, not just private educational institutions.[93]

(c)   Gender-Based Discrimination

While there is a recognized federal public policy against support for racial segregation in private schools (and, presumably, racial discrimination by other types

[85] Nat'l Alliance v. United States, 710 F.2d 868 (D.C. Cir. 1983).
[86] Allen v. Wright, 468 U.S. 737 (1984); Regan v. Wright, 468 U.S. 737 (1984).
[87] Virginia Educ. Fund v. Comm'r, 85 T.C. 743 (1985), aff'd, 799 F.2d 903 (4th Cir. 1986). Also, Estate of Clopton v. Comm'r, 93 T.C. 275 (1989).
[88] Norwood v. Harrison, 382 F. Supp. 921, 924–26 (N.D. Miss. 1984).
[89] Gen. Couns. Mem. 39525.
[90] Gen. Couns. Mem. 39524.
[91] Priv. Ltr. Rul. 200909064.
[92] Calhoun Academy v. Comm'r, 94 T.C. 284 (1990).
[93] Priv. Ltr. Rul. 8910001.

of educational entities),[94] a somewhat comparable federal public policy against support for private institutions that engage in gender-based discrimination may be developing.[95] The question is whether this is a sufficiently established federal policy so that its contravention would have an impact on the tax status of these institutions and other charitable organizations.[96] The issue has been raised, with the courts concluding that gender-based discrimination does not bar federal tax exemption.[97] One court, however, having concluded that the charitable contribution deduction is equivalent to a federal matching grant, found that by allowing the deduction of charitable contributions, the federal government has conferred a "benefit" on the recipient organization and that the Fifth Amendment is applicable.[98]

Nonetheless, the U.S. Supreme Court determined that a national nonprofit membership organization is compelled to accept women as regular members, by direction of a state human rights act, notwithstanding the organization's free speech and associational rights.[99] The organization's chapters were found to be "place[s] of public accommodations," the skills it develops were held to be "goods," and business contacts and employment promotions were ruled to be "privileges" and "advantages"—all so that the state's law banning gender-based discriminatory practices in access to places of public accommodation could be made applicable.[100]

(d) Other Forms of Discrimination

It may also be asserted that there is a federal public policy in the tax-exempt organization's context, either in existence at present or in the process of development, against other forms of discrimination, such as discrimination on the basis

---

[94] Bob Jones Univ. v. Simon, 416 U.S. 725 (1974); Crenshaw Cnty. Private School Found. v. Connally, 474 F.2d 1185 (3d Cir. 1973), *cert. denied*, 417 U.S. 908 (1973).

[95] E.g., McGlotten v. Connally, 388 F. Supp. 448 (D.D.C. 1972).

[96] E.g., Executive Order 11246, as amended, 30 Fed. Reg. 12319 (1965); Title VII of the Civil Rights Act of 1964, as amended, 42 U.S.C. § 2000e *et seq.*; Equal Employment Opportunity Commission regulations, 29 C.F.R. § 1604 *et seq.*; Title IX of the Education Amendments of 1972, 20 U.S.C. § 1681 *et seq.*; the Equal Pay Act of 1963, 29 U.S.C. § 206 *et seq.*; Califano v. Webster, 430 U.S. 313 (1977); Alexander v. Louisiana, 405 U.S. 625 (1972); Reed v. Reed, 404 U.S. 71 (1971).

[97] McCoy v. Shultz, 73-1 U.S.T.C. ¶ 9233 (D.D.C. 1973); Junior Chamber of Commerce of Rochester, Inc. v. U.S. Jaycees, 495 F.2d 883 (10th Cir. 1974), *cert denied*, 419 U.S. 1026 (1974); New York City Jaycees, Inc. v. United States Jaycees, Inc., 512 F.2d 856 (2d Cir. 1975).

[98] McGlotten v. Connally, 338 F. Supp. 448, 456–57, n.37 (D.D.C. 1972). Also, Stearns v. Veterans of Foreign Wars, 500 F.2d 788 (D.C. Cir. 1974) (remand).

[99] Roberts, Acting Comm'r, Minn. Dep't of Human Rights v. United States Jaycees, 468 U.S. 609 (1984). See § 1.7.

[100] *Id.* Also, New York State Club Ass'n v. New York City, 487 U.S. 1 (1987); Bd. of Directors of Rotary Int'l v. Rotary Club of Duarte, 481 U.S. 537 (1987). Cf. Trustees of Smith College v. Bd. of Assessors of Whately, 434 N.E.2d 182 (Mass. 1982) (successful defense of single-sex admissions policy at private college).

Where the educational institution is a governmental entity, the operation of it exclusively for the members of one gender is likely to be a violation of the equal protection doctrine (e.g., the operation by the Commonwealth of Virginia of the military college, Virginia Military Institute, exclusively for males) (United States v. Virginia, 518 U.S. 515 (1996)).

of marital status, national origin, religion, handicap, sexual preference, or age.[101] Thus, the law may develop to the point where a charitable organization will jeopardize its tax status if it engages in one or more of these forms of discrimination. The IRS has displayed some sensitivity to these matters, such as by including discrimination on the ground of national origin as being within the scope of racial discrimination for purposes of the nondiscrimination rules applicable to private educational institutions[102] and by evincing concern that guidance issued in 1965 carries overtones of condoning age discrimination.[103]

(e) Affirmative Action Principles

Tax-exempt organizations are often involved in affirmative action efforts, with benefits decisions based on race, gender, and the like, such as preferential social assistance and scholarship and award programs, designed to, in the words of the U.S. Supreme Court, "remedy disadvantages cast on minorities by past racial [or other] prejudice."[104] The dilemma in law, of course, with these policies is potential conflict with the public policy doctrine;[105] the Court also observed that "preferring members of any one group for no reason other than race or ethnic origin is discrimination for its own sake."[106] Nonetheless, the courts and the IRS have recognized, in the exempt organizations context, the distinction between "discrimination against" and "discrimination for." The former is what can be barred by the public policy doctrine; the latter can be tolerated as forms of affirmative action.

From a law standpoint, in addition to considerations as to impact on an organization's tax-exempt status, discrimination based on race can involve invocation of the equal protection doctrine (when governmental action is involved), Title VI of the Civil Rights Act of 1964,[107] and the Civil Rights Act of 1866.[108] One of the touchstone principles in this constitutional law setting is whether a government has a substantial *state interest* in conducting a program where race is an element as to classification or distribution of benefits; the law developed in this

---

[101] E.g., Title VII of the Civil Rights Act of 1964, as amended, 42 U.S.C. § 2000e *et seq.*; Executive Order 11246, as amended, 30 Fed. Reg. 12319 (1965); Title IX of the Education Amendments of 1972, 20 U.S.C. § 1681 *et seq.*; the Rehabilitation Act Amendments of 1974, 29 U.S.C. §§ 793, 794; the Age Discrimination in Employment Act, 29 U.S.C. § 621 *et seq.*; and the Age Discrimination Act of 1975, 89 Stat. 713.

For example, where a university was held by a court to be in violation of the District of Columbia human rights act, which prohibits an educational institution from discriminating against any individual on the basis of their sexual orientation (D.C. Code, Title 1 § 1-2520), the court wrote that the "eradication of sexual orientation discrimination is a compelling governmental interest" (Gay Rights Coalition of Georgetown Univ. Law Cent. & D.C. v. Georgetown Univ., 536 A.2d 1 (D.C. Ct. App. 1987)).

[102] Rev. Proc. 75-50, 1975-2 C.B. 587.

[103] Rev. Rul. 77-365, 1977-2 C.B. 192. The U.S. Supreme Court held, however, that a tax-exempt organization had the constitutional right, pursuant to the freedom of association principle (see § 1.7), to exclude gays from leadership positions because of their sexual orientation (Boy Scouts of America v. Dale, 530 U.S. 64 (2000)).

[104] Regents of Univ. of Cal. v. Bakke, 438 U.S. 265, 325 (1978).

[105] See § 6.2(b).

[106] Regents of Univ. of Cal. v. Bakke, 438 U.S. 265, 307 (1978).

[107] 42 U.S.C. § 2000e.

[108] 42 U.S.C. § 1981.

regard provides guidance as to what forms of discrimination are permissible in the larger context. Another fundamental principle is that racial classifications review-able pursuant to equal protection considerations must be strictly scrutinized; the Supreme Court wrote that "any person, of whatever race, has the right to demand that any governmental actor subject to the Constitution justify any racial classifi-cation subjecting that person to unequal treatment under the strictest of judicial scrutiny."[109] The Court stated that the "guarantee of equal protection cannot mean one thing when applied to an individual and something else when applied to a person of another color"; that is, "[i]f both are not accorded the same protection, then it is not equal."[110]

These competing principles have been examined by the Court in connection with admissions policies of public colleges and universities that are based, with varying degrees of emphasis, on race.[111] In a landmark case, the Court reviewed a race-based and ethnicity-based set-aside program that reserved 16 out of 100 seats in a public university's medical school class for members of certain minor-ity groups. The Court held that a state has a "substantial interest that legitimately may be served by a properly devised admissions program involving the competi-tive consideration of race and ethnic origin,"[112] thereby establishing the bedrock rule that a college or university may, as part of its admissions program, consider the race of applicants.

Subsequently, the Court upheld an admissions program of a public univer-sity's law school that considered race and ethnicity as "plus" factors affecting diversity, with a goal of attaining a "critical mass" of underrepresented minority students.[113] In this case, the Court emphasized that a "race-conscious admissions program [of a public university] cannot use a quota system—it cannot 'insulate each category of applicants with certain desired qualifications from competition with all other applicants.'"[114] Indeed, in a companion case, the Court found that a public university's undergraduate admissions policy, based on a system that auto-matically granted points to underrepresented minority individuals, was not nar-rowly tailored to achieve the university's asserted compelling interest in diversity; the policy was found to violate equal protection principles.[115]

The Court subsequently articulated a tougher strict scrutiny test that courts are to use in evaluating race-based affirmative action programs in the public higher education context.[116] The Court stated that, in reviewing an affirmative action pro-gram, a court must "verify that it is necessary for a university to use race to achieve the educational benefits of diversity."[117] This case was remanded, with the court of

[109] Adarand Constructors, Inc. v. Pena, 515 U.S. 200, 224 (1995).
[110] Regents of Univ. of Cal. v. Bakke, 438 U.S. 265, 289–90 (1978).
[111] As it happens, another clash of constitutional law principles occurs in the education context, by reason of academic freedom, that "long has been viewed as a special concern of the First Amendment" (*id.* at 314).
[112] *Id.* at 320.
[113] Grutter v. Bollinger, 539 U.S. 306, 316, 321 (2003).
[114] *Id.* at 334, quoting from Regents of the Univ. of Cal. v. Bakke, 438 U.S. 265, 315 (1978).
[115] Gratz & Hamacher v. Bollinger, 539 U.S. 244 (2003).
[116] Fisher v. Univ. of Texas at Austin, 133 S. Ct. 2411 (2013).
[117] *Id.* at 2421.

appeals holding that this race-influenced admissions program is constitutional.[118] The Court subsequently upheld this affirmative action program.[119]

In practice, the principles enunciated in the context of admissions programs of institutions of public higher education are not always followed by tax-exempt organizations. As noted, exempt organizations often conduct race-based, gender-based, and similar affirmative action programs. On occasion, affirmative action can be a primary purpose of an entity. For example, a court, in a fluid recovery case,[120] ordered the design of a scholarship program by which grants were to be awarded to African American high school students residing in two states.[121]

The IRS ruled that an organization formed to conduct an apprentice training program offering instruction in a skilled trade was a tax-exempt charitable entity, even though the benefits of its educational activities were confined to Native Americans.[122] Likewise, the IRS approved a scholarship program established by a private foundation, where these grants are required to be made on an "objective and nondiscriminatory basis,"[123] even though all of the grantees were students at a boys-only school.[124]

Nonetheless, in a Civil Rights Act of 1866 case,[125] a federal appellate court held that the admissions policy of a private school, which operated in practice as an absolute bar to admission to the school for those of a "non-preferred race," constituted unlawful race discrimination.[126] The district court had concluded that the admissions policy constituted a valid race-conscious remedial affirmative action program.[127] Nonetheless, following a review of this case by the full panel, this court of appeals held that the school's "preferential admissions policy is designed to counteract the significant, current educational deficits of Native Hawaiian children in Hawaii" (that is, it is an affirmative action program), and consequently concluded that the school's admissions policy is "valid" under the Civil Rights Act.[128]

It is thus clear that this aspect of the constitutional, civil rights, and federal tax law remains unsettled. The most that can be said is that tax-exempt organizations that engage in affirmative action programs should be prepared for strict scrutiny of their efforts, including the ability to articulate a compelling interest for taking this approach.

---

[118] Fisher v. Univ. of Texas at Austin, 758 F.3d 633 (5th Cir. 2014).

[119] Fisher v. Univ. of Texas at Austin, 136 S. Ct. 2198 (2016).

[120] See § 6.3(g).

[121] Powell v. Georgia-Pacific Corp., 119 F.3d 703 (8th Cir. 1997), aff'g 843 F. Supp. 491 (W.D. Ark. 1994).

[122] Rev. Rul. 77-272, 1977-2 C.B. 191.

[123] IRC § 4945(g)(1). See § 12.4(e); *Private Foundations* § 9.3(e).

[124] Priv. Ltr. Rul. 200603029. The policy of the IRS has long been that, where the effect of a racial focus or limitation in an exempt organization's program reduces the effects of discrimination, or lack of education or opportunity, the preference is allowable; that is, it is not contrary to public policy (e.g., Gen. Couns. Mems. 39082, 39792).

[125] See text accompanied by *supra* note 107.

[126] Doe v. Kamehameha Schools/Bernice Pauahi Bishop Estate, 416 F.3d 1025, 1027 (9th Cir. 2005).

[127] Doe v. Kamehameha Schools/Bernice Pauahi Bishop Estate, 295 F. Supp. 2d 1141 (D. Haw. 2003).

[128] Doe v. Kamehameha Schools/Bernice Pauahi Bishop Estate, 470 F.3d 827, 849 (9th Cir. 2006). The petition to the U.S. Supreme Court for a writ of certiorari was withdrawn in connection with settlement of the litigation on May 14, 2007.

§ 6.3 COLLATERAL CONCEPTS

Conceptually, the term *charitable* has a broad, wide-ranging, multifaceted meaning. The IRS observed that the provisions in the federal tax statutory law relating to charitable organizations "do not reflect any novel or specialized tax concept of charitable purposes, and . . . [those provisions] should be interpreted as favoring only those purposes which are recognized as charitable in the generally accepted legal sense."[129]

There are, however, some collateral principles derived from the law of charitable trusts with respect to the concept of charity as applied for federal income tax purposes that require distillation.

(a) Requirement of *Charitable Class*

The individuals who are to benefit from a purported charitable activity often must constitute a sufficiently large or indefinite class. Thus, tax exemption as a charitable entity will be precluded if the beneficiaries of the alleged charitable works are specifically named, are solely relatives of the donor or donors, or are organizations such as social clubs and fraternal organizations.[130] For example, a foundation established to award scholarships solely to members of a designated fraternity on a national basis was ruled exempt as an educational organization.[131] By contrast, the IRS ruled that a scholarship foundation affiliated with a local college fraternity alumni association could not be exempt as a charitable entity because it did not function for the benefit of a charitable class in that the group of potential recipients was "very limited."[132] Another foundation lost its exempt status because it expended a considerable portion of its funds on a scholarship grant to the son of a trustee of the foundation.[133] The IRS ruled that raising funds and operating a lottery for the purpose of paying student debt is not a charitable undertaking because the participants in the lottery, who would have their debt reduced, were not limited to members of a charitable class (e.g., low-income or distressed students).[134] Basically, where a class of persons is involved as beneficiaries, the sufficiency of the class for purposes of ascertaining whether charitable activities are being engaged in becomes a question of degree.[135] Current and former employees of a company can qualify as a charitable class for purposes of enabling a fund that provides emergency assistance to these beneficiaries to constitute a tax-exempt charitable entity.[136]

---

[129] Rev. Rul. 67-325, 1967-2 C.B. 113.

[130] Rev. Rul. 56-403, 1956-2 C.B. 307.

[131] *Id.*

[132] Priv. Ltr. Rul. 201017067.

[133] Charleston Chair Co. v. United States, 203 F. Supp. 126 (E.D.S.C. 1962). Also, Rev. Rul. 67-367, 1967-2 C.B. 188. Likewise, an organization that provided financial assistance to students at a for-profit school to cover their school-related expenses, regardless of need, was denied recognition of tax-exempt status because it was not aiding a charitable class of individuals (Priv. Ltr. Rul. 202351013).

[134] Priv. Ltr. Rul. 202105010.

[135] Rev. Rul. 67-325, 1967-2 C.B. 113, where the IRS discussed this concept in the context of ruling, following the decision in Peters v. Comm'r, 21 T.C. 55 (1953), that community recreational facilities may be classified as charitable if they are provided for the use of the general public in the community. Cf. Rev. Rul. 59-310, 1959-2 C.B. 146.

[136] E.g., Priv. Ltr. Rul. 200839034.

A case in point is classification by the IRS of the elderly. Until the 1970s, the IRS's position was that the aged were not a charitable class *per se*, even the unemployed aged.[137] There was some support for this stance from the courts.[138] When an organization operated to assist the elderly, any tax exemption as a charitable entity was tied to the concept that they were also impoverished, as illustrated by the charitable and educational status accorded an organization to aid elderly unemployed persons of limited means in obtaining employment by providing these persons with free counseling and placement services and by educating the general public in the employment capabilities of the elderly.[139]

This position of the IRS began to soften in the early 1970s, as evidenced by its change of heart with respect to homes for the aged, when the IRS first articulated the thought that the elderly face forms of distress other than financial distress and have special needs for housing, health care, and economic security in general.[140] Thereafter, the IRS held that charitable status could be extended to an organization that established a service center providing information, referrals, counseling services relating to health, housing, finances, education, employment, and recreational facilities for a particular community's senior citizens;[141] that operated a rural rest home to provide, at a nominal charge, two-week vacations for elderly poor people;[142] and that provided home delivery by volunteers of meals to elderly and handicapped people.[143]

In 1977, the IRS first recognized the elderly as a charitable class *per se*. The IRS observed: "Providing the elderly and the handicapped with necessary transportation within the community is an activity directed toward meeting the special needs of these charitable classes of individuals."[144] Subsequently, the IRS ruled that an organization that provided specially designed housing that is "within the financial reach of a significant segment of the community's elderly persons" qualified as a charitable entity.[145] Yet, somewhat inexplicably, the IRS ruled that a resident advisory council with respect to a retirement community must have its tax exemption revoked because it is operating for the private interests of its members, portrayed as a "private class of residents," and not functioning in ways that are "beneficial to the general public as a whole."[146]

The IRS ruled that a law library qualified as a tax-exempt educational organization, even though the organization's rules limited "access to and use of the library facilities . . . to a designated class of persons."[147] The IRS, on this point, said, "What is of importance is that the class benefited be broad enough to warrant a conclusion that the educational facility or activity is serving a broad public interest

---

[137] Rev. Rul. 68-422, 1968-2 C.B. 207; Rev. Rul. 56-138, 1956-1 C.B. 202.

[138] Watson v. United States, 355 F.2d 269 (3d Cir. 1965).

[139] Rev. Rul. 66-257, 1966-2 C.B. 212.

[140] Rev. Rul. 72-124, 1972-1 C.B. 145.

[141] Rev. Rul. 75-198, 1975-1 C.B. 157.

[142] Rev. Rul. 75-385, 1975-2 C.B. 205.

[143] Rev. Rul. 76-244, 1976-1 C.B. 155.

[144] Rev. Rul. 77-246, 1977-2 C.B. 190.

[145] Rev. Rul. 79-18, 1979-1 C.B. 194.

[146] Priv. Ltr. Rul. 201911016.

[147] Rev. Rul. 75-196, 1975-2 C.B. 155.

rather than a private interest." The rationale for the favorable ruling was that the library facilities were available to a "significant number" of people and that the restrictions were placed on use of the library because of the limited size and scope of the facilities.[148]

The use of trusts may conflict with the requirement of a charitable class, in that the concept is that an indefinite class of individual beneficiaries is to be served, rather than specified individuals.[149] A cluster of trusts will not satisfy the requirement, where there is no pooling of funds and/or assets. As the U.S. Supreme Court stated, trusts "may, and indeed must, be for the benefit of an indefinite number of persons; for if all the beneficiaries are personally designated, the trust lacks the essential element of indefiniteness, which is one characteristic of a legal charity."[150] Thus, the IRS denied recognition of tax-exempt status as a charitable entity to an organization, operated to serve individuals with disabilities, because its principal activity was management of special needs trusts, each of which was dedicated to the welfare of a specific disabled person.[151]

A charitable purpose may be served regardless of whether corpus is immediately distributed or is continued indefinitely, or whether the number of persons actually relieved is small as long as they are selected from a valid charitable class. Nor is the economic status of the individuals benefited necessarily a factor, except where relief of poverty is the basis for designation of the purpose as charitable. The essential requirement for achieving charitable status is that benefits be accorded the public or the community, or some sufficiently general subgroup thereof, such as students, patients, or the aged.[152] For example, the IRS determined that community

---

[148] Rev. Rul. 68-504, 1968-2 C.B. 211, and Rev. Rul. 65-298, 1965-2 C.B. 163, held that an organization formed to conduct educational programs for a specific group is entitled to IRC § 501(c)(3) classification.

An organization that provided sperm, received from one donor, without charge to women seeking to become pregnant by means of artificial insemination or in vitro fertilization was held to be ineligible for exemption as a charitable entity in part because the class of its beneficiaries was found to be "not sufficiently large to benefit the community as a whole," in that the class consists of only women who are interested in having him be the biological father of their children and who survive a "very subjective, and possibly arbitrary, selection process" (Free Fertility Found. V. Comm'r, 135 T.C. 21, 25 (2010)).

[149] An organization established for the benefit of a specified individual cannot constitute a tax-exempt charitable entity (e.g., Wendy L. Parker Rehabilitation Found., Inc. v. Comm'r, 52 T.C.M. 51 (1986)). The same is true in the case of a nonprofit organization established to provide assistance to three special-needs children in a family (Priv. Ltr. Rul. 201205011). A similar situation arose in the case of an organization formed to provide funding for the treatment, education, and therapies for an individual with autism (Priv. Ltr. Rul. 201519035). A nonprofit day-care center failed to achieve recognition of exemption where the only children (four) enrolled in the entity's programs were those of its board members (Priv. Ltr. Rul. 201218041). See § 20.6(i).

[150] Russell v. Allen, 107 U.S. 163, 167 (1882).

[151] Priv. Ltr. Rul. 200621025. An application of the charitable class requirement was provided by the IRS when it held that a bequest for scholarships at two universities failed to qualify for the estate tax charitable deduction inasmuch as the only other criterion for the grants was that the recipients have the same surname as the decedent; the IRS determined that only 603 families have that name (Priv. Ltr. Rul. 9631004).

[152] E.g., Rev. Rul. 68-422, 1968-2 C.B. 207. An organization was denied recognition of tax exemption as a charitable entity because those it was serving, "undocumented aliens" and "American workers," were not members of a charitable class (Priv. Ltr. Rul. 201527043), as was an organization formed to reduce the federal student loan debt held by U.S. individuals (Priv. Ltr. Rul. 201718036) and an organization established to assist "homeowners" (Priv. Ltr. Rul. 201519034).

recreational facilities are classifiable as charitable if they are provided for the use of the general public of a community.[153] As one court stated, "[r]elief of poverty is not a condition of charitable assistance. If the benefit conferred is of sufficiently widespread social value, a charitable purpose exists."[154] Likewise, another court accorded tax exemption to an organization that functioned primarily as a crop seed certification entity, despite the government's contention that its activities only incidentally benefit the public, with the court observing that the "fact that the majority of persons interested in seed technology may well come from the agricultural community does not mean that farmers and gardeners are not an important part of the general public."[155]

By contrast, the IRS ruled that a nonprofit corporation that develops and provides software that improves digital currency technology, allowing anyone access to the industry of cryptocurrency for any purpose, is ineligible for tax exemption as a charitable and educational entity.[156] This entity was organized to improve digital currency technology by coordinating a global community to collaboratively develop a freely available, user-driven, open-source software that may be used to allow access to the cryptocurrency industry. The organization described itself to the IRS as a "software developer toolkit of open-source libraries that organizes the essential components of [a digital currency] and prioritizes its stability, security, and accessibility." The IRS determined that these activities are "not conducted to exclusively benefit a charitable class, such as the poor, distressed and underprivileged, the aged, and the sick or handicapped." The IRS's concern was that the organization's software applications "can be used by anyone with an interest in" the currency.

(b)   Means-to-End/Instrumentality Rule

Persons may benefit from an organization's activities and the assistance will be considered to further charitable ends as long as the effect benefits the community or a charitable class rather than merely individual recipients. In these instances, the individuals benefited are frequently regarded as "means" or "instruments" to the accomplishment of a charitable end. As an illustration, an organization was ruled exempt as a charitable entity for providing substantially free legal services to low-income residents of economically depressed communities by according financial and other assistance to law interns; the IRS recognized that the interns themselves were not members of a charitable class but were "merely the instruments by which the charitable purposes are accomplished."[157] Likewise, proxy contests when conducted in the public interest are charitable activities, in that there is a "community benefit" (that is, the "beneficiary of this activity and educational process to promote socially responsible corporations will be the public"), even though the exempt organization's resources are being devoted to direct participation in the processes of corporate management.[158] Similarly,

---

[153] Rev. Rul. 67-325, 1967-2 C.B. 113.
[154] In re Estate of Henderson, 112 P.2d 605, 607 (Sup. Ct. Cal. 1941).
[155] Indiana Crop Improvement Ass'n, Inc. v. Comm'r, 76 T.C. 394, 400 (1981).
[156] Priv. Ltr. Rul. 202129016.
[157] Rev. Rul. 72-559, 1972-2 C.B. 247.
[158] Center on Corporate Responsibility, Inc. v. Shultz, 368 F. Supp. 863, 874, n. 21 (D.D.C. 1973).

a member of an organization may properly obtain financial benefit from the organization where the members are the means by which public purposes are served.[159] The same principle obtains with respect to the operation of public interest law firms.[160] The IRS has accepted the view that a charitable organization may provide services or make distributions to nonexempt organizations where done in furtherance of its exempt purpose.[161]

The IRS ruled that an organization did not fail to qualify as a charitable and educational entity because its tax-exempt function (the training of unemployed and underemployed individuals) was carried out through the manufacturing and selling of toy products.[162] The IRS observed that the facts in this instance "clearly support the conclusion that the manufacturing and merchandising operation is the means of accomplishing the organization's declared charitable objectives" and that there is a "clear and distinct causal relationship between the manufacturing activity and the training of individuals for the purpose of improving their individual capabilities." Similarly, the IRS stated that the "performance of a particular activity that is not inherently charitable may nonetheless further a charitable purpose. The overall result in any given case is dependent on why and how that activity is actually being conducted."[163]

Related to this concept of individuals as a means or instrument to tax-exempt ends is the matter of permissible private benefit[164] when it is unavoidable. For example, an exempt charitable organization that allocated Medicaid patients to physicians in private practice was held to provide qualitatively and quantitatively incidental private benefits to the physicians, including some on the organization's board of directors, inasmuch as it was "impossible" for the organization to accomplish its exempt purposes without providing some measure of benefit to these physicians.[165] Likewise, an exempt hospital's investment in a for-profit medical malpractice insurance company was ruled to further charitable purposes and not entail impermissible private benefit because the investment was required for the writing of insurance for the physicians, the physicians needed the insurance to practice at the hospital, and the hospital could not provide health care services to its communities without the physicians.[166] Similarly, an organization was ruled by the IRS to be exempt as a charitable entity because of the benefits it provided to the public through the maintenance and improvement of public recreational facilities; the IRS held that any private benefit derived by lakefront property owners did not lessen the public benefits flowing from

[159] Gen. Couns. Mem. 38459.

[160] See § 7.16(d).

[161] Rev. Rul. 81-29, 1981-1 C.B. 329; Rev. Rul. 68-489, 1968-2 C.B. 210. Where, however, a grant is for the improvement of a study room, the room must be used primarily for educational purposes, according to the IRS Chief Counsel, analogizing to IRC § 280A(c)(1)(A) (concerning the business deduction for a home office), in Gen. Couns. Mem. 39288, *as modified by* Gen. Couns. Mem. 39612.

[162] Rev. Rul. 73-128, 1973-1 C.B. 222.

[163] Rev. Rul. 69-572, 1969-2 C.B. 119. Also, Rev. Rul. 80-279, 1980-2 C.B. 176; Rev. Rul. 80-278, 1980-2 C.B. 175; Rev. Rul. 67-4, 1967-1 C.B. 121. Cf. Senior Citizens Stores, Inc. v. United States, 602 F.2d 711 (5th Cir. 1979).

[164] See § 20.13.

[165] Priv. Ltr. Rul. 9615030.

[166] Priv. Ltr. Rul. 200606042.

the organization's operations, and observed that "it would be impossible for the organization to accomplish its purposes without providing benefits" to these property owners.[167]

(c)   *Charity* as Evolving Concept

The concept of what is *charitable* is continually changing and evolving. This principle is illustrated by the abandonment by the IRS of its prior rule that homes for the aged may be exempt only where services are provided free or below cost, to be replaced by the requirement that housing, health care, and financial security needs be met.[168] Thus, the old law that focused solely on relief of financial distress of the aged has been supplanted by a recognition of other forms of "distress": need for housing, health care services, and financial security. Changes in the concept are expounded in constitutions, statutes, and, for the most part, court decisions. In the latter instance, the changes are "wrought by changes in moral and ethical precepts generally held, or by changes in relative values assigned to different and sometimes competing and even conflicting interests of society."[169]

The fact that a particular purpose requires efforts to bring about a change in the statutory law does not preclude the purpose from being charitable. Thus, the proscription on substantive legislative activities by charitable organizations is a statutory constraint on otherwise permissible charitable activities rather than a declaration of a feature of the term *charitable* in the common law.[170]

In conclusion, a frequently cited case is a venerable U.S. Supreme Court pronouncement, where the Court stated: "A charitable use, where neither law nor public policy forbids, may be applied to almost any thing that tends to promote the well-doing and well-being of social man."[171]

(d)   Motive

The motive of the founder in initiating the alleged charitable activity is immaterial in terms of ascertaining whether the activity is in fact charitable in nature. This principle was illustrated by the case of a decedent's bequest to a cemetery association formed to maintain a cemetery and sell burial plots. In the absence of proof that the cemetery was operated exclusively for charitable purposes or that the bequest was to be used exclusively for such purposes, a court held that the bequest was not a charitable bequest for federal estate tax purposes.[172] The court

---

[167] Rev. Rul. 70-186, 1970-1 C.B. 128. The IRS issued a similar ruling in conjunction with operation of a public park and unavoidable private benefit (Rev. Rul. 66-358, 1966-2 C.B. 218). Yet when the IRS ruled that most down payment assistance organizations could not be exempt as charitable entities (Rev. Rul. 2006-27, 2006-1 C.B. 915) (see § 7.5), it did so largely on the grounds of private benefit to the home sellers, refusing to recognize that, to provide charitable assistance to home buyers, the involvement of home sellers is unavoidable.

[168] Rev. Rul. 72-124, 1972-1 C.B. 145, *superseding* Rev. Rul. 57-467, 1957-2 C.B. 313.

[169] Green v. Connally, 330 F. Supp. 1150, 1159 (D.C.C. 1971), *aff'd sub nom.* Coit v. Green, 404 U.S. 997 (1971).

[170] See § 21.3.

[171] Ould v. Washington Hosp. for Foundlings, 95 U.S. 303, 311 (1877). Also, Peters v. Comm'r, 21 T.C. 55, 59 (1953). See §§ 6.2, 6.3(i).

[172] Estate of Amick v. Comm'r, 67 T.C. 924 (1977).

stated that it is the "use to which a bequest is to be applied that determines its deductibility and not the motive prompting the bequest."[173]

(e) Private Use

A charitable purpose cannot be served where the property involved or the income therefrom is directed to a private use. For example, a book publishing venture was denied exemption as a charitable and/or educational organization because a substantial purpose of the organization was found to be the derivation of substantial profits by the organization and the authors to which it made grants.[174] Other illustrations include an organization that was denied exemption because its principal activity was the making of research grants for the development of new machinery to be used in a commercial operation[175] and an association that was denied exemption as a business league because its "research program" benefited its members rather than the public.[176]

It was for this reason that the IRS refused to recognize an organization as being charitable where its primary purpose was to encourage individuals to contribute funds to charity and its primary activity was the offering of free legal services for personal tax and estate planning to individuals who wish to make current and planned gifts to charity as part of their overall tax and estate planning. Stating that "[a]iding individuals in their tax and estate planning is not a charitable activity in the generally accepted legal sense," the IRS ruled that the "benefits to the public are tenuous in view of the predominantly private purpose served by arranging individuals' tax and estate plans."[177]

The fact that individuals or organizations incidentally or unavoidably derive a benefit from a charitable undertaking does not, as noted, necessarily undermine the exempt, charitable nature of the endeavor. For example, an association of educational institutions that accredited schools and colleges was found to foster excellence in education and to qualify as a tax-exempt charitable and educational entity, even though its membership included a small number of proprietary schools, since any private benefit that "may accrue to the few proprietary members because of accreditation is incidental to the purpose of improving the quality of education."[178] Thus, the IRS, which accorded status as an exempt charitable entity to an organization formed and supported by residents of an isolated rural community to provide a medical building and facilities at reasonable rent to attract a physician who would provide medical services to the community, stated that "[i]n these circumstances, any personal benefit derived by the doctor . . . does not detract from the public purpose of the organization nor lessen the public benefit flowing from its activities."[179]

---

[173] *Id.* at 928. Also, Wilbur Nat'l Bank v. Comm'r, 17 B.T.A. 654 (1929); Estate of Wood v. Comm'r, 39 T.C. 1 (1962); Rev. Rul. 67-170, 1967-1 C.B. 272. Cf. Estate of Audenried v. Comm'r, 26 T.C. 120 (1956).

[174] Rev. Rul. 66-104, 1966-1 C.B. 135; Christian Manner Int'l, Inc. v. Comm'r, 71 T.C. 661 (1979).

[175] Rev. Rul. 65-1, 1965-1 C.B. 226.

[176] Rev. Rul. 69-632, 1969-2 C.B. 120.

[177] Rev. Rul. 76-442, 1976-2 C.B. 148.

[178] Rev. Rul. 74-146, 1974-1 C.B. 129. An IRS private letter ruling suggested that an association of this nature may receive up to 15 percent of its resources from for-profit members without endangering its tax-exempt status (Priv. Ltr. Rul. 9237034).

[179] Rev. Rul. 73-313, 1973-2 C.B. 174.

Likewise, the IRS ruled that the fact that lawyers use an exempt library to derive personal benefit in the practice of their profession is incidental to the exempt purpose of the library and is, in most instances, a "logical by-product" of an educational process.[180] Similarly, a court held that a day-care center qualified as an exempt educational organization and that the provision of custodial care was "merely a vehicle for or incidental to achieving petitioner's only substantial purpose, education of the children, and is not ground for disqualification from exemption."[181] This court subsequently reiterated this position, holding that an early childhood center is an exempt educational organization, "with custodial care being incidental only because of the needs of the children for such care if they are to receive the education offered."[182] Likewise, this court held that an organization may sell artwork without jeopardizing its exemption because the sales activities "are but a means to the end of increasing public appreciation of the arts."[183]

Still another illustration of this by-product doctrine is the ability of a tax-exempt organization to provide services (such as research) in furtherance of an exempt function where nonexempt entities are among the recipients of the services.[184] In still another illustration of this point, the IRS determined that a professional standards review organization can qualify as an exempt charitable entity as promoting health and lessening the burdens of government, because the benefits accorded by it to members of the medical profession were incidental to the charitable benefits it provided.[185]

(f) *Cy Pres* Doctrine

State law principles of equity include the doctrine of *cy pres*; its name reflects the Norman French expression "*cy pres comme possible*," which means "as near as possible." This doctrine, applied only in the charitable purposes context, is used by courts to preserve income and assets for charitable purposes in accordance with the donor's original intent.[186]

Pursuant to the doctrine of *cy pres*, courts may impose a public or constructive trust on the operations of a charitable organization if necessary to achieve the original purpose of the charitable entity. Application of this doctrine often causes a court to transfer charitable assets to one or more other charitable organizations when necessary to honor and sustain the intent underlying the formation of the organizations whose purposes or activities are at issue.[187] As a federal court of appeals stated, "[u]nder *cy pres*, if the testator had a general charitable intent, the court will look for an alternate recipient that will best serve the gift's original purpose."[188]

---

[180] Rev. Rul. 75-196, 1975-2 C.B. 155. Also, Rev. Rul. 75-471, 1975-2 C.B. 207; Rev. Rul. 78-85, 1978-1 C.B. 150.

[181] San Francisco Infant School, Inc. v. Comm'r, 69 T.C. 957, 966 (1978). See § 8.8.

[182] Michigan Early Childhood Cent., Inc. v. Comm'r, 37 T.C.M. 808, 810 (1978).

[183] Cleveland Creative Arts Guild v. Comm'r, 50 T.C.M. 272 (1985).

[184] Rev. Rul. 81-29, 1981-1 C.B. 329.

[185] Rev. Rul. 81-276, 1981-2 C.B. 128. Also, Fraternal Medical Specialist Servs., Inc. v. Comm'r, 49 T.C.M. 289 (1984).

[186] E.g., In re Airline Ticket Comm'n Antitrust Litigation, 268 F.3d 619, 625 (8th Cir. 2001).

[187] E.g., Blocker v. State, 718 S.W.2d 409 (Tex. Ct. App. 1986); Coffee v. William Marsh Rice Univ., 408 S.W.2d 269 (Tex. Ct. App. 1966).

[188] In re Airline Ticket Comm'n Antitrust Litigation, 307 F.3d 679, 682 (8th Cir. 2002).

A "cardinal principle" in this context is that construction of a trust instrument requires ascertainment of the original intent with the view of effectuating it.[189] A state court wrote that an entity's charitable purposes and "limitations" are *"defined by the donee's organizational purpose."*[190] This court added that any "limitations" imposed on a charity's assets are determined *"by reference to the stated purposes set forth in the articles of incorporation."*[191]

The rule that *cy pres* is to be invoked where the original purpose of the charitable entity has become illegal, impracticable, or impossible is, of course, not triggered where there is no legal or practical impediment to adherence to the original purpose.[192]

(g) Fluid Recovery Principles

Courts recognize the consumer class action as an "essential tool for the protection of consumers against exploitative business practices."[193] Distribution of damages, however, poses special problems in these actions; each individual's recovery may be too small to make traditional methods of proof worthwhile, and consumers are not likely to retain records of small purchases for long periods of time. When courts are faced with distributing unclaimed funds from a class action, they have four options: (1) a pro rata distribution to the class members who have already made claims, (2) escheat to the government, (3) reversion to the defendant, or (4) a *cy pres* distribution.[194] Often the solution crafted by the courts is the last of these options: allocation of funds to one or more charitable organizations.[195]

Cy pres principles[196] are invoked in the class action context in connection with the distribution of unclaimed funds. In these instances, the unclaimed funds "should be distributed for a purpose as near as possible to the legitimate objectives underlying the lawsuit, the interests of class members, and the interests of those similarly situated."[197] A court wrote that "[w]here settlement funds remain after distribution to class members, courts have approved charitable donations to organizations geared toward 'combating harms similar to those that injured the class members, [inasmuch as] [s]uch a donation may serve the *cy pres* principle of

---

[189] E.g., Coffee v. William Marsh Rice Univ., 408 S.W.2d 269, 273 (Tex. Ct. App. 1966).

[190] Blocker v. State, 718 S.W.2d 409, 415 (Tex. Ct. App. 1986).

[191] *Id.*

[192] Howard Hughes Medical Institute v. Neff, 640 S.W. 2d 942, 953 (Tex. Ct. App. 1982).

[193] California v. Levi Strauss & Co., 41 Cal. 3d 460, 471 (Sup. Ct. Cal. 1986).

[194] Kansas Ass'n of Private Investigators v. Mulvihill, 159 S.W. 3d 857, 860–861 (Mo. Ct. App. 2005).

[195] E.g., Powell v. Georgia-Pacific Corp., 843 F. Supp. 491 (W.D. Ark. 1994), *aff'd*, 119 F.3d 703 (8th Cir. 1997) (distribution of funds to the Georgia-Pacific Foundation to establish a scholarship program); In re Infant Formula Multidistrict Litigation, 2005 WL 2211312 (N.D. Fla. 2005) (distribution of funds to the American Red Cross to provide infant formula to individuals in areas affected by Hurricane Katrina). The rule of equity was applied in Kansas Ass'n of Private Investigators v. Mulvihill, 159 S.W.3d 857 (Mo. Ct. App. 2005), with the appellate court finding that the distributions to charities were not sufficiently related to the objectives underlying the lawsuit and the like. A similar finding was made in Cavalier v. Mobil Oil Corp., 898 So. 2d 584 (La. App. 2005), with the appellate court voiding 20 percent of the allocation. A court referred to distributions to appropriate charities in this context as "project funding" (Mace v. Van Ru Credit Corp., 109 F.3d 338 (7th Cir. 1997)).

[196] See § 6.3(f).

[197] In re Airline Ticket Comm'n Antitrust Litigation, 307 F.3d 679, 682 (8th Cir. 2002).

indirectly benefiting all class members.'"[198] Courts have, however, expanded the *cy pres* doctrine to permit distributions to charitable organizations the operations of which are not directly related to the original claims.[199] Indeed, a court wrote that the "absence of an obvious cause to support with the [settlement] funds does not bar a charitable donation."[200] Thus, another court observed that, although the "use of funds for purposes closely related to their origin is still the best *cy pres* application, the doctrine of *cy pres* and the courts' broad equitable powers now permit the use of funds for other public interest purposes by educational, charitable, and other public service organizations."[201]

In the class action context, the *cy pres* doctrine is generally denominated *fluid recovery*. Fluid recovery may, as a court stated, be "essential to ensure that the policies of disgorgement or deterrence are realized."[202] Another court wrote that "[w]ithout fluid recovery, defendants may be permitted to retain ill gotten gains simply because their conduct harmed large numbers of people in small amounts instead of small numbers of people in large amounts."[203] A court wrote that the *cy pres* doctrine "has been used to distribute proceeds of a class action lawsuit when the amounts owing to each individual plaintiff are exceedingly small and/or identification of the amount due each individual would be excessively difficult."[204] This court added that this type of distribution "does not subject defendants to greater liability or alter their substantive right, because it affects interests of silent class members only."[205]

An alternative in the fluid recovery context is formation of a charitable organization to receive the distributions and function in a manner that serves the interests of the class. A court termed such an entity a "consumer trust fund."[206] This court cautioned, nonetheless, that the consumer trust fund device "does entail the establishment of a new organization with its own administrative expenses" and observed that "[t]o avoid this additional cost, some courts have allocated the funds directly to responsible private [charitable] organizations."[207] A similar problem can arise if the new entity created in this type of context is, in the view of the court, underfunded.[208]

---

[198] In re Motorsports Merchandise Antitrust Litigation, 160 F. Supp. 2d 1392, 1394 (N.D. Ga. 2001), quoting Jones v. Nat'l Distillers, 56 F. Supp. 2d 355, 358 (S.D.N.Y. 1999).

[199] E.g., Superior Beverage Co. v. Owens-Illinois, 827 F. Supp. 477 (N.D. Ill. 1993).

[200] Jones v. Nat'l Distillers, 56 F. Supp. 2d 355, 359 (S.D.N.Y. 1999).

[201] In re Motorsports Merchandise Antitrust Litigation, 160 F. Supp. 2d 1392, 1394 (N.D. Ga. 2001).

[202] Simer v. Rios, 661 F.2d 655, 676 (7th Cir. 1981).

[203] California v. Levi Strauss & Co., 41 Cal. 3d 460, 472 (Sup. Ct. Cal. 1986).

[204] Cavalier v. Mobil Oil Corp., 898 So. 2d 584, 588 (La. Ct. App. 2005).

[205] *Id.*

[206] California v. Levi Strauss & Co., 41 Cal. 3d 460, 475 (Sup. Ct. Cal. 1986).

[207] *Id.* E.g., In re Folding Carton Antitrust Litigation, 557 F. Supp. 1091 (N.D. Ill. 1983), *aff'd in part and rev'd in part*, 744 F.2d 1252 (7th Cir. 1984).

[208] E.g., In re Microsoft Corp. Antitrust Litigation, 185 F. Supp. 2d 519 (D. Md. 2002). U.S. Supreme Court Chief Justice John Roberts wrote, in a statement respecting a denial of certiorari, that the Court may clarify the limits on the use of *cy pres* remedies in class action settlements (Marek v. Lane, 571 U.S. 1003 (2013)). The Chief Justice observed that a foundation established in the context of a fluid recovery case settlement has "disconcerting features," including board composition and grantmaking discretion (*id.*).

(h) Charging of Fees

A growing practice of the IRS is to deny recognition of tax exemption to an organization that is endeavoring to be classified as a charitable, educational, or like entity, on the ground that the entirety of its financial support is fee-based; this form of revenue is cast as evidence of undue commerciality.[209] This interpretation of the federal tax law is fundamentally incorrect; the concept of *charitable* rests on the inherent character of the activities involved and/or the nature of the program beneficiaries. Indeed, the public charity rules expressly provide for charitable organizations that are funded by means of exempt function revenue.[210]

For example, the IRS often uses the absence of a broad-based fundraising program as a basis to deny recognition of tax exemption to credit counseling organizations[211] and down payment assistance organizations.[212] This approach is also used in other contexts, as illustrated by the organization that failed to qualify as an exempt educational organization in part because it was supported by fees and did not have a fundraising program.[213] Thus, the IRS ruled that, because an organization charged fees for its services, it was operated for "substantial commercial purposes."[214]

(i) Illegal Activities

A charitable purpose cannot be one that is illegal or contrary to public policy.[215] The IRS determined that an organization formed to promote world peace and disarmament could not qualify as either a tax-exempt charitable organization or a social welfare organization, because its primary activity was the sponsorship of antiwar protest demonstrations where it urged its participants to commit violations of local ordinances and breaches of public order.[216] Likewise, the IRS ruled that, inasmuch as the practice of polygamy is illegal,[217] an organization attempting to be tax-exempt as an apostolic entity[218] could not be exempt, because its religious beliefs and practices include plural marriage, causing the organization to promote "illegal acts."[219] An organization engaged in activities to obstruct administration of the revenue laws, as detailed in a plea agreement entered into by its executive director, was also denied exemption.[220] Similarly, the IRS ruled that an organization that develops, manufactures, and distributes "dying medicines" cannot be exempt as a charitable entity, inasmuch as assisted suicides, euthanasia, and mercy killing are federal criminal offenses.[221]

---

[209] See § 4.9. Cf. § 24.2(e).
[210] IRC § 509(a)(2). See § 12.3(b)(iv).
[211] See § 7.3.
[212] See § 7.5.
[213] Priv. Ltr. Rul. 200622055.
[214] Priv. Ltr. Rul. 201019033.
[215] Tank Truck Rentals, Inc. v. Comm'r, 356 U.S. 30 (1958). See § 6.2.
[216] Rev. Rul. 75-384, 1975-2 C.B. 204.
[217] Reynolds v. United States, 98 U.S. 145 (1879).
[218] See § 10.8.
[219] Priv. Ltr. Rul. 201310047.
[220] Priv. Ltr. Rul. 201924018.
[221] Priv. Ltr. Rul. 202101007.

On one occasion, the IRS ruled that a charitable organization was engaged in "deceptive business practices," without stating what those practices were and without noting whether they were illegal; the IRS stated that these practices were "evidence of a substantial nonexempt purpose" and revoked the organization's tax exemption.[222] The IRS added: "Sharp business practices, including deceptive contracts and untrue statements about the law or an organization's business methods, are incompatible with the purpose of an organization claiming to be charitable," again without any explanation as to whether the "sharp" practices were illegal.

The IRS declined to recognize tax exemption as a charitable entity in the case of an organization whose principal purpose was the distribution of, and education with respect to, cannabis (marijuana) for medicinal purposes.[223] The organization operated a dispensary, much in the manner of a physician's office, and dispenses cannabis only in accordance with a doctor's recommendation and state law. The primary reason for the IRS's ruling was that federal law prohibits the manufacture, distribution, possession, or dispensation of a controlled substance, such as cannabis.[224] The fact that the state legalized the distribution of cannabis to a limited extent was said to not be "determinative," inasmuch as it is federal law that applies in this context.[225]

Likewise, the IRS denied recognition of exemption in a case involving an organization that had as its mission provision of a way for its members to collectively and cooperatively cultivate and distribute marijuana for medical purposes to qualified patients and primary caregivers who came together to cultivate physician-recommended marijuana.[226] The IRS adopted a similar stance in denying recognition of exemption to a nonprofit organization providing financial assistance to patients in need who are adversely affected by the costs of medical treatments using cannabis-based compounds,[227] a nonprofit organization with a program of fundraising and dissemination of funds to patients in a state program who had been approved to receive medical marijuana in the state,[228] and a nonprofit organization that provides its members with sacraments for use in religious services that entail federally illegal substances.[229] Similarly, the IRS declined to recognize a religious organization as an exempt entity because one of its activities was the cultivation and preparation of cannabis for "consecration" from "sacramental seeds" given to the organization's "Granger" by its members.[230] An organization was also denied recognition of exemption where its activities included promoting the medical benefits of various plants prohibited by federal law, funding research

---

[222] Priv. Ltr. Rul. 201734009.

[223] Priv. Ltr. Rul. 201224036.

[224] 21 U.S.C. §§ 812, 841(a). See § 25.5(c).

[225] This approach is not confined to the realm of charity. For example, the IRS denied recognition of exemption to a cooperative facilitating transactions among members involved in the medical use of marijuana, which was seeking classification as a crop operations finance organization (see § 19.10) in part on the ground that possession and distribution of marijuana was illegal and contrary to public policy (see § 6.2(a)) (Priv. Ltr. Rul. 201333014).

[226] Priv. Ltr. Rul. 201615018.

[227] Priv. Ltr. Rul. 201917008.

[228] Priv. Ltr. Rul. 201940008.

[229] Priv. Ltr. Rul. 202053019.

[230] Priv. Ltr. Rul. 202210022.

into novel uses of these plants, and persuading the public to support legalizing the plants "so they can be more easily studied and used by physicians."[231]

A court held that a church failed both the organizational and operational tests where its mission was to provide public access to ayahuasca, a psychedelic drink with an ingredient listed as a Schedule I substance under the Controlled Substances Act (CSA). The church had applied for, but not yet received, an exemption from the CSA from the Drug Enforcement Administration. Without the CSA exemption, the court held that the church's stated purpose in its articles of incorporation (distributing and facilitating the use of ayahuasca) and its primary mission (preparing for and conducting weekend ayahuasca ceremonies) were both illegal and therefore made it ineligible for exempt status. This court also held that the church lacked standing to assert a Religious Freedom Restoration Act of 1993[232] claim for impermissibly burdening the church's free exercise of religion by denying its tax-exemption application; any "chilling" effect on the church's sincerely held religious belief (i.e., the consumption of ayahuasca) was neither traceable to the IRS's denial of the church's application nor redressable with a favorable ruling.[233]

Matters in these regards are in some flux, however. About one-third of the states have revised their laws to permit marijuana distribution and use for medicinal and/or recreational purposes. The law change trend is likely to continue, placing pressure on the nature of the federal law in this regard. It is being said that the legality of polygamy is the "next frontier" in marriage law (following the controversies relating to same-sex marriage). A federal district court struck down a portion of a state's antipolygamy statute as being a violation of the Free Exercise Clause and principles of due process.[234] The court referenced the "much developed constitutional jurisprudence that now protects individuals from the criminal [law] consequences intended by legislatures to apply to certain personal choices," concluding that the state has been selectively prosecuting cases involving "religious cohabitation" but not those entailing "adulterous cohabitation."[235]

§ 6.4 WHAT TAX EXEMPTION DOES NOT CREATE

Litigants have asserted, without success in the courts, that an express or implied contract arises between an organization and the federal government once the IRS recognizes the tax-exempt status of the organization as a charitable entity. The principal contention in this regard has been that tax exemption accorded to hospitals gives rise to a contract obligating the exempt hospital to provide medical care to uninsured patients without regard to their ability to pay for the care. This assertion, however, has been repeatedly rejected.[236] This theory was also rejected

[231] Priv. Ltr. Rul. 202217009.

[232] Pub. L. No. 103-141, 107 Stat. 1488.

[233] Iowaska Church of Healing v. United States, 131 A.F.T.R. 2d 2023-1264 (D.D.C. 2023), aff'd, 105 F.4th 402 (D.C. Cir. 2024). The court also held that the church's illegal activities violated the public policy doctrine (see § 6.2(a)).

[234] Brown v. Buhman, 947 F. Supp. 2d 1170 (D. Utah 2013).

[235] Id. at 1222.

[236] E.g., Burton v. William Beaumont Hosp., 347 F. Supp. 2d 486 (E.D. Mich. 2004).

in connection with a claim that exempt status gave rise to a contract requiring a hospital system to continue operating one of its regional hospitals.[237]

Those who contended that recognition of tax-exempt status creates a contract between the federal government and the exempt organization then contended that they are third-party beneficiaries of this contract. This argument has been made, without success in the courts, by uninsured plaintiffs who claim that they were denied medical care by exempt hospitals, that this denial of care was a breach of this contract, and that they are entitled to relief as third-party beneficiaries of this contract.

Courts have held that the recognition of tax exemption of an organization as a charitable entity does not create a private right of action.

Courts have also repeatedly held that the recognition of an organization by the IRS as a charitable entity does not create a form of charitable trust.

---

[237] Jackson v. Cleveland Clinic Found., 2011 WL4007732 (N.D. Ohio 2011).

CHAPTER SEVEN

Charitable Organizations

Section 501(a) of the Internal Revenue Code provides federal income tax exemption for organizations described in IRC § 501(c)(3), including entities that are organized and operated exclusively for charitable purposes.

The term *charitable* has the most extensive history and the broadest meaning of any of the terms referencing categories of tax-exempt organizations in IRC § 501(c)(3). It is used in this context in its "generally accepted legal sense" and is, therefore, not construed as being limited by the other purposes stated in the section that may fall within the broad outlines of *charity* as developed by judicial decisions.[1] The various categories of purposes embraced by the term *charitable* in the federal tax law are the subject of this chapter.

§ 7.1   RELIEF OF POOR

The regulations underlying the federal tax statutory law concerning charitable organizations define the term *charitable* as including "[r]elief of the poor and distressed or of the underprivileged."[2] Nonetheless, the IRS, in three revenue rulings issued in 1979, changed this phraseology, so that the term *charitable* includes the relief of the poor *or* distressed.[3]

The relief of poverty is the most basic and historically founded form of charitable activity. The *poor* constitute a charitable class; the provision of nearly any type of aid to the poor constitutes a charitable undertaking. Indeed, in the minds of some, relief of the poor is the *only* function that warrants treatment as a charitable activity.[4]

The litigation that followed the issuance by the IRS of expanded criteria for defining a tax-exempt charitable hospital dramatically illustrated the fact that the term *charitable* embraces purposes and activities in addition to ways to assist the poor. The agency stated, on this occasion, that promotion of health is a discrete charitable purpose.[5] A lawsuit ensued, with a federal district court holding that, to be exempt, a hospital must significantly serve the poor for a reduced or forgone charge.[6] An appellate court, however, wrote, in upholding the IRS's criteria for

---

[1] Reg. § 1.501(c)(3)-1(d)(2). Also, Reg. § 1.501(c)(3)-1(d)(1)(i)(b).
[2] Reg. § 1.501(c)(3)-1(d)(2).
[3] See § 7.2(a), text accompanied by *infra* note 33.
[4] See § 6.1(a).
[5] See § 7.6(a).
[6] Eastern Ky. Welfare Rights Org. v. Shultz, 370 F. Supp. 325 (D.D.C. 1973).

exempt hospitals, that the term *charitable* is "capable of a definition far broader than merely relief of the poor."[7]

Organizations deemed tax-exempt because they relieve the poor (or under-privileged) may be categorized on the basis of the types of services they provide. Some organizations provide assistance to enable the impoverished to secure employment, such as vocational training,[8] establishment of a market for products of the needy,[9] or employment assistance for the elderly.[10] Others provide assistance to maintain employment, such as operation of a day-care center;[11] promotion of the rights and welfare of public housing tenants;[12] provision of technical and material assistance under foreign self-help programs;[13] provision of financial assistance in securing a private hospital room;[14] or operation of a service center providing information, referral, and counseling services relating to health, housing, finances, education, and employment, as well as a facility for specialized recreation for a community's senior citizens.[15]

Others of these types of tax-exempt organizations provide services more personal in nature, such as provision of low-income housing,[16] legal services,[17] money management advice,[18] vacations for the elderly poor at a rural rest home,[19] home delivery of meals to the elderly,[20] and transportation services for the elderly and handicapped.[21] Still others of these organizations seek to render assistance to the poor (or distressed) by helping them at a time when they are particularly needy, such as prisoners requiring rehabilitation,[22] the elderly requiring specially designed housing,[23] the physically handicapped requiring specially designed housing,[24] hospital patients needing the visitation and comfort provided by their relatives and friends,[25] and widow(er)s and orphans of police officers and firefighters killed in the line of duty.[26] Similarly, exemption on this basis was accorded

[7] Eastern Ky. Welfare Rights Org. v. Simon, 506 F.2d 1278, 1287 (D.C. Cir. 1974). The Supreme Court, in reviewing this case, did not address its merits, but found that the plaintiffs lacked standing to bring the action (Simon v. Eastern Ky. Welfare Rights Org., 426 U.S. 26 (1976)).

[8] Rev. Rul. 73-128, 1973-1 C.B. 222.

[9] Industrial Aid for the Blind v. Comm'r, 73 T.C. 96 (1979); Rev. Rul. 68-167, 1968-1 C.B. 255; Tech. Adv. Mem. 200021056.

[10] Rev. Rul. 66-257, 1966-2 C.B. 212.

[11] Rev. Rul. 70-533, 1970-2 C.B. 112; Rev. Rul. 68-166, 1968-1 C.B. 255.

[12] Rev. Rul. 75-283, 1975-2 C.B. 201.

[13] Rev. Rul. 68-165, 1968-1 C.B. 253; Rev. Rul. 68-117, 1968-1 C.B. 251.

[14] Rev. Rul. 79-358, 1979-2 C.B. 225.

[15] Rev. Rul. 75-198, 1975-1 C.B. 157. Also, Rev. Rul. 77-42, 1977-1 C.B. 142.

[16] See § 7.4.

[17] Rev. Rul. 78-428, 1978-2 C.B. 177; Rev. Rul. 72-559, 1972-2 C.B. 247; Rev. Rul. 69-161, 1969-1 C.B. 149.

[18] Rev. Rul. 69-441, 1969-2 C.B. 115.

[19] Rev. Rul. 75-385, 1975-2 C.B. 205.

[20] Rev. Rul. 76-244, 1976-1 C.B. 155.

[21] Rev. Rul. 77-246, 1977-2 C.B. 190.

[22] Rev. Rul. 70-583, 1970-2 C.B. 114; Rev. Rul. 67-150, 1967-1 C.B. 133.

[23] Rev. Rul. 79-18, 1979-1 C.B. 194.

[24] Rev. Rul. 79-19, 1979-1 C.B. 195.

[25] Rev. Rul. 81-28, 1981-1 C.B. 328.

[26] Rev. Rul. 55-406, 1955-1 C.B. 73.

to an organization that posted bail for individuals who were otherwise incapable of paying for bail, as part of its integrated program for their release and rehabilitation,[27] to a legal aid society that provided free legal services and funds to pay fees of commercial bondsmen for indigent persons who were otherwise financially unable to obtain these services,[28] and to an organization that provided rescue and emergency services to persons suffering because of a disaster.[29] Under appropriate circumstances, an organization can qualify as a charitable one where the impoverished being assisted are in countries other than the United States.[30]

§ 7.2 RELIEF OF DISTRESSED

The term *charitable* includes efforts to relieve the distressed.[31]

(a) General Principles

Tax-exempt charitable status is available for an organization solely on the ground that it relieves individuals who are *distressed*. The IRS considered the tax treatment of a nonprofit hospice that operated on both an inpatient and an outpatient basis to assist persons of all ages who have been advised by a physician that they are terminally ill in coping with the distress arising from their medical condition.[32] Thus, the classification of the organization as a charitable entity was predicated on the fact that the hospice "alleviat[ed] the mental and physical distress of persons terminally ill." What the IRS did, as noted, beginning with three rulings issued in 1979,[33] was change the phraseology from poor *and* distressed to poor *or* distressed.

The IRS sometimes refers to individuals who are distressed as being *needy*. In a ruling, the IRS observed that "basic need[s]" include "nutrition, safety, shelter, or minimum income."[34] This observation was made in the context of determining that "fill[ing] a gap in journalism which . . . ignores the less-than-affluent economic class"—known as *relational journalism*—does not rise to the level of addressing such a basic need.

(b) Disaster Relief Programs

The confusion inherent in the interplay between *relief of the poor* and *relief of the distressed*, as meanings of the term *charitable*, is vividly reflected in the IRS's policies with respect to disaster relief programs. Part of this confusion pertains to the eligibility of individuals for these programs' assistance; they need not be financially distressed but may be emotionally or physically distressed.

---

[27] Rev. Rul. 76-21, 1976-1 C.B. 147.

[28] Rev. Rul. 76-22, 1976-1 C.B. 148; Rev. Rul. 69-161, 1969-1 C.B. 149.

[29] Rev. Rul. 69-174, 1969-1 C.B. 149. Cf. Rev. Rul. 77-3, 1977-1 C.B. 140.

[30] E.g., Rev. Rul. 68-165, 1968-1 C.B. 253, Rev. Rul. 68-117, 1968-1 C.B. 251.

[31] Reg. § 1.501(c)(3)-1(d)(2).

[32] Rev. Rul. 79-17, 1979-1 C.B. 193.

[33] In addition to Rev. Rul. 79-17, 1979-1 C.B. 193, the IRS issued rulings concerning forms of distress facing the elderly, pertaining to homes for the aged (Rev. Rul. 79-18, 1979-1 C.B. 194) (see § 7.6(e)), and forms of distress confronting the physically disabled (Rev. Rul. 79-19, 1979-1 C. B. 195).

[34] Priv. Ltr. Rul. 201340020.

For many years, the IRS approved, as tax-exempt functions of charitable organizations, disaster relief and hardship programs, including those where the potential beneficiaries are employees (and perhaps also former employees) of related companies or other organizations, and the employees' families, where the potential recipients constituted a charitable class (that is, were distressed individuals).[35] In these situations, any private benefit[36] to the beneficiaries or any related entities was deemed by the IRS to be incidental and thus to not adversely affect the grantor's exempt status.[37] In the late 1990s, the IRS reversed this policy, concluding that company-related disaster and emergency relief programs were not exempt charitable functions and entailed private inurement[38] to the sponsoring company in the form of promotion of a loyal and stable employee base.[39]

This was the status of the IRS's policy on disaster relief programs in the tax-exempt organizations context at the time of the terrorist attacks on September 11, 2001. Considerable confusion, including misunderstanding of applicable federal tax law, ensued as to who was eligible for monetary relief and/or services provided by charitable organizations in the immediate aftermath of the attacks. This turmoil was compounded by the IRS's proclamations that, to be eligible for this aid, an individual must demonstrate a financial need. That, however, is not the law; the standard is whether the beneficiaries are distressed, as that term is defined in the federal tax law.[40]

Legislation enacted in 2001 introduced rules for provision of assistance by charitable organizations to individuals who are victims of terrorism.[41] Pursuant to this enactment, charitable organizations that make payments to individuals by reason of the death, injury, wounding, or illness of an individual incurred as a result of the terrorist attacks in 2001 or as the result of an attack involving anthrax in late 2001 are not required to make a specific assessment of need for the payments to be considered made for charitable purposes. The grantor organization must make the payments in good faith using a reasonable and objective formula that is consistently applied.

This legislation also excludes *qualified disaster relief payments* from gross income.[42] Such payments include amounts paid to or for the benefit of an individual to reimburse or pay reasonable and necessary personal, family, living, or funeral expenses incurred as a result of a qualified disaster.[43] A *qualified disaster* means a disaster that results from a terroristic or military action, a federally declared disaster, an accident involving a common carrier, and any other event

---

[35] E.g., Priv. Ltr. Rul. 9314058.

[36] See § 20.13.

[37] Where the grantor is a private foundation, there are also issues of self-dealing and taxable expenditures. See *Private Foundations*, Chapters 5, 9.

[38] See Chapter 20.

[39] E.g., Priv. Ltr. Ruls. 199914040, 199917079.

[40] In late 2001, the IRS shifted its position, stating that charities may provide assistance to those victimized by the terrorist attacks, without regard to financial need, as long as the payments are made "in good faith using objective standards" (Notice 2001-78, 2001-50 I.R.B. 576).

[41] Victims of Terrorism Tax Relief Act of 2001, Pub. L. No. 107-134, § 104(a)(1), 115 Stat. 2427, 2431.

[42] *Id.* at § 111(a).

[43] IRC § 139(b)(1).

that the IRS determines is catastrophic.[44] The legislative history stated that the IRS is expected to reconsider its ruling position in connection with disaster relief programs in light of this paradigm.

The IRS ultimately did so, issuing guidance by means of a publication on the matter of charitable organizations providing disaster relief.[45] This guidance recognizes that exempt charitable organizations can serve disaster victims and those facing emergency hardship needs by providing assistance to individuals and businesses.

(i) General Guidance. At the outset, the IRS observes that these charitable organizations must demonstrate that they serve a public rather than a private interest and assist a charitable class. The agency acknowledges that, in the past, employer-sponsored organizations were considered by it to "enhance employee recruitment and retention, resulting in private benefit to sponsoring employers," and there were "concerns that employers could exercise undue influence over the selection of recipients." It recognizes, however, that after the September 11 attacks, "Congress took the position that employer-sponsored private foundations should be able to provide assistance to employees in certain situations."

According to this publication, charitable organizations may provide assistance to individuals in this regard in the form of funds, services, or goods to ensure that victims have basic necessities, such as food, clothing, housing (including repairs), transportation, and medical assistance (including psychological counseling). The type of aid that is appropriate is dependent on each individual's needs and resources. The assistance may be for the short term, such as food, clothing, and shelter, but not for the long term if an individual has adequate financial resources. The publication states that individuals who are "financially needy or otherwise distressed are appropriate recipients of charity." Examples given are of individuals who are temporarily in need of food or shelter when stranded, injured, or lost because of a disaster; temporarily unable to be self-sufficient as a result of a sudden and severe personal or family crisis, such as victims of violent crimes or physical abuse; in need of long-term assistance with housing, childcare, or educational expenses because of a disaster; and in need of counseling because of trauma experienced as a result of a disaster or a violent crime.[46]

Disaster assistance may be provided to businesses to achieve these charitable purposes: to aid individual business owners who are financially needy or otherwise distressed, combat community deterioration,[47] and lessen the burdens of government.[48] A tax-exempt charitable organization can accomplish a

---

[44] IRC § 139(c). For example, on March 13, 2020, the president declared the COVID-19 pandemic a national emergency under the Robert T. Stafford Disaster Relief and Emergency Assistance Act, thereby bringing the pandemic within the statutory definition of a qualified disaster (IRC §§ 139(c)(2), 165(i)(5)(A)).

[45] Pub. 3833, *Disaster Relief: Providing Assistance through Charitable Organizations* (Dec. 2014).

[46] In a summary of the federal tax law concerning international grantmaking by charitable organizations, the IRS suggested that an individual must be "needy" to be an eligible recipient of financial assistance in the disaster relief context; the word *distressed* was not used (Chief Couns. Adv. Mem. 200504031).

[47] See § 7.11.

[48] See § 7.7.

charitable purpose by providing disaster assistance to a business if the assistance is a "reasonable means" of accomplishing a charitable purpose and any "benefit to a private interest" is incidental to the accomplishment of a charitable purpose.

The IRS guidelines invoke a *needy or distressed* test. They state that, generally, a disaster relief or emergency hardship organization must make a "specific assessment" that a potential recipient of aid is financially or otherwise in need. Individuals do not have to be "totally destitute" to be financially needy, "they may merely lack the resources to obtain basic necessities." Yet, the IRS continued, "charitable funds cannot be distributed to individuals merely because they are victims of a disaster." Therefore, a charitable organization's decision about how its funds will be distributed must be based on an objective evaluation of the victims' needs at the time the grant is made.

These guidelines state that "a charity may provide crisis counseling, rescue services, or emergency aid such as blankets or hot meals in the immediate aftermath of a disaster without a showing of financial need. That is, provision of these services to the distressed in the immediate aftermath of a disaster serves a charitable purpose regardless of the financial condition of the recipients." However, the IRS guidelines state that "as time goes on and people are able to call upon their individual resources, it may become increasingly appropriate for charities to conduct individual financial needs assessments." Said the IRS: "While those who may not have the resources to meet basic living needs may be entitled to such assistance, those who do not need continued assistance should not use charitable resources."

The IRS states that an individual who is eligible for assistance because the individual is a victim of a disaster or emergency hardship has "no automatic right" to a charity's funds. For example, a charitable organization that provides disaster or emergency hardship relief does not have to make an individual whole, such as by rebuilding the individual's uninsured home destroyed by a flood or replacing an individual's income after the individual becomes unemployed as the result of a civil disturbance. This "issue," the IRS writes, is "especially relevant when the volume of contributions received in response to appeals exceeds the immediate needs." The IRS states that a charitable organization "is responsible for taking into account the charitable purposes for which it was formed, the public benefit of its activities, and the specific needs and resources of each victim when using its discretion to distribute its funds."

The IRS guidelines address the matter of charitable organizations' documentation obligations. The rule is that a charitable organization in this context must maintain "adequate records" to show that the organization's payments further its charitable purposes and that the victims served are "needy or distressed." Moreover, these charities are required to maintain "appropriate records" to show that they have made distributions to individuals after making "appropriate needs assessments" based on the recipients' financial resources and their physical, mental, and emotional well-being.

The IRS states that this documentation should include a complete description of the assistance provided; the costs associated with provision of the assistance; the purpose for which the aid was given; the charity's objective criteria for disbursement of assistance under each program; how the recipients were selected; the name and address of, and the amount distributed to, each recipient; any relationship between a recipient and directors, officers, and/or key employees of, or substantial contributors to, the charitable organization; and the composition of the selection committee approving the assistance.

With respect to short-term emergency aid, the IRS guidelines recognize that charities proving that type of assistance are only expected to maintain records showing the type of assistance provided; the criteria for disbursing assistance; the date, place, and estimated number of victims assisted; the charitable purpose intended to be accomplished; and the cost of the aid. By contrast, organizations that are providing longer term assistance are required to keep more detailed records.

The IRS guidance differentiates among employer-sponsored programs utilizing public charities, donor-advised funds, and private foundations.

(ii) Public Charities. This guidance states that "[b]ecause public charities typically receive broad financial support from the general public," their operations are generally more transparent and are subject to greater public scrutiny.[49] Accordingly, the IRS states, public charities may provide a "broader range of assistance" to employees than can be provided by donor-advised funds or private foundations. The IRS writes that an employer can establish an employer-sponsored public charity to provide assistance programs to respond to any type of disaster or employee emergency hardship situations, as long as the employer involved does not exercise "excessive control" over the charitable organization. Generally, the IRS observes, employees contribute to the public charity, and rank and file employees constitute a "significant portion" of the organization's governing board.

The IRS states that "[t]o ensure the program is not impermissibly serving the related employer," these requirements must be met: (1) the class of beneficiaries must constitute a charitable class, (2) the recipients must be selected on the basis of an "objective determination of need," and (3) the recipients must be selected by an independent selection committee or adequate substitute procedures must be in place to ensure that any benefit to the employer is incidental and tenuous. As to this third requirement, the charity's selection committee is independent if a majority of its members consists of persons who are not in a position to exercise substantial influence over the affairs of the employer.

If these requirements are met, the public charity's payments to the employer-sponsor's employees and their family members in response to a disaster or emergency hardship are presumed to be made for charitable purposes and not to result in taxable compensation to the employees.

(iii) Donor-Advised Funds. As to donor-advised funds,[50] the IRS observes that, in general, grants cannot be made from these funds to individuals.[51] The agency recognizes, however, an exception for certain employer-related funds established to benefit employees and their family members who are victims of

---

[49] See § 12.3(b).
[50] See § 12.5.
[51] *Id.*

a qualified disaster.[52] Specifically, a donor-advised fund can make grants to employees and their family members where (1) the fund serves the single identified purpose of providing relief from one or more qualified disasters; (2) the fund serves a charitable class; (3) recipients of grants are selected on the basis of an objective determination of need; (4) the selection of recipients of grants is made using either an independent selection committee or adequate substitute procedures to ensure that any benefit to the employer is incidental and tenuous;[53] (5) no payment is made from the fund to, or for the benefit of, any trustee, director, or officer of the sponsoring organization, public charity, or members of the fund's selection committee; and (6) the fund maintains adequate records to demonstrate the recipients' need for the disaster assistance provided.

(iv) Private Foundations. Under current IRS policy, employer-sponsored private foundations may provide financial assistance to employees or family members affected by a qualified disaster,[54] as long as certain safeguards are in place to ensure that the assistance is serving charitable purposes, rather than the employer's business purposes.[55] Thus, the IRS will presume that payments in response to a qualified disaster made by a private foundation to employees or their family members of an employer that is a disqualified person with respect to the foundation are consistent with the foundation's charitable purposes if (1) the class of beneficiaries is "large or indefinite" (that is, is a charitable class), (2) the recipients are selected on the basis of an "objective determination of need," and (3) the selection is made using either an independent selection committee or "adequate substitute procedures" so as to ensure that any benefit to the employer is incidental and tenuous.[56] A foundation's selection committee is independent if a majority of the members of the committee consists of persons who are not in a position to exercise substantial influence over the affairs of the employer.

If these requirements are met, the private foundation's payments in response to a qualified disaster are treated as made for charitable purposes. The payments do not result in acts of self-dealing merely because the recipient is an employee, or family member of an employee, of the employer.[57] This presumption does not apply to payments that would otherwise constitute self-dealing, such as payments made to or for the benefit of individuals who are trustees, directors, or officers of the private foundation.

---

[52] Notice 2006-109, 2006-51 I.R.B. 1121. This exception is made pursuant to statutory authority granted to the IRS to exempt funds from treatment as donor-advised funds if the fund is advised by a committee not directly or indirectly controlled by the donor or any person appointed or designated by the donor for the purpose of advising with respect to distributions from such fund (and any related parties), or if such fund benefits a single identified charitable purpose (IRC § 4966(d)(2)(C)).

[53] The selection committee is considered independent if a majority of its members consists of individuals who are not in a position to exercise substantial influence over the employer's affairs.

[54] IRC § 139.

[55] It remains the IRS's position, however, that employer-sponsored private foundations may not make payments to employees or their family members affected by disasters other than qualified ones or in other emergency hardship situations.

[56] See *Private Foundations* § 9.3(c).

[57] These payments are not taxable compensation to the employees (IRC § 139(a)).

In this publication, the IRS states that, even if a private foundation fails to meet all of the requirements of this presumption, "other procedures and standards may be considered to constitute adequate substitutes to ensure that any benefit to the employer is incidental and tenuous, where all the facts and circumstances are taken into account." By contrast, even if a foundation does satisfy the presumption, the IRS reserves the right to review the facts and circumstances to ensure that any benefit to the employer is merely incidental and tenuous. For example, a program "may not be used to induce employees to follow a course of action sought by the employer or designed to relieve the employer of a legal obligation for employee benefits."

(v) Private Letter Rulings. The IRS has issued private letter rulings on this topic. In one of the first, the IRS ruled that a private foundation providing financial assistance to victims, or families of victims, of a natural disaster, violence, or terrorist acts of war; victims of discrimination, social injustice, or persecution; and artists was making qualifying distributions as long as the assistance was confined to "impoverished individuals with desperate financial needs."[58]

In another instance, an emergency assistance program was maintained by a system of health care institutions to provide grants and/or loans to current and former employees of the system and their families and those of system affiliates. Beneficiaries of the program were confined to individuals who were needy and suffered economic hardship due to accident, loss, or disaster; the pool of eligible grantees numbered approximately 5,000 individuals. A committee administered the program, which entailed an emergency assistance fund; there were a formal application process, objective criteria, committee review procedures, limits on allowable assistance, and elaborate record-keeping practices. The IRS ruled that operation of this fund would not adversely affect the tax-exempt status of the institutions in the system, holding that the class of eligible beneficiaries was "sufficiently large and open-ended to constitute a charitable class," observing that support for the fund would be derived only from employee contributions and gifts from the public.[59]

The IRS ruled that a financial assistance program was not a charitable undertaking because a substantial portion of the charitable class to be aided consisted of employees of a related for-profit corporation, thus causing unwarranted private benefit and self-dealing involving the private foundation that would be conducting the program.[60]

§ 7.3 CREDIT COUNSELING

Nonprofit credit counseling organizations emerged in the 1960s, sponsored by the consumer credit industry; they were initially funded by "fair share" payments based on a portion of the payments made by the counseling organizations' debtor clients. These organizations also often received government and private foundation grants, and contributions from federated public charities and the public.

---

[58] Priv. Ltr. Rul. 200634016.
[59] Priv. Ltr. Rul. 200839034.
[60] Priv. Ltr. Rul. 200926033.

Regarded as tax-exempt charitable and/or educational entities at the outset, this classification would eventually be lost as these entities reconstituted themselves as providers of debt-management plans on a fee basis.

(a) Initial Evolution of Exemption Law

The IRS has, from the outset, resisted the notion that nonprofit credit counseling agencies are, in general, eligible for tax-exempt status as charitable (and/or educational) organizations. The most the agency was willing to concede was that these entities are so exempt when they confine provision of their services to low-income individuals (who are members of a charitable class)[61] who have financial problems[62] and provide debt counseling without charge; when they provide the public with information on budgeting, buying practices, and the sound use of consumer credit;[63] and/or when they provide free or nominal-cost debt management plans (DMPs) for a small percentage of clients. Otherwise, the IRS was of the view that these agencies, if they are to be exempt at all, are properly classified as social welfare organizations, in that their activities contribute to the betterment of the community as a whole.[64]

Initially, it appeared that courts would take a broader view. For example, a court ruled that the IRS cannot condition a credit counseling organization's tax status solely on the extent to which it provides assistance to the indigent.[65] This court held that the classification of these organizations as exempt charitable entities cannot be made dependent on whether they confine their assistance to low-income individuals or provide their services without charge. Credit counseling organizations were found to be entitled to recognition as charitable and educational organizations as long as they can demonstrate that they satisfy at least one of the definitions of the term *charitable*[66] or qualify as *educational* organizations.[67] The IRS decided, at the time, not to pursue this matter in the courts, being of the view that "further litigation of this issue would be futile."[68]

The IRS, beginning in 2002, renewed its efforts to revoke or deny recognition of tax exemption of nonprofit credit counseling agencies, working in tandem with the Federal Trade Commission.[69] Congressional hearings encouraged the IRS in this regard.[70] Relying heavily on the private benefit doctrine[71] and the

---

[61] See § 6.3(a).

[62] See §§ 7.1, 7.2.

[63] See §§ 8.4, 8.5. Rev. Rul. 69-441, 1969-2 C.B. 115.

[64] Rev. Rul. 65-299, 1965-2 C.B. 165. Social welfare organizations are the subject of Chapter 13.

[65] Consumer Credit Counseling Serv. Of Ala., Inc. v. United States, 78-2 U.S.T.C. ¶ 9660 (D.D.C. 1978).

[66] For example, a credit counseling organization may be exempt as a charitable entity because it advances education or promotes social welfare (see §§ 7.8, 7.11).

[67] See Chapter 8. Also, Credit Counseling Centers of Okla., Inc. v. United States, 79-2 U.S.T.C. ¶ 9468 (D.D.C. 1979).

[68] Gen. Couns. Mem. 38881.

[69] IR-2003-120; FS-2003-17.

[70] House Committee on Ways and Means, Subcommittee on Oversight, Hearing on Non-Profit Credit Counseling Organizations (Nov. 20, 2003); Senate Committee on Finance, Hearing on Exempt Organizations: Enforcement Problems, Accomplishments, and Future Direction (April 5, 2005).

[71] See § 20.13.

commerciality doctrine,[72] the IRS started making the argument that contemporary credit counseling organizations are substantially different from their predecessors.[73] Adverse rulings in this context became the norm; they continue to be issued, although less frequently, inasmuch as the statutory criteria these types of organizations must meet to be exempt[74] has essentially eradicated exemption for these types of entities.[75] The IRS's policies in this regard are being extended to nonprofit organizations that assist homeowners in refinancing their mortgages[76] or that provide foreclosure-related services.[77]

(b) Statutory Criteria for Exemption

An organization that has provision of credit counseling services[78] as its substantial purpose may not be tax-exempt[79] under the general requirements unless it also (1) provides credit counseling services tailored to the specific needs and circumstances of consumers; (2) does not make loans to debtors (other than loans without fees or interest) and does not negotiate the making of loans on behalf of debtors; (3) provides services for the purpose of improving a consumer's credit record, credit history, or credit rating only to the extent that these services are incidental to provision of credit counseling services; and (4) does not charge a separately stated fee for services for the purpose of improving a consumer's credit record, credit history, or credit rating.[80] The organization may not refuse to provide credit counseling services to a consumer due to the inability of the consumer to pay, the ineligibility of the consumer for DMP enrollment, or the unwillingness of the consumer to enroll in a DMP.[81] Also, the organization must establish and implement a fee policy that requires that any fees charged to a consumer for services be reasonable, allows for the waiver of fees if the consumer is unable to pay, and, except to the extent allowed by state law, prohibits charging any fee based in whole or in part on a percentage of the consumer's debt, the consumer's payments to be made pursuant to a DMP, or the projected or actual savings to the consumer resulting from enrollment in a DMP.[82] Further, the organization's governing body must have certain characteristics.[83] Moreover, the organization may not own more than

---

[72] See § 4.9.

[73] Chief Couns. Adv. Mems. 200431023, 200620001.

[74] See § 7.3(b).

[75] E.g., Priv. Ltr. Rul. 200447046 (denying exempt status to an organization providing credit counseling services for failure to further charitable purposes); Priv. Ltr. Rul. 202416014 (denying exempt status to an organization providing credit counseling services that failed to meet the statutory requirements of IRC § 501(q)).

[76] E.g., Priv. Rul. 201213030.

[77] E.g., Priv. Ltr. Rul. 201205012.

[78] The phrase *credit counseling services* is defined as (1) provision of educational information to the public on budgeting, personal finance, financial literacy, saving and spending practices, and the sound use of consumer credit; (2) assisting individuals and families with financial problems by providing them with counseling; or (3) a combination of these activities (IRC § 501(q)(4)(A)).

[79] This refers to tax exemption by reason of IRC § 501(c)(3) or (4) (as to the latter, see Chapter 13).

[80] IRC § 501(q)(1)(A).

[81] IRC § 501(q)(1)(B).

[82] IRC § 501(q)(1)(C).

[83] IRC § 501(q)(1)(D). See § 5.6(d).

35 percent of the voting power of a corporation, the profits interest of a partnership, or the beneficial interest of a trust or estate that is in the business of lending money, repairing credit, or providing DMP services,[84] payment processing, or similar services.[85] Finally, this type of organization may not receive any amount for providing referrals for DMP services and may not pay for referrals of consumers.[86]

In addition, if a credit counseling organization is to qualify as a tax-exempt charitable entity, it may not solicit contributions from consumers during the initial counseling process or while the consumer is receiving services from the organization. Also, the aggregate revenues of the organization derived from payments of creditors of consumers of the organization and that are attributable to DMPs generally may not exceed 50 percent of its total revenues.[87] In addition, if a credit counseling organization is to qualify as an exempt social welfare entity, it must apply for recognition of exempt status.[88]

§ 7.4   PROVISION OF HOUSING

Provision of housing is not, in itself, a tax-exempt charitable function; usually for exemption to be available the housing must be primarily provided to low-income individuals.[89] This rule is predicated on the principle that charitable purposes include relief of the poor and/or distressed.[90] Other bases on which the provision of housing may be an exempt function are lessening the burdens of government[91] or promotion of social welfare (such as combating community deterioration or lessening racial tensions).[92]

In one instance, an organization carried on several activities directed to assisting low-income families in obtaining improved housing, including coordinating and supervising construction projects, purchasing building sites for resale at cost, and lending aid in obtaining home construction loans.[93] In another case,

---

[84] The phrase *debt management plan services* means services related to the repayment, consolidation, or restructuring of a consumer's debt, and includes the negotiation with creditors of lower interest rates, the waiver or reduction of fees, and the marketing and processing of DMPs (IRC § 501(q)(4)(B)). These services may be an unrelated trade or business (see § 24.5(p)).

[85] IRC § 501(q)(1)(E).

[86] IRC § 501(q)(1)(F). It is the position of the IRS that organizations that provide educational information on financial topics or provide financial counseling to homeowners who are at risk of foreclosure are providing *credit counseling services* within the meaning of IRC § 501(q)(4)(A); it is also the position of the agency that organizations that assist homeowners who are at risk of foreclosure by providing financial counseling and/or providing educational information to the public on financial topics as their substantial purpose are not in violation of the prohibition, in IRC § 501(q)(1)(A)(ii), regarding the *negotiating of the making of a loan*, where the organizations contact holders or servicers of homeowners' mortgages to try to modify the terms of mortgages so that individuals might avoid foreclosure (Program Manager Tech. Adv. 2010-011).

[87] IRC § 501(q)(2).

[88] IRC § 501(q)(3). See § 26.5.

[89] E.g., Priv. Ltr. Rul. 200534022.

[90] See §§ 7.1, 7.2. Low-income individuals are members of a charitable class (see § 6.3(a)).

[91] See § 7.7.

[92] See § 7.11.

[93] Rev. Rul. 67-138, 1967-1 C.B. 129.

an organization worked to educate the public about integrated housing and conducted programs to facilitate the integration of neighborhoods.[94] Likewise, an entity conducted investigations and research to obtain information regarding discrimination against minority groups in connection with housing and public accommodations.[95]

Combating community deterioration in furthering charitable purposes involves remedial action leading to the elimination of the physical, economic, and social causes of the deterioration,[96] such as by purchasing and renovating deteriorating residences and selling or leasing them to low-income families,[97] and by operating a self-help home-building program.[98]

The IRS discussed four examples of organizations providing housing.[99] An organization that constructed and renovated homes for sale to low-income families who could not obtain conventional financing was held to be charitable. Also ruled to be charitable was an organization that sold housing to low- and moderate-income minority groups who could not obtain housing because of discrimination. Another entity was found to be charitable inasmuch as its housing rehabilitation program combated community deterioration. However, an organization that rented housing at cost to moderate-income families was held to not further charitable purposes.[100]

An organization was denied tax exemption as a charitable entity, where its principal program is to acquire, renovate, and sell homes at their fair market value to low-income individuals, who must qualify for conventional financing.[101] In addition to stating that this entity is operated in a commercial manner,[102] the IRS faulted it for not ensuring that the homes will be habitable or that the buyers will be able to afford to maintain the homes over time, and for not providing any oversight or conducting any educational program or other activity to ensure that the buyers are purchasing properties that are safe, decent, sanitary, and affordable. Likewise, a nonprofit corporation, formed to purchase, rehabilitate, sell, and lease housing properties, that did not impose restrictions as to who may live in these properties, was ruled ineligible for exemption.[103]

The IRS is of the position that providing housing to students generally is not an exempt charitable activity. In one instance, students as such were not perceived by the agency as members of a charitable class;[104] the IRS wrote that, for

[94] Rev. Rul. 68-6, 968-2 C.B. 213.

[95] Rev. Rul. 68-438, 1968-2 C.B. 609.

[96] Rev. Rul. 67-6, 1967-1 C.B. 135.

[97] Rev. Rul. 68-17, 1968-1 C.B. 247.

[98] Rev. Rul. 67-138, 1967-1 C.B. 129.

[99] Rev. Rul. 70-585, 1970-2 C.B. 115.

[100] Nonetheless, inclusion of some individuals who are not poor, distressed, or underprivileged in a housing project for the poor may indirectly advance charitable purposes by providing stability, resource, and role-model functions; the IRS developed safe-harbor guidelines on the point. Rev. Proc. 96-32, 1996-1 C.B. 717 (e.g., Priv. Ltr. Rul. 200642009). An example of an organization that failed to achieve exempt status, in part because it did not satisfy this safe-harbor test, is in Priv. Ltr. Rul. 200450038.

[101] Priv. Ltr. Rul. 201039048.

[102] See § 4.9.

[103] Priv. Ltr. Rul. 201534020.

[104] See § 6.3(a).

a charitable class to be present, the students must be low-income individuals.[105] Likewise, the IRS denied recognition of exemption to an organization formed to provide housing on college campuses for Reserve Officer Training Corps students and returning veterans because these individuals did not constitute members of a charitable class.[106]

There is no case law pertaining to tax exemption for housing organizations. The IRS relies heavily in this context on the doctrine of commerciality[107] in denying exemption in instances where housing is provided to individuals and families who are not low-income. The IRS occasionally denies recognition of exemption to organizations operating housing programs that do not satisfy the agency's criteria as to what is charitable.[108]

§ 7.5 DOWN PAYMENT ASSISTANCE

A down payment assistance program is conducted by a nonprofit organization, either as its entire or primary focus or as one of several discrete programs, pursuant to which grants (in this context, sometimes termed *gifts*) are made to individuals to enable them to purchase a home. Down payment assistance programs offer prospective home buyers the opportunity to qualify for mortgages when they have sufficient earnings to make the monthly loan payments but cannot afford the down payment. A down payment assistance program provides this type of assistance to low-income individuals[109] and others who may be distressed;[110] some assistance may be provided to moderate-income individuals.[111]

The evolution of the law concerning tax exemption for down payment assistance organizations parallels law developments pertaining to credit counseling organizations,[112] in that the IRS originally deemed these entities to be exempt, and then abruptly reversed its policy and routinely issued adverse private letter rulings to organizations that provide down payment assistance to home buyers.[113] An anomaly is a ruling holding a type of down payment assistance to be a charitable activity where the assistance was in the form of a loan (second mortgage) rather than a grant.[114]

[105] Priv. Ltr. Rul. 201039035.

[106] Priv. Ltr. Rul. 201119036.

[107] See § 4.9.

[108] E.g., Priv. Ltr. Rul. 200444024. The IRS denied recognition of exemption to an organization formed to help homeowners struggling with mortgage debt in part because the entity did not confine its assistance to low-income individuals (Priv. Ltr. Rul. 201921019).

[109] See § 7.1.

[110] See § 7.2.

[111] The IRS, in a press release, stated that organizations that "provide seller-funded down-payment assistance to home buyers do not qualify as tax-exempt charities" (IR-2006-74); this document is titled "IRS Targets Down-Payment-Assistance Scams."

[112] See § 7.3.

[113] E.g., Priv. Ltr. Rul. 200444024. The IRS denied recognition of tax exemption to an organization that provided gift funds to low-income purchasers of automobiles (Priv. Ltr. Rul. 200623075).

[114] Priv. Ltr. Rul. 200721025.

The IRS's formal posture as to tax exemption for down payment assistance organizations is that, to be exempt, the entity must confine its services to low-income individuals and families, offer financial counseling and other educational activities, preclude its staff from knowing the identity of the home sellers, and conduct a broad-based fundraising program. Also, these organizations that combat community deterioration in economically depressed areas may be able to qualify as charitable entities. Seller-funded down payment assistance organizations cannot, according to IRS policy, qualify for exemption.[115] A court held that an organization maintaining a down payment assistance program was not operating for charitable purposes but rather in a commercial manner.[116]

The future of down payment assistance programs and organizations was significantly imperiled with the enactment of legislation in 2008[117] that bans seller-funded down payment assistance in connection with Federal Housing Administration (FHA)-insured mortgages. This prohibition, encompassing funds provided by the "seller or any other person or entity that financially benefits from the transaction," took effect on October 1, 2008.[118]

§ 7.6 PROMOTION OF HEALTH

The promotion of health as a charitable purpose includes the establishment or maintenance of hospitals, clinics, homes for the aged, and other providers of health care; advancement of medical and similar knowledge through research; and the maintenance of conditions conducive to health. The term *health*, for this purpose, includes mental health and would include, were it not for a separate enumeration in the federal tax law description of charitable organizations, the prevention of cruelty to children. The tax regulations defining the types of charitable entities do not contain any specific reference to the promotion of health as a charitable purpose, but this aspect of charitable activity has been reaffirmed by the courts and the IRS on several occasions.[119]

Not every activity that generally promotes health, however, furthers charitable purposes. For example, a hospital does not necessarily further charitable purposes solely by offering health care services to the public in exchange for fees.[120] Likewise, although the sale of prescription pharmaceuticals promotes health, pharmacies cannot qualify for recognition of tax exemption as charitable entities on that basis alone.[121] A tax-exempt hospital created a nonprofit organization to provide management, advisory, and consulting services, on a fee basis, to foreign

---

[115] Rev. Rul. 2006-27, 2006-1 C.B. 915.

[116] Partners In Charity, Inc. v. Comm'r, 141 T.C. 151 (2013).

[117] Housing and Economic Recovery Act of 2008, Pub. L. No. 110-289, 122 Stat. 2654 (title I of which is the FHA Modernization Act of 2008).

[118] *Id.* § 2113.

[119] E.g., Rev. Rul. 69-545, 1969-2 C.B. 117. Tax exemption in this context is often thwarted by application of the commerciality doctrine (see § 4.9) and/or the private benefit doctrine (see § 20.13) (e.g., Priv. Ltr. Rul. 201409012).

[120] See § 7.6(b).

[121] Federation Pharmacy Servs., Inc. v. Comm'r, 72 T.C. 687 (1979), *aff'd*, 625 F.2d 804 (8th Cir. 1980).

hospitals and foreign governments to assist them in designing, developing, and operating health care facilities; the IRS ruled that these activities did not constitute the promotion of health for exemption law purposes.[122] A nonprofit corporation providing outpatients with laboratory testing services, for fees, as requested by patients or health care providers, was denied recognition of exemption for engaging in noncharitable activities.[123]

(a) Hospital Law in General

The most common example of a type of tax-exempt organization established and operated for the promotion of health is a nonprofit hospital.[124] Law has accreted over the decades as to the requirements for exemption for these hospitals. Additional statutory requirements for exemption in this context were enacted in 2010.[125]

To qualify for tax exemption as a charitable organization, however, a nonprofit hospital must demonstrate that it serves a public rather than a private interest.[126] The Supreme Court observed that "[n]onprofit hospitals have never received these benefits [tax exemption and eligibility to receive deductible contributions] as a favored general category, but an individual nonprofit hospital has been able to claim them if it could qualify" as a charitable entity.[127] The Court added: "As the Code does not define the term charitable, the status of each nonprofit hospital is determined on a case-by-case basis by the IRS."[128] Also, to qualify for exemption, a nonprofit hospital must have hospital care, or medical education or medical research, as its "principal purpose or function."[129]

The initial position of the IRS in this regard was published in 1956, in which the IRS set forth requirements for tax exemption, including a rule requiring patient care without charge or below cost.[130] At that time, the IRS stated that a hospital, to be charitable, "must be operated to the extent of its financial ability for those not able to pay for the services rendered and not exclusively for those who are able and expected to pay."[131] This approach (the *charity care* standard) was a reflection of the charitable hospital as it once was—a health care provider emphasizing care more for the poor than for the sick.

Today's tax-exempt hospital provides health services for its community, funded by patient care revenue and charitable contributions. Prepayment plans cover hospital expenses for much of the citizenry, and reimbursement programs under Medicare and Medicaid have substantially reduced the number of patients who lack an ability to pay, directly or indirectly, for health care services. Because of these changes in the health care delivery system, in 1969 the IRS modified its 1956 position by

---

[122] Priv. Ltr. Rul. 201128028.

[123] Priv. Ltr. Rul. 202125020.

[124] IRC § 170(b)(1)(A)(iii).

[125] See § 7.6(b).

[126] Reg. § 1.501(c)(3)-1(d)(1)(ii).

[127] Simon v. Eastern Ky. Welfare Rights Org., 426 U.S. 26, 29 (1976).

[128] Id. at 29. The various types of nonprofit health care entities that qualify for tax-exempt status are discussed more fully in *Healthcare Organizations*, particularly Chapters 8–13.

[129] IRC § 170(b)(1)(A)(iii).

[130] Rev. Rul. 56-185, 1956-1 C.B. 202.

[131] Id. at 203.

recognizing that the promotion of health is inherently a charitable purpose and is not obviated by the fact that the cost of services is borne by patients or third-party payors.[132] Under the 1969 ruling, to be tax-exempt, a hospital must adhere to a *community benefit standard*; that is, it must promote the health of a class broad enough to benefit the community and must be operated to serve a public rather than a private interest.[133] In practical terms, this means that the emergency room must be open to all and that hospital care is provided to all who can pay, directly or indirectly. The hospital may generate a surplus of receipts over disbursements and nonetheless be exempt. The requirement that health care must be provided free or at reduced costs was abandoned.

Other factors that may indicate that a hospital is operating for the benefit of the public include control of the institution by a board of trustees composed of individuals who do not have any direct economic interest in the hospital; maintenance by the hospital of an open medical staff, with privileges available to all qualified physicians, consistent with the size and nature of the facilities; a hospital policy enabling any member of the medical staff to rent available office space; hospital programs of medical training, research, and education; and involvement by the hospital in various projects and programs to improve the health of the community. These and similar factors are of significance for tax exemption of hospitals that do not operate an emergency room, either because other institutions provide emergency care sufficient to adequately serve the community or because the hospital is a specialized institution (e.g., an eye hospital or cancer center) that offers medical care under conditions unlikely to necessitate emergency care.[134]

A nonprofit hospital need not satisfy all these factors to qualify for tax exemption. That is, the absence of any one factor, or the presence of others, may not necessarily be conclusive as to a hospital's community benefits. Charity care remains a significant factor indicative of community benefit. The IRS, however, considers all relevant facts and circumstances when determining whether a hospital's community benefits are sufficient to warrant tax exemption.[135]

For tax purposes, the term *hospital* includes federal government hospitals; state, county, and municipal hospitals that are instrumentalities of governmental units; rehabilitation institutions; outpatient clinics; extended care facilities; community mental health or drug treatment centers; and cooperative hospital service organizations,[136] if they otherwise qualify. The term does not, however, include convalescent homes, homes for children or the aged, or institutions whose principal

---

[132] Rev. Rul. 69-545, 1969-2 C.B. 117. This ruling was upheld in Eastern Ky. Welfare Rights Org. v. Simon, 506 F.2d 1278 (D.C. Cir 1974).

[133] The IRS occasionally denies tax-exempt status to a health care provider for failure to satisfy this standard (e.g., Ex. Den. and Rev. Ltr. 20044275E).

[134] Rev. Rul. 83-157, 1983-2 C.B. 94.

[135] As one court observed, the community benefit standard has evolved through a series of IRS pronouncements and cases to be "an inquiry focused on overall facts and circumstances that looks at the myriad ways in which a . . . hospital's fee-for-service operations and associated activities can confer a community benefit sufficient to distinguish it from taxable entities and to warrant a tax exemption" (Airlie Found. v. Internal Revenue Service, 283 F. Supp. 2d 58, 63 n.6 (D.D.C. 2003)).

[136] As to the latter, see § 11.4. Cf. Rev. Rul. 76-452, 1976-2 C.B. 60.

purpose or function is to train handicapped individuals to pursue a vocation;[137] nor does it include free clinics for animals.[138]

The term *medical care* includes the treatment of any physical or mental disability or condition, whether on an inpatient or an outpatient basis, as long as the cost of the treatment is eligible for deductibility[139] by the person treated.[140]

A four-entity reorganization resulted in the formation of a *federally qualified health center* (FGHC) as that term is defined in the Medicare and Medicaid law. A tax-exempt hospital transferred nine of its primary-care medical practices to a related supporting organization,[141] which thereafter began operating as an FQHC. A title-holding company[142] merged into the supporting organization. A for-profit company that provided support services to the hospital dissolved; the supporting organization absorbed its assets and liabilities. Noting that the FQHC will adopt a charity care policy and will have a board of directors that will be community controlled, the IRS ruled that the supporting organization remained tax-exempt as an organization that promotes health.[143]

(b)   Additional Statutory Requirements for Hospitals

To be tax-exempt, nonprofit hospitals are required to meet additional statutory requirements that were enacted in 2010.[144]

(i) Hospitals Subject to Requirements.   These rules apply to *hospital organizations*, namely, (1) an organization that operates a facility that is required by a state to be licensed, registered, or similarly recognized as a hospital, and (2) any other organization that the IRS determines has the provision of hospital care as its principal function or purpose constituting the basis for its tax exemption.[145]

The federal tax regulations utilize only the first of these definitions.[146] This definition does not contain any exceptions or special rules for government hospitals; the regulations apply to government hospitals that have been recognized as tax-exempt charitable hospitals. A facility located outside of the United States is not considered a hospital facility under the regulations.[147]

---

[137] Reg. § 1.170A-9(d)(1).

[138] Rev. Rul. 74-572, 1974-2 C.B. 82.

[139] IRC § 213.

[140] Reg. § 1.170A-9(d)(1). An organization will not fail to be treated as organized and operated exclusively for a charitable purpose solely because a hospital that is owned and operated by it participates in a provider-sponsored organization (as defined in § 1853(e) of the Social Security Act), irrespective of whether the provider-sponsored organization is tax-exempt (IRC § 501(o)). For purposes of private inurement (see Chapter 20), a person with a material financial interest in one of these provider-sponsored organizations is regarded as an insider with respect to the hospital (*id.*).

[141] See § 12.3(c).

[142] See § 19.2(a).

[143] Priv. Ltr. Rul. 200947064.

[144] IRC § 501(r), added by the Patient Protection and Affordable Care Act (Pub. L. No. 111-148, § 9007(a), 124 Stat. 119 (2010)) (PPA).

[145] IRC § 501(r)(2)(A).

[146] Reg. § 1.501(r)-1(b)(17).

[147] *Id.*

If a hospital organization operates more than one hospital facility, the organization must meet these requirements with respect to each facility and is not treated as exempt with respect to any facility not meeting the requirements.[148]

(ii) Community Health Needs Assessments. To be tax-exempt, a hospital organization must meet certain community health needs assessment requirements.[149] This assessment must be conducted at least every three years. The organization must adopt an implementation strategy to meet the community health needs that are identified by the assessment.

A community health needs assessment must (1) take into account input from persons who represent the broad interests of the community served by the hospital facility, including those with special knowledge of or expertise in public health, and (2) be made widely available to the public.[150]

An exempt hospital that fails to meet these community health needs assessment rules is subject to a $50,000 excise tax, potentially applicable annually.[151]

(iii) Financial Assistance Policy. To be tax-exempt, a hospital organization must meet certain financial assistance policy (FAP) requirements.[152] The organization must have a written FAP that includes (1) eligibility criteria for financial assistance; (2) a statement as to whether the assistance includes free or discounted care; (3) the basis for calculating amounts charged to patients; (4) the method for applying for the assistance; (5) in the case of an organization that does not have a separate billing and collections policy, the actions the organization may take in the event of nonpayment, including collections action and reporting to credit agencies; and (6) measures to widely publicize the policy within the community served by the organization.[153]

Although the FAP must generally include each of these items of information and must be made available on a website and without charge on request in public locations in hospitals and by mail, a hospital may widely publicize its FAP using summaries that do not contain all of the information in the FAP. Hospitals have the option of providing certain information separately from the FAP, as long as the FAP explains how members of the public can readily obtain this information free of charge on a website or in writing.

A hospital facility's FAP must apply to all emergency and other medically necessary care provided by the facility (or a substantially related entity), be widely publicized, and include the eligibility criteria for financial assistance, the basis for calculating amounts charged to patients, the method for applying for financial assistance, the actions that may be taken in the event of nonpayment (unless there is a separate billing and collections policy), and a list of any providers (other than the facility) delivering medically necessary care in the facility that specifies which

---

[148] IRC § 501(r)(2)(B).

[149] IRC § 501(r)(1)(A); Reg. § 1.501(r)-3.

[150] IRC § 501(r)(3).

[151] IRC § 4959. The IRS retroactively revoked the exempt status of a small rural hospital because it did not adopt an implementation strategy for its community health needs assessment and did not make its assessment report widely available to the public (Priv. Ltr. Rul. 201731014).

[152] IRC § 501(r)(1)(B).

[153] IRC § 501(r)(4)(A).

providers are covered by the FAP and which are not.[154] As to eligibility criteria and calculation of amounts charged, the FAP must specify all financial assistance available under it, the eligibility criteria an individual must satisfy, and the method[155] the facility uses to determine the amounts generally billed to individuals who have insurance covering emergency or other medically necessary care.[156]

As to the *widely publicized* requirement, a hospital facility must make the FAP, the application form, and a plain language summary of the policy widely available on a website; make paper copies of these documents available by mail and in public locations of the facility; inform members of the community about the FAP; and inform individuals who receive care from the facility about the FAP in a variety of ways.[157] An FAP is considered *established* only if an authorized body of the facility has adopted the policy and the facility has implemented it.[158]

(iv) Emergency Medical Care Policy. To be tax-exempt, a hospital organization must establish a written emergency medical care policy.[159] This policy must require the organization to provide, without discrimination, care for emergency medical conditions to individuals regardless of whether they are FAP-eligible.[160]

To qualify, a hospital's medical policy must prohibit the facility from engaging in actions that discourage individuals from seeking emergency medical care, such as by demanding that emergency department patients pay before receiving care.

(v) Limitation on Charges. To be tax-exempt, a hospital organization must meet certain requirements as to charges.[161] The organization (1) must limit amounts charged for emergency or other medically necessary care provided to individuals eligible for assistance under the financial assistance policy to not more than the amounts generally billed to individuals who have insurance coverage covering the care, and (2) must prohibit the use of gross charges.[162]

(vi) Billing and Collection. To be tax-exempt, a hospital organization must meet a billing and collection requirement.[163] The organization may not engage in extraordinary collection actions before it has made reasonable efforts to determine whether the individual is eligible for assistance under the financial assistance policy.[164]

(vii) Mandatory IRS Review of Tax Exemption. The IRS is required to "review" at least once every three years the community benefit activities of

---

[154] Reg. § 1.501(r)-4(b)(1). The IRS issued guidance providing hospital facilities with clarification as to how a facility may comply with this provider list requirement (Notice 2015-46, 2015-28 I.R.B. 64).
[155] Reg. § 1.501(r)-5(b).
[156] Reg. § 1.501(r)-4(b)(2).
[157] Reg. § 1.501(r)-4(b)(5).
[158] Reg. § 1.501(r)-4(d)(1).
[159] IRC § 501(r)(1)(B); Reg. § 1.501(r)-4(c).
[160] IRC § 501(r)(4)(B).
[161] IRC § 501(r)(1)(C); Reg. § 1.501(r)-5.
[162] IRC § 501(r)(5).
[163] IRC § 501(r)(1)(D); Reg. § 1.501(r)-6.
[164] IRC § 501(r)(6).

every tax-exempt hospital organization.[165] The IRS refers to these exercises as "community benefit activity reviews." This review is not an examination but rather a review of organizations' annual information returns. The purpose of these reviews is to determine if tax-exempt hospitals are complying with the community benefit standard and these statutory requirements. IRS agents conducting these reviews may refer a hospital for examination if it is determined there is potential noncompliance with either the community benefit standard or the IRC § 501(r) requirements.[166]

(viii) Effective Dates. Generally, these additional rules for hospital organizations took effect in tax years beginning after March 23, 2010. The community health needs assessment requirements, however, apply to tax years beginning two year after that date. The excise tax on failures to meet these requirements applies to failures that occur after that date.[167]

(c) Hospital Clinical Departments and Funds

Incorporated clinical departments of teaching hospitals associated with medical schools can be tax-exempt, charitable entities. For example, a court ruled that a professional corporation consisting of four departments of a medical school, which provided academic and clinical instruction for medical students, research, and administrative services for the benefit of the school and a teaching hospital, was exempt as a charitable, educational, and scientific entity in that it, in part, "delivers health care to the general public."[168]

On the basis of this and prior court decisions,[169] this type of corporate collective of physicians is tax-exempt, even though it generates fees for the performance of medical care services and pays the resulting earnings to individuals who are its stockholders. In these instances, of course, it is the close nexus with a medical school and teaching hospital that provides the underlying basis for the tax exemption.[170]

Occasionally the IRS will rule that an organization is a tax-exempt charitable entity because it is carrying out an *integral part* of the activities of another charitable organization.[171] The IRS used this rationale to find that a trust created by an exempt hospital to accumulate and hold funds for the settlement of malpractice claims against the hospital, and from which the hospital directed the trustee to make payments to claimants, is a charitable organization for federal tax purposes.[172]

---

[165] PPA, *supra* note 144, § 9007(c).

[166] GAO, "Tax Administration: Opportunities Exist to Improve Oversight of Hospitals' Tax-Exempt Status," Rep. No. GAO-20-679 (Sep. 2020), at 9.

[167] PPA, *supra* note 144, § 9007(f). Procedures for hospital organizations to use to correct and disclose failures to comply with IRC § 501(r) are the subject of Rev. Proc. 2015-21, 2015-13 I.R.B. 817.

[168] Univ. of Md. Physicians, P.A. v. Comm'r, 41 T.C.M. 732, 735 (1981).

[169] Univ. of Mass. Medical School Group Practice v. Comm'r, 74 T.C. 1299 (1980); B.H.W. Anesthesia Found. v. Comm'r, 72 T.C. 681 (1979).

[170] E.g., Priv. Ltr. Rul. 9434041, *superseded by* Priv. Ltr. Rul. 9442025.

[171] Rev. Rul. 75-282, 1975-2 C.B. 201; Rev. Rul. 78-41, 1978-1 C.B. 148. See § 26.15.

[172] Rev. Rul. 78-41, 1978-1 C.B. 148.

(d)   Medical Research Organizations

Charitable organizations that promote health include medical research organizations that are "directly engaged in the continuous active conduct of medical research in conjunction with a hospital."[173] The term *medical research* means the conduct of investigations, experiments, and studies to discover, develop, or verify knowledge relating to the causes, diagnosis, treatment, prevention, or control of physical or mental diseases and impairments of humans. To qualify, the organization must have the appropriate equipment and professional personnel necessary to carry out its principal function.[174] Medical research encompasses the associated disciplines spanning the biological, social, and behavioral sciences.

   This type of organization must have the conduct of medical research as its principal purpose or function[175] and be primarily engaged in the continuous active conduct of medical research in conjunction with a hospital that itself is a public charity. The organization need not be formally affiliated with a hospital to be considered primarily engaged in the active conduct of medical research in conjunction with a hospital. There must be, however, a joint effort on the part of the research organization and the hospital pursuant to an understanding that the two organizations will maintain continuing close cooperation in the active conduct of medical research.[176] An organization will not be considered to be "primarily engaged directly in the continuous active conduct of medical research" unless it, during the applicable computation period,[177] devoted more than one-half of its assets to the continuous active conduct of medical research or it expended funds equaling at least 3.5 percent of the fair market value of its endowment for the continuous active conduct of medical research.[178] If the organization's primary purpose is to disburse funds to other organizations for the conduct of research by them or to extend research grants or scholarships to others, it is not considered directly engaged in the active conduct of medical research.[179]

(e)   Homes for Aged

Another well-recognized health care provider is the home for the aged. Until 1972, the chief basis for tax exemption for a home for the aged as a charitable entity was that free or below-cost services must be provided, in conformance with the early IRS view of hospitals.[180] This approach was abandoned in that year and replaced with a requirement that the exempt charitable home for the aged be operated so

---

[173] IRC § 170(b)(1)(A)(iii).

[174] Reg. § 1.170A-9(d)(2)(iii).

[175] Reg. § 1.170A-9(d)(2)(iv).

[176] Reg. § 1.170A-9(d)(2)(vii).

[177] Reg. § 1.170A-9(d)(2)(vi)(A).

[178] Reg. § 1.170A-9(d)(2)(v)(B).

[179] Reg. § 1.170A-9(d)(2)(v)(C). For purposes of the charitable contribution deduction, the organization must be committed, during the calendar year in which the contribution is made, to expend the contribution for medical research before January 1 of the fifth calendar year that begins after the date the contribution is made (Reg. § 1.170A-9(d)(2)(ii)(C), (viii)).

[180] Rev. Rul. 56-185, 1956-1 C.B. 202. Also, Rev. Rul. 57-467, 1957-2 C.B. 313.

as to satisfy the primary needs of the aged: housing, health care, and financial security.[181]

The need for housing is generally satisfied if the home "provides residential facilities that are specifically designed to meet some combination of the physical, emotional, recreational, social, religious, and similar needs" of the aged. As for health care, that need is generally satisfied where the home "either directly provides some form of health care, or in the alternative, maintains some continuing arrangement with other organizations, facilities, or health personnel, designed to maintain the physical, and if necessary, mental well-being of its residents." Satisfaction of the financial security need has two aspects: The home must (1) maintain in the residence "any persons who become unable to pay their regular charges" and (2) provide its services "at the lowest feasible cost."

A home for the aged will qualify for tax-exempt status as a charitable organization, assuming it otherwise qualifies, if it operates in a manner designed to meet these primary needs of the aged. A home for the aged may, however, in the alternative, qualify under prior IRS rulings for exempt status if the home is primarily concerned with providing care and housing for financially distressed aged persons.[182]

(f) Health Maintenance Organizations

Many tax-exempt health maintenance organizations provide health care services by means of facilities and programs, in adherence to standards of what is *charitable* comparable to those followed by exempt hospitals. It is a membership organization; its services are provided to members on a prepaid basis and to nonmembers on a fee-for-service basis. In most instances, the HMO handles emergency cases without regard to whether the patient is a member and annually provides care either free or at reduced rates to a limited number of indigent patients. Frequently, HMOs sponsor education programs and research efforts to study ways to deliver better health care services. The HMO governing board is usually elected by and from its membership.

The position of the IRS originally was that an HMO may qualify for tax exemption as a social welfare organization[183] but cannot qualify for exemption as a charitable organization, on the ground that the preferential treatment accorded its member-subscribers constitutes the serving of private interests and because the prepayment feature constitutes a form of insurance that is not a charitable activity. This position was rejected in court, however, in connection with one model of an HMO, where it was held that (1) the persons benefited by an HMO represent a class large enough to constitute a requisite community;[184] (2) the HMO meets all of the IRS criteria applied to determine charitable status for nonprofit hospitals;[185] and (3) while the risk of illness is spread throughout its entire membership, the HMO operates not for commercial purposes but for charitable purposes, and thus

---

[181] Rev. Rul. 72-124, 1972-1 C.B. 145. Also, Rev. Rul. 75-198, 1975-1 C.B. 157.
[182] Rev. Rul. 64-231, 1964-2 C.B. 139; Rev. Rul. 61-72, 1961-1 C.B. 188.
[183] See Chapter 13.
[184] See § 6.3(b).
[185] Rev. Rul. 69-545, 1969-2 C.B. 117.

the risk-spreading feature[186] is not a bar to designation of an HMO as a charitable organization.[187]

Following the issuance of this court opinion, the IRS relented somewhat, agreeing that where an HMO possesses certain characteristics, it qualifies as a tax-exempt charitable entity.[188] Essentially, an HMO will qualify for charitable status in the eyes of the IRS when it operates primarily to benefit the community, rather than private interests. The IRS has determined, however, that certain HMOs cannot qualify as charitable organizations, because they are not operating for the benefit of a community. An IRS pronouncement distilled the key factors that, in the view of the agency, differentiate a tax-exempt HMO from a nonexempt HMO.[189]

A federal court of appeals held that a nonprovider HMO does not qualify as a tax-exempt charitable organization.[190] The government won this case by distinguishing the facts from those in the prior litigation.[191] In the previous case, the HMO provided health care services itself, rather than arranging for others to provide that care. It employed physicians and other health care providers who were not affiliated with the HMO to provide health care services. It provided services to both subscribers and members of the public through an outpatient clinic that it operated and through which it treated emergency patients, subscribers or not, regardless of ability to pay. It adjusted rates for and provided some free care to patients who were not subscribers. It offered public educational programs regarding health. The appellate court in the subsequent case held that a community benefit standard could be used; it went on to find, however, that the HMO did not provide any health services itself, it did not ensure that people who were not its subscribers had access to health care or information about health care, it did not conduct research, and it did not offer educational programs open to the public. In short, wrote the court, "it benefits no one but its subscribers."[192]

A court upheld the revocation by the IRS of the tax-exempt status of a nonprofit HMO, on the ground that it no longer provided the requisite community benefit.[193] One of the factors the court emphasized was the difference in treatment of the enrollees in the setting of premiums; the court inferred that this HMO was benefiting larger employers. Likewise, the composition of the HMO's board of trustees, "lacking in representation of the community at large, furthers the inference

---

[186] The IRS ruled that prepaid group practice plans are not insurance companies for federal tax law purposes (IRC Subchapter L) (Rev. Rul. 68-27, 1968-1 C.B. 315).

[187] Sound Health Ass'n v. Comm'r, 71 T.C. 158 (1978). This type of HMO is known as the *staff model HMO*; this test for qualification as a charitable entity is known as the *direct provider community benefit test* (or *rigid community benefit test*).

[188] Gen. Couns. Mem. 38735.

[189] Gen. Couns. Mem. 39828.

[190] Geisinger Health Plan v. Comm'r, 985 F.2d 1210 (3d Cir. 1993), *rev'g* 62 T.C.M. 1656 (1991).

[191] Sound Health Ass'n v. Comm'r, 71 T.C. 158 (1978).

[192] Geisinger Health Plan v. Comm'r, 985 F.2d 1210, 1219 (3d Cir. 1993). This approach was bolstered by a comparable finding in Vision Service Plan v. United States, 265 Fed. Appx. 650 (9th Cir. 2008). See § 13.2, text accompanied by note 77. The stance of the IRS in this regard is essentially the same with respect to HMOs attempting to qualify as exempt social welfare organizations (see Chapter 13) (e.g., Tech. Adv. Mem. 200245064), although the IRS reclassified an HMO (Medicaid-only type) from an IRC § 501(c)(3) entity to an IRC § 501(c)(4) HMO, after the plan merged with a commercial enrollment-based plan (Priv. Ltr. Rul. 201538027).

[193] IHC Health Plans, Inc. v. Comm'r, 82 T.C.M. 593 (2001), *aff'd*, 325 F.3d 1188 (10th Cir. 2003).

that [the HMO] predominantly served the private interests of the larger employers participating in its plans."[194] The court concluded that the HMO "failed to show that it provides any community benefit that accomplishes a charitable purpose."[195]

(g) Integrated Delivery Systems

Another type of organization eligible for tax exemption as charitable organizations because they promote health is the *integrated delivery system*. Private determination letters (from the National Office of the IRS) recognizing the exempt status of these entities first appeared in early 1993.

An IDS is a health provider (or a component entity of an affiliated network of providers) created to integrate the provision of hospital services with medical services provided by physicians. Previously, these services were provided (and paid for by patients, their insurers, or government programs) separately; the hospital provided its services and facilities (such as diagnostic services, surgery, nursing, emergency care, room, and board), while physicians provided medical services to patients by means of private medical practices, admitting and treating patients in hospital facilities. An IDS provides and bills for both hospital and physician services either itself or by contract with another organization.

There are several models of a tax-exempt IDS. In one, a charitable organization obtains (by purchase, lease, license, stock transfer, or contribution) all of the assets needed to operate one or more hospitals, clinics, and physician offices. (There is concern on this point about the potential for forms of private inurement or private benefit,[196] particularly in connection with leasing and licensing arrangements; the IRS prefers arrangements where the system's assets are purchased for fair market value and the IDS controls them.) It acquires the services of physicians, through direct employment or independent contract (the latter known as a professional services agreement). The organization is the provider of health care services—hospital and medical, inpatient and outpatient. It enters into all payor contracts, provides all nonprofessional personnel for the system, maintains all assets, and collects all revenues for services provided. Other models have the exempt IDS as a subsidiary of a hospital, hospital system, or clinic. Another type of IDS, which is jointly controlled by a health care provider and physicians, cannot qualify for exemption as a charitable entity because of the ownership and control by physicians.[197]

---

[194] *Id.* at 605.

[195] *Id.* Also, IHC Group, Inc. v. Comm'r, 82 T.C.M. 606 (2001); IHC Care, Inc. v. Comm'r, 82 T.C.M. 617 (2001).

[196] See Chapter 20.

[197] Somewhat similar to an IDS is a medical service organization (MSO). Typically, with the MSO structure, a hospital or affiliate, in return for a share of revenues, provides to an independent physician or group of physicians all real and personal property, support staff, and management and billing services required to manage an otherwise private medical practice. An MSO is not an IDS, because there is no one entity with responsibility for providing both types of services.

The IRS ruled that hospitals may form a health care delivery system, using a supporting organization (see § 12.3(c)) as the coordinating mechanism, pursuant to a joint operating agreement (JOA) (e.g., Priv. Ltr. Rul. 9651047). These hospitals ceded authority under the JOA to the governing body of the supporting organization to establish their budgets, including major expenditures, debts, contracts, managed care agreements, and capital expenditures; to direct their provision of health care services;

Tax exemption for an IDS is tested against the community benefit standard. In this connection, the exempt IDS can minimize or eliminate duplication of tests, procedures, and treatments, resulting in greater efficiency and reduced costs to the public; provide increased accessibility to Medicare, Medicaid, and charity care patients; undertake research in primary care or areas of specialization that benefit the public; and conduct health education programs open to the public. The IRS expects (as it does in the exempt hospital setting) the governing board, and most committees and subcommittees, of an IDS to be independent (that is, not controlled by the physicians) and reflective of the community.

(h) Peer Review Organizations

Another category of organization posing problems with regard to eligibility for tax exemption as a charitable entity is the *utilization and quality control peer review organization* (PRO), which was authorized by statute in 1972.[198] PROs are qualified groups of physicians that establish mandatory cost and quality controls for medical treatment rendered in hospitals and financed under Medicare and Medicaid, and that monitor this care. PROs were conceived as part of a larger effort to curb the rising costs of health care, in this instance by minimizing or eliminating unnecessary services (those services termed *overutilization*) by assuring that payments under these governmental health care programs are made only when and to the extent that the health care services provided are medically necessary.

Congress views PROs as entities that act in the public interest, their chief purpose being to generally improve the quality of medical care in the United States and to obtain maximum value for every federal health dollar expended.[199] Assuming that the tax law requirements for tax-exempt charitable organizations are otherwise satisfied, this purpose would seem to clearly constitute a charitable activity, the rationales being the promotion of health, lessening of the burdens of government,[200] and/or promotion of social welfare.[201] There may, however, be a private purpose served by PROs, namely, enhancement of and establishment of confidence in the medical profession (even though, ironically, much of the medical community initially was bitterly opposed to the PRO concept).

PROs must be nonprofit organizations; they are reimbursed by the federal government for administrative costs. Members of a PRO must be licensed practitioners of medicine or osteopathy. The basic question with respect to tax-exempt

and to monitor and audit their compliance with its directives. In addition, the governing body and its committees met regularly to exercise overall responsibility for operational decisions involving the day-to-day and long-range strategic management decisions delegated by the participating entities. The IRS concluded that this arrangement is analogous to circumstances where the hospitals are subsidiaries of the coordinating entity.

[198] Social Security Amendments of 1972, Pub. L. No. 92-603, § 249F, 86 Stat. 1329, 1429 (adding Title XI to the Social Security Act); 42 U.S.C. § 1320c *et seq.* These organizations were formerly known as professional standards review organizations.

[199] The law states that the purpose of these organizations is to perform medicine and osteopathy peer reviews of the "pattern of quality of care in an area of medical practice where actual performance is measured against objective criteria which define acceptable and adequate practice" (2 U.S.C. § 1320c-1(2)).

[200] See § 7.7.

[201] See § 7.11.

charitable status is whether a PRO functions primarily to benefit the general public or to serve the interests of the medical profession. The inclination of the IRS is to treat certain health care organizations as business leagues rather than as charitable organizations.[202] The IRS recognized that incidental benefit to physicians will not defeat exemption as a charitable organization,[203] but also made it clear that, when the IRS concludes that a profession is itself receiving substantial benefit from an organization's activities, status as a business league is the likely result.[204] If, however, the activity primarily benefiting a profession is an incidental portion of a charitable organization's activities, the activity may be regarded as an unrelated business, leaving tax-exempt status undisturbed.[205] Prior to litigation, it was the position of the IRS that the public benefits flowing from physician peer review activities were overshadowed by the benefits ostensibly accorded physicians in their professional capacities, and thus that these organizations could not qualify as exempt charitable entities.

By contrast, the IRS recognized a health systems agency (HSA), an organization established by federal law[206] to establish and maintain a system of health planning and resources development aimed at providing adequate health care for a specified geographic area, to be a tax-exempt charitable organization.[207] Among the functions of the HSA is the establishment of a health systems plan after appropriate consideration of the recommended national guidelines for health planning policy issued by the U.S. Department of Health and Human Services (HHS). The agency receives planning and matching grants from the federal government. Finding the basis of the designation of the agency as a charitable entity to be the promotion of health, the IRS observed that, by "establishing and maintaining a system of health planning and resources development aimed at providing adequate health care, the HSA is promoting the health of the residents of the area in which it functions."[208]

The adverse position of the IRS regarding PROs was rejected by a court in a case involving PRO support centers.[209] The court held that Congress's principal purpose in establishing PROs was to ensure the economical and effective delivery of health care services under Medicare and Medicaid, and that any benefits that physicians and others may derive (including reimbursement for services, limitation on tort liability, or promotion of esteem for the medical profession) have only a "tenuous, incidental, and non-substantial connection with the [PRO] scheme."[210] On this

[202] See Chapter 14.
[203] Rev. Rul. 73-313, 1973-2 C.B. 174.
[204] Rev. Rul. 74-553, 1974-2 C.B. 168; Rev. Rul. 73-567, 1973-2 C.B. 178; Rev. Rul. 70-641, 1970-2 C.B. 119. Cf. Kentucky Bar Found., Inc. v. Comm'r, 78 T.C. 1 (1982). This posture of the IRS may be contrasted with the fact that the medical profession instituted an (unsuccessful) action to enjoin implementation of the PSRO law (see supra note 198) and to declare the 1972 act unconstitutional (Ass'n of Amer. Physicians & Surgeons v. Weinberger, 395 F. Supp. 125 (N.D. Ill. 1975)). Cf. Amer. Ass'n of Councils of Medical Staffs v. Mathews, 421 F. Supp. 848 (E.D. La. 1976).
[205] E.g., Priv. Ltr. Rul. 200439043 (concerning a certification program).
[206] Nat'l Health Planning and Resources Development Act of 1974, 42 U.S.C. § 300k et seq.
[207] Rev. Rul. 77-69, 1977-1 C.B. 143.
[208] Id. at 144.
[209] Virginia Pro. Standards Review Found. v. Blumenthal, 466 F. Supp. 1164 (D.D.C. 1979).
[210] Id. at 1170.

latter point, the court added that the PRO support centers did not engage in financial transactions "designed to benefit the members of the organizations or the organizations themselves, activities in the nature of a patient referral service, or other potential money-making activities designed to benefit members or participants."[211]

As a sidelight of this PRO decision, the court found it "difficult to reconcile" the position of the IRS against PROs and the ruling granting classification as tax-exempt charitable entities to HSAs. Said the court: "The similarity between HSAs and PROs and [PRO] support centers is obvious. [PROs] collect and analyze data, establish regional norms and criteria of care, and coordinate activities with HSAs and other federal state health planning entities."[212]

In the aftermath of these two court decisions,[213] the IRS revised its position concerning physician peer review organizations and concluded that, in certain circumstances, this type of entity is a tax-exempt charitable organization because it is "promoting the health of the beneficiaries of governmental health care programs by preventing unnecessary hospitalization and surgery."[214] The IRS regards these factors as essential for exemption of a PRO as an exempt charitable entity: Membership in it is open by law to all physicians without charge; it is an organization mandated by federal statute as the exclusive method of assuring appropriate quality and utilization of care provided to Medicare and Medicaid patients; the composition of the board of directors of the PRO is not tied to any membership or association with any medical society; and the PRO has the authority to make final decisions regarding quality and utilization of medical care for purposes of payment under the Medicare and Medicaid programs. The fact that the activities of the PRO "may indirectly further the interests of the medical profession by promoting public esteem for the medical profession, and by allowing physicians to set their own standards for the review of Medicare and Medicaid claims and thus prevent outside regulation" was dismissed as being "incidental" to the charitable benefits provided by the organization.[215]

(i)   Fitness Centers

Fitness centers and similar facilities, whether freestanding or operated by institutions such as hospitals, can be tax-exempt organizations (or programs), considered charitable in nature because they promote health. In this setting, the IRS once again applies the community benefit doctrine. Thus, when the health facility provides a benefit for the entire community the organization serves, operation of the facility is an exempt function.[216] By contrast, if the fees for use of a health club are sufficiently high to restrict use of the club's facilities to a limited segment of a community, the club operation will be a nonexempt one.[217]

---

[211] Id. at 1173.

[212] Id. at 1172. Also, Professional Standards Review Org. of Queens Cnty., Inc. v. Comm'r, 74 T.C. 240 (1980).

[213] See supra notes 209, 212.

[214] Rev. Rul. 81-276, 1981-2 C.B. 128.

[215] Id. at 129. Analogous entities are the Medicaid service organizations, which can qualify as tax-exempt charitable organizations because they lessen the burdens of government (see § 7.7).

[216] Tech. Adv. Mem. 8505002.

[217] Rev. Rul. 79-360, 1979-2 C.B. 236.

In one instance, the IRS expressed the view that the standard as to tax exemption for a health club is whether its "operations promote health in a manner which is collateral to the providing of recreational facilities which advances the well-being and happiness of the community in general."[218] Similarly, a fitness center was held to be exempt inasmuch as it furthered the accomplishment of certain of the other programs of the health care organization that operated it (including an occupational and physical therapy program), its facilities and programs were specially designed for the needs of the disabled and the treatment plans of patients in other programs, its fee structure was designed to make it available to the public (its rates were comparable to those charged by similar fitness centers), and it offered a range of programs that focused on wellness.[219] Likewise, a freestanding state-of-the-art cardiovascular rehabilitation and heart disease prevention center, which included a fitness facility, was found to be a related activity of an exempt hospital, with the IRS emphasizing the existence of a nutrition program and a scholarship plan for those who could not afford the programs and services of the center.[220]

The IRS's treatment of fitness and health centers as tax-exempt charitable functions that promote health extends to the most elaborate of facilities. In one instance, exemption was accorded a hospital-run sports and fitness center, the components of which included exercise rooms, racquetball and tennis courts, a two-pool aquatic area, an indoor track, tanning beds, a roller-skating rink, and a juice bar. The agency held that the rehabilitation of hospital inpatients and outpatients in connection with treatment plans prescribed by physicians or other appropriate hospital personnel furthered the hospital's exempt purpose of serving the health care needs of the community involved.[221] Likewise, the IRS ruled that an "integrated medical fitness facility" was a related business; this facility included 69,000 square feet of cardiovascular and strength training areas, an indoor multipurpose gymnasium, a walking track, three swimming pools, a sauna, steam rooms, four group exercise studios, a youth fitness area, locker rooms, and a healing garden.[222]

(j) Other Health Care Organizations

There are various other types of health provider institutions that qualify as exempt charitable organizations for federal tax purposes. These include entities such as preferred provider organizations, drug rescue centers,[223] blood banks,[224] halfway houses,[225] organizations that minister to the nonmedical needs of patients in a

[218] Tech. Adv. Mem. 8505002.

[219] Priv. Ltr. Rul. 9329041.

[220] Priv. Ltr. Rul. 9736047. The IRS issued a similar ruling in the case of a university-based fitness center (Priv. Ltr. Rul. 9732032). The IRS held that a community recreational facility that operated an ice rink was engaged in charitable activity because its programs included physical education classes, provided for youth ice hockey, and charged nominal rates for public use of the facilities; this organization was found to combat community deterioration and juvenile delinquency (see § 7.11) (Tech. Adv. Mem. 201344009).

[221] Priv. Ltr. Rul. 200051049.

[222] Priv. Ltr. Rul. 201123045.

[223] Rev. Rul. 70-590, 1970-2 C.B. 1.

[224] Rev. Rul. 66-323, 1966-2 C.B. 216, *as modified by* Rev. Rul. 78-145, 1978-1 C.B. 169.

[225] Rev. Rul. 72-16, 1972-1 C.B. 143. Also, Rev. Rul. 75-472, 1975-2 C.B. 208.

proprietary hospital,[226] nursing bureaus,[227] senior citizens centers,[228] organizations that provide private hospital rooms when medically necessary,[229] and Christian Science medical care facilities.[230]

Moreover, recognition of tax-exempt status has been accorded to several types of organizations providing specialized health care services. Thus, for example, a home health agency that provides low-cost health care to patients in their homes can be an exempt charitable entity.[231] Similarly, an organization created to attract a physician to a medically underserved community by providing a medical building and facilities was ruled to be exempt, notwithstanding the fact that the physician charged for services provided and received some personal benefit (use of a building) under the arrangement.[232] Also, an organization was determined to be furthering the charitable purpose of promoting the health of its community where it built and leased a public hospital and related facilities to an exempt charitable association that operated the facilities for an amount sufficient only to retire indebtedness and meet necessary operating expenses.[233] Likewise, organizations that conduct medical research are frequently ruled to be exempt as charitable organizations, although these organizations may instead be considered as engaged in scientific research.[234] As another illustration, an organization that operated a free computerized donor authorization retrieval system to facilitate transplantation of body organs on the death of donors qualified as an exempt charitable organization engaged in the promotion of health.[235] Still another example is an organization that provided services (such as housing, transportation, and counseling) for relatives and friends who traveled to the organization's community to visit and comfort patients at local health care facilities.[236] Further, an organization that provided medical care to indigent individuals through five medical clinics, including the funding of emergency room care and related inpatient care to the indigent, was ruled by the IRS to be promoting health.[237]

The IRS stated that the term *charitable* includes the promotion of *public health*, in ruling that an organization formed to provide individual psychological and educational evaluations, as well as tutoring and therapy, for children and adolescents with learning disabilities qualified as a tax-exempt, charitable organization.[238] The organization's psychologists and other professionals administered tests designed

---

[226] Rev. Rul. 68-73, 1968-1 C.B. 251.

[227] Rev. Rul. 55-656, 1955-2 C.B. 262.

[228] Rev. Rul. 75-198, 1975-1 C.B. 157.

[229] Rev. Rul. 79-358, 1979-2 C.B. 225.

[230] Rev. Rul. 80-114, 1980-1 C.B. 115, *superseding* Rev. Rul. 78-4, 1978-2 C.B. 176. This determination is consistent with the IRS's position that payments to Christian Science practitioners for services rendered are deductible medical expenses (Rev. Rul. 55-261, 1955-1 C.B. 307).

[231] Rev. Rul. 72-209, 1972-1 C.B. 148.

[232] Rev. Rul. 73-313, 1973-2 C.B. 174. Also, In re Estate of Carlson, 358 P.2d 669 (Kan. 1961). Cf. Rev. Rul. 69-266, 1969-2 C.B. 151.

[233] Rev. Rul. 80-309, 1980-2 C.B. 183.

[234] E.g., Rev. Rul. 69-526, 1969-2 C.B. 115. See Chapter 9.

[235] Rev. Rul. 75-197, 1975-1 C.B. 156.

[236] Rev. Rul. 81-28, 1981-1 C.B. 328.

[237] Priv. Ltr. Rul. 200233024.

[238] Rev. Rul. 77-68, 1977-1 C.B. 142.

to determine intellectual capacity, academic achievement, psychological adjustment, speech and language difficulties, and perceptual-motor abilities. Therapy was available through staff professionals specially trained in the various areas of learning disabilities.

Despite the efforts of the IRS to deny tax-exempt status to nearly all forms of referral services,[239] a court held that an organization that operated a medical and dental referral service was a charitable entity because it promoted health.[240] Users of the service (subscribers) paid the organization an annual fee and were provided an array of information concerning the availability of health-related supplies, equipment, and services at a discount. The service providers did not pay any fees to be listed with the referral service, although many made contributions to the organization. Other program activities of the organization were the publication of a health care newsletter, sponsorship of a community health fair, the provision of speakers, and the presentation of an annual conference for physicians and dentists. The court said that the referral service "serves its charitable purpose by providing a resource whereby subscribers can be made aware of and referred to medical specialists who can serve their health care needs" and that any financial benefit inuring to the referral service is merely incidental to the overall charitable purposes being served.[241]

Thus, there are various types of nonprofit organizations that promote health. Many of these entities, including hospitals, operate as members of a health care provider system. Generally, an aggregation of organizations, even where they have a common purpose (sometimes termed a *system*), cannot itself qualify for tax exemption as a charitable entity.[242] Usually each organization must separately establish (if it can) a basis in law for its claim to exemption.[243] In this context, at least, the IRS resists the concept of "exemption by attachment" or "derivative exemption."[244] Nonetheless, the eligibility of a supporting organization for exemption often is determined by the nature of its relationship with one or more supported organizations.[245]

(k) Regional Health Information Organizations

The National Office of the IRS, in 2009, began issuing exemption rulings to regional health information organizations (RHIOs). The essential purpose of an RHIO is to facilitate the exchange of electronic health records. This information sharing is and will be occurring among health care providers, physicians, insurers, and others in the health care system. The overall purpose of these records-exchange programs

---

[239] Kentucky Bar Found., Inc. v. Comm'r, 78 T.C. 921 (1982).

[240] Fraternal Med. Specialist Servs., Inc. v. Comm'r, 49 T.C.M. 289 (1984).

[241] *Id.* at 292. An organization that provided sperm from one donor without charge to women seeking to become pregnant by means of artificial insemination or in vitro fertilization was held to be ineligible for exemption as a charitable entity in part because the court was not convinced that the "distribution of one man's . . . sperm to a small number of women . . . promotes health" (Free Fertility Found. v. Comm'r, 135 T.C. 21, 26 (2010)).

[242] Cf. § 7.13.

[243] Gen. Couns. Mem. 39508. See § 26.15.

[244] Gen. Couns. Mem. 31433.

[245] See § 12.3(c).

is promotion of health: improvement of the delivery of health care services and patient outcomes.

The federal government is promoting greater use of EHRs. This promotion was in President Bush's State of the Union address in 2006. The IRS, in 2007, issued a memorandum from the Director of the Exempt Organizations Division stating that the agency would not treat the benefits that a tax-exempt hospital provides to its medical staff physicians in the form of EHR software and technical support services as impermissible private benefit or private inurement if these benefits fall within the range of the EHR items and services that are permissible under the Department of Health and Human Services regulations promulgated in 2006.

Tax exemption for RHIOs was given a significant boost by enactment of legislation in 2009[246] that recognized that facilitation of health information exchange and technology is important to improvement of the delivery of health care and reduction in the costs of health care delivery and administration. The conference committee report accompanying this legislation stated that, as a result of the incentives for health information technology provided in the legislation, it is expected that "nonprofit organizations may be formed to facilitate the electronic use and exchange of health-related information consistent with standards adopted by HHS, and that such organizations may seek exemption from income tax as an organization described in IRC sec. 501(c)(3)."[247] Consequently, if a tax-exempt charitable organization "engages in activities to facilitate the electronic use or exchange of health-related information to advance the purposes of the bill, consistent with standards adopted by HHS, such activities will be considered activities that substantially further an exempt purpose under IRC sec. 501(c)(3), specifically the purpose of lessening the burdens of government."[248]

The conference report concluded with this observation: "Private benefit attributable to cost savings realized from the conduct of such activities will be viewed as incidental to the accomplishment of the nonprofit organization's exempt purpose."[249] That language was of considerable assistance to the IRS in enabling it to begin issuing favorable exemption rulings to qualified RHIOs.

(l)   Health Insurance Exchanges

States are required, by the health reform legislation enacted in 2010,[250] to establish health insurance exchanges, namely, American Health Benefit Exchanges for the individual market and Small Business Health Options Program Exchanges for the small employer market (those with no more than 100 employees), that will make available qualified health plans to individuals and employers who are eligible to purchase insurance through these exchanges. The exchanges can be

---

[246] American Recovery and Reinvestment Act of 2009, Pub. L. 111-5, 123 Stat. 114 (2009).

[247] H.R. Rep. No. 111-16, at 106 (2009).

[248] *Id.* See § 7.7. The IRS ruled that a program of a regional health information organization that promotes use of health information technology to improve health care quality and reduce health care costs is charitable because it is lessening the burdens of government (Priv. Ltr. Rul. 201250025).

[249] H.R. Rep. No. 111-16, at 106 (2009). See § 20.13(b).

[250] PPA, *supra* note 144, at §§ 1304, 1311, 1321.

operated by a governmental agency, a quasi-governmental entity, or a nonprofit organization established by a state.[251]

If a state elects to not establish an exchange, the federal government will operate one. A state may combine these two types of exchanges into one entity. The National Association of Insurance Commissioners and state insurance commissioners are heavily involved in securing funding for exchange planning and start-up activities.

The functions of these exchanges will be determined by the states based on minimum standards established by the legislation and after consultation with stakeholders. These functions include certification, recertification, and decertification of health plans as qualified health plans; maintenance of a toll-free hotline to respond to requests for assistance; maintenance of a website for enrollees and prospective enrollees to enable them to compare information regarding qualified health plans; use of a standardized format for presenting health benefit plan options in the exchange; establishment of, and electronic availability of, a calculator to determine the actual cost of coverage after application of any premium tax credit[252] and any applicable cost sharing; granting of certifications as to exemptions from the individual mandate or penalty;[253] transferring of information to the Treasury Department concerning exemptions from the mandate, employees eligible for the premium tax credit, and individuals who have changed employers or have ceased coverage under a qualified health plan during the year; provision of information to employers on employees eligible for the premium tax credit who cease coverage under a qualified health plan during the plan year; and establishment of a navigator program based on HHS standards and developed in collaboration with the states.

Plan offerings by means of these exchanges will be based on essential health benefits as defined by the HHS, based on a list of services in the legislation. A state may expand this list of essential health benefits; if a state does so, however, it is responsible for paying the associated costs.

Qualified health plans are required to implement a payment structure that provides increased reimbursement or incentives for quality improvement activities. These plans are required to report periodically to the appropriate exchange activities undertaken to implement the payment structure. Beginning on January 1, 2015, unless an exception is authorized by the exchange on the basis of rules developed by the HHS, a qualified health plan may contract with only (1) a hospital with more than 50 beds if the hospital uses a patient safety evaluation system and implements a mechanism ensuring that each patient receives information about a comprehensive program for hospital discharge, or (2) a health care provider if the provider implements mechanisms required by the HHS to improve health care quality. There is an opportunity for hospitals to participate in the development of guidelines for quality improvement and exceptions.

---

[251] An exchange that is a quasi-governmental entity may be tax-exempt in the sense that all of its income is excluded from taxation by reason of IRC § 115. See § 19.22(b).

[252] IRC § 36B. The Supreme Court held that these tax credits are available to qualified individuals irrespective of whether the health insurance is acquired from a state exchange or an exchange established by the federal government (King v. Burwell, 576 U.S. 473 (2015)).

[253] See *Healthcare Organizations* § 26.11(a).

States are required to develop a secure electronic interface that allows for the exchange of information to determine consumers' eligibility for public program coverage, tax credits, and other subsidies. Coordination is required between enrollment in the exchanges and state-funded health programs, such as Medicaid and the Children's Health Insurance Program. An exchange may contract with a Medicaid provider for enrollment, eligibility, and coordination of qualified health plans in an exchange.

A state may pursue federal funding to establish, expand, or provide support for offices of health insurance consumer assistance or ombudsman programs and, as a condition of receiving the grant, impose reporting and data collection requirements. A state may establish a risk-adjustment mechanism to assess issuers whose actuarial risk for a year is less than the average actuarial risk of all enrollees in the state and to pay issuers whose actuarial risk for a year is greater than average. The law requires states to adopt adjusted community rating, and limits premium variation for group and individual health insurance.[254]

(m)   Accountable Care Organizations

The health care reform legislation brought new law directing the HHS to establish a Medicare Shared Savings Program (MSSP) that promotes accountability for care of Medicare beneficiaries, improves the coordination of Medicare fee-for-service items and services, and encourages investment in infrastructure and redesigned care processes for high-quality and efficient health care service delivery.[255] Groups of health care service providers and suppliers that have established a mechanism for shared governance and that meet criteria specified by the HHS are eligible to participate as accountable care organizations (ACOs), which essentially are networks designed to reduce health care costs, under the MSSP.[256] ACOs will be rewarded with a share of the Medicare savings for providing quality care at a lower cost in relation to a spending benchmark.

(i) ACOs in General.   The Social Security Act provides examples of groups of service providers and suppliers that may form an ACO, including (1) physicians and other health care practitioners (collectively, ACO professionals) in a group practice, (2) a network of individual practices, (3) a partnership or joint venture agreement between hospitals and ACO professionals, and (4) a hospital employing ACO professionals. ACOs eligible to participate in the MSSP will manage and coordinate care for their assigned Medicare fee-for-service beneficiaries. Health care service providers and suppliers participating in an ACO will continue to receive Medicare fee-for-service payments in the same manner as these payments would otherwise be made. In addition, an ACO that meets quality performance standards established by the HHS and demonstrates that it has achieved savings against an appropriate benchmark of expected average per capita Medicare fee-for-service expenditures will be eligible to receive payments

---

[254] In general, see *Healthcare Organizations* § 13.4.
[255] PPA, *supra* note 144, § 3022 amended Title XVIII of the Social Security Act (42 U.S.C. § 1395 et seq.) (SSA) by adding SSA § 1899 (42 U.S.C. § 1395jjj).
[256] *Id.* § 1395jjj(b)(1).

for Medicare shared savings.[257] Other payment models that the HHS determines will improve the quality and efficiency of items and services for Medicare may also be used.[258]

The Centers for Medicare & Medicaid Services issued regulations in 2011 addressing the matter of ACOs. These rules contain eligibility criteria (including patient and program safeguards) that entities must meet to qualify as ACOs under the MSSP, and describe quality measures, reporting requirements, and monitoring by the CMS. An ACO must be an organization that is recognized under applicable state law and have a qualifying governing body. It must submit an application to the CMS and describe its participation in the MSSP. The CMS monitors and assesses the performance of ACOs and their participants. These ACOs must comply with public reporting and transparency requirements.

(ii) Tax-Exempt Organizations Issues. The IRS summarized some of the tax-exempt organizations' issues that may arise in the ACO setting.[259] These issues entail application of the private inurement doctrine,[260] application of the private benefit doctrine,[261] and the unrelated business rules.[262] Tax-exempt organizations are participating in the MSSP through an ACO along with private parties, including entities that are insiders[263] with respect to an exempt organization. An exempt organization's participation in the program may take a variety of forms, including membership in a nonprofit membership corporation, ownership of shares in a corporation, ownership of a partnership interest in a partnership, ownership of a membership interest in a limited liability company, and contractual arrangements with an ACO and/or its other participants.

The IRS advised, in this summary, that "[t]o avoid adverse tax consequences, the tax-exempt organization must ensure that its participation in the MSSP through an ACO is structured so as not to result in its net earnings inuring to the benefit of its insiders or in its being operated for the benefit of private parties participating in the ACO." The IRS added, however, that because of CMS regulation and

---

[257] *Id.* § 1395jjj(d)(2).

[258] *Id.* § 1395jjj(i).

[259] Notice 2011-20, 2011-16 I.R.B. 652.

[260] See Chapter 20.

[261] See § 20.13. The potential for application of the private benefit doctrine in this context is illustrated by the treatment accorded by the IRS to an organization establishing a "health delivery network." This entity did not directly provide medical services; it entered into payor agreements with purchasers of physician medical services on behalf of physicians with whom it has entered into "member agreements." The IRS, in denying this entity recognition of exemption as a charitable organization, ruled that it "merely facilitate[s] negotiations between physicians on the medical staff [of its member hospital] and to provide physician medical services to consumers of these services" (Priv. Ltr. Rul. 201145025). In a similar ruling, the IRS held that an organization formed to redesign health care delivery by utilization of the patient-centered medical home model was not entitled to recognition of exemption as a charitable entity because it is essentially providing consulting services of a commercial nature for the benefit of a group of medical practices (Priv. Ltr. Rul. 201315028). The IRS applied similar rationales to deny tax-exempt status as a social welfare organization (see Chapter 13) to an ACO that coordinated the care of patient populations between insurance companies and physicians, but that provided no direct health care services itself (Priv. Ltr. Rul. 202210023).

[262] See Chapters 24, 25.

[263] See § 20.3.

oversight of the MSSP, "as a general matter, the IRS expects that it will not consider a tax-exempt organization's participation in the MSSP through an ACO to result in inurement or impermissible private benefit to the private party ACO participants" in certain circumstances.

The IRS, on October 20, 2011, issued an update of its guidance, following issuance by the CMS's final regulations, concerning the participation of tax-exempt organizations in ACOs.[264] The IRS observed that, although the CMS's final regulations differ from the proposal in some respects, the discussion in the original guidance "continues to reflect IRS expectations regarding the application of existing IRS guidance to charitable organizations participating in the [Medicare] Shared Savings Program through ACOs." The agency said that, in the case of an ACO that has been accepted into the MSSP, it "expects that CMS's regulation and oversight of the ACO will be sufficient to ensure that the ACO's participation in the [MSSP] furthers the charitable purpose of lessening of the burdens of government."

The IRS said that it recognizes that certain non-MSSP activities involving an ACO may further a charitable purpose, such as those relieving the poor, distressed, and/or underprivileged. Also, an ACO's conduct of noncharitable activities will not jeopardize the tax-exempt status of one of its participants if the ACO's activities "are not attributed to that participant." Even if there is this type of attribution, such as because the ACO is a partnership, the participant's exempt status will not be jeopardized if the ACO's noncharitable activities "represent no more than an insubstantial part of the participant's total activities."

The IRS wrote that an ACO engaged exclusively in MSSP activities may qualify for tax exemption as a charitable organization "provided that it meets all of the requirements" for that exemption. An ACO that is constituted as a partnership or disregarded entity, however, may not apply for recognition of exemption.

One of the factors referenced by the IRS in its original guidance as to avoidance of private inurement or impermissible private benefit is that the exempt organization's share of economic benefits derived from the ACO is proportional to the benefits or contributions the organization provides to the ACO. That factor contains an example of proportionality based on existing IRS guidance. However, said the IRS, this factor "takes into account all contributions made by the charitable organization and other ACO participants to the ACO, in whatever form (cash, property, services), and all economic benefits received by ACO participants (including shares of Shared Savings payments and any ownership interests)."

An IRS memorandum issued in 2007 states that the agency will not treat the benefits that a tax-exempt hospital provides to its medical staff physicians as inurement or unwarranted private benefit if the benefits fall within the range of electronic health records software and technical support services that are permissible under HHS regulations and the hospital meets certain other requirements.[265] The IRS stated that it will continue to follow this memorandum with respect to charitable hospitals, including those participating in an ACO.[266]

---

[264] FS-2011-11.
[265] See § 20.13(b), note 403.
[266] In general, *Healthcare Organizations* § 13.5.

§ 7.7 LESSENING BURDENS OF GOVERNMENT

The regulations accompanying the federal tax law concerning exempt charitable organizations define the term *charitable* as including "lessening of the burdens of Government" and the "erection or maintenance of public buildings, monuments, or works."[267] This first concept relates more to the provision of governmental or municipal services rather than facilities, because of inclusion in the regulations of the exempt activity of erection or maintenance of public facilities.

According to the IRS, a determination of whether an organization is lessening the burdens of a government requires an analysis as to whether the organization's activities are functions that pertain to objectives that a governmental body considers to be its burden and whether these activities in fact lessen a government's burden.[268] For an activity to be a burden of a government, there must be an "objective manifestation" by a governmental body that it considers the activity to be part of its burden. It is insufficient that an organization engages in an activity that is sometimes undertaken by a government or that a government or a governmental official expresses approval of an organization and its activities. The interrelationship between a governmental unit and an organization may provide evidence that the governmental unit considers the activity to be its burden. All relevant facts and circumstances are considered in determining whether an organization is actually lessening the burdens of a government.

Thus, mere interaction with a governmental unit is insufficient to give rise to this category of tax exemption. For example, the fact that an organization provided services to a government pursuant to a contract does not mean that the organization is lessening a burden of that government.[269] Indeed, an organization that was planning on providing pipe products for use in infrastructure repair and building was denied recognition of exemption on the basis of lessening the burdens of government in part because it would not be working directly with government authorities.[270]

As the IRS stated, the "mere fact that a government agency has a policy or program to promote a certain outcome does not mean that the government has assumed the burden of engaging in that activity."[271] That observation was made in connection with denial of recognition of exemption to a nonprofit organization operating a lottery to help fund elimination of student debt, which asserted it was lessening the burdens of government because the lottery participants, who are not members of a charitable class,[272] deposit funds in special prize accounts made legal when maintained by federal savings banks and credit unions.

A favorable working relationship between a government agency or department and an organization is "strong evidence" that the organization is in fact lessening the burdens of the government. For example, an organization that provided

---

[267] Reg. § 1.501(c)(3)-1(d)(2). On one occasion, the IRS utilized this rationale to find ongoing tax exemption for a social welfare organization (see Chapter 13) (Priv. Ltr. Rul. 200624068).

[268] Rev. Rul. 85-1, 1985-1 C.B. 177; Rev. Rul. 85-2, 1985-1 C.B. 178.

[269] E.g., Priv. Ltr. Rul. 201741020.

[270] Priv. Ltr. Rul. 201726013, *aff'd*, New World Infrastructure Org. v. Comm'r, 122 T.C.M 88 (2021).

[271] Priv. Ltr. Rul. 202109008.

[272] See § 6.3(a), text accompanied by note 134.

funds to a county's law enforcement agencies to police illegal narcotic traffic was held to lessen the burdens of government and thus be charitable, in that governmental funds were not available to purchase the drugs used to apprehend drug traffickers.[273] Likewise, an organization that provided legal advice and training to guardians *ad litem* representing neglected or abused children before a juvenile court was found to lessen governmental burdens, inasmuch as otherwise the government would have to train the law volunteers or to appoint lawyers as guardians.[274] Conversely, an organization that contracted with governmental entities, but also other nonprofit and for-profit entities, to provide services relating to building codes, permits, and inspections was found not to be lessening the burdens of government because it was operated like any other for-profit entity that charges fees for its services.[275]

Some organizations that are tax-exempt under this category of *charitable* provide services directly in the context of governmental activity, such as assisting in the preservation of a public lake,[276] beautifying a city,[277] operating a prisoner correctional center,[278] assisting in the operation of a mass transportation system,[279] maintaining a volunteer fire company,[280] conserving natural resources,[281] or encouraging plantings of public lands.[282]

Other organizations that are charitable because they reduce a governmental burden provide services in tandem with the programs of one or more governmental agencies. As examples, tax exemption on this basis was ruled to be obtainable for an organization that made funds available to a police department for use as reward money;[283] an organization that assisted firefighters, police, and other personnel to perform their duties more efficiently during emergency conditions;[284] an organization that provided bus transportation to isolated areas of a community not served by the city bus system as a Model Cities demonstration project performed under the authority of the federal and local governments;[285] a community foundation that participated in an investment plan to retain a for-profit baseball team in a city (when the governmental units involved demonstrated an "intense and unique interest" in professional sports franchises);[286] an organization that provided expert opinions to local government officials

---

[273] Rev. Rul. 85-1, 1985-1 C.B. 177.

[274] Rev. Rul. 85-2, 1985-1 C.B. 178. In one instance, claims for tax exemption on this basis failed because the organization did not show that the entities ostensibly assisted were government agencies, that activities they undertook were those that a government considers its burden, and that the activities lessened any burdens (Univ. Med. Resident Servs., P.C. v. Comm'r, 71 T.C.M. 3130 (1996)).

[275] Priv. Ltr. Rul. 202221017.

[276] Rev. Rul. 70-186, 1970-1 C.B. 128.

[277] Rev. Rul. 68-14, 1968-1 C.B. 243. Cf. Rev. Rul. 75-286, 1975-2 C.B. 210.

[278] Rev. Rul. 70-583, 1970-2 C.B. 114.

[279] Rev. Rul. 71-29, 1971-1 C.B. 150.

[280] Rev. Rul. 74-361, 1974-2 C.B. 159.

[281] Rev. Rul. 67-292, 1967-2 C.B. 184.

[282] Rev. Rul. 66-179, 1966-1 C.B. 139.

[283] Rev. Rul. 74-246, 1974-1 C.B. 130.

[284] Rev. Rul. 71-99, 1971-1 C.B. 151.

[285] Rev. Rul. 78-68, 1978-1 C.B. 149. Cf. Rev. Rul. 78-69, 1978-1 C.B. 156.

[286] Priv. Ltr. Rul. 9530024.

concerning traffic safety;[287] an organization's program of arranging for pooled issuances of general obligation bonds for the benefit of its member governmental units;[288] an organization's operation of a health insurance plan for trainees associated with a government agency that it supports;[289] an organization's provision of medication services to other entities to lower the costs of a state's program for providing services to the mentally ill;[290] and an organization's conduct of stream mitigation activities in support of a government commission overseeing the operation of a nature preserve.[291]

A government internship program may likewise come within this category of charitable activities,[292] as does a program of awards to citizens for outstanding civic achievements.[293] Likewise, physician peer review organizations[294] can qualify as exempt charitable entities because they enable the medical profession to assume the government's responsibility for reviewing the appropriateness and quality of services provided under the Medicare and Medicaid programs.[295] An organization that functions as an independent system operator for the Federal Energy Regulatory Commission and thus is exempt because it lessens the burden of government was advised by the IRS that its establishment of a central counterparty structure for transactions taking place in a market it administers will be in furtherance of its exempt purposes.[296]

Congress established the MSSP to be conducted through ACOs in order to promote quality improvements and cost savings in health care.[297] Consequently, participation in the MSSP by an ACO furthers the charitable purpose of lessening the burdens of government.[298] By contrast, federal law does not provide an objective manifestation that the federal government considers non-MSSP-related ACO activities to be its burden, so that these types of ACOs are not tax-exempt by reason of lessening the burdens of government.[299]

In an application of these rules, an organization that certified crop seed within a state was found to be performing a service required by federal and state law—a service performed in other states by a governmental agency—and thus to be charitable because it was lessening the burdens of government. The organization, functioning in conjunction with one of the state's universities, was held to be protecting the "purchasing public—generally farmers and gardeners—from perceived abuses in the sale of agricultural and vegetable seed which is impure,

---

[287] Rev. Rul. 76-418, 1976-2 C.B. 145. Cf. Rev. Rul. 70-79, 1970-1 C.B. 127.
[288] Priv. Ltr. Rul. 200611033.
[289] Priv. Ltr. Rul. 200724034.
[290] Priv. Ltr. Rul. 200739012.
[291] Priv. Ltr. Rul. 201408031.
[292] Rev. Rul. 70-584, 1970-2 C.B. 114.
[293] Rev. Rul. 66-146, 1966-1 C.B. 136.
[294] See § 7.6(h).
[295] Rev. Rul. 81-276, 1981-2 C.B. 128.
[296] Priv. Ltr. Rul. 201209010. A similar ruling was issued to an organization that is a FERC-recognized regional transmission organization (Priv. Ltr. Rul. 201214034).
[297] See § 7.6(m).
[298] E.g., Notice 2011-20, 2011-6 I.R.B. 652.
[299] Priv. Ltr. Rul. 201615022.

mislabeled or adulterated," and therefore to be undertaking a "public service" and a "recognized governmental function."[300]

A private foundation proposed to build, maintain, and lease a public ice arena to promote the health and welfare of its community and to lessen the burdens of local government. This facility, in conformity with National Hockey League and college rink specifications, would include a pro shop, coffee shop, concession area, day-care center, and lounge; it might also include a conference center, a gymnastics facility, and an athletic medicine center. The arena would be leased at fair market value rates. The IRS ruled that the development, ownership, and leasing of this arena would further the foundation's charitable purposes.[301]

Organizations that qualify for *charitable* status because they perform functions for the benefit of a government also include those that supply a community with facilities ordinarily provided at the taxpayers' expense, or maintain the facilities, such as town halls, bridges, streets, parks, trees, and monuments.[302] Examples of organizations in this category include those that engage in activities such as solid waste recycling,[303] community improvement,[304] and community land-use analysis,[305] as well as those that provide public parks,[306] other recreational facilities,[307] and public parking lots.[308]

An organization may operate facilities on behalf of a city, county, or other governmental unit where the operations are not inherently charitable, yet nonetheless be a tax-exempt charitable entity because it is lessening the burdens of the government. In some instances, the facilities being operated are used for sports activities;[309] it is common for a charitable organization to operate a convention center as a way of lessening a government's burden.[310] An organization operating a complex of facilities for a city, including an aquarium, horticulture conservatories, a theater, and a hotel, was ruled to be an exempt charitable entity because it lessened the city's burdens.[311] Indeed, an economic development organization was found to be charitable by lessening the burdens of government, in part because it operated a quasi-grant program for the federal government and reported its investment activities to a state government.[312]

An organization claiming to be charitable because it is lessening the burdens of government had its tax exemption revoked.[313] The entity was established to purchase claims for refunds by fuel tank owners or contractors to clean up spillage

[300] Indiana Crop Improvement Ass'n, Inc. v. Comm'r, 76 T.C. 394, 398–99 (1981).
[301] Priv. Ltr. Rul. 200532058.
[302] *Restatement of Trusts* (2d ed. 1959) § 373, comment a.
[303] Rev. Rul. 72-560, 1972-2 C.B. 248.
[304] Rev. Rul. 68-15, 1968-1 C.B. 244.
[305] Rev. Rul. 67-391, 1967-2 C.B. 190.
[306] Rev. Rul. 66-358, 1966-2 C.B. 218.
[307] Rev. Rul. 70-186, 1970-1 C.B. 128; Rev. Rul. 59-310, 1959-2 C.B. 332.
[308] Monterey Pub. Parking Corp. v. United States, 481 F.2d 175 (9th Cir. 1973).
[309] See, e.g., text accompanied by *supra* notes 286, 301.
[310] E.g., Priv. Ltr. Rul. 200634036.
[311] Priv. Ltr. Rul. 200727020.
[312] Priv. Ltr. Rul. 201413012.
[313] Priv. Ltr. Rul. 201531022.

from underground storage tanks where approval for reimbursement was made by a state's department of environmental quality. The IRS stated that this organization failed to show that it was lessening the burden of a government, the fuel tank owners are not members of a charitable class,[314] and the financing program the organization developed was commercial in nature.[315]

A corollary of the foregoing law is that an organization that frustrates attempts to relieve the burdens of government and thereby increases these burdens cannot qualify as a charitable organization.[316] In accordance with this position, the IRS ruled that an organization could not qualify as a charitable entity in part because it may have engaged in an illegal act (possible violation of state law concerning promotion of raffles) that may have increased the burden of the state.[317] Likewise, where an organization engages in activities that are specifically proscribed under federal and applicable state law, it cannot be regarded as a charitable organization that is lessening the burdens of government.[318]

§ 7.8 ADVANCEMENT OF EDUCATION

(a) General Principles

The regulations accompanying the federal tax law concerning charitable organizations include among the definitions of the term *charitable* the "advancement of education."[319] The *advancement of education* includes the establishment or maintenance of nonprofit educational institutions, financing of scholarships and other forms of student assistance, making of awards, establishment or maintenance of institutions such as public libraries and museums, advancement of knowledge through research, and dissemination of knowledge by publications, seminars, lectures, and similar activities. Inasmuch as the federal tax law exemption for charitable organizations also contains the term *educational*,[320] organizations coming within one or both of the terms *charitable* or *educational* will qualify as tax-exempt organizations.

Thus, for federal income tax purposes, the more traditional forms of advancement of education, such as the establishment or maintenance of educational institutions, libraries, museums, and the like, will fall within the scope of the term *educational*, leaving to the broader term *charitable* related concepts of advancement of education in the collateral sense. Nonetheless, the IRS, in ruling that an organization is educational, frequently also finds it to be charitable.[321]

For example, while the operation of a college or university is an educational undertaking, many satellite endeavors are regarded as charitable in nature. Thus,

---

[314] See § 6.3(a).
[315] See § 4.9.
[316] Rev. Rul. 75-384, 1975-2 C.B. 204.
[317] Priv. Ltr. Rul. 200929019.
[318] Public Indus., Inc. v. Comm'r, 61 T.C.M. 1626 (1991).
[319] Reg. § 1.501(c)(3)-1(d)(2).
[320] See Chapter 8.
[321] E.g., Rev. Rul. 77-272, 1977-2 C.B. 191.

the provision of scholarships is a charitable activity,[322] as are the making of low-interest loans to attend college[323] and the provision of free housing, books, and/or supplies.[324] Other charitable activities that constitute the advancement of education include publication of student journals such as law review journals,[325] maintenance of a training table for athletes,[326] provision of assistance to law students to obtain experience with public interest law firms and legal aid societies,[327] operation of a foreign student center,[328] selection of students for enrollment at foreign universities,[329] operations of an alumni association,[330] provision of work experience in selected trades and professions to high school graduates and college students,[331] the operation of interscholastic athletic programs,[332] and the provision of housing for students of a college.[333] Still other activities that are charitable because they advance education are more institutionally oriented, such as bookstores,[334] as well as organizations that accredit schools, colleges, and universities[335] or provide financial and investment assistance[336] or computer services[337] to educational organizations. One type of organization operated closely with colleges and universities, however—fraternities and sororities—generally is not regarded as being charitable or educational in nature.[338] Similarly, an organization organized and operated to hold funds and then expend them for class reunions was found not to be furthering an exempt educational purpose.[339]

Although accreditation of educational institutions is a charitable activity, a similar function with respect to individuals—certification—is not. The IRS is of the view that the primary purpose of a program of certification of individuals is to benefit the profession or other field involved and the individuals in their private capacity, with any charitable, educational, or similar "public" benefit (e.g., consumer education and protection) secondary. Thus, an organization that was recognized by the IRS as a charitable and educational entity, then merged with

---

[322] Rev. Rul. 69-257, 1969-1 C.B. 151; Rev. Rul. 66-103, 1966-1 C.B. 134. See § 7.8(b).

[323] Rev. Rul. 63-220, 1963-2 C.B. 208; Rev. Rul. 61-87, 1961-1 C.B. 191.

[324] Rev. Rul. 64-274, 1964-2 C.B. 141.

[325] Rev. Rul. 63-235, 1963-2 C.B. 610.

[326] Rev. Rul. 67-291, 1967-2 C.B. 184.

[327] Rev. Rul. 78-310, 1978-2 C.B. 173.

[328] Rev. Rul. 65-191, 1965-2 C.B. 157.

[329] Rev. Rul. 69-400, 1969-2 C.B. 114.

[330] Rev. Rul. 60-143, 1960-1 C.B. 192; Rev. Rul. 56-486, 1956-2 C.B. 309; Estate of Thayer v. Comm'r, 24 T.C. 384 (1955).

[331] Rev. Rul. 75-284, 1975-2 C.B. 202; Rev. Rul. 70-584, 1970-2 C.B. 114.

[332] Rev. Rul. 55-587, 1955-2 C.B. 261.

[333] Rev. Rul. 76-336, 1976-2 C.B. 143.

[334] Squire v. Students Book Corp., 191 F.2d 1018 (9th Cir. 1951).

[335] Rev. Rul. 74-146, 1974-1 C.B. 129.

[336] Rev. Rul. 71-529, 1971-2 C.B. 234; Rev. Rul. 67-149, 1967-1 C.B. 133.

[337] Rev. Rul. 74-614, 1974-2 C.B. 164, *amplified by* Rev. Rul. 81-29, 1981-1 C.B. 329.

[338] Rev. Rul. 69-573, 1969-2 C.B. 125; Phinney v. Dougherty, 307 F.2d 357 (5th Cir. 1962); Davison v. Comm'r, 60 F.2d 50 (2d Cir. 1932); Alumnae Chapter Beta of Clovia v. Comm'r, 46 T.C.M. 297 (1983); Johnson v. Southern Greek Hous. Corp., 307 S.E.2d 491 (Ga. 1983); Alford v. Emory Univ., 116 S.E.2d 596 (Ga. 1960). Also, Rev. Rul. 64-118, 1964-1 C.B. 182 (fraternity housing corporations); Rev. Rul. 64-117, 1964-1 C.B. 180 (student clubs). These entities are tax-exempt social clubs (see Chapter 15).

[339] Priv. Ltr. Rul. 202232018.

another organization and became primarily a certification entity, had its exemption revoked.[340] Likewise, an organization that was recognized as a charitable entity, then implemented a program of certification of individuals and businesses in the travel industry, was deprived of its exemption because the program made "them more attractive to eco-friendly consumers."[341] The IRS ruled that an organization, primarily engaged in the certification of its members' conduct of an organic farming method, could not qualify as an exempt charitable entity because the certification service provided a "substantial benefit" to its members and enables them to "gain[] a benefit over other similarly situated commercial entities."[342] If a certification program is not a charitable organization's primary function, it may be classified as an unrelated business.[343] Certification programs are, however, suitable exempt activities for business leagues.[344]

Regarding college, university, or school bookstores, it is clear that the sale to students and faculty of books, supplies, materials, athletic wear necessary for participation in the institution's athletic and physical education programs, and other items that are required by or are otherwise necessary for courses at the institution (including computer hardware and software) is an activity that is charitable in nature. Some bookstores associated with educational institutions, however, sell items that are not related to education of the students; the sale of these items is likely to be an unrelated business activity,[345] unless the sales are within the scope of the *convenience doctrine*.[346]

Colleges and universities frequently utilize affiliated nonprofit organizations in connection with the carrying out of their charitable and educational programs. These related organizations can be charitable in character. As illustrations, the IRS recognized as tax-exempt an organization that operated a book and supply store that sold items only to students and faculty of a college,[347] one that operated a cafeteria and restaurant on the campus of a university primarily for the convenience of its students and faculty,[348] and one that provided housing and food service exclusively for students and faculty of a university.[349]

For this category of tax exemption to be available, the organization must in fact engage in advancement activities. In one instance, a court rejected two organizations' claims for tax exemption based on this ground, because they provided "minimal, if any" assistance to educational and other entities.[350]

The nature of the law regarding organizations whose functions represent assistance to other organizations that are tax-exempt can shift radically where the assistance is directed to two or more exempt entities. Exempt organizations, such

---

[340] Priv. Ltr. Rul. 201906010.
[341] Priv. Ltr. Rul. 201843016.
[342] Priv. Ltr. Rul. 201327014.
[343] See § 24.5(q).
[344] See § 14.1(g).
[345] See § 24.5(a), text accompanied by note 293.
[346] See § 25.2(b).
[347] Rev. Rul. 69-538, 1969-2 C.B. 116.
[348] Rev. Rul. 58-194, 1958-1 C.B. 240.
[349] Rev. Rul. 67-217, 1967-2 C.B. 181.
[350] Univ. Med. Resident Servs. P.C. v. Comm'r, 71 T.C.M. 3130 (1996).

as colleges and universities, often turn to cooperative ventures to reduce costs and improve the quality of performance. Colleges and universities often find it productive and more efficient to share, for example, data processing or library resources.[351]

Organizations not affiliated with an institution of learning but that provide instruction may also be deemed to advance education, such as those that teach industrial skills,[352] conduct work experience programs,[353] provide apprentice training,[354] act as a clearinghouse and course coordinator for instructors and students,[355] instruct in the field of business,[356] evaluate the public service obligations of broadcasters,[357] and provide services to relieve psychological tensions and improve the mental health of children and adolescents.[358]

The advancement of education can consist of making a grant to a tax-exempt fraternity or sorority[359] for the purpose of constructing or maintaining educational facilities, such as financing of allocable construction costs of the fraternity or sorority house, maintaining a library, and funding study facilities.[360] Likewise, a grant and loan program of an educational institution to enable fraternities and sororities on or near its campus to improve the safety of their housing was ruled to be advancement of education.[361] Where the grantor is a private foundation,[362] it should be certain that the grant is a qualifying distribution[363] and not a taxable expenditure.[364]

Education may be advanced through activities such as the publication and dissemination of research,[365] maintenance of collections,[366] the provision of anthropological specimens,[367] the operation of a foreign exchange program,[368] and the operation of an honor society.[369] Likewise, the IRS determined that the provision of bibliographic information by means of a computer network to researchers at both tax-exempt and nonexempt libraries constituted the advancement of education.[370] Similarly, the IRS held that an organization formed to preserve the natural environment by acquiring ecologically significant underdeveloped land and to

---

[351] See § 7.13.

[352] Rev. Rul. 72-101, 1972-1 C.B. 144. Cf. Rev. Rul. 78-42, 1978-1 C.B. 158.

[353] Rev. Rul. 78-310, 1978-2 C.B. 173; Rev. Rul. 76-37, 1976-1 C.B. 146; Rev. Rul. 75-284, 1975-2 C.B. 202; Rev. Rul. 70-584, 1970-2 C.B. 114.

[354] Rev. Rul. 67-72, 1967-1 C.B. 125.

[355] Rev. Rul. 71-413, 1971-2 C.B. 228.

[356] Rev. Rul. 68-16, 1968-1 C.B. 246.

[357] Rev. Rul. 79-26, 1979-1 C.B. 196.

[358] Rev. Rul. 77-68, 1977-1 C.B. 142.

[359] These entities are tax-exempt by reason of IRC § 501(c)(7). See Chapter 15.

[360] E.g., Priv. Ltr. Rul. 9014061.

[361] Priv. Ltr. Rul. 200839037.

[362] See Chapter 12.

[363] See § 12.4(b).

[364] See § 12.4(e).

[365] Rev. Rul. 67-4, 1967-1 C.B. 121.

[366] Rev. Rul. 70-321, 1970-1 C.B. 129.

[367] Rev. Rul. 70-129, 1970-1 C.B. 128.

[368] Rev. Rul. 80-286, 1980-2 C.B. 179.

[369] Rev. Rul. 71-97, 1971-1 C.B. 150.

[370] Rev. Rul. 81-29, 1981-1 C.B. 329.

maintain the land or transfer it to a government conservation agency qualified for exemption in part for the reason that it was advancing education.[371]

(b) Scholarship Grants

For purposes of scholarship awards granted by a private foundation to be used for study at an educational institution, the grants must be awarded on an "objective and nondiscriminatory basis" pursuant to a procedure approved in advance by the IRS.[372] Although public charities are not subject to these requirements, the IRS stated that a "scholarship program conducted by a public charity which conforms to these standards for objectivity and educational character will ordinarily be considered to be in furtherance of exempt purposes."[373]

In this context, for grants to be considered awarded on an objective and nondiscriminatory basis, the grantees must be selected from a group of individuals who are chosen on the basis of criteria that reasonably relate to the purpose of the grant and generally are from a group that is sufficiently broad so as to constitute a charitable class.[374] Selection from a group, however, is not necessary where, taking into account the purposes of the grant, one or several individuals are selected because they are exceptionally qualified to carry out the organization's purposes or it is otherwise evident that the selection is particularly calculated to effectuate the purpose of the grant rather than to benefit particular individuals or a particular class of individuals.[375]

As noted, the criteria used in selecting the grantees must be related to the purpose of the grant. For example, in granting academic scholarships, an organization's selection criteria might include prior academic performance, performance on aptitude tests, recommendations from instructors, financial need, and the conclusion a selection committee has drawn from a personal interview as to the prospective grantee's motivation, character, ability, and potential.[376] Moreover, the individuals or group of individuals who select recipients of the grants should not be in a position to derive a private benefit, directly or indirectly, if certain potential grantees are selected instead of others.[377]

The IRS's lawyers determined that educational grants are not awarded on an objective and nondiscriminatory basis if preference in awarding the grants is accorded to relatives of the charitable organization's grant makers.[378] In this determination, IRS counsel referenced the history of the private foundation taxable expenditures regulations, stating that it was "intended that grantees could not be selected for personal reasons but rather that the selection process, including the preliminary matter of determining the composition of the class of 'candidates' for grants from which the recipients are chosen, must be based on criteria which related to the 'educational' purpose of the grant."

---

[371] Rev. Rul. 76-204, 1976-1 C.B. 152. Cf. Rev. Rul. 78-384, 1978-2 C.B. 174.
[372] IRC § 4945(g). See § 12.4(e); *Private Foundations* § 9.3(e), (f).
[373] Priv. Ltr. Rul. 200332018.
[374] See § 6.3(a).
[375] Reg. 53.4945-4(b)(2).
[376] Reg. § 53.4945-4(b)(3).
[377] Reg. § 53.4945-4(b)(4).
[378] Gen. Couns. Mem. 38954.

§ 7.9 ADVANCEMENT OF SCIENCE

The regulations accompanying the federal tax law concerning charitable organizations include among the definitions of the term *charitable* the "advancement of science."[379] The *advancement of science* includes financing of scholarships and fellowships, making of awards, advancement of knowledge through research, and dissemination of knowledge by publications, seminars, lectures, and similar activities designed to further scientific endeavors and disseminate scientific knowledge. Inasmuch as the federal tax law exemption for charitable organizations also contains the term *scientific*,[380] organizations coming within one or both of the terms *charitable* or *scientific* will qualify as tax-exempt organizations.

Thus, the IRS ruled that an organization formed to preserve the natural environment by acquiring ecologically significant underdeveloped land and to maintain the land or transfer it to a government conservation agency qualified for tax exemption in part because it was advancing science.[381] Although an organization that is deemed to be a scientific entity is often engaged in scientific research, an organization may be classified as one that advances science (or education)[382] where it publishes or otherwise distributes scientific information without having performed the underlying research.[383]

§ 7.10 ADVANCEMENT OF RELIGION

The regulations accompanying the federal tax law concerning charitable organizations provide that the term *charitable* includes the "advancement of religion."[384]

The advancement of religion has long been considered a charitable purpose, although the scope of this category of charitable endeavors is imprecise because of the separate enumeration in the federal tax law of religious activities as being in furtherance of exempt purposes.[385] The concept of *advancement of religion* includes the construction or maintenance of a church building, monument, memorial window, or burial ground, and collateral services such as the provision of music, payment of salaries to employees of religious organizations, dissemination of religious doctrines, maintenance of missions, and distribution of religious literature.[386] This category of tax exemption includes organizations the works of which extend to the advancement of particular religions, religious sects, or religious doctrines, as well as religion in general.[387]

[379] Reg. § 1.501(c)(3)-1(d)(2).
[380] See Chapter 9.
[381] Rev. Rul. 76-204, 1976-1 C.B. 152. Cf. Rev. Rul. 78-384, 1978-2 C.B. 174.
[382] See § 7.8.
[383] E.g., Gen. Couns. Mem. 38459.
[384] Reg. § 1.501(c)(3)-1(d)(2).
[385] See Chapter 10.
[386] *Restatement of Trusts* (2d ed. 1959) § 371, comment a.
[387] *Id.*, comments b, d.

Organizations that are tax-exempt as charitable entities because they advance religion also include those maintaining a church newspaper,[388] providing material for a parochial school system,[389] providing young adults with counseling,[390] and undertaking genealogical research.[391] The IRS ruled that an organization that supervised the preparation and inspection of food products prepared commercially in a particular locality to ensure that they satisfy the dietary rules of a particular religion was exempt as advancing religion.[392] An organization that provided funds for the defense of members of a religious sect in legal actions involving a state's abridgement of religious freedom was ruled exempt as a charitable organization by virtue of "promoting social welfare by defending human and civil rights secured by law,"[393] although it seems that it was also advancing religion.[394]

An organization formed and controlled by an exempt conference of churches, which borrowed funds from individuals and made mortgage loans at less than the commercial rate of interest to affiliated churches to finance the construction of church buildings, qualified as a charitable organization because it advanced religion.[395] An organization that provided traditional religious burial services, which directly support and maintain basic tenets and beliefs of religion regarding burial of its members, was ruled to advance religion.[396] Likewise, an organization that conducted weekend religious retreats, open to individuals of diverse religious denominations, at a rural lakeshore site at which the participants may enjoy recreational facilities in their limited amount of free time, qualified as an organization that advances religion.[397]

Religion may be advanced by a tax-exempt organization that operates a noncommercial broadcasting station presenting programming on religious subjects.[398] Similarly, a nonprofit religious broadcasting entity may acquire classification as an exempt charitable organization even though it operates on a commercial license, as long as it does not sell commercial or advertising time[399] or, if it does so, sells the time as an incidental part of its activities.[400]

---

[388] Rev. Rul. 68-306, 1968-1 C.B. 257. Cf. Found. for Divine Meditation, Inc. v. Comm'r, 24 T.C.M. 411 (1965), aff'd sub nom. Parker v. Comm'r, 365 F.2d 792 (8th Cir. 1966), cert. denied, 385 U.S. 1026 (1967).

[389] Rev. Rul. 68-26, 1968-1 C.B. 272.

[390] Rev. Rul. 68-72, 1968-1 C.B. 250.

[391] Rev. Rul. 71-580, 1971-2 C.B. 235.

[392] Rev. Rul. 74-575, 1974-2 C.B. 161.

[393] See § 7.11.

[394] Rev. Rul. 73-285, 1973-2 C.B. 174.

[395] Rev. Rul. 75-282, 1975-2 C.B. 201.

[396] Rev. Rul. 79-359, 1979-2 C.B. 226; also, Passaic United Hebrew Burial Ass'n, v. United States, 216 F. Supp. 500 (1963). In contrast, cemetery activities such as selling plots, markers, evergreens, crypts, vaults, and perpetual and special care services to the public do not further a charitable purpose (Linwood Cemetery Ass'n v. Comm'r, 87 T.C. 1314 (1986)). Similarly, an organization that owned, operated, and maintained a cemetery in which only members of a certain family were entitled to be buried and that was supported by assessments and contributions of the family members was found not to be operated in furtherance of one or more purposes described in IRC § 501(c)(3) (Rev. Rul. 65-6, 1965-1 C.B. 229).

[397] Rev. Rul. 77-430, 1977-2 C.B. 194.

[398] Rev. Rul. 66-220, 1966-2 C.B. 209.

[399] Rev. Rul. 68-563, 1968-2 C.B. 212.

[400] Rev. Rul. 78-385, 1978-2 C.B. 174.

The IRS determined that an organization established to provide temporary low-cost housing and related services for missionary families on furlough for recuperation or training in the United States from their assignments abroad qualified as a charitable organization acting to advance religion because the assistance to the missionaries was provided to them in their official capacities for use in furtherance of and as part of the organized religious program with which they were associated.[401] The IRS cautioned, however, that the provision of "assistance to individuals in their individual capacities solely by reason of their identification with some form of religious endeavor, such as missionary work, is not a charitable use."[402]

§ 7.11   PROMOTION OF SOCIAL WELFARE

The promotion of social welfare is one of the more indefinite categories of charitable purposes. As was observed, "[n]o attempt . . . can successfully be made to enumerate all of the purposes which fall within the scope" of this category of charitable purpose, and the question in each case is whether the "purpose is one the accomplishment of which might reasonably be held to be for the social interest of the community."[403]

The federal tax regulations that define *charitable purpose* state five types of endeavors that constitute the promotion of social welfare: activities "designed to accomplish any of the above [charitable] purposes," "lessen neighborhood tensions," "eliminate prejudice and discrimination," "defend human and civil rights secured by law," and "combat community deterioration and juvenile delinquency."[404]

The types of organizations that are tax-exempt as charitable organizations because they operate to eliminate prejudice and discrimination are illustrated by three rulings issued by the IRS. One of these organizations worked to educate the public about integrated housing and conducted programs to facilitate the integration of neighborhoods.[405] Another entity conducted investigations and research to obtain information regarding discrimination against minority groups in connection with housing and public accommodations.[406] The third operated to advance equal job opportunities in a particular community for qualified workers discriminated against because of race or creed.[407]

An organization qualified as a tax-exempt charitable organization because it functioned to eliminate discrimination against members of minorities seeking employment in the construction trades by recruiting, educating, and counseling

---

[401] Rev. Rul. 75-434, 1975-2 C.B. 205. Also, World Family Corp. v. Comm'r, 81 T.C. 958 (1983).

[402] The IRS ruled that an organization formed to aid immigrants in the United States qualified as a tax-exempt charitable organization (Rev. Rul. 76-205, 1976-1 C.B. 154).

[403] *Restatement of Trusts* (2d ed. 1959) § 371, comment a. One of the sources of confusion in this area is use of the term *social welfare* to reference organizations that are tax-exempt by reason of IRC § 501(c)(4) (see Chapter 13).

[404] Reg. § 1.501(c)(3)-1(d)(2).

[405] Rev. Rul. 68-655, 1968-2 C.B. 213.

[406] Rev. Rul. 68-438, 1968-2 C.B. 609.

[407] Rev. Rul. 68-70, 1968-1 C.B. 248.

workers; providing technical assistance to lawyers involved in litigation to enforce workers' rights; and acting as a court-appointed monitor after successful lawsuits.[408] Combating community deterioration, in furthering charitable purposes, involves remedial action leading to the elimination of the physical, economic, and social causes of the deterioration,[409] such as by purchasing and renovating deteriorating residences and selling or leasing them to low-income families on a nonprofit basis,[410] and by operating a self-help home-building program.[411] Likewise, a nonprofit organization formed to relieve poverty, eliminate prejudice, reduce neighborhood tensions, and combat community deterioration through a program of financial assistance in the form of low-cost or long-term loans to, or the purchase of equity interests in, various business enterprises in economically depressed areas was held to be an exempt charitable entity,[412] as was a nonprofit organization that purchased blighted land in an economically depressed community, converted the land into an industrial park, and encouraged industrial enterprises to locate facilities in the park to provide employment opportunities for low-income residents in the area.[413] The charitable activity of combating community deterioration can be present "whether or not the community is in a state of decline."[414]

Discrimination in this context is not confined to racial discrimination. Thus, an organization formed to promote equal rights for women in employment and other economic contexts was ruled to be tax-exempt as promoting social welfare by eliminating prejudice and discrimination.[415] Also, an organization created to aid immigrants to the United States in overcoming social, cultural, and economic problems by personal counseling or referral to appropriate agencies was granted federal income tax exemption on this basis.[416]

The position of the IRS once was that the phrase "human and civil rights secured by law" refers only to the individual liberties, freedoms, and privileges involving human dignity that are specially guaranteed either by the U.S. Constitution or by a special statutory provision coming directly within the scope of the Thirteenth or Fourteenth Amendment or some other comparable constitutional

---

[408] Rev. Rul. 75-285, 1975-2 C.B. 203.

[409] Rev. Rul. 67-6, 1967-1 C.B. 135.

[410] Rev. Rul. 68-17, 1968-1 C.B. 247. Also, Rev. Rul. 76-408, 1976-2 C.B. 145 (nonprofit organization that provided interest-free home repair loans in a badly deteriorated urban residential area to low-income homeowners who are unable to obtain loans elsewhere was held to be charitable); Rev. Rul. 70-585, 1970-2 C.B. 115 (nonprofit housing organization created to aid low- and moderate-income families was ruled to be charitable).

[411] Rev. Rul. 67-138, 1967-1 C.B. 129.

[412] Rev. Rul. 74-587, 1974-2 C.B. 162.

[413] Rev. Rul. 76-419, 1976-2 C.B. 146. By contrast, an organization formed to increase business patronage in a deteriorated area by providing information on the area's shopping opportunities, local transportation, and accommodations was held to not be operated exclusively for charitable purposes (Rev. Rul. 77-111, 1977-1 C.B. 144).

[414] Rev. Rul. 76-147, 1976-1 C.B. 151. This line of law (this note and *supra*, notes 409–413) supports the concept that historic preservation (preserving the traditions, architecture, and appearance of a community) is a charitable undertaking. There are limits to this concept, as illustrated by an IRS ruling that promotion of a historical area for the purpose of benefiting the businesses within the area is not a charitable activity (Priv. Ltr. Rul. 202110031).

[415] Rev. Rul. 72-228, 1972-1 C.B. 148.

[416] Rev. Rul. 76-205, 1976-1 C.B. 154.

provision, or that otherwise fall within the protection of the Constitution by reason of their long-established recognition in the common law as rights that are essential to the orderly pursuit of happiness by free people. Consequently, tax exemption as a charitable organization was denied by the agency to an organization whose primary activity was providing legal assistance to employees whose rights were violated under compulsory unionization arrangements, on the theory that its criterion for intervention in a case is whether there is a grievance arising out of a compulsory union membership requirement, and that the right to work is not a protected constitutional right. A court disagreed, however, holding that the right to work is an individual liberty involving a human dignity that is guaranteed by the Constitution, and is therefore a human and civil right secured by law. The organization was thus ruled to be tax-exempt as a charitable entity.[417]

One of the ways in which an organization can qualify for tax exemption as a charitable entity is by preserving the historic or architectural character of a community, which promotes social welfare by combating community deterioration. This can be accomplished, for example, with a program of acquiring historic structures, restoring them, and selling them subject to restrictive covenants.[418]

Regarding the promotion of social welfare by combating juvenile delinquency, the IRS found the activity of an organization that promoted sports for children to be tax-exempt. This organization developed, promoted, and regulated a sport for individuals under 18 years of age, and generally provided a recreational outlet for young people.[419] Similarly, an organization that provided teaching of a particular sport to children by holding clinics conducted by qualified instructors and by providing free instruction, equipment, and facilities was found to be combating juvenile delinquency and thus to be charitable in nature.[420]

Obviously, these five categories of social welfare activities tend to overlap. Thus, one organization that was ruled to be engaged in the elimination of prejudice and discrimination was also found to operate to "lessen neighborhood tensions" and "prevent deterioration of neighborhoods,"[421] while another was ruled to also act to lessen neighborhood tensions and to defend "human and civil rights secured by law."[422] An organization that counseled residents of a community and city officials in the best use of vacant lots in order to eliminate potential gathering places for "unruly elements" was held to be engaged in combating juvenile

---

[417] Nat'l Right to Work Legal Defense & Educ. Found., Inc. v. United States, 487 F. Supp. 801 (E.D.N.C. 1979). An organization providing cyber security services to nongovernmental organizations and other entities in foreign countries tried to convince the IRS that its activities were charitable because they defend human and civil rights secured by law, but the IRS countered with the facts that (1) free speech rights under the U.S. Constitution do not extend to residents and citizens of foreign countries, and (2) the United Nations Universal Declaration of Human Rights, which encompasses international access to the Internet, is not law (Priv. Ltr. Rul. 201405022).

[418] Rev. Rul. 86-49, 1986-1 C.B. 243; Rev. Rul. 75-470, 1975-2 C.B. 207. A mobile home park is not a *community* for this purpose (Priv. Ltr. Rul. 201014068).

[419] Rev. Rul. 80-215, 1980-2 C.B. 174.

[420] Rev. Rul. 65-2, 1965-1 C.B. 227. Cf. Rev. Rul. 70-4, 1970-1 C.B. 126 (holding that an organization promoting and regulating a sport for amateurs qualified under IRC § 501(c)(4) (see Chapter 13) but not under IRC § 501(c)(3) because it directed its activities to all members of the public irrespective of age).

[421] Rev. Rul. 68-655, 1968-2 C.B. 613.

[422] Rev. Rul. 68-438, 1968-2 C.B. 609. Also, Rev. Rul. 73-285, 1973-2 C.B. 174.

delinquency, as well as, because of other activities, the elimination of prejudice and discrimination, the lessening of neighborhood tensions, and the combating of community deterioration.[423]

There can also be an overlap of categories of charitable organizations where they operate to eliminate prejudice and discrimination and to educate the public. Thus, an organization educating the public as to how to invest in housing made available to the public on a nondiscriminatory basis was ruled to be tax-exempt.[424] Similar illustrations include an organization that informed the public, through lectures and discussions, of the advantages of nondiscriminatory hiring[425] and an organization that operated programs to prevent panic selling from resulting integration of a neighborhood.[426]

As noted, the regulation defining *charitable* endeavors states that the promotion of social welfare includes activities that seek to accomplish otherwise charitable ends. By nature, these activities tend to be characterized as lessening the burdens of government.[427] Thus, an organization created to assist local governments of a metropolitan region by studying and recommending regional policies directed at the solution of mutual problems was held to be involved in both the combating of community deterioration and lessening of the burdens of government.[428] Yet, social welfare activities of this nature may traverse the gamut of charitable works, as illustrated by the case of an organization that made awards to individuals who have made outstanding contributions and achievements in the field of commerce, communications, creative arts and crafts, education, finance, government, law, medicine and health, performing arts, religion, science, social services, sports and athletics, technology, and transportation.[429]

§ 7.12 PROMOTION OF ARTS

Organizations devoted to promotion of the arts may qualify for tax exemption as charitable entities. For example, an organization that functioned to rouse and give direction to local interest in a community for the establishment of a repertory theater qualified as a charitable entity.[430] The repertory theater company itself can be charitable in nature.[431] This type of charitable activity was initially recognized by the IRS as being "cultural," with emphasis on the musical arts.[432]

---

[423] Rev. Rul. 68-15, 1968-1 C.B. 244. Also, Rev. Rul. 81-284, 1981-2 C.B. 130; Rev. Rul. 76-419, 1976-2 C.B. 146; Rev. Rul. 74-587, 1974-2 C.B. 162. Cf. Rev. Rul. 77-111, 1977-1 C.B. 144.

[424] Rev. Rul. 67-250, 1967-2 C.B. 182.

[425] Rev. Rul. 68-70, 1968-1 C.B. 248.

[426] Rev. Rul. 68-655, 1968-2 C.B. 613.

[427] See § 7.7.

[428] Rev. Rul. 70-79, 1970-1 C.B. 127.

[429] Rev. Rul. 66-146, 1966-1 C.B. 136; Bok v. McHugh, 42 F.2d 616 (3d Cir. 1930).

[430] Rev. Rul. 64-174, 1964-1 C.B. 183.

[431] Rev. Rul. 64-175, 1964-1 C.B. 185.

[432] S.M. 176, 1 C.B. 147 (1919); I.T. 1475, 1-2 C.B. 184 (1922).

One feature of this aspect of charitable endeavor is the effort akin to the advancement of education,[433] that is, to promote public appreciation of one or more of the arts. Thus, an organization formed to perpetuate group harmony singing and to educate the public as to this type of music was ruled to be tax-exempt.[434] Similarly, an organization formed to promote an appreciation of jazz music as an American art form was held to be an exempt organization,[435] as was a nonprofit school of contemporary dancing.[436] This exemption for charitable entities may likewise extend to an organization that seeks to encourage the creative arts and scholarship by making grants to needy artists,[437] by promoting interest in and appreciation of contemporary symphonic and chamber music,[438] or by sponsoring public exhibits of artworks by unknown but promising artists.[439]

Other organizations are tax-exempt because they function to promote and encourage the talent and ability of young artists. The scope of types of these activities include the training of young musicians in concert technique,[440] the promotion of filmmaking by conducting festivals to provide unknown independent filmmakers with opportunities to display their films,[441] and the encouragement of musicians and composers through commissions and scholarships and the opportunity for students to play with accomplished professional musicians.[442] Organizations in this category frequently promote (and finance) their charitable function through the sponsorship of public festivals, concerts, exhibits, and other productions.[443] In nearly all of these instances, the artists are amateurs, performing solely for the onstage experience or to enable the charitable organization to meet expenses.

Organizations operated to promote the arts, which otherwise qualify as charitable entities, may find themselves engaging in an activity the IRS regards as serving a private interest. Thus, while the preservation of classical music programming can be a charitable purpose,[444] an organization that undertook a variety of activities to enable a for-profit radio station to continue broadcasting classical music was denied tax exemption.[445] Likewise, although the displaying of artworks often is a charitable activity,[446] an organization will not achieve exemption as a charitable entity where it sells the artworks it exhibits and remits the proceeds to

[433] See § 7.8.
[434] Rev. Rul. 66-46, 1966-1 C.B. 133.
[435] Rev. Rul. 65-271, 1965-2 C.B. 161.
[436] Rev. Rul. 65-270, 1965-2 C.B. 160.
[437] Rev. Rul. 66-103, 1966-1 C.B. 134.
[438] Rev. Rul. 79-369, 1979-2 C.B. 226.
[439] Rev. Rul. 66-178, 1966-1 C.B. 138.
[440] Rev. Rul. 67-392, 1967-2 C.B. 191.
[441] Rev. Rul. 75-471, 1975-2 C.B. 207.
[442] Rev. Rul. 65-271, 1965-2 C.B. 161.
[443] E.g., Priv. Ltr. Rul. 9217001.
[444] Rev. Rul. 64-175, 1964-1 C.B. 185.
[445] Rev. Rul. 76-206, 1976-1 C.B. 154.
[446] Goldsboro Art League, Inc. v. Comm'r, 75 T.C. 337 (1980) (where the artworks displayed were selected by jury procedures and the organization maintained the only art gallery in the geographic area); Rev. Rul. 66-178, 1966-1 C.B. 138.

the artists.[447] The fact that exhibited artworks are available for sale, however, will not necessarily deprive the organization sponsoring the show of exemption as a charitable entity.[448]

Status as tax-exempt charitable organizations has been accorded organizations that sponsor professional presentations, such as plays, musicals, and concerts. The chief rationale for extending exemption to these organizations is that they operate to foster the development in a community of an appreciation for the dramatic and musical arts, such as by staging theatrical productions that are not otherwise available.[449] At the same time, these exempt theaters may be perceived as placing the commercial theaters in the same locale at a competitive disadvantage. Defenders of the exempt cultural centers claim that they champion theatrical presentations that otherwise would never be produced, while their critics insist that they are frequently presenting popular entertainment in unfair competition with privately owned theaters. A court discussed the distinctions between exempt performing arts organizations and commercial theaters.[450]

§ 7.13 CONSORTIA

Tax-exempt organizations frequently utilize cooperative ventures to further their purposes.

(a) General Principles

The early position of the IRS toward cooperative venturing by or for charitable (including educational) organizations was relatively favorable. This is reflected in an IRS ruling concerning an organization that was created to construct and maintain a building to house member agencies of a community chest.[451] Citing the concept that the "performance of a particular activity that is not inherently charitable may nonetheless further a charitable purpose,"[452] the IRS ruled that the organization was exempt as a charitable entity, emphasizing the low rental rates and the close relationship between its purposes and functions and those of the tenant organizations.[453]

The contemporary state of the law in this regard, however, is that these cooperative ventures are likely to be nonexempt entities, even where the venture

---

[447] St. Louis Science Fiction Ltd. v. Comm'r, 49 T.C.M. 1126 (1985) (where the organization did not apply any controls to ensure the quality of artworks sold, and the "tone" of its annual convention was predominantly social and recreational); Rev. Rul. 76-152, 1976-1 C.B. 151. Also, Rev. Rul. 71-395, 1971-2 C.B. 228.

[448] Cleveland Creative Arts Guild v. Comm'r, 50 T.C.M. 272 (1985) (where the organization's art sales activity was found to be a means to the end of increasing public appreciation of the arts); Rev. Rul. 78-131, 1978-2 C.B. 156.

[449] Rev. Rul. 73-45, 1973-1 C.B. 220.

[450] Plumstead Theatre Soc'y, Inc. v. Comm'r, 74 T.C. 1324, 1332–33 (1980), aff'd, 675 F.2d 244 (9th Cir. 1982).

[451] Rev. Rul. 69-572, 1969-2 C.B. 119.

[452] Rev. Rul. 67-4, 1967-1 C.B. 121. See, e.g., § 6.3(b).

[453] Also, Rev. Rul. 64-182, 1964-1 C.B. 186; Rev. Rul. 58-147, 1958-2 C.B. 275.

is controlled by and performs a function for its members that each tax-exempt institution would otherwise have to undertake for itself without adverse tax consequences. The IRS has two exceptions to this policy, in that exemption as a charitable organization will be granted where the consortium conducts substantive programs that are inherently exempt in nature[454] or where a substantial part of the organization's revenue is derived from outside sources thereby allowing the organization to provide services at substantially below cost (the *donative element test*).[455] The agency bases its position on a passage in the regulations accompanying the federal tax rules pertaining to feeder organizations.[456] The IRS policy toward cooperative ventures had, for many years, been rejected in the courts on nearly every occasion when it was considered,[457] and Congress had legislated in this area, contravening the IRS's policy three times.[458]

The direction of the law regarding tax exemption for consortia began to shift after the U.S. Tax Court considered the issue. A 1980 case involved a cooperative hospital laundry service owned and operated by exempt hospitals. Finding the regulations under the feeder organization rules to have the force of law because of long-standing congressional awareness of them, and concluding that the legislative history of related statutes evidenced congressional intent to not allow exemption for hospital-controlled laundries, the court found that the hospital laundry service organization was a feeder organization and thus not exempt from taxation.[459] Because of the emphasis placed on this legislative history, however, it was not clear whether consortia other than hospital laundry enterprises would receive like treatment by the Tax Court. Shortly after the Tax Court reached this decision, the Third,[460] Ninth,[461] and Sixth Circuit courts of appeal arrived at the same conclusion.[462]

Despite this policy, the IRS recognized the necessity and utility of cooperative endeavors in the field of higher education. Thus, the IRS stated that "[m]any activities normally carried on by colleges and universities can be more effectively

---

[454] Rev. Rul. 74-614, 1974-2 C.B. 164, *amplified by* Rev. Rul. 81-29, 1981-1 C.B. 329.

[455] Rev. Rul. 72-369, 1972-2 C.B. 245; Rev. Rul. 71-529, 1971-2 C.B. 234. A corollary policy of the IRS is that, where neither of the exceptions is present, the provision of services by one tax-exempt organization to one or more other exempt (or nonexempt) organizations may be the conduct of an unrelated trade or business (see Chapters 24, 25) (Rev. Rul. 69-528, 1969-2 C.B. 127). However, see § 24.5(k).

[456] Rev. Rul. 69-528, 1969-2 C.B. 127. The feeder organization rules are discussed in § 28.14.

[457] Hospital Bur. of Standards & Supplies v. United States, 158 F. Supp. 560 (Ct. Cl. 1958); United Hosp. Servs., Inc. v. United States, 384 F. Supp. 766 (S.D. Ind. 1974); Hospital Central Servs. Ass'n v. United States, 77-2 U.S.T.C. ¶ 9601 (W.D. Wash. 1977); Metropolitan Detroit Area Hosp. Servs., Inc. v. United States, 445 F. Supp. 857 (E.D. Mich. 1978); Northern Calif. Central Servs. Inc. v. United States, 591 F.2d 620 (Ct. Cl. 1979); Community Hosp. Servs., Inc. v. United States, 79-1 U.S.T.C. ¶ 9301 (E.D. Mich. 1979); HCSC-Laundry v. United States, 473 F. Supp. 250 (E.D. Pa. 1979).

[458] IRC §§ 501(e), 501(f), 513(e).

[459] Associated Hosp. Servs., Inc. v. Comm'r, 74 T.C. 213 (1980), *aff'd, unrep. dec.* (5th Cir. 1981).

[460] HCSC-Laundry v. United States, 624 F.2d 428 (3d Cir. 1980), *rev'g* 473 F. Supp. 250 (E.D. Pa. 1979), *aff'd*, 450 U.S. 1 (1981).

[461] Hospital Central Servs. Ass'n v. United States, 623 F.2d 611 (9th Cir. 1980), *cert. denied*, 450 U.S. 911 (1980), *rev'g* 77-2 U.S.T.C. ¶ 9601 (W.D. Wash. 1977). Also, Community Hosp. Servs., Inc. v. United States, 81-1 U.S.T.C. ¶ 9198 (6th Cir. 1981), *rev'g* 79-1 U.S.T.C. ¶ 9301 (E.D. Mich. 1979).

[462] Metropolitan Detroit Area Hosp. Servs. v. United States, 634 F.2d 330 (6th Cir. 1980), *cert. denied*, 450 U.S. 1031 (1980), *rev'g* 445 F. Supp. 857 (E.D. Mich. 1978).

accomplished through the combined efforts of a group of such institutions" and that these associations "aid and promote the educational endeavors of their members and interpret to the public the aims, functions, and needs of the institutions, with a view to better understanding and cooperation."[463] The IRS subscribed to this view in the intervening years.[464]

The IRS ruled that an organization whose members are educational (including some proprietary) institutions qualified as a tax-exempt charitable organization because it accredits these institutions.[465] The rationale for exemption was that the organization advanced education and thus was charitable in nature;[466] it engaged in activities that "support and advance education by providing significant incentive for maintaining a high quality educational program."

Similarly, the IRS accorded charitable entity status to an organization controlled by a tax-exempt conference of churches, where its purpose was to issue mortgages to the churches to enable them to finance the construction of church buildings.[467] The rationale for exemption was that the organization was advancing religion.[468] The making of loans is not, of course, an inherently religious activity; rather, exemption was derived from the fact that the loans were made at lower than commercial interest rates to churches of the conference to enable them to construct buildings for religious purposes at reduced cost.

Also, the IRS granted recognition of tax-exempt charitable status to a consortium of counties located in the same state.[469] This exemption was accorded on the ground that the organization's activities contribute to the "more efficient operation of county government." Efficiency of operation is, as noted, one of the principal reasons for the establishment and operation of consortia.

Further, it has long been the position of the IRS that an organization formed and operated for the purpose of providing financial assistance to organizations that are regarded as charitable is itself qualified for tax exemption as a charitable entity.[470]

(b) Adjunct Theory

A federal court had occasion to reaffirm its original position concerning consortia,[471] stating that "[t]his court has held in the past that where one organization provides a service which is necessary and indispensable to the operations of another, the first

---

[463] Rev. Rul. 63-15, 1963-1 C.B. 189.

[464] E.g., Rev. Rul. 63-208, 1963-2 C.B. 468; Rev. Rul. 63-209, 1963-2 C.B. 469 (where offices formed by a tax-exempt religious entity to administer its statewide parochial school system and a convent to house teachers in parochial schools organized by the religious institution were held to function as integral parts of the educational activities of the schools); Rev. Rul. 64-286, 1964-2 C.B. 401 (holding that the general board of a church that made purchases for the exclusive use of parochial schools and missions shared the exempt status of the primary educational organization); Rev. Rul. 71-553, 1971-2 C.B. 404 (where a student government association was ruled to be an integral part of a university).

[465] Rev. Rul. 74-146, 1974-1 C.B. 129.

[466] See § 7.8.

[467] Rev. Rul. 75-282, 1975-2 C.B. 201.

[468] See § 7.10.

[469] Rev. Rul. 75-359, 1975-2 C.B. 79.

[470] Rev. Rul. 67-149, 1967-1 C.B. 133; Rev. Rul. 78-310, 1978-2 C.B. 173.

[471] See *supra* note 457.

will take on the tax status of the second."[472] Invoking an *adjunct theory*, the court added that "[t]hese cases clearly indicate that where one organization serves as a mere adjunct for a primary organization by providing services which are essential to the functioning of the primary organization and which would be normally performed by it, the adjunct will acquire the tax status of the primary company."[473]

The adjunct theory was initially invoked by a federal court of appeals in 1934.[474] The first application of this theory to adjunct entities of charitable organizations occurred in 1951. In that year, another federal appellate court reviewed the tax status of a corporation organized to operate a bookstore and restaurant on the campus of a tax-exempt college. Despite the fact that these operations were not inherently charitable or educational activities, the court of appeals invoked the rationale of the adjunct theory, writing that the "business enterprise in which [the] taxpayer is engaged obviously bears a close and intimate relationship to the functioning of the [c]ollege itself."[475] The appellate court concluded that this corporation was entitled to exemption as an educational organization.

The adjunct theory was subsequently espoused by a court, which concluded that a museum was a tax-exempt educational organization because it was an integral part of and a valuable adjunct to a public school system.[476] At issue in this case was the availability of the pre-1969 additional charitable contribution deduction of 10 percent of a taxpayer's adjusted gross income for contributions to operating educational institutions that engage in the presentation of formal instruction.[477] The court concluded that gifts to the museum qualified for the bonus charitable contribution deduction, even though the museum itself did not satisfy the statutory requirements, because it was an integral part of the school system and thus was clothed with the educational status of the system.[478]

The adjunct theory, however, does not have broad application. As a court stated, the "adjunct doctrine has developed in unique factual settings which when reconciled do not stand for a general principle capable of eroding the statutory limitations on exemptions."[479]

(c)   Cooperative Arrangements

One of the principal reasons that the government has opposed tax-exempt status for a consortium entity is the fear that an organization that is not formed and controlled by charitable entities will by its own choice confine its services to charitable

---

[472] Trustees of Graceland Cemetery Improvement Fund v. United States, 515 F.2d 763, 770 (Ct. Cl. 1975).

[473] *Id.* at 771.

[474] Produce Exchange Stock Clearing Ass'n v. Helvering, 71 F.2d 142 (2d Cir. 1934).

[475] Squire v. Students Book Corp., 191 F.2d 1018, 1020 (9th Cir. 1951). Also, Rev. Rul. 78-41, 1978-1 C.B. 148.

[476] Brundage v. Comm'r, 54 T.C. 1468 (1970). Cf. Miller v. United States, 527 F.2d 231 (8th Cir. 1975).

[477] See IRC § 170(b)(1)(A)(ii).

[478] Also, Rosehill Cemetery Co. v. United States, 285 F. Supp. 21 (N.D. Ill. 1968); Industrial Aid for the Blind v. Comm'r, 73 T.C. 96 (1979).

[479] Knights of Columbus Bldg. Ass'n of Stamford, CT, Inc. v. United States, 88-1 U.S.T.C. ¶ 9336 (D. Conn. 1988) (holding that an organization, while closely affiliated with and principally holding title to property for a tax-exempt organization, could not qualify for exempt status under the adjunct theory because it failed to meet the requirements for exempt title-holding corporations under IRC § 501(c)(2); see § 19.2(a)).

entities and thereby itself acquire exempt charitable status, even where the provision of its services is in competition with commercial enterprises. Of course, this factual situation is easily distinguishable from the normal consortium arrangement, but this concern nonetheless persists.

The government's concerns in this regard were presumably largely alleviated by a court decision holding that an organization that planned to offer consulting services for a fee to a class of nonprofit (but not all tax-exempt) organizations did not qualify as an exempt charitable entity but was taxable as a business.[480] Nonetheless, the IRS reviewed the tax-exempt status of an organization whose members were exempt universities and municipal libraries; its operation of a computer network to facilitate exchange of information among its membership was ruled to be an exempt charitable function.[481] The IRS ruled that this organization could extend its services to private businesses in furtherance of its exempt information-sharing functions.[482]

The legislative history of the CommonFund provision[483] stated that it applies only to cooperative organizations formed and controlled by the participating institutions themselves, rather than to private organizations furnishing the same services, even where those services might be made available only to educational organizations. Congress stated that, in enacting this statute, "it is not intended that any inference be drawn as to the exempt status of other organizations formed by educational institutions or by other charities on their behalf to carry out their normal functions in a cooperative manner."[484]

Congress changed the law in this area in one respect in 1976.[485] It had been the position of the IRS that income derived by a tax-exempt hospital from providing services to other exempt hospitals constitutes unrelated business income to the hospital providing the services, on the rationale that the provision of services to other hospitals is not an activity that is substantially related to the exempt purposes of the provider hospital.[486] Congress acted to override this position in the case of small hospitals where an exempt hospital[487] provides services only to other exempt hospitals, as long as each of the recipient hospitals has facilities to serve no more than 100 inpatients and the services are consistent with the recipient hospitals' exempt purposes if performed by them on their own behalf.[488] This law change was implemented to enable a number of small hospitals to receive services from a single institution instead of providing them directly or creating an exempt organization to provide the services.

[480] B.S.W. Group, Inc. v. Comm'r, 70 T.C. 352 (1978).
[481] Rev. Rul. 74-614, 1974-2 C.B. 164.
[482] Priv. Ltr. Rul. 7951134.
[483] IRC § 501(f). See § 11.5.
[484] S. Rep. No. 93-888, at 3 (1974).
[485] IRC § 513(e). See § 25.2(g).
[486] Rev. Rul. 69-633, 1969-2 C.B. 121. The IRS, however, held that the provision by a tax-exempt organization of administrative services for unrelated exempt organizations constitutes the performance of an unrelated business (Tech. Adv. Mem. 8032039), which held open the possibility that services to related organizations may be considered related activities. This aspect of the law has been clarified (see § 24.5(k)).
[487] IRC § 170(b)(1)(A)(iii). See §§ 7.6(a), 12.3(a).
[488] The services provided must be confined to those described in IRC § 501(e)(1)(A). See § 11.4.

The U.S. Supreme Court held that a cooperative hospital laundry organization did not qualify for tax exemption as a charitable entity.[489] Such an organization is, of course, a type of consortium. The Court ruled in opposition to exemption in this context, however, because the facts necessitated application of the rules concerning cooperative hospital organizations[490]—a unique set of circumstances— and not because the tax law is generally in opposition to exemption for consortia. Thus, for example, a court held that an organization, operated on a cooperative basis, was entitled to exempt status as a charitable organization because it was controlled by its member exempt organizations (libraries) and provided indispensable program and administrative services to them.[491] The court stated that "where a group of tax exempt organizations forms a cooperative to provide services exclusively to those tax exempt organizations, and the services provided are necessary and indispensable to the operations of the tax exempt organizations, the cooperative is a tax exempt organization."[492]

§ 7.14 FUNDRAISING ORGANIZATIONS

Charitable activity is considered, by the IRS and the courts, to take place where contributions are made to an organization and that organization makes grants to other charities. That is, the law focuses on the grantmaking component rather than the process used to generate the grant funds. This is the basis of tax exemption for, as examples, private foundations and public charities that maintain donor-advised funds.[493]

(a) General Principles

The IRS observed that its records indicate that "over 12,000 exempt organizations are listed as having fund raising as a major purpose," adding that "it seems logical that there are tens of thousands of additional organizations that engage in fund raising programs to various degrees."[494] And that was written in 1982.

Indeed, it has been IRS policy since 1924 that a nonprofit organization that only carries on operations that involve receipt of contributions (and perhaps

---

[489] HCSC-Laundry v. United States, 450 U.S. 1 (1981).

[490] See § 11.4.

[491] Council for Bibliographic & Information Technologies v. Comm'r, 63 T.C.M. 3186 (1992).

[492] Id. at 3188. This court concluded that the Supreme Court decision, in HCSC-Laundry v. United States, 450 U.S. 1 (1981), is confined to cooperative hospital organizations, citing Chart, Inc. v. United States, 491 F. Supp. 10 (D.D.C. 1979), rev'd, 652 F.2d 195 (D.C. Cir. 1981).

This "necessary and indispensable" analysis was applied in a case involving an organization providing insurance services to its member charitable organizations; in denying tax exemption on this ground, the court wrote that "providing insurance to 487 unrelated exempt organizations is not an activity that is vital to each member's exempt purpose" and that such a service "neither goes to the essence of running each of . . . [the] member organizations nor constitutes an activity which would normally be performed by the member organizations" (Nonprofits' Ins. Alliance of Cal. v. United States, 94-2 U.S.T.C. ¶ 50,593 (Cl. Ct. 1994)). See, however, § 11.6.

[493] See §§ 12.1, 12.5.

[494] "Fund Raising," Topic L, IRS Exempt Organizations Continuing Professional Education Text for FY 1982 (1982 EO CPE Text), at 1.

investment income) and distributions of its income to public charities is eligible to receive recognition of tax exemption as a charitable entity.[495] This principle was restated in 1967, holding that an organization that meets this description qualifies for tax exemption as a charitable entity: "An organization was formed for the purpose of providing financial assistance to several different types of organizations which are exempt from Federal income tax under section 501(c)(3) of the Internal Revenue Code of 1954. It carries on no operations other than to receive contributions and incidental investment income and to make distributions of income to such exempt organizations at periodic intervals."[496]

In a 1960s case considered by the IRS, a resulting technical advice memorandum stated that "[c]haritable organizations have traditionally engaged in fund raising activities as a means of raising funds to carry out their charitable purposes." This TAM concluded: "The mere fact that an organization derives its income primarily from such fund-raising activity is not considered to defeat either the primary purposes or the substantial activity tests of section 1.501(c)(3)-1(c) of the Income Tax Regulations."[497]

Another case reviewed by the IRS in the 1970s involved a "social fund raiser," the objective of which was "to raise money for charity through members, family and friends sponsoring socials, lunches and dinners, and donations for the affairs to be given for various charitable organizations." The entity owned a clubhouse where these events (including birthday parties) took place. In a TAM, the IRS wrote: "Many charitable organizations do not engage in active charitable undertakings themselves, but rather assist the work of religious, charitable, educational or similar organizations by contributing money to them," adding that "[p]roviding financial assistance to such organizations is a charitable activity justifying exemption."[498]

In another case from the 1970s, an organization ran a beer "kegger" for the benefit of local charities. The parties produced a considerable profit. The IRS ruled that the organization qualified for exemption as a charitable entity.[499]

An early version of the *Exempt Organizations Handbook* contained this observation: "Many charitable foundations do not engage in active charitable undertakings themselves, but rather assist the work of religious, charitable, educational, or similar organizations by contributing money to them. The foundation's funds may be dedicated to purposes, as broad as but no broader than, the purposes set out in IRC [§] 501(c)(3). These foundations are charitable in the broad sense of the word."[500]

A court observed: "It seems well settled that an organization need not engage in a functional charitable activity to be organized and operated for charitable purposes within the meaning of section 501(c)(3). . . . Such charitable purposes may be accomplished solely by providing funds to other exempt organizations."[501]

---

[495] I.T. 1945, III-1 C.B. 273 (1924).

[496] Rev. Rul. 67-149, 1967-1 C.B. 133.

[497] 1982 EO CPE Text, *supra* note 494, at 6–7.

[498] *Id.* at 9.

[499] *Id.* at 9–10.

[500] *Id.* at 33.

[501] Golf Life World Entertainment Golf Championship, Inc. v. United States, 65-1 U.S.T.C. ¶ 9174 (S.D. Cal. 1964).

Another court stated: "In determining whether an activity is organized for educational purposes and so exempt from social security taxes, the purposes for which it spends its income and not the means whereby it obtains income are conclusive."[502]

(b)   Application of Commensurate Test

Because the IRS and the courts regard grantmaking to charities as charitable activity, the IRS has concerns where the grantor organization is distributing what it regards as insubstantial amounts. The IRS has termed these entities "unproductive" fundraising organizations.[503] The IRS measures this productivity by means of application of the *commensurate test.*

Pursuant to the commensurate test, the IRS assesses whether a charitable organization is maintaining program activities that are commensurate in scope with its financial resources.[504] In the facts underlying an IRS 1964 pronouncement, the organization derived most of its income from rents. The organization, nonetheless, was successful in preserving its tax-exempt status as a charity because it satisfied the test by engaging in sufficient charitable functions notwithstanding the extent of its rental activities.[505]

The IRS often combines application of the commensurate test with its consideration of the unrelated business rules, usually leading to a favorable outcome for the organization involved when the activity, considered by the organization to be fundraising, is protected from unrelated business income taxation by reason of a statutory exception.[506] As the IRS has said, taken in conjunction with these exceptions, the "Service has often granted IRC 501(c)(3) exemption status to the typical fund raiser if there has been a sufficient turnover of funds to charity."[507]

The IRS has said that, assuming the fundraising activity is not an unrelated business, tax exemption "cannot be legally denied under IRC [§] 501(c)(3)" if the agency "find[s] that the fund raising organizations through these events produce commensurately in scope with their financial resources." "This is true," the IRS added, "because a commensurately producing typical fund raising organization cannot be held to be organized or operated for the primary purpose of operating a trade or business for purposes of Reg. [§] 1.501(c)(3)-1(e)."[508]

If an organization engages in a form of fundraising but makes few or no distributions for charitable purposes, the organization cannot be exempt as a charitable entity, by reason of the commensurate test. For example, an organization conducted bingo games as its principal activity; its stated purpose was to conduct these games and provide financial assistance for the care of needy children and children's charities. The organization made grants to charitable entities that were insubstantial when compared to the gross receipts from the bingo games. A court held that this

---

[502] Southeastern Fair Ass'n v. United States, 52 F. Supp. 219 (Ct. Cl. 1943).

[503] 1982 EO CPE Text, *supra* note 494, at 54.

[504] See § 4.7.

[505] Rev. Rul. 64-182, 1964-1 C.B. 186.

[506] These exceptions are usually the ones for businesses conducted by volunteers (see § 25.2(a)) and for sales of donated items (see § 25.2(c)).

[507] 1982 EO CPE Text, *supra* note 494, at 2.

[508] *Id.*

organization did not qualify for exemption as a charitable entity because it did not engage in any charitable activities and principally operated the bingo game business.[509] Similarly, the IRS ruled that an organization conducting bingo games was not a charitable entity because it made no distributions for its ostensible exempt purpose, which was the making of scholarship grants.[510]

In sum, rather than following a set percentage formula, a threshold factor of charitable giving should be fully analyzed in context with all the operative facts. The IRS's lawyers have also written:

> The "commensurate test" does not lend itself to rigid numerical distribution formulas—there is no fixed percentage of income that an organization must pay out for charitable purposes. The financial resources of any organization may be affected by such factors as start-up costs, overhead, scale of operations, whether labor is volunteer or salaried, phone or postal rates, etc. In each case, therefore, the particular facts and circumstances of the fund-raising organization must be considered. Accordingly, a low payout percentage does not automatically mandate the conclusion that the fund-raising organization under consideration has a primary purpose that is not charitable. In each case, it should be ascertained whether the failure to make real and substantial contributions for charitable purposes is due to a reasonable cause.[511]

The IRS wrote that "[w]hether an organization is carrying on a real and substantial program reasonably commensurate in scope with its financial resources and capabilities is an essentially factual matter." In the fundraising context, the IRS stated that a "threshold consideration rests on an organization's production of funds distributed for charitable use."[512]

(c) Other Exemption Issues

As is the case in many aspects of the law, the general rules can be abused, leading, in this context, to denial of recognition of, or to revocation of, tax-exempt status. The abuses in the fundraising context include failure to meet the commensurate test (because of high administrative and fundraising expenses and/ or inadequate distributions for charitable purposes), violation of the private inurement doctrine (such as payment of excessive compensation to a service provider that is an insider or other inappropriate involvement of this type of service provider), and application of the doctrine of commerciality.

For example, the private inurement doctrine was found violated where a nonprofit organization was formed to raise money for a scholarship fund, where the fundraising medium consisted of the conduct of bingo games in a cocktail lounge

---

[509] Help the Children, Inc. v. Comm'r, 28 T.C. 1128 (1957).

[510] Priv. Ltr. Rul. 201103057.

[511] "Special Emphasis Program—Charitable Fund-Raising," Topic M, IRS Exempt Organizations Continuing Professional Education Text for FY 1989.

[512] 1982 EO CPE Text, *supra* note 494, at 47. Application of the commensurate test is not confined to the realm of public charities. For example, an organization was denied recognition of exemption as a fraternal beneficiary society (see § 19.4(a)) in part because more than 90 percent of the proceeds of fundraising campaigns were paid over to a fundraising company (Priv. Ltr. Rul. 201332015).

owned by a majority of the directors of the nonprofit entity. A court found that more than an insubstantial purpose of the nonprofit organization's activities was to attract customers, by way of the games, onto the premises of the lounge, expecting that they would purchase food and beverages while there, thus enhancing the profitability of the company operating the lounge. Tax exemption was denied in this instance.[513] A similar holding concerned the case of a nonprofit organization seeking to raise money for charities by selling lottery tickets in a bar.[514]

In another instance, a nonprofit entity, operating a "networking and fundraising" website, was denied recognition as a charitable entity by the IRS because its primary activity was advertising, which was considered commercial; the fact that a portion of the advertising revenue could be directed by users of the site to charities was deemed unavailing.[515] Likewise, a nonprofit organization selling coffee and hot chocolate products online, enabling customers to designate a portion of the "fundraising proceeds" for charity, was denied recognition of exemption, primarily on the grounds of commerciality.[516] Also, a nonprofit organization, formed to promote mobile giving and fundraising using other technology platforms to encourage charitable giving by younger donors, facilitating the distributions of contributions made by wireless mobile telephone customers to qualified charities, was denied recognition of exemption as a charitable entity largely because of private benefit provided to applications service provider companies and the participating wireless mobile telephone carriers.[517] The same fate befell an organization operating a website enabling individuals to volunteer to perform services in exchange for charitable contributions, with the IRS portraying this entity as a "facilitator of commerce" between the service providers and recipients.[518] Likewise, the IRS ruled that an organization was a "commercial fundraising service" that did not really engage in fundraising but merely facilitated the transfer of funds from donors to donees,[519] that fundraising by means of an online raffle was a commercial activity because the tickets were too highly priced,[520] that an organization providing fundraising and marketing services to unrelated charitable entities could not be exempt because it was primarily engaged in commercial activity,[521] and an organization selling shirts online, that planned to donate them to the needy and make grants to charitable organizations, could not be exempt.[522] The IRS revoked the exempt status of an organization that derived all its income from the sale of luxury travel packages to other exempt organizations to be used at their fundraising events, concluding that these activities demonstrated the characteristics of a commercial business and did not further educational purposes.[523]

---

[513] P.L.L. Scholarship Fund v. Comm'r, 82 T.C. 196 (1984).
[514] KJ's Fund Raisers, Inc. v. Comm'r, 166 F.3d 1200 (2d Cir. 1998).
[515] Priv. Ltr. Rul. 201309016.
[516] Priv. Ltr. Rul. 201310046.
[517] Priv. Ltr. Rul. 201429027.
[518] Priv. Ltr. Rul. 201323037.
[519] Priv. Ltr. Rul. 201407014.
[520] Priv. Ltr. Rul. 201410035.
[521] Priv. Ltr. Rul. 201507026.
[522] Priv. Ltr. Rul. 201702042.
[523] Priv. Ltr. Rul. 202245006.

It is the view of the IRS that fundraising activities by sports booster clubs, where the resulting payments directly benefit participating families rather than the organizations themselves, amount to a form of private inurement.[524] The government was successful in causing a court to agree in a case of a gymnastics booster club that facilitated fundraising by parents of children in the sports program; the parents earned points, which were used to reduce amounts owed for assessments for the expenses of competitions.[525] In this case, the court found that the fundraising practices caused private inurement to the participating parents[526] and conferred unwarranted private benefit to the children participating in the athletic activities.[527]

In recent years, the IRS has occasionally drifted away from the general principles discussed previously. That is, the agency may ignore the fundraising aspects of a particular case and focus instead on the nature of the underlying activity, finding that the activity is not an exempt function. For example, the tax-exempt status of an organization, formed to raise money for charitable purposes by holding motorcycle rallies and making grants to charities, was revoked on the ground that the activities conducted by this entity are "primarily social in nature."[528] Similarly, the IRS revoked the tax-exempt status of an organization that raised funds by engaging in bargain sales because this activity furthered a "substantial business purpose" and "bargain sales activity is not an exempt activity."[529] Both cases should have been resolved by application of the commensurate test.[530]

§ 7.15 GOVERNMENT ENTITIES AS CHARITABLE COUNTERPARTS

A wholly owned state or municipal instrumentality that is a separate entity may qualify for tax exemption as a charitable entity if it is a *clear counterpart* of a charitable, educational, religious, or like organization.[531] The test set by the IRS is based on the scope of the organization's purposes and powers—that is, whether the purposes and powers are beyond those of a charitable organization. For example, a state or municipality itself cannot qualify as a charitable organization, inasmuch as its purposes are not exclusively those inherent in charities, nor can an integral component of the state or municipality.[532]

---

[524] Priv. Ltr. Rul. 201245025.

[525] Capital Gymnastics Booster Club, Inc. v. Comm'r, 106 T.C.M. 154 (2013).

[526] See § 20.3, text accompanied by note 67.

[527] See § 20.13(b), text accompanied by note 419.

[528] Priv. Ltr. Rul. 202001018.

[529] Priv. Ltr. Rul. 202221013.

[530] See § 7.14(b).

[531] Rev. Rul. 60-384, 1960-2 C.B. 172; Rev. Rul. 55-319, 1955-1 C.B. 119; Estate of Slayton v. Comm'r, 3 B.T.A. 1343 (1926).

[532] Cf. IRC § 115(1). *Id.* Income accruing to a state or political subdivision is excluded from gross income, however, whether derived from an activity performed by the governmental entity directly (see § 19.22(a)) or from a separately organized entity that performs an essential governmental function (IRC § 115(1); see § 19.22(b)).

An otherwise qualified instrumentality meeting the *counterpart* requirement, such as a school, college, university, or hospital, can be deemed a charitable organization.[533] If, however, an instrumentality is clothed with powers other than those described in the federal tax rules for charitable organizations, such as enforcement or regulatory powers in the public interest (e.g., health, welfare, safety), it would not be a clear counterpart organization. For example, a public housing authority was denied exemption as a charitable organization because it had the power to conduct investigations, administer oaths, issue subpoenas, and make its findings available to other agencies.[534] By contrast, a public library was ruled to be an exempt charitable (counterpart) entity inasmuch as its power to determine the tax rate necessary to support its operations was deemed to not be regulatory or enforcement in nature.[535]

Until 1975, the IRS had not specifically distinguished between state instrumentalities and state political subdivisions.[536] In that year, the IRS made the distinction, ruling that an association of counties in a state constituted an instrumentality of the state or the counties (themselves political subdivisions) but not a political subdivision of the state.[537]

In 1957,[538] the IRS promulgated criteria for classification of an entity as an instrumentality of a state:

> In cases involving the status of an organization as an instrumentality of one or more states or political subdivisions, the following factors are taken into consideration: (1) whether it is used for a governmental purpose and performs a governmental function; (2) whether performance of its function is on behalf of one or more states or political subdivisions; (3) whether there are any private interests involved, or whether the states or political subdivision involved have the powers and interests of an owner; (4) whether control and supervision is vested in public authority or authorities; (5) if express or implied statutory or other authority is necessary for the creation and/or use of such an instrumentality and whether such authority exists; and (6) the degree of financial autonomy and the source of its operating expenses.

According to the government, however, an additional characteristic differentiates a political subdivision from a state instrumentality: The former has been delegated the right to exercise part of the sovereign government power of the governmental unit of which it is a division (or is a municipal corporation).[539] Thus, the association of counties referenced earlier was denied status as a political subdivision of the state because it was not delegated any of the counties' or state's sovereign powers. The IRS ruled that the association was nonetheless a qualified donee for charitable contribution purposes, however, with contributions deductible as

---

[533] E.g., Estate of Green v. Comm'r, 82 T.C. 843 (1984); Rev. Rul. 67-290, 1967-2 C.B. 183.
[534] Rev. Rul. 74-14, 1974-1 C.B. 125.
[535] Rev. Rul. 74-15, 1974-1 C.B. 126.
[536] See § 19.22.
[537] Rev. Rul. 75-359, 1975-2 C.B. 79.
[538] Rev. Rul. 57-128, 1957-1 C.B. 311.
[539] Reg. § 1.103-1(b).

being "for the use of" political subdivisions (that is, the counties), subject to the annual limitation of 20 percent of the donor's contribution base.[540]

A state law characterization of an entity's status as a governmental unit is overridden for federal tax purposes by the criteria established in 1957. For example, the University of Illinois has been determined by the supreme court of that state to be a "public corporation."[541] Because the university met the criteria promulgated in 1957 and has been delegated the right to exercise part of the sovereign power of the State of Illinois, it constitutes a political subdivision of the state. (The IRS and the courts have recognized that the education of its citizens is an essential governmental function of a state.)[542] Thus, a state college or university (and comparable entities such as state hospitals) may qualify as both a clear counterpart state instrumentality (and thus have tax exemption as a charitable entity) and a political subdivision because its activities, in addition to those described in the 1957 criteria, are neither regulatory nor enforcement powers.[543]

The foregoing analysis by the IRS did not take into account the consequence of operation of the adjunct theory.[544] By this theory, the association of counties could have been regarded as a political subdivision of the state rather than an instrumentality of the state, inasmuch as the characteristics of the counties are attributable to the association.[545]

The IRS ruled on several occasions as to whether an entity is a political subdivision or a state instrumentality. The IRS characterized a county board of education as an instrumentality of a state in the fact statement of a ruling, but then concluded that the board qualified as a political subdivision.[546] Similarly, the IRS ruled that a governor's conference was a political subdivision of a state.[547] Also, an organization created by the governors of 11 states to foster interstate cooperation and to otherwise coordinate action among these states was ruled to be an instrumentality of the states.[548] Likewise, the IRS held that an industrial commission established by a state legislature to study the problems of industrial life in a geographic area is qualified as a charitable donee.[549]

Reversing an earlier position, the IRS ruled that an incorporated integrated state bar did not qualify as an instrumentality or political subdivision of a state.[550] The IRS reasoned that the state bar was a "dual purpose" organization, in that it had public purposes (such as admission, suspension, disbarment, and reprimand of licensed lawyers) and private purposes (such as the protection of professional

---

[540] IRC § 170(b)(1)(B).

[541] People ex rel. The Bd. of Trustees of the Univ. of Ill. v. Barrett, 46 N.E.2d 951 (Ill. 1943).

[542] Rev. Rul. 75-436, 1975-2 C.B. 217; Gilliam v. Adams, 171 S.W.2d 813 (Tenn. 1943).

[543] Cf. Rev. Rul. 74-14, 1974-1 C.B. 125.

[544] See § 7.13(b).

[545] E.g., Brundage v. Comm'r, 54 T.C. 1468 (1970). Cf. Miller v. United States, 527 F.2d 231 (8th Cir. 1975); Puerto Rico Marine Mgt., Inc. v. Int'l Longshoremen's Ass'n, 398 F. Supp. 118 (D.P.R. 1975).

[546] Rev. Rul. 70-562, 1970-2 C.B. 63.

[547] Rev. Rul. 69-459, 1969-2 C.B. 35.

[548] Priv. Ltr. Rul. 7935043.

[549] Rev. Rul. 79-323, 1979-2 C.B. 106.

[550] Rev. Rul. 77-232, 1977-2 C.B. 71, *revoking* Rev. Rul. 59-152, 1959-1 C.B. 54. This change in classification also means that contributions to these state bars are not deductible under IRC §§ 170(c)(1), 2055(a)(1), and 2522(a)(1).

interests of its members), and thus that it was "not an arm of the state because it is a separate entity and has private as well as public purposes." The IRS also held that the state bar was "not a political subdivision because it has no meaningful sovereign powers."

A committee created by joint resolution of a state legislature, established to receive and expend contributions to provide state units for a parade incident to a presidential inauguration, was ruled to be a political subdivision.[551] A committee that was created by a governor's executive order to educate the public about the activities of the United Nations was considered a political subdivision of the state.[552] Under appropriate circumstances, a nonprofit corporation may qualify as a political subdivision of a state.[553]

The IRS considered the question of whether a nonprofit membership corporation qualified as a political subdivision.[554] The members of the corporation consisted of representatives of the local chambers of commerce and other private business groups in a particular county, the county commissioners, and officials of participating municipalities. There was no private inurement, and the corporation's articles provided that on any dissolution of the corporation the beneficial interest in any property owned by the corporation would pass to the county.

The IRS held that obligations of this type of corporation would be considered issued *on behalf* of the state or political subdivision of the state, provided each of the following requirements was met: The corporation engages in activities that are essentially public in nature; the corporation must be one that is not organized for profit (except to the extent of retiring indebtedness); the corporate income must not inure to any private person; the state or a political subdivision thereof must have a beneficial interest in the corporation while the indebtedness remains outstanding, and it must obtain full legal title to the property of the corporation with respect to which the indebtedness was incurred upon the retirement of such indebtedness; and the corporation must have been approved by the state or a political subdivision of the state.[555]

A federal court of appeals held that a *political subdivision* is any division of any state that has been delegated the right to exercise part of the sovereign power of the state.[556] The appellate court observed that the term *political subdivision* is "broad and comprehensive and denotes any division of the State made by the proper authorities thereof, acting within their constitutional powers, for the purpose of those functions of the State which by long usage and the inherent necessities of government have always been regarded as public."[557]

A state supreme court observed that the "[i]mportant factors, among others, which must be considered in determining that . . . [a]n agency is an instrument of government are [whether]: (1) [i]t was created by the government; (2) it is

---

[551] Rev. Rul. 58-265, 1958-1 C.B. 172.

[552] Rev. Rul. 62-66, 1962-1 C.B. 83.

[553] Rev. Rul. 59-41, 1959-1 C.B. 13; Rev. Rul. 54-296, 1954-2 C.B. 59.

[554] Rev. Rul. 63-20, 1963-1 C.B. 24.

[555] *Id.* Also, Rev. Rul. 60-243, 1960-2 C.B. 35; Rev. Rul. 57-187, 1957-1 C.B. 65.

[556] Comm'r v. Estate of Shamberg, 3 T.C. 131 (1944), *aff'd*, 144 F.2d 998 (2d Cir. 1944), *cert. denied*, 323 U.S. 792 (1944).

[557] *Id.*, 144 F.2d 1004.

wholly owned by the government; (3) it is not operated for profit; (4) it is primarily engaged in the performance of some essential governmental function; [and] (5) the proposed tax will impose an economic burden upon the government, or it serves to materially impair the usefulness or efficiency of the agency, or to materially restrict it in the performance of its duties."[558]

An organization may seek instrumentality status rather than tax exemption as a charitable entity to avoid the annual reporting requirements, the private foundation rules, and other federal tax limitations on charitable groups, or because it cannot qualify as charitable in nature. Contributions to instrumentalities are deductible as long as they qualify as a *governmental unit* and the gift is made for exclusively public purposes;[559] the interest they pay on their borrowings generally is exempt from the lender's gross income.[560]

A governmental entity may have a dual tax-exempt status; that is, it may be recognized as a "conventional" tax-exempt organization[561] as well as a governmental body. Usually, in this circumstance, the IRS will take the position that the entity must comply with the applicable law associated with the conventional exempt status, such as a government hospital's (with dual status) obligation to adhere to the special rules for exempt hospitals[562] and a state college or university's (with dual status) liability for the excise tax on excess compensation.[563]

§ 7.16 OTHER CATEGORIES OF CHARITY

There are several other categories of tax-exempt charitable organizations. Many of these do not fit within any of the traditional definitions of *charitable* function.

(a) Environmental Protection

An organization established to promote environmental conservancy is a tax-exempt charitable entity.[564] The IRS ruled that it is "generally recognized that efforts to preserve and protect the natural environment for the benefit of the public serve a charitable purpose."[565] The IRS, however, refused to classify an organization as an exempt charitable entity where it merely restricted land uses that did not change the environment, where the land lacked any "distinctive ecological

---

[558] Unemployment Compensation Comm'n of N.C. v. Wachovia Bank & Trust Co., 2 S.E.2d 592, 596 (N.C. 1939). Also, City of Bay Minette v. Quinly, 82 So.2d 192 (Ala. 1955); War Memorial Hosp. of District No. 1 v. Bd. of Cnty. Comm'rs of Cnty. of Park, 279 P.2d 472 (Wyo. 1955); City of Cincinnati v. Gamble, 34 N.E.2d 226 (Ohio 1941); Gebhardt v. Village of La Grange Park, 188 N.E. 372, 374 (Ill. 1933).
[559] IRC §§ 170(c)(1), 170(b)(1)(A)(v).
[560] IRC § 103(a)(1). Cf. State of S.C. v. Baker, 485 U.S. 505 (1988).
[561] That is, tax exemption by reason of IRC § 501(a) as an entity described in IRC § 501(c)(3).
[562] See § 7.6(b). The IRS revoked the tax exemption (IRC § 501(c)(3)) of a dual-status hospital for failure to comply with IRC § 501(r) (Priv. Ltr. Rul. 201829017).
[563] See § 20.5(c)(i). Consequently, a dual-status governmental entity may wish to relinquish its IRC § 501(c)(3) status (see § 26.16, text accompanied by notes 357–60).
[564] Rev. Rul. 80-279, 1980-2 C.B. 176; Rev. Rul. 80-278, 1980-2 C.B. 175; Rev. Rul. 75-207, 1975-1 C.B. 361; Rev. Rul. 70-186, 1970-1 C.B. 128; Rev. Rul. 67-292, 1967-2 C.B. 184.
[565] Rev. Rul. 76-204, 1976-1 C.B. 152.

significance," and where any public benefit was "too indirect and insignificant."[566] The IRS declined to accord recognition of exemption to a nonprofit corporation that proposed provision of "residential solar energy systems" to low- and middle-income households in a county, because the organization failed to provide "credible studies or research" showing that use of these systems "would have a measurable, significant impact in preserving and protecting the environment."[567] The IRS likewise did not recognize exemption of an alleged environment organization, finding that its program of mitigating carbon emissions was a nonexempt certification activity, with its selling of carbon offsets a commercial enterprise.[568]

Nonetheless, the position of the IRS that only land of "distinctive ecological significance" can qualify as a tax-exempt function holding of an environmental conservation organization was implicitly rejected by a court when it accorded classification as an exempt charitable organization to a model farm operated as a conservation project.[569] Rather than focus on the nature of the land as such, the court emphasized the use of the land: The organization's "agricultural program seeks to demonstrate the commercial viability of ecologically sound farming techniques not yet practiced in the surrounding community."[570]

This body of law is integrated with the rules in the charitable giving context pertaining to contributions of conservation easements.[571] For example, the IRS ruled that a nonprofit organization newly receiving gifts of conservation easements and incapable of enforcing them, and facilitating tax avoidance by allowing improper charitable contribution deductions, was not entitled to recognition of exemption as an environmental protection entity.[572] A similar situation occurred following observation by an IRS agent of illegal dumping, abandoned home appliances, and garbage on the ostensibly protected property, along with evidence of four-wheel-drive vehicles driven over sensitive wetlands and the development of recreational ponds.[573] Indeed, an organization had its exempt status as a charitable organization revoked when the IRS discovered that its function of receiving gifts of conservation easements was not being undertaken for the protection of open space or natural habitats but was done for the purpose of generating "sizeable deductions" for the donors, who were clients of the organization's president, an accountant.[574]

(b)   Promotion of Patriotism

The IRS concluded that the promotion of patriotism is a charitable objective. The ruling came in the case of a membership organization formed by citizens of a community to promote "civic pride in the community, state, and the country" by providing a color guard and conducting flag-raising and other ceremonies at patriotic

---

[566] Rev. Rul. 78-384, 1978-2 C.B. 174.

[567] Priv. Ltr. Rul. 201210044.

[568] Priv. Ltr. Rul. 201221023.

[569] Dumaine Farms v. Comm'r, 73 T.C. 650 (1980).

[570] Id. at 656.

[571] See Charitable Giving § 7.6.

[572] Priv. Ltr. Rul. 201048045.

[573] Priv. Ltr. Rul. 201109030.

[574] Priv. Ltr. Rul. 201405018.

and community functions.[575] As authority for this position, the IRS stated that trusts created for the purpose of "inculcating patriotic emotions have been upheld as charitable, as have trusts for the purchase and display of a flag, and for the celebration of a patriotic holiday."[576]

(c) Promotion of Sports

A court held that the promotion, advancement, and sponsoring of recreational and amateur sports is a charitable activity.[577] The organization involved owned and operated an amateur baseball team that played in a semiprofessional league, leased and maintained a baseball field used by its team and other teams, furnished instructors and coaches for a baseball camp, and provided coaches for Little League teams. The government's contention that the team was semiprofessional, and thus that the operation of it was a nonexempt activity, was rejected.[578] Where, however, the primary purpose of an organization is to promote recreational sports among adults, the entity does not provide instruction to youth, it lacks a regular program of teaching a sport and does not have a sports trainer, and/or it expends most of its funds on travel and meals for a team comprised of individuals 18 years of age or older, the organization will not qualify for exemption as a charitable entity.[579]

The IRS ruled that an organization that furthers recreational and amateur sports is a charitable entity; in this instance, the organization provides youth with learning facilities and educational programs that promote character-development and life-enhancing values by means of the playing of golf. The organization operates an 18-hole golf course, provides lessons, and sponsors golf clinics and youth tournaments. The IRS ruled that the operation of the golf course and the other functions, in this context, had a substantial causal relationship to the achievement of exempt functions.[580]

(d) Public Interest Law

Organizations structured as *public interest law firms*—nonprofit entities that provide legal representation in matters involving a broad public interest under circumstances where the financial interests at stake would not normally warrant representation from private legal sources—can qualify as tax-exempt charitable organizations where they provide a "service which is of benefit to the community as a whole," with "[c]haritability . . . also dependent upon the fact that the service

---

[575] Rev. Rul. 78-84, 1978-1 C.B. 150.
[576] Buder v. United States, 7 F.3d 1382 (8th Cir. 1993) (where a trust, established to foster and promote the cause of patriotism, loyalty, and fundamental constitutional government and to combat subversive activities, socialism, and communism, was held to qualify as a tax-exempt charitable entity).
[577] Hutchinson Baseball Enters., Inc. v. Comm'r, 73 T.C. 144 (1979), aff'd, 696 F.2d 757 (10th Cir. 1982). Where, however, the sports organization is primarily established to further social or recreational interests, tax exemption as a charitable organization will not be available (Wayne Baseball, Inc. v. Comm'r, 78 T.C.M. 437 (1999); North Am. Sequential Sweepstakes v. Comm'r, 77 T.C. 1087 (1981)).
[578] This case did not involve the IRC § 501(c)(3) provision for certain amateur sports organizations. See § 11.2. The IRS denied recognition of tax-exempt status to an organization representing that it would promote baseball for youth (Ex. Den. and Rev. Ltr. 20042708E).
[579] E.g., Priv. Ltr. Rul. 200849018.
[580] Priv. Ltr. Rul. 200536024.

provided by public interest law firms is distinguishable from that which is commercially available."[581] The recognition by the IRS that public interest law firms can be charitable in nature was significant, in that beforehand the agency would not recognize as exempt an organization operating in support of interests of a majority of the public since that segment of society does not constitute a charitable class.[582]

In guidelines containing criteria for these firms, the IRS stated that the engagement of public interest law firms in litigation "can reasonably be said to be in representation of a broad public interest rather than a private interest."[583] These guidelines "are not inflexible," in that an organization will be given the opportunity to demonstrate that, under the particular facts and circumstances, adherence to the guidelines is not required in certain respects in order to ensure that the charitable organization's operations are "totally charitable."

Litigation is considered to be in representation of a broad public interest if it is designed to present a position on behalf of the public at large on matters of public interest. This type of litigation includes class actions, in which resolution of the dispute is in the public interest, lawsuits for injunction against action by government or private interests broadly affecting the public, similar representation before administrative boards and agencies, and test suits where the private interest is small.

This type of litigation activity normally may not extend to direct representation of litigants in actions between private persons where the financial interests at stake would warrant representation from private legal sources. The organization may not attempt to achieve its objectives through a program of disruption of the judicial system, illegal activity, or violation of applicable canons of ethics. The policies and programs of the organization should be the responsibility of a board or committee representative of the public interest. The organization should not be operated in a manner that creates identification or confusion with a particular private law firm.

The organization may accept lawyers' fees in public interest cases if the fees are paid by opposing parties and are awarded by a court or administrative agency or approved by such a body in a settlement agreement. The organization may accept lawyers' fees in public interest cases if the fees are paid directly by its clients, if it adopts certain additional procedures concerning client-paid fees (see below). The likelihood or probability of a fee, whether court-awarded or client-paid, may not be a consideration in the organization's selection of cases.

The total amount of all lawyers' fees may not exceed 50 percent of the total cost of operation of the organization's legal functions. This percentage is calculated over a five-year period. Costs of legal functions include lawyers' and others' salaries, overhead, and costs directly attributable to the performance of the organization's legal functions. Staff lawyers and other employees are compensated on the basis of reasonable salaries that are not established by reference to fees received in connection with the cases they have handled.

---

[581] Rev. Rul. 75-74, 1975-1 C.B. 152.
[582] See § 6.3(a).
[583] Rev. Proc. 92-59, 1992-2 C.B. 411, which superseded Rev. Proc. 71-39, 1971-2 C.B. 575, modified and superseded Rev. Proc. 75-13, 1975-1 C.B. 662, revoked Rev. Rul. 75-75, 1975-1 C.B. 154, and amplified Rev. Rul. 75-76, 1975-1 C.B. 154.

Client-paid fees may not exceed the actual cost incurred in each case. These costs may be charged against a retainer, with any balance remaining after the conclusion of the litigation refunded to the litigant. Once having undertaken a representation, a public interest law firm may not withdraw from the case because the litigant is unable to pay the contemplated fee.

Other types of tax-exempt, charitable organizations engage in litigation activities in furtherance of their exempt functions. They are legal aid organizations,[584] human and civil rights organizations,[585] and still other organizations that attempt achievement of charitable goals by means of litigation.[586]

(e) Local Economic Development

A form of tax-exempt charitable organization is the *local economic development corporation* (LEDC). LEDCs engage in a variety of activities, including investment in local businesses; direct operation of job-training, housing, and other programs; business counseling; and encouragement to established national businesses to open plants or offices in economically depressed areas. A prime purpose of an LEDC is to alleviate poverty—clearly a charitable purpose.[587] By necessity, however, LEDCs render assistance to commercial business enterprises and make investments in businesses as part of their principal function. While these activities are not normally regarded as charitable in nature, there is authority for a determination that these LEDCs engage in charitable endeavors.

The IRS ruled that an organization is tax-exempt as a charitable entity (as promoting social welfare)[588] where it maintained a program of providing low-cost financial assistance and other aid designed to improve economic conditions and economic opportunities in economically depressed areas.[589] The organization undertook to combat these conditions by providing funds and working capital to business corporations or individual proprietors who were unable to obtain funds from conventional commercial sources because of the poor financial risks involved. The IRS noted that "these loans and purchases of equity interest are not undertaken for purpose of profit or gain but for the purpose of advancing the charitable goals of the organization and are not investments for profit in any conventional business sense."[590]

It is possible for an LEDC to qualify for tax exemption as a charitable entity even though it is licensed as a nonprofit small business investment company under the Small Business Investment Act (SBIC).[591] An SBIC licensee is required to comply with certain regulations promulgated by the Small Business Administration (SBA) that set requirements as to the level of interest rates charged by a licensee and impose various restrictions on the degree of financial support that may be offered to a prospective recipient. The difficulty is that an SBA-regulated SBIC

---

[584] E.g., Rev. Rul. 78-428, 1978-2 C.B. 177; Rev. Rul. 69-161, 1969-1 C.B. 149.
[585] See § 7.11, text accompanied by *supra* notes 417, 422.
[586] E.g., Rev. Rul. 80-278, 1980-2 C.B. 175.
[587] See § 7.1.
[588] See § 7.11.
[589] Rev. Rul. 74-587, 1974-2 C.B. 162.
[590] *Id.* at 163.
[591] 15 U.S.C. § 681(d).

may be prevented from engaging in certain loan transactions in which it would otherwise be able to engage in furtherance of charitable purposes. Although a "narrower range of permissible transactions" is available to an SBIC than to non-SBA-regulated LEDCs, the IRS concluded that the SBIC "may still provide loans to businesses that cannot secure financing through conventional commercial sources, the operation of which businesses will achieve charitable purposes."[592] Thus, although this ruling does not mean that all SBA-regulated SBICs are automatically exempt LEDCs, it does not mean that the mere fact that the organization is subject to the SBA regulations does not preclude it from exemption.

Subsequently, the IRS distinguished the situation involved in its prior ruling from that where the primary purpose of the organization is to promote business in general rather than to provide assistance only to businesses owned by minority groups or to businesses experiencing difficulty because of their location in a deteriorated section of the community. Thus, the IRS denied classification as a tax-exempt charitable entity to an organization formed to increase business patronage in a deteriorated area mainly inhabited by minority groups by providing information on the area's shopping opportunities, local transportation, and accommodations, and to an organization the purpose of which was to revive retail sales in an area suffering from continued economic decline by constructing a shopping center in the area to arrest the flow of business to competing centers in outlying areas.[593]

A public charity constructed an "innovation and incubator center," funded by commercial loans and government grants, to attract high-technology companies to a state for the purpose of creating employment opportunities and increase higher education in technology so as to build a skilled workforce. Small companies rent space at the center at below-market rates, thereby bringing more high-tech jobs into the area. Noting that the region where this center is located has been plagued by poverty, poor education, and low standards of living for over a century, the IRS ruled that this project furthers charitable purposes by providing economic development to this underprivileged area.[594]

A nonprofit corporation was established to revitalize and redevelop the central business district of a city. This entity informed the IRS that it would finance projects that "develop and promote the public good and general welfare, trade, commerce, industry, and employment opportunities" in the city, to the end of enhancing the city and creating a "climate favorable to the location of new industry, trade and commerce." The IRS responded that "[r]evitalizing a business district is not deemed charitable unless the area being revitalized is historical or blighted, or if the revitalization can lessen neighborhood tensions," adding that this organization had not established that it is lessening the burdens of government.[595] This organization failed to achieve recognition of exemption as a charitable entity.

[592] Rev. Rul. 81-284, 1981-2 C.B. 130. The IRS likewise recognized that an IRC § 501(c)(3) organization can provide funding for a minority enterprise small business investment company (Gen. Couns. Mem. 38497).
[593] Rev. Rul. 77-111, 1977-1 C.B. 144.
[594] Priv. Ltr. Rul. 200537038. The IRS also ruled that this organization was lessening the burdens of government (see § 7.7).
[595] Priv. Ltr. Rul. 202118021. See §§ 7.7, 7.11.

(f) Other Charitable Organizations

The IRS ruled that the term *charitable* includes the "care of orphans."[596] The occasion was consideration of the tax status of an organization that arranged for the placement of orphan children living in foreign countries with adoptive parents in the United States. The agency also determined that "facilitating student and cultural exchanges" is a charitable activity.[597]

Although a federal court allowed an estate tax charitable contribution deduction for a bequest to a "public" cemetery because of the "important social function" it performed and the "concurrent lessening of the burden of the public fisc,"[598] the decision was overturned on appeal on the grounds that Congress has not enacted an estate tax counterpart to the income tax exemption provision for cemetery companies[599] and that the common-law definition of the term *charity* in the income tax context cannot be imported into the estate tax field.[600] The appellate court was unable to discern why Congress elected to treat contributions to cemetery organizations differently for income and estate tax deduction purposes, regarding the matter as an "anomaly" that must be left to "congressional wisdom."[601] The attempt by the lower court to categorize public cemeteries as charities because the "maintenance of cemetery facilities by cemetery associations benefits the community both through its aesthetic effects and by the performance of a necessary social task"[602] thus failed.

A court concluded that the purpose of "maintain[ing] public confidence in the legal system" through "various means of improving the administration of justice" is charitable.[603] By contrast, a court refused to regard as charitable the object to "encourage, foster, promote and perpetuate outdoor activities."[604]

One of the many ways to qualify as a tax-exempt charitable entity is to engage in activities consisting of the "erection or maintenance of public buildings, monuments, or works."[605] An organization sought recognition of exemption as a charitable entity with a program of development and distribution of open-source software. The IRS declined to recognize exemption in this case because anyone can use the software for any purpose; the software was not considered the requisite "work."[606]

An agricultural research organization is a type of public charity.[607] This is an entity that is engaged in the continuous active conduct of agricultural research in

---

[596] Rev. Rul. 80-200, 1980-2 C.B. 173.

[597] Rev. Rul. 80-286, 1980-2 C.B. 179.

[598] Mellon Bank v. United States, 509 F. Supp. 160 (W.D. Pa. 1984).

[599] IRC § 501(c)(13). See § 19.6.

[600] Mellon Bank v. United States, 762 F.2d 283 (3d Cir. 1985), *cert. denied*, 475 U.S. 1031 (1986).

[601] *Id.* at 286. Also, Child v. United States, 540 F.2d 579 (2d Cir. 1976), *cert. denied*, 429 U.S. 1092 (1977).

[602] Mellon Bank v. United States, 509 F. Supp. 160, 164 (W.D. Pa. 1984).

[603] Kentucky Bar Found., Inc. v. Comm'r, 78 T.C. 921, 930 (1982).

[604] Greiss v. United States, 57-1 U.S.T.C. ¶ 11,659 (N.D. Ill. 1956) (where the court observed that such a "wide-sweeping, dragnet purpose would embrace many varied activities not contemplated by" the concept of charity).

[605] Reg. § 1.501(c)(3)-1(d)(2).

[606] Priv. Ltr. Rul. 201505040.

[607] See § 12.3(a), text accompanied by note 134.

conjunction with a land-grant college or university or non–land-grant college of agriculture.[608]

§ 7.17   QUALIFIED OPPORTUNITY ZONES

Qualified opportunity zones are designed to spur economic development and job creation in distressed communities throughout the nation and U.S. possessions by providing tax benefits to investors who invest capital in these communities. Taxpayers may defer tax on eligible capital gains by making an appropriate investment in a Qualified Opportunity Fund and meeting other requirements.[609]

A *qualified opportunity zone* is a population census tract that is a low-income community that is designated as such a zone.[610] The requisite designation occurs when the chief executive officer of the state in which the tract is located nominates the tract for the designation and the IRS certifies the nomination and designates the tract as an opportunity zone.[611]

Two principal tax incentives encourage investment in qualified opportunity zones. Deferral of inclusion in gross income for certain gains is provided to the extent the corresponding amounts are invested in a qualified opportunity fund.[612] There is an exclusion from gross income of the post-acquisition gains on investments in these funds that are held for at least 10 years.[613]

A *qualified opportunity fund* is an investment vehicle that is organized as a corporation or a partnership for the purpose of investing in qualified opportunity zone property that holds at least 90 percent of its assets in qualified opportunity zone property.[614] *Qualified opportunity zone property* is property that is qualified opportunity zone stock, a qualified opportunity zone partnership interest, or qualified opportunity zone business property.[615]

Although these opportunity zones are not necessarily discrete areas of charitable activity, "it is clear that philanthropies have a critical role in helping cities realize the full economic and social impact" of the zones.[616] This commentator

---

[608] IRC §§ 170(b)(1)(A)(ix), 509(a)(1). It is intended that this provision be interpreted in like manner to and consistent with the rules applicable to medical research organizations (see § 7.6(d)).

[609] IRC §§ 1400Z-1, 1400Z-2, added by the Tax Cuts and Jobs Act, Pub. L. No. 115-97, § 13823, 131 Stat. 2054, 2183-88 (2017). These zones and funds are not necessarily inherently charitable in nature but may involve nonprofit organizations and efforts that overlap with the concept of charity in economic development (see § 7.16(e)).

[610] IRC § 1400Z-1(a). The term *low-income community* is defined in IRC § 45D(e).

[611] IRC § 1400Z-1(b).

[612] IRC § 1400Z-2(a).

[613] IRC § 1400Z-2(b), (c).

[614] IRC § 1400Z-2(d)(1).

[615] IRC § 1400Z-2(d)(2). Final regulations provide guidance as to gains that may be deferred from an investment in a qualified opportunity fund (T.D. 9889, 85 Fed. Reg. 19082 (2020)). This body of law addresses the time by which corresponding amounts must be invested in these funds and the manner in which investors may elect to defer specified gains and includes rules for valuation of funds' assets and guidance on qualified opportunity zone businesses.

[616] Katz, "How Philanthropy Can Help Opportunity Zones Ensure Widespread Economic Renewal," 31 *Chron. of Phil.* (Issue 8) 34 (June 2019).

enumerated the ways charitable organizations can play important roles in advancing this program: to gather everyone with a stake in improving a poor neighborhood, to map out a region's assets, to build markets, to empower local residents, to bolster institutions, to encourage innovation, and to share information. He noted that this opportunity zone tax incentive has the potential to channel private capital to communities that have "suffered from neglect by financial institutions and government" but added that this "potential will be realized only if philanthropies and other players help shape this new incentive so that it provides at least as much benefit to the public as it provides in private gain—if not more."[617]

§ 7.18 CHARITABLE GRANTS TO INDIVIDUALS

There is little law directly pertaining to grantmaking to individuals by public charities; the IRS states that charitable organizations may distribute funds to individuals, as long as the distributions are made on a charitable basis in furtherance of exempt purposes and adequate records and case histories are maintained.[618] Private foundations are more restricted in their ability to make grants to individuals, largely because of the rules concerning taxable expenditures.[619]

A court upheld the IRS's denial of recognition of tax-exempt status to an organization that made grants purportedly "to assist the poor who were in need of food, clothing, shelter, and medical attention," because the organization failed to furnish any documented criteria "for the selection process of a deserving recipient, the reason for specific amounts given, or the purpose of the grant."[620] The organization's only documentation was a list of grants that included the name of the recipient, the amount of the grant, and a designation of "either unemployment, moving expenses, school scholarship, or medical expense" as the "reason" for the grant.[621] The court held that this information "clearly" precluded the IRS "from determining whether the grants were made in an objective and nondiscriminatory manner and whether the distribution of such grants was made in furtherance of an exempt purpose."[622]

[617] *Id.* at 35.
[618] Rev. Rul. 56-304, 1956-2 C.B. 306.
[619] See § 12.4(e). See *Private Foundations* § 9.3.
[620] Church in Boston v. Commissioner, 71 T.C. 102, 106–07 (1978).
[621] *Id.* at 107.
[622] *Id.*

CHAPTER EIGHT

Educational Organizations

Section 501(a) of the Internal Revenue Code provides federal income tax exemption for organizations described in IRC § 501(c)(3), including entities that are organized and operated exclusively for *educational* purposes.[1] There is overlap in this area with the classification of organizations as being charitable entities, inasmuch as the term *charitable* includes the *advancement of education*.[2]

§ 8.1   FEDERAL TAX LAW DEFINITION OF *EDUCATIONAL*

Federal tax law defines the term *educational* as encompassing far more than formal schooling. Basically, the concept of *educational* as used for federal tax law purposes is defined as relating to the "instruction or training of the individual for the purpose of improving or developing his capabilities" or the "instruction of the public on subjects useful to the individual and beneficial to the community."[3]

For many years, the definition accorded the term *educational* by the Treasury Department and the IRS was routinely followed. In 1980, however, a federal court of appeals found portions of the regulation defining the term unconstitutionally vague.[4] That segment of the regulation—pertaining to a *full and fair exposition test*[5]—permits materials that advocate a viewpoint to qualify as educational

---

[1] Also, Reg. § 1.501(c)(3)-1(d)(1)(i)(f).
[2] See § 7.8.
[3] Reg. § 1.501(c)(3)-1(d)(3)(i).
[4] Big Mama Rag, Inc. v. United States, 631 F.2d 1030 (D.C. Cir. 1980).
[5] See § 8.2.

in nature but only if the advocacy is preceded by an objective discussion of the issue or subject involved. Subsequently, this appellate court—albeit recognizing the "inherently general nature of the term 'educational' and the wide range of meanings Congress may have intended to convey," and stating that "[w]e do not attempt a definition" of the term—set forth some general criteria as to what material may qualify as educational.[6]

In the subsequent case, this federal appellate court decided that the materials there at issue "fall short" of being educational, "[e]ven under the most minimal requirement of a rational development of a point of view."[7] Said the court: "It is the fact that there is no reasoned development of the conclusions which removes it [the material at issue] from any definition of 'educational' conceivably intended by Congress."[8] The court wrote: "The exposition of propositions the correctness of which is readily demonstrable is doubtless educational. As the truth of the view asserted becomes less and less demonstrable, however, 'instruction' or 'education' must, we think, require more than mere assertion and repetition."[9] Thereafter, the court observed that, in "attempting a definition suitable for all comers, IRS, or any legislature, court, or other administrator is beset with difficulties which are obvious."[10]

Thus, the federal tax law does not contain a threshold, generic definition of the term *educational*, but rests on the concept that subjects spoken or written about must be objectively developed or founded.[11]

§ 8.2 *EDUCATION* CONTRASTED WITH *PROPAGANDA*

Inherent in the concept of *educational* is the principle that an organization is not educational in nature where it zealously propagates particular ideas or doctrines without presentation of them in any reasonably objective or balanced manner. The point is reflected in the income tax regulations that define the term *educational*, which state: "An organization may be educational even though it advocates a particular position or viewpoint so long as it presents a sufficiently full and fair exposition of the pertinent facts as to permit an individual or the public to form an independent opinion or conclusion. On the other hand, an organization is not educational if its principal function is the mere presentation of unsupported opinion."[12]

This requirement is designed to exclude from the concept of *educational* the dissemination of *propaganda*, a term that also is considered in the context of the

---

[6] Nat'l Alliance v. United States, 710 F.2d 868, 873 (D.C. Cir. 1983).
[7] *Id.*
[8] *Id.*
[9] *Id.*
[10] *Id.*
[11] In general, Congressional Research Service, "501(c)(3) Organizations: What Qualifies as 'Educational'?" Rep. No. R42673 (Aug. 21, 2012).
[12] Reg. § 1.501(c)(3)-1(d)(3)(i).

rules governing legislative activities by charitable organizations.[13] In this context, it can be said that the term *educational* does not extend to "public address with selfish or ulterior purpose and characterized by the coloring or distortion of facts."[14]

An organization may avoid the charge that its principal function is the mere presentation of unsupported opinion either by presenting a sufficiently full and fair exposition of the pertinent facts in the materials it prepares and disseminates or by circulating copies of materials that contain this type of an exposition.[15] As discussed below, this precept is now embodied in the IRS's *methodology* test, which bears that name in reflection of the point that the method used by an organization in advocating its position, rather than the position itself, is the standard for determining whether the organization has educational purposes. The IRS considered this aspect of the law in connection with an organization that educated the public about the public interest obligations of the broadcast media by evaluating the performance of broadcasters and reporting its findings to the public and government agencies; the agency ruled that these evaluations were "objective" and thus that the organization qualified as a tax-exempt educational entity.[16] This concept is reflected in the tax regulations, which allow an educational organization to advocate "social or civic changes" or present "opinion on controversial issues,"[17] as long as it refrains from functioning as an action organization.[18] Thus, the IRS ruled that an organization informing the public about homosexuality was an educational organization; the information disseminated by this organization was held to be "factual" and "independently compiled," with its materials containing a "full documentation of the facts relied upon to support conclusions contained therein."[19]

By contrast, an organization whose principal activity was publication of a feminist monthly newspaper was found by a federal district court to not qualify as a tax-exempt educational entity because it failed to meet the *full and fair exposition* standard.[20] The newspaper contained material designed to advance the cause of the women's movement; the organization refused to publish items it considered damaging to that cause. The court, characterizing the organization as an "advocate" that had eschewed a policy of offering any balancing facts, said that its holding "is not to say that a publication may not advocate a particular point of view and still be educational, or that it must necessarily present views inimical to its philosophy, only that in doing so it must be sufficiently

---

[13] See Chapter 22.

[14] Seasongood v. Comm'r, 227 F.2d 907, 911 (6th Cir. 1955).

[15] Nat'l Ass'n for the Legal Support of Alternative Schools v. Comm'r, 71 T.C. 118 (1978).

[16] Rev. Rul. 79-26, 1979-1 C.B. 196.

[17] Reg. § 1.501(c)(3)-1(d)(2).

[18] See Chapters 22, 23.

[19] Rev. Rul. 78-305, 1978-2 C.B. 172. By contrast, an employee caucus group recognized by a for-profit company, comprising individuals who are or who support gay, lesbian, bisexual, or transgender individuals, was denied recognition of exemption as an educational entity because it presents information to its members and the company, not the public (Priv. Ltr. Rul. 201120036).

[20] Big Mama Rag, Inc. v. United States, 494 F. Supp. 473 (D.D.C. 1979).

dispassionate as to provide its readers with the factual basis from which they may draw independent conclusions."[21] The court rejected the assertion that the standard is a *per se* violation of the First Amendment.[22]

On appeal, the court concluded that the *full and fair exposition* requirement was sufficiently vague so as to violate free speech rights, in that the test lacked the "requisite clarity, both in explaining which applicant organizations are subject to the standard and in articulating its substantive requirements."[23] The rule followed by the IRS was that organizations that are subject to the test are those that are "controversial."[24] That standard was determined to be too vague to pass First Amendment muster, inasmuch as the IRS did not apply an "objective standard by which to judge which applicant organizations are advocacy groups."[25] The court observed that the standards used by the IRS in processing applications for recognition of exemption "may not be so imprecise that they afford latitude to individual IRS officials to pass judgment on the content and quantity of an applicant's views and goals and therefore to discriminate against those engaged in protected First Amendment activities."[26]

In the aftermath of the voiding of the full and fair exposition test, the IRS advanced the *methodology test*, pursuant to which a communication is evaluated by that agency to determine whether it may be *educational*, as opposed to *propaganda*. Pursuant to the methodology test, initially unveiled in litigation, the federal government endeavors (because of the free speech considerations) to avoid being the "arbiter of 'truth'" and accordingly "test[s] the method by which the advocate proceeds from the premises he furnishes to the conclusion he advocates."[27]

Although a federal district court found the methodology test itself unconstitutionally vague,[28] on appeal, the appellate court did not reach the question of the constitutionality of the test, having concluded that the material at issue was not, in the first instance, educational in nature.[29] Nonetheless, the appellate court implicitly endorsed the methodology test by observing that "starting from the breadth of terms in the regulation, application by IRS of the methodology test would move in the direction of more specifically requiring, in advocacy material, an intellectually appealing development of the views advocated," that the "four criteria tend toward ensuring that the educational exemption be restricted to material which substantially helps a reader or listener in a learning process," and that the "test reduces the vagueness found" to be present in the full and fair exposition standard.[30]

The criteria of the methodology test as developed by the IRS rest on the predicate that the IRS "renders no judgment as to the viewpoint or position of

[21] *Id.* at 479.

[22] In so doing, the court relied largely on Cammarano v. United States, 358 U.S. 498 (1959), and Hannegan v. Esquire, 327 U.S. 146 (1946).

[23] Big Mama Rag, Inc. v. United States, 631 F.2d 1030, 1036 (D.C. Cir. 1980).

[24] E.g., Rev. Rul. 78-305, 1978-2 C.B. 172.

[25] Big Mama Rag, Inc. v. United States, 631 F.2d 1030, 1036 (D.C. Cir. 1980).

[26] *Id.* at 1040.

[27] Nat'l Alliance v. United States, 710 F.2d 868, 874 (D.C. Cir. 1983).

[28] Nat'l Alliance v. United States, 81-1 U.S.T.C. ¶ 9464 (D.D.C. 1981).

[29] Nat'l Alliance v. United States, 710 F.2d 868 (D.C. Cir. 1983).

[30] *Id.* at 875.

the organization." Under this test, the "method used by the organization will not be considered educational if it fails to provide a factual foundation for the viewpoint or position being advocated, or if it fails to provide a development from the relevant facts that would materially aid a listener or reader in a learning process."[31]

A court, when applying the methodology test, concluded that an organization's activities violated standards of the test and thus were not educational, including a finding that a significant portion of these activities consisted of the "presentation of viewpoints unsupported by facts."[32] It pronounced the methodology test constitutional, observing that its "provisions are sufficiently understandable, specific, and objective both to preclude chilling of expression protected under the First Amendment and to minimize arbitrary or discrimination application by the IRS," because the standard "focuses on the method rather than the content of the presentation."[33] This court subsequently concluded that, using these factors, messages were "indicative that the method used to communicate the position is not educational," such as distortion of facts and use of "inflammatory language and disparaging terms."[34]

The courts have applied the methodology test only to differentiate between *educational* and *advocacy* entities. The IRS, however, also uses the test to ascertain whether an organization is engaged in educational activities as a threshold matter. For example, the IRS's lawyers issued guidance as to when credit counseling organizations[35] can qualify for tax exemption as educational entities, heavily relying on the methodology test.[36] Likewise, an organization that conducted seminars and provided consulting services was ruled by the IRS to not qualify as an exempt educational organization, in part because it did not have a "tailored educational program with a structured educational methodology in place."[37]

§ 8.3 EDUCATIONAL INSTITUTIONS

Educational institutions can be classified as either *institutions* or other organizations engaged in some form of educational activity.[38] The former consists of schools, colleges, universities, museums, libraries, and the like.

---

[31] Rev. Proc. 86-43, 1986-2 C.B. 729.

[32] Nationalist Movement v. Comm'r, 102 T.C. 558, 592 (1994), *aff'd*, 37 F.3d 216 (5th Cir. 1994).

[33] *Id.* 102 T.C. at 589. A court, characterizing the administrative record in a case as consisting of "only irrelevant, unintelligible, and inflammatory statements, nonsensical distortions, and irrelevant photographs," concluded that the organization's activities "appear principally to involve the presentation to the public of unsupported opinions"; it utilized the methodology test to deny exemption as an educational organization (Families Against Government Slavery v. Comm'r, 93 T.C.M. 958, 959 (2007)).

[34] Parks v. Comm'r, 145 T.C. 278, 317-318 (2015), *aff'd*, Parks Found. v. Comm'r, 717 Fed. Appx. 712 (9th Cir., Dec. 15, 2017).

[35] See § 7.3.

[36] Chief Couns. Adv. Mem. 200620001.

[37] Priv. Ltr. Rul. 200622055. The IRS ruled that an organization could not qualify as an educational entity in part because it does not make its educational materials available to the public (Priv. Ltr. Rul. 201020021); this is not, however, a requirement of law.

[38] The latter are the subject of §§ 8.4, 8.5.

(a) Schools, Colleges, and Universities

Nonprofit educational institutions, such as primary, secondary, and postsecondary schools, colleges and universities, early childhood centers,[39] and trade schools, are educational organizations for federal tax law purposes.[40] These organizations all have, as required, a "regularly scheduled curriculum, a regular faculty, and a regularly enrolled body of students in attendance at the place where the educational activities are regularly carried on."[41] To be tax-exempt, however, the schools must, like all charitable organizations (as the term is used in its broadest sense), meet all of the tax law requirements pertaining to these entities, including a showing that they are operated for public, rather than private, interests.

According to the tax regulations, this type of institution must have as its *primary function* the presentation of formal instruction.[42] Thus, an organization that has as its primary function the presentation of formal instruction, has courses that are interrelated and given in a regular and continuous manner (thereby constituting a regular curriculum), normally maintains a regular faculty, and has a regularly enrolled student body in attendance at the place where its educational activities are regularly carried on qualifies as a tax-exempt educational institution.[43]

An organization may not achieve status as a tax-exempt operating educational institution where it is engaged in both educational and noneducational activities, unless the latter activities are *merely incidental* to the former.[44] Thus, the IRS denied status as an educational entity in the case of an organization whose primary function was not the presentation of formal instruction but the maintenance and operation of a museum.[45]

A court upended the foregoing requirements for qualification as an educational institution (and most of the other categories of public institutions), holding that the primary-function test and the merely incidental test in the regulations, as a matter of statutory construction, "exceed the bounds of authority" provided by the statute and thus are unlawful.[46] The court based this finding on its conclusion that Congress "unambiguously chose not to include a primary-function requirement in" the statutory definition of *educational organization*.[47] That conclusion was, in turn, based on the fact that, although absent from this definition, the

---

[39] Michigan Early Childhood Center, Inc. v. Comm'r, 37 T.C.M. 808 (1978); San Francisco Infant School, Inc. v. Comm'r, 69 T.C. 957 (1978); Rev. Rul. 70-533, 1970-2 C.B. 112. See § 8.8.

[40] Reg. § 1.501(c)(3)-1(d)(3)(ii), Example (1).

[41] *Id.* Also, IRC § 170(b)(1)(A)(ii). The IRS ruled that a private operating foundation could be expected to convert to an operating educational organization (Priv. Ltr. Rul. 200620036).

[42] Reg. § 1.170A-9(c). In one instance, an organization was held to not lose its classification as an operating educational institution where it made a grant of more than one-half of its annual income to another organization, because the grant did not affect its instructional activities and involved almost none of its employees' time and effort (Gen. Couns. Mem. 38437).

[43] Rev. Rul. 78-309, 1978-2 C.B. 123.

[44] Reg. § 1.170A-9(c).

[45] Rev. Rul. 76-167, 1976-1 C.B. 329.

[46] Mayo Clinic v. United States, 412 F. Supp. 3d 1038, 1057 (D. Minn. 2019).

[47] *Id.* at 1047.

"equivalent of that very requirement appears in the very next subsection of the statute,"[48] which relates to the tax law concerning public charity hospitals.[49]

On appeal, the appellate court agreed with the district court that the requirement in the regulations that an educational organization's "primary function" must be "the presentation of formal instruction" was unreasonable, and in this respect upheld the regulation as invalid.[50] The appellate court disagreed with the district court with respect to the validity of the merely incidental test in the regulations, however, stating that "it is valid to interpret the statute as requiring that a qualifying organization's primary purpose be 'educational' and that its noneducational activities be merely incidental to that primary purpose."[51] The case was remanded for a more detailed analysis of the organization's educational activities as compared to its noneducational ones, to determine whether the primary purpose of the organization is educational within the meaning of the statute and the portions of the regulation that remain valid. The appellate court stated that "it must be determined whether [the organization's] overall purpose and operations establish that it is 'organized and operated exclusively' for educational rather than other purposes." The appellate court added: "Separating out the wheat from the chaff—the educational from the noneducational—while difficult, is not impossible."[52]

On remand, the district court held that the activities of this system of organizations comprising a teaching hospital were primarily educational within the meaning of the statute. The court determined the organization's primary purpose by analyzing its system-wide activities, not merely those of its parent organization, and interpreted the term "primary" to mean a "substantial purpose" of the organization rather than its "most important purpose."[53] The court found that education, research, and clinical practice were inextricably intertwined at the organization and that providing health care, like the organization's other functions, also served educational functions, with education perfusing these other purposes "everywhere they occur."[54] As such, education was a substantial purpose of the organization and the court found no other substantial, noneducational purpose that would disqualify the organization from meeting the requirements to be an educational organization.

An organization may be regarded as presenting formal instruction even though it lacks a formal course program or formal classroom instruction. Thus, an organization that provided elementary education on a full-time basis to children at a facility maintained exclusively for that purpose, with a faculty and enrolled student body, was held to be an operating educational institution despite the absence of a formal course program.[55] Likewise, an organization that conducted a survival course was granted classification as an operating educational institution, although

---

[48] Id.

[49] See § 7.6(a).

[50] Mayo Clinic v. United States, 997 F.3d 789 (8th Cir. 2021). The IRS announced that it will not acquiesce in this decision to the extent it invalidates this requirement in the regulation (AOD 2021-04, 2021-47 I.R.B. 725).

[51] 997 F.3d at 800.

[52] 997 F.3d at 802.

[53] Mayo Clinic v. United States, 642 F. Supp. 3d 831, 870-71 (D. Minn. 2022).

[54] Id. at 876.

[55] Rev. Rul. 72-430, 1972-2 C.B. 105.

its course periods were only 26 days and it used outdoor facilities more than class-rooms, since it had a regular curriculum, faculty, and student body.[56] Similarly, an organization that operated a wilderness camping program to rehabilitate adolescents with emotional and behavioral problems was ruled to be an operating educational institution, notwithstanding the fact that its program comprised 26-day hiking and camping trips; other aspects of its program included daily demonstrations, group counseling sessions, and instruction in hiking and camping skills.[57]

By contrast, a tax-exempt organization whose primary activity was providing specialized instruction by correspondence and a 5-to-10-day seminar program of personal instruction for students who have completed the correspondence course was ruled to not be an operating educational organization "[s]ince the organization's primary activity consists of providing instruction by correspondence."[58] In another instance, tutoring on a one-to-one basis in the students' homes was ruled insufficient to make the tutoring organization an operating educational entity.[59]

The fact that an otherwise qualifying organization offers a variety of lectures, workshops, and short courses concerning a general subject area, open to the general public and to its members, is not sufficient for it to acquire nonprivate foundation status as an educational institution.[60] This is because this type of an "optional, heterogeneous collection of courses is not formal instruction" and does not constitute a "curriculum."[61] Where the attendees are members of the general public and can attend the functions on an optional basis, there is no "regularly enrolled body of pupils or students."[62] Further, where the functions are led by various invited authorities and personalities in the field, there is no "regular faculty."[63]

Even if an organization qualifies as a school or other type of formal educational institution, it will not be able to achieve tax-exempt status if it maintains racially discriminatory admissions policies[64] or if it benefits private interests to more than an insubstantial extent.[65] As an illustration of the latter point, an otherwise qualifying school, which trained individuals for careers as political campaign professionals, was denied exempt status because of the secondary benefit accruing to entities of a political party and its candidates, since nearly all of the school's graduates became employed by or consultants to these entities or candidates.[66]

One federal court rejected the contention of the IRS that a board of education cannot qualify as an operating educational organization. While this type of

---

[56] Rev. Rul. 73-434, 1973-2 C.B. 71. Also, Rev. Rul. 79-130, 1979-1 C.B. 332; Rev. Rul. 73-543, 1973-2 C.B. 343, *clarified by* Ann. 74-115, 1974-52 I.R.B. 29; Rev. Rul. 75-215, 1975-1 C.B. 335; Rev. Rul. 72-101, 1972-1 C.B. 144; Rev. Rul. 69-492, 1969-2 C.B. 36; Rev. Rul. 68-175, 1968-1 C.B. 83.

[57] Rev. Rul. 83-140, 1983-2 C.B. 185, *revoking* Rev. Rul. 80-21, 1980-1 C.B. 233.

[58] Rev. Rul. 75-492, 1975-2 C.B. 80.

[59] Rev. Rul. 76-384, 1976-2 C.B. 57. Also, Rev. Rul. 76-417, 1976-2 C.B. 58. In one case, the IRS classified an organization as a school although its primary activity was in fact "network marketing"; following an examination, this entity's exempt status was retroactively revoked (Priv. Ltr. Rul. 201038020).

[60] Rev. Rul. 78-82, 1978-1 C.B. 70.

[61] Rev. Rul. 62-23, 1962-1 C.B. 200.

[62] Rev. Rul. 64-128, 1964-1 C.B. 191.

[63] Rev. Rul. 78-82, 1978-1 C.B. 70.

[64] See § 6.2(b).

[65] See § 20.13.

[66] American Campaign Academy v. Comm'r, 92 T.C. 1053 (1989).

entity does not actually present formal instruction, it employs all of the teachers in a school system and maintains control over a community's school districts. The court viewed the board as an entity that merely delegated the conduct of the formal educational process to the schools administered by the school districts.[67]

One of the functions of a tax-exempt college or university is to provide housing for its students. Often this is accomplished by means of dormitories and other forms of institution-owned on-campus housing. Although, as noted in other contexts, fraternities and sororities are usually exempt social clubs,[68] colleges and universities may, under certain circumstances, permissibly utilize these organizations (including providing financing and renovating) to provide additional housing for their students.[69]

(b)   Museums and Similar Organizations

Museums and similar organizations may qualify as institutions that provide formal instruction and training, and therefore as tax-exempt educational entities.[70] Thus, a sports museum was held by the IRS to be an exempt educational institution, although the ruling lacked any discussion of the criteria for qualification.[71] Likewise, the agency concluded that an organization established to operate a museum, which offered, in sponsorship with an exempt university, a degree program in museology, was an exempt educational organization.[72]

The law as to what constitutes a tax-exempt *museum* is sparse. The IRS, relying on a dictionary, ruled that a museum is an institution "devoted to the procurement, care, and display of objects of lasting interest or value."[73] The agency ruled that, by obtaining items of lasting interest or value relating to a particular sport, caring for and displaying these items in an institution open to the general public, and sponsoring and carrying on activities that foster a better understanding of the history and development of the sport and people associated with it, the organization qualified as an exempt museum. Activities can include courses, seminars, and a lecture series.[74]

The IRS observed, in the context of issuance of a ruling preserving an organization's tax-exempt status, that the purpose of the organization was to "hold and manage" a "collection of works of art, artifacts, books, writings, materials and miscellaneous memorabilia pertaining to the historical and architectural heritage" of the organization's area, noting that, as part of its management of these assets, the entity will operate a museum.[75]

In another ruling, the IRS noted, in finding a museum to be tax-exempt, that it conducted the "usual activities of an art museum," namely, it maintained displays of the art for public viewing and operated a shop that offered related items

---

[67] Estate of Green v. Comm'r, 82 T.C. 843 (1984).
[68] See Chapter 15.
[69] E.g., Priv. Ltr. Rul. 200538026.
[70] Reg. § 1.501(c)(3)-1(d)(3)(ii), Example (4).
[71] Rev. Rul. 68-372, 1968-2 C.B. 205.
[72] Rev. Rul. 76-167, 1976-1 C.B. 329.
[73] Rev. Rul. 68-372, 1968-2 C.B. 205.
[74] Rev. Rul. 76-167, 1976-1 C.B. 329.
[75] Priv. Ltr. Rul. 8444097.

for sale, such as books, posters, reproductions, and art periodicals.[76] In still another ruling finding exempt status for an organization, the IRS stated that the entity "owns approximately 80 pieces of artwork in its permanent collection, and obtains for exhibition touring art collections."[77]

A court held that an organization was tax-exempt where it furnished "various educational and charitable services to the community."[78] These services were said to include the sponsorship of classes and demonstrations and the conduct of a lecture and film series. The organization owned pieces of art, which it held as a "permanent collection" and displayed in public buildings.

Still another IRS ruling involving a tax-exempt museum concerned the issue as to whether the museum could operate a gift shop and restaurant as related businesses.[79] In passing, the IRS observed that the purpose of the organization was to promote interest in and educate the public as to decoy carvings and baymen's artifacts. To that end, the organization operated a museum and acquired artifacts for display in it; it "will house, free to the public, a number of maritime exhibits and related literature." A floor of its building was used as classroom space. In addition to the exhibit, the organization engaged in "demonstrations, instructional classes, and workshops," all as educational activities.[80]

The IRS seems most concerned about the aspect of displays of objects and public access to them. In one instance, a private foundation placed paintings in the residence of a disqualified person, as part of a large private collection; although there were occasional tours of the premises, the IRS concluded that placement of the foundation's paintings in the residence amounted to self-dealing.[81] In another case, where there was a lack of publicity and public access to a museum, the IRS caused the museum to adopt regular open hours, provide detailed material as to its history and architecture to its visitors, offer tours, post adequate signage, and engage in marketing.[82]

An illustration of what the IRS regards as an institution *similar* to a museum was provided when the IRS categorized as a museum an organization formed to create and operate a replica of an early American village.[83] The organization, which held the village open to the public, was determined by the IRS to be "engaging in activities similar to those of a museum" and thus to be educational in nature. In so finding, the IRS relied on one of its prior determinations in which an organization was found to be educational because it promoted an appreciation of history through the acquisition, restoration, and preservation of homes, churches, and public buildings having special historical or architectural significance, and opened the structures for viewing by the public.[84]

[76] Priv. Ltr. Rul. 8040014.
[77] Priv. Ltr. Rul. 8634001.
[78] Goldsboro Art League, Inc. v. Comm'r, 75 T.C. 337, 339 (1980).
[79] See § 24.5(c).
[80] Priv. Ltr. Rul. 200222030.
[81] Rev. Rul. 74-600, 1974-2 C.B. 385. The self-dealing rules are the subject of § 12.4(a).
[82] Tech. Adv. Mem. 9646002.
[83] Rev. Rul. 77-367, 1977-2 C.B. 193.
[84] Rev. Rul. 75-470, 1975-2 C.B. 207.

(c)   Other Educational Organizations

Other tax-exempt educational institutions include zoos, planetariums, libraries, and symphony orchestras.[85] In this regard, a bird and animal sanctuary,[86] an international exposition,[87] and a bar association library[88] were ruled by the IRS to be educational organizations.

§ 8.4   INSTRUCTION OF INDIVIDUALS

As noted, the term *educational* for federal tax law purposes relates to the instruction or training of the individual for the purpose of improving or developing their capabilities.[89]

Within this category of tax-exempt educational organizations are entities whose primary function is to provide instruction or training for a general purpose or on a particular subject, although they may not have a regular curriculum, faculty, or student body. Thus, an organization that provided educational and vocational training and guidance to nonskilled persons to improve employment opportunity was ruled to be an exempt educational organization,[90] as were organizations that conducted an industrywide apprentice training program;[91] operated community correctional centers for the rehabilitation of prisoners;[92] provided a facility and program for the rehabilitation of individuals recently released from a mental institution;[93] provided apprentice training in a skilled trade to native Americans;[94] offered instruction in basic academic subjects, speech, perceptual motor coordination, and psychological adjustment for children and adolescents with learning disabilities;[95] provided room, board, therapy, and counseling for persons discharged from alcoholic treatment centers;[96] and operated a program offering financial management and literacy courses for low-income individuals.[97]

---

[85] Reg. § 1.501(c)(3)-1(d)(3)(ii), Example (4).
[86] Rev. Rul. 67-292, 1967-2 C.B. 184.
[87] Rev. Rul. 71-545, 1971-2 C.B. 235.
[88] Rev. Rul. 75-196, 1975-1 C.B. 155.
[89] See text accompanied by *supra* note 3.
[90] Rev. Rul. 73-128, 1973-1 C.B. 222.
[91] Rev. Rul. 67-72, 1967-1 C.B. 125. This conclusion was reached because the primary purpose (see § 4.4) of the organization was educational. If, however, the provision of education is secondary and the primary purpose of the organization is the betterment of the working conditions of the apprentices, the organization would be classified as a tax-exempt labor entity (see § 16.1) (Rev. Rul. 59-6, 1959-1 C.B. 121).
[92] Rev. Rul. 70-583, 1970-2 C.B. 114; Rev. Rul. 67-150, 1967-1 C.B. 133.
[93] Rev. Rul. 72-16, 1972-1 C.B. 143.
[94] Rev. Rul. 77-272, 1977-2 C.B. 191.
[95] Rev. Rul. 77-68, 1977-1 C.B. 142.
[96] Rev. Rul. 75-472, 1975-2 C.B. 208.
[97] Priv. Ltr. Rul. 201301014. If programs of this nature entail *credit counseling services*, additional rules must be satisfied (see § 7.3(b)). An example of an entity that was deemed to not be educational and not satisfy these rules is in Priv. Ltr. Rul. 201249016.

Similarly, the IRS ruled tax-exempt as educational in nature an organization that maintained a government internship program for college students,[98] one that provided high school graduates and college students with work experience in selected trades and professions,[99] one that provided assistance to law students to obtain experience with public interest law firms and legal aid societies,[100] and one that promoted student and cultural exchanges.[101] As for instruction on a particular subject, organizations that provided instruction in securities management,[102] dancing,[103] sailboat racing,[104] drag car racing,[105] and the promotion of sportsmanship[106] were ruled to be tax-exempt as educational entities. The training of animals is not an educational activity, however, even where the animals' owners also receive some instruction.[107]

Another category of tax-exempt educational organizations that relates to the instruction or training of individuals includes those that conduct discussion groups, panels, forums, lectures, and the like.[108] For example, the operation of a coffeehouse by a number of churches, where church leaders, educators, businesspersons, and young people discussed a variety of topics, was held to be an educational endeavor.[109] Comparable organizations include those that instruct individuals as to how to improve their business or professional capabilities, such as the conduct of seminars and training programs on the subject of managing credit unions (for individuals in developing nations),[110] the practice of medicine (for physicians),[111] and banking (for bank employees).[112] Other exempt organizations in this category include an organization that conducted discussion groups and panels in order to acquaint the public with the problems of ex-convicts and parolees,[113] an organization that sponsored public workshops for training artists in concert technique,[114] and an organization that conducted clinics for the

[98] Rev. Rul. 70-584, 1970-2 C.B. 114.

[99] Rev. Rul. 75-284, 1975-2 C.B. 202.

[100] Rev. Rul. 78-310, 1978-2 C.B. 173.

[101] Rev. Rul. 80-286, 1980-2 C.B. 179; Rev. Rul. 69-400, 1969-2 C.B. 114; Rev. Rul. 68-165, 1968-1 C.B. 253; Rev. Rul. 65-191, 1965-2 C.B. 157. By contrast, an organization that merely arranged group tours for students and faculty members of a university was ruled to not be tax-exempt as an educational organization (Rev. Rul. 67-327, 1967-2 C.B. 187).

[102] Rev. Rul. 68-16, 1968-1 C.B. 246.

[103] Rev. Rul. 65-270, 1965-2 C.B. 160.

[104] Rev. Rul. 64-275, 1964-2 C.B. 142.

[105] Lions Assoc. Drag Strip v. United States, 64-1 U.S.T.C. ¶ 9283 (S.D. Cal. 1963).

[106] Rev. Rul. 55-587, 1955-2 C.B. 261.

[107] Ann Arbor Dog Training Club, Inc. v. Comm'r, 74 T.C. 207 (1980); Rev. Rul. 71-421, 1971-2 C.B. 229.

[108] Reg. § 1.501(c)(3)-1(d)(3)(ii), Example (2).

[109] Rev. Rul. 68-72, 1968-1 C.B. 250.

[110] Rev. Rul. 74-16, 1974-1 C.B. 126.

[111] Rev. Rul. 65-298, 1965-2 C.B. 163.

[112] Rev. Rul. 68-504, 1968-2 C.B. 211. If this type of activity is or becomes more in the nature of business promotion, however, then the private benefit doctrine (see § 20.13) will preclude exemption (e.g., Priv. Ltr. Rul. 201927022).

[113] Rev. Rul. 67-150, 1967-1 C.B. 133.

[114] Rev. Rul. 67-392, 1967-2 C.B. 191.

purpose of teaching a particular sport.[115] Organizations that present courses of instruction by means of correspondence or through the utilization of television or radio (and presumably the Internet) may qualify as educational in nature.[116]

If the functions of a discussion group are to a significant extent fraternal or social in nature, and where the speeches and discussions are deemed subjective and more akin to the exchanges of personal opinions and experiences in the informal atmosphere of a social group or club, the organization will not qualify as organized and operated exclusively for educational purposes.[117] Likewise, an organization that does not employ any faculty and does not provide any classes, lectures, or instructional material may be regarded, for federal tax purposes, as a social or recreational group rather than an educational organization, as was the case with a flying club that merely provided its members with an opportunity for unsupervised flight time.[118] This conclusion was also reached in a case involving an organization that arranged chess tournaments for its members, provided chess magazines and books to libraries, and offered instruction in and sponsored exhibitions of the game of chess, yet was denied classification as an educational organization because a substantial activity of the organization was the promotion and conduct of the tournaments, which were found to serve "recreational interests."[119] In another instance, an organization that was originally classified as a tax-exempt social club was denied reclassification as a charitable or educational organization because of the "substantial social and personal aspects" of the organization.[120] Another application of this principle occurred when an organization, the principal function of which was an annual science fiction convention, was denied classification as an educational organization because of its substantial "social and recreational purposes."[121] Another instance of application of this rule occurred when it was held that an association of descendants of a settler from England in the United States in the 1600s did not qualify for exemption as an educational organization, in part because its annual meetings and other activities were held to be "family-focused" and "social and recreational."[122]

A third category of educational organizations that instruct individuals are those that primarily engage in study and research. As an illustration, educational status was accorded an organization that undertook a program of study, research, and assembly of materials relating to court reform in a particular state.[123] Other

---

[115] Rev. Rul. 65-2, 1965-1 C.B. 227, *as amplified by* Rev. Rul. 77-365, 1977-2 C.B. 192. Also, Hutchinson Baseball Enters., Inc. v. Comm'r, 73 T.C. 144 (1979), aff'd, 696 F.2d 757 (10th Cir. 1982). In contrast, exemption will be denied where an adult sports league primarily serves the social and recreational purposes of its members and does not provide formal or ongoing instruction (e.g., Priv. Ltr. Rul. 202316010). See § 4.4.

[116] Reg. § 1.501(c)(3)-1(d)(3)(ii), Example (3). An organization failed to achieve recognition of exemption under these rules, with the IRS observing that its activities "are best described as providing product information and are analogous to [publication of] a product manual" (Priv. Ltr. Rul. 201303018).

[117] North Am. Sequential Sweepstakes v. Comm'r, 77 T.C. 1087 (1981).

[118] Syrang Aero Club, Inc. v. Comm'r, 73 T.C. 717 (1980).

[119] Minnesota Kingsmen Chess Ass'n, Inc. v. Comm'r, 46 T.C.M. 1133, 1135 (1983). Also, Spanish Am. Cultural Ass'n of Bergenfield v. Comm'r, 68 T.C.M. 931 (1994).

[120] Alumnae Chapter Beta of Clovia v. Comm'r, 46 T.C.M. 297, 298 (1983).

[121] St. Louis Science Fiction Ltd. v. Comm'r, 49 T.C.M. 1126, 1129 (1985).

[122] Manning Ass'n v. Comm'r, 93 T.C. 596, 606 (1989).

[123] Rev. Rul. 64-195, 1964-2 C.B. 138.

organizations ruled to be tax-exempt under this category of *educational* include an organization that researched and studied Civil War battles[124] and one that conducted and published research in the area of career planning and vocational counseling.[125]

A subject of considerable controversy in this context is the tax-exempt status of organizations that conduct "study tours," with the IRS concerned that exemption not be attached to activities amounting to sightseeing or other forms of vacation travel. An organization that conducted study tours for the purpose of educating individuals about the culture of the United States and other countries was ruled to be exempt,[126] although the commercial travel industry challenged the policy of the IRS in granting exempt status to organizations that substantially provided commercial travel services, claiming a competitive disadvantage.[127]

Where a tax-exempt educational program involving travel (such as wintertime ocean cruises) is intermixed with substantial social and recreational activities, exempt status will not be forthcoming.[128] Thus, as noted, an organization whose sole purpose and activity was to arrange group tours for students and faculty members of a university was ruled to not be educational for federal tax purposes,[129] whereas an organization that arranged for and participated in the temporary exchange of children between families of a foreign country and the United States was found to be exempt because it was fostering the cultural and educational development of children.[130] According to the IRS, the tax status of travel tours is dependent on how they are structured, what they consist of, and what they accomplish. This amounts to a facts-and-circumstances test, which examines the "nature, scope and motivation for a tour in making a determination as to whether there is a connection between a particular tour and the accomplishment of an exempt purpose."[131]

The IRS was constrained to rule that the definition of the term *educational* relating to the instruction of individuals (and, presumably, also with respect to instruction of the public) "contains no limitation with regard to age in defining that term."[132] The issue arose when the IRS, in ruling that an organization organized and operated for the purpose of teaching a particular sport qualified as a tax-exempt educational entity,[133] observed in the facts that the program of

---

[124] Rev. Rul. 67-148, 1967-1 C.B. 132.

[125] Rev. Rul. 68-71, 1968-1 C.B. 249.

[126] Rev. Rul. 70-534, 1970-2 C.B. 113; Rev. Rul. 69-400, 1969-2 C.B. 114.

[127] American Soc'y of Travel Agents, Inc. v. Simon, 36 A.F.T.R. 2d 75-5142 (D.D.C. 1975) (complaint dismissed), aff'd, 566 F.2d 145 (D.C. Cir. 1977) (finding of no standing to sue), cert. denied, 435 U.S. 947 (1978).

[128] Rev. Rul. 77-366, 1977-2 C.B. 192. Also, Int'l Postgraduate Med. Found. v. Comm'r, 56 T.C.M. 1140 (1989).

[129] Rev. Rul. 67-327, 1967-2 C.B. 187.

[130] Rev. Rul. 80-286, 1980-2 C.B. 179.

[131] Tech. Adv. Mem. 9702004. These criteria are refinements of the IRS position articulated in 1990 (Tech. Adv. Mem. 9027003). The criteria the IRS follows in this regard were further clarified by the development of regulations in the unrelated business area (see § 24.5(j)).

[132] Rev. Rul. 77-365, 1977-2 C.B. 192.

[133] Rev. Rul. 65-2, 1965-1 C.B. 227.

instruction was offered only to children. This earlier ruling was amplified to make it clear that the concept of *educational* extends to the instruction of individuals "of all ages."[134]

The instruction of individuals is thus inherently a tax-exempt function, and tax exemption is not dependent on the subjects under instruction or the number or motives of those being instructed (unless the facts demonstrate the presence of a practice contrary to public policy or an unwarranted private benefit).[135] There is, then, no requirement that the public be directly instructed; in this context, there is nothing akin to any requirement that a charitable class be served.[136] For example, an organization may conduct a seminar for lawyers on some aspect of the law, and the lawyers may attend solely for the purpose of augmenting their law practices, yet the seminar is clearly an educational undertaking. The fact is that, generally, exempt educational activities provide direct benefits to parties in their private capacity. The dissemination of information and the training of individuals is seen as serving public purposes (and thus as being educational) in that the increased capabilities of those receiving the instruction serve to improve the public welfare. In one instance, the IRS advised that an "educational activity may be performed in the public interest even if members of the public have no access to the activity whatsoever."[137]

§ 8.5   INSTRUCTION OF PUBLIC

As noted, the income tax regulations state that the term *educational* as used for federal tax purposes relates, in part, to the "instruction of the public on subjects useful to the individual and beneficial to the community."[138]

One category of this type of tax-exempt educational organization is the one that provides certain personal services deemed beneficial to the general public. The IRS, under this rationale, ruled to be exempt organizations that disseminated information concerning hallucinatory drugs,[139] conducted personal money management instruction,[140] and educated expectant mothers and the public in a method of painless childbirth.[141] Similarly, an organization that functioned primarily as a crop seed certification entity was held to be educational because of its adult education classes, seminars, newsletter, and lending library.[142]

Another way an organization can be educational in this regard is by providing instruction in the form of counseling. The IRS wrote that "[p]ersonal

---

[134] Rev. Rul. 77-365, 1977-2 C.B. 192.

[135] See §§ 6.2, 20.13.

[136] Cf. § 6.3(a).

[137] Gen. Couns. Mem. 38459. In general, Rev. Rul. 75-196, 1975-1 C.B. 155. Cf. American Campaign Academy v. Comm'r, 92 T.C. 1053 (1989).

[138] See text accompanied by *supra* note 3.

[139] Rev. Rul. 70-590, 1970-2 C.B. 116.

[140] Rev. Rul. 69-441, 1969-2 C.B. 115.

[141] Rev. Rul. 66-255, 1966-2 C.B. 210.

[142] Indiana Crop Improvement Ass'n, Inc. v. Comm'r, 76 T.C. 394 (1981).

counseling has been recognized as a valid method of instruction for educational organizations."[143] For example, an organization that provided free counseling to men concerning methods of voluntary sterilization was held to be a tax-exempt educational entity.[144] Other exempt personal counseling organizations include those that offered group counseling to widows and widowers to assist them in legal, financial, and emotional problems caused by the deaths of their spouses;[145] counseling to women on methods of resolving unwanted pregnancies;[146] marriage counseling;[147] vocational counseling;[148] counseling of immigrants to the United States enabling them to overcome social, cultural, and economic problems;[149] and counseling as to personal health and fitness.[150]

Another category of tax-exempt educational organizations consists of those that endeavor to instruct the public in the field of civic betterment. This type of organization frequently also qualifies under one or more varieties of the concept of *charitable* or *social welfare*. Thus, an organization that disseminated information, in the nature of results of its investigations, in an effort to lessen racial and religious prejudice in the fields of housing and public accommodations was ruled to be exempt.[151] Other organizations in this category include ones that distributed information about the results of a model demonstration housing program for low-income families conducted by the organization,[152] disseminated information on the need for international cooperation,[153] educated the public as to the means of correcting conditions such as community tension and juvenile delinquency,[154] enlightened the public in a particular city as to the advantages of street planning,[155] developed and distributed a community land-use plan,[156] and educated the public regarding environmental deterioration due to solid waste pollution[157] and regarding the media, specifically radio and television programming[158] and accuracy of news coverage by newspapers.[159]

In the fourth category of tax-exempt educational organizations that exist to instruct the public are those that conduct study and research. The variety of efforts encompassed by these organizations is nearly limitless. As illustrations, these

---

[143] Rev. Rul. 73-569, 1973-2 C.B. 178.
[144] Rev. Rul. 74-595, 1974-2 C.B. 164.
[145] Rev. Rul. 78-99, 1978-1 C.B. 152.
[146] Rev. Rul. 73-569, 1973-2 C.B. 178.
[147] Rev. Rul. 70-640, 1970-2 C.B. 117.
[148] Rev. Rul. 68-71, 1968-1 C.B. 249.
[149] Rev. Rul. 76-205, 1976-1 C.B. 154.
[150] Priv. Ltr. Rul. 9732032.
[151] Rev. Rul. 75-285, 1975-2 C.B. 203; Rev. Rul. 68-438, 1968-2 C.B. 209; Rev. Rul. 68-70, 1968-1 C.B. 248; Rev. Rul. 67-250, 1967-2 C.B. 182.
[152] Rev. Rul. 68-17, 1968-1, C.B. 247; Rev. Rul. 67-138, 1967-1 C.B. 129.
[153] Rev. Rul. 67-342, 1967-2 C.B. 187.
[154] Rev. Rul. 68-15, 1968-1 C.B. 244.
[155] Rev. Rul. 68-14, 1968-1 C.B. 243.
[156] Rev. Rul. 67-391, 1967-2 C.B. 190.
[157] Rev. Rul. 72-560, 1972-2 C.B. 248.
[158] Rev. Rul. 64-192, 1964-2 C.B. 136.
[159] Rev. Rul. 74-615, 1974-2 C.B. 165.

organizations include those that conducted analyses, studies, and research into the problems of a particular region (pollution, transportation, water resources, waste disposal) and published the results;[160] instructed the public on agricultural matters by conducting fairs and exhibitions;[161] and published a journal to disseminate information about specific types of physical and mental disorders.[162]

The publication of printed material can be an educational activity in a variety of other contexts. For example, an organization that surveyed scientific and medical literature and prepared, published, and distributed abstracts of it was recognized as tax-exempt.[163] Similarly, an organization was ruled tax-exempt for assisting the National Park Service by preparing, publishing, and distributing literature concerning a park.[164] Likewise, a nonprofit corporation that compiled and published a manual on the standard library cataloging system was ruled to be engaged in educational activities.[165] By contrast, where a publication effort is operated by an entity akin to normal commercial practices, tax exemption as an educational organization will be denied.[166] Thus, the IRS held that an organization whose only activities were the preparation and publication of a newspaper of local, national, and international news articles with an ethnic emphasis, soliciting advertising and selling subscriptions to the newspaper in a manner indistinguishable from ordinary commercial publishing practices, was not operated exclusively for educational purposes.[167]

In general, an organization engaged in publishing can qualify as a tax-exempt educational entity where the content of the publication is inherently educational, the preparation of the material follows methods generally accepted as educational in character, the distribution of the materials is necessary or valuable in achieving the organization's exempt purposes, and the manner in which the distribution is accomplished is distinguishable from ordinary commercial publishing practices.[168] The IRS relied on these criteria in concluding that the recording and sale of musical compositions that were not generally produced by the commercial recording industry was educational because it was a means for presenting new works of unrecognized composers and the neglected works of more recognized composers.[169] By contrast, a publication of an exempt organization was held to not be educational because its contents were found to be primarily news concerning the organization's members and current events affecting the organization, with the information provided of limited interest to the general public.[170]

---

[160] Rev. Rul. 70-79, 1970-1 C.B. 127.

[161] Rev. Rul. 67-216, 1967-2 C.B. 180.

[162] Rev. Rul. 67-4, 1967-1 C.B. 121.

[163] Rev. Rul. 66-147, 1966-1 C.B. 137.

[164] Rev. Rul. 68-307, 1968-1 C.B. 258.

[165] Forest Press, Inc. v. Comm'r, 22 T.C. 265 (1954).

[166] Rev. Rul. 60-351, 1960-2 C.B. 169. See § 8.6.

[167] Rev. Rul. 77-4, 1977-1 C.B. 141. Also, Christian Manner Int'l, Inc. v. Comm'r, 71 T.C. 661 (1979).

[168] Rev. Rul. 67-4, 1967-1 C.B. 121.

[169] Rev. Rul. 79-369, 1979-2 C.B. 226.

[170] Phi Delta Theta Fraternity v. Comm'r, 90 T.C. 1033 (1988), *aff'd*, 887 F.2d 1302 (6th Cir. 1989).

The educational activities of organizations may be carried on through a tax-exempt club, such as a gem and mineral club[171] or a garden club,[172] or by means of public lectures and debates.[173] These organizations may function as broad-based membership organizations,[174] as organizations formed to promote a specific cause,[175] or as a transitory organization, such as one to collect and collate campaign materials of a particular candidate for ultimate donation to a university or public library.[176]

A somewhat controversial ruling from the IRS concerning this category of educational organization is one involving a society of heating and air-conditioning engineers and others having a professional interest in this field that was held to be educational in nature.[177] Its educational purposes were the operation of a library, dissemination of the results of its scientific research, and the making available of model codes of minimum standards for heating, ventilating, and air-conditioning. The IRS went to considerable lengths to distinguish this type of professional society from a business league.[178]

Organizations that are charitable, educational, or scientific societies have been recognized by the IRS as exempt organizations. Frequently, their membership base is composed of individuals (rather than organizations); these people share common professional and/or disciplinary interests. In most instances, these organizations satisfy the criteria for classification as charitable, educational, or like entities, but, because they provide services to individual members, the tendency of the IRS may be to categorize or reclassify them as business leagues, on the ground that they serve to enhance the professional development of the members rather than advance an educational purpose.[179]

An otherwise tax-exempt organization that produced and distributed, for free (or for small, cost-defraying fees), educational, cultural, and public interest programs for public viewing via public educational channels of commercial cable television companies was held to be operated for educational purposes and thus qualified for exemption because an organization may achieve its educational purposes through the production of television programs where it does so in a noncommercial manner.[180] Similarly, a nonprofit organization established to operate a noncommercial educational broadcasting station presenting educational, cultural, and public interest programs qualified as an exempt educational entity,[181] as did an

---

[171] Rev. Rul. 67-139, 1967-1 C.B. 129.
[172] Rev. Rul. 66-179, 1966-1 C.B. 139. In this ruling, a garden club qualified as an exempt charitable and educational where it operated a free library of horticultural materials, instructed the public on gardening and conservation through radio, television, and lectures, held public flower shows of a noncommercial nature, encouraged civic beautification projects, and made awards for achievement in conservation and horticulture; its membership was open to the general public and its activities were not restricted to members (*id.*). Cf. § 4.4, note 146.
[173] Rev. Rul. 66-256, 1966-2 C.B. 210.
[174] Rev. Rul. 68-164, 1968-1 C.B. 252.
[175] Rev. Rul. 72-228, 1972-1 C.B. 148.
[176] Rev. Rul. 70-321, 1970-1 C.B. 129.
[177] Rev. Rul. 71-506, 1971-2 C.B. 233.
[178] Cf. Rev. Rul. 70-641, 1970-2 C.B. 119.
[179] See § 14.1(e).
[180] Rev. Rul. 76-4, 1976-1 C.B. 145.
[181] Rev. Rul. 66-220, 1966-2 C.B. 209.

organization that produced educational films concerning a particular subject and that disseminated its educational material to the public by means of commercial television, where the films were presented in a noncommercial manner.[182]

With these three rulings as precedent, the IRS analyzed an organization that facilitated the dissemination of educational and cultural programs via the public and educational access channels of a commercial cable television company. Finding this entity to be educational, the IRS characterized these rulings as "clearly indicat[ing] that an organization may achieve its educational purposes through the production of television programs, regardless of whether the programs are to be broadcast over the airwaves or over a cable system, so long as the programs are presented in a noncommercial manner."[183]

Where an organization engages in educational programming by means of television to a substantial extent, however, it can be accorded designation as an educational entity, even though the organization owns and operates the station under a commercial broadcasting license.[184]

The IRS has ruled on several occasions that the development and making available of open-source software does not constitute "the instruction of the public on subjects useful to the individual and beneficial to the community," inasmuch as "anything learned is incidental" when people download the software for their own use.[185]

§ 8.6   EDUCATIONAL ACTIVITY AS COMMERCIAL BUSINESS

One of the most troublesome aspects of the law of tax-exempt organizations is differentiation between exempt and commercial functions.[186] While this aspect of the law is by no means confined to educational organizations,[187] much of the clashing of principles occurs in this setting because what may be an exempt educational activity in one context may be a commercial business in another. Certainly, for example, in the general world of commerce, operation of a restaurant, bookstore, broadcasting station, portfolio management service, publishing company, and the like is a trade or business. This type of operation may qualify as an exempt educational organization, however, as have, for example, a university restaurant,[188] a museum restaurant,[189] a university store,[190] a broadcasting station,[191] an

---

[182] Rev. Rul. 67-342, 1967-2 C.B. 187.

[183] Rev. Rul. 76-443, 1976-2 C.B. 149, 150.

[184] Rev. Rul. 78-385, 1978-2 C.B. 174.

[185] E.g., Priv. Ltr. Rul. 202221009.

[186] See § 4.9.

[187] Indeed, many of the difficulties in this area also occur in the health care field (see § 7.6).

[188] Rev. Rul. 67-217, 1967-2 C.B. 181.

[189] Priv. Ltr. Rul. 200222030. Inexplicably, however, the IRS does not follow this policy in settings other than colleges, universities, hospitals, and museums (e.g., Tech. Adv. Mem. 200021056). See § 24.5(c).

[190] Rev. Rul. 68-538, 1968-2 C.B. 116; Rev. Rul. 58-194, 1958-1 C.B. 240; Squire v. Students Book Corp., 191 F.2d 1018 (9th Cir. 1951).

[191] Rev. Rul. 66-220, 1966-2 C.B. 209.

endowment fund management service,[192] a retail sales enterprise,[193] a money lending operation,[194] and an organization publishing a law school journal.[195]

It is difficult to formulate guidelines to determine when a given purpose or activity is *educational* or is a commercial business. Of course, an exempt purpose or activity must be one that benefits the public or an appropriate segment of the public rather than any private individual or individuals, and the organization must not be operated for the benefit of private shareholders or individuals.[196] Nevertheless, even these rules, aside from the essential questions as to what constitutes an educational activity, require some subjective judgments.

The task of making these judgments befell a federal court in a case involving an organization created to disseminate knowledge of economics with a view to advancing the welfare of the American people. The court concluded that the primary purpose of the organization was not an educational but a commercial one.[197] The court, in concluding that the publications of the organization merely provided investment advice to subscribers for a fee, noted that the existence of profits, while not conclusive, is some evidence that the business purpose is primary[198] and that the services of the organization are those "commonly associated with a commercial enterprise."[199]

Subsequently, the IRS determined that an association of investment clubs, formed for the mutual exchange of investment information among its members and prospective investors to enable them to make sound investments, was not a tax-exempt educational organization, inasmuch as the association was serving private economic interests.[200] Likewise, an organization operated to protect the financial stability of a teachers' retirement system, and the contributions and pensions of retiree members of the system, was held to not be educational and to serve its members' private interests, notwithstanding its publication of a newsletter.[201]

The same result occurred with respect to a nonprofit organization that clearly engaged in educational activities, namely, the sponsorship of programs involving training, seminars, lectures, and the like in areas of intrapersonal awareness and communication.[202] The educational activities were conducted

---

[192] Rev. Rul. 71-529, 1971-2 C.B. 234.

[193] Rev. Rul. 68-167, 1968-1 C.B. 255. For this rationale to be successful, however, the business function must be related to exempt purposes. Thus, an organization wholly owned by an exempt college that manufactured and sold wood and metal products was ruled to not be exempt, notwithstanding the fact that the entity furnished employment to the students of the college (Rev. Rul. 69-177, 1969-1 C.B. 150).

[194] Rev. Rul. 63-220, 1963-2 C.B. 208; Rev. Rul. 61-87, 1961-1 C.B. 191.

[195] Rev. Rul. 63-235, 1963-2 C.B. 210. As noted, publishing can obviously be a commercial undertaking. Thus, even though an organization published "better teaching materials," it was found by the IRS to be an "enterprise conducted in an essentially commercial manner, in which all the participants expect to receive a monetary return" (Rev. Rul. 66-104, 1966-1 C.B. 135). Likewise, while a magazine had some educational aspects, it was published and sold to the "general public in accordance with ordinary commercial publishing practices" (Rev. Rul. 60-351, 1960-2 C.B. 169).

[196] Reg. § 1.501(c)(3)-1(c)(2), (d)(1)(ii).

[197] American Inst. for Economic Research v. United States, 302 F.2d 934 (Ct. Cl. 1962).

[198] Scripture Press Found. v. United States, 285 F.2d 800 (Ct. Cl. 1961), *cert. denied*, 368 U.S. 985 (1962).

[199] American Inst. for Economic Research v. United States, 302 F.2d 934, 938 (Ct. Cl. 1962).

[200] Rev. Rul. 76-366, 1976-2 C.B. 144.

[201] Retired Teachers Legal Defense Fund, Inc. v. Comm'r, 78 T.C. 280 (1982).

[202] est of Hawaii v. Comm'r, 71 T.C. 1067 (1979), *aff'd*, 647 F.2d 170 (9th Cir. 1981).

pursuant to licensing arrangements with for-profit corporations that amounted to substantial control over the functioning of the nonprofit organization. In rejecting tax-exempt status for the nonprofit organization, the court held that it is part of a "franchise system which is operated for private benefit and that its affiliation with this system taints it with a substantial commercial purpose."[203] Thus, the organization's entanglements with for-profit corporations were such that commercial ends were imputed to it, notwithstanding the inherently exempt nature of its activities.

Likewise, an organization, originally exempted from federal income tax as an educational and religious entity, had its tax exemption revoked as a result of evolution into a commercial publishing entity.[204] Both the IRS and a court concluded that the publishing activities had taken on a "commercial hue" and the organization had "become a highly efficient business venture."[205] In reaching this conclusion, the court noted that the organization followed publishing and sales practices used by comparable nonexempt commercial publishers, had generated increasing profits in recent years,[206] was experiencing a growth in accumulated surplus, and had been paying substantially increased salaries to its top employees.[207]

The IRS considered the status of an organization that operated a retail grocery store to sell food to residents in a poverty area at substantially lower-than-usual prices, that maintained a free delivery service for the needy, and that allocated about 4 percent of its earnings for use in a training program for the hard-core unemployed. The IRS held that the operation of the grocery store was a substantial nonexempt activity, since it was conducted on a scale larger than reasonably necessary for the training program (an exempt activity)[208] and since the operation could not be characterized as an investment or business undertaking for the production of income for use in carrying on qualified charitable purposes, and denied the exemption.[209] Similarly, the IRS ruled nonexempt an organization, wholly owned by an exempt college, that manufactured and sold wood products primarily to employ students of the college to enable them to continue their education, on the ground that the enterprise itself was not an instructional or training activity.[210] Conversely, the IRS recognized that an exempt organization may engage in a commercial activity without endangering its tax status where the business is not an end in itself but is a means by which charitable purposes are accomplished and where the endeavor is not conducted on a scale larger than is reasonably necessary to accomplish the organization's tax-exempt purpose.[211] Likewise, an organization that provided training of procurement officials for countries receiving United

---

[203] *Id.* at 1080.
[204] Incorporated Trustees of the Gospel Worker Soc'y v. United States, 510 F. Supp. 374 (D.D.C. 1981), *aff'd*, 672 F.2d 894 (D.C. Cir. 1981), *cert. denied*, 456 U.S. 944 (1982).
[205] *Id.* at 381.
[206] See § 4.9(d).
[207] See 20.4.
[208] See § 8.4.
[209] Rev. Rul. 73-127, 1973-1 C.B. 221.
[210] Rev. Rul. 69-177, 1969-1 C.B. 150.
[211] Rev. Rul. 73-128, 1973-1 C.B. 222.

States aid was found to be educational in nature, despite an IRS contention that procurement activity is not inherently exempt, since the procurement activity furthered the organization's educational and training program.[212]

A case involving an organization's tax-exempt status, where the IRS is claiming that the organization is operated for a substantial commercial purpose, may be dependent on the organization's charges for services or products in relation to its costs.[213] Where the fees are set at a level less than costs, the courts and sometimes the IRS will be spurred on to the conclusion that the organization is not operated in an ordinary commercial manner.[214] Other considerations govern where a nonprofit organization is experiencing net receipts.[215]

This aspect of the law is being greatly influenced by developments in the field of unrelated income taxation.[216] The courts have developed law concerning the scope of the phrase *trade or business* that ranges considerably beyond the criteria set forth in the statutory definition of the phrase.[217] As this aspect of the law is evolving, great consideration is being given to the concepts of *profit motive* and *unfair competition*.[218] More contemporaneously, the courts are focusing on the question of whether a particular activity is being operated in a *commercial* manner.[219]

Thus, some courts will, in characterizing an activity as a trade or business, place emphasis on the conclusion that the undertaking was conducted with a profit motive.[220] This conclusion is usually buttressed by a finding that the particular activity was in fact profitable. This approach is a reflection of the test for business expense deduction purposes,[221] which looks to determine whether the activity was entered into with the dominant hope and intent of realizing a profit.[222] One appellate court commented that where an activity is not substantially related to exempt purposes (the principal statutory test), is "conducted in a competitive profit seeking manner, and regularly earns significant profits, a heavy burden must be placed on the organization to prove profit is not its motive" for engaging in the activity.[223]

Other courts place more emphasis on the question as to whether the activity constitutes unfair competition with taxable business.[224] This is understandable,

---

[212] Afro-American Purchasing Center, Inc. v. Comm'r, 37 T.C.M. 184 (1978).

[213] See § 24.2(e).

[214] Peoples Translation Service/Newsfront Int'l v. Comm'r, 72 T.C. 42 (1979). Yet the IRS ruled that the conduct of seminars for the public without charge is not an educational (or charitable) activity (Priv. Ltr. Rul. 200844029).

[215] See § 4.9.

[216] See Chapter 24.

[217] See § 24.2(a).

[218] See § 24.2(b), (c).

[219] See § 4.9.

[220] E.g., Professional Ins. Agents of Mich. v. Comm'r, 726 F.2d 1097 (6th Cir. 1984); Carolinas Farm & Power Equip. Dealers Ass'n, Inc. v. United States, 699 F.2d 167 (4th Cir. 1983); Louisiana Credit Union League v. United States, 693 F.2d 525 (5th Cir. 1982); Professional Ins. Agents of Wash. v. Comm'r, 53 T.C.M. 9 (1987).

[221] IRC § 162.

[222] E.g., United States v. American Bar Endowment, 477 U.S. 105, 110 n.1 (1986).

[223] Carolinas Farm & Power Equip. Dealers Ass'n, Inc. v. United States, 699 F.2d 167, 171 (4th Cir. 1983).

[224] E.g., Disabled Am. Veterans v. United States, 650 F.2d 1178 (Ct. Cl. 1981); Hope School v. United States, 612 F.2d 298 (7th Cir. 1980); Carle Found. v. United States, 611 F.2d 1192 (7th Cir. 1979).

given the legislative history of the unrelated income rules, which clearly reflects the intent of Congress to eliminate unfair competitive advantages that tax-exempt organizations may otherwise have over for-profit business entities.[225]

The U.S. Supreme Court indicated a tendency to favor both of these lines of cases, noting the rationale for the profit motive approach[226] and that a focus should be on whether the activity under examination is the kind of activity that is "provided by private commercial entities in order to make a profit."[227] Lower courts are reflecting a willingness to utilize both of these lines of cases.[228]

§ 8.7   EDUCATIONAL ACTIVITY AS PRIVATE BENEFIT FUNCTION

The focus of an educational undertaking is the aspect of transmission of information or knowledge. What the recipient of the educational experience subsequently does with the newfound knowledge or training (such as obtain a degree and/or employment) is generally irrelevant.

Nonetheless, the IRS concluded that a certification program conducted by a tax-exempt educational and scientific organization was an unrelated business because it primarily advanced the interests of individuals in a particular profession. The agency wrote that seminars and publication of study guides developed in conjunction with the certification examination, "while educational, are designed primarily to assist candidates in passing the examination."[229] The inference is that this type of activity, though otherwise inherently educational, fails to qualify as an exempt function because the primary purpose of the activity is to serve the interests of the profession.[230]

§ 8.8   CHILD CARE ORGANIZATIONS

The term *educational* purposes includes "providing care of children away from their homes if—(1) substantially all of the care provided by the organization is for purposes of enabling individuals [their parents] to be gainfully employed, and (2) the services provided by the organization are available to the general public."[231] It is the view of the IRS that a child care facility will not qualify under these rules if it provides preference in enrollment for the children of employees of a specific employer.[232]

---

[225] See § 24.1.
[226] United States v. American Bar Endowment, 477 U.S. 105, 112–14 (1986).
[227] *Id.* at 111.
[228] E.g., Illinois Ass'n of Pro. Ins. Agents, Inc. v. Comm'r, 86-2 U.S.T.C. ¶ 9702 (7th Cir. 1986), *aff'g* 49 T.C.M. 925 (1985).
[229] Priv. Ltr. Rul. 200439043.
[230] E.g., Rev. Rul. 73-567, 1973-2 C.B. 178 (see § 14.1(g)).
[231] IRC § 501(k). The reference to the words *general public* means that the IRC § 501(k) organization cannot be racially discriminatory (see § 6.2(b)), although it does not have to satisfy the IRS guidelines on the subject (§ 6.2(b)(ii)) unless it is also classified under IRC § 170(b)(1)(A)(ii) (see § 12.3(a)) (Gen. Couns. Mem. 39757).
[232] Gen. Couns. Mem. 39613.

The Office of Chief Counsel of the IRS issued an opinion that the provision of day-care referrals and assistance information to the general public is not a charitable or educational activity but, rather, a commercial one.[233] In so doing, the IRS modified an earlier opinion from that office indicating that these activities were considered to not be unrelated business when undertaken by an organization the primary purpose of which was the operation of day-care centers.[234] In the earlier opinion, the IRS also took the position that the provision of specialized child care assistance to employers in the organization's locale is not a tax-exempt activity because of the substantial benefit provided the employers in connection with the operation of their qualified dependent care assistance programs.[235]

This statutory definition was enacted because of the reach of the ruling policy by the IRS in this area. This policy has been described as follows: "The IRS has recognized that nonprofit day care centers may be eligible for tax exemption and tax-deductible contributions where enrollment is based on the financial need of the family and the need of the child for the program, or where the center provides preschool-age children of working parents with an educational program through a professional staff of qualified teachers."[236]

This definition of *educational* purposes is "not intended to affect the meaning of terms 'educational' or 'charitable' for any purpose other than considering the child care organizations described in the provision as having educational purposes."[237]

[233] Gen. Couns. Mem. 39872.
[234] Gen. Couns. Mem. 39622.
[235] *Id.* These specialized child care assistance plans are operated pursuant to IRC § 129, which provides that the gross income of an employee does not include amounts paid or incurred by the employer for eligible dependent care assistance.
[236] H.R. Rep. No. 98-861, at 1100 (1984).
[237] *Id.*

CHAPTER NINE

Scientific Organizations

Section 501(c)(3) of the Internal Revenue Code provides that an organization may be exempt from federal income tax under IRC § 501(a) if it is organized and operated exclusively for *scientific* purposes.[1]

§ 9.1   FEDERAL TAX LAW DEFINITION OF *SCIENCE*

Neither the Internal Revenue Code nor any income tax regulation or IRS revenue ruling defines the term *scientific* as used in the tax-exempt organizations context. A dictionary definition states that *science* is a "branch of study that is concerned with observation and classification of facts and especially with the establishment . . . of verifiable general laws chiefly by induction and hypotheses."[2] Another dictionary defines *science* as "[k]nowledge, as of facts and principles, gained by systemic study."[3] A more technical definition of the term is that science is a "branch of study in which facts are observed, classified, and, usually, quantitative laws are formulated and verified; [or] involves the application of mathematical reasoning and data analysis to natural phenomena."[4]

A federal district court offered the view that "while projects may vary in terms of degree of sophistication, if professional skill is involved in the design and supervision of a project intended to solve a problem through a search for a demonstrable truth, the project would appear to be scientific research."[5] Another federal court was of the view that the term *science* means the "process by which

---

[1] Reg. § 1.501(c)(3)-1(d)(1)(i)(c).

[2] *Webster's Third New International Dictionary.*

[3] *Random House Dictionary of the English Language* (Stein, ed., 1967).

[4] *McGraw-Hill Dictionary of Scientific and Technical Terms* (Lapedes, ed., 2d ed. 1978).

[5] Midwest Research Inst. v. United States, 554 F. Supp. 1379, 1386 (W.D. Mo. 1983), *aff'd*, 744 F.2d 635 (8th Cir. 1984). Also, Oglesby v. Chandler, 288 P. 1034 (1930); *In re* Massachusetts General Hosp., 95 F. 973 (C.C. Mass. 1899).

knowledge is systematized or classified through the use of observation, experimentation, or reasoning."[6]

In one instance, concerning an organization whose exempt purpose was to provide multidisciplinary scientific research for government and industry, the court found all the contractual arrangements challenged by the government to consist of scientific research. The court observed that the organization was not involved in the commercialization of the products or processes developed from its research, nor did it conduct consumer or market research, social science research, or ordinary testing of the type carried on incident to commercial operations. Said the court: "The fact that research is directed towards solving a particular industrial problem does not necessarily indicate that the research is not scientific."[7]

Basically, then, a *scientific* organization is one engaged in scientific research or otherwise operated for the dissemination of scientific knowledge. A fundamental requirement underlying this form of tax exemption is that the organization must serve a public rather than a private interest.[8] Thus, the tax-exempt scientific organization must, among the other criteria for exemption, be organized and operated in the public interest.[9]

An organization composed of members of an industry to develop new and improved uses for products of the industry was ruled to not be a tax-exempt scientific organization on the ground that it was serving the private interests of its creators.[10] By contrast, an organization formed by a group of physicians specializing in heart disease to research the cause and publish treatments of heart defects was found to be an exempt scientific organization.[11] In the latter instance, any personal benefit (in the form of increased prestige and enhanced reputation) derived by the physician-creators was deemed not to lessen the public benefits flowing from the organization's operations.

§ 9.2 CONCEPT OF *RESEARCH*

With tax-exempt scientific organizations, the focus is largely on the concept of *research*. For research to be scientific, it must be carried on in furtherance of a scientific purpose. Thus, the term *scientific* includes the carrying on of scientific research in the public interest.[12]

Federal tax law excludes from unrelated business taxable income, in the case of an organization operated primarily for purposes of carrying on fundamental research the results of which are freely available to the public, all income derived

---

[6] IIT Research Inst. v. United States, 9 Cl. Ct. 13 (1985). The IRS held that a medical research organization that had a tissue specimen redistribution program was engaged in *scientific* activity because it involved "compiling experimentation data gathered from the residual tissue and assembling it into a useful central resource of effective targets for therapeutic intervention and indicators of unfavorable outcomes" (Priv. Ltr. Rul. 201114035).

[7] *Id.*

[8] Reg. §§ 1.501(a)-1(c), 1.501(c)(3)-1(c)(2).

[9] Reg. § 1.501(c)(3)-1(d)(5)(i).

[10] Rev. Rul. 69-632, 1969-2 C.B. 120. Also, Medical Diagnostic Ass'n v. Comm'r, 42 B.T.A. 610 (1940).

[11] Rev. Rul. 69-526, 1969-2 C.B. 115.

[12] E.g., Priv. Ltr. Rul. 200852036.

from research performed for any person and all deductions directly connected with the activity.[13] For purposes of the unrelated income rules, therefore, it is necessary to determine whether the organization is operated primarily for purposes of carrying on fundamental, as contrasted with applied, research.[14]

Consequently, scientific research does not include activities ordinarily carried on *incident to commercial operations*, as, for example, the testing or inspection of materials or products or the designing or construction of equipment or buildings.[15] For example, an organization that fostered the development of machinery in connection with a commercial operation, and was empowered to sell, assign, and grant licenses with respect to its copyrights, trademarks, trade names, or patent rights, was held by the IRS to not be engaged in scientific research.[16] Similarly, an organization that tested drugs for commercial pharmaceutical companies was held by the IRS to not qualify for tax exemption as a scientific organization because the testing was regarded as principally serving the private interests of the manufacturers.[17] Likewise, an organization that inspected, tested, and certified for safety shipping containers used in the transport of cargo, and engaged in related research activities, was determined by the IRS to not be undertaking scientific research because these activities were incidental to commercial or industrial operations.[18] Also, the promotion of blockchain technology for the benefit of payors, providers, and financial institutions in the health care context was ruled by the IRS to not be scientific research.[19] Further, the IRS ruled that a nonprofit corporation that provides research management software to the public cannot qualify as an exempt scientific research organization because it is merely engaged in "routine product development."[20] Similarly, the development, distribution, and maintenance of open-source software was ruled by the IRS to be an activity ordinarily carried on as support to a software company's commercial operation and therefore incident to commercial operations.[21] Scientific research is regarded as carried on in the public interest if the results of the research (including any patents, copyrights, processes, or formulas) are made available to the public on a nondiscriminatory basis, if the research is performed for the United States or any of its agencies or instrumentalities or for a state or political subdivision thereof, or if the research is directed toward benefiting the public.[22] Examples of scientific research that is

---

[13] IRC § 512(b)(9). See § 25.1(l).

[14] Reg. § 1.501(c)(3)-1(d)(5)(i). The IRS held that a medical research organization that had a tissue specimen redistribution program was engaged in scientific research because the activity consisted of "fundamental data gathering and analysis" (Priv. Ltr. Rul. 201114035).

[15] Reg. § 1.501(c)(3)-1(d)(5)(ii). Also, Rev. Rul. 68-373, 1968-2 C.B. 206. In one case, this type of activity was described as "generally repetitive work done by scientifically unsophisticated employees for the purpose of determining whether the item tested met certain specifications, as distinguished from testing done to validate a scientific hypothesis" (Midwest Research Inst. v. United States, 554 F. Supp. 1379, 1386 (W.D. Mo. 1983), *aff'd*, 744 F.2d 635 (8th Cir. 1984)).

[16] Rev. Rul. 65-1, 1965-1 C.B. 226.

[17] Rev. Rul. 68-373, 1968-2 C.B. 206.

[18] Rev. Rul. 78-426, 1978-2 C.B. 175.

[19] Priv. Ltr. Rul. 201918019.

[20] Priv. Ltr. Rul. 202129017.

[21] Priv. Ltr. Rul. 202221009.

[22] Reg. § 1.501(c)(3)-1(d)(5)(iii).

considered as meeting this last criterion include scientific research carried on for the purpose of aiding in the scientific education of college or university students, obtaining scientific information that is published in a form that is available to the interested public, discovering a cure for a disease, or aiding a community or geographical area by attracting new industry thereto or by encouraging the development of, or retention of, an industry in the community or area.[23] Publication of research results, consequently, is not the only means by which scientific research can be in the public interest.[24] Scientific research is regarded as carried on in the public interest even though research is performed pursuant to a contract or agreement under which the sponsor of the research has the right to obtain ownership or control of any patents, copyrights, processes, or formulas resulting from research.[25] Thus, an organization formed by physicians to research heart disease was ruled to be tax-exempt as a scientific organization.[26] An organization engaged in conducting research programs in the social sciences may qualify as an exempt scientific organization.[27] A court concluded that an organization that conducted research in seed technology and a crop seed certification program was entitled to tax exemption as a scientific entity because the research was undertaken in its capacity as the official seed certification agency for a state or in conjunction with the state's designated agency for agricultural research and experimentation.[28]

It is often difficult to ascertain whether a particular activity constitutes *scientific research* or *commercial testing*. This is particularly the case where the activity is conducted in the public interest.[29]

The IRS accorded categorization as a tax-exempt scientific organization to a membership organization formed to encourage and assist in the establishment of nonprofit regional health data systems; conduct scientific studies and propose improvements with regard to quality, utilization, and effectiveness of health care and health care agencies; and educate those involved in furnishing, administering, and financing health care.[30] The IRS observed that by "improving and enlarging the body of knowledge concerning current usage of health facilities and methods of treatment, the organization seeks to create a more efficient use of the nation's health facilities, and to aid in the planning of better care for future health needs."[31] The IRS also ruled that an organization formed to develop scientific methods for the diagnosis, prevention, and treatment of diseases, and to disseminate the results

---

[23] In one case, an organization that engaged in research projects for nongovernmental sponsors on a contract basis, in the fields of physics, chemistry, economic development, engineering, and biological sciences, was held to be a scientific entity (as defined; see *supra* notes 2–7), rather than engaged in commercial testing; it satisfied the public benefit test because the research was intended to attract and develop industry in a particular geographic area (Midwest Research Inst. v. United States, 554 F. Supp. 1379, 1386 (W.D. Mo. 1983), *aff'd*, 744 F.2d 635 (8th Cir. 1984)).

[24] IIT Research Inst. v. United States, 9 Cl. Ct. 13 (Ct. Cl. 1985).

[25] *Id.*

[26] Rev. Rul. 69-526, 1969-2 C.B. 115. Also, Comm'r v. Orton, 173 F.2d 483 (6th Cir. 1949).

[27] Rev. Rul. 65-60, 1965-1 C.B. 231.

[28] Indiana Crop Improvement Ass'n, Inc. v. Comm'r, 76 T.C. 394, 400 (1981).

[29] See § 9.3.

[30] Rev. Rul. 76-455, 1976-2 C.B. 150.

[31] *Id.*

of its developmental work to members of the medical profession and the general public, qualified for exemption as a scientific entity.[32]

In contrast, a court determined that an organization was not entitled to tax exemption as a scientific organization where its "prime function" was the maintenance of the sport of dog shows and field trials and its "chief aim" was to see that the dog shows were staffed by proper judges so that all entrants were fairly judged.[33] "However worthy this aim may be," this court wrote, "it is not scientific," notwithstanding that much of the data resulting from these activities could, and probably was, used scientifically by geneticists.[34]

§ 9.3   REQUIREMENT OF *PUBLIC INTEREST*

An organization is regarded as not organized or operated for the purpose of carrying on scientific research in the *public interest* and, consequently, will not qualify as a scientific organization for federal tax exemption purposes if (1) it performs research only for persons who are (directly or indirectly) its creators and not charitable organizations, or (2) it retains (directly or indirectly) the ownership or control of more than an insubstantial portion of the patents, copyrights, processes, or formulas resulting from its research and does not make the items available to the public on a nondiscriminatory basis.[35] In addition, although one person may be granted the exclusive right to the use of a patent, copyright, process, or formula, it is considered as made available to the public if the granting of the exclusive right is the only practicable manner in which the patent, copyright, process, or formula can be utilized to benefit the public. In this case, however, the research from which the patent, copyright, process, or formula resulted will be regarded as carried on in the public interest only if it is carried on for the United States (or instrumentality thereof) or a state (or political subdivision thereof) or if it is scientific research that is directed toward benefiting the public.[36]

An IRS ruling discussed the federal tax law treatment, in the tax-exempt organizations context, of research that is undertaken pursuant to contracts with for-profit industries (i.e., commercially sponsored research). Where the results and other relevant information of the commercially sponsored projects are "generally published in such form as to be available to the interested public either currently, as developments in the project warrant, or within a reasonably short time after completion of the project," the organization is considered to be engaging in

---

[32] Rev. Rul. 65-298, 1965-2 C.B. 163. Cf. Rev. Rul. 74-553, 1974-2 C.B. 168. The bodies of law concerning a tax deduction for research and experimental expenses (IRC § 174) and a tax credit for increasing research activities (IRC § 41) also include illustrations of what does and does not constitute research (e.g., Union Carbide Corp. & Subs. v. Comm'r, 97 T.C.M. 1207 (2009), *aff'd*, 697 F.3d 104 (2d Cir. 2012); Mayrath v. Comm'r, 41 T.C. 582 (1964), *aff'd*, 357 F.2d 209 (5th Cir. 1966); Max v. Comm'r, 121 T.C.M. 1250 (2021); Little Sandy Coal Co. v. Comm'r, 121 T.C.M. 61 (2021); Siemer Milling Co. v. Comm'r, 117 T.C.M. 1196 (2019)).

[33] American Kennel Club, Inc. v. Hoey, 148 F.2d 920 (2d Cir. 1945).

[34] *Id.*

[35] Reg. § 1.501(c)(3)-1(d)(5)(iv).

[36] *Id.*

scientific research in the public interest.[37] Publication of the research is not required in advance of the time at which it can be made public without jeopardy to the sponsor's right by reasonably diligent action to secure any patents or copyrights resulting from the research.[38] By contrast, the carrying on of sponsored research is considered the conduct of an unrelated trade or business[39] where the organization agrees, at the sponsor's request, to "forego [*sic*] publication of the results of a particular project in order to protect against disclosure of processes or technical data which the sponsor desires to keep secret for various business reasons" or where the research results are withheld beyond the time reasonably necessary to obtain patents or copyrights.[40]

§ 9.4 *SCIENTIFIC* AS *CHARITABLE* OR *EDUCATIONAL*

Organizations qualifying as tax-exempt scientific entities may also be tax-exempt as charitable and/or educational entities.[41] For example, an organization formed to survey scientific and medical literature published throughout the world and to prepare and distribute free abstracts of the literature was ruled to be both charitable and scientific in nature for federal tax purposes.[42] This is because the federal tax definition of the term *charitable* embraces the concept of *advancement of science*.[43]

An organization engaged in research on human diseases, developing scientific methods for treatment, and disseminating its results through physicians' seminars was determined to be a tax-exempt educational organization.[44] Also, an engineering society created to engage in scientific research in the areas of heating, ventilating, and air-conditioning for the benefit of the general public was deemed to qualify as an educational and scientific organization.[45]

§ 9.5 TECHNOLOGY TRANSFER

Tax-exempt colleges, universities, major scientific research institutions, and other exempt organizations frequently engage in *technology transfer*, that is, the transfer of certain results of scientific research conducted by them to for-profit entities for commercialization of the developed technology, including marketing and sale of products or services to the public.[46] As the IRS characterized the process

---

[37] Rev. Rul. 76-296, 1976-2 C.B. 141.

[38] *Id.*

[39] See Chapters 24, 25.

[40] Rev. Rul. 76-296, 1976-2 C.B. 141. In general, see § 9.5.

[41] See Chapters 7, 8.

[42] Rev. Rul. 66-147, 1966-1 C.B. 137. Also, Science & Research Found., Inc. v. United States, 181 F. Supp. 526 (S.D. Ill. 1960); Forest Press, Inc. v. Comm'r, 22 T.C. 265 (1954).

[43] See § 7.9.

[44] Rev. Rul. 65-298, 1965-2 C.B. 163.

[45] Rev. Rul. 71-506, 1971-2 C.B. 233.

[46] For example, a federal law encourages exempt universities and businesses to collaborate and "commercialize," and to license federally funded technology to U.S. businesses (Patent and Trademark Amendments of 1980, 35 U.S.C. § 200 *et seq.*).

on one occasion, the scientific organization "conducts research and development to the stage where the technical risk is reduced and the technology is acceptable to the private sector for commercialization."[47] From a federal tax law perspective, however, even though technology transfer is obviously an appropriate function for an exempt scientific entity, the relationships among these organizations, the researchers, and the licensees and other for-profit users of the technology can raise issues of commerciality,[48] private inurement,[49] private benefit,[50] and unrelated business[51] (as well as conflicts of interest).

The initial reaction of the IRS to technology transfer organizations was to resist granting them tax exemption as charitable entities.[52] In the one court case on the point, the IRS prevailed on the issue.[53] As technology transfer became more commonplace in the large colleges, universities, and scientific research institutions (and with much of the research activity protected from taxation[54]), however, the views of the IRS began to change. The first indication of this alteration in policy came when the IRS ruled that when a foundation, as its primary activity, assisted colleges and universities in bringing their scientific inventions into public use under the patent system, the foundation qualified for tax exemption as a charitable organization. Twelve years earlier, the activity, then much smaller in scope, was ruled to be an unrelated business.[55]

Subsequent rulings have involved organizations that were created in implementation of a state program; the basis for their exemption is the lessening of the burdens of a government.[56] Other organizations have transferred the technology they created through research to for-profit subsidiaries, which thereafter develop and manufacture the resulting products.[57] Still other organizations simply contract with unrelated commercial entities for the transfer of technology, often by means of a license agreement for a patent and technical information that results in tax-free royalties—the type of practice that the IRS found to be private inurement at the outset.[58]

The IRS seems particularly concerned about the financing associated with technology transfers. Thus, the agency ruled that a scientific technology transfer organization would not lose its tax exemption by taking title and copyright to

[47] Priv. Ltr. Rul. 9316052.

[48] See § 4.9.

[49] An organization failed to achieve tax exemption because its ostensible research was held to further its founder's "commercial goals" (David Muresan Scientific Research Found. v. Comm'r, 115 T.C.M. 1047 (2018)); an organization was denied recognition of exemption because it was engaged in technology transfer activities, involving technology as to which its CEO owned the patent (Priv. Ltr. Rul. 201818018). See Chapter 20.

[50] See § 20.13.

[51] See Chapters 24, 25.

[52] An IRS technical advice memorandum issued in 1970, discussed in Tech. Adv. Mem. 8306006, concluded that a technology transfer program constituted a business activity ordinarily carried on in a commercial manner for profit (and thus was an unrelated trade or business).

[53] Washington Research Found. v. Comm'r, 50 T.C.M. 1457 (1985).

[54] See § 25.1(l).

[55] Tech. Adv. Mem. 8306006 (see Chapters 24, 25).

[56] E.g., Priv. Ltr. Rul. 9243008. See § 7.7.

[57] E.g., Priv. Ltr. Rul. 8606056.

[58] E.g., Priv. Ltr. Rul. 9527031.

software developed at universities, introducing the software into public use by means of licenses, and paying the universities royalties from consumer use of the software. The IRS went out of its way to note that the software transfer program was incidental in relation to the other operations of the organization.[59]

An IRS ruling on technology transfer organizations concerned a tax-exempt scientific research entity that concentrated its efforts in biotechnology; its objective was regional economic development. It had shifted its focus from basic research to applied research, with emphasis on creating marketable technologies; it sought commercial application of resultant products. Although the IRS ruled that these new facts would not alter the organization's tax exemption, it did not do so by directly addressing the technology transfer issue. Instead, the organization's continuing exemption was predicated on the fact that it was "operated for the purpose of aiding a geographical area by attracting new industry to the area or by encouraging the development of, or retention of, an industry in the area"; the use of a subsidiary or of licensees was cast as the "only practicable manner" in which the organization's technology could be used to benefit the public.[60]

The most remarkable of the IRS rulings on technology transfer,[61] however, involved a tax-exempt medical research organization[62] that conducted basic biomedical research and focused on the discovery of a cure for a disease. A supporting organization[63] managed the intellectual property developed by the research organization; other tax-exempt organizations and governmental entities in the community ("research partners") would be added as supported organizations. The supporting organization had a wholly owned for-profit subsidiary[64] that commercialized the medical discoveries made by the medical research organization. The fundraising undertaken by the supporting organization and commercialization of the intellectual property were designed to build large endowments for future research. The IRS enthusiastically endorsed this structure, concluding that the management of the intellectual property by the supporting organization would "unlock and leverage" the value of the property for commercialization and endowment-building. The agency virtually celebrated the establishment of a "world-class technology transfer organization," which was destined to facilitate development of the medical research organization's community "into a leading center for basic biomedical research," thereby evidencing a complete reversal of its original position that technology transfer was a commercial undertaking precluding eligibility for exempt status.

Thus, the federal tax law as to technology transfer, and the underlying policies of the IRS now in support of it, has changed dramatically in the past few decades, in large part because persistent and growing practices in the higher education and other scientific communities eventually forced the agency to reverse its position.

---

[59] Priv. Ltr. Rul. 8512084.
[60] Priv. Ltr. Rul. 9316052.
[61] Priv. Ltr. Rul. 200326035.
[62] See § 7.6(d).
[63] See § 12.3(c).
[64] See Chapter 30.

CHAPTER TEN

Religious Organizations

Section 501(c)(3) of the Internal Revenue Code provides that an organization may be exempt from federal income tax if it is organized and operated exclusively for a *religious* purpose.[1] Because of policy and constitutional law constraints, the IRS and the courts are usually reluctant to enter, let alone dwell in, the realm of religion. The difficulties of enforcement of the law concerning tax-exempt religious organizations by the IRS are compounded by exceptions for churches and certain other religious organizations from the requirements of filing an application for recognition of exemption[2] and annual information returns,[3] and by rules making examinations of churches by the IRS more difficult to undertake and administer.[4]

---

[1] Also, Reg. § 1.501(c)(3)-1(d)(1)(i)(a).
[2] See § 26.2(b).
[3] See § 28.2(c)(i).
[4] See § 27.6(c).

RELIGIOUS ORGANIZATIONS

§ 10.1 CONSTITUTIONAL LAW FRAMEWORK

With few exceptions, the IRS, other governmental agencies, and the courts have either refused to or been quite cautious in attempting to define *religious* activities or organizations, or the word *religion*. This reticence by policy makers at the federal and state levels stems largely from First Amendment considerations, as articulated in opinions from the judiciary in tax law and other cases. Constitutional law principles in this context are imposed on the states by operation of the Fourteenth Amendment.[5]

(a) General Constitutional Law Principles

The First Amendment provides, in part, that "Congress shall make no law respecting an establishment of religion, or prohibiting the free exercise thereof." These two religion clauses are known as the *establishment clause* and the *free exercise clause*. The U.S. Supreme Court observed that the First Amendment "rests upon the premise that both religion and government can best work to achieve their lofty aims if each is left free from the other within its respective sphere."[6]

(i) Free Exercise Clause. Free exercise clause cases arise out of conflict between secular laws and individuals' religious beliefs. This clause was aptly characterized by the Supreme Court when it wrote that the "door of the Free Exercise Clause stands tightly closed against any governmental regulation of religious beliefs as such," and that "[g]overnment may neither compel affirmation of a repugnant belief, nor penalize or discriminate against individuals or groups because they hold religious views abhorrent to the authorities."[7] The Court also wrote that this aspect of First Amendment jurisprudence "requires the state to be neutral in its relations with groups of religious believers and nonbelievers."[8] Also, the "[s]tate must confine itself to secular objectives, and neither advance nor impede religious activity."[9]

Conversely, the Court rejected challenges under the free exercise clause to governmental regulation of "certain overt acts prompted by religious beliefs or principles, for 'even when the action is in accord with one's religious convictions, [it] is not totally free from legislative restrictions.'"[10] The Court added that "in this highly sensitive constitutional area, '[o]nly the gravest abuses, endangering paramount interest, give occasion for permissible limitation.'"[11]

The more significant free exercise clause cases relating to tax-exempt organizations include the clash between the secular law prohibiting polygamy and the precepts at the time of the Mormon religion,[12] military service requirements and conscientious objectors' principles,[13] state unemployment compensation

[5] E.g., Lee v. Weisman, 505 U.S. 577 (1992).
[6] Illinois ex rel. McCollum v. Bd. of Educ., 333 U.S. 203, 212 (1948).
[7] Sherbert v. Verner, 374 U.S. 398, 402 (1963).
[8] Everson v. Bd. of Educ., 330 U.S. 1, 18 (1947).
[9] Roemer v. Bd. of Pub. Works of Md., 426 U.S. 736, 747 (1976).
[10] Sherbert v. Verner, 374 U.S. 398, 403 (1963).
[11] *Id.* at 406, quoting from Thomas v. Collins, 323 U.S. 516, 530 (1937).
[12] Reynolds v. United States, 98 U.S. 145 (1878).
[13] Gillette v. United States, 401 U.S. 437 (1971).

law requiring Saturday work and the dictates of the Seventh-Day Adventists' religion,[14] compulsory school attendance laws and the doctrines of the Amish religion,[15] and a license tax on canvassing and the missionary evangelism objectives of Jehovah's Witnesses.[16] Where there is to be permissible government regulation notwithstanding free exercise of religion claims, there must be a showing by the government of "some substantial threat to public safety, place or order."[17] Thus, courts have upheld a compulsory vaccination requirement,[18] prosecution of faith healers practicing medicine without a license,[19] and a prohibition on snake handling as part of religious ceremonies.[20] The U.S. Supreme Court upheld the constitutionality of statutory law that endeavors to accommodate the religious interests of inmates by prison officials, as an illustration of the "play in the joints" between the free exercise clause and the establishment clause.[21]

Short of such a *substantial threat*, however, the government may not investigate or review matters of ecclesiastical cognizance. This principle frequently manifests itself in the area of alleged employment discrimination in violation of civil rights laws.[22] Thus, there must be a compelling governmental interest in regulation before free exercise of religion rights may be infringed. For example, a city ordinance prohibiting animal sacrifice for religious purposes was found to be violative of the constitutional right to the free exercise of religion.[23]

The Court recognized that there is "play in the joints" between the free exercise clause and the establishment clause.[24] This concept was illustrated by a case where a church was denied by a state the opportunity to compete for a state grant, for which it was otherwise qualified, merely because the organization was a church. The Court wrote that it "has repeatedly confirmed that denying a generally available benefit solely on account of religious identity imposes a penalty on the free exercise of religion that can be justified only by a state interest of the highest order."[25] The state's interest was found to be less than compelling, with the Court writing that the state's policy "expressly discriminates against otherwise

---

[14] Sherbert v. Verner, 374 U.S. 398 (1963).

[15] Wisconsin v. Yoder, 406 U.S. 205 (1972).

[16] Watchtower Bible & Tract Soc'y v. Village of Stratton, 536 U.S. 150 (2002); Murdock v. Pennsylvania, 319 U.S. 105 (1943).

[17] Sherbert v. Verner, 374 U.S. 398, 403 (1963).

[18] Jacobson v. Massachusetts, 197 U.S. 11 (1905).

[19] People v. Handzik, 102 N.E.2d 340 (Ill. 1964).

[20] Kirk v. Commonwealth, 44 S.E. 3d 409 (Va. 1947). However, the U.S. Supreme Court struck down a state executive order imposing restrictions on the size of gatherings in houses of worship, designed to control the spread of the coronavirus, because the limits were found excessively strict (Roman Catholic Diocese of Brooklyn v. Cuomo, 141 S. Ct. 63 (2020)).

[21] Cutter v. Wilkinson. 544 U.S. 709, 719 (2005).

[22] E.g., McClure v. Salvation Army, 460 F.2d 553 (5th Cir. 1972). The Supreme Court unanimously recognized a *ministerial exception* to employment discrimination laws, based on the religion clauses, writing that religious organizations are free to select and dismiss their ministers without interference by government (Hosanna-Tabor Evangelical Lutheran Church & School v. Equal Employment Opportunity Comm'n, 565 U.S. 171 (2012)).

[23] Church of the Lukumi Babalu Aye, Inc. v. City of Hialeah, 508 U.S. 520 (1993).

[24] Locke v. Davey, 540 U.S. 712, 718 (2004).

[25] Trinity Lutheran Church of Columbia, Inc. v. Comer, 137 S. Ct. 2012, 2019 (2017) (internal quotation omitted).

eligible recipients by disqualifying them from a public benefit solely because of their religious character."[26] This policy was held to be "odious to our Constitution"[27] and a violation of the free exercise clause.

In a similar holding, the Court held that states, once having implemented a program providing financial assistance (such as scholarships) for access to private schools, cannot exclude religious schools from participation in the program; a state supreme court's striking down such a program, on the ground that it violates the state's constitution, was held to transgress the free exercise clause.[28]

(ii) Establishment Clause. Establishment clause cases are usually more relevant to the law of tax-exempt organizations, inasmuch as they involve governmental regulation of religious organizations and institutions. These cases frequently arise in the form of attacks on the propriety of state aid to schools (including religious schools) or special treatment of religious entities (such as tax exemption).[29] For example, the Supreme Court held that a city's voucher plan, which funded private school tuition, was constitutional, notwithstanding the fact that some of the schools involved were religious entities.[30] Likewise, the proposed issuance by an industrial development board of tax-exempt revenue bonds for campus improvements to an exempt sectarian university was found to not be a violation of the establishment clause.[31]

This clause is designed to prohibit government from establishing a religion, aiding a religion, or preferring one religion over another. The Supreme Court observed that the establishment clause is intended to avoid "sponsorship, financial support, and active involvement of the sovereign in religious activity."[32] As will be discussed, the governing principle in this context is government *neutrality*.

The Supreme Court has repeatedly held that a function of the First Amendment is the avoidance of substantial entanglement of church–state relationships. In one case, where state aid to religious schools, conditioned on pervasive restrictions, was held to be excessive entanglement, the Court stated that "[t]his kind of state inspection and evaluation of religious content of a religious organization is fraught with the sort of entanglement that the Constitution forbids"; it is a "relationship pregnant with dangers of excessive government direction of church schools and hence of churches . . . and we cannot ignore here the danger that pervasive modern governmental power will ultimately intrude on religion and thus conflict with the Religion Clauses."[33]

The Court's establishment clause jurisprudence basically entails three tests: for a statute to be constitutional, it must have a "secular legislative purpose,"

---

[26] *Id.* at 2021.

[27] *Id.* at 2025.

[28] Espinoza v. Montana Department of Revenue, 140 S. Ct. 2246 (2020).

[29] E.g., Committee for Public Educ. v. Nyquist, 413 U.S. 756 (1973); Engle v. Vitale, 370 U.S. 421 (1962); Abington School Dist. v. Schempp, 374 U.S. 203 (1953); Zorach v. Clausen, 343 U.S. 306 (1952); Illinois ex rel. McCollum v. Bd. of Educ., 333 U.S. 203 (1948); Everson v. Bd. of Educ., 330 U.S. 1 (1947).

[30] Zelman v. Simmons-Harris, 536 U.S. 639 (2002).

[31] Steele v. Nashville Industrial Development Bd., 301 F.3d 401 (6th Cir. 2002)). Also, Johnson v. Economic Development Corp., 241 F.3d 501 (6th Cir. 2001); Hunt v. McNair, 413 U.S. 734 (1973).

[32] Lemon v. Kurtzman, 403 U.S. 602, 612 (1971).

[33] *Id.* at 619–20.

its "principal or primary effect must be one that neither advances nor inhibits religion," and it must not foster an "excessive government entanglement with religion."[34] Other tests applied by the Court are an *endorsement test*[35] and a *coercion test*.[36] Thus, where there is significant government investigation and/or surveillance of a religious institution, particularly analysis of the sincerity or application of religious beliefs, there is likely to be a violation of the establishment clause.[37]

Again, the essence of the standard applied in these cases is neutrality—the basis for the constitutionality of tax exemptions in general, albeit where religious organizations are benefited.[38] Thus, in the school voucher case, the Court wrote that "where a government aid program is neutral with respect to religion, and provides assistance directly to a broad class of citizens who, in turn, direct government aid to religious schools wholly as a result of their own genuine and independent private choice, the program is not readily subject to challenge under the Establishment Clause."[39] Similarly, in the case involving proposed issuance of exempt revenue bonds for the benefit of a sectarian university, the court wrote that, because the proposed bond issuance is "part of a neutral program to benefit education, including that provided by sectarian institutions, and confers at best only an indirect benefit to the school, we hold that the issuance of the bonds does not violate the First Amendment."[40]

Many cases decided by the Supreme Court find government assistance programs involving tax-exempt religious programs constitutional, including programs that provided educational materials and equipment to religious schools;[41] allowed remedial public school teachers and counselors to assist at religious schools;[42] provided printing facilities for all qualified student publications, including religious publications;[43] provided a sign-language interpreter for a deaf child in a religious secondary school;[44] funded abstinence-based family planning programs offered by a religious social welfare agency;[45] offered vocational education scholarship to a visually disabled seminarian;[46] reimbursed religious schools for performance of state-mandated standardized tests and record keeping;[47] provided textbook loans, vocational training, diagnostic services, therapeutic and remedial services, and

---

[34] *Id.* at 612–13. Other courts add refining tests, such as a measurement of whether a government "has directed a formal religious exercise in such a way as to oblige the participation of objectors" or a prohibition on a government "from conveying or attempting to convey a message that religion is preferred over nonreligion" (citations omitted) (Doe v. Beaumont Indep. School Dist., 240 F.3d 462, 468 (5th Cir. 2001)).

[35] E.g., County of Allegheny v. ACLU, 492 U.S. 573 (1989).

[36] E.g., Lee v. Weisman, 505 U.S. 577 (1992).

[37] E.g., Presbyterian Church v. Hull Church, 393 U.S. 440 (1969).

[38] See § 10.1(b).

[39] Zelman v. Simmons-Harris, 536 U.S. 639, 652 (2002).

[40] Steele v. Nashville Industrial Development Bd., 301 F. 3d 401, 416 (6th Cir. 2002).

[41] Mitchell v. Helms, 530 U.S. 793 (2000).

[42] Agostini v. Felton, 521 U.S. 203 (1997).

[43] Rosenberger v. Rector & Visitors of Univ. of Virginia, 515 U.S. 819 (1995).

[44] Zobrest v. Catalina Foothills Sch. Dist., 509 U.S. 1 (1993).

[45] Bowen v. Kendrick, 487 U.S. 598 (1988).

[46] Witters v. Washington Dept. of Servs. for the Blind, 474 U.S. 481 (1986).

[47] Committee for Pub. Educ. & Religious Liberty v. Regan, 444 U.S. 646 (1980).

standardized testing and scoring for religious schools;[48] provided subsidies on a per-student basis to a religious college;[49] provided construction grants to a religiously affiliated college;[50] provided loans of textbooks to children attending public and private (including religious) schools;[51] reimbursed parents for bus transportation costs to a religious school;[52] provided textbooks to children attending religious schools;[53] and allowed use of federal funds to build a religious hospital.[54]

Establishment clause cases also include Supreme Court decisions holding unconstitutional the practice of including invocations and benedictions in the form of ostensibly nonsectarian prayers in public school graduation ceremonies,[55] striking down a school district's policy of permitting student-led invocations before high school football games,[56] upholding the inclusion of a nativity scene in a city's Christmas display,[57] sanctioning a state legislature's practice of opening each day's session with a prayer by a state-paid chaplain,[58] finding unconstitutional a school district's wartime policy of punishing students who refused to recite the pledge of allegiance and salute the flag,[59] finding constitutional a monument concerning the Ten Commandments on the grounds of the Texas Capitol,[60] finding unconstitutional the display of framed copies of the Ten Commandments in two courthouses in Kentucky,[61] and holding constitutional a town's practice of opening its monthly board meetings with "ceremonial" prayer given by clergy serving congregations in the locality, even though nearly all of the participating prayer givers are Christian.[62] A federal court of appeals upheld the inscription of the phrase "In God We Trust" on the nation's coins and currency,[63] and found unconstitutional the practice of recitation in schools of the pledge of allegiance because of inclusion of the words "one nation under God."[64] By contrast, another federal appellate court concluded that recitation of the pledge in public schools is constitutional, being a

---

[48] Wolman v. Walter, 433 U.S. 229 (1977).

[49] Roemer v. Bd. of Pub. Works of Maryland, 426 U.S. 736 (1976).

[50] Tilton v. Richardson, 403 U.S. 672 (1971).

[51] Bd. of Educ. v. Allen, 392 U.S. 236 (1968).

[52] Everson v. Bd. of Educ., 330 U.S. 1 (1947).

[53] Cochran v. Louisiana State Bd. of Educ., 281 U.S. 370 (1930).

[54] Bradfield v. Roberts, 175 U.S. 291 (1899).

[55] Lee v. Weisman, 505 U.S. 577 (1992).

[56] Santa Fe Indep. School Dist. v. Doe, 530 U.S. 290 (2000).

[57] Lynch v. Donnelly, 465 U.S. 668 (1984).

[58] Marsh v. Chambers, 463 U.S. 783 (1983).

[59] West Virginia State Bd. of Educ. v. Barnette, 319 U.S. 624 (1943).

[60] Van Orden v. Perry, 545 U.S. 677 (2005).

[61] McCreary Cnty. v. American Civil Liberties Union, 545 U.S. 844 (2005).

[62] Town of Greece, New York v. Galloway, 572 U.S. 565 (2014). This decision has given rise to a historical significance test, where courts ascertain whether a statute is a continuation of a "historical practice" (id. at 576).

[63] Aronow v. United States, 432 F.2d 242 (9th Cir. 1970).

[64] Newdow v. U.S. Congress, 292 F.3d 597 (9th Cir. 2002). The U.S. Supreme Court granted certiorari to consider this case, as to the constitutionality of recitation of the pledge in public schools (540 U.S. 946 (2003)), only to conclude that the plaintiff lacked standing to bring the action (Elk Grove Unified School District v. Newdow, 542 U.S. 1 (2004)). A similar lawsuit was subsequently filed, leading a federal district court, bound by the Ninth Circuit decision, to conclude that the pledge is unconstitutional (Newdow v. Congress of the United States, 383 F. Supp. 2d 1229 (E.D. Cal. 2005)).

"patriotic activity."[65] A federal district court held that the regulations providing certain religious exemptions to the contraceptive mandate, enacted as part of the Patient Protection and Affordable Act, are not unconstitutional as violations of the Establishment Clause.[66]

(iii) Religious Freedom Restoration Act.   The Court, in 1990, held that the free exercise clause "does not relieve an individual of the obligation to comply with a valid and neutral law of general applicability."[67] Congress responded to that decision by enacting the Religious Freedom Restoration Act (RFRA),[68] which reinstated as a statutory matter the prior free exercise standard.[69] Thus, free exercise cases that predate the 1990 decision remain instructive when determining the RFRA's requirements.[70]

The RFRA provides that the federal government may not "substantially burden" a person's religious exercise, even if the burden results from a rule that applies generally to religious and nonreligious persons alike, unless the burden "(1) is in furtherance of a compelling governmental interest; and (2) is the least restrictive means of furthering that compelling governmental interest."[71] For example, the regulatory accommodation for religious nonprofit organizations that permits them to opt out of the contraceptive coverage requirement under the Patient Protection and Affordable Care Act was held to not impose an unjustified substantial burden on the plaintiff's religious exercise in violation of the RFRA.[72]

(iv) Free Speech Considerations.   Another aspect of this body of law, again from the perspective of tax-exempt religious and other organizations is First Amendment free speech principles, such as *viewpoint discrimination*. For example, the Supreme Court considered a case concerning the policy of a public school as to community use of its building, after school hours, for instruction in fields such as education, civics, and the arts. Use of the facilities by a nonprofit club—a Christian

[65] Myers v. Loudoun Cnty. Public Schools, 418 F. 3d 395 (4th Cir. 2005).
[66] Massachusetts v. U.S. Department of Health and Human Services, 513 F. Supp. 3d 215 (D. Mass. 2021). The court also held that these regulations do not contravene the Equal Protection Clause or the Administrative Procedure Act.
[67] Employment Division v. Smith, 494 U.S. 872 (1990).
[68] 42 U.S.C. § 2000bb *et seq.*
[69] This is the *compelling interest test* as set forth in cases such as Sherbert v. Verner, 374 U.S. 398 (1963), and Wisconsin v. Yoder, 406 U.S. 205 (1972). See text accompanied by *supra* notes 7, 15.
The Supreme Court ruled that the RFRA was unconstitutional as applied to the states, ostensibly by reason of the Fourteenth Amendment, because Congress exceeded its enumerated powers (City of Bourne v. Flores, 521 U.S. 507 (1997)). Congress responded by enacting the Religious Land Use and Institutionalized Persons Act of 2000 (42 U.S.C. § 2000cc), which the Court found constitutional (Cutter v. Wilkinson, 544 U.S. 709 (2005)).
[70] E.g., Kaemmerling v. Lappin, 553 F.3d 669, 678–80 (D.C. Cir. 2008).
[71] 42 U.S.C. § 2000bb-1.
[72] Real Alternatives, Inc. v. Sec'y, Dep't of Health and Human Servs., 867 F.3d 338 (3d Cir. 2017); Priests for Life v. Dep't of Health and Human Servs., 772 F.3d 229 (D.C. Cir. 2014). Yet a federal district court ruled that the contraceptive mandate violates the RFRA (and equal protection principles) because the mandate, as applied to a nonreligious, nonprofit organization and its employees with contrary religious views, is equally offensive to them as it is to those who are protected by the exemption for religious employers, resting that conclusion on the jurisprudence equating certain moral beliefs with religion (March for Life v. Burwell, 128 F. Supp. 2d 116 (D.D.C. 2015)). This position was rejected in *Real Alternatives*.

organization where children sang, heard Bible lessons, memorized scripture, and prayed—was denied on the ground that the club's program content was religious. The Court, however, concluded that the school violated the club's free speech rights by excluding it from conducting its meetings at the school.[73]

This school, assumed by the Court to be a limited public forum, was found by the Court to have acted in a discriminatory manner because the teaching of morals and character was permissible under the school's community use policy. The Court wrote that "speech discussing otherwise permissible subjects cannot be excluded from a limited public forum on the ground that the subject is discussed from a religious viewpoint."[74] For purposes of free speech rights, the Court saw "no logical difference in kind between the invocation of Christianity by the [c]lub and the invocation of teamwork, loyalty, or patriotism by other associations to provide a foundation for their lessons."[75]

Another case in this context involved *government speech*, which is not subject to conventional free speech considerations. (The First Amendment restricts government regulation of private speech.) A city maintaining a public park, which contains a privately donated monument to the Ten Commandments, refused a contribution by a religious group of a monument devoted to the group's Seven Aphorisms. The Court, rejecting a public forum analysis, wrote that governments generally have the discretion to determine when to accept gifts of permanent monuments; the practice was said to be "selective receptivity."[76] It was noted, however, that this case was litigated "in the shadow" of establishment-of-religion law, with the city "wary of associating itself too closely with the Ten Commandments monument displayed in the park, lest that be deemed a breach in the so-called wall of separation between church and State."[77]

The Court considered the constitutionality, from the standpoint of free speech principles, of a town's sign code. Signs concerning "qualifying events," including church services, were treated less favorably than other categories of signage. The Court held that this code was facially content-based; its provisions were said to be able to stand only if they could survive the strict scrutiny test. This required the town to prove that its restrictions, including those on churches, further a compelling governmental interest and are narrowly tailored to achieve that interest. The town was unable to meet its burden of proof; the sign code was struck down.[78]

(b) Constitutional Law and Tax Exemption

Income tax exemption and other types of tax exemption are accorded to a wide variety of nonprofit organizations, including religious entities. Tax exemptions for religious organizations, as part of exemptions for charitable organizations

---

[73] Good News Club v. Milford Central School, 533 U.S. 98 (2001). Litigation occurred over the issue as to whether the IRS acted improperly in its processing of an application for recognition of exemption by engaging in a review of eligibility for exemption in a manner that is viewpoint discrimination in violation of the First Amendment (Z Street, Inc. v. Koskinen, 44 F. Supp. 3d 48 (D.D.C. 2014)) (see § 26.17).
[74] Good News Club v. Milford Central School, 533 U.S. 98, 111–12 (2001)
[75] Id.
[76] Pleasant Grove City, Utah v. Summum, 555 U.S. 460, 471 (2009).
[77] Id. at 482.
[78] Reed v. Town of Gilbert, Arizona, 576 U.S. 155 (2015).

generally, are not unconstitutional, however, notwithstanding the fact that they are extended by government, inasmuch as this tax-advantaged status, like the deduction for charitable contributions, is neutral with respect to religion.

Thus, the Supreme Court, in the seminal case on the point, involving an attack on tax exemption for properties held by religious organization as being violative of the establishment clause, said that the government may become involved in matters relating to religious organizations in this regard so as to "mark boundaries to avoid excessive entanglement" and to adhere to the "policy of neutrality that derives from an accommodation of the Establishment and Free Exercise Clauses that has prevented that kind of involvement that would tip the balance toward government control of [c]hurch or governmental restraint on religious practice."[79] Recognizing that either tax exemption or taxation of churches "occasions some degree of involvement with religion," the Court held that "[g]ranting tax exemptions to churches necessarily operates to afford an indirect economic benefit and also gives rise to some, but yet a lesser, involvement than taxing them."[80]

The Court added that the "grant of a tax exemption is not sponsorship since the government does not transfer part of its revenues to churches but simply abstains from demanding that the church support the state."[81] Consequently, the Court concluded that "[t]here is no genuine nexus between tax exemption and establishment of religion."[82]

Although a general tax exemption for a variety of nonprofit organizations, including religious ones, is constitutional, a tax exemption solely for religious organizations violates the establishment clause. Thus, the Supreme Court held a state sales tax exemption "confined to religious organizations" to be a form of "state sponsorship of religion," and wrote that it should be struck down as "lacking a secular purpose and effect."[83] The Court added that "[w]hat is crucial [to sustaining the validity of a tax exemption] is that any subsidy afforded religious organizations be warranted by some overarching secular purpose that justifies like benefits for nonreligious groups."[84] In the aftermath of this decision, a federal district court held that another state's sales and use tax exemptions, available only to religious and faith-based organizations, violated the establishment clause and thus were unconstitutional,[85] although this decision was reversed on the ground that the district court lacked jurisdiction.[86] Thereafter, however, another federal district

---

[79] Walz v. Tax Comm'n of the City of New York, 397 U.S. 664, 669–70 (1970).

[80] Id. at 674.

[81] Id. at 675.

[82] Id. Also, Mueller v. Allen, 463 U.S. 388, 396 n.5 (1983) (where the Court upheld a tax deduction for amounts paid as school tuition, textbooks, and transportation, even though "religious institutions benefit very substantially from the allowance" of the deduction).

[83] Texas Monthly, Inc. v. Bullock, 489 U.S. 1, 11 (1989). A state's sales tax regime may violate the First Amendment's guarantee of freedom of the press. E.g., Arkansas Writers' Project, Inc. v. Ragland, 481 U.S. 221 (1987); Minneapolis Star & Tribune Co. v. Minnesota Comm'r of Revenue, 460 U.S. 575 (1983). It is possible, in this context, for both the establishment clause and the press-freedom guarantee to be violated. E.g., Finlator v. Powers, 902 F.2d 1158 (4th Cir. 1990).

[84] Texas Monthly, Inc. v. Bullock, 489 U.S. 1, 15, n. 4 (1989). As to the matter of a *subsidy*, see § 1.4.

[85] American Civil Liberties Union Found. of Louisiana v. Crawford, 2002 WL 461649 (E.D. La. 2002).

[86] American Civil Liberties Union Found. of Louisiana v. Bridges, 334 F.3d 416 (5th Cir. 2003).

court ruled that state sales tax exemptions provided only for religious organizations and transactions are unconstitutional.[87]

As regards nonprofit organizations seeking tax exemption as religious entities, it is difficult to mark the boundary between proper government regulation and unconstitutional entanglement. Not infrequently, for example, a religious organization will claim a violation of its constitutional rights when the IRS probes too extensively in seeking information about it in the context of evaluation of an application for recognition of exemption. The courts appear to agree that the IRS is obligated, when processing an exemption application, to make inquiries and gather information to determine whether the organization's purposes and activities are in conformance with the statutory requirements, and that this type of an investigation is not precluded by the First Amendment's guarantee of freedom of religion.[88]

(c) Internal Revenue Code Provisions

The Internal Revenue Code contains several provisions according a form of special tax treatment as to the law of tax-exempt organizations, with respect to various categories of religious organizations.

To be tax-exempt, nearly all charitable organizations are required to file an application for recognition of exemption with the IRS.[89] Churches, their integrated auxiliaries, and conventions and associations of churches, however, are excused from this filing requirement.[90]

Most tax-exempt organizations are required to file annual information returns or notices with the IRS.[91] Churches (including an interchurch organization of local units of a church), their integrated auxiliaries, and conventions or associations of churches, however, are exempt from this filing requirement.[92]

The federal tax law distinguishes, in the realm of charitable organizations, between classification as a public charity and as a private foundation.[93] For the

---

[87] Budlong v. Graham, 414 F. Supp. 2d 1222 (N.D. Ga. 2006).

[88] Church of Scientology of Calif. v. Comm'r, 83 T.C. 381 (1984), aff'd, 823 F.2d 1310 (9th Cir. 1987); United States v. Toy Nat'l Bank, 79-1 U.S.T.C. ¶ 9344 (N.D. Iowa 1979); General Conference of the Free Church of Am. v. Comm'r, 71 T.C. 920, 930–932 (1979); Coomes v. Comm'r, 572 F.2d 554 (6th Cir. 1978); United States v. Holmes, 614 F.2d 985 (5th Cir. 1980); United States v. Freedom Church, 613 F.2d 316 (1st Cir. 1980); Bronner v. Comm'r, 72 T.C. 368 (1979). Cf. United States v. Dykema, 80-2 U.S.T.C. ¶ 9735 (E.D. Wis. 1980). It is the position of the IRS that the tax-exempt status of a church is to be revoked where the church fails to produce its books and records following a proper request for them (Gen. Couns. Mem. 38248).

[89] IRC § 508(a).

[90] IRC § 508(c)(1)(A). See § 26.2(b).

[91] IRC § 6033(a)(1).

[92] IRC § 6033(a)(2)(A)(i). See § 28.2(c)(i). A lawsuit was filed contending that the IRS is violating the establishment clause and the equal protection clause by imposing different requirements on churches and certain other religious organizations, as opposed to nearly all other categories of nonprofit organizations in obtaining recognition of tax exemption and maintaining exemption, such as by filing annual information returns. The court denied the government's motion to dismiss on the ground that the plaintiffs lacked standing to sue, with respect to the claim that the exemption of religious organizations from annual information return filing is unconstitutional (Freedom From Religion Found. v. Werfel, 2013 WL 4501057 (W.D. Wis. 2013)).

[93] See Chapter 12.

most part, public charity status is more advantageous from a law perspective. Some charitable organizations (those of an institutional nature) are automatically classified as public charities. This preferential category of entities includes churches, conventions of churches, and associations of churches.[94]

Some tax-exempt organizations are required to report to the IRS when they have dissolved, liquidated, terminated, or substantially contracted.[95] Churches, their integrated auxiliaries, and conventions and associations of churches are, however, exempt from this requirement.[96]

An exemption is provided from the debt-financed property rules for interim income received by a tax-exempt organization from neighborhood real property acquired for an exempt purpose; there must be a plan to devote the property to exempt uses within 10 years of its acquisition.[97] A more generous 15-year rule, however, is available for churches; also, it is not required that the property be in the neighborhood of the church.[98]

The rules concerning commercial-type insurance preclude tax exemption for otherwise exempt charitable or social welfare organizations in certain circumstances, or treat the insurance activity as an unrelated business.[99] Of the five exceptions to the definition of *commercial-type insurance*, two are for property or casualty insurance provided by a church or a convention or association of churches for the church, convention, or association,[100] and the provision of retirement and/or welfare benefits by a church or a convention or association of churches for the employees of the church, convention, or association or for the employees' beneficiaries.[101]

The federal tax law includes the parsonage allowance, which excludes from gross income of ministers of the gospel the rental value of a home furnished to them as part of their compensation[102] and rental allowances.[103] The latter provision has been the subject of establishment clause challenges, with an appellate court ruling that this rental allowance is not unconstitutional as a violation of the establishment clause because the provision has secular purposes and it passed a historical significance test. The secular purposes were said to be elimination of discrimination against ministers, elimination of discrimination between ministers, and avoidance of excessive government entanglement with religion.[104]

---

[94] IRC § 170(b)(1)(A)(i). See § 12.3(a).

[95] IRC § 6043(b). See §§ 4.3(b), 30.7.

[96] IRC § 6043(b)(1).

[97] IRC § 514(b)(3)(A)-(C). See § 24.10(b).

[98] IRC § 514(b)(3)(E). This exception has a heading reading "special rule for churches."

[99] IRC § 501(m)(1), (2). See §§ 28.13(b), 24.9, respectively.

[100] IRC § 501(m)(3)(C).

[101] IRC § 501(m)(3)(D).

[102] IRC § 107(1). This rule somewhat parallels the exclusion for the value of housing provided to an employee for the convenience of the employer (IRC § 119).

[103] IRC § 107(2).

[104] Gaylor v. Mnuchin, 919 F.3d 420 (7th Cir. 2019), *rev'g* 278 F. Supp. 3d 1081 (W.D. Wis. 2017). As to the historical significance test, see *supra* note 62 and text accompanying it.

Generally, of course, the IRS has the authority to examine tax-exempt organizations.[105] Nonetheless, special rules impose restrictions on tax inquiries and examinations concerning churches.[106]

Donors to charitable organizations are required to adhere to the general charitable gift substantiation rules in order to obtain a charitable contribution deduction.[107] These rules are inapplicable, however, in connection with an intangible religious benefit that is provided by an organization organized exclusively for religious purposes and that generally is not sold in a commercial transaction outside the donative context.[108] Most charitable organizations are required to comply with the disclosure requirements relating to *quid pro quo contributions*.[109] Exempt from the definition of those contributions are payments made to an organization, organized exclusively for religious purposes, in return for an intangible religious benefit.[110]

§ 10.2 FEDERAL TAX LAW DEFINITION OF *RELIGION*

Although the federal income tax law provides tax exemption for religious organizations, there is no statutory or regulatory definition of the terms *religious* or *religion* for this purpose. Indeed, by reason of the religion clauses of the First Amendment, it would be unconstitutional for the federal government to adopt and apply a strict definition of these terms. As one court stated, the "lack of a precise definition [of the terms *religious* or *religion*] is not surprising in light of the fact that a constitutional provision is involved."[111]

(a) *Religion* Defined

Government officials, judges, and justices have, from time to time, grappled with the meaning of the term *religious*. The Supreme Court ventured the observation, authored well over a century ago, that the term *religion* has "reference to one's views of his relations to his Creator, and to the obligations they impose of reverence for his being and character, and of obedience to his will."[112] Subsequently, the Court wrote that the "essence of religion is belief in a relation to God involving duties superior to those arising from any human relation."[113] In other than the constitutional law and federal tax law contexts, these instances have arisen in cases concerning, for example, conscientious objector status,[114] employment

---

[105] See § 27.6(a).

[106] IRC § 7116. See § 27.6(c).

[107] IRC § 170(f)(8). See *Charitable Giving*, Chapter 19.

[108] IRC § 170(f)(8)(B), last sentence.

[109] IRC § 6115. See *Charitable Giving* § 20.2.

[110] IRC § 6115(b). In general, Hopkins, "Religious Organizations – Constitutionality of Code Provisions," 30 *Tax'n of Exempts* (No. 2) 17 (Sep./Oct. 2018).

[111] Malnak v. Yogi, 440 F. Supp. 1284, 1315 (D.N.J. 1977), *aff'd*, 592 F.2d 197 (3d Cir. 1979).

[112] Davis v. Beason, 133 U.S. 333, 342 (1890).

[113] United States v. Macintosh, 283 U.S. 605, 633 (1931).

[114] Welsh v. United States, 398 U.S. 333 (1970); United States v. Seeger, 380 U.S. 163 (1965); Berman v. United States, 156 F.2d 377 (9th Cir. 1946), *cert. denied*, 329 U.S. 795 (1946); United States ex rel. Phillips v. Downer, 135 F.2d 521 (2d Cir. 1943); United States v. Kauten, 133 F.2d 703 (2d Cir. 1943).

discrimination,[115] state and local real property tax exemptions,[116] Sunday closing laws,[117] and zoning restrictions.[118]

State courts have ventured into this area. One court stated that the term *religion* has "reference to man's relation to Divinity; to reverence, worship, obedience, and submission to the mandates and precepts of supernatural or superior beings" and in its broadest sense "includes all forms of belief in the existence of superior beings, exercising power over human beings by volition, imposing rules of conduct with future rewards and punishments."[119] Many courts have advanced definitions, including the following: "Religion as generally accepted may be defined as a bond uniting man to God and a virtue whose purpose is to render God the worship due to him as the source of all being and the principle of all government of things";[120] and the "Christian religion, in its most important ultimate aspect, recognizes, has faith in and worships a Divine Being or Spirit— one Father of all mankind—who has the power to and will forgive the transgressions of repentants and care for the immortal souls of the believers, and which belief brings earthly solace and comfort to and tends to induce right living in such believers."[121]

The courts, however, have generally been reluctant to take the position that a particular activity, function, or purpose is or is not religious in nature. As a court stated, "[n]either this Court, nor any branch of this Government, will consider the merits or fallacies of a religion," nor will the court "compare the beliefs, dogmas, and practices of a newly organized religion with those of an older, more established religion," or "praise or condemn a religion, however excellent or fanatical or preposterous it may seem," because to do so "would impinge upon the guarantees of the First Amendment."[122] Similarly, a federal court of appeals observed that it is not the "province of government officials or courts to determine religious orthodoxy."[123] Another court evidenced a like attitude when it wrote, "As a judicial body, we are loathe to evaluate and judge ecclesiastical authority and duties in the various religious disciplines."[124] Another court observed that Congress, in creating tax exemption for religious organizations, "left open the door of tax exemption to all corporations meeting the test, the restriction being not as to the species of religion, charity, science or education

[115] Johnson v. U.S. Postal Serv., 364 F. Supp. 37 (N.D. Fla. 1973); Powers v. State Dept. of Social Welfare, 493 P.2d 590 (Kan. 1972); Martin v. Industrial Accident Comm'n, 304 P.2d 828 (D.C. Cal. 1956).

[116] Walz v. Tax Comm'n of the City of New York, 397 U.S. 664 (1970); Washington Ethical Soc'y v. District of Columbia, 249 F. 2d 127 (D.C. Cir. 1957); American Bible Soc'y v. Lewisohn, 351 N.E.2d 697 (Ct. App. N.Y. 1976); Watchtower Bible & Tract Soc'y, Inc. v. Lewisohn, 315 N.E.2d 801 (N.Y. 1974); People ex rel. Watchtower Bible & Tract Soc'y, Inc. v. Haring, 170 N.E.2d 677 (Ct. App. N.Y. 1960); Fellowship of Humanity v. Cnty. of Alameda, 315 P.2d 394 (Cal. 1957).

[117] Braunfeld v. Brown, 366 U.S. 599 (1961).

[118] In re Community Synagogue v. Bates, 136 N.E.2d 488 (N.Y. 1956).

[119] McMasters v. State of Okla., 29 A.L.R. 292, 294 (Okla. Crim. App. 1922).

[120] Nikulnikoff v. Archbishop & Consistory of Russian Orthodox Greek Catholic Church, 255 N.Y.S. 653, 663 (Sup. Ct. N.Y. Cty. 1932).

[121] Taylor v. State, 11 So.2d 663, 673 (Miss. 1943).

[122] Universal Life Church, Inc. v. United States, 372 F. Supp. 770, 776 (E.D. Cal. 1974).

[123] Teterud v. Burns, 522 F.2d 357 (8th Cir. 1975).

[124] Colbert v. Comm'r, 61 T.C. 449, 455 (1974).

under which they might operate, but as to the use of its profits and the exclusive purpose of its existence."[125]

This approach has been sanctioned by the Supreme Court, which has repeatedly held[126] that freedom of thought and religious belief "embraces the right to maintain theories of life and of death and of the hereafter which are rank heresy to followers of the orthodox faiths," and that, if triers of fact undertake to examine the truth or falsity of the religious beliefs of a sect, "they enter a forbidden domain."[127] Subsequently, the Court observed that it is "not within the judicial ken to question the centrality of particular beliefs or practices to a faith, or the validity of particular litigants' interpretations of those creeds."[128] Yet some courts are not reluctant to attempt to separate secular beliefs from religious ones, as illustrated by a court opinion involving an organization that, in addition to lacking "external manifestations analogous to other religions," had as its major doctrine a "single-faceted doctrine of sexual preference and secular lifestyle."[129]

A court observed that, in "implementing the establishment clause, the Supreme Court has made clear that an activity may be religious even though it is neither part of nor derives from a societally recognized religious sect."[130] In another instance, a court held that an organization was a religious entity because it held regular prayer meetings and weekly services, and published a newsletter.[131] Yet another court concluded that an organization was not a religious entity in the absence of any "solid evidence of a belief in a supreme being, a religious discipline, a ritual, or tenets to guide one's daily existence."[132]

Another federal court reflected the same degree of caution when deciding a case involving an organization formed as the parent church of Scientology.[133] The court concluded that the organization was not exempt from tax—not because

---

[125] Unity School of Christianity v. Comm'r, 4 B.T.A. 61, 70 (1926), quoted in Saint Germain Found. v. Comm'r, 26 T.C. 648, 657 (1956). Also, Rev. Rul. 68-563, 1968-2 C.B. 212, *amplified by* Rev. Rul. 78-385, 1978-2 C.B. 174; Rev. Rul. 68-26, 1968-1 C.B. 272.

[126] See § 10.1(a).

[127] United States v. Ballard, 322 U.S. 78, 86, 87 (1943). Also, United States v. Seeger, 380 U.S. 163, 174–76 (1965).

[128] Hernandez v. Comm'r, 490 U.S. 680 (1989).

[129] Church of the Chosen People (North Am. Panarchate) v. United States, 548 F. Supp. 1247, 1252, 1253 (D. Minn. 1982).

[130] Malnak v. Yogi, 440 F. Supp. 1284, 1313 (D.N.J. 1977), *aff'd*, 592 F. 2d 197 (3d Cir. 1979).

[131] Church of the Visible Intelligence That Governs the Universe v. United States, 83-2 U.S.T.C. ¶ 9726 (Ct. Cl. 1983).

[132] United States v. Kuch, 288 F. Supp. 439, 443–44 (D.D.C. 1968). Also, Puritan Church of Am. v. Comm'r, 10 T.C.M. 485 (1951), *aff'd*, 209 F.2d 306 (D.C. Cir. 1953), *cert. denied*, 347 U.S. 975 (1954), 350 U.S. 810 (1955). Cf. People v. Woody, 394 P.2d 813 (Cal. 1964); Malnak v. Yogi, 440 F. Supp. 1284 (D.N.J. 1977), *aff'd*, 592 F.2d 197 (3d Cir. 1979); Clippinger v. Comm'r, 37 T.C.M. 484 (1978); Heller v. Comm'r, 37 T.C.M. 643 (1978); Baker v. Comm'r, 40 T.C.M. 983 (1980).

[133] Founding Church of Scientology v. United States, 412 F.2d 1197 (Ct. Cl. 1969), *cert. denied*, 397 U.S. 1009 (1970). Cf. Church of Scientology of Hawaii v. United States, 485 F.2d 313 (9th Cir. 1973); Church of Scientology of Calif. v. United States, 75-2 U.S.T.C. ¶ 9584 (9th Cir. 1975); Founding Church of Scientology of Washington, D.C. v. United States, 409 F.2d 1146 (D.C. Cir. 1968), *cert. denied*, 396 U.S. 963 (1969).

it was not religious (that issue was not even considered)—but because the net income of the entity inured to the founders in their private capacity.[134]

There are, nonetheless, some explicit discussions of what may constitute *religion* or *religious belief*. In one case, it was said that "[r]eligious belief . . . is a belief finding expression in a conscience which categorically requires the believer to disregard elementary self-interest and to accept martyrdom in preference to transgressing its tenets."[135] Another court found an activity religious because it was centered around belief in a higher being "which in its various forms is given the name 'god' in common usage" and because a form of prayer was involved.[136] Still another court formulated a three-part test for determining the religious nature of an organization's goals: whether the beliefs address fundamental and ultimate questions concerning the human condition, are comprehensive in nature and constitute an entire system of belief instead of merely an isolated teaching, and are manifested in external forms.[137] The Supreme Court placed emphasis on belief in a "supreme being," and looked to see whether a "given belief that is sincere and meaningful occupies a place in the life of its possessor parallel to that filled by the orthodox belief in God"[138] and whether the belief occupies in the life of the individual involved "'a place parallel to that filled by . . . God' in traditional religious persons."[139] Some courts have been reluctant, however, to confine the concept of *religious belief* to theistic beliefs.

For example, one court held that the permissible inquiry on this subject is "whether or not the belief occupies the same place in the lives of its holders that the orthodox beliefs occupy in the lives of believing majorities, and whether a given group that claims the exemption conducts itself the way groups conceded to be religious conduct themselves."[140] This court added that the appropriate test is whether the activities of the organization in question "serve the same place in the lives of its members, and occupy the same place in society, as the activities of the theistic churches."[141] Indeed, this court developed what is apparently the

---

[134] The U.S. Tax Court held that the expenses of Scientology processing and auditing are not deductible medical expenses in Brown v. Comm'r, 62 T.C. 551 (1974), *aff'd*, 523 F.2d 365 (8th Cir. 1975). Cf. Handeland v. United States, 75-2 U.S.T.C. ¶ 9586 (9th Cir. 1975); Rev. Rul. 78-188, 1978-1 C.B. 40; Rev. Rul. 78-190, 1978-1 C.B. 74. The Supreme Court held that payments to the Church of Scientology for auditing sessions are not deductible as charitable contributions, in Hernandez v. Comm'r, 490 U.S. 680 (1989). The IRS adopted the same position in 1978 (Rev. Rul. 78-189, 1978-1 C.B. 68), although it subsequently rendered that ruling obsolete (Rev. Rul. 93-73, 1993-2 C.B. 75). Also, the IRS recognized the tax-exempt status of 25 Church of Scientology organizations in rulings issued by the IRS National Office (61 *Tax Notes* 279, Oct. 18, 1993). A federal appellate court, in ruling that tuition payments made to a religious private school that the payors' children attend are not deductible as charitable gifts, questioned the constitutionality of the closing agreement between the IRS and the Church (Sklar v. Comm'r, 279 F.3d 697 (9th Cir. 2002)). In general, United States v. Moon, 718 F.2d 1210 (2d Cir. 1983), *cert. denied*, 466 U.S. 971 (1984).

[135] United States v. Kauten, 133 F. 2d 703, 708 (2d Cir. 1943).

[136] Malnak v. Yogi, 440 F. Supp. 1284, 1320, 1323 (D.N.J. 1977), *aff'd*, 592 F.2d 197 (3d Cir. 1979).

[137] Africa v. Pennsylvania, 662 F.2d 1025, 1032 (3d Cir. 1981), *cert. denied*, 456 U.S. 908 (1982).

[138] United States v. Seeger, 380 U.S. 163, 165–66 (1965).

[139] Welsh v. United States, 398 U.S. 333, 340 (1970).

[140] Fellowship of Humanity v. Cnty. of Alameda, 315 P.2d 394, 406 (Cal. 1957).

[141] *Id.*, 315 P.2d at 409–10.

most expansive, yet definitional, statement as to the general characteristics of the concept of *religion*: "Religion simply includes: (1) a belief, not necessarily referring to supernatural powers; (2) a cult, involving a gregarious association openly expressing the beliefs; (3) a system of moral practice directly resulting from an adherence to the belief; and (4) an organization within the cult designed to observe the tenets of belief."[142]

Indeed, the difficulties contemporary courts are having in grappling with a definition of the term *religion* can be seen in court holdings that the use in public schools of basic reader textbooks that are offensive to the religious beliefs of some does not advance "secular humanism" or inhibit theistic religion.[143]

An organization that is deemed to be a religious entity may well engage in activities that by themselves may not be regarded as religious, such as charitable, educational, social welfare, and community activities. It appears generally recognized that the conduct of these activities will not deprive an otherwise religious organization of its classification as a religious group. For example, one court held that "[s]trictly religious uses and activities are more than prayer and sacrifice" and includes social activities, study, and community service.[144]

(b) Bases for Denial of Tax Exemption

Typically, when a court finds an alleged religious organization to not be tax-exempt, it does so not on the ground that the organization's purpose is not religious but rather on a finding that the activity smacks too much of a commercial enterprise operated for private gain or that the organization engages in an inappropriate amount of lobbying or political activities.[145] In one case, a restaurant was operated as a private business for profit with the net profits going to a church, which itself was engaged in commercial activities; contributions to the church were held to not be deductible because the organization's business activities defeated the requisite tax status.[146] Another purported religious organization's exempt status was

---

[142] *Id.*, 315 P.2d at 406. This finding that secular humanism is a religion applied only to a particular group of humanists. The debate as to whether humanism is a *religion* or merely a *philosophy* has not been stilled. For example, an appellate court observed that "traditional notions of religion surely would not include humanism" (Kalka v. Hawk, 215 F.3d 90, 98 (D.C. Cir. 2000)) (holding that, even assuming humanism is a religion, that principle has not been clearly established, so that officials of the Federal Bureau of Prisons were qualifiedly immune from liability for refusing to allow a prisoner to promote humanism within prison chapels).

[143] Smith v. Bd. of School Comm'rs of Mobile Cnty., 827 F.2d 684, 688–89 (11th Cir. 1987), *rev'g* 655 F. Supp. 939 (S.D. Ala. 1987); also, Mozert v. Hawkins Cnty. Bd. of Educ., 827 F.2d 1058 (6th Cir. 1987), *rev'g* 647 F. Supp. 1194 (E.D. Tenn. 1986), where it was observed that "[a]lthough the Supreme Court has shied away from attempting to define religion, the past forty years has witnessed an expansion of the court's understanding of religious belief," so that the "concept of religion has shifted from a fairly narrow religious theism . . . to a broader concept providing protection for the views of unorthodox and nontheistic faiths" (concurring opinion, 827 F.2d at 1078).

[144] In re Community Synagogue v. Bates, 136 N.E.2d 488, 493 (N.Y. 1956).

[145] See § 4.9, Chapters 22, 23, respectively.

[146] Riker v. Comm'r, 244 F.2d 220 (9th Cir. 1957), *cert. denied*, 355 U.S. 839 (1957). Also, Parker v. Comm'r, 365 F.2d 792 (8th Cir. 1966), *cert. denied*, 385 U.S. 1026 (1967).

precluded because its primary activity was the operation of a (religious) publishing house.[147]

An illustration of the application of the legislative activities rules in this context was the government's successful revocation of the tax-exempt status of a national ministry organization; its exemption was lost on the grounds that a substantial part of its activities consisted of carrying on propaganda, attempting to influence legislation, and intervening in political campaigns.[148] Similarly, the IRS successfully revoked the exempt status of an organization whose purpose is to defend and maintain religious liberty in the United States by the dissemination of knowledge concerning the constitutional principle of the separation of church and state, on the ground that the organization engaged in a substantial amount of lobbying.[149]

A court found that an organization's social aspects were so predominant as to relegate any religious activities to secondary status.[150] The organization, formed to further the doctrine of "ethical egoism," was found to have as its principal purpose the social functions of sponsoring dinner meetings and publishing a newsletter. While "church meetings" were also held, the court believed they were in reality merely an extension of the social gatherings. In general, the court concluded that the "religious aspects of such conclaves seems . . . indistinct."[151] Likewise, an organization was found to not qualify as a religious organization because its primary activity was the investment and accumulation of funds, albeit for the purpose of eventually building a church.[152]

(c) Abuse of Tax Exemption

There is no question that the current state of the law on this subject poses perplexing and probably unresolvable burdens on regulatory officials and judges. These difficulties are exacerbated as new religions emerge and as new forms of approach to the practice of religion evolve (for example, the "electronic churches" and the "mail-order ministries").[153] In some instances, such as with

---

[147] Scripture Press Found. v. United States, 285 F.2d 800 (Ct. Cl. 1961), *cert. denied*, 368 U.S. 985 (1962). Also, Christian Manner Int'l, Inc. v. Comm'r, 71 T.C. 661 (1979); Fides Publishers Ass'n v. United States, 263 F. Supp. 924 (N.D. Ind. 1967); Unitary Mission Church of Long Island v. Comm'r, 74 T.C. 507 (1980), *aff'd*, 647 F.2d 163 (2d Cir. 1981); Bubbling Well Church of Universal Love, Inc. v. Comm'r, 74 T.C. 531 (1980), *aff'd*, 670 F.2d 104 (9th Cir. 1981); Loiler v. Comm'r, 53 T.C.M. 785 (1987). Cf. Elisian Guild, Inc. v. United States, 412 F.2d 121 (1st Cir. 1969); Rev. Rul. 68-26, 1968-1 C.B. 272.

[148] Christian Echoes Nat'l Ministry, Inc. v. United States, 470 F.2d 849 (10th Cir. 1972), *cert. denied*, 414 U.S. 864 (1973).

[149] Alexander v. "Americans United," Inc., 416 U.S. 752 (1974).

[150] First Libertarian Church v. Comm'r, 74 T.C. 396 (1980).

[151] *Id.* at 405.

[152] Western Catholic Church v. Comm'r, 73 T.C. 196 (1979), *aff'd*, 631 F.2d 736 (7th Cir. 1980), *cert. denied*, 450 U.S. 981 (1981).

[153] The IRS was particularly concerned with the tax status of mail-order ministries, such as those chartered by the Universal Life Church (ULC). In 1977, the IRS commenced a study of illegal tax protestor activities, which culminated in a report published in 1979. One finding of this report was that illegal protest schemes are increasingly employing the technique of establishing "bogus churches," where "a secularly employed individual places all of his or her wages in an organization created through the use

respect to personal churches,[154] the matter evolved away from the law of tax-exempt organizations and into the realm of criminal tax fraud.[155] Indeed, personal churches have been added to the concept of tax shelters, so that special penalties for substantial understatements of federal income tax[156] are applicable.[157] Other instances involving blatant abuses are generating numerous court opinions, which contribute to the shaping of the evolving law, often in ways not complimentary to the religious sector.[158] Yet policy makers are to tread carefully even when confronting the nontraditional, minority, and/or unorthodox religious groups; the First Amendment applies to them as well. As one court noted, "[n]ew religions appear in this country frequently and they cannot stand outside the first amendment merely because they did not exist when the Bill of Rights was drafted."[159] Nonetheless, the IRS's concerns about abuse in this area are leading to stringent decisions by the courts, so that the law is often shaping up as being appropriately tough with respect to the sham situations, but it is formulating some legal principles that are questionable when applied outside the areas of abuse.[160]

Still, church abuse cases abound, with tax avoidance clearly taking precedence over religion.[161] The U.S. Tax Court has been inundated with these cases; in 1983, the court wrote that "our tolerance for taxpayers who establish churches solely for tax avoidance purposes is reaching a breaking point."[162] The court added: "Not only do these taxpayers use the pretext of a church to avoid paying their fair share of taxes, even when their brazen schemes are uncovered many of them resort

---

of a mail-order charter whereby the organization pays for his or her living expense." To date, the courts have uniformly rejected claims for tax exemption for, or the deductibility of gifts to, these "organizations." E.g., Davis v. Comm'r, 81 T.C. 806 (1983), aff'd, 767 F.2d 931 (9th Cir. 1985), holding that the payment of personal expenses from a ULC congregation bank account constitutes private inurement (see Chapter 20) and that the transfer of funds to the account was not a bona fide gift. Courts have upheld summonses served on banks in connection with investigations into the legitimacy of deductions for contributions made to ULC congregations (e.g., LaMura v. Comm'r, 765 F.2d 974 (11th Cir. 1985)). In 1984, the IRS announced that it will no longer recognize the tax-exempt status of the "parent" Universal Life Church (Ann. 84-90, 1984-36 I.R.B. 32). This revocation was subsequently upheld by the U.S. Claims Court in Universal Life Church, Inc. v. United States, 87-2 U.S.T.C. ¶ 9617 (Cl. Ct. 1987), aff'd, 862 F.2d 321 (Fed. Cir. 1988). The practices represented by these cases can amount to tax fraud (e.g., Braswell v. Comm'r, 66 T.C.M. 627 (1993); Mobley v. Comm'r, 65 T.C.M. 1939 (1993), aff'd in unpublished opinion (11th Cir. 1994)).

[154] E.g., Rev. Rul. 81-94, 1981-1 C.B. 330; Rev. Rul. 78-232, 1978-1 C.B. 69.

[155] E.g., United States v. Daly, 756 F.2d 1076 (5th Cir. 1985).

[156] IRC § 6662.

[157] Rev. Rul. 89-74, 1989-1 C.B. 311; Tweeddale v. Comm'r, 92 T.C. 501 (1989).

[158] E.g., Southern Church of Universal Brotherhood Assembled, Inc. v. Comm'r, 74 T.C. 1223 (1980) (concerning a "religious" organization that held its "services" on a yacht in a large bay; the acronym for the entity is SCUBA).

[159] Malnak v. Yogi, 440 F. Supp. 1284, 1315 (D.N.J. 1977), aff'd, 592 F.2d 197 (3d Cir. 1979).

[160] E.g., Basic Bible Church v. Comm'r, 74 T.C. 846 (1980); Truth Tabernacle v. Comm'r, 41 T.C.M. 1405 (1981). Cf. McGahen v. Comm'r, 76 T.C. 468 (1981), aff'd, 720 F.2d 664 (3d Cir. 1983).

[161] E.g., Self-Realization Brotherhood, Inc. v. Comm'r, 48 T.C.M. 344 (1984); The Ecclesiastical Order of the Ism of Am v. Comm'r, 80 T.C. 833 (1983), aff'd, 740 F.2d 967 (6th Cir. 1984), cert. denied, 471 U.S. 1015 (1985). Also, King Shipping Consum, Inc. v. Comm'r, 58 T.C.M. 574 (1989) (alleged church operated for the purpose of selling illegal drugs held not tax-exempt); Baustert v. Comm'r, 54 T.C.M. 673 (1987).

[162] Miedaner v. Comm'r, 81 T.C. 272, 282 (1983).

to the courts in a shameless attempt to vindicate themselves."[163] Consequently, the court gave notice that it will impose sanctions in these cases for using the court for purposes of delay.[164] The Tax Court imposes the penalty for fraudulently intending to evade and defeat the payment of taxes legally due[165] in situations where an individual established a bogus church.[166] This aspect of the personal church has largely abated, although occasionally a case will still arise where an ostensible church is used as a vehicle for payment of personal expenses.[167]

There are several categories of institutions that are regarded, for federal tax purposes, as *religious* organizations. These include churches, conventions and associations of churches, integrated auxiliaries of churches, religious orders, and apostolic organizations. There are various church-administered organizations (usually tax-exempt but not necessarily religious in nature), such as schools, hospitals, orphanages, nursing homes, broadcasting and publishing entities, and cemeteries.

§ 10.3   CHURCHES AND SIMILAR INSTITUTIONS

A bona fide *church* (including institutions such as synagogues and mosques) is, of course, a religious entity. Yet, just as is the case with respect to the term *religious*, there is no definition in the Internal Revenue Code or in a currently applicable tax regulation of the term *church*. Again, a rigid regulatory definition of the term *church* would undoubtedly be unconstitutional. As one court observed: "We can only approach this question with care for all of us are burdened with the baggage of our own unique beliefs and perspectives."[168]

(a)   General Principles

The concept of a tax-exempt church is recognized in the Internal Revenue Code.[169] Federal tax law applies the term *church* in a variety of contexts. One of the oldest of these instances is reflected in tax regulations issued in 1958 and applicable for

---

[163] *Id.*

[164] IRC § 6673. Also, Sommer v. Comm'r, 45 T.C.M. 1271 (1983); Van Dyke v. Comm'r, 45 T.C.M. 1233 (1983); Noberini v. Comm'r, 45 T.C.M. 587 (1983).

[165] IRC § 6663.

[166] Butler v. Comm'r, 50 T.C.M. 218 (1985). Another approach used by the courts to deny tax-exempt status to a mail-order church is that it failed to keep adequate financial records to demonstrate entitlement to tax exemption as required by IRC § 6001 (Church of Gospel Ministry, Inc. v. United States (D.D.C. 1986)). See § 28.17.

[167] E.g., Cortes v. Comm'r, 108 T.C.M. 253 (2014). An individual selling religious merchandise by means of the Internet was found liable for federal income tax on the net proceeds, with a court rejecting his argument that he was functioning as a church (Lloyd v. Comm'r, T.C. Memo. 2020-92).

[168] Found. of Human Understanding v. Comm'r, 88 T.C. 1341, 1356–57 (1987).

[169] IRC § 170(b)(1)(A)(i). The term *church* has been defined for state law purposes in a variety of ways. One of the most straightforward definitions is that a church is "an organization for religious purposes, for the public worship of God" (Bennett v. City of La Grange, 112 S.E. 482, 485 (Ga. 1922)). Other definitions of the term *church* include the following: "A body or community of Christians, united under one form of government by the same profession of the same faith, and the observance of the same ritual and ceremonies" (McNeilly v. First Presbyterian Church in Brookline, 137 N.E. 691 (Mass. 1923)); "The term may denote either a society of persons who, professing Christianity, hold certain doctrines or observances which differentiate them from other like groups, and who use a common discipline, or the

tax years before 1970, which defined the term *church* (in the unrelated business and charitable contribution deduction settings).[170] Those regulations focused on the "duties" of a church, which were said to include the "ministration of sacerdotal [priestly] functions and the conduct of religious worship." The existence of these elements was said to depend on the "tenets and practices of a particular religious body."

The IRS formulated criteria to be used to ascertain whether an organization qualifies as a church. The IRS position was that, to be a church for tax purposes, an organization must satisfy at least some of the following criteria: a distinct legal existence, a recognized creed and form of worship, a definite and distinct ecclesiastical government, a formal code of doctrine and discipline, a distinct religious history, a membership not associated with any other church or denomination, a complete organization of ordained ministers ministering to their congregations and selected after completing prescribed courses of study, a literature of its own, established places of worship, regular congregations, regular religious services, Sunday schools for the religious instruction of the young, and schools for the preparation of its ministers. The then-Commissioner of Internal Revenue first made these criteria public in 1977.[171]

As discussed, the courts have been reluctant to define the concept of a religious organization, let alone what is a church. Nonetheless, some courts are becoming more willing to enunciate criteria for a church. Thus, in the view of the U.S. Tax Court, a church is an organization that, in addition to having a "religious-type function," holds services or meetings on a regular basis, has ministers or other "representatives," has a record of performance of "marriages, other ceremonies or sacraments," has a place of worship, ordains ministers, requires some financial support by its members, has a form of "formal operation," and satisfies all other requirements of the federal tax law rules for religious organizations.[172]

---

building in which such persons habitually assemble for public worship" (Baker v. Fales, 16 Mass. 488, 498, quoted in First Indep. Missionary Baptist Church of Chosen v. McMillan, 153 So.2d 337, 342 (Fla. 1963)); and "A church society is a voluntary organization whose members are associated together, not only for religious exercises, but also for the purpose of maintaining and supporting its ministry and providing the conveniences of a church home and promoting the growth and efficiency of the work of the general church of which it forms a co-ordinate part" (First Presbyterian Church of Mt. Vernon v. Dennis, 161 N.W. 183, 187 (Iowa 1917)). Thus, the term *church* carries many meanings, including the congregation and the physical facilities themselves. As one court observed, the term "may refer only to the church building or house of worship; it may mean in a more consecrated way the great body of persons holding the Christian belief, or in a restricted sense confined to those adhering to one of the several denominations of the Christian faith, at large or in a definite territory; and it may mean the collective membership of persons constituting the congregation of a single permanent place of worship" (Forsberg v. Zehm, 143 S.E. 284, 286 (Va. 1928)).

[170] Reg. §§ 1.170-2(b)(2), 1.511-2(a)(3)(ii) (inapplicable with respect to tax years after 1969).

[171] "Difficult Definitional Problems in Tax Administration: Religion and Race," remarks by then Commissioner Jerome Kurtz before the Practicing Law Institute Seventh Biennial Conference on Tax Planning for Foundations, Tax-Exempt Status and Charitable Contributions, on Jan. 9, 1977, reproduced at Bureau of Nat'l Affairs, *Daily Executive Report*, Jan. 11, 1977, at J8.

[172] Pusch v. Comm'r, 39 T.C.M. 838 (1980), *aff'd*, 628 F.2d 1353 (5th Cir. 1980). Also, Chambers v. Comm'r, 101 T.C.M. 1550 (2011); Pusch v. Comm'r, 44 T.C.M. 961 (1982); Abney v. Comm'r, 39 T.C.M. 965 (1980); Manson v. Comm'r, 40 T.C.M. 972 (1980); Lynch v. Comm'r, 41 T.C.M. 204 (1980). Cf. Morey v. Riddell, 205 F. Supp. 918 (S.D. Cal. 1962); Peek v. Comm'r, 73 T.C. 912 (1980); Chapman v. Comm'r, 48 T.C. 358 (1967).

In the first instance of a court's utilization of the IRS criteria as to the definition of the term *church*, a federal district court concluded that an organization, albeit religious, could not qualify as a church because there was no "congregation," nor requisite "religious instruction," nor "conduct of religious worship."[173] Laying down a "minimum" definition of a church as including a "body of believers or communicants that assembles regularly in order to worship," the court said that of "central importance" is the "existence of an established congregation served by an organized ministry, the provision of regular religious services and religious education for the young, and the dissemination of a doctrinal code."[174] In the case, no congregation was found present, in that the only communicants were the founder of the church and his wife, who "pray together in the physical solitude of their home"; the organization's religious instruction consisted of "a father preaching to his son"; and its organized ministry was a "single self-appointed clergyman."[175] Because the organization "does not employ recognized, accessible channels of instruction and worship" and was merely a "quintessentially private religious enterprise," the court concluded that it was not a church.[176] The U.S. Claims Court also endorsed these criteria, concluding that, while a "new religious organization should not be held to a standard only an established church can satisfy," "one man's publication of a newsletter and extemporaneous discussion of his beliefs, even when advertised, is not sufficient to constitute a church within the common understanding of that word."[177]

A federal court of appeals concluded that a social service agency, substantially connected with a particular faith, was not a church because it did not hold regular worship services, and because it provided services to individuals irrespective of their religious beliefs and counseling without any particular religious orientation.[178] Another appellate court held that an organization that did not meet enough of the IRS criteria could not qualify as a church.[179]

The U.S. Supreme Court offered a partial definition of the term *church* in the tax context, in an opinion construing an exemption from unemployment compensation taxes imposed by the Federal Unemployment Tax Act and complementary state law. The issue was the eligibility for the exemption for services performed for church-related schools that do not have a separate legal existence, pursuant to

---

[173] American Guidance Found., Inc. v. United States, 490 F. Supp. 304, 306 (D.D.C. 1980), *aff'd without opinion* (D.C. Cir. 1981).

[174] *Id.* at 306.

[175] *Id.* at 307.

[176] *Id.* Likewise, Church of Eternal Life & Liberty, Inc. v. Comm'r, 86 T.C. 916 (1986); Universal Bible Church, Inc. v. Comm'r, 51 T.C.M. 936 (1986).

[177] Church of the Visible Intelligence That Governs the Universe v. United States, 83-2 U.S.T.C. ¶ 9726 (Ct. Cl. 1983), at 88,597.

[178] Lutheran Social Servs. of Minn. v. United States, 758 F.2d 1283 (8th Cir. 1985). A court concluded that a "church is a coherent group of individuals and families that join together to accomplish the religious purposes of mutually held beliefs" and that a "church's principal means of accomplishing its religious purposes must be to assemble regularly a group of individuals related by common worship and faith" (Church of Eternal Life & Liberty, Inc. v. Comm'r, 86 T.C. 916, 924 (1986)). An organization unsuccessfully contested an IRS finding that it was not a church; a motion for summary judgment on the point, relying on dicta in a bankruptcy court opinion, failed (Gates Community Chapel of Rochester, Inc. d/b/a Freedom Village USA v. United States, 96-1 U.S.T.C. ¶ 50,093 (Cl. Ct. 1996)).

[179] Spiritual Outreach Soc'y v. Comm'r, 91-1 U.S.T.C. ¶ 50,111 (8th Cir. 1991).

provision of exemption for employees "of a church or convention or association of churches."[180] The Court held that the word *church* "must be construed, instead, to refer to the congregation or the hierarchy itself, that is, the church authorities who conduct the business of hiring, discharging, and directing church employees."[181] Thus, in one instance, a church-operated day school, financed by the church's congregation and controlled by a board of directors elected from that congregation, was considered part of the church, and a secondary school owned, supported, and controlled by a synod was considered part of a convention or association of churches; neither school was separately incorporated. Although the Court recognized that the issue carries with it potential constitutional law questions,[182] it also expressly "disavow[ed] any intimations in this case defining or limiting what constitutes a church under FUTA or under any other provision of the Internal Revenue Code."[183]

Traditionally, courts have enunciated only two guides as to what constitutes a church in the federal tax context: It must be a religious organization, and it must be the equivalent of a "denomination" or a "sect." For example, in 1967, a court held that "though every church may be a religious organization, every religious organization is not per se a church" and that the "concept of 'church' appears to be synonymous with the concept of 'denomination.'"[184] Then the court hastened to add that its holding "is not to imply that in order to be constituted a church, a group must have an organizational hierarchy or maintain church buildings."[185]

From this standpoint, a church is, in the absence of a statutory definition, an organization that is a church under the "common meaning and usage of the word."[186] Pursuant to this approach, an organization "established to carry out 'church' functions, under the general understanding of the term, is a 'church.'"[187] These functions, according to this view, principally are forms of conduct of religious worship (such as a mass or communion) but are not activities such as the operation of schools, religious orders, wineries, and missions, even where these "religious organizations . . . [or functions are] formed [or conducted] under church auspices."[188] If the latter categories of activities predominate, the organization cannot be a church, inasmuch as the "tail cannot be permitted to wag the dog" and the conduct of such "incidental activities" cannot make an organization a church.[189] Some subsequent cases follow this approach, such as the court finding that an organization is not a church because "there is no showing in the record of any marriages, other ceremonies or sacraments performed by any 'minister'

[180] IRC § 3309(b)(1)(A).

[181] St. Martin Evangelical Lutheran Church v. South Dakota, 451 U.S. 772, 784 (1981).

[182] *Id.* at 780.

[183] *Id.* at 784 n.15.

[184] Chapman v. Comm'r, 48 T.C. 358, 363 (1967). As to the latter element, the court observed that the organization involved is "merely a religious organization comprised of individual members who are already affiliated with various churches" (*id.* at 364).

[185] *Id.* at 363.

[186] De La Salle Inst. v. United States, 195 F. Supp. 891, 903 (N.D. Cal. 1961).

[187] *Id.* at 903.

[188] *Id.* at 902.

[189] *Id.* at 901.

or representative of the Church."[190] Other cases reject this narrow reading of the term and embrace within the ambit of church functions activities such as "mission or evangelistic program[s]" and efforts for the "care of the needy, the sick, or the imprisoned, traditionally the beneficiaries of the ministration of churches."[191]

(b) Associational Test

The IRS is adjusting its application of its criteria as to what constitutes a tax-exempt church. No longer is it the agency's position that only some of the criteria need be satisfied.[192] For example, the agency's lawyers are now of the view that a church, for federal tax law purposes, must meet certain "minimum" standards, such as "regular religious services," a "body of believers or communicants that assembles regularly in order to worship," a "defined congregation of worshippers," and an "established place of worship."[193] The principal activity of an organization was religious broadcasting and publication; the IRS termed these *nonassociational* activities, concluding that religious "programming" is not sufficient activity to enable an organization to constitute a church. Yet, thereafter, the IRS ruled that an international ministry qualified as a church, writing that it satisfied "most" of the IRS church criteria; the entity, however, lacked a place of worship and a membership, and ordination of its clergy was not a requirement.[194]

Subsequently, the IRS ruled that a religious organization, said by the agency to meet "several" of its criteria for church status, did not constitute a church for federal tax purposes in that the criteria it satisfied were not "distinctive characteristics" of a church but rather were "common to both churches and non-church religious organizations." The IRS wrote that this organization lacked a definite and distinct ecclesiastical government and did not have a "regular congregation of its own that engages in regular worship services in an established place of worship." Further, the organization did not have a code of discipline, it did not operate programs for the religious instruction of the young, and it did not publicly identify itself as a church. Consequently, the IRS concluded that this entity failed to qualify as a church.[195]

The IRS held that an online "seminary" did not qualify as a church, in that there was no regular place of worship and it did not hold regular worship services; the agency wrote that this organization did not satisfy the IRS's criteria that are

---

[190] Pusch v. Comm'r, 39 T.C.M. 838, 841 (1980), *aff'd*, 628 F.2d 1353 (5th Cir. 1980). An organization formed to promote "wellness" among its members, through education in exercise, nutrition, and stress management, was held to not qualify as a church (VIA v. Comm'r, 68 T.C.M. 212 (1994)).

[191] Bubbling Well Church of Universal Love, Inc. v. Comm'r, 74 T.C. 531, 536 (1980), *aff'd*, 670 F.2d 104 (9th Cir. 1981).

[192] See text accompanied by *supra* note 171.

[193] Tech. Adv. Mem. 200437040. A federal court of appeals wrote, in 2014, that the IRS "has developed a non-exhaustive, non-binding list of fourteen factors to consider when determining whether an entity is in fact a religious employer" (Priests for Life v. Dep't of Health and Human Servs., 772 F.3d 229 (D.C. Cir. 2014)), when in fact the factors relate to whether a religious organization is a church, the list of factors are no longer followed in their original form, and the subsequent approach of the IRS is indeed "binding."

[194] Priv. Ltr. Rul. 200530028.

[195] Priv. Ltr. Rul. 200727021. Also, Good v. Comm'r, 104 T.C.M. 595 (2012).

"considered the most important."[196] Likewise, the IRS refused to accord church status to an entity that conducted its religious services online, primarily because the organization lacked regularly held worship services, a regular place of worship, and a congregation.[197] Other IRS rulings state that an organization could not qualify as a church because its conduct of religious services occurred in a room in a commercial resort hotel[198] and because an entity conducted its worship services only by teleconference and thus those participating in its activities did so in solitude.[199]

The U.S. Court of Federal Claims more formally articulated this associational test when it held, in 2009, that the test is a "threshold" standard that religious organizations "must satisfy in order to obtain church status."[200] The court quoted another court's observation that, to qualify as a church, an organization "must serve an associational role in accomplishing its religious purpose."[201] The court credited another court opinion as having created the associational standard as the "minimum" requirement necessary for a "religious organization to gain church status."[202]

In this case, the organization's primary activities were radio and Internet broadcasts, which the court declined to characterize as religious services. The court wrote that the "weight of persuasive authority" holds that broadcasts of this nature "lack critical associational aspects characteristic of religious services and are therefore instead properly regarded simply as broadcasting and publishing services insufficient to qualify a religious organization for church status."[203] Also, the organization's services in the form of Sunday meetings, weddings, and seminars were held to not be sufficiently frequent to be characterized as "regular." The U.S. Tax Court had previously concluded that this organization was a church;[204] at that time, the organization provided religious services to an established congregation and otherwise had considerable associational activities.

---

[196] Priv. Ltr. Rul. 200912039. On that occasion, the IRS wrote that its 14-point criteria are "helpful in deciding what constitutes a church for federal tax purposes, although they are not a definitive test."

[197] Priv. Ltr. Rul. 201044019. The IRS subsequently wrote: "A website on the Internet does not qualify as a place of worship, nor do individuals accessing that website constitute a congregation assembled to worship" (Priv. Ltr. Rul. 201232034). In a similar ruling, the IRS denied an organization status as a church for the same reasons, referencing these elements as "associational requirements" (Priv. Ltr. Rul. 201251018). Thereafter, the IRS wrote that the "basic tenets required for obtaining status as a church [are] regular worship services conducted at a regular location with a regular congregation" (Priv. Ltr. Rul. 201325017).

[198] Priv. Ltr. Rul. 200926036.

[199] Priv. Ltr. Rul. 200926049.

[200] Found. of Human Understanding v. United States, 2009-2 U.S.T.C. ¶ 50,519 (U.S. Ct. Fed. Cl. 2009), aff'd, 614 F.3d 1383 (Fed. Cir. 2010), cert. denied, 562 U.S. 1286 (2011).

[201] Church of Eternal Life and Liberty, Inc. v. Comm'r, 86 T.C. 916, 924 (1986).

[202] Found. of Human Understanding v. United States, 2009-2 U.S.T.C. ¶ 50,519 (U.S. Ct. Fed. Cl. 2009), aff'd, 614 F.3d 1383 (Fed. Cir. 2010), cert. denied, 131 S. Ct. 1676 (2011), referencing American Guidance Foundation, Inc. v. United States, 490 F. Supp. 304, 306 (D.D.C. 1980).

[203] Id. The court quoted from another court's opinion, which stated that the "permissible purpose may be accomplished individually and privately in the sense that oral manifestation is not necessary, but it may not be accomplished in physical solitude" (Chapman v. Comm'r, 48 T.C. 358, 367 (1967)).

[204] Found. of Human Understanding v. Comm'r, 88 T.C. 1341 (1987).

An opinion by the U.S. Court of Federal Claims nicely synthesized the federal tax law as to what constitutes a church.[205] The court observed that several courts have recognized that "there is very little guidance for courts to use in making decisions" as to church status.[206] Also, a "coherent definition [of the term *church* does not] emerge from reviewing . . . the limited instances of judicial treatment."[207] Consequently, the court wrote, "[i]n the absence of Congressional guidance and without any guidance from within the [tax] regulations themselves, courts have developed at least three different approaches to determine whether" an organization qualifies as a church.[208]

The first approach is the "general or traditional understanding" of the term *church*, based on the "common meaning and usage of the word."[209] The court declined to adopt this approach, noting that "[t]here is no bright line beyond which certain organized activities undertaken for religious purposes coalesce into a 'church' structure . . . [a]nd the range of 'church' structures extant in the United States is enormously diverse and confusing."[210]

The second approach is application of the IRS criteria. Despite the court's concern about the constitutionality and applicability of these criteria[211] and about a "mechanical application of rigid criteria to a diverse set of religious organizations,"[212] the court applied the IRS criteria in this case, although not exclusively. In the case, the organization met some of these criteria, with the matter presenting a "close question" on that basis, but the organization's failure to satisfy the third approach, the associational test, precluded it from qualifying as a church.[213]

Thus, just as a tax law definition of the term *religion* cannot be formulated, a formal and consistent definition of the term *church* likewise appears incapable

[205] Found. of Human Understanding v. United States, 2009-2 U.S.T.C. ¶ 50,519 (U.S. Ct. Fed. Cl. 2009), *aff'd*, 614 F.3d 1383 (Fed. Cir. 2010), *cert. denied*, 562 U.S. 1286 (2011).

[206] *Id.* This quotation is from Spiritual Outreach Soc'y v. Comm'r, 927 F.2d 335, 338 (8th Cir. 1991).

[207] Found. of Human Understanding v. United States, 2009-2 U.S.T.C. ¶ 50,519 (U.S. Ct. Fed. Cl. 2009), *aff'd*, 614 F.3d 1383 (Fed. Cir. 2010), *cert. denied*, 562 U.S. 1286 (2011). This quotation is from American Guidance Foundation, Inc. v. United States, 490 F. Supp. 304, 306 (D.D.C. 1980).

[208] Found. of Human Understanding v. United States, 2009-2 U.S.T.C. ¶ 50,519 (U.S. Ct. Fed. Cl. 2009), *aff'd*, 614 F.3d 1383 (Fed. Cir. 2010), *cert. denied*, 562 U.S. 1286 (2011).

[209] *Id.* The court opinion most associated with this approach is De La Salle Institute v. United States, 195 F. Supp. 891 (N.D. Cal. 1961).

[210] Found. of Human Understanding v. United States, 2009-2 U.S.T.C. ¶ 50,519 (U.S. Ct. Fed. Cl. 2009), *aff'd*, 614 F.3d 1383 (Fed. Cir. 2010), *cert. denied*, 562 U.S. 1286 (2011). This quotation is from American Guidance Foundation, Inc. v. United States, 490 F. Supp. 304, 306 (D.D.C. 1980).

[211] See *supra* note 171.

[212] Found. of Human Understanding v. United States, 2009-2 U.S.T.C. ¶ 50,519 (U.S. Ct. Fed. Cl. 2009), *aff'd*, 614 F.3d 1383 (Fed. Cir. 2010), *cert. denied*, 562 U.S. 1286 (2011).

[213] *Id.* This court observed that there are a few cases that fall outside this tripartite analytical framework because they involve organizations primarily engaging in "secular functions" (e.g., Junaluska Assembly Housing, Inc. v. Comm'r, 86 T.C. 1114 (1986)) or are "individual or single-family private religious enterprises" (e.g., Richardson v. Comm'r, 70 T.C.M. 14 (1995)). This decision was affirmed, with the appellate court writing that the associational test "provide[s] individual congregants with the opportunity to interact and associate with each other in worship" (614 F.3d 1383, 1391 (Fed. Cir. 2010)). Thereafter, the U.S. Tax Court found a religious organization to be a church, based on the traditional IRS criteria and without reference to the Foundation of Human Understanding case (Chambers v. Comm'r, 101 T.C.M. 1550 (2011)).

of formulation. This is not surprising, in that the religion clauses preclude the strict application of definitions of this nature. Nonetheless, the IRS, from time to time, issues private letter rulings as to whether an organization qualifies as a church.[214]

(c) Principle of Respect for Autonomy

A federal court of appeals articulated a "historic principle of respect for the autonomy of genuine religions."[215] It stated that this principle provides the "legitimate purpose for the preferential treatment of religious organizations" and is predicated on the "long-established governmental desire to respect the autonomy of houses of worship."[216]

This court continued: "It is beyond dispute that respecting church autonomy is a legitimate purpose—one that . . . is enshrined in the constitutional fabric of this country."[217] Principles of noninterference were said to trace back to the "text of the First Amendment itself, which gives special solicitude to the rights of religious organizations" and recognizes their "independence from secular control or manipulation—in short, [their] power to decide for themselves, free from state interference, matters of church governance as well as those of faith and doctrine."[218] Accommodations of this nature, the court stated, "may be extended to houses of worship and religious denominations without applying to all nonprofit organizations"[219] in order to "alleviate significant governmental interference with the ability of religious organizations to define and carry out their religious missions."[220]

The U.S. Supreme Court recognized a ministerial exception, which precludes application of certain laws (in the case, employment discrimination laws) to claims concerning the relationship between a religious institution and its members.[221] The Court wrote that "government interference with an internal church decision that affects the faith and mission of the church" deprives the church of "control over the selection of those who will personify its beliefs."[222]

A related body of law, the ecclesiastical abstention doctrine, is based on courts' determination that the free exercise clause "restricts the government's ability to intrude into ecclesiastical matters or to interfere with a church's governance of its own affairs."[223] This doctrine is a qualified limitation, requiring that courts decide disputes involving churches without resolving underlying controversies over religious doctrine. A court held that the ministerial exception and the

---

[214] E.g., Priv. Ltr. Rul. 200502044.

[215] Real Alternatives, Inc. v. Sec'y, Dep't of Health & Human Servs., 867 F.3d 338, 351 (3d Cir. 2017).

[216] Id.

[217] Id. at 352.

[218] Hosanna-Tabor Evangelical Lutheran Church & School v. Equal Employment Opportunity Comm'n, 565 U.S. 171, 189, 186 (2012).

[219] Real Alternatives, Inc. v. Sec'y, Dep't of Health & Human Servs., 867 F.3d 338, 352 (3d Cir. 2017).

[220] Corp. of the Presiding Bishop of the Church of Jesus Christ of Latter-Day Saints v. Amos, 483 U.S. 327, 338 (1987).

[221] Hosanna-Tabor Evangelical Lutheran Church & School v. Equal Employment Opportunity Comm'n, 565 U.S. 171 (2012). See supra note 22. The Court expanded the ministerial exception to encompass teachers employed by religious schools (Our Lady of Guadalupe School v. Morrissey-Berru; St. James School v. Biel, 140 S. Ct. 2049).

[222] Id. at 188.

[223] E.g., Bollard v. California Province of the Soc'y of Jesus, 196 F.3d 940, 945 (9th Cir. 1999).

ecclesiastical abstention doctrine precluded it from resolving disputes concerning internal governance matters of religious organizations.[224]

§ 10.4   CONVENTIONS OR ASSOCIATIONS OF CHURCHES

Another type of religious organization is the *convention or association of churches*.[225] This phrase has a historical meaning generally referring to a cooperative undertaking by a church of the same denomination.[226] The IRS ruled that the term also applies to a cooperative undertaking by churches of differing denominations, assuming that the convention or association otherwise qualifies as a religious organization.[227]

The phrase *convention or association of churches* was used by Congress to refer to the organizational structures of congregational churches. The term was employed to accord them the comparable tax treatment granted to hierarchical churches.[228]

It is the position of the IRS that a convention of churches is a statewide, regional, or national group of churches of the same denomination. These conventions typically carry out such activities as the operation of schools for ministers, teachers, and missionaries; support of missions; holding of annual sessions; the setting of minimum standards of belief; and the conduct of religious workshops. An association of churches, according to the IRS, is a group of churches organized on a level usually less than statewide; these associations normally carry out many of the same activities as conventions of churches.[229]

An organization that otherwise is a convention or association of churches does not fail to qualify as such merely because the membership of the organization includes individuals as well as churches or because individuals have voting rights in the organization.[230]

§ 10.5   INTEGRATED AUXILIARIES OF CHURCHES

An integrated auxiliary of a church is a religious organization.[231] The phrase *integrated auxiliary of a church* means an organization that is a tax-exempt charitable

---

[224] Puri v. Khalsa, 321 F. Supp. 3d 1233 (D. Ore. 2018).

[225] IRC § 170(b)(1)(A)(i). A discussion of the legislative history of this phrase appears in De La Salle Inst. v. United States, 195 F. Supp. 891, 897–10 (N.D. Cal. 1961). See Reg. § 1.170A-9(b).

[226] Rev. Rul. 74-224, 1974-1 C.B. 61. Cf. Chapman v. Comm'r, 48 T.C. 358 (1957).

[227] Id.

[228] Lutheran Social Servs. of Minn. v. United States, 758 F.2d 1283, 1288 (8th Cir. 1985).

[229] Priv. Ltr. Rul. 8309092.

[230] IRC § 7701(n). The IRS ruled that employees of a tax-exempt elder care facility operated for the benefit of elderly and infirm members of a religious order are, by virtue of control of the facility by a church, deemed to be employees of a church or a convention or association of churches by reason of being employees of an organization that is exempt and controlled by or associated with a church or a convention or association of churches (Priv. Ltr. Rul. 201537025).

[231] IRC § 170(b)(1)(A)(i).

entity,[232] a public charity,[233] affiliated with a church or a convention or association of churches, and internally supported.[234]

An organization is *affiliated* with a church or a convention or association of churches, for this purpose, if the organization is covered by a group exemption letter issued to a church or a convention or association of churches;[235] the organization is operated, supervised, or controlled by or in connection with[236] a church or a convention or association of churches; or relevant facts and circumstances show that it has the requisite affiliation.[237]

The following factors are among those used to determine whether an organization is affiliated with a church or a convention or association of churches (although the absence of one or more of them does not necessarily preclude a finding of affiliation): the organization's enabling instrument[238] or bylaws affirm that the organization shares common religious doctrines, principles, disciplines, or practices with a church or a convention or association of churches; a church or a convention or association of churches has the authority to appoint or remove, or to control the appointment or removal of, at least one of the organization's officers or directors; the corporate name of the organization indicates an institutional relationship with a church or a convention or association of churches; the organization reports at least annually on its financial and general operations to a church or a convention or association of churches; an institutional relationship between the organization and a church or a convention or association of churches is affirmed by the church, or convention or association of churches, or a designee of one or more of them; and, in the event of dissolution, the organization's assets are required to be distributed to a church or a convention or association of churches, or to an affiliate (as defined by these rules) of one or more of them.[239]

An organization is *internally supported*, for these purposes, unless it both offers admissions, goods, services, or facilities for sale, other than on an incidental basis, to the general public (except goods, services, or facilities sold at a nominal charge or for an insubstantial portion of the cost) and normally receives more than 50 percent of its support from a combination of government sources, public solicitation of contributions, and receipts from the sale of admissions, goods, performance of services, or furnishing of facilities in activities that are not unrelated trades or businesses.[240]

Men's and women's organizations, seminaries, mission societies, and youth groups that meet all the criteria for qualification of an integrated auxiliary of a

---

[232] That is, an organization described in IRC § 501(c)(3).

[233] That is, an organization described in IRC §§ 509(a)(1), 509(a)(2), or 509(a)(3). See § 12.3.

[234] Reg. § 1.6033-2(h)(1).

[235] See § 26.11.

[236] This phraseology is similar to that used in connection with the supporting organization rules (see § 12.3(c), text accompanied by note 198).

[237] Reg. § 1.6033-2(h)(2).

[238] That is, its corporate charter, trust instrument, articles of association, constitution, or similar document. This is what the IRS refers to in other contexts as the *articles of organization* (e.g., § 4.2).

[239] Reg. § 1.6033-2(h)(3).

[240] Reg. § 1.6033-2(h)(4).

church or a convention or association of churches are such integrated auxiliaries, irrespective of whether these entities satisfy the internal support requirement.[241]

Under previous rules, the term *integrated auxiliary of a church* meant an organization that is a tax-exempt charitable organization, affiliated with a church, and engaged in a principal activity that is "exclusively religious."[242] An organization's principal activity was not considered to be exclusively religious, however, if that activity was of a nature other than religious that would serve as a basis for tax exemption (such as charitable, educational, or scientific activity).[243]

Litigation ensued as the consequence of issuance of these previous rules. A federal court of appeals invalidated the requirement that an organization must be exclusively religious to qualify as an integrated auxiliary of a church.[244] This court held that that portion of the regulation was inconsistent with clear congressional policy,[245] thus ruling that the organization involved—a social service agency that was affiliated with various synods of a church—was an integrated auxiliary of the church because it "performs functions of the church bodies to which it is related by satisfying the tenet of the . . . faith [of the church] which requires the stimulation of works of mercy through social action ministries developed to promote human welfare."[246] By contrast, a federal district court found these regulations to be valid, but only after finding an organization to be an integrated auxiliary of a church because the entity was exclusively religious.[247]

§ 10.6   MISSION SOCIETIES

A mission society is an entity sponsored by or affiliated with one or more churches or church denominations, more than one-half of the activities of which are

---

[241] Reg. § 1.6033-2(h)(5).

[242] Former Reg. § 1.6033-2(g)(5)(i).

[243] Former Reg. § 1.6033-2(g)(5)(ii).

[244] Lutheran Social Servs. of Minn. v. United States, 758 F. 2d 1283 (8th Cir. 1985), *rev'g* 583 F. Supp. 1298 (D. Minn. 1984). Also, Lutheran Children & Family Serv. of Eastern Pa. v. United States, 86-2 U.S.T.C. ¶ 9593 (E.D. Pa. 1986).

[245] The appellate court was particularly influenced by the fact that Congress specifically imposed the "exclusively religious" standard on religious orders (IRC § 6033(a)(2)(A)(iii)) but did not do so with respect to integrated auxiliaries of churches (IRC § 6033(a)(2)(A)(i)).

[246] Lutheran Social Servs. of Minn. v. United States, 758 F.2d 1283, 1291 (8th Cir. 1985).

[247] Tennessee Baptist Children's Homes, Inc. v. United States, 604 F. Supp. 210 (M.D. Tenn. 1984), *aff'd*, 790 F.2d 534 (6th Cir. 1986). Under prior law, for example, schools that were operated, supported, and controlled by a church or a convention or association of churches were integrated auxiliaries (St. Martin Evangelical Lutheran Church v. South Dakota, 451 U.S. 772 (1981)). An organization was held to not qualify as an integrated auxiliary because the church involved lacked any control over the assets or income of the organization (Parshall Christian Order v. Comm'r, 45 T.C.M. 488 (1983)), and a church-affiliated college that trained ministers and lay workers to serve religious functions in the church qualified as an integrated auxiliary (Rev. Rul. 77-381, 1977-2 C.B. 462). Private letter rulings issued by the IRS provided illustrations of organizations that were integrated auxiliaries of a church under prior law (e.g., Priv. Ltr. Rul. 8416065) and of those that did not qualify as an integrated auxiliary of a church (e.g., Priv. Ltr. Rul. 8402014).

conducted in or directed at persons in foreign countries.[248] The IRS uses the integrated auxiliary rules to define the *affiliation* requirement.[249]

An organization had as its primary activity the provision of humanitarian aid to individuals in a foreign country; it thus met the *foreign-activities* requirement. However, observing that mission societies that are sponsored by one or more churches "must have some institutional relationship with and provide some kind of financial accounting to the churches who are sponsoring them," the IRS denied mission society status to the organization since it could not meet the affiliation requirement.[250]

§ 10.7 RELIGIOUS ORDERS

Another type of religious organization is the *religious order*, a term that is not defined in the Internal Revenue Code or the tax regulations. The IRS promulgated guidelines for determining whether an organization qualifies as a religious order, utilizing a variety of characteristics drawn from the case law.[251] These characteristics are as follows: the organization is a charitable one;[252] the members of the organization vow to live under a strict set of rules requiring moral and spiritual self-sacrifice and dedication to the goals of the organization at the expense of their material well-being; the members of the organization, after successful completion of the organization's training program and probationary period, make a long-term commitment to the organization (normally more than two years); the organization is, directly or indirectly, under the control and supervision of a church or a convention or association of churches, or is significantly funded by a church or a convention or association of churches; the members of the organization normally live together as part of a community and are held to a significantly stricter level of moral and religious discipline than that required of lay church members; the members of the organization work or serve full-time on behalf of the religious, educational, or charitable goals of the organization; and the members of the organization participate regularly in activities such as public or private prayer, religious study, teaching, care of the aging, missionary work, or church reform or renewal.[253]

In determining whether an organization is a religious order, all the facts and circumstances must be considered. Generally, the presence of all these characteristics is determinative that the organization is a religious order. However,

---

[248] Reg. § 1.6033-2(g)(1)(iv).

[249] See § 10.5.

[250] Priv. Ltr. Rul. 201204016.

[251] Rev. Proc. 91-20, 1991-1 C.B. 524. The cases cited by the IRS in this regard are St. Joseph Farms of Indiana Bros. of the Congregation of Holy Cross, SW, Inc. v. Comm'r, 85 T.C. 9 (1985), *appeal dismissed* (7th Cir. 1986); De La Salle Inst. v. United States, 195 F. Supp. 891 (N.D. Cal. 1961); Eighth Street Baptist Church, Inc. v. United States, 295 F. Supp. 1400 (D. Kan. 1969), *aff'd*, 431 F.2d 1193 (10th Cir. 1970); Kelley v. Comm'r, 62 T.C. 131 (1974); Estate of Callaghan v. Comm'r, 33 T.C. 870 (1960).

[252] That is, it is described in IRC § 501(c)(3).

[253] Rev. Proc. 91-20, 1991-1 C.B. 524 § 3.

although the absence of the first of these characteristics is determinative that the organization is not a religious order, the absence of one or more of the other enumerated characteristics is not necessarily determinative in a particular case. If application of these characteristics to the facts of a particular case does not clearly indicate whether the organization is a religious order, the IRS's procedures call for it to contact the authorities affiliated with the organization for their views concerning the characterization of the organization, which views are to be "carefully considered."[254]

In one instance, a tax-exempt religious organization was inspired by Christian ideals and structured around daily religious observations and celebrations of festivals of the Christian year. The entity was dedicated to the care and well-being of adults with developmental disabilities—its residents. The community also included members who cared for the residents and the members' children. These three categories of individuals lived together on a full-time basis in extended family households and worked together maintaining the community. Members were individuals who had been in continuous residence at the organization's facility for at least three years, completed a course of studies, completed a discernment process regarding the suitability of their intended permanent commitment to the community, and been accepted into permanent residence at the community. Members agreed to strive to live in accordance with ideals requiring moral and spiritual self-sacrifice and dedication to the organization's goals, at the expense of their material well-being. The IRS ruled that this organization is a religious order, even though it is not under the control and supervision of a church or a convention or association of churches.[255]

§ 10.8   APOSTOLIC ORGANIZATIONS

Certain *religious or apostolic* organizations are exempt from federal income taxation, even though they are not embraced by the general reference to religious organizations. These are "religious or apostolic associations or corporations, if such associations or corporations have a common treasury or community treasury, even if such associations or corporations engage in business for the common benefit of the members, but only if the members thereof include (at the time of filing their returns) in their gross income their entire pro rata shares, whether distributed or not, of the taxable income of the association or corporation for such year."[256] Any amount so included in the gross income of a member is treated as a dividend received.[257] It is the position of the IRS that members of a religious or apostolic organization may not claim their minor children as dependents for tax purposes, because the organization provides their food, clothing, medical care, and the like;

[254] *Id.*

[255] Priv. Ltr. Rul. 201904008.

[256] IRC § 501(d).

[257] Reg. § 1.501(d)-1(a); Rev. Rul. 58-328, 1958-1 C.B. 327; Rev. Rul. 57-574, 1957-2 C.B. 161; Riker v. Comm'r, 244 F.2d 220 (9th Cir. 1957), *cert. denied*, 355 U.S. 839 (1957).

the members cannot claim the investment tax credit on their proportionate shares of property purchased by the organization;[258] the members cannot claim the fuel tax credit on fuels purchased by the organization; the costs of personal goods and services provided by such an organization for its members are not deductible business expenses; and the amounts distributed to the members of the organization do not constitute self-employment income.[259]

The requirement that there be a "common treasury or community treasury" does not mean that the members of the apostolic organization must take a vow of poverty and irrevocably contribute all of their property to the organization on becoming members and not be entitled to any part of that property on leaving the organization.[260] The concept of this type of treasury "connotes that the property of such organizations not be held by members individually but rather held in a 'community capacity' with all members having equal interests in the community property" and does not mean "that members are necessarily prohibited from owning property outside and apart from the organization."[261] This requirement is satisfied "when all of the income generated internally by community-operated business and any income generated from property owned by the organization is placed into a common fund that is maintained by such organization and is used for the maintenance and support of its members, with all members having equal, undivided interests in this common fund, but no right to claim title to any part thereof."[262]

For purposes of determining the pro rata shares of the taxable income of an apostolic organization (to be included in the members' gross income), the membership in the organization is to be determined in accordance with the rules of the organization itself and applicable state law. Individuals qualified to be members of this type of an organization must consent to this membership status; parents may consent to the membership on behalf of their minor children to the extent allowed under applicable state law.[263]

A federal court of appeals, in commenting on the type of organization contemplated by these rules, said: "One might assume, then, that Congress intended an association somewhat akin to the ordinary association or partnership in which each member has a definite, though undivided, interest in the business conducted for the common benefit of the members, as well as a common interest in

---

[258] The president of a tax-exempt apostolic organization was held by a federal court of appeals to be a common-law employee of the organization, thereby allowing the deductibility of medical and meal expenses at the corporate level, causing a reduction in the president's taxable income; the district court held that the faith-based nature of the relationship between the organization and its members was inconsistent with the concept of an employer/employee arrangement (Stahl v. United States, 2010-2 U.S.T.C. ¶ 50,744 (9th Cir. 2010), rev'g and remanding 2009-2 U.S.T.C. ¶ 50,785 (E.D. Wash. 2009)). On remand, the district court held that food and medical care provided by apostolic organizations to their members are in essence compensation and thus these organizations may deduct these expenses at the corporate level (Stahl v. United States, 861 F. Supp. 2d 1226 (E.D. Wash. 2012)).

[259] Priv. Ltr. Rul. 7740009. Nor are losses or charitable contributions passed through to members; instead, the charitable contribution deduction allowed to the organization reduces the amount of taxable income at the corporate level that is allocated to members (Priv. Ltr. Rul. 9434002).

[260] Twin Oaks Community, Inc. v. Comm'r, 87 T.C. 1233 (1986).

[261] Id. at 1248.

[262] Id. at 1254.

[263] Rev. Rul. 77-295, 1977-2 C.B. 196.

the community treasury and property."[264] Also, the statute's beginnings are traceable to the fact that apostolic organizations were early found to not qualify for tax exemption under the general rules for religious organizations because of the presence of commercial activities and private inurement, as discussed in the cases concerning the tax status of the Hutterische Church.[265] Few exemptions under this provision have been granted; the most notable example may be the 1939 determination of exemption thereunder accorded the Israelite House of David.[266] The courts appear to prefer to cope with organizations of this nature in the context of the law applicable to religious groups generally.[267]

Organizations contemplated by these rules are those that are supported by internally operated businesses in which all the members have an individual interest. In one instance, a communal religious organization did not conduct any business activities and instead was supported by the wages of some of its members who were engaged in outside employment and thus was ruled to not qualify as an apostolic organization.[268]

It is the position of the IRS (general counsel) that failure to qualify as an apostolic organization under these rules does not preclude the possibility that an organization may qualify as a communal religious organization.[269] In other words, the IRS does not believe that Congress occupied the field with respect to tax exemption of all communal religious organizations in enacting the rules for apostolic organizations.

§ 10.9 COMMUNAL GROUPS

The IRS invokes the private inurement doctrine in still another context involving religious organizations: the tax treatment of communal groups. The IRS position is that, generally, where individuals reside in a communal setting in the context of professing religious beliefs, with room, board, and other costs provided by the organization, the result is unwarranted private benefit to the individuals that precludes tax exemption. This position has been upheld by the courts.[270]

The IRS position—as manifested in a 1981 general counsel memorandum (overruling the IRS rulings division)[271]—is that communal groups can qualify as religious organizations where the facilities and benefits provided by the organization to its membership "do not exceed those strictly necessary to exist in a

---

[264] Riker v. Comm'r, 244 F. 2d 220, 230 (9th Cir. 1957), cert. denied, 355 U.S. 839 (1957).

[265] Hofer v. United States, 64 Ct. Cl. 672 (1928); Hutterische Bruder Gemeinde v. Comm'r, 1 B.T.A. 1208 (1925).

[266] Blume v. Gardner, 262 F. Supp. 405, 408 (W.D. Mich. 1966), aff'd, 397 F.2d 809 (6th Cir. 1968). Also, Israelite House of David v. United States, 58 F. Supp. 862 (W.D. Mich. 1945); People v. Israelite House of David, 225 N.W. 638 (Mich. 1929).

[267] Golden Rule Church Ass'n v. Comm'r, 41 T.C. 719 (1964); State v. King Colony Ranch, 350 P.2d 841 (Mont. 1960).

[268] Rev. Rul. 78-100, 1978-1 C.B. 162.

[269] Gen. Couns. Mem. 38827. See § 10.9.

[270] E.g., Canada v. Comm'r, 82 T.C. 973 (1984); Beth-El Ministries, Inc. v. United States, 79-2 U.S.T.C. ¶ 9412 (D.D.C. 1979); Martinsville Ministries, Inc. v. United States, 80-2 U.S.T.C. ¶ 9710 (D.D.C. 1979).

[271] Gen. Couns. Mem. 38827.

communal religious organization . . . "; references such as "primitive," "stark," and "deprivation in material terms of life" are used in the memorandum. Also, the IRS found a distinguishing feature in the fact that, in the case of the organization that achieved tax exemption, "few" of its members worked outside the community. (These allegedly "distinguishing" factors were not discussed in the court opinions, however, where the very fact of a communal existence was found to be the barrier to classification as a religious organization.)[272]

§ 10.10 RETREAT FACILITIES

Religious retreat facility or vacation resort? That is the issue that usually arises when a nonprofit retreat facility pursues recognition of tax exemption. In the principal case, the organization operating the facility claimed to be a religious entity, emphasizing prayer and contemplation opportunities, and optional daily devotions and occasional religious services. A court disagreed, concluding that tax exemption as a religious organization was not available, in that "[w]holesome family recreation or just sitting on a rock contemplating nature may well provide a family or an individual with a religious, or at least a spiritually uplifting experience, but it is difficult to see how that experience differs, if it does, from the same experience one can have at any quiet inn or lodge located in the beautiful mountains of Colorado."[273]

Nonetheless, retreat facilities can be regarded as tax-exempt religious organizations. For example, an organization, controlled by an auxiliary of a major church denomination, formed to contract for the construction of housing at a conference and retreat center owned and operated by the church, was held to be a religious organization, in that the housing it was to provide was predominantly to aid and enhance the religious purposes of the auxiliary and ultimately the church.[274] The court cautioned, however, that if the "housing units are in fact utilized substantially for vacation or recreational purposes, or otherwise by individuals who do not have active roles in the planning, organization, operation of or participation in the [auxiliary's] . . . programs and religious activities, then a substantial nonexempt purpose would be served" and the organization would not qualify for tax exemption.[275] As the court observed, the "tax law . . . does not require churches to hold their retreats or other gatherings for religious purposes in the wilderness or to eschew recreation incident to gatherings held primarily for religious activity."[276]

---

[272] The IRS held that a monastery of the Order of Cistercians of the Strict Observance, a Roman Catholic order, engages in an exempt function when it provides the monks "with food, shelter, clothing, and the other necessities of life" (Priv. Ltr. Rul. 7838028). Also, New Life Tabernacle v. Comm'r, 44 T.C.M. 309 (1982); Rev. Rul. 76-323, 1976-2 C.B. 18; Rev. Rul. 68-123, 1968-1 C.B. 35.

[273] Schoger Found. v. Comm'r, 76 T.C. 380, 388 (1981). Also, Petersen v. Comm'r, 53 T.C.M. 235 (1987).

[274] Junaluska Assembly Hous., Inc. v. Comm'r, 86 T.C. 1114 (1986).

[275] Id. at 1123.

[276] Id. at 1122–23. Previously, the Tax Court upheld the tax-exempt status of an organization that operated religious facilities in an idyllic setting, finding the social and recreational aspects of its program to be insubstantial (Alive Fellowship of Harmonious Living v. Comm'r, 47 T.C.M. 1134 (1984)).

Other Types of Charitable Organizations

Aside from the organizations discussed in the previous four chapters, Section 501(c)(3) of the Internal Revenue Code provides the basis for tax exemption for certain other types of organizations.

§ 11.1 CRUELTY PREVENTION ORGANIZATIONS

Charitable organizations include those that are organized and operated exclusively for the *prevention of cruelty to children or animals*.[1]

An organization that prevented the birth of unwanted animals and the eventual suffering of others by providing funds for pet owners who cannot afford the spaying or neutering operation was recognized by the IRS as tax-exempt as an animal cruelty prevention organization,[2] as was an organization that sought to secure humane treatment of laboratory animals.[3]

An organization to protect children from working in hazardous occupations in violation of state laws and in unfavorable work conditions was held by the IRS to be an organization established to prevent cruelty to children.[4]

§ 11.2 AMATEUR SPORTS ORGANIZATIONS

Another category of charitable organization is the *amateur athletic organization*. This exemption was established in 1976 by adding to the tax-exempt organizations

[1] Reg. § 1.501(c)(3)-1(d)(1)(i)(g).
[2] Rev. Rul. 74-194, 1974-1 C.B. 129.
[3] Rev. Rul. 66-359, 1966-2 C.B. 219.
[4] Rev. Rul. 67-151, 1967-1 C.B. 134.

rules[5] and the charitable contribution deduction rules[6] the following phraseology: "or to foster national or international amateur sports competition (but only if no part of its activities involve the provision of athletic facilities or equipment)."[7] Thus, an organization whose primary activities are conducted on a local level and/or are for the benefit of adults cannot qualify for tax exemption pursuant to this body of law.[8]

The legislative history of this provision contains the observation that, under prior law, organizations that "teach youth or which are affiliated with deductible organizations" may qualify as charitable entities and may receive charitable contributions but that organizations that foster national or international sports competition may be granted tax exemption as social welfare organizations[9] or business leagues[10] and be ineligible to receive deductible contributions. This history also states, as respects the parenthetical limitation, that this "restriction . . . is intended to prevent the allowance of these benefits for organizations which, like social clubs, provide facilities and equipment for their members."[11]

At issue in the first court case to interpret this parenthetical restriction was the tax-exempt status of an organization that promoted the building and use of a class of racing sailboats by, in part, maintaining the design character of the class. The organization maintained a full-size shape of the hull of the sailboat (the "master plug") and precisely measured pieces of aluminum or Mylar that represented the required shapes of parts of the boat (the "measurement templates"). Rejecting the IRS's contention that the master plug and measurement templates were proscribed athletic facilities or equipment, the court held that the items were "tools" necessary to standardize competitive categories in the amateur competition that the organization fostered.[12]

The parenthetical prohibition is a limitation only on the purpose added in 1976; that is, it is not a limitation on the tax exemption and charitable contribution provisions generally. Thus, a private foundation was advised by the IRS that it could make a grant to a state university–related foundation for the purpose of constructing an aquatic complex as an integral part of the university's educational program, with the grant constituting a qualifying distribution,[13] because it would be made to accomplish educational and charitable purposes.[14]

This aspect of the law of tax-exempt organizations was modified again in 1982.[15] Thus, in the case of a *qualified amateur sports organization*, the requirement

---

[5] IRC § 501(c)(3).

[6] IRC §§ 170(c)(2)(B), 2055(a)(2), 2522(a)(2).

[7] In general, Hutchinson Baseball Enters. v. Comm'r, 73 T.C. 144 (1979), *aff'd*, 696 F.2d 757 (10th Cir. 1982). Cf. Media Sports League, Inc. v. Comm'r, 52 T.C.M. 1093 (1986).

[8] E.g., Priv. Ltr. Rul. 200842055.

[9] IRC § 501(c)(4). See Chapter 13.

[10] IRC § 501(c)(6). See Chapter 14.

[11] Staff of Joint Comm. on Tax'n, 94th Cong., General Explanation of the Tax Reform Act of 1976, 423–24 (Comm. Print 1976).

[12] Int'l E22 Class Ass'n v. Comm'r, 78 T.C. 93, 98 (1982).

[13] See § 12.4(b).

[14] Priv. Ltr. Rul. 8037103.

[15] IRC § 501(j).

in the law that no part of the organization's activities may involve the provision of athletic facilities or equipment does not apply.[16] Also, a qualified amateur sports organization will not fail to qualify as a charitable entity merely because its membership is local or regional in nature.[17] A qualified amateur sports organization is any organization organized and operated exclusively to foster national or international amateur sports competition if the organization is also organized and operated primarily to conduct national or international competition in sports or to support and develop amateur athletes for national or international competition in sports.[18]

Booster clubs and other entities that provide financial support to tax-exempt amateur sports organizations are not likely to achieve exemption in accordance with these rules. In fact, they may not qualify for exemption at all. For example, if the fundraising is for the direct benefit of individual team members and their parents, the IRS will dismiss the organization as a mere "tool" for providing this form of private benefit to these individuals; the IRS may view the parents in these situations as insiders with respect to the organization and deny exemption on the basis of the private inurement doctrine.[19]

§ 11.3   PUBLIC SAFETY TESTING ORGANIZATIONS

A federal appellate court held that an organization that conducted tests, experiments, and investigations into the causes of losses against which insurance companies provided coverage was neither charitable, scientific, nor educational.[20] Congress responded by providing tax-exempt status for organizations that engage in *testing for public safety*.[21] This term includes the "testing of consumer products, such as electrical products, to determine whether they are safe for use by the general public."[22]

This provision was the basis for tax exemption for an organization that tested boating equipment and established safety standards for products used aboard pleasure craft by the boating public.[23] An organization that clinically tested drugs for commercial pharmaceutical companies was denied tax exemption under this

---

[16] IRC § 501(j)(1)(A).

[17] IRC § 501(j)(1)(B).

[18] IRC § 501(j)(2). The legislative history of this provision is discussed in Gen. Couns. Mem. 39775, which concluded that an organization that assists in securing and conducting state, regional, national, and international sports competitions in a particular geographic area and an organization that sponsors a postseason college football game are qualified amateur sports organizations. The IRS ruled that organizations conducting professional rodeos (Priv. Ltr. Rul. 201706019) and outboard motorboat races (without the participation of amateur athletes) open to the public (Priv. Ltr. Rul. 201933016) are not qualified amateur sports organizations.

[19] See Chapter 20 (e.g., Priv. Ltr. Rul. 201035034). The U.S. Tax Court agrees with this approach of the IRS (Capital Gymnastics Booster Club, Inc. v. Comm'r, 106 T.C. 154 (2013)). The IRS so ruled regarding an organization raising funds in connection with youth dance competitions (Priv. Ltr. Rul. 201037029).

[20] Underwriters' Laboratory, Inc. v. Comm'r, 135 F.2d 371 (7th Cir. 1943), *cert. denied*, 320 U.S. 756 (1943).

[21] IRC § 501(c)(3).

[22] Reg. § 1.501(c)(3)-1(d)(4). Also, Reg. § 1.501(c)(3)-1(d)(1)(i)(d).

[23] Rev. Rul. 65-61, 1965-1 C.B. 234.

provision, however, on the ground that the testing principally served the private interests of the manufacturer and that a drug is not a "consumer product" until it is approved for marketing by the Food and Drug Administration.[24] Similarly, an organization whose activities included the inspection, testing, and safety certification of cargo shipping containers and research, development, and reporting of information in the field of containerization was denied tax exemption under this provision because these activities served the private interests of manufacturers and shippers by facilitating their operations in international commerce.[25]

An organization that performed flammability tests and evaluations for manufacturers of building materials qualified under this category of tax exemption.[26] By contrast, an organization that had as its principal activity preservice and inservice examinations and evaluations of nuclear reactor power plants to ensure their safe operation did not qualify for this exemption because the examinations did not involve the testing of consumer products.[27] Likewise, an organization that tested various hydraulic and mechanical devices designed for the protection of a public water supply from contamination and pollution did not qualify because the devices were not consumer products.[28] This approach was also reflected in a ruling that held that testing performed for commercial entities of either products for premarket clearance or air samples or like substances for compliance with environmental laws is unrelated business activity.[29]

Public safety testing organizations are expressly exempted from classification as private foundations.[30] Contributions, bequests, or gifts to public safety testing organizations (as such) are not deductible as charitable gifts, however, inasmuch as provision has not been made for them in the charitable contribution deduction rules.[31]

§ 11.4 COOPERATIVE HOSPITAL SERVICE ORGANIZATIONS

Qualifying *cooperative hospital service organizations* are tax-exempt entities by virtue of being charitable organizations.[32] These organizations must be organized and operated solely for two or more exempt member hospitals and must be organized

---

[24] Rev. Rul. 68-373, 1968-2 C.B. 206.

[25] Rev. Rul. 78-426, 1978-2 C.B. 175.

[26] Priv. Ltr. Rul. 7930005.

[27] *Id.*

[28] Priv. Ltr. Rul. 7820007.

[29] Priv. Ltr. Rul. 8409055. An organization formed to provide carpool services for its members for a fee failed to qualify as a tax-exempt organization that tests for public safety; the IRS observed that, although this organization conducts background checks on its prospective members to ascertain whether they are safe to ride with, these individuals are not *consumer products* (Priv. Ltr. Rul. 200910060). An organization that developed and administered a program setting safety and other standards in a field of engineering qualified as a charitable organization because its quality control program lessened the burdens of a local government (see § 7.7) (Gen. Couns. Mem. 38577).

[30] IRC § 509(a)(4). See § 12.3(d).

[31] IRC §§ 170, 2055, 2106, 2522.

[32] IRC § 501(e).

and operated on a cooperative basis. They must perform certain specified services[33] on a centralized basis for their members, namely, data processing, purchasing (including the purchasing of insurance on a group basis),[34] warehousing, billing and collection (including the purchase of patron accounts receivable on a recourse basis), food, clinical, industrial engineering,[35] laboratory, printing, communications, records center, and/or personnel (including selection, testing, training, and education of personnel) services. To qualify, these services must constitute exempt activities if performed on their own behalf by a participating hospital.[36] Although this type of cooperative must have hospitals as members (patrons), its membership may include comparable entities, such as the outpatient component of a county health department.[37]

The IRS takes the position that, to qualify as a cooperative hospital service organization, the organization may provide only the services specified in the specific authorizing legislation.[38] This position is based on the legislative history of the provision.[39] Thus, the IRS ruled that a cooperative hospital laundry service cannot be tax-exempt as a charitable organization by reason of these rules, and observed that this type of an entity may qualify as a tax-exempt cooperative.[40] As discussed later, the IRS prevailed on this point. Thus, although it had been expressly held by a court that an organization that qualifies under the cooperative hospital service organization rules may nonetheless also qualify as a charitable organization generally,[41] this opinion was reversed, with the appellate court holding that these cooperatives can qualify (if at all) only under the cooperative hospital service organization rules.[42]

A court, in a case involving a centralized laundry service operated for tax-exempt hospitals, held that the organization qualified for status as a charitable entity, notwithstanding these specific rules.[43] Commenting on the rules for certain hospital cooperatives, the court said: "The clearly expressed Congressional purpose behind the enactment of [these rules] was to enlarge the category of charitable organizations under Section 501(c)(3) to include certain cooperative hospital service organizations, and not to narrow or restrict the reach of Section 501(c)(3)."[44]

---

[33] IRC § 501(e)(1)(A).

[34] An organization performs the service of *purchasing* when it buys equipment for one of its patron hospitals, even though it holds legal title to the equipment, where that arrangement is used merely as a convenience to the hospital, which remains the beneficial owner of and solely responsible for paying for the equipment (Rev. Rul. 80-316, 1980-2 C.B. 172).

[35] Rev. Rul. 74-443, 1974-2 C.B. 159.

[36] Rev. Rul. 69-633, 1969-2 C.B. 121.

[37] Gen. Couns. Mem. 39692.

[38] Rev. Rul. 69-160, 1969-1 C.B. 147.

[39] H.R. Rep. No. 90-1533, at 1, 20 (1968). Also, S. Rep. No. 90-744, at 200–201 (1967); H.R. Rep. No. 90-1030, at 73 (1967).

[40] Rev. Rul. 69-633, 1969-2 C.B. 121. (The rules concerning cooperative organizations are at IRC §§ 1381–1383.) Services performed in the employ of a cooperative hospital service organization described in IRC § 501(e) are exempted from "employment" for purposes of the FUTA (Rev. Rul. 74-493, 1974-2 C.B. 327).

[41] Chart, Inc. v. United States, 491 F. Supp. 10 (D.D.C. 1979).

[42] Chart, Inc. v. United States, 652 F.2d 195 (D.C. Cir. 1981).

[43] United Hosp. Servs., Inc. v. United States, 384 F. Supp. 776 (S.D. Ind. 1974).

[44] *Id.* at 781. Also, Northern Calif. Central Servs., Inc. v. United States, 591 F.2d 620 (Ct. Cl. 1979).

Following enactment of these rules in 1968,[45] controversy emerged as to the meaning and scope of the provision in relation to the general rules defining charitable entities.[46] There were two competing views: The hospital cooperative rules were enacted (1) to provide the exclusive and controlling means by which a cooperative hospital service organization can achieve tax exemption, so that this type of an organization that fails to satisfy the requirements of the rules thereby fails to qualify as a charitable organization,[47] or (2) to enlarge the category of charitable organizations to include certain types of cooperative hospital service organizations, so that it does not narrow or restrict the reach of the rules defining charitable organizations generally.[48]

Relying on legislative history[49] and using a statutory construction rationale (that a specific statute controls over a general provision), the Supreme Court ruled that the first of these two views is the correct one.[50] In this opinion, in a case involving a cooperative laundry organization serving tax-exempt entities, the Court wrote that "[i]nasmuch as laundry service was deliberately omitted from the statutory list and, indeed, was refused inclusion in that list, it inevitably follows that petitioner is not entitled to tax-exempt status."[51]

This provision pertains to hospital cooperative service organizations that perform qualified administrative and other services directly for hospitals. It is not controlling in situations where an organization provides patient care services to the public.[52]

§ 11.5 COOPERATIVE EDUCATIONAL SERVICE ORGANIZATIONS

Cooperative service organizations of operating educational organizations are regarded as charitable organizations.[53]

---

[45] Pub. L. No. 90-364, § 109(a), 82 Stat. 251, 269 (1968).

[46] RC § 501(c)(3).

[47] E.g., HCSC-Laundry v. United States, 624 F.2d 428 (3d Cir. 1980), *rev'g* 473 F. Supp. 250 (E.D. Pa. 1979); Metropolitan Detroit Area Hosp. Servs., Inc. v. United States, 634 F.2d 330 (6th Cir. 1980), *rev'g* 445 F. Supp. 857 (E.D. Mich. 1978); Community Hosp. Servs., Inc. v. United States, 47 AFTR 2d 81-999 (6th Cir. 1981), *rev'g* 43 AFTR 2d 79-934 (E.D. Mich. 1979): Hospital Central Servs. Ass'n v. United States, 623 F.2d 611 (9th Cir. 1980), *rev'g* 40 AFTR 2d 77-5646 (W.D. Wash. 1977).

[48] E.g., Northern Calif. Central Servs., Inc. v. United States, 591 F.2d 620 (Ct. Cl. 1979); United Hosp. Servs., Inc. v. United States, 384 F. Supp. 776 (S.D. Ind. 1974); Chart, Inc. v. United States, 491 F. Supp. 10 (D.D.C. 1979).

[49] See text accompanied by *supra* note 39.

[50] HCSC-Laundry v. United States, 450 U.S. 1 (1981).

[51] *Id.* at 8. Relying on this decision, the IRS ruled that, if an organization fails to qualify under a specific category of tax exemption, it is therefore precluded from qualifying under a more general category of exemption (Rev. Rul. 83-166, 1983-2 C.B. 96). The IRS revoked the exempt status of an organization providing services on a centralized basis for exempt hospitals because some of the services were not encompassed by these rules (Tech. Adv. Mem. 9542002).

[52] Tech. Adv. Mem. 200151045.

[53] IRC § 501(f).

These organizations must be organized and controlled by, and composed solely of, members that are private or public educational institutions.[54] They must be organized and operated solely to hold, commingle, and collectively invest and reinvest (including arranging for and supervising the performance by independent contractors of investment services), in stocks and other securities, the monies contributed to it by the members of the organization, and to collect income from the investments and turn over the entire amount, less expenses, to its members. While this type of organization may not invest in assets other than stocks and other securities, it may use a taxable subsidiary to make these investments.[55]

These rules were enacted to forestall the contemplated revocation by the IRS of the tax-exempt status of the CommonFund, a cooperative arrangement formed by a large group of colleges and universities for the collective investment of their funds. During its formative years, the management and administrative expenses of the fund were largely met by start-up grants from a private foundation. As the fund became more reliant on payments from its member institutions, however, the IRS decided that this factor alone disqualified the fund for exempt status.[56] In the face of loss of the fund's exemption, Congress made it clear that cooperative arrangements for investments of the type typified by the CommonFund are eligible for exemption as charitable entities.

§ 11.6 CHARITABLE RISK POOLS

Still another category of charitable organization is the *qualified charitable risk pool*.[57] This body of statutory law overrides otherwise applicable case law denying tax-exempt status to eligible charitable risk pools.[58]

A qualified charitable risk pool is an entity that is organized and operated solely to pool insurable risks of its members (other than medical malpractice risks) and to provide information to its members with respect to loss control and risk management.[59] No profit or other benefit may be accorded to any member of the organization other than through the provision of members with insurance coverage below the cost of comparable commercial coverage (and loss control and risk management information).[60] Only charitable organizations can be members of these pools.[61]

This type of pool is required to be organized as a nonprofit organization under state law authorizing risk pooling for charitable organizations, to be exempt from state income tax, to obtain at least $1 million in start-up capital[62] from nonmember

---

[54] That is, organizations defined in IRC § 170(b)(1)(A)(ii) or (iv). See § 12.3(a).
[55] Gen. Couns. Mem. 39776.
[56] See S. Rep. No. 93-888, at 2–3 (1974). See § 7.13.
[57] IRC § 501(n)(1)(A).
[58] See § 28.13(b).
[59] IRC § 501(n)(2)(A).
[60] H.R. Rep. No. 104-737, at 189 (1996).
[61] IRC § 501(n)(2)(B).
[62] This term means any capital contributed to and any program-related investments (see § 12.4(d)) made in the risk pool before the pool commences operations (IRC § 501(n)(4)(A)).

charitable organizations,[63] to be controlled by a board of directors elected by its members, and to provide three elements in its organizational documents: namely, that members must be tax-exempt charitable organizations at all times, that if a member loses that status it must immediately notify the organization, and that no insurance coverage applies to a member after the date of any final determination that the member no longer qualifies as an exempt charitable organization.[64]

The rule that a charitable organization cannot be exempt from tax if a substantial part of its activities consists of providing commercial-type insurance[65] is not applicable to charitable risk pools.[66] Because this category of tax exemption is based on qualification as a charitable organization, a risk pool must satisfy all of the other requirements for achievement of this exempt status.[67]

§ 11.7 LITERARY ORGANIZATIONS

Although there is a statutory basis for tax exemption as a *literary* organization,[68] there is no law on the subject. The concept is encompassed by the terms *charitable* and *educational*.[69]

---

[63] A *nonmember charitable organization* is a tax-exempt organization described in IRC § 501(c)(3) that is not a member of the risk pool and does not benefit, directly or indirectly, from the insurance coverage provided by the pool to its members (IRC § 501(n)(4)(B)).

[64] IRC §§ 501(n)(2)(C), (3). Examples of organizations that failed to qualify for exemption because they did not meet this start-up capital requirement are in Florida Indep. Colleges & Universities Risk Management Ass'n v. United States, 850 F. Supp. 2d 125 (D.D.C. 2012), and Priv. Ltr. Rul. 200941038.

[65] See § 28.13(b).

[66] IRC § 501(n)(1)(B).

[67] See Part Three.

[68] IRC § 501(c)(3); Reg. § 1.501(c)(3)-1(d)(1)(i)(e).

[69] See Chapters 7, 8.

Public Charities and Private Foundations

The federal tax law relating to charitable organizations[1] differentiates between *public charities* and *private foundations*. This is done for a variety of reasons, including

---

[1] That is, organizations described in IRC § 501(c)(3) and tax-exempt by reason of IRC § 501(a). See Part Three.

the fact that special regulatory requirements target private foundations.[2] Despite the relative scarcity of private foundations,[3] the extent and growth of the law governing them are extraordinary.[4]

§ 12.1 FEDERAL TAX LAW DEFINITION OF *PRIVATE FOUNDATION*

The federal tax law does not define the term *private foundation*. Rather, it enumerates the types of charitable organizations that are *not* private foundations.[5]

(a) Private Foundation Defined

From a statutory law perspective, a private foundation is a charitable organization, domestic or foreign, that does not qualify as a public charity; a public charity is an institution (such as a university or a hospital), an organization that has broad public support, or an organization that functions in a supporting relationship to one or more institutions or publicly supported entities.[6] A charitable entity is presumed to be a private foundation; this presumption may be rebutted by a showing that the entity is a public charity.[7]

A standard private foundation is a type of tax-exempt organization that has four characteristics: It is a charitable organization; it is funded from one source (usually an individual, married couple, family, or corporation); its ongoing funding is in the form of investment income (rather than from a flow of contributions and/or grants); and it makes grants for charitable purposes to other persons (rather than conducting its own programs). (In many respects, then, a private foundation is much like an endowment fund.)[8] The *private* aspect of a private foundation thus relates principally to the nature of its financial support.

(b) Private Operating Foundations

The *private operating foundation* is a private foundation that operates its own programs, in contrast to the standard private foundation that is a grantmaking entity.

---

[2] See § 12.4.

[3] There are about 145,000 private foundations, compared to approximately 1.85 million recognized charitable organizations (see § 2.1).

[4] The law in this area originated with the Tax Reform Act of 1969; it was written in an anti-private foundation environment. One of the principal stimuli for this legislation was a report prepared by the Treasury Department in 1965 ("Treasury Report on Private Foundations," Committee on Finance, United States Senate, 89th Cong., 1st Sess. (1969)). In the intervening years, however, the general perception is that private foundations are being properly operated and are in conformity with the tax law requirements. One court stated that Congress enacted these rules "to put an end, so far as it reasonably could, to the abuses and potential abuses associated with private foundations" (Hans S. Mannheimer Charitable Trust v. Comm'r, 93 T.C. 35, 39 (1989)). This objective of Congress seems to have been, in general, successfully reached. See *Private Foundations* for a more in-depth discussion of the law summarized in §§ 12.1–12.5.

[5] IRC § 509(a), the misleading heading of which is "Private Foundation Defined."

[6] Reg. § 1.509(a)-1. The term *public charity* is the subject of § 12.3.

[7] IRC § 508(b); Reg. § 1.508-1(b); Rev. Proc. 2024-5, 2024-1 I.R.B. 262 § 7.03.

[8] See § 12.6.

This type of foundation devotes most of its earnings and much of its assets directly to the conduct of its charitable programs.[9]

A private operating foundation must meet an *income test*.[10] To satisfy this test, a private foundation must expend an amount equal to substantially all[11] of the lesser of its adjusted net income or its minimum investment return,[12] in the form of qualifying distributions,[13] directly for the active conduct of its exempt charitable activities.[14]

The term *adjusted net income* means any excess of a private foundation's gross income for a year over the sum of deductions allowed to a taxable corporation.[15] This amount of gross income is determined using certain *income modifications*,[16] and the allowable deductions are determined using certain *deduction modifications*.[17]

The funds expended must be applied by the private foundation itself; these outlays are termed *direct expenditures*, while grants to other organizations are *indirect expenditures*.[18] Amounts paid to acquire or maintain assets that are used directly in the conduct of exempt activities are direct expenditures, as are administrative expenses and other operating costs necessary to conduct exempt activities. An amount set aside[19] by a foundation for a specific project involving the active conduct of exempt activities may qualify as a direct expenditure.[20] The making or awarding of grants or similar payments to individuals to support active tax-exempt programs constitutes direct expenditures only if the foundation maintains some significant involvement in the programs.[21]

To qualify as a private operating foundation, an organization must also satisfy an *assets test*,[22] an *endowment test*,[23] or a *support test*.[24]

A private foundation will satisfy the assets test where substantially more than one-half[25] of its assets is (1) devoted directly to the active conduct of its tax-exempt activities, to functionally related businesses,[26] or to a combination of these functions; (2) stock of a corporation that is controlled by the foundation and substantially all of the assets of which are devoted to charitable activities; or (3) in

---

[9] IRC § 4942(j)(3).

[10] IRC § 4942(j)(3)(A); Reg. § 53.4942(b)-1(a).

[11] Namely, at least 85 percent (Reg. § 53.4942(b)-1(c)).

[12] See § 12.4(b).

[13] *Id.*

[14] Reg. § 53.4942(b)-1(a)(1).

[15] IRC § 4942(f)(1); Reg. § 53.4942(a)-2(d)(1).

[16] IRC § 4942(f)(2); Reg. § 53.4942(a)-2(d)(2).

[17] IRC § 4942(f)(3); Reg. § 53.4942(a)-2(d)(4).

[18] Reg. § 53.4942(b)-1(b)(1).

[19] See § 12.4(b).

[20] Reg. § 53.4942(b)-1(b)(1). E.g., Rev. Rul. 74-450, 1974-2 C.B. 388.

[21] Reg. § 53.4942(b)-1(b)(2). E.g., "Miss Elizabeth" D. Leckie Scholarship Fund v. Comm'r, 87 T.C. 251 (1986); Rev. Rul. 78-315, 1978-2 C.B. 271.

[22] IRC § 4942(j)(3)(B)(i).

[23] IRC § 4942(j)(3)(B)(ii).

[24] IRC § 4942(j)(3)(B)(iii).

[25] Namely, at least 65 percent (Reg. § 53.4942(b)-2(a)(5)).

[26] 12.4(c).

part assets described in the first category and in part stock described in the second category.[27]

An asset, to qualify under this test, must actually be used by the foundation directly for the active conduct of its tax-exempt purpose. It can consist of real estate, physical facilities or objects, and intangible assets, but it cannot include assets held for the production of income, investment, or other similar use. Property used for both exempt and other purposes will meet the assets test (assuming it otherwise qualifies) as long as the exempt use represents at least 95 percent of total use.[28]

A private foundation will satisfy the endowment test where it normally expends its funds, in the form of qualifying distributions, directly for the active conduct of exempt activities, in an amount equal to at least two-thirds of its minimum investment return.[29] The concept of expenditures directly for the active conduct of exempt activities under the endowment test is the same as that under the income test.[30]

A private foundation will satisfy the support test if (1) substantially all of its support (other than gross investment income)[31] is normally received from the general public and from at least five tax-exempt organizations that are not disqualified persons[32] with respect to each other or the foundation involved; (2) not more than 25 percent of its support (other than gross investment income) is normally received from any one of these exempt organizations; and (3) not more than one-half of its support is normally received from gross investment income.[33]

An organization may satisfy the income test and either the assets, endowment, or support test by one of two methods: meeting the requirements for any three years during a four-year period consisting of the year involved and the three immediately preceding tax years, or on the basis of an aggregation of all pertinent amounts of income or assets held, received, or distributed during the four-year period. The same method must be used for satisfying the tests.[34] A foundation, to be regarded as a private operating foundation, generally must satisfy the income test and one of the other tests for its first year.[35]

Contributions to a private operating foundation are treated as if made to a public charity.[36]

(c) Exempt Operating Foundations

Another variant of private foundation is the *exempt operating foundation*.[37] This type of private foundation is termed an *exempt* entity because it does not have to pay the

---

[27] Reg. § 53.4942(b)-2(a)(1).
[28] Reg. § 53.4942(b)-2(a)(2).
[29] Reg. § 53.4942(b)-2(b)(1).
[30] Reg. § 53.4942(b)-2(b)(2).
[31] IRC § 509(e).
[32] See § 12.2.
[33] Reg. § 53.4942(b)-2(c)(1).
[34] Reg. § 53.4942(b)-3(a).
[35] Reg. § 53.4942(b)-3(b)(1).
[36] IRC §§ 170(b)(1)(A)(vii), 170(b)(1)(F)(i).
[37] IRC § 4940(d).

private foundation excise tax on investment income,[38] nor are grants to it subject to the expenditure responsibility requirement.[39] The reason this category of foundation was established is to provide organizations that are not, in a generic sense, private foundations (such as many museums and libraries) some of the attributes of public charities.[40]

To be an exempt operating foundation for a year, a private foundation is required to have these characteristics: It qualifies as a private operating foundation; it has been publicly supported[41] for at least 10 years; its governing body consists of individuals at least 75 percent of whom are not *disqualified individuals*[42] and is broadly representative of the public; and at no time during the year did it have an officer who is a disqualified individual.[43]

(d)   Conduit Foundations

A *conduit private foundation* is not a separate category of private foundation but is a standard private foundation that, under certain circumstances, is regarded as a public charity for charitable contribution deduction purposes.[44]

This type of foundation makes qualifying distributions that are treated as distributions from its corpus[45] in an amount equal in value to 100 percent of all contributions received in the year involved, whether as money or as property.[46] The distributions must be made not later than the 15th day of the third month after the close of the private foundation's year in which the contributions were received, and the foundation must not have any remaining undistributed income for the year.

The qualifying distribution may be of the contributed property or of the proceeds from its sale. In making the calculation in satisfaction of the 100 percent requirement, the amount distributed generally must be equal to the fair market value of the contributed property on the date of its distribution. The amount of this fair market value may, however, be reduced by any reasonable selling expenses incurred by the foundation in disposing of the contributed property. At the option of the private foundation, if the contributed property is sold or distributed within 30 days of its receipt by the foundation, the amount of the fair market value is either the gross amount received from the sale of the property (less reasonable selling expenses) or an amount equal to the fair market value of the property on the date of its distribution to a public charity.[47]

These distributions are treated as made first out of contributions of property and then out of contributions of money received by the private foundation in

---

[38] IRC § 4940(d)(1). See § 12.4(f).

[39] IRC § 4945(d)(4)(A). See § 12.4(e).

[40] H.R. Rep. No. 98-861, at 1084 (1984).

[41] IRC § 4940(d)(3)(A).

[42] Namely, substantial contributors (see § 12.2(a)) and certain related persons (IRC §§ 4940(d)(3)(B)–(E)).

[43] IRC § 4940(d)(2).

[44] IRC §§ 170(b)(1)(A)(vii), 170(b)(1)(F)(ii).

[45] IRC § 4942(h).

[46] IRC § 170(b)(1)(F)(ii); Reg. § 1.170A-9(h)(1).

[47] Reg. § 1.170A-9(h)(2)(iv).

the year involved. The distributions cannot be made to an organization controlled directly or indirectly by the private foundation or by one or more disqualified persons[48] with respect to the private foundation or to a private foundation that is not a private operating foundation.[49]

(e) Common Fund Foundations

A special type of standard private foundation (that is, it is not a private operating foundation) is one that pools contributions received in a common fund but allows the donor or their spouse (including substantial contributors[50]) to retain the right to designate annually the organizations to which the income attributable to the contributions is given (as long as the organizations qualify as certain types of entities that are not private foundations)[51] and to direct (by deed or will) the organizations to which the corpus of the contributions is eventually to be given. Moreover, this type of private foundation must pay out its adjusted net income to public charities by the 15th day of the third month after the close of the tax year in which the income is realized by the fund, and the corpus must be distributed to these charities within one year after the death of the donor or their spouse.[52]

Contributions to this type of private foundation are treated as if made to a public charity.[53]

(f) Other Types of Foundations

There are various types of tax-exempt charitable organizations that are termed *foundations* although they are not private foundations. For example, a form of publicly supported charity is the *community foundation*, which is a fund established to support charitable organizations in an identified geographical area.[54] Various *supporting organizations* are termed foundations, although they are public charities.[55] Public colleges and universities often have related "foundations" that are in fact public charities.[56]

One of the types of organizations eligible to receive funding that qualifies for the scientific research tax credit[57] is a fund organized and operated exclusively to make basic research grants to qualified institutions of higher education.[58] This type of fund must be a charitable organization that is not a private foundation and must make its grants pursuant to written research contracts. A fund must elect this

---

[48] See § 12.2.
[49] Reg. § 1.170A-9(h)(1).
[50] See § 12.2(a).
[51] IRC § 509(a)(1). See §§ 12.3(a), (b).
[52] Reg. § 170A-9(i).
[53] IRC §§ 170(b)(i)(A)(vii), 170(b)(i)(F)(iii).
[54] This entity is a publicly supported charity by reason of IRC §§ 170(b)(1)(A)(vi) and 509(a)(1). See § 12.3(b)(iii).
[55] See § 12.3(c).
[56] See § 12.3(b)(v).
[57] IRC § 41.
[58] IRC § 41(e)(6)(D).

status; by doing so, it becomes treated as a private foundation, although the tax on net investment income[59] is not applicable.[60]

(g) Organizational Test

An organization must satisfy the applicable organizational test in order to achieve tax-exempt status.[61] There are organizational rules for private foundations, which must be met in addition to the organizational test applicable for charitable organizations generally.[62]

A private foundation cannot be exempt from tax (nor will contributions to it be deductible as charitable gifts) unless its governing instrument includes provisions the effects of which are to require distributions at such time and in such manner as to comply with the payout rules and to prohibit the foundation from engaging in any act of self-dealing, retaining any excess business holdings, making any jeopardizing investments, and making any taxable expenditures.[63] Generally, these elements must be in the foundation's articles of organization and not solely in its bylaws.[64]

The provisions of a foundation's governing instrument must require the foundation to act (or refrain from acting) so that the foundation, and any foundation managers or other disqualified persons with respect to it, will not be liable for any of the private foundation excise taxes.[65] The governing instrument of a nonexempt split-interest trust[66] must make comparable provision with respect to any of the applicable private foundation excise taxes.[67] Specific reference in the governing instrument to the appropriate sections of the Internal Revenue Code is generally required, unless equivalent language is used that is deemed by the IRS to have the same full force and effect. A governing instrument that contains only language sufficient to satisfy the requirements of the organizational test for charitable entities generally does not meet the specific requirements applicable with respect to private foundations, regardless of the interpretation placed on the language as a matter of law by a state court, and a governing instrument does not meet the organizational requirements if it expressly prohibits the distribution of capital or corpus.[68]

A foundation's governing instrument is deemed to conform with the organizational requirements if valid provisions of state law have been enacted that require the foundation to act (or refrain from acting) so as to not subject it to any

---

[59] See § 12.4(f).

[60] IRC § 41(e)(6)(D)(iv).

[61] The law contains an express organizational test for charitable organizations; there is an implied test of this nature for other categories of exempt organizations. For the latter, the requirement essentially is that the organizational document be reflective of the organization's primary exempt purposes (see § 4.4).

[62] See § 4.3.

[63] IRC § 508(e)(1).

[64] Reg. § 1.508-3(c).

[65] Rev. Rul. 70-270, 1970-1 C.B. 135, contains sample governing instrument provisions.

[66] That is, entities described in IRC § 4947(a)(1).

[67] Reg. § 1.508-3(e). Rev. Rul. 74-368, 1974-2 C.B. 390, contains sample governing instrument provisions.

[68] Reg. § 1.508-3(b).

of the private foundation excise taxes or that treat the required provisions as contained in the foundation's governing instrument.[69] A private foundation is responsible for verifying that the required provisions are satisfied by applicable state law if its governing instrument does not include them.[70]

Any provision of state law is presumed valid as enacted, and in the absence of state law provisions to the contrary, applies with respect to any foundation that does not specifically disclaim coverage under state law (either by notification to the appropriate state official or by commencement of judicial proceedings).[71] If a state law provision is declared invalid or inapplicable with respect to a class of foundations by the highest appellate court of the state or by the U.S. Supreme Court, the foundations covered by the determination must meet certain requirements[72] within one year from the date on which the time for perfecting an application for review by the Supreme Court expires. If such an application is filed, these requirements must be met within a year from the date on which the Supreme Court disposes of the case, whether by denial of the application for review or by decision on the merits. In addition, if a provision of state law is declared invalid or inapplicable with respect to a class of foundations by any court of competent jurisdiction, and the decision is not reviewed by the highest state appellate court or by the Supreme Court, and the IRS notifies the general public that the provision has been so declared invalid or inapplicable, then all foundations in the state must meet these requirements, without reliance on the statute to the extent declared invalid or inapplicable by the decision, within one year from the date such notice is made public. These rules do not apply to any foundation that is subject to a final judgment entered by a court of competent jurisdiction, holding the law invalid or inapplicable with respect to the foundation.[73]

§ 12.2 DISQUALIFIED PERSONS

A basic concept of the tax laws relating to private foundations is that of the *disqualified person*. Essentially, a disqualified person is a person (including an individual, corporation, partnership, trust, or estate) that has a particular relationship with respect to a private foundation.[74]

---

[69] Reg. § 1.508-3(d)(1).

[70] Rev. Rul. 2024-10, 2024-22 I.R.B. 1240, *obsoleting* Rev. Rul. 75-38, 1975-1 C.B. 161.

[71] Reg. § 1.508-3(b)(6).

[72] IRC § 508(e).

[73] Reg. § 1.508-3(d)(2).

[74] The term *disqualified person* is defined, for these purposes, in IRC § 4946(a). The term is defined somewhat differently in the setting of excess benefit transactions involving applicable tax-exempt organizations (see § 21.3). The principal difference is that brothers and sisters are not, in the private foundation setting, disqualified persons. Thus, in one instance, the IRS ruled that sale of property to a disqualified person with respect to a private foundation would not result in direct or indirect self-dealing, the latter avoided in part because of the rule that brothers and sisters are not disqualified persons (Priv. Ltr. Rul. 201510050).

(a)   Substantial Contributors

A category of disqualified person[75] is a substantial contributor to a private foundation.[76] A *substantial contributor* generally is any person who contributed or bequeathed an aggregate amount of more than $5,000 to the private foundation involved, where the amount is more than 2 percent of the total contributions and bequests received by the foundation before the close of its year in which the contribution or bequest is received by the foundation from that person.[77] In making this computation, all contributions and bequests to the private foundation made since its establishment are taken into account.[78]

In the case of a trust, the term *substantial contributor* also means the creator of the trust.[79] The term *person* includes tax-exempt organizations[80] (except as discussed later) but does not include governmental units.[81] The term *person* also includes a decedent, even at the point in time preceding the transfer of any property from the estate to the private foundation.[82] With one exception, once a person becomes a substantial contributor to a private foundation, it can never escape that status,[83] even though it might not be so classified if the determination were first made at a later date.[84]

Only one exception enables a person's status as a substantial contributor to terminate in certain circumstances after 10 years with no connection with the private foundation.[85] This requires that, during the 10-year period, (1) the person (and any related persons) did not make any contributions to the private foundation, (2) neither the person (nor any related person) was a foundation manager of the private foundation, and (3) the aggregate contributions made by the person (and any related person) are determined by the IRS "to be insignificant when compared to the aggregate amount of contributions to such foundation by one other person,"[86] taking into account appreciation on contributions while held by the private foundation. For these purposes, the term *related person* means related disqualified persons, and in the case of a corporate donor includes the officers and directors of the corporation.[87]

For certain purposes,[88] the term *substantial contributor* does not include most organizations that are not private foundations[89] or an organization wholly owned

---

[75] IRC § 4946(a)(1)(A); Reg. § 53.4946-1(a)(1)(i).

[76] IRC §§ 4946(a)(2), 507(d)(2).

[77] IRC § 507(d)(2)(A).

[78] Reg. § 1.507-6(a)(1). In the only case on the point, a court concluded that an individual was not a substantial contributor to a private foundation (Graham v. Comm'r, 83 T.C.M. 1137 (2002)).

[79] IRC § 507(d)(2)(A); Reg. § 1.507-6(a)(1).

[80] That is, organizations encompassed by IRC § 501(a).

[81] That is, entities described in IRC § 170(c)(1).

[82] Rockefeller v. United States, 572 F. Supp. 9 (E.D. Ark. 1982), aff'd, 718 F.2d 290 (8th Cir. 1983), cert. denied, 466 U.S. 962 (1984).

[83] IRC § 507(d)(2)(B)(iv).

[84] Reg. § 1.507-6(b)(1).

[85] IRC § 507(d)(2)(C).

[86] IRC § 507(d)(2)(C)(i)(III).

[87] IRC § 507(d)(2)(C)(ii).

[88] IRC §§ 170(b)(1)(D)(iii), 507(d)(1), 508(d), 509(a)(1), 509(a)(3), and IRC Chapter 42.

[89] That is, organizations described in IRC §§ 509(a)(1), 509(a)(2), or 509(a)(3).

by a public charity. Moreover, for purposes of the self-dealing rules,[90] the term does not include any charitable organization,[91] since to require inclusion of charitable organizations for this purpose would preclude private foundations from making large grants to or otherwise interacting with other private foundations.[92] In computing the support fraction for purposes of one category of publicly supported organization,[93] however, the term *substantial contributor* includes service provider public charities where the $5,000/2 percent test is exceeded, although the support may qualify as a material change in support or an unusual grant.

In determining whether a contributor is a substantial contributor, the total of the amounts received from the contributor and the total contributions and bequests received by the private foundation must be ascertained as of the last day of each tax year commencing with the first year ending after October 9, 1969.[94] Generally, all contributions and bequests made before October 9, 1969, are deemed to have been made on that date, and each contribution or bequest made after that is valued at its fair market value on the date received, with an individual treated as making all contributions and bequests made by their spouse.[95]

(b) Foundation Managers

Another category of disqualified person[96] is the foundation manager. A *foundation manager* is an officer, director, or trustee of a private foundation, or an individual having powers or responsibilities similar to one or more of these three positions.[97] An individual is considered an *officer* of a private foundation if they are specifically designated as such under the documents by which the foundation was formed or if they regularly exercise general authority to make administrative or policy decisions on behalf of the foundation.[98] Independent contractors acting in that capacity—such as lawyers, accountants, and investment managers and advisers—are not officers.[99]

An organization such as a bank, a similar financial institution, or an investment adviser can be a foundation manager.[100]

(c) Twenty Percent Owners

An owner of more than 20 percent of the total *combined voting power* of a corporation, the *profits interest* of a partnership, or the *beneficial interest* of a trust or

---

[90] See § 12.4(a).

[91] For these purposes, an organization described in IRC § 501(c)(3), other than an organization that tests for public safety (IRC § 509(a)(4)). See § 12.3(a)–(c).

[92] Reg. § 1.507-6(a)(2). This exception also applies to IRC § 4947(a)(1) trusts (Rev. Rul. 73-455, 1973-2 C.B. 187).

[93] IRC § 509(a)(2)(A). See § 12.3(b)(iv).

[94] Reg. § 1.507-6(b)(i).

[95] IRC § 507(d)(2)(B)(i)–(iii).

[96] IRC § 4946(a)(1)(B); Reg. § 53.4946-1(f)(1).

[97] IRC § 4946(b)(1).

[98] Reg. § 53.4946-1(f)(1). An example of the latter is in Rev. Rul. 74-287, 1974-1 C.B. 327.

[99] Reg. § 53.4946-1(f)(2).

[100] E.g., Priv. Ltr. Rul. 9535043.

unincorporated enterprise, any of which is (during the ownership) a substantial contributor to a private foundation, is a disqualified person.[101]

The term *combined voting power*[102] includes voting power represented by holdings of voting stock, actual or constructive,[103] but does not include voting rights held only as a director or trustee.[104]

The term *voting power* includes outstanding voting power and does not include voting power obtainable but not obtained, such as voting power obtainable by converting securities or nonvoting stock into voting stock, by exercising warrants or options to obtain voting stock, and voting power that will vest in preferred stockholders only if and when the corporation has failed to pay preferred dividends for a specified period or has otherwise failed to meet specified requirements.[105]

The profits interest[106] of a partner is that equal to their distributive share of income of the partnership as determined under special federal tax rules.[107] The term *profits interest* includes any interest that is outstanding but not any interest that is obtainable but has not been obtained.[108]

The beneficial interest in an unincorporated enterprise (other than a trust or estate) includes any right to receive a portion of distributions from profits of the enterprise or, in the absence of a profit-sharing agreement, any right to receive a portion of the assets (if any) on liquidation of the enterprise, except as a creditor or an employee.[109] A right to receive distribution of profits includes a right to receive any amount from the profits other than as a creditor or an employee, whether as a sum certain or as a portion of profits realized by the enterprise. Where there is no agreement fixing the rights of the participants in an enterprise, the fraction of the respective interests of each participant therein is determined by dividing the amount of all investments or contributions to the capital of the enterprise made or obligated to be made by the participant by the amount of all investments or contributions to capital made or obligated to be made by all of them.[110]

A person's beneficial interest in a trust is determined in proportion to the actuarial interest of the person in the trust.[111]

The term *beneficial interest* includes any interest that is outstanding but not any interest that is obtainable but has not been obtained.[112]

---

[101] IRC § 4946(a)(1)(C).
[102] IRC § 4946(a)(1)(C)(i).
[103] See IRC § 4946(a)(3).
[104] Reg. § 53.4946-1(a)(5).
[105] Reg. § 53.4946-1(a)(6).
[106] IRC § 4946(a)(1)(C)(ii).
[107] IRC §§ 707(b)(3), 4946(a)(4); Reg. § 53.4946-1(a)(2).
[108] Reg. § 53.4946-1(a)(6).
[109] IRC § 4946(a)(1)(C)(iii).
[110] Reg. § 53.4946-1(a)(3).
[111] Reg. § 53.4946-1(a)(4).
[112] Reg. § 53.4946-1(a)(6).

(d) Family Members

Another category of disqualified person is a member of the family of an individual who is a substantial contributor, a foundation manager, or one of the previously discussed 20 percent owners.[113] The term *member of the family* is defined to include an individual's spouse, ancestors, children, grandchildren, and great-grandchildren, and the spouses of children, grandchildren, and great-grandchildren.[114] Thus, these family members are themselves disqualified persons.

A legally adopted child of an individual is treated for these purposes as a child of the individual by blood.[115] A brother or sister of an individual is not, for these purposes, a member of the family.[116] However, as noted, the spouse of a grandchild of an individual is a member of their family for these purposes.[117]

(e) Corporations

A corporation is a disqualified person if more than 35 percent of the total combined voting power in the corporation (including constructive holdings)[118] is owned by substantial contributors, foundation managers, 20 percent owners, or members of the family of any of these individuals.[119]

(f) Partnerships

A partnership is a disqualified person if more than 35 percent of the profits interest in the partnership (including constructive holdings)[120] is owned by substantial contributors, foundation managers, 20 percent owners, or members of the family of any of these individuals.[121]

(g) Trusts or Estates

A trust or estate is a disqualified person if more than 35 percent of the beneficial interest in the trust or estate (including constructive holdings)[122] is owned by substantial contributors, foundation managers, 20 percent owners, or members of the family of any of these individuals.[123]

(h) Private Foundations

A private foundation may be a disqualified person with respect to another private foundation but only for purposes of the excess business holdings rules.[124] The

---

[113] IRC § 4946(a)(1)(D).
[114] IRC § 4946(d).
[115] Reg. § 53.4946-1(h).
[116] *Id.*
[117] *Id.*
[118] IRC § 4946(a)(3).
[119] IRC § 4946(a)(1)(E).
[120] IRC § 4946(a)(4).
[121] IRC § 4946(a)(1)(F).
[122] IRC § 4946(a)(4).
[123] IRC § 4946(a)(1)(G).
[124] IRC § 4946(a)(1)(H). See § 12.4(c).

disqualified person private foundation must be effectively controlled,[125] directly or indirectly, by the same person or persons (other than a bank, trust company, or similar organization acting only as a foundation manager) who control the private foundation in question, or must be the recipient of contributions substantially all of which were made, directly or indirectly, by substantial contributors, foundation managers, 20 percent owners, and members of their families who made, directly or indirectly, substantially all of the contributions to the private foundation in question.[126] One or more persons are considered to have made *substantially all* of the contributions to a private foundation for these purposes if the persons have contributed or bequeathed at least 85 percent of the total contributions and bequests that have been received by the private foundation during its entire existence, where each person has contributed or bequeathed at least 2 percent of the total.[127]

(i)   Governmental Officials

A governmental official may be a disqualified person with respect to a private foundation but only for purposes of the self-dealing rules.[128] The term *governmental official* means (1) an elected public official in the U.S. Congress or executive branch, (2) presidential appointees to the U.S. executive or judicial branches, (3) certain higher-compensated or ranking employees in one of these three branches, (4) House of Representatives or Senate employees earning at least $15,000 annually, (5) elected or appointed public officials in the U.S. or D.C. governments (including governments of U.S. possessions or political subdivisions or areas of the United States) earning at least $20,000 annually, or (6) the personal or executive assistant or secretary to any of the foregoing.[129]

§ 12.3   CATEGORIES OF PUBLIC CHARITIES

A *public charity* is a charitable organization[130] that does not constitute a private foundation. There are, in essence, four categories of charitable organizations that are not private foundations: *institutions, publicly supported charities, supporting organizations,* and *organizations that test for public safety.*

(a)   Institutions

There are types of charitable organizations that generally are recognized as entities that are not private foundations, under any reasonable definition of that term, by virtue of the nature of their programs, how they are structured, and their relationship with the public. These are the *public institutions.*

---

[125] Reg. § 1.482-1(a)(3).
[126] Reg. § 53.4946-1(b)(1).
[127] Reg. § 53.4946-1(b)(2).
[128] IRC § 4946(a)(1)(I).
[129] IRC § 4946(c).
[130] That is, an organization described in IRC § 501(c)(3) and tax-exempt by reason of IRC § 501(a). See Part Three.

The category of public institutions comprises churches, and conventions and associations of churches;[131] educational organizations that normally maintain a regular faculty and curriculum, and normally have a regularly enrolled body of pupils or students in attendance at the place where the educational activities are regularly carried on (that is, schools, colleges, and universities);[132] hospitals and medical research organizations;[133] agricultural research organizations;[134] and governmental units,[135] including a state, a possession of the United States, a political subdivision of either of the foregoing, the United States, or the District of Columbia.[136]

(b) Publicly Supported Charities

There are essentially two types of publicly supported charities: the donative publicly supported charity and the service provider publicly supported charity.

(i) Donative Publicly Supported Charities in General. A charitable organization qualifies as a *donative* type of publicly supported charity if it normally receives a substantial part of its support (other than exempt function revenue) from a governmental unit[137] or from direct or indirect contributions or grants from the public.[138]

The principal requirement for a charitable organization to qualify as a donative publicly supported organization is that it normally derives at least one-third of its financial support from qualifying contributions and grants.[139] This type of entity must maintain a *support fraction*, the denominator of which is total eligible support received during the computation period and the numerator of which is the amount of eligible public support for the period.

The term *support* means amounts received as contributions, grants, net income from unrelated business activities,[140] gross investment income,[141] tax revenues levied for the benefit of the organization and either paid to or expended on behalf of it, and the value of services or facilities (exclusive of services or facilities generally furnished to the public without charge) furnished by a governmental unit to the organization without charge.[142] All of these items are amounts that, if received by the organization, represent the denominator of the support fraction.

Support does not include any gain from the disposition of property that would be considered gain from the sale or exchange of a capital asset, or the value

---

[131] IRC §§ 170(b)(1)(A)(i), 509(a)(1). See §§ 10.3, 10.4.

[132] IRC §§ 170(b)(1)(A)(ii), 509(a)(1). See § 8.3.

[133] IRC §§ 170(b)(1)(A)(iii), 509(a)(1). See § 7.6. The IRS observed that a nonprofit hospital's ongoing public charity and tax-exempt (see § 7.6(a)) status is dependent on its provision of medical care to its community, not on the relationship between its board of directors and the governing board of its parent entity operating a health care delivery system (Priv. Ltr. Rul. 201314044).

[134] IRC §§ 170(b)(1)(A)(ix), 509(a)(1). See § 7.16(f), text accompanied by notes 607, 608.

[135] IRC §§ 170(b)(1)(A)(v), 509(a)(1). See § 7.15.

[136] IRC § 170(c)(1).

[137] *Id.*

[138] IRC §§ 170(b)(1)(A)(vi), 509(a)(1).

[139] Reg. § 1.170A-9(f)(2).

[140] See Chapters 24, 25.

[141] IRC § 509(e).

[142] IRC § 509(d).

of exemption from any federal, state, or local tax or any similar benefit.[143] A loan is not a form of support; however, should the lender forgive the debt, the amount becomes support in the year of the forgiveness.[144]

In general, contributions and grants constitute public support to the extent that the total amount of gifts or grants from a source during the computation period does not exceed an amount equal to 2 percent of the organization's total includible support for the period.[145] Where a contributor or grantor provides an amount that is in excess of the 2 percent threshold, the portion that does not exceed the threshold qualifies as public support. Therefore, the total amount of support from a donor or grantor is included in full in the denominator of the support fraction, while the amount determined by application of the 2 percent threshold is included in the numerator of the support fraction. Persons who have a defined relationship with one another (such as spouses) are considered as one source for purposes of computing the 2 percent threshold amount.

Qualifying gifts and grants constitute support in the form of *direct* contributions from the public. Support received from governmental units and other donative publicly supported organizations, in the form of grants, are forms of *indirect* contributions from the public (in that these grantors are considered conduits of direct public support).

This 2 percent threshold does not generally apply to support received by a donative publicly supported charity from other donative publicly supported charities nor to support from governmental units. That is, this type of support is, in its entirety, public support.[146] This is also the case concerning grants from a public institution, the support of which satisfies the rules for donative publicly supported charities.[147]

In constructing the support fraction, an organization must exclude from the numerator and denominator of it amounts that constitute *exempt function revenue*, which are amounts received from the exercise or performance of its exempt purpose or function and contributions of services for which a deduction is not allowable.[148] The organization is not treated as meeting the support test, however, if it receives almost all of its support in the form of exempt function revenue and an insignificant amount of its support from governmental units and the public.[149] The organization also may exclude from the support fraction an amount equal to one or more qualifying *unusual grants*.[150]

The determination of whether a payment is a contribution rather than exempt function revenue, or whether a payment is a grant rather than an amount paid pursuant to a contract (the latter being a form of exempt function revenue) can be controversial. As to the former, a membership fee is not a contribution.[151]

---

[143] *Id.*

[144] Priv. Ltr. Rul. 9608039.

[145] Reg. § 1.170A-9(f)(6)(i).

[146] *Id.*

[147] E.g., Rev. Rul. 78-95, 1978-1 C.B. 71 (concerning grants by a church).

[148] Reg. § 1.170A-9(f)(7)(i).

[149] Reg. § 1.170A-9(f)(7)(ii).

[150] Reg. §§ 1.170A-9(f)(6)(ii), (iii) and 1.509(a)-3(c)(3), (4). See text accompanied by *infra* notes 185–186.

[151] Reg. § 1.170A-9(f)(7)(iii). E.g., Williams Home, Inc. v. United States, 540 F. Supp. 310 (W.D. Va. 1982) (monies paid to a home for the aged by incoming residents as a condition of admission are not contributions but are a form of exempt function revenue).

As to the latter, an amount paid by a governmental unit to an organization is not regarded as received from the exercise or performance of its exempt functions, and thus is a grant, if the purpose of the payment is primarily to enable the organization to provide a service to the direct benefit of the public rather than to serve the direct and immediate needs of the payor.[152] By contrast, for example, Medicare and Medicaid payments to tax-exempt health care organizations constitute gross receipts derived from the performance of exempt functions and thus are not forms of public support, inasmuch as the patients control the ultimate recipients of the payments by their choice of a health care provider, so that they, not the governmental units, are the payors.[153]

Calculation of the support fraction entails an assessment of the charitable organization's financial support that it has *normally* received. This means that the organization must satisfy the one-third support test during the course of a multiyear public support measuring period, in the aggregate. The measuring period is the five-year period that includes the current tax year; an organization that meets this public support test for its current year is treated as a publicly supported entity for that year and the immediately succeeding tax year.[154] A five-year computation period for meeting this support test is used for organizations in the initial years of their existence.[155]

A tax-exempt charitable organization with more than one unrelated business may aggregate its net income and net losses from all unrelated business activities for purposes of determining whether the organization is publicly supported under these rules.[156] That is, the bucketing rule[157] does not apply in this context. Nonetheless, organizations have the option of determining public support using their unrelated business taxable income calculated under the bucketing rule or in the aggregate.

Previously, when an exempt charitable organization computed its public support, it was required to use the cash basis method of accounting to report its public support,[158] even if it used the accrual basis method of accounting in keeping its books and otherwise reporting on its annual information returns. Now, however, when a charitable entity computes its public support and reports the information on its annual information return, it must use the same accounting method that it uses in keeping its books and its annual information return reporting.[159]

An organization that generally uses the accrual method of accounting will not be able to use the support information reported on its annual information returns for prior years—because that support was reported using the cash method—in computing its public support ratio for the current year. Rather, it must revise its

---

[152] Reg. § 1.170A-9(f)(8)(ii). E.g., payments by the federal government to a professional standards review organization were held to not be excludable gross receipts but instead includable public support because the payments compensated the organization for a function that promoted the health of the beneficiaries of government health care programs in the areas in which the organization operated (Rev. Rul. 81-276, 1981-2 C.B. 128).

[153] Rev. Rul. 83-153, 1983-2 C.B. 48.

[154] Reg. § 1.170A-9(f)(4)(i).

[155] See § 26.3(b).

[156] Reg. § 1.170A-9(f)(7)(v).

[157] See § 25.5.

[158] This support is reported on Form 990, Schedule A.

[159] Reg. § 1.170A-9(f)(13).

reporting for the prior years in the computation period so that it is reporting all support for the computation period on the accrual method.

(ii) Facts-and-Circumstances Test.   There are some charitable organizations that are not private foundations in the generic sense yet are not publicly supported under the general rules. Organizations in this position include entities such as museums and libraries that rely principally on endowments for their financial support. The *facts-and-circumstances test* offers a way for an organization of this type to qualify as a donative publicly supported charity, even though it does not receive at least one-third of its support from the public.

An organization may qualify as a publicly supported donative organization—where it cannot satisfy the one-third public support requirement—as long as the amount normally received from governmental and/or public sources is *substantial*.[160] To meet this test, the organization must demonstrate the existence of three elements: (1) the total amount of public support normally received by the organization being at least 10 percent of its total support normally received;[161] (2) the organization having a continuous and bona fide program for solicitation of funds from the general public, governmental units, or public charities; and (3) all other pertinent facts and circumstances, including the percentage of its support from governmental and public sources, the public nature of the organization's governing board, the extent to which its facilities or programs are publicly available, its membership dues rates, and whether its activities are likely to appeal to persons having some broad common interest or purpose.[162]

Concerning the governing board factor, the organization's nonprivate foundation status will be enhanced where it has a governing body that represents the interests of the public, rather than the personal or private interests of a limited number of donors. This can be accomplished by the election of board members by a broadly based membership or otherwise by having the board composed of public officials, persons having particular expertise in the field or discipline involved, community leaders, and the like.

(iii) Community Foundations.   A community trust (or community foundation) may qualify as a donative publicly supported charity if it attracts, receives, and depends on financial support from members of the general public on a regular, recurring basis. Community foundations are designed primarily to attract large contributions of a capital or endowment nature from a small number of donors, with the gifts often received and maintained in the form of separate trusts or funds. They are generally identified with a particular community or area and are controlled by

---

[160] Reg. § 1.170A-9(f)(3). An illustration of an organization that failed both the general rules and the facts-and-circumstances test appears in Collins v. Comm'r, 61 T.C. 693 (1974). By contrast, the IRS ruled that a private operating foundation could be expected to convert to a publicly supported charitable organization by qualifying under this test (Priv. Ltr. Rul. 200623068).

[161] The 10 percent public support element is calculated using the methodology of the general one-third support test (see § 12.3(b)(i)), including the five-year measuring period (Reg. § 1.170A-9(f)(4)(ii)).

[162] Reg. § 1.170A-9(f)(3). In a case concerning the public charity status of a home for the elderly, a court held that the practice of the home to encourage lawyers to mention to their clients the possibility of bequests to the home was inadequate compliance with the requirement of an ongoing development program (Trustees for the Home for Aged Women v. United States, 86-1 U.S.T.C. ¶ 9290 (D. Mass. 1986)).

a representative group of persons from that community or area. Individual donors relinquish control over the investment and distribution of their contributions and the income generated from them, although donors may designate the purposes for which the assets are to be used, subject to change by the governing body of the community trust.[163]

A community foundation, to qualify as a publicly supported organization, must meet the support requirements for a donative publicly supported charity[164] or meet a facts-and-circumstances test.[165] As to the latter, the requirement of attraction of public support will generally be satisfied if a community foundation seeks gifts and bequests from a wide range of potential donors in the community or area served, through banks or trust companies, through lawyers or other professional individuals, or in other appropriate ways that call attention to the community foundation as a potential recipient of gifts and bequests made for the benefit of the community or area served.

A community foundation wants to be treated as a single entity, rather than as an aggregation of funds. To be regarded as a component part of a community foundation, a trust or fund must be created by gift or like transfer to a community foundation that is treated as a separate entity and may not be subjected by the transferor to any material restriction[166] with respect to the transferred assets.[167] To be treated as a separate entity, a community foundation must be appropriately named, be so structured as to subject its funds to a common governing instrument, have a common governing body, and prepare periodic financial reports that treat all funds held by the community foundation as its funds.[168] The governing body of a community foundation must have the power to modify any restriction on the distribution of funds where it is inconsistent with the charitable needs of the community, must commit itself to the exercise of its powers in the best interests of the community foundation, and must commit itself to seeing that the funds are invested pursuant to accepted standards of fiduciary conduct.[169]

(iv) Service Provider Publicly Supported Organizations. A charitable organization qualifies as a *service provider* type of publicly supported charity[170] if it satisfies two tests.[171] One test requires that the charity normally receive more than one-third of its support from any combination of (1) contributions, grants, or membership fees, and/or (2) gross receipts from admissions, sales of merchandise, performance of services, or furnishing of facilities in activities related to its exempt

---

[163] Reg. § 1.170A-9(f)(10).

[164] See § 12.3(b)(i).

[165] See § 12.3(b)(ii).

[166] See Reg. §§ 1.507-2(a)(7), (8).

[167] Reg. § 1.170A-9(f)(11)(ii).

[168] Reg. §§ 1.170A-9(f)(11)(iii)–(vi).

[169] Reg. § 1.170A-9(f)(11)(v). Illustrations of organizations satisfying these requirements are the subject of Priv. Ltr. Ruls. 201307008, 201936002, and 201936003.

[170] This term was adopted by the U.S. Supreme Court in Camps Newfound/Owatonna, Inc. v. Town of Harrison, 520 U.S. 564, 572 (1997).

[171] IRC § 509(a)(2).

purposes, as long as the support is from *permitted sources*.[172] (As discussed later, there is an additional limitation on the qualification of exempt function revenue as public support.) Thus, an organization seeking to qualify under this set of rules must construct a *support fraction*, with the amount of qualified support received from these two sources constituting the numerator of the fraction and the total amount of support received being the denominator.[173]

Permitted sources are public institutions, donative publicly supported charitable organizations, and persons other than disqualified persons with respect to the organization.[174] The term *support* means the two types of public support, along with net income from unrelated business activities,[175] gross investment income,[176] tax revenues levied for the benefit of the organization and either paid to or expended on behalf of it, and the value of services or facilities (exclusive of services or facilities generally furnished to the public without charge) furnished by a governmental unit to the organization without charge.[177] All of these items are amounts that, if received by the organization, comprise the denominator of the support fraction.

Support does not include any gain from the disposition of property that would be considered gain from the sale or exchange of a capital asset, or the value of exemption from any federal, state, or local tax or any similar benefit.[178] A loan is not a form of support; however, should the lender forgive the debt, the amount becomes support in the year of the forgiveness.[179]

The second test requires that an organization, to qualify as a service provider publicly supported charity, normally receive not more than one-third of its support from the sum of gross investment income[180] and any excess of the amount of unrelated business taxable income over the amount of the tax imposed on that income.[181] This entails the construction of a *gross investment income fraction*, with the amount of gross investment income and any unrelated income (less the tax paid on it) received constituting the numerator of the fraction and the total amount of support received being the denominator.[182]

Calculation of the support and investment income fractions entails an assessment of the charitable organization's financial support, including investment income, that it has *normally* received. This means that the organization must satisfy the one-third permitted sources support test and less-than-one-third gross investment income test over a multiyear public support measuring period, in the aggregate. The measuring period is the five-year period that includes the current

---

[172] IRC § 509(a)(2)(A). Revenue derived from the sale of pickle cards (a form of gambling) is not public support (Education Athletic Ass'n. v. Comm'r, 77 T.C.M. 1525 (1999)).
[173] Reg. § 1.509(a)-3(a)(2).
[174] IRC § 509(a)(2)(A).
[175] See Chapters 24, 25.
[176] IRC § 509(e).
[177] IRC § 509(d).
[178] Id.
[179] Priv. Ltr. Rul. 9608039.
[180] IRC § 509(e).
[181] IRC § 509(a)(2)(B).
[182] Reg. § 1.509(a)-3(a)(3).

tax year; an organization that meets these tests for its current year is treated as a publicly supported entity for that year and the immediately succeeding tax year.[183] (A five-year computation period for meeting these tests is used for organizations in the initial years of their existence.)[184] Substantial contributions and bequests that are unusual or unexpected in terms of the amount—termed *unusual grants*—may be excluded from these calculations.[185] The IRS promulgated "safe harbor" criteria that automatically cause a contribution or grant to be considered *unusual*.[186]

In computing the amount of support received from gross receipts that is allowable toward the one-third support requirement, gross receipts from related activities (other than from membership fees) received from any person or from any bureau or similar agency of a governmental unit are includable in a year to the extent that the receipts do not exceed the greater of $5,000 or 1 percent of the organization's support for the year.[187]

A tax-exempt charitable organization with more than one unrelated business may aggregate its net income and net losses from all unrelated business activities for purposes of determining whether the organization is publicly supported under these rules.[188] That is, the bucketing rule[189] does not apply in this context. Nonetheless, organizations have the option of determining public support using their unrelated business taxable income calculated under the bucketing rule or in the aggregate.

A charitable entity computes its public support and reports the information on its annual information return[190] using the same accounting method that it uses in keeping its books and its annual information return reporting.[191]

(v) Public Colleges and Universities Support Foundations. Public charity status is accorded to certain organizations providing support for public colleges and universities.[192] The organization must normally receive a substantial part of its support (exclusive of income received in the exercise or performance of its tax-exempt activities) from the United States or from direct or indirect contributions from the general public. It must be organized and operated exclusively to receive, hold, invest, and administer property and to make expenditures to or for the benefit of a college or university (including a land grant college or university) that is a public charity and that is an agency or instrumentality of a state or political subdivision thereof, or that is owned or operated by a state or political subdivision thereof or by an agency or instrumentality of one or more states or political subdivisions.

These expenditures include those made for any one or more of the regular functions of colleges and universities, such as the acquisition and maintenance of

---

[183] Reg § 1.509(a)-3(c)(1)(i).

[184] See § 26.3(b).

[185] Reg. § 1.509(a)-3(c)(3), (4). E.g., Rev. Rul. 76-440, 1976-2 C.B. 58.

[186] Rev. Proc. 2018-32, 2018-23 I.R.B. 739 § 7.03. See *Private Foundations* § 15.5(c).

[187] IRC § 509(a)(2)(A)(ii); Reg. § 1.509(a)-3(b)(1). E.g., Rev. Rul. 83-153, 1983-2 C.B. 48; Rev. Rul. 75-387, 1975-2 C.B. 216.

[188] Reg. § 1.509(a)-3(a)(3)(i), (4).

[189] See § 25.5.

[190] This support is reported on Form 990, Schedule A.

[191] Reg. § 1.509(a)-3(k).

[192] IRC §§ 170(b)(1)(A)(iv), 509(a)(1).

real property representing part of the campus area; the construction of college or university buildings; the acquisition and maintenance of equipment and furnishings used for, or in conjunction with, regular functions of colleges and universities; or expenditures for scholarships, libraries, and student loans.[193]

Another frequently important feature of the foundation is its ability to borrow money for or on behalf of the supported state college or university, with the indebtedness bearing tax-excludable interest.[194]

(c) Supporting Organizations

A category of organization that is a public charity is the supporting organization.[195] A qualified supporting organization must satisfy an organizational test, an operational test, a relationship test,[196] and a disqualified person control test.

A supporting organization must be organized and operated exclusively for the benefit of, to perform the functions of, or to carry out the purposes of one or more qualified supported organizations.[197] This type of organization must be operated, supervised, or controlled by one or more qualified supported organizations, supervised or controlled in connection with one or more such organizations, or operated in connection with one or more such organizations.[198] These organizations are referred to as Type I, Type II, or Type III supporting organizations, respectively.[199] Inasmuch as Type III supporting organizations are classified as either functionally integrated Type III supporting organizations or nonfunctionally integrated Type III supporting organizations,[200] there are four types of supporting organizations. A supporting organization may not be controlled, directly or indirectly, by one or more disqualified persons with respect to the organization (other than foundation managers and supported organizations).[201]

An organization is not considered to be a Type III entity unless the organization (1) annually provides to each supported organization sufficient information to ensure that the organization is responsive to the needs or demands of the supported organization(s) (the *notification requirement*)[202] and (2) is not operated in connection with any supported organization that is not organized in the

---

[193] Reg. § 1.170A-9(c).

[194] IRC § 103.

[195] IRC § 509(a)(3). In general, see *Private Foundations* § 15.6.

[196] A supporting organization must support one or more qualified supported organizations (IRC § 509(f) (3)), which usually are institutions (see § 12.3(a)) and/or publicly supported organizations (see § 12.3(b)). Reg. § 1.509(a)-4(a)(5).

[197] IRC § 509(a)(3)(A); Reg. § 1.509(a)-4(a)(2). Supported organizations are the subject of IRC § 509(f)(3).

[198] IRC § 509(a)(3)(B). In general, Reg. §§ 1.509(a)-4(a)(3), (f)(2), (f)(4), (g)(1)(i).

[199] The Type III supporting organization is defined in IRC § 4943(f)(5)(A).

[200] See text accompanied by *infra* notes 224–227.

[201] IRC § 509(a)(3)(C); Reg. § 1.509(a)-4(a)(4). A charitable organization failed to achieve status as a supporting organization, in part because disqualified persons controlled it (Polm Family Found., Inc. v. United States, 2009-2 U.S.T.C. ¶ 50,638 (D.D.C. 2009), *aff'd*, 644 F.3d 406 (D.C. Cir. 2011)).

[202] Reg. § 509(a)-4(i)(2). Specifically, a Type III supporting organization annually must provide the following documents to each of its supported organizations: (1) a written notice, addressed to a principal officer of the supported organization, describing the type and amount of all of the support (including

United States.[203] An organization is not considered to be a Type I or Type III entity if the organization accepts a contribution from a person (other than a qualified supported organization) who, directly or indirectly, controls, either alone or with family members or certain controlled entities, the governing body of a supported organization.[204]

To meet the operational test, a supporting organization must engage solely in activities that support or benefit one or more supported organizations.[205] These activities may include making payments to or for the use of, or providing services or facilities for, individual members of the charitable class benefited by one or more supported charitable organizations. If this type of payment is made indirectly through another unrelated organization, however, then the payment must constitute a grant to an individual rather than a grant to an organization.[206] A supporting organization may also provide support (in the form or grants or the provision of services or facilities) to other supporting organizations that also support or benefit one or more of its supported organizations. If neither of these exceptions applies, a supporting organization may not make a grant to another organization that is not one of its supported organizations.[207]

A supporting organization (other than a nonfunctionally integrated Type III supporting organization)[208] may, but need not, distribute income to a supported organization. It may carry on an independent program that supports or benefits one or more supported organizations.[209] A supporting organization must be

---

all distributions) the supporting organization provided to the supported organization during the prior tax year; (2) a copy of the supporting organization's annual information return that was most recently filed as of the date the notification is provided; and (3) a copy of the supporting organization's governing documents as in effect on the date the notification is provided (unless previously provided and not subsequently amended) (Reg. § 1.509(a)-4(i)(2)(i)). The written notice must include a brief narrative description of the support provided and sufficient financial detail for the recipient to identify the types and amounts of support (Reg. § 1.509(a)-4(i)(2)(i)(A)). All the notification documents must be delivered or transmitted electronically by the last day of the fifth calendar month of the organization's tax year (Reg. § 1.509(a)-4(i)(2)(iii)). For purposes of this notification requirement, a *principal officer* includes, but is not limited to, a person who, regardless of title, has ultimate responsibility for implementing the decisions of the governing body of a supported organization; for supervising the management, administration, or operation of the supported organization; or for managing the finances of the supported organization (Reg. § 1.509(a)-4(i)(2)(iv)).

[203] IRC § 509(f)(1). Reg. § 1.509(a)-4(i)(10).

[204] IRC § 509(f)(2). The governing body of a supporting organization is considered *controlled* by one or more such persons if that person, alone or by aggregating their votes or positions of authority with other such persons, may require the governing body of the supported organization to perform any act that significantly affects its operations or may prevent the governing body of the supported organization from performing any such act (Reg. § 1.509(a)-4(f)(5)(ii)). Thus, the requisite control exists if such persons in the aggregate possess 50 percent or more of the total voting power of the governing body or one or more such persons possesses a veto power over actions of the governing body (*id.*).

[205] Reg. §§ 1.509(a)-4(e)(1), (2). The operational test specific to supporting organizations is in addition to the general operational test that all charitable organizations are required to meet (see § 4.5).

[206] Reg. § 1.509(a)-4(e)(1). In determining whether a grant is indirectly to an individual rather than to an organization, the earmarking rules for private foundation grants to individuals in Reg. § 53.4945-4(a)(4) are applied. See *Private Foundations* § 9.3(g).

[207] Reg. § 1.509(a)-4(e)(1).

[208] See text accompanied by *infra* notes 224–227.

[209] Reg. § 1.509(a)-4(e)(2).

organized and operated to support or benefit one or more specified supported organizations, with the manner of the specification being dependent on which type of supporting organization is involved.[210]

A supporting organization is *operated in connection with* one or more supported organizations (and thus is a Type III entity) only if it satisfies the notification requirement, the responsiveness test, and an integral part test.[211]

An organization satisfies the *integral part test* if it is significantly involved in the operations of the supported organization and the supported organization is dependent upon the supporting organization for the type of support the supporting organization provides.[212] An organization is an integral part of a supported organization only if it satisfies the requirements for functionally integrated Type III supporting organizations or for nonfunctionally integrated Type III supporting organizations.[213]

A supporting organization meets the *responsiveness test* if it is "responsive to the needs or demands" of each of its supported organizations.[214] This test is generally satisfied if (1) one or more trustees, directors, or officers of the supporting organization are elected or appointed by the supported organization; (2) one or more members of the governing body of the supported organization are also trustees, directors, or officers of, or hold other important offices in, the supporting organization; or (3) the trustees, directors, or officers of the supporting organization maintain a "close and continuous" working relationship with the trustees, directors, or officers of the supported organization.

Also, by reason of one of these three elements, the trustees, directors, or officers of the supported organization must, for the responsiveness test to be satisfied, have a "significant voice" in the investment policies of the supporting organization, the timing of grants, the manner of making them, and the selection of recipients by the supporting organization, and in otherwise directing the use of the income or assets of the supporting organization.[215]

A supporting organization meets the integral part test as a functionally integrated Type III supporting organization in one of three ways. One way to meet this test is for the organization to engage in activities (1) substantially all of which directly further the exempt purposes of the supported organization(s), by performing the functions of, or carrying out the purposes of, the supported organization(s), and (2) that, but for the involvement of the supporting organization, would normally be engaged in by the supported organization(s).[216] Fundraising, investing, and managing non–exempt-use property, and making grants (to the supported organization or elsewhere) are *not* activities that meet the *directly further* standard.[217]

---

[210] Reg. § 1.509(a)-4(c)(1).

[211] Reg. § 1.509(a)-4(i)(1).

[212] Reg. § 1.509(a)-4(i)(1)(iii).

[213] *Id.*

[214] Reg. § 1.509(a)-4(i)(3).

[215] *Id.* The IRS revoked the supporting organization status of a Type III entity because none of the three required elements for meeting the responsiveness test were present and the supported organization did not have a significant voice in the Type III entity's investment policies, timing of grants, manner of making grants, selection of recipients of grants, or the like (Priv. Ltr. Rul. 202238018).

[216] Reg. § 1.509(a)-4(i)(4)(i)(A).

[217] Reg. § 1.509(a)-4(i)(4)(ii).

Another way this test is met is for the supporting organization to be the parent of each of its supported organizations.[218] This relationship exists where (1) the supporting organization and its supported organizations are part of an integrated system (such as, for example, a hospital system); (2) the supporting organization directs the overall policies, programs, and activities of the supported organizations (such as, for example, coordinating the activities of the supported organizations and engaging in overall planning, policy development, budgeting, and resource allocation); and (3) the supporting organization has the power to appoint or elect a majority of the officers, directors, or trustees of each supported organization, and has the power to remove and replace them, or otherwise has an ongoing power to appoint them with reasonable frequency.[219]

The third way for this test to be met is for the supporting organization to support a governmental entity.[220] This test is met where (1) the supporting organization supports only one or more governmental supported organizations and (2) a substantial part of the supporting organization's total activities are activities that directly further the exempt purposes of at least one governmental supported organization. Additionally, in any case in which there is more than one governmental supported organization, they all must either operate within the same city, county, or metropolitan area or work in close coordination or collaboration with one another to conduct a service, program, or activity that the supporting organization supports.[221] A *governmental supported organization* is a governmental unit,[222] including all of its agencies, departments, and divisions, all of which are treated as one governmental supported organization.[223]

A supporting organization meets the integral part test as a nonfunctionally integrated Type III supporting organization in one of two ways. One way to meet this test is to satisfy a distribution requirement and an attentiveness requirement.[224]

---

[218] Reg. § 1.509(a)-4(i)(4)(i)(B).

[219] Reg. § 1.509(a)-4(i)(4)(iii)(A). A supporting organization may meet the third of these requirements with respect to a second-tier (or lower) subsidiary if, by control of its first-tier subsidiary, the supporting organization has the power to appoint or elect a majority of the officers, directors, or trustees of the lower-tier subsidiary (Reg. § 1.509(a)-4(i)(4)(iii)(B)).

[220] Reg. § 1.509(a)-4(i)(4)(i)(C).

[221] Reg. § 1.509(a)-4(i)(4)(iv)(A). To satisfy the close coordination or collaboration requirement, the supporting organization must maintain on file a letter from each of the governmental supported organizations (or a joint letter from all of them) describing their coordination or collaboration efforts with respect to the service, program, or activity (Reg. § 1.509(a)-4(i)(4)(iv)(C)). All pertinent facts and circumstances are taken into consideration in determining whether a substantial part of a supporting organization's activities directly further the exempt purposes of its governmental supported organization(s) (Reg. § 1.509(a)-4(i)(4)(iv)(D). Although the regulations provide no fixed percentage for determining what constitutes a substantial part of an organization's activities, an example in the regulations indicates that a governmental supporting organization simultaneously may have direct furtherance activities and grantmaking activities, each as a *substantial part* of its activities (Reg. § 1.509(a)-4(i)(4)(v), Example (6)).

[222] IRC § 170(c)(1). See § 7.15.

[223] Reg. § 1.509(a)-4(i)(4)(iv)(B)(1). The term also includes an organization described in IRC § 170(c)(2) and (b)(1)(A) (other than in clauses (vii) and (viii)) that is an instrumentality (see § 7.15) of one or more governmental units (Reg. § 1.509(a)-4(i)(4)(iv)(B)(2)).

[224] Reg. § 1.509(a)-4(i)(5)(i)(A).

Pursuant to this *distribution requirement*, a supporting organization must distribute, for each of its years, to or for the use of one or more supported organizations, amounts equaling or exceeding its annual distributable amount on or before the last day of the year involved. This annual *distributable amount* is equal to the greater of 85 percent of adjusted net income or 3.5 percent of the fair market value of the supporting organization's non-exempt-use assets for the immediately preceding tax year.[225]

Pursuant to the *attentiveness requirement*, a supporting organization must distribute at least one-third of its annual distributable amount to one or more supported organizations that are attentive to the operations of the supporting organization.[226]

The second way to meet this test is for the organization to be a trust that, on November 20, 1970, met and continues to meet certain requirements if, for years beginning after October 16, 1972, the trustee makes annual written reports containing certain information to the supported organizations.[227]

For the purposes of the distribution requirement, the amount of a distribution made to a supported organization is the fair market value of the property as of the date the distribution is made.[228] This amount is determined using the cash receipts and disbursements method of accounting. Distributions that qualify for the distribution requirement are limited to amounts (1) paid to a supported organization to accomplish its exempt purposes; (2) paid by the supporting organization to perform an activity that directly furthers a supported organization's exempt purposes, but only to the extent such amount exceeds any income derived by the supporting organization from the activity; (3) paid by the supporting organization for reasonable and necessary administrative expenses (excluding expenses incurred in the production of investment income or fundraising activities, other than certain solicitation expenses);[229] (4) paid to acquire an asset used (or held for use) to carry out the exempt purposes of the supported organization(s); and (5) set aside for a specific project that accomplishes the exempt purposes of a supported organization, with such set-aside counting toward the distribution requirement

---

[225] Reg. § 1.509(a)-4(i)(5)(ii). *Adjusted net income* for the immediately preceding taxable year is determined by applying the principles of IRC § 4942(f) and Reg § 53.4942(a)-2(d) (Reg. § 1.509(a)-4(i)(5)(ii)(B)). The IRS proposed the revocation of a Type III entity's supporting organization status for failure to meet this distribution requirement (Priv. Ltr. Rul. 202151008).

[226] Reg. § 1.509(a)-4(i)(5)(iii)(A). One way for a supporting organization to satisfy the attentiveness requirement with respect to a supported organization is to distribute amounts equaling or exceeding 10 percent of the supported organization's total annual support (or, in the case of a particular department or school of a university, hospital, or church, the total annual support of the department or school) (Reg. § 1.509(a)-4(i)(5)(iii)(B)). The regulations provide two other alternatives for demonstrating that a supported organization is attentive to the operations of a supporting organization (*id.*). Distributions held by a supported organization in a donor-advised fund are disregarded for purposes of determining whether the attentiveness requirement is met (Reg. § 1.509(a)-4(i)(5)(iii)(C)).

[227] Reg. §§ 1.509(a)-4(i)(5)(i)(B), (9).

[228] Reg. § 1.509(a)-4(i)(6).

[229] Includible solicitation expenses are those incurred to solicit contributions that are received directly by a supported organization (rather than by the supporting organization), but only to the extent the amount incurred for each solicitation does not exceed the amount of contributions that are actually received by the supported organization directly from donors as a result of each such solicitation (Reg.

for the taxable year in which the amount is set aside but not in the year in which it is actually paid, provided certain additional requirements are met.[230]

Generally, if with respect to a year an excess distributed amount is created, the excess amount may be used to reduce the annual distributable amount in any of the five years immediately following the year in which the excess amount was created.[231] An *excess amount* is created where the total distributions made by a supporting organization to its supported organization(s) for a year exceed the supporting organization's annual distributable amount for the year.

The regulations include extensive rules for ascertaining whether an asset is used or held for use to carry out exempt purposes of a supporting organization, determining the fair market value of various types of non–exempt-use assets of a supporting organization, and the timing of valuations.[232]

The private foundation excess business holdings rules[233] are applicable to Type III supporting organizations, other than functionally integrated Type III supporting organizations.[234] These excess business holdings rules also apply to a Type II supporting organization if the organization accepts a contribution from a person (other than a public charity, not a supporting organization) who controls, either alone or with family members and/or certain controlled entities, the governing body of a supported organization of the supporting organization.[235] Nonetheless, the IRS has the authority to not impose the excess business holdings rules on a supporting organization if the organization establishes that the holdings are consistent with the organization's tax-exempt status.[236]

A nonoperating private foundation may not treat as a qualifying distribution[237] an amount paid to a Type III supporting organization that is not a functionally integrated Type III supporting organization or to any other type of supporting organization if a disqualified person with respect to the foundation directly or indirectly controls the supporting organization or a supported organization of the supporting organization.[238] An amount that does not count as a qualifying distribution under this rule is regarded as a taxable expenditure unless the private foundation exercises expenditure responsibility over the payment.[239] Additional rules

---

§ 1.509(a)-4(i)(6)(iii)(B)). For this exception to apply, the supported organization must substantiate the amount of such contributions in a written report to the supporting organization before the due date for the supporting organization's annual information return (*id.*).

[230] Reg. § 1.509(a)-4(i)(6)(v). The supporting organization must obtain a written statement from the supporting organization approving the project and the need for a set-aside, obtain an advance ruling from the IRS (see § 28.1(d)), and appropriately account for the set-aside on its books and records.

[231] Reg. § 1.509(a)-4(i)(7).

[232] Reg. § 1.509(a)-4(i)(8).

[233] See § 12.4(c).

[234] IRC §§ 4943(f)(1), (3)(A).

[235] IRC § 4943(f)(1), (3)(B).

[236] IRC § 4943(f)(2).

[237] See § 12.4(b).

[238] IRC § 4942(g)(4). As to the second element of this rule, a payment also is not a qualifying distribution if the IRS determines by regulation that the distribution "otherwise is inappropriate" (IRC § 4942(g)(4)(ii)(II)).

[239] IRC § 4945(d)(4). See § 12.4(e). Because a distribution by a private foundation to these types of supporting organizations is not a qualifying distribution and may be a taxable expenditure, and a

pertaining to supporting organizations concern their annual information returns and the applicability of the intermediate sanctions rules.[240]

A supporting organization may operate to support and benefit a social welfare organization,[241] a labor or agricultural organization,[242] or a business league.[243] The principal requirement in this regard is that the beneficiary organization meet the one-third public support test of the rules concerning the service provider publicly supported charitable organization.[244]

An organization that fails the tests to be classified as a supporting organization will be reclassified as a private foundation unless it can qualify as another type of public charity.[245] Loss of supporting organization status does not, however, *per se* result in loss of tax-exempt status, although the IRS occasionally gets this wrong.[246]

A court discussed the fiduciary duties owed by a supporting organization, formed as a trust, to its supported organization, with an emphasis on the duties of loyalty and disclosure.[247] In a subsequent decision, this court held that the trustees of the supporting organization repeatedly breached fiduciary duties to the supported organization, to the end that the trustees of the supporting organization were required to pay personally the fees and costs owed to the supported organization, a trustee was removed, and an institutional trustee selected.[248] These decisions were affirmed, with the appellate court writing that "[w]e do not think it necessary to add to the district court's explanation of these decisions, all of which are either compelled by law (including the law of contracts and the Internal Revenue Code) or within the scope of remedial discretion allowed to a court by Wisconsin's law of trusts."[249]

(d) Public Safety Testing Organizations

Another category of organization that is deemed to not be a private foundation is an organization that is organized and operated exclusively for testing for public safety.[250] These entities are described in the analysis of charitable organizations.

---

distribution from individual retirement accounts to any type of supporting organization is not eligible for exclusion from the IRA holder's income (IRC § 408(d)(8)(B)(i)), an organization may seek a reclassification of its status from a supporting organization to another category of public charity. See § 28.1(d).

[240] See § 28.2(b)(x) and § 21.4(d), respectively.

[241] See Chapter 13.

[242] See Chapter 16.

[243] See Chapter 14.

[244] IRC § 509(a), last sentence; Reg. § 1.509(a)-4(k). This matter is referenced in the statute as follows: "For purposes of [IRC § 509(a)(3)], an organization described in paragraph (2) [see § 12.3(b)(iv)] shall be deemed to include an organization described in section 501(c)(4), (5), or (6) which would be described in paragraph (2) if it were an organization described in section 501(c)(3)." An illustration of a situation where a tax-exempt business league should have placed its substantial charitable and educational activities in a supporting organization is provided in Priv. Ltr. Rul. 202017035.

[245] See §§ 12.1(a), 12.3.

[246] E.g., Priv. Ltr. Rul. 202405012, in which the IRS erroneously conflated supporting organization status with exempt status and proposed revocation of an organization's exempt status because it "does not continue to qualify for exemption . . . as a supporting organization."

[247] Cohen v. Minneapolis Jewish Fed'n, 286 F. Supp. 3d 949 (W.D. Wis. 2017).

[248] Cohen v. Minneapolis Jewish Fed'n, 346 F. Supp. 3d 1274 (W.D. Wis. 2018).

[249] Cohen v. Minneapolis Jewish Fed'n, 776 Fed. Appx. 912, 913 (7th Cir. 2019).

[250] IRC § 509(a)(4). See § 11.3.

§ 12.4 PRIVATE FOUNDATION RULES

The federal tax law governing the operations of private foundations is a composite of rules pertaining to self-dealing, mandatory payout requirements, business holdings, investment practices, various types of expenditures, and more. The sanctions for violation of these rules are five sets of excise taxes, with each set entailing three tiers of taxation. The three tiers are known as the *initial tax*,[251] the *additional tax*,[252] and the *involuntary termination tax*.[253] In general, when there is a violation, the initial tax must be paid; the additional tax is levied only when the initial tax is not timely paid and the matter not timely corrected; the termination tax is levied when the other two taxes have been imposed and there continues to be willful, flagrant, or repeated acts or failures to act, giving rise to one or more of the initial or additional taxes.

The IRS generally has the authority to abate these initial taxes, where the taxable event was due to reasonable cause and not to willful neglect, and the event was timely corrected.[254] This abatement authority, however, does not extend to initial taxes imposed in the context of self-dealing.[255] Where a taxable event is timely corrected, any additional taxes that may have been assessed or paid are abated.[256]

Because of the stringency of these rules, the sanctions are far more than merely taxes, being essentially a system of absolute prohibitions.

(a) Self-Dealing

In general, the federal tax law prohibits acts of self-dealing between a private foundation and a disqualified person.[257] An act of self-dealing may be direct or indirect. The latter generally is a self-dealing transaction between a disqualified person and an organization controlled by a private foundation.[258]

The sale or exchange of property between a private foundation and a disqualified person generally constitutes an act of self-dealing.[259] The transfer of real or personal property by a disqualified person to a private foundation is treated as a sale or exchange if the property is subject to a mortgage or similar lien that the foundation assumes or if it is subject to a mortgage or similar lien that a disqualified person placed on the property within the 10-year period ending on the date of transfer.[260]

The leasing of property between a private foundation and a disqualified person generally constitutes self-dealing.[261] The leasing of property by a disqualified person to a private foundation without charge is not, however, an act of self-dealing.[262]

---

[251] IRC §§ 4941(a), 4942(a), 4943(a), 4944(a), 4945(a).
[252] IRC §§ 4941(b), 4942(b), 4943(b), 4944(b), 4945(b).
[253] IRC § 507(a)(2).
[254] IRC § 4962(a).
[255] IRC § 4962(b).
[256] IRC § 4961.
[257] IRC § 4941.
[258] Reg. § 53.4941(d)-1(b).
[259] IRC § 4941(d)(1)(A); Reg. § 53.4941(d)-2(a)(1). E.g., Rev. Rul. 76-18, 1976-1 C.B. 355.
[260] IRC § 4941(d)(2)(A); Reg. § 53.4941(d)-2(a)(2).
[261] IRC § 4941(d)(1)(A); Reg. § 53.4941(d)-2(b)(1).
[262] Reg. § 53.4941(d)-2(b)(2).

The lending of money or other extension of credit between a private foundation and a disqualified person generally constitutes an act of self-dealing.[263] This
rule does not apply to an extension of credit by a disqualified person to a private
foundation if the transaction is without interest or other charge and the proceeds
of the loan are used exclusively for charitable purposes.[264]

The furnishing of goods, services, or facilities between a private foundation
and a disqualified person generally constitutes an act of self-dealing.[265] The furnishing of goods, services, or facilities by a disqualified person to a private foundation is not an act of self-dealing, however, if they are furnished without charge
and used exclusively for charitable purposes.[266] The furnishing of goods, services,
or facilities by a private foundation to a disqualified person is not self-dealing if
the furnishing is made on a basis no more favorable than the basis on which the
goods, services, or facilities are made available to the public.[267]

The payment of compensation (or payment or reimbursement of expenses)
by a private foundation to a disqualified person generally constitutes an act of
self-dealing.[268] Except in the case of a governmental official, however, the payment of compensation (or payment or reimbursement of expenses) by a private
foundation to a disqualified person for the performance of personal services that
are reasonable and necessary to carrying out the charitable purpose of the foundation is not self-dealing if the compensation (or payment or reimbursement) is
not excessive.[269]

The transfer to, or use by or for the benefit of, a disqualified person of the
income or assets of a private foundation generally constitutes self-dealing.[270]
Unlike the other sets of rules describing specific categories of acts of self-dealing,
this one is a catch-all provision designed to sweep into the ambit of self-dealing a
variety of transactions that might otherwise technically escape the discrete transactions defined to be self-dealing ones. The fact that a disqualified person receives
an incidental or tenuous benefit from the use by a private foundation of its income
or assets will not, by itself, make the use an act of self-dealing.[271]

An agreement by a private foundation to make a payment of money or other
property to a government official generally constitutes self-dealing, unless the
agreement is to employ the individual for a period after termination of their government service if they are terminating service within a 90-day period.[272] In the
case of a government official, the self-dealing rules do not apply to the receipt of

---

[263] IRC § 4941(d)(1)(B): Reg. § 53.4941(d)-2(c)(1).

[264] IRC § 4941(d)(2)(B); Reg. § 53.4941(d)-2(c)(2).

[265] IRC § 4941(d)(1)(C); Reg. § 53.4941(d)-2(d)(1).

[266] IRC § 4941(d)(2)(C); Reg. § 53.4941(d)-2(d)(3).

[267] IRC § 4941(d)(2)(D); Reg. § 53.4941(d)-3(b).

[268] IRC § 4941(d)(1)(D); Reg. § 53.4941(d)-2(e).

[269] IRC § 4941(d)(2)(E); Reg. § 53.4941(d)-3(c).

[270] IRC § 4941(d)(1)(E); Reg. § 53.4941(d)-2(f)(1). There are special rules concerning indemnification
and the purchase of insurance by private foundations for the benefit of foundation managers (Reg. §
53.4941(d)-2(f)(3)–(8)).

[271] Reg. § 53.4941(d)-2(f)(2).

[272] IRC § 4941(d)(1)(F); Reg. § 53.4941(d)-2(g).

certain prizes and awards, scholarship and fellowship grants, annuities, gifts, and traveling expenses.[273]

There are several other exceptions to the self-dealing rules, one of which holds that a transaction between a private foundation and a corporation that is a disqualified person with respect to the foundation is not an act of self-dealing if the transaction is engaged in pursuant to a liquidation, merger, redemption, recapitalization, or other corporate adjustment, organization, or reorganization.[274] For this exception to apply, all the securities of the same class as that held by the foundation prior to the transfer must be subject to the same terms, and these terms must provide for receipt by the foundation of no less than fair market value.[275]

An act of self-dealing *occurs* on the date on which all of the terms and conditions of the transaction and the liabilities of the parties have been fixed.[276] The *amount involved* generally is the greater of the amount of money and the fair market value of the other property given or the amount of money and the fair market value of the other property received.[277] *Correction* of an act of self-dealing means undoing the transaction that constituted the act to the extent possible, but in no case may the resulting financial position of the private foundation be worse than would be the case if the disqualified person was dealing under the highest fiduciary standards.[278]

An initial tax is imposed on each act of self-dealing between a disqualified person and a private foundation; the tax is imposed on the self-dealer at a rate of 10 percent of the amount involved with respect to the act for each year in the taxable period or part of a period.[279] Where this initial tax is imposed, a tax of 5 percent of the amount involved is imposed on the participation of any foundation manager in the act of self-dealing, where the manager knowingly participated in the act.[280] This tax is not imposed, however, where the participation is not willful and is due to reasonable cause.[281] This tax, which must be paid by the foundation manager, may not exceed $20,000 per act of self-dealing.[282]

Where an initial tax is imposed and the self-dealing act is not timely corrected, an additional tax is imposed in an amount equal to 200 percent of the amount involved; this tax must be paid by the disqualified person (other than a foundation manager) who participated in the act of self-dealing.[283] An additional

---

[273] IRC § 4941(d)(2)(G); Reg. § 53.4941(d)-3(e).

[274] IRC § 4941(d)(2)(F); Reg. § 53.4941(d)-3(d).

[275] Reg. § 53.4941(d)-3(d)(1).

[276] Reg. § 53.4941(e)-1(a)(2).

[277] IRC § 4941(e)(2); Reg. § 53.4941(e)-1(b)(1).

[278] IRC § 4941(e)(3); Reg. § 53.4941(e)-1(c).

[279] IRC § 4941(a)(1); Reg. § 53.4941(a)-1(a)(1). The *taxable period* is the period beginning with the date on which the transaction occurred and ending on the earliest of the date of mailing of a notice of deficiency with respect to the initial tax, the date on which the initial tax is assessed, or the date on which correction of the transaction is completed (IRC § 4941(e)(1); Reg. § 53.4941(e)-1(a)). The calculation of the initial self-dealing tax in the case of a multiyear loan to a disqualified person is illustrated in Rev. Rul. 2002-43, 2002-2 C.B. 85.

[280] IRC § 4941(a)(2); Reg. § 53.4941(a)-1(b).

[281] *Id.*

[282] IRC § 4941(c)(2); Reg. § 53.4941(c)-1(b).

[283] IRC § 4941(b)(1); Reg. § 53.4941(b)-1(a).

tax equal to 50 percent of the amount involved, up to $20,000,[284] is imposed on a foundation manager (where the additional tax is imposed on the self-dealer) who refuses to agree to all or part of the correction.[285]

In a case where more than one person is liable for any initial or additional tax with respect to any one act of self-dealing, all the persons are jointly and severally liable for the tax or taxes.[286]

Willful repeated violations of these rules will result in involuntary termination of the private foundation's status and the imposition of additional taxes.[287] The termination tax thus serves as a third-tier tax.

(b) Mandatory Distributions

A private foundation is required to distribute, for each year, at least a minimum amount of money and/or property for charitable purposes.[288] The amount that must annually be distributed by a private foundation is the *distributable amount*.[289] That amount must be in the form of *qualifying distributions*, which essentially are grants, outlays for administration, and payments made to acquire charitable assets.[290] Generally, the distributable amount for a private foundation is an amount equal to 5 percent of the value of the noncharitable assets of the foundation;[291] this is the *minimum investment return*.[292] The distributable amount also includes amounts equal to repayments to a foundation of items previously treated as qualifying distributions (such as scholarship loans), amounts received on disposition of assets previously treated as qualifying distributions, and amounts previously set aside for a charitable project but not so used.[293]

The charitable assets of a private foundation are those actually used by the foundation in carrying out its charitable objectives or assets owned by the foundation where it has convinced the IRS that its immediate use of them for exempt purposes is not practical and that definite plans exist to commence a related use within a reasonable period.[294] Thus, the assets that are in the minimum investment

---

[284] IRC § 4941(c)(2); Reg. § 53.4941(c)-1(b).

[285] IRC § 4941(b)(2); Reg. § 53.4941(b)-1(b).

[286] IRC § 4941(c)(1); Reg. § 53.4941(c)-1(a).

[287] IRC § 507(a)(2).

[288] IRC § 4942.

[289] IRC § 4942(d).

[290] IRC § 4942(g)(1); Reg. §§ 53.4942(a)-3(a), (c). Private foundations generally confine their grants to public charities. If the prospective grantee is a foreign charity, the foundation will usually want to make a good-faith determination that the grantee is a qualifying public charity so as to not require expenditure responsibility (see text accompanied by *infra* notes 360, 361); the procedure for foundations to follow in this regard is the subject of Rev. Proc. 2017-53, 2017-40 I.R.B. 263.

[291] Reg. §§ 53.4942(a)-2(c)(1), (5). A private foundation is required to ascertain the aggregate fair market value of its assets, although those used or held for use for charitable purposes are not considered when determining its minimum investment return (IRC § 4942(e)(1)(A)).

[292] IRC §§ 4942(d)(1), 4942(e)(1)(A); Reg. § 53.4942(a)-2(b)(1). The minimum investment return is reduced by any acquisition indebtedness (see § 24.10(c)) with respect to the assets (IRC § 4942(e)(1)(B)).

[293] IRC §§ 4942(d)(1), (f)(2)(C).

[294] Reg. § 53.4942(a)-2(c)(3). These assets include interests in a functionally related business (see text accompanied by *infra* notes 311, 312) and in a program-related investment (see text accompanied by *infra* notes 327, 328).

return base are those held for the production of income or for investment (such as stocks, bonds, interest-bearing notes, endowment funds, and leased real estate).[295] Where property is used for both exempt and other purposes, it is considered to be used exclusively for tax-exempt purposes where the exempt use represents at least 95 percent of the total use; otherwise, a reasonable allocation between the two uses is required.[296]

An exception to the timing of distributions by a private foundation for mandatory payout purposes is the *set-aside*, where funds are credited for a charitable purpose, rather than immediately granted; where the requirements are met, the set-aside is regarded as a qualifying distribution.[297] One type of set-aside is that referenced in the *suitability test*; this requires a specific project, a payment period not to exceed 60 months, and a ruling from the IRS.[298] The other type of set-aside is that of the *cash distribution test*; this test entails set percentages of distributions over a multiyear period and does not require an IRS ruling.[299]

An initial tax of 30 percent is imposed on the undistributed income of a private foundation for any year that has not been distributed on a timely basis in the form of qualifying distributions.[300] In a case in which an initial tax is imposed on the undistributed income of a private foundation for a year, an additional tax is imposed on any portion of the income remaining undistributed at the close of the taxable period.[301] This tax is equal to 100 percent of the amount remaining undistributed at the close of the period.[302]

Payment of these taxes is required in addition to, rather than in lieu of, making the required distributions.[303]

The termination taxes[304] serve as third-tier taxes.

(c) Excess Business Holdings

Private foundations are limited as to the extent to which they can own interests in commercial business enterprises.[305] A private foundation and all disqualified persons with respect to it generally are permitted to hold no more than 20 percent of a corporation's voting stock or other interest in a business enterprise; these are *permitted holdings*.[306] If effective control of the business can be shown to be elsewhere, a 35 percent limit may be substituted for the 20 percent limit.[307] A private

---

[295] IRC § 4942(e)(1)(A).
[296] Reg. § 53.4942(a)-2(c)(3).
[297] Reg. § 53.4942(a)-3(b)(1).
[298] Reg. § 53.4942(a)-3(b)(2), (7)(i).
[299] IRC § 4942(g)(2); Reg. § 53.4942(a)-3(b)(3)–(7)(ii).
[300] IRC § 4942(a); Reg. § 53.4942(a)-1(a)(1).
[301] IRC § 4942(b); Reg. § 53.4942(a)-1(a)(2). The *taxable period* is the period beginning with the first day of the year involved and ending on the date of mailing of a notice of deficiency with respect to the initial tax or the date on which the initial tax is assessed (IRC § 4942(j)(1); Reg. § 53.4942(a)-1(c)(1)).
[302] IRC § 4942(b); Reg. § 53.4942(a)-1(a)(2).
[303] Reg. § 53.4942(a)-1(a)(3).
[304] IRC § 507(a)(2).
[305] IRC § 4943.
[306] IRC §§ 4943(c)(2)(A), (c)(3); Reg. §§ 53.4943-1, 53.4943-3(b)(1), 53.4943-3(b)(2), 53.4943-3(b)(3)(c).
[307] IRC § 4943(c)(2)(B); Reg. § 53.4943-3(b)(3).

foundation must hold, directly or indirectly, more than 2 percent of the value of a business enterprise before these limitations become applicable.[308]

There are four principal exceptions to these rules. One is for a business at least 95 percent of the gross income of which is derived from passive sources.[309] These sources generally include dividends, interest, annuities, royalties, and capital gain.[310] The second exception is for holdings in a *functionally related business*.[311] This is a business that is substantially related to the achievement of the foundation's exempt purposes (other than merely providing funds for the foundation's programs); in which substantially all the work is performed for the private foundation without compensation; that is carried on by a private foundation primarily for the convenience of its employees; that consists of the selling of merchandise, substantially all of which was received by the foundation as contributions; or that is carried on within a larger aggregate of similar activities or within a larger complex of other endeavors that is related to the exempt purposes of the foundation.[312] The third exception is for program-related investments.[313] The fourth exception pertains to holdings in a philanthropic business.[314]

If a private foundation obtains holdings in a business enterprise, in a transaction that is not a purchase by the foundation or by disqualified persons with respect to it, and the additional holdings would result in the foundation having an excess business holding, the foundation has five years to reduce the holdings to a permissible level without penalty.[315] The IRS has the authority to allow an additional five-year period for the disposition of excess business holdings in the case of an unusually large gift or bequest of diverse business holdings or holdings with complex corporate structures.[316] This latter rule entails several requirements, including a showing that diligent efforts were made to dispose of the holdings within the initial five-year period and that disposition within that five-year period was not possible (except at a price substantially below fair market value) by reason of the size and complexity or diversity of the holdings.

An initial excise tax is imposed on the excess business holdings of a private foundation in a business enterprise for each tax year that ends during the taxable period.[317] The amount of this tax is 10 percent of the total value of all of the private foundation's excess business holdings in each of its business enterprises.[318]

---

[308] IRC § 4943(c)(2)(C); Reg. § 53.4943-3(b)(4).

[309] IRC § 4943(d)(3)(B).

[310] Reg. § 53.4943-10(c).

[311] IRC § 4943(d)(3)(A).

[312] IRC § 4942(j)(4), Reg. § 53.4943-10(b).

[313] Reg. § 53.4943-10(b) (see text accompanied by *infra* notes 327, 328).

[314] IRC § 4943(g).

[315] IRC § 4943(c)(6); Reg. § 53.4943-6(a).

[316] IRC § 4943(c)(7).

[317] IRC § 4943(a)(1); Reg. § 53.4943-2(a)(1). The *taxable period* is the period beginning on the first day on which there are excess business holdings and ending on the earlier of the date of mailing of a notice of deficiency with respect to the initial tax or the date on which the initial tax is assessed (IRC § 4943(d)(2); Reg. § 53.4943-9(a)(1)).

[318] IRC § 4943(a)(1); Reg. § 53.4943-2(a)(1).

If the excess business holdings are not disposed of during the period, an additional tax is imposed on the private foundation; the amount of this tax is 200 percent of the value of the excess business holdings.[319]

The termination taxes[320] serve as third-tier taxes.

(d) Jeopardizing Investments

There are rules governing the type of investments that a private foundation is allowed to make.[321] In general, a private foundation cannot invest any amount—income or principal—in a manner that would jeopardize the carrying out of any of its tax-exempt purposes.[322] An investment is considered to jeopardize the carrying out of the exempt purposes of a private foundation if it is determined that the foundation managers, in making the investment, failed to exercise ordinary business care and prudence, under the facts and circumstances prevailing at the time of the investment, in providing for the long-term and short-term financial needs of the foundation in carrying out its charitable activities.[323]

A determination as to whether the making of a particular investment jeopardizes the exempt purposes of a private foundation is made on an investment-by-investment basis, in each case taking into account the private foundation's portfolio as a whole.[324] Although the IRS will not rule as to a procedure governing investments to be made in the future, it will rule as to a currently proposed investment.[325]

No category of investments is treated as a *per se* violation of these rules. The types or methods of investment that are closely scrutinized to determine whether the foundation managers have met the requisite standard of care and prudence include trading in securities on margin, trading in commodity futures, investments in oil and gas syndications, the purchase of puts and calls (and straddles), the purchase of warrants, and selling short.[326]

A *program-related investment* is not a jeopardizing investment. This is an investment whose primary purpose is to accomplish one or more charitable purposes and no significant purpose of which is the production of income or the appreciation of property.[327] No purpose of the investment may be the furthering of substantial legislative or political campaign activities.[328]

Also, outside the context of program-related investments, private foundations may take their charitable purposes into account in formulating investment policy; this is termed *mission-related investing*. That is, when exercising ordinary business care and prudence in deciding whether to make an investment,

---

[319] IRC § 4943 (b); Reg. § 53.4943-2(b).
[320] IRC § 507(a)(2).
[321] IRC § 4944.
[322] IRC § 4944(a)(1).
[323] Reg. § 53.4944-1(a)(2)(i).
[324] *Id.*
[325] E.g., Priv. Ltr. Rul. 9451067.
[326] Reg. § 53.4944-1(a)(2)(i).
[327] IRC § 4944(c); Reg. § 53.4944-3(a).
[328] Reg. § 53.4944-3(a)(1)(iii).

foundation managers may consider all relevant facts and circumstances, including the relationship between an investment and the foundation's charitable purposes. Foundations are not required to select only investments that offer the highest rate of return, the lowest risks, or the greatest liquidity as long as the foundation managers exercise the requisite ordinary business care and prudence under the facts and circumstances prevailing at the time of the investment in making investment decisions that support, and do not jeopardize, the furtherance of the private foundation's charitable purposes.[329]

If a private foundation invests an amount in a manner as to jeopardize the carrying out of any of its charitable purposes, an initial tax is imposed on the foundation on the making of the investment, at the rate of 10 percent of the amount invested for each year or part of a year in the taxable period.[330]

In any case in which this initial tax is imposed, a tax is imposed on the participation of any foundation manager making an investment with the knowledge that it jeopardizes the carrying out of any of the foundation's exempt purposes; the tax is equal to 10 percent of the amount so invested for each year of the foundation (or part of the year) in the period.[331] With respect to any one investment, the maximum amount of this tax is $10,000.[332] This tax, which must be paid by any participating foundation manager, is not imposed where the participation was not willful and was due to reasonable cause.[333]

An additional tax is imposed in any case in which this initial tax is imposed and the investment is not removed from jeopardy within the period; this tax, which is to be paid by the private foundation, is at the rate of 25 percent of the amount of the investment.[334] In any case in which this additional tax is imposed and a foundation manager has refused to agree to all or part of the removal of the investment from jeopardy, a tax is imposed at the rate of 5 percent of the amount of the investment.[335] With respect to any one investment, the maximum amount of this tax is $20,000.[336]

Where more than one foundation manager is liable for an initial tax or an additional tax with respect to a jeopardizing investment, all of the managers are jointly and severally liable for the taxes.[337]

The termination taxes[338] serve as third-tier taxes.

---

[329] Notice 2015-62, 2015-39 I.R.B. 411.

[330] IRC § 4944(a)(1); Reg. § 53.4944-1(a)(1). The *taxable period* is the period beginning with the date of the jeopardizing investment and ending on the earliest of the date of mailing of a notice of deficiency with respect to the initial tax, the date on which the initial tax is assessed, or the date on which the amount invested is removed from jeopardy (as defined in IRC § 4944(e)(2); Reg. § 53.4944-5(b) (IRC § 4944(e)(1)); Reg. § 53.4944-5(a)).

[331] IRC § 4944(a)(2); Reg. § 53.4944-1(b)(1).

[332] IRC § 4944(d)(2); Reg. § 53.4944-4(b).

[333] IRC § 4944(a)(2); Reg. § 53.4944-1(b)(1).

[334] IRC § 4944(b)(1); Reg. § 53.4944-2(a).

[335] IRC § 4944(b)(2); Reg. § 53.4944-2(b).

[336] IRC § 4944(d)(2); Reg. § 53.4944-4(b).

[337] IRC § 4944(d)(1); Reg. § 53.4944-4(a).

[338] IRC § 507(a)(2).

(e) Taxable Expenditures

The federal tax law provides restrictions, in addition to those discussed previously, on the activities and purposes for which private foundations may expend their funds.[339] These rules pertain to matters such as legislative activities, electioneering, grants to individuals, and grants to noncharitable organizations. Improper and, in effect, prohibited expenditures are termed *taxable expenditures*.

One form of taxable expenditure is an amount paid or incurred by a private foundation to carry on propaganda or otherwise attempt to influence legislation.[340] Thus, the general rule by which charitable organizations can engage in a certain amount of legislative activity[341] is inapplicable to private foundations.

Attempts to influence legislation generally include certain communications with a member or employee of a legislative body or with an official or employee of an executive department of a government who may participate in formulating legislation or efforts to affect the opinion of the general public or a segment of it.[342] An expenditure is an attempt to influence legislation if it is for a *direct lobbying communication* or a *grassroots lobbying communication*.[343]

Engaging in nonpartisan analysis, study, or research and making the results of this type of an undertaking available to the general public (or a segment of it) or to governmental bodies or officials is not a prohibited form of legislative activity.[344] Likewise, amounts paid or incurred in connection with the provision of technical advice or assistance to a governmental body or committee (or other subdivision of it) in response to a written request from the entity do not constitute taxable expenditures.[345] Another exception is that the taxable expenditures rules do not apply to any amount paid or incurred in connection with an appearance before or communication to a legislative body with respect to a possible decision of that body that might affect the existence of the private foundation, its powers and duties, its tax-exempt status, or the deductibility of contributions to the foundation.[346] Expenditures for examinations and discussions of broad social, economic, and similar issues are not taxable even if the problems are of the types that government would be expected to deal with ultimately.[347]

The term *taxable expenditure* includes an amount paid or incurred by a private foundation to influence the outcome of a specific public election or to conduct, directly or indirectly, a voter registration drive.[348] The first of these prohibitions generally parallels the prohibition on political campaign activities by all charitable organizations.[349] A private foundation may engage in electioneering activities

---

[339] IRC § 4945.
[340] IRC § 4945(d)(1).
[341] See Chapter 22.
[342] IRC § 4945(e).
[343] Reg. § 53.4945-2(a)(1).
[344] IRC § 4945(e); Reg. § 53.4945-2(d)(1).
[345] IRC § 4945(e)(2); Reg. § 53.4945-2(d)(2).
[346] IRC § 4945(e) (last sentence); Reg. § 53.4945-2(d)(3).
[347] Reg. § 53.4945-2(d)(4).
[348] IRC § 4945(d)(2); Reg. § 53.4945-3(a)(1).
[349] Reg. § 53.4945-3(a)(2). See Chapter 23.

(including voter registration drives), however, without making a taxable expenditure, where a variety of criteria are satisfied, such as not confining the activity to one election period and carrying it on in at least five states.[350]

The term *taxable expenditure* includes an amount paid or incurred by a private foundation as a grant to an individual for travel, study, or other similar purposes.[351] This type of grant is not prohibited, however, if it is awarded on an objective and nondiscriminatory basis pursuant to a procedure approved in advance by the IRS and the IRS is satisfied that the grant is one of three specified types: (1) a scholarship or fellowship grant that is excludable from the recipient's gross income and used for study at an educational institution; (2) a prize or award that is excludable from the recipient's gross income, where the recipient is selected from the general public; or (3) a grant the purpose of which is to achieve a specific objective, produce a report or similar product, or improve or enhance a literary, artistic, musical, scientific, teaching, or other similar capacity, skill, or talent of the grantee.[352]

The requirement as to objectivity and nondiscrimination generally requires that the group from which grantees are selected be chosen based on criteria reasonably related to the purposes of the grant. The group must be sufficiently broad so that the making of grants to members of the group would be considered to fulfill a charitable purpose.[353] The individual or group of individuals who select grant recipients should not be in a position to derive a private benefit as a result of the selection process.[354]

These rules as to individual grants generally require (1) the receipt by a private foundation of an annual report from the beneficiary of a scholarship or fellowship;[355] (2) that a foundation investigate situations indicating that all or a part of a grant is not being used in furtherance of its purposes;[356] and (3) recovery or restoration of any diverted funds, and withholding of further payments to a grantee in an instance of improper diversion of grant funds.[357] A private foundation must maintain certain records pertaining to grants to individuals.[358]

A private foundation may make grants to an organization that is not a public charity;[359] however, when it does so, it must exercise *expenditure responsibility* with respect to the grant.[360] A private foundation is considered to be exercising expenditure responsibility in connection with a grant as long as it exerts all reasonable efforts and establishes adequate procedures to see that the grant is spent solely

---

[350] IRC § 4945(f); Reg. § 53.4945-3(b).

[351] IRC § 4945(d)(3); Reg. § 53.4945-4(a)(1), (2).

[352] IRC § 4945(g); Reg. § 53.4945-4(a)(3)(ii).

[353] Reg. § 53.4945-4(b)(2).

[354] Reg. § 53.4945-4(b)(4).

[355] Reg. § 53.4945-4(c)(2), (3).

[356] Reg. § 53.4945-4(c)(4).

[357] Reg. § 53.4945-4(c)(5).

[358] Reg. § 53.4945-4(c)(6).

[359] See § 12.3.

[360] IRC § 4945(d)(4); Reg. § 53.4945-5(a). For this purpose, exempt operating foundations (see § 12.1(c)) are regarded the same as public charities.

for the purpose for which it was made, obtains full and complete reports from the grantee on how the funds are spent, and makes full and detailed reports to the IRS with respect to the expenditures.[361]

The term *taxable expenditure* includes an amount paid or incurred by a private foundation for a *noncharitable* purpose.[362] Ordinarily, only an expenditure for an activity that, if it were a substantial part of the organization's total activities, would cause loss of tax exemption is a taxable expenditure.[363]

Expenditures ordinarily not treated as taxable expenditures under these rules are (1) expenditures to acquire investments entered into for the purpose of obtaining income or funds to be used in furtherance of charitable purposes; (2) reasonable expenses with respect to investments; (3) payment of taxes; (4) any expenses that qualify as deductions in the computation of unrelated business income tax;[364] (5) any payment that constitutes a qualifying distribution[365] or an allowable deduction pursuant to the investment income tax rules;[366] (6) reasonable expenditures to evaluate, acquire, modify, and dispose of program-related investments;[367] or (7) business expenditures by the recipient of a program-related investment. Conversely, expenditures for unreasonable administrative expenses, including compensation, consultants' fees, and other fees for services rendered, are ordinarily taxable expenditures, unless the private foundation can demonstrate that the expenses were paid or incurred in the good-faith belief that they were reasonable and that the payment or incurrence of the expenses in amounts was consistent with ordinary business care and prudence.[368]

An excise tax is imposed on each taxable expenditure of a private foundation, which is to be paid by the private foundation at the rate of 20 percent of the amount on each taxable expenditure.[369] An excise tax is imposed on the agreement of any foundation manager to the making of a taxable expenditure by a private foundation.[370] This latter initial tax is imposed only where the private foundation initial tax is imposed, the manager knows that the expenditure to which they agreed was a taxable one, and the agreement is not willful and not due to reasonable cause. This initial tax, which is at the rate of 5 percent of each taxable expenditure, must be paid by the foundation manager.[371]

An excise tax is imposed in any case in which an initial tax is imposed on a private foundation because of a taxable expenditure and the expenditure is not corrected within the taxable period; this additional tax is to be paid by the

---

[361] IRC § 4945(h); Reg. § 53.4945-5(b)–(d).
[362] IRC § 4945(d)(5).
[363] Reg. § 53.4945-6(a).
[364] See § 25.7.
[365] IRC § 4942(g). See § 12.4(b).
[366] IRC § 4940.
[367] See § 12.4(d).
[368] Reg. § 53.4945-6(b).
[369] IRC § 4945(a)(1); Reg. § 53.4945-1(a)(1).
[370] IRC § 4945(a)(2).
[371] Reg. § 53.4945-1(a)(2).

private foundation and is at the rate of 100 percent of the amount of each taxable expenditure.[372] An excise tax in any case in which an initial tax has been levied is imposed on a foundation manager because of a taxable expenditure and the foundation manager has refused to agree to part or all of the correction of the expenditure; this additional tax, which is at the rate of 50 percent of the amount of the taxable expenditure, is to be paid by the foundation manager.[373]

Where more than one foundation manager is liable for an excise tax with respect to the making of a taxable expenditure, all the foundation managers are jointly and severally liable for the tax.[374] The maximum aggregate amount collectible as an initial tax from all foundation managers with respect to any one taxable expenditure is $10,000, and the maximum aggregate amount so collectible as an additional tax is $20,000.[375]

The termination taxes[376] serve as third-tier taxes.

(f) Other Provisions

For decades, private foundations generally were subject to an annual excise tax of 2 percent on their net investment income, which could be reduced to 1 percent under certain circumstances; for tax years beginning after December 20, 2019, however, this tax is imposed at a single rate of 1.39 percent.[377] Capital gains from appreciation are included in this tax base.[378] This tax must be estimated and paid quarterly, generally following the estimated tax rules for corporations.[379] Under certain circumstances, this tax rate is reduced to 1 percent in a year where the foundation's payout for charitable purposes is increased by an equivalent amount.[380] Exempt operating foundations[381] are exempt from this tax on investment income.[382]

As to certain of the private foundation rules, nonexempt charitable trusts[383] and split-interest trusts[384] are treated as private foundations.[385] A 4 percent tax is

---

[372] IRC §§ 4945(b)(1), 4945(i); Reg. § 53.4945-1(b)(1). The *taxable period* begins with the event giving rise to the expenditure tax and ends on the earlier of the date a notice of deficiency with respect to the first-tier tax is mailed or the date the first-tier tax is assessed if there has not been a mailing of a deficiency notice (IRC § 4945(i)(2); Reg. § 53.4945-1(e)(1)).

[373] IRC § 4945(b)(2); Reg. § 53.4945-1(b)(2).

[374] IRC § 4545(c)(1); Reg. § 53.4945-1(c)(1).

[375] IRC § 4545(c)(2); Reg. § 53.4945-1(c)(2).

[376] IRC § 507(a)(2).

[377] IRC § 4940(a). This law change was made by the Taxpayer Certainty and Disaster Tax Relief Act of 2019, enacted as part of the Further Consolidated Appropriations Act, 2020 (Pub. L. No. 116-94, div. Q, tit. II, § 206, 133 Stat. 2534, 3246).

[378] IRC § 4940(c)(4)(A).

[379] IRC § 6655.

[380] IRC § 4940(e)(1).

[381] See § 12.1(c).

[382] IRC § 4940(d)(1).

[383] That is, entities described in IRC § 4947(a)(1).

[384] That is, entities described in IRC § 4947(a)(2), including charitable remainder trusts (IRC § 664) and pooled income funds (IRC § 642(c)(5)).

[385] IRC § 4947.

imposed on the gross investment income derived from sources within the United States by foreign organizations that constitute private foundations.[386]

§ 12.5 DONOR-ADVISED FUNDS

An account may be maintained within a charitable organization that is classified as a public charity, such as a community foundation, a college, a university, a church, or a charitable gift fund.[387] These accounts are usually referred to as *funds*; the most common of them is known as the *donor-advised fund*.

The donor-advised fund is to be contrasted with the *donor-directed fund*. In the case of a donor-directed fund, the donor or a designee of the donor retains the right to direct investment of the fund's assets and/or to direct grants from the fund for charitable purposes.[388] By contrast, with the donor-advised fund, the donor has the ability (but not a legal right) to make recommendations (proffer advice) as to investment policy and/or the making of grants.

The IRS challenged the donor-advised fund concept in court, as part of its efforts to deny recognition of tax exemption to a public charity that main-tained these funds. The agency claimed that the entity was merely an associa-tion of donors for which commercial services were being performed for fees, the donors retained control of the funds, and it was violating the prohibitions on private inurement and private benefit.[389] The court, however, found that donors to the organization "relinquish all ownership and custody of the donated funds or property" and that the organization is "free to accept or reject any suggestion or request made by a donor."[390] Indeed, the court enthused that the "goal" of the organization "is to create an effective national network to respond to many worthy charitable needs at the local level which in many cases might go unmet" and that its activities "promote public policy and represent the very essence of charitable benevolence as envisioned by Congress in enacting" exempt status for charitable organizations.[391]

A statutory definition of the term *donor-advised fund* provides that it is a fund or account (1) that is separately identified by reference to contributions of one or more donors, (2) that is owned and controlled by a sponsoring organization, and

---

[386] IRC § 4948.

[387] See § 12.3.

[388] A court held that an organization that operated a donor-directed fund program could not be tax-exempt as a charitable entity, in part because of unwarranted private benefit (see § 20.13); the decision in fact principally turned on the rampant extent of federal tax law abuse promoted by the founder of the program (New Dynamics Found. v. United States, 2006-1 U.S.T.C. ¶ 50,286 (U.S. Ct. Fed. Cl. 2006)). A similar situation was presented in a case in which a charitable deduction for ostensible gifts to a donor-advised fund was denied in part because the donor retained dominion and control over the transferred property; the donor used the predominant portion of the fund's income and assets for private ends (Viralam v. Comm'r, 136 T.C. 151 (2011)).

[389] See Chapter 20.

[390] Nat'l Found., Inc. v. United States, 87-2 U.S.T.C. ¶ 9602 (Ct. Cl. 1987), at 89,831.

[391] Id. at 89,832. Also, Fund for Anonymous Gifts v. Internal Revenue Serv., 99-1 U.S.T.C. ¶ 50,440 (D.C. Cir. 1999).

(3) as to which a donor or a donor advisor[392] has, or reasonably expects to have, advisory privileges with respect to the distribution or investment of amounts held in the fund or account by reason of the donor's status as a donor.[393] A *sponsoring organization* is a public charity that maintains one or more donor-advised funds.[394] A donor-advised fund does not include funds that make distributions only to a single identified organization or governmental entity, or certain funds where a donor or donor advisor provides advice as to which individuals receive grants for travel, study, or other similar purposes.[395]

A distribution from a donor-advised fund is a *taxable distribution* if it is to (1) a natural person, (2) any other person for a noncharitable purpose, or (3) any other person (for a charitable purpose) unless expenditure responsibility is exercised with respect to the distribution.[396] A tax of 20 percent of the amount involved is imposed on the sponsoring organization.[397] Another tax, of 5 percent, is imposed on the agreement of a fund manager[398] to the making of a taxable distribution where the manager knew that the distribution was a taxable one.[399] The tax on fund management is subject to a joint and several liability requirement.[400] This tax does not apply to a distribution from a donor-advised fund to most public charities,[401] the fund's sponsoring organization, or another donor-advised fund.[402]

If a donor, donor advisor, or a person related to a donor or donor advisor with respect to a donor-advised fund provides advice as to a distribution that results in any of those persons receiving, directly or indirectly, a benefit that is more than incidental, an excise tax equal to 125 percent of the amount of the benefit is imposed on the person who advised as to the distribution and on the recipient of the benefit.[403] Also, if a manager of the sponsoring organization agreed to the making of the distribution knowing that the distribution would confer more than

---

[392] That is, a person appointed or designated by a donor.

[393] IRC § 4966(d)(2)(A). The IRS provided this prestatute definition of the term: It "was understood to refer to separate funds or accounts established and maintained by public charities to receive contributions from a single donor or a group of donors. The charities had ultimate authority over how the assets in each account were invested and distributed, but the donors, or individuals selected by the donors, were permitted to provide nonbinding recommendations regarding account distributions and/or investments" (Priv. Ltr. Rul. 201313034).

[394] IRC § 4966(d)(1).

[395] IRC § 4966(d)(2)(B). The IRS has the authority to exempt a fund or account from treatment as a donor-advised fund under certain circumstances (IRC § 4966(d)(2)(C)).

[396] IRC § 4966(c)(1). This is termed a *taxable distribution*. The expenditure responsibility rules are the subject of § 12.4(e).

[397] IRC § 4966(a)(1).

[398] This term embraces trustees, directors, officers, and executive employees of a sponsoring organization (IRC § 4966(d)(3)).

[399] IRC § 4966(a)(2). This tax is confined to $10,000 per transaction (IRC § 4966(b)(2)).

[400] IRC § 4966(b)(1).

[401] That is, organizations described in IRC § 170(b)(1)(A), other than a *disqualified supporting organization*, which is a Type III supporting organization (other than a functionally integrated one) and certain Type I and II supporting organizations (IRC § 4966(d)(4)). See § 12.3(c).

[402] IRC § 4966(c)(2).

[403] IRC § 4967(a)(1).

an incidental benefit on a donor, donor advisor, or related person, the manager is subject to an excise tax equal to 10 percent of the amount of the benefit.[404] These taxes are subject to a joint and several liability requirement.[405]

The private foundation excess business holdings rules[406] apply to donor-advised funds.[407] For this purpose, the term *disqualified person* means, with respect to a donor-advised fund, a donor, donor advisor, member of the family of either, or a 35 percent–controlled entity of any such person.[408]

Contributions to a sponsoring organization for maintenance in a donor-advised fund are not eligible for a charitable deduction for federal income tax purposes if the sponsoring organization is a fraternal society, a cemetery company, or a veterans' organization.[409] Contributions to a sponsoring organization for such maintenance are not eligible for a charitable deduction for federal estate or gift tax purposes if the sponsoring organization is a fraternal society or a veterans' organization.[410] Contributions to a sponsoring organization for such maintenance are not eligible for a charitable deduction for income, estate, or gift tax purposes if the sponsoring organization is a Type III supporting organization (other than a functionally integrated Type III supporting organization).[411] A donor must obtain, with respect to each charitable contribution to a sponsoring organization to be maintained in a donor-advised fund, a contemporaneous written acknowledgment from the sponsoring organization that the organization has exclusive legal control over the funds or assets contributed.[412]

The IRS and the Treasury Department are in the process of drafting regulations to accompany these statutory rules.[413]

---

[404] IRC § 4967(a)(2). The maximum amount of this tax per distribution is $10,000 (IRC § 4967(c) (2)). This tax and the tax referenced in *supra* note 403 may not be imposed if a tax with respect to the distribution has been imposed pursuant to the intermediate sanctions rules (IRC § 4967(b); see Chapter 21).

[405] IRC § 4967(c)(1). The Tax Technical Corrections Act of 2007 added references to the donor-advised funds excise taxes to the definition of *qualified first-tier taxes* (IRC § 4962) for purposes of tax abatement (Pub. L. No. 110-172, § 3(h), 121 Stat. 2473, 2475).

[406] See § 12.4(c).

[407] IRC § 4943(e)(1).

[408] IRC § 4943(e)(2). A supporting organization maintaining donor-advised funds received an IRS ruling holding that its ownership of certain nonvoting stock constitutes permitted holdings, and thus it did not have any excess business holdings, because all disqualified persons do not own more than 20 percent of the voting stock of the corporation (IRC § 4943(c)(2)) (Priv. Ltr. Rul. 201311035).

[409] IRC § 170(f)(18)(A)(i). See §§ 19.4, 19.6, and 19.11, respectively.

[410] IRC §§ 2055(e)(5)(A)(i), 2522(c)(5)(A)(i).

[411] IRC §§ 170(f)(18)(A)(ii), 2055(e)(5)(A)(ii), 2522(c)(5)(A)(ii).

[412] IRC §§ 170(f)(18)(B), 2055(e)(5)(B), 2522(c)(5)(B). This requirement is in addition to other charitable giving substantiation requirements (see *Charitable Giving*, Chapter 19).

Additional rules pertaining to donor-advised funds concern their applications for recognition of exemption, annual information returns (see § 28.2(b)(ix)), and applicability of the intermediate sanctions rules (see § 21.4(e)). A sponsoring organization must indicate in its application for recognition of exemption (see § 26.1) whether it maintains or intends to maintain donor-advised funds and how it plans to operate the funds (IRC § 508(f)).

[413] Department of the Treasury, 2024-2025 Priority Guidance Plan (Oct. 3, 2024); Notice 2017-73, 2017-51 I.R.B. 562. See *Private Foundations*, Chapter 16, and the supplements accompanying that book for a discussion of these proposed regulations.

§ 12.6   ENDOWMENT FUNDS

Interest in federal tax law issues surrounding endowment funds maintained by or for the benefit of public charities[414] (such as colleges, universities, hospitals, and museums) and certain other tax-exempt organizations, particularly social welfare organizations,[415] and associations and other business leagues,[416] is increasing.

(a)   Definition of *Endowment Fund*

An *endowment fund* is a form of investment fund; money and property (usually derived from contributions or the organization's existing resources) are placed in and invested by means of the fund, some or all of the income of which is used by the organization to satisfy costs of operations, cover capital expenditures, and/ or fund special projects or programs. These funds either are part of the exempt organization or are held in a separate organization, such as a supporting organization,[417] which is either controlled by or independent of the organization that is the beneficiary of the fund. An endowment fund is an exempt organization, either as a fund within an exempt organization[418] or as an exempt entity itself, contributions to which are deductible as charitable gifts.

(b)   College and University Endowment Tax

The federal tax law imposes an annual excise tax of 1.4 percent on the net investment income of each applicable educational institution and its related entities.[419] This tax is not applicable to income derived from assets that are used directly in carrying out exempt purposes.[420]

An *applicable educational institution* is a college, university, or school that had at least 500 tuition-paying students during the preceding tax year (where more than 50 percent of them are located in the United States), is a private institution, and had an aggregate fair market value of investment assets, and those of related entities, that is at least $500,000 per student.[421]

The number of students of an institution (including for purposes of determining the number of students at a particular location) is based on the daily average

---

[414] See § 12.3.

[415] See Chapter 13.

[416] See Chapter 14.

[417] See § 12.3(c).

[418] See § 26.15(b).

[419] IRC § 4968(a), added by the Tax Cuts and Jobs Act (Pub. L. No. 115-97, § 13701(a), 131 Stat. 2054, 2167–68 (2017); Reg. § 53.4968-1(a)). The concept of *net investment income* is similar to that used in the private foundation context (IRC § 4940(c)) (see *Private Foundations* § 10.4). Just as private foundations were accorded, in computing net investment income, a step-up in basis to 1969 values, the basis of property in determining gain under these rules was fixed as of December 31, 2017 (Notice 2018-55, 2018-26 I.R.B. 773). An educational organization that owes this tax must file Form 4720 to report the liability and pay the tax (see § 21.14).

[420] IRC § 4968(b)(1)(D); Reg. § 53.4968-1(b)(5).

[421] IRC § 4968(b)(1); Reg. § 53.4968-1(b)(1).

number of full-time students attending the institution (with part-time students taken into account on a full-time student equivalent basis).[422]

A *related organization* is, with respect to an educational institution, any organization that controls or is controlled by the institution, is controlled by one or more persons that also control the institution, is a supported organization[423] with respect to the institution, or is a supporting organization[424] with respect to the institution.[425]

The term *student* means an individual who is enrolled and attending a course for academic credit from the educational institution and who is being charged tuition at a rate that is commensurate with the tuition rate charged to students enrolled for a degree.[426] The standards for determining full-time and part-time students, full-time equivalents, and daily average are determined by each institution.[427] (This subjective definition of the term *student* may enable some institutions to sidestep this excise tax by reason of the $500,000-per-student ratio.) Federal, state, and local grants or financial aid are not considered *tuition*, but grants and scholarships provided by a nongovernmental party other than the educational institution are considered to be tuition.[428] A student is considered to be *located in the United States* on the basis of each institution's reasonable approach on the point, as long as the rule is consistently applied.[429]

Excluded from the tax base are certain intangible assets and nonfinancial assets used in a functionally related business.[430] An asset of a related organization that is treated as an asset of an educational institution and that is used directly in carrying out an educational institution's exempt purpose, or that is used directly in carrying out the exempt purpose of a related charitable organization, is considered used directly by the educational institution in carrying out its exempt purpose.[431]

Net investment income is determined using the law similar to that concerning the net investment income of private foundations.[432] *Gross investment income* includes most items of investment income,[433] but excludes interest income from student loans, certain royalties, and certain rental income from the provision of housing to students and faculty.[434] Capital loss carryovers may be used by educational institutions with more flexibility than private foundations.[435]

---

[422] IRC § 4968(b)(2).

[423] IRC § 509(f)(3).

[424] See § 12.3(c).

[425] IRC § 4968(d)(2); Reg. § 53.4968-3(a)(1).

[426] Reg. § 53.4968-1(b)(2).

[427] *Id.* The standards determined by the institution may not, however, be lower than the minimum applicable standards established by the Department of Education under the Higher Education Act of 1965 (20 U.S.C. 1088), as amended (Reg. § 53.4968-1(b)(2)).

[428] Reg. § 53.4968-1(b)(3).

[429] Reg. § 53.4968-1(b)(4).

[430] Reg. § 53.4968-1(b)(5); Reg. § 53.4968-2(b)(2)(iii).

[431] Reg. § 53.4968-1(b)(5)(iv).

[432] Reg. § 53.4968-2(a). See *supra* note 419.

[433] Reg. § 53.4968-2(b)(1).

[434] Reg. § 53.4968-2(b)(2).

[435] Reg. § 53.4968-2(d).

As noted, the assets and net investment income of a related organization with respect to an educational institution are generally treated as assets and net investment income of the institution. The term *related organization* means an organization that (1) controls the institution, (2) is controlled by the institution, (3) is controlled by one or more persons that also control the institution, (4) is a supported organization with respect to the institution, or (5) is a supporting organization with respect to the institution.[436]

The term *related organization* does not include a grantor charitable lead trust, a charitable remainder trust, or a decedent's estate.[437] Taxable corporations and certain taxable trusts are excluded from the definition of *related organization*.[438] Similarly excluded are partnerships, S corporations, and other pass-through entities a portion of the income of which flows through to an educational institution.[439]

An organization *controls* an educational institution if (1) the organization owns (by vote or value) more than 50 percent of the voting and nonvoting stock or membership interest of the institution or (2) the organization (or one or more of its managers) can (a) appoint or elect more than 50 percent of the members of the institution's governing body or otherwise has the ongoing power to appoint or elect more than 50 percent of the members with reasonable frequency, (b) require the institution to make an expenditure or prevent the institution from making an expenditure, or (c) require the institution to perform any act that significantly affects its operations or prevent it from performing an act.[440]

A tax-exempt corporation is *controlled by* an educational organization if the institution owns (by vote or value) more than 50 percent of the voting and nonvoting stock or membership interest of the corporation.[441] A trust is controlled by an educational institution only (1) if the educational institution is substantially the sole permissible trust beneficiary or appointee of both income and principal, (2) if the trust is a pooled income fund, (3) to the extent the assets of the trust were contributed to the trust by the institution or a controlled entity, or (4) to the extent the institution or a controlled entity has the right to demand or otherwise cause distribution of principal from the trust to the institution or controlled entity.[442]

A nonstock organization is controlled by an educational institution if the institution (or one or more of its managers) can (1) appoint or elect more than 50 percent of the members of the organization's governing body or otherwise appoint or elect that majority with reasonable frequency, (2) require the organization to make an expenditure or prevent it from making an expenditure, or (3) require the organization to perform any act that significantly affects its operations or prevent it from

---

[436] IRC § 4968(d)(2); Reg. § 53.4968-3(a)(1).

[437] Reg. § 53.4968-3(a)(2).

[438] *Id.*

[439] *Id.* These rules recognize that because some types of entities that might be related organizations may be taxed, then provide after-tax funds to an educational institution, taxation of these distributions again pursuant to this excise tax would lead to double taxation.

[440] Reg. § 53.4968-3(b)(1).

[441] Reg. § 53.4968-3(b)(2)(i).

[442] Reg. § 53.4968-3(b)(2)(ii)(A).

performing such an act.[443] Employee benefit funds are not related organizations for these purposes.[444]

An organization (other than an entity that is not a related one) is controlled by one or more persons who also control the educational institution if more than 50 percent of the members of the governing body of the other organization are directly or indirectly controlled by persons that comprise more than 50 percent of the members of the governing body of the institution.[445]

A related organization's assets and net investment income are generally taken into account, for purposes of calculation of the excise tax, in determining whether an institution is an *applicable educational institution* and in computing the net investment income of an educational institution. If an organization is a related organization with respect to an institution under more than one of these definitions, the rule that attributes the largest amount of assets and net investment income to the institution must be applied.[446]

There are three exceptions to this attribution rule, one being the above-referenced rule that assets that are used directly in carrying out the institution's exempt purpose are not part of the excise tax base. In determining the attributions, assets and net investment income of a related organization are not taken into account with respect to more than one educational institution; there is to be an allocation "in a reasonable manner" between or among the institutions.[447] Unless a related organization is controlled by the educational institution or is a supporting organization with respect to the institution, assets and net investment income of a related organization that are not intended or available for the use or benefit of the institution are not taken into account by the institution.[448]

(c) Form 990 Reporting

The annual information return[449] includes a section by which filing tax-exempt organizations report on their endowment funds.[450] An organization is required to report the beginning-of-the-year balance in its endowment fund, contributions to the fund during the reporting period, investment earnings or losses during the period, grants from the fund during the period, other expenditures for facilities and programs, administrative expenses during the period, and the end-of-the-year balance.

The filing organization is required to provide the estimated percentage of the year-end balances held as board-designated or quasi-endowment, permanent endowment, and/or term endowment. The organization must indicate whether there are endowment funds not in the possession of the organization that are held and administered for the organization by related or unrelated organizations. Also, the organization must describe the "intended uses" of its endowment fund(s).

---

[443] Reg. § 53.4968-3(b)(2)(iii).

[444] Reg. § 53.4968-3(a)(3).

[445] Reg. § 53.4968-3(b)(3).

[446] Reg. § 53.4968-3(d)(1).

[447] IRC § 4968(d)(1)(A); Reg. § 53.4968-3(d)(2)(i).

[448] IRC § 4968(d)(1)(B); Reg. § 4968-3(d)(2)(ii).

[449] See § 28.2(a)(i).

[450] Form 990, Schedule D, Part V.

CHAPTER THIRTEEN

Social Welfare Organizations

The federal tax law provides tax exemption for "[c]ivic leagues or organizations not organized for profit but operated exclusively for the promotion of social welfare."[1] An entity will not be exempt as a social welfare organization if any part of the net earnings of the entity inures to the benefit of any private shareholder or individual.[2] Thus, the private inurement doctrine is a statutory criterion for exemption for these types of organizations.[3]

§ 13.1 CONCEPT OF *SOCIAL WELFARE*

(a) General Rules

A precise definition of the term *social welfare* for federal law tax exemption purposes does not exist.[4] However, the regulations amplifying the law concerning this category of tax-exempt organizations offer two basic precepts: (1) "Social welfare" is commensurate with the "common good and general welfare" and "civic betterments and social improvements,"[5] and (2) the promotion of social welfare does not include activities that primarily constitute "carrying on a business with the general public in a manner similar to organizations which are operated for

---

[1] IRC § 501(c)(4)(A); Reg. § 1.501(c)(4)-1(a)(1). In certain circumstances, organizations that promote the social welfare may also qualify as *charitable* organizations (see Chapter 7). Thus, an organization providing fire, ambulance, and rescue services to a community could qualify as either type of organization (Rev. Rul. 74-361, 1974-2 C.B. 159). Similarly, a charitable organization that lessens the burdens of government (see § 7.7) may also qualify as a social welfare organization (Tech. Adv. Mem. 8923001).
[2] IRC § 501(c)(4)(B).
[3] See § 20.9.
[4] Gen. Couns. Mem. 39574.
[5] Reg. § 1.501(c)(4)-1(a)(2)(i).

profit."[6] The regulations also include a prohibition on political campaign activity[7] and state that an organization is not operated primarily for the promotion of social welfare "if its primary activity is operating a social club for the benefit, pleasure, or recreation of its members."[8] The conduct of social functions for the benefit of its members will not defeat social welfare status for an organization, however, where these activities are something less than primary,[9] or are otherwise incidental to a primary function.[10]

Like all tax-exempt organizations, the social welfare organization, to be operated *exclusively* for the promotion of social welfare, must be operated *primarily* for that purpose.[11] The key principle is that, to qualify as an exempt social welfare organization, the activities of the organization must be those that benefit a community, rather than merely benefit the organization's membership or other select group of individuals or organizations.[12]

Thus, an organization that restricted its membership to individuals of good moral character and health belonging to a particular ethnic group residing in a geographical area and that provided sick benefits to members and death benefits to their beneficiaries was ruled to not be exempt as a social welfare organization, inasmuch as it was essentially a mutual, self-interest type of organization.[13] Likewise, an individual practice association was denied categorization as an exempt social welfare organization because its primary beneficiaries were its member-physicians, in that it provided an available pool of physicians who abided by its fee schedule when rendering medical services to the subscribers of a health maintenance organization and provided its members with access to a large group of patients (the subscribers) who generally may not be referred to non–member-physicians.[14] Social welfare status was also denied to an accountable care organization[15] because its non-Medicare-related activities were found by a court to primarily benefit its commercial payor health care and provider patient participants rather than the public; only 18 percent of this organization's patient participants were Medicare beneficiaries, with the remaining 82 percent receiving health coverage from private payors.[16] Organizations that primarily engage in gaming activities cannot qualify as exempt social welfare entities.[17]

---

[6] Reg. § 1.501(c)(4)-1(a)(2)(ii).

[7] See § 23.6.

[8] Reg. § 1.501(c)(4)-1(a)(2)(ii). A separate category of tax exemption for social clubs (see Chapter 15) can encompass entities that do not qualify as social welfare organizations (e.g., Ye Mystic Krewe of Gasparilla v. Comm'r, 80 T.C. 755 (1983); Polish Am. Club v. Comm'r, 33 T.C.M. 925 (1974)).

[9] Rev. Rul. 66-179, 1966-1 C.B. 139; Rev. Rul. 63-190, 1963-2 C.B. 212.

[10] Rev. Rul. 74-361, 1974-2 C.B. 159. Also, Rev. Rul. 68-224, 1968-1 C.B. 262 (annual festival); Priv. Ltr. Rul. 9220010 (recreational activities).

[11] See § 4.4.

[12] Reg. § 1.501(c)(4)-1(a)(2)(i). See § 13.1(b).

[13] Rev. Rul. 75-199, 1975-1 C.B. 160, *modifying* Rev. Rul. 55-495, 1955-2 C.B. 259, and *amplified by* Rev. Rul. 81-58, 1981-1 CB 331.

[14] Rev. Rul. 86-98, 1986-2 C.B. 74.

[15] See § 7.6(m).

[16] Memorial Hermann Accountable Care Org. v. Comm'r, T.C. Memo. 2023-62.

[17] E.g., Priv. Ltr. Rul. 202015036.

As an additional example, a nonprofit organization, incorporated for the purpose of furnishing television reception to its members on a cooperative basis in an area not adaptable to ordinary reception, where the members contracted for services and the payment of installment fees, was deemed to not be a tax-exempt social welfare organization because it was "operate[d] for the benefit of its members rather than for the promotion of the welfare of mankind."[18] Yet a similar organization, which obtained memberships and contributions on a voluntary basis, was found to be an exempt social welfare organization, since it "operate[d] its system for the benefit of all television owners in the community."[19]

Similarly, because of the lack of sufficient benefit to the entire community, a trust to provide group life insurance only for members of an association was not considered a tax-exempt social welfare organization.[20] Likewise, a resort operated for a school's faculty and students was held to not be an exempt social welfare organization.[21] In the latter instance, a federal court of appeals wrote that the "exemption granted to social welfare organizations is made in recognition of the benefit which the public derives from their social welfare activities."[22] Conversely, a consumer credit counseling service that assisted families and individuals with financial problems was ruled to qualify as an exempt social welfare organization because its objectives and activities "contribute to the betterment of the community as a whole" by curbing the rising incidence of personal bankruptcy in the community.[23] Also, exempt social welfare status was accorded an organization that processed consumer complaints concerning products and services provided by businesses, met with the parties involved to encourage resolution of the problem, and recommended an appropriate solution, and (where the solution was not accepted) informed the parties about the administrative or judicial remedies available to resolve the dispute.[24] Likewise, an organization created to maintain a system for the storage and distribution of water to raise the underground water level in a community was ruled to be an exempt social welfare organization because of the benefits to those whose wells were thereby supplied.[25]

Organizations that operate in a manner inimical to principles of what constitutes the common good and the general welfare of the people in a community will not, of course, qualify as a tax-exempt social welfare organization. In part for that reason, the IRS denied tax exemption to an antiwar protest organization that urged demonstrators to commit violations of local ordinances and breaches of public order.[26] Said the IRS: "Illegal activities, which violate the minimum standards of

---

[18] Rev. Rul. 54-394, 1954-2 C.B. 131. Also, Rev. Rul. 55-716, 1955-2 C.B. 263, *modified by* Rev. Rul. 83-170, 1983-2 C.B. 97.

[19] Rev. Rul. 62-167, 1962-2 C.B. 142.

[20] New York State Ass'n of Real Estate Bds. Group Ins. Fund v. Comm'r, 54 T.C. 1325 (1970).

[21] People's Educ. Camp Soc'y, Inc. v. Comm'r, 331 F.2d 923 (2d Cir. 1964), *aff'g* 39 T.C. 756 (1963), *cert. denied*, 379 U.S. 839 (1964).

[22] *Id.* at 932.

[23] Rev. Rul. 65-299, 1965-2 C.B. 165. Cf. § 7.3.

[24] Rev. Rul. 78-50, 1978-1 C.B. 155.

[25] Rev. Rul. 66-148, 1966-1 C.B. 143.

[26] Rev. Rul. 75-384, 1975-2 C.B. 204.

acceptable conduct necessary to the preservation of an orderly society,. . .are not a permissible means of promoting social welfare."[27]

Other examples of tax-exempt social welfare organizations include an organization that provided a community with supervised facilities for the teaching of the safe handling and proper care of firearms,[28] encouraged industrial development to relieve unemployment in an economically depressed area,[29] helped to secure accident insurance for the students and employees in a school district,[30] provided bus transportation between a community and the major employment centers in a metropolitan area during rush hours when the regular bus service was inadequate,[31] conducted a community art show for the purpose of encouraging interest in painting, sculpture, and other art forms,[32] provided assistance to low-income farm families in a particular state,[33] conducted a free public radio forum for the dissemination of progressive social views,[34] maintained parking for visitors to a downtown business district,[35] provided low-cost rural electrification,[36] and established and maintained a roller-skating rink for residents of a particular county.[37] Junior chambers of commerce usually qualify as exempt social welfare organizations.[38]

Organizations formed to promote sports frequently are a type of nonprofit organization likely to gain status as tax-exempt social welfare organizations. A corporation formed to initiate programs designed to stimulate the interest of youth in organized sports, by furnishing youths virtually free admission and encouraging their attendance at sporting events, was considered an exempt social welfare organization because it provided "wholesome entertainment for the social improvement and welfare of the youths of the community."[39] Sports organizations can fall short of the requisite criteria in this regard, however, as illustrated by the fate of a nonprofit corporation that was organized to provide facilities for training individuals and horses for use in emergencies, and obtained recognition as an exempt social welfare organization, only to subsequently lose its exemption because it evolved into a commercial riding stable.[40] The court said that "the few persons eligible to use. . .[the organization's] facilities as members or on any basis other than by paying a regular commercial fee for such use causes. . .[the] operation (no matter how laudable) to be such as not to come within the meaning of 'social welfare.'"[41]

[27] Id.

[28] Rev. Rul. 66-273, 1966-2 C.B. 222.

[29] Rev. Rul. 67-294, 1967-2 C.B. 193.

[30] Rev. Rul. 61-153, 1961-2 C.B. 114. Cf. Rev. Rul. 66-354, 1966-2 C.B. 207.

[31] Rev. Rul. 78-69, 1978-1 C.B. 156. Cf. Rev. Rul. 78-68, 1978-1 C.B. 149; Rev. Rul. 55-311, 1955-1 C.B. 72.

[32] Rev. Rul. 78-131, 1978-1 C.B. 156. Cf. § 7.12.

[33] Scofield v. Rio Farms, Inc., 205 F.2d 68 (5th Cir. 1953).

[34] Debs Memorial Radio Fund, Inc. v. Comm'r, 148 F.2d 948 (2d Cir. 1945).

[35] Rev. Rul. 81-116, 1981-1 C.B. 333. Cf. Rev. Rul. 78-86, 1978-1 C.B. 151.

[36] United States v. Pickwick Elec. Membership Corp., 158 F.2d 272 (6th Cir. 1946).

[37] Rev. Rul. 67-109, 1967-1 C.B. 136.

[38] Rev. Rul. 65-195, 1965-2 C.B. 164.

[39] Rev. Rul. 68-118, 1968-1 C.B. 261. Also, Rev. Rul. 70-4, 1970-1 C.B. 126; Rev. Rul. 69-384, 1969-2 C.B. 122. As discussed in § 11.2, Congress amended IRC § 501(c)(3) to provide tax exemption for organizations whose primary purpose is to foster national or international sports competition.

[40] Los Angeles Cnty. Remount Ass'n v. Comm'r, 27 T.C.M. 1035 (1968).

[41] Id. at 1044. Also, Rev. Rul. 55-516, 1955-2 C.B. 260.

The IRS, from time to time, denies recognition of tax exemption of an organization as a social welfare organization and revokes the exempt status of a social welfare organization.[42]

(b) Benefits to Members

A related criterion of the tax-exempt social welfare organization is that it must not be operated primarily for the economic benefit or convenience of its members. As the IRS nicely summarized the law, the "concept of social welfare implies a service or program directed at benefiting the community as a whole, rather than a private group of individuals."[43]

Thus, a corporation that purchased and sold unimproved land, invested proceeds received from the sales, and distributed profits to members, was deemed to not be a tax-exempt social welfare organization.[44] Similarly, an organization formed to manage low- and moderate-income housing property for a fee was ruled to not qualify for exempt social welfare status.[45] Likewise, a federal court of appeals held that a consumer and producer membership cooperative that rebated a percentage of net income to members as patronage dividends made the disbursements "primarily to benefit the taxpayer's membership economically" and not exclusively for promotion of social welfare,[46] and that a membership corporation composed of buyers of ready-to-wear apparel and accessories was not an exempt social welfare organization, since its functions were largely social and many of its activities were designed to enable presently employed members to earn more money.[47] Subsequently, another federal court of appeals denied exempt social welfare status to a mutual assistance association established by a church in furtherance of its "mutual aid" practices, because its practices and policies were found to benefit only its members, rather than the requisite community.[48]

Similarly, an association of police officers primarily engaged in providing retirement benefits to members and death benefits to beneficiaries of members was held to not qualify for exemption as a social welfare organization because the primary benefits from the organization were limited to its members,[49] although the

---

[42] E.g., Priv. Ltr. Rul. 200531025.

[43] Priv. Ltr. Rul. 202105008, denying social welfare organization status to a nonprofit organization formed to provide business referrals to its members by means of networking.

[44] Rev. Rul. 69-385, 1969-2 C.B. 123. Using this rationale, the IRS denied recognition of exemption to an organization that had the primary activity of negotiating contracts with vendors, receiving rebates, and passing them on to its members (Priv. Ltr. Rul. 200742022). As the IRS stated in this ruling, an organization that "primarily benefits a private group of citizens cannot qualify for exemption."

[45] Rev. Rul. 70-535, 1970-2 C.B. 117. Also, Priv. Ltr. Rul. 202331004, denying social welfare organization status to an organization administering a pharmaceutical benefit program for its members for a fee.

[46] Consumer-Farmer Milk Coop. v. Comm'r, 186 F.2d 68, 71 (2d Cir. 1950), *aff'g* 13 T.C. 150 (1949), *cert. denied*, 341 U.S. 931 (1951).

[47] American Women Buyers Club, Inc. v. United States, 338 F.2d 526 (2d Cir. 1964).

[48] Mutual Aid Ass'n of the Church of the Brethren v. United States, 759 F.2d 792 (10th Cir. 1985), *aff'g* 578 F. Supp. 1451 (D. Kan. 1983). Also, American Ass'n of Christian Schools Voluntary Employees Beneficiary Ass'n Welfare Plan Trust v. United States, 850 F.2d 1510 (11th Cir. 1988), *aff'g* 663 F. Supp. 275 (M.D. Ala. 1987); El Paso Del Aguila Elderly v. Comm'r, 64 T.C.M. 376 (1992).

[49] Rev. Rul. 81-58, 1981-1 C.B. 331, *amplifying* Rev. Rul. 75-199, 1975-1 C.B. 160. Also, Police Benevolent Ass'n of Richmond, Va. v. United States, 661 F. Supp. 765 (E.D. Va. 1987).

exemption may be available where this type of an association is established and is maintained by, and where the benefits provided are funded primarily by, a government.[50] Likewise, an individual practice association providing health services through written agreements with health maintenance organizations was ruled to not qualify as an exempt social welfare organization because the primary beneficiaries were its member physicians,[51] an organization carrying on a business with the public was found to not qualify as an exempt social welfare entity because it was operated primarily for the benefit of its members,[52] and an organization providing assistance to those owning recreational residences in a natural forest had its exemption as a social welfare entity revoked because its activities were almost exclusively for the benefit of its membership.[53] An organization that received and contributed excess funds to the Social Security Administration from use-it-or-lose-it employee benefit plans, to be credited to employee accounts of specific employers, was denied recognition as a social welfare organization because it served the pecuniary interests of the select group of employees and employers participating in its program.[54] As still another illustration, it was held that, although an exempt social club was entitled to retain its exempt status, the club's operation of a beach club and parking lots was not substantially related to the promotion of community welfare because they are not open to the public.[55]

Many other types of membership service groups have been denied categorization as tax-exempt social welfare organizations, such as an automobile club,[56] an organization that operated a dining room and bar for the exclusive use of its members,[57] and a national sorority controlled by a business corporation that furnished the member chapters with supplies and services.[58]

In another instance, an organization formed to purchase groceries for its membership at the lowest possible prices on a cooperative basis was denied exempt social welfare status.[59] The rationale: "The organization. . .is a private cooperative enterprise [operated primarily] for the economic benefit or convenience of the members."[60] Similarly, the IRS denied recognition as an exempt social welfare entity to a cooperative organization providing home maintenance services to its members, even though payments for the services were made in kind.[61] In another instance, an organization whose membership was limited to persons who

---

[50] Rev. Rul. 87-126, 1987-2 C.B. 150.

[51] Rev. Rul. 86-98, 1986-2 C.B. 74.

[52] Santa Cruz Bldg. Ass'n v. United States, 411 F. Supp. 871 (D. Mo. 1976).

[53] Priv. Ltr. Rul. 201518018.

[54] Priv. Ltr. Rul. 202214013.

[55] Ocean Pines Ass'n, Inc. v. Comm'r, 135 T.C. 276 (2010), aff'd, 672 F.3d 284 (4th Cir. 2012).

[56] Smyth v. California State Automobile Ass'n, 175 F.2d 752 (9th Cir. 1949), cert. denied, 338 U.S. 905 (1949). Also, Automobile Club of St. Paul v. Comm'r, 12 T.C. 1152 (1949).

[57] Rev. Rul. 61-158, 1961-2 C.B. 115.

[58] Rev. Rul. 66-360, 1966-2 C.B. 228.

[59] Rev. Rul. 73-349, 1973-2 C.B. 179.

[60] Id.

[61] Rev. Rul. 78-132, 1978-1 C.B. 157. The IRS applied the rationale of this ruling to deny recognition as a social welfare organization to an organization that coordinated the employment and payment of its member baseball and softball umpires (Priv. Ltr. Rul. 202023008).

owned shares of public utility companies was ruled to not qualify as an exempt social welfare entity because it was operated to serve private interests, in that it promoted the interests of the public utility industry and its stockholders by preparing and filing statements concerning public utility matters pending before state and federal agencies and legislative bodies, and by publishing a newsletter about matters affecting the stockholders.[62] Likewise, an organization was denied recognition of exemption as a social welfare organization because its activities consisted of provision of maintenance services to its members, which were businesses owning lots in a commercial shopping property, in exchange for assessments.[63]

The rendering of services to members does not, however, necessarily work a denial or loss of tax-exempt social welfare status. For example, a memorial association formed to develop methods of achieving simplicity and dignity in funeral services and to maintain a registry for the wishes of its members in regard to funeral arrangements qualified for exemption as a social welfare organization,[64] as did an organization engaged in rehabilitation and job placement of its members.[65] Likewise, an organization that promoted the legal rights of all tenants in a particular community and occasionally initiated litigation to contest the validity of legislation adversely affecting tenants was held to qualify as an exempt social welfare organization because its activities were directed toward benefiting all tenants in the community.[66] By contrast, a tenants' rights group was denied exempt social welfare organization status because its activities were directed primarily toward benefiting only tenants who were its members.[67]

Also, qualification as a tax-exempt social welfare entity will not be precluded where an organization's services are equally available to members and nonmembers. As an illustration of this point, the IRS accorded exempt social welfare classification to an organization formed to prevent oil and other liquid spills in a city port area, and to contain and clean up any spills that occur.[68] Had the organization confined its repairs to property damaged by its members, this exemption would not have been available.[69]

Veterans' organizations may qualify as tax-exempt social welfare organizations;[70] however, the IRS has ruled to the contrary.[71] Organizations that have a membership of veterans may qualify as exempt social welfare groups,[72] although exemption is more likely to be available under a separate category of exemption

---

[62] Rev. Rul. 80-107, 1980-1 C.B. 117.

[63] Priv. Ltr. Rul. 201907013.

[64] Rev. Rul. 64-313, 1964-2 C.B. 146.

[65] Rev. Rul. 57-297, 1957-2 C.B. 307.

[66] Rev. Rul. 80-206, 1980-2 C.B. 185.

[67] Rev. Rul. 73-306, 1973-2 C.B. 179. This organization would not have qualified as a charitable organization under IRC § 501(c)(3) either (e.g., Priv. Ltr. Rul. 202245009).

[68] Rev. Rul. 79-316, 1979-2 C.B. 228.

[69] Contracting Plumbers Coop. Restoration Corp. v. United States, 488 F.2d 684 (2d Cir. 1973), *cert. denied*, 419 U.S. 827 (1974).

[70] Rev. Rul. 66-150, 1966-1 C.B. 147. Cf. Rev. Rul. 58-117, 1958-2 C.B. 196.

[71] Rev. Rul. 68-46, 1968-1 C.B. 260. Also, Veterans Found. v. United States, 281 F.2d 912 (10th Cir. 1960).

[72] Rev. Rul. 68-455, 1968-2 C.B. 215; Rev. Rul. 68-45, 1968-1 C.B. 259; Rev. Rul. 55-156, 1955-1 C.B. 292; Polish Army Veterans Post 147 v. Comm'r, 236 F.2d 509 (3d Cir. 1956), *vacating and remanding* 24 T.C. 891 (1956).

enacted for the benefit of veterans' groups.[73] The IRS, from time to time, reviews the status of a veterans' organization and concludes that the entity cannot qualify for this category of exemption.[74] A subsidiary organization must establish exempt status on its own rather than on the basis of the functions of the parent veterans' organization.[75]

§ 13.2 REQUIREMENT OF *COMMUNITY*

As discussed, a social welfare organization may not—if it is to qualify for tax exemption—operate for the benefit of a select group of individuals but must be engaged in the promotion of the common good and general welfare of those in a *community*.[76]

Thus, an organization operating a vision care plan by contracting with subscribers was held to not qualify for tax-exempt status as a social welfare organization, in part because the membership-based structure caused the entity to not serve the requisite community.[77] Likewise, an organization claiming to be an agency providing home health care services to residents of five facilities in various locations was found by the IRS to be merely a registry, matching the needs of residents with independent service providers for a fee; the organization was denied recognition of exemption as a social welfare entity primarily because it did not serve the requisite community.[78] An organization established for the purpose of developing and distributing dental benefit products was denied recognition of exemption as a social welfare organization, in part because it was not promoting the welfare of a community.[79]

(a) Homeowners' Associations

The IRS has struggled with the concept of *community* in relation to the advent of homeowners' associations, other community associations, and condominium associations. A homeowners' association, for example, typically maintains common

---

[73] IRC § 501(c)(19). See § 19.11(a).

[74] E.g., Tech. Adv. Mem. 199912033.

[75] Rev. Rul. 66-150, 1966-1 C.B. 147.

[76] Reg. § 1.501(c)(4)-1(a)(2)(i). Also, Rev. Rul. 76-147, 1976-1 C.B. 151; Erie Endowment v. United States, 316 F.2d 151 (3d Cir. 1963).

A court held that a vacation home for "working girls and women of proper character" served a "broad community need" because, when "one segment or slice" of the community is served, the "community as a whole benefits" (Eden Hall Farm v. United States, 389 F. Supp. 858 (W.D. Pa. 1975)); not surprisingly, the IRS does not follow this decision (Rev. Rul. 80-205, 1980-2 C.B. 184).

[77] Vision Service Plan v. United States, 2006-1 U.S.T.C. ¶ 50,173 (E.D. Cal. 2005)), *aff'd*, 2008-1 U.S.T.C. ¶ 50,173 (9th Cir. 2008), *cert. denied*, 555 U.S. 1097 (2009). A court thereafter held, in the context of multi-district litigation, that a subsidiary of this organization (there were six) was collaterally estopped from asserting entitlement to exemption because of the prior litigation (*In re* Vision Service Plan Tax Litigation, 2010-1 U.S.T.C. ¶ 50,486 (S.D. Ohio 2010)).

[78] Priv. Ltr. Rul. 200544020.

[79] Priv. Ltr. Rul. 201351024. Tax exemption was also denied in this instance on a private benefit rationale because these products were being developed for for-profit companies.

areas for the use of all residents; enforces covenants for preservation of the architecture and general appearance of the development; and participates in the formulation of public policies impacting the development, such as road expansion, land development, and encroachment of commercial enterprises. In this latter capacity, an association of this nature is functioning much like a conventional civic league.[80]

The IRS ruled that an association performing the first two of these functions is exempt from federal income tax as a social welfare organization.[81] The association was found to be "serving the common good and the general welfare of the people of the entire development," with the IRS noting that a "neighborhood, precinct, subdivision, or housing development" may constitute the requisite community.[82] Even though the association was established by the developer and its existence may have aided the developer in selling housing units, any benefit to the developer was dismissed as incidental. Also deemed incidental were the benefits that accrued to the individual members, such as the preservation and protection of property values.[83]

Following issuance of this ruling in 1972, the IRS concluded that its "increasing experience" with homeowners' associations demonstrated that the ruling was being misconstrued as to its scope. Consequently, in 1974, the IRS issued a "clarifying" ruling.[84] The IRS said that homeowners' associations, as described in the 1972 ruling, are *prima facie* presumed to be essentially and primarily formed and operated for the benefit of the individual members and, accordingly, to not be tax-exempt.[85] Subsequently, however, the IRS ruled that an organization with membership limited to the residents and business operators within a city block and formed to preserve and beautify the public areas in the block, thereby benefiting the community as a whole as well as enhancing the members' property rights, may qualify as an exempt social welfare entity.[86] Moreover, a membership organization formed to help preserve, beautify, and maintain a public park was ruled to qualify as an exempt charitable organization.[87]

The position of the IRS as to the definition of the word *community*, as stated in this 1974 ruling, is that the term has "traditionally been construed as having reference to a geographical unit bearing a reasonably recognizable relationship to an area ordinarily identified as a governmental subdivision or a unit or district thereof."[88] Thus, the IRS held that a community is "not simply an aggregation of homeowners bound together in a structured unit formed as an integral part of a plan for the development of a real estate subdivision and the sale and purchase of homes therein."[89]

---

[80] Rev. Rul. 67-6, 1967-1 C.B. 135, *modified by* Rev. Rul. 76-147, 1976-1 C.B. 151.

[81] Rev. Rul. 72-102, 1972-1 C.B. 149, *modified by* Rev. Rul. 74-99, 1974-1 C.B. 131.

[82] Rev. Rul. 72-102, 1972-1 C.B. 149.

[83] Cf. Rev. Rul. 69-280, 1969-1 C.B. 152.

[84] Rev. Rul. 74-99, 1974-1 C.B. 131.

[85] This position of the IRS is reflected in a ruling concerning an organization that excluded the public from a development by means of a security gate (Priv. Ltr. Rul. 200706014).

[86] Rev. Rul. 75-286, 1975-2 C.B. 210. Cf. Rev. Rul. 68-14, 1968-1 C.B. 243.

[87] Rev. Rul. 78-85, 1978-1 C.B. 150.

[88] Rev. Rul. 74-99, 1974-1 C.B. 131.

[89] *Id.*

The IRS, in this 1974 ruling, also held that, where the association's activities include those directed to exterior maintenance of private residences, the above *prima facie* presumption is reinforced. Moreover, the 1974 ruling stated that, as far as ownership and maintenance of common areas are concerned, the IRS's approval is extended only to those areas "traditionally recognized and accepted as being of direct governmental concern in the exercise of the powers and duties entrusted to governments to regulate community health, safety, and welfare."[90] That is, the IRS's "approval" was extended only to ownership and maintenance by a homeowners' association of areas such as "roadways and parklands, sidewalks and street lights, access to, or the use and enjoyment of which is extended to members of the general public, as distinguished from controlled use or access restricted to the members of the homeowners' association."[91]

Thereafter, the IRS somewhat moderated its position in these regards by stating that whether a homeowners' association meets the requirements of conferring benefit on a community must be determined according to the facts and circumstances of each case. The agency continues to insist, however, that exemption as a social welfare organization is not available to a homeowners' association (that does not represent a community) if it restricts the use of its facilities (such as parking and recreational facilities) to its members.[92] This position of the IRS is generally being accepted by the courts.[93] Nonetheless, a federal district court rejected some of the positions of the IRS concerning the eligibility of homeowners' associations for tax-exempt status as social welfare organizations, holding that the association in the case represented a development that is an "independent community" (with 3,000 members and 6,100 acres of land), so that its benefits were provided to persons within the requisite community.[94] The court stated: "Thus, only where an association represents less than the entire community is it a concern whether the benefits of the association are made available to the general public, because in that situation the benefits which are restricted to association members are not benefiting the community as a whole."[95]

As noted, another court was in agreement with the IRS position in these regards, holding that an association of homeowners, which owned, controlled, leased, and sold real estate and built, maintained, and operated recreational facilities for the pleasure and convenience of its members, did not qualify as a tax-exempt social welfare organization.[96] Holding that a "private association of homeowners which restricts its facilities to the exclusive use of its members" cannot be exempt, the court observed that in other court holdings to the contrary there was "availability of taxpayer's facilities to the general public."[97]

---

[90] *Id.*
[91] *Id.*
[92] Rev. Rul. 80-63, 1980-1 C.B. 116, *clarifying* Rev. Rul. 74-99, 1974-1 C.B. 131.
[93] E.g., Flat Top Lake Ass'n, Inc. v. United States, 86-2 U.S.T.C. ¶ 9756 (S.D. W. Va. 1986), *rev'd*, 89-1 U.S.T.C. ¶ 9180 (4th Cir. 1989); Lake Petersburg Ass'n v. Comm'r, 33 T.C.M. 259 (1974).
[94] Rancho Santa Fe Ass'n v. United States, 84-2 U.S.T.C. ¶ 9536 (S.D. Cal. 1984).
[95] *Id.* at 84,530.
[96] Flat Top Lake Ass'n, Inc. v. United States, 86-2 U.S.T.C. ¶ 9756 (S.D. W. Va. 1986), *rev'd*, 89-1 U.S.T.C. ¶ 9180 (4th Cir. 1989).
[97] *Id.* at 85,865. Cf. Columbia Park & Recreation Assn, Inc. v. Comm'r, 88 T.C. 1 (1987).

The position of the IRS is that condominium management corporations do not qualify as tax-exempt social welfare organizations inasmuch as the organizations' activities are for the private benefit of the members.[98] The IRS's rationale underlying this position is of two parts. First, the IRS ruled that, because of the essential nature and structure of the condominium system of ownership, the rights, duties, privileges, and immunities of the members are "inextricably and compulsorily tied to the owner's acquisition and enjoyment of his property in the condominium."[99] Second, the IRS noted that "condominium ownership necessarily involves ownership in common by all condominium unit owners of a great many so-called common areas, the maintenance and care of which necessarily constitutes the provision of private benefits for the unit owners."[100]

The IRS traces its position as to condominium management organizations to a 1962 federal court of appeals opinion.[101] In 1965, the IRS ruled that a cooperative organization operating and maintaining a housing development and providing housing facilities did not qualify as an exempt social welfare organization.[102] Again, in 1969, the IRS ruled that a nonprofit organization formed to provide maintenance of exterior walls and roofs of members' homes in a development was not exempt as a social welfare entity.[103]

A homeowners' association or condominium management organization may, if attempts to qualify as a tax-exempt social welfare organization fail, qualify as an exempt social club.[104] That is, an organization may have as its primary purpose the establishment and operation of social facilities, such as a swimming pool, for the benefit of the homeowners in a community.[105]

Also, a tax-exempt homeowners' association may establish a separate but affiliated organization to own and maintain recreational facilities and restrict their use to members of the association, as long as the organization is operated totally separate from the association.[106]

Congress, in 1976, brought some clarification of the tax law concerning homeowners' associations.[107] This provision provides an elective tax exemption for condominium management and residential real estate management associations.[108]

The IRS from time to time denies recognition of social welfare organization status to, or revokes the exempt status of, homeowners', condominium management, and residential real estate management associations, along with other

---

[98] Rev. Rul. 74-17, 1974-1 C.B. 130. Cf. Rev. Rul. 70-604, 1970-2 C.B. 9.

[99] Rev. Rul. 74-17, 1974-1 C.B. 130.

[100] *Id.*

[101] See *infra* note 110.

[102] Rev. Rul. 65-201, 1965-2 C.B. 170.

[103] Rev. Rul. 69-280, 1969-1 C.B. 152. Cf. Rev. Rul. 74-563, 1974-2 C.B. 38. Also, Eckstein v. United States, 452 F.2d 1036 (Ct. Cl. 1971). A mobile home park is not a *community* for this purpose (Priv. Ltr. Rul. 201014068).

[104] See Chapter 15.

[105] Rev. Rul. 69-281, 1969-1 C.B. 155. Cf. Rev. Rul. 75-494, 1975-2 C.B. 214.

[106] Rev. Rul. 80-63, 1980-1 C.B. 116.

[107] IRC § 528.

[108] See § 19.14.

organizations similarly restricting their services or facilities to a limited group of property owners.[109]

(b) Broader Requirement of *Community*

The IRS subsequently adopted a far more expansive view of the concept of a *community* in this context, equating it essentially to the entirety of the nation's public. This position largely rested on a federal court of appeals decision issued in 1962.[110] The court rejected the claim that a nonprofit organization operated to provide low-cost housing for veterans was a tax-exempt social welfare entity, portraying it as merely an "economic and private cooperative undertaking."[111] This appellate court wrote that an exempt social welfare organization must "offer a service or program for the direct betterment or improvement of the community as a whole"; these organizations must, added the court, function on a "community basis."[112] The IRS's lawyers characterized this opinion as meaning that *social welfare* is the "well-being of persons of a community" and that the "benefits provided by a social welfare organization must be municipal or public."[113] The IRS also relies on an appellate court decision rendered in 1964.[114] In this case, the court characterized the promotion of social welfare as involving the serving of "purposes beneficial to the community as a whole" or the promotion of the "welfare of mankind."[115] The IRS ruled that a state-approved discharge cleanup organization that worked to prevent oil spills and had pollution-control programs was a tax-exempt social welfare organization.[116] Certain members of the organization could meet part of the state's licensing requirements for their facilities. The IRS concluded that, by cleaning up spills of members and nonmembers, however, the organization acted to prevent deterioration of a port community and not merely to prevent damage to its members' facilities. The agency thus ruled that this organization was primarily engaged in activities designed to benefit all inhabitants of the community served by it.[117] In reliance on this ruling, the IRS held that an organization that promoted uniform codes and otherwise provided programs concerning hazardous situations supported the "public sector" and generally worked to "ensure the public safety," and therefore qualified as an exempt social welfare organization because it benefited the "community as a whole."[118] By contrast, the IRS ruled that an entity could not qualify as an exempt social welfare organization inasmuch as its sole function was maintenance of a private road that was essentially a common driveway for its four members' homes.[119]

---

[109] E.g., Priv. Ltr. Rul. 202344018.
[110] Comm'r v. Lake Forest, Inc., 305 F.2d 814 (4th Cir. 1962), *rev'g and remanding* 36 T.C. 510 (1962).
[111] *Id*. at 820.
[112] *Id*. at 818.
[113] Tech. Adv. Mem. 200829029.
[114] People's Educ. Camp Soc'y, Inc. v. Comm'r, 331 F.2d 923 (2d Cir. 1964), *aff'g* 39 T.C. 756 (1963), *cert. denied*, 379 U.S. 839 (1964).
[115] *Id*. at 933.
[116] Rev. Rul. 79-316, 1979-2 C.B. 228.
[117] In this instance, the community involved was a discrete local community, rather than the public.
[118] Tech. Adv. Mem. 200829029.
[119] Priv. Ltr. Rul. 201623013.

§ 13.3 CONDUCT OF BUSINESS

As noted, the promotion of social welfare does not include activities that primarily constitute "carrying on a business with the general public in a manner similar to organizations which are operated for profit."[120] In the charitable organization setting, the IRS generally equates the charging of fees with the conduct of unwarranted business.[121] This concept also is being imported into the law of tax-exempt social welfare organizations. For example, the IRS denied recognition of exemption to a nonprofit credit counseling organization seeking exempt social welfare status, in part because it was engaging in business with the public because it charged fees for its services.[122] Likewise, the IRS decided that a nonprofit dog rescue organization did not qualify as an exempt social welfare organization because it charged a fee for receiving dogs; dogs had to have recent veterinary records as to vaccinations, spay/neuter, and heartworm test results; the organization was selective as to the breed of dogs taken in; and there was no waiver or reduction of fees based on income or need for the surrender and adoption of dogs.[123]

An organization was formed to operate a "holistic medicine establishment" selling medicinal marijuana products to patients with prescriptions from licensed physicians; it conducted a storefront business, being licensed by the state as a retailer of recreational-use cannabis. The IRS denied recognition of exemption as a social welfare organization to this entity, on the ground that its primary activity was carrying on a business with the public in a manner similar to for-profit organizations.[124] The IRS applied the commerciality doctrine[125] in reaching this conclusion, finding that the organization "use[s] promotional policies to enhance sales," "advertises goods and services," sets margins at a level that "enables [it] to replace merchandise inventory," and "maintain[s] a retail outlet with hours of operation that are competitive with other retail establishments." Notably, the IRS did not deploy the arguments that it uses in the charitable setting: namely, that the activity is illegal under federal law and is contrary to federal public policy.[126]

§ 13.4 ADVOCACY ORGANIZATIONS

As noted at the outset, the contemporary tax-exempt social welfare organization often is an advocacy organization. The term *advocacy* in this context is used to

---

[120] Reg. § 1.501(c)(4)-1(a)(2)(ii). E.g., Industrial Addition Ass'n v. Comm'r, 149 F.2d 294 (6th Cir. 1945); Club Gaona, Inc. v. United States, 167 F. Supp. 741 (S.D. Cal. 1958); Harvey v. Campbell, 107 F. Supp. 757 (N.D. Tex. 1952); Interneighborhood Housing Corp. v. Comm'r, 45 T.C.M. 115 (1982).

[121] See, e.g., §§ 6.3(h), 24.2(e).

[122] Priv. Ltr. Rul. 201325016. This, however, is not the law. If it were, there would not be any exempt schools, colleges, universities, hospitals, associations, clubs, theaters, symphony orchestras, opera companies, and the like. Also, the statutory rules for exempt credit counseling organizations provide that they can charge reasonable fees (IRC § 501(q)(1)(C)). See § 7.3(b), text accompanied by note 82.

[123] Priv. Ltr. Rul. 201749020.

[124] Priv. Ltr. Rul. 201941028.

[125] See § 4.9(g).

[126] See §§ 6.2(a), 6.3(i).

embrace attempts to influence legislation and involvement in political campaign activities. Thus, a social welfare organization can be what a charitable organization may not be—an *action organization*.[127]

(a) Legislative Activities

In general, a tax-exempt social welfare organization is permitted to engage in unlimited legislative activity, as long as the primary purpose[128] for these activities is achievement of the organization's exempt purposes.[129]

(b) Political Campaign Activities

A tax-exempt social welfare organization can engage in political campaign activity without jeopardizing its exemption, as long as this type of activity is not its primary purpose or function.[130]

---

[127] See §§ 4.5(d), 22.5.
[128] See § 4.4.
[129] See § 22.5.
[130] See § 23.6.

CHAPTER FOURTEEN

Business Leagues and Similar Organizations

Federal income tax exemption is provided for "[b]usiness leagues. . .not organized for profit and no part of the net earnings of which inures to the benefit of any private shareholder or individual."[1] Exemption is also available for chambers of commerce, boards of trade, real estate boards, and professional sports leagues.[2]

§ 14.1 CONCEPT OF *BUSINESS LEAGUE*

The term *business league* is rather antiquated; at best, the word *league* suggests an association of persons united by common interests or for the achievement

---

[1] IRC § 501(c)(6). The second component of this provision is a recitation of the doctrine of private inurement (see § 20.10).
[2] See §§ 14.3, 14.4, 14.5, 19.21, respectively.

of common ends. Synonyms include *alliance, association, coalition, federation,* and *network*; from a historical standpoint, another synonym is *guild.*

As the Supreme Court observed, the phrase *business league* "has no well-defined meaning or common usage outside the perimeters" of the federal tax law.[3] An appellate court wrote that these two words do not have a "special significance."[4] On another occasion, the Supreme Court wrote that *business league* is a term "so general. . .as to render an interpretive regulation appropriate."[5]

(a) General Principles

A court held that a business league is an association of persons having some common business interest; it quickly added, nonetheless, that "[a]ll business leagues are not exempt."[6] Those that are tax-exempt have six discrete characteristics.[7]

(i) Tax Law Characteristics. A tax-exempt business league is an association of persons having some common business interest, the purpose of which is to promote that common interest and not to engage in a regular business of a kind ordinarily carried on for profit. Its activities must be directed to the improvement of business conditions of one or more lines of business, as distinguished from the performance of particular services for individual persons. An organization whose purpose is to engage in a regular business of a kind ordinarily carried on for profit, even though the business is conducted on a cooperative basis or produces only sufficient income to be self-sustaining, cannot be an exempt business league.[8]

This definition of a tax-exempt business league, "[h]aving been left undisturbed despite numerous reenactments" of the exemption provision, "is deemed to have been given the imprimatur of Congress and is thus entitled to the effect of law."[9] A parsing of this definition shows that a business league, to be exempt, must be (1) an association of persons having a common business interest; (2) the purpose of which is to promote that common business interest; (3) that is not organized for profit; (4) that does not engage (other than incidentally) in a business ordinarily conducted for profit;[10] (5) the activities of which are directed to the improvement of business conditions of one or more lines of business, as distinguished from the

---

[3] Nat'l Muffler Dealers Ass'n, Inc. v. United States, 440 U.S. 472, 476 (1979).

[4] Retailers Credit Ass'n of Alameda Cnty. v. Comm'r, 90 F.2d 47, 50 (9th Cir. 1937).

[5] Helvering v. Reynolds Co., 306 U.S. 110, 114 (1939).

[6] Retailers Credit Ass'n of Alameda Cnty. v. Comm'r, 90 F.2d 47, 50 (9th Cir. 1937).

[7] An illustration of an organization that did not meet any of these criteria (other than being a nonprofit entity) appears in ABA Retirement Funds v. United States, 2013-1 U.S.T.C. ¶ 50,306 (N.D. Ill. 2013), *aff'd,* 759 F.3d 718 (7th Cir. 2014). Occasionally, a tax-exempt organization, such as a charitable entity, will have its operations evolve from activities originally established into those of an exempt business league (e.g., Priv. Ltr. Rul. 201907011).

[8] Reg. § 1.501(c)(6)-1.

[9] Engineers Club of San Francisco v. United States, 791 F.2d 686, 689 (9th Cir. 1986). Also, United States v. Oklahoma City Retailers Ass'n of Alameda Cnty., 331 F.2d 328 (10th Cir. 1964).

[10] Although the tax regulation is absolute on the point, it has been held that a business undertaken by a business league will not lead to revocation of its exemption if the activity is "merely incidental" to the organization's main purposes (e.g., Retailers Credit Ass'n of Alameda Cnty. v. Comm'r, 90 F.2d 47, 51 (9th Cir. 1937)).

performance of particular services for individual persons; and (6) that is of the same general class as a chamber of commerce, board of trade, or the like.[11]

To be exempt as a business league, an organization must meet all six of these criteria. For example, an entity that satisfied only the first four of these elements was held to not be entitled to tax exemption as a business league.[12] If, however, an otherwise disqualifying activity is merely incidental or subordinate to an entity's principal purpose, exemption as a business league will not be defeated.[13]

The IRS is discouraging use of small boards, in the case of public charities, by portraying the practice as an inherent form of private benefit.[14] The agency has made an attempt to import that proposition into the law concerning tax exemption for business leagues, ruling that an organization did not qualify as an exempt business league, in part because the organization had a self-perpetuating board; in that instance, the IRS lamented the absence of "oversight of an independent board."[15] Nonetheless, among the federal tax law criteria for exempt business leagues, there is no requirement of an independent board.

Even though it is almost always essential to qualification as a tax-exempt business league that the organization be an association of persons having a common business interest, the persons do not necessarily have to be engaged in a business at the time they are acting in association. As an illustration of this point, an organization of persons studying for a degree in a particular profession can qualify as an exempt business league if the purpose of the organization is to promote their common business interests as future members of that profession.[16] Also, an exempt association will not jeopardize its business league status if it characterizes as nonvoting associate members those persons who are merely sponsors of the organization and lack a common business interest with the regular members.[17]

(ii) Members.   The typical tax-exempt business league has a membership; this element is reflected in the above six-part definition that references "an association of persons." The IRS is likely to deny recognition of exemption as a business league where the entity does not have a membership.[18] Usually this membership comprises individuals, for-profit businesses, or both. An exempt business league may,

---

[11] E.g., Credit Union Ins. Corp. v. United States, 896 F. Supp. 1166 (D. Md. 1995), *aff'd*, 86 F.3d 1326 (4th Cir. 1996).

[12] Engineers Club of San Francisco v. United States, 791 F.2d 686 (9th Cir. 1986).

[13] E.g., Comm'r v. Chicago Graphic Arts Fed'n, Inc., 128 F.2d 424 (7th Cir. 1942); Retailers Credit Ass'n of Alameda Cnty. v. Comm'r, 90 F.2d 47 (9th Cir. 1937).

[14] See § 5.7(c).

[15] Priv. Ltr. Rul. 201349021.

[16] Rev. Rul. 77-112, 1977-1 C.B. 149.

[17] In one instance, the requirement that there be an *association of persons* was deemed met solely because the organization was created by three incorporators and had a board of directors (North Carolina Ass'n of Ins. Agents, Inc. v. United States, 83-2 U.S.T.C. ¶ 9445 (E.D.N.C. 1983)), although that decision was reversed (739 F.2d 949 (4th Cir. 1984)).

[18] E.g., Priv. Ltr. Rul. 201222050. On another occasion, the IRS wrote that an exempt business league "must be a membership organization and have a meaningful extent of membership support" (Priv. Ltr. Rul. 201242016). Thereafter, the IRS denied recognition of exemption as a business league, in part because the organization did not have a voting membership, it had a self-perpetuating board, and its members were not involved in its operations "at a meaningful level" (Priv. Ltr. Rul. 201349021).

however, have exempt organizations as members, even where there are only two entities as members. For example, the IRS held that a trust created by an exempt labor union and an exempt business league qualified as an exempt business league.[19] Likewise, a trust created pursuant to collective bargaining agreements between an exempt labor union and several exempt business leagues was ruled to be exempt as a business league.[20]

There can be situations, however, where an exempt business league does not have members. For example, an association of individuals that is exempt as a charitable organization and that wants a certification program should place the program in a separate entity, which would be a business league. This type of business league can gain tax-exempt status, even though it lacks a membership. Of course, for this purpose, the membership of the association may be imputed to the business league.[21]

(iii) Dues. Inherent in the concept of a membership organization is the expectation that the organization is primarily supported by dues, although this requirement is not among the formal elements of the definition of a business league. Nonetheless, the IRS has observed that an exempt business league must be "financed, at least in part, through membership dues."[22] The agency, notwithstanding the absence of the point in the tax regulations, wrote that an organization "which is not in fact membership supported lacks the most significant characteristics common to" exempt business leagues. An organization that has "demonstrated a pattern of nonmembership support must necessarily fail a critical test of exemption" for business leagues, the IRS added. Nonetheless, the IRS, in contemplating the exempt status of a membership organization, nearly all of the revenue of which was certification fees, concluded that the certification function was a substantially related activity and that this revenue was "therefore considered to be membership support."[23]

An exempt business league is not required to promote the betterment of general commercial welfare.[24]

(b) Meaning of *Business*

The term *business* is broadly construed and includes nearly every activity carried on for the production of income.[25] In this context, distinctions between trades, businesses, and professions are not, as such, observed. Thus, the fact that the membership

---

[19] Rev. Rul. 70-31, 1970-1 C.B. 130.

[20] Rev. Rul. 82-138, 1982-2 C.B. 106.

[21] Thus, the IRS overstated the point when it wrote: "Without members, an organization cannot be an association of persons having a common business interest and must fail as a business league" (Priv. Ltr. Rul. 201024066).

[22] Tech. Adv. Mem. 200020056. As to certification programs, see § 14.1(g). In one instance, the IRS ruled that grants from one exempt trade association to another to fund legislative and regulatory activities formerly conducted by the transferor would not affect either organization's IRC § 501(c)(6) status; it was expected that in its early years the grantee organization would not be able to receive sufficient dues income to fund the conduct of its legislative and regulatory activities (Priv. Ltr. Rul. 9517036).

[23] Id.

[24] Rev. Rul. 59-391, 1959-2 C.B. 151.

[25] See § 24.2(a).

of an organization is composed of individuals from different professions does not preclude tax exemption as a business league, as long as the members all have a common business interest in a field.[26] The membership of an exempt business league may be individuals and/or other persons. Thus, an association of nonprofit consumer cooperatives that promoted the cooperative method of doing business was ruled to be an exempt business league,[27] as was an organization of individuals who advanced their spouses' profession.[28] The IRS concluded that an association that promoted a certain philosophy as to the conduct of business was an exempt business league, writing that "[u]pholding the integrity of a particular industry/profession is an activity properly engaged in by" exempt business leagues.[29]

Of course, if a group of persons is not engaged in a business at all, exemption in this context is not available, such as an association of motorists[30] and an association of dog owners most of whom were not in the business of raising dogs.[31] Thus, organizations that promote the common interests of hobbyists do not qualify as exempt business leagues.[32]

At a minimum, to qualify as an exempt business league, an organization must have some substantive program directed to the improvement of business conditions; for example, the mere provision of bar and luncheon facilities is insufficient.[33]

(c) Line-of-Business Requirement

The fundamental requirement for operation as a tax-exempt business league is that the organization engage in activities that are directed to the improvement of business conditions of one or more lines of business.

(i) Concept of Line of Business.   A *line of business* is a trade, business (industry), or profession, or a segment of a trade, business, or profession. The IRS defines the phrase as a "trade or occupation, entry into which is not restricted by a patent, trademark, or similar device which would allow private parties to restrict the right to engage in the business."[34] A critical component of the line of business is that it is composed of competitors within a trade, industry, or profession. Thus, tax exemption as a business league has been denied for lack of a sufficient common business interest in situations involving an organization of individuals engaged in different trades or professions not in competition who exchanged business information.[35]

(ii) Supreme Court Pronouncement.   This line-of-business requirement was upheld by the Supreme Court as being consistent with the intent of Congress in

---

[26] Rev. Rul. 70-641, 1970-2 C.B. 119.
[27] Rev. Rul. 67-264, 1967-2 C.B. 196.
[28] Rev. Rul. 67-343, 1967-2 C.B. 198.
[29] Priv. Ltr. Rul. 200223067.
[30] American Automobile Ass'n v. Comm'r, 19 T.C. 1146 (1953).
[31] American Kennel Club v. Hoey, 148 F.2d 920 (2d Cir. 1945).
[32] Rev. Rul. 66-179, 1966-1 C.B. 144.
[33] Rev. Rul. 70-244, 1970-1 C.B. 132.
[34] E.g., Priv. Ltr. Rul. 202010004.
[35] Rev. Rul. 59-391, 1959-2 C.B. 151. See text accompanied by *infra* notes 88–90.

granting tax exemption to business leagues. The occasion for the Court's review of the requirement was a case involving the exempt status of a trade organization of muffler dealers that confined its membership to dealers franchised by a particular company and that had as its principal activity bargaining with the company on behalf of its members. The Court held that the franchisees did not represent a line of business, in that their efforts did not benefit a sufficiently broad segment of the business community involved, as would the efforts of an organization functioning on behalf of the entire muffler dealer industry.[36]

The Court observed that "[m]ost trade associations fall within" one of two categories.[37] They either represent an "entire industry"[38] or "all components of an industry within a geographic area."[39] This characterization of the essence of tax-exempt associations was seen by the Court as "[t]rue to the representations made by the Chamber of Commerce, in its statement to the Senate [Finance Committee] in 1913," that benefits would be received "in common with all other members of their communities or of their industries."[40]

The Court wrote that, while the view of the IRS as to the necessity of the line-of-business requirement "perhaps is not the only possible one, it does bear a fair relationship to the language of the statute, it reflects the views of those who sought its enactment, and it matches the purpose they articulated."[41] Also, the agency "infrequently but consistently has interpreted [the definition] to exclude an organization. . .that is not industrywide" and therefore the IRS's view "merits serious deference."[42] The Court noted that the IRS "consistently has denied exemption to business groups whose membership and purposes are narrower,"[43] such as entities composed of businesses that market a single brand of automobile,[44] have licenses to a single patented product,[45] or bottle one type of soft drink.[46] The Court wrote that the IRS "has reasoned that these groups are not designed to better conditions in an

---

[36] Nat'l Muffler Dealers Ass'n, Inc. v. United States, 440 U.S. 472 (1979), aff'g 565 F.2d 845 (2d Cir. 1977). The Supreme Court thus rejected the contrary view of the U.S. Court of Appeals for the Seventh Circuit, which held that an association composed solely of bottlers of a single brand of soft drink was an exempt business league (Pepsi-Cola Bottlers' Ass'n, Inc. v. United States, 369 F.2d 250 (7th Cir. 1966)).

[37] Nat'l Muffler Dealers Ass'n, Inc. v. United States, 440 U.S. 472, 528 (1979).

[38] Id., citing American Plywood Ass'n v. United States, 267 F. Supp. 830 (W.D. Wash. 1967); Nat'l Leather & Shoe Finders Ass'n v. Comm'r, 9 T.C. 121 (1947). The Court noted that the U.S. Court of Appeals for the Second Circuit earlier observed that an organization was not entitled to classification as an exempt business league because "[n]othing is done to advance the interests of the community or to improve the standards or conditions of a particular trade" (Produce Exchange Stock Clearing Ass'n v. Helvering, 71 F.2d 142, 144 (2d Cir. 1934)).

[39] Nat'l Muffler Dealers Ass'n, Inc. v. United States, 440 U.S. 472, 528 (1979), citing Comm'r v. Chicago Graphic Arts Fed'n, Inc., 128 F.2d 424 (7th Cir. 1942); Crooks v. Kansas City Hay Dealers' Ass'n, 37 F. 83 (8th Cir. 1929); Washington State Apples, Inc. v. Comm'r, 46 B.T.A. 64 (1942).

[40] Nat'l Muffler Dealers Ass'n, Inc. v. United States, 440 U.S. 472, 528 (1979).

[41] Id. at 529.

[42] Id.

[43] Id. at 528.

[44] Rev. Rul. 67-77, 1967-1 C.B. 138.

[45] Rev. Rul. 58-294, 1958-1 C.B. 244.

[46] Rev. Rul. 68-182, 1968-1 C.B. 263 (announcing nonacquiescence in Pepsi-Cola Bottlers' Ass'n v. United States, 369 F.2d 250 (7th Cir. 1966)).

entire industrial 'line,' but, instead, are devoted to the promotion of a particular product at the expense of others in the industry."[47]

(iii) Other Developments. In the aftermath of this Supreme Court opinion, the IRS ruled that tax exemption as a business league is not available for organizations that endeavor to improve business conditions in only "segments" of lines of business.[48] This development occurred when the agency, reviewing the status of an organization of users of a manufacturer's computers, formed to discuss computer use operational and technical problems (a computer users' group), ruled that the organization did not qualify as an exempt business league, in part because the organization helped provide a competitive advantage to the manufacturer and its customers.[49] This position of the IRS was endorsed by a federal district court, holding that a computer users' group did not constitute an exempt business league because it promoted a single manufacturer's computers, in that the group's activities "advance the interests of [the vendor] and fail to bestow a benefit upon either an entire industry or all components of an industry within a geographic area."[50] This decision was thereafter mirrored in another federal district court decision, finding a computer users' group to not be an exempt business league because the single manufacturer involved represented only a segment of the industry and because a group that "promotes a particular product at the expense of others in the industry necessarily fails the line of business requirement."[51] The second of these cases was affirmed, with the appellate court writing that the organization seeking exempt status was functioning as a "powerful marketing tool" for the computer manufacturer involved.[52]

By contrast, an association was ruled by the IRS to be a tax-exempt business league where its diverse members own, rent, or lease computers of various manufacturers and its purpose is to facilitate their data processing; the primary objective of the organization was to provide a forum for the exchange of information that will lead to more efficient utilization of digital computers by its members.[53] Likewise, the IRS held that an organization formed by members of an industry that contracted with research organizations to develop new and improved uses for existing products was an exempt business league, in part because none of the organization's patents and trademarks was licensed to any member on an exclusive basis.[54]

The IRS ruled that an organization did not qualify as a tax-exempt business league because its membership of fraternal and veterans' organizations did not constitute an *industry*, so that the requisite *line of business* was not being represented.[55] In another instance, exempt business league status was not extended to

---

[47]Nat'l Muffler Dealers Ass'n, Inc. v. United States, 440 U.S. 472, 528 (1979), citing Rev. Rul. 76-400, 1976-2 C.B. 153, and Rev. Rul. 61-177, 1961-2 C.B. 117.

[48]Rev. Rul. 83-164, 1983-2 C.B. 95.

[49]E.g., Priv. Ltr. Rul. 201038015. Another rationale is that this type of computer users' group is serving the private interests of its members (Rev. Rul. 74-116, 1974-1 C.B. 127).

[50]Nat'l Prime Users Group, Inc. v. United States, 667 F. Supp. 250 (D. Md. 1987).

[51]Guide Int'l Corp. v. United States, 90-1 U.S.T.C. ¶ 50,304 (N.D. Ill. 1990).

[52]Guide Int'l Corp. v. United States, 948 F.2d 360, 362 (7th Cir. 1991).

[53]Rev. Rul. 74-147, 1974-1 C.B. 136.

[54]Rev. Rul. 69-632, 1969-2 C.B. 120.

[55]Priv. Ltr. Rul. 200505024.

an organization inasmuch as it was not composed of persons with a common business interest "but rather consists of persons desiring to increase their own personal wealth."[56] Similarly, an organization had its exempt status revoked because it was operating "solely as a leads/referrals group which only benefits uncommon business members," and its activities were "providing a direct benefit to the members rather than for the improvement of business conditions as a whole."[57] Likewise, a court held that the Bluetooth (a radio-based technology that supports wireless communications) specification and accompanying trademark, created and marketed by an association, is a brand being sold by the association in a "garden-variety" business rather than an effort to promote a common business interest.[58] A classic example of violation of the line-of-business requirement was provided when the IRS ruled that an organization serving as an association for the independent restaurant industry had as its primary activity the marketing of an "identifiable brand" as a way of public promotion of the member restaurants; the IRS ruled that the marketing effort was intended to provide the association's members a competitive advantage over other independent restaurants.[59]

A nonprofit organization was formed to promote and facilitate the operation and use of tax-qualified master retirement plans for members of an exempt business league. This entity created and maintains these plans for adoption by lawyers and law firms. This organization failed to qualify as an exempt business league itself, largely because its activities were, as a court wrote, "directed principally to individual lawyers and law firms rather than promoting the well-being of the legal industry generally."[60] The organization maintained that providing retirement services to legal professionals, in its words, "advances the common business interests of the legal profession by assisting lawyers in more efficiently managing their practices so that they can concentrate more on serving the interests of their clients," instead of managing retirement plans.[61] The "foremost problem," observed the court, is that the organization's position "lacks any limiting principle," in that the logic of this position is that the offering of "virtually any product or service" could therefore be deemed to advance the common business interests of the legal profession.[62]

(d) Membership Services

As noted, nearly every exempt business league has a membership; the members pay dues in exchange for the services that the league provides. Services provided by exempt business leagues, which promote a common business interest, typically

---

[56] Priv. Ltr. Rul. 200536026.

[57] Priv. Ltr. Rul. 200709070.

[58] Bluetooth SIG, Inc. v. United States, 2008-1 U.S.T.C. ¶50,177 (W.D. Wash. 2008), aff'd, 611 F.3d 617 (9th Cir. 2010); the appellate court wrote that a "benefit to non-members is a key characteristic of [tax-exempt] business leagues" (611 F.3d at 624).

[59] Priv. Ltr. Rul. 200837035. Likewise, the IRS denied exempt status as a business league to an organization formed to promote the business interests of its members, all of whom were franchise owners of stores selling a particular brand of pizza (Priv. Ltr. Rul. 201231013).

[60] ABA Retirement Funds v. United States, 2013-1 U.S.T.C. ¶ 50,306 (N.D. Ill. 2013), aff'd, 759 F.3d 718 (7th Cir. 2014).

[61] 2013-1 U.S.T.C. ¶ 50,306 (N.D. Ill. 2013), at 84,041.

[62] Id.

are or include the following activities: conduct of annual conventions, educational seminars, and the like;[63] development and distribution of publications (such as journals and newsletters) of pertinence to the interests of an organization's members;[64] attempts to influence legislation germane to the members' common business interests;[65] presentation of information and opinions to government agencies; dissemination by other means of information (including advocacy) pertaining to the field involved; conduct of public relations and community relations programs; maintenance of a library; promotion of improved business standards and methods and uniform business practices;[66] holding of luncheon meetings for the purpose of discussing the problems of a particular industry;[67] conduct of an industry advertising program;[68] conduct of negotiations for members and nonmembers in an industry;[69] sponsorship of other events, such as forums, sports tournaments, and holiday parties;[70] mediation and settlement of disputes affecting an industry;[71] operation of a bid registry;[72] investigation of criminal aspects of claims against members;[73] initiation and subsidizing of litigation;[74] operation of an insurance rating bureau;[75] negotiation of the sale of broadcast rights;[76] conduct of fire patrols and salvage operations for insurance companies;[77] provision for equitable distribution of high-risk insurance policies among member insurance companies;[78] provision of credit information;[79] engagement in research activities;[80] conduct of a trade show;[81] and conduct of one or more certification programs.[82]

---

[63] American Refractories Inst. v. Comm'r, 6 T.C.M. 1302 (1947); Atlanta Master Printers Club v. Comm'r, 1 T.C.M. 107 (1942). An organization gained exemption by advocating the open shop principle (Associated Indus. of Cleveland v. Comm'r, 7 T.C. 1449 (1946)).

[64] E.g., Nat'l Leather & Shoe Finders Ass'n v. Comm'r, 9 T.C. 121 (1947).

[65] Rev. Rul. 61-177, 1961-2 C.B. 117.

[66] Rev. Rul. 68-657, 1968-2 C.B. 218.

[67] Rev. Rul. 67-295, 1967-2 C.B. 197.

[68] Rev. Rul. 67-344, 1967-2 C.B. 199.

[69] American Fishermen's Tuna Boat Ass'n v. Rogan, 51 F. Supp. 933 (S.D. Cal. 1943).

[70] Priv. Ltr. Rul. 9550001.

[71] Rev. Rul. 65-164, 1965-1 C.B. 238.

[72] Rev. Rul. 66-223, 1966-2 C.B. 224.

[73] Rev. Rul. 66-260, 1966-2 C.B. 225.

[74] Rev. Rul. 67-175, 1967-1 C.B. 139.

[75] Oregon Casualty Ass'n v. Comm'r, 37 B.T.A. 340 (1938).

[76] Priv. Ltr. Rul. 7922001.

[77] Minneapolis Bd. of Fire Underwriters v. Comm'r, 38 B.T.A. 1532 (1938).

[78] Rev. Rul. 71-155, 1971-1 C.B. 152.

[79] Oklahoma City Retailers Ass'n v. United States, 331 F.2d 328 (10th Cir. 1964); Rev. Rul. 70-591, 1970-2 C.B. 118; Rev. Rul. 68-265, 1968-1 C.B. 265.

[80] Rev. Rul. 69-106, 1969-1 C.B. 153; Glass Container Indus. Research Corp. v. United States, 70-1 U.S.T.C. ¶ 9214 (W.D. Pa. 1970).

[81] E.g., Texas Mobile Home Ass'n v. Comm'r, 324 F.2d 691 (5th Cir. 1963); American Woodworking Mach. & Equip. Show v. United States, 249 F. Supp. 392 (M.D.N.C. 1966); Nat'l Ass'n of Display Indus. v. United States, 64-1 U.S.T.C. ¶ 9285 (S.D.N.Y. 1964); American Inst. of Interior Designers v. United States, 204 F. Supp. 201 (N.D. Cal. 1962); Orange Cnty. Builders Ass'n, Inc. v. United States, 65-2 U.S.T.C. ¶ 9679 (S.D. Cal. 1956); Men's & Boys' Apparel Club of Fla. v. United States, 64-2 U.S.T.C. ¶ 9840 (Ct. Cl. 1964); Rev. Rul. 67-219, 1967-2 C.B. 212; Rev. Rul. 58-224, 1958-1 C.B. 242.

[82] See § 14.1(g).

In other instances, the IRS ruled that an organization formed to promote the acceptance of women in business and the professions was an exempt business league because it attempted to seek to improve conditions in one or more lines of business,[83] as was an organization formed to attract conventions to a city for the benefit of the economic interest of business throughout the community[84] and a self-regulatory organization with authority to promulgate and enforce business conduct and certain ethical rules with respect to an industry.[85]

(e) Professional Organizations

Some nonprofit membership organizations operate for the benefit of members of a profession rather than a trade or business. These entities are often known as *professional societies*. This can cause tax exemption classification tensions, inasmuch as there may be controversy as to whether the organization is properly cast as an exempt business league or an exempt charitable, educational, scientific, or like organization.

In many instances, a professional society will have as the basis for its tax exemption classification as a business league. For example, the IRS presumes that bar associations, medical societies, accounting institutes, and similar organizations are business leagues, notwithstanding their conduct of activities that are charitable, educational, scientific, and the like. The IRS applies the primary purpose test,[86] usually concluding that these organizations' activities, considered in the aggregate, are directed primarily at the promotion of the interests of members of the profession involved and thus that the entities are operated to further the common business purpose of their members.[87] Some organizations, however, are structured to serve members from a variety of professions, often for networking or other marketing purposes; entities of this nature cannot qualify as exempt business leagues,[88] principally because they do not represent a line of business[89] and provide particular services to the membership.[90]

A tax-exempt medical society may engage in the following charitable and educational activities: meetings where technical papers are presented, maintenance of a library, publication of a journal, provision of lectures and counseling services at medical schools, and support of public health programs. An exempt medical society may also convene an annual conference where members discuss practice issues, publish a membership journal and/or newsletter, provide a patient referral service, operate a grievance committee, conduct meetings concerned with the administration and enhancement of the practice of medicine, attempt to influence legislation, utilize an ethics committee, and conduct a public relations program. Where the latter category of activities predominates, the

---

[83] Rev. Rul. 76-400, 1976-2 C.B. 153.

[84] Rev. Rul. 76-207, 1976-1 C.B. 158.

[85] Priv. Ltr. Rul. 200723029.

[86] See § 4.4.

[87] It is because of this tax law outcome that many associations transfer their educational and similar functions to a separate organization (see § 29.2).

[88] Rev. Rul. 59-391, 1959-2 C.B. 151; e.g., Priv. Ltr. Rul. 201424023. This type of referral group cannot qualify as a tax-exempt social welfare organization (see Chapter 13) either (e.g., Priv. Ltr. Rul. 202009025).

[89] See text accompanied by *supra* note 35.

[90] See § 14.2.

organization is deemed to have the essential characteristics and purposes of an exempt business league.[91]

A tax-exempt bar association may engage in charitable and educational activities, such as law institutes, moot court programs, speakers' bureaus, and provision of legal assistance to indigents. The bar association may also convene an annual membership conference, publish a membership journal and/or newsletter, publish studies on the economics of law office administration, conduct programs on enhancement of law practice profitability, and enforce standards of members' conduct.[92] Again, where the latter activities are primary, the organization is considered to have the purposes of and classification as an exempt business league. Some courts have implied, however, that bar associations may qualify as exempt charitable organizations.[93] Notably, a court held that the maintenance of "public confidence in the legal system" is a "goal of unquestionable importance in a civil and complex society" and that activities such as the operation of a client security fund, an inquiry tribunal, a fee arbitration plan, and a lawyer referral service are "devoted to that goal through various means of improving the administration of justice."[94]

If a professional society's dominant activities are noncommercial research, maintenance of a library, publication of a journal, and the like, it may qualify for tax exemption as being charitable, educational, scientific, or the like, as long as no substantial activities are directed at or are concerned with the protection or promotion of the professional practice or business interests of its membership.[95] A professional society, then, may fail to qualify as an exempt charitable organization and will be considered an exempt business league (or perhaps still another type of exempt entity) where it, other than incidentally, engages in public relations activities, polices a profession, seeks to improve the conditions of its members, seeks to develop goodwill or fellowship among its members, engages in social and recreational activities, maintains facilities (such as a restaurant, lounge, or club house) for its members, or engages in advocacy activities.[96] In one instance, an organization of individuals from various public health and welfare professions (seemingly charitable in nature) was ruled by the IRS to be an exempt business league, inasmuch as its activities "promote the business and professional interests of the members by increasing the effectiveness of the interaction among the various professions, by developing greater efficiency in the professions, and by solving problems common to the professions."[97]

---

[91] Rev. Rul. 71-504, 1971-2 C.B. 231. Also, Rev. Rul. 77-232, 1977-2 C.B. 71.

[92] Rev. Rul. 71-505, 1971-2 C.B. 232. Also, Hammerstein v. Kelly, 349 F.2d 928 (8th Cir. 1965); Colonial Trust Co. v. Comm'r, 19 B.T.A. 174.

[93] St. Louis Union Trust Co. v. United States, 374 F.2d 427 (8th Cir. 1967); Dulles v. Johnson, 273 F.2d 362 (2d Cir. 1959); Rhode Island Hosp. Trust Co. v. United States, 159 F. Supp. 204 (D.R.I. 1958).

[94] Kentucky Bar Found., Inc. v. Comm'r, 78 T.C. 921 (1982). Also, Fraternal Med. Specialist Servs., Inc. v. Comm'r, 59 T.C.M. 289 (1984).

[95] Rev. Rul. 71-506, 1971-2 C.B. 233.

[96] If advocacy activities are political campaign activities, even an incidental amount of these functions may preclude exempt status as a charitable (IRC § 501(c)(3)) organization. See Chapter 23.

[97] Rev. Rul. 70-641, 1970-2 C.B. 119.

It is the position of the IRS that activities such as the operation of certification programs and the maintenance of a code of ethics for members[98] are suitable programs for professional organizations that are business leagues but not for professional organizations that are charitable, educational, scientific, and like organizations, because these programs are designed and operated to achieve professional standing for the line of business represented by the profession and to enhance the respectability of those who are certified.[99]

(f) Varieties of Business Leagues

Varieties of tax-exempt business leagues abound:

- An organization that made recommendations concerning the establishment and revision of regulations and rates for its members who were regulated by a federal agency.[100]

- An organization that provided its member small loan companies with information concerning borrowers.[101]

- An organization composed of advertising agencies that verified the advertising claims of publications selling advertising space and made reports available to members of the advertising industry generally.[102]

- An organization composed of members of a particular industry formed to develop new and improved uses for existing products of the industry.[103]

- An organization formed to improve the business conditions of financial institutions by offering rewards for information leading to the arrest and conviction of individuals committing crimes against its members.[104]

- An organization that operated a "plan room" and published a news bulletin that contained information about plans available at the plan room, bid results, and activities of concern to persons in the industry.[105]

- An organization created pursuant to state statute to pay claims against (act as guarantor for) insolvent insurance companies, where the companies were mandatory members of the organization was ruled to be an exempt business league, with the IRS holding that the organization is serving a "quasi-public function imposed by law which is directed at relieving a common cause of hardship and distress of broad public concern in the field of insurance protection."[106]

---

[98] See § 14.1(g).
[99] Gen. Couns. Mem. 39721.
[100] *Id.*
[101] Rev. Rul. 67-394, 1967-2 C.B. 201.
[102] Rev. Rul. 69-387, 1969-2 C.B. 124.
[103] Rev. Rul. 69-632, 1969-2 C.B. 120.
[104] Rev. Rul. 69-634, 1969-2 C.B. 124.
[105] Rev. Rul. 72-211, 1972-1 C.B. 150, *clarifying* Rev. Rul. 56-65, 1956-1 C.B. 199. Also, Builder's Exch. of Tex., Inc. v. Comm'r, 31 T.C.M. 844 (1972).
[106] Rev. Rul. 73-452, 1973-2 C.B. 183.

- Exempt business league status was accorded by the IRS to an organization of representatives of diversified businesses that own or lease one or more digital computers produced by various manufacturers; the IRS found that the "primary objective of the organization is to provide a forum for the exchange of information which will lead to the more efficient utilization of computers by its members and other interested users, and thus improves the overall efficiency of the business operations of each."[107]

- An organization, the members of which were involved in the commercial fishing industry in a state, that published a monthly newspaper of commercial fishing technical information and news, and that derived its income primarily from membership dues and sales of advertising, may qualify as an exempt business league.[108]

- An association of insurance companies created pursuant to a state's no-fault insurance statute to provide personal injury protection for residents of the state who sustain injury and are not covered by any insurance was ruled to qualify as an exempt business league because its activities "promote the common business interests of its members by fulfilling an obligation that the state has imposed upon the insurance industry as a prerequisite for doing business within the state and by enhancing the image of the industry."[109]

- An organization that collected contributions to further an industry's programs,[110] an organization that promoted convention and tourism business in a town,[111] and an organization that effected improvement in public awareness of Thoroughbred racing[112] also qualified as exempt business leagues.

A merger, consolidation, or other reorganization of business leagues can result in one or more exempt business leagues.[113]

(g)   Certification Programs

As noted, some appropriate functions of an exempt business league are, when considered alone, charitable, educational, and/or scientific activities.[114] There can be a dispute, nonetheless, as to what the primary purpose[115] of a particular activity is—that is, for example, whether the primary purpose of an activity is charitable or otherwise, such as promotion of a common business interest. This dichotomy of view is amply apparent in connection with programs of exempt organizations that

[107] Rev. Rul. 74-147, 1974-1 C.B. 136.
[108] Rev. Rul. 75-287, 1975-2 C.B. 211.
[109] Rev. Rul. 76-410, 1976-2 C.B. 155.
[110] Priv. Ltr. Rul. 8422170.
[111] Priv. Ltr. Rul. 9032005.
[112] Priv. Ltr. Rul. 9050002.
[113] E.g., Priv. Ltr. Rul. 9003045.
[114] See Chapters 7, 8, 9.
[115] See § 4.4.

entail the certification of individuals. This type of certification, product testing, and the like are tax-exempt functions for a business league.[116]

It is the view of the IRS, however, that certification programs are inconsistent with tax-exempt status for charitable, educational, and scientific organizations, due to the extent of private benefit conferred on the certified individuals.[117] For example, the IRS revoked the tax-exempt status of a public charity that evolved to the point that its primary functions were the certification of travel professionals; the agency rejected the argument that an eco-certification program was charitable in nature.[118] Likewise, a public charity lost its exemption because, due to a merger, it undertook a substantial new program of certifying individuals in a health care field.[119]

The IRS ruled that an organization formed by physicians who are members of a state medical society to operate peer review boards for the purpose of establishing and maintaining standards for quality, quantity, and reasonableness of the costs of medical services qualified as a tax-exempt business league.[120] Nonetheless, ruled the IRS, "[a]lthough this activity may result in a measurable public benefit, its primary objective is to maintain the professional standards, prestige, and independence of the organized medical profession and thereby further the common business interest of the organization's members."[121] The promotion of health, however, is a charitable purpose,[122] and some courts are of the view that improvements in the delivery of health care is a charitable undertaking, even if the medical profession is somewhat benefited.[123] A tax-exempt business league's purpose may be the creation and maintenance of various industry standards.[124]

§ 14.2 DISQUALIFYING ACTIVITIES

There are five principal bases pursuant to which tax-exempt status may be denied an organization that otherwise qualifies as an exempt business league.

(a) Line-of-Business Requirement

One basis for nonqualification as a tax-exempt business league is a finding that the organization failed to satisfy the line-of-business requirement.[125] The IRS, from time to time, issues private letter rulings holding that an organization cannot qualify as a tax-exempt business league because it does not represent a line of business.[126]

---

[116] Rev. Rul. 73-567, 1973-2 C.B. 178.
[117] See § 7.8, text accompanied by notes 340–344; as to private benefit, see § 20.13(a).
[118] Priv. Ltr. Rul. 201843016.
[119] Priv. Ltr. Rul. 201906010.
[120] Rev. Rul. 74-553, 1974-2 C.B. 168.
[121] Id. at 169.
[122] See § 7.6.
[123] E.g., San Antonio District Dental Soc'y v. United States, 340 F. Supp. 11 (W.D. Tex. 1972); Huron Clinic Found. v. United States, 212 F. Supp. 847 (S.D. 1962).
[124] Priv. Ltr. Rul. 201426029.
[125] See § 14.1(c).
[126] E.g., Priv. Ltr. Rul. 201203018.

For example, this outcome occurred in the case of an organization confined to a limited group of franchisees;[127] an organization that, claiming to serve the Internet media industry, provided software without charge, thereby promoting its interest, not the common business interest of the entire industry;[128] an organization providing a forum for the exchange of information to assist users and potential users of a particular software application;[129] an organization, styled as an "angel investment network," that performed analyses of early-stage tech companies for its members to determine the potential of these investments;[130] an organization that functioned as a cooperative to promote its members' businesses;[131] an organization of businesses that provided housing but excluded hotel and motel operations from its membership;[132] an organization with the primary activity of marketing a software program with the objective of taking a market share at the expense of others in the same industry;[133] an organization with the primary activity of establishing a technology standard to be used only by its members, who consist of a segment of an industry, giving them a competitive edge;[134] an organization of medical professionals with the primary activity of negotiating managed-care contracts on behalf of its members;[135] an association of agents licensed to sell financial products offered by a company;[136] an organization providing advertising services for its automobile dealers members who sell a brand of vehicles;[137] an organization providing mass-market advertising for its "brand partners" members.[138]

(b)   For-Profit Business Activities

As noted, one of the fundamental elements of the definition of an exempt business league is that it may not engage (other than incidentally) in a regular business of a kind ordinarily carried on for profit.[139]

(i) General Rule.   One of the hallmarks of a for-profit business is that it is operated to generate profits for its owners.[140] Thus, an organization that issued shares of stock carrying the right to dividends was denied exemption as a business league.[141] Also, an association of insurance companies that provided medical malpractice insurance to physicians, nurses, hospitals, and other health care providers in a particular state, where that type of insurance was not available from for-profit

---

[127] Priv. Ltr. Rul. 202017028.
[128] Priv. Ltr. Rul. 201024066.
[129] Priv. Ltr. Rul. 202013016.
[130] Priv. Ltr. Rul. 201045034.
[131] Priv. Ltr. Rul. 201107028.
[132] Priv. Ltr. Rul. 201147034.
[133] Priv. Ltr. Rul. 201347022.
[134] Priv. Ltr. Rul. 201349019.
[135] Priv. Ltr. Rul. 201411040.
[136] Priv. Ltr. Rul. 201715003.
[137] Priv. Ltr. Rul. 201717045.
[138] Priv. Ltr. Rul. 201718040.
[139] See § 14.1(a)(i).
[140] See § 1.1(a).
[141] Northwestern Jobbers Credit Bur. v. Comm'r, 37 F.2d 83 (8th Cir. 1930). Cf. Crooks v. Kansas City Hay Dealers Ass'n, 37 F.2d 83 (8th Cir. 1929).

insurers, was denied classification as an exempt business league on the ground that the provision of medical malpractice insurance is a business of a kind ordinarily carried on for profit.[142] Similarly, an association of insurance companies that accepted for reinsurance high-risk customers who would ordinarily be declined for coverage by the member companies was ruled to not qualify as an exempt business league, inasmuch as reinsurance is a business ordinarily carried on by commercial insurance companies.[143]

In one instance, a court held that an organization did not qualify as a tax-exempt business league because it engaged in a regular business of a kind ordinarily carried on for profit.[144] The court distinguished this insurance activity from that conducted by associations only on a passive basis (that is, mere sponsorship of the insurance program) and where a self-insurance program was not involved.[145] A court concluded that a nonprofit organization that itself functioned as an insurance agent was a tax-exempt business league. The organization's sole client was a state, which it served in the purchase of all insurance and bonding coverage required by the state and its agencies.[146] On appeal, however, it was held that the organization was not an exempt business league because it conducted a business of a kind ordinarily carried on for profit and did so more than incidentally.[147]

As noted, the association that created and marketed the Bluetooth technology was held to be conducting for-profit business activities.[148] As the district court viewed the matter, while an exempt business league can advance a common and *preexisting* interest among its members, the association at issue was formed to *create* a common business interest among its members. This court wrote that the "collective enterprise of the [a]ssociation derives from the fact that it has created a thing of value, which its members can then use to enhance the value of the products they sell."[149]

(ii) Incidental Business Activity. Notwithstanding the general rule, if the for-profit business activity is merely incidental to the organization's overall activities, the organization can be an exempt business league. Instead, the business activity is treated as one or more unrelated businesses.[150]

(c) Performance of Particular Services

As noted, an exempt business league may not (other than incidentally) perform particular services for individual persons.[151] This aspect of the law is one

---

[142] Rev. Rul. 81-174, 1981-1 C.B. 335.

[143] Rev. Rul. 81-175, 1981-1 C.B. 337.

[144] Associated Master Barbers & Beauticians of Am., Inc. v. Comm'r, 69 T.C. 53 (1977).

[145] Oklahoma Cattlemen's Ass'n, Inc. v. United States, 310 F. Supp. 320 (W.D. Okla. 1969); San Antonio District Dental Soc'y v. United States, 340 F. Supp. 11 (W.D. Tex. 1972).

[146] North Carolina Ass'n of Ins. Agents, Inc. v. United States, 83-2 U.S.T.C. ¶ 9445 (E.D.N.C. 1983).

[147] North Carolina Ass'n of Ins. Agents, Inc. v. United States, 739 F.2d 949 (4th Cir. 1984).

[148] See text accompanied by *supra* note 58.

[149] Bluetooth SIG, Inc. v. United States, 2008-1 U.S.T.C. ¶ 50,177 (W.D. Wash. 2008), *aff'd*, 611 F.3d 617 (9th Cir. 2010).

[150] See Chapter 24.

[151] See § 14.1(a)(i).

of the most developed of the bases for nonqualification of an organization as an exempt business league. Usually, for this purpose, these *individual persons* are, or are among, the organization's membership. Rather, an exempt business league is expected to function to improve business conditions in the trade, business, or profession involved.[152]

(i) Particular Services.   The term *particular services* generally means services that are provided to an organization's membership that are either in addition to those that are exempt functions funded by dues (particularly where there is separate payment for them) or that provide what is sometimes termed a *convenience or economy* in connection with operation of members' businesses. In one instance, an association of life insurance companies that operated an insurance underwriting information exchange among its members was ruled by a court to not qualify as a tax-exempt business league, despite its contention that its primary purpose was to benefit the entire life insurance industry by deterring fraud in the application process and that any benefits to its members were incidental.[153]

A court, in addressing this issue, concluded that an activity of a tax-exempt business league was an exempt function where the activity benefited its membership as a group, rather than the members in their individual capacities.[154] Subsequently, the IRS grappled with these distinctions, differentiating between an "industry-wide benefit or a particular service to members." The agency held that activities that provide a benefit across an industry "usually possess certain characteristics," such as being an "activity for which individual members could not be expected to bear the expense and thus lends itself to cooperative effort" and the fact that the benefits are "intangible and only indirectly related to the individual business."[155] Consequently, for example, the agency held that the operation, by an exempt association of members in the trucking industry, of an alcohol and drug testing program for members and nonmembers was a particular service for individual persons (as opposed to an incident of membership), notwithstanding the fact that the prevention of alcohol and drug abuse is a "legitimate goal" of trucking companies.[156] It is frequently difficult in a specific instance to distinguish between the performance of particular services and activities directed to the improvement of business conditions.[157]

(ii) General Rule.   Courts have, on several occasions, applied the rule that an organization cannot be an exempt business league if it provides particular services to individual persons. In one instance, an organization that operated a cold storage warehouse for its members on a cooperative basis was denied exemption as a business league because the organization's primary activities were found to constitute the performance of particular services for individual persons.[158]

---

[152] Southern Hardware Traffic Ass'n v. United States, 283 F. Supp. 1013 (W.D. Tenn. 1968), *aff'd*, 411 F.2d 563 (6th Cir. 1969).

[153] MIB, Inc. v. Comm'r, 734 F.2d 71 (1st Cir. 1984).

[154] Professional Ins. Agents of Mich. v. Comm'r, 726 F.2d 1097 (6th Cir. 1984).

[155] Priv. Ltr. Rul. 8524006.

[156] Tech. Adv. Mem. 9550001.

[157] E.g., Rev. Rul. 72-211, 1972-1 C.B. 150, *clarifying* Rev. Rul. 56-65, 1956-1 C.B. 199.

[158] Growers Cold Storage Warehouse Co. v. Comm'r, 17 B.T.A. 1279 (1929).

The court concluded that, even though the organization was not organized for profit and did not violate the private inurement doctrine, this combination of its members—done in order to save money—was not an appropriate function of an exempt business league.

A stock clearing association was denied exemption as a business league where its purpose was to provide a business economy or convenience for individual traders.[159] Noting that serving as a convenience to members is not a characteristic of entities seeking recognition of exemption as a business league, the court stated that it could not find a reason to exempt an association that serves each member as a convenience or economy in the member's business.

Tax exemption as a business league was denied an organization formed to facilitate the purchase of supplies and equipment for, and to supply management services to, its members.[160] This court found that the organization did not appear to answer the description of an exempt business league. The association performed particular services for individual persons, as evidenced by activities that included the furnishing of credit information, the supplying of an apartment shopping service, and the making of arrangements for direct purchases by members at discount.

A court held that a real estate board, whose primary purpose and activity were the operation of a multiple listing service for its members, did not qualify for this exemption.[161] It was stated that where this type of a service is "operated primarily for individual members as a convenience and economy in the conduct of their respective businesses, rather than for the improvement of business conditions within the [industry] generally. . ., the operation is not an activity warranting an exemption under the statute."[162]

An organization formed to facilitate the purchase of supplies and equipment and to provide management services for its membership was found to not be tax-exempt. A court held that the high percentage of income obtained by the organization from performing particular services for individuals as a convenience and economy in their business, along with its other income-producing activities, and the amount of time devoted by employees of the organization to the performance of these services were sufficiently substantial so that the income-producing activities could not be said to be merely incidental activities of the organization.[163] Another case involved a business league formed to promote the common business interest of its members by advancing the credit union movement. According to the court involved, it was the "distinctiveness of the activity that cements the substantial relationship" between the activity and the exempt function.[164] In denying tax exemption as a business league to an organization whose activities consisted of

[159] Produce Exchange Stock Clearing Ass'n v. Helvering, 71 F.2d 142 (2d Cir. 1934).
[160] Apartment Operators Ass'n v. Comm'r, 136 F.2d 435 (9th Cir. 1943).
[161] Evanston-North Shore Bd. of Realtors v. United States, 320 F.2d 375 (Ct. Cl. 1963), cert. denied, 376 U.S. 931 (1964).
[162] Id. at 378.
[163] Indiana Retail Hardware Ass'n, Inc. v. United States, 366 F.2d 998 (Ct. Cl. 1966). Essentially the same result occurred in Uniform Printing & Supply Co. v. Comm'r, 33 F.2d 445 (7th Cir. 1929), cert. denied, 280 U.S. 69 (1929).
[164] Louisiana Credit Union League v. United States, 693 F.2d 525, 535 (5th Cir. 1982).

providing particular services to its members in the form of transmittal of information that would be used in decisions affecting their business operations, a court held that the ultimate inquiry was whether the association's activities advanced the members' interests generally by virtue of their membership in the industry or whether they assisted members in the pursuit of their individual businesses.[165]

In another instance, a court held that an organization did not qualify as a tax-exempt business league because its activities were directed to the performance of particular services for individual members.[166] The court observed that the organization offered its members, in addition to many insurance programs, an eyeglass and prescription lens replacement service, and sold its local chapters and members various supplies, charts, books, shop emblems, and association jewelry.

In other court decisions, the performance of particular services for individual persons was found (and thus the organizations were denied tax exemption as a business league) in instances of operation of a laundry and dry cleaning plant,[167] performance of services in connection with bond investments,[168] appraisal of properties,[169] promotion of the exchange of orders by wire,[170] estimation of quantities of building materials for an organization's members' projects,[171] and the provision of food and beverage service by an engineering society to its members.[172]

The IRS likewise has not, over the decades, been reticent in applying this principle of law, holding that organizations were providing services to individual persons and thus denying tax exemption as a business league in the following instances: an organization acting as a receiver and trustee for a fee;[173] an organization operating commodity and stock exchanges;[174] an organization whose principal activity consisted of furnishing particular information and specialized individual service to its individual members through publications and other means to effect economies in the operation of their businesses;[175] an organization promoting and selling national advertising in members' publications;[176] an organization promoting its members' writings;[177] an organization operating a multiple listing service;[178] a nurses' registry that was denied categorization as an exempt business league on the basis of a finding that it was no more than an employment service for the benefit of its members;[179] an organization conducting a trading stamp program;[180]

---

[165] MIB, Inc. v. Comm'r, 734 F.2d 71 (1st Cir. 1984).
[166] Associated Master Barbers & Beauticians of America, Inc. v. Comm'r, 69 T.C. 53 (1977).
[167] A-1 Dry Cleaners & Dyers Co. v. Comm'r, 14 B.T.A. 1314 (1929).
[168] Northwestern Mun. Ass'n, Inc. v. United States, 99 F.2d 460 (8th Cir. 1938).
[169] Central Appraisal Bur. v. Comm'r, 46 B.T.A. 1281 (1942).
[170] Florists' Telegraph Delivery Ass'n v. Comm'r, 47 B.T.A. 1044 (1942).
[171] General Contractors Ass'n v. United States, 202 F.2d 633 (7th Cir. 1953).
[172] Engineers Club of San Francisco v. United States, 791 F.2d 686 (9th Cir. 1986).
[173] O.D. 786, 4 C.B. 269 (1921).
[174] Reg. § 501(c)(6)-1. Cf. Rev. Rul. 55-715, 1955-2 C.B. 263.
[175] Rev. Rul. 56-65, 1956-1 C.B. 199.
[176] Rev. Rul. 56-84, 1956-1 C.B. 201.
[177] Rev. Rul. 57-453, 1957-2 C.B. 310.
[178] Rev. Rul. 59-234, 1959-2 C.B. 149.
[179] Rev. Rul. 61-170, 1961-2 C.B. 112.
[180] Rev. Rul. 65-244, 1965-2 C.B. 167.

an organization that provided its members with an economy and convenience in the conduct of their individual businesses by enabling them to secure supplies, equipment, and services at less cost than if they had to secure them on an individual basis;[181] an organization ensuring the discharge of an organization's members' obligations to pay taxes;[182] an organization maintaining a library for its members' use;[183] an organization providing services to members and nonmembers, principally operating a traffic bureau, which resulted in savings and simplified operations;[184] an organization whose principal activity was to provide its members with group workers' compensation insurance that was underwritten by a private insurance company (thereby relieving its members of the burden of having to obtain insurance on an individual basis, resulting in a convenience in the conduct of their businesses);[185] an organization appointing travel agents to sell passage on members' ships;[186] a telephone answering service for tow truck operators, on the ground that it provided its members with economy and convenience in the conduct of their individual businesses;[187] an organization making interest-free loans to member credit unions;[188] an organization publishing and distributing a directory of an organization's members to businesses likely to require the members' services;[189] an organization administering a welfare benefit plan pursuant to a collective bargaining agreement;[190] an organization matching the needs of nonprofit and governmental entities with services provided by its members;[191] an "angel investment network" that performed analyses of early-stage tech companies for its members to determine the potential of these investments;[192] an organization of beverage industry members that essentially provides them services in negotiating with suppliers;[193] an organization the membership of which is confined to franchisees affiliated with a business;[194] an organization operating a farmers' market;[195] and an organization serving its members as a negotiating agent to get better pricing from vendors, suppliers, and service providers and disburse rebates to members;[196] an organization operating a scheduling service for its member food truck operators;[197] an association of bridal salons where its primary activity was advertising;[198] an organization formed to facilitate transfers, by sale or lease, of certain

[181] Rev. Rul. 66-338, 1966-2 C.B. 226.
[182] Rev. Rul. 66-354, 1966-2 C.B. 207.
[183] Rev. Rul. 67-182, 1967-1 C.B. 141.
[184] Rev. Rul. 68-264, 1968-1 C.B. 264.
[185] Rev. Rul. 74-81, 1974-1 C.B. 135.
[186] Rev. Rul. 74-228, 1974-1 C.B. 136.
[187] Rev. Rul. 74-308, 1974-2 C.B. 168.
[188] Rev. Rul. 76-38, 1976-1 C.B. 157.
[189] Rev. Rul. 76-409, 1976-2 C.B. 154.
[190] Gen. Couns. Mem. 39411 (*revoking* Gen. Couns. Mem. 38458).
[191] Priv. Ltr. Rul. 201012051.
[192] Priv. Ltr. Rul. 202420028.
[193] Priv. Ltr. Rul. 201105048.
[194] Priv. Ltr. Rul. 201540017.
[195] E.g., Priv. Ltr. Rul. 201639016.
[196] Priv. Ltr. Rul. 201726014.
[197] Priv. Ltr. Rul. 202015022.
[198] Priv. Ltr. Rul. 202034010.

land and water rights from a particular company to individuals, businesses, or other interested parties for a fee;[199] and property owners' associations.[200]

An independent practice association that provided health services through written agreements with health maintenance organizations was ruled to not qualify as an exempt business league. The IRS concluded that the principal functions of the association were to provide an available pool of physicians who would abide by its fee schedule when rendering medical services to the subscribers of an HMO and to provide its members with access to a large group of patients who generally may not be referred to nonmember physicians.[201]

A network of physicians entered into contracts with self-insured employers for the provision of health care benefits, with the major goal of minimizing administrative costs. The IRS ruled that this organization engaged in activities that provide a "convenience through an economy of scale" and relieved its member-physicians of "having to conduct certain aspects of their businesses on their own."[202] By contrast, a certification function was held to benefit an industry in its entirety and not merely provide particular services to its members.[203] The IRS held that a lawyer referral service was a tax-exempt business league, since (because of the manner in which it was operated) it was more than a mere business referral service and served to improve the image and functioning of the legal profession in general.[204]

The IRS denied tax exemption as a business league in the case of two types of associations of insurance companies because they were performing particular services for their members.[205] In one of these instances, an association of insurance companies in a state that provided medical malpractice insurance to health care providers where the insurance was not available from for-profit insurers in the state was held to be performing particular services for its member companies and policyholders because its "method of operation involves it in its member companies' insurance business, and since the organization's insurance activities serve as an economy or convenience in providing necessary protection to its policy-holders engaged in providing health care."[206] This rationale was applied to the activities of an association of insurance companies that accepted for reinsurance high-risk customers who would ordinarily be declined for coverage by its member companies.[207] An association of insurance companies that assigns applications for insurance to member companies that perform the actual insurance functions can, however, qualify as an exempt business league inasmuch as it does not assume the risk on the policies.[208]

---

[199] Priv. Ltr. Rul. 202221016.

[200] E.g., Priv. Ltr. Rul. 202232020.

[201] Rev. Rul. 86-98, 1986-2 C.B. 74.

[202] Priv. Ltr. Rul. 200522022.

[203] Priv. Ltr. Rul. 200536023.

[204] Rev. Rul. 80-287, 1980-2 C.B. 185.

[205] In these instances, the IRS also concluded that the associations were engaged in a business of a kind ordinarily carried on for profit (see § 14.2(b)).

[206] Rev. Rul. 81-174, 1981-1 C.B. 335.

[207] Rev. Rul. 81-175, 1981-1 C.B. 337.

[208] Rev. Rul. 71-155, 1971-1 C.B. 152.

The IRS has been unabashed in applying the particular services rule to deny recognition of business league status to associations of umpires and referees. Although these organizations provide education and training for their membership, their primary function is to schedule, assign, and pay their members for their officiating services. The IRS rejects these organization's efforts to be recognized as tax-exempt business leagues on the ground that they are providing particular services to their members by arranging employment opportunities for them, resulting in impermissible private benefit. The IRS has so ruled in cases involving baseball umpires,[209] tennis umpires,[210] soccer referees,[211] volleyball officials,[212] football officials,[213] and hockey officials.[214]

Under limited circumstances, a business league can operate a "warranty or guarantee" program, which is a program designed to assure purchasers of a product that it meets acceptable standards and to provide insurance and arbitration services, and be tax-exempt on the ground that it is providing services for the common benefit of its membership. The IRS favors an enforced policy of a business league of obtaining reimbursement from the members responsible for defects.[215] The IRS is likely to conclude, however, that unwarranted private benefits are being conferred to an organization's members in this setting where only a small portion of the eligible sellers participate in the program.[216]

In the case referenced earlier concerning the Bluetooth technology,[217] the district court found that the association was providing particular services for individual persons, thereby not qualifying as an exempt business league on that basis. The court wrote: "It is undisputed that use of the Bluetooth trademark is absolutely limited to members who pay the appropriate listing fee."[218] Also: "[S]omething of value is offered to all comers on the condition that they pay for it, and the benefits are in proportion to the contribution," and "[f]rom the standpoint of manufacturers, Bluetooth quite simply benefits those who use it, which is why it is for sale."[219]

The IRS, from time to time, issues private letter rulings holding that an organization cannot qualify as a tax-exempt business league on the ground that it provides particular services to some or all of its members.[220]

(iii) Particular Services for Nonmembers.   In most instances, the *individual persons* in this context are, or are among, the entity's membership. Occasionally, however, the *particular services* are provided not only to an organization's

---

[209] E.g., Priv. Ltr. Rul. 201810011.

[210] Priv. Ltr. Rul. 201820020. This ruling involved classification as a social welfare organization (see § 13.1(b)).

[211] Priv. Ltr. Rul. 201924019.

[212] Priv. Ltr. Rul. 201931010.

[213] Priv. Ltr. Rul. 202103015.

[214] Priv. Ltr. Rul. 201820019.

[215] Gen. Couns. Mem. 34608.

[216] Gen. Couns. Mem. 39105.

[217] See text accompanied by *supra* notes 58, 148.

[218] Bluetooth SIG, Inc. v. United States, 2008-1 U.S.T.C. ¶ 50,177 (W.D. Wash. 2008), *aff'd*, 611 F.3d 617 (9th Cir. 2010).

[219] *Id.* at ¶ 50,177.

[220] E.g., Priv. Ltr. Rul. 202110021.

members, but also to others. For example, in an instance of a physicians' network that was denied exempt status as a business league, particular services were provided, not only to the member physicians, but also to employers and an insurance company.[221]

In some instances, the particular services are provided only to nonmembers. For example, the IRS concluded that the sale of discount certificates by an exempt business league that promotes interest in a particular sport, to enable individuals to play the sport at participating sports facilities, was providing a particular service for individual persons, even though the facilities are not members.[222] As another illustration, the IRS denied recognition of exemption as a business league, in part because the organization was providing particular services to clients of a for-profit company that is wholly owned by the organization's founder.[223] Likewise, an organization of individuals servicing automobiles built by a particular manufacturer failed to qualify as an exempt business league because its activities were directed to the performance of services for the manufacturer.[224]

(iv) Unrelated Business Activities. Despite express prohibition as stated in the regulations, a tax-exempt business league will lose its exemption (or an organization will fail to gain exemption in the first instance) because it performs particular services for individual members only where the services are a principal or sole undertaking of the organization.[225] Where these services are less than a primary function of an exempt business league, the IRS will characterize them as a business of a kind ordinarily carried on for profit and treat the business as an unrelated activity.[226]

For example, the IRS concluded that an executive referral service conducted by an exempt association constituted the performance of particular services for individual persons but, because other activities were the organization's primary ones, the agency ruled that the service was an unrelated business.[227] Similarly, a compensation consulting service, while amounting to the performance of a particular service, did not jeopardize an association's exemption because it was not a primary activity of the organization.[228] Likewise, as noted, an exempt association that promotes a sport was ruled to have unrelated business income from the sale of discount certificates, which enable members of the public to play the sport at various facilities, on the ground that the marketing and sales activities constitute the performance of particular services primarily for the benefit of the participating facilities; the association's tax exemption was not disturbed.[229]

---

[221] Priv. Ltr. Rul. 200522022.
[222] Tech. Adv. Mem. 201005061.
[223] Priv. Ltr. Rul. 201242016.
[224] Priv. Ltr. Rul. 201431032.
[225] E.g., Rev. Rul. 68-265, 1968-1 C.B. 265; Rev. Rul. 68-264, 1968-1 C.B. 264. In general, Retailers Credit Ass'n of Alameda Cnty. v. Comm'r, 90 F.2d 47 (9th Cir. 1937).
[226] See Chapter 24.
[227] Priv. Ltr. Rul. 8524006.
[228] Priv. Ltr. Rul. 9128003.
[229] Tech. Adv. Mem. 201005061.

(d) Private Inurement and Private Benefit

Still another basis for failure to qualify as a tax-exempt business league is violation of the doctrine of private inurement. That is, none of the income or assets of an exempt business league may be permitted to directly or indirectly unduly benefit an individual or other person who has a close relationship with the organization, when the person is in a position to exercise a significant degree of control over it.[230]

It is rare that the IRS denies recognition of, or revokes, the exempt status of a business league on the ground of private inurement;[231] it is far more likely to apply the particular services rule[232] rather than the private inurement doctrine in these situations.

The IRS occasionally invokes the private benefit doctrine[233] when denying recognition of tax exemption to an organization seeking to be an exempt business league. This doctrine is more likely to be applied than the private inurement doctrine because most of these organizations' memberships lack the status of insiders.[234] Use of the private benefit doctrine is often made in tandem with application of the particular services rule.[235]

For example, an organization that pursued tax exemption as a business league was operated primarily to provide cooperative services for its members, acting as a bargaining agent to negotiate for better terms and conditions of doing business with vendors, suppliers, and service providers with whom its members do business. In addition to invoking the particular services rule, the IRS held that this entity was providing a private economic benefit to its members.[236]

(e) Commerciality

As part of its ongoing efforts to expand the reach of the commerciality doctrine,[237] the IRS is increasing application of the doctrine in the business league context. In its fullest explication of this use of the doctrine to date, the IRS was compelled to proclaim that an exempt business league is a "membership organization characteristically supported by dues."[238] The IRS continued: "While such an organization may receive a substantial portion or even the primary part of its income from non-member sources, membership support, both in the form of dues and involvement in the organization's activities, must be at a meaningful level."[239]

In this case, the IRS observed that the organization's revenue from dues and assessments had "steadily declined" while revenue from its branded services and certain other activities had "steadily increased," giving its overall operations a

---

[230] See § 20.10.

[231] E.g., Priv. Ltr. Rul. 201701019.

[232] See § 14.2(c).

[233] See § 20.13(a).

[234] See § 20.3.

[235] See § 14.2(c)(i), (ii).

[236] Priv. Ltr. Rul. 201931013.

[237] See, in general, § 4.9.

[238] Priv. Ltr. Rul. 201321026. This is an accurate statement as a matter of fact, although the Internal Revenue Code and tax regulations are silent on the point as a matter of law.

[239] Id.

"commercial hue." The agency stated that this organization's activities "do not promote a common business interest with inherently group benefits," but rather it offers its branded services only to individual members in a manner that is "commercial in nature."[240]

§ 14.3   CHAMBERS OF COMMERCE

A tax-exempt chamber of commerce is a nonprofit association of individuals and businesses organized and operated to promote the commercial and industrial interests of a community, state, or nation. This type of business network, which usually has an advocacy component, typically functions to improve the business climate and advance the general economic welfare of a community. Thus, a chamber of commerce's efforts are directed at promoting the common economic interests of all of the commercial enterprises in a trade community.

A federal court of appeals noted, by reference to dictionaries, two similar definitions of the term *chamber of commerce*. One of these definitions is that a chamber of commerce is an association that promotes the commercial interests of a locality, country, or the like. The other definition is that such an organization is a society of a city that strives to promote the general trade and commerce of that community.[241]

The IRS observed, in a ruling, that a function of a local chamber of commerce was attempting to attract new industry to a community.[242] Similarly, the IRS recognized an organization formed for the purpose of encouraging national organizations to hold their conventions in a city as an exempt chamber of commerce.[243] Membership in an exempt chamber of commerce must be voluntary and open to all business and professional persons in a community.[244]

The IRS ruled that a tenants' association—in this instance, an association of shopping center merchants—did not qualify as a tax-exempt chamber of commerce.[245] The agency noted that membership in the association was compulsory, imposed by the landlord owner of the shopping center, and that the requisite *community* was not being served, as the "community represented by the membership of the. . .organization is a closed, non-public aggregation of commercial enterprises having none of the common characteristics of a community in the usual geographic or political sense."[246] Moreover, the IRS invoked a private inurement

---

[240] The organization's primary activity was operation of a call center for consumers of member financial institutions who are victims of suspected identity theft; its membership was confined to the top 50 banks, credit card issuers, and other nonbank financial services companies. The IRS also ruled that this entity did not represent a line of business (see § 14.2(a)) and provided particular services to its members (see § 14.2(c)).

[241] Retailers Credit Ass'n of Alameda Cnty. v. Comm'r, 90 F.2d 47, 51 (9th Cir. 1937). The second of these definitions was also cited in Crooks v. Kansas City Hay Dealers' Ass'n, 37 F.2d 83, 85 (8th Cir. 1929).

[242] Rev. Rul. 70-81, 1970-1 C.B. 131, *amplified by* Rev. Rul. 81-138, 1981-1 C.B. 358.

[243] Rev. Rul. 76-207, 1976-1 C.B. 158.

[244] A self-insurer guaranty trust fund was held to be tax-exempt by reason of IRC § 501(c)(6) because it was "of the same general class" as a chamber of commerce or board of trade (Georgia Self-Insurers Guar. Trust Fund v. United States, 78 A.F.T.R. 2d 6552 (N.D. Ga. 1996)).

[245] Rev. Rul. 73-411, 1973-2 C.B. 180.

[246] *Id.* Also, Rev. Rul. 59-391, 1959-2 C.B. 151.

doctrine rationale,[247] holding that the organization was designed to serve the tenants' business interests in the shopping center. Exempt status as a business league was denied because the association was not structured along particular industry or business lines.

A neighborhood community association may qualify for tax exemption in this context where the organization has a voluntary membership, it is not concerned with tenants' matters, and the organization is operated to improve the business conditions of a community (rather than a single one-owner shopping mall).[248] This may be the case even though a majority of the association's member businesses is located in one shopping center.

Consequently, the principal distinction between a business league and a chamber of commerce is that the former must promote the common business interests of persons within a line of business, whereas the latter must promote the common business interests of persons within a community or similarly defined geographic area.

The IRS, from time to time, issues private letter rulings as to whether an organization qualifies as a tax-exempt chamber of commerce.[249]

§ 14.4 BOARDS OF TRADE

A tax-exempt board of trade is a nonprofit organization organized and operated to regulate, promote, supervise, or protect commercial or business enterprises or interests in a community.

A federal court of appeals observed that the terms *chamber of commerce* and *board of trade* are "nearly synonymous," although there is a "slight distinction" between their meanings. The court explained: "The former relates to all businesses in a particular geographic location, while the latter may relate to only one or more lines of business in a particular geographic location, but need not relate to all."[250] This court noted that a board of trade is an organization operated for the "advancement and protection of business interests."[251]

The previously referenced association of shopping center merchants was also denied tax-exempt status as a board of trade, essentially for the same reasons it failed to achieve exempt status as a chamber of commerce.[252] Similarly, an organization was precluded from exempt status as a board of trade principally because its predominant activity was the provision of services to individuals, in the form of grain analysis laboratory services to both members and nonmembers, and because the entity was supported almost entirely from the substantial profits of the laboratory.[253] Likewise, the concept of an exempt board of trade does not encompass

---

[247] See Chapter 20.
[248] Rev. Rul. 78-225, 1978-1 C.B. 159.
[249] E.g., Ex. Den. and Rev. Ltr. 20044001E.
[250] Retailers Credit Ass'n of Alameda Cnty. v. Comm'r, 90 F.2d 47, 51 (9th Cir. 1937).
[251] Id.
[252] Rev. Rul. 73-411, 1973-2 C.B. 180.
[253] Rev. Rul. 78-70, 1978-1 C.B. 159. Also, Fort Wayne Grain & Cotton Exch. v. Comm'r, 27 B.T.A. 983 (1933).

organizations that "provide conveniences or facilities to certain persons in connection with buying, selling, and exchanging goods."[254] By contrast, an organization regulating the sale of an agricultural commodity to assure equal treatment of producers, warehousers, and purchasers was ruled to be an exempt board of trade.[255]

As is the case with tax-exempt business leagues and chambers of commerce, membership in an exempt board of trade must be voluntary, and open to all trades and businesses in the particular community.

§ 14.5   REAL ESTATE BOARDS

Tax exemption for real estate boards came into being as an overturning of a court decision. The court had denied exemption as a business league to a corporation organized by associations of insurance companies to provide printing services for member companies.[256] Thereafter, the law was revised to specifically exempt real estate boards from federal income taxation.[257]

[254] L.O. 1123, III-1 C.B. 275 (1924).
[255] Rev. Rul. 55-715, 1955-2 C.B. 263.
[256] Uniform Printing & Supply Co. v. Comm'r, 33 F.2d 445 (7th Cir. 1929), *cert. denied*, 280 U.S. 69 (1929).
[257] IRC § 501(c)(6).

CHAPTER FIFTEEN

Social Clubs

Tax-exempt social clubs have as the essential requirement of their exemption the provision of pleasure and recreation to their members.

§ 15.1 SOCIAL CLUBS IN GENERAL

The federal tax law provides tax exemption for qualified social clubs, which are "organized for pleasure, recreation, and other nonprofitable purposes, substantially all of the activities of which are for such purposes and no part of the net earnings of which inures to the benefit of any private shareholder."[1] Generally, this exemption extends to social and recreation clubs that are supported primarily by membership fees, dues, and assessments.[2] An organization that otherwise qualifies as an exempt social club will not, however, be denied exemption solely because it adopts a method of raising revenue from members by means other than fees, dues, and assessments.[3]

(a) Rationale for Tax Exemption

Social clubs are tax-exempt because Congress recognized that these organizations are generally not appropriate subjects of taxation: that is, that the operation of a social club does not involve the requisite shifting of income.[4] Thus, a court wrote that "Congress has determined that in a situation where individuals have banded

---

[1] IRC § 501(c)(7). As to private inurement, see § 20.11. Notwithstanding the prohibition on private inurement in the statute, a social club may liquidate its assets and distribute the net proceeds thereof to its members upon dissolution without affecting its exemption in the year of liquidation and distribution, even when the amount distributed exceeds the basis of the interests of the members in the organization's assets (Mill Lane Club v. Comm'r, 23 T.C. 433 (1954), *acq.* 1955-1 C.B. 5; Rev. Rul. 58-501, 1958-2 C.B. 262; Gen. Couns. Mem. 33210). See § 15.5.
[2] Reg. § 1.501(c)(7)-1(a); Maryland Country Club, Inc. v. United States, 539 F.2d 345 (4th Cir. 1976).
[3] Rev. Rul. 53-44, 1953-1 C.B. 109.
[4] See § 1.5.

together to provide recreational facilities on a mutual basis, it would be conceptually erroneous to impose a tax on the organization as a separate entity" and that "[n]o income of the sort usually taxed has been generated; the money has simply been shifted from one pocket to another, both within the same pair of pants."[5] These observations were presaged in a Treasury Department report, which stated that where the "sources of income of the organization are limited to receipts from the membership. . .the individual is in substantially the same position as if he had spent his income on pleasure and recreation without the intervening separate organization."[6] Reflecting on this rationale, the U.S. Supreme Court concluded that the federal tax exemption for social clubs has a "justification fundamentally different from that which underlies the grant of tax exemption to other nonprofit entities."[7]

(b) Club Functions

To qualify as a tax-exempt social club, an organization not only must be a non-profit entity[8] but must meet an organizational test and an operational test.[9] To satisfy the requirement of a pleasure, recreation, or other nonprofitable purpose, a club must have an established membership of individuals, personal contacts, and fellowship.[10] A mingling of the members must play a material part in the life of the organization.[11] For these reasons, a club, organized only because that form was required by state law to enable a restaurant of which it is a part to serve alcoholic beverages, was denied recognition of exemption as a social club on the grounds that it is not operated exclusively for pleasure and recreation, there is no mingling of members, there was private inurement regarding the owners of the restaurant, and the sole function of this ostensible club was to sell alcohol to the public.[12] Similarly, an organization engaged primarily in operating and maintaining a web-site for its members failed to achieve exemption as a social club; its members-only forum was the sole means of membership interaction.[13] Likewise, a national online sorority was denied recognition of exemption as a social club because min-gling and promotion of fellowship were not a material part of its operations.[14]

---

[5] McGlotten v. Connally, 338 F. Supp. 448, 458 (D.D.C. 1972).

[6] Department of the Treasury, *Tax Reform Studies and Proposals* 317 (Comm. Print 1969). The federal tax law was changed in 1969 to require taxation of social clubs where they receive non-membership revenue (e.g., S. Rep. No. 91-552, at 71 (1969)); Staff of Joint Comm. on Internal Revenue Tax'n, *General Explanation of Tax Reform Act of 1969* 66–67 (Comm. Print 1970). See § 15.4.

[7] Portland Golf Club v. Comm'r, 497 U.S. 154, 161 (1990).

[8] West Side Tennis Club v. Comm'r, 111 F.2d 6 (2d Cir. 1940), *cert. denied*, 311 U.S. 674 (1940).

[9] E.g., Rev. Rul. 70-32, 1970-1 C.B. 132.

[10] Kanawha-Roane Lands, Inc. v. United States, 136 F. Supp. 631 (D. W. Va. 1956); Barstow Rodeo & Riding Club v. Comm'r, 12 T.C.M. 1351 (1953).

[11] Rev. Rul. 58-589, 1958-2 C.B. 266. Thus, an organization was denied exempt social club status in part because its "core business function" was providing winemaking services and products, where a substantial portion of its activities were "one on one" between a member and the winemaker (Priv. Ltr. Rul. 201025078).

[12] Priv. Ltr. Rul. 201515035.

[13] Priv. Ltr. Rul. 201043042. In this ruling, the IRS observed: "Face-to-face interaction is important for members of a social club."

[14] Priv. Ltr. Rul. 201434022.

As still other examples, a membership organization of football officials functioning in public school districts was denied recognition of tax exemption in part
because of lack of "social commingling or fellowship" among its members; the
only gatherings were training sessions, which were not mandatory.[15] The same
held for a membership entity whose members met weekly to make decisions and
take advantage of opportunities within its local business region,[16] an organization maintaining a private road in a gated community as its sole activity;[17] and a
buying club that secured for its members reasonably priced, non-GMO, organic
foods and products that are safe for families and the environment.[18] An organization operating a trailer park was also found to fail the commingling requirement
where any member of the public had a right to park their trailer upon purchase
of a single share of the organization's stock.[19] Where the requisite degree of fellowship is absent, tax exemption may be denied, as occurred with respect to an
organization formed to furnish television antenna service to its members[20] and
associations composed primarily of "artificial" persons or other clubs.[21] Thus, a
club operated to assist its members in their business endeavors through study and
discussion of problems and similar activities at weekly luncheon meetings was
denied exemption as a social club on the ground that any social activities at the
meetings were merely incidental to the business purpose of the organization.[22] A
related concept is that a club, to be exempt, must have members actively sharing
interests or goals, as evidenced, for example, by appropriate prerequisite conditions or limitations on members.[23] It is insufficient, for purposes of exemption, for
an organization to be able to demonstrate a common objective or interest of the
members. Consequently, for example, most nonprofit automobile clubs are denied
exemption as social clubs.[24]

  To the IRS, the criterion of providing pleasure or recreation by a tax-exempt
social club to its members is paramount to the qualification of the club for tax
exemption. Thus, gambling can be an exempt purpose for a social club, even

---

[15] Priv. Ltr. Rul. 201845030. Likewise, an organization formed to provide funding for student athletes
did not receive recognition of exempt status where its membership was composed of anyone who
donated to it and there was "no co-mingling or fellowship between members unless by happenstance
at a sporting event" (Priv. Ltr. Rul. 202310012).

[16] Priv. Ltr. Rul. 201848017.

[17] Priv. Ltr. Rul. 202124011.

[18] Priv. Ltr. Rul. 202215016.

[19] Priv. Ltr. Rul. 202213011.

[20] Rev. Rul. 55-716, 1955-2 C.B. 263, *modified by* Rev. Rul. 83-170, 1983-2 C.B. 97; also, Gen. Couns. Mem.
39063. Cf. Rev. Rul. 62-167, 1962-2 C.B. 142.

[21] Rev. Rul. 67-428, 1967-2 C.B. 204.

[22] Rev. Rul. 69-527, 1969-2 C.B. 125. Thus, an organization that operated to foster networking among
vendors and prospective clients within the legal profession failed to qualify as an exempt social club
(Priv. Ltr. Rul. 200906057).

[23] Arner v. Rogan, 40-2 U.S.T.C. ¶ 9567 (S.D. Cal. 1940).

[24] Warren Automobile Club v. Comm'r, 182 F.2d 551 (6th Cir. 1950); Keystone Automobile Club v.
Comm'r, 181 F.2d 402 (3d Cir. 1950); Chattanooga Automobile Club v. Comm'r, 182 F.2d 551 (6th Cir.
1950); Smyth v. California State Automobile Ass'n, 175 F.2d 752 (9th Cir. 1949), *cert. denied*, 338 U.S. 905
(1949); Automobile Club of St. Paul v. Comm'r, 12 T.C. 1152 (1949); Rev. Rul. 69-635, 1969-2 C.B. 126;
Rev. Rul. 67-249, 1967-2 C.B. 179.

where substantial income is derived from the practice, as long as the source of the revenue is the club's members and their guests. The IRS will refrain from denying or revoking an organization's exemption on this basis, notwithstanding the fact that the gambling activities are illegal under state or local law.[25]

In determining whether a club is being operated for tax-exempt purposes, the IRS will test each of its activities to determine if it is a *traditional* one (furthering pleasure, recreation, or other nonprofitable purposes) or a *nontraditional* one (that will likely preclude tax exemption or cause loss of exemption).[26] Traditional activities are those that are "normal and usual" activities for an exempt social club,[27] and permitted *other nonprofitable purposes* include only those purposes of the same general character as pleasure and recreation.[28] Thus, the payment of sick and death benefits is not considered a traditional function of a social club.[29]

While country clubs, dinner clubs, variety clubs, swim, golf, and tennis clubs, and the like set the norm for the tax-exempt social club,[30] the concept of an exempt social club is considerably broader. Thus, a flying club was ruled to qualify for exemption, where the members were interested in flying as a hobby, commingled in informal meetings, maintained and repaired aircraft owned by the club, and flew together in small groups,[31] as opposed to a club that was operated primarily to provide flying facilities suitable for members' individual business or personal use.[32] Social club status was accorded an organization composed solely of persons who were members of a political party and those interested in party affairs,[33] and of members of a specific family to bring them into closer communication through social, family history, and newsletter activities.[34] Gem and mineral clubs or a federation of these clubs may qualify as exempt social clubs.[35] Other illustrations of exempt social clubs include pet clubs,[36] garden clubs,[37] fraternities

---

[25] Rev. Rul. 69-68, 1969-1 C.B. 153.

[26] The IRS sometimes refers to this as the *activities test* (e.g., Tech. Adv. Mem. 201430019). See § 4.5(b).

[27] S. Rep. No. 94-1318, at 4 (1976); H.R. Rep. No. 94-1353, at 4 (1976).

[28] Allgemeiner Arbeiter Verein v. Comm'r, 25 T.C. 371, 375 (1955), *aff'd per curiam*, 237 F.2d 604 (3d Cir. 1956). Not surprisingly, a corporation engaged in trading securities was found not to meet this statutory requirement (Associates v. Comm'r, 28 B.T.A. 521 (1933)).

[29] Allied Trades Club, Inc. v. Comm'r, 23 T.C. 1017 (1955), *aff'd*, 228 F.2d 906 (3d Cir. 1956); Polish Army Veterans Post 147 v. Comm'r, 24 T.C. 891 (1955), *rev'd on other grounds*, 236 F.2d 509 (3d Cir. 1956); St. Albert's American-Polish Citizens & Social Club v. Comm'r, 14 T.C.M. 196 (1955); Spokane Commercial Travelers v. United States, 126 F. Supp. 424 (W.D. Wash. 1954); Rev. Rul. 63-190, 1963-2 C.B. 212.

[30] Hillcrest Country Club, Inc. v. United States, 152 F. Supp. 896 (D. Mo. 1957); Slovene Workers Home v. Dallman, 56-1 U.S.T.C. ¶ 9205 (S.D. Ill. 1956); Coeur D'Alene Athletic Round Table, Inc. v. Comm'r, 21 T.C.M. 1430 (1962); Rev. Rul. 69-281, 1969-1 C.B. 155.

[31] Rev. Rul. 74-30, 1974-1 C.B. 137. Also, Syrang Aero Club, Inc. v. Comm'r, 73 T.C. 717 (1980).

[32] Rev. Rul. 70-32, 1970-1 C.B. 132. Also, Rev. Rul. 56-475, 1956-2 C.B. 308. Thus, the IRS denied recognition of exempt status to a flying club where the members (totaling four) each used the aircraft one week each month with the other members not present (Priv. Ltr. Rul. 200450041).

[33] Rev. Rul. 68-266, 1968-1 C.B. 270. Cf. Thomas J. McGee Regular Democratic Club, Inc. v. Comm'r, 1 T.C.M. 18 (1942) (where public use was extensive).

[34] Rev. Rul. 67-8, 1967-1 C.B. 142.

[35] Rev. Rul. 67-139, 1967-1 C.B. 129.

[36] Rev. Rul. 73-520, 1973-2 C.B. 180; Rev. Rul. 71-421, 1971-2 C.B. 229.

[37] Rev. Rul. 66-179, 1966-1 C.B. 139.

and sororities,[38] a sponsor of bowling tournaments,[39] a promoter of golf,[40] a horse-riding club,[41] and clubs affiliated with exempt lodges.[42]

A tax-exempt social club may provide social and recreational facilities to its members who are limited to homeowners of a housing development and nonetheless qualify for tax exemption. This exemption will be precluded, however, where any of the following services are provided by the club: owning and maintaining residential streets, administering and enforcing covenants for the preservation of the architecture and appearance of the housing development, or providing police and fire protection and a trash collection service to residential areas.[43] Thus, an organization that maintained privately owned residential streets, boat docks, and ramps in a neighborhood and paid for property liability insurance for its members was found not to qualify as an exempt social club.[44]

(c)   Other Tax Law Matters

A social club constitutes a *welfare benefit fund*,[45] and therefore a *disqualified benefit*[46] provided by the organization will give rise to tax liability.[47]

There is no business expense or other tax deduction for amounts paid or incurred for membership in a social club, whether or not tax-exempt.[48]

§ 15.2   PUBLIC USE AND INVESTMENT INCOME LIMITATIONS

Under the income tax regulations (which antedate the 1976 statutory revision, discussed below), a "club which engages in business, such as making its social and recreational facilities available to the general public. . ., is not organized and operated exclusively for pleasure, recreation, and other nonprofitable purposes, and is not exempt" from federal income tax.[49] Solicitation of the public to utilize club

---

[38] Rev. Rul. 69-573, 1969-2 C.B. 125; Rev. Rul. 64-118, 1964-1 C.B. 182; Phinney v. Dougherty, 307 F.2d 357 (5th Cir. 1962); Alumnae Chapter Beta of Clovia v. Comm'r, 46 T.C. 297 (1983). The IRS said this about college sororities: "Although the typical college sorority does in some degree contribute to the cultural and educational growth of its members during their student years[,] that is not its primary purpose," in that "[s]uch an organization is primarily a social club in that its major functions are to provide a meeting place for its members, living quarters, and the headquarters for their entertainment" (Priv. Ltr. Rul. 201213036).

[39] Rev. Rul. 74-148, 1974-1 C.B. 138.

[40] Augusta Golf Ass'n v. United States, 338 F. Supp. 272 (S.D. Ga. 1971).

[41] Clements Buckaroos v. Comm'r, 21 T.C.M. 83 (1962).

[42] Rev. Rul. 66-150, 1966-1 C.B. 164; Rev. Rul. 56-305, 1956-2 C.B. 307.

[43] Rev. Rul. 75-494, 1975-2 C.B. 214.

[44] Priv. Ltr. Rul. 202327017.

[45] IRC § 419(e)(3)(A).

[46] IRC § 4976(b).

[47] IRC § 4976(a).

[48] IRC § 274(a)(3).

[49] Reg. § 1.501(c)(7)-1(b). In 1976, Congress changed the reference to *exclusively* in the statute (which continues to appear in the regulations) to *substantially*, thereby relaxing somewhat the restrictions on an exempt social club's ability to earn nonmember and investment income (see text accompanied by *infra* notes 73–78).

facilities prima facie evidence that the club is engaging in business and typically will disqualify the social club for tax exemption.[50]

The IRS promulgated guidelines for determining the effect on a social club's tax exemption of gross receipts derived from nonmember use of the club's facilities.[51] The concern in this regard is not with the situation where a club member entertains a few guests at their club, but where a club's facilities are made available to the public on a regular and recurring basis, thereby removing that segment of the public from the marketplace of competing commercial operations.[52] Infrequent use of an exempt social club by the public is permissible, since it is an incidental use.[53] Thus, for example, a club cannot be exempt when a significant portion of its revenue is derived from greens fees charged to the public,[54] yet can be exempt where fees of this nature are incidental.[55]

This matter concerning the permissible extent of public use of the facilities of social clubs has long been the subject of debate. In perhaps the most well-known case on the point, a tennis club was held not to be entitled to tax exemption because it received more than one-half of its income from the conduct of national championship tennis matches. The court mused that, were it not for limitations on nonmember income, a club would be able to maintain "as large and luxurious a plant as the members might like without the payment of burdensome dues."[56]

In another instance, a court nicely stated the consequence arising from a situation when a club derives substantial income from nonmember sources: The club "has eschewed that mutuality which is the basis for its exemption."[57] "In such a situation," the court continued, "revenue derived from nonmembers is used to benefit members since the outside revenue permits the club to assess lower dues than would otherwise be required to support the club's facilities and operations."[58]

A corporation may pay for individual club memberships without jeopardizing the club's tax exemption,[59] although an organization whose membership is

[50] Id. Keystone Automobile Club v. Comm'r, 181 F.2d 402 (3d Cir. 1950); United States v. Fort Worth Club of Fort Worth, Texas, 345 F.2d 52 (5th Cir. 1965), modified and aff'd, 348 F.2d 891 (5th Cir. 1965); Polish American Club, Inc. v. Comm'r, 33 T.C.M. 925 (1974).

[51] Rev. Proc. 71-17, 1971-1 C.B. 683. Also, Minnequa Univ. Club v. Comm'r, 30 T.C.M. 1305 (1971). Litigation concerning these guidelines is reflected in Pittsburgh Press Club v. United States, 388 F. Supp. 1269 (W.D. Pa. 1975), rev. and remanded, 536 F.2d 572 (3d Cir. 1976), on remand, 426 F. Supp. 553 (W.D. Pa. 1977), remanded, 579 F.2d 751 (3d Cir. 1978), on remand, 462 F. Supp. 322 (W.D. Pa. 1978), rev'd, 615 F.2d 600 (3d Cir. 1980).

[52] Rev. Rul. 60-324, 1960-2 C.B. 173. Also, Rev. Rul. 69-220, 1969-1 C.B. 154; Rev. Rul. 69-217, 1969-1 C.B. 115; Rev. Rul. 68-638, 1968-2 C.B. 220; Rev. Rul. 65-63, 1965-1 C.B. 240; United States v. Fort Worth Club of Fort Worth, Texas, 345 F.2d 52 (5th Cir. 1965), modified and aff'd, 348 F.2d 891 (5th Cir. 1965); Spokane Motorcycle Club v. United States, 222 F. Supp. 151 (E.D. Wash. 1963); Sabers of Denver, Inc. v. United States, 65-2 U.S.T.C. ¶ 9670 (D. Col. 1965); Matter of The Breakfast Club, Ltd., 35-1 U.S.T.C. ¶ 9265 (D. Cal. 1935).

[53] Rev. Rul. 60-323, 1960-2 C.B. 173; Rev. Rul. 66-149, 1966-1 C.B. 146; Town & Country Club v. Comm'r, 1 T.C.M. 334 (1942).

[54] Rev. Rul. 69-219, 1969-1 C.B. 153.

[55] Coeur d'Alene Country Club v. Viley, 64 F. Supp. 540 (N.D. Idaho 1946).

[56] West Side Tennis Club v. Comm'r, 111 F.2d 6, 8 (2d Cir. 1940).

[57] Pittsburgh Press Club v. United States, 579 F.2d 751, 761 (3d Cir. 1978).

[58] Id.

[59] Rev. Rul. 74-168, 1974-1 C.B. 139.

entirely in corporations' names does not qualify for exemption.[60] To the extent that an exempt social club has corporate members, however, the individuals who use the club's facilities under the memberships are treated as part of the public for these purposes.[61] Amounts paid to an exempt social club by visiting members of another exempt social club, pursuant to a reciprocity arrangement, are forms of nonmember income.[62]

Where the group includes eight or fewer individuals at least one of whom is a member, the IRS will assume any nonmembers are the guests of the member, provided that the tax-exempt social club maintains records that substantiate that the group includes no more than eight individuals, at least one of whom is a member, and that payment was received from the member or their employer.[63] Where 75 percent or more of the group are members of the club, records must be maintained that substantiate that at least 75 percent of the group are club members and that payment was received directly from members or members' employers.[64]

On all other occasions involving nonmembers, the tax-exempt social club must maintain records showing each use and the income derived from the use, even though a member pays initially for the use. The club's records must also include the following: the date, the total number in the party, the number of nonmembers in the party, the total charges, the charges attributable to nonmembers, and the charges paid by nonmembers. If a member pays all or part of the charges, there must be a statement signed by the member as to whether they have been or will be reimbursed and to what extent by the nonmembers.

Further, where a member's employer reimburses the member or pays the social club directly for nonmember charges, there must be a statement indicating the name of the employer, the amount attributable to nonmember use, the nonmember's name and business or other relationship to the member, and the business, personal, or social purpose of the member served by the nonmember use. If a nonmember (other than a member's employer) makes payment to the club or reimburses a member and claims the amount was paid gratuitously, the member must sign a statement indicating the donor's name, relationship to the member, and information demonstrating the gratuitous nature of the payment.[65]

Excessive use of tax-exempt social club facilities by the public is not the only way in which a club may be considered as engaging in business. In one instance, a swim club was held to be operated as a commercial venture for the financial benefit of its manager and thus was denied exemption.[66] (A club may, however, without jeopardizing its exemption, enter into a management and lease agreement for the operation of its facilities.)[67] In another case, a club had such a large number of "associate members" that the IRS treated it as selling services for profit to these individuals.[68]

---

[60] Rev. Rul. 67-428, 1967-2 C.B. 204.

[61] Rev. Rul. 74-489, 1974-2 C.B. 169.

[62] Gen. Couns. Mem. 39343.

[63] Rev. Proc. 71-17, 1971-1 C.B. 683 §§ 3.01, 4.01.

[64] Id. §§ 3.02, 4.02.

[65] Id. § 4.03.

[66] Rev. Rul. 65-219, 1965-2 C.B. 168.

[67] Rev. Rul. 67-302, 1967-2 C.B. 203.

[68] Rev. Rul. 58-588, 1958-2 C.B. 265.

As part of the change in rules in this context occasioned by the development of legislative history,[69] in general, no more than 15 percent of the gross receipts of a tax-exempt social club can be derived from the use of a club's facilities or services by the public. Thus, for example, the IRS revoked the exempt status of a club, formed to provide sport parachuting facilities, because more than 40 percent of its gross receipts was derived from students (nonmembers) paying for training services and participation in jumps.[70]

The IRS occasionally rules that a particular activity or flow of money is not a violation of the public use limitation. For example, the agency held that a tax-exempt social club operating a golf course and other sports facilities may provide limited public access to the course pursuant to an agreement with a municipality while its public course is being renovated; the club was ruled to not be opening its facilities to the public in a manner that would endanger its exempt status.[71] Also, the IRS ruled that a social club's exemption would not be jeopardized because of its support of a program of an exempt social welfare organization; it was held that the gross receipts of the social welfare entity are not attributable to the club for purposes of the nonmember income limitation and that reimbursements from the entity are not nonmember gross receipts.[72]

Congress, in 1976, changed the original statutory requirement that a social club be organized and operated *exclusively* for pleasure, recreation, and similar purposes so that *substantially all* of a club's activities must be for these purposes.[73] This change allows an exempt social club to receive some outside income, including investment income and income from nonmembers using its facilities or services, without losing its exempt status. The underlying rationale was that the extension of the unrelated business income tax to social clubs[74] meant that the "extent to which a club can obtain income from nonmember sources can be somewhat liberalized."[75]

These rules are formulated as "safe-harbor" guidelines: A tax-exempt social club generally can receive as much as 35 percent of its *gross receipts*,[76] including investment income, from sources outside of its membership without losing exempt status; however, as noted previously, generally no more than 15 percent of its gross receipts can be derived from the use of a social club's facilities or services by the public.[77]

---

[69] See text accompanied by *infra* notes 73–78.

[70] Priv. Ltr. Rul. 200623072.

[71] Priv. Ltr. Rul. 201414029.

[72] Priv. Ltr. Rul. 201428009.

[73] Pub. L. No. 94-568, 90 Stat. 2697 (1976).

[74] See § 15.4.

[75] S. Rep. No. 94-1318, at 3 (1976); H.R Rep. No. 94-1353, at 3 (1976). Also, I.R. 1731 (Jan. 11, 1977). The guidelines created by Congress in 1976 effectively supersede the criteria in Rev. Proc. 71-17, 1971-1 C.B. 683 (see text accompanied by *supra* note 51) with respect to the safe harbor gross receipts amounts that a social club may receive from nonmembers. The revenue procedure otherwise remains valid as a basis for record-keeping requirements and its assumptions as to the guest status of nonmembers (Gen. Couns. Mem. 39773; see text accompanied by *supra* notes 63-65).

[76] Case law embodying prior law as to the nonmember income issue loosely used words like *income*, *revenue*, and *subsidy*. As to the concept of *subsidy*, for example, see Pittsburgh Press Club v. Comm'r, 579 F.2d 751 (3d Cir. 1978). These words have been replaced by the term *gross receipts*.

[77] S. Rep. No. 94-1318, at 4 (1976); H.R. Rep. No. 94-1353, at 4 (1976).

It is not intended that social clubs be permitted to receive, within either percentage allowance, income from the active conduct of businesses not traditionally carried on by these organizations.[78]

The term *gross receipts*, for this purpose, means those receipts from normal and usual activities of these clubs (that is, those activities they have traditionally conducted), including charges, admissions, membership fees, assessments, investment income, and normal recurring gain. Initiation fees and capital contributions are excluded.[79] The concept of gross receipts entails some form of tangible economic benefit, such as revenue derived from a club's sale of cookbooks;[80] revenue derived by a club from the sale of fox hounds;[81] revenue derived from a club's conduct of a sports tournament;[82] revenue derived from commercial advertising appearing in a club's periodicals;[83] fees paid by "apprentice members";[84] revenue derived by a club from the conduct of luncheons, banquets, and receptions;[85] and revenue derived from the sale of timber by a club.[86] Court opinions likewise reflect this view, including in gross receipts income from concessions and the sale of souvenirs,[87] revenue from the conduct of nonmember golf tournaments,[88] and revenue from the sale of food and beverages to nonmembers.[89]

The IRS has not been bashful over the years in revoking the exempt status of a social club for violation of the public use and investment income limitations and related rules.[90]

§ 15.3 EXCEPTIONS TO LIMITATIONS

In computing the public use and investment income percentages, a tax-exempt social club need not take into consideration "unusual amounts of income."[91]

---

[78] *Id.*

[79] The rule as to capital contributions does not reference any categories of providers of capital; presumably, then, excludable capital contributions can come from members and nonmembers. As a practical matter, it is uncommon for a social club to receive contributions to its capital from any source other than its members, although it does happen. An analogy may be made to the law concerning contributions of capital to for-profit corporations by shareholders and non-shareholders (IRC § 118(a); Reg. § 1.118-1). The principal cases on the law pertaining to non-shareholder contributions to capital are Brown Shoe Co. v. Comm'r, 339 U.S. 583 (1950), and United States v. Chicago, Burlington & Quincy Railroad Co., 412 U.S. 401 (1973). An IRS ruling on non-shareholder capital contributions is Priv. Ltr. Rul. 200133036.

[80] Priv. Ltr. Rul. 8141019.

[81] Priv. Ltr. Rul. 8242003.

[82] Priv. Ltr. Rul. 8426001.

[83] Priv. Ltr. Rul. 8446008.

[84] Priv. Ltr. Rul. 8541008.

[85] Priv. Ltr. Rul. 8542003.

[86] Priv. Ltr. Rul. 9533015.

[87] Ye Mystic Krewe of Gasparilla v. Comm'r, 80 T.C. 755 (1983).

[88] North Ridge Country Club v. Comm'r, 877 F.2d 750 (9th Cir. 1989), *rev'g* 89 T.C. 563 (1987).

[89] The Cleveland Athletic Club, Inc. v. United States, 779 F.2d 1160 (6th Cir. 1985); Inter-Com Club, Inc. v. United States, 721 F. Supp. 1112 (D. Neb. 1989); The Brook, Inc. v. Comm'r, 50 T.C.M. 959 (1985); Polish American Club v. Comm'r, 33 T.C.M. 925 (1974).

[90] E.g., Priv. Ltr. Rul. 202249017. An organization supported exclusively by gifts, donations, and contributions will also fail to qualify as a social club under these rules (Priv. Ltr. Rul. 202442008).

[91] S. Rep. No. 94-1318, at 4 (1976); H.R. Rep. No. 94-1353, at 4 (1976).

This rule is generally intended to cover receipts from the sale of a clubhouse or similar facility. Presumably, the rule is also applicable to receipts from a major sporting event (such as a golf or tennis tournament) that is open to the public but is held by the club on an irregular basis. This interpretation would be in conformity with prior case law.[92]

Some tax-exempt social clubs hold tournaments on a regularly recurring basis (for example, annually). In this situation, the exclusion for unusual amounts is presumably unavailable. Thus, the exemption of a social club in this circumstance would be adversely affected if the 15 percent limitation was exceeded[93] but, even if the level of receipts did not trigger revocation of exemption, the return from the tournament would nonetheless be subject to taxation as unrelated business income.[94]

The tax-exempt status of a social club is not automatically lost, however, if these percentages are exceeded, because the guidelines are, as noted, a safe harbor. If the guidelines are exceeded, then all of the facts and circumstances are taken into account in determining whether the organization qualifies for exempt status. The overarching standard used in application of this facts-and-circumstances test is whether the activity or support is "necessary to preserve the assets of the club used for exempt purposes."[95] On another occasion, when a club exceeded the percentage guidelines, the IRS used the facts-and-circumstances test to enable the club to retain its tax exemption because of a "lack of profits."[96] Remarkably, in one instance, the IRS applied the test (the safe-harbor guidelines having been exceeded), concluding that revocation was inappropriate because the "officers and [other] representatives [of the club] held a good faith belief that the income from the functions at issue constituted member income."[97]

Nonetheless, this safe-harbor rule notwithstanding, there is *some* limit as to the amount of investment income a social club can receive and still remain tax-exempt. Thus, a court held that a club could not be tax-exempt when it received 100 percent of its gross receipts in the form of investment income.[98] This court referenced an appellate court opinion (albeit one issued before 1976) that contained the observation that the "source of a club's revenues, as well as their destination, is crucial in determining the purpose for which the club is 'organized and operated.'"[99]

It is the view of the Chief Counsel of the IRS, however, that the revision of the law in 1976 did not modify the preexisting rule that revenue derived by an activity that does not advance tax-exempt purposes, whether engaged in for the benefit of members or nonmembers, will lead to revocation of a social club's exempt status.

---

[92] E.g., Santee Club v. White, 87 F.2d 5 (1st Cir. 1936).
[93] West Side Tennis Club v. United States, 111 F.2d 6 (2d Cir. 1940), *cert. denied*, 311 U.S. 674 (1940); Rev. Rul. 68-638, 1968-2 C.B. 220.
[94] E.g., Priv. Ltr. Rul. 8426001. See § 15.4.
[95] Priv. Ltr. Rul. 9533015.
[96] Priv. Ltr. Rul. 8426001.
[97] Priv. Ltr. Rul. 8542003.
[98] Skillman Family Reunion Fund, Inc. v. Comm'r, 196 F. Supp. 2d 543 (N.D. Ohio 2002).
[99] United States v. Fort Worth Club of Fort Worth, Texas, 345 F.2d 52, 56 (5th Cir. 1965), *modified and aff'd*, 348 F.2d 891 (5th Cir. 1965).

These activities, known as *nontraditional* activities,[100] may not cause loss of tax-exempt status if the income from them represents only *de minimis* amounts of income. In one instance, the IRS's lawyers considered the tax status of a social club that rented rooms as temporary principal residences, rented offices, operated a barbershop, provided a take-out service, operated a service station and a parking garage, and maintained in its lobby a commercial ticket agency, a flower and gift shop, and a liquor store. The sales of petroleum products and services and of take-out food were found to be nontraditional activities; the rental of rooms, operation of the barbershop and parking garage, and maintenance of the ticket agency were termed "questionable."[101] In another instance, the IRS ruled that income from the sale of emission credits will not disturb a social club's tax exemption because the sale will be a new source of income for the club and the sale activity will be a nonrecurring event.[102] The IRS also found boat storage and retrieval, boat maintenance, rentals, and fuel sales provided to residents of a boat condominium to be nontraditional activities.[103]

§ 15.4   TAXATION OF SOCIAL CLUBS

The income tax regulations disallow tax exemption for a social club that "engages in business, such as by selling real estate, timber or other products," unless a sale of property is incidental.[104] Nonetheless, abuses were prevalent, perhaps fostered by the courts' willingness to salvage a social club's exemption. For example, a federal court of appeals held that two golf clubs did not lose exemption because of the execution of oil leases on their properties that generated substantial income, on the theory that the leases were "incidental" to club operations.[105] Of course, the profits from the oil leases went untaxed.[106]

In 1969, Congress adhered to the Treasury Department's recommendation for reform in this area. The Treasury Department had, in effect, relied on the basic rationale for the tax exemption of social clubs and ran the rationale in reverse, contending that the investment income of social clubs was equivalent to income earned by the club members in their individual capacity.[107] In that year, Congress

---

[100] See text accompanied by *supra* notes 26-29.

[101] Gen. Couns. Mem. 39115. The IRS made clear in an information letter that it continues to adhere to its position that exempt social clubs may not utilize for-profit subsidiaries (see Chapter 30) to provide club facilities for use by nonmembers (INFO 2003-0115).

[102] Priv. Ltr. Rul. 202019027.

[103] Priv. Ltr. Rul. 202242013.

[104] Reg. § 1.501(c)(7)-1(b); Rev. Rul. 69-232, 1969-1 C.B. 154.

[105] Scofield v. Corpus Christi Golf & Country Club, 127 F.2d 452 (5th Cir. 1942); Koon Kreek Klub v. United States, 108 F.2d 616 (5th Cir. 1940). Cf. Coastal Club, Inc. v. Comm'r, 43 T.C. 783 (1965), *aff'd*, 368 F.2d 231 (5th Cir. 1966), *cert. denied*, 386 U.S. 1032 (1967).

[106] Another case involving a social club that was a nonexempt business is Aviation Club of Utah v. Comm'r, 162 F.2d 984 (10th Cir. 1947), *cert. denied*, 332 U.S. 837 (1947). Where the business activity was incidental, however, tax exemption was permitted (e.g., Town & Country Club v. Comm'r, 1 T.C.M. 334 (1942); Aviation Country Club, Inc. v. Comm'r, 21 T.C. 807 (1954)).

[107] S. Rep. No. 91-552, at 71 (1969); H.R. Rep. No. 91-413, pt. 1, at 47 (1969); Rev. Rul. 69-220, 1969-1 C.B. 154. Applying this doctrine, a federal court of appeals held that the regular drawings with the public

subjected income unrelated to the normal operation of a social club to the tax on unrelated business income.

For most types of tax-exempt organizations, revenue is nontaxable other than net income from unrelated business activities.[108] Thus, for nearly all exempt organizations, nontaxable revenue embraces gifts, grants, income from the performance of exempt functions, and passive (investment) income. The income of a tax-exempt social club, however, is taxed in a significantly different manner: Rather than isolate and tax unrelated business taxable income (the general rule), the law isolates the exempt function income of social clubs and subjects the balance of its revenue (including investment income) to taxation. (Thus, one of the principal disadvantages of classification as a "tax-exempt" social club is that all of its investment income—including passive income—generally is taxable.)

Specifically, a tax-exempt social club's *unrelated business taxable income* is defined as "gross income (excluding any exempt function income), less the deductions allowed. . .[for business expenses] which are directly connected with the production of the gross income (excluding exempt function income)."[109] This income is computed for tax purposes by deducting all expenses directly connected with production of the income and by applying certain of the modifications generally used in determining unrelated business taxable income.[110]

There had been a substantial dispute (eventually resolved by the U.S. Supreme Court, as discussed below) as to the extent to which deductions may be taken in determining a tax-exempt social club's taxable income, leading to differing positions by federal appellate courts. This dispute was stimulated by the practice of social clubs of deducting from investment income losses incurred in connection with the sale of meals and beverages to nonmembers. Thus, an effort commenced to develop a theory to preclude an exempt social club from generating losses from the performance of nonexempt functions that could be offset against gross investment income.

The IRS announced in 1981 that, when a tax-exempt social club operates a food and beverage concession catering to nonmembers and has consistently sold the food and beverages at prices insufficient to recover the cost of sales, the club "may not, in determining its unrelated business taxable income. . ., deduct from its net investment income its losses from such sales to nonmembers."[111] The concept

---

by a Knights of Columbus council, an IRC § 501(c)(8) fraternal society (see § 19.4(a)), were subject to the wagering excise and occupational taxes (IRC § 4421), in that the exception from the taxes for activities where there is no inurement of net earnings was ruled to not apply, on the theory that the revenues derived from the gaming are used to preclude dues increases, so that the "subsidization" constitutes a form of private inurement to the council's members (Knights of Columbus Council No. 3660 v. United States, 83-2 U.S.T.C. ¶ 16,410 (S.D. Ind. 1983), aff'd, 783 F.2d 69 (7th Cir. 1986)).

[108] See Chapters 24, 25.

[109] IRC § 512(a)(3)(A). Thus, in one case, the interest earned by a tax-exempt social club on deposits required for its charter flights was held taxable as unrelated income (Council of British Societies in S. Calif. v. United States, 78-2 U.S.T.C. ¶ 9744 (C.D. Cal. 1978), aff'd, 587 F.2d 931 (9th Cir. 1978)). Also, Deer Park Country Club v. Comm'r, 70 T.C.M. 1445 (1995); Confrerie De La Chaine Des Rotisseuers v. Comm'r, 66 T.C.M. 1845 (1993); Inter-Com Club, Inc. v. United States, 721 F. Supp. 1112 (D. Neb. 1989).

[110] IRC §§ 162, 512(b). The foregoing rules are also applicable to organizations described in IRC §§ 501(c)(9) and 501(c)(17). See Chapter 18.

[111] Rev. Rul. 81-69, 1981-1 C.B. 351.

underlying this position was that, where an exempt social club does not endeavor to realize a profit from the sales to nonmembers, the expenses cannot be deductible as business expenses under the general rules for that deduction.[112]

This position was tested in the U.S. Tax Court and was upheld, albeit on a different theory. The Tax Court, relying on the statutory language that states that a social club's taxable income is gross nonexempt income less the deductions that are "directly connected" with the production of gross income, held that a tax-exempt social club's expenses may be offset only against income it directly helped to generate, thereby precluding a club from deducting the expenses of service to nonmembers against investment income.[113] On appeal, however, it was held that the Tax Court's interpretation of the statute was incorrect and that federal tax law "authorizes deductions to be taken from the sum total of a club's non-exempt gross income, not merely from the portion of the income connected to the particular deduction."[114] This appellate court returned to the IRS position and concluded that exempt social clubs can deduct only the expenses of activities engaged in with the intention of making a profit, thereby precluding the club in the case from reducing its taxable investment income with nonmember service expenses.

The stance of the IRS in this regard was initially upheld in another case[115] but was rejected on appeal by the U.S. Court of Appeals for the Sixth Circuit. This appellate court's position, which is founded on the difference in tax treatment of social clubs in the unrelated income context,[116] was that a social club has a business expense deduction for outlays associated with activities engaged in with "a basic purpose of economic gain."[117] Under this principle, with which the Second Circuit disagreed, a club could deduct, as business expenses against investment income, all expenses of providing food and beverages to nonmembers.

The U.S. Court of Appeals for the Ninth Circuit sided with the Second Circuit on this point, holding that a tax-exempt social club must pursue a nonmember activity with a profit motive before it can properly deduct its losses.[118] The appellate court agreed with the IRS that the omission of the term *trade or business* from the definition of *unrelated business taxable income* as applied to tax-exempt social clubs[119] does not allow social clubs to deduct losses in nonmember activities that are not businesses, writing that it is "well-established" that, to qualify as a trade or business, an activity must be "regular and profit-seeking."[120] In the case, the club's nonmember food and bar activity was held to not be profit-seeking,

[112] IRC § 162. Thus, a tax-exempt social club was permitted to deduct the donations of the net proceeds of beano games it conducted, where the payments were a condition of its license for the games (South End Italian Indep. Club, Inc. v. Comm'r, 87 T.C. 168 (1986)).

[113] The Brook, Inc. v. Comm'r, 50 T.C.M. 959 (1985), 51 T.C.M. 133 (1985).

[114] The Brook, Inc. v. Comm'r, 799 F.2d 833 (2d Cir. 1986).

[115] The Cleveland Athletic Club, Inc. v. United States, 588 F. Supp. 1305 (N.D. Ohio 1984).

[116] See text accompanied by *supra* notes 108–110.

[117] The Cleveland Athletic Club, Inc. v. United States, 779 F.2d 1160, 1165 (6th Cir. 1985).

[118] North Ridge Country Club v. Comm'r, 877 F.2d 750 (9th Cir. 1989), *rev'g* 89 T.C. 563 (1987).

[119] IRC § 512(a)(3)(A). See text accompanied by *infra* note 125.

[120] North Ridge Country Club v. Comm'r, 877 F.2d 750, 753 (9th Cir. 1989), citing Comm'r v. Groetzinger, 480 U.S. 23 (1987) (see § 24.2(a)).

because of consistent losses for six years.[121] As noted, this matter was resolved by the U.S. Supreme Court in 1990, when it held that a tax-exempt social club may use losses incurred in connection with sales to nonmembers to offset investment income only if the sales were motivated by an intent to generate a profit.[122]

Under the general rules of unrelated income taxation,[123] unrelated business taxable income is defined as the "gross income derived by any organization from any unrelated trade or business. . .regularly carried on by it, less the deductions. . .which are directly connected with the carrying on of such trade or business."[124] The *trade or business* requirement is not in the definition of unrelated business taxable income applicable to social clubs, thereby, as noted, subjecting these organizations to, in the words of the Second Circuit Court of Appeals, a "much more far-reaching tax than" most other categories of tax-exempt organizations.[125]

Exempt function income is gross income from dues, fees, charges, or similar amounts paid by members of the tax-exempt organization in connection with the purposes constituting the basis for the exemption of the club.[126] Also, the passive income of an exempt social club is generally not taxed if it is set aside to be used for charitable and similar purposes.[127] In one instance, an attempted set-aside failed

---

[121] Cf. Portland Golf Club v. Comm'r, 55 T.C.M. 212 (1988); West Va. State Med. Ass'n v. Comm'r, 91 T.C. 651 (1988), *aff'd*, 882 F.2d 123 (4th Cir. 1989), *cert. denied*, 493 U.S. 1044 (1990).

[122] Portland Golf Club v. Comm'r, 497 U.S. 154, 165 (1990). Thereafter, the U.S. Tax Court ruled that a tax-exempt social club was not entitled to offset losses from its nonmember activities against investment income because it did not undertake the activities with the requisite profit motive (Atlanta Athletic Club v. Comm'r, 61 T.C.M. 2011 (1991), *rev'd on other grounds*, 980 F.2d 1409 (11th Cir. 1993)).

[123] See Chapter 24.

[124] IRC § 512(a)(1).

[125] The Brook, Inc. v. Comm'r, 799 F.2d 833, 841 (2d Cir. 1986).

[126] IRC § 512(a)(3)(B).

[127] IRC § 170(c)(4). In 1926, the U.S. District Court for the Southern District of New York had occasion to review a set-aside provision contained in the Revenue Act of 1918, in Slocum v. Bowers, 15 F.2d 400 (S.D.N.Y. 1926), the classic opinion on the subject of set-asides. Noting that the "policy of exempting" charitable and similar organizations "is firmly established," the court wrote that the set-aside rule should be read "in such a way as to carry out this policy and not to make the result turn on accidental circumstances or legal technicalities" (*id*. at 403). The tax consequences depend, said the court, "upon who is ultimately entitled to the property constituting [the] income" (*id*. at 404). Consequently, the court interpreted the set-aside rule to exempt from taxation the income of an estate that was destined for charitable purposes even though the representative of the estate still held legal title to the underlying property during the period of administration and even though there was no entry made on the books of the representative crediting the charitable organizations with the income. This decision was affirmed on appeal, with the U.S. Court of Appeals for the Second Circuit holding that it was the intent of Congress to not tax income going to charitable entities and that the designation made by the decedent in the will was the "most effective method" of setting the income aside (Bowers v. Slocum, 20 F.2d 350, 352-53 (2d Cir. 1927)).

Comparable case law invokes the law of trusts, where the courts have concluded that the segregated funds are housed in a constructive trust, an implied trust, or a resulting trust. For example, the U.S. Tax Court, having found in the facts a "reasonable certainty as to the property, the objects and the beneficiaries," held that funds transferred to an organization for the purpose of carrying out the objects "were impressed with a trust upon their receipt" (Broadcast Measurement Bur., Inc. v. Comm'r, 16 T.C. 988, 997 (1951)). "No express words of trust were used, but none are necessary," wrote the court in concluding that the recipient organization "was merely a designated fiduciary" (*id*. at 997, 1000). In finding that the funds did not constitute gross income to the organization, this court singled out the essential criteria for what is also known as the set-aside: The organization's "books showed the

to immunize net investment income from taxation because the activity funded by the investment income, which was publication of a magazine, was found to not be educational.[128]

In an illustration of these rules, the Tax Court ruled that a tax-exempt social club, the principal activity of which was to annually stage a mock pirate invasion and a parade, incurred taxable income from the sale of refreshments along the parade route, souvenirs, and advertising, inasmuch as the concession and other income was derived from dealings with nonmembers. The court also held that the expenses of staging the invasion and parade could not be used to offset concession revenue, because the expenses did not have the requisite "direct" relationship with the income.[129]

The U.S. Tax Court held that a tax-exempt country club could not offset its taxable investment income with losses from nonmember sales, because the sales activity was not entered into for profit, due to losses in each of the years at issue.[130] In affirming this decision, the court of appeals stated that "demonstrating profit motive without profitability proves difficult."[131] Entities in this position, the appellate court continued, "generally must show that their intent to profit was thwarted somehow."[132] It added: "When an organization is *consistently* unprofitable, even tougher."[133] The court then stated this telltale observation: "Although courts review holistically all relevant facts and circumstances when deciding whether an activity is a business or hobby, a long history of consistent and unexplained losses can overwhelm all other factors."[134] This club, the appellate court concluded, "never adduced any evidence that it attempted to stem its flood of losses, or that it expected to eventually profit."[135]

It is the view of the Treasury Department that the dividends-received deduction[136] is not allowed in computing the taxable income of these organizations.[137] Believing that the reason for this deduction is inapplicable in the context of these organizations, Congress clarified this point by agreeing to the Treasury Department's position.[138] (A similar law change was made for nonexempt membership organizations.)[139] Although the statutory revision took effect in 1976, it has been held that tax-exempt social clubs are not entitled to the dividends-paid deduction

---

total amount of such fees it received and the unexpended balance thereof at all times" (*id.* at 1001). A commingling of the funds with other receipts was expressly held to "not destroy their identity as a trust fund" (*id.*; also, Seven-Up Co. v. Comm'r, 14 T.C. 965 (1950)). Further, Reg. § 1.512(a)-4(b)(5); Phi Delta Theta Fraternity v. Comm'r, 887 F.2d 1302 (6th Cir. 1989), *aff'g* 90 T.C. 1033 (1988) (set-aside not found)).

[128] Phi Delta Theta Fraternity v. Comm'r, 887 F.2d 1302 (6th Cir. 1989), *aff'g* 90 T.C. 1033 (1988).

[129] Ye Mystic Krewe of Gasparilla v. Comm'r, 80 T.C. 755 (1983).

[130] Losantiville Country Club v. Comm'r, 114 T.C.M 198 (2017), *aff'd*, 906 F.3d 468 (6th Cir. 2018).

[131] *Id.* at 474.

[132] *Id.*

[133] *Id.*

[134] *Id.*

[135] *Id.*

[136] IRC § 243.

[137] Prop. Reg. § 1.512(a)-3(b)(2) (withdrawn).

[138] IRC § 512(a)(3)(A), last sentence (Pub. L. No. 94-568, 90 Stat. 2697 (1976)). See H.R. Rep. 94-1353, at 6 (1976).

[139] IRC § 277. See § 19.25.

for prior years (back to 1970) because the deduction is not for an expense incurred in the production of income but comes into being as a consequence of the existence of the income.[140]

§ 15.5 SALE OF CLUB ASSETS

Congress, in 1969, relegated to statute the law governing nonrecurring sales of club assets. A common example of this is a country club that sells land that has become encroached on by developers to buy land farther out in the countryside for new facilities.[141] Where the purpose of this type of a sale is not profit but to facilitate relocation or a comparable purpose, the law provides a carryover of basis, that is, nonrecognition of gain.[142] Specifically, where property used directly in the performance of the club's tax-exempt function is sold and the proceeds reinvested in exempt function property, within a period beginning one year before the sale date and ending three years thereafter, any gain from the sale is recognized only to the extent that the sale price of the old property exceeds the purchase price of the new property.[143]

Applying this rule, the IRS held that the gain received by an exempt social club on the sale of an exempt function painting qualified for this exclusion from unrelated income taxation, where the proceeds were used in furtherance of the club's exempt purposes.[144] Likewise, the IRS ruled that an exempt social club could sell some exempt function acreage to finance a substantial renovation of its recreational facilities, without payment of unrelated income tax.[145] The IRS adhered to this rule in an instance where an exempt social club terminated and relinquished a parcel of long-term leased property in exchange for a larger parcel of land to be used in furtherance of its exempt purposes.[146] Similarly, the rule was held applicable to a club's sale of timber in a forest, pursuant to a state's forest and wildlife resources plan, where the resulting income will be used to acquire real or personal property in furtherance of the club's exempt functions.[147] The IRS has issued

[140] Rolling Rock Club v. United States, 85-1 U.S.T.C. ¶ 9374 (W.D. Pa. 1985) aff'd, 785 F.2d 93 (3d Cir. 1986). An exempt social club that has paid Social Security taxes on all tips earned by its employees (paid by members and nonmembers) may claim the general business credit (IRC § 38) for these taxes paid, in calculating its unrelated business income (Rev. Rul. 2003-64, 2003-1 C.B. 1036).

[141] Rev. Rul. 69-232, 1969-1 C.B. 154; Rev. Rul. 65-64, 1965-1 C.B. 241; Rev. Rul. 58-501, 1958-2 C.B. 262; Santee Club v. White, 87 F.2d 5 (1st Cir. 1936); Mill Lane Club v. Comm'r, 23 T.C. 433 (1954); Anderson Country Club, Inc. v. Comm'r, 2 T.C. 1238 (1943); Juniper Hunting Club, Inc. v. Comm'r, 28 B.T.A. 525 (1933).

[142] IRC § 512(a)(3)(D). The IRS twice ruled that gain need not be recognized, by reason of this provision, in the case of an exempt club selling its assets to members in connection with its dissolution and liquidation, and then decided that ruling position was in error, revoking the rulings and holding that the gain was taxable (Priv. Ltr. Rul. 201213035, revoking Priv. Ltr. Rul. 200314030; Priv. Ltr. Rul. 201213034, revoking Priv. Ltr. Rul. 200451031).

[143] IRC § 512(a)(3)(D). E.g., Tamarisk Country Club v. Comm'r, 84 T.C. 756 (1985).

[144] Priv. Ltr. Rul. 200051046.

[145] Priv. Ltr. Rul. 200532056.

[146] Priv. Ltr. Rul. 200826038.

[147] Priv. Ltr. Rul. 201002043.

rulings allowing social clubs to sell a conservation easement to a governmental unit, with the (nontaxable) proceeds used to improve club grounds and facilities; the sale of the easement is considered to be the sale of property used directly for exempt purposes.[148] Where, however, a club is disbanding, this exclusion rule is not available; the property was used for the club's exempt purposes but the sales proceeds will not be reinvested in exempt function property.[149]

There can be controversy over the meaning of the term *used directly*. In one case, the government argued that there must be "actual, direct, continuous, and regular usage" and that the property involved must form an "integral part of the exempt functions of a social club"; it lamented the club's "desultory activities" on the property, which it regarded as essentially investment property. But the court involved held that these requirements are not in the statute and, if they should be, Congress should expand the statute.[150]

By contrast, where the sale of tax-exempt social club assets occurs more than once, the IRS is likely to resist application of this special rule, particularly in any case where the sale transactions substantially deplete the club of its assets and the club has not evidenced an intention to replace the property that is being sold.[151] Also, where a club derives revenue as the result of a grant of an option on the sale of the property, rather than from the sale of the property itself, this nonrecognition rule is inapplicable, so that the option income is taxable as unrelated business income.[152]

---

[148] E.g., Priv. Ltr. Rul. 201235024.

[149] Priv. Ltr. Rul. 201003022.

[150] Atlanta Athletic Club v. Comm'r, 980 F.2d 1409, 1414 (11th Cir. 1993). By contrast, in another instance, the government prevailed in a case involving the *used directly* requirement (Deer Park Country Club v. Comm'r, 70 T.C.M. 1445 (1995)).

[151] E.g., Priv. Ltr. Rul. 8337092.

[152] Framingham Country Club v. United States, 659 F. Supp. 650 (D. Mass. 1987). Occasionally, the IRS will address the question as to whether an asset sale will adversely affect a club's exempt status (e.g., Priv. Ltr. Rul. 201032045).

Labor, Agricultural, and Horticultural Organizations

The federal tax law provides tax exemption for qualified labor, agricultural, and horticultural organizations. No part of the net earnings of this type of an organization may inure to the benefit of any member.[1] This category of organization must have as its principal object the betterment of the conditions of those engaged in the exempt pursuits, the improvement of the grade of their products, and the development of a higher degree of efficiency in the particular occupation.[2]

§ 16.1 LABOR ORGANIZATIONS

The principal purpose of a tax-exempt labor organization is to engage in collective action to better the working conditions of individuals engaged in a common pursuit. The most common example of the exempt labor entity is labor unions that negotiate with employers on behalf of workers for improved wages, fringe benefits, hours, and working conditions. Nonetheless, the exempt labor organization category encompasses a broader range of entities, including union-controlled organizations that provide benefits to workers that enhance the union's ability to bargain effectively. This classification includes, for example, an organization of exempt labor unions representing public employees,[3] an organization to provide strike and lockout benefits (strike funds),[4] the "labor temple" (offices, meeting rooms, auditoriums, and the like for labor union members),[5] an organization

---

[1] Reg. § 1.501(c)(5)-1(a)(1). The pro rata refund of excess dues to members by an exempt agricultural organization does not constitute private inurement and thus does not disqualify the organization from continuing tax exemption (Rev. Rul. 81-60, 1981-1 C.B. 335). See Chapter 20.

[2] Reg. § 1.501(c)(5)-1(a)(2).

[3] Rev. Rul. 74-596, 1974-2 C.B. 167. A public-sector union, however, cannot constitutionally extract fees from nonmembers to be expended in furtherance of certain collective bargaining activities (Janus v. American Fed'n of State, Cnty., and Mun. Employees, Council 31, 138 S. Ct. 2448 (2018)).

[4] Rev. Rul. 67-7, 1967-1 C.B. 137.

[5] Portland Co-Operative Labor Temple Ass'n v. Comm'r, 39 B.T.A. 450 (1939).

publishing a labor newspaper,[6] and a nonprofit apprenticeship and training committee conducting educational courses and programs in various aspects of a trade for local union members, employees, or associates of the industry.[7]

A court characterized the term *labor organization* as "bespeak[ing] a liberal construction to embrace the common acceptation of the term, including labor unions and councils and groups which are ordinarily unions and councils and the groups which are ordinarily organized to protect and promote the interests of labor."[8] Subsequently, another court observed that a tax-exempt labor organization is a "voluntary association of workers which is organized to pursue common economic and social interests."[9]

Thus, a tax-exempt labor organization must have authority to represent or speak for its members in matters relating to their employment, such as wages, hours of labor, conditions, or economic benefits. For example, an organization (controlled by individuals in their private capacity) that provided weekly income to its members in the event of a lawful strike by the members' labor union by reason of its contractual agreements with and payments from the workers was ruled to not qualify as an exempt labor organization.[10]

A tax-exempt labor organization is generally composed of employees or representatives of the employees (such as collective bargaining agents) and similar groups. An organization whose membership is composed principally of laborers will not, for that reason alone, however, qualify as an exempt labor organization.[11] For example, an organization whose members were independent contractors and entrepreneurs (persons engaged in harness racing in a specific geographical area as drivers, trainers, and horse owners) was held to not qualify as an exempt labor organization because the members were not employees.[12] Likewise, an organization that provided and assigned officials to youth football games failed to qualify as an exempt labor entity inasmuch as all of its members were dues-paying independent contractors.[13]

A case concerned the appropriateness of the membership of a tax-exempt labor organization (a union), with the government asserting that certain associate members were not bona fide members. The court disagreed, holding that the "membership of a union is a matter of self-definition, found in the organization's constitution or other governing documents."[14] This court observed that

---

[6] Rev. Rul. 68-534, 1968-2 C.B. 217.

[7] Rev. Rul. 78-42, 1978-1 C.B. 158.

[8] Portland Co-Operative Labor Temple Ass'n v. Comm'r, 39 B.T.A. 450, 455 (1939).

[9] American Postal Workers Union, AFL-CIO v. United States, 90-1 U.S.T.C. ¶ 50,013 (D.D.C. 1989). An organization of individuals servicing automobiles built by a particular manufacturer failed to qualify as an exempt labor organization because its activities were training services for its members, their employer dealerships, and the manufacturer rather than the betterment of conditions for those engaged in labor (Priv. Ltr. Rul. 201431032).

[10] Rev. Rul. 76-420, 1976-2 C.B. 153.

[11] Workingmen's Co-Op. Ass'n of the United States Ins. League of N.Y. v. Comm'r, 3 B.T.A. 1352 (1978). Cf. Rev. Rul. 78-287, 1978-2 C.B. 146.

[12] Rev. Rul. 78-288, 1978-2 C.B. 179. On this point, the IRS will look to see whether the members are self-employed for purposes of IRC § 1402.

[13] Priv. Ltr. Rul. 201121027, in which the IRS likened the organization to an "employment agency."

[14] American Postal Workers Union, AFL-CIO v. United States, 90-1 U.S.T.C. ¶ 50,013 (D.D.C. 1989), at 83,055.

"neither the Congress, the Treasury, the Internal Revenue Service nor the courts have made exemption for labor organizations dependent on the identity of the particular group or groups of employees represented or the types of economic benefits provided" and that "[t]here is no authority for limiting a labor union's exempt purposes to representing a particular classification of employees or providing particular kinds of benefits to its members."[15] The court added that "[t]here is no requirement in the Internal Revenue Code that a union member receive any particular quantum of benefit in order to be considered a bona fide member," so that a union or other type of labor organization can have different classes of membership.[16] The consequence of these findings was that the dues revenue from the associate members was held nontaxable.

By contrast, another case, on essentially the same facts, produced the opposite conclusion of law. The court involved found taxable the income paid to the organization by its "limited benefit members" for the opportunity to obtain insurance under its health plan.[17] The organization operated for the economic well-being of its regular and associate members, the court found, but these operations were held to benefit the limited benefit members only incidentally and indirectly. The court held that the provision of the insurance to limited benefit members, who could not vote or hold office in the organization, was not related to the organization's tax-exempt purposes (which were to serve the regular and associate members) and thus was taxable as income from the performance of unrelated services.

Labor organizations may also meet the requirements of exemption by providing benefits that directly improve working conditions or compensate for unpredictable hazards that interrupt work. Thus, the IRS recognized as a tax-exempt labor organization a committee formed pursuant to a collective bargaining agreement to improve working conditions for apprentices in various skilled crafts and to aid in the settlement of disputes between employers and apprentices.[18] The agency so held, even though the committee's membership consisted of an equal number of employer and employee representatives, and the committee was financed primarily by employer and union contributions. Another example was an organization that operated a dispatch hall to match union members with work assignments.[19] Exempt labor organization classification was also recognized in the case of a trust organized pursuant to a collective bargaining agreement, funded and administered solely by the employers in an industry, because the purpose of the trust was to compensate a multiemployer steward who was under a union's direct control with responsibility to settle disputes, investigate complaints, and otherwise encourage compliance with the agreement throughout the entire industry.[20] Similarly, the IRS determined that a nurses' association, which had as its primary purposes acting as a collective bargaining agent for its members in contract negotiations between various institutions and the nurses

---

[15] *Id.*

[16] *Id.* This opinion was reversed, on the issue of unrelated income taxation (925 F.2d 480 (D.C. Cir. 1991)) (see § 25.2(l)).

[17] Nat'l Ass'n of Postal Supervisors v. United States, 90-2 U.S.T.C. ¶ 50,445 (Cl. Ct. 1990).

[18] Rev. Rul. 59-6, 1959-1 C.B. 121. Also, Rev. Rul. 78-42, 1978-1 C.B. 158.

[19] Rev. Rul. 75-473, 1975-2 C.B. 213.

[20] Rev. Rul. 77-5, 1977-1 C.B. 148.

employed by them and operating a health and welfare fund for its membership, constituted an exempt labor organization.[21]

In another illustration, the IRS ruled that an association of city school teachers was a tax-exempt labor organization.[22] The organization was formed to improve the professional abilities of its members and to secure for them better salaries and working conditions. It sponsored seminars and courses for its members, participated in teacher conventions, bargained collectively and processed grievances, and kept its members informed of its activities through regular meetings and a newsletter.

Generally, a tax-exempt labor organization is one that operates to better the conditions of those (frequently its members) engaged in a particular trade, such as by striking for better wages and working conditions. Where the labor organization has members, they will mostly be employees, although the inclusion of some self-employed persons in the membership will not deprive the organization of its classification as an exempt labor group if it otherwise qualifies.[23] Similarly, the payment by a labor organization of death, sickness, accident, and similar benefits to its members generally will not preclude exemption, even in circumstances in which a majority of the organization's members are retired.[24] Likewise, the payment by an organization of law enforcement officers for its members' legal defense in actions brought against them in connection with the performance of their official duties did not adversely affect the organization's exempt status as a labor organization.[25]

The IRS had occasion to consider the tax status of a nonprofit organization that was established pursuant to a collective bargaining agreement between a union and an employers' association to enable members of the union to save money under a plan by which a fixed amount was withheld from their pay and deposited in a bank account. In determining that this organization did not qualify as a tax-exempt labor organization, the IRS noted that, to so qualify, the activities of this type of an organization must be those "commonly or historically recognized as characteristic of labor organizations, or be closely related and necessary to accomplishing the principal purposes of exempt labor organizations."[26] Thus, the IRS concluded that "savings plans that disburse money on an annual basis are not closely related to the labor organization's principal activities of negotiating wages, hours, and working conditions nor are such savings plans closely related and necessary to providing the mutual benefits characteristically associated with labor organizations."[27]

As noted, one of the purposes of a tax-exempt labor organization may be the development among its members of a higher degree of efficiency in their occupations. To this end, an exempt labor organization may administer bona fide

[21] Rev. Rul. 77-154, 1977-1 C.B. 148.

[22] Rev. Rul. 76-31, 1976-1 C.B. 157.

[23] Rev. Rul. 77-154, 1977-1 C.B. 148; Rev. Rul. 74-167, 1974-1 C.B. 134.

[24] Rev. Rul. 62-17, 1962-1 C.B. 87. This position represents a reversal of the IRS's prior stance, as stated in Rev. Rul. 58-143, 1958-1 C.B. 239. Also, American Postal Workers Union, AFL-CIO v. United States, 90-1 U.S.T.C. ¶ 50,013 (D.D.C. 1989).

[25] Rev. Rul. 75-288, 1975-2 C.B. 212.

[26] Rev. Rul. 77-46, 1977-1 C.B. 147.

[27] Id.

skill-improvement or self-improvement programs as part of its exempt activity, if the programs are administered by the organization specifically for, and involve substantial participation by, its members. For example, a labor organization was advised that its conduct of travel tours for nonmembers and members who do not substantially participate in educational programs administered by it was not an exempt activity.[28]

An organization cannot qualify as a tax-exempt labor organization if its principal activity is to receive, hold, invest, disburse, or otherwise manage funds associated with savings or investment plans or programs, including pension or other retirement savings plans or programs.[29] For example, a trust organized pursuant to a collective bargaining agreement between a labor union and multiple employers that, as most of its activities, (1) receives funds from the employers who are subject to the agreement, (2) invests the funds and uses them and accumulated earnings to pay retirement benefits to union members as specified in the agreement, (3) provides information to union members about their retirement benefits and assists them with administrative tasks associated with the benefits, and (4) participates in the renegotiation of the agreement, cannot qualify as an exempt labor organization.[30] This position is a reflection of the view of the IRS that, a decision of an appellate court[31] notwithstanding, managing saving and investment plans for workers, including retirement plans, does not bear directly on working conditions.[32]

A company owned and controlled by a labor union organized to provide employment to the union's members did not qualify for tax exemption, even though its net profits were turned in to the union's treasury.[33] Exemption was also denied an organization established by an employer and a union under a collective bargaining agreement to ensure the efficient discharge of the employer's obligation to pay withheld employment taxes to federal and state authorities.[34] An organization of farmers formed to furnish farm laborers for individual farmers also did not qualify for exemption as a labor organization.[35] With the advent of the unrelated business income taxation regime,[36] exempt labor organizations may engage in some nonexempt activities, in the nature of "business" functions or services, and nonetheless continue to remain exempt from federal income taxation.[37]

---

[28] Priv. Ltr. Rul. 7944018.

[29] Reg. § 1.501(c)(5)-1(b)(1). There is an exception for certain dues-financed pension plans that do not have any employer involvement (Reg. § 1.501(c)(5)-1(b)(2)).

[30] Reg. § 1.501(c)(5)-1(b)(2).

[31] Morganbesser v. United States, 984 F.2d 560 (2d Cir. 1993). The court relied heavily on IRS Gen. Couns. Mems. 37942, 37726, and 35862 in its decision. The IRS Office of Chief Counsel recommended nonacquiescence in this case (AOD 1995-016).

[32] Rev. Rul. 77-46, 1977-1 C.B. 147. A federal district court subsequently refused to follow the *Morganbesser* rationale, holding that the term *labor organization* does not encompass a pension fund that exists only to provide retirement benefits for its members (Stichting Pensioenfonds Voor de Gezondheid v. United States, 950 F. Supp. 373 (D.D.C. 1996), *aff'd*, 129 F.3d 195 (D.C. Cir. 1997)). Also, Tupper v. United States, 134 F.3d 444 (1st Cir. 1998).

[33] Rev. Rul. 69-386, 1969-2 C.B. 123.

[34] Rev. Rul. 66-354, 1966-2 C.B. 207.

[35] Rev. Rul. 72-391, 1972-2 C.B. 249.

[36] See Chapter 24.

[37] E.g., Rev. Rul. 62-191, 1962-2 C.B. 146; Rev. Rul. 59-330, 1959-2 C.B. 153.

The effectiveness of labor organizations, particularly unions, on the legislative and political fronts continually generates controversy. The matter came before the courts in a case brought by aerospace workers covered by compulsory union-shop contracts and thus required to pay union dues, to enjoin the government from continuing to recognize tax exemption in the case of any labor organization that expended membership dues for partisan political campaigns.[38] The court rejected the idea that exemption of unions should be terminated where union dues are used in political campaigns, stating that Congress has considered and not adopted that result.[39] The court also rejected the argument that the exemption amounts to a federal subsidy and consequently that general political activity of labor organizations should be proscribed, finding that the exemption is "benevolent neutrality" and that there is not the requisite "nexus" between the exemption and any government "involvement" in union activities.[40]

§ 16.2 AGRICULTURAL ORGANIZATIONS

Regarding agricultural organizations, the principal tax issue is likely to be the scope of the term *agricultural*. For many years, the IRS relied on the narrow dictionary definition of the term *agriculture* as meaning the "science or art of cultivating the soil, harvesting crops and raising livestock."[41] In this context, *livestock* refers to animals typically considered to be farm animals.[42] Thus, an organization formed to promote and protect a particular breed of dog did not qualify as an agricultural organization,[43] nor did an organization formed to care for homeless cats.[44]

Prior to 1976, neither the federal statutory tax law nor the income tax regulations defined the term *agricultural*. There was a body of law holding that this term must, for tax purposes, be given its normal and customary meaning.[45] This approach did not entail mere reference to dictionary definitions, inasmuch as statutes are to be interpreted in effectuation of intended congressional policy, which may not be identical to the meaning of certain words in lay terms. Certainly, the principal dictionary meaning of *agriculture* is the cultivation of land, as in the raising of crops. *Agriculture*, however, also means *husbandry*, which connotes *farming* as well as *agriculture*. *Agriculture* means "farming (in a broad sense, including. . .stock raising, etc.)."[46] Certainly, *stock* raising can be interpreted as broader

---

[38] Marker v. Schultz, 485 F.2d 1003 (D.C. Cir. 1973), *aff'g* 337 F. Supp. 1301 (D.D.C. 1972).

[39] E.g., 18 U.S.C. § 610.

[40] Marker v. Schultz, 485 F.2d 1003, 1006 (D.C. Cir. 1973), citing Walz v. Tax Comm'n of the City of New York, 397 U.S. 664 (1970). Tax exemption was, however, held to be "a form of subsidy that is administered through the tax system" in Regan v. Taxation With Representation of Washington, 461 U.S. 540, 544 (1983).

[41] Citing *Webster's Third New Int'l Dictionary*. Also, Dorrell v. Norida Land & Timber Co., 27 P.2d 960 (Id. 1933).

[42] Rev. Rul. 73-520, 1973-2 C.B. 180.

[43] *Id.*

[44] Priv. Ltr. Rul. 202345010.

[45] United States v. Byrum, 408 U.S. 125, 136 (1972). Also, Comm'r v. Caulkins, 144 F.2d 482, 484 (6th Cir. 1944), *aff'g* 1 T.C. 656 (1944).

[46] *The American College Dictionary*.

than the raising of *livestock*.[47] Thus, it was contended that the meaning reflected in the statutory scheme should be relied on, rather than dictionary definitions.[48]

An illustration of the foregoing was the IRS's refusal to accord tax-exempt status to organizations engaged in the harvesting of aquatic resources (often termed *aquaculture*). Yet it appeared that, in the face of contemporary food, health, and related needs, any distinction in this context between land farming and sea-resource gathering was artificial. In other statutory and regulatory contexts, this distinction has disappeared. For example, the Farm Credit Act, as amended, provided that those engaging in commercial fishing may qualify for the benefits of the Act as "producers or harvesters of aquatic products." The Rural Development Act of 1972 authorized individuals involved in producing fish and fishery products to obtain loans in the same manner as farmers. Additionally, the Federal Energy Office's Petroleum Allocation and Price Regulations included fishing under the definition of *agricultural production*. In other contexts, the IRS has readily turned, in the process of assessing organizations' claims to exemption, to nontax statutes to divine congressional intent or the basis for federal public policy bearing on the organizations' activities.[49]

Unlike the term *farmer*,[50] it is clear that the term *agriculture*, for federal tax purposes, is to be liberally construed. Thus, for example, an organization that annually hosted a rodeo was recognized as being a tax-exempt agricultural organization.[51] An organization that was concerned with methods of raising fur-bearing animals and marketing pelts was ruled to be an exempt agricultural organization,[52] as was an organization that tested soil for farmers and nonfarmers and furnished test results for educational purposes.[53] It is not mandatory that the membership of the organization desiring tax categorization as an agricultural entity be engaged in agricultural pursuits.[54] For example, an organization of women who had no relationship to agriculture other than the fact that their husbands were farmers in a particular state was ruled to be an exempt agricultural organization.[55]

Efforts were made to invest the law in this area with a broader interpretation of the term *agriculture*. A federal court of appeals provided precedent for this undertaking, writing that "[a]ccording to the lexicographers, agriculture is defined as the art or science of cultivating the ground including the harvesting of crops and *in a broader sense the science or art of the production of plants and animals useful to man*, including in a variable degree the preparation of these products for man's use."[56] The IRS did not, however, accept this broader view, conceding only that an organization formed for the purpose of encouraging better and more

---

[47] Fromm Bros., Inc. v. United States, 35 F. Supp. 145 (W.D. Wis. 1940); Rev. Rul. 57-588, 1957-2 C.B. 305.
[48] Mitchell v. Cohn, 333 U.S. 411 (1948).
[49] E.g., Rev. Rul. 76-204, 1976-1 C.B. 152.
[50] IRC § 521. See § 19.12.
[51] Campbell v. Big Spring Cowboy Reunion, 210 F.2d 143 (5th Cir. 1954).
[52] Rev. Rul. 56-245, 1956-1 C.B. 204.
[53] Rev. Rul. 54-282, 1954-2 C.B. 126.
[54] Rev. Rul. 60-86, 1960-1 C.B. 198.
[55] Rev. Rul. 74-118, 1974-1 C.B. 134.
[56] Sancho v. Bowie, 93 F.2d 323, 324 (1st Cir. 1937) (emphasis added).

economical methods of fish farming was an agricultural organization.[57] Also, the IRS determined that an organization, the members of which were involved in the commercial fishing industry in a state, that published a monthly newspaper of commercial fishing technical information and news, and that derived its income primarily from membership dues and sale of advertising, did not qualify as a tax-exempt agricultural organization but instead as an exempt business league.[58]

In an attempt to settle this controversy, Congress, in 1976, authored a rule[59] providing that, for purposes of tax exemption as an agricultural organization, the term *agriculture* includes (but is not limited to) "the art or science of cultivating land, harvesting crops or aquatic resources, or raising livestock." The insertion of the phrase "harvesting crops or aquatic resources" was designed to encompass fishing and related pursuits (such as the taking of lobsters and shrimp), the cultivation of underwater vegetation, and the cultivation or growth of any edible organism. This change resulted from Congress's realization that there is no tax policy to be served under the provision for exempt agricultural groups for differentiating between occupations devoted to the production of foodstuffs and other items from the earth and from the waters. The statutory definition became effective for tax years beginning after 1975, although inasmuch as the statute may be declaratory of what Congress perceived the law should have been beforehand,[60] it can be contended that the definition is of utility with respect to pre-1976 tax years as well.[61]

Another dimension of this dilemma for organizations engaged in or associated with aquatic harvesting is that the Postal Service followed the position of the IRS and categorized them as business leagues rather than agriculture organizations, thereby depriving them of the preferential postal rates under the second and third classes. Congress also remedied this aspect of the problem in 1976, when it enacted the Postal Reorganization Act Amendments of 1976.[62] This law added a definition of the term *agriculture* to the postal laws, as including the "art or science of cultivating land, harvesting crops or marine resources, or raising of livestock," thereby removing these organizations from business league status under the postal laws as well.[63] For postal law purposes, this definition also extends to "any organization or association which collects and disseminates information or materials relating to agricultural pursuits."

[57] Rev. Rul. 74-488, 1974-2 C.B. 166. Cf. Rev. Rul. 76-241, 1976-1 C.B. 131.

[58] Rev. Rul. 75-287, 1975-2 C.B. 211. See Chapter 14.

[59] IRC § 501(g).

[60] 121 Cong. Rec. 34442 (1975).

[61] Applying this definition of the term *agricultural*, the IRS denied recognition of exemption to an organization that educates the public as to the values and benefits of the horse and greyhound racing industries to its state's economy and the benefits of permitting electronic gaming alongside pari-mutuel betting at racing facilities (Priv. Ltr. Rul. 201905005).

[62] Pub. L. No. 94-421, 90 Stat. 1303 (1976).

[63] 39 U.S.C. § 3626(d). While the tax law definition of the term *agricultural* encompasses the "harvesting. . .[of] aquatic resources," the postal law definition of the term includes the "harvesting. . .[of] marine resources." The dictionary definition of *aquatic* is "of or pertaining to water," whereas the dictionary definition of *marine* is "of or pertaining to the sea," thereby holding open the possibility that an organization engaged in or associated with the harvesting of freshwater will acquire classification as an agricultural organization for federal tax purposes but as a business league for postal law purposes.

Other tax-exempt agricultural organizations include an organization engaged in ways to improve the breed of cattle,[64] an association engaged in the promotion of the artificial insemination of cattle,[65] an association formed to guard the purity of Welsh ponies,[66] an organization established to advance agriculture that purchased supplies and equipment for resale to its members,[67] a local association of dairy farmers that participated in the U.S. Department of Agriculture's National Cooperative Dairy Herd Improvement Program,[68] a local association of farmers formed to promote more effective agricultural pest control,[69] an organization that produced and distributed certified seed to a state's corn producers,[70] an organization of agricultural growers and producers formed principally to negotiate with processors for crop prices,[71] and an organization that participated in furthering research, sales, and distribution of seed stock.[72]

A tax-exempt agricultural organization usually has a membership; those served by the entity must represent a significant portion of the interested agricultural community.[73] The performance of services directly on behalf of an individual member, however, is not improving the grade of the person's product or developing a higher degree of efficiency in the person's agriculture-related pursuits.[74] Thus, an organization operating a certification and marketing program for high-quality, branded, value-added products of its members did not qualify as an exempt agricultural entity because it did not benefit the producers in the particular field generally; indeed, the IRS concluded that this organization was merely a "sales agent" for its members.[75] Likewise, a nonprofit organization operating a plan, protecting its member breeding farms from significant losses if their deer herds are dissipated by disease, by means of member contributions to offset the losses, was denied recognition of exemption as an agricultural organization because, in the absence of this plan, the members would have to insure themselves.[76] Yet, where an activity benefits agriculture as a whole and only incidentally benefits individual members, tax exemption is available.[77]

The IRS will not recognize as a tax-exempt agricultural entity an organization whose principal purpose is to provide a direct business service for its members' economic benefit. Thus, an organization engaged in the management, grazing, and sale of its members' cattle was denied exempt status as an agricultural entity.[78]

---

[64] Minnesota Holstein-Friesian Breeders Ass'n v. Comm'r, 64 T.C.M. 1319 (1992). Also, California Thoroughbred Breeders Ass'n v. Comm'r, 57 T.C.M. 962 (1989).

[65] East Tenn. Artificial Breeders Ass'n v. United States, 63-2 U.S.T.C. ¶ 9748 (E.D. Tenn. 1963).

[66] Rev. Rul. 55-230, 1955-1 C.B. 71.

[67] Rev. Rul. 57-466, 1957-2 C.B. 311. Cf. Rev. Rul. 67-252, 1967-2 C.B. 195.

[68] Rev. Rul. 74-518, 1974-2 C.B. 166, *clarifying* Rev. Rul. 70-372, 1970-2 C.B. 118.

[69] Rev. Rul. 81-59, 1981-1 C.B. 334.

[70] Priv. Ltr. Rul. 8429010.

[71] Rev. Rul. 76-399, 1976-2 C.B. 152.

[72] Priv. Ltr. Rul. 9732022.

[73] *Id.*

[74] Rev. Rul. 70-372, 1970-2 C.B. 118; Rev. Rul. 66-105, 1966-1 C.B. 145; Rev. Rul. 57-466, 1957-2 C.B. 311.

[75] Priv. Ltr. Rul. 200644043.

[76] Priv. Ltr. Rul. 201716049.

[77] Rev. Rul. 81-59, 1981-1 C.B. 334; Rev. Rul. 74-518, 1974-2 C.B. 166.

[78] Rev. Rul. 74-195, 1974-1 C.B. 135.

The same fate befell an organization composed of agricultural producers whose principal activity was marketing livestock for its members.[79] Similarly, the IRS denied an organization classification as an exempt agricultural entity where it furnished farm laborers for individual farmers, ruling that the organization was "merely providing services to individual farmers that they would have to provide for themselves or get someone else to provide for them."[80] In another illustration of this rule, the IRS denied exempt agricultural status to an organization that owned and operated a livestock facility and leased it to local members of a nonexempt national association of farmers for use in implementing the association's collective bargaining program with processors. The facility was used to collect, weigh, sort, grade, and ship livestock marketed through the program. The IRS determined that the operation and leasing of the facility was the "providing of a business service to those members who make use of the national association's collective bargaining program" and that this service "merely relieves the members of the organization of work they would either have to perform themselves or have performed for them."[81] By reason of this rationale, organizations operating farmers' markets cannot qualify as tax-exempt agricultural entities.[82]

As noted, to be tax-exempt as an agricultural organization, the organization must have as its objective the betterment of the conditions of those *engaged in* agricultural pursuits. The IRS on one occasion used this rule as the rationale for denying exempt agricultural status to an institute of butter and cheese manufacturers, concluding that those who benefit directly from its activities were not engaged in agricultural pursuits (allowing, however, that it may qualify as a business league).[83] Similarly, the IRS was successful, using the rationale that activities only remotely promoting the interests of those engaged in agricultural pursuits cannot qualify an organization for this exemption, in refusing an organization exemption where it was organized to hold agricultural fairs, stock shows, and horse race meets but actually devoted itself solely to horse racing.[84]

As was pointed out, the IRS may conclude that an organization is being operated in the furtherance of interests other than agriculture and that, consequently, it is more properly classifiable as a tax-exempt business league rather than as an agricultural organization.[85] The exemptions for agricultural and charitable organizations may also overlap, such as where an organization conducts a state or county fair or otherwise presents expositions and exhibitions in an educational manner.[86]

---

[79] Rev. Rul. 66-105, 1966-1 C.B. 145. Also, Rev. Rul. 70-372, 1970-2 C.B. 118.

[80] Rev. Rul. 72-391, 1972-2 C.B. 249.

[81] Rev. Rul. 77-153, 1977-1 C.B. 147.

[82] E.g., Priv. Ltr. Rul. 202405015.

[83] Rev. Rul. 67-252, 1967-2 C.B. 195.

[84] Forest City Live Stock & Fair Co. v. Comm'r, 26 B.T.A. 1494 (1932).

[85] E.g., Rev. Rul. 67-252, 1967-2 C.B. 195; Rev. Rul. 56-245, 1956-1 C.B. 204.

[86] Rev. Rul. 67-216, 1967-2 C.B. 180. Also, Indiana Crop Improvement Ass'n, Inc. v. Comm'r, 76 T.C. 394 (1981).

§ 16.3 HORTICULTURAL ORGANIZATIONS

Horticulture is the art or science of cultivating fruits, flowers, and vegetables.[87]

Tax exemption as a horticultural organization was determined by the IRS to be appropriate for a garden club formed for the purpose of bettering the conditions of persons engaged in horticultural pursuits and improving their products, by publishing a monthly journal, reporting new developments in horticultural products to its members, and encouraging the development of these types of products through a system of awards.[88]

---

[87] Guerrero v. United States Fidelity & Guar. Co., 98 S.W.2d 796 (Tex. 1936).
[88] Rev. Rul. 66-179, 1966-1 C.B. 139.

Political Organizations

Until 1974, there were no rules as to whether political campaign committees and similar organizations were appropriate subjects of taxation. This absence of tax exposure resulted from the belief that virtually all of the receipts of political organizations were in the form of gifts and that, consequently, these organizations would not have taxable income.[1]

For many years, the IRS either failed or refused to assert tax liability against political campaign committees.[2] In 1974, however, the IRS ruled that an unincorporated campaign committee was not exempt from federal income taxation and must file tax returns, showing, as elements of gross income, items such as interest, dividends, and net gains from the sale of securities and related deductions (although contributions to the organization remained nontaxable).[3] This ruling was superseded by the enactment in 1974 of a tax law provision on the point[4] and related rules (including a per donee gift tax exclusion).[5]

---

[1] S. Rep. No. 93-1357, at 25 (1974). The philosophy underlying the enactment of the tax rules concerning political organizations is much the same as that for social clubs (see Chapter 15) and homeowners' associations (see § 19.14). That is, in the case of social clubs and homeowners' associations, the law is designed to preclude income from sources other than members (i.e., nonmember and investment income) from subsidizing the members in their personal capacity.

[2] See Ann. 73-84, 1973-2 C.B. 461, which noted that it had been the historical practice of the IRS not to require the filing of tax returns by political parties and organizations, and that this policy had been previously communicated to the field offices of the IRS more than 25 years beforehand but was never made public.

[3] Rev. Rul. 74-21, 1974-1 C.B. 14. Also, Rev. Rul. 74-23, 1974-1 C.B. 17, *modified and clarified by* Rev. Rul. 74-475, 1974-2 C.B. 22.

[4] IRC § 527.

[5] IRC §§ 84, 2501(a)(4). IRC § 84 and Reg. § 1.84-1 provide that if any person transfers appreciated property to a political organization, the transferor is treated as having sold the property to the political organization on the date of the transfer and as having realized an amount equal to the property's fair market value on that date.

Nonetheless, even after its 1974 ruling, the IRS continued to uphold the per donee gift tax exclusion for separate fundraising campaign committees,[6] despite opposition in the courts.[7] Later in 1974, as noted, Congress exempted contributions to political parties or committees from the gift tax.[8] This gift tax exclusion was later extended to transfers of money or other property to tax-exempt social welfare organizations, business leagues, and labor organizations.[9]

The granting of tax exemption to political organizations by Congress in 1974 resulted from a congressional belief that "political activity (including the financing of political activity) as such is not a trade or business that is appropriately subject to tax."[10]

§ 17.1 POLITICAL ORGANIZATIONS IN GENERAL

This category of tax exemption is available for the *political organization*.[11] A political organization is a party, committee, association, fund, or other organization (whether or not incorporated) organized and operated primarily for the purpose of directly or indirectly accepting contributions[12] or making expenditures[13] for an exempt function.[14]

---

[6] Rev. Rul. 72-355, 1972-2 C.B. 532; Rev. Rul. 74-199, 1974-1 C.B. 285.

[7] E.g., Tax Analysts & Advocates v. Schultz, 376 F. Supp. 889 (D.D.C. 1974), *vacated*, 75-1 U.S.T.C. ¶ 13,052 (D.C. Cir. 1975).

[8] IRC § 2501(a)(4); Reg. § 25.2501-1(a)(5). The IRS contended that gifts to political organizations made before May 8, 1974 (the effective date of the statutory revision) were subject to the gift tax. Litigation ensued, with the U.S. Tax Court holding that the gift tax did not apply to amounts contributed for political purposes during the period there at issue (1967–1971) (Carson v. Comm'r, 71 T.C. 252 (1978), *aff'd*, 641 F.2d 864 (10th Cir. 1981)). A similar decision had been reached by the U.S. Court of Appeals for the Fifth Circuit, for the years 1959 to 1961 (Stern v. United States, 426 F.2d 1327 (5th Cir. 1971)). The *Carson* decision rejected the government's contention that the enactment of this gift tax exclusion represented a change in the law. The IRS subsequently acquiesced in the *Carson* decision (Rev. Rul. 82-216, 1982-2 C.B. 220). This acquiescence was as to the result of, and not necessarily in the rationale of, the decision. That is, in the acquiescence ruling, the IRS stated that it "continues to maintain that gratuitous transfers to persons. . .[other than political organizations] are subject to the gift tax absent any specific statute to the contrary, even though the transfers may be motivated by a desire to advance the donor's own social, political or charitable goals" (*id.* at 220). For example, the IRS stated that the gift tax exclusion in the charitable gift context (IRC § 2522(a)) is not available for transfers to organizations that have been disqualified from classification under IRC § 501(c)(3) for engaging in legislative or political campaign activities (*id.* at 220).

[9] IRC § 2501(a)(6), added as part of the Protecting Americans from Tax Hikes Act of 2015 (Pub. L. No. 114-113, div. Q, tit. IV § 408, 129 Stat. 2242, 3120-21). As to tax-exempt social welfare organizations, business leagues, and labor organizations, see Chapters 13 and 14 and § 16.1, respectively.

[10] S. Rep. No. 93-1357, at 26 (1974).

[11] Political organizations generally cannot qualify under any of the other categories of tax-exempt organizations, such as IRC § 501(c)(3) (e.g., Lonsdale v. Comm'r, 41 T.C.M. 1106 (1981); Cavell v. Comm'r, 40 T.C.M. 395 (1980), *aff'd*, 661 F.2d 71 (5th Cir. 1981)).

[12] The term *contribution* includes a gift, subscription, loan, advance, or deposit of money, or anything of value, and includes a contract, promise, or agreement to make a contribution, whether or not legally enforceable (IRC § 527(e)(3), which incorporated the definition in IRC § 271(b)(2)).

[13] The term *expenditures* includes a payment, distribution, loan, advance, deposit, or gift of money or anything of value, and includes a contract, promise, or agreement to make an expenditure, whether or not legally enforceable (IRC § 527(e)(4), which incorporated the definition in IRC § 271(b)(3)).

[14] IRC § 527(e)(1).

(a) Political Organizations Defined

Although the *political action committee* is perhaps the most recognized form of the political organization, the term includes a much broader range of entities. For example, it has been held that a bank account used by a candidate for depositing political contributions and disbursing bona fide political campaign expenses qualifies as a tax-exempt political organization.[15] Additionally, a candidate's newsletter fund can constitute an exempt political organization.[16]

As noted, a political organization is exempt from taxation when it accepts contributions or makes expenditures for an exempt function. An *exempt function* is the activity of influencing or attempting to influence the selection, nomination, election, or appointment of any individual to any federal, state, or local public office[17] or office in a political organization, or the election of presidential or vice-presidential electors, whether or not these individuals or electors are selected, nominated, elected, or appointed.[18] The term includes the making of expenditures relating to an eligible office that, if incurred by the individual, would be a deductible business expense.[19]

The term *exempt function* has been construed by the IRS to encompass a wide range of activities. For example, the IRS ruled that exempt function expenditures include expenses for parties and like celebrations given on election night by a candidate's campaign committee for the candidate's campaign workers;[20] cash awards to campaign workers after the election, if the amounts are reasonable;[21] amounts expended to enable an elected legislator to attend a political party's national convention as a delegate;[22] amounts expended for voter research, public opinion polls, and voter canvasses on behalf of an elected legislator who becomes a candidate for another political office;[23] payments made for a direct mail campaign (for grassroots lobbying[24] purposes) in support of a nonbinding referendum promoting fiscal responsibility where a potential candidate's name, picture, and

---

[15] Rev. Rul. 79-11, 1979-1 C.B. 207. Also, Rev. Rul. 79-12, 1979-1 C.B. 208; Rev. Rul. 79-13, 1979-1 C.B. 208. A nonprofit and nonpartisan committee organized to provide a corporation's employees, shareholders, and their families an opportunity to financially support candidates for public office was ruled to be a political organization (Tech. Adv. Mem. 7742008).

[16] See § 17.1(b).

[17] The facts and circumstances of each case determine whether a particular federal, state, or local office is a *public office*. In making the determination, the IRS uses principles consistent with those found in Reg. § 52.4946-1(g)(2) (Reg. § 1.527-2(d)). This regulation, which is part of the private foundation rules, contains a definition of *public office* for purposes of determining who is a government official under IRC § 4946(c) (see §§ 12.2(i), 12.4(a)).

[18] IRC § 527(e)(2).

[19] *Id.*, last sentence.

[20] Rev. Rul. 87-119, 1987-2 C.B. 151. An exempt function does not, however, include the payment of an elected official's trade or business expenses; payment of these expenses is gross income to the official (*id.*).

[21] *Id.* The amount of the cash award, however, is includible in the campaign worker's gross income.

[22] Rev. Rul. 79-12, 1979-1 C.B. 208. The delegate's expenses were paid from surplus funds from an earlier campaign maintained in a separate bank account; these expenses are not includible in the delegates' gross income.

[23] Rev. Rul. 79-13, 1979-1 C.B. 208.

[24] See § 22.3(d)(i).

political philosophy were included in the mailing;[25] payments of salary to a candidate who took a leave of absence from their employment to campaign on a fulltime basis, where the amounts are reasonable;[26] disbursements for the distribution of voter guides and incumbents' voting records;[27] expenditures for grassroots lobbying where the lobbying is of a dual character,[28] in that the targeting of materials and the timing of their distribution are in relation to one or more elections, so that there is a link between issues and candidates;[29] disbursements for distribution of incumbents' voting records, voter guides, and information about incumbents and other candidates or potential candidates;[30] and contributions and advertising in support of particular candidates, mass media campaigns, initiative campaigns, and litigation.[31]

The income tax regulations also contain several examples of exempt function expenditures[32] and state that the individual for whom these expenditures are made does not have to be an announced candidate, "nor is it critical that [they] ever become a candidate for an office."[33] Even activities engaged in "between elections" can be exempt function activities, as long as they are directly related to the process of selection, nomination, or election of an individual in the next applicable political campaign.[34] Also, *indirect expenses*[35] and *terminating activities*[36] fall within the definition of *exempt function*.

The IRS will look at all the facts and circumstances in determining whether an expenditure constitutes an exempt function.[37] For example, a proper exempt function expenditure includes expenses for "voice and speech lessons to improve [a candidate's] skills," but does not include expenses of a political incumbent for "periodicals of general circulation in order to keep [themself] informed on national and local issues."[38]

---

[25] Tech. Adv. Mem. 9130008.

[26] Priv. Ltr. Rul. 9516006.

[27] Priv. Ltr. Rul. 9652026.

[28] See § 22.3(d)(i).

[29] E.g., Priv. Ltr. Rul. 9652026.

[30] Priv. Ltr. Rul. 9808037.

[31] Priv. Ltr. Rul. 199925051.

[32] Reg. § 1.527-2(c)(5).

[33] Reg. § 1.527-2(c)(1).

[34] *Id.* For example, funds held by a political organization and expended at the direction of a public officeholder after the individual had assumed office were found to be exempt function expenditures because the funds were expended for activities that were directly related to the process of influencing or attempting to influence the reelection of the individual (Tech. Adv. Mem. 8650001).

[35] Indirect expenses include items such as overhead, record keeping, and expenses incurred in soliciting contributions to the political organization (Reg. § 1.527-2(c)(2)).

[36] Terminating activities expenses are expenses incurred in furtherance of the process of terminating a political organization's existence. They can include payment of campaign debts after the conclusion of a campaign (Reg. § 527-2(c)(3)).

[37] Reg. § 1.527-2(c)(1); Tech. Adv. Mem. 8147009 (the determining factor in categorizing an activity as an exempt function is the character and nature of the activity itself and not the identity of the organization that is conducting the activity).

[38] Reg. §§ 1.527-2(c)(5)(iii), (v). These rules should be read against the backdrop of campaign finance and regulation law generally. For example, the Supreme Court held that it is constitutional, in application of free speech principles, to bar tax-exempt advocacy organizations from contributing directly to

(b)   Newsletter Funds

A newsletter fund is treated as if the fund constituted a political organization.[39] A *newsletter fund* is a fund established and maintained by an individual who holds, has been elected to, or is a candidate[40] for nomination or election to any federal, state, or local elective public office, for use by the individual exclusively for the preparation and circulation of the individual's newsletter.[41] The exempt function of a newsletter fund is limited to the preparation and circulation of the news-letter, which includes secretarial services, printing, addressing, and mailing.[42] Thus, unlike other types of political organizations, newsletter fund assets may not be used for campaign activities.[43] Furthermore, newsletter fund assets used for purposes other than the preparation and circulation of the newsletter must be included in the gross income of the individual who established and maintains the fund.[44]

§ 17.2   ORGANIZATIONAL TEST

A political organization satisfies the requisite organizational test if its articles of organization provide that the primary purpose of the organization is to carry on one or more exempt functions. If the organization has no formal arti-cles of organization, consideration will be given to statements of the organi-zation's members at the time it was formed that they intend to carry on an exempt function.[45]

---

candidates for federal office (Federal Election Comm'n v. Beaumont, 539 U.S. 146 (2003)). The Court, however, held that these financing restrictions are unconstitutional as applied to advertisements that an exempt social welfare organization (see Chapter 13) intended to run before an election, because the advertisements were not expressing advocacy or its functional equivalent (Federal Election Comm'n v. Wisconsin Right to Life, 551 U.S. 449 (2007)). Also, the Court ruled that corporations, including non-profit corporations, may make expenditures from their general treasuries in support of or in opposition to political candidates in furtherance of their free speech rights (Citizens United v. Federal Election Comm'n, 588 U.S. 310 (2010)). A summary of the federal law regulating political campaign financing is at *Fundraising* § 6.15.

[39] IRC § 527(g). The exempt function of a newsletter fund, however, is narrower (see text accompanied by *infra* notes 42 and 43) and the $100 specific deduction allowed to other political organizations is not applicable to a newsletter fund (Reg. § 1.527-7(b)).

[40] For purposes of newsletter funds, the term *candidate* means an individual who "publicly announces" that they are a candidate for nomination or election to an office and who meets the qualifications prescribed by law to hold such office (IRC § 527(g)(3)). This differs from the definition of *candidate for public office* contained in Reg. § 1.501(c)(3)-1(c)(3)(iii), which does not require public announcement of a candidacy. (For a discussion of this term, see § 23.2(d).)

[41] IRC § 527(g)(1).

[42] Reg. § 1.527-7(c).

[43] Reg. § 1.527-7(d). Thus, a newsletter fund cannot transfer assets to another political organization, unless that organization also is a newsletter fund.

[44] Reg. § 1.527-7(a). Additionally, any future contributions to the fund also are treated as income to that individual (*id.*).

[45] Reg. § 1.527-2(a)(2).

§ 17.3 OPERATIONAL TEST

To satisfy an operational test, a political organization does not have to engage exclusively in exempt function activities.[46] For example, a political organization may sponsor nonpartisan educational workshops, carry on social activities unrelated to an exempt function, support the enactment or defeat of a ballot proposition, or pay an incumbent's office expenses, as long as these are not the organization's primary activities.[47] In contrast, an organization that engages wholly in legislative activities cannot qualify as a political organization.[48]

§ 17.4 PUBLIC POLICY ADVOCACY ACTIVITIES

An expenditure by a tax-exempt organization, other than a political organization, for issue advertising may be a political expenditure (an exempt function).[49] The IRS provided guidance for determining when an expenditure by a tax-exempt organization[50] for an advocacy communication relating to a public policy issue is for an exempt function.[51] When an advocacy communication explicitly advocates the election or defeat of an individual to public office, the expenditure for the communication obviously is for an exempt function.[52] Otherwise (that is, where an advocacy communication is not so explicit as to a candidacy), all of the facts and circumstances must be considered in determining whether the expenditure is for an exempt function.

The IRS stated that factors that tend to show that an advocacy communication on a public policy issue is for an exempt function include, but are not limited to, the following: (1) The communication identifies a candidate for public office; (2) the timing of the communication coincides with a political campaign; (3) the communication targets voters in a particular election; (4) the communication identifies that candidate's position on the public policy issue that is the subject of the communication; (5) the position of the candidate on the public policy issue has been raised as distinguishing the candidate from others in the campaign, either

---

[46] Reg. § 1.527-2(a)(3).

[47] *Id.* As noted, the payment of an incumbent's office expenses is not an exempt function and will be treated as gross income to the incumbent (*supra* note 20).

[48] E.g., Priv. Ltr. Rul. 9244003.

[49] See § 17.1(a).

[50] This guidance focused on advocacy activities by exempt social welfare organizations (see Chapter 13), labor organizations (see § 16.1), and business leagues (see Chapter 14). Its principles, however, are generally applicable to nearly any category of organization that is tax-exempt under IRC § 501(a) by reason of being described in IRC § 501(c).

[51] Rev. Rul. 2004-6, 2004-1 C.B. 328. A court ruled that this revenue ruling is not unconstitutionally vague and/or overbroad in violation of the First Amendment or void for vagueness in violation of the due process clause of the Fifth Amendment (Freedom Path, Inc. v. Internal Revenue Service, 2017 BL 234957(N.D. Tex. 2017)). On appeal, however, the organization lacked standing to bring the action in that it did not make a sufficient claim of chilled speech; even if it had, its injury (denial of recognition of exemption) was not traceable to the allegedly vague ruling (Freedom Path, Inc. v. Internal Revenue Service, 913 F.3d 503 (5th Cir. 2019)).

[52] See text accompanied by *supra* notes 32–34.

in the communication involved or in other public communications; and (6) the communication is not part of an ongoing series of substantially similar advocacy communications by the organization on the same issue.

Factors that tend to show that an advocacy communication on a public policy issue is not for an exempt function include, but are not limited to, the following: (1) Any one or more of the foregoing six factors are absent; (2) the communication identifies specific legislation, or a specific event outside the control of the organization, that the organization hopes to influence; (3) the timing of the communication coincides with a specific event outside the control of the organization that the organization hopes to influence, such as a vote on legislation or other major legislative action (for example, a hearing before a legislative committee on the issue that is the subject of the communication); (4) the communication identifies a candidate solely as a governmental official who is in a position to act on the public policy issue in connection with the specific event (such as a legislator who is eligible to vote on the legislation); and (5) the communication identifies a candidate solely in the list of key or principal sponsors of the legislation that is the subject of the communication.

This guidance posits six illustrations of these rules; in three of them, the amounts expended by the exempt organizations are not exempt function expenditures, and in the other three, the amounts expended are these types of expenditures (and thus are subject to tax). In all of these situations, the advocacy communication identifies a candidate in an election, appears shortly before that election, and targets the voters in that election.

Each of these situations assumes that all payments for the activity are from the general treasury of the organization (that is, not from a separate fund), the organization would continue to be tax-exempt because the organization's activities continue to meet the appropriate primary purpose test, and all advocacy communications also include a solicitation of contributions to the organization.

§ 17.5   TAXATION OF POLITICAL ORGANIZATIONS

As stated earlier, although political organizations are generally tax-exempt, they are subject to the corporate tax on their political organization taxable income.[53] A political organization's *taxable income* is its gross income,[54] less *exempt function income* and allowable deductions directly connected with the production of gross income (other than exempt function income).[55]

---

[53] IRC § 527(b).

[54] *Gross income* can include amounts expended for other than an exempt function, if the expenditure results in direct or indirect financial benefit to the political organization. For example, a political organization must include in its gross income amounts expended for improvements to its facilities or for equipment that is not necessary for or used in carrying out an exempt function (Reg. § 1.527-5(a)(1)). Amounts expended for illegal activities also must be included in the political organization's taxable income (Reg. § 1.527-5(a)(2)).

[55] IRC § 527(c). A specific deduction of $100 is also allowed but net operating loss deductions and special deductions for corporations may not be taken (IRC § 527(c)). The IRS ruled that state income taxes paid by a political organization on its nonexempt function income are deductible in computing its

A political organization's exempt function income is any amount received as (1) contributions[56] of money or other property;[57] (2) membership dues, fees, or assessments[58] from members of the organization; (3) proceeds from political fund-raising or entertainment events;[59] (4) proceeds from the sale of political campaign materials[60] that are not received in the ordinary course of conduct of a trade or business;[61] or (5) proceeds from the conduct of a bingo game,[62] to the extent the amount is segregated for use only for the exempt function of the political organization.[63]

taxable income (Rev. Rul. 85-115, 1985-2 C.B. 172). A political organization's tax return is Form 1120-POL (IRC § 6012(a)(6); Reg. § 1.6012-6). See § 28.6.

[56] Generally, money or other property solicited personally, by mail, or through advertising will qualify as a *contribution*. Additionally, to the extent a political organization receives federal, state, or local funds under the "check-off" provisions of IRC § 9001 *et seq.* or other provisions for campaign financing, those amounts are also treated as a contribution (Reg. § 1.527-3(b)).

[57] Some businesses establish "charity-PAC" matching programs, which allow employees of the business to designate a charitable organization to be the recipient of a contribution from the corporate employer; the contribution made by the corporation is an amount equal to the sum of the contributions that the employee made to the corporation's political action committee during the previous year. The Federal Election Commission is of the view that this type of matching is not a means of exchanging corporate funds for voluntary contributions, which is illegal (11 C.F.R. 114.5(b)), but instead is a permissible solicitation expense (2 U.S.C. 441b(b)(2) (Federal Election Commission Advisory Opinion 1989-7)). It is the position of the IRS, as expressed by its Chief Counsel's office, however, that a business corporation's contribution to a charitable organization, designated by an employee of the corporation, is not deductible as a charitable gift by the corporation where the contribution is made under a charity-PAC matching program (Gen. Couns. Mem. 39877). The reason for this lack of deduction is the fact that the corporation received a *quid pro quo* for the payment to the charity, in the form of the contribution to the political action committee. In general, see *Charitable Giving* § 2.1(c).

[58] For example, filing fees paid by an individual directly or indirectly to a political party to enable the individual to run as a candidate in a primary or general election as a candidate of that party are treated as exempt function income (Reg. § 1.527-3(c)).

[59] Events intended to rally and encourage support for an individual for public office would be proper political fundraising events. Examples of these events are dinners, breakfasts, receptions, picnics, dances, and athletic exhibitions (Reg. § 1.527-3(d)(1)). By contrast, the IRS ruled that the mere use of funds generated by an event for political purposes does not transform the event into a political event; thus, for example, the sale of raffle tickets by a political organization did not result in exempt function revenue (Tech. Adv. Mem. 9847006). In response to outcries from the political fundraising community, the IRS (in a memorandum from the Exempt Organizations Division to the regional chief compliance officers, dated Dec. 1, 1999) clarified this matter by stating that raffle proceeds can escape taxation as long as the sponsors of the raffle make the political purpose clear to those who purchase tickets (such as by placing a sign to that effect in the place where the tickets are sold).

[60] Proceeds from the sale of political memorabilia, bumper stickers, campaign buttons, hats, shirts, political posters, stationery, jewelry, or cookbooks are related to political activity as long as these items can be identified as relating to distributing political literature or organizing voters to vote for a candidate for public office (Reg. § 1.527-3(e)).

[61] The IRS looks at all the facts and circumstances in determining whether an activity is in the ordinary course of a trade or business. Usually, proceeds from "casual, sporadic fund raising or entertainment events" are not considered in the ordinary course of a trade or business (Reg. § 1.527-3(d)(2)). However, the IRS ruled that the proceeds received by a political organization from the sales of art reproductions did not qualify as exempt function income, because the sales activity was considered to be a trade or business (Rev. Rul. 80-103, 1980-1 C.B. 120).

[62] This term uses the definition in IRC § 513(f)(2). See § 25.2(h).

[63] IRC § 527(c)(3). As noted previously, exempt function income must be segregated. Reg. § 1.527-2(b) defines a *segregated fund* as any fund that is established and maintained by a political organization or an individual separately from the assets of the organization or the personal assets of the individual.

By contrast, where a political organization expends money that results in a direct or indirect benefit to the organization itself[64] or expends money for an illegal activity,[65] the entire amount of the expenditure will be included in the political organization's gross income. Further, where a political organization makes a dual use of facilities or personnel (that is, use for both an exempt function and for the production of political organization taxable income), the expenses, depreciation, and similar items attributable to the facility or personnel must be allocated between the two uses on a "reasonable and consistent basis."[66]

In addition to the aforementioned activities, which result in gross income to the political organization, certain activities by political organizations can result in gross income to a candidate or other individual affiliated with the political organization.[67] For example, where a political organization expends any amount for the personal use of any individual, such as for paying a candidate's income tax liability, the amount expended is included in the individual's gross income.[68] Also, excess funds controlled by a political organization or other person after a campaign or an election are treated as expended for the personal use of the person having control over the ultimate use of the funds, unless the funds are held in reasonable anticipation of use by the political organization for future exempt functions or the funds are transferred within a reasonable period of time to certain political, tax-exempt, or governmental organizations described in the regulations.[69]

The purpose of the fund must be to receive and segregate exempt function income (and earnings on this income) for use only for an exempt function or for an activity necessary to fulfill an exempt function. If an organization that has a segregated fund for purposes of segregating amounts referred to in IRC § 527(c) expends more than an insubstantial amount from the segregated fund for activities that are not for an exempt function during the taxable year, the fund will not be treated as a segregated fund for that tax year (*id.*).

[64] An illustration is the expenditure of exempt function income to purchase building improvements or equipment not necessary to carry on an exempt function.

[65] Although expenses for illegal activity are includable in the organization's gross income, expenses incurred in the defense of civil or criminal suits against the organization are not taxable to the organization (Reg. § 1.527-5(a)(2)). In addition, voluntary reimbursement to the participants in the illegal activity for similar expenses incurred by them are not taxable to the organization if it can demonstrate that such payments were not a part of the inducement to engage in the illegal activity or part of the agreed-upon compensation for such activity (*id.*).

[66] Reg. § 1.527-4(c)(3).

[67] Activities that will not be treated as income to a candidate or other person affiliated with a political organization include contributions to another political organization or newsletter fund; contributions to organizations described in IRC §§ 509(a)(1) or 509(a)(2) (see § 12.3(a), (b)); and deposits in the general fund of the U.S. Treasury or the general fund of any state or local governments (IRC § 527(d); Reg. § 1.527-5(b)).

[68] Reg. § 1.527-5(a)(1).

[69] Reg. § 1.527-5(c)(1). The organizations to which funds can be transferred are described in Reg. § 1.527-5(b). For example, a political organization can contribute amounts "to or for the use of" a public or publicly supported charitable organization (that is, those entities described in IRC § 509(a)(1) or § 509(a)(2) (see § 12.3(a), (b)) (Reg. § 1.527-5(b)(2)). The IRS ruled that campaign committees could transfer funds to a private foundation and remain within this exception, where the foundation was obligated by its corporate documents to make grants only to these types of charitable entities; the foundation was characterized as a "trust" under state law, with the funds transferred "for the use of" the charitable organizations (Priv. Ltr. Rul. 9425032). Contributions to these organizations are not deductible (Reg. § 1.527-5(b)(2), last sentence). Where excess funds are held by an individual who dies before the funds

§ 17.6 TAXATION OF OTHER EXEMPT ORGANIZATIONS

Although a political organization is exempt from taxation on amounts expended for an exempt function, if another type of tax-exempt organization[70] expends any amount during a tax year, either directly[71] or through another organization,[72] for what would be a political organization exempt function, it must include in its gross income for the year an amount equal to the lesser of (1) its net investment income[73] for the year or (2) the aggregate amount expended during the year for the exempt function.[74] Generally, this amount is taxed at the highest corporate tax rate.[75]

The foregoing rules are not intended to change the prohibition on political activities applicable to charitable organizations and the limitation on such activities imposed on social welfare organizations.[76] Indeed, charitable organizations engaging to any extent in political campaign intervention stand to lose their tax-exempt status, in addition to facing the political organization tax.[77] The concept of political organization exempt function, however, is broader than the political campaign intervention limitation.[78] For example, an exempt function includes an attempt to influence the appointment of an individual to a federal public office, such as a presidential nomination of a Supreme Court justice.[79] Since the effort to secure Senate confirmation of a Supreme Court nominee does not involve a political campaign, however, a charitable organization is not precluded from participating in that process.[80]

have been properly transferred, the funds are generally considered income of the decedent and will be included in the decedent's gross estate, unless the estate transfers the funds within a reasonable period to an eligible organization in accordance with Reg. § 1.527-5(b) (Reg. § 1.527-5(c)(2)).

[70] That is, an organization described in IRC § 501(c) that is exempt from tax under IRC § 501(a).

[71] See Tech. Adv. Mem. 8502003 (contributions made by an exempt labor organization from its general checking fund directly to state and local candidates were taxable expenditures).

[72] Although an expenditure can be made for an exempt function "through another organization" (for example, by making a contribution to another organization, which then uses the contribution for an exempt function), an IRC § 501(c) organization will not be absolutely liable for tax under IRC § 527(f)(1) for amounts transferred to an organization, as long as "reasonable steps" are taken to ensure that the transferee does not use these amounts for an exempt function (Reg. § 1.527-6(b)(1)(ii)).

[73] Net investment income is defined as the excess of gross income from interest, dividends, rents, and royalties, plus the excess of gains from the sale or exchange of assets over losses from the sale or exchange of assets, over allowable deductions directly connected with the production of investment income (IRC § 527(f)(2)). To avoid double taxation, however, items taken into account for purposes of the unrelated business income tax imposed by IRC § 511 are not taken into account when calculating net investment income (id., last sentence).

[74] IRC § 527(f)(1).

[75] IRC § 527(b). Special rules apply, however, in cases where the organization has a net capital gain (IRC § 527(b)(2)).

[76] S. Rep. No. 93-1357, at 27 (1974); Reg. § 1.527-6(g).

[77] Thus, for example, a charitable organization that has its tax-exempt status revoked for engaging in political campaign intervention (see § 23.2), but without retroactive effect pursuant to IRC § 7805(b) (see § 28.1, note 1), would be subject to taxation on any political activity during the IRC § 7805(b) relief period (Gen. Couns. Mem. 39811).

[78] In general, § 23.2.

[79] See text accompanied by supra notes 17–18.

[80] See § 23.2(iv), text accompanied by note 43.

The purpose of taxing exempt organizations on their exempt function activity is to treat them on an equal basis for tax purposes with political organizations and, at the same time, to ensure that they are taxed only to the extent they actually operate in a fashion similar to political organizations.[81] Tracing of funds is not required, and the tax will apply even though the tax-exempt organization uses its investment income exclusively for nonpolitical purposes and makes its political expenditures entirely out of other funds.[82]

Not all politically related expenditures by exempt organizations, however, are considered exempt function expenditures subject to taxation. For example, expenditures for nonpartisan activities are not considered exempt function expenditures. *Nonpartisan activities* include voter registration and "get-out-the-vote" campaigns, as long as they are not specifically identified with any candidate or political party.[83] Additionally, where an exempt organization appears before a legislative body in response to a "written request. . .for the purpose of influencing the appointment or confirmation of an individual to a public office," expenditures related to the appearance are not treated as exempt function expenditures.[84] Also, the IRS ruled that an exempt social welfare organization is not subject to the political activities tax when it provides administrative services to a related political action committee in exchange for a fee based on fair market value.[85]

§ 17.7   AVOIDING POLITICAL ORGANIZATIONS TAX

Although tax-exempt organizations are subject to tax on their exempt function expenditures, these entities can avoid this political activities tax in a number of ways.

First, it may be possible for a tax-exempt organization to establish a related political organization (usually a political action committee). From a tax law perspective, the law on this point is sparse. It is clear that tax-exempt organizations, such as social welfare organizations, trade and business associations, labor unions, and chambers of commerce can establish related PACs.[86] Presumably this is also true with respect to other types of exempt organizations, such as social clubs and veterans' organizations.

---

[81] S. Rep. No. 93-1357, at 29 (1974). For example, the IRS ruled that a tax-exempt social welfare (IRC § 501(c)(4)) organization may, without adversely affecting its exempt status, participate in political campaign activities if it is primarily engaged in the promotion of social welfare but that the amounts expended for the activities may be treated as political organization taxable income (Rev. Rul. 81-95, 1981-1 C.B. 332) (see § 23.6(a)). The U.S. Tax Court held that a tax-exempt labor organization (see § 16.1) was liable for the IRC § 527(f) tax as the result of the transfer of monies to its political action committee (Alaska Pub. Serv. Employees Local 71 v. Comm'r, 67 T.C.M. 1664 (1991)).

[82] S. Rep. No. 93-1357, at 29 (1974).

[83] Reg. § 1.527-6(b)(5).

[84] Reg. § 1.527-6(b)(4).

[85] Priv. Ltr. Rul. 9850025.

[86] E.g., Priv. Ltr. Rul. 9652026. The Senate Finance Committee stated that "generally, a section 501(c) organization that is permitted to engage in political activities would establish a separate organization that would operate primarily as a political organization, and directly receive and disburse all funds related to nomination, etc. activities. In this way, the campaign-type activities would be taken entirely

Also, a tax-exempt organization will not be taxed where it merely receives contributions from its members for political action and promptly and directly[87] transfers the funds to the political organization that solicited them.[88] Furthermore, the IRS ruled that, where an exempt organization deposits political contributions into an interest-bearing checking account for administrative efficiency before their transfer to a PAC, it has still satisfied the regulation's requirements to promptly and directly transfer the funds to the PAC.[89]

A separate segregated fund that is maintained by an eligible tax-exempt organization is treated as a separate entity from that organization for purposes of the rules pertaining to political organizations.[90] Thus, an exempt organization that engaged in a political organization exempt function as a relatively small part of its operations may have much or all of its net investment income taxed, while the exempt organization that maintains a separate segregated fund can segregate contributions for use in an exempt function, with the result that only the net investment income of the fund is subject to tax.[91]

A tax-exempt organization can make *soft-dollar* expenditures (that is, expenditures for indirect expenses allowed by the federal election law) in support of a separate segregated fund. These expenditures generally are not considered an exempt function outlay and, thus, will not subject an exempt organization to the political activities tax. It is important to note, however, that this type of expenditure is an exempt function outlay when made by a political organization.[92] There is some confusion on this point because of the dual use of the term *exempt function expenditure*, and the IRS has indicated that, if it should conclude in the future that

out of the section 501(c) organization, to the benefit both of the organization and the administration of the tax laws" (S. Rep. No. 93-1357, at 30 (1974)).

[87] A transfer is considered *promptly and directly made* if the organization's procedures satisfy requirements of applicable federal or state campaign laws, the organization maintains adequate records to demonstrate that amounts transferred are in fact political contributions or dues (rather than investment income), and the political contributions or dues transferred were not used to earn investment income for the organization (Reg. § 1.527-6(e)(3)).

[88] Reg. § 1.527-6(e).

[89] Tech. Adv. Mems. 9105001, 9105002; Gen. Couns. Mem. 39837. The IRS stated that the primary objective of the test stated in Reg. § 1.527-6(e)(3) is to prevent tax-exempt organizations from needlessly retaining the PAC funds in order to invest those funds. In this case, even though a small amount of interest was earned and retained by the organization when it briefly held the PAC funds in its interest-bearing checking account, the PAC funds were placed in the checking account primarily for administrative efficiency, rather than for investment purposes (*id.*; also, Tech. Adv. Mem. 9042004, reaching the same result with respect to a business league; Tech. Adv. Mem. 8628001, reaching the same result with respect to a labor union).

[90] IRC § 527(f)(3); Reg. § 1.527-6(f). A *separate segregated fund* is defined as a fund within the meaning of 18 U.S.C. § 610 or any similar state statute, or within the meaning of any state statute that permits the segregation of dues moneys for political organization exempt functions (IRC § 527(f)(3)). However, 18 U.S.C. § 610 was repealed by the Federal Election Campaign Act Amendments of 1976, Pub. L. No. 94-382. § 112, 90 Stat. 490, and was recodified at 2 U.S.C. § 441b. The term *separate segregated fund* is not further defined in the recodified section. Although the focus of IRC § 527(f)(3) is on separate segregated funds that are maintained by an IRC § 501(c) organization, the IRS stated that there is nothing in the legislative history to indicate that was to be the only type of segregated fund to which amounts could be transferred (Tech. Adv. Mem. 8147008).

[91] Ann. 88-114, 1988-37 I.R.B. 26; S. Rep. No. 93-1357, at 30 (1974).

[92] Reg. § 1.527-6(b)(1).

some or all of the indirect expenses allowed by the federal election law constitute exempt function expenditures for purposes of the political activities tax, that interpretation of the law will apply only on a prospective basis.[93]

Although charitable organizations are not permitted to engage in political campaign activities,[94] they may establish and use a political organization (such as a PAC) if the purpose of the PAC is to engage in political activities[95] that are not political campaign activities.[96] In other words, a noncampaign PAC affiliated with a charitable organization may be used to promote the organization's viewpoint on particular issues. In the view of the IRS, however, a corporate sponsor of a PAC may not deduct the organizational and administrative costs of the PAC.[97] In the instance under review, the expenses sought to be deducted were legal fees and interest expenses. The IRS concluded that the expenditures for the PAC were for intervention in political campaigns on behalf of candidates for public office and/or in connection with attempts to influence the general public, and thus were nondeductible.[98]

§ 17.8 INDEPENDENT POLITICAL ACTION COMMITTEES

It is possible for the managers of a charitable organization and/or others, acting as individuals, to establish and use an *independent* political action committee, even if the PAC has the function of supporting a candidate's political campaign. While the IRS has yet to address this topic, the Federal Election Commission (FEC) published an advisory opinion[99] sanctioning the concept of what the federal campaign law recognizes as a nonconnected political committee.[100]

According to the FEC, a *nonconnected political committee* has the following characteristics: (1) It is established by the members of the governing board of the charitable organization acting in their individual capacities, (2) the committee operates and is governed independently of the charitable organization, (3) the committee is not financially supported by the charitable organization, (4) the committee appropriately reimburses the charitable organization for expenses incurred on behalf of

---

[93] Tech. Adv. Mem. 8516001. A soft-dollar expenditure by a tax-exempt membership organization, which is not an exempt function expenditure, may nevertheless cause a portion of its members' dues to be nondeductible as a business expense (IRC § 162(e)(2)) (Tech. Adv. Mem. 8202019). The same may be the case in connection with certain types of lobbying expenditures (Tech. Adv. Mem. 7946009). The business expenses deduction is disallowed where either of these disqualifying activities is substantial in relation to total activities (Reg. § 1.162-20(c)(3)).

[94] See §§ 23.1, 23.2.

[95] That is, IRC § 527 exempt functions.

[96] Ann. 88-114, 1988-37 I.R.B. 26.

[97] Priv. Ltr. Rul. 8202019. The IRS also held that the portion of the salaries of the corporation's officers and employees allocable to work on the PAC (including time spent after regular working hours) was nondeductible. Further, the IRS also ruled as nondeductible the corporation's overhead expenses relating to the withholding of contributions to the PAC from employees' salaries and agents' commissions.

[98] IRC § 162(e)(2).

[99] FEC Advisory Opinion 1984-12.

[100] Cf. 2 U.S.C. §§ 431(7), 411b.

the committee, (5) the committee pays a fair rent to the charitable organization for the use of any office space and/or facilities, (6) the committee pays a "commercially reasonable" consideration for the services of individuals who are employees or agents of the charitable organization, (7) the charitable organization does not engage in conduct that favors or appears to favor the solicitation activity of the committee, and (8) neither the charitable organization nor the committee asserts a proprietary interest in or control over use of the name of the political committee.[101]

[101] *Id.*

CHAPTER EIGHTEEN

Employee Benefit Funds

The law of tax-exempt organizations and the law of employee benefits are inextricably intertwined. This is because the funding underlying the various forms of employee benefit plans is derived from assets contributed to and held for investment in a trust or fund; the law provides for federal income tax exemption for these funds, so as to maximize the resources available to provide the benefits.

This interrelationship is also reflected in the organization of the IRS. A component of the agency is the Tax Exempt and Government Entities Division. This division serves three IRS "customer segments": tax-exempt organizations, government entities, and employee (public and private retirement) plans.

The tax-exempt organizations aspect of the law of employee benefits is reflected in the opening passage of the statutory law of tax-exempt organizations, where it is provided that organizations referenced in the rules concerning retirement, profit-sharing, and similar plans[1] are exempt from federal income taxation.[2] That section makes reference to trusts that are part of qualified stock bonus, pension, or profit-sharing plans.

§ 18.1 OVERVIEW

Employees—whether of nonprofit, for-profit, or governmental employers—are individuals who provide services to an employer. That is, these individuals are provided compensation, in a context where they are not functioning as independent contractors, in exchange for their services. There are employees of nonprofit, tax-exempt organizations who choose to earn less than what they would receive were they working in the for-profit sector, but for the most part those who work for nonprofit organizations (other than volunteers) expect and must have remuneration

[1] IRC § 401(a).
[2] IRC § 501(a).

for their services. Indeed, the law is clear that an individual need not necessarily accept reduced compensation merely because they render services to a tax-exempt, as opposed to a taxable, organization.[3]

Compensation in general is provided in three forms: current, deferred, and retirement. Each of these forms of compensation is available to employees of tax-exempt organizations. Whatever the mode of compensation—be it wages, salaries, bonuses, commissions, fringe benefits, deferred compensation, and/or retirement benefits—most exempt organizations are constrained by the doctrines of private inurement, private benefit, and/or the intermediate sanctions rules.[4] This essentially means that all compensation, no matter how determined or whatever the form, must, for the employer to be or remain exempt, be *reasonable*.

Some of the vehicles by which employee benefits are provided are conventional tax-exempt organizations.[5]

§ 18.2 SPECIAL RULES FOR WELFARE BENEFIT FUNDS

There are several categories of tax-exempt organizations, other than those entities that are exempt as retirement or profit-sharing plans, that are funds underlying employee benefit plans, or are otherwise principally concerned with employee compensation. Two of these are termed *welfare benefit funds*:[6] the voluntary employees' beneficiary association (VEBA) and the supplemental unemployment benefit (SUB) trust.

(a) Nondiscrimination Requirements

A VEBA cannot be tax-exempt unless it meets certain nondiscrimination requirements.[7] In general, a plan meets these requirements only if (1) each class of benefits under the plan is provided to a classification of employees that is set forth in the plan and that is found by the IRS not to be discriminatory in favor of employees who are highly compensated individuals, and (2) in the case of each class of benefits, the benefits do not discriminate in favor of employees who are highly compensated individuals.[8]

The following categories of employees may be excluded from consideration in this regard: employees who have not completed three years of service,

---

[3] H. R. Rep. 104-506, at 56, n. 5 (1996). See § 21.4(a).

[4] See Chapters 20, 21. In this regard, public charities, social welfare organizations, and certain nonprofit health insurers must take into account the rules concerning excess benefit transactions (see § 21.4), and private foundations must take into account the self-dealing rules (see § 12.4(a)).

[5] That is, the organizations are tax-exempt pursuant to IRC § 501(a) because they are described in a subsection of IRC § 501(c).

[6] IRC § 505.

[7] IRC § 505(a)(1). This rule does not apply to any organization that is part of a plan maintained pursuant to an agreement between employee representatives and one or more employers if the IRS finds that the agreement is a collective bargaining agreement and that the plan was the subject of good faith bargaining between the employee representatives and the employer or employers (IRC § 505(a)(2)).

[8] IRC § 505(b)(1). A life insurance, disability, severance pay, or supplemental unemployment compensation benefit will not fail the second of these requirements merely because the benefits available bear a uniform relationship to the total compensation, or the basic or regular rate of compensation, of

employees who have not attained age 21, seasonal employees or less than half-time employees, employees covered by a collective bargaining agreement that was the subject of good-faith bargaining, and employees who are nonresident aliens and who do not receive earned income from U.S. sources.[9]

(b)   Tax-Exempt Status

A VEBA or SUB is not an organization that is tax-exempt for federal income purposes unless it has made timely application to the IRS for recognition of exempt status.[10]

§ 18.3   VOLUNTARY EMPLOYEES' BENEFICIARY ASSOCIATIONS

The federal tax law accords tax-exempt status to voluntary employees' beneficiary associations "providing for the payment of life, sick, accident or other benefits to the members of such association or their dependents or designated beneficiaries," as long as there is no private inurement.[11]

One of the basic requirements for achievement of tax exemption as a VEBA is that the organization must be an association of employees.[12] Thus, a trust that provides benefits to only one employee cannot qualify as an exempt VEBA.[13] Typically, those eligible for membership in a VEBA are defined by reference to a common employer (or affiliated employers), to coverage under one or more collective bargaining agreements (with respect to benefits provided by reason of the agreement or agreements), to membership in a labor union, or to membership in one or more locals of a national or international labor union. Employees of one or more employers engaged in the same line of business in the same geographic locale are considered to share an employment-related bond for purposes of an organization through which their employers provide benefits. Employees of a labor union are considered to share an employment-related common bond with members of the union, and employees of a VEBA are considered to share an employment-related common bond with members of the VEBA. Whether a group of individuals is defined by reference to a permissible standard or standards is a question to be determined with regard to all the pertinent facts and circumstances.[14] For example, the IRS allowed an exempt VEBA to expand its membership base because the

---

employees covered by the plan (*id.*, last sentence). The term *compensation* is defined in IRC § 414(s); the term *highly compensated individual* is defined in IRC § 414(q).

[9] IRC § 505(b)(2).

[10] IRC § 505(c). The concept of *recognition* of tax-exempt status by the IRS is the subject of § 3.2.

[11] IRC § 501(c)(9); Reg. § 1.501(c)(9)-1. See § 20.12.

[12] Reg. § 1.501(c)(9)-2(b).

[13] Rev. Rul. 85-199, 1985-2 C.B. 163.

[14] Reg. § 1.501(c)(9)-2(a)(1). A proposal of a VEBA established by state and local affiliates of a national labor union to provide welfare benefits to certain actively employed and retired nonmember staff of the establishing entities was held to not adversely affect the VEBA's exemption because the proposed participants shared an employment-related common bond with members of affiliates who were also members of the VEBA (Priv. Ltr. Rul. 201422025).

present and prospective members are engaged in the same line of business and are in the same geographic locale, and thus share an employment-related common bond.[15] By contrast, the IRS ruled that an entity could not qualify as an exempt VEBA because employees of any small business that is a member of one of more than 100 chambers of commerce in an area are not employees whose eligibility for membership is defined by reference to objective standards that constitute an employment-related common bond.[16]

Tax exemption is not imperiled merely because the membership of a VEBA includes individuals who are not employees, as long as these individuals share an employment-related bond with the employee members. These individuals may include, for example, the proprietor of a business whose employees are members of the VEBA. For these purposes, a VEBA is considered to be composed of employees if at least 90 percent of its total membership on one day of each quarter of the VEBA's tax year consists of employees.[17]

Despite the foregoing criteria, a federal court of appeals declared the tax regulations invalid to the extent of the *same geographic locale* requirement. The court reviewed the legislative history of the statute and the phraseology of other tax exemption provisions and concluded that Congress intentionally elected to not place a geographic restriction on exempt VEBAs. Noting that the "quintessential element" of an exempt VEBA is the "commonality of interests among its employee members," the court wrote that the "relatedness among a group of employees is neither established nor dissipated upon the geographic locale of the group's members."[18]

Eligibility for membership in a VEBA may nevertheless be restricted by geographic proximity, or by objective conditions or limitations reasonably related to employment, such as a limitation as to a reasonable classification of workers, a limitation based on a reasonable minimum period of service, a limitation based on maximum compensation, or a requirement that members be employed on a full-time basis. Also, eligibility for benefits may be restricted by objective conditions relating to the type or amount of benefits offered.[19] Any objective criteria used to restrict eligibility for membership or benefits may not, however, be selected or administered in a manner that limits membership or benefits to officers, shareholders, or highly compensated employees of an employer contributing to or otherwise funding a VEBA. Similarly, eligibility for benefits may not be subject to conditions or limitations that have the effect of entitling officers, shareholders, or highly compensated employees of an employer contributing to or otherwise funding the

---

[15] Priv. Ltr. Rul. 201221030.

[16] Priv. Ltr. Rul. 201224037.

[17] Reg. § 1.501(c)(9)-2(a)(1). An organization's expansion of its eligible membership to include all former employees of an employer is permissible under this regulation (Priv. Ltr. Rul. 202236004).

[18] Water Quality Ass'n Employees' Benefit Corp. v. United States, 795 F.2d 1303, 1310–11 (7th Cir. 1986), *rev'g* 609 F. Supp. 91 (N.D. Ill. 1985).

[19] A plan of a VEBA, covering employees pursuant to collective bargaining agreements, to add nonunion common-law employees of industry league members as participants was ruled to not adversely affect the VEBA's exemption (Priv. Ltr. Rul. 201415008). A VEBA's plan to extend health care benefits to nondependent domestic partners was ruled to not adversely affect exemption, as long as these (impermissible) benefits did not exceed 3 percent of total annual benefits paid (Priv. Ltr. Rul. 201415011).

VEBA to benefits that are disproportionate in relation to benefits to which other members of the VEBA are entitled.[20] Whether the selection or administration of objective conditions has the effect of providing disproportionate benefits to officers, shareholders, or highly compensated employees generally is determined on the basis of all the facts and circumstances.[21] This tax exemption does not apply to pension funds distributing benefits to partners.[22]

Membership in a VEBA must be voluntary. Membership is *voluntary* if an affirmative act is required on the part of an employee to become a member rather than the designation as a member being due to employee status. A VEBA is considered voluntary even though membership is required of all employees, however, as long as the employees do not incur a detriment (such as deductions from compensation) as a result of membership in the VEBA. An employer is not deemed to have imposed involuntary membership on the employees if membership is required as the result of a collective bargaining agreement or as an incident of membership in a labor organization.[23]

A tax-exempt VEBA must be controlled either by its membership, by an independent trustee (such as a bank), or by trustees, at least some of whom are designated by or on behalf of the membership.[24] Loose forms of affiliation are insufficient.[25]

The life, sick, accident, or other benefits provided by a VEBA must be payable to its members, their dependents, or their designated beneficiaries.[26] Life, sick, accident, or other benefits may take the form of cash or noncash benefits. To be tax-exempt, the VEBA must function so that substantially all of its operations are in furtherance of the provision of the requisite benefits.[27] The income tax regulations define the terms *life benefit*[28] and *sick and accident benefit*,[29] and provide that the term *other benefits* includes only benefits that are similar to life, sick, or accident benefits—namely, a benefit that is intended to safeguard or improve the health of a member or a member's dependents, or that protects against a contingency that interrupts or impairs a member's earning power.[30] Other benefits include paying

---

[20] E.g., Lima Surgical Assocs., Inc. Voluntary Employees' Beneficiary Ass'n Plan Trust v. United States, 90-1 U.S.T.C. ¶ 50,329 (Cl. Ct. 1990), *aff'd*, 944 F.2d 885 (Fed. Cir. 1991).

[21] Reg. § 1.501(c)(9)-2(a)(2)(i). The income tax regulations enumerate certain generally permissible restrictions or conditions (Reg. § 1.501(c)(9)-2(a)(2)(ii); also Reg. § 1.501(c)(9)-4(b)).

[22] Nelson v. Joyce, 404 F. Supp. 489 (N.D. Ill. 1975); Rev. Rul. 70-411, 1970-2 C.B. 91; Rev. Rul. 69-144, 1969-1 C.B. 115.

[23] Reg. § 1.501(c)(9)-2(c)(2).

[24] Reg. § 1.501(c)(9)-2(c)(3)(iii). E.g., Lima Surgical Assocs., Inc. Voluntary Employees' Beneficiary Ass'n Plan Trust v. United States, 90-1 U.S.T.C. ¶ 50,329 (Cl. Ct. 1990), *aff'd*, 944 F.2d 885 (Fed. Cir. 1991).

[25] E.g., American Ass'n of Christian Schools Voluntary Employees Beneficiary Ass'n Welfare Plan Trust v. United States, 663 F. Supp. (N.D. Ala. 1987), *aff'd*, 850 F.2d 1510 (11th Cir. 1988).

[26] E.g., Milwaukee Sign Painters Welfare Fund v. United States, 66-1 U.S.T.C. ¶ 9170 (E.D. Wis. 1965).

[27] Reg. § 1.501(c)(9)-3(a). The IRS appears to apply a *de minimis* standard to determine whether less than substantially all of a VEBA's assets are used to provide permissible benefits to members (Gen. Couns. Mems. 39873, 39817).

[28] Reg. § 1.501(c)(9)-3(b). In the case of an employee-funded association, the provision of group whole life insurance to its members is a permissible life benefit (Priv. Ltr. Rul. 202039003).

[29] Reg. § 1.501(c)(9)-3(c).

[30] Reg. § 1.501(c)(9)-3(d).

vacation benefits, providing vacation facilities, reimbursing vacation expenses, subsidizing recreational activities, the provision of child care facilities for pre-school and school-age dependents, and personal legal service benefits.[31] A VEBA may provide identity theft insurance to its participants and their dependents.[32]

Other benefits do not include the payment of commuting expenses, the provision of accident or homeowner's insurance benefits for damage to property, the provision of malpractice insurance,[33] the provision of loans to members (except in times of distress), the provision of pension and annuity benefits payable at the time of mandatory or voluntary retirement, universal life insurance coverage (because the policies have provisions for period payments to the insured as a settlement option),[34] or the provision of savings facilities for members.[35] An activity may fail to qualify as an "other" benefit but not endanger the VEBA's exempt status if it is merely incidental in relation to its total activities.[36]

An illustration of VEBAs, under the law prior to the promulgation of the pertinent income tax regulations, was an organization that reimbursed its members for premiums paid under the Medicare program.[37] An association that merely ensured the discharge of an obligation imposed by law on an employer corporation (for example, workers' compensation benefits) was held to not qualify for tax exemption as a VEBA because the employees did not receive any additional benefits.[38]

VEBAs may merge, with the successor entity retaining its status as a tax-exempt VEBA.[39] Following a merger, the VEBA can provide benefits to participants employed by any member of the acquiring group.[40] Likewise, a VEBA may be divided, with its assets apportioned to successor VEBAs.[41] Surplus assets may be transferred from a trust to a VEBA without altering the exempt status of the VEBA.[42] A transfer of assets from a subsidiary's VEBA to a parent's VEBA will not disqualify either entity for exempt status,[43] nor will the transfer of assets to, and use by, the VEBA of an acquiring corporation from the VEBA of a corporation

---

[31] Reg. § 1.501(c)(9)-3(e). Certain health insurance (IRC § 35) may be provided under an employee benefit plan funded by a VEBA, in the case of eligible coverage months beginning before Jan. 1, 2011, where the VEBA was established pursuant to an order of a bankruptcy court or by agreement with an authorized representative (IRC § 35(e)(1)(K), enacted by the American Recovery and Reinvestment Act of 2009, Pub. L. No. 111-5, § 1899G, 123 Stat. 115, 430).

[32] Priv. Ltr. Rul. 200911037.

[33] E.g., Anesthesia Serv. Med. Group, Inc., Employee Protective Trust, San Diego Trust & Sav. Bank, Trustee v. Comm'r, 85 T.C. 1031 (1985).

[34] Priv. Ltr. Rul. 200950049.

[35] Reg. § 1.501(c)(9)-3(f). This regulation was upheld in Canton Police Benevolent Ass'n of Canton, Ohio v. United States, 658 F. Supp. 411 (N.D. Ohio 1987), aff'd, 88-1 U.S.T.C. ¶ 9285 (6th Cir. 1988); Bricklayers Benefit Plans of Delaware Valley, Inc. v. Comm'r, 81 T.C. 735 (1983).

[36] E.g., Priv. Ltr. Rul. 202125002 (concerning provision of an online student loan servicing benefit).

[37] Rev. Rul. 66-212, 1966-2 C.B. 230.

[38] Rev. Rul. 74-18, 1974-1 C.B. 139. Also, Rev. Rul. 66-354, 1966-2 C.B. 207.

[39] E.g., Priv. Ltr. Rul. 200009051.

[40] Priv. Ltr. Rul. 200111046.

[41] Priv. Ltr. Rul. 200301047.

[42] Priv. Ltr. Rul. 9840050.

[43] Priv. Ltr. Rul. 200211053.

acquired in a merger.[44] A VEBA may return excess assets to its tax-exempt sponsor without loss of exempt status.[45] Where the exempt sponsor is dissolving, the VEBA's assets may be distributed as taxable lump-sum payments among the participants without triggering excise tax.[46] This type of entity may use excess assets to provide welfare benefits to affiliates of a sponsoring employer.[47] Indeed, a VEBA, without any remaining participants and that has paid all benefits that were due, may terminate by distributing its remaining assets to charitable organizations.[48] The use of reserves to provide postretirement benefits will not cause a VEBA to lose its exempt status.[49]

A VEBA cannot be tax-exempt unless it meets certain nondiscrimination requirements.[50] For example, the IRS, having determined that a welfare plan's membership was not voluntary, because the plan excluded certain employees from participating in it, held that the plan cannot qualify as an exempt VEBA because it is discriminatory.[51] This rule is inapplicable, however, to a VEBA that is part of a plan maintained pursuant to one or more collective bargaining agreements between one or more employee organizations and one or more employers.[52] The exempt status of a VEBA will not be adversely affected if the plan is amended to permit nonspousal, nondependent domestic partner beneficiaries.[53]

A VEBA constitutes a *welfare benefit fund*.[54] Therefore, a *disqualified benefit*[55] provided by a VEBA will give rise to tax liability.[56]

VEBAs are subject to the unrelated income rules,[57] including the special rules by which only exempt function revenue is excluded from taxation.[58] Employer contributions to VEBAs are contributions to capital rather than forms of gross income.[59] Net passive income of VEBAs constitutes unrelated business income, unless it is properly set aside for charitable purposes or to provide for the payment of life, sick, accident, or other benefits.[60]

---

[44] Priv. Ltr. Rul. 200225041.

[45] Priv. Ltr. Rul. 200126034.

[46] Priv. Ltr. Rul. 201528038. This excise tax (IRC § 4976(a)) was avoided inasmuch as the amounts to be distributed did not give rise to a disqualified benefit (IRC § 4976(b)(1)(C)), in part because these amounts were not the subject of an employer plan deduction (IRC § 419) in any year, since the employer had been tax-exempt.

[47] Priv. Ltr. Rul. 200204045.

[48] Priv. Ltr. Rul. 201545026.

[49] Priv. Ltr. Rul. 200302052.

[50] IRC § 505(a)(1), (b).

[51] Priv. Ltr. Rul. 201515036. The statute on which the IRS relied (IRC § 50(b)(1)) addresses discrimination only in favor of employees who are highly compensated.

[52] IRC § 505(a)(2).

[53] Priv. Ltr. Rul. 200953029.

[54] IRC § 419(e)(3)(A). See § 18.2.

[55] IRC § 4976(b).

[56] IRC § 4976(a).

[57] See Chapters 24, 25.

[58] See § 25.4(c).

[59] Priv. Ltr. Rul. 8512058.

[60] IRC § 512(a)(3)(B). See § 25.4(c). These limits are, however, inapplicable to collectively bargained plans (IRC § 419A(f)(5)(A)). Thus, there are no set-aside limits where the VEBA is a plan that is collectively bargained for (e.g., Priv. Ltr. Ruls. 9216033, 200003053).

Congress, in 1969, removed a limitation that no more than 15 percent of a VEBA's annual receipts could be in the form of investment income, thereby enabling VEBAs to accumulate reserves at reasonable levels. (VEBAs must conform to the requirements of the Employee Retirement Income Security Act, however, including those governing investment practices.) With this restriction eliminated, business corporations are utilizing VEBAs to provide employee benefits on a self-insurance basis, because the benefits program can be fashioned to meet the employers' desires and because it is less expensive than insurance premium costs.

§ 18.4 SUPPLEMENTAL UNEMPLOYMENT BENEFIT TRUSTS

The federal tax law provides tax exemption for certain trusts forming part of a plan providing for the payment of supplemental unemployment compensation benefits.[61] Among other criteria, the supplemental unemployment benefit trust must be part of a plan whose eligibility conditions and benefits do not discriminate in favor of supervisory or highly compensated employees and that requires that benefits be determined according to objective standards.[62] Also, the SUB must be a part of a plan that provides that the corpus and income of the SUB cannot (before the satisfaction of all liabilities to employees covered by the plan) be used for, or be diverted to, any purpose other than the provision of supplemental unemployment compensation benefits. Termination of a SUB, with distribution of its remaining assets to employees covered by the plan (after the satisfaction of all liabilities), will not result in loss of its exempt status (even though technically the assets will not be used solely for the purpose of providing benefits).[63] Moreover, the excess assets of a SUB, after paying all benefits and outstanding administrative costs, may be transferred to, and the SUB effectively merged with, a VEBA without threatening the exempt status of either.[64]

SUBs are intended to provide benefits to laid-off (or perhaps ill) employees, frequently in conjunction with other payments such as state unemployment benefits.

The term *supplemental unemployment compensation benefits* means separation-from-employment benefits and sick and accident benefits that are subordinate to the separation benefits.[65] These benefits encompass short-week benefits paid to employees not wholly separated from employment[66] and relocation payments to employees who would otherwise be separated from employment.[67] In one case, however, payments from a SUB to union members to compensate them for

[61] IRC § 501(c)(17); Reg. § 1.501(c)(17)-1(a).

[62] Thus, a single trust intended to provide benefits to employees of multiple employers was ruled ineligible for tax exemption (Priv. Ltr. Rul. 201411041).

[63] Rev. Rul. 81-68, 1981-1 C.B. 349.

[64] Priv. Ltr. Rul. 200206056.

[65] IRC § 501(c)(17)(D); Reg. § 1.501(c)(17)-1(b)(1).

[66] Rev. Rul. 70-189, 1970-1 C.B. 134. Also, Rev. Rul. 80-124, 1980-1 C.B. 212; Rev. Rul. 56-249, 1956-2 C.B. 488.

[67] Rev. Rul. 70-188, 1970-1 C.B. 133.

anticipated lost wages because of the adoption of a new industrial process were ruled to not qualify as this type of benefit since there was no showing that all union members receiving the benefits were involuntarily separated from employment or actually incurred a reduction in the number of hours worked because of the new process.[68]

An otherwise qualified SUB can invest in low-risk, income-producing investments that serve social purposes, do not accrue for the benefit of related parties, and are not contrary to the employees' interests without jeopardizing its tax exemption.[69] Distribution to employees of funds representing contributions in excess of maximum funding will, however, adversely affect a SUB's exempt status.[70] The trustee of an exempt plan may, upon authorization from an employee, deduct and pay the employee's union dues from their benefit payments.[71]

A SUB constitutes a *welfare benefit fund*.[72] Accordingly, a *disqualified benefit*[73] provided by a SUB will give rise to tax liability.[74]

§ 18.5 BLACK LUNG BENEFITS TRUSTS

Another type of tax-exempt organization is the black lung benefits trust (BLBT).[75] The purpose of this body of law is to provide income tax exemption for a qualifying trust used by a coal mine operator to self-insure for liabilities under federal and state black lung benefits laws. Under the federal black lung benefits statute, a coal mine operator in a state not deemed to provide adequate workers' compensation coverage for pneumoconiosis must secure the payment of benefits for which the operator may be found liable under the statute, either by means of commercial insurance or through self-insuring. Since state laws are deemed inadequate for this purpose, all operators subject to this liability must obtain insurance or self-insure. Because this insurance is unavailable or is of high cost, Congress established this form of self-insurance program, with similar tax consequences (from the point of view of the operator) as would result if the operator had purchased noncancellable accident and health insurance.[76]

A qualified BLBT must be irrevocable, must be established by a written instrument, must be created or organized in the United States, and may be contributed to by any person (other than an insurance company). The trust instrument may be amended or restated for appropriate purposes, such as to enable

---

[68] Rev. Rul. 77-43, 1977-1 C.B. 151.

[69] Rev. Rul. 70-536, 1970-2 C.B. 120.

[70] Rev. Rul. 71-156, 1971-2 C.B. 153.

[71] Rev. Rul. 73-307, 1973-2 C.B. 185.

[72] IRC § 419(e)(3)(A).

[73] IRC § 4976(b).

[74] IRC § 4976(a). Also, an organization described in IRC § 501(c)(17) cannot be tax-exempt if it engages in a prohibited transaction as defined in IRC § 503(b) (IRC § 503(a)(1)(A), (B)).

[75] IRC § 501(c)(21).

[76] S. Rep. No. 95-336, at 11–12 (1978).

subsidiaries of the corporation that initially created the BLBT to self-insure their obligations under the black lung benefits law.[77]

The tax-exempt BLBT has as its exclusive purpose (1) the satisfaction, in whole or in part, of the liability of a contributor to the trust for, or with respect to, claims for compensation for disability or death due to pneumoconiosis under Black Lung Acts;[78] (2) the payment of premiums for insurance exclusively covering this type of liability; and (3) the payment of administrative and other incidental expenses of the trust (including legal, accounting, actuarial, and trustee expenses) in connection with the operation of the trust and the processing of claims under Black Lung Acts against a contributor to the trust.[79]

No part of the assets of a tax-exempt BLBT may be used for, or diverted to, any purpose other than the foregoing three purposes or investment.[80] Investment can, however, occur only to the extent that the trustee determines that the invested assets are not currently needed for the trust's exempt purposes. Moreover, the investment may only be in (1) public debt securities of the United States, (2) obligations of a state or local government that are not in default as to principal or interest, or (3) time or demand deposits in a bank[81] or an insured credit union located in the United States.[82] A division of a BLBT and the transfer of its assets to one or more new BLBTs is not a prohibited diversion of assets.[83]

The assets of a qualified BLBT also may be paid into the Black Lung Disability Trust Fund[84] or into the general fund of the U.S. Treasury (other than in satisfaction of any tax or other civil or criminal liability of the person who established or contributed to the trust). In certain circumstances, the *excess assets* of an exempt BLBT may be distributed for non–black lung health benefits for coal miners.[85]

The income of a qualified BLBT is not taxable to the operator making contributions to it. Similarly, the trust's income is not taxable to the trust, except that the trust is subject to tax on any unrelated business taxable income.[86] The trust must, however, file annual information returns with the IRS.[87]

---

[77] E.g., Priv. Ltr. Rul. 9428030.

[78] These laws are Part C, Title IV, of the Federal Coal Mine Health and Safety Act of 1969 and any state law providing compensation for disability or death due to pneumoconiosis.

[79] IRC § 501(c)(21)(A).

[80] IRC § 501(c)(21)(B).

[81] As defined in IRC § 581.

[82] As defined in the Federal Credit Union Act, 12 U.S.C. § 1752(b).

[83] E.g., Priv. Ltr. Ruls. 200102056, 9428029.

[84] See Black Lung Benefits Revenue Act of 1977, Pub. L. No. 95-227, § 3, 92 Stat. 11, 12 (1978).

[85] IRC § 501(c)(21)(C). The statutory scheme for computing excess assets takes into account assets in a trust in tax years ending prior to the effective date of the rules (IRC § 501(c)(21)(C)(ii)). A BLBT was held to not be required to distribute assets for this purpose because the trust did not have any tax years ending prior to that effective date and thus did not have any excess assets to distribute (PNC Bank, N.A. v. PPL Utilities Corp., 2006-2 U.S.T.C. ¶ 50,376 (3d Cir. 2006)).

[86] See Chapters 24, 25.

[87] See § 28.2(a). Although the exemption application and annual information returns of an IRC § 501(c)(21) trust are subject to the public disclosure requirements (IRC § 6104(a)(1), 6104(b); see §§ 28.9(a)(ii), 28.10), disclosure is not required of confidential business information of a coal mine operator who establishes and contributes to such a trust (Pub. L. No. 95-488, § (e), 92 Stat. 1637, 1638 (1978); H.R. Rep. No. 95-1656, at 6 (1978)).

The contributions by a coal mine operator to a tax-exempt BLBT are deductible by the operator for federal income tax purposes.[88] This provision imposes alternative limitations on the deductibility of these contributions for a tax year, based on actual benefit claims approved or filed during the taxable year, as well as on the amount of anticipated liabilities for claims filed or expected to be filed in the future by past or present employees of the operator determined by using reasonable actuarial methods and assumptions, and any excess contributions may be taxable.[89] A contribution of property will be treated as a sale or exchange of the property for tax purposes, unless it is transferred without consideration and is not subject to a mortgage or similar lien.

A trust that is tax-exempt under these rules is subject to prohibitions on self-dealing[90] and the making of certain expenditures.[91] These prohibitions are similar to those imposed on private foundations and are sanctioned by excise taxes on the trust, its trustees, and/or the disqualified person(s) involved. The Senate Finance Committee observed that the investment limitations imposed on these trusts "are intended to preclude speculative or other investments of corpus or income which might jeopardize the carrying out of the trust's exempt purposes and permit the [C]ommittee [which authored these provisions] to simplify the self-dealing restrictions and avoid the necessity of certain other restrictions to prevent potential abuses."[92]

§ 18.6 RETIREMENT PLAN TRUST FUNDS

The federal tax law provides that an organization "described in. . .[IRC] section 401(a) shall be exempt from taxation under this subtitle." This provision of the Internal Revenue Code defines the qualified trust fund that is part of a stock bonus, pension, or profit-sharing plan[93] maintained by an employer for the exclusive benefit of its employees or their beneficiaries. While the fund is the tax-exempt organization, the principal focus of the law in this area is on the terms, conditions, and provided benefits of the retirement plan.[94]

The law of retirement plans was substantially modified by the Employee Retirement Income Security Act of 1974.[95] Government supervision of retirement plans is largely the responsibility of the IRS and the Department of Labor. This body of law imposes requirements relating to employee participation, coverage, vesting of interests, funding, portability of benefits, fiduciary responsibility, prohibited transactions, preparation of plan summaries, and annual reporting and disclosure to the Department of Labor.

---

[88] IRC § 192.
[89] IRC § 4953.
[90] IRC § 4951. Cf. § 12.4(a).
[91] IRC § 4952. Cf. § 12.4(e).
[92] S. Rep. No. 95-336, at 14 (1978).
[93] IRC § 501(a).
[94] E.g., IRC §§ 403(b), 457(b), 457(f).
[95] 29 U.S.C. § 1001 *et seq.*

§ 18.7 OTHER BENEFIT FUNDS

Another type of tax-exempt organization is a trust established by the sponsors of a multiemployer pension plan as a vehicle to accumulate funds in order to provide withdrawal liability payments to the plan.[96]

Also, a type of tax-exempt organization is a trust described in section 4049 of the Employee Retirement Income Security Act of 1974 (as in effect on the date of the enactment of the Single-Employer Pension Plan Amendments Act of 1986).[97]

The federal tax law references a trust or trusts, created before June 25, 1959, forming part of a plan providing for the payment of benefits under a pension plan funded only by employees' contributions, where three requirements are satisfied.[98]

Tax exemption is provided for teachers' retirement fund associations of a purely local character, if there is no private inurement (other than through payment of retirement benefits)[99] and the organization's income consists wholly of amounts received from public taxation, amounts received from assessments on the teaching salaries of members, and income from investments.[100] Tax regulations have not been issued under this provision, nor have there been any IRS rulings or court opinions concerning it. Consequently, it may be concluded that this category of exemption has limited application. The phrase *of a purely local character* has the same meaning in this context as it does with respect to benevolent or mutual organizations.[101]

---

[96] IRC § 501(c)(22).

[97] IRC § 501(c)(24). Section 4049 was repealed on Dec. 22, 1987 (Pub. L. No. 100-203, § 9312(a), 101 Stat. 1330, 1361).

[98] IRC § 501(c)(18); Reg. § 1.501(c)(18)-1. An organization described in IRC § 501(c)(18) cannot be tax-exempt if it engaged in a prohibited transaction as defined in IRC § 503(b) (IRC § 503(a)(1)(C)).

[99] See Chapter 20.

[100] IRC § 501(c)(11).

[101] See § 19.5(a), text accompanied by notes 120–124.

CHAPTER NINETEEN

Other Categories of Tax-Exempt Organizations

Many categories of organizations are exempt from federal income tax in addition to those that are the subject of the previous chapters. The law as to these categories of entities is summarized in this chapter, in order of the accompanying Internal Revenue Code section provisions, followed by law summaries as to other types of exempt organizations.

§ 19.1 INSTRUMENTALITIES OF THE UNITED STATES

The federal income tax law references "[c]orporations organized under Act of Congress, if such corporations are instrumentalities of the United States and if it is specifically provided in this title [Internal Revenue Title] (or under such Act as amended and supplemented before. . .[July 18, 1984]) that such corporations are exempt from Federal income taxes."[1] This third criterion was added to the Internal Revenue Code in 1984 to stipulate that tax exemptions for *United States instrumentalities* must be specified in the Code or in a revenue act. Under prior law (and for pre-1984 instrumentalities), it was sufficient to have tax exemption provided in any act of Congress.

Organizations exempt from federal income tax as U.S. instrumentalities include the Federal Deposit Insurance Corporation, the Reconstruction Finance Corporation, Federal Land Banks, the Federal National Mortgage Association, Federal Reserve Banks, the Federal Savings and Loan Insurance Corporation, the Pennsylvania Avenue Development Corporation, and the Pension Benefit Guaranty Corporation.[2]

Federal credit unions organized and operated under the Federal Credit Union Act are instrumentalities of the United States[3] and therefore are entitled to tax exemption under this body of law. These credit unions are included in a group exemption ruling[4] issued to the National Credit Union Administration.[5] Certain other credit unions that fail to qualify under this provision may secure tax exemption as nonstock mutual credit unions.[6]

In other illustrations, the Supreme Court held that the concept of a *federal instrumentality* includes army post exchanges[7] and the American National Red Cross.[8] While neither is directly controlled by the United States, both have an "unusual relationship" with the federal government, such as operation pursuant to a federal charter, federal government audit, involvement of a presidential appointee or government employees, and government funding or provision of

---

[1] IRC § 501(c)(1).

[2] Tax exemption as a U.S. instrumentality extends to the Central Liquidity Facility established under the Federal Credit Union Act, and the Resolution Trust Corporation and the Resolution Funding Corporation established under the Federal Home Loan Bank Act (IRC § 501(l)).

[3] Rev. Rul. 55-133, 1955-1 C.B. 138.

[4] See § 26.11.

[5] Rev. Rul. 89-94, 1989-2 C.B. 233.

[6] Rev. Rul. 69-283, 1969-1 C.B. 156. See § 19.7.

[7] Standard Oil Co. v. Johnson, 316 U.S. 481 (1942).

[8] Department of Employment v. United States, 85 U.S. 355 (1966). Also, United States v. Livingston, 179 F. Supp. 9 (E.D.S.C. 1959), *aff'd*, 364 U.S. 281 (1960).

services. Applying these criteria, a federal court found the U.S. Capital Historical Society to be a federal instrumentality, also finding that it performs an essential function for the federal government (with the result that the District of Columbia was held to lack the power to tax sales by the Historical Society).[9] An organization that was created by Congress to coordinate, support, and facilitate programs of the federal government and state and local governments, along with other entities, in commemoration of a war was ruled to be an activity of the federal government and thus tax-exempt, with contributions to it deductible as charitable gifts.[10]

§ 19.2   TITLE-HOLDING CORPORATIONS

The *title-holding corporation* is an entity that serves one or more tax-exempt organizations. Its purpose, as the name indicates, is to function as a subsidiary organization, holding title to property that would otherwise be held by the parent exempt organization or organizations and remitting any net income from the property to the parent or parents. Originally designed to circumvent state law restrictions on the holding of property by nonprofit organizations, the title-holding company today is used to house the title to property in the subsidiary for the purpose of reducing the exposure to liability from use of the property by the parent entity, otherwise facilitate administration, and increase borrowing power.

Title-holding corporations are most useful where—for management and/or law reasons—it is deemed appropriate that the title to an item of property be held in the name of another (albeit related) organization. There is no limitation on the type of property whose title may be held by a title-holding corporation; it may be real property, such as an office building, or an item of personal property, such as capital equipment. As the IRS observed, the title-holding corporation is "by its nature responsive to the needs and purposes of its exempt parent which established it mainly to facilitate the administration of properties."[11] Wherever the administration of one or more organizations may be so served, the title-holding corporation is available as a useful tax planning mechanism.

Should the organization to which a tax-exempt title-holding corporation makes income distributions cease to qualify for tax exemption, the holding company would, in turn, lose its entitlement to tax exemption on this basis.[12] Likewise, the sale of all of the stock of an exempt title-holding company to a private person would cause the organization to no longer qualify for tax-exempt status.[13]

(a)   Single-Parent Organizations

The federal tax law references "[c]orporations organized for the exclusive purpose of holding title to property, collecting income therefrom, and turning over the

[9] United States v. District of Columbia, 558 F. Supp. 213 (D.D.C. 1982).
[10] Priv. Ltr. Rul. 201228026.
[11] Rev. Rul. 77-429, 1977-2 C.B. 189.
[12] Rev. Rul. 68-371, 1968-2 C.B. 204.
[13] Priv. Ltr. Rul. 9414002.

entire amount thereof, less expenses, to an organization that itself is" tax-exempt.[14] This is the *single-parent title-holding organization*. For this purpose, the term *expenses* includes a reasonable allowance for depreciation.[15]

In general, this type of organization cannot accumulate income.[16] That is, as a general rule, its function is to transfer the entire amount of its income, less expenses, to a tax-exempt parent.[17] If the organization is not specifically organized to do this, it cannot qualify as an exempt title-holding corporation.[18] Moreover, if the entity does not operate in this fashion, it cannot constitute this type of exempt organization.[19]

Despite the general prohibition on income accumulation, however, a tax-exempt title-holding corporation may retain part of its income each year to apply to indebtedness on property to which it holds title.[20] The transaction is treated as if the income had been transferred to the parent organization and that entity had used the income to make a capital contribution to the title-holding corporation, which, in turn, applied the contribution to the indebtedness.[21]

The IRS ruled that an organization formed as a subsidiary of a tax-exempt title-holding corporation, organized for the exclusive purpose of holding title to investment property that would otherwise be held by the parent, itself qualified as an exempt title-holding corporation, inasmuch as it collected the income from the property and transferred it to its parent (which was, of course, an exempt organization).[22] In other words, an exempt title-holding organization can be the beneficiary of the functions of another exempt title-holding organization.

These organizations can be put to creative uses. In one instance, a tax-exempt title-holding corporation was utilized to hold and administer a scholarship and loan fund for a fraternity.[23] In another case, a stock corporation organized and operated to hold title to a chapter house of a college fraternity was held to qualify as an exempt title-holding organization, even though the stock was owned by members of the fraternity.[24] (Where, however, an exempt organization has no control over the title-holding organization, the latter cannot qualify for tax-exempt status.)[25]

---

[14] IRC § 501(c)(2). The IRS ruled, quite understandably, that an organization could no longer qualify as an exempt title-holding corporation because it ceased to own any property; without property, the IRS reasoned, there cannot be any holding of title (Priv. Ltr. Rul. 201309014).

[15] Rev. Rul. 66-102, 1966-1 C.B. 133.

[16] E.g., Kanawha-Roane Lands v. United States, 136 F. Supp. 631 (S.D. W. Va. 1955).

[17] Reg. § 1.501(c)(2)-1(b).

[18] E.g., Banner Bldg. Co., Inc. v. Comm'r, 46 B.T.A. 857 (1942).

[19] E.g., Eddie Cigelman Corp. v. Comm'r, 15 T.C.M. 1259 (1955); Davenport Found. v. Comm'r, 6 T.C.M. 1335 (1947).

[20] Rev. Rul. 77-429, 1977-2 C.B. 189.

[21] *Id.* at 189-190.

[22] Rev. Rul. 76-335, 1976-2 C.B. 141.

[23] N.P.E.F. Corp. v. Comm'r, 5 T.C.M. 313 (1946).

[24] Rev. Rul. 68-222, 1968-1 C.B. 243. This stock was the type that did not provide any rights to receive profits (either as dividends or as liquidating distributions). See § 1.1(a), note 7.

[25] Rev. Rul. 71-544, 1971-2 C.B. 227; Citizens Water Works, Inc. v. Comm'r, 33 B.T.A. 201 (1935). Cf. Return Realty Corp. v. Ranieri, 359 N.Y.S.2d 611 (N.Y. Cty. 1974).

While the renting of real estate generically is a business, the IRS determined that income from the rental of realty is a permissible source of income for tax-exempt title-holding corporations.[26] That is, this rental activity is not an unrelated business. The rental of personal property (unless leased with realty), however, is treated as the conduct of an unrelated business.[27] Thus, title-holding organizations engaging in business activity—other than rental of real property—may be denied or lose tax exemption.[28]

Consequently, the characterization of the nature of the property being rented can be determinative of an organization's status as a tax-exempt title-holding corporation. In one instance, a corporation that otherwise qualified for exemption as a title-holding entity held a leasehold interest in an office building, with all of its income derived from the subleasing of space in the building to the general public. Even though a leasehold of real property is generally classified as personal property, income derived from subleasing an office building was treated as income derived from the rental of real property.[29] The IRS reasoned that this type of income is similarly treated as rental income from real property for purposes of qualification for exemption as a title-holding corporation,[30] thereby concluding that the corporation was tax-exempt.[31]

A title-holding corporation that derives income from the rental of real property to the general public is not precluded from tax exemption. In one instance, a corporation held title to a building containing offices that were rented to the public. It collected the rents, paid the expenses incident to operation and maintenance of the building, and turned over the balance of the income to its exempt parent. The rents were not forms of unrelated business income, because there were no substantial services to the tenants.[32] The IRS wrote that the "statutory language that requires them [tax-exempt title-holding corporations] to turn over the income from the property to an exempt organization contemplates that income will be received from parties other than the exempt organization for which they hold title."[33]

A tax-exempt title-holding corporation may receive unrelated business taxable income in an amount up to 10 percent of its gross income for a tax year, where the unrelated income is incidentally derived from the holding of real property.[34]

---

[26] Rev. Rul. 69-381, 1969-2 C.B. 113. Also Reg. § 1.512(b)-1(c)(2); Rev. Rul. 66-295, 1966-2 C.B. 207.

[27] Rev. Rul. 69-278, 1969-1 C.B. 148. See § 25.1(h)(i).

[28] Stanford Univ. Bookstore v. Comm'r, 29 B.T.A. 1280 (1934); Sand Springs Ry. Co. v. Comm'r, 21 B.T.A. 1291 (1931).

[29] IRC § 512(b)(3). See § 25.1(h)(i).

[30] This reasoning unfolded as follows: An IRC § 501(c)(2) corporation generally cannot have unrelated business taxable income (Reg. § 1.501(c)(2)-1(a)). (This aspect of the law, however, has been altered (see *infra* note 34).) For unrelated income purposes, the term *real property* includes property described in IRC § 1250(c) (Reg. § 1.512(b)-1(c)(3)(i)). That provision encompasses certain real property that is or has been property of a character subject to the depreciation allowance rules of IRC § 167. Qualifying depreciable real property includes intangible real property, which in turn includes a leasehold of land of IRC § 1250 property. Accordingly, this type of a leasehold is IRC § 1250 property and thus is real property for purposes of the tax law concerning title-holding companies.

[31] Rev. Rul. 81-108, 1981-1 C.B. 327.

[32] See § 25.1(h)(i).

[33] Rev. Rul. 69-381, 1969-2 C.B. 113.

[34] See § 25.4(d).

A tax-exempt title-holding corporation is subject to the unrelated business income tax if one of its parent organizations is subject to that tax. In one instance, a title-holding entity with two parents, one subject to the tax, the other not, found itself in this position.[35]

Where a tax-exempt title-holding corporation holds title to property for the benefit of its parent exempt organization, the property is encumbered with a debt, and the property is not utilized for the exempt purposes of the parent organization, the title-holding corporation will be subject to the tax on unrelated debt-financed income.[36]

As noted, a title-holding corporation must, to be tax-exempt, not engage in any business other than that of holding title to property and collecting and remitting any resulting income to its parent organization.[37] For example, an organization that held title to a building housing its exempt parent, maintained the property, and operated social facilities located in the building was held to not qualify for this tax exemption, because the social activities were "outside the scope of" those allowed to an exempt title-holding entity.[38] Likewise, a title-holding corporation had its exempt status revoked because it operated a bar and buffet in the building it maintained.[39]

A title-holding corporation may file a consolidated return with a parent entity for a tax year. When this occurs and the title-holding entity pays net income to the parent, or would pay net income but for the fact that the expenses of collecting the income exceed its income, the title-holding corporation is deemed, for purposes of the unrelated business income tax, as being organized and operated for the same purposes as the parent, as well as its title-holding purposes.[40]

Generally, contributions to a title-holding corporation are not deductible as charitable gifts. Where a tax-exempt title-holding entity engages in a charitable activity, however, contributions to it for the express purpose of funding that activity are deductible as charitable gifts for federal income tax purposes.[41] Indeed, if a title-holding corporation has a charitable organization as its parent and the corporation engages in one or more activities that the parent itself could undertake without loss of tax exemption, the title-holding entity itself may be eligible to be recognized as a charitable organization or can convert its basis for tax exemption from that as a title-holding organization to that of a charitable entity.[42]

---

[35] Rev. Rul. 68-490, 1968-2 C.B. 241.

[36] Priv. Ltr. Rul. 8145011. See § 24.10. An instance of the use of tax-exempt entities to hold title to property acquired with borrowed funds, prior to adoption of the unrelated debt-financed income rules, appears in Rev. Rul. 66-295, 1966-2 C.B. 207; the rationale was that this type of activity was not a trade or business engaged in for profit, under the approach adopted in court opinions such as Bright Star Found., Inc. v. Campbell, 191 F. Supp. 845 (N.D. Tex. 1960).

[37] Reg. § 1.501(c)(2)-1(a).

[38] Rev. Rul. 66-150, 1966-1 C.B. 147.

[39] Knights of Columbus Bldg. Ass'n of Stamford, Conn., Inc. v. United States, 88-1 U.S.T.C. ¶ 9336 (D. Conn. 1988). Occasionally the IRS or a court will not allow an organization to qualify under this category of tax exemption because of a violation of the private inurement doctrine (see Chapter 20) (e.g., Rev. Rul. 58-566, 1958-2 C.B. 261; Davenport Found. v. Comm'r, 6 T.C.M. 1335 (1947)).

[40] IRC § 511(c).

[41] Priv. Ltr. Rul. 8705041.

[42] E.g., Priv. Ltr. Rul. 9242002. For example, a supporting organization (see § 12.3(c)) often can be utilized in this regard instead of a title-holding entity, as can a single-member limited liability company (see § 4.1(b)).

It was the position of the IRS that a title-holding company is ineligible for tax exemption under these rules if it has multiple unrelated parents, inasmuch as that is evidence of a pooling of assets for an active corporate venture, not a mere holding of title.[43] This matter was, however, resolved by legislation.[44]

(b) Multiple-Parent Organizations

The *multiple-parent title-holding organization* was added in 1986 to the categories of tax-exempt organizations.[45] This is an otherwise eligible corporation or trust that is organized for the exclusive purposes of acquiring and holding title to real property, collecting income from the property, and remitting the entire amount of income from the property (less expenses) to one or more qualified tax-exempt organizations that are shareholders of the title-holding corporation or beneficiaries of the title-holding trust.[46] For this purpose, the term *real property* does not include any interest as a tenant in common (or similar interest) and does not include any indirect interest; this requirement means that the title-holding entity must hold real property directly, rather than, for example, as a partner in a partnership.[47] The term *real property* also includes any personal property that is leased under, or in connection with, a lease of real property, although this rule applies only if the rent attributable to the leasing of the personal property for a year does not exceed 15 percent of the total rent for the year attributable to both the real and personal property under the lease.[48]

Tax exemption under this category of organization is available only if the corporation or trust has no more than 35 shareholders or beneficiaries, and has only one class of stock or beneficial interest.[49] Also, to be exempt as this type of title-holding organization, the corporation or trust must permit its shareholders or beneficiaries to (1) dismiss the corporation's or trust's investment adviser, following reasonable notice, on a vote of the shareholders or beneficiaries holding a majority of interest in the corporation or trust, and (2) terminate their interest in the corporation or trust by either (or both), as determined by the corporation or the trust, selling or exchanging their stock in the corporation or interest in the trust (subject

---

[43] Gen. Couns. Mems. 39341, 37351.

[44] See § 19.2(b).

[45] IRC § 501(c)(25).

[46] IRC § 501(c)(25)(A)(iii). In 1988, the IRS modified and supplemented an earlier pronouncement (Notice 87-18, 1987-1 C.B. 455) concerning certain provisions that must be included in the articles of incorporation or trust document of an organization seeking recognition of federal tax exemption as an organization described in IRC § 501(c)(25) (Notice 88-121, 1988-2 C.B. 457). If state law prevents a corporation from including the required provisions in its articles of incorporation, the provisions must be included in the bylaws of the corporation. A nonstock corporation may qualify under IRC § 501(c)(25) if its articles of incorporation or bylaws provide members with the same rights as is required for other qualifying entities. The 1988 pronouncement also stated that a multiple-parent title-holding organization may, under certain circumstances, acquire options to purchase real estate, hold reasonable cash reserves, and receive debt-financed income (see § 24.10) without loss of tax-exempt status.

An organization failed to qualify as this type of title-holding company because it was in the business of issuing loans, which is an impermissible activity; it did not hold title to real property; and it did not have a qualified parent (Priv. Ltr. Rul. 201133011).

[47] IRC § 501(c)(25)(A).

[48] IRC § 501(c)(25)(F).

[49] IRC § 501(c)(25)(A)(i), (ii).

to federal or state securities law) to any qualified organization as long as the sale or exchange does not increase the number of shareholders or beneficiaries in the corporation or trust to more than 35, or having their stock or interest redeemed by the corporation or trust after the shareholder or beneficiary has provided 90 days' notice to the corporation or trust.[50]

Organizations that are eligible to acquire or hold interests in this type of title-holding organization are charitable organizations;[51] qualified pension, profit-sharing, or stock bonus plans;[52] governmental plans;[53] and governments and agencies and instrumentalities of them.[54]

For these purposes, a corporation that is a *qualified subsidiary* (wholly owned) of a tax-exempt multiple-parent title-holding organization is not treated as a separate organization.[55] In this instance, all assets, liabilities, and items of income, deduction, and credit of the qualified subsidiary are treated as assets, liabilities, and like items of the title-holding organization.[56] These rules allow a title-holding company to hold properties in separate corporations so as to limit liability with respect to each property.

This category of tax-exempt organization was, as noted, created in response to the position of the IRS that a title-holding company otherwise eligible for tax exemption under preexisting law[57] cannot be tax-exempt if two or more of its parent organizations are unrelated. This body of law does not modify the preexisting law concerning the exempt status of single-parent or related-parent title-holding corporations.[58]

§ 19.3 LOCAL ASSOCIATIONS OF EMPLOYEES

Federal income tax law provides exemption for "local associations of employees, the membership of which is limited to the employees of a designated person or persons in a particular municipality, and the net earnings of which are devoted exclusively to charitable, educational or recreational purposes."[59] The word *local* has the same meaning as is applicable with respect to certain benevolent organizations.[60]

A *local association of employees* can assume a variety of forms. For example, an association that operated a gasoline station on property owned by its members' employer qualified,[61] as did an organization that engaged only in social

---

[50] IRC § 501(c)(25)(D).
[51] That is, organizations that are tax-exempt pursuant to IRC § 501(a) as entities described in IRC § 501(c)(3).
[52] That is, plans that meet the requirements of IRC § 401(a). See Chapter 18.
[53] That is, plans that are described in IRC § 414(d).
[54] See § 19.22.
[55] IRC § 501(c)(25)(E)(i)(I).
[56] IRC § 501(c)(25)(E)(i)(II).
[57] See § 19.2(a).
[58] H.R. Rep. 99-841, at II-824 (1986).
[59] IRC § 501(c)(4).
[60] Reg. §§ 1.501(c)(4)-1(b), 1.501(c)(12)-1. These benevolent organizations are the subject of § 19.5(a).
[61] Rev. Rul. 66-180, 1966-1 C.B. 144.

and recreational activities that met the approval of the members' employer.[62] By contrast, a local employees' association whose membership was limited to the employees of a particular employer and that operated a bus for the convenience of its members was denied recognition of tax exemption,[63] as was an organization whose purpose was to pay lump-sum retirement benefits to its members or death benefits to their survivors.[64] Employees can include retirees who were members of the association at the time of retirement.[65] An exempt local association of employees may allow family and friends of its members to participate in the organization's recreational activities as long as those uses of the facilities are not so extensive as to deter the association from adhering to its primary function of providing means of recreation to its members.[66]

The IRS considered the tax status of an organization whose membership was limited to the employees of an employer in a particular municipality. The organization arranged with businesses to extend discounts to its members on their purchases of specified goods and services, and sold tickets to recreational and entertainment activities to them at a discount. Basing its position on the legislative history for this category of tax-exempt organization,[67] the IRS dismissed the organization as merely a "cooperative buying service for members" and denied it tax exemption as an employees' association.[68]

The IRS took the position that a voluntary employees' beneficiary association[69] that could not meet the 85 percent source-of-income test (repealed in 1969)[70] could not qualify for tax exemption as an employees' association.[71] Thus, the IRS does not follow a case holding that a cooperative electric company is exempt as an employees' association even though it met the requirements for exemption under the rules for certain benevolent and mutual organizations,[72] except for the 85 percent source-of-income test.[73]

There is no statutory law or regulation standard concerning the qualification of members in the case of tax-exempt employees' associations. The IRS, however, informally applies the 90 percent threshold that is part of the law in the context of voluntary employees' beneficiary associations.[74] Thus, a health club available only to salaried

---

[62] Rev. Rul. 70-202, 1970-1 C.B. 130. Also, T. J. Moss Tie Co. v. Comm'r, 18 T.C. 188 (1952), *aff'd*, 201 F.2d 512 (8th Cir. 1953); Weil Clothing Co. v. Comm'r, 13 T.C. 873 (1949).

[63] Rev. Rul. 55-311, 1955-1 C.B. 72.

[64] Rev. Rul. 66-59, 1966-1 C.B. 142.

[65] Rev. Rul. 74-281, 1974-1 C.B. 133.

[66] Priv. Ltr. Rul. 8018073.

[67] Hearings before House Ways and Means Committee on Revenue Revision of 1924, 68th Cong., 5-12 (1924); 65 Cong. Rec. 2905-2906 (1924).

[68] Rev. Rul. 79-128, 1979-1 C.B. 197.

[69] See § 18.3.

[70] *Id.*, last paragraph.

[71] Rev. Rul. 57-494, 1957-2 C.B. 315, *obsoleted by* Rev. Rul. 82-148, 1982-2 C.B. 401.

[72] See § 19.5.

[73] United States v. Pickwick Elec. Membership Corp., 158 F.2d 272 (6th Cir. 1946).

[74] See § 18.3, text accompanied by note 17. This restriction may be alleviated somewhat if the IRS is persuaded to also follow a loosening of the rules that is included in the law in the context of benevolent life insurance associations (see § 19.5(a), text accompanied by *infra* note 122).

employees qualified as an exempt employees' association.[75] If, however, the membership criteria are too exclusive, the organization may not qualify as a local employees' association because it may "not really [be] an association of employees at all."[76]

§ 19.4 FRATERNAL ORGANIZATIONS

There are two general types of tax-exempt fraternal organizations: fraternal beneficiary societies and domestic fraternal societies.

(a) Fraternal Beneficiary Societies

Federal income tax law provides tax exemption for fraternal beneficiary societies, orders, or associations operating under the lodge system or for the exclusive benefit of the members of a fraternity itself operating under the lodge system and providing for the payment of life, sickness, accident, or other benefits to the members of the society, order, or association or their dependents.[77] These are, collectively, *fraternal beneficiary societies*.[78]

A federal court of appeals wrote that a fraternal beneficiary society is an organization "whose members have adopted the same, or a very similar, calling, avocation, or profession, or who are working in unison to accomplish some worthy object, and who for that reason have banded themselves together as an association or society to aid and assist one another and to promote the common cause," and these entities have been formed for the purpose of "promoting the social, moral, and intellectual welfare of the members of such associations, and their families, as well as for advancing their interests in other ways and in other respects."[79] On the basis of this definition, an organization of employees of a railroad company was denied tax exemption as a fraternal beneficiary society.[80]

Thus, an organization will not be classified as fraternal in nature for these purposes where the only common bond between the majority of its members is the fact of membership in the organization.[81] Moreover, mere recitation of common ties and objectives in an organization's governing instrument is insufficient; there must be specific activities in implementation of the appropriate purposes.[82]

As noted, a fraternal beneficiary organization, to qualify for tax exemption, must operate under the lodge system or for the exclusive benefit of members that operate in that manner. The phrase *operating under the lodge system* means

---

[75] Gen. Couns. Mem. 39357.

[76] *Id.*

[77] IRC § 501(c)(8); Reg. § 1.501(c)(8)-1; Banner Bldg. Co., Inc. v. Comm'r, 46 B.T.A. 857 (1942); Royal Highlanders v. Comm'r, 1 T.C. 184 (1942).

[78] In the absence of a statutory definition of the term *fraternal beneficiary association*, the courts and the IRS presume that Congress used the term in its ordinary sense. E.g., United States v. Cambridge Loan & Building Co., 278 U.S. 55 (1923).

[79] Nat'l Union v. Marlow, 74 F. 775, 778 (8th Cir. 1896). Also, Employees Benefit Ass'n of Am. Steel Foundries v. Comm'r, 14 B.T.A. 1166 (1929).

[80] Philadelphia & Reading Relief Ass'n v. Comm'r, 4 B.T.A. 713 (1926).

[81] Polish Army Veterans Post 147 v. Comm'r, 24 T.C. 891 (1955), *aff'd*, 236 F.2d 509 (3d Cir. 1956).

[82] Fraternal Order of Civitans of Am. v. Comm'r, 19 T.C. 240 (1952).

that an organization is "carrying on its activities under a form of organization that comprises local branches, chartered by a parent organization and largely self-governing, called lodges, chapters, or the like."[83] Therefore, an organization without a parent organization or subordinate branches does not operate under the lodge system and cannot qualify for tax exemption as a fraternal beneficiary society.[84] (Moreover, this type of a mutual, self-interest type of organization that may otherwise qualify as an exempt fraternal beneficiary society cannot qualify as an exempt social welfare organization.)[85] Further, the parent and local organizations must be active; mere provision for them in governing instruments is insufficient.[86] Notwithstanding this requirement, however, an organization that did not operate under the lodge system was granted exemption as a fraternal beneficiary society because it operated exclusively for the benefit of the members of a fraternal beneficiary society that itself operated under the lodge system, by providing life, sickness, and accident benefits to the members of the society or their dependents.[87]

Also, as noted, a tax-exempt fraternal beneficiary society must have an established system for the payment to its members or their dependents of life, sickness, accident, or other benefits. While not every member of a society need be covered by the benefits program,[88] this type of coverage must be extended to a substantial number of members.[89] A common way benefits are provided by an exempt fraternal beneficiary society is by means of insurance programs.[90] According to a federal court of appeals, the term *benefits* in this context is not confined to insurance for members against personal risks such as disability or death but may also extend to insuring them against property loss.[91] This decision overruled a lower court's determination that permissible benefits include only those insuring members against mishap to the person.[92] The IRS concluded that the term *other benefits* embraces the provision of legal expenses to defend members accused of criminal, civil, or administrative misconduct arising in the course of their employment (by a fraternal beneficiary society composed of law enforcement officers)[93] and the operation by a fraternal beneficiary society of an orphanage for children of deceased members.[94] The IRS ruled that whole life insurance constitutes a life benefit that fraternal domestic societies can provide to members, even though the policies contain investment features such as cash surrender value and policy loans.[95]

---

[83] Reg. § 1.501(c)(8)-1. Also, Western Funeral Benefit Ass'n v. Hellmich, 2 F.2d 367 (E.D. Mo. 1924).

[84] Rev. Rul. 55-495, 1955-2 C.B. 259.

[85] Rev. Rul. 75-199, 1975-1 C.B. 160, *modifying* Rev. Rul. 55-495, 1955-2 C.B. 259. Also, Police Benevolent Ass'n of Richmond, Va. v. United States, 87-1 U.S.T.C. ¶ 9238 (E.D. Va. 1987); Rev. Rul. 81-58, 1981-1 C.B. 331.

[86] I.T. 1516, 1-2 C.B. 180 (1922).

[87] Rev. Rul. 73-192, 1973-1 C.B. 224.

[88] Rev. Rul. 64-194, 1964-2 C.B. 149.

[89] Polish Army Veterans Post 147 v. Comm'r, 24 T.C. 891 (1955), *aff'd*, 236 F.2d 509 (3d Cir. 1956).

[90] E.g., Order of United Commercial Travelers of America v. Wolfe, 331 U.S. 586 (1947); Van de Water v. Order of United Commercial Travelers of America, 77 F.2d 331 (2d Cir. 1935).

[91] Grange Ins. Ass'n of Calif. v. Comm'r, 317 F.2d 222 (9th Cir. 1963).

[92] Grange Ins. Ass'n of Calif. v. Comm'r, 37 T.C. 582 (1961).

[93] Rev. Rul. 84-48, 1984-1 C.B. 133.

[94] Rev. Rul. 84-49, 1984-1 C.B. 134; Gen. Couns. Mem. 39212.

[95] Rev. Rul. 86-75, 1986-1 C.B. 245; Gen. Couns. Mem. 39510.

Consequently, a tax-exempt fraternal beneficiary organization must both operate under the lodge system and provide for the payment of benefits to members or their dependents—although one of these features does not have to predominate over the other.[96] Both of these features, however, must be present in substantial form; neither may be a sham.[97]

As noted, the tax-exempt fraternal beneficiary society must be operated for the exclusive benefit of its members. Where benefits provided to others are incidental to the accomplishment of the society's exempt purpose, however, the organization's exemption will not be jeopardized. For example, a society that conducted an insurance operation for its members in all of the states was found not to have lost its exemption because it participated in a state-sponsored reinsurance pool that protected participating insurers from excessive losses on major medical health and accident insurance, since any benefit derived by other insurers from participation in the pooling arrangement was "incidental to" the society's exempt purpose.[98] Similarly, the reinsurance of its policies is a fraternal beneficiary society's exempt function.[99]

A federal district court held that fraternal organizations that are otherwise tax-exempt that practice racial discrimination as to entry into membership may not be exempt.[100] This holding was based on the fact that, unlike organizations that are exempt as social clubs or voluntary employees' beneficiary associations,[101] the passive investment income of fraternal beneficiary organizations is not taxed; this the court found to be a governmental benefit warranting invocation of the Fifth Amendment.

Individuals' gifts to a domestic fraternal beneficiary organization are deductible where the gift is to be used exclusively for religious, charitable, scientific, literary, or educational purposes, or for the prevention of cruelty to children and animals.[102]

(b) Domestic Fraternal Societies

Federal income tax law provides tax exemption for domestic fraternal societies, orders, or associations, operating under the lodge system, whose net earnings are devoted exclusively to religious, charitable, scientific, literary, educational, and fraternal purposes, and that do not provide for the payment of life, sickness, accident, or other benefits to their members.[103] These are, collectively, *domestic fraternal societies.*

An organization not providing these benefits but otherwise qualifying as a fraternal beneficiary society[104] qualifies as a tax-exempt domestic fraternal society.

---

[96] Rev. Rul. 73-165, 1973-1 C.B. 224.
[97] Commercial Travelers Life & Accident Ass'n v. Rodway, 235 F. 370 (N.D. Ohio 1913).
[98] Rev. Rul. 78-87, 1978-1 C.B. 160.
[99] Priv. Ltr. Rul. 7937002.
[100] McGlotten v. Connally, 338 F. Supp. 448, 459 (D.D.C. 1972).
[101] See IRC § 512(a)(3); § 25.4(c).
[102] IRC § 170(c)(4).
[103] IRC § 501(c)(10); Reg. § 1.501(c)(10)-1.
[104] See § 19.4(a).

Thus, for example, a domestic fraternal beneficiary society of farmers, which met the fraternal beneficiary society rules except that it did not provide for the payment of the requisite benefits, although it did make its members eligible for favorable insurance rates, was denied classification as an exempt fraternal beneficiary society and was ruled to be an exempt domestic fraternal society.[105] A social welfare organization,[106] however, does not qualify for tax exemption under these rules.[107]

A domestic fraternal society meeting these basic requirements was organized to provide a fraternal framework for social contact among its members who were interested in the use of and the philosophy behind a method used in attempting to divine the future. The net income of the organization was used to provide instruction on the use of the method, supply information on the method to the public, and maintain a reference library—all charitable and educational uses. The IRS ruled that the organization qualified for tax exemption under these rules.[108]

The IRS ruled that an organization formed by a local lodge of a fraternal beneficiary society, both tax-exempt as domestic fraternal societies, to carry on the activities of the society in a particular geographical area, was itself exempt as a domestic fraternal society.[109] Because the organization was chartered and supervised by the local lodge and was subject to the laws and edicts of the parent society, it was deemed to function as "part of the lodge system" of the fraternal society and hence qualify for exemption.

The IRS also ruled that an organization that did not conduct any fraternal activities and did not operate under the lodge system, but operated exclusively for the benefit of the members of certain related domestic fraternal societies operating under the lodge system, could not qualify as a tax-exempt domestic fraternal society.[110] The rationale for this denial of exemption was that the tax law requirements for domestic fraternal societies lack the language in the tax rules for fraternal beneficiary societies providing exemption for an organization operating for the benefit of the members of a tax-exempt fraternity (a provision enacted to cover the separately organized insurance branches of a fraternal beneficiary society). The IRS likewise ruled that an organization operating a public tavern and conducting gaming did not qualify for this exemption, in that the only common bond among the ostensible membership was the membership itself; there was no lodge system or rituals.[111] Similarly, the IRS declined to recognize a membership organization composed of soccer referees as a domestic fraternal society because it did not operate under the lodge system and lacked the rituals, ceremonies, or regalia necessary to evidence a fraternal purpose.[112]

[105] Rev. Rul. 76-457, 1976-2 C.B. 155.
[106] See Chapter 13.
[107] Reg. § 1.501(c)(10)-1. This distinction was upheld by the U.S. Tax Court in Zeta Beta Tau Fraternity, Inc. v. Comm'r, 87 T.C. 421 (1986).
[108] Rev. Rul. 77-258, 1977-2 C.B. 195.
[109] Rev. Rul. 73-370, 1973-2 C.B. 184. In Hip Sing Ass'n, Inc. v. Comm'r, 43 T.C.M. 1092 (1982), an organization was found to be operating under the lodge system, even though the parent organization was established after creation of the branch organizations.
[110] Rev. Rul. 81-117, 1981-1 C.B. 346.
[111] Priv. Ltr. Rul. 201002040.
[112] Priv. Ltr. Rul. 202222006.

§ 19.5 BENEVOLENT OR MUTUAL ORGANIZATIONS

Federal income tax law references tax-exempt benevolent life insurance associations of a purely local character, mutual ditch or irrigation companies, mutual or cooperative telephone companies, or like organizations.[113] These are, collectively, *benevolent or mutual organizations*. In general, 85 percent or more of the income of these entities must consist of amounts collected from members for the sole purpose of meeting losses and expenses.[114] As discussed later in this section, there are some exceptions to this rule in the case of mutual or cooperative telephone companies.[115]

(a) Local Life Insurance Associations

Thus, one type of organization described in these rules is the benevolent life insurance association of a purely local character. These associations basically operate to provide life insurance coverage to their members, albeit at cost because of the requirement that income be collected solely for the purpose of meeting losses and expenses. Organizations *like* benevolent life insurance associations include burial and funeral benefit associations that provide benefits in cash,[116] but not in the form of services and supplies (although the latter type of organization may qualify for exemption as a mutual insurance company),[117] and an organization furnishing light and water to its members on a cooperative basis.[118] IRS rulings and court decisions provide examples of organizations considered not like benevolent life insurance associations.[119]

The phrase *of a purely local character* means "confined to a particular community, place, or district, irrespective, however, of political subdivisions,"[120] that is, a single identifiable locality.[121] This requirement does not mean that members of an otherwise qualifying benevolent life insurance association must continually reside in the local area to retain membership; it only means that persons applying for membership in the association must reside in the local geographic area at the time of application.[122] An organization is not local in character where

---

[113] IRC § 501(c)(12)(A).

[114] Reg. § 1.501(c)(12)-1(a); Consumers Credit Rural Elec. Coop. Corp. v. Comm'r, 37 T.C. 136 (1961), *aff'd in pertinent part*, 319 F.2d 475 (6th Cir. 1963). This 85-percent-of-income test is applied annually; a cooperative can be taxable for one year and tax-exempt for another (Rev. Rul. 65-99, 1965-1 C.B. 242). In addition to meeting this test, these organizations must operate according to cooperative principles to be eligible for tax exemption (Buckeye Countrymark, Inc. v. Comm'r, 103 T.C. 547 (1994); Puget Sound Plywood, Inc. v. Comm'r, 44 T.C. 305 (1965); Rev. Rul. 72-36, 1972-1 C.B. 151).

[115] IRC § 501(c)(12)(A).

[116] Thompson v. White River Burial Ass'n, 178 F.2d 954 (8th Cir. 1950), *aff'g* 81 F. Supp. 18 (E.D. Ark. 1948).

[117] See § 19.9.

[118] Rev. Rul. 67-265, 1967-2 C.B. 205.

[119] Rev. Rul. 65-201, 1965-2 C.B. 170; Consumers Credit Rural Elec. Coop. Corp. v. Comm'r, 37 T.C. 136 (1961), *aff'd in pertinent part*, 319 F.2d 475 (6th Cir. 1963); Shelby Cnty. Mut. Relief Ass'n v. Schwaner, 21 F.2d 252 (S.D. Ill. 1927); New Jersey Automobile Club v. United States, 181 F. Supp. 259 (Ct. Cl. 1960), *cert. denied*, 366 U.S. 964 (1961); Swedish Mission Friends' Aid Ass'n v. Comm'r, 12 B.T.A. 1152 (1928).

[120] Reg. § 1.501(c)(12)-1(b).

[121] Hardware Underwriters & Nat'l Hardware Serv. Corp. v. United States, 65 Ct. Cl. 267 (1928).

[122] Rev. Rul. 83-43, 1983-1 C.B. 108.

its activities are limited only by the borders of a state,[123] although state lines are not controlling as to what constitutes a single locality. One organization lost its tax exemption as a benevolent life insurance association by advertising in four states.[124] Another organization was denied tax exemption because it operated in 14 counties, as did another conducting its affairs in 32 counties, including three separate metropolitan trade centers.[125]

(b)   Mutual Organizations

The other type of organization exempt from federal income tax by virtue of these rules encompasses mutual ditch or irrigation companies, mutual or cooperative telephone companies, and similar organizations. The IRS issued criteria as to cooperative operation in 1972.[126] These organizations are commonly mutual or cooperative electric companies and water companies.[127] Tax exemption was accorded an organization established to protect certain riverbanks against erosion,[128] an organization that provided and maintained a two-way radio system for its members,[129] an electric generation and transmission cooperative that sold and serviced electric appliances,[130] an electric utility that provided Internet service to its members on a cooperative basis,[131] and a mutual telephone exchange that provided telecommunications/broadband services to its members.[132] The membership of cooperative companies need not be restricted to ultimate consumers,[133] nonmembers may be charged a higher rate for service than members,[134] and a government agency may be a member of a cooperative.[135] The IRS, ruling that a cooperative organization furnishing cable television service to its members qualified for tax exemption as a like organization under these rules, observed that this category of tax exemption is applicable "only to those mutual or cooperative organizations that are engaged in activities similar in nature to the benevolent life insurance or public utility type of

---

[123] Reg. § 1.501(c)(12)-1(b).

[124] Huff-Cook Mut. Burial Ass'n, Inc. v. United States, 327 F. Supp. 1209 (W.D. Va. 1971).

[125] Rev. Rul. 64-193, 1964-2 C.B. 151.

[126] Rev. Rul. 72-36, 1972-1 C.B. 151, *modified by* Rev. Rul. 81-109, 1981-1 C.B. 347; Rev. Rul. 65-174, 1965-2 C.B. 169. Also, Puget Sound Plywood v. Comm'r, 44 T.C. 305 (1965). The IRS concluded that amendment of the bylaws of an exempt cooperative to implement an equity discounting program (Priv. Ltr. Rul. 200602035), acceleration of the retirement of patronage allocations to members (Priv. Ltr. Rul. 200634048), or adoption of a capital credit retirement program (Priv. Ltr. Rul. 200625033) would not adversely affect the entity's operations as a cooperative.

[127] Rev. Rul. 67-265, 1967-2 C.B. 205. Also, Rev. Rul. 73-453, 1973-2 C.B. 185.

[128] Rev. Rul. 68-564, 1968-2 C.B. 221.

[129] Rev. Rul. 57-420, 1957-2 C.B. 308.

[130] Priv. Ltr. Rul. 8109002.

[131] Priv. Ltr. Rul. 200504035.

[132] Priv. Ltr. Rul. 201002042. An electric cooperative's proposed revisions to its method for retiring former members' capital credit accounts, which permitted offsetting amounts in these accounts against outstanding debts for electrical service, were held to not adversely affect the organization's exempt status (Priv. Ltr. Rul. 201340017).

[133] Rev. Rul. 65-174, 1965-2 C.B. 169.

[134] Rev. Rul. 70-130, 1970-1 C.B. 133.

[135] Rev. Rul. 68-75, 1968-1 C.B. 271.

service or business customarily conducted by the specified organizations."[136] IRS rulings also, by contrast, provide examples of organizations considered not like mutual and cooperative organizations.[137]

A mutual ditch company, created in 1874, qualified for this tax exemption, even though it did not satisfy all of the IRS criteria at the time. The IRS gave consideration to the "historical context" in which these entities were created, in that they were operating in the manner under review at the time legislation providing for their exemption was adopted.[138] (These requirements were modified accordingly.) In another instance, a court held that a mutual company did not have to credit or distribute its net gains on a patronage basis to maintain its exemption.[139]

As noted,[140] the general rule is that all organizations, to be exempt from tax under these rules, must obtain at least 85 percent of their income from amounts collected from members for the sole purpose of meeting losses and expenses.[141] This requirement is applied on the basis of annual accounting periods[142] and by taking into account only income actually received each year.[143] Income from all sources is taken into account, including capital gains from the sale of assets[144] and investments.[145] Amounts received as gifts or contributions are not regarded as income.[146] In one instance, the IRS ruled that, where an electric cooperative leased power facilities to a nonmember power company that in turn sold power to the cooperative, the entire rental income was income from a nonmember for purposes of the 85-percent-of-income requirement, rather than an offset against the cost of acquiring power.[147] In another case, an organization in good faith failed to elect the installment method of treating gain from the sale of real property, with the result that the receipt of the entire gain caused less than 85 percent of its income to be derived from its members; over the government's objection, a court allowed the organization to amend its annual information return to make the election and thus preserve its tax exemption.[148]

[136] Rev. Rul. 83-170, 1983-2 C.B. 97, *modifying* Rev. Rul. 55-716, 1955-2 C.B. 263. A tax-exempt rural electric cooperative developed a new line of business, consisting of the sale of natural gas to its members; the IRS ruled that this service "clearly" is a public utility type of service and thus "fits squarely" within the definition of a *like organization* (Priv. Ltr. Rul. 200717020).

[137] Rev. Rul. 65-201, 1965-2 C.B. 170; Rev. Rul. 55-311, 1955-1 C.B. 72.

[138] Rev. Rul. 81-109, 1981-1 C.B. 347.

[139] Peninsula Light Co., Inc. v. United States, 552 F.2d 878 (9th Cir. 1977). The IRS does not follow this decision (Rev. Rul. 78-238, 1978-1 C.B. 161).

[140] See text accompanied by *supra* note 110.

[141] IRC § 501(c)(12)(A).

[142] Rev. Rul. 65-99, 1965-1 C.B. 242.

[143] Priv. Ltr. Rul. 9809055.

[144] Cate Ditch Co. v. United States, 194 F. Supp. 688 (S.D. Cal. 1961); Mountain Water Co. of La Crescenta v. Comm'r, 35 T.C. 418 (1960).

[145] Reg. § 1.501(c)(12)-1(a).

[146] Gen. Couns. Mem. 35921.

[147] Rev. Rul. 65-174, 1965-2 C.B. 169. It was held that income from a cooperative's sale of discretionarily supplied power to a member entity constituted member income (Buckeye Power, Inc. v. United States, 38 Fed. Cl. 154 (1997)).

[148] Sunny Slope Water Co. v. United States, 78-2 U.S.T.C. ¶ 9685 (C.D. Cal. 1978).

By contrast, the IRS determined that the income derived by an exempt electric cooperative from the annual sale of its excess fuel to a commercial pipeline company that was not a member of the cooperative was not to be taken into account in determining compliance with the 85-percent-of-income requirement, in that the excess fuel was sold at cost and thus gross income was not derived from the sales.[149] A federal district court held that the 85-percent-of-income requirement was satisfied where income from tenants of members of a mutual water and electric company was considered member income; the IRS took the position that the tenants did not have any participation in the management of the company and thus could not be regarded as *members*.[150] Court decisions provide examples of organizations that failed to meet the 85-percent-of-income requirement.[151]

Some exceptions to this 85-percent-of-income requirement are applicable in the case of mutual or cooperative telephone companies. One of these exceptions is that the requirement does not apply to income received or accrued from a nonmember telephone company for the performance of communication services that involve members of the mutual or cooperative telephone company.[152]

---

[149] Rev. Rul. 80-86, 1980-1 C.B. 118. The IRS ruled that an IRC § 501(c)(12) cooperative's calculation of nonmember income can be based on its net income from interest rate swaps and hedges of fuel price risks (Priv. Ltr. Rul. 200634043) and that income received by an exempt telephone cooperative from federal and state universal service funds is income excluded from the 85-percent-member-income test (Priv. Ltr. Rul. 201105045).

[150] Modern Elec. Water Co. v. United States, 88-2 U.S.T.C. ¶ 9523 (E.D. Wash. 1988).

[151] Allgemeiner Arbeiter Verein v. Comm'r, 237 F.2d 604 (3d Cir. 1956), aff'g 25 T.C. 371 (1956); Family Aid Ass'n of the United States House of Prayer for All People v. United States, 36 F. Supp. 1017 (Ct. Cl. 1941). In Dial-Cab Taxi Owners Guild Ass'n, Inc. v. Comm'r, 42 T.C.M. 590 (1981), aff'd in unpublished opinion. (2d Cir. May 4, 1982), the organization was held to not qualify under IRC § 501(c)(12) because it was unable to carry its burden of proving that 85 percent of its income in the tax years involved was collected solely to cover losses and expenses.

A court held that certain bond proceeds and items of interest were not income for this purpose but were "capital investment funds" and thus that the 85-percent-of-income rule was not transgressed (Lockwood Water Users Ass'n v. United States (unreported) (D. Mont. 1990)), but the holding was reversed, with the appellate court finding that the monies were items of gross income for purposes of IRC § 501(c)(12)(A) (Lockwood Water Users Ass'n v. United States, 935 F.2d 274 (9th Cir. 1991)). The IRS ruled that a government grant to a tax-exempt electric power cooperative was excluded from the 85-percent member-income fraction because it was excluded from income as a nonshareholder contribution to the capital of the cooperative (under IRC § 118(a)) (Priv. Ltr. Rul. 9401035).

The IRS held that income received by a cooperative telephone company from charges to third parties (such as interexchange carriers, local exchange carriers, or other exchange carriers) for billing or collecting intrastate, interstate, or international revenues was income from the provision of a service to nonmembers (Tech. Adv. Mems. 9110041, 9111001). Thus, this income was not member source income for purposes of the requirement that 85 percent of the cooperative's income must be derived from members. The IRS also ruled that the income was not excludable from the computation of the percentage of nonmember income under the rule that includes income from nonmember sources where the provision of the services involves members of the cooperative (IRC § 501(c)(12)(B)(i)). Thus, the cooperative involved did not qualify for tax exemption for the year unless the 15 percent limit was not exceeded, in which case this income would be unrelated business income (see Chapters 24, 25). Subsequently, however, the IRS announced that these positions will apply for all tax years beginning after December 31, 1990 (Notice 92-33, 1992-2 C.B. 363). Income received by a telephone cooperative allocable to billing and collection services performed in respect of long-distance calls was held to qualify as income from communication services, enabling the organization to be exempt under these rules (Golden Belt Telephone Ass'n, Inc. v. Comm'r, 108 T.C. 23 (1997)).

[152] IRC § 501(c)(12)(B)(i).

These services pertain to the completion of long-distance calls to, from, or between members of the company.[153] This exception was legislated to supplant a ruling by the IRS holding that a cooperative telephone company, providing only local telephone service to its members but obtaining connecting long-distance service by agreement with a nonmember company, could not adjust its gross income by offsetting income from long-distance tolls collected by both companies against expenses for services rendered by the nonmember company to the cooperative's members, but had to include as part of its gross income all of the member and nonmember income from the long-distance service to determine whether member income met the 85-percent-of-income requirement.[154] This statutory revision reflects the view that the performance of the "call-completion services" is a related activity and that the "payments" from another telephone company for the services should not disqualify otherwise eligible mutual or cooperative telephone cooperatives from this tax-exempt status.[155]

Another exception is that this requirement does not apply to income received or accrued from qualified pole rentals.[156] A *qualified pole rental* is any rental of a utility pole (or other structure used to support wires) if the pole (or other structure) is used by the telephone or electric company to support one or more wires needed to provide telephone or electric services to its members and is used pursuant to the rental to support one or more additional wires for use in connection with the transmission by wire of electricity or of telephone or other communications.[157] For this purpose, the word *rental* includes any sale of the right to use the pole (or other structure).[158]

There are two other exceptions. One exception is for income received or accrued from the sale of display listings in a directory furnished to the members of the mutual or cooperative telephone company.[159] The other exception is for income received or accrued from the prepayment of certain loans.[160]

Exceptions are also available in the case of an exempt mutual or cooperative electric company,[161] in that the 85-percent-of-income requirement does not apply in connection with income received or accrued from (1) qualified pole rentals; (2) the provision or sale of electric energy transmission services or ancillary services if these services are provided on a nondiscriminatory open access basis under an open access transmission tariff approved or accepted by the Federal Energy Regulatory Commission (FERC)[162] or under an independent transmission provider

---

[153] H.R. Rep. 95-742 (1977); S. Rep. 95-762 (1978).

[154] Rev. Rul. 74-362, 1974-2 C.B. 170.

[155] Consequently, Rev. Rul. 74-362, 1974-2 C.B. 170, was declared obsolete by the IRS with respect to tax years beginning after December 31, 1974 (Rev. Rul. 81-291, 1981-2 C.B. 131).

[156] IRC § 501(c)(12)(B)(ii), (C)(i).

[157] IRC § 501(c)(12)(D).

[158] IRC § 501(c)(12), last sentence.

[159] IRC § 501(c)(12)(B)(iii).

[160] IRC § 501(c)(12)(B)(iv), (C)(ii).

[161] IRC § 501(c)(12)(C).

[162] This reference to the FERC includes, in the case of any utility with respect to which all of the electricity generated, transmitted, or distributed by such utility is generated, transmitted, distributed, and consumed in the same state, the state agency of such state with the authority to regulate electric utilities (IRC § 501(c)(12)(E)).

agreement approved or accepted by the FERC (other than income received or accrued directly or indirectly from a member); (3) the provision or sale of electric energy distribution services or ancillary services if the services are provided on a nondiscriminatory open-access basis to distribute electric energy not owned by the mutual or cooperative electric company (a) to end users who are served by distribution facilities not owned by the company or any of its members (other than income received or accrued directly or indirectly from a member) or (b) generated by a generation facility not owned or leased by the company or any of its members and which is directly connected to distribution facilities owned by the company or any of its members (other than income received or accrued directly or indirectly from a member); (4) any nuclear decommissioning transaction;[163] or (5) any asset exchange or conversion transaction.[164]

The income of a wholly owned subsidiary of a tax-exempt cooperative is not included for purposes of determining whether the exempt cooperative satisfies the 85-percent-member-income test.[165] (This rule assumes that the subsidiary is recognized as an entity validly separate from the cooperative.)[166] Any payments a cooperative receives from its wholly owned subsidiary must, however, be included in the calculation of the member income test.

The IRS is of the opinion that an organization that meets all of the requirements for tax exemption under these rules except for the 85-percent-of-income test cannot qualify for exemption as a social welfare organization.[167] Also, an organization carrying on two functions, one qualifying under the social club rules[168] and the other under these rules, cannot qualify for exemption under either category.[169]

§ 19.6   CEMETERY COMPANIES

The federal income tax law exemption rules reference *cemetery companies* that are owned and operated exclusively for the benefit of their members and that are not operated for profit.[170] This tax exemption also extends to a corporation chartered solely for the purpose of the disposal of bodies by burial or cremation; it may not engage in any business not necessarily incident to that purpose. Thus, there are three types of cemetery companies that may gain exemption under these rules.

According to the courts, a tax-exempt cemetery company is generally one that owns a cemetery, sells lots therein for burial purposes, and maintains these and the unsold lots in a state of repair and upkeep appropriate to a final resting

---

[163] This phrase is defined in IRC § 501(c)(12)(F).

[164] This phrase is defined in IRC § 501(c)(12)(G). Also, see IRC § 501(c)(12)(H).

[165] Rev. Rul. 2002-55, 2002-2 C.B. 529. This was a reversal of the IRS's initial position, which was that the revenue received by a for-profit subsidiary should be regarded as revenue of the parent cooperative for purposes of determining the cooperative's tax-exempt status (Tech. Adv. Mem. 9722006).

[166] See § 30.2.

[167] Cf. United States v. Pickwick Elec. Membership Corp., 158 F.2d 272 (6th Cir. 1946). Tax-exempt social welfare organizations are the subject of Chapter 13.

[168] See Chapter 15.

[169] Allgemeiner Arbeiter Verein v. Comm'r, 237 F.2d 604 (3d Cir. 1956), *aff'g* 25 T.C. 371 (1956).

[170] IRC § 501(c)(13).

place.[171] With respect to the membership category of cemetery companies, its members are those who are its "lot owners who hold such lots for bona fide burial purposes and not for purpose of resale."[172] A mutual cemetery company that also engages in charitable activities, such as the burial of paupers, is regarded as operating in conformity with this rule.[173] According to a court, an exempt cemetery company need not serve exclusively public interests but may be a family cemetery organization.[174] Under certain circumstances, a cemetery company may be exempt even though it has private preferred stockholders.[175] This category of exemption applies only to organizations providing for the burial or cremation of the remains of human bodies—not pets.[176]

An organization receiving and administering funds for the perpetual care of a nonprofit cemetery itself qualifies as a tax-exempt cemetery company.[177] A nonprofit organization that provides for the perpetual care of a burial area in a community may also become so classified, even though it is not associated with a nonprofit cemetery.[178]

One of the requirements for tax exemption as a cemetery company is that the company may not be permitted by its charter to engage in any business not necessarily incident to its tax-exempt (burial) purposes.[179] The IRS construed this requirement to extend to activities, thereby ruling, for example, that operation by a cemetery company of a mortuary will deprive the company of this exemption.[180] Under this approach, the IRS also held that operation of a crematorium would likewise adversely affect the exemption,[181] although this determination was withdrawn in view of modification of the exemption statute.[182] A cemetery company may, however, sell monuments, markers, vaults, and flowers solely for use in the cemetery, where the sales proceeds are used for maintenance of the cemetery.[183]

No part of the net earnings of a tax-exempt cemetery company may inure to the benefit of any private shareholder or individual.[184] The private inurement

---

[171] E.g., Resthaven Memorial Park & Cemetery Ass'n v. United States, 155 F. Supp. 539 (W.D. Ky. 1957); Forest Lawn Memorial Park Ass'n, Inc. v. Comm'r, 5 T.C.M. 738 (1946).

[172] Reg. § 1.501(c)(13)-1(a)(1). Also, West Laurel Hill Cemetery Co. v. Rothensies, 139 F.2d 50 (3d Cir. 1943).

[173] Id. The IRS ruled that a grant of property, including a historic cemetery, to an exempt charitable organization was a charitable activity for purposes of cemetery company tax law (Priv. Ltr. Rul. 201605019).

[174] John D. Rockefeller Family Cemetery Corp. v. Comm'r, 63 T.C. 355 (1974); Du Pont de Nemours Cemetery Co. v. Comm'r, 33 T.C.M. 1438 (1974). Cf. Rev. Rul. 65-6, 1965-1 C.B. 229; Provident Nat'l Bank v. United States, 325 F. Supp. 1187 (E.D. Pa. 1971).

[175] Reg. § 1.501(c)(13)-1(b).

[176] Rev. Rul. 73-454, 1973-2 C.B. 185. A tax-exempt cemetery company can, however, establish and utilize a for-profit subsidiary (see Chapter 30) to operate a pet cemetery and mortuary (Priv. Ltr. Rul. 200162048).

[177] Rev. Rul. 58-190, 1958-1 C.B. 15.

[178] Rev. Rul. 78-143, 1978-1 C.B. 161.

[179] Reg. § 1.501(c)(13)-1(b).

[180] Rev. Rul. 64-109, 1964-1 C.B. 190.

[181] Rev. Rul. 69-637, 1969-2 C.B. 127.

[182] Rev. Rul. 71-300, 1971-2 C.B. 238.

[183] Rev. Rul. 72-17, 1972-1 C.B. 151.

[184] Reg. § 1.501(c)(13)-1(b). E.g., Branson v. Comm'r, 50 T.C.M. 1056 (1985). In general, see Chapter 20.

doctrine frequently is involved in the case of a newly organized cemetery company, in relation to payments to and other relationships with the organizers. The reasoning of the IRS is that (1) where a cemetery company acquires land at an indeterminable price, to be paid for on the basis of a percentage of the proceeds from the sale of individual lots from the tract, the vendor of the land has a continuing interest in the land; (2) any appreciation in value, whether it is due to the state of the market generally or to the cemetery's own efforts in undertaking capital improvements and the like, will result in a benefit to the vendor of the land; and (3) continuing participation in the earnings of the cemetery company will also ordinarily result in receipt by the vendor of a total price substantially in excess of the reasonable value of the land at the time of its sale to the cemetery company.[185]

Perhaps the most important issue in relation to these rules is one that emerged as many American cemeteries became transformed from noncommercial operations (such as by religious institutions and municipal governments) to commercial businesses. As part of that process, profit-oriented enterprises sought favorable tax consequences from bootstrap sales of assets to ostensibly tax-exempt cemetery companies. When this issue was first litigated, the courts were highly tolerant of these transactions,[186] thereby generating substantial criticism. Subsequently, the courts began to scrutinize the substance of these transactions more carefully, concluding that some cemetery companies were causing private inurement of net earnings by the creation of equity interests.[187] Thus, the IRS ruled that a nonprofit cemetery company that acquired land from a for-profit cemetery company, under an agreement providing payment to the former owners on the basis of a percentage of the sales price of each cemetery lot sold, was not a tax-exempt cemetery company, because the transferors acquired an equity interest in the cemetery company, which constituted private inurement.[188]

Another issue concerns the ability of a commercial cemetery to sequester funds in a perpetual care trust fund that would qualify as a tax-exempt cemetery company. The matter seemed to have been resolved when a court, enunciating an adjunct theory,[189] held in 1975 that this type of tax exemption was available by reason of the fact that the fund, which rendered services normally provided by the cemetery company, had the same tax status as the cemetery company itself.[190]

---

[185] Rev. Rul. 61-137, 1961-2 C.B. 118; Butler Cnty. Memorial Park, Inc. v. Comm'r, 45 T.C.M. 181 (1982).

[186] Forest Lawn Memorial Park Ass'n, Inc. v. Comm'r, 45 B.T.A. 1091 (1941); Kensico Cemetery v. Comm'r, 35 B.T.A. 498 (1937), aff'd, 96 F.2d 594 (2d Cir. 1938). Also, Rose Hill Memorial Park, Inc. v. Comm'r, 23 T.C.M. 1434 (1964); Washington Park Cemetery Ass'n, Inc. v. Comm'r, 22 T.C.M. 1345 (1963).

[187] Restland Memorial Park of Dallas v. United States, 509 F.2d 187 (5th Cir. 1975); Evergreen Cemetery Ass'n v. United States, 375 F. Supp. 166 (W.D. Ky. 1974); Rose Hill Memorial Park Ass'n v. United States, 463 F.2d 425 (Ct. Cl. 1972), cert. denied, 414 U.S. 822 (1973); Arlington Memorial Park Ass'n v. United States, 327 F. Supp. 344 (W.D. Ark. 1971); Knollwood Memorial Gardens v. Comm'r, 46 T.C. 764 (1966).

[188] Rev. Rul. 77-70, 1977-1 C.B. 150.

[189] See § 7.13(b).

[190] Trustees of Graceland Cemetery Improvement Fund v. United States, 515 F.2d 763 (Ct. Cl. 1975). Also, Laurel Hill Cemetery Ass'n v. United States, 427 F. Supp. 679 (E.D. Mo. 1977), aff'd, 566 F.2d 630 (8th Cir. 1977); Endowment Care Trust Fund of Inglewood Park Cemetery Ass'n Bd. of Trustees v. United States, 76-2 U.S.T.C. ¶ 9516 (Ct. Cl. 1976); Au v. United States, 76-1 U.S.T.C. ¶ 9370 (Ct. Cl. 1976); Albuquerque Nat'l Bank v. United States, 75-1 U.S.T.C. ¶ 9294 (D.N.M. 1975).

The IRS had espoused this rationale earlier.[191] Congress the next year, however, enacted a law providing a deduction for amounts distributed by perpetual care trust funds to taxable cemetery companies for the care and maintenance of gravesites.[192] To qualify under this provision, the fund must be a trust established pursuant to local law by a taxable cemetery for the care and maintenance of the cemetery.[193]

Contributions to tax-exempt cemetery companies are deductible for federal income tax purposes.[194] The contributions must be voluntary and made to or for the use of a nonprofit cemetery, the funds of which are irrevocably dedicated to the care of the cemetery as a whole. Contributions made to a cemetery company for the perpetual care of a particular lot or crypt are, however, not deductible.[195] While bequests or gifts to exempt cemetery companies are generally not deductible for federal estate or gift tax purposes,[196] a court allowed the estate tax deduction for a bequest to a public nonprofit cemetery because of its ostensible characteristics as a charitable entity.[197] This decision was, however, reversed.[198]

§ 19.7 CREDIT UNIONS

The federal income tax law exemption rules reference *credit unions* without capital stock organized and operated for mutual purposes and without profit.[199] As noted, federal credit unions organized and operated in accordance with the Federal Credit Union Act are tax-exempt as instrumentalities of the United States.[200] Credit unions otherwise exempt from federal income tax generally are those chartered under state law,[201] although in one instance the IRS recognized tax exemption

---

[191] Rev. Rul. 64-217, 1964-2 C.B. 153; Rev. Rul. 58-190, 1958-1 C.B. 15. Cf. Washington Trust Bank v. United States, 444 F.2d 1235 (9th Cir. 1971), *cert. denied*, 404 U.S. 1059 (1972); Evergreen Cemetery Ass'n of Seattle v. United States, 444 F.2d 1232 (9th Cir. 1971), *cert. denied*, 404 U.S. 1050 (1971); Mercantile Bank & Trust Co. v. United States, 441 F.2d 364 (8th Cir. 1971); Arlington Memorial Park Ass'n v. United States, 327 F. Supp. 344 (W.D. Ark. 1971).

[192] Pub. L. No. 94-528 (1976). Also, H.R. Rep. No. 94-1344 (1976).

[193] IRC § 642(j); Reg. § 1.642(j). A trust established for the care of two cemetery lots for a family was held to not qualify for tax-exempt status (Cave Hill Investment Co. v. United States, 2002-2 U.S.T.C. ¶ 50,722 (W.D. Ky. 2002)).

[194] IRC § 170(c)(5).

[195] Rev. Rul. 58-190, 1958-1 C.B. 15.

[196] Rev. Rul. 67-170, 1967-1 C.B. 272.

[197] Mellon Bank v. United States, 590 F. Supp. 160 (W.D. Pa. 1984).

[198] Mellon Bank v. United States, 762 F.2d 283 (3d Cir. 1985). A court held that a cemetery association cannot qualify as a charitable organization for estate tax deduction purposes because of its function of selling burial plots and maintenance of grounds (Smith v. United States, 84-2 U.S.T.C. ¶ 13,595 (W.D. Mo. 1984)). Also, Linwood Cemetery Ass'n v. Comm'r, 87 T.C. 1314 (1986).

[199] IRC § 501(c)(14)(A); Reg. § 1.501(c)(14)-1. Also, United States v. Cambridge Loan & Bldg. Co., 278 U.S. 55 (1923). The IRS ruled that equity shares issued by a credit union solely for the purpose of raising capital do not constitute capital stock for this purpose because they do not provide an equity interest in, or participation in the management of, the credit union (Priv. Ltr. Rul. 200530030).

[200] Rev. Rul. 55-133, 1955-1 C.B. 138. See § 19.1.

[201] Rev. Rul. 69-282, 1969-1 C.B. 155. An organization, formed under and operated in accordance with the laws of a foreign country, applied for recognition of exemption as a state-chartered credit union; the IRS denied recognition, in part by observing that this country "is not a state" (Priv. Ltr. Rul. 201416009).

under this body of law for the benefit of an organization formed by a group at a U.S. military base in a foreign country.[202] In addition to being chartered under a state credit union law, however, a credit union, to qualify under these rules, must, as noted, operate without profit and for the mutual benefit of its members.[203]

The first credit union in the United States had its tax exemption recognized in 1935; the government attempted to revoke its exempt status in 1966, contending it was operating in a commercial manner. Courts found that the organization did not lose its exempt credit union status because it offered services such as checking accounts and real estate loans, and that the members of the credit union in fact had a common bond even though this commonality was not reduced to a written requirement.[204] A federal court of appeals used the occasion of its decision in this case to define a *credit union* as a "democratically controlled, cooperative, nonprofit society organized for the purpose of encouraging thrift and self-reliance among its members by creating a source of credit at a fair and reasonable rate of interest in order to improve the economic and social conditions of its members."[205]

§ 19.8   MUTUAL RESERVE FUNDS

Tax exemption is extended to certain *mutual organizations* organized before September 1, 1957.[206] Prior to 1951, all savings and loan associations were exempt from taxation, as were the nonprofit corporations that insured these savings institutions. In that year, the tax exemption for savings and loan associations was repealed because Congress determined that the purpose of the exemption, which was to afford savings institutions that had no capital stock the benefit of an exemption so that a surplus could be accumulated to provide the depositors with greater security, was no longer applicable because the savings and loan industry had developed to the point where the ratio of capital account to total deposits was comparable to that of commercial banks.

Tax exemption for the insurers of these associations was, however, continued for those that were organized prior to September 1, 1951.[207] In 1960, Congress extended the expiration date to September 1, 1957, to accommodate a particular organization, inasmuch as that entity had been organized at a time when the savings and loan associations were essentially not taxed, due to generous bad debt reserve provisions.[208]

In 1962, a nonprofit corporation was established by a state legislature for the purpose of insuring the accounts of depositors in savings and loan associations doing business in the state that were not insured by the Federal Savings and

---

[202] Rev. Rul. 69-283, 1969-1 C.B. 156.

[203] Rev. Rul. 72-37, 1972-1 C.B. 152.

[204] La Caisse Populaire Ste. Marie v. United States, 425 F. Supp. 512 (D.N.H. 1976), *aff'd*, 563 F.2d 505 (1st Cir. 1977).

[205] *Id.*, 563 F.2d at 509.

[206] IRC § 501(c)(14)(B).

[207] At that time, Congress understood that the exemption would be limited to four private insurers (two in Massachusetts, one in Connecticut, and one in New Hampshire). S. Rep. No. 82-781, at 22-29 (1951).

[208] S. Rep. No. 87-1881, at 40 (1962).

Loan Insurance Corporation (FSLIC). Legislation to extend the termination date was not enacted, in part because Congress did not want to discriminate (again) in favor of these financial institutions.[209] (This nonaction on the part of Congress was challenged, with the U.S. Supreme Court holding that Congress did not function in an arbitrary and unconstitutional manner in declining to extend the exemption beyond 1957.)[210] Similar legislation to extend the cutoff period was considered but not enacted. Thereafter, one of the organizations that would have been benefited by the legislation attempted to secure a judicial determination that it was entitled to a deduction from its income for an addition to its loss reserves, but this was rejected on the ground that the deduction would be the equivalent of exemption of the income from tax—a result Congress had rejected.[211]

It is the position of the IRS that the only way that organizations providing insurance for shares or deposits can qualify for tax exemption is to satisfy the rules as to this category of exemption.[212] This position is predicated on the rule of statutory construction that a specific statutory provision must prevail over more general provisions.[213] Thus, for example, the type of organization that cannot satisfy the requirements for exemption of these mutual organizations (for example, because it was organized after 1957) cannot be exempt as a business league.[214] Therefore, generally, credit unions cannot be categorized as exempt business leagues.[215]

§ 19.9 INSURANCE COMPANIES AND ASSOCIATIONS

A property and casualty insurance company generally is a taxable organization.[216] The taxable income of a property and casualty insurance company is determined as the sum of its underwriting income and its investment income (including gains and other income items), reduced by allowable deductions.[217]

Nonetheless, federal law provides tax exemption for insurance companies[218] other than life insurance companies (including interinsurers and reciprocal

---

[209] Savings and loan associations, like other financial institutions, were entitled to establish tax-free reserves from their earnings for losses on loans; there was opposition to exemption of these insurers from tax on the earnings of their members' capital deposits because it would, in effect, provide a method whereby the associations could accumulate reserves free of tax. Also, there was concern about the financial stability of the FSLIC.

[210] Maryland Sav.-Share Ins. Corp. v. United States, 400 U.S. 4 (1970).

[211] Maryland Sav.-Share Ins. Corp. v. United States, 644 F.2d 16 (Ct. Cl. 1981).

[212] Rev. Rul. 83-166, 1983-2 C.B. 96.

[213] E.g., HCSC-Laundry v. United States, 450 U.S. 1 (1981).

[214] See Chapter 14.

[215] Credit Union Ins. Corp. v. United States, 95-1 U.S.T.C. ¶ 50,286 (D. Md. 1995), aff'd, 96-2 U.S.T.C. ¶ 50,323 (4th Cir. 1996).

[216] IRC § 831(a).

[217] IRC § 832.

[218] The term *insurance company* is defined in IRC § 816(a) to mean a company, more than one-half of the business of which during the tax year involved is the issuance of insurance or annuity contracts or the reinsurance of risks underwritten by insurance companies (also, IRC § 831(c)). A company whose investment activities outweigh its insurance activities is not an insurance company (e.g., Inter-American Life Ins. Co. v. Comm'r, 56 T.C. 497 (1971), aff'd, 469 F.2d 697 (9th Cir. 1972)).

underwriters) if the gross receipts of the company for the tax year involved do not exceed $600,000 and more than 50 percent of the receipts consists of premiums.[219] For a mutual insurance company to be exempt, however, its gross receipts for the tax year cannot exceed $150,000, and more than 35 percent of the receipts[220] must consist of premiums. Exemption is available for mutual insurance companies only if no employee of the company or member of the employee's family is an employee of another company that is exempt under these rules.[221]

For purposes of determining gross receipts, the gross receipts of all members of a controlled group of corporations of which the company is a part are taken into account.[222] This controlled group rule[223] takes into account the gross receipts of foreign and tax-exempt corporations.[224]

The IRS is issuing rulings that organizations failed to qualify as tax-exempt insurance companies because they did not function as an insurance company in the first instance.[225]

§ 19.10   CROP OPERATIONS FINANCE CORPORATIONS

Federal income tax law provides tax exemption for corporations organized by an exempt farmers' cooperative or association[226] or members of these organizations, for the purpose of financing the ordinary crop operations of the members or other producers, and operated in conjunction with this type of an association.[227] The *crop operations finance corporation* may retain its exemption even though it issues capital stock, where certain statutory conditions are met, or it accumulates and maintains a reasonable reserve. A tax-exempt crop financing corporation may own all the stock of a business corporation without jeopardizing its exempt status.[228]

---

[219] E.g., Priv. Ltr. Rul. 200830025. A court rejected an argument that "purchase payments" an entity received in consideration for annuity contracts sold to its customers were not premiums for purposes of the $600,000 gross receipts limitation and observed further that if these payments were not premiums the entity would have had insufficient premiums to pass the 50 percent minimum premiums test required for IRC § 501(c)(15) status (Commonwealth Underwriting & Annuity Services Inc. v. Comm'r, T.C. Memo. 2023-27).

[220] The term *gross receipts* means premiums (including deposits and assessments) without reduction for return premiums or premiums paid for reinsurance, items constituting gross investment income of a non–life insurance company (IRC § 834(b)), and other items properly includible in this type of organization's gross income (Notice 2006-42, 2006-19 I.R.B. 878).

[221] IRC § 501(c)(15)(A). Although an insolvent insurance company does not lose its exemption due to liquidation (e.g., Priv. Ltr. Rul. 200552021), an insurance company, formerly a life insurance company, was ruled to be ineligible for this exemption, even if in liquidation under the auspices of a state's director of insurance (Priv. Ltr. Rul. 200642011).

[222] IRC § 501(c)(15)(B).

[223] This term is defined in IRC § 831(b)(2)(B)(ii).

[224] IRC § 501(c)(15)(C).

[225] E.g., Priv. Ltr. Rul. 200520035. Likewise, Reserve Mechanical Corp. v. Comm'r, T.C. Memo. 2018-86 (2018), *aff'd*, 34 F.4th 881 (10th Cir. 2022).

[226] See § 19.12.

[227] IRC § 501(c)(16); Reg. § 1.501(c)(16)-1.

[228] Rev. Rul. 78-434, 1978-2 C.B. 179.

A court denied tax exemption under these rules to a crop financing corporation that was organized by fruit growers who were members of tax-exempt cooperatives, because the growers were not engaging in their activities in the capacity of members of the cooperatives.[229]

§ 19.11 VETERANS' ORGANIZATIONS

(a) General Rules

Federal income tax law provides tax exemption for a post or organization of past or present members of the armed forces of the United States, or an auxiliary unit or society of these entities, or a trust or foundation operated for these entities, where (1) it is organized in the United States or any of its possessions; (2) at least 75 percent of its members are past or present members of the U.S. armed forces, and substantially all of the other members are individuals who are cadets or spouses, widows, or widowers of these past or present members or of cadets; and (3) there is no private inurement.[230] The IRS, from time to time, issues rulings as to whether organizations adhere to these membership requirements.[231] Indeed, in one instance, the IRS revoked the exemption of an ostensible veterans' organization because it did not have a bona fide membership.[232] Some veterans' groups may have exemption as social welfare organizations.[233]

Presumably, a veterans' organization, to qualify for tax exemption under these rules, must operate exclusively to (1) promote the social welfare of a community; (2) assist disabled and needy veterans and members of the U.S. armed forces and their dependents, and the widows, widowers, and orphans of deceased veterans; (3) provide entertainment, care, and assistance to hospitalized veterans or members of the U.S. armed forces; (4) carry on programs to perpetuate the memory of deceased veterans and members of the armed forces and comfort their survivors; (5) conduct programs for religious, charitable, scientific, literary, or educational purposes; (6) sponsor or participate in activities of a patriotic nature; (7) provide insurance benefits for their members or dependents thereof, or both; and/or (8) provide social and recreational activities for their members.[234]

---

[229] Growers Credit Corp. v. Comm'r, 33 T.C. 981 (1970).

[230] IRC § 501(c)(19). See Chapter 20.

[231] E.g., Priv. Ltr. Rul. 200540012.

[232] Priv. Ltr. Rul. 201035035.

[233] See Chapter 13.

[234] Reg. § 1.501(c)(19)-1(c). The IRS's legal counsel concluded, on the basis of federal tax law in the social club context (see Chapter 15), that a veterans' organization is operating to provide social and recreational activities to its members when it provides these services to "nonmembers who are guests or dependents," but if a "substantial amount" of the services are provided to other categories of nonmembers the veterans' organization would not qualify for exemption (Chief Couns. Adv. Mem. 200936027). The IRS held that a veterans' organization engaged in unrelated activities when it rented its hotel to nonmembers, sold bottled liquor, and provided banquet services to civic groups (Priv. Ltr. Rul. 8539091).

Income derived from members of these organizations attributable to payments for life, accident, or health insurance with respect to the members or their dependents, where the net profits are set aside for charitable purposes, is exempt from the unrelated business income tax.[235] The enactment of this general income tax exemption thus provides a category of organizations entitled to use the unrelated business income tax exemption.

The IRS, from time to time, issues rulings as to whether organizations qualify as tax-exempt veterans' organizations.[236]

A contribution to a post or organization of war veterans, or an auxiliary unit or society of, or trust or foundation for, any of these posts or organizations is deductible as a charitable gift, if the donee is organized in the United States or any of its possessions and none of its net earnings inures to the benefit of any private shareholder or individual.[237]

There is no federal tax law restriction on the extent of lobbying by veterans' organizations. This feature was characterized by the U.S. Supreme Court as a "subsidy" enacted by Congress as part of the nation's long-standing policy of compensating veterans for their contributions by providing them with numerous advantages.[238] Presumably tax exemption for their organizations is likewise a subsidy, for those who have "been obliged to drop their own affairs and take up the burdens of the nation"[239] and have subjected themselves to the "mental and physical hazards as well as the economic and family detriments which are peculiar to military service and which do not exist in normal life."[240] "This policy [of subsidization]," wrote the Court, "has 'always been deemed to be legitimate.'"[241]

(b) Pre-1880 Organizations

In 1982, Congress established another category of tax-exempt veterans' organizations, which is available for any association organized before 1880, more than 75 percent of the members of which are present or past members of the U.S. armed forces, and a principal purpose of which is to provide insurance and other benefits to veterans or their dependents.[242]

---

[235] IRC § 512(a)(4); Reg. § 1.512(a)-4. See § 25.4(b).

[236] E.g., Priv. Ltr. Rul. 200519084.

[237] IRC § 170(c)(3). Also, Rev. Rul. 84-140, 1984-2 C.B. 56, *modifying and superseding* Rev. Rul. 59-151, 1959-1 C.B. 53. A federal court of appeals concluded that a contribution to a qualified veterans' organization by an individual of long-term capital gain appreciated property was subject to the 30-percent-of-contribution-base limitation, because the donee satisfied the publicly supported organization test of (that is, is "described in") IRC § 509(a)(2) (see § 12.3(b)(iv)) and thus was described in IRC § 170(b)(1)(A)(viii) (Weingarden v. Comm'r, 825 F.2d 1027 (6th Cir. 1987)). The appellate court thus rejected the conclusion of the U.S. Tax Court that the gift was limited by the 20-percent-of-contribution-base limitation on the ground that Congress intended that only organizations described in IRC § 501(c)(3) are charitable donees eligible for the more liberal limitation (Weingarden v. Comm'r, 86 T.C. 669 (1986)).

[238] Regan v. Taxation with Representation of Wash., 461 U.S. 540, 550 (1983).

[239] Boone v. Lightner, 319 U.S. 561, 575 (1943).

[240] Johnson v. Robison, 415 U.S. 361, 380 (1974).

[241] Personnel Admin. v. Feeney, 442 U.S. 256, 279 n.25 (1979).

[242] IRC § 501(c)(23).

§ 19.12 FARMERS' COOPERATIVES

An eligible *farmers' cooperative organization* is exempt from federal income taxation.[243] These farmers' cooperatives are farmers', fruit growers', or like associations organized and operated on a cooperative basis for the purpose of (1) marketing the products of members or other producers and returning to them the proceeds of sales, less the necessary marketing expenses, on the basis of either the quantity or the value of the products furnished by them, or (2) purchasing supplies and equipment for the use of members or other persons and turning over the supplies and equipment to them at actual cost plus necessary expenses.[244] A farmers' cooperative may pay dividends on its capital stock in certain circumstances,[245] permit proxy voting by its shareholders,[246] and maintain a reasonable reserve.[247] The earnings of cooperatives are generally taxed to them or their patrons; these rules give tax-exempt farmers' cooperatives certain advantages in computing their tax that are not available to other cooperatives.[248]

Farmers' cooperatives came into being because of the economic fact that a farmer sells products in a producers' market and makes purchases in a retail market. Thus, a farmers' marketing cooperative markets farmers' products at a price nearer retail price and makes its purchases at wholesale rather than retail. A farmers' purchasing cooperative sells supplies and equipment to its patrons at a price that leaves a balance after expenses. The cooperative's net earnings or savings are distributed to the patrons on the basis of the amount of business transacted by them, in the form of patronage dividends. *Patronage dividends* are the profits of a cooperative that are rebated to its patrons pursuant to a preexisting obligation of the cooperative to do so; the rebate must be made in an equitable fashion on the basis of the quantity or value of business done with the cooperative.

Farmers' cooperatives are associations of individuals such as farmers, fruit growers, livestock growers, and operators of dairies. Illustrations of these organizations include associations operated to facilitate the artificial breeding of members' livestock,[249] acquire and apportion the beneficial use of land for the grazing of members' livestock,[250] furnish its members a place to market their farm products,[251] process and market poultry for members and other producers,[252] market

[243] IRC § 521.
[244] Reg. § 1.521-1. In general, Liberty Warehouse Co. v. Burley Tobacco Growers' Coop. Mktg. Ass'n, 276 U.S. 71, 92-96 (1928).
[245] IRC § 521(b)(2); Reg. § 1.521-1(a)(2). Also, Agway, Inc. v. United States, 524 F.2d 1194 (Ct. Cl. 1975); Rev. Rul. 75-388, 1975-2 C.B. 227; Rev. Rul. 73-148, 1973-1 C.B. 294.
[246] Rev. Rul. 75-97, 1975-1 C.B. 167.
[247] IRC § 521(b)(3); Reg. § 1.521-1(a)(3). Also, Rev. Rul. 76-233, 1976-1 C.B. 173.
[248] According to the U.S. Tax Court, in determining the amount to be paid as patronage dividends, a cooperative may allocate all of its gain from the sale of equipment to its patrons in the year of the sale in proportion to their patronage during that year (Lamesa Coop. Gin v. Comm'r, 78 T.C. 894 (1982)).
[249] Rev. Rul. 68-76, 1968-1 C.B. 285.
[250] Rev. Rul. 67-429, 1967-2 C.B. 218.
[251] Rev. Rul. 67-430, 1967-2 C.B. 220.
[252] Rev. Rul. 58-483, 1958-2 C.B. 277.

farm-raised fish,[253] operate a grain elevator and feed yard and process soybeans,[254] purchase raw materials for processing into completed products before their transfer to patrons,[255] and produce and market range grasses.[256] The term *like association* is limited to associations that market agricultural products or purchase supplies and equipment for those engaged in producing agricultural products.[257] Thus, the admission to membership of a substantial number of nonproducers in an otherwise tax-exempt producers' cooperative would destroy the association's exemption.[258] This, in turn, raises questions as to what constitutes a *farm*[259] and a *farmer*.[260]

The specific rules in this area of the federal tax law do not define these terms. These terms are, however, referenced elsewhere in the federal tax law.[261] On the basis of these other definitions, the IRS concluded that these terms do not apply to forestry, so that a federated cooperative marketing newsprint and its member cooperatives supplying pulpwood cut from timber grown by the patron members did not qualify as tax-exempt farmers' cooperatives.[262]

Examples of organizations denied this category of tax exemption as not being like a farmers' cooperative include an association that maintained its patrons' orchards and harvested their crops,[263] an association that marketed lumber for the independent lumber-producing companies that controlled it,[264] an association that marketed building materials on a cooperative basis,[265] an association of advertising agencies[266] and one of garbage collectors,[267] and a cooperative that processed and marketed brine shrimp cysts where the harvesting of the cysts occurred in a publicly owned lake.[268] An organization may be recognized as a cooperative association under state law and still be denied this form of exemption.[269]

Other requirements must be met in order to achieve this category of tax exemption, including the requirements that the association be organized and operated on a cooperative basis,[270] there be bona fide members,[271] and (where

---

[253] Rev. Rul. 64-246, 1964-2 C.B. 154.
[254] Rev. Rul. 74-567, 1974-2 C.B. 174.
[255] Rev. Rul. 54-12, 1954-1 C.B. 93.
[256] Rev. Rul. 75-5, 1975-1 C.B. 166.
[257] Sunset Scavenger Co., Inc. v. Comm'r, 84 F.2d 453 (9th Cir. 1936).
[258] Cooperative Cent. Exch. v. Comm'r, 27 B.T.A. 17 (1932).
[259] Rev. Rul. 64-246, 1964-2 C.B. 154.
[260] Rev. Rul. 55-611, 1955-2 C.B. 270.
[261] IRC §§ 61 (Reg. § 1.61-4(d)), 175 (Reg. § 1.175-3), 180, 182 (Reg. § 1.182-2), 464(e)(1).
[262] Rev. Rul. 84-81, 1984-1 C.B. 135.
[263] Rev. Rul. 66-108, 1966-2 C.B. 154.
[264] Rev. Rul. 73-570, 1973-2 C.B. 195.
[265] Rev. Rul. 73-308, 1973-2 C.B. 193.
[266] Nat'l Outdoor Advertising Bur., Inc. v. Helvering, 89 F.2d 878 (2d Cir. 1937).
[267] Sunset Scavenger Co., Inc. v. Comm'r, 84 F.2d 453 (9th Cir. 1936).
[268] Priv. Ltr. Rul. 200841038. This organization differed from the one referenced in *supra* note 253, inasmuch as, in the facts in the prior ruling, the harvesting was in privately owned waters (i.e., a fish farm).
[269] Lyeth v. Hoey, 305 U.S. 188 (1938).
[270] Reg. § 1.521-1(a)(1); Eugene Fruit Growers Ass'n v. Comm'r, 37 B.T.A. 993 (1938); Rev. Rul. 71-100, 1971-1 C.B. 159; Rev. Rul. 68-496, 1968-2 C.B. 251; Rev. Rul. 55-558, 1955-2 C.B. 270.
[271] Reg. § 1.521-1(a)(3); Producers Livestock Mktg. Ass'n of Salt Lake City v. Comm'r, 45 B.T.A. 325 (1941).

appropriate) there be producers.[272] A federal court of appeals held that a person who merely stores items in the cooperative's facilities but does not market any products or purchase any supplies from the cooperative is not a *producer*.[273]

To be tax-exempt as a farmers' cooperative, an organization must establish that it does not have any taxable income for its own account other than that reflected in an authorized reserve or surplus.[274] An organization engaged in both marketing farm products and purchasing supplies and equipment is exempt as this type of cooperative if it meets the tax law requirements as to each of its functions.[275] An organization cannot be exempt under these rules if it nets losses between the marketing function and the purchasing function.[276]

With respect to a farmers' cooperative that issues stock, for the cooperative to be tax-exempt substantially all of the capital stock must be owned by producers who market their products or purchase their supplies and equipment through the cooperative.[277] Also, the farmers' cooperative must be able to demonstrate that the ownership of its capital stock has been restricted to participating shareholders "as far as possible."[278] While the phrase *substantially all* is not defined in the statute or regulations, it is the view of the IRS that, for this rule to be satisfied, at least 85 percent of the capital stock must be held by producers;[279] a court held that a 91 percent holding satisfied the requirement[280] and that neither a 78 percent nor a 72 percent holding met the requirement.[281]

Subsequently, a court agreed with the IRS's 85-percent-of-stock test "in concept," emphasizing that the "favorable tax treatment offered cooperatives is intended to benefit the member producers, not the cooperative as a business entity."[282] A federal court of appeals twice concluded that the test is reasonable.[283] This appellate court wrote that, inasmuch as this form of tax exemption is available "only to those cooperatives in which participation in the direction and decision making process of the cooperative is strictly limited to patrons," of "primary importance, therefore, is a shareholder's right to vote."[284] Consequently, the court of appeals enunciated

[272] Farmers Coop. Creamery Ass'n of Cresco, Iowa v. United States, 81-1 U.S.T.C. ¶ 9457 (N.D. Iowa 1981); Dr. P. Phillips Coop. v. Comm'r, 17 T.C. 1002 (1951); Rev. Rul. 72-589, 1972-2 C.B. 282; Rev. Rul. 67-422, 1967-2 C.B. 217; Rev. Rul. 58-483, 1958-2 C.B. 277.
[273] West Cent. Coop. v. United States, 758 F.2d 1269 (8th Cir. 1985), *aff'g per curiam* (N.D. Iowa 1983).
[274] Reg. § 1.521-1(c).
[275] Id.
[276] Union Equity Coop. Exch. v. Comm'r, 481 F.2d 812 (10th Cir. 1973), *cert. denied*, 414 U.S. 1028 (1973).
[277] IRC § 521(b)(2).
[278] Reg. § 1.521-1(a)(2).
[279] Rev. Rul. 73-248, 1973-1 C.B. 295.
[280] Farmers Co-Op. Creamery v. Comm'r, 21 B.T.A. 265 (1930). Also, Farmers' Co-Op. Milk Co. v. Comm'r, 9 B.T.A. 696 (1927).
[281] Co-Op. Grain & Supply Co. v. Comm'r, 32 T.C.M. 795 (1973), *on remand*, 407 F.2d 1158 (8th Cir. 1969), *rev'g in part and rem'g*, 26 T.C.M. 593 (1967); Petaluma Co-Op. Creamery v. Comm'r, 52 T.C. 457 (1969).
[282] Farmers Coop. Co. v. Comm'r, 85 T.C. 601, 613-614 (1985).
[283] Farmers Coop. Co. v. Comm'r, 87-2 U.S.T.C. ¶ 9404 (8th Cir. 1987); West Cent. Coop. v. United States, 758 F.2d 1269 (8th Cir. 1985), *aff'g per curiam* (N.D. Iowa 1983).
[284] Farmers Coop. Co. v. Comm'r, 87-2 U.S.T.C. ¶ 9404 (8th Cir. 1987), at 89,116.

the rule that "if a producer who sufficiently patronizes a cooperative during the tax year to become entitled to a share of capital stock is actually entitled to vote that share at the annual shareholders' meeting following the close of that tax year, that producer should be counted as both a shareholder and as a patron for the tax year in which the right to vote the share accrued," while "if a shareholder, by failing to patronize a cooperative, ceases to be entitled to own a share and thereby actually loses the right to vote at the annual shareholders' meeting following the close of the tax year, that shareholder should not be counted as a shareholder or patron for the tax year in which the right to the share was lost."[285]

The law provides that tax exemption "shall not be denied any such association because it has capital stock. . .if substantially all such stock. . .is owned by producers who market their products or purchase their supplies and equipment through the association."[286] It is, as noted, the position of the IRS that at least 85 percent of capital stock must be held by producers to satisfy the *substantially all* test.[287] This requirement has been upheld by the courts, with the courts agreeing that, as noted, a person who merely stores items in the cooperative's storage facilities but does not market any products or purchase any supplies from the cooperative is not a producer.[288]

The IRS issued guidelines[289] to determine whether a patron is a producer patron of a tax-exempt farmers' cooperative for purposes of applying these stock ownership requirements. These guidelines, which were subsequently abandoned, stated that the qualifying stockholders will be persons who, during the cooperative's tax year, market through the cooperative more than 50 percent of their products, who purchase from the cooperative more than 50 percent of their products, or who purchase from the cooperative more than 50 percent of their supplies and equipment of the type handled by the cooperative. A person who did not meet this 50 percent requirement could nonetheless be considered a producer for purposes of the ownership requirements if certain facts and circumstances, as stated in a 1977 IRS ruling, were present.[290] A court, however, voided the 50-percent-patronage requirement,[291] causing the IRS to revoke the test[292] and the ruling.[293] Thus, stock owned by persons who transact any amount of current and active patronage with an exempt cooperative during the cooperative's tax year will be considered stock that is counted toward the stock ownership requirement. Moreover, a person who does not transact any patronage during the cooperative's tax year may still be considered a producer for these purposes if, on the basis of all the facts and circumstances, it is determined that the person was unable to transact any patronage during the year because (1) the person encountered a crop failure and had nothing to market; (2) sickness, disability, death, or other hardship prevented the person

---

[285] *Id.*

[286] IRC § 521(b)(2).

[287] Rev. Rul. 73-248, 1973-C.B. 295.

[288] West Cent. Coop. v. United States, 758 F.2d 1269 (8th Cir. 1985), *aff'g per curiam* (N.D. Iowa 1983).

[289] Rev. Proc. 73-39, 1973-2 C.B. 502.

[290] Rev. Rul. 77-440, 1977-2 C.B. 199.

[291] Farmers Coop. Co. v. Comm'r, 89 T.C. 682 (1987).

[292] Rev. Proc. 90-29, 1990-1 C.B. 533.

[293] Rev. Rul. 90-42, 1990-1 C.B. 117.

from transacting any patronage; or (3) the cooperative deals in items (such as farm machinery) that are not normally purchased on an annual basis.[294]

Still other requirements concern the nature of permissible activities of these tax-exempt cooperatives. With respect to marketing cooperatives, questions have been raised as to what constitutes *marketing*.[295] The IRS has a long-standing policy of allowing exempt farmers' cooperatives, in connection with their marketing function, to manufacture or otherwise change the basic form of their members' products, as illustrated by the exempt farmers' cooperative that operated a cannery and facilities for drying fruit and a cooperative that operated a textile mill, both of which marketed the processed or unprocessed products of their member growers and distributed the proceeds to them on the basis of the quantity of product furnished, less a charge to cover the cost of processing.[296] Subsequently, this policy was illustrated by an IRS ruling allowing qualification as an exempt farmers' cooperative of a cooperative association that, in connection with its marketing function, processed its members' agricultural products into alcohol.[297]

As to the tax-exempt purchasing cooperative, the issue may be what is encompassed by the term *supplies and equipment*.[298] Business done for or with the federal government is disregarded in determining the right to this category of exemption.[299] Because hedging is an activity that is incidental to the marketing function of an exempt farmers' cooperative, it may establish a commodity trading division to serve as a commodity broker to facilitate hedging transactions for its marketing patrons without adversely affecting its exemption.[300]

Tax exemption for a farmers' cooperative may not be denied because it has capital stock, if the dividend rate of the stock is fixed at a rate not to exceed the legal rate of interest in the state of incorporation or 8 percent annually, whichever is greater, on the value of the consideration for which the stock was issued, and if substantially all of the stock (other than nonvoting preferred stock, the owners of which are not entitled or permitted to participate, directly or indirectly, in the profits of the organization on dissolution or otherwise, beyond the fixed dividends) is owned by producers who market their products or purchase their supplies and equipment through the organization.[301] It is the position of the IRS that this *substantially all* test can be satisfied only where at least 85 percent of the capital stock (other than the nonvoting preferred stock) is held by producers.[302] This test was upheld by a federal court of appeals.[303]

---

[294] See Rev. Proc. 90-29, 1990-1 C.B. 533; Rev. Rul. 90-42, 1990-1 C.B. 117.

[295] Treasure Valley Potato Bargaining Ass'n v. Ore-Ida Foods, Inc., 497 F.2d 203 (9th Cir. 1974); Rev. Rul. 67-430, 1967-2 C.B. 220; Rev. Rul. 66-108, 1966-2 C.B. 154.

[296] Rev. Rul. 77-384, 1977-2 C.B. 198.

[297] Rev. Rul. 81-96, 1981-1 C.B. 359.

[298] Farmers Union Coop. Ass'n, Fairbury, Neb. v. Comm'r, 44 B.T.A. 34 (1941); Rev. Rul. 68-76, 1968-1 C.B. 285; Rev. Rul. 67-429, 1967-2 C.B. 218; Rev. Rul. 54-12, 1954-1 C.B. 93; S.M. 2288, III-2 C.B. 223 (1924).

[299] IRC § 521(b)(5); Rev. Rul. 65-5, 1965-1 C.B. 244.

[300] Rev. Rul. 76-298, 1976-2 C.B. 179.

[301] IRC § 521(b)(2).

[302] Rev. Rul. 73-248, 1973-1 C.B. 295.

[303] West Cent. Coop. v. United States, 758 F.2d 1269 (8th Cir. 1985), *aff'g per curiam* (N.D. Iowa 1983). Also, Co-Op. Grain & Supply Co. v. Comm'r, 32 T.C.M. 795 (1973), *on remand*, 407 F.2d 1158 (8th Cir. 1969), *rev'g in part and rem'g*, 26 T.C.M. 593 (1967).

A tax-exempt farmers' cooperative may establish and control a subsidiary corporation as long as the activities of the subsidiary are activities that the cooperative itself might engage in as an integral part of its operations without adversely affecting its exempt status.[304] For this reason, the IRS ruled that a cooperative may establish and control a domestic international sales corporation.[305]

A rule that has generated considerable attention is the limitation on the purchasing of supplies and equipment for nonmembers and nonproducers to 15 percent of the value of all of the tax-exempt cooperative's purchase of supplies and equipment.[306] By contrast, a marketing cooperative will generally not qualify for this exemption if it markets the goods of nonproducers.[307] There are exceptions to the limitation on marketing nonproducer goods, however, which may be categorized into sideline,[308] ingredient,[309] and emergency[310] purchases from nonproducers.

Still another requisite for qualification for this category of tax exemption is that any excess of gross receipts over expenses and payments to patrons (termed *earnings*) must be returned to the patrons in proportion to the amount of business done for them. The income and expenses for each function (primarily marketing and purchasing) must be accounted for separately.[311] In computing earnings, the exempt cooperative must experience only necessary expenses associated with marketing and purchasing (frequently undertaken in different departments or branches), rather than for items such as the purchase of life insurance for members.[312] Nonpatronage income may be allocated to the appropriate department of the cooperative.[313]

Also, a tax-exempt farmers' cooperative must treat its nonmember patrons the same as member patrons with respect to patronage dividends. There are several cases where an association was denied tax exemption under these rules because of this type of discrimination,[314] as well as a number of instances where inequality among patrons was deemed to not be present.[315]

---

[304] Rev. Rul. 69-575, 1969-2 C.B. 134.

[305] Rev. Rul. 73-247, 1973-1 C.B. 294.

[306] IRC § 521(b)(4). Also, Rev. Rul. 69-417, 1969-2 C.B. 132; Rev. Rul. 67-346, 1967-2 C.B. 216; Rev. Rul. 67-223, 1967-2 C.B. 214. As to the effect of the use of subsidiaries in relation to this limitation, see Rev. Rul. 73-148, 1973-1 C.B. 294; Rev. Rul. 69-575, 1969-2 C.B. 134.

[307] IRC § 521(b)(1). Also, Rev. Rul. 67-152, 1967 C.B. 147.

[308] Rev. Proc. 67-37, 1967-2 C.B. 668; Land O'Lakes, Inc. v. United States, 362 F. Supp. 1253 (S.D. Minn. 1973), *rev'd and rem.*, 514 F.2d 134 (8th Cir. 1975), *cert. denied.*, 423 U.S. 926 (1975); Eugene Fruit Growers Ass'n v. Comm'r, 37 B.T.A. 993 (1938).

[309] Rev. Rul. 75-4, 1975-1 C.B. 165; Rev. Rul. 67-152, 1967-1 C.B. 147; Dr. P. Phillips Coop. v. Comm'r, 17 T.C. 1002 (1951).

[310] Rev. Rul. 69-222, 1969-1 C.B. 161; Producer's Produce Co. v. Crooks, 2 F. Supp. 969 (W.D. Mo. 1932).

[311] Rev. Rul. 67-253, 1967-2 C.B. 214; Rev. Rul. 75-110, 1975-1 C.B. 167.

[312] Rev. Rul. 55-558, 1955-2 C.B. 270. Also, Rev. Rul. 73-93, 1973-1 C.B. 292.

[313] Rev. Rul. 67-128, 1967-1 C.B. 147; Juanita Farmers Coop. Ass'n v. Comm'r, 43 T.C. 836 (1965). Cf. Rev. Rul. 75-228, 1975-1 C.B. 278; Rev. Rul. 74-327, 1974-2 C.B. 66.

[314] E.g., Farmers Coop. Creamery Ass'n of Cresco, Iowa v. United States, 81-1 U.S.T.C. ¶ 9457 (N.D. Iowa (1981)); Fertile Coop. Dairy Ass'n v. Huston, 119 F.2d 274 (8th Cir. 1951); Farmers Coop. Co. of Wahoo, Neb. v. United States, 23 F. Supp. 123 (Ct. Cl. 1938); Rev. Rul. 73-59, 1973-1 C.B. 292.

[315] E.g., Rev. Rul. 69-52, 1969-1 C.B. 161; Rev. Rul. 66-152, 1966-1 C.B. 155. Also, Rev. Rul. 76-388, 1976-2 C.B. 180.

A discussion of the circumstances under which a federated farmers' coopera-tive (an association whose membership includes tax-exempt farmers' cooperative associations) may qualify for this form of exemption was the subject of an IRS ruling.[316] Two revenue procedures set forth methods acceptable for a federated cooperative and its members to establish exemption (involving the look-through principle)[317] and setting forth the general requirements in this regard.[318]

The federal tax law provisions for cooperatives generally[319] operate to treat these organizations more like a conduit than a separate taxable business enter-prise. The primary reason for this treatment is to avoid penalizing (by taxing) a group of persons for collectivizing their marketing or purchasing efforts in order to take advantage of economies of scale. The conduit treatment is derived from the ability of a cooperative to deduct from its taxable income patronage dividends paid. (A farmers' cooperative generally may deduct patronage dividends to the full extent of its net income and may also deduct, to a limited extent, dividends on common stock.)

A tax-exempt cooperative may make purchases and/or market goods in several product lines and/or several geographic areas. Many cooperatives of this type will calculate net income on an aggregate basis, netting gains from profitable products or geographic areas with losses from unprofitable ones, and thus pay patronage dividends based on the net income so computed. The position of the IRS is that a cooperative may not net gains and losses from different operations in any manner it chooses and that netting is not permitted unless it is equitable under the circumstances.[320]

§ 19.13 SHIPOWNERS' PROTECTION AND INDEMNITY ASSOCIATIONS

The federal tax law provides that "[t]here shall not be included in gross income the receipts of shipowners' mutual protection and indemnity associations not organ-ized for profit, and no part of the net earnings of which inures to the benefit of any private shareholder; but such corporations shall be subject as other persons to the tax on their taxable income from interest, dividends, and rents."[321] This law, in essence, provides federal income tax exemption for the *shipowners' protection and indemnity association*.

The return of excess dues by a fishing vessel owners' association to its members was ruled by the IRS to not be inurement of earnings to the mem-bers; therefore, the dues paid to the association were not includable in its gross

---

[316] Rev. Rul. 69-651, 1969-2 C.B. 135.

[317] Rev. Ruls. 72-50, 72-51, 72-52, 1972-1 C.B. 163, 164, 165.

[318] Rev. Procs. 72-16, 72-17, 1972-1 C.B. 738, 739.

[319] IRC § 1381 *et seq.*

[320] The case law is more supportive of the cooperatives', rather than the government's, position. E.g., Ford-Iroquois FS v. Comm'r, 74 T.C. 1213 (1980); Lamesa Coop. Gin v. Comm'r, 78 T.C. 894 (1982); Asso-ciated Milk Producers v. Comm'r, 68 T.C. 729 (1977).

[321] IRC § 526.

income.[322] The amount paid by a member of a tax-exempt association of this type to its reserve fund to provide certain insurance protection was deemed deductible.[323]

§ 19.14   HOMEOWNERS' ASSOCIATIONS

For decades, tax-exempt *homeowners' associations* were treated as a form of exempt social welfare organization.[324] It is common for these associations to be formed as part of the development of a real estate subdivision, a condominium project, or a cooperative housing project. These associations enable their members (usually individual homeowners) to act together in managing, maintaining, and improving areas where they live. The associations' purposes include the administration and enforcement of covenants for preserving the physical appearance of the development, the ownership and management of common areas (for example, sidewalks and parks), and the exterior maintenance of property owned by the members.

Originally, as noted, the IRS regarded homeowners' associations as tax-exempt social welfare organizations.[325] The agency, however, concerned that the requisite *community* was not being served, issued a countervailing ruling in 1974.[326] Most homeowners' associations found it difficult to meet the requirements of this policy change. The IRS also ruled that condominium management associations did not qualify for this category of exemption.[327]

Congress responded to this dilemma with an elective tax exemption provision for most of these associations.[328] This provision is in the mode of the tax treatment of exempt social clubs[329] and political organizations,[330] in that only *exempt function income* escapes unrelated business income taxation.

To qualify as a tax-exempt homeowners' association, an organization must be a condominium[331] management association or a residential real estate management association.[332] Generally, membership in these associations is confined to the

---

[322] Rev. Rul. 70-566, 1970-1 C.B. 128.

[323] Rev. Rul. 55-189, 1955-1 C.B. 265.

[324] See Chapter 13.2(a).

[325] Rev. Rul. 72-102, 1972-1 C.B. 149.

[326] Rev. Rul. 74-199, 1974-1 C.B. 131.

[327] Rev. Rul. 74-17, 1974-1 C.B. 130.

[328] IRC § 528; Reg. § 1.528-8. This election (IRC § 528(c)(1)(E)) is a year-to-year one (Reg. § 1.528-8(a)); a homeowners' association may thus alternate between taxable and tax-exempt status.

In one instance, the IRS refused to excuse a homeowners' association from the requirement of filing a timely refund claim, under the mitigation rules of IRC §§ 1311-1314, in the face of the argument that the claim is dependent on a future event, namely, the granting of permission to revoke the IRC § 528 election on the ground of inadequate accounting advice (Priv. Ltr. Rul. 8429049). The IRS ruled that a homeowners' association may revoke an election because of incorrect tax advice provided by a professional tax adviser (Rev. Rul. 83-74, 1983-1 C.B. 112). There is an automatic 12-month extension to make the election (Instructions for Form 1120-H).

[329] IRC § 512(a)(3). See § 15.4.

[330] IRC § 527(b). See § 17.5.

[331] The term *condominium* is defined for these purposes in Reg. § 1.528-1(b).

[332] Reg. § 1.528-1(a). The term *residential real estate management association* is defined in Reg. § 1.528-1(c).

developers and the owners of the units, residences, or lots.[333] Membership in either type of association is normally required as a condition of this ownership.[334]

A tax-exempt homeowners' association must meet certain requirements: (1) It must be organized and operated primarily to provide for the acquisition, construction, management, maintenance, and care of association property;[335] (2) it must pass an income test, by which at least 60 percent of the association's gross income for a tax year consists of exempt function income;[336] (3) it must pass an expenditure test, by which at least 90 percent of the annual expenditures of the association must be to acquire, construct, manage, maintain, and care for or improve its property;[337] (4) no part of the association's net earnings may inure to the benefit of any private shareholder or individual;[338] and (5) substantially all of the dwelling units in the condominium project or lots and buildings in a subdivision, development, or similar area must be used by individuals for residences.[339] The acts of acquiring, constructing, or providing management, maintenance, and care of association property, and of rebating excess membership dues, fees, or assessments, do not constitute private inurement. *Association property* means not only property held by it but also property commonly held by its members, property within the association privately held by the members, and property owned by a governmental unit and used for the benefit of residents of the unit.[340]

In this context, *exempt function income* means any amount received as membership dues, fees, or assessments from persons who are members of the association, namely, owners of condominium housing units (in the case of a condominium management association) or owners of real property (in the case of a residential real estate management association).[341] Taxable income includes investment income and payments by nonmembers for the use of the association's facilities, subject to a specific $100 deduction and deductions directly connected with the production of gross income (other than exempt function income).[342] The taxable income of a qualified homeowners' association is taxable at the rate of 21 percent.[343]

The House version of the Tax Reform Act of 1969 would have applied the foregoing rules to cooperative housing corporations,[344] but the 1969 act in its final

---

[333] Reg. § 1.528-1(a).

[334] *Id.* Associations of holders of time-share interests (IRC § 528(c)(4)) are treated as homeowners' associations.

[335] Reg. § 1.528-2.

[336] Reg. § 1.528-5.

[337] Reg. § 1.528-6.

[338] Reg. § 1.528-7. See Chapter 20.

[339] Reg. § 1.528-4.

[340] Reg. § 1.528-3.

[341] Reg. § 1.528-9. Annual assessments paid to a homeowners' association by its members are not deductible as real property taxes (Rev. Rul. 76-495, 1976-2 C.B. 43). An amount received by a homeowners' association in settlement of litigation on behalf of individual lot owners was deemed to constitute *membership fees* for this purpose (Rev. Rul. 88-56, 1988-1 C.B. 126). By contrast, interest earned by a homeowners' association on funds received in settlement of a pending lawsuit and held for certain repairs was ruled to be taxable (Priv. Ltr. Rul. 9042036).

[342] Reg. § 1.528-10. Qualified homeowners' associations that elect to be taxed under IRC § 528 file tax return Form 1120-H (IRC § 6012(a)(7)); Reg. § 1.528-8(a)).

[343] IRC § 528(b).

[344] IRC § 216(b).

form followed the Senate bill in not allowing the exemption for these corporations.[345] Instead, the act clarified existing law to ensure that a cooperative housing corporation is entitled to a deduction for depreciation[346] with respect to property it leases to a tenant-stockholder even though the tenant-stockholder may be entitled to depreciate their stock in the corporation to the extent that the stock is related to a proprietary lease or right of tenancy that is used by the tenant-stockholder in a trade or business or for the production of income.[347]

§ 19.15   HIGH-RISK INDIVIDUALS' HEALTH CARE COVERAGE ORGANIZATIONS

Tax-exempt status is available for a membership organization established by a state exclusively to provide coverage for medical care[348] on a nonprofit basis to high-risk individuals through insurance issued by the organization or a health maintenance organization under an arrangement with the organization.[349]

The individuals, who must be residents of the state, must be—by reason of the existence or history of a medical condition—unable to acquire medical care coverage for the medical condition through insurance or from a health maintenance organization, or able to acquire the coverage only at a rate that is substantially in excess of the rate for the coverage through the membership organization.[350] The composition of the membership in the organization must be specified by the state.[351] For example, a state can mandate that all organizations that are subject to insurance regulation by the state must be members of the organization.[352] The private inurement doctrine[353] is applicable to this type of organization.[354]

§ 19.16   WORKERS' COMPENSATION REINSURANCE ORGANIZATIONS

Tax-exempt status under federal law is available for a membership organization established before June 1, 1996, by a state exclusively to reimburse its members for losses arising under workers' compensation acts.[355]

Tax exemption is also available to any organization (including a mutual insurance company) if it is created by state law and is organized and operated under state law exclusively to (1) provide workers' compensation insurance that is

---

[345] Thus, "[c]ooperative housing corporations and organizations based on a similar form of ownership are not eligible to be taxed as homeowners' associations" (Reg. § 1.528-1(a)).

[346] IRC § 167(a).

[347] Park Place, Inc. v. Comm'r, 57 T.C. 767 (1972).

[348] This term is defined in IRC § 213(d).

[349] IRC § 501(c)(26)(A).

[350] IRC § 501(c)(26)(B).

[351] IRC § 501(c)(26)(C).

[352] H.R. Rep. 104-736 (1996).

[353] See Chapter 20.

[354] IRC § 501(c)(26)(D).

[355] IRC § 501(c)(27)(A)(i). An organization failed to qualify for tax exemption on this basis because it could not prove that it was created by a state (Priv. Ltr. Rul. 200536025).

required by state law or with respect to which state law provides significant disincentives if the insurance is not purchased by an employer, and (2) provide related coverage that is incidental to workers' compensation insurance.[356]

(a) State-Sponsored Organizations

The state must require that the membership of the organization consist of all persons who issue insurance covering workers' compensation losses in the state, and all persons and governmental entities that self-insure against these losses. The organization must "operate as a nonprofit organization" by returning surplus income to its members or workers' compensation policyholders on a periodic basis and by reducing initial premiums in anticipation of investment income.[357]

(b) Certain Insurance Companies

The organization must provide workers' compensation insurance to any employer in the state (for employees in the state or temporarily assigned out of state) that seeks the insurance and meets other reasonable requirements.[358] The state must make a financial commitment with respect to the organization, either by extending the full faith and credit of the state to the initial debt of the organization or by providing the organization its initial operating capital.[359] The assets of the organization must revert to the state on dissolution, unless state law does not permit the dissolution of the organization.[360] The majority of the board of directors or oversight body of the organization must be appointed by the chief executive officer or other executive branch official of the state, by the state legislature, or by both.[361]

§ 19.17 NATIONAL RAILROAD RETIREMENT INVESTMENT TRUST

Federal income tax law provides tax exemption for the National Railroad Retirement Investment Trust, which was established by enactment of the Railroad Retirement Act of 1974.[362]

§ 19.18 QUALIFIED HEALTH INSURANCE ISSUERS

Federal income tax law provides tax exemption for qualified nonprofit health insurance issuers.[363] In general, this type of organization is one that has received

---

[356] IRC § 501(c)(27)(B)(i).

[357] IRC § 501(c)(27)(A)(i).

[358] IRC § 501(c)(27)(B)(ii).

[359] IRC § 501(c)(27)(B)(iii)(I).

[360] IRC § 501(c)(27)(B)(iii)(II).

[361] IRC § 501(c)(27)(B)(iv). Inasmuch as this basis for exemption is effective only for tax years beginning after 1997, these organizations may be able to qualify as a form of exempt quasi-governmental entity (see § 19.22) in prior years, although in one instance the IRS took the position that status as a political subdivision was not available (Field Serv. Adv. 200041007).

[362] IRC § 501(c)(28).

[363] IRC § 501(c)(29), added by the Patient Protection and Affordable Care Act (as to this section, Act) (Pub. L. No. 111-148, § 1322(h), 124 Stat. 119, 191 (2010)).

a loan or grant under the Consumer Operated and Oriented Plan (CO-OP) program[364] but only with respect to periods for which the issuer is in compliance with the requirements of that program[365] and any agreement with respect to the loan or grant. In addition, to be exempt, the issuer must seek recognition of exemption from the IRS,[366] be in compliance with the private inurement doctrine,[367] not engage in legislative activities to a substantial extent,[368] and not participate in or intervene in political campaigns on behalf of or in opposition to candidates for public office.[369]

The aspects of the CO-OP program that fall outside the tax law are administered by the Department of Health and Human Services, which has published a rule to implement the program.[370] There is to be at least one CO-OP in every state in order to expand the number of health plans available in Affordable Insurance Exchanges. There may be funding for multiple CO-OPs in a state, if there is sufficient funding to foster the creation of a CO-OP in each state; $3.8 billion has been authorized for this program.

The executive summary of the rules states that individuals and small businesses will be able to purchase health insurance through the Exchanges (which the summary terms "state-based competitive marketplaces"). The summary states that the Exchanges will "offer Americans competition, choice, and clout . . . . Insurance companies will compete for business on a level playing field, driving down costs" and "[c]onsumers will have a choice of health plans to fit their needs."

These rules set forth eligibility standards for the CO-OP program, establish terms for the loans, and provide basic standards that organizations must meet to participate in the program and become a CO-OP. A CO-OP will be expected to implement policies and procedures to ensure member control (by a majority) of the organization. The members will select a board of directors in a contested election. Each director must meet ethical, conflict-of-interest, and disclosure standards, "protecting against insurance industry involvement and interference." A CO-OP will have to "operate with a strong consumer focus, including timeliness, responsiveness, and accountability to members." These entities must "demonstrate financial viability and the ability to meet all other statutory, legal, or other requirements." An organization that was an insurance issuer on July 16, 2009, is ineligible for this classification.

---

[364] This CO-OP program was established by enactment of Act § 1322(a)(1).

[365] The purpose of the CO-OP program is to foster the creation of qualified nonprofit health insurance issuers to offer qualified health plans in the individual and small group markets in the states in which the issuers are licensed to offer the plans (Act § 1322(a)(2)).

[366] See § 26.8. Also, Rev. Proc. 2015-17, 2015-7 I.R.B. 599, which provides information regarding procedures for organizations seeking to qualify for exemption as qualified nonprofit health insurance issuers (Rev. Proc. 2024-5, 2024-1 I.R.B. 262 §§ 2.02(3), 6.08(3)).

[367] See Chapter 20.

[368] See Chapter 22.

[369] See Chapter 23.

[370] 45 C.F.R. Part 156 (76 Fed Reg. 77392 (2011)).

§ 19.19 QUALIFIED TUITION PROGRAMS

Tax-exempt status is accorded certain types of *qualified tuition programs*.[371] States may be the sponsors of *college savings plans* or may offer *prepaid tuition plans*. Eligible private institutions of higher education may offer the second type of qualified tuition programs.

(a) State-Sponsored Programs

State-sponsored tuition programs include programs established and maintained by a state (or an agency or instrumentality of a state) under which individuals may (1) purchase tuition credits or certificates on behalf of a designated beneficiary that entitle the beneficiary to the waiver or payment of qualified higher education expenses of the beneficiary or (2) make contributions to an account that is established for the sole purpose of meeting qualified higher education expenses of the designated beneficiary of the account.[372] The phrase *qualified higher education expenses* means tuition, fees, and outlays for books, supplies, and equipment (including computer or peripheral equipment, computer software, and Internet access and related services) required for the enrollment or attendance at a college, university, or certain vocational schools.[373]

  This type of program must provide that purchases or contributions may be made only in cash.[374] Contributors and beneficiaries are not allowed to direct any investments made on their behalf by the program more than two times in any calendar year.[375] The program is required to maintain a separate accounting for each designated beneficiary.[376] A specified individual must be designated as the beneficiary at the commencement of participation in a qualified tuition program (that is, when contributions are first made to purchase an interest in the program), unless interests in the program are purchased by a state or local government or a tax-exempt charitable organization as part of a scholarship program operated by the government or charity under which beneficiaries to be named in the future will receive the interests as scholarships.[377] A transfer of credits (or other amounts) from one account benefiting one designated beneficiary to another account benefiting a different beneficiary is considered a distribution (as is a change in the designated beneficiary of an interest in a qualified tuition program) unless the beneficiaries are members of the same family.[378]

  Earnings on an account may be refunded to a contributor or beneficiary, but the state or instrumentality must impose a more than *de minimis* monetary penalty unless the refund is used for qualified higher education expenses of the beneficiary, made on account of the death or disability of the beneficiary, or made on

---

[371] IRC § 529(a).

[372] IRC § 529(b)(1).

[373] IRC § 529(e)(3).

[374] IRC § 529(b)(2).

[375] IRC § 529(b)(4).

[376] IRC § 529(b)(3).

[377] IRC § 529(e)(1). An interest in a qualified tuition program is not regarded as a debt for purposes of the unrelated debt-financed income rules (see § 24.10) (IRC § 529(e)(4)).

[378] The phrase *member of the family* is defined in IRC § 529(e)(2).

account of a scholarship received by the designated beneficiary to the extent the amount refunded does not exceed the amount of the scholarship used for higher education expenses.[379] These programs may not allow any interest in the program or any portion of it to be used as security for a loan.[380]

A program cannot be treated as a qualified tuition program unless it provides adequate safeguards to prevent contributions on behalf of a designated beneficiary in excess of those necessary to provide for the qualified higher education expenses of the beneficiary.[381]

(b)   Educational Institution–Sponsored Programs

Pursuant to this body of law as originally enacted, these tuition programs could be established and maintained only by a state or an agency or instrumentality of a state. Prepaid tuition plans, however, now may be established and maintained by eligible educational institutions, including private institutions.[382] In order for a tuition program of a private eligible educational institution to be a qualified tuition program, assets of the program must be held in a *qualified trust*.[383] This is a trust that is organized in the United States for the exclusive benefit of designated beneficiaries, where its trustee is a bank or other person or entity that demonstrates that it will administer the trust in accordance with certain requirements; the assets of the trust may not be commingled with other property except in a common trust fund or common investment fund.[384] The tuition program of a private educational institution must receive a determination from the IRS that the program meets these requirements.[385]

(c)   Other Rules

Amounts from qualified tuition programs can be distributed, up to $10,000, for tuition incurred during a tax year in connection with the enrollment or attendance of a designated beneficiary at a public, private, or religious elementary or secondary school.[386]

In general, no amount is includable in the gross income of a designated beneficiary under a qualified tuition program or a contributor to the program on behalf of a designated beneficiary with respect to any distribution or earnings under the program.[387] A contribution to a qualified tuition program on behalf of a designated

---

[379] IRC § 529(b)(3).

[380] IRC § 529(b)(5).

[381] IRC § 529(b)(6).

[382] IRC § 529(b)(1). The term *eligible educational institution* means an institution described in section 481 of the Higher Education Act of 1965 (20 U.S.C. 1088), as in effect on June 7, 2001, and that is eligible to participate in Department of Education student aid programs (IRC § 529(e)(5)). These institutions generally are accredited postsecondary educational institutions offering credit toward an associate's, bachelor's, graduate-level, or professional degree, another recognized postsecondary credential, and certain proprietary institutions and postsecondary vocational institutions (Prop. Reg. § 1.529-1(c)).

[383] IRC § 529(b)(1).

[384] IRC § 408(a)(2), (5).

[385] IRC § 529(b)(1).

[386] IRC § 529(c)(7), (e)(3)(A).

[387] IRC § 529(c)(1). The IRS clarified in an information letter that an employer may make a contribution on behalf of an employee or an employee's family member to a qualified tuition program (subject to

beneficiary is not a taxable gift.[388] A distribution under a qualified tuition program not made for qualified higher educational expenses is includable in the gross income of the distributee in the manner as prescribed under the annuity taxation rules[389] to the extent not excluded from gross income under other federal tax law.[390] Thus, if matching-grant amounts are distributed to or on behalf of a beneficiary as part of a qualified tuition program, the matching grant amounts still may be excluded from the gross income of the beneficiary as a scholarship.[391]

An exclusion from gross income is provided, however, for distributions from qualified state tuition programs to the extent that the distribution is used to pay for qualified higher education expenses. This exclusion from gross income was extended to distribution from qualified tuition programs established and maintained by an entity other than a state (or agency or instrumentality of a state).[392]

In the case of a designated beneficiary who receives a refund of any higher education expenses, any distribution that was used to pay the refunded expenses is not subject to tax if the beneficiary recontributes the refunded amount to the qualified tuition program within 60 days of receiving the refund, only to the extent that the recontribution is not in excess of the refund.[393]

Amounts contributed to a qualified tuition program (and earnings on those amounts) are included in the contributor's estate for federal estate tax purposes in the event that the contributor dies before the amounts are distributed under the program.[394]

The IRS issues private letter rulings on an ongoing basis as to plans that do or do not qualify as qualified tuition programs.[395] The IRS approved a prepaid tuition plan structured for participation by private colleges and universities throughout the United States; it is organized as a limited liability company,[396] with the institutions functioning as members pursuant to a consortium agreement.[397] The IRS subsequently ruled that, when an institution of higher education receives a distribution from the plan of proceeds reflecting a "tuition certificate" in consideration for the provision of educational services to a qualified beneficiary, the proceeds will not be unrelated business income[398] to the institution.[399]

---

the IRC § 529(b)(6) contribution limit), with the contribution treated as a taxable fringe benefit to the employee and deductible as wages or compensation by the employer (INFO 2023-0007).

[388] IRC § 529(c)(2).

[389] IRC § 72.

[390] IRC § 529(c)(3).

[391] H.R. Rep. 104-737 (1996).

[392] IRC § 529(c)(3)(B).

[393] IRC § 529(c)(3)(D).

[394] IRC § 529(c)(4). The proposed regulations concerning these programs issued in 1998 have yet to be finalized. The IRS provided interim guidance regarding the restriction on investment direction (see text accompanied by *supra* note 375) (Notice 2001-55, 2001-39 I.R.B. 299 and Notice 2009-1, 2009-2 I.R.B. 250) and guidance on changes to record keeping, reporting, and other requirements applicable to these programs (Notice 2001-81, 2001-52 I.R.B. 617).

[395] E.g., Priv. Ltr. Rul. 9812037.

[396] See § 4.3(e).

[397] Priv. Ltr. Rul. 200311034.

[398] See Chapters 24, 25.

[399] Priv. Ltr. Rul. 200313024. The Congressional Research Service published a report titled "Saving for College Through Qualified Tuition (Section 529) Programs" (September 13, 2010). Thereafter, the CRS

§ 19.20   ABLE PROGRAMS

One of the newest categories of tax-exempt organization, modeled somewhat on the state-sponsored qualified tuition program,[400] is the qualified ABLE Program.[401] This is a program established and maintained by a state, or agency or instrumentality of a state, under which a person may make contributions for a tax year, for the benefit of an eligible individual, to an ABLE account that is established for the purpose of meeting the qualified disability expenses of the designated beneficiary of the account.[402] The term *ABLE account* means an account established by an eligible individual, owned by the individual, and maintained under a qualified ABLE program.[403]

A designated beneficiary may have only one ABLE account.[404] A beneficiary is not required to be a resident of the state that established the account. An interest in an ABLE program may not be pledged as security for a loan.[405]

An *eligible individual* is an individual entitled to benefits based on blindness or disability under the Social Security Act, where the blindness or disability occurred before the date on which the individual attained age 26,[406] or a disability certification[407] with respect to the individual is filed with the IRS.[408] A *designated beneficiary* in connection with an ABLE account established under a qualified ABLE program is the eligible individual who established an ABLE account and is the owner of the account.[409] The term *qualified disability expenses* means expenses related to the eligible individual's blindness or disability that are made for the benefit of an eligible individual who is the designated beneficiary, including expenses for education, housing, transportation, health, financial management services, and legal fees.[410]

Contributions to an ABLE account generally must be in the form of money.[411] There is an annual per account funding limit equal to the annual gift tax exclusion.[412] A qualified ABLE program must provide a separate accounting for each designated beneficiary.[413] A beneficiary may, directly or indirectly, direct the

---

published a report titled "Tax-Preferred College Savings Plans: An Introduction to 529 Plans" (November 2, 2012).

[400] See § 19.19(a).

[401] IRC § 529A(a); Reg. §§ 1.529A-1(a), 1.511-2(e), 1.529A-2. This acronym is in reference to the Achieving a Better Life Experience Act of 2014, Pub. L. 113-295, div. B, 128 Stat. 4010, 4056.

[402] IRC § 529A(b)(1)(A).

[403] IRC § 529A(e)(6).

[404] IRC § 529A(b)(1)(B). This type of account is defined in IRC § 529A(e)(6).

[405] IRC § 529A(b)(5).

[406] For tax years beginning after December 31, 2025, this age limitation is increased to age 46 (Secure 2.0 Act of 2022, enacted as part of the Consolidated Appropriations Act, 2023, Pub. L. No. 117-328, div. T, tit. I, § 124, 136 Stat. 4459, 5314).

[407] IRC § 529A(e)(2).

[408] IRC § 529A(e)(1).

[409] IRC § 529A(e)(3).

[410] IRC § 529A(e)(5).

[411] IRC § 529A(b)(2)(A).

[412] IRC § 529A(b)(2)(B).

[413] IRC § 529A(b)(3).

investment of contributions to the program, and earnings thereon, no more than two times in any calendar year.[414] Distributions from a qualified program are not includible in the beneficiary's gross income to the extent they do not exceed the amount of qualified disability expenses.[415]

Each officer or employee having control of the qualified ABLE program or their designee must make reports regarding the program to the IRS and to designated beneficiaries with respect to matters such as contributions, distributions, and the return of excess contributions.[416] For research purposes, the IRS must make available to the public reports containing aggregate information, by diagnosis and other relevant characteristics, on contributions and distributions from qualified ABLE programs.[417]

§ 19.21 PROFESSIONAL SPORTS LEAGUES

Tax exemption is available for professional football leagues.[418] This category of exemption exists to forestall a claim that an exempt football league's pension plan is a means of conferring private inurement to individuals.[419] This addition to the law was enacted as part of a larger legislative package that facilitated a merger that created an "industry-wide" professional football league.[420] This category of exemption has been extended to other categories of professional sports leagues.[421]

§ 19.22 GOVERNMENTAL AND QUASI-GOVERNMENTAL ENTITIES

The concept of federal tax exemption extends to a variety of governmental and quasi-governmental entities. These entities range from the states to nonprofit organizations that have a unique relationship with one or more governmental departments, agencies, and/or instrumentalities. There are essentially four ways an organization can achieve tax exemption or its equivalent in this context: (1) by constituting a state or political subdivision of a state; (2) by reason of having its income excluded from federal income taxation, when the income is derived from the exercise of an essential governmental function and the income accrues to a state or a political subdivision of the state; (3) by reason of being an integral part

---

[414] IRC § 529A(b)(4).

[415] IRC § 529A(c)(1)(B)(i); Reg. § 1.529A-3. Amounts from qualified tuition programs (see § 19.19) can be rolled over to an ABLE account, without penalty, provided that the ABLE account is owned by the designated beneficiary or a member of the beneficiary's family (IRC § 529(c)(3)(C)(i)(III)). This provision is currently set to expire on December 31, 2025 (see Staff of Joint Comm. on Taxation, List of Expiring Federal Tax Provisions 2024-2034 9 (Comm. Print JCX-1-24)).

[416] IRC § 529A(d)(1); Reg. § 1.529A-6.

[417] IRC § 529A(d)(2).

[418] IRC § 501(c)(6).

[419] Nat'l Muffler Dealers Ass'n v. United States, 440 U.S. 472 (1979).

[420] Id.; Gen. Couns. Mem. 37595.

[421] Gen. Couns. Mem. 38179; e.g., Priv. Ltr. Rul. 9040030.

of a state, city, or similar governmental entity; or (4) by classification as an instrumentality of a state.

(a)   Intergovernmental Immunity

The states, the District of Columbia, and U.S. territories are, in a loose sense of the term, tax-exempt entities. This tax exemption does not derive from any specific provision in the federal tax statutory law, but rather is a consequence of the doctrine of *intergovernmental immunity*—the doctrine implicit in the U.S. Constitution that the federal government will not tax the states.

This tax exemption extends not only to the states as such but to component parts thereof: political subdivisions, instrumentalities, agencies, and other integral parts. These entities are sometimes referred to as *governmental units*.[422] The general principle is that the "United States may not tax instrumentalities which a state may employ in the discharge of her essential governmental duties."[423] The IRS recognizes this general principle,[424] albeit with the caveat that it may be superseded by a specific statutory authorization of taxation.[425]

The constitutional law basis for this tax exemption is not unlimited; however, its scope has not been delineated. The position of the U.S. Supreme Court initially was that all "governmental" functions of a state were encompassed by the exemption and that only its "proprietary" activities could be taxed by the federal government.[426] Subsequently, the Court ruled that Congress could tax any "source of revenue by whomsoever earned and not uniquely capable of being earned only by a State," even though the tax "incidence falls also on a State."[427] Apparently, the *uniquely capable* test remains the standard.[428]

The IRS, though it had for some time been regularly issuing private letter rulings concerning organizations that do or do not qualify for tax exemption by reason of the intergovernmental immunity doctrine,[429] has ceased doing so.[430]

(b)   Income Exclusion Rule

Notwithstanding the existence of this constitutional law tax exemption, Congress in 1913 enacted a provision providing a statutory immunity from taxation in the form of an exclusion from gross income. In its relevant portions, this statutory immunity is available only for entities that exercise an *essential governmental function*, and where the income thereby generated accrues to a state or political subdivision of the state.[431] The IRS has long maintained that, by enacting the statutory

---

[422] E.g., IRC §§ 170(b)(1)(A)(v), 170(c)(1). See §§ 7.15, 12.3(a).

[423] Helvering v. Therrell, 303 U.S. 218, 223 (1938).

[424] Rev. Rul. 87-2, 1987-1 C.B. 18; Rev. Rul. 71-132, 1971-1 C.B. 29; Rev. Rul. 71-131, 1971-1 C.B. 28.

[425] E.g., IRC § 511(a)(2)(B). See § 24.1, text accompanied by note 22.

[426] South Carolina v. United States, 199 U.S. 437 (1905).

[427] New York v. United States, 326 U.S. 572, 582 (1946).

[428] Massachusetts v. United States, 435 U.S. 44 (1978); Willmette Park Dist. v. Campbell, 388 U.S. 411 (1949). Cf. Davis v. Michigan Dept. of Treasury, 89-2 U.S.T.C. ¶ 9456 (Mich. Ct. App. 1989); State of S.C. v. Baker, 485 U.S. 505 (1988). Also, Flint v. Stone Tracy Co., 220 U.S. 107, 172 (1911).

[429] E.g., Priv. Ltr. Rul. 8842071.

[430] The most recent private letter ruling on this subject is Priv. Ltr. Rul. 200238001.

[431] IRC § 115(1).

immunity, "Congress did not desire in any way to restrict a State's participation in enterprises which might be useful in carrying out those projects desirable from the standpoint of the State Government."[432] This body of law applies with respect to a governmental entity that is separately organized from a state or political subdivision of a state.[433]

Thus, the IRS ruled that the income of an investment fund established by a state was excludable from gross income; even though more than one governmental entity participated in the fund, the requisite accrual was found.[434] Likewise, the IRS held that the income of an organization formed, operated, and funded by one or more political subdivisions (or by a state and one or more political subdivisions) to pool their risks in lieu of purchasing insurance to cover their public liability, workers' compensation, or employees' health obligations was excluded from gross income, as long as private interests did not, except for incidental benefits to employees of the participating state and political subdivisions, participate in or benefit from the organization.[435] Similarly, this status was accorded an integrated faculty group practice corporation, formed to deliver high-quality, cost-effective patient care, established by a state university and the state's teaching hospital facility to provide a more strategically, financially, and clinically integrated enterprise.[436]

As to the type of entity that can avail itself of the broader immunity based on income accruing to a state, it appears that only a state or political subdivision of a state, and not a private corporation, may invoke this immunity, because only the former can perform an essential governmental function. The courts have reached this conclusion, albeit for a different reason—namely, on the theory that the interposition of a corporation operates to prevent the requisite *accrual* from taking place.[437] These analyses, however, leave unanswered the question of whether a corporation, such as a nonprofit one, can qualify for federal tax purposes as a political subdivision. The answer to this question has several ramifications, not the least of which is the ability of this type of entity to incur debt the interest on which is excludable from the recipient's gross income.[438]

In its narrowest sense, the term *political subdivision* connotes a jurisdictional or geographical component of a state, such as counties, cities, and sewer districts. Perhaps a more realistic definition of the term was provided by a federal court of

---

[432] Rev. Rul. 77-261, 1977-2 C.B. 45.

[433] That is, IRC § 115(1) does not apply to income from an activity that the state conducts directly, rather than through a separate entity (Rev. Rul. 71-131, 1971-1 C.B. 28; Rev. Rul. 77-261, 1977-2 C.B. 45). Income accruing to a state or political subdivision resulting from its own participation in activities, rather than from an entity engaged in the performance of an essential governmental function, is excluded from gross income pursuant to the doctrine of intergovernmental immunity (see § 19.22(a); e.g., Priv. Ltr. Rul. 8832056). Income accruing to the government of any possession of the United States, or any political subdivision thereof, is excluded from gross income under IRC § 115(2) (e.g., Priv. Ltr. Rul. 202405002).

[434] Rev. Rul. 77-261, 1977-2 C.B. 45, *as clarified by* (on another point) Rev. Rul. 78-316, 1978-2 C.B. 304.

[435] Rev. Rul. 90-74, 1990-2 C.B. 34.

[436] Priv. Ltr. Rul. 201528010.

[437] E.g., Troy State Univ. v. Comm'r, 62 T.C. 493 (1974).

[438] IRC § 103. The U.S. Supreme Court ruled that the federal income tax exemption for mutual bond interest is not mandated by the Tenth Amendment to the U.S. Constitution or by the doctrine of intergovernmental immunity (South Carolina v. Baker, 485 U.S. 505 (1988)).

appeals: The term *political subdivision* is broad and comprehensive, and denotes any division of a state made by the proper authorities thereof, acting within their constitutional powers, for the purpose of carrying out a portion of these functions of the state that by long usage and the inherent necessities of government have always been regarded as public.[439]

The term *political subdivision* has been defined as denoting a division of a state or local governmental unit that is a municipal corporation or that has been delegated the right to exercise part of the sovereign power of the unit.[440] Under that definition, a political subdivision of a state or local governmental unit may or may not include special assessment districts so created, such as road, water, sewer, gas, light, reclamation, drainage, irrigation, levee, school, harbor, port improvement, and similar districts and divisions of these units.[441] The three generally acknowledged sovereign powers are the power to tax, the power of eminent domain, and the police power.[442]

An entity may nonetheless be a *division* of a state without being a political subdivision. In that determination, consideration is given to factors that indicate that it will be a governmental rather than a private entity. These factors include its public purposes and attributes, whether its assets or income will inure to private interests,[443] and the degree of control by the state.[444] For example, the IRS ruled that an association formed by state statute to fund no-fault compensation for certain medical procedures was not a political subdivision of the state because it was not delegated the right to exercise a sovereign power, yet was a division of the state because it was established for a "public purpose," its plan was funded by the state, it was granted sovereign immunity, its board is appointed by the state's chief financial officer, and it is operated in accordance with a plan of operation approved by a department of the state.[445] The IRS also ruled that an employee benefit fund, although it could not qualify for exemption as a social welfare organization (in part because it was not serving a community),[446] was an instrumentality of the state involved and its income derived from an essential governmental function, so that its income is excludible under this rule.[447]

These considerations take on greater coloration when applied in the context of organizations that are state-owned but have charitable organization counterparts, such as state schools, colleges, universities, hospitals, and libraries.[448]

---

[439] Comm'r v. Estate of Shamberg, 3 T.C. 131 (1944), *aff'd*, 144 F.2d 998 (2d Cir. 1944), *cert. denied*, 323 U.S. 792 (1944). Cf. Rev. Rul. 76-550, 1976-2 C.B. 331; Rev. Rul. 76-549, 1976-2 C.B. 330. Also, Crilly v. Southeastern Pa. Transp. Auth., 529 F.2d 1355 (3d Cir. 1976); Popkin v. New York State Health & Mental Hygiene Facilities Improvement Corp., 409 F. Supp. 430 (S.D.N.Y. 1976).

[440] Reg. § 1.103-1(b).

[441] Rev. Rul. 78-276, 1978-2 C.B. 256.

[442] Comm'r v. Estate of Shamberg, 3 T.C. 131 (1944), *aff'd*, 144 F.2d 998 (2d Cir. 1944), *cert. denied*, 323 U.S. 792 (1944).

[443] See Chapter 20.

[444] E.g., Rev. Rul. 83-131, 1983-2 C.B. 184.

[445] Priv. Ltr. Rul. 201050017.

[446] See § 13.2.

[447] Priv. Ltr. Rul. 201710034.

[448] See Chapters 7, 8.

Certainly these entities are generally exempt from tax; the tax exemption derives in part from the constitutional immunity accorded the revenue of integral units of states. The exemption may likewise be traced to this statutory immunity. Presumably, there is the requisite accrual; for example, the provision of education has been regarded as the exercise of an essential governmental function.[449] By contrast, courts have held that, under certain circumstances, operation of a hospital is not an essential governmental function.[450] There is no case that specifically holds that, for example, a state college or university is a political subdivision, although this conclusion may be reached by a process of negative implication.[451] The IRS, however, asserted that a state university cannot qualify as a political subdivision because it fails to possess a substantial right to exercise the power to tax, the power of eminent domain, or the police power.[452]

The IRS issues private letter rulings on an ongoing basis as to organizations that do or do not qualify as entities eligible for the exclusion.[453]

(c) Integral Parts of States

As noted,[454] one way for an organization to qualify for this type of tax-exempt status is to be an integral part of a state (or political subdivision of a state). Generally, income earned by an enterprise that is an integral part of a state (or political subdivision thereof) is not subject to federal income taxation in the absence of specific statutory authorization to tax that income. If an enterprise is deemed to be an integral part of a state (or political subdivision), that enterprise will not be treated as a separate entity for federal tax purposes. By contrast, when a state conducts an enterprise through a separate entity, the income of the entity may be excluded from gross income.[455]

---

[449] Page v. Regents of Univ. Sys. of Ga., 93 F.2d 887 (5th Cir. 1937), *rev. on other grounds sub nom.*, Allen v. Regents of the Univ. Sys. of Ga., 304 U.S. 339 (1938).

[450] Liggett & Myers Tobacco Co. v. United States, 13 F. Supp. 143 (Ct. Cl. 1936), *aff'd*, 299 U.S. 383 (1937), *reh'g denied*, 300 U.S. 686 (1937); Cook v. United States, 26 F. Supp. 253 (D. Mass. 1939).

[451] Troy State Univ. v. Comm'r, 62 T.C. 493 (1974); Iowa State Univ. of Science & Technology v. United States, 500 F.2d 508 (Ct. Cl. 1974).

[452] Rev. Rul. 77-165, 1977-1 C.B. 21. In Tech. Adv. Mem. 8119061, the IRS held that a state university was not a political subdivision of the state (for purposes of eligibility for the interest exclusion for the university's obligations) because the university possessed no more than an insubstantial part of any sovereign power. The university did not have the power to tax or the power of eminent domain, and the IRS concluded that the possession of certain powers to promulgate and enforce regulations in the areas of health and safety on the university's campus did not constitute the police power (citing Manigault v. Springs, 119 U.S. 473 (1905); Barbier v. Connelly, 113 U.S. 27 (1885)). The IRS noted that the campus police operated at the university under a scope of authority defined by state law rather than by the university and that the campus police had the power to make arrests only for violations of the state's criminal law and not for violations of the university's rules and regulations that are not criminal in nature. The university also failed with its argument that the interest on its obligations should be tax-excludable because the obligations were issued "on behalf of" the state (principally inasmuch as the university was a state instrumentality and a land grant institution), with the IRS determining that the requisite degree of control by the state was absent, in that fewer than one-third of the university's board of trustees were government officials or appointees of the governor of the state (see § 7.15).

[453] E.g., Priv. Ltr. Rul. 202102003.

[454] See § 19.22(a).

[455] See § 19.22(b).

The IRS ruled that a trust fund created by a state supreme court to hold amounts advanced to lawyers in the state by their clients was an integral part of the state.[456] This ruling was based on the state court's creation of the fund and its ability to select and remove the fund's governing body, to control the fund's investments and expenditures, to monitor the fund's daily operation, and to abolish the fund.

In one case, a state formed a corporation to insure the customer accounts of state-chartered savings and loan associations. Under this entity's charter, the full faith and credit of the state was not pledged for the organization's operations. State officials selected only 3 of 11 directors. The trial court rejected the organization's claim of intergovernmental tax immunity because the state did not make any financial contribution to the entity and did not have a present interest in its income. Thus, it was held that the imposition of the federal income tax on this corporation would not burden the state. The U.S. Supreme Court, though it reversed the decision on other grounds, agreed with the lower court's analysis on this point.[457]

The rules as to whether an entity is a political subdivision, instrumentality, agency, or integral part of a state continue to become more inconsistent and confusing. A court of appeals evaluated the tax status of an organization established to receive advance payments of college tuition, invest the money, and ultimately make disbursements under a program that allows its beneficiaries to attend any of the state's public colleges and universities without further tuition cost. The appellate court, having found that the entity was an instrumentality of the state, concluded that it was also an integral part of the state, so that its investment income was not taxable.[458] The court ruled that a state or political subdivision of a state is not a corporation for purposes of the federal corporate income tax.[459] It wrote that the "broad constitutional immunity from federal taxation once thought to be enjoyed by states and their instrumentalities has been severely eroded by the passage of time."[460] As to the law concerning the exclusion from taxation of income accruing to the state, the court characterized the rules as "very old and somewhat cryptic."[461]

An organization created in the aftermath of a major hurricane as a vehicle for property and casualty insurers to share insurance coverage for property owners unable to obtain coverage in the "voluntary" market was held to be an integral

---

[456] Rev. Rul. 87-2, 1987-1 C.B. 18. Also, Rev. Rul. 71-131, 1971-1 C.B. 28.

[457] Maryland Sav.-Share Ins. Corp. v. United States, 308 F. Supp. 761 (D. Md. 1970), *rev'd on other grounds*, 400 U.S. 4 (1970).

[458] Michigan v. United States, 40 F.3d 817 (6th Cir. 1994). The district court in this case ruled that this entity was not tax-exempt under the doctrine of intergovernmental immunity because it was not an integral part of the state and that its income could not be excluded from taxation pursuant to IRC § 115 because there was no accrual of income to the state (Michigan v. United States, 802 F. Supp. 120 (W.D. Mich. 1992)).

[459] IRC § 11.

[460] Michigan v. United States, 40 F.3d 817, 822 (6th Cir. 1994).

[461] *Id.* at 829. Further confusing aspects of this opinion include the court's reliance on Rev. Rul. 57-128, 1957-1 C.B. 311 (see § 7.15), which applies to entities that are separate from a state (see § 19.22(d)); the factors enumerated in the revenue ruling do not determine whether an enterprise is a separate entity or an integral part of a state. Also, Rose v. Long Island R.R. Pension Plan, 828 F.2d 910 (2d Cir. 1987). Subsequently, a statutory basis for tax-exempt status for tuition programs of this nature was enacted (see § 19.19).

part of a state.[462] The court considered the factors used in this context by the IRS to determine instrumentality status,[463] and concluded that the organization "bears a much closer resemblance to being an integral part of the state than to being a private insurance company."[464] The court also noted the state's financial commitment to the enterprise. Overall, wrote the court, the "determinative test with respect to the financial arrangements" regarding this organization is "whether it is the [s]tate or the participating private insurance companies who ultimately may profit from its operations, and the undisputed evidence is that only the state may receive any financial benefit."[465]

The check-the-box regulations support the position that an entity that is recognized as separate from a state (or political subdivision) for local law purposes may nonetheless be an integral part of that state (or political subdivision). These regulations state: "An entity formed under local law is not always recognized as a separate entity for federal tax purposes. For example, an organization wholly owned by a State is not recognized as a separate entity for federal tax purposes if it is an integral part of the State."[466]

The policy of the IRS, in determining whether an enterprise is an integral part of a state, is to consider all the facts and circumstances, including the state's degree of control over the enterprise and the state's financial commitment to the enterprise. For example, a multiemployer insurance program established by a state, when the participants include the state and its political subdivisions, was held to be an integral part of the state because the state exerted significant control and influence over the program and the state made a substantial financial commitment to the program.[467] Also, an entity established by legislation to educate the citizens of a state about a historical event was found to be an integral part of the state, because the state exerted significant control over and made a substantial financial commitment to the entity.[468] Likewise, a nonprofit public corporation formed by a state legislature for the purpose of insuring the existence of an orderly market of types of insurance offered by two plans for state residents and businesses was held to be an integral part of the state because the entity was to be supervised and controlled by the state and the state was to exercise a significant degree of control over it.[469]

(d) State Instrumentalities

The IRS rarely issues rulings that an entity is tax-exempt by reason of being an instrumentality of a state.[470] An entity can, however, have its income excluded from taxation because it exercises an essential governmental function and its income

---

[462] Florida Residential Property & Casualty Joint Underwriting Ass'n v. United States, 2002-1 U.S.T.C. ¶ 50,280 (N.D. Fla. 2002).

[463] Rev. Rul. 57-128, 1957-1 C.B. 311.

[464] Florida Residential Property & Casualty Joint Underwriting Ass'n v. United States, 2002-1 U.S.T.C. ¶ 50,280 (N.D. Fla. 2002).

[465] Id. at 83,641.

[466] Reg. § 301.7701-1(a)(3). See § 4.1(b)(ii), text accompanied by note 28.

[467] Priv. Ltr. Rul. 200210024.

[468] Priv. Ltr. Rul. 200307065.

[469] Priv. Ltr. Rul. 200427016.

[470] E.g., Priv. Ltr. Rul. 9424024.

accrues to a state or political subdivision,[471] and be classified as an instrumentality of a state for other purposes.[472]

The IRS takes the following factors into account in determining whether an entity is an instrumentality of one or more governmental units: whether the organization is used for a governmental purpose and performs a governmental function; whether performance of its function is on behalf of one or more states or political subdivisions; whether any private interests are involved or whether the states or political subdivisions have the power and interests of an owner; whether control and supervision of the organization are vested in a public authority or authorities; whether express or implied statutory or other authority is necessary for the creation and/or use of the organization, and whether this authority exists; and the degree of financial autonomy of the entity and the source of its operating expenses.[473] The IRS used these criteria in ruling, for example, that a charter school did not qualify as a state instrumentality.[474]

(e)   Related Considerations

Some governmental entities are tax-exempt because they have a clear counterpart in the conventional realm of tax-exempt organizations.[475] Some organizations are exempt because they are instrumentalities of the federal government.[476] A governmental unit can qualify as a public charity.[477] Exempt organizations can be excused from the requirement of filing an annual information return if they can be classified as an affiliate of a governmental unit.[478]

This aspect of the law of tax-exempt organizations has become somewhat of a jumble, if only because of the variety and inconsistency of the nomenclature: a state, city, and similar governmental entity; political subdivision; governmental department, agency, and/or instrumentality; clear counterpart entity; governmental unit; and affiliate of a governmental unit.

§ 19.23   NATIVE AMERICAN TRIBES

Native American tribes generally are not taxable entities for federal income tax purposes.[479] These tribes generally have governing instruments, a council, operational

---

[471] See § 19.22(b).

[472] Other purposes for which an entity may be classified as an instrumentality of a state or political subdivision include the income exclusion for state or local bond interest (IRC § 103) (e.g., Priv. Ltr. Rul. 200314024), the deductibility of contributions to the entity (IRC § 170(c)(1) (e.g., Priv. Ltr. Rul. 200530016), or the federal unemployment tax exemption (IRC § 3306(c)(7)) (e.g., Priv. Ltr. Rul. 200428021).

[473] Rev. Rul. 57-128, 1957-1 C.B. 311.

[474] Priv. Ltr. Rul. 201519027.

[475] See § 7.15.

[476] See § 19.1.

[477] See § 12.3(a).

[478] See § 28.2(c)(iii).

[479] Rev. Rul. 67-284, 1967-2 C.B. 55, *modified on another issue*, Rev. Rul. 74-13, 1974-1 C.B. 14. Cf. Lummi Indian Tribe v. Whatcom Cnty., Wash., 5 F.3d 1355 (9th Cir. 1993) (real property of a tribe was held to not be exempt from state property tax).

rules, a formal membership arrangement, and various governmental powers, such as the rights to levy taxes, enact ordinances, and maintain a police force. The assets of an Indian tribe are owned by the tribe as a community (rather than by the individual members), and the right to participate in the enjoyment of tribal property depends on continuing membership in the tribe.[480]

Any income earned by an unincorporated tribe (including that from gambling and other commercial business activities), regardless of the location of the business activities that produced the income (that is, whether on or off the tribe's reservation), is not subject to federal income tax.[481] Tribal income not otherwise exempt from federal income tax is includable in the gross income of the Indian tribal member when distributed to, or constructively received by, the member.[482]

Native American tribal corporations organized under the Indian Reorganization Act of 1934[483] share the same tax status as the Native American tribe and are not taxable on income from activities carried on within the boundaries of the reservation.[484] Thus, any income earned by this type of corporation, regardless of the location of the business activities that produced the income, is not subject to federal income tax.[485] Tribal corporations organized under the Oklahoma Welfare Act[486] have the same tax status.[487]

A corporation organized by a Native American tribe under state law is not the same as a Native American tribal corporation organized under the Indian Reorganization Act and does not share the same tax status as the Native American tribe for federal income tax purposes. This type of corporation is subject to federal income tax on any income earned, regardless of the location of the income-producing activities.[488]

§ 19.24 OTHER CATEGORIES OF TAX-EXEMPT ORGANIZATIONS

There are several other types of organizations or entities that may be regarded as tax-exempt organizations in the broadest sense of the term.

---

[480] Gritts v. Fisher, 224 U.S. 640 (1912).

[481] Rev. Rul. 94-16, 1994-1 C.B. 19.

[482] Id. E.g., Beck v. Comm'r, 67 T.C.M. 2469 (1994) (income received by a member of the Eastern Band of Cherokee Indians from the rental of apartment buildings located on a Cherokee reservation was held to not be exempt from federal income taxation).

[483] 25 U.S.C. § 5124.

[484] Rev. Rul. 81-295, 1981-2 C.B. 15, which relied on Mescalero Apache Tribe v. Jones, 411 U.S. 145 (1973).

[485] Rev. Rul. 94-16, 1994-1 C.B. 19.

[486] 25 U.S.C. § 5203.

[487] Rev. Rul. 94-65, 1994-2 C.B. 14. Earlier law was clear that the fact that a Native American tribe was incorporated did not alter its federal tax status (Maryland Cas. Co. v. Citizens Nat'l Bank of W. Hollywood, 361 F.2d 517 (5th Cir. 1966), cert. denied, Maryland Cas. Co. v. Seminole Tribe of Fla., Inc., 385 U.S. 918 (1966); Parker Drilling Co. v. Metlakatla Indian Community, 451 F. Supp. 1127 (D. Alaska 1978); Rev. Rul. 81-295, 1981-2 C.B. 15).

[488] Rev. Rul. 94-16, 1994-1 C.B. 19. IRC § 7871 provides that a qualified Native American tribal government is treated as a state for certain federal income tax purposes, including the private foundation rules, unrelated business income rules, and the charitable contribution deductions. Although Native American tribal governments do not have an inherent exemption from federal excise taxes, the IRS

Some organizations are tax-exempt as a matter of practice, not because of any specific grant of exemption but because of the ability to utilize sufficient deductions to effectively eliminate taxation. As noted, this is the principle on which the general tax exemption for cooperatives is premised.[489] Likewise, a pooled income fund[490] is generally a nontaxpaying entity because it is entitled to a deduction for distributions to beneficiaries and for long-term capital gain set aside.[491] A charitable remainder trust[492] is an organization that is exempt from federal income tax, although it has to pay a tax in years in which it has unrelated business taxable income.[493] As discussed earlier, this approach also provides "tax exemption" for perpetual care trust funds operated in conjunction with taxable cemeteries.[494]

Other entities achieve federal income tax exemption because the law regards them as organizations that, while they may have to file tax returns, do not have taxable income but instead pass that liability on to others. It is this principle that operates to exempt partnerships,[495] small business ("S") corporations,[496] and limited liability companies[497] from federal income taxation.

§ 19.25   NONEXEMPT MEMBERSHIP ORGANIZATIONS

An organization can be a nonprofit entity without qualifying for tax exemption; an organization can be a nonprofit entity and not be tax-exempt even though it is eligible for exemption.[498] That is, a nonprofit organization can be a taxable organization. It is possible for a taxable organization to, in fact, not pay taxes because its deductible expenses are equal to or exceed its gross income. Indeed, occasionally, the management of a tax-exempt organization contemplates forfeiture of its exemption,[499] to avoid the regulatory requirements, believing that its expenses will offset its income.

Special rules apply, however, in situations where the nonprofit organization that is not exempt from federal income tax is a membership entity. Where this type of organization is operated primarily to furnish goods or services to its members, these rules allow deductions for a tax year attributable to the furnishing of services, insurance, goods, or other items of value to the organization's membership

issued a ruling, founded on IRC § 7871, granting limited exemptions from some of these taxes (Rev. Rul. 94-81, 1994-2 C.B. 412).

[489] See § 19.12.

[490] IRC § 642(c)(5). See *Charitable Giving*, Chapter 11.

[491] Reg. § 1.642(c)-5(a)(2).

[492] IRC § 664. See *Charitable Giving*, Chapter 10.

[493] This rule (IRC §§ 664(c)(1), (2)) is effective for years beginning after December 31, 2006; previously, tax exemption for these trusts was lost for years in which there was unrelated business taxable income (Reg. § 1.664-1(c)).

[494] See § 19.6. Also, IRC § 852(a) (concerning regulated investment companies).

[495] IRC § 701. See § 31.1(a).

[496] IRC § 1372.

[497] See §§ 4.1(b)(i), 32.3, 32.4.

[498] See § 1.1.

[499] See § 26.16.

only to the extent of income derived during the year from members or transactions with members (including income derived during the year from institutes and trade shows that are primarily for the education of members).[500, 501] If, in a tax year in these circumstances, deductions exceed income, the excess is treated as a deduction attributable to furnishing services, insurance, goods, or other items of value to members paid or incurred in the succeeding tax year.[502]

The purpose of these rules is to preclude a result earlier sanctioned by a federal court of appeals, which held that the investment income of a nonexempt water company could be offset by its losses in supplying water to its members.[503] (Other courts, however, were not permitting this result.)[504] That is, the rules prevent a taxable membership organization from offsetting its business and investment income with deductions created by the provision of related services to members. Stated another way, these rules are designed to cause taxable membership organizations to allocate and confine their deductions to the corresponding sources of income.[505] As a result, an organization that operated in a year at an overall loss may still have to pay tax if its unrelated business and investment activities produced net income. These rules are intended to deter the abandonment of tax-exempt status by membership organizations by entities that are serving their members at less than cost.[506]

The principal issue in this context pivots on the concept of *membership income*. The seminal court opinion on this point held that the term means only gross income *received directly* from an organization's members or transactions with members.[507] In that case, the court addressed the issue of whether interest income earned on statutorily mandated cash reserves held by a taxable membership organization was income derived from members or transactions with members for

---

[500] See § 25.2(f).

[501] IRC § 277(a).

[502] There are relatively narrow exceptions to this rule as provided by IRC § 277(b). For example, certain nonprofit membership organizations that receive prepaid dues income (such as the American Automobile Association) are not subject to the IRC § 277(a) restrictions on deductions (IRC §§ 277(b)(2), 456(c)). IRC § 277(a) is applicable to any nonexempt membership organization that otherwise meets the requirements of the section and was previously tax-exempt by reason of description in IRC § 501(c).

IRC § 277 does not apply to cooperatives subject to IRC subchapter T (IRC §§ 1381–1388) (Buckeye Countrymark, Inc. v. Comm'r, 103 T.C. 547 (1994); Landmark, Inc. v. United States, 25 Ct. Cl. 100 (1992)).

[503] Anaheim Union Water Co. v. Comm'r, 321 F.2d 253 (9th Cir. 1963), rev'g 35 T.C. 1972 (1961). (IRC § 277 was enacted in 1969.) Also, San Antonio Water Co. v. Riddell, 285 F. Supp. 297 (C.D. Cal. 1968), aff'd, 427 F.2d 713 (9th Cir. 1970); Bear Valley Mut. Water Co. v. Riddell, 283 F. Supp. 949 (C.D. Cal. 1968), aff'd, 427 F.2d 713 (9th Cir. 1970).

The IRS applied IRC § 277 to a nonprofit membership organization that failed to qualify for tax-exempt status, either as a social club (see Chapter 15) or as a homeowners' association (see § 19.14) (Priv. Ltr. Rul. 200528008).

[504] Adirondack League Club v. Comm'r, 55 T.C. 796 (1971), aff'd, 458 F.2d 506 (2d Cir. 1972); Five Lakes Outing Club v. United States, 468 F.2d 443 (8th Cir. 1972); Iowa State Univ. of Science & Technology v. United States, 500 F.2d 508 (Ct. Cl. 1974).

[505] These rules are comparable to those for social clubs and certain other tax-exempt organizations (IRC § 512(a)(3)). See § 25.4(c). E.g., Armour-Dial Men's Club, Inc. v. Comm'r, 77 T.C. 1 (1981); Rev. Rul. 90-36, 1990-1 C.B. 59.

[506] H.R. Rep. No. 91-413, pt. 1, at 49 (1969); S. Rep. No. 91-552, at 74 (1969).

[507] Concord Consumer Hous. Coop. v. Comm'r, 89 T.C. 105 (1987).

these purposes. The court wrote that it found "nothing to indicate that Congress intended that phrase [income derived from members] to include all income from sources substantially related to the function of the organization."[508] Consequently, this court concluded that because the interest income at issue was not received from members or came to the organization in a transaction with members, the income constituted nonmembership income in this setting. Similarly, a court ruled that a taxable insurance trust could not deduct an expense incurred for insurance for its members inasmuch as it failed to convince the court that the gain realized from the sale of shares of stock was member income, which held that the income was not derived from its members or transactions with its members.[509]

---

[508] *Id.* at 121.

[509] Texas Med. Ass'n Ins. Trust v. United States, 391 F. Supp. 2d 529 (W.D. Tex. 2005). Also, Buckeye Countrymark, Inc. v. Comm'r, 103 T.C. 547 (1994); Associated Master Barbers & Beauticians of Am., Inc. v. Comm'r, 69 T.C. 53 (1977); Shore Drive Apts., Inc. v. United States, 1976 WL 1181 (M.D. Fla. 1976) (unpublished order).

CHAPTER TWENTY

Private Inurement and Private Benefit Doctrines

PRIVATE INUREMENT AND PRIVATE BENEFIT DOCTRINES

The doctrine of *private inurement* is one of the most important sets of rules constituting the law of tax-exempt organizations; indeed, it is the fundamental defining principle of law that distinguishes *nonprofit organizations* from *for-profit organizations*.[1] The private inurement doctrine is a statutory criterion for federal income tax exemption for charitable organizations,[2] social welfare organizations,[3] business leagues,[4] chambers of commerce,[5] boards of trade,[6] real estate boards,[7] social clubs,[8] voluntary employees' beneficiary associations,[9] teachers' retirement fund associations,[10] cemetery companies,[11] veterans' organizations,[12] state-sponsored organizations providing health care to high-risk individuals,[13] qualified health insurance issuers,[14] and professional football leagues.[15] Nearly all of the law concerning the private inurement doctrine has been developed in connection with transactions involving charitable organizations.

The oddly phrased and thoroughly antiquated language of the private inurement doctrine requires that the tax-exempt organization be organized and operated so that "no part of. . .[its] net earnings. . .inures to the benefit of any private shareholder or individual." This provision reads as if it were proscribing the payment of dividends. In fact, it is rare for an exempt organization to have shareholders; it would certainly, however, be a violation of the doctrine to make payments of dividends to them.[16] Moreover, the private inurement doctrine can be triggered by the involvement of persons or entities other than individuals, such as corporations, partnerships, limited liability companies, estates, and trusts. The contemporary meaning of this statutory language is barely reflected in its literal form and transcends the over 100-year-old formulation; what the doctrine means today is that none of the income or assets of an exempt organization subject to the private inurement doctrine may be permitted to directly or indirectly unduly benefit an individual or other person who has a close relationship with the organization, when they are in a position to exercise a significant degree of control over the organization.

The *private benefit doctrine* is considerably different from, although it subsumes, the private inurement doctrine. Being an extrapolation of the operational

---

[1] See § 1.1.
[2] See Part Three.
[3] See § 20.9.
[4] See § 20.10.
[5] See § 14.3.
[6] See § 14.4.
[7] See § 14.5.
[8] See § 20.11.
[9] See §§ 18.3, 20.12.
[10] See § 18.7.
[11] See §§ 19.6, 20.12.
[12] See § 19.11(a).
[13] See § 19.15.
[14] See § 19.18.
[15] See § 19.21.
[16] The law in a few states permits a nonprofit corporation to issue stock. This type of stock, however, does not carry with it rights to receive dividends. Thus, these rare bodies of law are not in conflict with the private inurement doctrine, although the IRS appears to believe they are.

test applicable to tax-exempt charitable organizations,[17] this doctrine seemingly is applicable only to these entities. Nonetheless, the IRS is of the view that the private benefit doctrine is applicable in connection with other categories of exempt organizations; the agency has so ruled in instances involving social welfare organizations.[18]

§ 20.1 CONCEPT OF *PRIVATE INUREMENT*

The concept of *private inurement* lacks precision. A court wrote that the "boundaries of the term 'inures' have thus far defied precise definition."[19] The case law teaches that the doctrine is broad and wide-ranging. The rules concerning excess benefit transactions[20] have introduced some exactitude to, albeit perhaps less application of, the doctrine. Further, the rules as to self-dealing involving private foundations[21] continue to bring many examples of private inurement transactions, as does the private benefit doctrine.

A pronouncement from the IRS stated that private inurement is "likely to arise where the financial benefit represents a transfer of the organization's financial resources to an individual solely by virtue of the individual's relationship with the organization, and without regard to accomplishing exempt purposes."[22] Another of these observations, this one more bluntly expressed, was that the "inurement prohibition serves to prevent anyone in a position to do so from siphoning off any of a charity's income or assets for personal use."[23]

The purpose of the private inurement rule is to ensure that the tax-exempt organization involved is serving exempt rather than private interests. It is thus necessary for an organization subject to the doctrine to be in a position to establish that it is not organized and operated for the benefit of persons in their private capacity, such as the organization's founders, trustees, directors, officers, members of their families, entities controlled by these individuals, or any other persons having a personal and private interest in the activities of the organization.[24]

In ascertaining the presence of private inurement, the law looks to the ultimate purpose of the organization involved. If its basic purpose is to benefit individuals in their private capacity—without thereby serving exempt purposes—then it cannot be tax-exempt, even though exempt activities may also be performed. Thus, a court, in concluding that an organization that purchased and sold products

---

[17] See § 4.5.

[18] See § 20.13(d).

[19] Variety Club Tent No. 6 Charities, Inc. v. Comm'r, 74 T.C.M. 1485, 1494 (1997).

[20] See Chapter 21.

[21] IRC § 4941. See § 12.4(a).

[22] Gen. Couns. Mem. 38459.

[23] Gen. Couns. Mem. 39862. As noted, this summary applies, not just to charitable organizations, but also to other tax-exempt organizations subject to the doctrine. A most puzzling explanation of the doctrine is this: "Inurement involves an expenditure of organizational funds resulting in a benefit which is beyond the scope of the benefits which logically flow from the organization's performance of its exempt function" (Priv. Ltr. Rul. 201347023).

[24] Reg. §§ 1.501(a)-1(c), 1.501(c)(3)-1(c)(2). Also, Ginsberg v. Comm'r, 46 T.C. 47 (1966); Rev. Rul. 76-206, 1976-1 C.B. 154.

manufactured by blind individuals constituted an exempt charitable organization, was not deterred in reaching this finding because of the fact that the organization distributed a portion of its "net profits" to qualified workers at a state agency; the court in essence held that these distributions were in furtherance of exempt purposes.[25] Conversely, in some contexts, incidental benefits to individuals in their private capacity will not defeat an exemption, as long as the organization otherwise qualifies for exempt status.[26]

The doctrine of private inurement does not prohibit transactions between a tax-exempt organization subject to the doctrine and those who have a close relationship with it. As the IRS wrote, "[t]here is no absolute prohibition against an exempt section 501(c)(3) organization dealing with its founders, members, or officers in conducting its economic affairs."[27] It "does not matter," the IRS wrote, whether the recipient of compensation paid by an exempt organization is a trustee, director, officer, or founder of the entity, as long as the compensation is reasonable.[28] Thus, as is the case with the excess benefit transactions rules and the doctrine of private benefit, the private inurement doctrine requires that these transactions be tested against a standard of *reasonableness*.[29] The standard calls for an approximately equal exchange of benefits between the parties; the law is designed to discourage what the IRS termed a "disproportionate share of the benefits of the exchange" flowing to an insider.[30]

The reasonableness standard focuses essentially on comparability of data— that is, on how similar organizations, acting prudently, transact their affairs in comparable instances. Thus, the regulations pertaining to the business expense deduction, addressing the matter of the reasonableness of compensation, provide that it is generally "just to assume that reasonable and true compensation is only such amount as would ordinarily be paid for like services by like enterprises under like circumstances."[31] Consequently, the terms of these transactions are, in resolution of a private inurement issue, analyzed in relation to comparable practices at comparable exempt or for-profit organizations.

The core of the private inurement doctrine is the several ways to impermissibly confer private inurement.[32] Indeed, the IRS, applying the doctrine, frequently

---

[25] Industrial Aid for the Blind v. Comm'r, 73 T.C. 96 (1979).

[26] Reg. § 1.501(c)(3)-1(d)(1)(ii).

[27] Priv. Ltr. Rul. 9130002. Trustees and directors are also included in this group.

[28] Priv. Ltr. Rul. 200944055. Sometimes, however, the IRS applies the private benefit doctrine in contexts where only the private inurement doctrine need be applied, finding impermissible benefit even though the terms of the transaction or arrangement are reasonable (see § 20.13(d), text accompanied by *infra* notes 470–475).

[29] By contrast, the private foundation self-dealing rules (IRC § 4941) generally and essentially forbid these types of transactions (see § 12.4(a)). In general, *Private Foundations*, Chapter 5. Occasionally, the IRS applies the private inurement doctrine to a transaction or arrangement involving an insider, without making a judgment as to the reasonableness of the matter (e.g., Priv. Ltr. Rul. 201548021).

[30] Priv. Ltr. Rul. 9130002.

[31] Reg. § 1.162(b)(3).

[32] See §§ 20.4, 20.6. In one instance, however, the IRS refused to grant recognition of tax exemption, in part because the agency, while acknowledging that "there is no evidence of any inurement," speculated that the prospective "actual operations" of the organization may give rise to private inurement (Priv. Ltr. Rul. 200535029).

denies an organization recognition of tax exemption[33] or revokes the exemption of an organization.[34]

§ 20.2   DEFINITION OF *NET EARNINGS*

The term *net earnings* means gross earnings minus related expenses—a meaning that, as noted, seemingly applies the term, in the private inurement setting, in a technical, accounting sense. For example, a state supreme court addressed this definition at length in the early years of the federal tax law. In one opinion, this court wrote that, since the term is not defined in the statute, it "must be given its usual and ordinary meaning of what is left of earnings after deducting necessary and legitimate items of expense incident to the corporate business."[35] This approach was followed in the early years by other state courts as well as by federal courts.[36]

From the perspective of the law of tax-exempt organizations, however, this technical definition of the term was never quite adequate as to its sole meaning. Some courts applied the term in this constricted manner, where the facts particularly lent themselves to this approach,[37] but most court opinions on the point reflect the broader, and certainly contemporary, view that there can be inurement of net earnings in the absence of blatant transfers of all of an exempt organization's net income in the nature of dividend payments.[38]

An early proponent of this expansive view was another state supreme court, which observed that the *net earnings* phraseology "should not be given a strictly literal construction, as in the accountant's sense" and that the "substance should control the form," so that tax exemption should not be available where private inurement is taking place, "irrespective of the means by which that result is accomplished."[39] Likewise, early in the evolution of this body of law, a federal court foresaw today's application of the term when it held that private inurement "may include more than the term net profits as shown by the books of the organization or than the difference between the gross receipts and disbursements in dollars," and that "[p]rofits may inure to the benefit of shareholders in ways other than dividends."[40] This view certainly represents the current application of the private inurement doctrine—as an overall standard assessing the use of a

---

[33] E.g., Priv. Ltr. Rul. 202113009.

[34] E.g., Priv. Ltr. Rul. 202421008. Cf. § 21.16.

[35] Bank of Commerce & Trust Co. v. Senter, 260 S.W. 144, 151 (Sup. Ct. Tenn. 1924). Likewise, Southern Coal Co. v. McCanless, 192 S.W. 2d 1003, 1005 (Sup. Ct. Tenn. 1946); Nat'l Life & Accident Ins. Co. v. Dempster, 79 S.W. 2d 564 (Sup. Ct. Tenn. 1935).

[36] E.g., United States v. Riely, 169 F.2d 542 (4th Cir. 1948); Winkelman v. General Motors Corp., 44 F. Supp. 960 (S.D.N.Y. 1942); Inscho v. Mid-Continent Development Co., 146 P. 1014 (Kan. 1915).

[37] E.g., Birmingham Business College, Inc. v. Comm'r, 276 F.2d 476 (5th Cir. 1960); Gemological Inst. of America v. Comm'r, 17 T.C. 1604 (1952), aff'd, 212 F.2d 205 (9th Cir. 1954); Putnam v. Comm'r, 6 T.C. 702 (1946).

[38] E.g., Edward Orton, Jr., Ceramic Found. v. Comm'r, 9 T.C. 533 (1947), aff'd, 173 F.2d 483 (6th Cir. 1949); Gemological Inst. of America v. Riddell, 149 F. Supp. 128 (S.D. Cal. 1957).

[39] Virginia Mason Hosp. Ass'n v. Larson, 114 P.2d 978, 983 (Wash. 1941).

[40] Northwestern Mun. Ass'n v. United States, 99 F.2d 460, 463 (8th Cir. 1938).

tax-exempt organization's income and assets[41]—although there is an occasional somewhat contrary (literal) interpretation.[42] Thus, a tax-exempt organization was advised by the IRS that, if it entered into a proposed service agreement with a for-profit company (an insider with respect to it), it would lose its exemption because of violation of the private inurement doctrine; the package of special benefits that would flow to the company, measured in relation to the organization's standard agreement, was viewed by the IRS as a price reduction constituting the inurement of the organization's net earnings.[43]

§ 20.3 DEFINITION OF *INSIDER*

A potential private inurement transaction is one that is between a tax-exempt organization that is subject to the doctrine and a person (or persons) who has a special, close relationship with the organization. To put a name to the latter, the federal tax law appropriated the term *insider* from the federal securities laws.[44]

Generally, an *insider* is an individual who has a unique relationship with the tax-exempt organization involved, by which that individual can cause application of the organization's funds or assets for the private purposes of the individual by reason of the individual's exercise of control or influence over, or being in a position to exercise that control or influence over, the organization.[45] Insiders include an organization's trustees, directors, officers, key employees, family members of these individuals, and entities controlled by them.[46] All of these persons have been swept into the insider category, from the starting point of the statutory language with its peculiar and incomplete reference to *private shareholder or individual*.

The case law is replete with court opinions concerning the involvement of insiders in private inurement transactions. A group of insiders engaged in private inurement transactions with a tax-exempt school in the form of excessive rent

[41] E.g., Harding Hosp., Inc. v. United States, 505 F.2d 1068 (6th Cir. 1974).
[42] A federal court found that the term net earnings signified funds used for expenses over and above expenses that are "ordinary and necessary" in the operation of a charitable organization (Carter v. United States, 973 F.2d 1479, 1487 (9th Cir. 1992); also, Hall v. Comm'r, 729 F.2d 632, 634 (9th Cir. 1984)).
  A less-than-literal interpretation of these rules occurred when a court held that "paying over a portion of gross earnings to those vested with the control of a charitable organization constituted private inurement as well," adding that "all in all, taking a slice off the top should be no less prohibited than a slice out of the net" (People of God Community v. Comm'r, 75 T.C. 127, 133 (1980)).
[43] Priv. Ltr. Rul. 201317013.
[44] These laws prohibit, for example, insider trading. The IRS, however, from time to time issues private letter rulings, asserting the presence of private inurement, when it is by no means clear that any of the persons involved are insiders (e.g., Priv. Ltr. Rul. 201028042). See, e.g., § 20.10.
[45] American Campaign Academy v. Comm'r, 92 T.C. 1053 (1989). It was subsequently stated that the "case law [as to private inurement] appears to have drawn a line between those who have significant control over the organization's activities and those who are unrelated third parties" (Variety Club Tent No. 6 Charities, Inc. v. Comm'r, 74 T.C.M. 1485, 1492 (1997)).
[46] In the excess benefit transaction context (see § 21.3) and in the private foundation context (IRC § 4946), the term *disqualified person* is used to describe an insider.
  The IRS expressed the view that all persons performing services for a tax-exempt organization are insiders with respect to that organization (Gen. Couns. Mem. 39670); this obviously is an overly

and school-funded property improvements on land owned by them.[47] A charitable organization made loans to its founder and his family members, made expenditures to advance his hobby, and invested in a corporation owned by a friend—all of which were found to be private inurement.[48] A radio entertainer received "great benefit" from a charitable organization bearing his name in the form of services it provided to individuals who appeared on his programs.[49] Tax exemption was denied to a college that had five family members as its board of trustees, with three of them its shareholders, because of private inurement in the form of "constant commingling" of funds.[50] A court found private inurement in the form of benefits to a physician in his practice due to use of a neighboring scientific research foundation.[51] Private inurement was found where a church disbursed substantial sums to its founder and his family members as fees, commissions, royalties, compensation, rent, expense reimbursements, and maintenance of a personal residence.[52] A court barred tax exemption for a hospital because of the "virtual monopoly" of it by its founding physicians.[53]

The IRS revoked, on private inurement grounds, the tax-exempt status of a hospital organized and operated by a physician that was held to have distributed its earnings to the physician in the form of direct payments (compensation and loans), improvements to the property of a corporation he owned, administrative services relating to his private practice, and the free use of its facilities.[54] The same fate befell an organization established to study chiropractic methods, where the founding chiropractor sold his home, automobile, and medical equipment to the entity, and caused it to pay his personal expenses and a salary while he continued his private practice.[55] Likewise, the exemption of an organization was revoked because of several transactions, including the receipt of property from the founder's mother and payment to her of an annuity, payment of costs of a child's college education, payment of the founder's personal expenses, and purchasing and leasing real estate owned by the founder.[56]

Private inurement precluded an ostensible religious organization from achieving tax-exempt status inasmuch as its founder's ministry was considered "more personal than church oriented."[57] A court rejected an organization's claim

---

expansive interpretation of the concept. It was the position of the IRS, for example, that all physicians on the medical staff of an exempt hospital are insiders in relation to the hospital (Gen. Couns. Mem. 39498); however, this stance was ameliorated in the aftermath of enactment of the intermediate sanctions law.

[47] Texas Trade School v. Comm'r, 30 T.C. 642 (1958), *aff'd*, 272 F.2d 168 (5th Cir. 1959).

[48] Best Lock Corp. v. Comm'r, 31 T.C. 1217 (1959).

[49] Horace Heidt Found. v. United States, 170 F. Supp. 634, 638 (Ct. Cl. 1959).

[50] Birmingham Business College, Inc. v. Comm'r, 276 F.2d 476, 479 (5th Cir. 1960).

[51] Cranley v. Comm'r, 20 T.C.M. 20 (1961).

[52] Founding Church of Scientology v. United States, 412 F.2d 1197 (Ct. Cl. 1969), *cert. denied*, 397 U.S. 1009 (1970).

[53] Harding Hosp., Inc. v. United States, 505 F.2d 1068, 1078 (6th Cir. 1974).

[54] Kenner v. Comm'r, 33 T.C.M. 1239 (1974).

[55] Labrenz Found., Inc. v. Comm'r, 33 T.C.M. 1374 (1974).

[56] Rueckwald Found., Inc. v. Comm'r, 33 T.C.M. 1383 (1974).

[57] Western Catholic Church v. Comm'r, 73 T.C. 196, 211 (1979), *aff'd*, 631 F.2d 736 (7th Cir. 1980), *cert. denied*, 450 U.S. 981 (1981).

of exemption because it provided its founder and his family with housing, food, transportation, clothing, and "other proper needs."[58] A court's finding that a church was ineligible for exemption was based in part on private inurement in the form of unreasonable compensation, payments in support of its founder's family, book marketing on his behalf, and "unfettered control over millions of dollars" belonging to church-affiliated entities.[59] A community association was held to be engaging in private inurement transactions by providing "comfort and convenience" to its residents who were cast as the "beneficiaries" of its facilities and services, and thus had a "personal interest" in the entity.[60] An individual who was the founder, president, chief executive officer, and executive director of an exempt school caused revocation of the exemption because she had "control...over the entity's funds, assets, and disbursements; use of entity moneys for personal expenses; payment of salary or rent to [her] without any accompanying evidence or analysis of the reasonableness of the amounts; and purported loans to [her] showing a ready private source of credit."[61]

The focus on the concept of the *insider* in the private inurement context over the years has been on founders, trustees, directors, officers, and their family members. In part due to the intermediate sanctions rules, however, this concept has been expanded to encompass key employees[62] and vendors of services, such as management and fundraising companies.[63] As to the latter, a trial court found a fundraising firm to be an insider with respect to a charitable organization due to the extent to which the firm controlled and manipulated the organization for its private ends; the firm was portrayed as "in many ways analogous to that of a founder and major contributor to a new organization."[64] This decision was reversed, with the appellate court unable to find anything in the facts of this case to support the "theory" that this firm "seized control" of the charity and thus "by doing so became an insider."[65] This court of appeals concluded that "[t]here is nothing [in the facts of this case] that corporate or agency law would recognize as control" and that the lower court used the word *control* in a "special sense not used elsewhere, so far as we can determine, in the law, including the federal tax law."[66]

[58] Parshall Christian Order v. Comm'r, 45 T.C.M. 488, 492 (1983).

[59] Church of Scientology of Cal. v. Comm'r, 83 T.C. 381, 492 (1984), aff'd, 823 F.2d 1310 (9th Cir. 1987).

[60] Columbia Park & Recreation Ass'n, Inc. v. Comm'r, 88 T.C. 1, 24, 26 (1987), aff'd, 838 F.2d 465 (4th Cir. 1988).

[61] Rameses School of San Antonio, Texas v. Comm'r, 93 T.C.M. 1092, 1097 (2007). A trust with a reversionary interest in the trustor was ruled to entail private inurement (Rev. Rul. 66-259, 1966-2 C.B. 214). The IRS ruled that private inurement was not involved when an exempt hospital compensated a radiologist in part because the physician did not control the hospital (Rev. Rul. 69-383, 1969-2 C.B. 113).

[62] E.g., Form 990, Part VII.

[63] See § 21.3.

[64] United Cancer Council, Inc. v. Comm'r, 109 T.C. 326, 387 (1997). This court wrote that, for purposes of the private inurement doctrine, an *insider* is a person who has "significant control of the [exempt] organization's activities" (id.). Congress adopted the essence of this approach when it wrote the definition of *disqualified person* for purposes of the intermediate sanctions rules (see § 21.3).

[65] United Cancer Council, Inc. v. Comm'r, 165 F.3d 1173, 1178 (7th Cir. 1999).

[66] Id. The intermediate sanctions rules, embodying precisely that concept, had been in existence for more than three years at the time of these observations.

Courts can be zealous, when applying the private inurement doctrine, in finding the involvement of one or more insiders. This point was nicely illustrated in the case of a sports booster club, which lost its tax exemption in part because a court found private inurement accruing to the parents of children participating in sports competitions in the form of fundraising opportunities, which enabled the parents to generate funds that were applied to reduce the parents' assessments to cover the cost of participation in the competitions. The court concluded that the fundraising members of the club were insiders with respect to it, in that they "exerted direct or indirect control over the organization."[67]

Consequently, a tax-exempt organization subject to the private inurement doctrine should be concerned with the doctrine only where there is a transaction or transactions involving one or more *insiders* with respect to the organization. The overall rule on this point was expressed this way: the "concept of private benefit [inurement]. . .[is] limited to the situation in which an organization's *insiders*. . .[are] benefited."[68] A modern definition of the term *insider* is a person who has a "significant formal voice in [an exempt organization's] activities generally and. . .substantial formal and practical control over most of [the organization's] income."[69]

At the same time, however, the IRS may elect to apply the intermediate sanctions penalties (when applicable) against the insider[70] rather than revoke tax-exempt status.[71] Moreover, even if it turns out that a transaction involving an exempt organization does not involve a person who is an insider, the analysis should not necessarily end, inasmuch as the transaction could nonetheless operate for the use or benefit of an insider/disqualified person or be a transgression of the private benefit doctrine.[72]

§ 20.4 COMPENSATION ISSUES

The concept of the private inurement transaction has many manifestations. The most common instance of private inurement is excessive compensation.

---

[67] Capital Gymnastics Booster Club, Inc. v. Comm'r, 106 T.C.M. 154 (2013). The court offered no analysis in support of this conclusion. Yet, it is hard to believe that a nonprofit corporation can be controlled, even indirectly, by the adult members of about 110 families, particularly when it has a board of directors. As to the parents who are board members, their excess benefit (about $300 per family) should have been taxed under the intermediate sanctions rules (see the text accompanied by *infra* notes 70–71), rather than found the basis for revocation.

[68] Sound Health Ass'n v. Comm'r, 71 T.C. 158, 185 (1978). In one instance, the IRS ruled that private inurement was not taking place because insiders were not involved (Priv. Ltr. Rul. 201250025). Occasionally, the overwhelming domination of a tax-exempt organization and wrongdoing by an insider can lead a court to a finding of private inurement, when in fact inurement is not present because the terms and conditions of the transactions involved were reasonable (e.g., Airlie Found., Inc. v. United States, 826 F. Supp. 537 (D.D.C. 1993), aff'd, 55 F.3d 684 (D.C. Cir. 1995)).

[69] Variety Club Tent No. 6 Charities, Inc. v. Comm'r, 74 T.C.M. 1485, 1493 (1997). A tax-exempt social welfare organization (see Chapter 13) had an exempt business league (see Chapter 14) as its sole member and thus its parent; a for-profit company that was a member of the league had a representative on the league's board of directors, leading the IRS to rule that the company was an insider with respect to the social welfare organization (Priv. Ltr. Rul. 201317013).

[70] As discussed, in the intermediate sanctions area, an insider is termed a *disqualified person* (see § 21.3). The terms *insider* and *disqualified person* are essentially synonymous.

[71] See § 21.16.

[72] See § 20.13.

A tax-exempt organization subject to the private inurement doctrine can, of course, make ordinary and necessary expenditures in furtherance of its operations without forfeiting its exempt status.[73] This includes the payment of compensation for services rendered, whether to an employee or to a vendor, consultant, or other independent contractor. As a court observed, the law "places no duty on individuals operating charitable [or, for that matter, other exempt] organizations to donate their services; they are entitled to reasonable compensation for their efforts."[74] The legislative history of the intermediate sanctions rules states that an individual "need not necessarily accept reduced compensation merely because he or she renders services to a tax-exempt, as opposed to a taxable, organization."[75]

(a) Meaning of *Compensation*

The concept of *compensation* paid to an individual or other person by a tax-exempt organization is not confined to items such as a salary. All forms of compensation (economic benefits) are aggregated for this purpose; in the case of an employee, the elements include salary, wages, bonuses, commissions, royalties, fringe benefits, deferred compensation, severance payments, retirement and pension benefits, expense allowances, and insurance coverages,[76] and in the case of an independent contractor, the payment of advances, fees, and expense reimbursements.[77]

[73] E.g., Birmingham Business College, Inc. v. Comm'r, 276 F.2d 476 (5th Cir. 1960); Mabee Petroleum Corp. v. United States, 203 F.2d 872 (5th Cir. 1953); Broadway Theatre League of Lynchburg, Va., Inc. v. United States, 293 F. Supp. 346 (W.D. Va. 1968); Enterprise Railway Equipment Co. v. United States, 161 F. Supp. 590 (Ct. Cl. 1958).

[74] World Family Corp. v. Comm'r, 81 T.C. 958, 969 (1983). In its zeal to punish tax-exempt organizations for engaging in acts of private inurement (or private benefit (see § 20.13)), the IRS sometimes overlooks this point and, in so doing, omits any analysis of whether an insider is involved (see § 20.3) and/or whether the compensation is reasonable (see § 20.4(b)). Indeed, the IRS may find the very payment of compensation to be private inurement (or private benefit) (e.g., Priv. Ltr. Rul. 202127041, retroactively revoking an organization's tax exemption for functioning as a "staffing agency"), which, of course, is not the law.

[75] H.R. Rep. 104-506, at n.3 (1996).

[76] E.g., Priv. Ltr. Rul. 9539016 (where the IRS discussed the coverage provided by a split-dollar life insurance plan as compensation).

[77] In a compliance questionnaire sent by the IRS to colleges and universities (Form 14018, Compliance Questionnaire Colleges and Universities (Sept. 2008)), the agency identified the various types of remuneration it perceives as *compensation*, including salary; bonus; contributions to employee benefit plans (e.g., health benefit plans); incentives (short-term and long-term); contributions to life, disability, and/or long-term care insurance; split-dollar life insurance (where the organization pays the premiums); loans or other extensions of credit (in the case of forgone interest or debt forgiveness); stock or stock options (equity-based compensation); severance or change-of-control payments; personal use of the organization's credit card (where there is no reimbursement); personal use of the organization's owned or leased vehicles; personal travel for the individual and/or spouse/other family member (where there is no reimbursement); expense reimbursements pursuant to a nonaccountable plan; value of organization-provided housing and utilities; value of organization-provided vacation home; personal services provided at individual's residence (e.g., housekeeper, lawn service, maintenance or repair services); other personal services provided (e.g., legal, financial, retirement services); payment of health and/or social club dues; personal use of organization's aircraft or boat; first-class travel; scholarship and/or fellowship grants (if taxable); executive fringe benefits; and contributions to deferred compensation plans.

In one instance, private inurement was found where a nonprofit organization was conducting ostensible research on dietary supplements, where the supplements were manufactured by a related entity and related entities funded the
research; a director received "substantial" compensation and made considerable
sums selling shares of stock in a related corporation that were purchased at a discount from another related entity.[78]

(b) Determining Reasonableness of Compensation

The private inurement doctrine mandates that the compensation amount paid by
most tax-exempt organizations to insiders with respect to them be *reasonable*. In
other words, the payment of *excessive* compensation can result in a finding of private inurement.[79] Whether an amount of compensation is reasonable is a question
of *fact*, to be decided in the context of each case;[80] it is not an issue of *law*.

The process for determining the reasonableness of compensation is conceptually
much like that entailed when valuing an item of property. It requires an appraisal—an
evaluation of factors that lead to a determination of the value. It is an exercise of
comparing a mix of variables pertaining to the compensation of others in similar circumstances. The basic standard has been in the federal tax law for years; it is cited
in the business expense regulations[81] and the intermediate sanctions regulations[82] as
follows: Reasonable compensation is that amount as would ordinarily be paid for
like services by like enterprises under like circumstances. This alchemy—what the
intermediate sanctions rules refer to as an accumulation and assessment of data as to
comparability[83]—yields the conclusion as to whether a particular item of compensation or a compensation package is *reasonable* or it is *excessive*.[84]

Traditionally, case law has dictated the criteria to be used in ascertaining the
reasonableness of compensation. This approach has come to be known as utilization of the *multifactor test*. The elements—factors—to be utilized in a particular case can vary, depending on the court. (Even though the reasonableness of

---

[78] Priv. Ltr. Rul. 201144032.

[79] E.g., Harding Hosp., Inc. v. United States, 505 F.2d 1068 (6th Cir. 1974); Birmingham Business College,
Inc. v. Comm'r, 276 F.2d 476 (5th Cir. 1960); Mabee Petroleum Corp. v. United States, 203 F.2d 872 (5th
Cir. 1953); Texas Trade School v. Comm'r, 30 T.C. 642 (1958), *aff'd*, 272 F.2d 168 (5th Cir. 1959); Northern
Illinois College of Optometry v. Comm'r, 2 T.C.M. 664 (1943).

[80] E.g., Jones Brothers Bakery, Inc. v. United States, 411 F.2d 1282 (Ct. Cl. 1969); Home Oil Mill v. Will-
ingham, 68 F. Supp. 525 (N.D. Ala. 1945), *aff'd*, 181 F.2d 9 (5th Cir. 1950), *cert. denied*, 340 U.S. 852 (1950).

[81] Reg. § 1.162-7(b)(3).

[82] Reg. § 53.4958-4 (b)(1)(ii)(A). See § 21.4(a).

[83] Reg. § 53.4958-6(c)(2). See § 21.9(b).

[84] The IRS wrote that "exemption from federal income tax of an organization is not jeopardized where
agreements on compensation [with insiders] are entered into through negotiations conducted at arm's-
length and are not considered to be excessive based on persons having similar responsibilities and
comparable duties"; the governing board of the organization involved adopted a "Policy Against
Inurement," which the IRS referenced with approval (Priv. Ltr. Rul. 200944055).

The process of determining reasonable compensation may include obtaining a report from an independent consultant and/or a ruling from the IRS. Nonetheless, these arrangements are, by definition,
reviewed from the standpoint of hindsight, which may obviate the effectiveness of these documents.
An excellent illustration of this process appeared in Priv. Ltr. Rul. 200020060, concerning the valuation
of a compensation package paid to the executive of a tax-exempt charitable organization.

compensation is a matter of fact, the selection and application of the appropriate factors are a matter of law.) Much of the law in this field is based on case law concerning payments by for-profit corporations to their chief executives. This is because a payment of compensation, to be deductible as a business expense,[85] must be an *ordinary and necessary* outlay; the concepts of *reasonable* and *ordinary and necessary* are essentially identical.[86] Also, as will be discussed, the advent of the intermediate sanctions rules has greatly informed this aspect of the law of tax-exempt organizations.

The factors commonly applied in the private inurement setting (and similar settings) to ascertain the reasonableness of compensation are the levels of compensation paid by similar organizations (tax-exempt and taxable) for functionally comparable positions, with emphasis on comparable entities in the same community or region; the need of the organization for the services of the individual whose compensation is being evaluated; the individual's background, education, training, experience, and responsibilities; whether the compensation resulted from arm's-length bargaining, such as whether it was approved by an independent board of directors; the size and complexity of the organization, in terms of elements such as assets, income, and number of employees; the individual's prior compensation arrangement; the individual's performance; the relationship of the individual's compensation to that paid to other employees of the same organization; whether there has been a sharp increase in the individual's compensation (a spike) from one year to the next; and the amount of time the individual devotes to the position.[87]

If the issue is litigated, the individual whose compensation is being challenged and the IRS are both likely to have expert witnesses, who produce reports and testimony incorporating some or all of these factors. The judge in the case is called on to determine whether there has been payment of excessive compensation. Most of these cases originate in the U.S. Tax Court. A federal court of appeals observed (articulating a fact that, until then, no court had ventured to mention), however, that the "judges of the Tax Court are not equipped by training or experience to determine the salaries of corporate officers; no judges are."[88]

This appellate court excoriated the multifactor test, characterizing it as "redundant, incomplete, and unclear."[89] The test was found to "not provide adequate

---

[85] IRC § 162(a).

[86] If the IRS or a court finds that a portion of a payment by a for-profit corporation constitutes excessive compensation, that amount is treated as a dividend and thus is not deductible by the payor corporation (e.g., Rapco, Inc. v. Comm'r, 85 F.3d 950 (2d Cir. 1996); Leonard Pipeline Contractors, Ltd. v. Comm'r, 72 T.C.M. 83 (1996), *rev'd and remanded* (on other issue), 142 F.3d 1133 (9th Cir. 1998)).

[87] E.g., Miller & Son Drywall, Inc. v. Comm'r, 89 T.C. 1279 (2005). In one instance of a finding of private inurement, the IRS noted that the initial aggregate fixed compensation of an organization's directors exceeded 50 percent of its projected revenues (Priv. Ltr. Rul. 201121021). In another such instance, the IRS faulted an organization for not using national surveys to determine compensation levels, not imposing caps on fixed income, and not having written employment agreements with those it compensated (Priv. Ltr. Rul. 201141021). In general, the importance of sufficient comparability data was highlighted by a case in which a court found private inurement, where an individual working 250 hours annually was paid $70,000, because adequate data were not in the evidentiary record (Family Trust of Mass., Inc. v. United States, 892 F. Supp. 2d 149 (D.D.C. 2012), *aff'd*, 722 F.3d 355 (D.C. Cir. 2013)). Also, K&K Veterinary Supply, Inc. v. Comm'r, 105 T.C.M. 1522 (2013).

[88] Exacto Spring Corp. v. Comm'r, 196 F.3d 833, 835 (7th Cir. 1999).

[89] *Id.*

guidance to a rational decision."[90] Rather, wrote the court, the test to be applied when determining the reasonableness of an individual's compensation package paid by a for-profit business is the *independent investor test*.[91] This test establishes a presumption that an executive's compensation is reasonable if the investors in the company (actual or hypothetical) believe that the return on their investment is reasonable, with the investment return percentage determined by an expert witness. This court proclaimed that, when these investors are obtaining a "far higher return than they had any reason to expect," the executive's salary is "presumptively reasonable," even if the compensation may otherwise be considered "exorbitant."[92] Under this approach, the presumption can be rebutted if the government shows that, although the executive's salary was reasonable, the company did not in fact intend to pay them that amount as salary, their salary "really did include a concealed dividend though it need not have."[93] Also, according to this court, if the executive's salary is approved by the other owners of the corporation, who are independent of the executive—that is, who lacked an incentive to disguise a dividend as a salary—that approval "goes far" to rebut any evidence of "bad faith."[94]

It initially appeared that a federal court of appeals would use either the multifactor test or the independent investor test in determining the reasonableness of executive compensation. For example, a federal appellate court, considering this issue for the first time, elected to utilize the multifactor test.[95] In one instance, a court used the independent investor test to find an executive's compensation reasonable, portraying the individual as the "locomotive" of the company.[96] However, another federal court of appeals, in one of these cases, applied a multifactor test and then used the independent investor test to interpret one of the factors.[97] On another occasion, a court used the independent investor test to establish the presumption that an individual's compensation was reasonable, and then applied the multifactor test to rebut the presumption and determine that the compensation was unreasonable.[98] The independent investor test will not be applied in determining the reasonableness of the compensation of executives of tax-exempt organizations; rather, ongoing application of that test will provide additional illustrations of use of the multifactor test.[99]

---

[90] *Id.*

[91] This approach was first advanced in Dexsil Corp. v. Comm'r, 147 F.3d 96 (2d Cir. 1998). This test subsequently has been characterized as the *hypothetical investor test* and the *hypothetical inactive independent investor test*.

[92] Exacto Spring Corp. v. Comm'r, 196 F.3d 833, 835, 838 (7th Cir. 1999).

[93] *Id.* at 839.

[94] *Id.* at 839.

[95] Haffner's Service Stations, Inc. v. Comm'r, 326 F.3d 1 (1st Cir. 2003).

[96] Beiner, Inc. v. Comm'r, 88 T.C.M. 297, 325 (2004). The court observed that this business would not have succeeded without this executive's "devotion, dedication, intelligence, foresight, and skill" (*id.* at 324). Likewise Multi-Pak Corp. v. Comm'r, 99 T.C.M. 1567 (2010) (where the executive was the "driving force" behind the company's success, with the court recognizing his "dedication and hard work").

[97] Labelgraphics, Inc. v. Comm'r, 221 F.3d 1091 (9th Cir. 2000).

[98] Menard, Inc. v. Comm'r, 88 T.C.M. 229 (2004).

[99] The hypothetical investor test may prove to be no more rational than the multifactor test. In one case, the Tax Court found, using the test, that the reasonable compensation for an executive for a year was $98,000; revisiting the case following a partial reversal, the court concluded that the reasonable

A large salary paid by a tax-exempt organization can be considered private inurement, particularly where the employee is concurrently receiving other forms of compensation from the organization (for example, fees, commissions, and/or royalties) and more than one member of the same family is compensated by the same organization.[100] Thus, where the control of an organization was in two ministers whose contributions were its total receipts, all of which were paid to them as housing allowances, the exemption of the organization was revoked; the court said that the compensation was not "reasonable" although it may not be "excessive."[101] Yet large salaries and noncash benefits received by an exempt organization's employees can be reasonable, considering the nature of their services and skills, such as payments to physicians by a nonprofit entity that was an incorporated department of anesthesiology of a hospital.[102]

Another basis for finding private inurement is where the compensation paid annually is reasonable but the year-to-year increases of it are not justifiable. In one case, salary increases were found to be "abrupt," resulting in a "substantial" amount of compensation, leading the court to the conclusion that the salaries were "at least suggestive of a commercial rather than nonprofit operation."[103] Spikes in compensation amounts of this nature can also be seen in large bonuses.[104] Yet it is also possible to cast salary increases, abrupt or otherwise, as payments, in whole or in part, for prior years' services, where the executive was undercompensated in those years.[105]

Other forms of compensation are subject to the private inurement doctrine. For example, although a court held that an excessive parsonage allowance may constitute private inurement,[106] the same court subsequently ruled that another parsonage allowance was "not excessive as a matter of law."[107] The IRS revoked

compensation amount was $500,000 (E.J. Harrison & Sons, Inc. v. Comm'r, 86 T.C.M. 240 (2003), rev'd and remanded, 2005-2 U.S.T.C. ¶ 50,493 (9th Cir. 2005), on rem., 91 T.C.M. 1301 (2006), aff'd, 2008-1 U.S.T.C. ¶ 50,244 (9th Cir. 2008)).

[100] E.g., Founding Church of Scientology v. United States, 412 F.2d 1197 (Ct. Cl. 1969), cert. denied, 397 U.S. 1009 (1970); Bubbling Well Church of Universal Love, Inc. v. Comm'r, 74 T.C. 531 (1980), aff'd, 670 F.2d 104 (9th Cir. 1981); Unitary Mission Church of Long Island v. Comm'r, 74 T.C. 507 (1980), aff'd, 647 F.2d 163 (2d Cir. 1981).

[101] Church of the Transfiguring Spirit, Inc. v. Comm'r, 76 T.C. 1, 6 (1981). Cf. Universal Church of Scientific Truth, Inc. v. United States, 74-1 U.S.T.C. ¶ 9360 (N.D. Ala. 1973) (where the organization retained its tax exemption in part because its revenue was derived from fees for publications and its expenses included items other than the compensation of its ministers).

[102] B.H.W. Anesthesia Found., Inc. v. Comm'r, 72 T.C. 681 (1979). Also, Univ. of Mass. Medical School Group Practice v. Comm'r, 74 T.C. 1299 (1980). A court upheld executive compensation arrangements for two executives (related parties) who were "absolutely integral" to a company's "successful performance, a performance that included remarkable growth in revenues, assets, and gross profits" during the tax years at issue (H.W. Johnson, Inc. v. Comm'r, 111 T.C.M. 1418, 1424 (2016)).

[103] Incorporated Trustees of the Gospel Worker Soc'y v. United States, 510 F. Supp. 374, 379 (D.D.C. 1981), aff'd, 672 F.2d 894 (D.C. Cir. 1981), cert denied, 456 U.S. 944 (1982).

[104] E.g., Haffner's Service Stations, Inc. v. Comm'r, 326 F.3d 1 (1st Cir. 2003); Midwest Eye Center, S.C. v. Comm'r, 109 T.C.M. 1245 (2015).

[105] E.g., Aries Communications, Inc. & Subs. v. Comm'r, 105 T.C.M. 1585 (2013); Devine Brothers, Inc. v. Comm'r, 85 T.C.M. 768 (2003). In some circumstances, in the intermediate sanctions context (see Chapter 21), a determination of the reasonableness of compensation for a year may take into account services performed by a disqualified person in prior years (Reg. § 53.4958-4(a)(1)).

[106] Hall v. Comm'r, 729 F.2d 632 (9th Cir. 1984).

[107] Carter v. United States, 973 F.2d 1479, 1487 (9th Cir. 1992).

the tax-exempt status of a health care institution on the ground of several instances of private inurement, including various forms of compensation.[108]

(c) Percentage-Based Compensation

Some compensation arrangements are not fixed payments based on a salary, wage, or (perhaps) bonus but, in whole or in part, on a percentage of the tax-exempt organization's revenue. (In the intermediate sanctions setting, these forms of services are often revenue-sharing arrangements.)[109] The law on this point is unclear and inconsistent. In one case, a court held that a percentage compensation arrangement involving an exempt organization amounted to private inurement, because there was no upper limit as to total allowable compensation.[110] This court subsequently restricted the import of this decision when it held that private inurement did not occur when an exempt organization paid its president a commission determined by a percentage of the contributions obtained by him. The court in the second of these cases held that the standard is whether the compensation is reasonable, rather than the manner in which it is ascertained. Fundraising commissions that are "directly contingent on success in procuring funds" were held by this court to be an "incentive well suited to the budget of a fledgling [charitable] organization."[111] Another court subsequently introduced more confusion in this area when it ruled that "there is nothing insidious or evil about a commission-based compensation system" and thus that an arrangement by which those who successfully secured contributions for a charitable organization were paid a percentage of the gift amounts is "reasonable," despite the absence of any limit as to an absolute amount of compensation (and despite the fact that the law requires compensation to be reasonable, not the percentage by which it is determined).[112]

The IRS will likely closely scrutinize compensation programs of tax-exempt organizations that are predicated on an incentive feature by which compensation is a function of revenue received by the organization, is guaranteed, or is otherwise outside the boundaries of conventional compensation arrangements. These programs—sometimes termed *gainsharing arrangements*—have developed largely in the health care context. For example, the IRS concluded that the establishment of incentive compensation plans for the employees of an exempt hospital, with payments determined as a percentage of the excess of revenue over a budgeted level, will not constitute private inurement, where the plans are not devices to distribute profits to principals, are the result of arm's-length bargaining, and do not result in unreasonable compensation.[113] Employing similar reasoning, the agency approved guaranteed minimum annual salary contracts pursuant to which physicians'

---

[108] Tech. Adv. Mem. 9451001. Litigation ensued (LAC Facilities, Inc. v. United States (No. 94-604T, U.S. Ct. Fed. Cl.)); the case was settled.

[109] See § 21.4(b).

[110] People of God Community v. Comm'r, 75 T.C. 1053 (1989).

[111] World Family Corp. v. Comm'r, 81 T.C. 958, 970 (1983).

[112] Nat'l Found., Inc. v. United States, 87-2 U.S.T.C. ¶ 9602 (Ct. Cl. 1987). Thus, the IRS was incorrect in ruling that the payment of percentage-based compensation "with no stated limit" is a practice amounting to private inurement (Priv. Ltr. Rul. 201820019).

[113] Gen. Couns. Mem. 39674. Also, Rev. Rul. 69-383, 1969-2 C.B. 113; Lorain Avenue Clinic v. Comm'r, 31 T.C. 141 (1958); INFO 2002-0021.

compensation was subsidized so as to induce them to commence employment at a hospital.[114] The IRS promulgated guidance concerning the tax law consequences of physician recruitment incentives.[115]

The agency has explored other forms of productivity incentive programs[116] and contingent compensation plans.[117] Outside the health care field, the IRS concluded that a package of compensation arrangements for the benefit of coaches of sports for schools, colleges, and universities, including deferred compensation plans, payment of life insurance premiums, bonuses, and moving expense reimbursements, did not constitute private inurement.[118] In one instance, the IRS approved of a "sharable income policy" by which a tax-exempt scientific research organization provided one-third of the revenue derived from patents, copyrights, processes, or formulas to the inventors and 15 percent of the revenue received from the licensing or other transfer of the organization's technology to valuable employees.[119]

(d) Multiple Payors

An individual may receive compensation (including fringe benefits) and/or other payments from more than one organization, whether or not tax-exempt. A determination as to the reasonableness of this compensation or other payments must be made in the aggregate.

(e) Role of Board

The law surrounding the private inurement doctrine does not mandate any particular conduct by the governing board of a tax-exempt organization. The contemporary trend, however, is imposition by regulators of corporate governance principles that include involvement by these boards in transactions and arrangements that may have private inurement implications. For example, the IRS prefers that a board of directors or trustees of an exempt organization, particularly a charitable one, be involved in deciding the compensation amounts of at least an organization's key employees. The IRS also is actively encouraging the boards of exempt organizations to adopt conflict-of-interest policies, in part to help bring relationships that have the potential for private inurement to the fore.[120]

(f) Board Member Compensation

The private inurement doctrine, to date, when applied to members of the board of a tax-exempt organization, tends to be focused on the compensation of board members for rendering services in an additional capacity, such as an officer or key employee. As the duties and responsibilities (and potential for liability) of exempt organization board

---

[114] Gen. Couns. Mem. 39498.

[115] Rev. Rul. 97-21, 1997-1 C.B. 121. In general, see *Healthcare Organizations*, Chapter 25.

[116] E.g., Gen. Couns. Mem. 36918.

[117] E.g., Gen. Couns. Mem. 32453.

[118] Gen. Couns. Mem. 39670. Cf. Copperweld Steel Co.'s Warren Employees' Trust v. Comm'r, 61 T.C.M. 1642 (1991) (where an organization was denied tax-exempt status on the basis of IRC § 501(c)(3) because its primary purpose was the provision of compensatory fringe benefits).

[119] Priv. Ltr. Rul. 9316052.

[120] See Form 990, Part VI, line 12.

members increases (due in part to emerging corporate governance principles),[121] so too does the propensity of board members to consider compensation for their services as board members. Also, some exempt organizations have board members who expend considerable time managing the affairs of the organization; these are becoming known as *executive trustees*. These practices are contrary to the culture of most charitable and many other types of exempt organizations; thus, there is little experience or documentation of compensation amounts in this context.[122]

From the standpoint of the private inurement doctrine, the test again is whether such compensation is reasonable; nonetheless, inasmuch as this type of board member compensation is so uncommon, it is nearly impossible to gauge the reasonableness of this compensation by means of the multifactor test, which stresses comparables.[123] A federal court of appeals remanded a case, finding "clearly erroneous" the conclusion of the trial court that most of an individual's compensation was unreasonable, where the appellate court concluded that her services to a corporation were extensive and critical to its survival; the trial court had determined that her role in the affairs of the corporation was equivalent to that of "outside board chair."[124]

(g)   Actuality of Services Rendered

Aside from the reasonableness of compensation, it is axiomatic that a tax-exempt organization subject to the private inurement doctrine may not, without transgressing the doctrine, pay compensation where services are not actually rendered. For example, an organization was denied exempt status because it advanced funds to telephone solicitors, to be offset against earned commissions, where some of the solicitors resigned and kept the funds before earning commissions equal to or exceeding their advances.[125]

(h)   Illegal Payments

Aside from the matter of reasonableness, private inurement can arise where the payment of compensation is contrary to law. In one instance, the IRS revoked the tax-exempt status of an organization that was subject to the private inurement doctrine, where state law required workers in the particular field to be volunteers yet the organization nonetheless compensated them.[126]

§ 20.5   EXCESS EXECUTIVE COMPENSATION TAX

(a)   Overview

An excise tax of 21 percent is imposed on most categories of tax-exempt organizations paying annual compensation in excess of $1 million, and paying separation

---

[121] See § 5.3.
[122] In the rules stipulating the type of governing board a tax-exempt credit counseling organization must have, there are two references to the allowable receipt of reasonable directors' fees (see § 5.6(d)).
[123] See § 20.4(b).
[124] E.J. Harrison & Sons, Inc. v. Comm'r, 2005-2 U.S.T.C. ¶ 50,493 (9th Cir. 2005).
[125] Senior Citizens of Missouri, Inc. v. Comm'r, 56 T.C.M. 479 (1988).
[126] Priv. Ltr. Rul. 200842051.

amounts, where the employee is one of the five highest-compensated employees.[127] The tax base is the "excess" compensation amount. Most tax-exempt organizations (and related nonexempt organizations) are unaffected by this body of law simply because they do not pay any employees remuneration at the level that triggers the tax. That is, there is no excess remuneration[128] if an exempt organization (and any related organization) does not pay more than $1 million of remuneration to any employee for a tax year, and there is no excess parachute payment[129] if the employer does not have any highly compensated employees (for 2022, individuals earning more than $135,000)[130] for the year.

(b) Definition of Applicable Tax-Exempt Organization

This tax is imposed on an *applicable tax-exempt organization*,[131] which is a conventional exempt organization,[132] a farmers' cooperative,[133] a governmental entity that has income excluded from taxation,[134] and a political organization.[135]

A state college or university with a determination letter recognizing exempt status as an educational institution[136] is an applicable tax-exempt organization.[137] By contrast, a state college or university that does not have such a determination letter and that does not utilize the income exclusion rule[138] (that is, is exempt by reason of the doctrine of implied statutory immunity)[139] is not an applicable tax-exempt organization.

A state college or university may, however, be liable for the tax if it is a related organization with respect to an applicable tax-exempt organization.[140]

(c) Definition of *Covered Employee*

A *covered employee* is an individual who is one of the five highest compensated employees of an applicable tax-exempt organization for a tax year or was a covered

---

[127] IRC § 4960, added by the Tax Cuts and Jobs Act (Pub. L. No. 115-97, § 13602(a), 131 Stat. 2054, 2157–59 (2017)).

[128] IRC § 4960(a)(1).

[129] IRC § 4960(a)(2), (c)(5).

[130] IRC § 414(q)(1)(B); Notice 2021-61, 2021-47 I.R.B. 738.

[131] IRC § 4960(c)(1).

[132] That is, an organization that is tax-exempt by reason of IRC § 501(a).

[133] See § 19.12.

[134] See § 19.22(b).

[135] See Chapter 17.

[136] That is, under IRC § 501(c)(3). See § 8.3(a).

[137] 85 Fed. Reg. 35746, 35747 (2020) (preamble to proposed regulations). Also, according to the staff of the Joint Committee on Taxation, in its general explanation of the contents of the Tax Cuts and Jobs Act, the term *applicable tax-exempt organizations* is "intended to include State colleges and universities" (Staff of Joint Comm. on Tax'n, 115th Cong., General Explanation of Public Law 115-97 264 (Comm. Print JCS-1-18 (2018))); this summary adds that a technical correction "may be necessary to reflect this intent" (*id.* at n.1251).

[138] IRC § 115(1). See § 19.22(b).

[139] See § 19.22(a).

[140] IRC § 4960(c)(4)(B). See § 20.5(e).

employee for a preceding year (beginning in 2017).[141] The regulations contain rules for identifying these five highest paid individuals.[142]

Whether an employee is a covered employee is determined separately for each tax-exempt organization. An employee may be a covered employee of more than one exempt organization in a related group of organizations for a year. Once an employee is a covered employee of an exempt organization, the employee continues to be a covered employee of the entity.[143]

(d) Definition of *Remuneration*

For purposes of this tax, *remuneration*[144] generally includes wages,[145] other than a designated Roth contribution,[146] and deferred compensation required to be included in gross income.[147] Remuneration does not, however, include the portion of any remuneration paid to a licensed medical practitioner, including a veterinarian, which is for the performance of medical or veterinary services by the professional.[148] A substantially similar exception applies in connection with the definition of parachute payment.[149]

The regulations define *medical services* as the diagnosis, cure, mitigation, treatment, or prevention of disease in humans or animals; services provided for the purpose of affecting any structure or function of the human or animal body; and other services integral to providing these medical services, that are directly performed by a licensed medical professional.[150] Compensation for teaching or research services does not qualify for the exclusion.[151] The phrase *licensed medical professional* means an individual who is licensed under state or local law to perform medical services, namely, a doctor, nurse, nurse practitioner, dentist, veterinarian, or other licensed medical professional.[152]

(e) Definition of Related Organization

Compensation of a covered person by a related organization or governmental entity is also taken into account for these purposes.[153]

The term *related organization* means any person or governmental entity (domestic or foreign) that meets one or more of these tests: the person or governmental entity (1) controls, or is controlled by, the applicable tax-exempt organization; (2) is controlled by one or more persons that control the exempt organization;

---

[141] IRC § 4960(c)(2); Reg. § 53.4960-1(d)(1).

[142] Reg. § 53.4960-1(d)(2)(i).

[143] Reg. § 53.4960-1(d); T.D. 9938, 86 Fed. Reg. 6196, 6198 (2021).

[144] IRC § 4960(c)(3)(A); Reg. § 53.4960-2(a)(1).

[145] As defined in IRC § 3401(a).

[146] As defined in IRC § 402A(c).

[147] Under IRC § 457(f).

[148] IRC § 4960(c)(3)(B).

[149] IRC § 4960(c)(5)(C)(iii).

[150] Reg. § 53.4960-1(g)(1)(i).

[151] *Id.*

[152] Reg. § 53.4960-1(g)(2).

[153] IRC § 4960(c)(4)(A).

(3) is a supported organization[154] with respect to the exempt organization; or (4) is a supporting organization[155] with respect to the applicable tax-exempt organization.[156] A separate rule applies in connection with voluntary employees' beneficiary associations.[157]

The regulations generally utilize the definition of *control* used in the context of controlling organizations in the unrelated business income setting.[158] The regulations set forth a rule of control in the context of nonstock organizations, entailing a *more-than-50-percent test*, a *removal-power test*, and a *representatives test*.[159] There is a control test for brother-sister arrangements.[160] Constructive ownership rules[161] apply.[162]

(f) Parachute Payments

The regulations capaciously address the matter of the excise tax on excess parachute payments.[163]

A *parachute payment* generally is any payment in the nature of compensation to, or for the benefit of, a covered employee if the payment is contingent on the employee's separation from employment and the aggregate present value of the payments in the nature of compensation to, or for the benefit of, the individual that are contingent on the separation equals or exceeds an amount equal to three times a base amount.[164] There are exclusions, such as compensation for medical services.[165] An excess parachute payment is an amount equal to the excess of a parachute payment over the portion of the base amount allocated to the payment.[166]

The regulations address the requirement of involuntary separation from employment,[167] summarize when a payment is *contingent*,[168] provide a *three-times-base-amount test*,[169] and supply rules for calculating excess parachute payments.[170]

(g) For-Profit Executives as Volunteers

Because of the way in which an applicable tax-exempt organization's five highest compensated may be identified, an issue may arise as to whether for-profit

---

[154] IRC § 509(f)(3). See § 12.3(c).

[155] IRC § 509(a)(3). See § 12.3(c).

[156] IRC § 4960(c)(4)(B); Reg. § 53.4960-1(i)(1).

[157] *Id.*

[158] IRC § 512(b)(13)(D) (see §§ 29.7, 30.6(b)); Reg. § 53.4960-1(i)(2)(ii)-(iv). A person controls a stock corporation if they own, by vote or value, more than 50 percent of the stock in the corporation (Reg. § 53.4960-1(i)(2)(ii)).

[159] Reg. § 53.4960-1(i)(2)(v).

[160] Reg. § 53.4960-1(i)(2)(vi).

[161] IRC § 318.

[162] Reg. § 53.4960-1(i)(2)(vii).

[163] IRC § 4960(a)(2); Reg. § 53.4960-3.

[164] IRC § 4960(c)(5)(B); Reg. § 53.4960-3(a)(1).

[165] Reg. § 53.4960-3(a)(2)(iii). See § 20.5(d).

[166] IRC § 4960(c)(5)(A).

[167] Reg. § 53.4960-3(e).

[168] Reg. § 53.4960-3(d).

[169] Reg. § 53.4960-3(g).

[170] Reg. § 53.4960-3(h)-(l).

businesses are subject to this excise tax because their executives are volunteers at related tax-exempt organizations.

The regulations include two exceptions to the definition of the terms *employee* and *covered employee*, and the rules for identifying the five highest compensated employees, intended to ensure that certain employees of a related nonexempt entity providing services as an employee of an exempt organization are not treated as one of the five highest compensated employees of the exempt organization—as long as certain conditions are satisfied.

One of these exceptions is the *limited hours exception*, which entails two requirements.[171] For purposes of determining an exempt organization's five highest paid employees for a year, an individual is disregarded if neither the exempt organization nor a related exempt organization paid remuneration to the individual for services the individual performed as an employee of the exempt organization during the year. Also, for the individual to be disregarded, the individual must have performed services as an employee of the exempt organization and any related exempt organizations for no more than 10 percent of the total hours the individual worked as an employee of the exempt organization and any related organizations during the year. The second element of this exception is deemed met if the employee performed no more than 100 hours of service as an employee of the exempt organization and any related exempt organization during the year.

The other exception is the *nonexempt funds exception*, which has three requirements.[172] One, neither the exempt organization nor any related exempt organization nor any taxable related organization controlled by the exempt organization or by one or more related exempt organizations, either alone or together with the exempt organization, paid remuneration to the individual for services the individual performed as an employee of an exempt organization during the year and the preceding year. Two, the individual performed services as an employee of the exempt organization and any related exempt organizations for not more than 50 percent of the total hours worked as an employee of the exempt organization and any related organizations during the year and the preceding year. Three, no related organization that paid remuneration to the individual during the year and the preceding year provided services for a fee to the exempt organization, a related exempt organization, or a taxable related organization controlled by the exempt organization or by one or more related exempt organizations, either alone or together with the exempt organization, during the year and the preceding year.

The limited hours and nonexempt funds exceptions thus exclude certain employees who may be viewed as volunteers (even though, under law, they are employees) from status as one of an applicable tax-exempt organization's five highest compensated employees.

Additionally, a *limited-services exception* allows an individual to be disregarded for these purposes where the tax-exempt organization paid less than 10 percent of the individual's total compensation for services performed as an employee of the exempt organization and all related organizations during the year.[173] This exception,

---

[171] Reg. § 53.4960-1(d)(2)(ii).
[172] Reg. § 53.4960-1(d)(2)(iii).
[173] Reg. § 53.4960-1(d)(2)(iv).

however, may be of limited utility inasmuch as it requires that the applicable tax-exempt organization have at least one related organization.

Finally, the regulations include rules that a member of a board of directors of a corporation or trustee of a trust is not an employee of the corporation or trust (in that capacity).[174]

(h) Additional Law

The regulations include definitions of various other terms relevant to the tax on excess tax-exempt organization executive compensation, such as *applicable year*,[175] *employee*,[176] *employer*,[177] and *predecessor*.[178]

The regulations provide rules regarding when compensation is paid, the entity that is liable for the excise tax, and how that tax is calculated, both as to excess remuneration and excess parachute payments, and allocation of liability for the tax among related organizations.[179]

For each tax year, with respect to each covered employee, the taxpayer is liable for tax on the sum of the excess remuneration allocated to the taxpayer with respect to an applicable year and, if the taxpayer is an applicable tax-exempt organization, any excess parachute payment paid by the taxpayer or a predecessor during the tax year.[180]

For example, if remuneration paid during a year by more than one employer to a covered employee is taken into account in determining the tax imposed on excess remuneration, the taxpayer is liable for the tax in an amount that bears the same ratio to the total tax as the amount of compensation paid by the taxpayer bears to the total amount of compensation involved.[181]

§ 20.6 OTHER FORMS OF PRIVATE INUREMENT

Although the precepts of private inurement and self-dealing in the private foundation setting are by no means precisely the same, the following summary of self-dealing transactions offers a useful sketch of the scope of transactions that, in appropriate circumstances, amount to instances of private inurement:[182] (1) sale or exchange, or leasing, of property between a tax-exempt organization and an insider; (2) lending of

---

[174] Reg. § 53.4960-1(e)(2), (3).

[175] Reg. § 53.4960-1(c).

[176] Reg. § 53.4960-1(e). Generally, an *employee* is an individual performing services if the relationship between the individual and the person for whom the individual performs services is the legal relationship of employer and employee, including common-law employees (Reg. § 53.4960-1(e)(1)).

[177] Reg. § 53.4960-1(f).

[178] Reg. § 53.4960-1(h).

[179] Reg. § 53-4960-4.

[180] Reg. § 53.4960-4(a)(1).

[181] Reg. § 53.4960-4(c)(1).

[182] The definition of *self-dealing* as applied in the private foundation setting, written in 1969, is, in essence, a codification of much of the case law concerning private inurement. Yet more than 35 years later, Congress believed its specificity in this regard to be too limiting and chose, when once again legislating on the subject, to use an overarching definition when creating the concept of the *excess benefit transaction* (see § 21.4(a)).

money or other extension of credit between an exempt organization and an insider; (3) furnishing of goods, services, or facilities between an exempt organization and an insider; (4) payment of compensation (or payment or reimbursement of expenses) by an exempt organization to an insider; and (5) transfer to, or use by or for the benefit of, an insider of the income or assets of an exempt organization.[183]

The principal forms of private inurement, other than excessive compensation,[184] involve rental arrangements, lending arrangements, sales of assets, capital improvements, equity distributions, assumptions of liability, provision of employee benefits, a variety of tax avoidance schemes, the rendering of services, business referral operations, the provision of goods or refreshments, and certain retained interests, but not embezzlement.

(a) Rental Arrangements

A tax-exempt organization subject to the doctrine of private inurement generally may lease property and make rental payments for the use of property in a transaction involving an insider. The rent payments, and other terms and conditions of the arrangement, must, however, be reasonable; the arrangement should be beneficial for the exempt organization. That is, an inflated rent amount favoring the insider is private inurement.[185] For example, an organization striving to be a tax-exempt church was ruled ineligible for exemption because a substantial portion of its revenue was paid to lease a currently unusable warehouse, to ultimately be used for religious purposes, from its president.[186]

The factors to be considered in the rental arrangement context in determining reasonableness include the duration of the lease and the amount and frequency of the rent payments, with all elements of the relationship evaluated in relation to comparable situations in the community. In one instance, the IRS found private inurement, and thus denied recognition of tax exemption, in part because the organization was leasing land from an insider, without consideration as to whether the lease arrangement was reasonable.[187]

(b) Lending Arrangements

A loan involving the assets of a tax-exempt organization subject to the doctrine of private inurement, made to an insider, is likely to be closely scrutinized by the IRS. It is the view of courts that the "very existence of a private source of loan credit from an [exempt] organization's earnings may itself amount to inurement of benefit."[188]

---

[183] IRC § 4941(d)(1)(A)–(E). The IRS applied the self-dealing rationale in one public pronouncement in an instance of a transaction involving a public charity and its directors (Rev. Rul. 76-441, 1976-2 C.B. 147); a court essentially did the same (without expressly using the term) in a case concerning a church and its ministers (Church by Mail, Inc. v. Comm'r, 48 T.C.M. 471 (1984), aff'd, 765 F.2d 1387 (9th Cir. 1985)).

[184] See § 20.4.

[185] E.g., Founding Church of Scientology v. United States, 412 F.2d 1197 (Ct. Cl. 1969), cert. denied, 397 U.S. 1009 (1970); Texas Trade School v. Comm'r, 30 T.C. 642 (1958), aff'd, 272 F.2d 168 (5th Cir. 1959).

[186] Priv. Ltr. Rul. 201411037.

[187] Priv. Ltr. Rul. 201849012.

[188] Founding Church of Scientology v. United States, 412 F.2d 1197, 1202 (Ct. Cl. 1969), cert. denied, 397 U.S. 1009 (1970). Also, Unitary Mission Church of Long Island v. Comm'r, 74 T.C. 507 (1980), aff'd, 647

The terms of this type of loan should be reasonable, that is, financially advantageous to the exempt organization (or at least not be disadvantageous) and should be commensurate with the organization's purposes (including investment policies).[189] The factors to be considered when assessing reasonableness in this setting include the duration of the indebtedness, the rate of interest paid, the security underlying the loan, and the amount involved—all evaluated in relation to similar circumstances in the commercial setting. If such a loan is not repaid on a timely basis, questions as to private inurement may well be raised.[190] Thus, for example, the tax exemption of a school was revoked, in part because two of its officers were provided by the school with interest-free, unsecured loans that subjected the school to uncompensated risks for no business purpose.[191]

A court found private inurement resulting from a loan where a nonprofit organization, formed to assume the operations of a school conducted up to that point by a for-profit corporation, required parents of its students to make interest-free loans to the corporation. Private inurement was detected in the fact that the property to be improved using the loan proceeds would revert to the for-profit corporation after a 15-year term; the interest-free feature of the loans was held to be an unwarranted benefit to individuals in their private capacity.[192] Earlier, this court found private inurement in a situation where a tax-exempt hospital made a substantial number of unsecured loans to a nursing home owned by the founding physician at below-market interest rates; this arrangement reduced his financial risk in and lowered the interest costs for the home.[193]

The IRS found private inurement in a lending transaction where a charitable organization borrowed money from two of its board members, at a rate of interest that was twice the rate the organization subsequently obtained from a bank.[194]

(c) Sales of Assets

Another application of the private inurement doctrine involves the sale of assets of tax-exempt organizations to those who are insiders with respect to them. A charitable or other exempt organization may, for example, decide to sell assets relating to a program activity because the organization no longer wishes to engage in that activity. Sometimes, for a variety of reasons, these assets are sold to one or more individuals who are insiders (usually directors or officers). As with other manifestations of these transactions, they are not prohibited; the requirement is that their terms and conditions be reasonable.

An illustrative case identified some of the difficulties and complexities that can arise in this context. The matter concerned the sale of the assets of an exempt hospital to an entity controlled by insiders with respect to the hospital. The court concluded that the transaction gave rise to private inurement because the sale was

---

F.2d 163 (2d Cir. 1981); Western Catholic Church v. Comm'r, 73 T.C. 196 (1979), *aff'd*, 631 F.2d 736 (7th Cir. 1980), *cert. denied*, 450 U.S. 981 (1981); Church in Boston v. Comm'r, 71 T.C. 102 (1978).

[189] Griswold v. Comm'r, 39 T.C. 620 (1962).

[190] Best Lock Corp. v. Comm'r, 31 T.C. 1217 (1959); Rev. Rul. 67-5, 1967-1 C.B. 123.

[191] John Marshall Law School v. United States, 81-2 U.S.T.C. ¶ 9514 (Ct. Cl. 1981).

[192] Hancock Academy of Savannah, Inc. v. Comm'r, 69 T.C. 488 (1977).

[193] Lowry Hospital Ass'n v. Comm'r, 66 T.C. 850 (1976).

[194] Priv. Ltr. Rul. 202004012.

not at arm's length, which caused the assets to be sold for less than their fair market value. The purchase price (as determined by the court) was $6.6 million; the court, noting an array of elements that either were not taken into account or were inadequately taken into account in arriving at the price, concluded that the fair market value of the hospital's assets was $7.8 million.[195]

The court, however, rejected the claim of the IRS that it is necessary to determine a "precise amount" representing the fair market value of property in a private inurement case.[196] All that is required is an amount that is "sufficiently close to the fair market value of the property at the time of the sale."[197] The court wrote that, when the amount is within a "reasonable range" of what could be considered fair market value, there cannot be private inurement.[198]

An open issue is whether, in assigning a value to an item of property for private inurement purposes, a single valuation will suffice.[199] Moreover, there is no mandated valuation method. The IRS wrote that "no single valuation method is necessarily the best indicator of value in a given case."[200] Yet the agency has signaled its preference for various appraisal methodologies in valuing property, observing in one instance that "it would be logical to assume that an appraisal that has considered and applied a variety of approaches in reaching its 'bottom line' is more likely to result in an accurate valuation than an appraisal that focused on a single valuation method."[201]

(d) Capital Improvements

Some nonprofit organizations, principally those seeking public charity status, find themselves using real property provided by an insider, perhaps for little or no rent. This type of organization may intend, once recognition of exemption is obtained, to seek funding to make substantial capital improvements to the land. This type of property improvement constitutes private inurement, precluding tax exemption.[202]

(e) Equity Distributions

With the emphasis of the federal tax law in the private inurement area on *net earnings* and the reference to *private shareholders*, the most literal and obvious form of private inurement is the parceling out of an exempt organization's net income to those akin to shareholders, such as members of its board of directors. It is rare, however, that private inurement is this blatant. In one instance, nonetheless, where the assets of a tax-exempt hospital relating to a pharmacy were sold to a corporation, which then sold pharmaceuticals to the hospital at higher prices, a court held

---

[195] Anclote Psychiatric Center, Inc. v. Comm'r, 76 T.C.M. 175 (1998).

[196] *Id*. at 182.

[197] *Id*.

[198] *Id*. A similar case unfolded in the intermediate sanctions setting (Caracci v. Comm'r, 118 T.C. 379 (2002), *rev'd*, 456 F.3d 444 (5th Cir. 2006)); see § 21.4(a).

[199] In the charitable giving setting, where an appraisal of property is required, only a single appraisal is called for; see *Charitable Giving* § 19.8.

[200] Priv. Ltr. Rul. 9130002.

[201] *Id*.

[202] E.g., Priv. Ltr. Rul. 201417017.

that this practice amounted to the "siphoning off" of the hospital's income for the benefit of the corporation's stockholders.[203]

A limited dividend housing corporation, under close supervision of a state, was denied tax exemption as a social welfare entity[204] because it was operated on a for-profit basis (the private inurement doctrine not being expressly applicable at the time).[205] Similarly, a "sweat equity housing cooperative association," formed to engage in restoration of historic properties, was denied recognition of exemption as a charitable entity because its board members held possessory interests in properties owned by the organization and were potentially eligible for cash distributions on dissolution.[206]

In nearly all the states, nonprofit corporations may not be organized as entities with the ability to issue stock. Even in the few instances where tax-exempt organizations may have stockholders, the organizations may not pay dividends.[207] In one instance, memberships in a tax-exempt hospital were found to not entitle the members to a beneficial interest in the capital or earnings of the hospital because the law of the state prohibited the corporation from paying any part of its income to members and required transfer of the assets on dissolution for charitable purposes.[208] Of course, an organization issuing voting stock with rights in the form of equity interests is violating the doctrine of private inurement.[209]

(f) Assumptions of Liability

Generally, a tax-exempt organization can incur debt to purchase an asset at its fair market value, thereafter retire the debt with its receipts, and not thereby violate the private inurement proscription.[210] As is the case with the sale of an asset, however, if the purchase price for an asset acquired from an insider is in excess of the property's fair market value (debt-financed or not), private inurement may result.[211] In one instance, a nonprofit organization, in taking over operation of a school conducted by a for-profit corporation, assumed a liability for goodwill; this assumption was found to be private inurement because it was an excessive amount and benefited the owners of the corporation.[212]

(g) Employee Benefits

A tax-exempt organization can provide reasonable compensation, including standard benefits, to its employees.[213] For example, a court found that payments

---

[203] Maynard Hospital, Inc. v. Comm'r, 52 T.C. 1006, 1032 (1969).
[204] See Chapter 13.
[205] Amalgamated Housing Corp. v. Comm'r, 37 B.T.A. 817 (1938), aff'd, 108 F.2d 1010 (2d Cir. 1940).
[206] Priv. Ltr. Rul. 201640022.
[207] See § 1.1(a), note 7.
[208] Estate of Scharf v. Comm'r, 316 F.2d 625 (7th Cir. 1963), aff'g 38 T.C. 15 (1962).
[209] E.g., Priv. Ltr. Rul. 201918020.
[210] E.g., Shiffman v. Comm'r, 32 T.C. 1073 (1959); Estate of Howes v. Comm'r, 30 T.C. 909 (1958), aff'd sub nom., Comm'r v. Johnson, 267 F.2d 382 (1st Cir. 1959); Ohio Furnace Co., Inc. v. Comm'r, 25 T.C. 179 (1955), appeal dismissed (6th Cir. 1956). The acquisition of property by means of debt financing may, however, generate unrelated business income (IRC § 514) (see § 24.10).
[211] E.g., Kolkey v. Comm'r, 27 T.C. 37 (1956), aff'd, 254 F.2d 51 (7th Cir. 1958).
[212] Hancock Academy of Savannah, Inc. v. Comm'r, 69 T.C. 488 (1977).
[213] See § 20.4(b).

for medical insurance are an "ordinary and necessary" expense of an exempt employer.[214] An organization may not be able to qualify as an exempt charitable one, however, where the provision of employee benefits is its purpose. For example, a trust created by an employer to pay pensions to retired employees failed to qualify as a charitable entity.[215] This would be the result where the recipients are still employees providing services, in part because they do not constitute a charitable class.[216] Thus, a foundation lost its tax-exempt status because it devoted its funds to the payment of the expenses of young performers employed by the foundation's founder, who was in show business.[217] Organizations such as these may, however, qualify for tax exemption under other provisions of the federal tax law.[218]

A school's tax exemption was revoked because, for one or more of its officers, it provided interest-free, unsecured loans, paid for household items and furnishings used in their residences, made scholarship grants to their children, paid personal travel expenses, paid their personal automobile expenses, paid the premiums on life and health insurance policies (where the premiums were not paid for other employees), and purchased season tickets for them to sports events.[219] Yet in another instance, a court concluded that the payment by a church of medical expenses for its minister and family did not constitute private inurement.[220]

The IRS came around to the view that charitable and other tax-exempt organizations may establish profit-sharing and similar compensation plans without causing private inurement,[221] having earlier taken the position that the establishment of qualified profit-sharing plans resulted in *per se* private inurement.[222] This shift in position was based on the reasoning that the principles of qualification of pension and profit-sharing plans,[223] and the protections afforded by the Employee Retirement Income Security Act (enacted in 1974), are sufficient to ensure that operation of these plans would not jeopardize the tax-exempt status of the non-profit organizations involved. Thereafter, legislation enacted in 1986 amended the employee plan rules to make it clear that tax-exempt organizations can, without jeopardy, maintain qualified profit-sharing plans,[224] and extended deferred compensation rules[225] to make them applicable to tax-exempt organizations.

Tax-exempt organizations may maintain the qualified cash or deferral arrangements known as 401(k) plans.[226] A charitable organization may maintain a

---

[214] Carter v. United States, 973 F.2d 1479, 1487 (9th Cir. 1992).
[215] Rev. Rul. 56-138, 156-1 C.B. 202.
[216] Rev. Rul. 68-422, 1968-2 C.B. 207. Also, Watson v. United States, 355 F.2d 269 (3d Cir. 1965).
[217] Horace Heidt Foundation v. United States, 170 F. Supp. 634 (Ct. Cl. 1959).
[218] E.g., IRC §§ 401, 501(c)(9), (c)(17).
[219] John Marshall Law School v. United States, 81-2 U.S.T.C. ¶ 9514 (Ct. Cl. 1981). Also, Chase v. Comm'r, 19 T.C.M. 234 (1960).
[220] Brian Ruud Int'l v. United States, 733 F. Supp. 396 (D.D.C. 1989).
[221] Gen. Couns. Mem. 39674.
[222] E.g., Gen. Couns. Mem. 35869.
[223] IRC § 401.
[224] IRC § 401(a)(27).
[225] IRC § 457.
[226] IRC § 401(k)(4)(B)(i).

tax-sheltered annuity program for its employees.[227] In general, exempt organizations may pay pensions, where the terms are reasonable, to their retired employees without adversely affecting their exempt status.[228]

(h) Tax Avoidance Schemes

Tax-exempt organizations can be used impermissibly as vehicles to avoid income taxation. In one instance, a physician transferred his medical practice and other assets to a controlled organization, which hired him to conduct "research," which amounted to the ongoing examination and treatment of patients; recognition of exemption for this organization was denied.[229] In another case, an organization, ostensibly a church, was formed by a professional nurse, who was the organization's minister, director, and principal officer; the organization did not qualify as an exempt organization, the IRS ruled, because it "serve[d] as a vehicle for handling the nurse's personal financial transactions."[230] In another instance, a court found that "tax avoidance" was a "substantial nonexempt purpose" of an organization, as evidenced by its promotional literature and seminars, and for that reason revoked the organization's exempt status.[231] In still another of these situations, an exempt organization founded and managed by an accountant had its exemption revoked because the accountant concealed receipts from his practice to avoid payment of federal income tax, by treating some payments as having been made to the charitable entity.[232]

A court, unwilling to recognize an organization as a church because most of the organization's support was derived from the founder, whose living expenses were paid by the organization, wrote that private "inurement is strongly suggested where an individual or small group is the principal contributor to an organization and the principal recipient of the distributions of the organization, and that individual or small group has exclusive control over the management of the organization's funds."[233] Another "church" failed to gain exemption because of the transfer to it of funds used to furnish a sports car to its donor and pastor.[234]

(i) Services Rendered

An organization whose primary purpose is to render services to individuals in their private capacity, generally cannot qualify as a tax-exempt, charitable entity. There are exceptions to this general rule, of course, such as where the individuals

---

[227] IRC § 403(b).

[228] Rev. Rul. 73-126, 1973-1 C.B. 220.

[229] Rev. Rul. 69-266, 1969-1 C.B. 151. Also, Nittler v. Comm'r, 39 T.C.M. 422 (1979); Walker v. Comm'r, 37 T.C.M. 1851 (1978); Boyer v. Comm'r, 69 T.C. 521 (1977).

[230] Rev. Rul. 81-94, 1981-1 C.B. 330. Also, Rev. Rul. 78-232, 1978-1 C.B. 69. These two rulings pertain to the *personal church* (see § 10.2(c)).

[231] Freedom Church of Revelation v. United States, 588 F. Supp. 693 (D.D.C. 1984).

[232] Priv. Ltr. Rul. 201544028. An organization had its tax exemption retroactively revoked because a lawyer who dominated it promoted a scheme involving ostensible charitable gifts, where in fact little or no economic benefits were transferred to charities (Priv. Ltr. Rul. 201834013).

[233] Church of Eternal Life & Liberty, Inc. v. Comm'r, 86 T.C. 916 (1986).

[234] McFall v. Comm'r, 58 T.C.M. 175 (1989). Also, Good Friendship Temple v. Comm'r, 55 T.C.M. 1310 (1988); Church of Modern Enlightenment v. Comm'r, 55 T.C.M. 1304 (1988); Petersen v. Comm'r, 53 T.C.M. 235 (1987).

benefited constitute members of a charitable class, the individual beneficiaries are considered merely instruments or means for advancement of a charitable objective, or the private benefit involved is incidental and/or unavoidable.

This type of private inurement takes many forms and involves judgments in specific cases that are difficult to quantify or generalize. For example, even though furtherance of the arts can be a charitable activity, a cooperative art gallery that exhibited and sold only its members' works was ruled to be serving their private ends—a "vehicle for advancing their careers and promoting the sale of their work"—and hence to not be tax-exempt, notwithstanding the fact that the exhibition and sale of works of art may sometimes be an exempt purpose.[235] Similarly, although the provision of housing assistance for low-income families may qualify as an exempt purpose, an organization that provided this form of assistance but gave preference for housing to employees of a farm proprietorship operated by the individual who controlled the organization was ruled to not qualify as a charitable organization.[236] Also, a school's exemption was revoked, in part because it awarded scholarships to the children of two of its officers yet did not make scholarship grants to anyone else.[237]

The provision of services to individuals, as precluded by the private inurement proscription, takes several forms. For example, an organization created to provide bus transportation for schoolchildren to a tax-exempt private school was ruled to not be eligible for exemption.[238] The IRS said that the organization served a private rather than a public interest, in that it enabled the participating parents to fulfill their individual responsibility of transporting children to school. The IRS applied this rationale to deny recognition of tax exemption to an organization providing a cooperative education for homeschooled students; the organization's members were the students' parents and although the IRS conceded that there was an "educational aspect" to the organization's activities, it impermissibly served a private benefit rather than a public interest.[239] A testamentary trust established to make payments to charitable organizations and to use a fixed sum from its annual income for the perpetual care of the testator's burial lot was ruled to be serving a private interest and thus to not qualify for exemption.[240] Further, an organization that operated a subscription "scholarship" plan, by which "scholarships" were paid to preselected, specifically named individuals designated by subscribers, was ruled to not be exempt, since it was operated for the benefit of designated individuals.[241] Likewise, the furnishing of farm laborers for individual farmers, as part of the operation of a labor camp to house transient workers, was held to not be an agricultural purpose under the federal tax law but rather the provision of services to individual farmers that they would otherwise have to provide for themselves.[242]

---

[235] Rev. Rul. 71-395, 1971-2 C.B. 228.

[236] Rev. Rul. 72-147, 1972-1 C.B. 147.

[237] John Marshall Law School v. United States, 81-2 U.S.T.C. ¶ 9514 (Ct. Cl. 1981).

[238] Rev. Rul. 69-175, 1969-1 C.B. 149. Also, Chattanooga Automobile Club v. Comm'r, 182 F.2d 551 (6th Cir. 1950).

[239] Priv. Ltr. Rul. 202224013.

[240] Rev. Rul. 69-256, 1969-1 C.B. 150.

[241] Rev. Rul. 67-367, 1967-2 C.B. 188.

[242] Rev. Rul. 72-391, 1972-2 C.B. 249.

Also, a nonprofit corporation was deemed to be serving private purposes where it was formed to dredge a navigable waterway, little used by the public, fronting the properties of its members.[243] Further, an organization that provided travel services, legal services, an insurance plan, an antitheft registration program, and discount programs to its members was held to be serving the interests of the members, thereby precluding the organization from qualifying as an exempt educational organization.[244] Moreover, an organization was denied exempt status because a substantial portion of its funds was to be used to pay for the medical and rehabilitative care of an individual who was related to each of the trustees of the organization.[245] Thus, a trust established to raise funds for an individual's legal defense, including bail, was denied recognition of tax exemption as a charitable organization because it is benefiting a preselected, designated individual and is serving private interests.[246] Likewise, private inurement was found where a nonprofit organization primarily funded the continuing education of its founder, president, and director, including payment for airfare and other transportation, apartment and furnishings, tuition, school supplies, and training seminars, plus paid this individual a salary while studying.[247]

Charitable organizations frequently provide services to individuals in their private capacity when they dispense financial planning advice in the context of designing major gifts. This type of personal service made available by tax-exempt organizations has never been regarded as jeopardizing the organizations' tax exemption, when undertaken by institutions such as churches, universities, colleges, and hospitals. The IRS, however, refused to accord tax exemption to an organization that engaged in financial counseling by providing tax planning services (including charitable giving considerations) to wealthy individuals referred to it by subscribing religious organizations. The court that subsequently heard the case upheld the agency's position, finding that tax planning is not an exempt activity (which, of course, it is not—outside of this context) and that the primary effect of the advice is to reduce individuals' liability for income taxes—a private benefit.[248] The court rejected the contention that the organization was merely doing what the

---

[243] Ginsberg v. Comm'r, 46 T.C. 47 (1966). Cf. Rev. Rul. 70-186, 1970-1 C.B. 128.

[244] U.S. C.B. Radio Ass'n, No. 1, Inc. v. Comm'r, 42 T.C.M. 1441 (1981).

[245] Wendy L. Parker Rehabilitation Found., Inc. v. Comm'r, 52 T.C.M. 51 (1986). Likewise, a nonprofit organization established to negotiate, receive funds, organize, and manage support for three special needs children of a family was denied recognition of exemption (Priv. Ltr. Rul. 201205011). Similarly, a trust was held ineligible for exemption as a charitable entity because its function was to pay a family's medical expenses in the aftermath of an automobile accident (Priv. Ltr. Rul. 201428026). Also, a nonprofit organization was ruled unqualified for exemption because it provided health care services to one individual for several years, despite requests from others for services and referrals (Priv. Ltr. Rul. 202109007).

Congress, from time to time, overrides this rule. For example, the Slain Officer Family Support Act of 2015 (Pub. L. 114-7, 129 Stat. 83), which facilitates deductible contributions for the benefit of the families of two police detectives, states that distributions to the families shall "not be treated as inuring to the benefit of any private individual," as long as the payments are made in good faith in accordance with a reasonable and objective formula (id. at 84).

[246] Priv. Ltr. Rul. 202014015.

[247] Priv. Ltr. Rul. 202117023.

[248] Christian Stewardship Assistance, Inc. v. Comm'r, 70 T.C. 1037 (1978).

subscribing members can do for themselves without endangering their tax exemption: fundraising.

The private inurement proscription may apply not only to individuals in their private capacity but also to corporations, industries, professions, and the like. Thus, an organization primarily engaged in the testing of drugs for commercial pharmaceutical companies was ruled to not be engaged in scientific research or testing for public safety but to be serving the private interests of the manufacturers.[249] Similarly, an organization composed of members of a particular industry to develop new and improved uses for existing products of the industry was ruled to be operating primarily to serve the private interests of its creators and thus not be tax-exempt.[250] Further, an association of professional nurses that operated a nurses' registry was held to be affording greater employment opportunities for its members and thus to be substantially operating for private ends.[251] A nonprofit organization organized and operated to provide scholarships to students to enable them to enroll in online educational study and coursework programs that prepare the students to earn higher education credits was denied recognition of exemption, in part because the programs were conducted by a related for-profit business; the business was said to be "in a position to profit from" this arrangement.[252] Likewise, a nonprofit organization formed to provide scholarships to public educational institutions offered prospective donors, in exchange for their gifts, the right to niches in a columbarium located on their campuses; the organization was denied recognition of exemption as a charitable entity on the ground that this activity amounted to a "valuable inducement" for the purchase of niches from a related company.[253]

A court held that a genealogical society, the membership of which was composed of persons interested in the migration of individuals with a common name to and within the United States, failed to qualify as an exempt charitable entity on the ground that its activities served the private interests of its members.[254] Following this court's holding, the IRS acted to contain the reach of the decision. The agency ruled that a genealogical society may qualify as a tax-exempt educational organization by conducting lectures, sponsoring public displays and museum tours, providing written materials to instruct members of the general public on genealogical research, and compiling a geographical area's pioneer history.[255] By contrast, the IRS also ruled that an organization cannot qualify as a charitable or educational entity where its membership is limited to descendants of a particular family, it compiled family genealogical research data for use by its members for reasons other

---

[249] Rev. Rul. 68-373, 1968-2 C.B. 206. Also, Rev. Rul. 65-1, 1965-1 C.B. 266.

[250] Rev. Rul. 69-632, 1969-2 C.B. 120.

[251] Rev. Rul. 61-170, 1961-2 C.B. 112.

[252] Priv. Ltr. Rul. 201148008.

[253] Priv. Ltr. Rul. 201910022.

[254] Callaway Family Ass'n, Inc. v. Comm'r, 71 T.C. 340 (1978). This opinion presumably reinforces an IRS ruling that nonprofit genealogical societies qualify as tax-exempt social clubs (Rev. Rul. 67-8, 1967-1 C.B. 142) (see Chapter 15). Just prior to this decision, the court recognized that a membership organization can qualify under IRC § 501(c)(3) where it provides information and services to members and nonmembers (Nat'l Ass'n for the Legal Support of Alternative Schools v. Comm'r, 71 T.C. 118 (1978)). The approach in *Callaway* was followed in Benjamin Price Genealogical Ass'n v. Internal Revenue Service, 79-1 U.S.T.C. ¶ 9361 (D.D.C. 1979); Manning Ass'n v. Comm'r, 93 T.C. 596 (1989).

[255] Rev. Rul. 80-301, 1980-2 C.B. 180.

than to conform to the religious precepts of the family's denomination, it presented the data to designated libraries, it published volumes of family history, and it promoted occasional social activities among family members.[256]

The rendering of services to individuals may also violate the private benefit doctrine.[257] Rather than decide whether the individuals to whom services are rendered are insiders, thereby resulting in private inurement, courts and the IRS may apply the private benefit doctrine to support the revocation or denial of exempt status. Thus, while acknowledging that the private inurement doctrine was potentially applicable, a court instead applied the private benefit doctrine to uphold the revocation of exempt status in the case of an organization that provided funds to defray or pay for its members' funeral and burial costs.[258] The IRS often applies the same approach in the case of organizations providing services to its members.[259] Thus, for example, an organization operating a membership-based barter system that uses "time banked" volunteer hours instead of money as currency for goods and services was found to be operating primarily for the private benefit of its members.[260]

(j) Business Referral and Networking Operations

A nonprofit organization may seek recognition of exemption, usually as an educational entity, where, although it provides some educational benefits, its principal purpose is to serve as a means for generating business opportunities for its insiders. For example, an organization represented to the IRS that its educational activity was the conduct of workshops to provide first-time home buyers with information to help them achieve home ownership in an informed manner. In fact, the entity was operated by a team consisting of two real estate agents, a mortgage banker, an insurance agent, and a lawyer. No fee was charged for the workshops; the operation was funded by the team members. Finding the organization to be a "medium to enrich the private businesses" of its insiders, the IRS found private inurement as the consequence of "client referrals" to the insiders' "private business ventures."[261] Similarly, the IRS found private inurement in a situation where a nonprofit corporation, formed to help homeowners struggling with mortgage debt, was providing referrals to a for-profit company owned by two of the corporation's officers.[262]

Likewise, an organization providing services for foreclosure mitigation was found by the IRS to be a "conduit" linking potential customers to its founders in the nature of a "consulting referral service."[263]

---

[256] Rev. Rul. 80-302, 1980-2 C.B. 182.

[257] See § 20.13.

[258] Korean-American Senior Mut. Ass'n, Inc. v. Comm'r, T.C. Memo. 2020-129.

[259] Rev. Rul. 67-367, 1967-2 C.B. 188; Rev. Rul. 69-175, 1969-1 C.B. 149. E.g., Priv. Ltr. Rul. 202421009.

[260] Priv. Ltr. Rul. 202308012.

[261] Priv. Ltr. Rul. 201039046.

[262] Priv. Ltr. Rul. 201921019.

[263] Priv. Ltr. Rul. 201121021. Similarly, Abovo Found., Inc. v. Comm'r, 115 T.C.M. 1277 (2018), finding the organizations seeking exempt status was a façade for its founder's quality management consulting activities.

(k)　Provision of Goods or Refreshments

A tax-exempt organization subject to the private inurement doctrine cannot have as its primary purpose the provision of goods or refreshments (in the nature of social or recreational activities) to individuals in their private capacity. Of course, an organization of this nature may incidentally bear the expense of meals, refreshments, and the like (such as working luncheons and annual banquets), but, in general, "[r]efreshments, goods and services furnished to the members of an exempt corporation from the net profits of the business enterprise are benefits inuring to the individual members."[264] Thus, a discussion group that held closed meetings at which personally oriented speeches were given, followed by the serving of food and other refreshments, was ruled to not be tax-exempt, inasmuch as the public benefits were remote at best and the "functions of the organization are to a significant extent fraternal and designed to stimulate fellowship among the membership."[265]

(l)　Retained Interests

A charitable organization may not be organized so that one or more individuals retain a reversionary interest, by which the principal would flow to an individual on the entity's dissolution or liquidation; instead, in this event, net assets and income must be transferred to one or more other charitable or governmental entities.[266]

By contrast, a charitable organization may, in appropriate circumstances, accept an asset subject to a life estate or other income interest for one or more individuals; the fact that only a charitable remainder interest is acquired is not private inurement. Thus, there are bodies of law concerning permissible partial interest gifts to charitable organizations of income and remainder interests.[267] Likewise, annuity payments made in exchange for a gift of property are not a form of private inurement to the annuitants, inasmuch as the payment of the annuity merely constitutes satisfaction of the charge on the transferred asset.[268]

(m)　Embezzlements

Private inurement does not occur when an insider steals money from a charitable or other tax-exempt organization (even though the insider has derived an economic benefit from the entity). In a case where insiders stole proceeds from a charity's bingo games, private inurement was not found. The court wrote: "[W]e do not believe that the Congress intended that a charity must lose its exempt status merely because a president or a treasurer or an executive director of a charity has skimmed or embezzled or otherwise stolen from the charity, at least where the charity has a real-world existence apart from the thieving official."[269] It would be

---

[264] Spokane Motorcycle Club v. United States, 222 F. Supp. 151, 153 (E.D. Wash. 1963).

[265] Rev. Rul. 73-439, 1973-2 C.B. 176.

[266] Reg. § 1.501(c)(3)-1(c)(2); Rev. Rul. 66-259, 1966-2 C.B. 214.

[267] See *Charitable Giving*, Chapters 10 (charitable remainder trusts), 11 (pooled income funds), 13 (other gifts of remainder interests), and 14 (charitable lead trusts).

[268] Rev. Rul. 69-176, 1969-1 C.B. 150. See *Charitable Giving*, Chapter 12 (charitable gift annuities).

[269] Variety Club Tent No. 6 Charities, Inc. v. Comm'r, 74 T.C.M. 1485, 1494 (1997).

anomalous, indeed, for an exempt organization to suffer the loss and indignity of an embezzlement, only to then incur additional suffering in the form of revocation of its exemption because it was the victim of the crime.[270]

(n)   Successors to For-Profit Companies

One or more individuals may establish an enterprise as a for-profit company, operate it for a period of time, and then discover that a mistake was made: the entity should have been formed as a nonprofit organization. Under the law in most states, a "conversion" of an entity from for-profit to nonprofit status requires formation of a new entity. Usually, for this new entity to be tax-exempt, it must successfully seek recognition of tax exemption.[271]

The IRS, however, has a harsh policy in this regard, by which tax-exempt status is uniformly denied to this type of successor entity on the grounds of private inurement, private benefit, or commerciality.[272]

This matter fared even worse in a U.S. Tax Court case, when the court ruled that a nonprofit corporation, a successor to a for-profit corporation, cannot qualify for tax exemption as a scientific or charitable entity because it is engaging in the same activities as its predecessor did, none of which qualify for exemption.[273] The court also found private inurement, writing that the nonprofit entity "appears to be a façade" for the for-profit corporation.[274] It noted that the two individuals who founded and directed the for-profit corporation are the nonprofit organization's only directors, officers, and paid employees. The court concluded that the nonprofit entity is "owned and controlled exclusively by [these individuals]; consequently, the benefits relating to [the nonprofit entity] would inure to [them]."[275]

(o)   Other Forms of Inurement

Promotion of the career advancement of an individual (an insider) within a nonprofit entity was ruled by the IRS to be a form of private inurement; an entity seeking classification as a charitable and religious organization was supporting the candidacy of its pastor for the position of bishop of a church.[276] The IRS denied recognition of tax exemption to an organization, in part on the ground that

---

[270] In the intermediate sanctions setting, an economic benefit that a disqualified person obtains by theft or fraud cannot be treated as consideration for the performance of services (see § 21.4(c)).

[271] See Chapter 26.

[272] See § 32.7(b).

[273] New World Infrastructure Org. v. Comm'r, 122 T.C.M. 88 (2021). The organization's primary activity was the manufacture and sale of metal pipe to contractors for use in infrastructure projects such as roads and bridges.

[274] Id.

[275] Id. The court's approach to use of the private inurement doctrine was plain error in two respects. First, nonprofit organizations are not owned by anyone (unless they are stock based, which was not the case here). Second, the court's invocation of the private inurement doctrine is based on a definition of the doctrine that has no basis in the law. The court essentially held that any "benefits relating" to the organization "would inure" to those who control it (here, the couple). Just because a benefit accrues to an organization does not mean it automatically accrues to its directors, officers, and/or employees. Even if there is such an attenuation, there must be a finding that the terms and conditions of the benefit render it unreasonable (see § 20.4(b); cf. § 20.13).

[276] Priv. Ltr. Rul. 201523022.

it was engaging in activities constituting unwarranted private benefit.[277] Because members of this entity's governing board were recipients of this benefit, the IRS converted the private benefit to private inurement.[278] Payment by an ostensible charitable organization for exhumation of the remains of a parent of an insider was held to be private inurement.[279]

§ 20.7   *PER SE* PRIVATE INUREMENT

As discussed, most instances of private inurement arise in that a payment—such as compensation for services, rent, or interest—to one or more insiders is unreasonable or excessive. There are forms of private inurement, however, that have that designation because they constitute *per se private inurement*. This means that the structure of the transaction is inherently deficient; private inurement is embedded in the very nature of the transaction. It is thus irrelevant, in this context, that the economic benefit conferred on an insider in some way also furthers the organization's exempt purposes and/or that the amount paid is reasonable.

The doctrine of *per se* private inurement was most notably applied when the IRS articulated its view as to the impact on the tax-exempt status of a hospital involved in a joint venture with members of its medical staff, where the hospital sold to the venture the gross or net revenue stream derived from operation of a department of the hospital for a defined period.[280] The agency ruled that the hospital jeopardized its tax exemption, on the basis of private inurement, simply by entering into the venture.[281]

In the facts underlying one of these rulings, a limited partnership purchased the net revenue stream of a tax-exempt hospital's outpatient surgical program and gastroenterology laboratory.[282] The partnership consisted of a subsidiary of the hospital as the general partner; the limited partners were members of the hospital's medical staff. A limited partnership involving an exempt hospital and members of its medical staff, in the facts of another ruling, acquired the gross revenue stream derived from operation of the hospital's outpatient surgery facility.[283] This was done to provide an investment incentive to the physicians to use the hospital's facilities. In one of these instances, a for-profit venture had established a competing ambulatory surgery center near the nonprofit hospital and was offering physicians on that hospital's staff ownership interests in the surgery center, attempting to lure their practices.

The IRS recognized that "there often are multiple reasons why hospitals are willing to engage in joint ventures and other sophisticated financial arrangements with [their] physicians."[284] Two of these reasons are the "need to raise capital and to

---

[277] See § 20.13.
[278] Priv. Ltr. Rul. 201731012.
[279] Ass'n for Honest Attorneys v. Comm'r, 115 T.C.M. 1183 (2018).
[280] Gen. Couns. Mem. 39862.
[281] Priv. Ltr. Ruls. 8942099, 8820093.
[282] Priv. Ltr. Rul. 8820093 (subsequently withdrawn (Priv. Ltr. Rul. 9231047)).
[283] Priv. Ltr. Rul. 8942099 (subsequently withdrawn (Priv. Ltr. Rul. 9233037)).
[284] Gen. Couns. Mem. 39862.

give physicians a stake in the success of a new enterprise or service." The hospital, in addition to the "hope for or expectation of additional admissions and referrals," may act "out of fear that a physician will send patients elsewhere or, worse, establish a new competing provider." The IRS nonetheless added: "Whenever a charitable organization engages in unusual financial transactions with private parties, the arrangements must be evaluated in light of applicable tax law and other legal standards."

Its analysis of these net revenue stream ventures led the IRS to conclude that there "appears to be little accomplished that directly furthers the hospitals' charitable purposes of promoting health." The IRS wrote that "[g]iving (or selling) medical staff physicians a proprietary interest in the net profits of a hospital under these circumstances creates a result that is indistinguishable from paying dividends on stock."[285] Thus, the agency considered the prohibition on private inurement violated because "[p]rofit distributions are made to persons having a personal and private interest in the activities of the organization and are made out of the net earnings of the organization." The IRS added that, in these cases, the "hospital's profit interests in those [charitable] assets have been carved out largely for the benefit of the physician-investors." The IRS's lawyers opined that "[t]his is enough to constitute inurement and is per se inconsistent with exempt status."

§ 20.8 INCIDENTAL PRIVATE INUREMENT

It is the position of the IRS that there is no *de minimis* exception to the doctrine of private inurement.[286] That is, the agency will generally not accept a defense to an allegation of private inurement that it was merely *incidental*.[287]

Nonetheless, even though private inurement is present in a set of facts, a reasonable argument can be made that tax exemption should not be denied or revoked for that reason if the inurement was incidental or insignificant. As an illustration, the IRS, having reversed an initial decision, ruled that an organization of accredited educational institutions was exempt as a charitable entity because the development of standards for accreditation of colleges and universities constitutes the advancement of education.[288] The pertinence of this ruling is that, although "very few" schools that had been approved for membership in the organization were proprietary institutions, the IRS ruled that any benefit that may accrue to them because of accreditation was incidental to the purpose of improving the quality of education.

Similarly, where a business donated land and money to a charitable organization to establish a public park, its tax exemption was not jeopardized by reason of the fact that the donor retained the right to use a scenic view of the park as a brand symbol.[289] Also, in a situation involving a business that provided a

---

[285] See text accompanied by *supra* note 16.

[286] E.g., Gen. Couns. Mem. 39862.

[287] E.g., Gen. Couns. Mem. 35855. There is no formal standard as to an incidental excess benefit transaction, either; by contrast, the law in the self-dealing context recognizes self-dealing that is "incidental and tenuous," as does the private benefit doctrine (see § 20.13(b)).

[288] Rev. Rul. 74-146, 1974-1 C.B. 129. Also, Rev. Rul. 74-575, 1974-2 C.B. 161. Cf. Rev. Rul. 81-29, 1981-1 C.B. 329.

[289] Rev. Rul. 66-358, 1966-2 C.B. 218.

substantial portion of the support of a charitable organization operating a replica of a nineteenth-century village, where the business benefited from the village being named after it by having its name associated with the village in conjunction with its own advertising program and by having its name mentioned in each publication of the organization, the IRS ruled that "such benefits are merely incidental to the benefits flowing to the general public."[290]

Likewise, the IRS determined that a children's day-care center, operated in conjunction with an industrial company that enrolled children on the basis of financial need and the children's needs for the care and development program of the center, was tax-exempt because any benefit derived by the company or the parents of enrolled children was incidental to the public benefit resulting from operation of the center.[291] In another example, the agency concluded that an otherwise exempt educational organization may produce public interest programs for viewing via public educational channels of commercial cable television companies because any benefit to the companies was "merely incidental."[292] Further, the IRS concluded that the sale of items on consignment by an exempt thrift shop did not result in loss of its exempt status, in that any benefit to the consignors was "clearly incidental" in relation to the organization's charitable purposes.[293] Also, an exempt consortium of exempt universities and libraries was advised by the IRS that it may, without endangering its exemption, make its information dissemination services available to private businesses, since "[a]lthough there is some benefit to the private institutions, such benefit is incidental to this activity and, in fact, may be said to be a logical by-product of it."[294] In still another example, the IRS determined that the provision of tickets and/or admission passes to an exempt organization's shareholders, to enable them to attend an agricultural fair conducted by the organization, did not rise to the level of private inurement, with the agency emphasizing the fact that only 3 percent of the free passes were given to shareholders.[295]

The U.S. Tax Court is in agreement with the IRS that any element of private inurement can cause an organization to lose or be deprived of tax exemption. For example, this court stated that "even if the benefit inuring to the members is small, it is still impermissible."[296] Likewise, a federal district court wrote that "any inurement, however small the benefit to the individual, is impermissible."[297] A federal court of appeals observed that "[w]e have grave doubts that the de minimis doctrine, which is so generally applicable, would not apply in this situation [that is, in the private inurement setting]."[298] This appellate court cited cases where a civil rights plaintiff was held to not be a prevailing party for purposes of an award of lawyers' fees where

---

[290] Rev. Rul. 77-367, 1977-2 C.B. 193.
[291] Rev. Rul. 70-533, 1970-2 C.B. 112.
[292] Rev. Rul. 76-4, 1976-1 C.B. 145.
[293] Rev. Rul. 80-106, 1980-1 C.B. 113.
[294] Priv. Ltr. Rul. 7951134.
[295] Tech. Adv. Mem. 9835003.
[296] McGahen v. Comm'r, 76 T.C. 468, 482 (1981), aff'd, 720 F.2d 664 (3d Cir. 1983). Also, Unitary Mission Church of Long Island v. Comm'r, 74 T.C. 507 (1980), aff'd, 647 F.2d 163 (2d Cir. 1981).
[297] Gookin v. United States, 707 F. Supp. 1156, 1158 (N.D. Cal. 1988). Also, Beth-El Ministries, Inc. v. United States, 79-2 U.S.T.C. ¶ 9412 (D.D.C. 1979).
[298] Carter v. United States, 973 F.2d 1479, 1486 n.5 (9th Cir. 1992).

the success was considered technical or *de minimis*,[299] where it was held that only if a state's noncompliance with statutorily prescribed time periods for an administrative action was *de minimis* does a court have the discretion to not issue an injunction,[300] where a court concluded that if the role of illegally obtained leads in the discovery of evidence was *de minimis* the suppression of the evidence was inappropriate,[301] and where it was held that the *de minimis* rule applies in relation to the total sum involved in litigation, thereby precluding the recovery of compensation for overtime for tasks otherwise compensable under the federal labor laws where the time spent on the tasks was *de minimis*.[302]

The state of the law in this regard is probably that articulated by another federal court of appeals, looking at a set of facts from the standpoint of the primary purpose test.[303] That court wrote that nonexempt activity of a tax-exempt charitable organization will not result in loss or denial of exemption where it is "only incidental and less than substantial" and that a "slight and comparatively unimportant deviation from the narrow furrow of tax approved activity is not fatal."[304]

As a practical matter, it is now clear that there is the concept of incidental private inurement, in the sense of private inurement that will not lead to denial or revocation of tax-exempt status. This is because of instances of application of the intermediate sanctions rules, rather than the private inurement doctrine. Regulations promulgated by the IRS illustrate when the existence of private inurement only has the consequence of application of the intermediate sanctions rules.[305]

§ 20.9 PRIVATE INUREMENT AND SOCIAL WELFARE ORGANIZATIONS

The private inurement doctrine is among the statutory criteria for tax-exempt status for social welfare organizations.[306] Even before this addition to the statute (in 1996), however, the IRS and the courts were utilizing a generic version of the doctrine in connection with these organizations. For example, a social welfare organization was found to have engaged in private benefit practices when it conferred most of its benefits on the employees of a corporation with which the organization's founder had been affiliated, and the board of directors of which was composed solely of employees of the same corporation.[307] A related body of

[299] Texas State Teachers Ass'n v. Garland Indep. School District, 489 U.S. 782 (1989).

[300] Withrow v. Concannon, 942 F.2d 1385 (9th Cir. 1991).

[301] United States v. Johns, 891 F.2d 243 (9th Cir. 1989).

[302] Lindow v. United States, 738 F.2d 1057 (9th Cir. 1984).

[303] See § 4.4.

[304] St. Louis Union Trust Co. v. United States, 374 F.2d 427, 431–32 (8th Cir. 1967).

[305] See § 21.16.

[306] IRC § 501(c)(4)(B), added by Pub. L. No. 104-168, §§ 1311(b)(1), 110 Stat. 1452, 1477-78 (1996) and effective for inurement occurring on or after September 14, 1995 (*id.* § 1311(d)(3), 110 Stat. at 1478-79). Prior to this statutory revision, the IRS had ruled that pro rata distributions to its members of proceeds from the sale of a social welfare organization's assets as part of a plan of dissolution would not jeopardize its exempt status, "[b]ecause there is no express provision . . . that states that the income . . . [of a social welfare organization] may not be distributed to its members" (Priv. Ltr. Rul. 8738075). Social welfare organizations are the subject of Chapter 13.

[307] Eden Hall Farm v. United States, 389 F. Supp. 858 (W.D. Pa. 1975).

law requires that a tax-exempt social welfare organization not be operated primarily for the economic benefit or convenience of its members.[308]

The IRS retroactively revoked the exempt status of a social welfare organization in part on private inurement grounds, inasmuch as it was owned by its members as stockholders, public patronage revenue inured to these individuals, and the net assets of the organization were dedicated to the members on dissolution.[309] An organization was ruled ineligible for exemption as a social welfare entity because its primary purpose was qualification of a referendum to overturn legislation adversely affecting its primary donor; its activities were held to be forms of private inurement.[310]

§ 20.10   PRIVATE INUREMENT AND BUSINESS LEAGUES

The private inurement doctrine is applicable with respect to tax-exempt business leagues.[311] The doctrine is related to the proscription on unwarranted services to associations' members.[312] Thus, private inurement was deemed present with respect to an organization that used its funds to provide financial assistance and welfare benefits to its members,[313] one that paid its members for expenses incurred in malpractice litigation,[314] and one that distributed royalties to its members.[315] The private inurement doctrine was applied by the IRS to deny recognition of exemption to an organization seeking qualification as a business league, where the agency concluded that its founder will benefit by means of its operations and expanded business to a founder-owned company.[316] By contrast, private inurement was not found in connection with a payment by a business league to its members, where the source of the funding was a publicly traded company that paid the money in satisfaction of a condition to a merger transaction, which was a change in the business league's governance structure.[317] Likewise, the IRS ruled that a return of contributions by an exempt business league on a pro rata basis, where the funds were given to finance litigation following a lucrative settlement, was not private inurement.[318] Similarly, the IRS ruled that an exempt business league may procure health and pension benefits for its members and their employees, using funds provided by a state, without causing inurement of the league's net earnings (while improving the image of the industry involved).[319]

---

[308] See § 13.1(b).

[309] Priv. Ltr. Rul. 201013060.

[310] Priv. Ltr. Rul. 201411039.

[311] These organizations are the subject of Chapter 14.

[312] Reg. § 1.501(c)(b)-1. See § 14.2(c). The private inurement doctrine is often applied in the business league context, without consideration as to whether the members of the association involved are insiders (see § 20.3).

[313] Rev. Rul. 67-251, 1967-2 C.B. 196.

[314] Nat'l Chiropractor Ass'n v. Birmingham, 96 F. Supp. 874 (N.D. Iowa 1951).

[315] Wholesale Grocers Exchange v. Comm'r, 3 T.C.M. 699 (1944).

[316] Priv. Ltr. Rul. 201242016.

[317] Priv. Ltr. Rul. 200723029.

[318] Priv. Ltr. Rul. 200917042.

[319] Priv. Ltr. Rul. 201246039. The IRS revisited this ruling and concluded that the activity of providing pension and health benefits to a business league's members constitutes the conduct of an unrelated

The doctrine can apply in the context of the level of members' dues in relation to an organization's receipt of nonmember income. Today this is an unrelated business issue,[320] although prior to the advent of those rules (in 1950), it had been held that a dues reduction subsidized by the earnings of a business constituted private inurement.[321] The IRS considered taking the position that a tiered dues structure of a tax-exempt association, with some members paying certain amounts and other members who were making payments to a related business league paying less, amounted to undue private benefit, but elected to not get into that policy thicket.[322] Likewise, the IRS explored the matter of whether association members are being inappropriately subsidized when they pay less for publications, seminars, and the like than do nonmembers but chose not to pursue it.

A tax-exempt business league may receive income from nonmember sources without endangering its exemption where the income-producing activity is related to the exempt purposes of the association, such as a sports organization operating public championship tournaments,[323] a veterinarians' association operating a public rabies clinic,[324] an insurance agents' association receiving commissions from handling insurance programs,[325] and a professional association conducting a training program for nonmembers.[326] Thus, an otherwise qualified exempt business league was able to derive its support primarily from the sale of television broadcasting rights to the tournaments it sponsored, without imperiling its exemption, because this sponsorship and sale of broadcasting rights by the organization "directly promotes the interests of those engaged in the sport and by enhancing awareness of the general public of the sport as a profession."[327]

Another private inurement issue of pertinence to tax-exempt associations concerns the tax consequences of cash rebates to exhibitors who participate in their trade shows.[328] As a general principle, a qualified business league may make cash distributions to its members without loss of exemption where the distributions represent no more than a reduction in dues or contributions previously paid to the organization in support of its activities.[329] The IRS extrapolated from this principle in ruling that an association may, without adversely affecting its exempt status, make cash rebates to member and nonmember exhibitors who participate in the association's annual trade show, where the rebates represent a portion of an advance floor deposit paid by each exhibitor to insure the show against financial loss, are made to all exhibitors on the same basis, and may not exceed the amount of the deposit.[330] Because the

trade or business (see Chapter 24) and does not further business league purposes because it amounts to providing particular services (see § 14.2(c)) and constitutes a regular business of a kind ordinarily carried on for profit (see § 14.2(b)) (Program Manager Tech. Adv. 2022-004).

[320] See Chapters 24, 25.
[321] Nat'l Automobile Dealers Ass'n v. Comm'r, 2 T.C.M. 291 (1943).
[322] Priv. Ltr. Rul. 9448036.
[323] Rev. Rul. 58-502, 1958-2 C.B. 271.
[324] Rev. Rul. 66-222, 1966-2 C.B. 223.
[325] Rev. Rul. 56-152, 1956-1 C.B. 56.
[326] Rev. Rul. 67-296, 1967-2 C.B. 22.
[327] Rev. Rul. 80-294, 1980-2 C.B. 187.
[328] See § 25.2(f).
[329] E.g., King Cnty. Insurance Ass'n v. Comm'r, 37 B.T.A. 288 (1938).
[330] Rev. Rul. 77-206, 1977-1 C.B. 149. Also, Rev. Rul. 81-60, 1981-1 C.B. 335.

"effect of refunding a portion of the floor deposits is to reduce the exhibitors' cost of participating in the trade show," the IRS concluded that the return of funds would not constitute private inurement.[331] If, however, an exempt business league sponsoring an industry trade show involving both member and nonmember exhibitors who are charged identical rates makes space rental rebates only to its member-exhibitors, the rebates are considered proscribed inurement of income.[332]

§ 20.11   PRIVATE INUREMENT AND SOCIAL CLUBS

The private inurement doctrine is applicable with respect to tax-exempt social clubs.[333] For the most part, the application of the doctrine to exempt clubs focuses on the question as to whether nonmember use is generating revenue, the use of which (such as for maintenance and improvement of club facilities) redounds inappropriately to the personal advantage of the members (as reflected in reduced or not-increased dues, improved facilities, and the like).[334] Even in this context, however, use of club facilities by the general public may not constitute proscribed inurement where the club contributes net profits from a function (for example, a steeplechase)[335] to charity.[336] Infrequent public use is permissible as long as it is incidental and basically in furtherance of the club's purposes.[337] Much of this law as to private inurement has been eclipsed by guidelines on permissible nonmember income that social clubs can receive that were subsequently developed by Congress (in 1976).[338]

These clubs must be organized and operated for pleasure, recreation, and other nonprofit purposes. They must have an established membership of individuals, personal contacts, and fellowship, and a mingling of members must play a material part in the life of the organization.[339] For example, this commingling requirement was satisfied in the case of a membership organization that provided bowling tournaments and recreational bowling competition for its members.[340] In this instance, the IRS ruled that the awarding of cash prizes paid from entry fees did not constitute inurement of the organization's net income because the payments were in furtherance of the members' pleasure and recreation.

An organization that failed in its attempt to gain recognition of tax exemption as a social club rented a facility from its founders at fair market value rent. The IRS

[331] Rev. Rul. 77-206, 1977-1 C.B. 149.

[332] Michigan Mobile Home & Recreational Vehicle Inst. v. Comm'r, 66 T.C. 770 (1976).

[333] These organizations are the subject of Chapter 15.

[334] E.g., Knights of Columbus Council 3660 v. United States, 83-2 U.S.T.C. ¶ 16,410 (S.D. Ind. 1983), aff'd, 783 F.2d 69 (7th Cir. 1986); Aviation Club of Utah v. Comm'r, 162 F.2d 984 (10th Cir. 1947); Rev. Rul. 69-220; 1969-1 C.B. 154. See § 15.2. The private inurement doctrine is often applied in the social club context without consideration as to whether members of the club involved are insiders (e.g., Priv. Ltr. Rul. 201028042).

[335] Rev. Rul. 68-119, 1968-1 C.B. 268.

[336] Rev. Rul. 69-636, 1969-2 C.B. 126.

[337] Rev. Rul. 60-323, 1960-2 C.B. 173.

[338] See § 15.2.

[339] Rev. Rul. 58-589, 1958-2 C.B. 266.

[340] Rev. Rul. 74-148, 1974-1 C.B. 138.

nonetheless[341] found private inurement in that this rental "relieved [the founders] of the expense of marketing the facility to an unknown, unrelated tenant." Payment of reasonable compensation[342] to one of the founders was also determined to be private inurement, in that "this arrangement relieves [the founder] of the time, effort, and expense of seeking employment from an unrelated employer."[343]

The private inurement doctrine can also be applicable where an otherwise tax-exempt social club has more than one class of members. It is the position of the IRS that, where individuals are in membership classes in a club that enjoy the same rights and privileges in the club facilities but are treated differently with respect to dues and initiation fees, there is private inurement because those who pay lower dues and fees are subsidized by the others.[344] Similarly, private inurement can arise where an exempt club increases the scope of its services without a corresponding increase in dues or other fees paid to the club.[345]

Another dimension to application of the private inurement doctrine in the tax-exempt social club setting involves undue dealings between a club and its members. For example, a social club was denied tax exemption because it regularly sold liquor to its members for consumption off the club premises.[346] Likewise, a club that leased building lots to its members in addition to providing them with recreation facilities was deemed not entitled to exemption.[347] Also, an organization was denied exemption as a social club in part because its purpose was a pooling of the financial resources of its members in advancement of their litigation against a city in a dispute over ownership of waterfront real estate; this use of the entity was ruled to be private inurement with the membership.[348] Similarly, an organization failed to qualify as an exempt social club in part because, acting as a craft guild, it was facilitating the sales of its members' products.[349] In a somewhat comparable set of circumstances, the IRS ruled that a club, operating a cocktail lounge and café as an integral part of a motel and restaurant business, was not an exempt organization; about one-fourth of the club's "membership" consisted of individuals temporarily staying at the motel.[350] Private inurement was ruled to not be involved, however, where an exempt social club paid a fixed fee to each member who brought a new member into the club, as long as the payments are "reasonable compensation for performance of a necessary administrative service."[351]

A tax-exempt social club may provide social and recreational facilities to its members who are limited to homeowners of a housing development and nonetheless qualify for tax exemption. This exemption will be precluded, however, where

---

[341] See § 20.6(a).

[342] See § 20.4(b).

[343] Priv. Ltr. Rul. 201025078.

[344] Rev. Rul. 70-48, 1970-1 C.B. 133.

[345] Rev. Rul. 58-589, 1958-2 C.B. 266.

[346] Rev. Rul. 68-535, 1968-2 C.B. 219. Also, Santa Barbara Club v. Comm'r, 68 T.C. 200 (1972).

[347] Rev. Rul. 68-168, 1968-1 C.B. 269. Also, Lake Petersburg Ass'n v. Comm'r, 33 T.C.M. 259 (1974).

[348] Priv. Ltr. Rul. 201213033.

[349] Priv. Ltr. Rul. 201219032. The IRS, in these rulings, often does not make a determination as to whether the members are insiders with respect to the organization (see § 20.3).

[350] Rev. Rul. 66-225, 1966-2 C.B. 227.

[351] Rev. Rul. 80-130, 1980-1 C.B. 117.

any of the following services are provided by the club: owning and maintaining residential streets, administering and enforcing covenants for the preservation of the architecture and appearance of the development, or providing police and fire protection and/or a trash collection service to residential areas.[352]

§ 20.12   PRIVATE INUREMENT AND OTHER CATEGORIES OF EXEMPT ORGANIZATIONS

As noted at the outset of this chapter, the doctrine of private inurement is applicable to nearly every category of tax-exempt organization. For example, the IRS ruled that a tax-exempt cemetery company[353] may purchase property from trusts whose beneficiaries include several of its board members, without engaging in private inurement transactions, because the property will be sold at its fair market value as reflected in an independent appraisal.[354]

As to assessment of the reasonableness of compensation,[355] the IRS ruled that the transfer, by the trustee of a voluntary employees' beneficiary association,[356] of the trust's administration business to a for-profit company would not result in private inurement as long as the fees paid by the trustee to the company did not exceed the administrative fees paid by other entities to the company for comparable services.[357]

The private inurement doctrine as applied to VEBAs means not only a prohibition on matters such as unreasonable compensation and self-dealing but also the payment to any member of disproportionate benefits.[358] Thus, a plan was held to be merely a separate fund controlled by a company's sole shareholder for his own benefit, with coverage of other employees incidental, in part because deducted contributions were found to be excessive in relation to amounts paid out for insurance premiums and costs and because funds of the plan were invested in a speculative manner.[359] The rebate of excess insurance premiums, based on the mortality or morbidity experience of the insurer to which the premiums were paid, to the person or persons whose contributions were applied to the premiums is not prohibited inurement.[360] Also, the termination of a VEBA, with the remaining assets used to provide permissible benefits, such as a transfer of assets from one VEBA to another,[361] or certain distributions to members on dissolution of a VEBA, are not forms of prohibited inurement.[362]

---

[352] Rev. Rul. 75-494, 1975-2 C.B. 214.

[353] See § 19.6.

[354] Priv. Ltr. Rul. 201428011.

[355] See § 20.4(b).

[356] See § 18.3.

[357] Priv. Ltr. Rul. 200503027.

[358] Reg. § 1.501(c)(9)-4(a), (b). E.g., Lima Surgical Assocs., Inc. Voluntary Employees' Beneficiary Ass'n Plan Trust v. United States, 90-1 U.S.T.C. ¶ 50,329 (Ct. Cl. 1990), aff'd, 944 F.2d 885 (Fed. Cir. 1991); Ex. Den. and Rev. Ltr. 20042704E.

[359] Sunrise Constr. Co. v. Comm'r, 52 T.C.M. 1358 (1987).

[360] Reg. § 1.501(c)(9)-4(c).

[361] E.g., Priv. Ltr. Rul. 9414044.

[362] Reg. § 1.501(c)(9)-4(d). The IRS ruled that dedication of a portion of VEBA assets that is vested and can be willed to a beneficiary by a member is private inurement (Priv. Ltr. Rul. 200638027). An

A tax-exempt VEBA provided medical benefits to employees of its members. It was required by state law to maintain a certain fund balance. In its first year of operation, the premiums it collected from its members were insufficient to maintain the balance. Thus, it assessed additional contributions, a substantial portion of which were memorialized in the form of interest-free promissory notes. The VEBA thereafter became adequately funded; it proposed to extinguish the notes over a five-year period by applying the amount of the notes to the contributions that the members would otherwise be required to pay to it. The IRS ruled that this proposed transaction will not result in private inurement.[363]

§ 20.13 PRIVATE BENEFIT DOCTRINE

An organization cannot qualify as a tax-exempt charitable entity if it has transgressed the *private benefit doctrine*. The tax regulations state that an organization is not organized or operated exclusively for one or more charitable purposes "unless it serves a public rather than a private interest."[364] Private interests include "designated individuals, the creator or [their] family, shareholders of the organization, or persons controlled, directly or indirectly, by such private interests."[365]

The concept of private benefit is a derivative of the operational test;[366] as one court put the matter, the private benefit proscription "inheres in the requirement that [a charitable] organization operate exclusively for exempt purposes."[367] The private benefit doctrine is separate from the private inurement doctrine yet is broader than and thus subsumes that doctrine.[368]

(a) General Rules

The private benefit doctrine differs from the private inurement doctrine in two significant respects. One is that the law formally recognizes the concept of *incidental* private benefit—that is, types of private benefit that will not cause loss or denial of tax-exempt status.[369] The other is that the private benefit doctrine is applied in the absence of undue benefit to insiders.[370] As to the latter, a court noted that the private benefit doctrine embraces benefits provided to "disinterested persons."[371]

---

insurance-based scheme to utilize tax-exempt VEBAs to generate business expense deductions and tax-free income has been thwarted by courts, with the excess contributions treated as taxable disguised dividends and the individuals involved held liable for the accuracy-related negligence penalties (e.g., Neonatology Assocs. P.A. v. Comm'r, 299 F.3d 221 (3d Cir. 2002)); these cases do not concern the exempt status of the VEBAs involved, although presumably private inurement occurred.
[363] Priv. Ltr. Rul. 201817008.
[364] Reg. § 1.501(c)(3)-1(d)(1)(ii).
[365] *Id.*
[366] See § 4.5.
[367] Redlands Surgical Services v. Comm'r, 113 T.C. 47, 74 (1999), *aff'd*, 242 F.3d 904 (9th Cir. 2001).
[368] E.g., Church of Ethereal Joy v. Comm'r, 83 T.C. 20 (1984); Canada v. Comm'r, 82 T.C. 973 (1984); Goldsboro Art League, Inc. v. Comm'r, 75 T.C. 337 (1980); Aid to Artisans, Inc. v. Comm'r, 71 T.C. 202 (1978).
[369] See § 20.13(b). Cf. § 20.7.
[370] Cf. § 20.3.
[371] American Campaign Academy v. Comm'r, 92 T.C. 1053, 1069 (1989).

Subsequently, this court wrote that impermissible private benefit can be conferred on "unrelated" persons.[372] As the IRS characterized the point, the private benefit doctrine applies to "all kinds of persons and groups."[373]

A principal case in the private benefit context concerned an otherwise tax-exempt school that trained individuals for careers as political campaign professionals. Nearly all of the school's graduates became employed by or consultants to Republican Party organizations or candidates. A court ruled that this school could not be exempt because it was substantially benefiting the private interests of these entities and candidates, in the form of secondary private benefit flowing to those who hired the graduates.[374] The school unsuccessfully presented as precedent several IRS rulings holding tax-exempt, as educational organizations, entities that provide training to individuals in a particular industry or profession.[375] The court accepted the IRS's characterization of these rulings, which was that the "secondary benefit provided in each ruling was broadly spread among members of an industry. . ., as opposed to being earmarked for a particular organization or person."[376] The court said that the secondary benefit in each of these rulings was, because of the spread, "incidental to the providing organization's exempt purpose."[377]

The IRS frequently applies the private benefit doctrine as well. In one striking example, the IRS applied the doctrine in the private foundation setting. An individual requested access to an archive of materials held by a foundation, concerning a distant and famous relative who had recently died, for the purpose of writing a book about the decedent. The book project was to be a commercial one; the foundation was not to be compensated for the author's use of the collection. The IRS ruled that, although provision of the materials to the author would not constitute self-dealing,[378] because the individual was not a disqualified person,[379] it would amount to substantial private benefit, which could endanger the tax-exempt status of the private foundation.[380]

A nonprofit organization applied for recognition of tax exemption as a charitable and educational entity, stating that its purpose is to "provide safe, adequate, and maintained housing" for special-needs children and "improve their quality of life." The founders of this organization, a married couple, used their personal residence as the home for the children, soliciting contributions for renovation of their home and finding individuals to care for the children; the couple adopted the children involved. The IRS denied recognition on the ground of substantial private benefit.[381]

---

[372] Redlands Surgical Services v. Comm'r, 113 T.C. 47, 74 (1999), aff'd, 242 F.3d 904 (9th Cir. 2001).

[373] Priv. Ltr. Rul. 200635018.

[374] American Campaign Academy v. Comm'r, 92 T.C. 1053 (1989).

[375] E.g., Rev. Rul. 75-196, 1975-1 C.B. 155; Rev. Rul. 72-101, 1972-1 C.B. 144; Rev. Rul. 68-504, 1968-2 C.B. 211; Rev. Rul. 67-72, 1967-1 C.B. 125.

[376] American Campaign Academy v. Comm'r, 92 T.C. 1053, 1074 (1989).

[377] Id.

[378] IRC § 4941. See § 12.4(a); Private Foundations, Chapter 5.

[379] IRC § 4946. That is, this individual was not a member of the family of the decedent (IRC § 4946(a)(1) (D)). See § 12.2(d); Private Foundations § 4.4.

[380] Priv. Ltr. Rul. 200114040.

[381] Priv. Ltr. Rul. 201907014. Inasmuch as the couple adopted the children, this should have been processed as a private inurement case.

The IRS revoked the tax-exempt status of an organization formed to advance renewable and sustainable home energy products and practices, increase awareness and educate the public about ways to conserve valuable natural resources, and provide assistance to homeowners who may wish to make improvements that conserve resources. On examination, the IRS found that grants by the organization to homeowners were used to hire the same contractor, who was also a primary donor. The IRS concluded that private benefit, not environmental conservation, was the primary purpose of the organization based on the benefits to the contractor (primary donor), in the form of increased business, and to his homeowner clients, in the form of a reduction in their home improvement costs.[382]

The private benefit doctrine is sometimes applied in connection with activities involving an organization's members. (These individuals, as such, are rarely insiders with respect to an organization.) In general, the provision of unwarranted or excessive benefits, including death benefits, to members of an organization claiming to be a charitable entity will give rise to forms of private benefit that are more than insubstantial.[383] In one instance, the IRS concluded that an organization that functioned as a "bartering exchange" could not qualify for exemption because it was operated only for the private benefit of its members.[384] Likewise, an organization failed to gain recognition as a tax-exempt charitable organization in part because its extensive social and networking activities, its mentoring and scholarship programs (where only members or their family members were eligible recipients), and the fact that it charged nonmembers more than its members for its events were considered forms of private benefit to the members.[385] Similarly, a nonprofit organization, formed to provide training to softball and baseball umpires, and to coordinate games and tournaments, was also involved in assigning umpires to games and promoting ethical standards among baseball officials; this organization was denied recognition of exemption as a charitable or educational entity, in part because it was serving the private interests of the umpires, who are compensated for their services.[386] Likewise, a membership organization cannot qualify as a tax-exempt charitable entity if its principal function is a program by which individuals are certified.[387]

(b) Incidental Private Benefit

As noted, the federal tax law recognizes the concept of *incidental* private benefit, that is, private benefit that does not jeopardize or preclude a charitable organization's tax exemption.[388]

---

[382] Priv. Ltr. Rul. 202216020.

[383] E.g., Priv. Ltr. Rul. 202011008. See text accompanied by *supra* note 259.

[384] Priv. Ltr. Rul. 201042040. For much the same reason, an entity operating a farmers' market cannot qualify for tax exemption by reason of IRC § 501(c)(3) (Priv. Ltr. Rul. 201752012). For that matter, organizations with this purpose cannot qualify as exempt business leagues (see § 14.2(c)(ii), text accompanied by note 195) or exempt agricultural entities (see § 16.2, text accompanies by note 82).

[385] Priv. Ltr. Rul. 201143020.

[386] Priv. Ltr. Rul. 201617012.

[387] See § 7.8, text accompanied by notes 340–344.

[388] On occasion, a private benefit is disregarded for tax exemption purposes as being *unavoidable*. See § 6.3(b).

Although tax-exempt charitable organizations may permissibly provide benefits to persons in their private capacity, benefits of this nature must—to avoid jeopardizing exempt status—be both quantitatively and qualitatively incidental in relation to the furthering of exempt purposes. To be *quantitatively incidental*, the private benefit must be insubstantial, measured in the context of the overall exempt benefit conferred by the activity.[389] For example, the IRS ruled that an organization was not entitled to exemption where it turned over 90 percent of sales proceeds to local artists whose works the organization exhibited and sold; this extensive benefit "served the private interests of the artists and could not be dismissed as being merely incidental to its other purposes and activities."[390] To be *qualitatively incidental*, private benefit must be a necessary concomitant of the exempt activity, in that the exempt objectives cannot be achieved without necessarily benefiting certain individuals privately.[391] For example, the IRS ruled that an organization formed to preserve a lake as a public recreational facility was exempt notwithstanding that its activities provided some benefit to private individuals owning lakefront property. The organization's activities principally benefitted the public at large through the improvement and maintenance of public recreational facilities, and it would have been impossible to accomplish the exempt purpose without benefiting the lakefront property owners.[392]

In a generic legal advice memorandum, the IRS Office of Chief Counsel concluded that an organization that develops paid name, image, and likeness opportunities for student athletes will, in many cases, be operating for the substantial nonexempt purpose of serving the private interests of student athletes. The IRS observed that where these organizations pay out substantially all their contributions to student athletes, they are serving private interests more than incidentally in a quantitative sense. They are also serving private interests more than incidentally in a qualitative sense because they provide direct benefits to student athletes by compensating them for the use of their names, images, or likenesses, and in a manner that is not a necessary concomitant to achieving its exempt activities.[393] The IRS has applied the rationale of this memorandum to deny exempt status to collectives formed to engage student athletes of a university to lend their names, images, and likenesses to other charitable organizations.[394]

In contrast, a tax-exempt charitable organization that allocated Medicaid patients to physicians in private practice was held to provide qualitatively and quantitatively incidental private benefit to the physicians, including some on the organization's board of directors (where the private inurement rules would properly come into play), inasmuch as it was "impossible" for this organization to accomplish its exempt purposes without providing some measure of benefit to these physicians.[395] Likewise, an exempt hospital received a ruling that it, having

---

[389] E.g., Ginsberg v. Comm'r, 46 T.C. 47 (1966); Rev. Rul. 75-286, 1975-2 C.B. 210; Rev. Rul. 68-14, 1968-1 C.B. 243.

[390] Rev. Rul. 76-152, 1976-1 C.B. 151.

[391] Gen. Couns. Mem. 37789.

[392] Rev. Rul. 70-186, 1970-1 C.B. 128.

[393] Adv. Mem. 2023-004.

[394] E.g., Priv. Ltr. Rul. 202414007.

[395] Priv. Ltr. Rul. 9615030.

constructed new facilities, had the only economically viable alternative of transferring its prior facilities to an unrelated for-profit organization, at a below-market price, for the purpose of leasing space in the renovated facility to community businesses; the IRS held that this rental activity would create new jobs in the hospital's economically depressed community[396] and entail only incidental economic benefit to the for-profit company.[397] Similarly, the IRS ruled that an exempt hospital's investment in a for-profit medical malpractice insurance company, using funds paid by its staff physicians, furthered charitable purposes[398] and was deemed to not extend impermissible private benefit, because the investment was required for the writing of insurance for the physicians, the physicians needed the insurance to practice at the hospital, and the hospital needed the physicians to provide health care services in its communities.[399]

Likewise, the IRS held that a supporting organization operating for the benefit of a tax-exempt college[400] may make grants to a capital fund for advancement of a business incubator program, with the business thus created contributing importantly to the college's teaching program; the benefit conferred to the companies by the incubator investments was considered incidental to the advancement of the college's educational purposes.[401] A public charity that educated the public about the history and architecture of a cemetery was allowed to participate in a burial lot exchange with a donor, with the IRS observing that "any benefit to the donor in connection with the exchange will not lessen the public benefits" flowing from the organization's operations, and dismissing any adverse application of the private benefit doctrine.[402] The IRS announced that it does not treat the benefits an exempt hospital provides to its medical staff physicians—in the form of electronic health records software and technical support services—as impermissible private benefit if the benefits fall within the range of electronic health records items and services that are allowable under Department of Health and Human Services regulations, and if the hospital operates in a certain manner.[403] The IRS began issuing favorable ruling letters to regional health information organizations after being reassured by Congress that the private benefit necessarily involved was incidental.[404]

Also, a research agreement between an exempt scientific organization and a for-profit business was held to not jeopardize this tax exemption because the resulting private benefit, to overlapping directors involving the exempt organization and another for-profit business, was considered by the IRS to be incidental in

[396] See §§ 7.11, 7.16(e).
[397] Priv. Ltr. Rul. 200103083.
[398] See § 7.6.
[399] Priv. Ltr. Rul. 200606042.
[400] See § 12.3(a), (c), respectively.
[401] Priv. Ltr. Rul. 200614030.
[402] Priv. Ltr. Rul. 200708087.
[403] Memorandum dated May 11, 2007, from the Director, Exempt Organizations Division, to the Directors, EO Examinations and Rulings and Agreements. The Department of Health and Human Services earlier promulgated regulations permitting hospitals to provide, within certain parameters, such electronic health records services to their medical staff physicians without violating the federal anti-kickback and physician self-referral laws.
[404] See § 7.6(k).

relation to the benefit accruing to the scientific organization.[405] The IRS's lawyers ruled that construction and maintenance of a recreational path on an island was charitable activity, with any resulting private benefit accruing to the residents of the island and a private corporation owning property there dismissed as being incidental.[406] The IRS ruled, in connection with the operations of a regional health information organization,[407] that the participating physicians' access to a database and clinical quality reports confer private benefit on the physicians that is "qualitatively incidental because those benefits are a necessary concomitant of the activities that benefit the general public."[408] A public charity's administrative services agreement with a for-profit corporation was ruled to provide only incidental private benefit to the corporation, which provides the charity with seconded employees, because the corporation does not control the charity, the minuscule amount of business to the corporation, and the corporation's waiver of fees.[409] The IRS ruled that a public charity may restore a tax-exempt social club's historic building, where the public will be given substantial access to the facility, with the resulting private benefit to the club and its members being incidental.[410] In what appears to be its most generous interpretation of incidental private benefit, the IRS ruled that a public charity may provide its research results to a major for-profit global media corporation for fees, format the information specifically for the company, license rights to derivative works to the company, allow the company to use the charity's information for its internal business purposes, agree to not deliver information to the company's competitors, and agree that the company may have a perpetual license to use the information, with this package of private benefits considered incidental.[411]

By contrast, a nonprofit organization was formed to generate community interest in retaining classical music programming on a commercial radio station, by seeking sponsors for the programs, urging listeners to patronize the sponsors, and soliciting listener subscriptions to promote the programs; the IRS ruled that the organization could not qualify for tax exemption as a charitable and educational entity because these activities increased the station's revenues and thus benefited it in more than an insubstantial manner.[412] Likewise, an inventor was ruled to receive unwarranted private benefit when he licensed a patent on one of his inventions to a would-be charitable organization, which would then employ him; the organization was seen by the IRS as merely a vehicle to enable him to complete his work on the patent and thereafter be "richly compensated."[413] Similarly, an organization formed to improve the quality of health care available to consumers, with its first priority being promotion of adoption of standardized performance measures of health care quality and efficiency, was ruled by the IRS to not

---

[405] Priv. Ltr. Rul. 200905033.
[406] Tech. Adv. Mem. 201151028.
[407] See § 7.6(k).
[408] Priv. Ltr. Rul. 201250025.
[409] Priv. Ltr. Rul. 201419015.
[410] Priv. Ltr. Rul. 201442066.
[411] Priv. Ltr. Rul. 201440023.
[412] Rev. Rul. 76-206, 1976-1 C.B. 154.
[413] Priv. Ltr. 200849017.

constitute an exempt charitable and educational entity in part because it was characterized as a "cooperative enterprise" that primarily benefited its members, who were large for-profit businesses and health care insurance companies.[414] Also, the IRS ruled that a nonprofit organization, by allowing its members to advertise and sell property in its magazine, was operating for their private benefit.[415] An organization participating in a "health delivery network," where it "merely facilitate[d] negotiations between physicians on the medical staff [of its member hospital] to provide physician medical services to consumers," was held to be "serving private interests" by operating primarily for the benefit of the physicians.[416] A nonprofit organization was ruled to be in violation of the private benefit doctrine where its purpose was provision of scholarships for students attending an art academy, as well as funding acquisition of equipment for the school; the academy was structured as a for-profit entity.[417] Unwarranted private benefit was also found where a scholarship-granting organization was making grants only to members of one family; a court allowed revocation of this entity's tax exemption.[418]

Courts can be overly exuberant when applying the private benefit doctrine, in slipping past the element of the law that incidental private benefit is permissible. This point was nicely illustrated in the case of a sports booster club that lost its tax exemption in part because a court found unwarranted private benefit to the children participating in the sports program because the club facilitated fundraising by their parents to help defray competition costs.[419] The offensive private benefit amounted to about $33,000 accorded to 110 families—$300 per family.

The private benefit doctrine is nearly boundless.[420] The doctrine's use by the IRS is pliant; the IRS can be generous in dismissing private benefit as incidental. Yet when the agency embarks on a massive campaign to eradicate tax exemption in a particular field, such as exemption for employee hardship assistance funds,[421] credit counseling organizations,[422] housing provider entities,[423] or down payment assistance organizations,[424] the IRS will swiftly and strictly apply the private benefit doctrine.

(c) Joint Venture Law

The private benefit doctrine has been repeatedly invoked in a line of cases concerning the involvement of tax-exempt charitable organizations in partnerships and other joint ventures. The IRS has an ongoing concern that some of these ventures may constitute a means for conferring unwarranted private benefit on nonexempt participants.[425]

---

[414] Priv. Ltr. Rul. 200944053.

[415] Priv. Ltr. Rul. 201144030.

[416] Priv. Ltr. Rul. 201145025.

[417] Priv. Ltr. Rul. 201514011.

[418] Educational Assistance Found. for the Descendants of Hungarian Immigrants in the Performing Arts, Inc. v. United States, 111 F. Supp. 3d 34 (D.D.C. 2015).

[419] Capital Gymnastics Booster Club, Inc. v. Comm'r, 106 T.C.M. 154 (2013).

[420] See § 20.13(c), (d).

[421] See § 7.2(b).

[422] See § 7.3.

[423] See § 7.4.

[424] See § 7.5.

[425] See Chapter 31.

Originally the IRS was of the view that involvement by a tax-exempt charitable organization as a general partner in a limited partnership would automatically lead to revocation of its exempt status, irrespective of the organization's purpose for joining the venture. This *per se* rule[426] surfaced when the IRS ruled that participation by a charitable organization in a partnership, where the organization would be the general partner and private investors would be limited partners, would be inconsistent with eligibility for exempt status in that private economic benefit would flow to the limited partners. The agency wrote that, if the charity "entered [into] the proposed partnership, [it] would be a direct participant in an arrangement for sharing the net profits of an income producing venture with private individuals and organizations of a noncharitable nature." By serving as the general partner in the project, the IRS said, the charity would be furthering the "private financial interests" of the limited partners, which would "create a conflict of interest that is legally incompatible with [the charity] being operated exclusively for charitable purposes."[427] This was the position of the IRS, even though the purpose of the partnership was to advance a charitable objective—the development and operation of a low-income housing project.

The *per se* rule was followed again the next year, when the IRS issued an adverse ruling to a charitable organization that was the general partner in a limited partnership, also created for the purpose of maintaining a low-income housing development. As before, the agency declared that the organization was a "direct participant in an arrangement for sharing the net profits of an income producing venture" with private individuals, so that the organization was "further[ing] the private financial interest of the [limited] partners."[428] The organization took the matter to court; the case was settled.[429]

Another IRS ruling, concerning whether certain fees derived by a tax-exempt lawyer referral service were items of unrelated business income,[430] reflected this IRS position. The agency ruled that, while flat counseling fees paid by clients and registration fees paid by lawyers were not taxable, the fees paid by lawyers to the organization based on a percentage of the fees received by the lawyers for providing legal services to clients referred to them constituted unrelated business income. The reason: The subsequently established lawyer-client relationship was a commercial undertaking, and the ongoing fee arrangement with the percentage feature placed the exempt organization in the position of being in a joint venture in furtherance of these commercial objectives.[431]

The first of the court decisions concerning a charitable organization in a joint venture sanctioned the involvement of a charitable organization as a general partner in a limited partnership. The case concerned an arts organization that, to generate funds to pay its share of the capital required to produce a play with a tax-exempt theater, sold a portion of its rights in the play to outside investors, utilizing the limited partnership. The arts organization was the general partner, with

---

[426] See § 20.7.
[427] Priv. Ltr. Rul. 7820058.
[428] Unnumbered private letter ruling dated Feb. 6, 1979.
[429] Strawbridge Square, Inc. v. United States (Ct. Cl. No. 471-79T).
[430] See Chapter 24.
[431] Priv. Ltr. Rul. 7952002.

two individuals and a for-profit corporation as limited partners. Only the limited partners were required to contribute capital; they collectively received a share of the profits or losses resulting from the production. In disagreeing with the IRS's position that the organization, solely by involvement in the limited partnership, was being operated for private interests, the court noted that the sale of the interest in the play was for a reasonable price, the transaction was at arm's length, the organization was not obligated for the return of any capital contributions made by the limited partners, the limited partners lacked control over the organization's operations, and none of the limited partners nor any officer or director of the for-profit corporation was an officer or director of the arts organization.[432]

Around that same time, the IRS approved an undertaking between a tax-exempt blood plasma fractionation facility and a commercial laboratory, by which the parties acquired a building and constructed a blood fractionation facility. This arrangement enabled the facility to become self-sufficient in its production of blood fractions, to reduce the cost of fractionating blood, and thus to be able to more effectively carry out its charitable blood program. Each party had an equal ownership of, and shared equally in the production capacity of, the facility. The IRS concluded that the exempt organization's participation in this venture was substantially related to its exempt purposes and that there was no private benefit.[433]

One of the most significant of the private benefit court cases[434] concerned the matter of whole-entity joint ventures, where a health care facility places its entire operations in a venture with a for-profit entity, perhaps ceding authority over all of its resources to the co-venturer.[435] A fundamental concept in this context is control, with the IRS and the courts examining relationships between public charities and for-profit organizations to ascertain whether the former have lost control of their facilities and programs to the latter. Examples include relationships reflected in management agreements, leases, fundraising contracts, and, of course, partnership, limited liability company, or other joint venture agreements.[436] In this setting, it can be irrelevant if the public charity is in fact engaging substantially in exempt activities[437] and if fees (if any) paid by the exempt organization to a for-profit entity are reasonable.[438]

The sweeping rule of law in this regard was articulated, in one of the two most extreme of these cases, by a federal court of appeals, which wrote that the "critical inquiry is not whether particular contractual payments to a related for-profit

[432] Plumstead Theatre Society, Inc. v. Comm'r, 74 T.C. 1324 (1980). Cf. Broadway Theatre League of Lynchburg, Va., Inc. v. United States, 293 F. Supp. 346 (W.D. Va. 1968).
[433] Priv. Ltr. Rul. 7921018.
[434] Redlands Surgical Services v. Comm'r, 113 T.C. 47 (1999), aff'd, 242 F.3d 904 (9th Cir. 2001).
[435] See § 31.3.
[436] In St. David's Health Care System, Inc. v. United States, 2002-1 U.S.T.C. ¶ 50,452 (W.D. Tex. 2002), the court purportedly followed the rationale of Redlands Surgical Services v. Comm'r, 113 T.C. 47 (1999), aff'd, 242 F.3d 904 (9th Cir. 2001), although it concluded that private benefit was not present in the case. This summary judgment opinion, however, was vacated by a federal court of appeals, and the case was remanded for trial (349 F.3d 232 (5th Cir. 2003)). The district court conducted a trial before a jury, which voted that the entity should retain its tax-exempt status (No. 101CV-046 (W.D. Tex., Mar. 4, 2004)).
[437] See § 4.4.
[438] See § 20.4.

organization are reasonable or excessive, but instead whether the entire enterprise is carried on in such a manner that the for-profit organization benefits substantially from the operation of" the tax-exempt organization.[439] In this case, the court found that the organization was operated for the substantial nonexempt purpose of providing a market for a for-profit advertising agency owned and controlled by the same individuals who controlled the organization.

In the other of these cases, two for-profit corporations that did not have any formal structural control over the nonprofit entity whose tax exemption was at issue nevertheless were found to have exerted "considerable control" over its activities.[440] The trial court, in this case, concluded that the nonprofit organization was "part of a franchise system which is operated for private benefit and. . .its affiliation with this system taints it with a substantial commercial purpose."[441] The "ultimate beneficiaries" of the nonprofit organization's activities were found to be the for-profit corporations; the nonprofit organization was "simply the instrument to subsidize the for-profit corporations and not vice versa."[442] The nonprofit organization was held to not be operating exclusively for charitable purposes.

As an example of application of this opinion, an organization providing health care services was denied recognition of exemption because it was "effectively controlled" by two for-profit medical practices and because the provision of the services "enhances these businesses [the medical practices] and improves their reputation in the community."[443] In another illustration, an organization was denied recognition of exemption because it was "totally dependent" on its for-profit creator for material and operations, the two entities are "functionally inseparable," and the organization "ceded control to a for-profit [organization] that has an independent financial interest in your activities and no obligation to operate for exempt purposes."[444]

Matters worsen in this context when there is actual control. This is the principal message of the decision concerning whole-entity joint ventures. In that case, a tax-exempt subsidiary of a public charity (hospital) became a co–general partner with a for-profit organization in a partnership that owned and operated a surgery center. A for-profit management company affiliated with the for-profit co–general partner managed the arrangement. The subsidiary's sole activity was participation in the partnership. The court termed this relationship "passive participation

---

[439] Church by Mail, Inc. v. Comm'r, 765 F.2d 1387, 1392 (9th Cir. 1985). "When a for-profit organization benefits substantially from the manner in which the activities of a related organization are carried on, the latter organization is not operated exclusively for exempt purposes . . . even if it furthers other exempt purposes" (Int'l Postgraduate Med. Found. v. Comm'r, 56 T.C.M. 1140 (1989)).

[440] est of Hawaii v. Comm'r, 71 T.C. 1067, 1080 (1979), aff'd, 647 F.2d 170 (9th Cir. 1981).

[441] Id., 71 T.C. at 1080.

[442] Id. The IRS denied tax-exempt status, as a charitable entity, to a nonprofit organization that was controlled by two for-profit organizations, in part by application of a private benefit doctrine analysis relying heavily on the *est of Hawaii* opinion (Priv. Ltr. Rul. 200635018). Likewise, an organization was denied recognition of exemption as a charitable entity for violating the private benefit doctrine inasmuch as it was formed as the "nonprofit arm" of a for-profit company with both entities promoting a brand that is owned by the company (Priv. Ltr. Rul. 202041016).

[443] Priv. Ltr. Rul. 200635018.

[444] Priv. Ltr. Rul. 200702042. The private inurement doctrine was invoked in a case concerning a charitable organization in a partnership (Housing Pioneers, Inc. v. Comm'r, 65 T.C.M. 2191 (1993)).

[by the charitable subsidiary] in a for-profit health-service enterprise."[445] The court concluded that it was "patently clear" that the partnership was not being operated in an exclusively charitable manner. The income-producing activity of the partnership was characterized as "indivisible" between the nonprofit and for-profit organizations. No "discrete part" of these activities was "severable from those activities that produce income to be applied to the other partner's profit."[446]

The heart of the whole-entity joint venture decision is this: To the extent a public charity "cedes control over its sole activity to for-profit parties [by, in this case, entering into the joint venture] having an independent economic interest in the same activity and having no obligation to put charitable purposes ahead of profit-making objectives," the charity cannot be assured that the partnership will in fact be operated in furtherance of charitable purposes.[447] The consequence is the conferring on the for-profit party in the venture "significant private benefits."[448] In application of this decision, the IRS refused to recognize exemption in a case of a nonprofit corporation with four directors who were also the directors of a for-profit entity; the IRS ruled that the nonprofit entity was "totally dependent upon your for-profit creator" and that it "ceded control" to the for-profit company.[449]

Overall, today, a tax-exempt charitable organization can participate as a general partner in a limited partnership without endangering its exempt status, if the organization is serving a charitable purpose by means of the partnership, the organization is insulated from the day-to-day responsibilities as general partner, and the limited partners are not receiving an undue economic benefit from the partnership.[450]

(d) Perspective

The IRS is making much of the private benefit doctrine. Indeed, the agency has evolved to the point where the doctrine may be more significant to it than the private inurement doctrine, writing that "inurement is a subset of private benefit."[451] Two examples illustrate this phenomenon. The agency is of the view that private benefit is present when the founders of an otherwise tax-exempt school also are directors of a for-profit company that manages the school; the nature of the benefit is largely financial, and the IRS asserted that the educational activities of the school could be undertaken without conferring the benefit (such as by use of employees or volunteers).[452] It also believes that certain scholarship-granting foundations are ineligible for exemption, by reason of the private benefit doctrine, because the recipients are individuals who are participants in beauty pageants

---

[445] Redlands Surgical Services v. Comm'r, 113 T.C. 47, 77 (1999).

[446] Id.

[447] Id. at 78.

[448] Id.

[449] Priv. Ltr. Rul. 200702042.

[450] E.g., Gen. Couns. Mems. 39862. See § 31.2.

[451] Priv. Ltr. Rul. 201044025. This observation is correct, however, only in the context where both doctrines are applicable, which essentially is the charitable (IRC § 501(c)(3)) field.

[452] "Private Benefit Under IRC 501(c)(3)," Topic H, IRS Exempt Organizations Continuing Professional Education Text for FY 2001.

operated by exempt social welfare organizations; private benefit is thought to be bestowed on the social welfare organizations because the grant programs serve to attract contestants to enter the pageants and on the for-profit entities that are corporate sponsors of the pageants.[453]

In other instances of application of the private benefit doctrine, the IRS ruled that a public charity engaging in litigation activities in furtherance of its exempt purposes should have its exemption retroactively revoked because the law firm it used acted independently of the organization and received what was deemed to be excessive contingent fees;[454] an organization of members of a nationality formed as a networking group to provide business referrals to its members is serving private interests;[455] an organization disbursing gifts provided by the residents of a retirement community for its employees was engaging in private benefit activities;[456] and impermissible private benefit occurred in an instance where an organization was held to be acquiring land for the purpose of preparing it for farming and then leasing it to a for-profit company owned by the organization's president.[457] The IRS also found impermissible private benefit in the case of an organization providing a market for a for-profit corporation's therapy services where the corporation was owned by the organization's founder and was the sole provider of therapy services in the state;[458] an organization requiring the needy and distressed to participate in a multilevel marketing company as a condition of receiving transitional housing;[459] an organization training individuals in various computer services where the trainees performed services for a fee for a for-profit company owned by the organization's founder;[460] and an organization that engaged in several bargain sale transactions with a "disinterested" third party under an exclusive contract with a "highly unfavorable fee structure" that resulted in high fees to the third party and low net proceeds to the organization.[461]

The IRS promulgated regulations that include examples of application of the private benefit doctrine.[462] One example concerns an educational organization whose purpose is to study history and immigration; the focus of this entity's studies is the genealogy of one family, tracing the descent of its current members. It solicits for membership only individuals who are members of this family. Its research is directed toward publishing a history of this family that will document the pedigrees of family members. A major objective of the research is to identify and locate living descendants of this family to enable them to become acquainted with each other. These educational activities primarily (according to the example) serve the private interests of members of a single family. This is held to be a

---

[453] "Beauty Pageants: Private Benefit Worth Watching," Topic B, IRS Exempt Organizations Continuing Professional Education Text for FY 2002.
[454] Priv. Ltr. Rul. 201217026.
[455] Priv. Ltr. Rul. 202036008.
[456] Priv. Ltr. Rul. 202040008.
[457] Priv. Ltr. Rul. 202041016.
[458] Priv. Ltr. Rul. 202118022.
[459] Priv. Ltr. Rul. 202141027.
[460] Priv. Ltr. Rul. 202145029.
[461] Priv. Ltr. Rul. 202319018.
[462] T.D. 9390.

violation of the private benefit doctrine; thus, this organization does not qualify for exemption as an educational entity.[463]

Another example pertains to a museum whose sole activity is exhibition of art created by a group of unknown but promising local artists. The museum's board members are unrelated to the artists whose work is exhibited. The art is for sale at prices set by the artists; the artists have a consignment agreement with the museum, pursuant to which the artist receives 90 percent of the sales price. This, too, is a transgression of the private benefit doctrine, precluding exemption.[464]

The third of these examples involves an educational organization whose purpose is to train individuals in a program developed by its president. A for-profit company owned by this individual owns the rights to this program. Prior to the existence of the educational entity, the for-profit company conducted the training function. The educational organization licenses rights to the program in exchange for the payment of royalties. The educational entity may develop course materials, but they must be assigned to the for-profit company without consideration if the license agreement is terminated. This arrangement is said to constitute substantial private benefit conferred on the organization's president and the for-profit company, barring tax exemption for the educational organization, even if the royalty amounts are reasonable.[465]

The courts had traditionally applied the private benefit doctrine only to situations involving charitable organizations. Over the decades, the IRS had done the same. In 2004, however, the IRS suggested that the private benefit doctrine is applicable with respect to tax-exempt status for social welfare organizations.[466] This position has been asserted multiple times since.[467] Therefore, the agency could take the position that this doctrine is applicable with respect to exempt business leagues and similar organizations.

A decision from the U.S. Tax Court, issued in 2000, is of considerable interest (and should be of immense concern) to the association community, in that it

[463] Reg. § 1.501(c)(3)-1(d)(1)(iii), Example (1); Callaway Family Ass'n, Inc. v. Comm'r, 71 T.C. 340 (1978) (on which this example is based); and Rev. Rul. 80-302, 1980-2 C.B. 182. Also, Manning Ass'n v. Comm'r, 93 T.C. 596 (1989); Benjamin Price Genealogical Ass'n v. Internal Revenue Serv., 79-1 U.S.T.C. ¶ 9361 (D.D.C. 1979). Thus, on this basis, an organization maintaining a family cemetery was denied recognition of exemption (Priv. Ltr. Rul. 201847011), as was an organization providing scholarships only to descendants of a particular family (Priv. Ltr. Rul. 201846006) and an organization that coordinated family reunions and awarded scholarships to members of one family (Priv. Ltr. Rul. 202304014).

[464] Reg. § 1.501(c)(3)-1(d)(1)(iii), Example (2). See St. Louis Science Fiction Ltd. v. Comm'r, 49 T.C.M. 1126 (1985). See § 7.12.

[465] Reg. § 1.501(c)(3)-1(d)(1)(iii), Example (3).

[466] Ex. Den. and Rev. Ltr. 20044008E. The organization involved in this matter was found by the IRS to be partisan in nature; the authority relied on by the IRS was American Campaign Academy v. Comm'r, 92 T.C. 1053 (1989). Inasmuch as the private benefit doctrine is a derivative of the operational test applicable only with respect to IRC § 501(c)(3) entities (see § 4.5), this reasoning by the agency seems incorrect.

[467] The IRS ruled that organizations that conduct recruitment and training programs for individuals who are members of a political party, with emphasis on encouraging them to seek public office, did not qualify as exempt social welfare organizations because of violation of the private benefit doctrine, citing American Campaign Academy v. Comm'r, 92 T.C. 1053 (1989) (Priv. Ltr. Ruls. 201128032, 201128034, 201128035). In a subsequent similar ruling, the IRS wrote that the "standard for determining what constitutes private benefit described in *American Campaign Academy* applies to both sections," referencing

invoked the private benefit doctrine in connection with a "foundation" seeking recognition of exemption that was related to a tax-exempt business league.[468] The court held that a nonprofit organization that audited structural steel fabricators in conjunction with a quality certification program conducted by a related trade association did not constitute a charitable organization that lessens the burdens of government, and yielded private benefit to the association and to the fabricators who were inspected. This was the first court case in which the private benefit doctrine was applied with respect to a benefit conferred on a tax-exempt, noncharitable organization.[469]

Sometimes, the IRS conflates the private inurement and private benefit doctrines, leading to confusing (and incorrect) outcomes. For example, the long-standing rule is that a tax-exempt organization, subject to the private inurement doctrine, may pay compensation to an insider as long as the compensation is reasonable.[470] But, in one instance, even though that rule was satisfied, the IRS still found private inurement because this "arrangement relieves [the insider] of the time, effort, and expense of seeking employment from an unrelated employer."[471] Similarly, the rule is that an exempt organization may lease property from an insider, as long as the rental arrangement is reasonable.[472] Yet, even though that rule was satisfied, the IRS nonetheless found private inurement because the arrangement relieved the insider of the "expense of marketing the facility to an unknown, unrelated tenant."[473] Likewise, in connection with a set of facts that clearly warranted application of the private inurement doctrine (and thus the standard of reasonableness), the IRS found private benefit in that a nonprofit organization that will conduct research may contract for services with a for-profit company operating in the same field, where the owner of the company is the founder of the nonprofit entity.[474] Also, in connection with an organization that had its exempt status as a charity revoked because it was not a conservation easement-enforcing entity but a "conduit" for its president (an accountant) to help his clients claim "sizeable" charitable deductions, the IRS applied the private benefit doctrine in connection with the officer and the clients, even though the private inurement doctrine should have been applied in conjunction with the president.[475]

Traditionally, then, the private benefit doctrine has been largely applied in cases concerning relationships between public charities and individuals. The

---

IRC §§ 501(c)(3) and 501(c)(4)(B) (Priv. Ltr. Rul. 201142027). IRC § 501(c)(4)(B), however, pertains to the private *inurement* doctrine, not the private benefit doctrine. See § 20.9.

[468] Quality Auditing Co. v. Comm'r, 114 T.C. 498 (2000).

[469] Congress expressly endorsed this type of in-tandem operating relationship involving tax-exempt organizations. The supporting organizations rules (see § 12.3(c)) permit an exempt business league to utilize a related charitable organization. The court failed to acknowledge even the existence, let alone applicability, of this law. It is an anomaly that Congress would authorize such a relationship, only to have a court nullify it by application of the private benefit doctrine.

[470] See § 20.4(b).

[471] Priv. Ltr. Rul. 201025078.

[472] See § 20.6(a).

[473] Priv. Ltr. Rul. 201025078.

[474] Priv. Ltr. Rul. 201128030.

[475] Priv. Ltr. Rul. 201405018.

application of this doctrine, however, is being expanded to encompass arrangements between charitable organizations and for-profit entities and between charitable organizations and other categories of tax-exempt organizations.[476]

The IRS frequently issues rulings denying recognition of, or revoking, tax exemption on the basis of the private benefit doctrine.[477]

---

[476] The court of appeals that reversed the Tax Court in *United Cancer Council, Inc. v. Comm'r*, 165 F.3d 1173 (7th Cir. 1999), also remanded the case for consideration in light of the private benefit doctrine. Inasmuch as an act of private inurement is also an act of private benefit (see § 20.0), the *United Cancer Council* case was shaping up to be a significant private benefit case. The case, however, was settled before the Tax Court could rule on the private benefit law aspects.

[477] E.g., Priv. Ltr. Rul. 200447050.

CHAPTER TWENTY-ONE

Intermediate Sanctions

The rules pertaining to *excess benefit transactions* in many ways parallel and overlap the private inurement doctrine.[1] The tax penalties underlying these rules are termed *intermediate sanctions*.[2]

---

[1] See Chapter 20.

[2] The effective date of these rules is September 14, 1995 (Reg. § 53.4958-1(f)(1)). In the first of the reported intermediate sanctions cases, the effective date of the transactions was October 1, 1995 (Caracci v. Comm'r, 118 T.C. 379 (2002), *rev'd*, 456 F.3d 444 (5th Cir. 2006)). In the second of the reported intermediate sanctions cases, the effective date of one of the contracts involved was January 12, 1995; the court held that transactions that took place during the term of this contract were "preempted from [these] excess benefit taxes" (Dzina v. United States, 2004-2 U.S.T.C. ¶ 50,133 (N.D. Ohio 2004)).

§ 21.1 CONCEPT OF *INTERMEDIATE SANCTIONS*

The intermediate sanctions rules emphasize the taxation of individuals who engaged in impermissible private transactions with certain types of tax-exempt organizations, rather than revocation of the exempt status of these entities. With this approach, tax law sanctions—structured as penalty excise taxes—may be imposed on those persons who improperly benefited from the transaction and on certain managers of the organization who participated in the transaction knowing that it was improper.[3]

The penalties in this context are termed *intermediate sanctions* because, when the IRS determines that a form of private inurement has occurred, these penalties stand between the two extremes of the absence of action by the agency (other than perhaps an examination and a warning) and revocation of the tax-exempt status of the organization (often with the principal impact of harming the organization's programs and beneficiaries).

§ 21.2 TAX-EXEMPT ORGANIZATIONS INVOLVED

The law as to excess benefit transactions applies with respect to tax-exempt public charities,[4] exempt social welfare organizations,[5] and exempt health insurance issuers.[6] These entities are collectively termed, for this purpose, *applicable tax-exempt organizations*.[7] Organizations of this nature include any organization described in one of these three categories of exempt organizations at any time during the five-year period ending on the date of the transaction.[8]

There are no exemptions from these rules.[9] That is, all tax-exempt public charities, social welfare organizations, and health insurance issuers are applicable tax-exempt organizations. A foreign organization that receives substantially all of its support from sources outside the United States, however, is not an applicable tax-exempt organization.[10]

A social welfare organization is embraced by these rules if it has received recognition of tax exemption from the IRS, has filed an application for recognition of exemption, has filed an information return with the IRS as a social

---

[3] The excess benefit transactions rules are the subject of IRC § 4958. The report of the House Committee on Ways and Means, dated March 28, 1996 (H.R. Rep. 104-506 (1996)), constitutes the totality of the legislative history underlying these rules.

[4] A *public charity* is an organization that is tax-exempt for federal income tax purposes (IRC § 501(a)) because it is a charitable, educational, scientific, and/or like organization (that is, it is described in IRC § 501(c)(3) (see Part Three)); this type of charitable organization is not (by reason of IRC § 509(a)) a private foundation (see §§ 12.1, 12.3). The excess benefit transactions rules do not apply to private foundations because of application to them of the self-dealing rules (see § 12.4(a)).

[5] See Chapter 13.

[6] See § 19.18.

[7] IRC § 4958(e)(1); Reg. § 53.4958-2(a)(1).

[8] IRC § 4958(e)(2); Reg. § 53.4958-2(b)(1).

[9] In other areas of the law of tax-exempt organizations, by contrast, there are exemptions from the rules for entities such as, for example, small organizations and religious organizations (e.g., §§ 26.2(b), 28.2(c)).

[10] Reg. § 53.4958-2(b)(2).

welfare organization, or has otherwise held itself out as an exempt social welfare organization.[11]

The tax regulations contain an example concerning a nonprofit corporation that timely filed an application for recognition of exemption as a charitable entity.[12] This application includes a description of the organization's plans to purchase property from some of its directors for excessive prices. The IRS denied recognition of exemption; the organization engaged in the transactions. Inasmuch as this organization was never recognized as a charitable entity, it never became an applicable tax-exempt organization. Therefore, the transactions are not subject to the intermediate sanctions taxes, even though they generically are excess benefit transactions.[13]

A second example in these regulations involves a charitable organization that received a favorable IRS determination as to its tax exemption. In its fifth year of operation, the organization engages in excess benefit transactions that also constitute private inurement. The IRS revokes this exemption, effective in the fifth year. Tax exemption remained for the organization's first four years. By reason of the five-year look-back rule,[14] this organization was an applicable tax-exempt organization and its directors are, as to year five, subject to the intermediate sanctions taxes.[15]

§ 21.3 DISQUALIFIED PERSONS

For these purposes,[16] the term *disqualified person* means (1) any person who was, at any time during the five-year period ending on the date of the transaction involved, in a position to exercise substantial influence over the affairs of the organization (whether by virtue of being an organization manager or otherwise),[17] (2) a member of the family of an individual described in the preceding category,[18] and (3) an entity in which individuals described in the preceding two categories own more than a 35 percent interest.[19]

A person is in a position to exercise substantial influence over the affairs of an applicable tax-exempt organization if that person is a voting member of the organization's governing body or is (or has the powers or responsibilities of) the organization's president, chief executive officer, chief operating officer, or chief

---

[11] Reg. § 53.4958-2(a)(3). These distinctions are required because, unlike nearly all public charities, an entity can be a tax-exempt social welfare organization without applying for recognition of exemption (see § 3.2).

[12] See §§ 26.1, 26.2.

[13] Reg. § 53.4958-2(a)(6), Example (1). Also, Reg. § 1.501(c)(3)-1(f)(1).

[14] See text accompanied by *supra* note 8.

[15] Reg. § 53.4958-2(a)(6), Example (2).

[16] The definition of the term *disqualified person* for purposes of the private foundation rules is the subject of IRC § 4946 (see § 12.2). Also, *Private Foundations*, Chapter 4.

[17] IRC § 4958(f)(1)(A); Reg. § 53.4958-3(a)(1).

[18] IRC § 4958(f)(1)(B); Reg. § 53.4958-3(b)(1).

[19] IRC § 4958(f)(1)(C); Reg. § 53.4958-3(b)(2).

financial officer.[20] Certain facts and circumstances tend to show this substantial influence, such as being the organization's founder, being a substantial contributor to it, having managerial control over a discrete segment of the organization, or serving as a key adviser to a person who has managerial authority.[21]

An individual who was convicted of defrauding a public charity was found in a subsequent civil proceeding to be a disqualified person with respect to the organization by reason of being in a position to exercise substantial influence over the entity's affairs.[22] Although this individual had no formal position or job title with the charity, the court in the intermediate sanctions case held him to be, in substance, the entity's founder and to have had the authority to control or determine a substantial portion of the organization's capital expenditures or operating budget. The court in the criminal case found that the benefits he "extracted" from the charity caused it to "suffer a cumulative loss" of $1,165,317, with the court in the intermediate sanctions case observing that he "could not have achieved this feat without possessing 'substantial influence' over the organization and its personnel."[23] The court added to the list of facts and circumstances tending to show substantial influence the fact that the individual was the "chief fundraiser" for the organization. It was held that the word *position* includes a "location or condition in which one has the advantage" and is not confined to "office" or "job title."

Certain facts and circumstances tend to show a lack of substantial influence, such as service as an independent contractor (for example, as a lawyer, accountant, or investment adviser).[26] Certain persons are deemed not to have the requisite substantial influence, such as an employee who receives economic benefits that are less than the compensation referenced for a highly compensated employee,[27] and public charities.[28] An *organization manager* is a trustee, director, or officer of the applicable tax-exempt organization, as well as an individual having powers or responsibilities similar to those of trustees, directors, or officers of the organization.[29]

The term *member of the family* is defined as being (1) spouses, ancestors, children, grandchildren, great-grandchildren, and the spouses of children, grandchildren,

---

[20] Reg. § 53.4958-3(c). The legislative history of the intermediate sanctions rules, however, states that an individual having the title of "trustee," "director," or "officer" is not automatically considered a disqualified person (H.R. Rep. 104-506, at 58 (1996)).

[21] Reg. § 53.4958-3(e)(2).

[22] Fumo v. Comm'r, 121 T.C.M. 1475 (2021).

[23] *Id.*

[24] *Id.*

[25] *Id.*

[26] Reg. § 53.4958-3(e)(3).

[27] IRC § 414(q)(1)(B)(i). An individual is a *highly compensated employee* with respect to a year if they received compensation in excess of a dollar limitation, which is indexed for inflation, in the immediately prior year. This limitation for 2025 is $160,000 (Notice 2024-80, 2024-47 I.R.B. 1120).

[28] Reg. § 53.4958-3(d). As to this last point, other types of tax-exempt organizations can be disqualified persons in this context, such as an association (see Chapter 14) in relation to a supporting organization (see § 12.3(c)). The IRS ruled that a physician, paid by a tax-exempt health care network on the basis of a fixed salary plus compensation based on productivity (and, due to his hard work, was the highest-paid individual at the facility), was not a disqualified person with respect to the network because he was not in a position to exercise substantial influence over the affairs of the network or any of its affiliated applicable tax-exempt organizations (Priv. Ltr. Rul. 201336020).

[29] IRC § 4958(f)(2); Reg. § 53.4958-1(d)(2)(i).

and great-grandchildren, namely, those individuals so classified under the private foundation rules,[30] and (2) the brothers and sisters (whether by whole or half blood) of the individual, and their spouses.[31]

The entities that are disqualified persons because one or more disqualified persons own more than a 35 percent interest in them are termed *35-percent-controlled entities*. These are (1) corporations in which one or more disqualified persons own more than 35 percent of the total combined voting power, (2) partnerships in which one or more disqualified persons own more than 35 percent of the profits interest, and (3) trusts or estates in which one or more disqualified persons own more than 35 percent of the beneficial interest.[32] The term *voting power* includes voting power represented by holdings of voting stock, actual or constructive, but does not include voting rights held only as a director or trustee.[33] In general, constructive ownership rules apply for purposes of determining whether an entity is a 35-percent-controlled entity.[34]

Also, a disqualified person is a person who was, at any time during the above-referenced five-year period, in a position to exercise substantial influence over the affairs of an organization, a member of the family of any such individual, or a 35-percent-controlled entity with respect to a supporting organization[35] and organized and operated exclusively for the benefit of, to perform the functions of, or to carry out the purposes of an applicable tax-exempt organization.[36]

Further, in connection with a transaction involving a donor-advised fund,[37] a disqualified person is a donor or donor advisor with respect to the fund.[38] This category of persons embraces (1) a donor or any person appointed or designated by a donor who has, or reasonably expects to have, advisory privileges with respect to the distribution or investment of amounts held in an account of the fund, (2) a member of the family of an individual described in the foregoing category, or (3) an entity in which persons described in the preceding two categories own more than a 35 percent interest.[39]

Moreover, in connection with a transaction involving a sponsoring organization,[40] an investment adviser with respect to the organization is a disqualified person.[41] This category of persons encompasses an (1) investment adviser, (2) a member of the family of an investment adviser, or (3) an entity in which persons described in the preceding two categories own more than a 35 percent interest.[42]

---

[30] IRC § 4946(d). See § 12.2(d).

[31] IRC § 4958(f)(4); Reg. § 53.4958-3(b)(1).

[32] IRC § 4958(f)(3)(A); Reg. § 53.4958-3(b)(2)(i).

[33] Reg. § 53.4958-3(b)(2)(ii).

[34] IRC § 4958(f)(3)(B); Reg. § 53.4958-3(b)(2)(iii).

[35] See § 12.3(c).

[36] IRC § 4958(f)(1)(D). Thus, a person that is a disqualified person with respect to a supporting organization in most cases is also a disqualified person with respect to the supported organization (*id.*).

[37] IRC § 4966(d)(2). See § 12.5.

[38] IRC § 4958(f)(1)(E).

[39] IRC § 4958(f)(7).

[40] IRC § 4966(d)(1). See § 12.5.

[41] IRC § 4958(f)(1)(F).

[42] IRC § 4958(f)(8)(A).

In this context, an investment adviser means, with respect to a sponsoring organization, any person (other than an employee of a sponsoring organization) who is compensated by the organization for managing the investment of, or providing investment advice with respect to, assets maintained in donor-advised funds owned by the sponsoring organization.[43]

§ 21.4 EXCESS BENEFIT TRANSACTIONS

This tax law regime has as its heart the excess benefit transaction.

(a) General Rules

An *excess benefit transaction* is any transaction in which an economic benefit is provided by an applicable tax-exempt organization directly or indirectly to or for the use of any disqualified person, if the value of the economic benefit provided by the exempt organization exceeds the value of the consideration (including the performance of services) received for providing the benefit.[44] This type of benefit is known as an *excess benefit*.[45]

Payment of compensation that is not reasonable to a disqualified person is a type of excess benefit transaction. Compensation for the performance of services is reasonable if it is only such "amount that would ordinarily be paid for like services by like enterprises under like circumstances."[46] Generally, the circumstances to be taken into consideration are those existing at the date when the contract for services was made. When reasonableness cannot be determined on that basis, the determination is made based on all facts and circumstances, up to and including circumstances as of the date of payment. The IRS may not consider "circumstances existing at the date when the payment is questioned" in making a determination of the reasonableness of compensation.[47]

Compensation for these purposes means all items of compensation provided by an applicable tax-exempt organization in exchange for the performance of services. This includes (1) forms of cash and noncash compensation, such as salary, fees, bonuses, and severance payments; (2) forms of deferred compensation that

---

[43] IRC § 4958(f)(8)(B).

[44] IRC § 4958(c)(1)(A); Reg. § 53.4958-4(a)(1). Thus, the definition of *excess benefit transaction* encompasses not only transactions where a benefit is provided *to* a disqualified person but also transactions where a benefit provided to a person who is not disqualified results in a benefit *for the use of* a disqualified person (see § 21.7). A variety of excess benefit transactions were found to occur where an organization's chief executive officer used its bank account to make purchases at department stores and grocery stores, automobile-related purchases, and home-related purchases, and to pay her son's school tuition (Farr v. Comm'r, T.C. Memo. 2018-2, *aff'd*, 738 Fed. Appx. 969 (10th Cir. 2018), *cert. denied*, 139 S. Ct. 1263 (2019)). The IRS ruled that an annual monetary award presented by a public charity was an exempt activity and did not involve an excess benefit transaction, where disqualified persons were excluded from receiving the award (Priv. Ltr. Rul. 9802045).

[45] IRC § 4958(c)(1)(B).

[46] Reg. § 53.4958-4(b)(1)(ii)(A). See § 20.4(b).

[47] Reg. § 53.4958-4(b)(2)(i). By contrast, the U.S. Tax Court is of the view that, in the private inurement setting, circumstances occurring after the transaction in question can be considered in determining reasonableness (e.g., Anclote Psychiatric Center, Inc. v. Comm'r, 76 T.C.M. 175 (1998) (see § 20.6(c))).

are earned and vested, whether or not funded and whether or not the plan is a qualified one; (3) the amount of premiums paid for insurance coverage (including liability), as well as payment or reimbursement by the organization of charges, expenses, fees, or taxes not ultimately covered by the insurance coverage; and (4) other benefits, whether or not included in income for federal income tax purposes, including payments to welfare benefit plans on behalf of the individuals being compensated, such as plans providing medical, dental, life insurance, severance pay, and disability benefits, and taxable and nontaxable fringe benefits,[48] including expense allowances or reimbursements or forgone interest on loans that the recipient must report as income for tax purposes.[49]

The criteria for determining the reasonableness of compensation and fair market value of property are not stated in the intermediate sanctions statute or regulations. (As to the former, however, some of the criteria are provided in connection with the rebuttable presumption of reasonableness.)[50] Preexisting law standards apply in determining reasonableness of this nature.[51] An individual need not necessarily accept reduced compensation merely because they renders services to a tax-exempt, as opposed to a taxable, organization.[52]

Excess benefit transactions can also include a rental arrangement,[53] borrowing arrangement, and/or sales of assets between an applicable tax-exempt organization and a disqualified person. Thus, a court held that the transfers of assets by public charities to disqualified persons, where the value of the assets "far exceeded" the consideration paid for them, were excess benefit transactions.[54]

The phraseology *directly or indirectly* means the provision of an economic benefit directly by the tax-exempt organization or indirectly by means of a controlled entity. Thus, an applicable tax-exempt organization cannot avoid involvement in an excess benefit transaction by causing a controlled entity to engage in the transaction.[55] An economic benefit may also be provided by an applicable tax-exempt organization indirectly to a disqualified person through an intermediary entity.[56] All consideration and benefits exchanged between a disqualified person and an applicable tax-exempt organization, and all entities the organization controls, are taken into account to determine whether an excess benefit transaction has occurred. The following economic benefits are disregarded for these purposes: (1) the payment of reasonable expenses for members of the governing body of an organization to attend board meetings, (2) an economic benefit received by a disqualified person solely as a member of (if the membership

---

[48] This item, however, does not include working condition fringe benefits (IRC § 132(d)) or *de minimis* fringe benefits (IRC § 132(e)) (Reg. § 53.4958-4(a)(4)(i)).

[49] Reg. § 53.4958-4(b)(1)(ii)(B).

[50] See § 21.9(b).

[51] H.R. Rep. 104-506, at 56 (1996).

[52] *Id.* at n.5.

[53] The IRS held that an office-sharing arrangement involving public charities and other persons was not an excess benefit transaction (Priv. Ltr. Rul. 200421010).

[54] Caracci v. Comm'r, 118 T.C. 379, 415 (2002), *rev'd* (because of a "cascade" of legal and factual errors committed by the IRS and the trial court), 456 F.3d 444, 456 (5th Cir. 2006).

[55] H.R. Rep. 104-506, at 56, n.3 (1996). See § 21.5.

[56] Reg. § 53.4958-4(a)(2). See § 21.6.

fee does not exceed $75) or volunteer for the organization, and (3) an economic benefit provided to a disqualified person solely as a member of a charitable class.[57]

The IRS ruled that economic benefits provided to disqualified persons that are "incidental and tenuous" are not violative of the excess benefit transactions rules.[58]

(b)   Revenue-Sharing Arrangements

To the extent to be provided in tax regulations, the term *excess benefit transaction* includes any transaction in which the amount of any economic benefit provided to or for the use of a disqualified person is determined in whole or in part by the revenues generated by one or more activities of the organization, but only if the transaction results in private inurement.[59] In this context, the excess benefit is the amount of the private inurement.[60] This type of arrangement is known as a *revenue-sharing arrangement*. The Treasury Department was instructed to promptly issue guidance providing examples of revenue-sharing arrangements that violate the private inurement prohibition.[61] The tax regulations that were issued in 2002 are silent on the subject.[62]

Under the law in existence before the enactment of the intermediate sanctions rules, certain revenue-sharing arrangements have been determined by the IRS to not constitute private inurement.[63] It continues to be the case that not all revenue-sharing arrangements are private inurement transactions. The legislative history of the intermediate sanctions rules, however, states that the IRS is not bound by any of its prior rulings in this area.[64]

(c)   Automatic Excess Benefit Transactions in General

An economic benefit may not be treated as consideration for the performance of services unless the organization providing the benefit clearly indicates its intent to treat the benefit as compensation when the benefit is paid.[65] In determining whether payments or transactions of this nature are in fact forms of compensation, the relevant factors include whether (1) the appropriate decision-making body approved the transfer as compensation in accordance with established procedures or (2) the organization provided written substantiation (such as treatment of the

---

[57] Reg. § 53.4958-4(a)(4). With respect to the third category of disregarded benefits, the IRS ruled that a health care organization, which will provide a bus service as an exempt function, will not confer unwarranted benefits on disqualified persons (namely, the physicians treating patients served by this means of transportation) (Priv. Ltr. Rul. 200247055). The IRS also ruled, in applying this charitable class exception, that a statewide scholarship program administered by a public charity and local community foundations did not cause any excess benefit transactions merely because some scholarship recipients may be related to members of a community foundation's directors or officers, or to members of a nominating committee (Priv. Ltr. Rul. 200332018).

[58] Priv. Ltr. Rul. 200335037.

[59] IRC § 4958(c)(4).

[60] *Id.*

[61] H.R. Rep. 104-506, at 56 (1996).

[62] A section in the regulations is reserved for these rules (Reg. § 53.4958-5).

[63] E.g., Gen. Couns. Mems. 39674, 38905, 38283. See H.R. Rep. 104-506, at 56, n.4 (1996).

[64] *Id.*

[65] IRC § 4958(c)(1)(A); Reg. § 53.4958-4(c)(1).

payment as compensation on an IRS return or other form) that is contemporaneous with the transfer of the economic benefit at issue.[66] If an organization fails to provide this documentation, any services provided by the disqualified person will not be treated as provided in consideration for the economic benefit for purposes of determining the reasonableness of the transaction.[67] These transactions are thus known as *automatic excess benefit transactions.*[68] These rules do not apply to nontaxable fringe benefits[69] and certain other types of nontaxable transfers (such as employer-provided health benefits and contributions to qualified pension plans).[70]

A transaction can be an automatic excess benefit transaction even though its terms and conditions show that it is, in fact, reasonable. Transactions of this nature include the provision by an applicable tax-exempt organization to a disqualified person, for personal purposes, of residential real property, use of a vehicle, access to exempt organization charge accounts, and use of a computer.[71] Payment for the expenses of spousal travel and no-interest loans (resulting in imputed income)[72] can also constitute automatic excess benefit transactions.

(d)   Automatic Excess Benefit Transactions and Supporting Organizations

If a supporting organization[73] makes a grant, loan, payment of compensation, or similar payment (such as an expense reimbursement) to a substantial contributor[74] or related person of the supporting organization, the substantial contributor is regarded, for purposes of the intermediate sanctions rules, as a disqualified person.[75] This type of payment is treated as an automatic excess benefit transaction; that is, the entire amount of the payment is treated as an excess benefit.[76]

Accordingly, a substantial contributor in this position is subject to the initial intermediate sanctions excise tax[77] on the amount of the payment. An organization

---

[66] Reg. § 53.4958-4(c)(1). These returns or forms include the organization's annual information return filed with the IRS (usually Form 990) (see § 28.2(a)), the information return provided by the organization to the recipient (Form W-2 or Form 1099), and the individual's income tax return (Form 1040) (Reg. § 53.4958-4(c)(3)(i)(A)(1); also, H.R. Rep. 104-506, at 57 (1996)).

[67] Reg. § 53.4958-4(c)(1). An economic benefit that a disqualified person obtains by theft or fraud cannot be treated as consideration for the performance of services (*id.*). See § 20.6(m).

[68] For example, the IRS, having found substantial private inurement in the form of personal use by an insider of a charitable organization's funds and debit card, and having determined that the organization lacked any intent to treat these economic benefits as compensation, ruled that the provision of these benefits was an automatic excess benefit transaction (Priv. Ltr. Rul. 202024016). Likewise, the U.S. Tax Court ruled that an individual (an impoverished and abandoned mother of eight children), in her capacity as a disqualified person with respect to a public charity, owed $258,750 in excise taxes, plus tax penalties, as the consequence of engaging in excess benefit transactions in the form of payments that could not be characterized as compensation (Ononuju v. Comm'r, 122 T.C.M. 109 (2021)).

[69] IRC § 132.

[70] Reg. § 53.4958-4(c)(2).

[71] E.g., Tech. Adv. Mem. 200435018.

[72] IRC § 7872.

[73] See § 12.3(c).

[74] As defined in IRC § 4958(c)(3)(C).

[75] IRC § 4958(f)(1)(D).

[76] IRC § 4958(c)(3).

[77] See § 21.10.

manager[78] that knowingly participated in the making of the payment is also subject to an excise tax.[79] The second-tier taxes and the other excess benefit transaction excise tax rules are also applicable to these payments.[80]

Loans by a supporting organization to a disqualified person with respect to the supporting organization are treated as excess benefit transactions; the entire amount of this type of loan is regarded as an excess benefit.[81]

(e)   Automatic Excess Benefit Transactions and Donor-Advised Funds

A grant, loan, compensation, or other similar payment from a donor-advised fund[82] to a person that, with respect to the fund, is a donor, donor advisor, or person related to a donor or donor advisor automatically is treated as an excess benefit transaction for intermediate sanctions law purposes.[83] Again, this means that the entire amount paid to any of these persons is an excess benefit.

Donors and donor advisors with respect to a donor-advised fund, and related persons, are disqualified persons for intermediate sanctions law purposes with respect to transactions with the donor-advised fund (although not necessarily with respect to transactions with the sponsoring organization generally).[84]

§ 21.5 CONTROLLED ENTITIES

As noted, an applicable tax-exempt organization may provide an excess benefit indirectly through the use of one or more entities it controls. Economic benefits provided by a controlled entity are treated as provided by the applicable tax-exempt organization.[85]

Control by an applicable tax-exempt organization means, in the case of (1) a stock corporation, ownership (by vote or value) of more than 50 percent of the stock of the corporation; (2) a partnership, ownership of more than 50 percent of the profits interests or capital interests in the partnership; (3) a nonstock corporation (namely, an entity in which no person holds a proprietary interest), where at least 50 percent of the trustees or directors of the organization are either representatives (including trustees, directors, employees, or agents) of, or directly or indirectly controlled by, an applicable tax-exempt organization; or (4) any other entity, ownership of more than 50 percent of the beneficial interest in the entity.[86]

---

[78] See § 21.3, text accompanied by *supra* note 29.

[79] See § 21.10.

[80] *Id*. These rules generally do not apply to a transaction between a supporting organization and a supported organization with respect to it. IRC § 4958(c)(3)(C)(ii).

[81] IRC § 4958(c)(3)(A)(i)(I).

[82] IRC § 4966(d)(2). See § 12.5.

[83] IRC § 4958(c)(2).

[84] IRC § 4958(f)(1)(D), (E).

[85] Reg. § 53.4958-4(a)(2)(ii)(A).

[86] Reg. § 53.4958-4(a)(2)(ii)(B)(1).

Constructive ownership rules relating to constructive ownership of stock[87] apply in connection with the determination of ownership of stock in a corporation for purposes of this rule. Similar principles apply for purposes of determining ownership of interests in any other entity.[88]

§ 21.6   INTERMEDIARIES

An applicable tax-exempt organization may provide an excess benefit indirectly through an intermediary. An *intermediary* is any person (an individual or a taxable or tax-exempt entity) who participates in a transaction with one or more disqualified persons of an applicable tax-exempt organization. Economic benefits provided by an intermediary are treated as provided by the applicable tax-exempt organization when the organization provides an economic benefit to an intermediary and, in connection with the receipt of the benefit by the intermediary, (1) there is evidence of an oral or written agreement or understanding that the intermediary will provide economic benefits to or for the use of[89] a disqualified person, or (2) the intermediary provides economic benefits to or for the use of a disqualified person without a significant business purpose or exempt purpose of its own.[90]

§ 21.7   *FOR THE USE OF* TRANSACTIONS

To date, nothing in the law of intermediate sanctions addresses the matter of situations in which an economic benefit is provided, by an applicable tax-exempt organization, *for the use of* a disqualified person.[91] In nearly all excess benefit transactions, the excess benefit is provided *to* the disqualified person.[92]

There is parallel law in the private foundation self-dealing context, however, that provides some insight as to the reach of this rule. In that setting, the transfer to or for use by or for the benefit of a disqualified person of the income or assets of a private foundation generally constitutes self-dealing.[93]

Thus, the purchase or sale of securities by a private foundation is an act of self-dealing if the purchase or sale is made in an attempt to manipulate the price of the securities to the advantage of a disqualified person with respect to the foundation.[94] Likewise, self-dealing occurs if a private foundation makes a grant that satisfies a disqualified person's legally enforceable pledge to pay the amount.[95]

[87] IRC § 318.
[88] Reg. § 53.4958-4(a)(2)(ii)(B)(2).
[89] See § 21.7.
[90] Reg. § 53.4958-4(a)(2)(iii).
[91] IRC § 4958(c)(1)(A); Reg. § 53.4958-4(a)(1).
[92] This element may be overlooked in a set of facts. For example, the IRS concluded that certain grants by a public charity were not excess benefit transactions; the agency neglected to take into consideration the *for the use of* aspect (Priv. Ltr. Rul. 200335037).
[93] IRC § 4941(d)(1)(E). See *Private Foundations* § 5.8.
[94] Reg. § 53.4941(d)-2(f)(1).
[95] *Id.*

Payment of church membership dues by a private foundation for a disqualified person was found, for example, to be self-dealing when the membership provided a personal benefit to the individual.[96]

In one instance, disqualified persons with respect to a private foundation had assets in an investment company that had a collateralization obligation used to satisfy margin requirements. The foundation also had investments assets placed with the same company, which were taken into account in determining compliance by the disqualified persons with the collateralization requirement. This was found by the IRS to constitute self-dealing, inasmuch as the assets of the foundation were being used for the benefit of disqualified persons.[97]

As this example and subsequent ones indicate, the IRS maintains an expansive view of the scope of the for the use of (or benefit of) rule. On one occasion, the agency observed that this prohibition is intended to be "extremely broad."[98]

An issue on which the IRS has not directly ruled concerns the sale of securities by a private foundation in a redemption (where the purchasing corporation is not a disqualified person)[99] or in a secondary public offering (where the offering would not take place but for the involvement of the private foundation), where one or more disqualified persons also desire to participate in the securities transaction. To allow the disqualified person(s) to participate in the transaction would be an act of self-dealing, either as an attempt to manipulate the price of the stock to the advantage of the disqualified person(s) or as a use of the foundation's assets for the benefit of the disqualified person(s). This conclusion is sustained by IRS determinations involving fact situations where the disqualified persons were precluded from participation in the transactions. In one instance, a public offering of stock made to enable a private foundation to sell its shares, where disqualified persons were excluded from the transaction, was ruled to not be an act of self-dealing.[100] Likewise, where the managers of a private foundation were not allowed to deal in the stock of a disqualified person corporation during the planning and implementation of a stock redemption, the stock transaction was ruled to not entail self-dealing.[101] Similarly, the sale of limited partnership interests by charitable remainder trusts (which are subject to the self-dealing rules)[102] was held to not constitute an act of self-dealing as long as the trustee of the trusts acted "independently" of the disqualified persons holding similar interests.[103]

---

[96] Rev. Rul. 77-160, 1977-1 C.B. 351.

[97] Tech. Adv. Mem. 9627001.

[98] Tech. Adv. Mem. 9825001. Yet on that occasion the IRS held that the purchase by a charitable remainder trust of deferred annuity contracts from a commercial life insurance company, where the named annuitants were disqualified persons, did not constitute self-dealing pursuant to this rule because, under the facts (including an assignment of the disqualified persons' interest in the policy to the trust), the disqualified persons did not receive any present value under the policies.

[99] An exception from the self-dealing rules is available for certain redemptions and other corporation transactions where the purchasing corporation is a disqualified person (IRC § 4941(d)(2)(F)).

[100] Priv. Ltr. Rul. 9016003.

[101] Priv. Ltr. Rul. 8944007.

[102] IRC § 4947(a)(2).

[103] Priv. Ltr. Rul. 9114025.

The payment of a pledge by a private foundation, which was legally binding on a disqualified person with respect to the foundation, constitutes self-dealing.[104]

In a matter involving a lawyer who was the sole trustee of a private foundation, the IRS ruled that the benefit to the lawyer from a loan by the foundation to an individual who had substantial dealings with the lawyer and his firm was more than an incidental benefit, because the loan enhanced the lawyer's image in the view of his client and thus provided an economic benefit to him; the lawyer's procurement of the loan was determined to be an act of self-dealing.[105]

The IRS found that a bank, in extending credit to large for-profit corporations and tax-exempt organizations, where the notes were to be purchased by private foundations for which the bank acted as trustee (and thus with respect to which was a disqualified person), was engaging in a substantial activity that enhanced the bank's reputation and significantly increased its goodwill, so that the transactions would be acts of self-dealing.[106] On another occasion, the IRS suggested that marketing benefits provided by means of a transaction of this nature could amount to self-dealing.[107]

These last two IRS determinations may mark the outer edge of the for-the-use-of (or benefit-of) transaction; indeed, the line may have been crossed, with the holding unduly stringent. There is, as noted, recognition in the realm of self-dealing, and in the area of intermediate sanctions as well,[108] that the fact that a disqualified person receives an incidental or tenuous benefit from the use by a private foundation of its income or assets will not, by itself, make the use an act of self-dealing.[109]

This exemption usually manifests itself in the area of public recognition. Thus, the public recognition a person may receive, arising from the charitable activities of a private foundation as to which the person is a substantial contributor, does not in itself result in an act of self-dealing.[110] The IRS ruled that an incidental or tenuous benefit occurs when the general reputation or prestige of a disqualified person is enhanced by public acknowledgment of a specific contribution by that person, when a disqualified person receives some other relatively minor benefit of an indirect nature, or when a disqualified person merely participates to a wholly incidental degree in the fruits of a charitable program that is of broad public interest.[111]

As an example, a private foundation grant to a tax-exempt hospital for modernization, replacement, and expansion was deemed to not be an act of self-dealing, even though two of the trustees of the private foundation served on the board of trustees of the hospital.[112] Likewise, a grant by a private foundation to a public charity does not constitute an act of self-dealing, notwithstanding the fact

---

[104] E.g., Priv. Ltr. Rul. 9703020.

[105] Tech. Adv. Mem. 8719004.

[106] Gen. Couns. Mem. 39107.

[107] Priv. Ltr. Rul. 9726006.

[108] See § 21.4(a), text accompanied by *supra* note 58.

[109] Reg. § 53.4941(d)-2(f)(2).

[110] *Id.*

[111] Rev. Rul. 77-331, 1977-2 C.B. 388.

[112] Rev. Rul. 75-42, 1975-1 C.B. 359.

that the grant is conditioned on the agreement of the public charity to change its name to that of a substantial contributor to the foundation.[113]

In another illustration of what may be the outer reaches of the for the use of exception, the IRS ruled that impermissible self-dealing will not occur when a private foundation establishes, funds, and operates an educational institute that has a name similar to that of a company owned by disqualified persons with respect to the foundation, who will plan the programs of the institute.[114]

The IRS sometimes overlooks (or at least does not discuss) this issue. As an illustration, the IRS ruled that a private foundation that owns a parking garage may lease excess parking spaces in the garage to tenants renting space in a building owned by a disqualified person without engaging in acts of self-dealing because the disqualified person is not involved in the transaction.[115] In this type of situation, there may well be an increment of benefit accruing to the disqualified person. That benefit is the additional parking provided using the charitable organization's assets, thereby enhancing the disqualified person's building in the view of its tenants and the market in general. For example, the disqualified person's building may be less desirable to prospective tenants without the parking spaces provided by the use of charity's property.[116]

§ 21.8 INITIAL CONTRACT EXCEPTION

The intermediate sanctions rules do not apply to any fixed payment made to a person pursuant to an initial contract.[117] A *fixed payment* is an amount of money or other property specified in the contract, or determined by a fixed formula specified in the contract, which is to be paid or transferred in exchange for the provision of specified services or property.[118] An *initial contract* is a binding written contract between an applicable tax-exempt organization and a person who was not a disqualified person immediately prior to entering into the contract.[119] A compensation package can be partially sheltered by this initial contract exception; for example, an individual can have a base salary that is a fixed payment pursuant to an initial contract and also have an annual performance-based bonus that is subject to excess benefit transaction analysis.

The IRS crafted the initial contract exception in the aftermath of a federal appeals court decision issued in 1999.[120] (Thus, this decision was handed down between the time of issuance of proposed intermediate sanctions regulations and issuance of temporary regulations.) Indeed, the IRS believes that the exception was compelled by the decision. For example, in the preamble to the final regulations, the IRS wrote that this appellate court held that private inurement "cannot

---

[113] Rev. Rul. 73-407, 1973-2 C.B. 383.

[114] Priv. Ltr. Rul. 199939049.

[115] Priv. Ltr. Rul. 201301015.

[116] This benefit may, however, be incidental.

[117] Reg. § 53.4958-4(a)(3)(i).

[118] Reg. § 53.4958-4(a)(3)(ii).

[119] Reg. § 53.4958-4(a)(3)(iii).

[120] United Cancer Council, Inc. v. Comm'r, 165 F.3d 1173 (7th Cir. 1999).

result from a contractual relationship negotiated at arm's length with a party having no prior relationship with the organization, regardless of the relative bargaining strength of the parties or resultant control over the tax-exempt organization created by the terms of the contract."[121]

§ 21.9   REBUTTABLE PRESUMPTION OF REASONABLENESS

This body of law includes a *rebuttable presumption of reasonableness* with respect to compensation arrangements and other transactions between an applicable tax-exempt organization and a disqualified person.[122] This presumption arises where the transaction was approved by a board of directors or trustees (or a committee of the board) of an applicable tax-exempt organization that was composed entirely of individuals who were unrelated to and not subject to the control of the disqualified person or persons involved in the transaction, the board obtained and relied on appropriate data as to comparability, and the board adequately documented the basis for its determination.[123]

(a)   Independent Body

The first of these criteria essentially requires an independent board. The standard as to independence for governing bodies and committees is based on the concept of an absence of a *conflict of interest*.[124] An individual is not regarded as a member of a governing body or committee when the body or committee is reviewing a transaction if that individual meets with the members only to answer questions, otherwise recuses themself from the meeting, and is not present during debate and voting on the transaction.[125] A committee of a governing body may be composed of any individuals permitted under state law to serve on the committee and may act on behalf of the governing body to the extent permitted by state law.[126]

(b)   Appropriate Data

As to the second of these criteria, an authorized body has appropriate data as to comparability if, given the knowledge and expertise of its members, it has information sufficient to determine whether the compensation arrangement in its entirety is reasonable or the property transfer is at fair market value.[127] In the case of compensation, the term *appropriate data* includes compensation levels paid by similarly situated organizations, both tax-exempt and taxable, for functionally comparable positions; the location of the organization, including the availability

---

[121] 67 Fed. Reg. 3076, 3079-80 (2002).

[122] This rebuttable presumption is not provided for in the Internal Revenue Code; it was created by the legislative history (H.R. Rep. 104-506, at 56–57 (1996)) and is reflected in and amplified by the regulations (Reg. § 58.4958-6).

[123] Reg. § 53.4958-6(a).

[124] Reg. § 53.4958-6(c)(1)(iii).

[125] Reg. § 53.4958-6(c)(1)(ii).

[126] Reg. § 53.4958-6(c)(1)(i)(B).

[127] Reg. § 53.4958-6(c)(2)(i).

of similar services in the geographic area; independent compensation surveys by nationally recognized independent firms; and written offers from similar institutions competing for the services of the disqualified person.[128] In the case of property, *relevant information* includes current independent appraisals of the value of the property to be transferred and offers received as part of an open and competitive bidding process.[129]

In the case of an organization with annual gross receipts of less than $1 million, when reviewing compensation arrangements, the governing body or committee is considered to have appropriate data as to comparability if it has data on compensation paid by three comparable organizations in the same or similar communities for similar services.[130]

(c) Adequate Documentation

As to the third of these criteria, adequate documentation includes an evaluation of the individual whose compensation level and terms were being established and the basis for the determination that the individual's compensation was reasonable in light of that evaluation and data.[131] The fact that a state or local legislative or agency body may have authorized or approved a particular compensation package paid to a disqualified person is not determinative of the reasonableness of the compensation paid.[132]

For a decision to be documented adequately, the written or electronic records of the governing body or committee must note the terms of the transaction that was approved, the date it was approved, the members of the governing body or committee who were present during debate on the transaction or arrangement that was approved and those who voted on it, the comparability data obtained and relied on by the governing body or committee and how it was obtained, and the actions taken with respect to consideration of the transaction by anyone who was otherwise a member of the governing body or committee but who had a conflict of interest with respect to the transaction or arrangement.[133] If the governing body or committee determines that reasonable compensation for a specific arrangement or fair market value in a specific transaction is higher or lower than the range of comparable data received, the governing body or committee must record the basis for that determination.[134]

The documentation must be made concurrently with the determination.[135] This means that records must be prepared by the next meeting of the governing body or committee occurring after the final action or actions of the body or

---

[128] H.R. Rep. 104-506, at 57 (1996); Reg. § 53.4958-6(c)(2)(i).

[129] Reg. § 53.4958(c)(2)(i). The IRS concluded that a process established for setting the coupon rate for the bonds of a tax-exempt hospital constituted an offer received as part of an open competitive bidding procedure (Priv. Ltr. Rul. 200413014).

[130] Reg. § 53.4958-6(c)(2)(ii).

[131] H.R. Rep. 104-506, at 57 (1996).

[132] *Id.* at n.7. Likewise, this type of authorization or approval is not determinative of whether a revenue-sharing arrangement violates the private inurement proscription (*id.*).

[133] Reg. § 53.4958-6(c)(3)(i).

[134] Reg. § 53.4958-6(c)(3)(ii).

[135] *Id.*

committee are taken. Records must be reviewed and approved by the governing body or committee as reasonable, accurate, and complete within a reasonable time thereafter.[136]

If these three criteria are satisfied, penalty excise taxes can be imposed only if the IRS develops sufficient contrary evidence to rebut the probative value of the comparability data relied on by the authorized governing body.[137] For example, the IRS could establish that the compensation data relied on by the parties was not for functionally comparable positions or that the disqualified person in fact did not substantially perform the responsibilities of the position.[138]

§ 21.10   EXCISE TAX REGIME

A disqualified person who benefited from an excess benefit transaction is subject to and must pay an excise tax—termed the *initial tax*—equal to 25 percent of the amount of the excess benefit.[139]

An organization manager who participated in an excess benefit transaction, knowing that it was such a transaction, is subject to and must pay an excise tax of 10 percent of the excess benefit (subject to a maximum amount of tax as to a transaction of $20,000),[140] where an initial tax is imposed on a disqualified person and if there was no correction of the excess benefit transaction within the taxable period.[141] This tax is not imposed, however, where the participation in the transaction was not willful and was due to reasonable cause.[142]

Another tax—the *additional tax*—may be imposed on a disqualified person where the initial tax was imposed and if there was no correction of the excess benefit within a specified period. This period is the *taxable period*, which means—with respect to an excess benefit transaction—the period beginning with the date on which the transaction occurred and ending on the earlier of (1) the date of mailing of a notice of deficiency[143] as to the initial tax or (2) the date on which the initial tax

---

[136] *Id.* If reasonableness of compensation cannot be determined based on circumstances existing as of the date when a contract for services was made, this rebuttable presumption cannot arise until circumstances exist so that reasonableness of compensation can be determined and the three requirements for the presumption are satisfied (Reg. § 53.4958-6(d)(1)).

The fact that a transaction between an applicable tax-exempt organization and a disqualified person does not qualify for this presumption does not create an inference that the transaction is an excess benefit transaction (Reg. § 53.4958-6(e)). (An instance of nonqualification for this presumption is in Priv. Ltr. Rul. 200244028.) The fact that a transaction qualifies for the presumption does not exempt or relieve any person from compliance with any federal or state law imposing any obligation, duty, responsibility, or other standard of conduct with respect to the operation or administration of any applicable tax-exempt organization (Reg. § 53.4958-6(e)).

[137] Reg. § 53.4958-6(b).

[138] H.R. Rep. 104-506, at 57 (1996).

[139] IRC § 4958(a)(1); Reg. § 53.4958-1(a), (c)(1).

[140] IRC § 4958(d)(2); Reg. § 53.4958-1(d)(7).

[141] IRC § 4958(a)(2); Reg. § 53.4958-1(d)(1). The concepts of *participation* (see § 21.12(a)) and *knowing* (see § 21.12(b)) are the subject of Reg. § 53.4958-1(d)(3), (4).

[142] IRC § 4958(a)(2); Reg. § 53.4958-1(d)(1). The concepts of *willful* and *reasonable cause* are the subject of Reg. § 53.4958-1(d)(5), (6). See § 21.12(d).

[143] IRC § 6212.

is assessed.[144] In this situation, the disqualified person is subject to and must pay a tax equal to 200 percent of the excess benefit involved.[145]

If more than one organization manager or other disqualified person is liable for an excise tax, then all such persons are jointly and severally liable for the tax.[146] The IRS possesses the usual collection techniques in this context, including levies.[147]

The IRS has the authority to abate an intermediate sanctions excise tax penalty if it is established that the violation was due to reasonable cause and not due to willful neglect, and the transaction was corrected within the appropriate taxable period.[148]

In one instance, the IRS concluded that the first-tier excise tax due under these rules, in connection with an automatic excess benefit transaction,[149] should not be abated, because the disqualified person did not exercise ordinary business care and prudence when it relied on the oral advice of a public charity's legal counsel.[150]

§ 21.11 CORRECTION REQUIREMENT

The term *correction* means undoing the excess benefit transaction to the extent possible and taking any additional measures necessary to place the applicable tax-exempt organization involved in the excess benefit transaction in a financial position that is not worse than the position it would be in if the disqualified person were dealing under the highest fiduciary standards.[151] This phraseology is taken from the private foundations self-dealing rules.[152] There is almost no law on this point. Phrases such as *to the extent possible* and *additional measures* are unexamined. Presumably they are applied in the context of the facts and circumstances of each case. The phrase *highest fiduciary standards* was the subject of a solitary appellate court analysis, with the court concluding that these standards were not adhered to in the correction process.[153]

Generally, a disqualified person corrects an excess benefit transaction only by making a payment in cash or cash equivalents, excluding payment by a promissory note, to the applicable tax-exempt organization equal to the correction amount.[154]

---

[144] IRC § 4958(f)(5); Reg. § 53.4958-1(c)(2)(ii).

[145] IRC § 4958(b); Reg. § 53.4958-1(c)(2)(i).

[146] IRC § 4958(d)(1); Reg. § 53.4958-1(c)(1), (d)(8).

[147] E.g., Archer v. Comm'r, 112 T.C.M. 675 (2016).

[148] IRC § 4962; Reg. § 53.4958-1(c)(2)(iii).

[149] See § 21.4(c).

[150] Tech. Adv. Mem. 201503019.

[151] IRC § 4958(f)(6); Reg. § 53.4958-7. The lawyers for the IRS wrote that the primary purpose of the intermediate sanctions rules is to "require insiders who are receiving excess benefits to make their exempt organizations whole, with the goal of keeping them operating for the benefit of the public" (Chief Couns. Adv. Mem. 200431023).

[152] IRC § 4941(e)(3).

[153] Oliff v. Exchange Int'l Corp., 669 F.2d 1162 (7th Cir. 1980), *cert. denied*, 450 U.S. 915 (1981).

[154] Reg. § 53.4958-7(b)(1).

A disqualified person will not satisfy the correction requirement, however, if the IRS determines that the disqualified person engaged in one or more transactions with the applicable tax-exempt organization in order to circumvent the requirement and, as a result, the disqualified person effectively transferred property other than cash or cash equivalents.[155]

An exception to this general rule applies in the context of nonqualified deferred compensation. If an excess benefit transaction results, in whole or in part, from the vesting of benefits provided under a nonqualified deferred compensation plan, then, to the extent that the benefits have not yet been distributed to the disqualified person, the disqualified person may correct the portion of the excess benefit resulting from the undistributed deferred compensation by relinquishing any right to receive the excess portion of the undistributed deferred compensation (including any earnings generated by it).[156]

A disqualified person may, with the agreement of the applicable tax-exempt organization, make a correction by returning to the organization the specific property previously transferred to the disqualified person in the excess benefit transaction. In this type of situation, the disqualified person is treated as making a payment to the organization equal to the lesser of (1) the fair market value of the property determined on the date the property is returned to the organization or (2) the fair market value of the property on the date the excess benefit transaction occurred.[157] If the payment made by this type of return of property is less than the correction amount, the disqualified person must make an additional payment of cash to the organization equal to the difference. Conversely, if the payment made by this type of return of property exceeds the correction amount, the organization may make a cash payment to the disqualified person equal to the difference.[158]

In the first of the intermediate sanctions cases decided by a court, the court, although not deciding the point, indicated that correction of the excess benefit transactions involved could be accomplished by a transfer of the assets, by the recipient disqualified persons, back to the applicable tax-exempt organizations.[159]

A disqualified person who received an excess benefit from an excess benefit transaction may not participate in the decision process of the applicable tax-exempt organization as to whether to accept the return of specific property in enabling the disqualified person to correct the excess benefit transaction in this manner.[160] The regulations do not state the consequence of such a participation by the disqualified person, but it may be presumed that this exception would be voided, so that the necessary correction was not made. Also, it may be that, under a particular set of facts and circumstances, the transaction would constitute another excess benefit transaction.

If the excess benefit transaction arises under a contract that has been partially performed, termination of the contractual relationship between the organization and the disqualified person is not required to correct the transaction. The parties,

---

[155] Reg. § 53.4958-7(b)(2).

[156] Reg. § 53.4958-7(b)(3).

[157] Reg. § 53.4958-7(b)(4)(i).

[158] Reg. § 53.4958-7(b)(4)(ii).

[159] Caracci v. Comm'r, 118 T.C. 379 (2002), *rev'd on other grounds*, 456 F.3d 444 (5th Cir. 2006).

[160] Reg. § 53.4958-7(b)(4)(iii).

however, may need to modify the terms of any ongoing contract to avoid future excess benefit transactions.[161]

A disqualified person must correct an excess benefit transaction even though the applicable tax-exempt organization that engaged in the transaction no longer exists or is no longer eligible for tax-exempt status.[162] The rules in this regard are somewhat different as to the type of applicable tax-exempt organization involved.

In the case of an excess benefit transaction with a charitable organization, the disqualified person must pay the correction amount to another tax-exempt charitable organization in accordance with the dissolution clause contained in the constitutive documents of the applicable tax-exempt organization involved in the excess benefit transaction, as long as (1) the organization receiving the correction amount is a public charity[163] and has been in existence with that status for a continuous period of at least 60 calendar months ending on the correction date, (2) the disqualified person involved is not a disqualified person with respect to the organization receiving the correction amount, and (3) the organization receiving the correction amount does not allow the disqualified person (or family members[164] or controlled entities)[165] to make or recommend any grants or other distributions by the organization.[166]

In the case of an excess benefit transaction with a social welfare organization,[167] the disqualified person must pay the correction amount to a successor tax-exempt social welfare organization or, if there is no tax-exempt successor, to any tax-exempt charitable organization or other tax-exempt social welfare organization, as long as the three conditions (other than that the recipient be a public charity) are satisfied.[168]

With respect to an excess benefit transaction, the correction amount equals the sum of the excess benefit and interest on the excess benefit. The amount of the interest charge for this purpose is determined by multiplying the excess benefit by the appropriate interest rate. Interest is compounded annually and is computed for the period from the date the excess benefit transaction occurred[169] to the date of correction.[170]

The interest rate used for this purpose must be a rate that equals or exceeds the applicable federal rate,[171] compounded annually, for the month in which the excess benefit transaction occurred. The period from the date the excess benefit transaction occurred to the date of correction is used to determine whether the appropriate federal rate is the federal short-term rate, the federal midterm rate, or the federal long-term rate.[172]

[161] Reg. § 53.4958-7(d).
[162] Reg. § 53.4958-7(e)(1).
[163] That is, a public charity described in IRC § 170(b)(1)(A)(i)–(vi). See § 12.3(a), (b).
[164] See § 21.3.
[165] See § 21.5.
[166] Reg. § 53.4958-7(e)(2).
[167] That is, an organization described in IRC § 501(c)(4). See Chapter 13.
[168] Reg. § 53.4958-7(e)(3).
[169] See § 21.12(e).
[170] Reg. § 53.4958-7(c).
[171] IRC § 1274(d)(1)(A).
[172] Reg. § 53.4958-7(c).

The IRS is of the view that a proper correction also requires a change in the policies or practices of the organization involved, to accord the agency some assurance that the infraction or infractions will not be repeated.

§ 21.12   DEFINITIONS

Aside from the terms defined elsewhere, the intermediate sanctions law includes several other defined terms.

(a)   Participation

In general, a person *participates* in a transaction when they take some affirmative action with respect to it. Also, in this context, *participation* includes silence or inaction on the part of an organization manager where the manager is under a duty to speak or act. An organization manager is not considered to have participated in an excess benefit transaction, however, where the manager has opposed the transaction in a manner consistent with the fulfillment of the manager's responsibilities to the applicable tax-exempt organization.[173]

(b)   Knowing

An organization manager participates in a transaction *knowingly* only if the individual (1) has actual knowledge of sufficient facts so that, based solely on those facts, the transaction would be an excess benefit transaction; (2) is aware that the transaction under these circumstances may violate the provisions of federal law governing excess benefit transactions; and (3) negligently fails to make reasonable attempts to ascertain whether the transaction is an excess benefit transaction; or (4) is in fact aware that it is an excess benefit transaction.[174]

Knowing does not mean *having reason to know*. Evidence tending to show that an organization manager has reason to know of a particular fact or particular rule, however, is relevant in determining whether the manager had actual knowledge of the fact or rule. Thus, for example, evidence tending to show that a manager has reason to know of sufficient facts so that, based solely on those facts, a transaction would be an excess benefit transaction is relevant in determining whether the manager had actual knowledge of the facts.[175]

(c)   Reliance on Professional Advice

Even though a transaction subsequently is determined to be an excess benefit transaction, participation of an organization manager in the transaction is ordinarily not considered *knowing* for these purposes to the extent that, after making full disclosure of the factual situation to an appropriate professional, the organization manager relied on a reasoned written opinion of that professional with respect to elements of the transaction that were within the professional's expertise.[176]

---

[173] Reg. § 53.4958-1(d)(3).
[174] Reg. § 53.4958-1(d)(4)(i).
[175] Reg. § 53.4958-1(d)(4)(ii).
[176] Reg. § 53.4958-1(d)(4)(iii).

A written opinion is *reasoned* even though it reaches a conclusion that is subsequently determined to be incorrect, as long as the opinion addresses itself to the facts and the applicable standards. A written opinion is not reasoned, however, if it does nothing more than recite the facts and express a conclusion.[177]

Appropriate professionals on whose written opinion an organization manager may rely are confined to legal counsel, including house counsel; certified public accountants or accounting firms with expertise regarding the relevant tax law matters; and independent valuation experts who (1) hold themselves out to the public as appraisers or compensation consultants, (2) perform the relevant valuations on a regular basis, (3) are qualified to make valuations of the type of property or services involved, and (4) include in the written opinion a certification that the foregoing three requirements are met.[178]

The absence of a written opinion of an appropriate professional with respect to a transaction does not, by itself, give rise to any inference that an organization manager participated in the transaction knowingly.[179]

Also, participation of an organization manager in a transaction ordinarily is not considered knowing, even though the transaction subsequently is determined to be an excess benefit transaction, if the appropriate authorized body has met the requirements of the rebuttable presumption of reasonableness[180] with respect to the transaction.[181]

(d) Willful and Reasonable Cause

Participation by an organization manager in an excess benefit transaction is *willful* if it is "voluntary, conscious, and intentional." A motive to avoid the restrictions of the law or the incurrence of any tax is not necessary to make a participation willful. Participation by an organization manager is not willful, however, if the manager does not know that the transaction in which they are participating is an excess benefit transaction.[182]

An organization manager's participation is due to *reasonable cause* if the manager has exercised responsibility on behalf of the organization with ordinary business care and prudence.[183]

(e) Occurrence

Generally, an excess benefit transaction *occurs* on the date on which the disqualified person receives the economic benefit from the applicable tax-exempt organization for federal income tax purposes. When a single contractual arrangement provides for a series of compensation or other payments to (or for the use of)[184] a disqualified person over the course of the disqualified person's tax year (or part

---

[177] *Id.*
[178] *Id.*
[179] *Id.*
[180] See § 21.9.
[181] Reg. § 53.4958-1(d)(4)(iv).
[182] Reg. § 53.4958-1(d)(5).
[183] Reg. § 53.4958-1(d)(6).
[184] See § 21.7.

of a tax year), any excess benefit transaction with respect to these aggregate payments is deemed to occur on the last day of the tax year (or, if the payments continue for part of the year, the date of the last payment in the series).[185]

There are, however, some variants on this general rule. In the case of benefits provided pursuant to a qualified pension, profit-sharing, or stock bonus plan, the transaction occurs on the date the benefit becomes vested. In the case of a transfer of property by an applicable tax-exempt organization to a disqualified person that is subject to a substantial risk of forfeiture, or in the case of rights to future compensation or property (including benefits under a nonqualified deferred compensation plan), the transaction occurs on the date the property, or the rights to future compensation or property, is no longer subject to a substantial risk of forfeiture. Where the disqualified person elects to include an amount in gross income in the tax year of transfer pursuant to the election rules in the case of property transferred in connection with the performance of services,[186] however, the excess benefit transaction occurs when the disqualified person received the economic benefit from the applicable tax-exempt organization for federal income tax purposes. Any excess benefit transaction involving benefits under a deferred compensation plan that vest during any tax year of the disqualified person is deemed to occur on the last day of that tax year.[187]

§ 21.13   INDEMNIFICATION AND INSURANCE

Any reimbursement by an applicable tax-exempt organization of excise tax liability of a disqualified person is treated as an excess benefit transaction itself, unless it is included in the disqualified person's compensation for the year in which the reimbursement is made.[188] The total compensation package, including the amount of any reimbursement, must be reasonable. Similarly, the payment by an applicable tax-exempt organization of premiums for an insurance policy providing liability insurance to a disqualified person for excess benefit taxes is an excess benefit transaction itself, unless the amounts of the premiums are treated as part of the compensation paid to the disqualified person and the total compensation, including the premiums, is reasonable.[189]

§ 21.14   RETURN FOR PAYMENT OF EXCISE TAXES

Under the law in existence prior to enactment of the excess benefit transactions rules, charitable organizations and other persons liable for certain excise taxes are required to file returns—Form 4720 (Schedule I)—by which the taxes due are calculated and reported. These taxes are those imposed on public charities

---

[185] Reg. § 53.4958-1(e)(1).
[186] IRC § 83(b).
[187] Reg. § 53.4958-1(e)(2).
[188] H.R. Rep. 104-506, at 58 (1996).
[189] Id.

for excessive lobbying expenditures[190] and for political campaign expenditures,[191] and on private foundations and/or other persons for a range of impermissible activities.[192]

Disqualified persons and organization managers liable for payment of an intermediate sanctions excise tax are required to file Form 4720 as the return by which these taxes are paid.[193] In general, returns on Form 4720 for a disqualified person or organization manager liable for an excess benefit transaction tax are required to be filed on or before the 15th day of the fifth month following the close of the tax year of that person.[194] Additions to tax are imposed for failure to timely file a Form 4720 or to pay an amount of tax shown (or required to be shown) on Form 4720, unless it is shown that the failure is due to reasonable cause and not to willful neglect.[195]

If a disqualified person is an entity and is required to file at least 10 returns of any type during the calendar year, it must file Form 4720 electronically.[196]

§ 21.15 STATUTE OF LIMITATIONS

In general, the statute of limitations for assessment by the IRS of an intermediate sanctions excise tax is the same as the general statute of limitations rules with

---

[190] IRC § 4911 or § 4912. See §§ 22.3(d)(iii), 22.4.

[191] IRC § 4955. See § 23.3.

[192] IRC §§ 4940–4948. This return is also used to pay excise taxes on failure to meet the community health needs assessment requirements (IRC § 4959) (see § 7.6(b)(ii)), for being a party to a prohibited tax shelter transactions, and on entity managers (IRC § 4965) (see § 28.16); taxes on taxable distributions by sponsoring organizations and on fund managers (IRC § 4966) (see § 12.5); taxes on prohibited benefits distributed from donor-advised funds (IRC § 4967) (*id.*); and taxes on the net investment income of certain colleges and universities (IRC § 4968) (see § 12.6(b)).

[193] Reg. § 53.6011-1(b).

[194] Reg. § 53.6071-1(f)(1). It is the view of the IRS's lawyers that interest begins to accrue on intermediate sanctions excise taxes as of the date the return reporting the tax was due (Chief Couns. Adv. Mem. 200819017), with this position based on the conclusion that these taxes are indeed taxes and not penalties (where interest starts accruing following notice and demand for payment by the IRS), in adherence to Latterman v. United States, 872 F.2d 564 (3d Cir. 1989).

[195] IRC § 6651(a)(1), (2); see § 28.8(b). The IRS may also seek to impose an accuracy-related penalty on an underpayment of excise taxes that is attributable to negligence or disregard of rules or regulations (IRC § 6662(b)(1); see § 28.8(b)).

On the face of the statute, the accuracy-related penalty for a substantial understatement of income tax (see § 28.8(b)) does not apply to excise taxes (IRC § 6662(b)(2), (d)(1)(A); e.g., Drummond v. Comm'r, 73 T.C.M. 1959 (1997)). The applicable regulations also limit the application of the accuracy-related penalty for negligence or disregard of rules and regulations to income taxes (Reg. § 1.6662-3(a)), but the statute does not contain any such limitation (IRC § 6662(b)(1), (c)). Thus, the IRS may attempt to apply this penalty to an understatement of excise tax that is attributable to negligence or disregard of rules or regulations on the ground that the regulations conflict with the statute (e.g., Program Manager Tech. Adv. 2007-00205).

[196] Reg. § 301.6011-12(a)(1). A "return" for these purposes is a return of "any type," including information returns (for example, Forms W-2 and Forms 1099), income tax returns, employment tax returns, and excise tax returns (Reg. § 301.6011-12(d)(3)). This electronic filing rule applies to Form 4720 required to be filed for tax years ending on or after December 31, 2023 (Reg. § 301.6011-12(f)). The addition to tax (see *supra* note 195) also may apply if Form 4720 is submitted on paper when required to be filed electronically (Reg. § 301.6011-12(c)).

respect to the assessment of taxes,[197] that is, three years.[198] The general rule in this regard is that the statute of limitations begins to run as of the date the return involved was filed or the due date of the return, whichever is later, and ends three years after that date. Thus, in the intermediate sanctions context, the statute begins to run on the later of the date when the applicable tax-exempt organization filed its annual information return[199] or the due date of the return.

The intermediate sanctions taxes are excise taxes. In the case of a return involving an excise tax, if the return omits an amount of tax properly includable on the return that exceeds 25 percent of the amount of the reported tax, the tax may be assessed (or a court proceeding commenced) at any time within six years after the return is filed.[200] The tax-exempt organizations annual information return, however, does not provide for the payment of any tax.[201] Thus, in determining the amount of tax "omitted" on the return, an intermediate sanctions tax is not taken into account if the excess benefit transaction that gave rise to the tax is disclosed in the return in a manner adequate to apprise the IRS of the existence and nature of the transaction.[202] The IRS has the burden of proving that the disclosure of information on an exempt organization's annual information return was insufficient to apprise it of the existence and nature of the excess benefit transaction involved.[203]

The IRS, when investigating the possibility of an excess benefit transaction, may send a summons to the applicable tax-exempt organization involved; this summons may be sent after the three-year statute of limitations pertaining to the exempt organization expired. A court held that an IRS summons is valid, even when sent after expiration of a statute of limitations, as long as the investigation is being conducted for a legitimate purpose, the inquiry is relevant to that purpose, the information sought is not already within the IRS's possession, and the administrative steps required by the federal tax law are being followed.[204]

§ 21.16   INTERRELATIONSHIP WITH PRIVATE INUREMENT DOCTRINE

The intermediate sanctions penalties may be imposed by the IRS in lieu of or in addition to revocation of the tax-exempt status of an applicable tax-exempt organization.[205] In general, these sanctions are the sole penalty imposed in cases in which the excess benefit does not rise to such a level as to call into question whether, on

[197] IRC § 6501(a); Reg. § 301.6501(a)-1(a).
[198] Reg. § 53.4958-1(e)(3).
[199] See § 28.2.
[200] IRC § 6501(e)(3); Reg. § 301.6501(e)-1(c)(3)(ii).
[201] See IRC §§ 6501(b)(4), 6501(l)(1); Reg. § 301.6501(n)-1(a)(1), (c).
[202] Id.
[203] Rev. Rul. 69-247, 1969-1 C.B. 303.
[204] Lintzenich v. United States, 371 F. Supp. 2d 972 (S.D. Ind. 2005). These criteria are from United States v. Powell, 379 U.S. 48 (1964). See § 27.6(a)(ii), text accompanied by note 255.
[205] H.R. Rep. 104-506, at 59 (1996).

the whole, the organization functions as an exempt charitable or social welfare organization or health insurance issuer.[206]

Revocation of tax-exempt status, with or without the imposition of intermediate sanctions taxes, is to occur only when the applicable tax-exempt organization no longer operates as an exempt charitable or social welfare organization or health insurance issuer (as the case may be).[207] Existing law principles apply in determining whether an applicable tax-exempt organization no longer operates as an exempt organization. For example, the loss of tax-exempt status would occur in a year, or as of a year, the entity was involved in a transaction constituting a substantial amount of private inurement.

The tax regulations provide that, in determining whether to continue to recognize the tax exemption of a charitable entity that engages in an excess benefit transaction that violates the private inurement doctrine, the IRS will consider all relevant facts and circumstances, including (1) the size and scope of the organization's regular and ongoing activities that further exempt purposes before and after one or more excess benefit transactions occurred, (2) the size and scope of one or more excess benefit transactions in relation to the size and scope of the organization's regular and ongoing exempt functions, (3) whether the organization has been involved in multiple excess benefit transactions, (4) whether the organization has implemented safeguards that are reasonably calculated to prevent future violations, and (5) whether the excess benefit transaction has been corrected or the organization has made good-faith efforts to seek correction from the disqualified person or persons who benefited from the excess benefit transaction.[208]

The fourth and fifth of these factors "weigh more heavily" in favor of continuing exemption where the organization has discovered the excess benefit transaction and takes corrective action before the IRS learns of the matter. Correction of an excess benefit transaction after the IRS discovers it, by itself, is never a sufficient basis for continuing recognition of exemption.[209]

An example concerns a newly created art museum (public charity) that, in its first two years, engaged in fundraising and preparation of its facilities. In its third year, a new board of trustees consisting of local art dealers was elected. Thereafter, the organization used almost all of its funds to purchase art from its trustees at excessive prices. This organization exhibits and offers for sale all of the purchased art. The purchasing of art from its trustees was not disclosed in the organization's application for recognition of exemption. These transactions violate the private inurement doctrine and are excess benefit transactions. The foregoing factors dictate that this museum is no longer tax-exempt, effective as of the third year.[210]

---

[206] The tax regulations essentially state the matter this way: The intermediate sanctions law does not affect the substantive standards for tax exemption for applicable tax-exempt organizations; these entities qualify for exemption only if no part of their net earnings inures to the benefit of insiders (Reg. § 53.4958-8(a); also, Reg. § 1.501(c)(3)-1(f)(2)(i)).

[207] H.R. Rep. 104-506, at 59, n.15 (1996). In one instance, the IRS's lawyers concluded that, although the intermediate sanctions rules should be applied, revocation of tax exemption on the ground of private inurement was "not appropriate" (Tech. Adv. Mem. 200437040).

[208] Reg. § 1.501(c)(3)-1(f)(2)(ii).

[209] Reg. § 1.501(c)(3)-1(f)(2)(iii).

[210] Reg. § 1.501(c)(3)-1(f)(2)(iv), Example (1).

Continuing with this illustration, in the fourth year, the entire museum board resigns and is replaced by members of the community who have experience operating educational institutions. The museum promptly discontinues the selling of exhibited art, ceases to purchase art from its trustees, adopts a conflict-of-interest policy, adopts art valuation guidelines, retains the services of a lawyer to recover the excess payments to the former trustees, and implements a program of educational activities. Even though the payments were excess benefit transactions and private inurement, this implementation of safeguards and efforts to pursue correction enables the museum to remain exempt.[211]

As another example, a public charity conducts educational programs for the benefit of the public. In its fifth year, the organization's chief executive officer began causing the entity to divert substantial funds to the executive for personal use. The organization's board of directors did not authorize this practice, although some board members were aware of these diversions. The CEO claimed, despite a lack of documentation and no repayment amounts, that the diverted funds were loans. These diversions of funds were excess benefit transactions and private inurement. By application of the factors, this organization's tax exemption was lost in its fifth year.[212]

In a third example, a public charity uses several buildings in the conduct of its exempt activities. This charitable organization sold one of its buildings for an amount that was substantially below fair market value; the sale was a significant event in relation to the entity's other activities. The building was sold to a company that is wholly owned by the charity's CEO. At the time of the transaction, the governing board of the charity did not undertake due diligence that could have made it aware that the sales price was below fair value. Nonetheless, prior to an IRS examination of the charity, the board determined that the company underpaid for the property. Realizing that an excess benefit transaction (and a private inurement transaction) occurred, the board promptly terminated the employment of the CEO, hired legal counsel to recover the excess benefit, and adopted a conflict-of-interest policy and new contract review procedures. This organization continues to be tax-exempt.[213]

Another example concerns a large public charity that, during a year, paid $2,500 of the personal expenses of its chief financial officer. These payments constitute an automatic excess benefit transaction and private inurement. However, inasmuch as only a *de minimis* portion of the organization's revenues were so diverted, this organization's tax exemption is not disturbed.[214]

A public charity, with substantial assets and revenues, furthers its exempt purposes by providing social services in a geographical area. The organization's board of directors adopted written procedures for setting of executive compensation, modeled on the procedures for establishing the rebuttable presumption of reasonableness.[215] On the basis of recommendations from its compensation

---

[211] *Id.*, Example (2).
[212] *Id.*, Example (3).
[213] *Id.*, Example (4).
[214] *Id.*, Example (5).
[215] See § 21.9.

committee, the board approved compensation packages for the organization's top executives and timely documented the basis for its decision in board meeting minutes. The IRS, on examination, determined that the requirements of the presumption were not met and that the executives' compensation packages in a year were excessive. The board thereafter appointed additional members to the compensation committee, amended its procedures, and renegotiated the executives' compensation on a going-forward basis. The compensation payments as to the year involved thus were excess benefit and private inurement transactions. In part because the size and scope of the excess benefit transactions were not significant in relation to the size and scope of the organization's charitable functions, the organization continued to be tax-exempt, even though it engaged in multiple excess benefit transactions, did not void the compensation contracts for the year, and did not seek correction from the top executives for the excessive compensation.[216]

In recent instances, the IRS has applied the factors described earlier to revoke a charitable organization's tax-exempt status where the organization engaged in multiple excess benefit transactions.[217]

The coming years will bring interpretations and amplification of the intermediate sanctions rules, with emphasis on what does and does not constitute an excess benefit transaction; this process will draw heavily on the law as shaped by the private inurement doctrine. Likewise, application of the intermediate sanctions rules will meaningfully inform the substance and boundaries of the doctrines of private inurement and private benefit. Thus, a development in one of these three bodies of law is likely to directly affect the evolution of the other two bodies of law. The intermediate sanctions rules probably will be invoked more frequently than revocation of tax-exempt status by application of the private inurement doctrine to public charities and social welfare organizations.

The law concerning self-dealing in the private foundation context[218] also will be heavily interrelated with the intermediate sanctions rules. Indeed, the very structure of these rules is, in many ways, patterned after the private foundation rules. Of greater substance, however, is that a significant amount of the private foundation self-dealing law is directly usable in discerning the contours of the intermediate sanctions law. Likewise, a development in the intermediate sanctions area is likely to be applicable in the private foundation context.

Thus, as the years unfold, the law of tax-exempt organizations will be enriched by the process and outcomes resulting from the interrelationships and fertilization of the intermediate sanctions, private inurement, private benefit, and self-dealing rules.

---

[216] Reg. § 1.501(c)(3)-1(f)(2)(iv), Example (6).
[217] E.g., Priv. Ltr. Rul. 201816012.
[218] See § 12.4(a).

CHAPTER TWENTY-TWO

Legislative Activities by Tax-Exempt Organizations

The federal tax law imposes limitations on the extent to which tax-exempt charitable organizations[1] and health care issuers[2] can engage in lobbying and impedes lobbying by membership associations[3] by curbing the deductibility of dues paid to them.

---

[1] That is, organizations described in IRC § 501(c)(3) and exempt from federal income taxation by reason of IRC § 501(a). See Part Three. These rules are principally applicable to public charities (see § 12.3); private foundations are governed by somewhat more restrictive rules (see § 12.4(e)). As to the latter, see *Private Foundations* § 9.1.

[2] That is, organizations described in IRC § 501(c)(29) and exempt from federal income taxation by reason of IRC § 501(a). See § 19.18.

[3] E.g., organizations described in IRC § 501(c)(6) and exempt from federal income taxation by reason of IRC § 501(a). See Chapter 14.

§ 22.1 LEGISLATIVE ACTIVITIES LAW FOR EXEMPT ORGANIZATIONS— INTRODUCTION

At the federal level, there are six discrete bodies of law that can pertain to attempts to influence legislation by tax-exempt organizations: two sets of rules applicable to public charities,[4] rules applicable to private foundations,[5] rules pertaining to membership associations,[6] law concerning lobbying by recipients of federal grants and similar payments,[7] and rules established by the Office of Management and Budget concerning the use of federal funds for lobbying by nonprofit organizations.[8] These various sets of rules contain law by which terms such as *legislation* and *influencing legislation* are defined, and costs associated with lobbying are ascertained.

§ 22.2 MEANING OF *LEGISLATION*

A threshold concept in this setting is the meaning of the term *legislation*.

(a) Substantial Part Test

The term *legislation*, as defined for purposes of the substantial part test, includes action by Congress, a state legislature, a local council or similar governing body, and the general public in a referendum, initiative, constitutional amendment, or similar procedure.[9]

Legislation generally does not include action by an executive branch of a government, such as the promulgation of rules and regulations, nor does it include action by independent regulatory agencies. Appropriations bills are items of legislation for federal tax purposes. Also, the term *legislation* includes proposals for the making of laws in countries other than the United States.[10]

An attempt to influence the confirmation by the U.S. Senate of a federal judicial nominee constitutes, for these purposes, an attempt to influence legislation.[11] This position is based on the definition of the term *legislation* found in the expenditure test, where the term is defined to include resolutions and similar items.[12]

(b) Expenditure Test

The statute in connection with the expenditure test states that the term *legislation* includes "action with respect to Acts, bills, resolutions, or similar items by the Congress, any State legislature, any local council, or similar governing body, or by the public in a referendum, initiative, constitutional amendment, or similar procedure."[13]

---

[4] See § 22.3.
[5] See § 12.4(e).
[6] See § 22.6.
[7] 31 U.S.C. § 1352 (Byrd Amendment).
[8] Circular A-122, "Cost Principles for Nonprofit Organizations."
[9] Reg. § 1.501(c)(3)-1(c)(3)(ii). Cf. Smith v. Comm'r, 3 T.C. 696 (1944).
[10] Rev. Rul. 73-440, 1973-2 C.B. 177.
[11] Notice 88-76, 1988-2 C.B. 392.
[12] IRC § 4911(e)(2).
[13] *Id.* Also, Reg. § 56.4911-2(d)(1).

An attempt to influence the confirmation by the U.S. Senate of a federal judicial nominee, as constituting an attempt to influence legislation, is reflected in the expenditure test by means of examples in the regulations.[14]

(c) Associations' Dues Deductibility Test

The term *legislation*, as defined for purposes of the rules concerning the deductibility of associations' members' dues, means the same as is the case with respect to the expenditure test.[15] Thus, the term includes any action with respect to acts, bills, resolutions, or other similar items by a legislative body.[16] Also, legislation includes a "proposed treaty required to be submitted by the President to the Senate for its advice and consent from the time the President's representative begins to negotiate its position with the prospective parties to the proposed treaty."[17]

Because of the breadth of these rules,[18] however, legislative bodies are "Congress, state legislatures, and other similar governing bodies, excluding local councils (and similar governing bodies), and executive, judicial, or administrative bodies."[19] The term *administrative bodies* includes "school boards, housing authorities, sewer and water districts, zoning boards, and other similar Federal, State, or local special purpose bodies, whether elective or appointive."[20]

§ 22.3 LOBBYING BY CHARITABLE ORGANIZATIONS

As noted, one of the criteria for qualification as a tax-exempt charitable organization is that "no substantial part of the activities" of the organization may constitute "carrying on propaganda, or otherwise attempting, to influence legislation."[21] It is irrelevant, for purposes of classification of an organization as a charitable entity under the federal tax law, that the legislation that is advocated or opposed would advance the charitable purposes for which the organization was created to promote.[22] This position should be contrasted with the state of the law prior to enactment of statutory law on the point in 1934.[23]

(a) Legislative History

The provision limiting the extent of lobbying by charitable organizations was added to the federal tax law in 1934, without benefit of congressional hearings,

[14] Reg. § 56.4911-2(b)(4)(ii)(B), Example (6). Also, Reg. § 53.4945-2(d)(2)(iii), Examples (5)–(7).
[15] IRC § 162(e)(4)(B).
[16] Reg. § 1.162-29(b)(4).
[17] *Id.*
[18] These rules encompass certain lobbying efforts with respect to the federal executive branch but do not apply with respect to direct lobbying in connection with local legislation (see § 22.6(a)).
[19] Reg. § 1.162-29(b)(6).
[20] *Id.*
[21] IRC § 501(c)(3).
[22] Rev. Rul. 67-293, 1967-2 C.B. 185. Also, Cammarano v. United States, 358 U.S. 498 (1959).
[23] There is nothing in the English common law of charity that prohibits a charitable organization from engaging in legislative activities. A federal court opinion, which sparked development of contemporary

as the result of a floor amendment adopted by the Senate. During consideration of the legislation that became the Revenue Act of 1934, there was debate on an amendment to restrict "partisan politics" and lobbying by charitable organizations.[24] The amendment was adopted two days later;[25] it was changed in conference, with deletion of reference to "partisan politics."

(b) Concept of *Lobbying*

Although legislative activities take many forms, the federal tax law distinguishes between communications that are *direct* lobbying and indirect, or *grassroots*, lobbying. Direct lobbying includes the presentation of testimony at public hearings held by legislative committees, correspondence and conferences with legislators and their staffs, communications by electronic means, and publication of documents advocating specific legislative action.[26] Grassroots lobbying consists of appeals to the general public or segments of the general public to contact legislators or take other specific action regarding legislative matters.[27]

(c) Substantial Part Test

The essence of the substantial part test is that a tax-exempt charitable organization can engage in attempts to influence legislation to the extent that the lobbying is not substantial. The term *substantial*, however, has never been defined in this context.

(i) Action Organizations. Pursuant to the substantial part test, a charitable organization will not be precluded from tax exemption because of lobbying as long as it avoids classification as an action organization. An organization is regarded as attempting to influence legislation if it (1) contacts, or urges the public to contact, members of a legislative body for the purpose of proposing, supporting, or opposing legislation, or (2) advocates the adoption or rejection of legislation.[28] If a substantial part of a charitable organization's activities is attempting to influence legislation, the organization is designated an *action organization* and hence cannot qualify as a tax-exempt charitable entity.[29] For example, a fund was held to be an action organization on the ground that it functioned in a partisan manner as part of its efforts to further the cause of tax reform.[30]

tax policy, held that charitable organizations may not engage in "[p]olitical agitation" (Slee v. Comm'r, 42 F.2d 184, 185 (2d Cir. 1930)).

[24] 78 Cong. Rec. 5861 (Apr. 2, 1934).

[25] 78 Cong. Rec. 5959 (Apr. 4, 1934).

[26] It is often the position of charitable organizations that, when a representative of it "speaks directly with a legislator, it is for educational purposes only, helping legislators understand the effect of proposed legislation" (Priv. Ltr. Rul. 201908024); the IRS is not likely to agree with this assertion.

[27] Roberts Dairy Co. v. Comm'r, 195 F.2d 948 (8th Cir. 1952), *cert. denied*, 344 U.S. 865 (1952); American Hardware & Equip. Co. v. Comm'r, 202 F.2d 126 (4th Cir. 1953), *cert. denied*, 346 U.S. 814 (1953). In certain circumstances, grassroots lobbying is also exempt function (see § 17.1(a)) or political campaign activity (see § 23.2) (e.g., Priv. Ltr. Rul. 9652026).

[28] Reg. § 1.501(c)(3)-1(c)(3)(ii).

[29] See § 4.5(d). Also, Reg. § 1.501(h)-1(a)(4).

[30] Fund for the Study of Economic Growth & Tax Reform v. Internal Revenue Service, 997 F. Supp. 15 (D.D.C. 1998), *aff'd*, 161 F.3d 755 (D.C. Cir. 1999). This appellate court opinion included a curious and oblique footnote (*id.*, 161 F.3d at 760 n.9). There the court observed that its holding in the case is "quite

For an organization to be denied or lose tax-exempt status because of lobbying activity, the legislative activity must be undertaken as an act of the organization itself. Thus, for example, the IRS recognized that the legislative activities of a student newspaper were not attributable to the sponsoring university.[31] Similarly, during the course of the anti-Vietnam War efforts on many college and university campuses, which included legislative activities, the principle was established that the activities by students and faculty were not official acts of the particular institutions.[32]

(ii) Allowable Lobbying.   A determination as to whether a specific activity or category of activities of a charitable organization is *substantial* basically is a factual one. Until enactment of the expenditure test,[33] the law did not offer any formula for computing substantial or insubstantial legislative undertakings. (It was once suggested that 5 percent of an organization's time and effort that involves legislative activities is not substantial.)[34] In reflection of this state of affairs, the Senate Finance Committee, in its report accompanying the Tax Reform Act of 1969, said that the "standards as to the permissible level of [legislative] activities under the present law are so vague as to encourage subjective application of the sanction."[35] In its report accompanying the Tax Reform Act of 1976, the Senate Finance Committee portrayed the dilemma this way: "Many believe that the standards as to the permissible level of [legislative] activities under present law are too vague and thereby tend to encourage subjective and selective enforcement."[36]

One approach to attempting to measure substantiality in this context is to determine what percentage of an organization's expenditures is devoted on an annual basis to efforts to influence legislation. Yet the limitation on influencing legislation involves more than simply a curb on spending or diversions of funds; it includes restrictions on levels of activity as well (expenditures of time). A portion of an organization's activities devoted to legislative pursuits may be regarded as more important than the organization's expenditures of funds for the purpose.[37] Indeed, particularly with the advent of lobbying by means of the Internet, in some circumstances neither of these elements is particularly relevant; the even more subjective factor of *influence* may have to be taken into consideration.[38]

Thus, a tax-exempt organization enjoying considerable prestige and influence might be considered as having a substantial impact on a legislative process solely on the basis of a single official position statement, an activity considered

narrow." The court wrote that it was "not holding that any organization which studies an issue touching on legislation, reaches a conclusion with respect to that issue, and then argues the merits of that conclusion must necessarily be characterized" as an action organization. It continued: "We are simply holding that an organization which assumes a conclusion with respect to a highly public and controversial legislative issue and then goes into the business of selling that conclusion may properly be designated" an action organization.

[31] Rev. Rul. 72-513, 1972-2 C.B. 246.

[32] American Council on Education Guidelines, CCH Stand. Fed. Tax Rep. ¶ 3033.197.

[33] See § 22.3(d).

[34] Seasongood v. Comm'r, 227 F.2d 907, 912 (6th Cir. 1955).

[35] S. Rep. No. 91-552, at 47 (1969).

[36] S. Rep. No. 94-938, pt. 2, at 80 (1976).

[37] League of Women Voters v. United States, 180 F. Supp. 379 (Ct. Cl. 1960), *cert. denied*, 364 U.S. 822 (1960).

[38] See § 22.8.

negligible when measured according to a percentage standard of time or money expended.[39] A standard such as this, however, tends to place undue emphasis on whether a particular legislative effort was successful, inasmuch as this evaluation is usually made on the basis of hindsight.[40]

In 1972, a federal court of appeals provided a new dimension to the concept of attempting to influence legislation, when it upheld the revocation of tax exemption of a ministry organization.[41] The court found the following substantial legislative activities: articles constituting appeals to the public to react to certain issues, support or opposition to specific terms of legislation and enactments, and efforts to cause members of the public to contact members of Congress on various matters. Of particular consequence was the court's explicit rejection of a percentage test in determining substantiality, which was dismissed as obscuring the "complexity of balancing the organization's activities in relation to its objectives and circumstances."[42]

A subsequent court decision offered authority for the proposition that *substantiality* is not always measured by the factor of funds or time expended. The court observed, albeit reviewing the term in a different context,[43] that "[w]hether an activity is substantial is a facts-and-circumstances inquiry not always dependent upon time or expenditure percentages."[44]

(iii) Exceptions. A charitable organization found to have engaged in legislative activities to a prohibited extent is deemed an action organization and thus is not entitled to continuing tax exemption.[45] Likewise, legislative activities may preclude tax exemption. One form of action organization is one as to which a "substantial part of its activities is attempting to influence legislation by propaganda or otherwise."[46] Another type of action organization is one whose "main or primary objective or objectives (as distinguished from its incidental or secondary objectives) may be attained only by legislation or a defeat of proposed legislation," and "it advocates, or campaigns for, the attainment of such main or primary objective or objectives as distinguished from engaging in nonpartisan analysis, study or research and making the results thereof available to the public."[47]

The IRS stated that a charitable organization that does not initiate any action with respect to pending legislation but merely responds to a request from a legislative committee to testify is not, solely because of this activity, an action organization.[48]

---

[39] Kuper v. Comm'r, 332 F.2d 562 (3d Cir. 1964), *cert. denied*, 379 U.S. 920 (1964).

[40] Haswell v. United States, 500 F.2d 1133, 1142 (Ct. Cl. 1974), *cert. denied*, 419 U.S. 1107 (1974); Dulles v. Johnson, 273 F.2d 362, 367 (2d Cir. 1959), *cert. denied*, 364 U.S. 834 (1960).

[41] Christian Echoes Nat'l Ministry, Inc. v. United States, 470 F.2d 849 (10th Cir. 1972), *cert. denied*, 414 U.S. 864 (1973).

[42] *Id.*, 470 F.2d at 855.

[43] See § 8.2.

[44] Nationalist Movement v. Comm'r, 102 T.C. 558, 589 (1994), *aff'd*, 37 F.3d 216 (5th Cir. 1994).

[45] See § 4.5(d).

[46] Reg. § 1.501(c)(3)-1(c)(3)(iii).

[47] Reg. § 1.501(c)(3)-1(c)(3)(iv). In general, McClintock-Trunkey Co. v. Comm'r, 19 T.C. 297 (1952), *rev'd on other grounds*, 217 F.2d 329 (9th Cir. 1955).

[48] Rev. Rul. 70-449, 1970-2 C.B. 111.

An organization may engage in nonpartisan analysis, study, and research, and publish its results (that is, undertake activities that are educational in nature),[49] without being an action organization, as long as it does not advocate the adoption of legislation or legislative action to implement its findings.[50] That is, an organization may evaluate a subject of proposed legislation or a pending item of legislation and present to the public an objective analysis of it, as long as it does not participate in the presentation of one or more bills to a legislature and does not engage in any campaign to secure enactment of any proposals.[51] If, however, the organization's primary objective can be attained only by legislative action, it is an action organization.[52] In general, promoting activism instead of promoting educational activities can deny an organization classification as a charitable entity.[53]

As for the specific connotation of the term *propaganda*, the term is not as expansive as merely spreading particular beliefs, opinions, or doctrines. Rather, the word "connotes public address with selfish or ulterior purpose and characterized by the coloring or distortion of facts."[54] To avoid stigmatization as propaganda, therefore, a presentation must be fairly well balanced as to stating alternative viewpoints and solutions, and be motivated more by a purpose to educate than by a "selfish" purpose.[55]

(iv) Reporting Rules. The required contents of annual information returns filed by tax-exempt organizations[56] include a section designed to make information about the legislative activities of charitable organizations, which are subject to the substantial part test, accessible to the public.[57] Thus, an organization subject to this test must disclose in its annual information return any attempts to influence legislation through the use of volunteers or paid individuals; media advertisements; mailings to members, legislators, or the public; publications or broadcast statements; grants to other organizations for lobbying purposes; direct contact with legislators, their staffs, government officials, or a legislative body; and/or rallies, demonstrations, seminars, conventions, speeches, lectures, or any other means.

(d)   Expenditure Test

Under the expenditure test, the definition of *legislation* includes the term *action.* The term *action* is "limited to the introduction, amendment, enactment, defeat, or repeal of Acts, bills, resolutions, or similar items."[58]

---

[49] See Chapter 8.

[50] Reg. § 1.501(c)(3)-1(c)(3)(iv); Weyl v. Comm'r, 48 F.2d 811 (2d Cir. 1931); Rev. Rul. 70-79, 1970-1 C.B. 127.

[51] Rev. Rul. 64-195, 1964-2 C.B. 138; I.T. 2654, XI-2 C.B. 39 (1932).

[52] Fund for the Study of Economic Growth & Tax Reform v. Internal Revenue Service, 997 F. Supp. 15 (D.D.C. 1998), aff'd, 161 F.3d 755 (D.C. Cir. 1999); Haswell v. United States, 500 F.2d 1133, 1143–45 (Ct. Cl. 1974), *cert. denied*, 419 U.S. 1107 (1974); Rev. Rul. 62-71, 1962-1 C.B. 85. Thus, for example, the IRS denied recognition of tax exemption as a charitable and educational organization to an entity because its primary objective is achieving statehood for a "political unit," which can be attained only by the enactment of legislation (Priv. Ltr. Rul. 201932017).

[53] Rev. Rul. 60-193, 1960-1 C.B. 195, *as modified by* Rev. Rul. 66-258, 1966-2 C.B. 213.

[54] Seasongood v. Comm'r, 227 F.2d 907, 910–12 (6th Cir. 1955). Also, Cochran v. Comm'r, 78 F.2d 176, 179 (4th Cir. 1935).

[55] Rev. Rul. 68-263, 1968-1 C.B. 256. In general, see § 8.2.

[56] See § 28.2(a).

[57] Form 990, Schedule C, Part II-B.

[58] IRC § 4911(e)(3); Reg. § 56.4911-2(d)(2).

(i) Influencing Legislation. These rules define the term *influencing legislation* in two ways. One is any attempt to influence any legislation through communication with any member or employee of a legislative body[59] or with any other governmental official or employee who may participate in the formulation of the legislation (a *direct lobbying communication*).[60] The other is any attempt to influence any legislation through an attempt to affect the opinions of the general public or any segment of the public (a *grassroots lobbying communication*).[61]

A communication with a legislator or government official is a direct lobbying communication only where the communication refers to *specific legislation* and reflects a view on the legislation.[62] Where a communication refers to and reflects a view on a measure that is the subject of a referendum, ballot initiative, or similar procedure, and is made to the members of the general public in the jurisdiction where the vote will occur, the communication is a direct lobbying communication (unless certain exceptions apply).[63] On the basis of the principles illustrated in examples in the tax regulations, a court held that a communication refers to a ballot measure "if it either refers to the measure by name or, without naming it, employs terms widely used in connection with the measure or describes the content or effect of the measure."[64]

A communication is regarded as a grassroots lobbying communication only where the communication refers to specific legislation, reflects a view on the legislation, and encourages the recipient of the communication to take action with respect to the legislation.[65] The phrase *encouraging the recipient to take action* with respect to legislation (also known as a *call to action*) means that the communication (1) states that the recipient should contact a legislator or an employee of a legislative body, or should contact any other government official or employee who may participate in the formulation of legislation (but only if the principal purpose of urging contact with the government official or employee is to influence legislation); (2) states the address, telephone number, or similar information of a legislator or an employee of a legislative body; (3) provides a petition, tear-off postcard, or similar material for the recipient to communicate with a legislator or an employee of a legislative body, or with any other government official or employee who may participate in the formulation of legislation (but only if the principal purpose of so facilitating contact with the government official or employee is to influence legislation); or (4) specifically identifies one or more legislators who will vote on the legislation as opposing the communication's view with respect to the legislation, being undecided with respect to the legislation, being the recipient's representative in the legislature, or being a member of the legislative committee

---

[59] This term is defined in Reg. § 56.4911-2(d)(3).

[60] IRC § 4911(d)(1)(B); Reg. § 56.4911-2(b)(1)(i).

[61] IRC § 4911(d)(1)(A); Reg. § 56.4911-2(b)(2)(i).

[62] Reg. § 56.4911-2(b)(1)(ii).

[63] Reg. § 56.4911-2(b)(1)(iii). This type of communication may be treated as nonpartisan analysis, study, or research (see text accompanied by *infra* note 115).

[64] Parks v. Comm'r, 145 T.C. 278, 309 (2015), *aff'd*, Parks Found. v. Comm'r, 717 Fed. Appx. 712 (9th Cir. 2017).

[65] Reg. § 56.4911-2(b)(2)(ii).

or subcommittee that will consider the legislation.[66] The IRS considers this definition of a grassroots lobbying communication to be "very lenient," because it "will permit many clear advocacy communications to be treated as NONlobbying."[67]

The term *specific legislation* is defined as (1) legislation that has already been introduced in a legislative body and (2) a specific legislative proposal that the organization supports or opposes.[68] In the case of a referendum, ballot initiative, constitutional amendment, or other measure that is placed on the ballot by petitions, an item becomes specific legislation when the petition is first circulated among the voters for signature.[69] The term specific legislation is accorded, despite use of the word *specific*, a rather expansive definition due to use of the term *proposal*. For example, an item of legislation that has passed a state's legislature can be a legislative proposal with respect to another state's legislature.[70] Summaries of "plans" can be a legislative proposal,[71] as can a request for an increase in appropriations,[72] or submission of a proposed budget to a legislative body.[73]

The regulations contain a rebuttable presumption that a *paid mass media advertisement*[74] is grassroots lobbying if it (1) is made within two weeks before a vote by a legislative body or committee of a legislative body on highly publicized legislation, (2) reflects a view on the general subject of the legislation, and (3) either refers to the legislation or encourages the public to communicate with legislators on the general subject of the legislation. The presumption is rebutted either by showing that the charitable organization regularly makes similar mass media communications without regard to the timing of legislation or that the timing of the communication was unrelated to the upcoming vote.[75]

Expenses incurred for nonlobbying communications can subsequently be characterized as grassroots lobbying expenditures where the materials or other communications are later used in a lobbying effort. For this result to occur, the materials must be *advocacy communications or research materials*, where the primary purpose of the organization in undertaking or preparing the communications or materials was for use in lobbying; in the case of subsequent distribution of the materials by another organization, there must be "clear and convincing" evidence of collusion between the two organizations to establish that the primary purpose for preparing the communication was for use in lobbying. In any event, this subsequent-use rule applies only to expenditures paid less than six months before the first use of the nonlobbying material in the lobbying campaign.[76]

A communication between an organization and any bona fide member of the organization made to directly encourage the member to engage in direct lobbying

[66] Reg. § 56.4911-2(b)(2)(iii). A naming of the main sponsor(s) of the legislation for purposes of identifying it is not considered an encouragement of the recipient to take action (*id.*).
[67] 55 Fed. Reg. 35580 (Aug. 31, 1990).
[68] Reg. § 56.4911-2(d)(1)(ii).
[69] *Id.*
[70] Reg. § 56.4911-2(d)(1)(iii), Example (2).
[71] Reg. § 56.4911-2(b)(4)(ii)(B), Examples (1)–(3).
[72] Reg. § 56.4911-2(b)(4)(ii)(B), Example (5).
[73] Reg. § 56.4911-2(d)(4).
[74] Certain large-scale in-house publications and broadcasts are considered *paid mass media advertisements*.
[75] Reg. § 56.4911-2(b)(5).
[76] Reg. § 56.4911-2(b)(2)(v).

is itself considered direct lobbying.[77] A communication between an organization and any bona fide member of the organization made to directly encourage the member to urge persons other than members to engage in direct or grassroots lobbying is considered grassroots lobbying.[78]

A transfer is a grassroots expenditure to the extent it is earmarked[79] for grassroots lobbying purposes.[80] A transfer that is earmarked for direct lobbying purposes, or for both direct lobbying and grassroots lobbying purposes, is regarded as a grassroots expenditure in full, unless the transferor can demonstrate that all or part of the amounts transferred were expended for direct lobbying purposes, in which case that part of the amounts transferred is a direct lobbying expenditure by the transferor.[81] There are rules for treating as a lobbying (direct or grassroots) expenditure transfers for less than fair market value from a public charity that has elected the expenditure test to any noncharity that makes lobbying expenditures.[82]

(ii) Allocation Rules. There are two allocation rules for communications that have both a lobbying purpose and a bona fide nonlobbying purpose.

One rule requires that the allocation be *reasonable*. This rule applies to an electing public charity's communications primarily with its bona fide members. More than one-half of the recipients of the communication must be members of the electing public charity for this rule to apply.[83]

The other allocation rule is for nonmembership communications. Where a nonmembership lobbying communication also has a bona fide nonlobbying purpose, an organization must include as lobbying expenditures all costs attributable to those parts of the communication that are on the same specific subject as the lobbying message. The rules define the phrase *same specific subject.*[84]

If a communication (other than to an organization's members) is both a direct lobbying communication and a grassroots lobbying communication, the communication is treated as a grassroots lobbying expenditure, unless the electing public charity demonstrates that the communication was made primarily for direct lobbying purposes, in which case a reasonable allocation is permitted.[85]

(iii) Allowable Lobbying. The expenditure test utilizes a mechanical standard for measuring permissible and impermissible ranges of lobbying expenditures[86] by eligible charitable organizations, and does so in terms of the expenditure of funds and sliding scales of percentages. (The basic concept that legislative activities cannot be a substantial portion of the undertakings of a charitable organization was not altered by enactment of the expenditure test.)

---

[77] IRC § 4911(d)(3)(A).
[78] IRC § 4911(d)(3)(B).
[79] Reg. § 56.4911-4(f)(4).
[80] Reg. § 56.4911-3(c)(1).
[81] Reg. § 56.4911-3(c)(2).
[82] Reg. § 56.4911-3(c)(3).
[83] Reg. § 56.4911-3(a)(2)(ii).
[84] Reg. § 56.4911-3(a)(2)(i).
[85] Reg. § 56.4911-3(a)(3).
[86] IRC § 4911(c)(1); Reg. § 1.501(h)-3(c)(1).

These standards are formulated in terms of declining percentages of total *exempt purpose expenditures*.[87] In general, an expenditure is an exempt purpose expenditure for a tax year if it is paid or incurred by an electing public charity to accomplish the organization's exempt purposes.[88] These expenditures include (1) those expended for one or more charitable purposes, including most grants made for charitable ends; (2) amounts paid as compensation (current or deferred) of one or more employees in furtherance of a charitable purpose; (3) the portion of administrative expenses allocable to a charitable purpose; (4) lobbying expenditures; (5) amounts expended for nonpartisan analysis, study, or research;[89] (6) amounts expended for examinations of broad social, economic, and similar problems;[90] (7) amounts expended in response to requests for technical advice;[91] (8) amounts expended pursuant to the *self-defense exception*;[92] (9) amounts expended for communications to members that are not lobbying expenditures; (10) a reasonable allowance for straight-line depreciation or amortization of charitable assets;[93] and (11) certain fundraising expenditures.[94]

The term *exempt purpose* expenditure does not include (1) amounts expended that are not for purposes described in the preceding items (1) through (9), or (11); (2) the amount of transfers to members of an affiliated group,[95] made to artificially inflate the amount of exempt purpose expenditures, or to certain noncharitable organizations; (3) amounts paid to or incurred for a separate fundraising unit of the organization or an affiliated organization; (4) amounts paid to or incurred for any person who is not an employee or any organization that is not an affiliated organization, if paid primarily for fundraising, but only if the person or organization engages in fundraising, fundraising counseling, or the provision of similar advice or services; (5) amounts paid or incurred that are properly chargeable to a capital account with respect to an unrelated trade or business;[96] (6) amounts paid or incurred for a tax that is not imposed in connection with the organization's efforts to accomplish charitable purposes (such as the unrelated business income tax); and (7) amounts paid or incurred for the production of income, where the income-producing activity is not substantially related to exempt purposes (such as the costs of maintaining an endowment).[97]

For this purpose, the term *fundraising* embraces (1) the solicitation of dues or contributions from members of the organization, from persons whose dues are in arrears, or from the general public; (2) the solicitation of gifts from businesses or gifts or grants from other organizations, including charitable entities; or (3) the

---

[87] IRC § 4911(e)(1); Reg. § 56.4911-4(a).
[88] IRC § 4911(e)(1)(A).
[89] See § 22.3(d)(v), text accompanied by *infra* note 115.
[90] See § 22.3(d)(v), text accompanied by *infra* note 126.
[91] See § 22.3(d)(v), text accompanied by *infra* note 116.
[92] See § 22.3(d)(v), text accompanied by *infra* note 117.
[93] IRC § 4911(e)(4).
[94] IRC § 4911(e)(1)(B); Reg. § 56.4911-4(b). Cf. Reg. § 56.4911-3(a)(1).
[95] See § 22.3(d)(viii).
[96] See Chapters 24, 25.
[97] IRC § 4911(e)(1)(C); Reg. § 56.4911-4(c).

solicitation of grants from governmental units or any agency or instrumentality of the units.[98]

A *separate fundraising unit* of an organization "must consist of either two or more individuals a majority of whose time is spent on fundraising for the organization, or any separate accounting unit of the organization that is devoted to fundraising." In addition, "amounts paid to or incurred for a separate fundraising unit include all amounts incurred for the creation, production, copying, and distribution of the fundraising portion of a separate fundraising unit's communication."[99]

The basic permitted annual level of expenditures for legislative efforts (the *lobbying nontaxable amount*)[100] is determined by using a sliding scale percentage of the organization's exempt purpose expenditures, as follows: 20 percent of the first $500,000 of an organization's expenditures for an exempt purpose, plus 15 percent of the next $500,000, 10 percent of the next $500,000, and 5 percent of any remaining expenditures. These calculations generally are made based on a four-year average.[101] The total amount spent for legislative activities in any one year by an eligible charitable organization may not exceed $1 million.[102] A separate limitation—amounting to 25 percent of the foregoing amounts—is imposed on attempts to influence the general public on legislative matters[103] (the *grassroots nontaxable amount*).[104]

A charitable organization that has elected the expenditure test[105] and that exceeds either or both of these limitations becomes subject to an excise tax in the amount of 25 percent of the excess lobbying expenditures,[106] which tax falls on the greater of the two excesses.[107] If an electing organization's lobbying expenditures normally (that is, on an average over a four-year period)[108] exceed 150 percent of either limitation (the *lobbying ceiling amount*[109] and the *grassroots ceiling amount*),[110] it will lose its tax-exempt status as a charitable entity.[111] A charitable organization in this circumstance is not able to convert to a tax-exempt social welfare organization.[112]

(iv) Nonearmarked Grants. The federal tax lobbying rules concerning nonearmarked grants by private foundations[113] are applicable to like grants by public charities that have elected the expenditure test.[114] Thus, a general support grant by

---

[98] Reg. § 56.4911-4(f)(1).

[99] Reg. § 56.4911-4(f)(2).

[100] Reg. §§ 1.501(h)-3(c)(2), 56.4911-1(c)(1).

[101] IRC § 501(h)(1). This averaging is used as the consequence of the word *normally*; the general measuring period is termed the *base years* (Reg. § 1.501(h)-3(c)(7)).

[102] IRC § 4911(c)(2); Reg. § 56.4911-1(c)(1).

[103] IRC § 4911(c)(3); Reg. §§ 56.4911-1(c)(2), 1.501(h)-3(c)(4).

[104] IRC § 4911(c)(4); Reg. §§ 1.501(h)-3(c)(5), 56.4911-1(c)(2).

[105] See § 22.3(d)(vi).

[106] IRC § 4911(a); Reg. §§ 56.4911-1(a), 1.501(h)-1(a)(3).

[107] IRC § 4911(b); Reg. § 56.4911-1(b). A tax paid under this section is reported on Form 4720 (Schedule G).

[108] Reg. § 1.501(h)-3(c)(7).

[109] Reg. § 1.501(h)-3(c)(3).

[110] Reg. § 1.501(h)-3(c)(6).

[111] IRC §§ 501(h)(1), 501(h)(2); Reg. § 1.501(h)-3(b).

[112] IRC § 504; Reg. §§ 1.504-1, 1.504-2. See Chapter 13. Cf. Reg. § 1.501(c)(3)-1(c)(3)(v).

[113] Reg. § 53.4945-2(a)(6)(i). See *Private Foundations* § 9.1(c).

[114] Priv. Ltr. Rul. 200943042.

an electing public charity to another public charity may be treated as a nonlobbying expenditure as long as it is not earmarked for lobbying, even if some or all of the funds are expended by the grantee for lobbying. Likewise, an electing public charity's grant restricted for use for a specific project of a grantee public charity will not, solely by reason of the restriction, be considered earmarked for lobbying. Grants to a public charity for a specific purpose will not be considered earmarked for lobbying as long as all the grants by the grantor during the year involved do not exceed the amounts budgeted for nonlobbying activities. If, however, the public charity's grants exceed the amount budgeted for nonlobbying activities, the amount in excess of the nonlobbying activities amount will be considered a lobbying expenditure.

(v) Exceptions.   Five categories of activities are excluded by statute from the term *influencing legislation* for purposes of the expenditure test: (1) making available the results of nonpartisan analysis, study, or research;[115] (2) providing technical advice or assistance to a governmental body or legislative committee in response to a written request by that body or committee;[116] (3) appearances before or communications to any legislative body with respect to a possible decision of that body that might affect the existence of the organization, its powers and duties, its tax-exempt status, or the deduction of contributions to it (the *self-defense exception*);[117] (4) communications between the organization and its bona fide members[118] with respect to legislation or proposed legislation of direct interest to it and them, unless the communications directly encourage the members to influence legislation or directly encourage the members to urge nonmembers to influence legislation;[119] and (5) routine communications with government officials or employees.[120]

In amplification of the fourth exception, expenditures for a communication that refers to, and reflects a view on, specific legislation are not lobbying expenditures if the communication satisfies the following requirements: (1) The communication is directed only to members of the organization; (2) the specific legislation the communication refers to, and reflects a view on, is of direct interest to the organization and its members; (3) the communication does not directly encourage the member to engage in direct lobbying;[121] and (4) the communication does not directly encourage the member to engage in grassroots lobbying.[122] An expenditure that meets all of these requirements, other than the third one, is treated as an expenditure for direct lobbying.[123] An expenditure that satisfies all of these requirements, other than the fourth one, is treated as an expenditure for

---

[115] IRC § 4911(d)(2)(A); Reg. § 56.4911-2(c)(1). See text accompanied by *supra* notes 49–53.

[116] IRC § 4911(d)(2)(B); Reg. § 56.4911-2(c)(3).

[117] IRC § 4911(d)(2)(C); Reg. § 56.4911-2(c)(4).

[118] Reg. §§ 56.4911-5(f)(1)-(4). The IRS ruled that, for purposes of this exception, subordinate organizations in a group exemption arrangement (see § 26.11) are members of the central organization, as are the paid and volunteer staff, agents, officers, and board and committee members of the affiliates (Priv. Ltr. Rul. 201347024).

[119] IRC § 4911(d)(2)(D).

[120] IRC § 4911(d)(2)(E).

[121] Reg. § 56.4911-5(f)(6).

[122] Reg. § 56.4911-5(b).

[123] Reg. § 56.4911-5(c).

grassroots lobbying.[124] The regulations provide rules for treatment as expenditures for either direct or grassroots lobbying, of expenditures for any written communication that is designed primarily for members of an organization and that refers to and reflects a view on specific legislation of direct interest to the organization and its members.[125]

The regulations create a sixth exception, excusing examinations and discussions of broad social, economic, and similar problems from the ambit of direct lobbying communications and grassroots lobbying communications, even if the problems are of the type with which government would be expected to deal ultimately.[126]

(vi) Election of Test. An eligible charitable organization[127] that desires to avail itself of the expenditure test must elect to come within these standards; it can do so on a year-to-year basis.[128] Charitable organizations that may not or that choose not to make the election are governed by the substantial part test.[129] Churches, conventions or associations of churches, integrated auxiliaries of churches, certain supporting organizations of noncharitable entities,[130] and private foundations may not elect to come under these rules[131]—foundations being subject to more stringent regulation in this regard.[132]

If a charitable organization has its tax exemption revoked by reason of the expenditure test and thereafter is again recognized as an exempt charitable organization, it may again elect the expenditure test.[133]

(vii) Evaluating Election. Consequently, a charitable organization (that is not a private foundation) may attempt to influence a legislative process as long as the organization stays within the bounds of insubstantiality. Thus, a charitable organization desiring to engage in attempts to influence legislation must, in assessing the basis for insubstantiality, decide whether to utilize the substantial part test or elect the expenditure test, and must determine whether one or more exceptions provided by either test are available. In an optimum situation, a charitable organization can expend 20 percent or more of its total expenditures on attempts to influence legislation.[134]

---

[124] Reg. § 56.4911-5(d).

[125] Reg. § 56.4911-5(e).

[126] Reg. § 56.4911-2(c)(2).

[127] Reg. §§ 1.501(h)-2(b), 1.501(h)-2(e).

[128] IRC §§ 501(h)(3), 501(h)(4), 1.501(h)(6). This election, and any revocation or reelection of it, is made by filing Form 5768 with the IRS (Reg. §§ 1.501(h)-2(a), (c), (d)).

[129] Reg. § 1.501(h)-1(a)(4).

[130] See § 12.3(c).

[131] IRC § 501(h)(5).

[132] IRC § 4945(d)(1), (e). See § 12.4(e).

[133] Reg. § 1.501(h)-3(d)(4).

[134] Presumably, a 20 percent lobbying expenditure, allowed by the expenditure test, is greater than what would be allowed under the substantial part test. Whether lobbying can exceed 20 percent in any one year (disregarding the expenditure test's averaging rule) without adversely affecting a charitable organization's tax-exempt status will essentially depend on the availability and use of one or more of the exceptions from the limitation.

There are many variables a charitable organization should consider when deciding whether to elect the expenditure test. For example, a charitable organization that seeks to engage in a considerable amount of grassroots lobbying is undoubtedly best advised to not make the election, because the limitation on that type of lobbying is probably more stringent under the expenditure test than under the substantial part test. Other factors to consider are (1) the relative certainty as to allowable lobbying afforded by the expenditure test, (2) the possibility that the IRS may enforce the substantial part test using one or more standards other than the volume of legislative activity, (3) the fact that the time expended by volunteers for lobbying is taken into account for purposes of the substantial part test and is disregarded for purposes of the expenditure test, (4) the fact that the extent of lobbying is assessed annually pursuant to the substantial part test and over a four-year average under the expenditure test, (5) the potential impact of the affiliation rules in the expenditure test, (6) the additional record-keeping and reporting responsibilities imposed by the expenditure test, (7) the potential of applicability of the taxes that may be imposed in instances of substantial lobbying,[135] (8) the fact that a public charity that has elected the expenditure test may report lobbying expenses to Congress by using the tax law definition of lobbying expenses, (9) the exceptions that are available under the expenditure test (such as the self-defense exception), (10) a difficulty in staying below the expenditure test's $1 million limitation on annual lobbying expenditures, and (11) avoidance, by electing the expenditure test, of the taxes imposed on charitable organizations and their managers that are under the substantial part test.

Moreover, a charitable organization remaining under the substantial part test and desiring to engage in a substantial amount of lobbying can convert to a social welfare organization[136] to pursue those activities.

(viii) Affiliated Organizations. The expenditure test contains methods of aggregating the expenditures of related organizations, so as to forestall the creation of numerous organizations for the purpose of avoiding the limitations of the expenditure test. Where two or more charitable organizations are members of an affiliated group[137] and at least one of the members has elected coverage under the expenditure test, the calculations of lobbying and exempt purpose expenditures must be made by taking into account the expenditures of the group.[138] If these expenditures exceed the permitted limits, each of the electing member organizations must pay a proportionate share of the penalty excise tax, with the non-electing members treated under the substantial part test.[139]

A publicly supported charity became the sole member of a tax-exempt university. The charity had made the expenditure test lobbying election. As a result of this restructuring, the charity became a member of an affiliated group. This made the charity potentially liable for excise tax on the group's excess lobbying expenditures. The lawyer representing the charity in the restructuring missed this issue,

---

[135] See § 22.4.
[136] See § 22.5.
[137] Reg. § 56.4911-7(e).
[138] IRC § 4911(f)(1); Reg. §§ 56.4911-8, -10.
[139] IRC § 4911(f)(1)(B).

as did the accounting firm that prepared the charity's next annual information return. The accounting firm caught this matter while preparing the next year's return. The charity petitioned the IRS for an extension of time to file a revocation of the lobbying election. Finding that the charity acted reasonably and in good faith, and that the interests of the government were not being prejudiced, the IRS granted the extension.[140]

Generally, under these rules, two organizations are deemed *affiliated* where (1) one organization is bound by decisions of the other on legislative issues pursuant to its governing instrument,[141] or (2) the governing board of one organization includes enough representatives of the other (an *interlocking governing board*)[142] to cause or prevent action on legislative issues[143] by the first organization.[144] Where a number of organizations are affiliated, even in chain fashion, all of them are treated as one group of affiliated organizations.[145] If a group of autonomous organizations controls an organization but no one organization in the controlling group alone can control that organization, however, the organizations are not an affiliated group by reason of the interlocking directorates rule.[146]

(ix) Record-Keeping Requirements. A public charity that is under the expenditure test must keep a record of its lobbying expenditures. These records must include (1) expenditures for grassroots lobbying, (2) amounts paid for direct lobbying, (3) the portion of amounts paid or incurred as compensation for an employee's services for direct lobbying, (4) amounts paid for out-of-pocket expenditures incurred on behalf of the organization and for direct lobbying, (5) the allocable portion of administration, overhead, and other general expenditures attributable to direct lobbying, (6) expenditures for publications or for communications with members to the extent the expenditures are treated as expenditures for direct lobbying, and (7) expenditures for direct lobbying of a controlled organization[147] to the extent included by a controlling organization[148] in its lobbying expenditures.[149] Identical record-keeping requirements apply with respect to grassroots expenditures.[150]

(x) Reporting Rules. The required contents of annual information returns filed by tax-exempt organizations[151] include a section designed to make information about the legislative activities of electing charitable organizations accessible to the public.[152] Thus, an organization subject to the expenditure test must disclose in

---

[140] Priv. Ltr. Rul. 201239012.
[141] Reg. § 56.4911-7(c).
[142] Reg. § 56.4911-7(b).
[143] Reg. § 56.4911-7(a)(3).
[144] IRC § 4911(f)(2); Reg. § 56.4911-7(a)(1).
[145] Reg. § 56.4911-7(d).
[146] IRC § 4911(f)(3).
[147] Reg. § 56.4911-10(c).
[148] *Id.*
[149] Reg. § 56.4911-6(a).
[150] Reg. § 56.4911-6(b).
[151] See § 28.2(a).
[152] Form 990, Schedule C, Part II-A.

its information return the amount of its lobbying expenditures (direct and grass-roots), together with the amount that it could have spent for legislative purposes without becoming subject to the 25 percent excise tax. The organization generally must also report its annual lobbying expenditures in connection with the four-year averaging period rules. An electing organization that is a member of an affiliated group must provide this information with respect to both itself and the entire group.[153]

§ 22.4 LOBBYING EXPENDITURES AND TAX SANCTIONS

If a charitable organization, otherwise tax-exempt, that has not elected to come under the expenditure test or that is ineligible to make the election, fails to meet the federal tax law requirements for exemption because of attempts to influence legislation, a tax in the amount of 5 percent of the lobbying expenditures for each year involved may be imposed on the organization.[154] A *lobbying expenditure* is an amount paid or incurred by a charitable organization in carrying on propaganda or otherwise attempting to influence legislation.[155]

A separate tax is applicable to each of the organization's managers (basically, its officers and directors) who agreed to the making of the lobbying expenditures (knowing that they were likely to result in revocation of the organization's tax exemption), unless the agreement was not willful and was due to reasonable cause.[156] This tax is also an amount equal to 5 percent of the lobbying expenditures and can be imposed only where the tax on the organization is imposed.

§ 22.5 LEGISLATIVE ACTIVITIES OF SOCIAL WELFARE ORGANIZATIONS

There are no federal tax law statutory limitations on attempts to influence legislation by tax-exempt social welfare organizations, other than the general requirement that the organization primarily engage in efforts to promote social welfare.[157] In other words, a social welfare organization can be what a charitable organization cannot be—an action organization.[158]

---

[153] IRC § 6033(b)(8).

[154] IRC § 4912(a). A tax paid under this section is reported on Form 4720 (Schedule H). For the excise tax on excess lobbying expenditures by an organization that has elected the expenditure test (IRC § 4911), see § 22.3(d)(iii).

[155] IRC § 4912(d)(1).

[156] IRC § 4912(b). The burden of proof as to whether a manager knowingly participated in the lobbying expenditure is on the IRS, and the fact that the excise tax is imposed on an organization does not itself establish that any manager of the organization is subject to the excise tax (H.R. Rep. No. 100-495, at 1024 (1987)).

[157] See § 4.4.

[158] A social welfare organization that meets the definition of *charitable* in Reg. § 1.501(c)(3)-1(d)(2) (see Chapter 7) and is not an *action organization* (see § 4.5(d)) can qualify for exemption under IRC § 501(c)(3) (Reg. § 1.501(c)(4)-1(a)(2)); conversely, an action organization can qualify for exemption under IRC § 501(c)(4) where it otherwise meets the requirements for social welfare organization status (Reg. § 1.501(c)(3)-1(c)(3)(v)).

Thus, a tax-exempt social welfare organization may draft legislation, present petitions for the purpose of having legislation introduced, and circulate speeches, reprints, and other material concerning legislation.[159] This type of organization may appear before a federal or state legislative body or a local council, administrative board, or commission, and may encourage members of the community to contact legislative representatives in support of its programs.[160]

The IRS ruled that a tax-exempt social welfare organization can operate to inform the public on controversial subjects, "even though the organization advocates a particular viewpoint."[161] Likewise, the IRS extended exempt status as a charitable entity to an organization formed to educate the public on the subject of abortions, promote the rights of the unborn, and support legislative and constitutional changes to restrict women's access to abortions, recognizing that the organization "advocates objectives that are controversial."[162]

Similarly, an organization that engaged in attempts to influence legislation intended to benefit animals, animal owners, persons interested in the welfare of animals, and the community at large was considered a tax-exempt social welfare organization, although it was denied tax-exempt status as a charitable entity (as an organization operated for the prevention of cruelty to animals) because it was deemed to be an action organization.[163]

§ 22.6 LEGISLATIVE ACTIVITIES OF BUSINESS LEAGUES

There is no restriction, from the standpoint of the tax exemption for membership associations and other business leagues, on the amount of legislative activity these organizations may conduct. Indeed, the IRS recognized attempts to influence legislation as a valid function for a tax-exempt business league.[164]

The federal tax law rules stringently restricting the deductibility of business expenses for legislative activities[165] have, however, meaningful consequences in this context, in that they can operate as an indirect limitation on lobbying activities by business leagues. The inability to fully deduct membership dues may have an impact on the extent of an association's membership.

(a) Business Expense Deduction Disallowance Rules

Under these rules, generally there is no business expense deduction for any amount paid or incurred in connection with[166] influencing legislation (whether by

---

[159] Rev. Rul. 68-656, 1968-2 C.B. 216.

[160] Rev. Rul. 67-6, 1967-1 C.B. 135.

[161] Rev. Rul. 68-656, 1968-2 C.B. 216.

[162] Rev. Rul. 76-81, 1976-1 C.B. 156.

[163] Rev. Rul. 67-293, 1967-2 C.B. 185.

[164] Rev. Rul. 61-177, 1961-2 C.B. 117.

[165] IRC § 162(e).

[166] The IRS is of the view that this phrase should be broadly construed (e.g., Priv. Ltr. Rul. 201616002), citing Snow v. Comm'r, 416 U.S. 500 (1974); Conopco v. United States, 572 F.3d 162 (3d Cir. 2009); and General Mills v. United States, 554 F.3d 727 (8th Cir. 2009); a court of appeals ruled it should be read narrowly (Boise Cascade v. United States, 329 F.3d 751 (9th Cir. 2003)).

direct or by grassroots lobbying); any attempt to influence the general public, or segments of it, with respect to legislative matters or referendums; or any direct communication with a covered executive branch official in an attempt to influence the official actions or positions of the official.[167] This deduction disallowance rule, however, does not apply with respect to Indian tribal governments.[168]

In this setting, *influencing legislation* means (1) any attempt to influence legislation through a lobbying communication and (2) all activities, such as research, preparation, planning, and coordination, including deciding whether to make a lobbying communication, engaged in for a purpose of making or supporting a lobbying communication, even if not yet made.[169] A *lobbying communication* is any communication (other than one compelled by subpoena or otherwise compelled by federal or state law) with any member or employee of a legislative body or any other government official or employee who may participate in the formulation of the legislation[170] that (1) refers to specific legislation and reflects a view on that legislation or (2) clarifies, amplifies, modifies, or provides support for views reflected in a prior lobbying communication.[171] The term *specific legislation* includes a specific legislative proposal that has not been introduced in a legislative body.[172]

Covered executive branch official describes the President, the Vice President, any officer or employee of the White House Office of the Executive Office of the President, the two most senior-level officers of each of the other agencies within the Executive Office of the President, any individual serving in a position in level I of the Executive Schedule (for example, a member of the Cabinet),[173] any other individual designated by the President as having Cabinet-level status, and an immediate deputy of an individual in the preceding two categories.[174]

The purposes for engaging in an activity are determined on the basis of all the facts and circumstances, including whether the activity and the lobbying communication are proximate in time; whether the activity and the lobbying communication relate to similar subject matter; whether the activity is performed at the request of, under the direction of, or on behalf of a person making the lobbying communication; whether the results of the activity are also used for a nonlobbying purpose; and whether, at the time the person engages in the activity, there is specific legislation to which the activity relates.[175] In instances of activities involving lobbying and nonlobbying purposes, costs must be allocated.[176] Certain activities, such as determining the status of legislation or summarizing legislation, do not constitute lobbying.[177]

Any amount paid or incurred for research for, or preparation, planning, or coordination of, any lobbying activity subject to the general disallowance rule is

---

[167] IRC § 162(e)(1)(A), (C), (D).
[168] IRC § 162(e)(7).
[169] Reg. § 1.162-29(b)(1).
[170] The term *legislation* is the subject of § 22.2.
[171] IRC § 162(e)(4)(A); Reg. § 1.162-29(b)(3).
[172] Reg. § 1.162-29(b)(5).
[173] 5 U.S.C. § 5312.
[174] IRC § 162(e)(6).
[175] Reg. § 1.162-29(c)(1).
[176] Reg. § 1.162-29(c)(2). See text accompanied by *infra* note 183.
[177] Reg. § 1.162-29(c)(3).

treated as paid or incurred in connection with the lobbying activity.[178] The intent of this rule is to convert what might otherwise be a function constituting nonpartisan analysis, study, or research[179] into a lobbying undertaking where the research is subsequently used in an attempt to influence legislation. It is not clear how this rule is to be applied where the research is performed by one organization and the lobbying using that research is done by another, particularly where the two organizations are related.[180]

A *de minimis* exception applies in connection with certain in-house expenditures where the organization's total amount of these expenditures for a tax year does not exceed $2,000 (computed without taking into account general overhead costs otherwise allocable to most forms of lobbying).[181] The term *in-house expenditures* means expenditures for lobbying (such as labor and materials costs) other than payments to a professional lobbyist to conduct lobbying for the organization and dues or other similar payments that are allocable to lobbying (such as association dues).[182]

An organization, although able to use any reasonable method of allocation of labor costs and general and administrative costs to lobbying activities, is authorized to use a *ratio method*, a *gross-up method*, or tax rules concerning allocation of service costs.[183] An organization may disregard time spent by an individual on lobbying activities if less than 5 percent of their time was so spent, although this *de minimis* test is not applicable with respect to *direct contact lobbying*, which is a meeting, telephone conversation, letter, or other similar means of communication with a federal or state legislator or a covered executive branch official and which otherwise qualifies as a lobbying activity.[184]

Other than a general exclusion for charitable organizations, there are no specific statutory exceptions to these rules. As noted, however, any communication compelled by subpoena, or otherwise compelled by federal or state law, does not constitute an attempt to influence legislation or an official's actions.[185]

A provision prevents a cascading of the lobbying expense disallowance rule to ensure that, when multiple parties are involved, the rule results in the denial of a deduction at only one level. Thus, in the case of an individual engaged in the trade or business of providing lobbying services or an individual who is an employee and receives employer reimbursements for lobbying expenses, the disallowance rule does not apply to expenditures of the individual in conducting the activities directly on behalf of a client or an employer. Instead, the lobbying payments made by the client or employer to the lobbyist or employee are nondeductible under the general disallowance rule.[186]

---

[178] IRC § 162(e)(5)(C).

[179] See § 22.3(c)(iii), text accompanied by *supra* notes 49–53; § 22.3(d)(v), text accompanied by *supra* note 115.

[180] See, by contrast, § 22.3(d)(i), text accompanied by *supra* note 76.

[181] IRC § 162(e)(5)(B)(i).

[182] IRC § 162(e)(5)(B)(ii).

[183] Reg. § 1.162-28(a)-(f). The third of these methods is the subject of IRC § 263A.

[184] Reg. § 1.162-28(g).

[185] See text accompanied by *supra* note 170. Also, H.R. Rep. No. 103-213, at 607 (1993).

[186] IRC § 162(e)(5)(A).

This anticascading rule applies where there is a direct, one-on-one relationship between the taxpayer and the entity conducting the lobbying activity, such as a client or employment relationship. It does not apply to dues or other payments to membership organizations that act to further the interests of all of their members rather than the interests of any one particular member. These organizations are themselves subject to the general disallowance rule, based on the amount of their lobbying expenditures.[187]

An anti-avoidance rule is designed to prevent donors from using charitable organizations[188] as conduits to conduct lobbying activities, the costs of which would be nondeductible if conducted directly by the donor. That is, no deduction is allowed as a charitable contribution deduction (nor as a business expense deduction) for amounts contributed to a charitable organization if (1) the charitable organization's lobbying activities regard matters of direct financial interest to the donor's trade or business, and (2) a principal purpose of the contribution is to avoid the general disallowance rule that would apply if the contributor directly had conducted the lobbying activities.[189] The application of this anti-avoidance rule to a contributor would not adversely affect the tax-exempt status of the charitable organization as long as the activity qualified as nonpartisan analysis, study, or research[190] or was not substantial under either the substantial part test or the expenditure test[191] of the rules limiting the legislative activities of charitable organizations.[192]

The determination regarding a *principal purpose* of the contribution is to be based on the facts and circumstances surrounding the contribution, including the existence of any formal or informal instructions relating to the charitable organization's use of the contribution for lobbying efforts (including nonpartisan analysis), the "temporal nexus" between the making of the contribution and the conduct of the lobbying activities, and any historical pattern of contributions by the donor to the charity.[193]

(b)   Flow-Through Rules

A flow-through rule applicable with respect to membership associations disallows a business expense deduction for the portion of the membership dues (or voluntary payments or special assessments) paid to a tax-exempt organization that engages in lobbying activities.[194] Trade, business, and professional associations, and similar organizations, generally are required to provide annual information disclosure to their members, estimating the portion of their dues that is allocable to lobbying and thus nondeductible.

The organization must disclose in its annual information return both the total amount of its lobbying expenditures and the total amount of dues (or similar

---

[187] H.R. Rep. No. 103-213, at 610 (1993).

[188] See Part Three.

[189] IRC § 170(f)(9).

[190] See § 22.3(c)(iii), text accompanied by *supra* notes 49–53; § 22.3(d)(v), text accompanied by *supra* note 115.

[191] See § 22.3(c), (d).

[192] H.R. Rep. No. 103-213, at 610, n. 70 (1993).

[193] *Id.* at 610.

[194] IRC § 162(e)(3).

payments) allocable to these expenditures.[195] For this purpose, an organization's lobbying expenditures for a taxable year are allocated to the dues received during the taxable year.[196] Any excess amount of lobbying expenditures is carried forward and allocated to dues received in the following taxable year.[197]

The organization also is generally required to provide notice to each person paying dues (or similar payments), at the time of assessment or payment of the dues, of the portion of dues that the organization reasonably estimates will be allocable to the organization's lobbying expenditures during the year and that is, therefore, not deductible by the member.[198] This estimate must be reasonably calculated to provide organization members with adequate notice of the nondeductible amount. The notice must be provided in conspicuous and easily recognizable format.[199] These requirements of annual disclosure and notice to members are applicable to all tax-exempt organizations other than those that are charitable entities.[200]

(c) Proxy Tax Rules

If an organization's actual lobbying expenditures for a tax year exceed the estimated allocable amount of the expenditures (either because of higher-than-anticipated lobbying expenses or lower-than-projected dues receipts), the organization must pay a *proxy tax* on the excess amount[201] or seek permission from the IRS to adjust the following year's notice of estimated expenditures.[202] The proxy tax rate is equal to the corporate tax rate in effect for the taxable year;[203] the corporate tax rate is 21 percent.[204] If an organization does not provide its members with reasonable notice of anticipated lobbying expenditures allocable to dues, the organization is subject to the proxy tax on its aggregate lobbying expenditures for the year.

If an organization elects to pay the proxy tax rather than provide the requisite information disclosure to its members, no portion of any dues or other payments made by members of the organization is rendered nondeductible because of the organization's lobbying activities. That is, if the organization pays the tax, the dues payments are fully deductible by the members as business expenses (assuming they otherwise qualify).

---

[195] IRC § 6033(e)(1)(A)(i). An organization that is subject to these rules may satisfy its requirement to report lobbying activities to Congress using the definition of lobbying under these rules and may satisfy its requirement to report lobbying expenses to Congress by using the amounts that are nondeductible under these rules (Lobbying Disclosure Act of 1995, 2 U.S.C. § 1610(b)).

[196] IRC § 6033(e)(1)(C)(i).

[197] IRC § 6033(e)(1)(C)(ii).

[198] IRC § 6033(e)(1)(A)(ii).

[199] H.R. Rep. No. 103-213, at 608, n. 65 (1993). As to the standard of "conspicuous and easily recognizable," the IRC § 6113 rules are used (see § 28.12).

[200] IRC § 6033(e)(1)(B). The term *charitable* in this context means all organizations that are tax-exempt by reason of IRC § 501(c)(3).

[201] IRC § 6033(e)(2)(A)(ii).

[202] IRC § 6033(e)(2)(B).

[203] IRC § 6033(e)(2)(A).

[204] IRC § 11.

This disclosure and notice element is not required, however, in the case of an organization that (1) incurs only *de minimis* amounts of in-house lobbying expenditures, (2) elects to pay the proxy tax on its lobbying expenditures incurred during the tax year,[205] or (3) establishes, pursuant to an IRS regulation or procedure, that substantially all of its dues monies are paid by members who are not entitled to deduct the dues in computing their taxable income. The concept of *de minimis* in-house expenditures in this setting is the same as that in the disallowance rules (including the $2,000 maximum).[206] Amounts paid to outside lobbyists, or as dues to another organization that lobbies, do not qualify for this exception.

Regarding this third component, if an organization establishes, to the satisfaction of the IRS, that substantially all of the dues monies it receives are paid by members who are not entitled to deduct their dues in any event (and obtains a waiver from the IRS), the organization is not subject to the disclosure and notice requirements (or the proxy tax).[207] In this context, the term *substantially all* means at least 90 percent.[208] Examples of organizations of this nature are (1) an organization that receives at least 90 percent of its dues monies from members that are tax-exempt charitable organizations and (2) an organization that receives at least 90 percent of its dues monies from members who are individuals not entitled to deduct the dues payments because the payments are not ordinary and necessary business expenses.[209] Indeed, by IRS pronouncement,[210] there is a complete exemption from the reporting and notice requirements (and proxy tax) for all tax-exempt organizations, other than social welfare organizations that are not veterans' organizations;[211] agricultural organizations;[212] horticultural organizations;[213] and trade, business, and professional associations, other business leagues, chambers of commerce, and boards of trade.[214]

If the amount of lobbying expenditures exceeds the amount of dues or other similar payments for the taxable year, the proxy tax is imposed on an amount

---

[205] IRC § 6033(e)(2)(A)(i).

[206] IRC § 6033(e)(1)(B)(ii). See text accompanied by *supra* note 181.

[207] IRC § 6033(e)(3).

[208] H.R. Rep. No. 103-213, at 609 (1993).

[209] E.g., Priv. Ltr. Rul. 9534021.

[210] Rev. Proc. 98-19, 1998-1 C.B. 547 § 4.01.

[211] See § 13.1(b).

[212] See § 16.2.

[213] See § 16.3.

[214] See Chapter 14. There are, however, exemptions for these four categories of organizations based on refinements of the 90-percent-of-dues test. For example, social welfare, agricultural, and horticultural organizations are treated as satisfying the exemption requirements if either (1) more than 90 percent of all annual dues are received from persons who each pay less than $75 or (2) more than 90 percent of all annual dues are received from certain tax-exempt entities (Rev. Proc. 98-19, 1998-1 C.B. 547, § 4.02). This $75 amount is indexed for inflation; for tax years beginning in 2025, the amount is $147 or less (Rev. Proc. 2024-40, 2024-45 I.R.B. 1100, § 3.47). The IRS occasionally issues rulings as to the availability of the exemption (e.g., Priv. Ltr. Rul. 9429016). Additionally, these four types of organizations may also claim exemption from the disclosure and notice requirements (and the proxy tax) by satisfying certain record-keeping and annual return filing requirements or by obtaining a private letter ruling from the IRS on the point (Rev. Proc. 98-19, 1998-1 C.B. 547, § 5.06).

equal to the dues and similar payments; any excess lobbying expenditures are carried forward to the next taxable year.[215]

§ 22.7 LEGISLATIVE ACTIVITIES OF OTHER TAX-EXEMPT ORGANIZATIONS

As is the case with tax-exempt social welfare organizations and business leagues,[216] with one exception, there is no restriction in the federal tax law concerning attempts to influence legislation by any other category of exempt organization, other than the general requirement that the organization primarily engage in efforts to advance its exempt purpose.[217] The one exception is for exempt health insurance issuers,[218] which are subject to the same constraint on substantial legislative activities as are exempt charitable organizations. Thus, for example, if the primary activities of an entity classified as a political organization[219] became attempts to influence legislation, it could not continue to qualify as an exempt political organization. Likewise, the IRS ruled that a voluntary employees' beneficiary association[220] may engage in legislative activities, particularly if the efforts are with respect to decisions that might affect the continued existence of the organization, its powers and duties, and/or its exempt status,[221] as long as substantially all of the association's operations are the provision of the requisite benefits.[222] Consequently, within these parameters, exempt social clubs, credit unions, and labor, agricultural, horticultural, fraternal, veterans', and other exempt organizations[223] can engage in lobbying; that is, they can function as action organizations.

§ 22.8 INTERNET COMMUNICATIONS

Tax-exempt organizations engage in legislative activities by means of the Internet and/or are affiliated with organizations that conduct Internet-based lobbying. As the IRS saliently observed, the "use of the Internet to accomplish a particular task does not change the way the tax laws apply to that task."[224] Thus, the rules applicable to exempt organizations in the legislative activities context, including the substantial part test and the expenditure test, embrace lobbying using websites.

Substantiality in the expenditure test context is, as noted, measured solely in terms of expenditures of funds. The Internet is far more cost-effective than other forms of communication. Consequently, it is obvious that a charitable organization

---

[215] H.R. Rep. No. 103-213, at 608-609 (1993).

[216] See §§ 22.5, 22.6.

[217] See § 4.4.

[218] See § 19.18.

[219] See Chapter 17.

[220] See § 18.3.

[221] See text accompanied by *supra* note 117.

[222] Priv. Ltr. Rul. 201027058.

[223] See Chapters 15, 16, and 19.

[224] "Tax Exempt Organizations and World Wide Web Fundraising and Advertising on the Internet," Topic I, IRS Exempt Organization Continuing Professional Education Text for FY 2000.

that has elected the expenditure test is in a position to engage in considerably more lobbying activity when the attempts to influence legislation are made by means of the Internet.

The IRS issued an announcement in 2000 seeking public comment on a number of questions pertaining to use of the Internet in the context of lobbying activity by charitable organizations. On that occasion, the IRS wrote that "[w]hen a charitable organization engages in advocacy on the Internet, questions arise as to whether it is conducting. . .lobbying activity, and if so, to what extent." The agency added: "This situation is further complicated by the affiliation of charitable organizations with other organizations engaging in. . .lobbying activities on the Internet. The ease with which different websites may be linked electronically (through a 'hyperlink') raises a concern about whether the message of a linked website is attributable to the charitable organization."[225]

§ 22.9   CONSTITUTIONAL LAW FRAMEWORK

It has been repeatedly asserted that the proscription on substantial legislative activities applicable to public charities is violative of constitutional law principles. Although the issues were often presented to the courts, it was not until 1982 that a litigant was successful in securing a decision finding that this provision is constitutionally deficient. Nonetheless, even that remarkable occurrence ultimately failed—almost with unintended consequences for other categories of tax-exempt organizations.

Representative of these decisions was one handed down in 1979.[226] The issues involved were the following: Does this tax law limitation on legislative activities (1) impose an unconstitutional condition on the exercise of First Amendment rights (that is, the right to engage in legislative activity), (2) restrict the exercise of First Amendment rights as being a discriminatory denial of tax exemption for engaging in speech, (3) deny organizations so restricted the equal protection of the laws in violation of the Fifth Amendment, and/or (4) lack a compelling governmental interest that would justify the restrictions on First Amendment rights?

The approach of the courts on the First Amendment question has been to recognize that the lobbying of legislators constitutes an exercise of the First Amendment right of petition[227] and thus that the amendment protects legislative activities. Often cited in this context is the Supreme Court declaration that the general advocacy of ideas is constitutionally protected as part of this nation's "profound national commitment to the principle that debate on public issues should be uninhibited, robust, and wide-open."[228] The courts inevitably press on to observe, however, that the federal tax law limitation on exempt charitable organizations'

---

[225] Ann. 2000-84, 2000-42 I.R.B. 385.

[226] Taxation With Representation of Washington v. Blumenthal, 79-1 U.S.T.C. ¶ 9185 (D.D.C. 1979), aff'd, 81-1 U.S.T.C. ¶ 9329 (D.C. Cir. 1981), rev. en banc sub nom., Taxation With Representation of Washington v. Regan, 676 F.2d 715 (D.C. Cir. 1982).

[227] E.g., Eastern R.R. Presidents Conference v. Noerr Motor Freight, Inc., 365 U.S. 127 (1961); Liberty Lobby, Inc. v. Pearson, 390 F.2d 489 (D.C. Cir. 1968).

[228] New York Times Co. v. Sullivan, 376 U.S. 254, 270 (1964).

lobbying does not violate First Amendment rights because it does not on its face prohibit organizations from engaging in substantial efforts to influence legislation.[229] This position is fundamentally based on a Supreme Court pronouncement upholding the constitutionality of a tax regulation that excluded from deduction as business expenses amounts expended for the promotion or defeat of legislation.[230]

With respect to the second aspect of the First Amendment question, this argument is premised in part on the fact that several categories of tax-exempt organizations are free to lobby without jeopardizing their exempt status.[231] Thus, the proposition has been that the restraint on lobbying by charitable organizations is a discriminatory revocation or denial of a tax exemption for engaging in protected speech. The courts hold that this principle relates to legislative efforts "aimed at the suppression of dangerous ideas"[232] and not to denials or revocations of tax exemptions for charitable organizations.

Similar short shrift has been given to the equal protection challenge, which is premised on the fact that similarly situated (that is, tax-exempt) organizations are accorded different treatment with respect to lobbying activities. The courts usually concede that this involves a classification that imposes differing treatment to classes but that it is permissible inasmuch as the classification does not affect a "fundamental" right nor involve a "suspect" class.[233] The applicable standard of scrutiny—which this statutory limitation has been repeatedly ruled to satisfy—is whether the challenged classification is reasonably related to a legitimate governmental purpose.[234]

This standard is also deemed met where the courts evaluate the constitutionality of the proscription on substantial legislative activities in relation to the requirement that the restraint be rationally related to a legitimate government purpose.[235] Several of these purposes are usually found served: "assurance of governmental neutrality with respect to the lobbying activities of charitable organizations; prevention of abuse of charitable lobbying by private interests; and preservation of a balance between the lobbying activities of charitable organizations and those of non-charitable organizations and individuals."[236]

Thus, until 1982, all courts that considered the matter had made it clear that there is no constitutional imperfection in the federal tax anti-lobbying clause

---

[229] Taxation With Representation v. United States, 585 F.2d 1219 (4th Cir. 1978), *cert. denied*, 441 U.S. 905 (1979).

[230] Cammarano v. United States, 358 U.S. 498 (1959).

[231] See §§ 22.5–22.7.

[232] Speiser v. Randall, 357 U.S. 513, 519 (1958), where the U.S. Supreme Court struck down a state statute that required veterans to take a loyalty oath as a condition to the receipt of a veterans' property tax exemption.

[233] E.g., San Antonio Indep. School District v. Rodriguez, 411 U.S. 1 (1973); Dunn v. Blumstein, 405 U.S. 330 (1972); Shapiro v. Thompson, 394 U.S. 618 (1969).

[234] E.g., United States Department of Agriculture v. Moreno, 413 U.S. 528 (1973); Frontiero v. Richardson, 411 U.S. 677 (1973).

[235] E.g., United States v. O'Brien, 391 U.S. 367 (1968); Schenk v. United States, 249 U.S. 47 (1919).

[236] Taxation With Representation of Washington v. Blumenthal, 79-1 U.S.T.C. ¶ 9185 (D.D.C. 1979), *aff'd* 81-1 U.S.T.C. ¶ 9329 (D.C. Cir. 1981), *rev'd. en banc sub nom.*, Taxation With Representation of Washington v. Regan, 676 F.2d 715 (D.C. Cir. 1982).

applicable to tax-exempt charitable organizations.[237] In that year, however, a federal court of appeals temporarily changed the complexion of the constitutional law concerning the anti-lobbying rule applicable to charitable entities. This appellate court agreed that this restriction on legislative activities is not violative of free speech (First Amendment) rights but—after concluding that an organization that acquires recognition of tax exemption and charitable donee status is thereby receiving a government subsidy—held that this subsidy cannot constitutionally be accorded on a discriminatory basis and that to do so is violative of equal protection (Fifth Amendment) rights.[238] Therefore, the court held, the fact that tax-exempt charitable organizations are required to limit their lobbying to an insubstantial extent, while certain other exempt organizations—such as veterans' organizations—can lobby without these limits, is an unconstitutionally discriminatory allocation of this "government subsidy."[239] This appellate court held that "[b]y subsidizing the lobbying activities of veterans' organizations while failing to subsidize the lobbying of. . .charitable groups, Congress has violated the equal protection guarantees of the Constitution."[240]

The Supreme Court reacted swiftly in 1983, unanimously reversing the court of appeals.[241] In so holding, the Court reiterated its position that the lobbying restriction on charitable organizations does not infringe First Amendment rights or regulate any First Amendment activity, that Congress did not violate the equal protection doctrine in the Fifth Amendment, and that Congress acted rationally in subsidizing (by means of tax exemption and charitable deductions) lobbying by veterans' organizations while not subsidizing lobbying by charitable organizations generally.

Constitutional law challenges in the lobbying context have not been confined to the realm of charitable organizations, although the success rate of these other challenges is no better than those initiated by charities. The business league/association community challenged the constitutionality of the rules by which the deductibility, as a business expense, of the dues paid by members of an association is limited as a consequence of lobbying (or political campaign activity) by the association. This challenge—on free speech and equal protection grounds—failed for the same basic reasons that the challenges in the charitable setting failed: Congress has broad latitude in creating classifications and distinctions in tax statutes and Congress did not preclude associations from lobbying, but instead lawfully eliminated a tax subsidy underlying the lobbying activity. As the court stated in its conclusion, the "challenged provisions do not impose 'penalties' on tax-exempt associations that engage in lobbying, but merely enforce the

---

[237] Haswell v. United States, 500 F.2d 1133, 1147–1150 (Ct. Cl. 1974), *cert. denied*, 419 U.S. 1107 (1974); Tax Analysts & Advocates v. Shultz, 74-2 U.S.T.C. ¶ 9601 (D.D.C. 1974), *aff'd*, 512 F.2d 992 (D.C. Cir. 1975) (where a lawsuit to declare the legislative activities provision of IRC § 501(c)(3) unconstitutional was dismissed).

[238] Taxation With Representation of Washington v. Regan, 676 F.2d 715 (D.C. Cir. 1982).

[239] Charitable organization are those that are tax-exempt by reason of IRC § 501(c)(3) and that are charitable donees by reason of IRC § 170(c)(2); veterans' organizations are tax-exempt by reason of IRC § 501(c)(4) or (19) and are charitable donees by reason of IRC § 170(c)(3).

[240] Taxation With Representation of Washington v. Regan, 676 F.2d 715, 717 (D.C. Cir. 1982).

[241] Regan v. Taxation With Representation of Washington, 461 U.S. 540 (1983).

decision of Congress to eliminate the lobbying subsidy."[242] The speech involving legislation (i.e., lobbying) was found to encompass the "entire spectrum of possible viewpoints and is, therefore, viewpoint neutral"[243]—a finding that blunted the claim that the challenged provisions discriminate on the basis of the content of the speech. These tax provisions were held to be rationally related to a legitimate government interest and thus constitutional, in relation to both free speech and equal protection principles.[244]

[242] American Soc'y of Ass'n Executives v. United States, 23 F. Supp. 2d 64 (D.D.C. 1998).
[243] Id. at 70. This opinion was affirmed (195 F.3d 47 (D.C. Cir. 1999), cert. denied, 529 U.S. 1108 (2000)).
[244] Also, American Soc'y of Ass'n Executives v. Bentsen, 848 F. Supp. 245 (D.D.C. 1994).

CHAPTER TWENTY-THREE

Political Campaign Activities by Tax-Exempt Organizations

With one exception—the political organization[1]—the federal tax laws concerning tax-exempt organizations do not encourage their involvement in political campaign activities. The limitations with respect to exempt charitable organizations and health insurance issuers[2] are particularly stringent. The tax law in this regard concerning other types of exempt organizations is uncertain.

[1] See Chapter 17.
[2] Exempt charitable organizations are the entities described in IRC § 501(c)(3) and exempt from federal income taxation by reason of IRC § 501(a). These rules are aimed primarily at public charities (see § 12.3); private foundations are also governed by more specific rules (see § 12.4(e); *Private Foundations* § 9.2). Exempt health care insurance issuers are the entities described in IRC § 501(c)(29) and exempt from federal income taxation by reason of IRC § 501(a) (see § 19.18).

§ 23.1 POLITICAL CAMPAIGN ACTIVITIES BY CHARITABLE ORGANIZATIONS—INTRODUCTION

One of the criteria for qualification as a tax-exempt charitable organization is that it must "not participate in, or intervene in (including the publishing or distributing of statements), any political campaign on behalf of (or in opposition to) any candidate for public office."[3] The prohibition on political campaign activity is applicable to campaigns at the federal, state, and local levels; it is also applicable with respect to political activities in foreign countries. If a charitable organization engages in a political campaign activity, it becomes classified as an *action organization*[4] and thus may be disqualified for exempt status.[5]

This provision forbidding political campaign activity by charitable organizations was added to the federal tax law in 1954, without benefit of congressional hearings, in the form of a floor amendment adopted in the Senate.[6] During consideration of the legislation that became the Revenue Act of 1954, Senator Lyndon B. Johnson of Texas, on July 2, 1954, offered the amendment out of concern that funds provided by a charitable foundation were being used to help finance the campaign of an opponent in a primary election. Senator Johnson said only that the purpose of the amendment is to "deny[] tax-exempt status to not only those people who influence legislation but also to those who intervene in any political campaign on behalf of any candidate for any public office."[7] The phrase "(or in opposition to)" was added to the provision in 1987.

§ 23.2 PROHIBITION ON CHARITABLE ORGANIZATIONS

The prohibition on political campaign activities applicable to tax-exempt charitable organizations embodies four basic elements, all of which must be present for the proscription to be operative.[8]

(a) Scope of the Proscription

The prohibition on involvement by a tax-exempt charitable organization in a political campaign is generally considered to be absolute.[9] The Chief Counsel of the IRS opined that "an organization described in section 501(c)(3) is precluded from engaging in *any* political campaign activities."[10]

---

[3] IRC § 501(c)(3).

[4] Reg. § 1.501(c)(3)-1(c)(3)(iii).

[5] E.g., Priv. Ltr. Rul. 202316011.

[6] 100 Cong. Rec. 9604 (1954).

[7] *Id*. There is no analysis of this provision (sometimes referred to as the Johnson Amendment) in the conference report (H.R. Rep. No. 83-2543, at 46 (1954)).

[8] A court observed: "It should be noted that exemption is lost . . . by participation in any political campaign on behalf of [or in opposition to] *any* candidate for public office" (United States v. Dykema, 666 F.2d 1096, 1101 (7th Cir. 1981), *cert. denied*, 456 U.S. 983 (1982)).

[9] Reg. § 1.501(c)(3)-1(c)(iii).

[10] Gen. Couns. Mem. 39694 (emphasis added).

Nonetheless, analogy may be made to a comparable statute that was also absolute on its face: section 610 of the Federal Corrupt Practices Act. That act made it "unlawful for . . . any corporation whatever . . . to make a contribution or expenditure in connection with" various federal elections. Despite this phraseology, the courts read an insubstantiality threshold into the absolute proscription of this law.[11] Further, it has been stated that a "slight and comparatively unimportant deviation from the narrow furrow of tax approved activity is not fatal."[12] It was also observed that "courts recognize that a nonexempt purpose, even 'somewhat beyond a de minimis level,' may be permitted without loss of exemption."[13] Thus, the Commissioner of Internal Revenue stated, in congressional testimony describing the political campaign limitation: "If political intervention is involved, the prohibition is absolute; however, some consideration may be given to whether, qualitatively or quantitatively, the organization is in the circumstance where the activity is so trivial it is without legal significance and, therefore, de minimis."[14]

There is an anomaly in this aspect of the federal tax law. The IRS has the discretion to deny recognition of or revoke tax exemption for violation of the prohibition on political campaign activities or, in instances of insubstantial campaign activity, only impose a tax on political expenditures as an alternative.[15] Thus, political activities that only give rise to a tax may be considered incidental, much as are certain forms of private inurement that do not result in revocation of exemption but merely are treated as excess benefit transactions.[16]

(b)   *Participation* or *Intervention*

The requirement that a charitable organization, to be tax-exempt, must refrain from engaging in political campaign activity appears, on its face, to be relatively clear as to its meaning, if only because of the absoluteness of the proscription. This prohibition is repeatedly violated, however, with IRS enforcement of this aspect of the law of tax-exempt organizations historically erratic and not particularly vigorous.

(i) Terminology.   The statute employs the words *participate* and *intervene.* The prohibition is simply that a tax-exempt charitable organization must avoid issuing a communication or performing any other function that would cause it to be involved in a political campaign.

(ii) Political Campaign Intervention.   Political campaign intervention involves an activity that favors or opposes one or more candidates for public office. The most obvious way for an organization to participate in a political campaign is to

---

[11] United States v. Painters Local 481, 172 F.2d 854 (2d Cir. 1949); United States v. Construction Local 264, 101 F. Supp. 873 (W.D. Mo. 1951). The repeal of the Federal Corrupt Practices Act does not alter the analysis on this point.

[12] St. Louis Union Trust Co. v. United States, 374 F.2d 427, 431–32 (8th Cir. 1967).

[13] Living Faith, Inc. v. Comm'r, 950 F.2d 365, 370 (7th Cir. 1991).

[14] Statement of Lawrence B. Gibbs before the House Subcommittee on Oversight, March 12, 1987, in "Lobbying and Political Activities of Tax-Exempt Organizations," Hearings before the Subcommittee on Oversight, Committee on Ways and Means, House of Representatives, Serial 100-5, 96–97, 100th Cong., 1st Sess. (1987).

[15] See §§ 23.3, 23.4.

[16] See § 20.8; Chapter 21.

make a contribution to the political campaign of a candidate for public office (or a contribution in opposition to such a candidate). Other ways by which an organization can participate in a political campaign include distribution of statements, other communications to the public (such as endorsements or get-out-the-vote drives), provision of facilities, use of other assets, lending of employees, voter registration efforts, hosting of debates, and establishment and use of a political action committee. Aside from the federal tax law rules, however, many of these political campaign efforts are prohibited by federal and/or state campaign financing laws.[17]

(iii) Ascertaining Intervention. The standard to apply in determining whether an organization is involved in a political campaign should be amply clear by this time (if only because this prohibition applicable to charitable entities has been in the law for over 60 years), but it is not. There are essentially two choices when framing the standard: *express advocacy*, where participation in a political campaign by a charitable organization is considered to occur only where there is an explicit communication or other direct and obvious manifestation as to the organization's position with respect to a candidate, or a *facts-and-circumstances test*, where political campaign activity (or the absence of it) can be inferred from the particular circumstances.

By the close of 2005, the IRS or a court had yet to articulate a substantive view as to the appropriate standard for ascertaining the presence of an organization's participation in a political campaign. Utilization of the facts-and-circumstances approach by the IRS in this context is reflected in revenue rulings issued in the voter education setting.[18] For example, this statement appears in two of these rulings: "Whether an organization is participating or intervening, directly or indirectly, in any political campaign on behalf of or in opposition to any candidate for public office depends upon all of the facts and circumstances of each case."[19] In one instance, voter guides were found to be violative of the rule inasmuch as they either emphasized "one area of concern" that indicated the purpose was not nonpartisan or some questions in a questionnaire "evidence[d] a bias on certain issues."[20] In the other instance, an organization's publication was held to be "not

---

[17] In the context of campaign finance laws, the U.S. Supreme Court held unconstitutional restrictions on independent political expenditures by corporations, including nonprofit corporations (Citizens United v. Federal Election Comm'n, 558 U.S. 310 (2010)). This decision overruled Austin v. Michigan State Chamber of Commerce, 494 U.S. 652 (1990), and the portion of McConnell v. Federal Election Comm'n, 540 U.S. 93 (2003), that facially upheld these limits on electioneering communications. The Court reaffirmed its decision in *Citizens United* in American Tradition P'ship, Inc. v. Bullock, 567 U.S. 516 (2012). In the aftermath of the *Citizens United* decision, a federal district court ruled that the federal law absolute ban on political contributions to candidates by corporations is unconstitutional, because individuals can make these types of contributions (within limits); the court held that "corporations and human beings are entitled to equal political speech rights" (United States v. Danielczwk, Jr. & Biagi, 788 F. Supp. 2d 472, 791 F. Supp. 2d 513 (E.D. Va. 2011)). This decision was, however, reversed (683 F.3d 611 (4th Cir. 2012)). A decision by the Court, striking down a cap on the aggregate amount an individual can contribute to federal candidates in a two-year election cycle (McCutcheon v. Federal Election Comm'n, 572 U.S. 185 (2014)), may somewhat shift the flow of political contributions away from politically involved exempt organizations and to political party officials and senior members of Congress. In general, see *Constitutional Law*, Chapter 5; *Fundraising*, § 6.15.
[18] See § 23.2(c).
[19] Rev. Rul. 80-282, 1980-2 C.B. 178; Rev. Rul. 78-248, 1978-1 C.B. 154.
[20] Rev. Rul. 78-248, 1978-1 C.B. 154.

neutral," yet other factors led to the conclusion that distribution of the publication was not prohibited political campaign activity.[21] A fuller explication of the standard, however, was not provided. Then, in a private letter ruling made public at the outset of 2006, the IRS wrote that, for these purposes, "one looks to the effect of the communication as a whole, including whether support for, or opposition to, a candidate for public office is express or implied."[22]

Thereafter, the IRS issued more formal guidance on this subject, indicating whether, in 21 factual situations, a tax-exempt charitable organization violated the federal income tax law proscription on participation or intervention in a political campaign on behalf of or in opposition to a candidate for public office.[23] This guidance addresses voter education and registration, action by organizations' leaders, candidate appearances, issue advocacy, and activity on websites.

(iv) Summary of Law.   The IRS ruled that a charitable organization may not—without loss of tax-exempt status—evaluate the qualifications of potential candidates in a school board election and then support particular slates in the campaign.[24] The agency also ruled that a charitable organization violated the prohibition on political campaign activities when it made an interest-bearing loan to an organization that used the funds for political purposes.[25] Also, a court held that an organization established with the dominant aim of bringing about world government as rapidly as possible did not qualify as a charitable organization because the activity was political in nature.[26]

Conversely, the IRS ruled that a tax-exempt university did not intervene in a political campaign by conducting a political science course that required the students' participation in political campaigns of their choice,[27] nor by the provision of faculty advisers and facilities for a campus newspaper that published the students' editorial opinions on political matters.[28] Also, an exempt broadcasting station that provided equal airtime to all electoral candidates in compliance with the Federal Communications Act was ruled to not be in violation of the proscription against partisan political activities.[29]

The IRS ruled that a charitable organization's administration of a payroll deduction plan to collect contributions from its employees and remit the contributions to unions representing its employees for transfer to union-sponsored political action committees would not violate the prohibition on participating in political campaigns, in part because the charity's expenses would be reimbursed.[30] The IRS's lawyers, however, subsequently concluded that administration of a payroll deduction plan by a public charity in support of a political action committee

---

[21] Rev. Rul. 80-282, 1980-2 C.B. 178.
[22] Priv. Ltr. Rul. 200602042.
[23] Rev. Rul. 2007-41, 2007-1 C.B. 1421.
[24] Rev. Rul. 67-71, 1967-1 C.B. 125.
[25] Tech. Adv. Mem. 9812001.
[26] Estate of Blaine v. Comm'r, 22 T.C. 1195 (1954).
[27] Rev. Rul. 72-512, 1972-2 C.B. 246.
[28] Rev. Rul. 72-513, 1972-2 C.B. 246.
[29] Rev. Rul. 74-574, 1974-2 C.B. 160.
[30] Priv. Ltr. Rul. 200151060.

constituted prohibited participation or intervention in political campaigns, in that charitable organizations "may not provide or solicit financial or other forms of support to political organizations."[31] Nonetheless, the IRS thereafter ruled that a public charity may form and control a tax-exempt social welfare organization that, in turn, forms and maintains a political action committee, and may maintain a payroll deduction plan for its employees for contributions to political action committees, without the activity of the political action committee attributed to it and without operation of the plan constituting participation in political campaign activity, inasmuch as the recipients of the political contributions are selected solely by the employees.[32] These arrangements can, however, be doomed by the attribution principle,[33] as illustrated by the situation where the operation of a political action committee by a for-profit subsidiary of a public charity was considered by the IRS to be operation of the political action committee by the charity itself, where the subsidiary lacked employees, office space, equipment, and the like.[34]

Despite the requirement of a political campaign and a candidate for public office, the IRS denominated as an action organization (and thus denied recognition of tax exemption to) an organization formed for the purpose of implementing an orderly change of administration of the office of governor of a state in the most efficient and economical fashion possible by assisting the governor-elect during the period between his election and inauguration.[35] Without any statement of its reasoning, the IRS ruled that a presidential inaugural committee that sponsored inaugural activities, some of which were open to the public and some by invitation only, where donations to it were commingled with the proceeds from various fundraising affairs and activities, was not an organization organized and operated exclusively for charitable purposes.[36]

An expansive reading of this prohibition on political activities was provided by a federal court of appeals in denying tax-exempt status to a religious ministry organization for engaging in legislative activities and intervening in political campaigns.[37] The court summarized the offenses: "These attempts to elect or defeat certain political leaders reflected . . . [the organization's] objective to change the composition of the federal government."[38] The IRS Chief Counsel's office "reluctantly" concluded in 1989 that an organization "probably" did not intervene in a political campaign on behalf of or in opposition to a candidate for public office, even though the organization ran a political advertising program that (1) was, in the words of the IRS, "mostly broadcast during a two week period around

[31] Tech. Adv. Mem. 200446033.
[32] Priv. Ltr. Rul. 201127013. This distinction is found in Rev. Rul. 62-156, 1962-2 C.B. 47, which held that the employer's costs of administration of a payroll deduction plan for employees for political gifts were deductible as business expenses (IRC § 162) because the arrangement improved employee morale and enhanced the reputation of the employer; the donee political action committees were of the employees' choosing.
[33] See § 30.2.
[34] Priv. Ltr. Rul. 202005020.
[35] Rev. Rul. 74-117, 1974-1 C.B. 128.
[36] Rev. Rul. 77-283, 1977-2 C.B. 72.
[37] Christian Echoes National Ministry, Inc. v. United States, 470 F.2d 849 (10th Cir. 1972), cert. denied, 414 U.S. 864 (1973).
[38] Id. at 856. Also, Monsky v. Comm'r, 36 T.C.M. 1046 (1977); Giordano v. Comm'r, 36 T.C.M. 430 (1977).

the Reagan/Mondale foreign and defense policy debate on October 21, 1984," (2) contained statements that "could be viewed as demonstrating a preference for one of the debating candidates" (Mondale), (3) "could be viewed" as having content such that "individuals listening to the ads would generally understand them to support or oppose a candidate in an election campaign," (4) involved statements that were released so close to the November vote as to be "troublesome," and (5) was clearly in violation of the IRS's voter education rules.[39]

A charitable organization was found to have engaged in prohibited political campaign activity because of language in and the timing of mailing of fundraising letters.[40] Likewise, a charitable organization was held to have improperly intervened in a political campaign because its fundraising letters were signed by an individual who was a candidate for political office at the time; language in the letters was found to be "very much like [the candidate's] campaign statements, positions, and rhetoric."[41] By contrast, the IRS concluded that two direct-mail fundraising letters sent by a public charity that were signed by members of Congress who were candidates for public office did not entail participation in their political campaigns because the letters were not mailed to the jurisdictions represented by the two candidates, nothing in the letters suggested that contributions be made to the campaigns, and the results of a survey contained in the letters were not made available to the candidates.[42]

It is the view of the IRS that an attempt to influence the confirmation, by the U.S. Senate, of a federal judicial nominee does not constitute participation or intervention in a political campaign, inasmuch as the individual involved is not a contestant for elective public office.[43]

It is common for a tax-exempt charitable organization to be related to another exempt organization that is permitted to engage in some political campaign activity or that is permitted to establish and maintain a political action committee. If the arrangement is properly structured, the campaign activities of the other organization or organizations will not be attributed to the charitable entity for purposes of the political campaign prohibition. For example, a business league established a political action committee; that fact was ruled by the IRS to not jeopardize the exempt status of a charitable organization related to the business league.[44]

The IRS stated, without explanation or citation of any authority for the proposition, that a tax-exempt organization that violates the regulatory requirements of the Federal Election Campaign Act may well "jeopardize its exemption or be subject to other tax consequences."[45]

---

[39] Tech. Adv. Mem. 8936002. See § 23.2(c).

[40] Tech. Adv. Mem. 9609007.

[41] Tech. Adv. Mem. 200044038.

[42] Priv. Ltr. Rul. 200602042.

[43] Notice 88-76, 1988-2 C.B. 392.

[44] Priv. Ltr. Rul. 200103084. Business leagues are the subject of Chapter 14; political organizations are the subject of Chapter 17.

[45] Rev. Rul. 2004-6, 2004-1 C.B. 328; IR-2003-146. A public charity had its tax exemption retroactively revoked for engaging in political campaign activity in the form of numerous statements on its website and in fundraising solicitations; its "defenses"—that the statements were "unimportant" or made solely for fundraising purposes—failed (Priv. Ltr. Rul. 201416011).

(v) Candidate Appearances. When a candidate is invited to speak at a charitable organization's event as a political candidate, the organization should ensure that it provides an equal opportunity to other political candidates seeking the same public office, it does not indicate support for or opposition to the candidate, and political fundraising does not take place. A public forum involving several candidates for public office may qualify as an exempt educational activity.[46] If, however, the forum is operated in a manner showing bias for or against a candidate, the forum is political campaign intervention.[47]

(vi) Individual Participation. Inasmuch as organizations function only by means of the acts of individuals, who retain their civil rights to engage in political campaign activities in their personal capacity and/or serve as government officials, the law differentiates between activities that are undertaken in connection with "official" responsibilities on behalf of a tax-exempt charitable organization and those that are "personal"; only the former category of activities is relevant in assessing a charitable organization's qualification for exemption in the face of political campaign efforts.[48] Likewise, the leaders and managers of a charitable organization are not prohibited from speaking about issues of public policy. Political campaign activities of individuals (such as directors, officers, or key employees) will be attributed to an exempt organization if it has, directly or indirectly, authorized or ratified their acts (such as comments at official functions or in official organization publications) or reimbursed them for contributions or other similar expenditures.[49] Charitable organization leaders who speak or write in their individual capacity are well advised to clearly indicate that their comments are personal and not intended to represent the views of the organization.[50]

(c) Voter Education Activities

A charitable organization may instruct the public on matters useful to the individual and beneficial to the community.[51] In carrying out this form of an educational purpose, an organization may operate in a political milieu, albeit cautiously. Thus, organizations have been permitted to assemble and donate to libraries the campaign speeches, interviews, and other materials of an individual who was a candidate for a "historically important elective office";[52] conduct public forums

---

[46] See Chapter 8.

[47] E.g., Priv. Ltr. Rul. 201020021.

[48] Gen. Couns. Mem. 34631.

[49] Gen. Couns. Mem. 33912.

[50] This distinction between political campaign involvement by tax-exempt organizations and the free expression on political matters by organizations' leaders speaking only for themselves often arises with respect to religious organizations. The IRS stated that for their organizations to remain tax exempt, "religious leaders can't make partisan comments in official organization publications or at official church functions." Therefore, "religious leaders who speak or write in their individual capacity are encouraged to clearly indicate that their comments are personal and not intended to represent the views of the organization" (Pub. 1828, *Tax Guide for Churches and Other Religious Organizations* (Aug. 2015) at 8).

[51] Reg. § 1.501(c)(3)-1(d)(3). See §§ 8.4, 8.5.

[52] Rev. Rul. 70-321, 1970-1 C.B. 129.

involving debates and lectures on social, political, and international questions;[53] and conduct public forums involving congressional candidates, where there is a "fair and impartial treatment of the candidates."[54] By contrast, the organization will imperil its tax exemption if it solicits the signing or endorsing of a fair campaign practices code by political candidates.[55]

In performing activities such as these, however, the organization must present a sufficiently full and fair exposition of pertinent facts to permit the public to form its own opinion or conclusion independent of that presented by the organization, although the organization may also advocate a particular position or viewpoint.[56] Thus, while a charitable organization may seek to educate the public on patriotic, political, and civic matters and even alert the citizenry to the dangers of an extreme political doctrine, it may not do so by the use of disparaging terms, insinuations, innuendoes, and suggested implications drawn from incomplete facts.[57]

There is, not surprisingly, tension between the concepts of political campaign activities and voter education activities. This is illustrated by a case involving the practice of a tax-exempt bar association (otherwise qualified as a charitable organization) of rating candidates for public office in a state's judiciary. The candidates were rated as "approved," "not approved," or "approved as highly qualified"; more than one candidate for the same office may receive the same rating. The ratings were disseminated to the public in press releases and by means of the publications of the association. A court held that this rating process did not constitute prohibited participation or intervention in political campaigns on behalf of or in opposition to candidates; the court found that the "ratings do not support or oppose the candidacy of any particular individual or recommend that the public vote for or against a specific candidate."[58] This opinion was reversed, however, with the appellate court concluding that the rating activity constituted participation or intervention in the political campaigns for the judgeships.[59] The court of appeals characterized the ratings as "[p]ublished expressions of . . . opinion, made with an eye toward imminent elections."[60]

The IRS published a ruling allowing organizations that operate broadcast stations to provide equal airtime to political candidates.[61] The import of this

---

[53] Rev. Rul. 66-256, 1966-2 C.B. 210. The IRS ruled that a nonprofit organization planning on conducting a series of ostensibly educational symposia failed to qualify for tax exemption because representatives of only one political party, some of whom were candidates for public office, were invited to participate as speakers (Priv. Ltr. Rul. 201523021).

[54] Rev. Rul. 86-95, 1986-1 C.B. 332. In one instance, the IRS approved of a forum where less than all of the candidates were invited because the decision "accentuate[d] the educational nature of the forums and still ensure[d] a meaningful field of candidates for worthwhile forums, while allocating for the organization's limited space and time" (Tech. Adv. Mem. 9635003).

[55] Rev. Rul. 76-456, 1976-2 C.B. 151; Rev. Rul. 66-258, 1966-2 C.B. 213. Also, Rev. Rul. 60-193, 1960-1 C.B. 195.

[56] Reg. § 1.501(c)(3)-1(d)(3). Also, Haswell v. United States, 500 F.2d 1133, 1143-1145 (Ct. Cl. 1974), cert. denied, 419 U.S. 1107 (1974).

[57] Rev. Rul. 68-263, 1968-1 C.B. 256.

[58] Ass'n of the Bar of the City of New York v. Comm'r, 89 T.C. 599, 609-610 (1987).

[59] Ass'n of the Bar of the City of New York v. Comm'r, 858 F.2d 876 (2d Cir. 1988), cert. denied, 490 U.S. 1030 (1989).

[60] Id., 858 F.2d at 880.

[61] Rev. Rul. 74-574, 1974-2 C.B. 160.

POLITICAL CAMPAIGN ACTIVITIES BY TAX-EXEMPT ORGANIZATIONS

ruling as a matter of tax policy is uncertain, however, in that these organizations were required by federal communications law to provide free airtime to political candidates.[62]

The IRS ruled that a charitable organization may publish a newsletter containing the voting records of congressional incumbents on selected issues without prohibited involvement in political campaigns.[63] The IRS indicated that the format and content of the publication need not be neutral, in that each incumbent's votes and the organization's views on selected legislative issues can be reported, and the publication may indicate whether the incumbent supported or opposed the organization's view.

The position of the IRS on this issue in general is that "in the absence of any expressions of endorsement for or opposition to candidates for public office, an organization may publish a newsletter containing voting records and its opinions on issues of interest to it provided that the voting records are not widely distributed to the general public during an election campaign or aimed, in view of all the facts and circumstances, towards affecting any particular elections."[64]

The IRS concluded that the use by a charitable organization of panels of citizens to review and rate political candidates is a form of intervention or participation in the candidates' campaigns.[65] The organization viewed these processes as forms of issue education and means to stimulate public dialogue, but the IRS determined that the candidates' ratings provided "political editorial opinions to the general public and went beyond the neutral forums" that are permissible.

(d) Requirement of *Candidate*

The Internal Revenue Code does not define the term *candidate* for purposes of the prohibition on political campaign activities by charitable organizations. The income tax regulations provide a definition of the term in the context of defining the phrase *candidate for public office*, as an individual who offers themself, or is proposed by others, "as a contestant for an elective public office, whether such office be national, State, or local."[66]

An analysis of the political campaign intervention rules by the staff of the Joint Committee on Taxation stated that "[c]lear standards do not exist for determining precisely at what point an individual becomes a candidate for purposes of the rule."[67] This analysis continued: "On the one hand, once an individual declares his candidacy for a particular office, his status as a candidate is clear."[68] The analysis added: "On the other hand, the fact that an individual is a prominent political figure does not automatically make him a candidate, even if there is speculation regarding his possible future candidacy for particular offices."[69]

---

[62] See Rev. Rul. 78-160, 1978-1 C.B. 153, *rev'd*, Rev. Rul. 78-248, 1978-1 C.B. 154.
[63] Rev. Rul. 80-282, 1980-2 C.B. 178.
[64] Gen. Couns. Mem. 38444.
[65] Tech. Adv. Mem. 9635003.
[66] Reg. § 1.501(c)(3)-1(c)(3)(iii).
[67] Staff of Joint Comm. on Tax'n, Lobbying and Political Activities of Tax-Exempt Organizations 14 (Comm. Print JCS-5-87).
[68] *Id.*
[69] *Id.*

221

(e) Requirement of *Campaign*

A federal court of appeals observed that a "campaign for a public office in a public election merely and simply means running for office, or candidacy for office, as the word is used in common parlance and as it is understood by the man in the street."[70] The term *campaign* is not otherwise defined in the federal tax law.

(f) Requirement of *Public Office*

The Internal Revenue Code and the federal tax regulations do not define the term *public office* for purposes of the political campaign activity prohibition applicable to charitable organizations.

The private foundation law, however, utilizes the term *elective public office*.[71] The accompanying tax regulations state that the term *public office* "must be distinguished from mere public employment" and that the "essential element" in determining whether a public employee holds a public office is "whether a significant part of the activities of a public employee is the independent performance of policymaking functions."[72] Also, in the rules concerning political organizations, the term *public office* is used in the definition of a political organization exempt function.[73] A related regulation uses the same definition of the term *public office* as is used in the private foundation law setting.[74] The IRS's lawyers took the position that precinct committee members in a state were holders of a public office, conceding nonetheless that, if the definition of the term in these two sets of regulations was applied, the members of the committee "would not be considered as holding public office because their duties entail no independent policymaking functions."[75]

A state court of appeals held that an individual who is a candidate for delegate to a county political convention is a candidate for state law purposes but is not a candidate for a public office.[76] Another federal appellate court has held that the phrase *candidate for office* is "used in common parlance and as it is understood by the man in the street."[77] Relying on this observation, the above IRS pronouncement stated that, to the "average person, the appearance of precinct candidates on the general election ballot indicates that the position is a public office."[78]

(g) Activist Organizations

Aside from substantial legislative activities[79] and political campaign activities, there is a broad range of advocacy undertakings that may be described as the type of speech or activity protected by free speech principles. These undertakings may

---

[70] Norris v. United States, 86 F.2d 379, 382 (8th Cir. 1936), *rev'd on other grounds*, 300 U.S. 564 (1937).

[71] IRC § 4946(c)(1), (5).

[72] Reg. § 53.4946-1(g)(2)(i).

[73] IRC § 527(e)(2). See § 17.1(a).

[74] Reg. § 1.527-2(d).

[75] Gen. Couns. Mem. 39811.

[76] Templin v. Oakland City Clerk, 387 N.W.2d 156 (Mich. Ct. App. 1986).

[77] Ass'n of the Bar of the City of New York v. Comm'r, 858 F.2d 876, 880 (2d Cir. 1988), *cert. denied*, 490 U.S. 1030 (1989).

[78] Gen. Couns. Mem. 39811.

[79] See Chapter 22.

be manifested in a variety of ways, such as writings, demonstrations, boycotts, strikes, picketing, and litigation, all protected by the rights of free speech and association and the right to petition (assuming the absence of any illegal activities). These activities frequently give the IRS pause in evaluating the status of an organization as a charitable entity, but, unless the activities may be fairly characterized as being impermissible lobbying or electioneering, there is no basis in the law concerning action organizations (as that term is used in its technical sense) for denying an organization engaging in these activities recognition of tax-exempt status or for revoking this type of organization's tax-exempt status.

The position of the IRS on this point apparently is that this type of activity can be a permissible method by which to further tax-exempt purposes.[80] These activities will jeopardize exemption, however, where they are illegal or otherwise contrary to public policy.[81] Nonetheless, where an activity is legal, the IRS generally will not deem it contrary to public policy.[82]

The tolerance of the courts in this area in general was classically illustrated by a federal district court finding that the anticonvention boycott orchestrated by the National Organization for Women in the 1970s, in states whose legislatures had not ratified the proposed Equal Rights Amendment, was not in violation of antitrust laws, even though the boycott or concerted refusal to deal has been held to be an unlawful combination in restraint of trade.[83] Because the objective of NOW's convention boycott campaign was the ratification of the proposed amendment by means of demonstrating support and generating widespread publicity for the proposed amendment, the court found that the boycott activities "were not intended as punitive . . . and were not motivated by any type of anti-competitive purpose."[84] NOW was successful in asserting that the antitrust laws do not apply to boycotts that take place in a political rather than a commercial context.[85]

At the same time that the NOW litigation was unfolding, the IRS had before it the tax status of an organization that conducted a consumer boycott. Prior to the decision in the NOW case, the IRS concluded that the organization, which conducted a national campaign against the purchase of products from companies that manufacture infant formula and market it in developing countries by means of allegedly unethical business practices, could not qualify as a charitable entity because it was an action organization. Consequently, the organization took the matter into court,[86] but just before the case reached the briefing stage, the IRS suddenly reversed its position and issued a favorable ruling, thereby mooting the case.

Presumably, therefore, the case stands for the proposition that an organization may conduct a boycott in furtherance of charitable ends.[87] The operative legal

---

[80] Gen. Couns. Mem. 37858.

[81] See §§ 6.2, 6.3(i).

[82] Id.

[83] Missouri v. Nat'l Org. for Women, Inc., 467 F. Supp. 289 (W.D. Mo. 1978).

[84] Id. at 296.

[85] Also, Eastern R.R. Presidents Conf. v. Noerr Motor Freight, Inc., 365 U.S. 127 (1961); Register of Wills for Baltimore City v. Cook, 216 A.2d 542 (Md. 1966).

[86] Infant Formula Action Coalition v. United States (D.D.C. No. 79-0129).

[87] Some organizations, already possessing IRC § 501(c)(3) classification, engage in consumer boycotts (relating to, for example, the purchase of tuna, products that exploit animals, and products produced

principle appears to be that, while the conduct of a boycott may not inherently be an exempt function, a boycott can further an exempt purpose and thereby lead to charitable status. As the IRS recognized, the "performance of a particular activity that is not inherently charitable may nonetheless further a charitable purpose [and the] . . . overall result in any given case is dependent on why and how that activity is actually being conducted."[88]

Moreover, the IRS recognized that an otherwise tax-exempt charitable organization can further its exempt purposes by instituting litigation, even where the organization employs private lawyers to represent it in bringing and maintaining the litigation.[89] The IRS insists, however, that an organization's litigation activities be a "reasonable means" of accomplishing its exempt purposes, and that the program of litigation not be illegal, contrary to a clearly defined and established public policy, or violative of express statutory provisions.

This means-to-an-end principle has also been recognized by the courts. One court discussed the point that the purpose toward which an organization's activities are directed, and not the nature of the activities themselves, is ultimately dispositive of the organization's right to be classified as a charitable organization.[90] In a similar case, this court found that an activity (sale of handicrafts) was "neither an exempt purpose nor a nonexempt purpose but an activity carried on by . . . [the organization] in furtherance of its exempt purposes."[91]

The U.S. Supreme Court applied this principle in analogous contexts. Perhaps the most applicable of the Court's opinions in this setting is the holding that litigation activities as conducted in the public interest context of that case are modes of expression and association protected by constitutional law, and may not be barred by state authority to regulate the legal profession.[92] In that case, litigation activities were perceived as neutral activities, engaged in as a means for accomplishment of the organization's ends. Likewise, as discussed, boycotts, demonstrations, and the like can serve as the basis for advancing charitable purposes. As the Court has repeatedly observed, the First Amendment protects advocacy, certainly of lawful ends, against governmental intrusion.[93]

---

in whaling nations), but the *Infant Formula Action Coalition* case, *supra* note 86, involved an organization that conducted a boycott as its primary activity and that had its tax status reviewed by the IRS at the outset of its existence.

[88] Rev. Rul. 69-572, 1969-2 C.B. 119.

[89] Rev. Rul. 80-278, 1980-2 C.B. 175. The IRS, in Rev. Rul. 80-279, 1980-2 C.B. 176, took a like stance with respect to an organization that conducted mediation of environmental disputes.

[90] Pulpit Resource v. Comm'r, 70 T.C. 594 (1978). See § 4.4.

[91] Aid to Artisans, Inc. v. Comm'r, 71 T.C. 202, 214 (1978).

[92] N.A.A.C.P. v. Button, 371 U.S. 415 (1963).

[93] E.g., Thomas v. Collins, 323 U.S. 516 (1945); Herndon v. Lowry, 301 U.S. 242 (1937). Also, Pratt v. Robert S. Odell & Co., 122 P.2d 684, 692 (Cal. Dist. Ct. App. 1942), where it was held that a corporation may expend funds in the prosecution of litigation to which it is not a party where the expenditure is a means for furthering its objects; and Register of Wills for Baltimore City v. Cook, 216 A.2d 542, 546 (Md. 1966), where it was held that advocacy of passage of the Equal Rights Amendment is one method of accomplishing the charitable objectives of a tax-exempt trust. In this context, it should be noted that, in Village of Schaumburg v. Citizens for a Better Environment, 444 U.S. 620 (1980), the Supreme Court held that acts of fundraising are among the most protected forms of free speech. Also, as to the latter point, Riley v. Nat'l Federation of the Blind of N.C., 487 U.S. 781 (1988); Secretary of State of Maryland v. Joseph H. Munson Co., Inc., 467 U.S. 947 (1984). In general, *Fundraising*, § 4.5.

A court held that litigation is an "appropriate vehicle for an organization to accomplish" its tax-exempt purpose, in a case involving the exempt status of an organization that provided legal assistance to employees whose rights were violated under compulsory unionism arrangements.[94]

In one case, the IRS had taken the position that engaging in proxy contests was not a charitable activity. There was no dispute over the obvious fact that proxy contests are not inherently charitable or educational endeavors. On review, however, the court involved placed the organization's activities in context—that is, in light of its overall purposes.[95] The court recognized that the mission of the organization "is to make corporate management, and thus corporations, responsible."[96] The court proclaimed that it is "incumbent upon corporations to use their substantial economic power for the community good, rather than solely for self-enrichment" and that the "need for a swift re-orientation of the corporate perspective to its community responsibilities is imperative."[97]

Thus, certain activities—activist in nature—can avoid classification as political campaign activities, thereby enabling the organizations involved to qualify for tax-exempt status as public charities.[98]

§ 23.3 POLITICAL CAMPAIGN EXPENDITURES AND TAX SANCTIONS

The federal tax law authorizes the levy of taxes in situations where a charitable organization makes a political expenditure.[99] Generally, a *political expenditure* is any amount paid or incurred by a charitable organization in any participation in, or intervention in (including the publication or distribution of statements), any political campaign on behalf of or in opposition to any candidate for public office.[100] The IRS has the discretion, in a situation where a charitable organization engages in political campaign activity, to revoke the organization's tax-exempt status,[101] impose this tax,[102] or do both.

The IRS's lawyers wrote that these taxes were enacted "not so much as an intermediate sanction to replace revocation, but primarily as an additional tax, and secondarily, as a sanction to apply instead of revocation in certain limited instances."[103] On that occasion, the tax was imposed on a tax-exempt church for

---

[94] Nat'l Right to Work Legal Defense & Education Found., Inc. v. United States, 487 F. Supp. 801 (E.D.N.C. 1979). Cf. Retired Teachers Legal Defense Fund, Inc. v. Comm'r, 78 T.C. 280 (1982).

[95] Center on Corporate Responsibility, Inc. v. Shultz, 368 F. Supp. 863 (D.D.C. 1973).

[96] *Id.* at 874, n.21.

[97] *Id.* at 874–75, n.21.

[98] E.g., Priv. Ltr. Rul. 8936002.

[99] IRC § 4955.

[100] Reg. § 53.4955-1(c)(1).

[101] E.g., Branch Ministries, Inc. v. Rossoti, 40 F. Supp. 2d 15 (D.D.C. 1999), *aff'd*, 211 F. 3d 137 (D.C. Cir. 2000).

[102] E.g., Tech. Adv. Mem. 9635003. In one instance, the IRS evaluated the matter of a charitable organization's involvement in political campaign activity solely from the standpoint of the IRC § 4955 rules; that is, the issue of revocation of tax-exempt status was not raised (Priv. Ltr. Rul. 200602042).

[103] Tech. Adv. Mem. 200437040.

engaging in political campaign activity that was considered incidental. In another instance, the tax was imposed in lieu of exemption revocation when a public charity administered a payroll deduction plan that facilitated contributions by its employees to a political action committee maintained by an exempt association.[104]

In an effort to discourage the use of ostensibly educational organizations operating in tandem with political campaigns, the concept of a political expenditure was expanded, so as to apply with respect to an organization "which is formed primarily for purposes of promoting the candidacy (or prospective candidacy) of an individual for public office (or which is effectively controlled by a candidate or prospective candidate and which is availed of primarily for such purposes)." In these circumstances, the term *political expenditure* includes any of the following amounts paid or incurred by the organization: (1) amounts paid to or incurred by the individual for speeches or other services; (2) the travel expenses of the individual; (3) the expenses of conducting polls, surveys, or other studies, or the preparation of papers or other materials, for use by the individual; (4) the expenses of advertising, publicity, and fundraising for the individual; and (5) any other expense "which has the primary effect of promoting public recognition, or otherwise primarily accruing to the benefit, of" the individual.

A political expenditure can trigger an *initial tax*, payable by the organization, of 10 percent of the amount of the expenditure. An initial tax of 2½ percent of the expenditure can also be imposed on each of the organization's managers (such as directors and officers) who knew it was a political expenditure, unless the agreement to make the expenditure was not willful and was due to reasonable cause.[105] The IRS has the discretion to abate these initial taxes where the organization can establish that the violation was due to reasonable cause and not to willful neglect, and corrects the violation in a timely fashion.[106]

An *additional tax* can be imposed on a charitable organization, at a rate of 100 percent of the political expenditure. This tax is levied where the initial tax was imposed and the expenditure was not timely corrected. An additional tax can be imposed on the organization's manager, at a rate of 50 percent of the expenditure. This tax is levied where the additional tax was imposed on the organization and where the manager refused to agree to part or all of the correction.

As to management and as to any one political expenditure, the maximum initial tax is $5,000 and the maximum additional tax is $10,000.[107]

In this context, the concept of *correction* means "recovering part or all of the expenditure to the extent recovery is possible, establishment of safeguards to prevent future political expenditures, and where full recovery is not possible, such additional corrective action" as may be prescribed by federal tax regulations.[108]

---

[104] Tech. Adv. Mem. 200446033.

[105] Reg. § 53.4955-1(b).

[106] IRC § 4962; Reg. § 53.4955-1(d).

[107] A tax paid under this section is reported on Form 4720 (Reg. §§ 53.6011-1(b), 53.6071-1(e)).

[108] Reg. § 53.4955-1(e). The conference report noted that the "adoption of the excise tax sanction does not modify the present-law rule that an organization is not tax-exempt under [IRC] section 501(c)(3), eligible to receive tax-deductible charitable contributions, if the organization engages in any political campaign activity" (H.R. Rep. No. 100-495, at 1020 (1987)). Also, Reg. § 53.4955-1(a).

If a tax is imposed with respect to a political expenditure under these rules, the expenditure will not be treated as a taxable expenditure under the private foundation rules.[109]

An organization that loses its federal tax-exempt status as a charitable organization because of political campaign activities is precluded from becoming exempt as a social welfare organization.[110]

Under certain circumstances, the IRS is empowered to commence an action in federal district court to enjoin a charitable organization from the further making of political expenditures and for other relief to ensure that the assets of the organization are preserved for tax-exempt purposes.[111] If the IRS finds that a charitable organization has flagrantly violated the prohibition against the making of political expenditures, the IRS is required to determine and assess any income and/or excise tax(es) due immediately, by terminating the organization's tax year.[112]

§ 23.4 TAXATION OF POLITICAL EXPENDITURES

A tax-exempt organization[113] that makes an expenditure for a political activity is subject to a tax.[114] This tax is determined by computing an amount equal to the lesser of the organization's net investment income[115] for the year involved or the amount expended for the political activity. This amount constitutes *political organization taxable income*[116] and is taxed[117] at the highest corporate rate.[118]

The concept of *political activity* for purposes of this tax is the same as that used for defining the exempt functions of political organizations.[119] Thus, political activity includes the function of influencing or attempting to influence the selection, nomination, election, or appointment of any individual to any federal, state, or local public office.[120] Consequently, this concept of *political activity* is broader than the concept of *political campaign activity* made applicable, as a prohibition, to charitable organizations.[121]

---

[109] See § 12.4(e); *Private Foundations* § 9.2.

[110] IRC § 504.

[111] IRC § 7409; Reg. § 301.7409-1.

[112] IRC § 6852; Reg. § 301.6852-1. The IRS, in one instance, assessed this tax, then abated and refunded it, yet refused to expressly concede that political campaign activity did not occur; a complaint filed by the organization to force the agency to make that concession was dismissed on the ground that the tax refund mooted the case (Catholic Answers, Inc. v. United States, 2009-2 U.S.T.C. ¶ 50,697 (S.D. Cal. 2009), aff'd, 438 Fed. Appx. 640 (9th Cir. 2011), *cert. denied*, 565 U.S. 1178 (2012)).

[113] That is, an organization described in IRC § 501(c) and exempt from federal income taxation by reason of IRC § 501(a).

[114] IRC § 527(f)(1).

[115] This term is defined in IRC § 527(f)(2).

[116] IRC § 527(c)(1), (2).

[117] IRC § 527(b).

[118] IRC § 11(b).

[119] IRC § 527(e)(2). In general, see Chapter 17.

[120] *Id.*

[121] This chapter, *passim*. (The term *charitable organization* means an organization described in IRC § 501(c)(3).)

Political activity that is not political campaign activity can constitute a charitable, educational, religious, or like activity, undertaken in furtherance of the tax-exempt functions of a charitable organization. Thus, the income tax regulations state that, where the prohibited activities are not engaged in as a "primary objective," the organization is not an action organization but can be regarded as "engaging in nonpartisan analysis, study, or research and making the results thereof available to the public."[122]

§ 23.5 "RELIGIOUS LIBERTY" EXECUTIVE ORDER

The White House issued an executive order containing guidance for the executive branch of the federal government "in formulating and implementing policies with implications for the religious liberty of persons and organizations in America," and "to further compliance with the Constitution and with applicable statutes and Presidential Directives."[123]

The overarching policy of the executive branch is said in this order to be "to vigorously enforce Federal law's robust protections for religious freedom." Thus, the order states that "[a]ll executive departments and agencies (agencies) shall, to the greatest extent practicable and to the extent permitted by law, respect and protect the freedom of persons and organizations to engage in religious and political speech."

From the standpoint of the law of tax-exempt organizations, here is the operative sentence: "In particular, the Secretary of the Treasury shall ensure, to the extent permitted by law, that the Department of the Treasury does not take any adverse action against any individual, house of worship, or other religious organization on the basis that such individual or organization speaks or has spoken about moral or political issues from a religious perspective, where speech of similar character has, consistent with law, not ordinarily been treated as participation or intervention in a political campaign on behalf of (or in opposition to) a candidate for public office by the Department of the Treasury."

For these purposes, the term *adverse action* means the "imposition of any tax or tax penalty; the delay or denial of [recognition of] tax-exempt status; the disallowance of tax deductions for contribution made to entities exempted from taxation under section 501(c)(3) of title 26, United States Code; or any other action that makes unavailable or denies any tax deduction, exemption, credit, or benefit."

The order states that it shall be implemented "consistent with applicable law." It concludes with the observation that it "is not intended to, and does not, create any right or benefit, substantive or procedural, enforceable at law or in equity by any party against the United States, its departments, agencies, or entities, its officers, employees, or agents, or any other person."

§ 23.6 POLITICAL ACTIVITIES OF SOCIAL WELFARE ORGANIZATIONS

A tax-exempt social welfare organization is an entity that is primarily operated for the promotion of social welfare; it must be engaged in promoting the common

---

[122] Reg. § 1.501(c)(3)-1(c)(3)(iv).
[123] Executive Order No. 13798 (May 4, 2017).

good and general welfare of the people of a community.[124] An organization is an exempt social welfare organization if it is operated primarily for the purpose of bringing about civic betterments and social improvement.[125] Thus, exemption for this type of organization—like exempt organizations generally—fundamentally hinges on satisfaction of a primary purpose test.[126]

(a) Allowable Campaign Activity

The promotion of social welfare does not include direct or indirect participation or intervention in political campaigns on behalf of or in opposition to a candidate for public office.[127] Whether an organization is participating or intervening, directly or indirectly, in any political campaign activity on behalf of or in opposition to a candidate for public office depends on the facts and circumstances of each case.[128]

Although political campaign activities do not promote social welfare, the IRS has recognized that there is not a "complete ban" on such activities by tax-exempt social welfare organizations; this type of organization may engage in such activities as long as it is primarily engaged in activities that promote social welfare.[129] Subsequently, however, the IRS stated that exempt social welfare organizations may engage in "limited" political campaign activity.[130]

In private letter rulings, the IRS has ruled that exempt social welfare organizations can engage in political campaign activity as long as that function is not its primary activity.[131] This approach suggests that a social welfare entity can expend up to 49 percent of its time and funds on political activity. For example, the IRS denied recognition of exemption as a social welfare organization to an entity because it expended about 60 percent of its revenue in its first year and more than 87 percent of its revenue in its second year on political campaign activity.[132] The IRS denied recognition as a social welfare organization because it devoted 90 percent of its time and resources to the conduct of political campaign activities.[133] An entity was held not entitled to recognition of exemption as a social welfare organization because a "substantial" portion of its activities consisted of direct or indirect political campaign involvement.[134]

(b) Political Campaign Activities

The IRS has traditionally been strict in applying the restriction on political campaign activity by tax-exempt social welfare organizations, as illustrated by the

[124] Reg. § 1.501(c)(4)-1(a)(2)(i). See Chapter 13.
[125] Id.
[126] See §§ 4.4, 4.6.
[127] Reg. § 1.501(c)(4)-1(a)(2)(ii).
[128] See § 23.2(b).
[129] Rev. Rul. 81-95, 1981-1 C.B. 332. Amounts expended for political campaign activities within the meaning of IRC § 527(e)(2), however, will be subject to tax (Rev. Rul. 81-95, *supra*). See § 23.4.
[130] Rev. Rul. 2004-6, 2004-1 C.B. 328; IR-2003-146.
[131] E.g., Priv. Ltr. Rul. 200833021.
[132] Priv. Ltr. Rul. 201403019.
[133] Priv. Ltr. Rul. 201403020.
[134] Priv. Ltr. Rul. 201424028. The Department of the Treasury and the IRS, in 2013, issued proposed regulations concerning political campaign activities conducted by exempt social welfare organizations

denial of classification as an exempt social welfare organization to a group that rated candidates for public office on a nonpartisan basis and disseminated its ratings to the general public, on the theory that its rating process was intervention or participation on behalf of those candidates favorably rated and in opposition to those less favorably rated.[135] The IRS denied recognition of exemption as a social welfare organization to an entity having the objective of increasing the number of women involved in government service, including elected positions; the agency said that this organization conducted its activities for the benefit of a political party and thus was unduly partisan.[136] The IRS also denied recognition of exemption as a social welfare organization to an entity the principal functions of which were the recruitment of individuals to become active in politics at the precinct level and the distribution of voter guides that were not nonpartisan educational materials.[137]

Nor will objectivity necessarily ward off an unfavorable determination, as evidenced by the nonprofit group that selected slates of candidates for school board elections and engaged in campaigns on their behalf, and that was accordingly denied tax exemption as a charitable organization (and thus presumably as a social welfare organization) because of these political activities, "even though its process of selection may have been completely objective and unbiased and was intended primarily to educate and inform the public about the candidates."[138]

An organization whose activities were primarily directed, on a nonprofit and nonpartisan basis, toward encouraging individuals in business to become more active in politics and government and toward promoting business, social, or civic action was held to qualify for tax exemption as a social welfare organization.[139] Likewise, a group that engaged in nonpartisan analysis, study, and research, made the results available to the public, and publicized the need for a code of fair campaign practices was ruled to be an exempt educational organization.[140] Also, an organization that recruited college students for an internship program providing employment with local municipal agencies qualified as an exempt educational and charitable organization.[141] Thus, an exempt social welfare organization could similarly undertake these activities.

(c)   Political Activities

Notwithstanding the fact that political campaign activity of a tax-exempt social welfare organization may be permissible from the standpoint of tax exemption,

---

(REG-134417-13); in the face of intense criticism, this proposal was withdrawn. Congress, beginning with the federal government's budget legislation for fiscal year 2016, has prohibited the Department of the Treasury and the IRS from issuing guidance concerning candidate-related political activity. Most recently, the Consolidated Appropriations Act, 2023, provides that no funds may be used by the Treasury Department or the IRS to issue or finalize any regulation or other guidance related to the standard used to determine whether an organization is operated exclusively for the promotion of social welfare for purposes of IRC § 501(c)(4) (Pub. L. No. 117-328, div. E, tit. I, § 123, 136 Stat. 4459, 4660).

[135] Rev. Rul. 67-368, 1967-2 C.B. 194.
[136] Ex. Den. and Rev. Ltr. 20044008E.
[137] Priv. Ltr. Rul. 200833021.
[138] Rev. Rul. 67-71, 1967-1 C.B. 125.
[139] Rev. Rul. 60-193, 1960-1 C.B. 145.
[140] Rev. Rul. 66-258, 1966-2 C.B. 213.
[141] Rev. Rul. 70-584, 1970-2 C.B. 114.

expenditures associated with the activity may be taxable, with the taxable amount equal to the lesser of the organization's net investment income or the amount expended for the political activity.[142]

The IRS provided guidance for determining when expenditures by exempt social welfare organizations for issue advocacy are taxable as political expenditures pursuant to the political organizations rules.[143] In general, the agency applies a facts-and-circumstances test in assessing whether an expenditure by a social welfare organization for an advocacy communication relating to a public policy issue is for a political organization exempt function.[144]

For purposes of the tax rule that disallows a tax deduction for worthless debt where the debt is owed by a political party, the IRS ruled that a tax-exempt social welfare organization that makes expenditures in support of a candidate for elective public office is a political party.[145]

§ 23.7 POLITICAL ACTIVITIES BY LABOR ORGANIZATIONS

The federal tax law essentially is silent as to the extent to which tax-exempt labor organizations[146] can engage in political campaign activities. The IRS has observed that exempt labor organizations may engage in "limited" political campaign activity.[147] This is the case as long as these organizations are primarily engaged in exempt labor functions.[148]

The IRS guidance for determining when expenditures by exempt social welfare organizations for issue advocacy are taxable as political expenditures pursuant to the political organizations rules[149] is applicable to exempt labor organizations.

§ 23.8 POLITICAL ACTIVITIES BY BUSINESS LEAGUES

The federal tax law is essentially silent as to the extent to which tax-exempt associations (business leagues)[150] can engage in political campaign activities, in relation to their eligibility for exempt status. (The rules concerning the impact of this type of activity on the deductibility of members' dues are the same as those in the lobbying context.)[151] The IRS has observed that exempt associations may engage in

---

[142] IRC § 527(f)(1). See §§ 17.6, 23.4.

[143] See § 17.4.

[144] See § 23.10.

[145] Chief Couns. Adv. Mem. 201842006. In general, a tax deduction is allowed for a debt that becomes worthless (IRC § 166(a)(1)). This deduction is disallowed, however, for any debt that is owed by a political party (IRC § 271).

[146] See § 16.1.

[147] IR-2003-146.

[148] See § 4.4.

[149] See § 23.6(c).

[150] See Chapter 14.

[151] IRC § 162(e)(1)(B). See § 22.6. Citing this IRC provision, the IRS ruled that a business corporation maintaining a political action committee may not deduct as a business expense charitable contributions

"limited" political campaign activity.[152] This is the case as long as these organizations are primarily engaged in exempt business league functions.[153]

The IRS guidance for determining when expenditures by exempt social welfare organizations for issue advocacy are taxable as political expenditures pursuant to the political organizations rules[154] is applicable to exempt associations (business leagues).

§ 23.9   POLITICAL ACTIVITIES BY OTHER CATEGORIES OF EXEMPT ORGANIZATIONS

With one exception, the federal tax law is silent as to the extent to which tax-exempt organizations other than the foregoing categories[155] can engage in political campaign activities, in relation to their eligibility for exempt status. Presumably, the general rules applicable to these types of exempt organizations are likewise applicable to other types of exempt entities (other than charitable ones).[156] The one exception is for exempt health insurance issuers,[157] which are subject to the same constraint on political campaign activities are as exempt charitable organizations.

§ 23.10   ADVOCACY COMMUNICATIONS

The IRS provided guidance for determining when expenditures by certain types of tax-exempt organizations for issue advocacy are taxable as political expenditures pursuant to the political organizations rules.[158] An expenditure by an exempt organization for an advocacy communication relating to a public policy issue may be for an exempt function (as that term is used in the political organizations context). When an advocacy communication explicitly advocates the election or defeat of an individual to public office, the expenditure for the communication obviously is for an exempt function. Otherwise (that is, when an advocacy communication is not so explicit as to a candidacy), all of the facts and circumstances must be considered in determining whether the expenditure is for an exempt function.

The agency stated that factors that tend to show that an advocacy communication on a public policy issue is for an exempt function include the following: (1) The communication identifies a candidate for public office; (2) the timing of the communication coincides with a political campaign; (3) the communication targets

made to match its employees' charitable gifts, inasmuch as its charitable gifts are intended to incentivize political contributions by its employees to the PAC; the agency stated that the corporation's gifts to its PAC and its matching charitable gifts are "inextricably linked," so that the latter types of gifts are being made in connection with political campaigns (Priv. Ltr. Rul. 201616002).

[152] IR-2003-146.

[153] See § 4.4.

[154] See § 23.6(c).

[155] See §§ 23.6–23.8.

[156] See § 23.1.

[157] See § 19.18.

[158] See § 17.4.

voters in a particular election; (4) the communication identifies that candidate's position on the public policy issue that is the subject of the communication; (5) the position of the candidate on the public policy issue has been raised as distinguishing the candidate from others in the campaign, either in the communication involved or in other public communications; and (6) the communication is not part of an ongoing series of substantially similar advocacy communications by the organization on the same issue.

Factors that tend to show that an advocacy communication on a public policy issue is not for an exempt function include these: One or more of the foregoing six factors are absent; the communication identifies specific legislation, or a specific event outside the control of the organization, that the organization hopes to influence; the timing of the communication coincides with a specific event outside the control of the organization that the organization hopes to influence, such as a vote on legislation or other major legislative action (for example, a hearing before a legislative committee on the issue that is the subject of the communication); the communication identifies a candidate solely as a governmental official who is in a position to act on the public policy issue in connection with the specific event (such as a legislator who is able to vote on the legislation); and the communication identifies a candidate solely in the list of key or principal sponsors of the legislation that is the subject of the communication.

§ 23.11 INTERNET COMMUNICATIONS

Charitable and other tax-exempt organizations may engage in political campaign activities by means of the Internet. This practice is raising questions as to the application of the federal tax law to this form of advocacy. Moreover, some charitable entities are affiliated with organizations that conduct political campaign activity using the Internet. A message concerning this type of activity may be on an organization's website, which is linked to a charity's website.

Political campaign activity can constitute a form of communication, and the Internet is a medium of communication. As is the case in other contexts, however, the federal tax law does not provide any unique treatment to transactions or activities of exempt organizations involving political campaign activities simply because the Internet is the medium of communication.

As the IRS saliently observed, the "use of the Internet to accomplish a particular task does not change the way the tax laws apply to that task." The IRS continued: "Advertising is still advertising and fundraising is still fundraising."[159] The agency also could have said: "Political campaign activity is still political campaign activity."

There are four forms of Internet communications in this setting: (1) a communication published on a publicly accessible Web page; (2) a communication posted on a password-protected portion of a website; (3) a communication on a listserv (or by means of other methods such as a news group, chat room, and/or

[159] "Tax Exempt Organizations and World Wide Web Fundraising and Advertising on the Internet," Topic I, IRS Exempt Organization Continuing Professional Education Text for FY 2000.

forum); and (4) a communication by means of e-mail. The IRS recognized that, by "publishing a webpage on the Internet, an exempt organization can provide the general public with information about the organization, its activities, and issues of concern to the organization."[160] The agency added: "An exempt organization can provide information to subscribers about issues of concern to the organization as well as enable people with common interests to share information via the Internet through a variety of methods," referencing mailing lists and the methods referred to previously in the third category of Internet communication.[161]

An e-mail communication from a tax-exempt organization clearly can constitute a political campaign activity (such as an endorsement). If an exempt organization were to send an e-mail message or messages urging the election of an individual to a public office, that would constitute a political campaign activity. An exempt organization may post a political campaign message on the portion of its website that is publicly accessible. That also would be a political campaign activity. The IRS Chief Counsel's office concluded that a public charity intervened in political campaigns where its website included candidate questionnaires and endorsements. This came about because the material on the site of an affiliated social welfare organization that permissibly contained these items[162] was integrated with the public charity's site. The charitable organization asserted that this was a "shared site" with the Web pages containing the political campaign material "separate" by reason of a previous reimbursement arrangement; the IRS nonetheless concluded that the website pages were "virtually indistinguishable."[163] An organization was held to not qualify as a public charity because it posted a statement in opposition to a political candidate on its website.[164]

---

[160] Ann. 2000-84, 2000-42 I.R.B. 385.
[161] Id.
[162] See § 23.6.
[163] Tech. Adv. Mem. 200908050.
[164] Priv. Ltr. Rul. 200928045.

Unrelated Business: Basic Rules

One of the most significant components of the law of tax-exempt organizations is the body of law that defines, and taxes the net income from, exempt organizations' unrelated trade or business activities. Exempt organizations are permitted to engage in some activities that are not related to their exempt purposes. This type of undertaking is termed an *unrelated business*. Nearly all of what exempt organizations otherwise do is considered *related business* activity.

§ 24.1 INTRODUCTION TO UNRELATED BUSINESS RULES

Taxation of the unrelated business income of tax-exempt organizations, a feature of the federal tax law since 1950, is predicated on the precept that this approach is a more effective and workable sanction for enforcement of this aspect of the law of exempt organizations than denial or revocation of exempt status because of unrelated business activity. The unrelated business law rests on two concepts: Activities that are unrelated to an exempt organization's purposes are to be segregated from related business activities, and the net income from unrelated business activities is taxed essentially in the same manner as the net income earned by for-profit organizations.

The primary objective of the unrelated business rules is to eliminate a source of unfair competition with for-profit businesses, by placing the unrelated business activities of tax-exempt organizations on the same tax basis as the nonexempt business endeavors with which they compete.[1] The House Ways and Means Committee report that accompanied the Revenue Act of 1950 contains the observation that the "problem at which the tax on unrelated business income is directed here is primarily that of unfair competition," in that exempt organizations can "use their profits tax-free to expand operations, while their competitors can expand only with the profits remaining after taxes."[2] The Senate Committee on Finance

---

[1] Reg. § 1.513-1(b).
[2] H.R. Rep. No. 81-2319, at 36–37 (1950). Also, S. Rep. No. 81-2375, at 28–29 (1950).

reaffirmed this position nearly three decades later when it noted that one "major purpose" of the unrelated business rules "is to make certain that an exempt organization does not commercially exploit its exempt status for the purpose of unfairly competing with taxpaying organizations."[3]

This rationale for the unrelated business rules has been subjected to revisionist theories, namely, the view that other objectives of this law are equally important. Thus, a federal appellate court observed that "although Congress enacted the [unrelated business income rules] to eliminate a perceived form of unfair competition, that aim existed as a corollary to the larger goals of producing revenue and achieving equity in the tax system."[4] Another appellate court, electing more reticence, stated that "while the equalization of competition between taxable and tax-exempt entities was a major goal of the unrelated business income tax, it was by no means that statute's sole objective."[5] At a minimum, however, elimination of this type of competition clearly was Congress's principal aim; the tax regulations proclaim that it was the federal legislature's "primary objective."[6]

Generally, unrelated business activities must be confined to something less than a substantial portion of a tax-exempt organization's overall activities.[7] This is a manifestation of the *primary purpose test*.[8] According to traditional analysis, if a substantial portion of an exempt organization's income is from unrelated sources, the organization cannot qualify for tax exemption.[9] The IRS may deny or revoke the exempt status of an organization where it regularly derives over one-half of its annual revenue from unrelated activities.[10]

Although there generally are no specific percentage limitations in this area,[11] it is common to measure substantiality and insubstantiality in terms of percentages of expenditures or time.[12] For example, a court barred an organization from achieving exempt status where the organization received about one-third of its revenue from an unrelated business.[13]

---

[3] S. Rep. No. 94-938, at 601 (1976).

[4] Louisiana Credit Union League v. United States, 693 F.2d 525, 540 (5th Cir. 1982).

[5] American Medical Ass'n v. United States, 887 F.2d 760, 772 (7th Cir. 1989).

[6] Reg. § 1.513-1(b). In the course of upholding the California tax on unrelated business taxable income against a claim that that state law was preempted by the Employee Retirement Income Security Act to the extent that the tax is imposed on the income of pension plan trusts, a federal court of appeals observed that the unrelated business laws "serve to even the playing field among tax-exempt organizations and their for-profit rivals. They accomplish this by ensuring that tax-exempt entities pay taxes on revenue unrelated to their tax-exempt purpose. That way, tax-exempt organizations do not receive an unfair advantage in the market based on an unrelated-tax-exempt purpose" (Hattem v. Schwarzenegger, 449 F.3d 423, 426 (2d Cir. 2006)).

[7] Rev. Rul. 66-221, 1966-2 C.B. 220 (holding that a volunteer fire department was tax-exempt, notwithstanding an incidental amount of unrelated business activities).

[8] See § 4.4.

[9] E.g., People's Educ. Camp Soc'y, Inc. v. Comm'r, 331 F.2d 923 (2d Cir. 1964), *cert. denied*, 379 U.S. 839 (1964); Indiana Retail Hardware Ass'n v. United States, 366 F.2d 998 (Ct. Cl. 1966); Rev. Rul. 69-220, 1969-1 C.B. 154.

[10] E.g., Gen. Couns. Mem. 39108.

[11] See, however, § 25.4(d).

[12] See § 4.5(c).

[13] Orange Cnty. Agric. Soc'y, Inc. v. Comm'r, 893 F.2d 647 (2d Cir. 1990), *aff'g* 55 T.C.M. 1602 (1988).

Still, this is not the approach always taken by the IRS or the courts. As the IRS framed the matter, there is no "quantitative limitation" on the amount of unrelated business in which a tax-exempt organization may engage.[14] Likewise, a court wrote that "[w]hether an activity [of an exempt organization] is substantial is a facts-and-circumstances inquiry not always dependent upon time or expenditure percentages."[15]

Yet there are countervailing principles. The IRS, from time to time, applies the *commensurate test*, which compares the extent of a tax-exempt organization's resources to its program efforts.[16] Pursuant to this test, an organization may derive a substantial portion of its revenue in the form of unrelated business income, yet nonetheless be exempt because it also expends a significant amount of time on exempt functions. Thus, in one instance, although a charitable organization derived 98 percent of its income from an unrelated business, it remained exempt because 41 percent of the organization's activities, as measured in terms of expenditure of time, constituted exempt programs.[17] Utilizing another approach, the IRS permitted an organization to remain exempt, even though two-thirds of its operations were unrelated businesses, inasmuch as the purpose for the conduct of these businesses was achievement of charitable purposes.[18] On that occasion, the IRS said that one way in which a business may be in furtherance of exempt purposes "is to raise money for the exempt purpose of the organization, notwithstanding that the actual trade or business activity may be taxable." The agency reiterated that the "proper focus is upon the purpose of [the organization's] activities and not upon the taxability of its activities."

In determining the nature of a primary purpose, all of the circumstances must be considered, including the size and extent of the trade or business and of the activities that are in furtherance of one or more exempt purposes.[19] For example, an organization that purchased and sold at retail products manufactured by blind individuals was held by a court to qualify as an exempt charitable organization because its activities resulted in employment of the blind, notwithstanding its receipt of net profits and its distribution of some of these profits to qualified workers.[20]

The unrelated business rules are applicable to nearly all categories of tax-exempt organizations.[21] These rules are inapplicable to governmental entities, other than colleges and universities that are agencies or instrumentalities of a government or political subdivision of a government, or that are owned or operated by a government or such political subdivision or by any agency or instrumentality of one or more governments or political subdivisions of them; the rules also apply to any corporation wholly owned by one or more of these colleges or universities.[22]

---

[14] Tech. Adv. Mem. 200021056.
[15] Nationalist Movement v. Comm'r, 102 T.C. 558, 589 (1994), *aff'd*, 37 F.3d 216 (5th Cir. 1994). Also, Manning Ass'n v. Comm'r, 93 T.C. 596 (1989); Church in Boston v. Comm'r, 71 T.C. 102 (1978).
[16] See § 4.7.
[17] Tech. Adv. Mem. 9711003.
[18] Tech. Adv. Mem. 200021056.
[19] Reg. § 1.501(c)(3)-1(e)(1).
[20] Industrial Aid for the Blind v. Comm'r, 73 T.C. 96 (1979).
[21] IRC § 511(a)(2)(A).
[22] IRC § 511(a)(2)(B).

These rules also do not apply to instrumentalities of the federal government,[23] certain religious and apostolic organizations,[24] farmers' cooperatives,[25] and ship-owners' protection and indemnity associations.[26] These rules are applicable to charitable trusts.[27]

The portion of a tax-exempt organization's gross income that is subject to the tax on unrelated business income is generally includable in the computation of unrelated business taxable income when three factors are present:[28] The income is from a *trade or business*,[29] the business is *regularly carried on* by the exempt organization,[30] and the conduct of the business is not *substantially related* to the performance by the organization of its exempt functions.[31] In addition, there are certain types of income and certain types of activities that are exempt from unrelated business income taxation.[32]

Over the years, considerable attention has been accorded the phenomenon of tax-exempt organizations that are considered to be operating in a commercial manner or unfairly competing with for-profit organizations.[33] Some of the activities that are under review as being ostensibly commercial or competitive, however, are those that are *related*, rather than *unrelated*, businesses.[34]

§ 24.2   DEFINITION OF *TRADE OR BUSINESS*

As noted, some or all of the gross income of a tax-exempt organization may be includable in the computation of unrelated business income where it is income from a *trade or business*.

(a)   General Principles

The statutory definition of the term *trade or business*, used for unrelated business law purposes, states that it includes "any activity which is carried on for the

---

[23] See § 19.1.

[24] See § 10.8.

[25] See § 19.12. The sweep of this definition reflects a much earlier observation by the Supreme Court that the word *business* is a "very comprehensive term and embraces everything about which a person can be employed" (Flint v. Stone Tracy Co., 220 U.S. 107, 171 (1911)).

[26] See § 19.13.

[27] IRC § 511(b)(2).

[28] IRC § 513(a).

[29] See § 24.2.

[30] See § 24.3.

[31] See § 24.4. Thus, the IRS ruled that income to be received by a private foundation on satisfaction of debts of legal fees earned by its founder, now deceased, will not be unrelated business income because the foundation will be a passive recipient of the income; the fee-generating business that was regularly carried on was conducted by the founder's law firm, not the foundation (Priv. Ltr. Rul. 201626004). In general, Reg. § 1.513-1(a).

[32] See §§ 25.1, 25.2.

[33] E.g., At Cost Services, Inc. v. Comm'r, 80 T.C.M. 573 (2000). See §§ 4.9, 24.2(c).

[34] E.g., Priv. Ltr. Rul. 200051049 (concerning the operation by exempt hospitals and universities of fitness centers that compete with for-profit health clubs).

production of income from the sale of goods or the performance of services."[35] This definition is sweeping and encompasses nearly every activity that a tax-exempt organization may undertake. Indeed, the federal tax law views an exempt organization as a cluster of businesses, with each discrete activity susceptible to evaluation independently from the others.[36]

The definition of the term *trade or business*, however, also embraces an activity that otherwise possesses the characteristics of a business as that term is defined by the federal income tax law in the business expense deduction setting.[37] This definition, then, is even more expansive than the statutory one, being informed by the considerable body of law as to the meaning of the word *business* that has accreted in the federal tax law generally.

There is a third element to consider in this regard, stemming from the view that, to constitute a business, an income-producing activity of a tax-exempt organization must have the general characteristics of a trade or business. Some courts of appeals have recognized that an exempt organization must carry out extensive business activities over a substantial period of time to be considered engaged in a trade or business.[38] In one case, a court held that the proceeds derived by an exempt organization from gambling operations were not taxable as unrelated business income, inasmuch as the organization's functions in this regard were considered insufficiently "extensive" to warrant treatment as a business.[39] In another instance, the receipt of payments by an exempt association pursuant to involvement in insurance plans was ruled to not constitute a business because the association's role was not extensive and did not possess the general characteristics of a trade or business.[40] This aspect of the analysis, however, is close to a separate test altogether, which is whether the business activities are regularly carried on.[41]

Where an activity carried on for profit constitutes an unrelated business, no part of the business may be excluded from classification as a business merely because it does not result in profit.[42]

(b) Requirement of Profit Motive

The most important element in the federal tax law as to whether an activity is a trade or business, for purposes of the business expense deduction (aside from the underlying statutory definition), is the presence of a *profit motive*. The courts have exported the profit objective standard into this aspect of the law of tax-exempt organizations.

The Supreme Court held that the principal test in this regard is that the "taxpayer's primary purpose for engaging in the activity must be for income or

---

[35] IRC § 513(c).

[36] See § 24.2(f).

[37] Reg. § 1.513-1(b). The business expense deduction is the subject of IRC § 162.

[38] E.g., in the tax-exempt organizations context, Professional Ins. Agents v. Comm'r, 726 F.2d 1097 (6th Cir. 1984). E.g., in the business expense deduction context, Zell v. Comm'r, 763 F.2d 1139 (10th Cir. 1985); McDowell v. Ribicoff, 292 F.2d 174 (3d Cir. 1961), *cert. denied*, 368 U.S. 919 (1961).

[39] Vigilant Hose Co. of Emmitsburg v. United States, 2001-2 U.S.T.C. ¶ 50,458 (D. Md. 2001).

[40] American Academy of Family Physicians v. United States, 91 F.3d 1155 (8th Cir. 1996).

[41] See § 24.3.

[42] IRC § 513(c).

profit."[43] In the tax-exempt organizations context, the Court said that the inquiry should be whether the activity "was entered into with the dominant hope and intent of realizing a profit."[44] An appellate court stated that the "existence of a genuine profit motive is the most important criterion for . . . a trade or business."[45]

Various federal courts of appeal have applied the profit motive element to ascertain whether an activity of a tax-exempt organization is a business for purposes of the unrelated business rules. For example, an appellate court employed an *objective profit motivation test* to ascertain whether an exempt organization's activity is a business. This court wrote that "there is no better objective measure of an organization's motive for conducting an activity than the ends it achieves."[46] Subsequently, this court held that an activity of an exempt organization was a business because it "received considerable financial benefits" from performance of the activity, which was found to be "persuasive evidence" of a business endeavor.[47] On this latter occasion, the court defined as a business the situation where a "nonprofit entity performs comprehensive and essential business services in return for a fixed fee."[48] Thereafter, this appellate court wrote simply that for an activity of a tax-exempt organization to be a business, it must be conducted with a "profit objective."[49] Another appellate court observed that an insurance company's payments to an exempt association were not taxable, in that "it does not matter whether the payments were brokerage fees, gratuities, to promote goodwill, or interest," since the association was not engaging in business activity for a profit.[50] Other courts of appeals have adopted this profit motive test.[51]

A court concluded, in the case of a tax-exempt labor union[52] that collected per capita taxes from unions affiliated with it, that, other than the services the union provided its members and affiliated unions in furtherance of its exempt purposes, the union "provide[d] no goods or services for a profit and therefore cannot be [engaged in] a trade or business."[53]

The IRS applies the profit motive test in this context. In one example, a tax-exempt health care provider sold a building to another provider organization; it was used to operate a skilled nursing and personal care home. The selling entity provided food service to the patients for about seven months, at a net loss; the IRS

---

[43] Comm'r v. Groetzinger, 480 U.S. 23, 35 (1987).

[44] United States v. American Bar Endowment, 477 U.S. 105, 110, n.1 (1986). The Court cited for this proposition the appellate court opinion styled Brannen v. Comm'r, 722 F.2d 695 (11th Cir. 1984).

[45] Professional Ins. Agents v. Comm'r, 726 F.2d 1097, 1102 (6th Cir. 1984).

[46] Carolinas Farm & Power Equipment Dealers Ass'n, Inc. v. United States, 699 F.2d 167, 170 (4th Cir. 1983).

[47] Steamship Trade Ass'n of Baltimore, Inc. v. Comm'r, 757 F.2d 1494, 1497 (4th Cir. 1985).

[48] *Id.* This latter statement, however, is a mischaracterization of the law. For an activity to be a business, there is no requirement that the endeavor be *comprehensive*, nor is there a requirement that the activity be *essential*. Also, the mode of payment is irrelevant; whether the payment is by fixed fee, commission, or some other standard has no bearing on whether the income-producing activity is a business.

[49] West Va. State Med. Ass'n v. Comm'r, 882 F.2d 123, 125 (4th Cir. 1989), *cert. denied*, 493 U.S. 1044 (1990).

[50] American Academy of Family Physicians v. United States, 91 F.3d 1155, 1159–60 (8th Cir. 1996).

[51] E.g., Louisiana Credit Union League v. United States, 693 F.2d 525 (5th Cir. 1982); Professional Ins. Agents v. Comm'r, 726 F.2d 1097 (6th Cir. 1984).

[52] See § 16.1.

[53] Laborers' Int'l Union of North America v. Comm'r, 82 T.C.M. 158, 160 (2001).

characterized the food service operation as merely an "accommodation" to the purchasing entity.[54]

On another occasion, the IRS concluded that, although the development of a housing project and sales of parcels of land was an unrelated business of an exempt planned community, the provision of water, sewer, and garbage services in conjunction with the project lacked a profit motive, so that the income received for the services was not taxable as unrelated business income.[55] The IRS ruled that a tax-exempt college or university is not engaged in an unrelated business when it enables charitable remainder trusts,[56] as to which it is trustee and remainder interest beneficiary, to participate in the investment return generated by the institution's endowment fund, inasmuch as the institution is not receiving any economic return by reason of the arrangement.[57] Likewise, the IRS held that the sharing of money, assets, and personnel among supported organizations and the supporting organization[58] did not amount to a form of business regularly carried on for the production of income.[59]

(c) Competition

The presence or absence of competition—fair or unfair—is not among the criteria applied in assessing whether an activity of a tax-exempt organization is an unrelated business. This is the case notwithstanding the fact that concern about competition between exempt and for-profit organizations is the principal reason for and underpinning of the unrelated business rules.[60]

Thus, an activity of a tax-exempt organization may be wholly noncompetitive with an activity of a for-profit organization and nonetheless be an unrelated business. For example, in an opinion finding that the operation of a bingo game by an exempt organization was an unrelated business, a court wrote that the "tax on unrelated business income is not limited to income earned by a trade or business that operates in competition with taxpaying entities."[61] Yet, in a case concerning an exempt labor union that collected per capita taxes from unions affiliated with it, a court concluded that the imposition of these taxes, which enabled the union to perform its exempt functions, "simply is not conducting a trade or business," in part because the union was not providing any services in competition with taxable entities.[62]

---

[54] Tech. Adv. Mem. 9719002.

[55] Tech. Adv. Mem. 200047049.

[56] See *Charitable Giving*, Chapter 12.

[57] E.g., Priv. Ltr. Rul. 200703037. A similar arrangement involved a religious organization and a charitable remainder trust of which it is the remainder interest beneficiary (Priv. Ltr. Rul. 201636042). These arrangements also do not give rise to unrelated business income because they entail transactions between related organizations (see § 24.5(k)).

[58] See § 12.3(c).

[59] Priv. Ltr. Rul. 201222040. Cf. § 24.3.

[60] See § 24.1, text accompanied by *supra* notes 1–6.

[61] Clarence LaBelle Post No. 217 v. United States, 580 F.2d 270, 272 (8th Cir. 1978). Also, Smith-Dodd Businessman's Ass'n, Inc. v. Comm'r, 65 T.C. 620 (1975); Rev. Rul. 59-330, 1959-2 C.B. 153.

[62] Laborers' Int'l Union of North America v. Comm'r, 82 T.C.M. 158, 160 (2001).

(d)   Commerciality

Where there is competition, a court may conclude that the activity of a tax-exempt organization is being conducted in a commercial manner[63] and thus is an unrelated business. For example, the operation of a television station by an exempt university was held to be an unrelated business because it was operated in a commercial manner; the station was an affiliate of a national television broadcasting company.[64]

Historically, the IRS has used the commerciality doctrine in assessing an organization's qualification for tax-exempt status; the doctrine was not used to ascertain the presence of an unrelated business. This approach is changing, however, with the IRS employing the doctrine in rationalizing that a business is an unrelated one. For example, the operation of an eating facility that helped attract visitors to a tax-exempt museum was held by the IRS to contribute importantly to the accomplishment of the museum's exempt purposes and thus constitute a related business.[65] Yet, subsequently, the IRS ruled that a tearoom operated by an exempt organization in conjunction with a consignment shop and a gift shop was a nonexempt function because of competition with commercial restaurants and the use of profit-making pricing formulas and advertising.[66] Indeed, on one occasion, the IRS ruled that an exempt organization was engaged in an unrelated business, determining that the business was unrelated by solely applying the commerciality doctrine.[67]

(e)   Charging of Fees

Many tax-exempt organizations charge fees for the services they provide; where the business generating this revenue is a related one, the receipts are characterized as *exempt function revenue*.[68] Universities, colleges, hospitals, museums, planetariums, orchestras, and like institutions generate exempt function revenue without adverse impact as to their exempt status.[69] Organizations such as medical clinics, homes for the aged, and blood banks impose charges for their services and are not subject to unrelated income taxation (or deprived of exemption) as a result.[70] Indeed, the IRS, in a ruling discussing the tax status of homes for the aged as charitable organizations, observed that the "operating funds [of these homes] are derived principally from fees charged for residence in the home."[71] Similarly, the IRS ruled that a nonprofit theater may charge admission for its performances and nonetheless qualify as an exempt charitable organization.[72] Other fee-based

---

[63] See § 4.9.

[64] Iowa State Univ. of Science & Technology v. United States, 500 F.2d 508 (Ct. Cl. 1974).

[65] Rev. Rul. 74-399, 1974-2 C.B. 172.

[66] Tech. Adv. Mem. 200021056.

[67] Priv. Ltr. Rul. 201814009.

[68] See, e.g., § 12.3(b)(iv).

[69] IRC § 170(b)(1)(A)(ii), (iii); Reg. § 1.501(c)(3)-1(d)(3)(ii), Example (4).

[70] E.g., Rev. Rul. 72-124, 1972-1 C.B. 145; Rev. Rul. 70-590, 1970-2 C.B. 116; Rev. Rul. 66-323, 1966-2 C.B. 216, *modified by* Rev. Rul. 78-145, 1978-1 C.B. 169.

[71] Rev. Rul. 72-124, 1972-1 C.B. 145.

[72] Rev. Rul. 73-45, 1973-1 C.B. 220.

exempt charitable entities include hospices,[73] organizations providing specially designed housing for the elderly,[74] and organizations providing housing for the disabled.[75] Moreover, for some types of publicly supported charities, exempt function revenue is regarded as support enhancing public charity status.[76] Several categories of exempt organizations, such as business associations, unions, social clubs, fraternal groups, and veterans' organizations, are dues-based entities.

Yet the receipt of fee-for-service revenue is repeatedly regarded by the IRS as evidence of the conduct of an unrelated business. In one instance, the IRS opposed tax exemption for nonprofit consumer credit counseling agencies. The IRS sought to deny these agencies exempt status on the ground that they charged a fee for certain services, even though the fee was nominal and waived in instances of economic hardship. This effort was rebuffed in court.[77] Thereafter, the IRS's Office of Chief Counsel advised that if the "activity [of consumer credit counseling] may be deemed to benefit the community as a whole, the fact that fees are charged for the organization's services will not detract from the exempt nature of the activity" and that the "presence of a fee is relevant only if it inhibits accomplishment of the desired result."[78] (Earlier, the Chief Counsel's office wrote that the fact that a charitable organization charges a fee for a good or service "will be relevant in very few cases," that the "only inquiry" should be whether the charges "significantly detract from the organization's charitable purposes," and that the cost issue is pertinent only where the activities involved are commercial in nature.)[79] At about the same time, the IRS ruled that an organization that is operated to provide legal services to indigents may charge, for each hour of legal assistance provided, a "nominal hourly fee determined by reference to the client's own hourly income."[80]

The IRS has become quite adamant, albeit inconsistent, on this point. Frequently, the agency will take the position that the charging of fees is evidence of substantial commercial activity or purpose,[81] thus precluding exemption as a charitable entity.[82] An organization was denied recognition of exemption as a charitable and educational entity because it charged "substantial fees,"[83] even though the federal tax law does not preclude exemption on that basis. A consumer care organization was denied recognition of exemption in part because of its "funding mechanism," cast by the IRS as "essentially a fee-for-service structure similar to the manner in which for-profit businesses charge their clients in proportion to the services they receive."[84] Yet the agency held that the sale of grantmaking services by a community foundation to charitable organizations in its community was a

---

[73] Rev. Rul. 79-17, 1979-1 C.B. 193.
[74] Rev. Rul. 79-18, 1979-1 C.B. 194.
[75] Rev. Rul. 79-19, 1979-1 C.B. 195.
[76] IRC § 509(a)(2). See § 12.3(b)(iv).
[77] Consumer Credit Counseling Service of Ala., Inc. v. United States, 78-2 U.S.T.C. ¶ 9660 (D.D.C. 1978).
[78] Gen. Couns. Mem. 38459.
[79] Gen. Couns. Mem. 37257.
[80] Rev. Rul. 78-428, 1978-2 C.B. 177.
[81] See § 4.9.
[82] E.g., Priv. Ltr. Rul. 201019033.
[83] Priv. Ltr. Rul. 201007060.
[84] Priv. Ltr. Rul. 200944053.

related business, notwithstanding the fact that the foundation charged a fee, based on staff hourly rates, for its services.[85]

There have been instances where the IRS determined that an organization is charitable in nature, and thus tax-exempt, because it provides services that are free to the recipients. This is, however, an independent basis for finding a charitable activity, usually invoked where the services, assistance, or benefits provided are not inherently charitable in nature. In one instance, a computer services sharing organization was ruled to be an exempt charitable organization because the IRS concluded that the services provided to the participating institutions of higher education were charitable as advancing education; no requirement was imposed that the services be provided without charge.[86] In another instance, a similar organization was found to be charitable even though the services it rendered to the participating educational institutions were regarded as nonexempt functions (being "administrative"); the distinguishing feature was that the organization received less than 15 percent of its financial support from the colleges and universities that received the services.[87]

(f)   Fragmentation Rule

The IRS has the authority to tax net income from an activity as unrelated business taxable income where the activity is an integral part of a cluster of activities that is in furtherance of a tax-exempt purpose. To ferret out unrelated business, the IRS regards an exempt organization as a bundle of activities and evaluates each of the activities in isolation to determine if one or more of them constitute a trade or business. This assessment process is known as *fragmentation*.

The *fragmentation rule* states that an "activity does not lose identity as trade or business merely because it is carried on within a larger aggregate of similar activities or within a larger complex of other endeavors which may, or may not, be related to the exempt purpose of the organization."[88] Thus, as noted, the IRS is empowered to fragment the operations of a tax-exempt organization, operated as an integrated whole, into its component parts in search of one or more unrelated businesses.

The fragmentation rule was fashioned to tax the net income derived by a tax-exempt organization from the soliciting, selling, and publishing of commercial advertising, even where the advertising is published in a publication of an exempt organization that contains editorial matter related to the exempt purposes of the organization.[89] That is, the advertising functions constitute an unrelated business even though the overall set of publishing activities amounts to one or more related businesses; the advertising is an integral part of the larger publication activity.[90]

Applications of the fragmentation rule abound. A tax-exempt blood bank, which sold blood plasma to commercial laboratories, was found by the IRS to not

---

[85] Priv. Ltr. Rul. 200832027.

[86] Rev. Rul. 74-614, 1974-2 C.B. 164, *amplified by* Rev. Rul. 81-29, 1981-1 C.B. 329.

[87] Rev. Rul. 71-529, 1971-2 C.B. 234.

[88] IRC § 513(c); Reg. § 1.513-1(b).

[89] The caption of IRC § 513(c), which also contains the basic definition of the term *business* (see § 24.2(a)), is "Advertising, etc." See § 24.5(h).

[90] Reg. § 1.512(a)-1(f).

be engaging in unrelated business when it sold by-product plasma and salvage plasma, because these plasmas were produced in the conduct of related businesses, but was ruled to be engaged in unrelated business when it sold plasma-pheresed plasma and plasma it purchased from other blood banks.[91] An exempt organization, whose primary purpose was to retain and stimulate commerce in the downtown area of a city where parking facilities were inadequate, was ruled to be engaged in related businesses when it operated a fringe parking lot and shuttle service to the downtown shops, and an unrelated business by conducting a park-and-shop plan.[92]

Likewise, the use of a tax-exempt university's golf course by its students and employees was ruled to not be unrelated businesses, while use of the course by alumni of the university and major donors to it was found to be unrelated businesses.[93] The fragmentation rule was applied to differentiate between related and unrelated travel tours conducted by an educational and religious organization.[94] An exempt charitable organization was held to be a dealer in certain parcels of real property and thus engaged in unrelated business with respect to those properties, even though the principal impetus for the acquisition and sale of real property by the organization was achievement of exempt purposes.[95] An exempt monastery whose members made and sold caskets was ruled to be engaged in a related business as long as the caskets were used in funeral services conducted by churches that were part of the religious denomination supporting the monastery, but was held to be conducting an unrelated business where the caskets were used in services conducted by other types of churches.[96] An exempt organization established to benefit deserving women, in part by enabling them to sell foodstuffs and handicrafts, was held to operate a consignment shop as a related business, but a retail gift shop and a small restaurant were found to be unrelated businesses.[97] The IRS ruled that the sale of grantmaking services by a community foundation[98] to charitable organizations, principally small private foundations in its community, was a related business, although sales of administrative and clerical services to them were held to be unrelated businesses.[99]

(g) Nonbusiness Activities

Not every activity of a tax-exempt organization that generates a financial return is a trade or business for purposes of the unrelated business rules. As the Supreme Court observed, the "narrow category of trade or business" is a "concept which falls far short of reaching every income or profit making activity."[100] Specifically in the exempt organizations context, an appellate court wrote that "there are

---

[91] Rev. Rul. 78-145, 1978-1 C.B. 169, *modifying* Rev. Rul. 66-323, 1966-2 C.B. 216.
[92] Rev. Rul. 79-31, 1979-1 C.B. 206.
[93] Tech. Adv. Mem. 9645004.
[94] Tech. Adv. Mem. 9702004. See § 24.5(j).
[95] Priv. Ltr. Rul. 200119061.
[96] Priv. Ltr. Rul. 200033049.
[97] Tech. Adv. Mem. 200021056.
[98] See § 12.3(b)(iii).
[99] Priv. Ltr. Rul. 200832027.
[100] Whipple v. Comm'r, 373 U.S. 193, 197, 201 (1963).

instances where some activities by some exempt organizations to earn income in a noncommercial manner will not amount to the conduct of a trade or business."[101]

The most obvious of the types of nonbusiness activities is the management by a tax-exempt organization of its own investment properties. Under the general rules concerning the business expense deduction defining *business activity*, the management of an investment portfolio composed wholly of the manager's own securities and other assets does not constitute the carrying on of a trade or business. The Supreme Court held that the mere derivation of income from securities and other assets and keeping of related records is not the operation of a business.[102] On that occasion, the Court sustained the government's position that "mere personal investment activities never constitute carrying on a trade or business."[103] Subsequently, the Court stated that "investing is not a trade or business."[104] Likewise, a court of appeals observed that the "mere management of investments . . . is insufficient to constitute the carrying on of a trade or business."[105]

This principle of law is applicable in the tax-exempt organizations context. For example, the IRS ruled that the receipt of income by an exempt employees' trust from installment notes purchased from the employer-settlor was not income from the operation of a business, noting that the trust "merely keeps the records and receives the periodic payments of principal and interest collected for it by the employer."[106] Likewise, the agency held that a reversion of funds from a qualified plan to a charitable organization did not "possess the characteristics" required for an activity to qualify as a business.[107] For a time, there was controversy over whether the practice, engaged in by some tax-exempt organizations, of lending securities to brokerage houses for compensation was an unrelated business; the IRS ultimately arrived at the view that securities lending is a form of "ordinary or routine investment activities" and thus is not a business.[108] A court held that certain investment activities conducted by a charitable organization were not businesses.[109]

Other similar activities do not rise to the level of a business. In one instance, a tax-exempt association of physicians was held to not be taxable on certain payments it annually received by reason of its sponsorship of group insurance plans that were available to its members and their employees, with the court writing that

---

[101] Steamship Trade Ass'n of Baltimore, Inc. v. Comm'r, 757 F.2d 1494, 1497 (4th Cir. 1985). Also, Adirondack League Club v. Comm'r, 458 F.2d 506 (2d Cir. 1972); Blake Constr. Co., Inc. v. United States, 572 F.2d 820 (Ct. Cl. 1978); Monfore v. United States, 77-2 U.S.T.C. ¶ 9528 (Ct. Cl. 1977); Oklahoma Cattlemen's Ass'n, Inc. v. United States, 310 F. Supp. 320 (W.D. Okla. 1969); McDowell v. Ribicoff, 292 F.2d 174 (3d Cir. 1969), *cert. denied*, 368 U.S. 919 (1961).

[102] Higgins v. Comm'r, 312 U.S. 212 (1941).

[103] *Id.* at 215.

[104] Whipple v. Comm'r, 373 U.S. 193, 202 (1963).

[105] Continental Trading, Inc. v. Comm'r, 265 F.2d 40, 43 (9th Cir. 1959), *cert. denied*, 361 U.S. 827 (1959). Also, Van Wart v. Comm'r, 295 U.S. 112 (1935); Deputy v. du Pont, 308 U.S. 488 (1940) (concurring opinion); Moller v. United States, 721 F.2d 810 (Fed. Cir. 1983); Comm'r v. Burnett, 118 F.2d 659 (5th Cir. 1941); Rev. Rul. 56-511, 1956-2 C.B. 170.

[106] Rev. Rul. 69-574, 1969-2 C.B. 130.

[107] Priv. Ltr. Rul. 200131034.

[108] Rev. Rul. 78-88, 1978-1 C.B. 163. This issue was subsequently further resolved by statute (see § 25.1(d)).

[109] Marion Found. v. Comm'r, 19 T.C.M. 99 (1960).

the payments "were neither brokerage fees nor other compensation for commercial services, but were the way the parties decided to acknowledge the . . . [association's] eventual claim to the excess reserves while . . . [the insurance company involved] was still holding and using the reserves."[110] In another case, an exempt dental society that sponsored a payment plan to finance dental care was held to not be taxable on refunds for income taxes and interest on amounts paid as excess reserve funds from a bank and as collections on defaulted notes.[111] A comparable position was taken by a court in concluding that an exempt organization did not engage in an unrelated business by making health insurance available to its members, in that the organization did not control the financial result of the insurance activities.[112]

In still another case, a court held that the proceeds derived by a tax-exempt organization from gambling operations were not taxable as unrelated business income, in that the economic activity did not constitute a business.[113] The operations involved the use of "tip jars," with the exempt organization's role confined to applying for gambling permits and purchasing the tip-jar tickets; the significant and substantial portion of the gambling activities was the sale of the tickets at participating taverns. The exempt organization's functions in this regard were considered insufficiently "extensive" to warrant treatment as a business.[114]

(h) Real Estate Development Activities

Tax-exempt organizations acquire real property, by purchase or contribution, for a variety of reasons, usually to advance exempt purposes or for investment. There may come a time when an exempt organization decides to maximize the value of its property by selling or developing it. A federal tax issue in this context is whether the organization is liquidating the investment, resulting in capital gain,[115] or selling property in the ordinary course of business, as a dealer, resulting in ordinary income that is often regarded as unrelated business income.[116]

The elements considered in this evaluation are many. One is the purpose for which the property was acquired. Others are the purpose for which it was held; the length of time it was held; the proximity of the sale to the purchase of the property; the activities of the exempt organization in improving and

---

[110] American Academy of Family Physicians v. United States, 91 F.3d 1155, 1159 (8th Cir. 1996). Nonetheless, the IRS remains of the view that these types of oversight and like activities with respect to insurance programs constitute unrelated business (e.g., Tech. Adv. Mem. 9612003, concerning a charitable organization, fostering competition in a sport (see § 11.2), that provided certain administrative services in connection with an insurance program covering its members for practices and other sports activities).

[111] San Antonio Dist. Dental Soc'y v. United States, 340 F. Supp. 11 (W.D. Tex. 1972).

[112] Carolinas Farm & Power Equip. Dealers Ass'n, Inc. v. United States, 541 F. Supp. 86 (E.D.N.C. 1982), aff'd, 699 F.2d 167 (4th Cir. 1983). Cf. § 24.5(e).

[113] Vigilant Hose Co. of Emmitsburg v. United States, 2001-2 U.S.T.C. ¶ 50,458 (D. Md. 2001).

[114] On occasion, as an alternative argument, the IRS will assert that the tax-exempt organization is involved in a joint venture with one or more for-profit entities and will attempt to tax net revenues received by the exempt organization on that basis (see § 31.1(c)). Cf. § 24.2(j).

[115] See § 25.1(j). E.g., Farley v. Comm'r, 7 T.C. 198 (1946); Rymer v. Comm'r, 52 T.C.M. 964 (1986).

[116] E.g., Brown v. Comm'r, 143 F.2d 468 (5th Cir. 1944); Rev. Rul. 55-449, 1955-2 C.B. 599.

disposing of the property; and the frequency, continuity, and size of the sales of the property.[117]

In the absence of use of the property for exempt functions, the factor of frequency of sales tends to be the most important of the criteria.[118] Even in this context, the activity may not be characterized as a business if the sales activity results from unanticipated, externally introduced factors that make impossible the continued preexisting use of the property. The IRS places emphasis on the presence of and the reasons for improvements on the land.

The standard followed in making these determinations, as to whether property is held primarily for sale in the ordinary course of business or is held for investment, is a primary purpose test. In this setting, the word *primary* has been interpreted to mean "of first importance" or "principally."[119] By this standard, the IRS ruled, ordinary income would not result unless a "sales purpose" is "dominant."[120]

In a typical instance, the IRS accorded capital gain treatment to the sale of real estate by a public charity, where the property had been acquired by bequest and held for a significant period, and where there was no advertising of the transaction.[121] Likewise, a public charity sold a parcel of unimproved real estate, preceded by improvements mandated by a city; the IRS ruled that the organization made a "passive and gradual" disposition of the property, with the sales proceeds not taxable as unrelated business income.[122] The IRS reached the same conclusion in connection with a "liquidity challenged" charitable trust that wanted to sell leased fee interests in three condominium properties; the underlying land had been acquired by gift nearly 100 years beforehand, and most of it had been maintained to produce rental income in support of the trust's exempt activities.[123] Thus, the ideal circumstances—for preservation of the capital gains exclusion—are acquisition of the real estate by gift or devise, a long holding period, little or no development of the property, little or no marketing of the availability of the property, and a valid reason for its sale.[124] Occasionally, land development and sales are activities in furtherance of an exempt purpose.[125]

Even if the primary purpose underlying the acquisition and holding of real property is advancement of exempt purposes, the IRS may apply the fragmentation

---

[117] E.g., Adam v. Comm'r, 60 T.C. 996 (1973). Also, Houston Endowment, Inc. v. United States, 606 F.2d 77 (5th Cir. 1979); Biedenharn Realty Co., Inc. v. United States, 526 F.2d 409 (5th Cir. 1976); Buono v. Comm'r, 74 T.C. 187 (1980).

[118] In part, this is due to the *regularly carried on* test (see § 24.3).

[119] Malat v. Riddell, 383 U.S. 569, 572 (1966).

[120] Priv. Ltr. Rul. 9316032. The IRS applied this concept in holding that a public charity's liquidation of its holding of rights in millions of intellectual property addresses would not be unrelated business income (Priv. Ltr. Rul. 201407022).

[121] *Id.*

[122] Priv. Ltr. Rul. 200619024.

[123] Priv. Ltr. Rul. 200728044.

[124] E.g., Priv. Ltr. Rul. 201049047. By contrast, the IRS concluded that the development and sale of parcels of real estate by an exempt organization were undertaken in a manner "similar to [that of] a for-profit residential land development company" (Tech. Adv. Mem. 200047049).

[125] E.g., Junaluska Assembly Housing, Inc. v. Comm'r, 86 T.C. 1114 (1986).

rule[126] in search of unrelated business. As the IRS stated the matter in one instance, a charitable organization "engaged in substantial regularly carried on unrelated trade [or] business as a component of its substantially related land purchase activity."[127]

(i) Occasional Sales

Another illustration of a transaction involving a tax-exempt organization that is not a business undertaking is the occasional sale of an item of property. For example, the IRS held that a sale of property by an exempt entity was not under circumstances where the property was held primarily for sale to customers in the ordinary course of business.[128] Similarly, a one-time transfer of assets by a group insurance trust affiliated with an exempt association to its supporting organization, triggered by the unexpected demutualization of an insurance company, was ruled by the IRS to not cause unrelated business income taxation.[129] By contrast, as noted, the subdivision, development, and sale of real estate parcels by an exempt organization was held by the IRS to be a business carried on in a manner similar to the activities of for-profit residential land development companies.[130] This aspect of the law, however, is closely analogous to the *regularly carried on* test.[131]

(j) Concept of *Investment Plus*

Activities that solely (or perhaps substantially) give rise to passive income, usually investment income, are generally not considered active businesses and thus not unrelated businesses.[132] A set of activities may, of course, entail more than passive investing and thus are considered one or more businesses. This concept has been dubbed by a court *investment plus*.

A federal court of appeals held that a private equity fund was engaged in a trade or business as that phrase is applied in the context of the multiemployer pension termination liability law.[133] This definition of the term *trade or business* may be applicable in the unrelated business setting, serving as a reminder that activities that go beyond conventional investing can be considered, for federal tax purposes, a business.

The appellate court concluded that at least one private equity fund, which operated a business (through layers of fund-related activities), was not merely a passive investor but was "sufficiently operated, managed, and was advantaged by its relationship with its portfolio company,"[134] a business that became bankrupt.

[126] See § 24.2(f).
[127] Priv. Ltr. Rul. 200119061.
[128] Priv. Ltr. Rul. 9316032.
[129] Priv. Ltr. Rul. 200328042.
[130] Tech. Adv. Mem. 200047049. See § 24.2(h).
[131] See § 24.3.
[132] See § 25.1(a). Also, private foundations are not concerned about the amount of holdings in an organization that is not functioning as a *business enterprise*, that is, an entity where 95 percent of its income is derived from passive sources (see § 12.4(c)).
[133] Sun Capital Partners III, LP v. New England Teamsters & Trucking Industry Pension Fund, 724 F.3d 129 (1st Cir. 2013), *cert. denied*, 571 U.S. 1244 (2014).
[134] *Id.*, 724 F.3d at 133.

The court characterized the funds' activities, engaged in once they acquired controlling interests in struggling companies (called "portfolio companies"), as "implement[ing] restructuring and operational plans, build[ing] management teams, becom[ing] intimately involved in company operations, and otherwise caus[ing] growth in the portfolio companies in which the [funds] invest."[135]

As the court observed, these funds "engaged in a particular type of investment approach, to be distinguished from mere stock holding or mutual fund investments."[136] The court found that "[n]umerous individuals with affiliations to various [funds'] entities . . . exerted substantial operational and managerial control over [the company], which at the time of the acquisition had 208 employees and continued as a [manufacturing] trade or business."[137]

In the unrelated business area, two Supreme Court opinions stand for the proposition that mere investing is not a trade or business.[138] The funds relied on these opinions in asserting that they were only investing, not engaging in business activities. But the court invoked an investment plus test. Under this test, more than investing with the objective of making a profit is needed to cause a set of activities to be a business. In this case, the appellate court held, the funds are "actively involved in the management and operation of the companies in which they invest."[139]

Thus, as noted, this opinion should be instructive to tax-exempt organizations with large endowment funds, private foundations, and the like, in that what may appear to be mere investing (a passive undertaking) can be more than that. Where there is a form of investment plus, the bundle of activities may, for tax law purposes, be considered an active business, which is to say an unrelated business.

§ 24.3 DEFINITION OF *REGULARLY CARRIED ON*

As noted, gross income of a tax-exempt organization may be includable in the computation of unrelated business income where the trade or business that produced the income is *regularly carried on* by the organization.

(a) General Principles

In determining whether a trade or business from which a particular amount of gross income is derived by a tax-exempt organization is *regularly carried on*,[140] the frequency and continuity with which the activities productive of the income are conducted and the manner in which they are pursued must be considered. This

---

[135] *Id.* at 134.

[136] *Id.*

[137] *Id.* at 136.

[138] Whipple v. Comm'r, 373 U.S. 193 (1963); Higgins v. Comm'r, 312 U.S. 212 (1941). See § 24.2(g).

[139] Sun Capital Partners III, LP v. New England Teamsters & Trucking Industry Pension Fund, 724 F.3d 129, 139 (1st Cir. 2013), *cert. denied*, 571 U.S. 1244 (2014). The concept of investment plus was subsequently applied by another court, which embellished the arrangement by referring to it as a "partnership-in-fact" (Sun Capital Partners III, LP v. New England Teamsters & Trucking Industry Pension Fund, 2016 WL 1253529 (D. Mass. 2016)).

[140] IRC § 512(a).

requirement is applied in light of the purpose of the unrelated business income rules, which is to place tax-exempt organization business activities on the same tax basis as the nonexempt business endeavors with which they compete.[141] Thus, for example, specific business activities of a tax-exempt organization will ordinarily be deemed to be *regularly carried on* if they manifest a frequency and continuity and are pursued in a manner generally similar to comparable commercial activities of nonexempt organizations.[142]

For example, the IRS ruled that a tax-exempt organization that published a yearbook for its membership was regularly engaging in unrelated business because, by means of a contract with a commercial firm, it was "engaging in an extensive campaign of advertising solicitation" and thus to be conducting "competitive and promotional efforts typical of commercial endeavors."[143] By contrast, an exempt health care organization that developed a series of computer programs concerning management and administration, and sold some of the programs to another health care entity, was ruled to have engaged in a "one-time only operation," so that the sales proceeds were not taxable as unrelated business income.[144] Similarly, a commission received by a public charity's chief executive, functioning as its agent, was held to be a "one-time, unique event," so that the brokerage activity that generated the income was not regularly carried on and the commission thus was not taxable as unrelated business income.[145] Also, the sale of software by an exempt church did not give rise to unrelated income because it was not a "continuous and consistent income-producing activity" inasmuch as the church "performed or carried on this activity once."[146] Likewise, the transfer of investment assets from an exempt organization to its supporting organization[147] is exempt from unrelated business taxation under this rule,[148] as is the infrequent sale of parcels of real estate.[149]

(b) Determining Regularity

Where income-producing activities are of a kind normally conducted by nonexempt organizations on a year-round basis, the conduct of the activities by a tax-exempt organization over a period of only a few weeks does not constitute the regular carrying on of a business.[150] For example, the operation of a sandwich

---

[141] See § 24.1. This is one of only two aspects of the unrelated business rules where the commerciality doctrine (see § 4.9) is expressly taken into account in the statute or tax regulations. The other aspect is the subject of §§ 24.9, 28.13.

[142] Reg. § 1.513-1(c)(1).

[143] Rev. Rul. 73-124, 1973-2 C.B. 190.

[144] Priv. Ltr. Rul. 7905129.

[145] Priv. Ltr. Rul. 201015037.

[146] Priv. Ltr. Rul. 201024069. Similarly, a sale of stock in a subsidiary to another newly created tax-exempt organization, as a "one-time, fortuitous event involving a unique asset," was held not to be an activity that was regularly carried on and therefore did not result in unrelated business income (Priv. Ltr. Rul. 202133014).

[147] See § 12.3(c).

[148] E.g., Priv. Ltr. Rul. 9425030.

[149] The gain from transactions of this nature may be protected from unrelated income taxation by the exclusion for capital gain (see § 25.1(j)).

[150] Reg. § 1.513-1(c)(2)(i).

stand by a hospital auxiliary organization for two weeks at a state fair is not the regular conduct of a business.[151] The conduct of year-round business activities for one day each week, such as the operation of a commercial parking lot once a week, however, constitutes the regular carrying on of a business.[152] On one occasion, the IRS stated that the conduct of a business for "approximately seven months out of a year would be considered to be regularly carried on by almost any measure."[153]

If income-producing activities are of a kind normally undertaken by non-exempt commercial organizations only on a seasonal basis, the conduct of the activities by a tax-exempt organization during a significant portion of the season ordinarily constitutes the regular conduct of a business.[154] For example, the operation of a track for horse racing for several weeks in a year is the regular conduct of a business where it is usual to carry on the business only during a particular season.[155] Likewise, where a distribution of greeting cards celebrating a holiday was deemed to be an unrelated business, the IRS measured regularity in terms of that holiday's season.[156]

In determining whether intermittently conducted activities are regularly carried on, the manner of conduct of the activities must, as noted, be compared with the manner in which commercial activities are normally pursued by nonexempt organizations.[157] In general, tax-exempt organization business activities that are engaged in only discontinuously or periodically will not be considered regularly carried on if they are conducted without the competitive and promotional efforts typical of commercial endeavors.[158] As an illustration, the publication of advertising in programs for sports events or music or drama performances will not ordinarily be deemed to be the regular carrying on of a business.[159] Conversely,[160] where the nonqualifying sales are not merely casual but are systematically and consistently promoted and carried on by the organization, they meet the requirement of regularity.

The functions of a service provider with which a tax-exempt organization has contracted may be attributed to the exempt organization for these purposes. This is likely to be the case where the contract denominates the service provider as an agent of the exempt organization, in that the activities of an agent are attributed to the principal for law analysis purposes. In such a circumstance, the time expended by the service provider is attributed to the exempt organization for purposes of determining regularity.[161]

[151] *Id.*
[152] S. Rep. No. 81-2375, at 106–07 (1950).
[153] Tech. Adv. Mem. 9822006.
[154] *Id.*
[155] *Id.* Also, Rev. Rul. 68-505, 1968-2 C.B. 248.
[156] Priv. Ltr. Rul. 8203134.
[157] Reg. § 1.513-1(c)(1), (2)(ii).
[158] Reg. § 1.513-1(c)(2)(ii). Also, Adam v. Comm'r, 60 T.C. 996 (1973).
[159] *Id.*
[160] *Id.* A leasing arrangement that was "one-time, completely fortuitous" was held to involve a business not regularly carried on (Museum of Flight Found. v. United States, 63 F. Supp. 2d 1257 (W.D. Wash. 1999)), whereas a lease of extended duration can constitute a business that is regularly carried on (Cooper Tire & Rubber Co. Employees' Retirement Fund v. Comm'r, 306 F.2d 20 (6th Cir. 1962)).
[161] Nat'l Collegiate Athletic Ass'n v. Comm'r, 92 T.C. 456 (1989), *aff'd*, 914 F.2d 1417 (10th Cir. 1990).

Noncompetition under a covenant not to compete, characterized as a "one-time agreement not to engage in certain activities," is not a taxable business inasmuch as the "activity" is not "continuous and regular."[162]

(c) Preparatory Time

The IRS occasionally asserts that the time expended by a tax-exempt organization in preparing for the conduct of an unrelated business must be taken into account in assessing whether the activity is regularly carried on, even if the event itself occurs only one or two days a year.[163] In one instance, an exempt organization sponsored a concert series occupying two weekends each year; the preparatory time (including ticket sales) per concert, which usually occupied up to six months, was held by the IRS to be the basis for holding that the concerts were unrelated businesses that were regularly carried on.[164]

This preparatory time argument, however, has been rejected in court.[165] In the principal case, a federal court of appeals held that the argument is inconsistent with the tax regulations, which do not mention the concept. This court referenced the example concerning operation of a sandwich stand at a state fair,[166] denigrating the thought that preparatory time should be taken into consideration, observing that the regulations "do not mention time spent in planning the activity, building the stand, or purchasing the alfalfa sprouts for the sandwiches."[167]

Application of the preparatory time rule does not, however, always lead to the conclusion by the IRS that the activity is an unrelated business. For example, an exempt organization engaged in substantial year-round promotional activities for an annual literacy event held during the weekends of two months; the IRS ruled that, inasmuch as the event was substantially related to the organization's exempt purpose, the revenue involved was not subject to the unrelated business income tax.[168]

§ 24.4 DEFINITION OF *SUBSTANTIALLY RELATED*

As noted, gross income of a tax-exempt organization may be includable in the computation of unrelated business income where it is income from a trade or business that is regularly carried on and that is not *substantially related* to the exempt purposes of the organization.[169] (The fact that the organization needs or uses the

---

[162] Ohio Farm Bureau Fed., Inc. v. Comm'r, 106 T.C. 222, 234 (1996). This opinion caused the IRS to issue Gen. Couns. Mem. 39891, *revoking* Gen. Couns. Mem. 39865 (which held that refraining from competition in this context was a business activity).

[163] E.g., Tech. Adv. Mem. 9147007.

[164] Tech. Adv. Mem. 9712001.

[165] E.g., Suffolk Cnty. Patrolmen's Benevolent Ass'n, Inc. v. Comm'r, 77 T.C. 1314 (1981).

[166] See text accompanied by *supra* note 151.

[167] Nat'l Collegiate Athletic Ass'n v. Comm'r, 914 F.2d 1417, 1423 (10th Cir. 1990). The IRS generally disagrees with these holdings (AOD No. 1991-015). The IRS acquiesced in the Suffolk Cnty. Ass'n case (see *supra* note 165) (AOD No. 1984-1249); this was not seen as inconsistent with the IRS's general position in this regard inasmuch as the preparatory time period in that case was "much shorter."

[168] Priv. Ltr. Rul. 201251019.

[169] IRC § 513(a); Reg. § 1.513-1(a).

funds for an exempt purpose does not make the underlying activity a related business.) Thus, it is necessary to examine the relationship between the business activity that generates the income in question—the activity, that is, of producing or distributing the goods or performing the services involved—and the accomplishment of the organization's exempt purposes.[170]

Where the primary purpose behind the conduct of the activity is to further an exempt purpose, the activity meets the substantially related test. According to the IRS, this exercise entails examination of the "nature, scope and motivation" for conducting the activity.[171] As an example, the IRS concluded that the construction and operation of a regulation-size 18-hole golf course, replete with warm-up area, snack bar, and pro shop, was substantially related to the purposes of an exempt school operated to rehabilitate court-referred juveniles, inasmuch as the course was utilized primarily as part of the school's vocational education and career development department.[172]

(a)   General Principles

A trade or business is *related* to tax-exempt purposes of a tax-exempt organization only where the conduct of the business activity has a causal relationship to the achievement of an exempt purpose (again, other than through the production of income); it is *substantially related* only if the causal relationship is a substantial one.[173] Thus, for the conduct of a business from which a particular amount of gross income is derived to be substantially related to exempt purposes, the production or distribution of the goods or the performance of the services from which the gross income is derived must contribute importantly to the accomplishment of these purposes.[174] A court wrote that resolution of the substantial relationship test requires an examination of the "relationship between the business activities which generate the particular income in question . . . and the accomplishment of the organization's exempt purposes."[175]

Certainly, gross income derived from charges for the performance of a tax-exempt function does not constitute gross income from the conduct of an unrelated business.[176] Thus, income is not taxed when it is generated by functions such as performances by students enrolled in an exempt school for training children in the performing arts, the conduct of refresher courses to improve the trade skills of members of a union, and the presentation of a trade show for exhibiting industry products by a trade association to stimulate demand for the products.[177] Also, dues paid by bona fide members of an exempt organization are forms of related income.[178]

---

[170] Reg. § 1.513-1(d)(1).

[171] Priv. Ltr. Rul. 200151061.

[172] *Id.*

[173] Reg. § 1.513-1(d)(2).

[174] *Id.*

[175] Louisiana Credit Union League v. United States, 693 F.2d 525, 534 (5th Cir. 1982).

[176] Reg. § 1.513-1(d)(4)(i).

[177] *Id.*

[178] E.g., Rev. Rul. 67-109, 1967-1 C.B. 136. Certain forms of associate-member dues are, however, taxable as unrelated business income (see §§ 24.5(e)(iii), 25.2(l)).

Whether activities productive of gross income contribute importantly to the accomplishment of an organization's exempt purpose depends in each case on the facts and circumstances involved.[179] A court observed that each of these instances requires a case-by-case identification of the exempt purpose involved and an analysis of how the activity contributed to the advancement of that purpose.[180] By reason of court opinions and IRS rulings, there have been many determinations over the years as to whether particular activities are related businesses[181] or unrelated businesses.[182]

In one instance, a tax-exempt charitable organization whose purpose was enabling needy women to support themselves operated three businesses. The IRS concluded that a consignment shop was a business that was substantially related to the achievement of this exempt purpose. The agency determined that there was a causal relationship between the operation of a gift shop and the exempt purpose but that the relationship was not substantial. A tearoom was classified as an unrelated business.[183]

In a series of technical advice memoranda, the IRS entered the ongoing fray over whether tax-exempt credit unions should retain their exempt status or lose it because of competition with commercial banks,[184] by holding that various insurance products and financial services provided by exempt credit unions to their members constituted unrelated businesses (and thus are not exempt functions but rather are businesses directly competing with for-profit banks). These unrelated products and services included the sale of accidental death and dismemberment, dental, cancer, guaranteed automobile protection, and credit disability insurance.[185] Thereafter, the agency's lawyers concluded that funds in the form of nonmember automated teller machine fees also are unrelated business income.[186] Nonetheless, thereafter, in a jury trial, a court concluded that an exempt credit union's sales of credit life and credit disability insurance, and guaranteed automobile protection insurance, were related businesses, in that they improved the social and economic life of the credit union's members.[187] Thereafter, a court held that revenue derived by an exempt credit union from the provision of credit life and credit disability insurance, and accidental death and dismemberment insurance, was not unrelated business income.[188] The IRS's ruling policy continued for a period, as illustrated by a determination that the sales of financial management services and of credit life and credit disability insurance were unrelated businesses; then the government's policy shifted.[189]

---

[179] Reg. § 1.513-1(d)(2).
[180] Hi-Plains Hosp. v. United States, 670 F.2d 528 (5th Cir. 1982). Also, Huron Clinic Found. v. United States, 212 F. Supp. 847 (D.S.D. 1962).
[181] See § 24.4(f).
[182] See § 24.4(g).
[183] Tech. Adv. Mem. 200021056.
[184] See § 19.7.
[185] Tech. Adv. Mem. 200709072. The sale of checks to members was held to be a related business.
[186] Tech. Adv. Mem. 200717031.
[187] Community First Credit Union v. United States, 2009-2 U.S.T.C. ¶ 50,496 (E.D. Wis. 2009).
[188] Bellco Credit Union v. United States, 2010-1 U.S.T.C. ¶ 50,343 (D. Col. 2010).
[189] Tech. Adv. Mem. 200931064. See § 24.5(g).

(b)   Size and Extent Test

In determining whether an activity contributes importantly to the accomplishment of a tax-exempt purpose, the *size and extent* of the activity must be considered in relation to the nature and extent of the exempt function that it purportedly serves.[190] Thus, where income is realized by an exempt organization from an activity that is generally related to the performance of its exempt functions, but the activity is conducted on a scale that is larger than reasonably necessary for performance of the functions, the gross income attributable to the portion of the activity that is in excess of the needs associated with exempt functions constitutes gross income from the conduct of an unrelated business.[191] This type of income is not derived from the production or distribution of goods or the performance of services that contribute importantly to the accomplishment of any exempt purpose of the organization.[192]

For example, the IRS ruled that an activity of a tax-exempt association, which was the supplying of companies (members and nonmembers) with employment injury histories on prospective employees, was an unrelated business, in that the activity went "well beyond" any promotion of efficient business practices.[193] Likewise, a retail grocery store operation, established to sell food in a poverty area at below-market prices and to provide job training for unemployed individuals, failed to qualify for exemption because the activity was conducted on a "much larger scale than reasonably necessary" for the training program.[194] Similarly, the provision of private-duty nurses to unrelated exempt organizations by an exempt health care entity, which provided nurses to patients of related organizations as a related business, was ruled to be an activity performed on a scale much larger than necessary for the achievement of exempt purposes.[195]

By contrast, a tax-exempt organization formed to provide a therapeutic program for emotionally disturbed adolescents was the subject of a ruling from the IRS that a retail grocery store operation, almost fully staffed by adolescents to secure their emotional rehabilitation, was not an unrelated business because it was operated on a scale no larger than reasonably necessary for its training and rehabilitation program.[196] A like finding was made in relation to the manufacture and marketing of toys, which was the means by which an exempt organization accomplished its charitable purpose of training unemployed and underemployed individuals.[197]

---

[190] Reg. § 1.513-1(d)(3). A court discussed the point that, in a search for unrelated activity, there should be an examination of the scale on which the activity is conducted (Hi-Plains Hosp. v. United States, 670 F.2d 528 (5th Cir. 1982)).

[191] Reg. § 1.513-1(d)(3).

[192] *Id.* In essence, the size and extent test is an application of the fragmentation rule (see § 24.2(f)).

[193] Rev. Rul. 73-386, 1973-2 C.B. 191.

[194] Rev. Rul. 73-127, 1973-1 C.B. 221. In a similar factual situation, a nonprofit organization that operated restaurants and health food stores in accordance with certain religious tenets was denied tax-exempt status as a charitable entity on the ground that it was primarily operated for commercial purposes (Living Faith, Inc. v. Comm'r, 60 T.C.M. 710 (1990), *aff'd*, 950 F.2d 365 (7th Cir. 1991)). See § 24.2(d).

[195] Priv. Ltr. Rul. 9535023.

[196] Rev. Rul. 76-94, 1976-1 C.B. 171.

[197] Rev. Rul. 73-128, 1973-1 C.B. 222.

(c)   Same State Rule

Ordinarily, gross income from the sale of items that result from the performance of tax-exempt functions does not constitute gross income from the conduct of an unrelated business if the item is sold in substantially the *same state* it is in on completion of the exempt functions.[198] Thus, in the case of a charitable organization engaged in a program of rehabilitation of disabled individuals, income from the sale of items made by them as part of their rehabilitation training was not gross income from the conduct of an unrelated business. The income in this instance was from the sale of products, the production of which contributed importantly to the accomplishment of the organization's exempt purposes, namely, rehabilitation of the disabled.[199] Conversely, if an item resulting from an exempt function is utilized or exploited in further business endeavors beyond that reasonably appropriate or necessary for disposition in the state it is in on completion of exempt functions, the gross income derived from these endeavors is from the conduct of unrelated business.[200]

As an illustration, a tax-exempt scientific organization maintained an experimental dairy herd; the sale of milk and cream produced in the ordinary course of the program is a related business, while the sale of food items made from the milk and cream, such as ice cream and pastries, generally is an unrelated business.[201] Similarly, an exempt organization that operated a salmon hatchery as an exempt function sold some of its harvested and unprocessed salmon stock to fish processors as a related business; however, sale by this organization of salmon nuggets (fish that was seasoned and breaded, formed into nugget shape, and deep-fried) was ruled by the IRS to be an unrelated business.[202]

(d)   Dual Use Rule

An asset or facility of a tax-exempt organization that is necessary for the conduct of exempt functions may also be utilized for nonexempt purposes. In these *dual use* instances, the mere fact of the use of the asset or facility in an exempt function does not, by itself, make the income from the nonexempt endeavor gross income from a related business. The test is whether the activities producing the income in question contribute importantly to the accomplishment of exempt purposes.[203] For example, an exempt museum shows educational films in its theater during its normal hours of operation in furtherance of its public education program; use of the theater for public entertainment in the evening hours when the museum is otherwise closed is an unrelated business.[204] Similarly, a mailing service operated by an exempt organization was ruled to be an unrelated trade or business even though the mailing equipment was also used for exempt purposes.[205]

---

[198] Reg. § 1.513-1(d)(4)(ii).
[199] *Id.*
[200] *Id.*
[201] *Id.*
[202] Priv. Ltr. Rul. 9320042.
[203] Reg. § 1.513-1(d)(4)(iii).
[204] *Id.*
[205] Rev. Rul. 68-550, 1968-2 C.B. 249.

Another illustration is the athletic facilities of a college or university, which, while used primarily for educational purposes, may also be made available for members of the faculty, other employees of the institution, and members of the public. Income derived from the use of the facilities by those who are not students or employees of the institution is likely to be unrelated business income.[206] For example, the IRS ruled that the operation by a tax-exempt school of a ski facility for the public was the conduct of an unrelated business, while use of the facility by the students of the school for recreational purposes and in its physical education program was a related activity.[207] Likewise, a college that made available its facilities and personnel to an individual not associated with the institution for the conduct of a summer tennis camp was ruled to be engaged in the conduct of an unrelated business.[208]

The provision of athletic or other activities by an educational institution to outsiders may be a tax-exempt function, inasmuch as the instruction of individuals on the subject of a sport can be an educational activity.[209] As illustrations, the IRS held that the following were exempt educational activities: the conduct of a summer hockey camp for youths by a college,[210] the conduct of four summer sports camps by a university,[211] and the operation of a summer sports camp by a university-affiliated athletic association.[212] Similarly, the IRS determined that a college may operate a professional repertory theater on its campus that is open to the public[213] and that a college may make its facilities available to outside organizations for the conduct of conferences[214]—both activities being in furtherance of exempt purposes.

This area of the law intertwines with the exclusion from unrelated income taxation for rent received by tax-exempt organizations.[215] For example, a college may lease its facilities to a professional sports team for the conduct of a summer camp and receive nontaxable lease income, as long as the college does not provide food or cleaning services to the team.[216] By contrast, where the institution provides services, such as cleaning, food, laundry, security, and grounds maintenance, the exclusion for rent is defeated.[217]

This dichotomy is reflected in an IRS analysis of a tax-exempt school that used its tennis facilities, operated during the academic year as a related activity, in the summer as a public tennis club operated by employees of the school. The IRS, in ruling that the operation of this club was an unrelated business not sheltered by the exclusion for rental income, observed that if the school had leased the facilities

---

[206] E.g., Tech. Adv. Mem. 9645004 (concerning dual use of a university's golf course).
[207] Rev. Rul. 78-98, 1978-1 C.B. 167.
[208] Rev. Rul. 76-402, 1976-2 C.B. 177.
[209] E.g., Rev. Rul. 77-365, 1977-2 C.B. 192. In general, see § 8.4.
[210] Priv. Ltr. Rul. 8024001.
[211] Priv. Ltr. Rul. 7908009.
[212] Priv. Ltr. Rul. 7826003.
[213] Priv. Ltr. Rul. 7840072.
[214] Priv. Ltr. Rul. 8020010.
[215] See § 25.1(h).
[216] Priv. Ltr. Rul. 8024001.
[217] Priv. Ltr. Rul. 7840072.

to an unrelated party without the provision of services for a fixed fee, the exclusion would have been available.[218] In a comparable ruling, the IRS determined that, when a university that leased its stadium to a professional sports team for several months of the year and provided the utilities, grounds maintenance, and dressing room, linen, and stadium security services, it was engaged in an unrelated business and was not entitled to the rental income exclusion.[219]

(e) Exploitation Rule

Activities carried on by a tax-exempt organization in the performance of exempt functions may generate goodwill or other intangibles that are capable of being exploited in commercial endeavors. Where an exempt organization exploits this type of intangible in commercial activities, the fact that the resultant income depended in part on the conduct of an exempt function of the organization does not make it gross income from a related business. In these cases, unless the activities contribute importantly to the accomplishment of an exempt purpose, the income that they produce is gross income from the conduct of an unrelated business.[220]

Thus, the rules with respect to taxation of advertising revenue received by tax-exempt organizations treat advertising as an exploitation of exempt publication activity.[221] As another illustration of this *exploitation rule*, where access to athletic facilities of an educational institution by students is covered by a general student fee, outside use may trigger the exploitation rule; if separate charges for use of the facilities are imposed on students, faculty, and outsiders, any unrelated income is a product of the dual use rule.[222]

(f) Related Business Activities

A myriad of determinations by the courts and the IRS conclude that activities conducted by tax-exempt organizations are related businesses, including these: operation of a furniture shop by an exempt halfway house;[223] sale of computer-based cataloging services to libraries maintained by for-profit organizations;[224] conduct of a product certification program as part of an effort to prevent trade abuses in the automobile racing business;[225] sale of products to encourage wildlife preservation;[226] operation of restaurants and cocktail lounges by social clubs and veterans' organizations for their members;[227] operation of a beauty shop and barber shop by a senior citizens' center;[228] conduct of an employment program providing training

---

[218] Rev. Rul. 80-297, 1980-2 C.B. 196.
[219] Rev. Rul. 80-298, 1980-2 C.B. 197. The dual use rule is, in some ways, an application of the fragmentation rule (see § 24.2(f)).
[220] Reg. § 1.513-1(d)(4)(iv).
[221] See § 24.5(h).
[222] E.g., Priv. Ltr. Rul. 7823062.
[223] Rev. Rul. 75-472, 1975-2 C.B. 208.
[224] Priv. Ltr. Rul. 7816061.
[225] Priv. Ltr. Rul. 7922001.
[226] Priv. Ltr. Rul. 8107006.
[227] Priv. Ltr. Rul. 8120006.
[228] Rev. Rul. 81-61, 1981-1 C.B. 355.

and work experience for the disabled;[229] loan organization and servicing activities;[230] facilitation of court proceedings by telephone;[231] provision of veterinary services by a tax-exempt humane society;[232] operation of a health club for individuals reflective of the community;[233] sale of computer software by an organization formed to make new scientific technology widely available for the benefit of the public;[234] sale of life memberships in a rural lodge used only for religious and educational purposes;[235] management of a project to restore historic property;[236] operation of golf courses to promote rehabilitation of disadvantaged youths;[237] performance of art conservation services for private collectors;[238] sale of posters and other promotional items carrying the organization's program message;[239] publication and sale by a shipowners' and ship operators' organization of common tariffs;[240] operation of a mobile cancer screening program;[241] licensing of an educational institution's curriculum to other colleges and universities;[242] cleaning up of spills of oil and oil products;[243] operation of a birthing center by a church;[244] sponsorship of gospel concerts by a broadcast ministry;[245] and operation by a charitable organization of a parking garage for the benefit of its member charities.[246]

Also: provision of services by a community development organization to a community development bank;[247] conduct by a public charity of market development and investment programs intended to promote investment in foreign countries;[248] operation of a center for regional economic development, and for educational and cultural activities;[249] sale of caskets by an exempt cemetery company;[250] conduct of national amateur athletic contests;[251] lease of the assets of a hospital district to a charitable organization that was to operate the hospital;[252] operation by a charitable organization of a mushroom growing and processing

---

[229] Priv. Ltr. Rul. 8349072.
[230] Priv. Ltr. Rul. 8349051.
[231] Priv. Ltr. Rul. 8351160.
[232] Tech. Adv. Mem. 8450006.
[233] Tech. Adv. Mem. 8505002.
[234] Priv. Ltr. Rul. 8518090.
[235] Priv. Ltr. Rul. 8523072.
[236] Priv. Ltr. Rul. 8628049.
[237] Priv. Ltr. Rul. 8626080.
[238] Priv. Ltr. Rul. 8606074.
[239] Priv. Ltr. Rul. 8633034.
[240] Priv. Ltr. Rul. 8709072.
[241] Priv. Ltr. Rul. 8749085.
[242] Priv. Ltr. Rul. 8824018.
[243] Priv. Ltr. Rul. 9242035.
[244] Priv. Ltr. Rul. 9252037.
[245] Priv. Ltr. Rul. 9325062.
[246] Priv. Ltr. Rul. 9401031.
[247] Priv. Ltr. Rul. 9539015.
[248] Priv. Ltr. Rul. 9651046.
[249] Priv. Ltr. Rul. 9810038.
[250] Priv. Ltr. Rul. 9814051.
[251] Priv. Ltr. Rul. 9821049.
[252] Priv. Ltr. Rul. 9825030.

facility predominantly to employ poor and drug-addicted individuals;[253] provision of credit enhancement services to developers of, and predevelopment and construction lending to projects that result in, affordable housing;[254] conduct by a library of a remote access project, fee-based services, research assistance for library users, business information collection, and library management training;[255] operation by a public charity of noncommercial television and radio stations;[256] sale of cat-related merchandise by an organization that educates the public about the ownership of cats;[257] use by a charitable organization of a vessel to provide ferry service for a limited time in the context of an emergency;[258] leasing of industrial buildings by a charitable organization to promote development of an economically distressed county;[259] renovation of a conference center and redevelopment of commercial rental property;[260] carrying out of student loan securitization transactions by a supporting organization for the benefit of the supported organization that undertakes a variety of exempt student loan programs;[261] delivery by an exempt business league of an online legal information service to its members;[262] the conduct of public outreach events by a charitable organization in cooperation with exempt and nonexempt sponsoring organizations;[263] the operation by a union of a pharmacy program for the benefit of its members;[264] the promotion of the enjoyment of and involvement in a sports game;[265] and the undertaking of stream mitigation activities by charity managing a nature preserve.[266]

Private letter rulings from the IRS provide additional illustrations of related business activity.[267]

(g) Unrelated Business Activities

Many determinations by the courts and the IRS conclude that activities conducted by tax-exempt organizations are unrelated businesses, including these: operation of dining facilities for the public by exempt social clubs and veterans' organizations;[268] sale of membership lists to commercial companies by educational organizations;[269] provision of pet boarding and grooming services to the public by an

[253] Priv. Ltr. Rul. 199920041.
[254] Priv. Ltr. Rul. 199929049.
[255] Priv. Ltr. Rul. 199945062.
[256] Priv. Ltr. Rul. 200151047.
[257] Priv. Ltr. Rul. 200126033.
[258] Priv. Ltr. Rul. 200204051 (time limit extended by Priv. Ltr. Rul. 200301048).
[259] Priv. Ltr. Rul. 200213027.
[260] Priv. Ltr. Rul. 200225044.
[261] Priv. Ltr. Rul. 200345041.
[262] Priv. Ltr. Rul. 200506025.
[263] Priv. Ltr. Rul. 200733030.
[264] Priv. Ltr. Rul. 201222043.
[265] Priv. Ltr. Rul. 201406020.
[266] Priv. Ltr. Rul. 201408031.
[267] E.g., Priv. Ltr. Rul. 8640007.
[268] Rev. Rul. 68-46, 1968-1 C.B. 260.
[269] Rev. Rul. 72-431, 1972-2 C.B. 141.

animal cruelty prevention organization;[270] carrying on of commercially sponsored research, where publication of the research is withheld or delayed significantly beyond the time reasonably necessary to establish ownership rights;[271] presentation of commercial programs by an exempt broadcasting station;[272] operation of a miniature golf course in a commercial manner, by an organization working to provide for the welfare of youths;[273] management of health and welfare plans by a business league for a fee;[274] sale of heavy-duty appliances to senior citizens by a senior citizens' center;[275] and provision of veterinary services for a fee by an animal cruelty prevention society.[276]

Also: operation of a commuting program by a labor union for its members;[277] sale of work uniforms by a union;[278] sale of a computer-based information retrieval and message service provided by a for-profit business;[279] sale of information about real estate used to prepare market evaluations and house appraisals;[280] provision of arbitration, mediation, and other alternative dispute resolution services for the benefit of consumers;[281] sale of herbs and herb products by an exempt scientific research organization to private practitioners and the public;[282] operation by a low-income housing corporation of a temporary storage business open to the public;[283] storage by an agricultural organization of trailers, campers, motor homes, boats, and automobiles;[284] use by the public of a golf course maintained by an exempt planned community;[285] and sale of life insurance policies by an exempt fraternal beneficiary society to the nonmember widows of deceased insured members within one year following the member's death where the widows can name as a beneficiary someone other than a dependent of a member.[286]

Private letter rulings from the IRS provide additional illustrations of unrelated business activity.[287]

---

[270] Rev. Rul. 73-587, 1973-2 C.B. 192.

[271] Rev. Rul. 76-296, 1976-2 C.B. 141.

[272] Rev. Rul. 78-385, 1978-2 C.B. 174.

[273] Rev. Rul. 79-361, 1979-2 C.B. 237.

[274] Rev. Rul. 66-151, 1966-1 C.B. 152. Also, Cooper Tire & Rubber Co. Employees' Retirement Fund v. Comm'r, 306 F.2d 20 (6th Cir. 1962); Rev. Rul. 69-633, 1969-2 C.B. 121; Rev. Rul. 69-69, 1969-1 C.B. 159; Rev. Rul. 68-505, 1968-2 C.B. 248; Rev. Rul. 68-267, 1968-1 C.B. 284; Duluth Clinic Found. v. United States, 67-1 U.S.T.C. ¶ 9226 (D. Minn. 1967); Rev. Rul. 66-47, 1966-1 C.B. 149; Rev. Rul. 62-191, 1962-2 C.B. 146; Rev. Rul. 60-228, 1960-1 C.B. 200; Rev. Rul. 60-86, 1960-1 C.B. 198; Rev. Rul. 58-482, 1958-2 C.B. 273; Rev. Rul. 57-466, 1957-2 C.B. 311; Rev. Rul. 57-313, 1957-2 C.B. 316; Rev. Rul. 55-449, 1955-2 C.B. 599.

[275] Rev. Rul. 81-62, 1981-1 C.B. 355.

[276] Priv. Ltr. Rul. 8303001.

[277] Tech. Adv. Mem. 8226019.

[278] Tech. Adv. Mem. 8437014.

[279] Priv. Ltr. Rul. 8814004.

[280] Priv. Ltr. Rul. 9043001.

[281] Priv. Ltr. Rul. 9145002.

[282] Tech. Adv. Mem. 9550001.

[283] Tech. Adv. Mem. 9821067.

[284] Tech. Adv. Mem. 9822006.

[285] Tech. Adv. Mem. 200047049.

[286] Tech. Adv. Mem. 201320023.

[287] E.g., Priv. Ltr. Rul. 9128003.

Occasionally, a situation will arise where monies are paid to an agent of a tax-exempt organization, who in turn pays the monies over to the organization, with the monies taxable as unrelated business income. This situation occurs, for example, in connection with an exempt religious order, which requires its members to provide services for a component of the supervising church and to turn over their remuneration to the order under a vow of poverty. Under these circumstances, the payments for services are income to the order and not to the member.[288] Where the individual is not acting as agent for the order and is performing services (as an employee) of the type ordinarily required by members of the religious order, however, the income is to the individual, and the unrelated income tax is avoided, because the monies are received by the order as charitable contributions.

§ 24.5 CONTEMPORARY APPLICATIONS OF UNRELATED BUSINESS RULES

Myriad activities undertaken by various types of tax-exempt organizations provide contemporary applications of the unrelated business income rules.

(a) Educational Institutions

Tax-exempt colleges, universities, and schools[289] have as their principal function the education of their students; consequently, income generated by the conduct of this related activity in the form of tuition, fees, assessments, and food service revenue is not taxable.[290] Another major exempt function conducted by these institutions is research; this type of activity is not normally taxed, either because it is inherently an exempt function or because it is sheltered from tax by statute.[291] Other exempt functions of these institutions are sports programs,[292] operation of bookstores,[293] operation of a university press,[294] publication of scholarly works by

---

[288] Rev. Rul. 76-323, 1976-2 C.B. 18, *clarified by* Rev. Rul. 77-290, 1977-2 C.B. 26. Also, Rev. Rul. 77-436, 1977-2 C.B. 25; Rev. Rul. 68-123, 1968-1 C.B. 35.

[289] These are essentially institutions referenced in IRC § 170(b)(1)(A)(ii). See § 12.3(a).

[290] When an institution of higher education receives a distribution from a qualified tuition plan (see § 19.19) of proceeds reflecting a "tuition certificate" in consideration for the provision of educational services to a qualified beneficiary, the proceeds constitute revenue from a related business (Priv. Ltr. Rul. 200313024).

[291] See §§ 9.2, 25.1(l).

[292] H.R. Rep. No. 81-2319, at 37, 109 (1950); S. Rep. No. 81-2375, at 29, 107 (1950). Broadcasting revenues generated by these sports events are not taxable (Tech. Adv. Mem. 7851004). In general, attendance at exempt educational institutions' sports events "enhances student interest in education generally and in the institution because such interest is whetted by exposure to the school's athletic activities" (Priv. Ltr. Rul. 7930043).

[293] Squire v. Students Book Corp., 191 F.2d 1018 (9th Cir. 1951); Rev. Rul. 58-194, 1958-1 C.B. 240. Sales of many items in these bookstores that are not inherently educational (such as sundries and health and beauty aids) are rendered nontaxable by virtue of the convenience doctrine (see § 25.2(b)). This doctrine does not, however, shelter the sales of items having a useful life of more than one year (Gen. Couns. Mem. 35811), such as appliances (e.g., Priv. Ltr. Rul. 8025222).

[294] S. Rep. No. 81-2375, at 107 (1950).

their faculty and students,[295] sale of handicraft articles (in the case of an exempt vocational school),[296] operation of a health and physical fitness center,[297] and operation of a farm (in the case of an exempt agricultural college).[298] By contrast, an activity such as the manufacture and sale of automobile tires by an exempt college is almost certain to be an unrelated business, even if students performed minor clerical or bookkeeping functions as part of their educational program.[299]

Provision by a tax-exempt educational institution of campus housing and related services to its students, such as in dormitories, is a substantially related business.[300] It is not clear whether the provision of housing by an exempt educational institution to its faculty members is a related or an unrelated business.[301] Otherwise, revenue generated from the renting of rooms by an educational institution to individuals other than its students is unrelated business income; this includes rentals to potential students, family members of potential students, guest speakers, performers, and guests of nonaffiliated nonprofit organizations in the institution's immediate geographic area who are speakers or performers at the institution.[302]

Educational organizations can engage in activities that are exempt functions in that they facilitate or otherwise support the accomplishment of the institutions' educational purposes and major functions, such as student housing. Thus, a public charity that constructed, owned, and leased a college's student housing project was ruled to be engaged in related business activities (that is, operated to advance education).[303, 304] Likewise, a public charity was held to be engaging in related business activities when it commenced establishment of student housing facilities in college communities, with emphasis on housing for low-income students.[305]

As to the sports programs of tax-exempt educational institutions, the IRS ruled that an exempt organization that sponsored a postseason all-star college football game for the benefit of a state university did not jeopardize its exempt status because of, nor realize unrelated income from the sale of, television broadcast rights of the games since broadcasting of the games "contributes importantly" to the accomplishment of its exempt purposes;[306] that payments received by a state university for the sale of radio and television broadcasting rights to its basketball and football games were not unrelated business income because carrying on the sporting events was substantially related to the university's exempt purposes;[307] that income received by an exempt organization that promoted professional automobile

---

[295] Priv. Ltr. Rul. 9036025.
[296] Rev. Rul. 68-581, 1968-2 C.B. 250.
[297] Priv. Ltr. Rul. 9732032.
[298] S. Rep. No. 81-2375, at 107 (1950).
[299] Id.
[300] Id. at 29.
[301] Priv. Ltr. Rul. 201106019, *revoking in part and modifying in part* Priv. Ltr. Rul. 200625035.
[302] Id.
[303] See § 7.8.
[304] Priv. Ltr. Rul. 200249014.
[305] Priv. Ltr. Rul. 200304036.
[306] Priv. Ltr. Rul. 7948113 (which also held that the proceeds from admissions to the game, sales of the program of the game, and sales of advertising in the program were not taxable as unrelated income).
[307] Priv. Ltr. Rul. 7930043.

racing from the sale of television broadcast rights to the races it sanctioned did not constitute unrelated income because the television coverage effectively popularized automobile racing;[308] that income derived from the sale by an exempt organization that sponsored and sanctioned amateur athletics of television rights to broadcast its athletic events was not unrelated income because the television medium was used to disseminate its goals and purposes to the public;[309] that an exempt organization promoting interest in a particular sport that sold television rights to championship golf tournaments that it sponsored did not incur unrelated income because the grant of the rights was directly related to its exempt purposes;[310] that the income received by an exempt amateur sports organization for the licensing of television broadcasting rights was not unrelated income because the broadcasting of the sports events was substantially related to the organization's exempt purpose of promoting international goodwill;[311] and that payments to be received from the sale of radio and television broadcasting rights to an athletic event were not items of unrelated income because the promotion of the event (the organization's exempt purpose) was furthered by the broadcasting of it.[312]

The IRS issued a ruling holding that the sale of exclusive television and radio broadcasting rights to athletic events to an independent producer by a tax-exempt national governing body for amateur athletics was not unrelated business because the "broadcasting of the organization's sponsored, supervised, and regulated athletic events promotes the various amateur sports, fosters widespread public interest in the benefits of its nationwide amateur athletic program, and encourages public participation," and, therefore, the sale of the broadcasting rights and the broadcasting of the events was an exempt function.[313] The IRS issued a similar ruling with respect to the sale of broadcasting rights to a national radio and television network by an organization created by a regional collegiate athletic conference composed of exempt universities to hold an annual athletic event.[314]

The IRS asserted that the payment by a business of a sponsorship fee to a college, university, or bowl association in connection with the telecasting or radio broadcasting of an athletic event was unrelated business income because the package of "valuable services" received by the business was not substantially related to exempt purposes and amounted to advertising services.[315] This matter was generally resolved by the enactment of legislation concerning the *qualified sponsorship payment*.[316]

A tax-exempt educational institution may provide athletic facilities, dormitories, and other components of the campus to persons other than its students, such as for seminars or the training of professional athletes. The income derived from the provision of the facilities in these circumstances is likely to be regarded by

[308] Priv. Ltr. Rul. 7922001.
[309] Priv. Ltr. Rul. 7851003.
[310] Priv. Ltr. Rul. 7845029.
[311] Priv. Ltr. Rul. 8303078.
[312] Priv. Ltr. Rul. 7919053.
[313] Rev. Rul. 80-295, 1980-2 C.B. 194.
[314] Rev. Rul. 80-296, 1980-2 C.B. 195.
[315] Tech. Adv. Mem. 9147007.
[316] See § 24.6. The taxation of advertising revenue is the subject of § 24.5(h).

the IRS as unrelated business income where the institution is providing collateral services such as meals or maintenance; a mere leasing of facilities would likely generate passive rental income excluded from taxation.[317] The provision of dormitory space may be an activity that is substantially related to an exempt purpose, however, as the IRS ruled in an instance of rental of dormitory rooms primarily to individuals under age 25 by an exempt organization whose purpose was to provide for the welfare of young people.[318]

(b) Health Care Organizations

Hospitals and other health care providers[319] have as their principal business the promotion of health; income generated by this related activity in the form of revenue from patients (whether by means of Medicare, Medicaid, insurance, or private pay) is not taxable.[320] Other organizations operating in the health care context have varieties of related businesses.

(i) Various Related Businesses. Tax-exempt hospitals operate many businesses that are necessary to their exempt function. Thus, an exempt hospital may operate a gift shop, which is patronized by patients, visitors making purchases for patients, and its employees, without incurring the unrelated business income tax.[321] The IRS observed: "By providing a facility for the purchase of merchandise and services to improve the physical comfort and mental well-being of its patients, the hospital is carrying on an activity that encourages their recovery and therefore contributes importantly to its exempt purposes."[322] The same rationale is extended to the hospital's operation of a cafeteria and coffee shop primarily for its employees and medical staff,[323] its operation of a parking lot for its patients and visitors,[324] and its operation of a guest accommodation facility.[325] Other related businesses conducted by exempt hospitals include the sale of hearing aids as an integral part of the hospital's provision of various rehabilitation services,[326] providing physicians and facilities to read and diagnose electrocardiogram tests,[327] providing staffing services to hospitals and nursing homes,[328] and operation of outpatient clinics.[329]

---

[317] See § 25.1(h).

[318] Rev. Rul. 76-33, 1976-1 C.B. 169.

[319] These are essentially institutions referenced in IRC § 170(b)(1)(A)(iii). See § 12.3(a).

[320] S. Rep. No. 81-2375, at 107 (1950).

[321] Rev. Rul. 69-267, 1969-1 C.B. 160.

[322] *Id.*

[323] Rev. Rul. 69-268, 1969-1 C.B. 160.

[324] Rev. Rul. 69-269, 1969-1 C.B. 160. Also, Ellis Hosp. v. Fredette, 279 N.Y.S. 925 (N.Y. 1967); Rev. Rul. 81-29, 1981-1 C.B. 329.

[325] Priv. Ltr. Rul. 9404029. In holding that the operation of a motel by a supporting organization of a university's medical center (including a hospital), for the benefit of patients and their relatives and friends, was a related business, the IRS observed that "[p]roviding a temporary living facility for patients and their friends or family members . . . advances one of the purposes of the hospital which is to provide health care for members of the community" (Tech. Adv. Mem. 9847002).

[326] Rev. Rul. 78-435, 1978-2 C.B. 181.

[327] Priv. Ltr. Rul. 8004011.

[328] Tech. Adv. Mem. 9405004.

[329] Priv. Ltr. Rul. 200211051.

The *convenience doctrine*—applicable with respect to businesses that are conducted for the benefit of patients—is of considerable import in the health care setting.[330] The IRS defined the term *patient* of a health care provider.[331]

A hospital may be able to develop real estate by constructing condominium residences to be used as short-term living quarters by its patients, as a related business.[332] The provision of ancillary health care services by charitable health care providers by means of a health maintenance organization (an exempt social welfare entity),[333] with income in the form of capitated payments for the services of employee-physicians and physicians who are independent contractors, was ruled to be a related business.[334]

(ii) Sales of Pharmaceuticals.   The sale of pharmaceutical supplies by a tax-exempt hospital to private patients of physicians who have offices in a medical building owned by the hospital is considered by the IRS to constitute the conduct of an unrelated business.[335] The IRS also outlined the circumstances in which an exempt hospital derives unrelated business income from the sale of pharmaceutical supplies to the general public.[336] By contrast, the sale of pharmaceutical supplies by a hospital pharmacy to its patients is not the conduct of an unrelated trade or business.

The case law on this point is uneven. A federal court of appeals concluded that the sale of pharmaceuticals by an exempt hospital to the public was an unrelated business, in part because of the competition with commercial pharmacies.[337] By contrast, another appellate court held that sales of this nature were not unrelated business, because the activity attracted and held physicians in a community that previously lacked medical services.[338]

The IRS ruled that the operation by a public charity of a national Internet-based specialty pharmacy that sells prescription pharmaceuticals, durable medical equipment, and nonprescription vitamins and other supplements, all pertaining to a disease, is a substantially related business.[339]

(iii) Testing Services.   It is the view of the IRS that a tax-exempt hospital's performance of diagnostic laboratory testing, otherwise available in the community, on specimens from private office patients of the hospital's staff physicians generally constitutes an unrelated business.[340]

Nonetheless, the IRS noted that there may exist "unique circumstances" that cause the testing to be related activities, such as emergency laboratory diagnosis

---

[330] See § 25.2(b).

[331] Rev. Rul. 68-376, 1968-2 C.B. 246.

[332] Priv. Ltr. Rul. 8427105.

[333] See Chapter 13.

[334] Priv. Ltr. Rul. 9837031.

[335] Rev. Rul. 68-375, 1968-2 C.B. 245. Cf. Rev. Rul. 69-463, 1969-2 C.B. 131.

[336] Rev. Rul. 68-374, 1968-2 C.B. 242.

[337] Carle Found. v. United States, 611 F.2d 1192 (7th Cir. 1979), *cert. denied*, 449 U.S. 824 (1980).

[338] Hi-Plains Hosp. v. United States, 670 F.2d 528 (5th Cir. 1982), *rev'g and remanding* 81-1 U.S.T.C. ¶ 9214 (N.D. Tex. 1981).

[339] Priv. Ltr. Rul. 200723030.

[340] Rev. Rul. 85-110, 1985-2 CB. 166.

of blood samples from nonpatient drug overdose or poisoning victims in order to identify specific toxic agents, where referral of these specimens to other locations would be detrimental to the health of the victims, or in situations where other laboratories are not available within a reasonable distance from the area served by the hospital or are clearly unable or inadequate to conduct the needed tests.[341] Thus, the IRS ruled that laboratory testing services provided by an exempt university's dental school were related activities because a unique type of diagnostic dental service and testing was provided; there were no commercial laboratories that provided a comparable service.[342] Likewise, the performance by an exempt hospital of laboratory testing services with respect to patients of private-practice physicians was held to be the conduct of a related business, inasmuch as the testing took place in the hospital's rural area where alternative testing services were not available.[343]

A court held that income received by a tax-exempt teaching and research hospital for the performance of pathological diagnostic tests on samples submitted by physicians associated with the hospital was not unrelated business taxable income.[344] The court found that the performance and interpretation of these outside pathology tests by the hospital's pathology department were substantially related to the performance by the hospital of its exempt functions because the tests contributed importantly to the teaching functions of the hospital. Further, the court concluded that the testing was a related activity because it increased the doctors' confidence in the quality of the work performed by the pathology department and it was convenient in the event of surgery, in that the pathologist who interpreted the test could interpret the biopsy.[345]

From time to time, the IRS rules that analysis and testing activities conducted by hospitals and other health care entities in laboratories are the conduct of exempt functions.[346]

(iv) Fitness Centers. Fitness centers operated as programs of tax-exempt hospitals generally are related businesses. In this setting, the IRS looks to the scope of the group of individuals being served and the center's fee structure. If the fees for use of a fitness center are sufficiently high so as to limit use of the center's facilities to a narrow segment of the community, the center's operation will be a nonexempt one—an unrelated business in the nature of a commercial health club.[347] By contrast, where the fitness center provides a benefit for the general community served by the hospital (which usually is the case), operation of the center is an exempt function—a related business. Thus, in one instance, the IRS concluded that a fitness center was an exempt function because its "operations promote health in a manner which is collateral to the providing of recreational facilities which advances the well-being and happiness of the community in general."[348] Similarly, a fitness

[341] *Id.* at 168.

[342] Priv. Ltr. Rul. 9739043.

[343] Tech. Adv. Mem. 201428030.

[344] St. Luke's Hosp. of Kansas City v. United States, 494 F. Supp. 85 (W.D. Mo. 1980). The IRS agreed to follow this aspect of the decision (Rev. Rul. 85-109, 1985-2 C.B. 165).

[345] Also, Anateus Lineal 1948, Inc. v. United States, 366 F. Supp. 118 (W.D. Ark. 1973).

[346] E.g., Priv. Ltr. Rul. 9851054.

[347] Rev. Rul. 79-360, 1979-2 C.B. 236.

[348] Tech. Adv. Mem. 8505002.

center was held to be exempt inasmuch as it advanced other programs of the health care organization involved (including an occupational and physical therapy program), its facilities and programs were specially designed for the needs of the handicapped and the treatment plans of patients in other programs, its fee structure was designed to make it available to the public (its rates were comparable to those charged by other similar local fitness centers), and it offered a range of programs focusing on wellness.[349]

Likewise, a freestanding state-of-the-art cardiovascular rehabilitation and heart disease prevention center, which included a fitness facility, was found to be a related activity of an exempt hospital, with the IRS emphasizing a nutrition program and a scholarship plan for those who could not afford the programs and services of the center.[350] In another instance, a full-service, state-of-the-art preventive health care and rehabilitation facility, with community education programs and a pricing policy suitable for its community, was ruled to be a charitable and educational undertaking.[351] Indeed, the operation of an "integrated medical fitness facility," which included cardiovascular and strength training areas, an indoor multipurpose gymnasium, a walking track, three swimming pools, a sauna, steam rooms, four group exercise studios, a youth fitness area, locker rooms, and a healing garden, was ruled to be an exempt hospital's related business.[352]

(v) Physical Rehabilitation Programs. Organizations that maintain physical rehabilitation programs often provide housing and other services that are available commercially. Yet the IRS ruled that an organization that provided specially designed housing to physically handicapped individuals at the lowest feasible cost and maintained in residence those tenants who subsequently became unable to pay the monthly fees was a tax-exempt charitable entity.[353] The IRS similarly ruled that the rental to individuals under age 25 and low-income individuals of all ages of dormitory rooms and similar residential accommodations was a related business.[354] The IRS likewise ruled that a halfway house, organized to provide room, board, therapy, and counseling for individuals discharged from alcoholic treatment centers, was an exempt charitable organization; its operation of a furniture shop to provide full-time employment centers for its residents was considered a related business.[355] Also, the IRS ruled that an organization that provided a residence facility and therapeutic group living program for individuals recently released from a mental institution was an exempt charitable organization.[356] An organization with the purpose of providing rehabilitative and prevocational counseling to the handicapped and developmentally disabled received a ruling that its residential and day-care facilities were related activities.[357] Another entity,

---

[349] Priv. Ltr. Rul. 9329041.

[350] Priv. Ltr. Rul. 9736047. A similar facility operated by a tax-exempt university was ruled to entail related business activities (Priv. Ltr. Rul. 9732032).

[351] Priv. Ltr. Rul. 200101036.

[352] Priv. Ltr. Rul. 201123045.

[353] Rev. Rul. 79-19, 1979-1 C.B. 195.

[354] Rev. Rul. 76-33, 1976-1 C.B. 169.

[355] Rev. Rul. 75-472, 1975-2 C.B. 208.

[356] Rev. Rul. 72-16, 1972-1 C.B. 143.

[357] Priv. Ltr. Rul. 9335061.

a charitable organization that maintained nursing homes and ancillary health facilities, was ruled to be engaged in the following related businesses: programs offering physical therapy, occupational therapy, speech therapy, injury prevention, pediatric services, and adult care, as well as the provision of day-care services for its employees.[358]

Lifestyle rehabilitation programs can also present this dichotomy. For example, the IRS ruled that the operation of a miniature golf course in a commercial manner by a tax-exempt organization, the purpose of which was to provide for the welfare of young people, constituted an unrelated trade or business.[359] The IRS also ruled, however, that an exempt organization, formed to improve the lives of abused and otherwise disadvantaged youths by means of the sport and business of golf, did not conduct an unrelated activity in operation of a golf course, because the opportunity to socialize and master skills through the playing of the game was "essential to the building of self-esteem and the ultimate rehabilitation of the young people" in the organization's programs.[360]

(vi) Administrative Services. The IRS reviewed the operations of a tax-exempt charitable organization that contracts with employer groups (commercial and governmental) to provide comprehensive, coordinated health care services for enrollees in a variety of prepaid health care plans operating in several states through a network of subordinate exempt and nonexempt organizations. The organization is establishing an *administrative services only program* primarily for large, self-insured employers, which will contract with a for-profit subsidiary to receive certain administrative services, including claims adjudication, utilization management, disease management, quality assurance, eligibility and enrollment, and access to the organization's integrated health care delivery system. The exempt organization will also provide administrative services. The IRS ruled that these administrative services will be provided as "necessary and integral parts" of the organization's overall arrangements with employer groups, and thus will be substantially related to the organization's exempt purposes.[361]

(vii) Other Health Care Activities. In other instances, the IRS ruled that the rental of pagers to staff physicians by a hospital is not an unrelated business;[362] the sale by a hospital of silver recovered from x-ray film is not an unrelated activity;[363] and the leasing of space and the furnishing of services to practitioners is not an unrelated activity by the lessors.[364] Still other related businesses in the health care setting are operation of mobile cancer screening units;[365] sales and rentals of durable medical equipment to patients of a health care organization;[366] the provision by an exempt hospital of services such as ultrasound and general radiology,

---

[358] Priv. Ltr. Rul. 9241055.
[359] Rev. Rul. 79-361, 1979-2 C.B. 237.
[360] Priv. Ltr. Rul. 8626080.
[361] Priv. Ltr. Rul. 201012052.
[362] Tech. Adv. Mem. 8452011.
[363] Tech. Adv. Mem. 8452012.
[364] Priv. Ltr. Rul. 8452099.
[365] Priv. Ltr. Rul. 8749085.
[366] Priv. Ltr. Rul. 8736046.

outpatient dialysis, acute dialysis, critical life support, home health, occupational health, electrocardiogram computer, wellness and prevention, employee physicals, and storage of medical and administrative records;[367] the operation of home care services;[368] the operation of an adult foster care home;[369] the operation of nursing homes by an exempt health care organization;[370] the operation of physical, occupational, and speech therapy, injury prevention, pediatric services, and adult day-care programs;[371] the receipt of income from Medicare, Medicaid, or private insurance programs for the operation of intermediate care facilities;[372] the provision by an exempt health care entity of temporary nurses to a related exempt organization;[373] the sale of medical diagnostic literature and equipment;[374] the transfer to and operation of blood-related clinical service programs by a charitable organization;[375] and the operation of an assisted living facility.[376]

The provision of services by and among organizations within a hospital system, such as the leasing of property and the sale of services, generally will not give rise to unrelated business taxable income.[377] Designation of a health care provider as the preferred provider of services for patients of another charitable organization and its statewide affiliates is not the creation of an unrelated business.[378] The operation of a call center by an exempt ambulance service provider was ruled to be a related business.[379]

(c) Museums

Tax-exempt museums operate related businesses when they maintain collections and make them accessible to the general public; admissions fees and the like are income from related business. Some museum business operations are nontaxable by reason of the lines of law referenced previously, pertaining to parking lots, snack bars, and the like. The operation of a dining room, cafeteria, and/or snack bar by an exempt museum for use by its staff, employees, and members of the public usually is a related activity.[380] Food service operations of this nature are considered related businesses when they are merely "convenient eating places" for visitors and employees, as opposed to endeavors "designed to serve as a public restaurant."[381]

---

[367] E.g., Priv. Ltr. Rul. 8736046.

[368] Priv. Ltr. Rul. 9822039.

[369] Priv. Ltr. Rul. 199943053.

[370] Priv. Ltr. Rul. 9237090.

[371] Priv. Ltr. Rul. 9241055.

[372] Priv. Ltr. Rul. 9335061.

[373] Priv. Ltr. Rul. 9535023.

[374] Priv. Ltr. Rul. 9821063.

[375] Priv. Ltr. Rul. 199946036.

[376] Priv. Ltr. Rul. 199946037.

[377] E.g., Priv. Ltr. Rul. 8822065.

[378] Priv. Ltr. Rul. 9839040.

[379] Priv. Ltr. Rul. 200222031.

[380] Rev. Rul. 74-399, 1974-2 C.B. 172. Cf. Rev. Rul. 69-268, 1969-1 C.B. 160.

[381] E.g., Priv. Ltr. Rul. 200222030. The IRS, however, is not this tolerant outside the museum setting (e.g., Tech. Adv. Mem. 200021056, holding that a gift shop and a tearoom operated in conjunction with an exempt craft and foodstuff business were unrelated activities).

The most difficult issues in the unrelated trade or business context presented by museum operations relate to sales to the public. Where, for example, a tax-exempt museum sells to the public greeting cards that display printed reproductions of selected works from the museum's collection and from other art collections, the sales activity is substantially related to the museum's exempt purpose.[382] The rationale for this conclusion is that (1) the sale of the cards "contributes importantly to the achievement of the museum's exempt educational purposes by stimulating and enhancing public awareness, interest, and appreciation of art," and (2) a "broader segment of the public may be encouraged to visit the museum itself to share in its educational functions and programs as a result of seeing the cards."[383]

The fragmentation rule[384] is applied to segment the retailing activities of tax-exempt museums.[385] Where an item sold by an exempt museum is "low-cost"[386] and bears the museum's logo, the sales activity is likely to be considered a related business. As the prices of items increase, so too does the likelihood that the IRS will find the sales activity to be substantially unrelated to the museum's exempt purposes (with the possible exception of clothing bearing reference to the museum).

A difficult issue in this context is the distinction drawn by the IRS between museum *reproductions* and *adaptations*. Generally, the sales of reproductions of items in the museum's collection will be considered related activity. The relatedness of sales of adaptations, which are items that incorporate or reflect original art but differ significantly from the original work, may be more difficult to ascertain (unless the item encourages the public to visit the museum).

Application of the fragmentation rule may depend on whether the primary purpose of an article sold is *utilitarian*. The position of the IRS's lawyers is that if the "primary purpose of the article is utilitarian and the utilitarian aspects are the predominant reasons for the production and sale of the article, it should not be considered related." Conversely, if the "utilitarian or ornamental aspects are merely incidental to the article's relation to an exempt purpose, then the article should be considered related." Under this standard, sales of "items of a souvenir, trivial, or convenience nature" are unrelated business.[387] Museum sales of original art or craft may be unrelated business, in that the sales activity is inconsistent with the purpose of exhibiting art for the benefit of the public.[388]

In another of these instances, a tax-exempt museum, which sponsored programs for children, maintained a shop; the IRS found that the sale of certain tots' and children's items constituted an unrelated business. Nonetheless, items that were reproductions or adaptations of articles displayed in the collections and exhibits were held salable in related business. The IRS reiterated its general view that, where the primary purpose behind the production and sale of an item is

---

[382] Rev. Rul. 73-104, 1973-1 C.B. 263.

[383] *Id.*

[384] See § 24.2(f).

[385] Rev. Rul. 73-105, 1973-1 C.B. 264.

[386] Reg. § 1.513-1(b). See § 25.2(j).

[387] Gen. Couns. Mem. 38949. A discussion of the factors to consider in applying this primary purpose test is in Tech. Adv. Mem. 9550003. An excellent example of detailed fragmentation in the museum setting is in Tech. Adv. Mem. 8605002.

[388] Priv. Ltr. Rul. 8326008. Cf. Goldsboro Art League v. Comm'r, 75 T.C. 337 (1980).

utilitarian, ornamental, and/or souvenir in nature, or only generally educational, the matter entails unrelated business activity.[389]

The IRS ruled that a tax-exempt museum may operate an art conservation laboratory and perform conservation work for other institutions and collectors for a fee without incurring unrelated business income.[390] Likewise, the agency ruled that a museum store may sell items in furtherance of the exempt museum's exempt purpose, other than those that have utilitarian purposes.[391] The IRS ruled that the sale of merchandise by an exempt museum, in its gift shop, contributed importantly to its exempt purpose and thus that the resulting income was not unrelated business income; the items sold included books and documentary videos.[392]

(d) Social Welfare Organizations

The few IRS public and private letter rulings and court opinions that apply the unrelated business rules to tax-exempt social welfare organizations conclude that related activities include the conduct of weekly dances by a volunteer fire company,[393] the tax collection activities by a social welfare organization on behalf of its member municipalities,[394] the provision of group insurance and workers' compensation self-insurance for member counties by a social welfare entity,[395] and the provision of workers' compensation insurance to county government employees by a social welfare organization.[396]

The weekly operation of a bingo game by an exempt social welfare organization was found to be an unrelated business.[397]

(e) Business Leagues

A tax-exempt association (or, technically, an exempt business league)[398] is subject to the unrelated income rules. The basic related business function of an exempt association is the provision of services to its members in exchange for dues; thus, this type of dues income is related revenue.

(i) Services to Members. The IRS ruled that a variety of services performed by tax-exempt associations for their members are unrelated businesses.[399] Illustrations of this approach include the sale of equipment by a tax-exempt association to its members;[400] the management of health and welfare plans for

---

[389] Tech. Adv. Mem. 9720002.

[390] Priv. Ltr. Rul. 8432004.

[391] Tech. Adv. Mem. 8605002.

[392] Priv. Ltr. Rul. 201429029.

[393] Rev. Rul. 74-361, 1974-2 C.B. 159. Also, Maryland State Fair & Agric. Soc'y, Inc. v. Chamberlin, 55-1 U.S.T.C. ¶ 9399 (D. Md. 1955); Rev. Rul. 68-225, 1968-1 C.B. 283; Rev. Rul. 67-296, 1967-2 C.B. 212; Rev. Rul. 67-219, 1967-2 C.B. 210; Rev. Rul. 64-182, 1964-1 C.B. 186.

[394] Kentucky Mun. League v. Comm'r, 81 T.C. 156 (1983).

[395] Priv. Ltr. Rul. 8442092.

[396] Tech. Adv. Mem. 8443009.

[397] Clarence LaBelle Post No. 217 v. United States, 580 F.2d 270 (8th Cir. 1978); Smith-Dodd Businessman's Ass'n, Inc. v. Comm'r, 65 T.C. 620 (1975). Also, Rev. Rul. 59-330, 1959-2 C.B. 153.

[398] See Chapter 14.

[399] See § 14.2(c).

[400] Rev. Rul. 66-338, 1966-2 C.B. 226.

a fee by an exempt business league;[401] the provision of insurance for the members of an exempt association;[402] the operation of an executive referral service;[403] the publication of ordinary commercial advertising for products and services used by the legal profession in an exempt bar association's journal;[404] the conduct of a language translation service by an exempt trade association that promoted international trade relations;[405] the publication and sale, by an association of credit unions to its members, of a consumer-oriented magazine designed as a promotional device for distribution to the members' depositors;[406] the sale of members' horses by a horsebreeders' association;[407] the operation of a lawyer referral service by a bar association;[408] the provision of mediation and arbitration services by an exempt business league;[409] the advertising and administrative services provided by an exempt business league with respect to a for-profit discount purchasing service;[410] the operation by an exempt association of members in the trucking industry of an alcohol and drug testing program for members and nonmembers;[411] the provision of lobbying services by a business league for the benefit of its member health care providers;[412] and the sale of various items to the association's membership.[413]

By contrast, the IRS ruled that the sale of television time to governmental and nonprofit organizations at a discount by an exempt association was a related business.[414]

The sale of standard legal forms by a bar association to its members was ruled by the IRS to be an unrelated business because the activity did not contribute importantly to the accomplishment of the association's exempt purpose.[415] A court held, however, that the sale of standard real estate legal forms to lawyers and law students by an exempt bar association was an exempt function because it promoted the common business interests of the legal profession and improved the relationships among the bench, bar, and public.[416] Similarly, a court decided that the sale of preprinted lease forms and landlord's manuals by an exempt association of apartment owners and managers was a related activity.[417]

---

[401] Rev. Rul. 66-151, 1966-1 C.B. 152. The IRS reached the same conclusion with respect to the management of retirement plans for members for a fee (Program Manager Tech. Adv. 2022-004).

[402] Rev. Rul. 74-81, 1974-1 C.B. 135.

[403] Tech. Adv. Mem. 8524006.

[404] Rev. Rul. 82-139, 1982-2 C.B. 108. In this ruling, the IRS also held that the publication of legal notices by a bar association was not an unrelated trade or business.

[405] Rev. Rul. 81-75, 1981-1 C.B. 356.

[406] Rev. Rul. 78-52, 1978-1 C.B. 166.

[407] Priv. Ltr. Rul. 8112013.

[408] Priv. Ltr. Rul. 8417003. Cf. Rev. Rul. 80-287, 1980-2 C.B. 185; Priv. Ltr. Rul. 9645027.

[409] Priv. Ltr. Rul. 9408002.

[410] Tech. Adv. Mem. 9440001.

[411] Tech. Adv. Mem. 9550001.

[412] Priv. Ltr. Rul. 199905031.

[413] Priv. Ltr. Rul. 7902006.

[414] Priv. Ltr. Rul. 9023081.

[415] Rev. Rul. 78-51, 1978-1 C.B. 165.

[416] San Antonio Bar Ass'n v. United States, 80-2 U.S.T.C. ¶ 9594 (W.D. Tex. 1980).

[417] Texas Apartment Ass'n v. United States, 869 F.2d 884 (5th Cir. 1989).

(ii) Insurance Programs. Where a tax-exempt association endorses, sponsors, or manages, for compensation, an insurance program for the benefit of its members, the undertaking is almost certain to be regarded as an unrelated business, pursuant to the IRS's position[418] and court decisions.[419] At the outset of development of the law in this area, it was held that mere sponsorship by an exempt association of an insurance program was a sufficiently passive involvement that did not rise to the level of a business,[420] but that rationale could not be sustained.[421] The IRS initially permitted exempt associations to escape taxation of income derived from insurance programs by structuring the payments as royalties,[422] but then reversed that position.[423] Should the provision of insurance be an association's sole or principal activity, it cannot be tax-exempt.[424]

One approach to avoidance of unrelated business income taxation in this context may be to have the insurance program conducted by a separate entity, such as a trust or corporation, albeit controlled by the parent tax-exempt association. This approach requires care that the separate entity is in fact a true legal entity, with its own governing instruments, governing board, and separate tax return filing obligation.[425] If it is a mere trusteed bank account or the like of the association, the IRS will regard the program as an integral part of the association itself.[426] If it is an authentic separate legal entity, any tax liability would be confined to that imposed on the net income of the entity, which presumably would have no basis for securing tax exemption.[427] If the entity transfers funds to the parent association, however, the funds may be taxable to the association as unrelated business income.[428] Likewise, the funds may be taxable to the association if the separate entity is regarded as an agent of the association.[429]

---

[418] Rev. Rul. 66-151, 1966-1 C.B. 152. Also, Rev. Rul. 60-228, 1960-1 C.B. 200.

[419] Louisiana Credit Union League v. United States, 693 F.2d 525 (5th Cir. 1982); Professional Ins. Agents of Mich. v. Comm'r, 726 F.2d 1097 (6th Cir. 1984); Illinois Ass'n of Pro. Ins. Agents, Inc. v. Comm'r, 86-2 U.S.T.C. ¶ 9702 (7th Cir. 1986); Indiana Retail Hardware Ass'n v. United States, 366 F.2d 998 (Ct. Cl. 1966); Texas Farm Bur. v. United States, 822 F. Supp. 371 (W.D. Tex. 1993), *aff'd and rev'd*, 95-1 U.S.T.C. ¶ 50,297 (5th Cir. 1995); Associated Master Barbers & Beauticians of America, Inc. v. Comm'r, 69 T.C. 53 (1977); Long Island Gasoline Retailers Ass'n, Inc. v. Comm'r, 43 T.C.M. 815 (1982); Professional Ins. Agents of Wash. v. Comm'r, 53 T.C.M. 9 (1987); Indep. Ins. Agents of Huntsville, Inc. v. Comm'r, 63 T.C.M. 2468 (1992), *aff'd*, 998 F.2d 898 (11th Cir. 1993).

[420] E.g., Oklahoma Cattlemen's Ass'n v. United States, 310 F. Supp. 320 (W.D. Okla. 1969).

[421] E.g., Carolinas Farm & Power Equip. Dealers Ass'n, Inc. v. United States, 699 F.2d 167 (4th Cir. 1983); San Antonio Dist. Dental Soc'y v. United States, 340 F. Supp. 11 (W.D. Tex. 1972).

[422] Priv. Ltr. Rul. 8828011. See § 25.1(g).

[423] Priv. Ltr. Rul. 9029047. In reaching this conclusion, the IRS took into consideration both the insurance-related activities of associations and their agents, the latter attributable to the associations under the authority of Nat'l Water Well Ass'n, Inc. v. Comm'r, 92 T.C. 75 (1989).

[424] E.g., Rev. Rul. 74-81, 1974-1 C.B. 135; Rev. Rul. 67-176, 1967-1 C.B. 140.

[425] See § 28.2.

[426] Priv. Ltr. Rul. 7847001.

[427] North Carolina Oil Jobbers Ass'n, Inc. v. United States, 78-2 U.S.T.C. ¶ 9658 (E.D.N.C. 1978); New York State Ass'n of Real Estate Bds. Group Ins. Fund v. Comm'r, 54 T.C. 1325 (1970).

[428] See § 30.6.

[429] See § 24.3(b), text accompanied by *supra* note 161.

A court recognized that the acquisition and provision of insurance can be an exempt function of a tax-exempt business league.[430] In this instance, the organization's purposes included counseling governmental agencies with regard to insurance programs, accepting and servicing insurance written by the agencies, and otherwise acting as an insurance broker for the governmental agencies. In so holding, the court placed some reliance on an IRS ruling that the provision for equitable distribution of high-risk insurance policies among member insurance companies is an exempt undertaking.[431]

Separate consideration must be given the insurance programs of tax-exempt fraternal beneficiary societies,[432] as their exempt purpose is to provide for the payment of qualifying benefits to their members and their dependents.[433] The IRS recognized that these benefits are in the nature of insurance, in holding that a society may not, as an exercise of an exempt function, provide additional insurance for terminated members.[434]

(iii) Associate Member Dues.   Dues derived from associate (or affiliate or patron) members may be taxable as unrelated business income.[435] In some instances, these dues will be taxable on the ground that these members are paying for a specific service, such as insurance coverage.[436] In other instances, these dues will be cast as *access fees* and be taxable because they were paid to gain access to an association's regular members for marketing and sales purposes.[437]

The IRS stated that, in the case of tax-exempt labor, agricultural, and horticultural organizations,[438] dues payments from associate members will not be regarded as unrelated business income unless, for the relevant period, the membership category was formed or availed of for the principal purpose of producing unrelated income.[439] This aspect of the law was subsequently altered by statute, however, in that certain dues payments to exempt agricultural or horticultural organizations are exempt from unrelated business income taxation.[440] Nonetheless, this IRS position continues to be its view with respect to labor organizations (and to agricultural and horticultural entities that do not qualify for the exception); indeed, the IRS indicated that it will follow this approach with respect to associations generally.[441]

---

[430] Indep. Ins. Agents of N. Nev., Inc. v. United States, 79-2 U.S.T.C. ¶ 9601 (D. Nev. 1979). This position of the IRS extends to insurance programs maintained by tax-exempt social welfare membership organizations (see Chapter 13) (e.g., Priv. Ltr. Rul. 9441001).

[431] Rev. Rul. 71-155, 1971-1 C.B. 152.

[432] See § 19.4(a).

[433] *Id.*

[434] Priv. Ltr. Rul. 7937002.

[435] E.g., Nat'l League of Postmasters v. Comm'r, 69 T.C.M. 2569 (1995), *aff'd*, 86 F.3d 59 (4th Cir. 1996).

[436] E.g., Tech. Adv. Mem. 9416002.

[437] E.g., Tech. Adv. Mem. 9345004.

[438] See Chapter 16.

[439] Rev. Proc. 95-21, 1995-1 C.B. 686.

[440] See § 25.2(l).

[441] Rev. Proc. 97-12, 1997-1 C.B. 631, *modifying* Rev. Proc. 95-21, 1995-1 C.B. 686.

(iv) Other Association Business Activities. It is the position of the IRS that a tax-exempt business league can engage in charitable activities without incurring an unrelated income tax even though the activities are technically unrelated to the business league's purposes.[442]

However, the position of the IRS is that the operation of an employment service by a tax-exempt association is an unrelated activity.[443] This approach embraces registry programs[444] but not job training programs.[445] The IRS also ruled that the operation by an exempt business league of a recycling facility is an unrelated business.[446]

A federal court of appeals applied three factors in resolving the issue of whether an activity is substantially related to an association's exempt purposes: (1) whether the fees charged are directly proportionate to the benefits received, (2) whether participation is limited to members and thus is of no benefit to those in the industry who are nonmembers, and (3) whether the service provided is one commonly furnished by for-profit entities.[447] In subsequent application of these criteria, the court found that an association's administration of vacation pay and guaranteed annual income accounts for its members under a collective bargaining agreement was unrelated to its exempt negotiation and arbitration activities, because each member benefited in proportion to its participation in the activity, only the association's members were eligible to participate in the service, and the functions could be performed by for-profit entities.[448]

Other instances of related activities by tax-exempt associations are the sponsorship of championship tournaments by an association operated to promote a sport;[449] the conduct of research and counseling activities to promote business in foreign countries;[450] the operation of a medical malpractice peer review program by an exempt medical society;[451] the activities of an association as a "certified frequency coordinator" (as designated by the federal government) for its industry;[452] the development and operation by a business league of a tracking system for alimony and support payments;[453] and administration of a program to control and assign a form of messaging technology, along with other activities, including clearinghouse services, maintenance of a database, and functions amounting to a centralized registry.[454]

---

[442] Tech. Adv. Mem. 8418003.

[443] Rev. Rul. 61-170, 1961-2 C.B. 112.

[444] Priv. Ltr. Rul. 8503103.

[445] Rev. Rul. 67-296, 1967-2 C.B. 22.

[446] Tech. Adv. Mem. 9848002.

[447] Carolinas Farm & Power Equip. Dealers Ass'n, Inc. v. United States, 699 F.2d 167, 171 (4th Cir. 1983).

[448] Steamship Trade Ass'n of Baltimore, Inc. v. Comm'r, 757 F.2d 1494 (4th Cir. 1985), where the appellate court endorsed Rev. Rul. 66-151, 1966-1 C.B. 152. Cf. Rev. Rul. 82-138, 1982-2 C.B. 106; Rev. Rul. 65-164, 1965-1 C.B. 238.

[449] Rev. Rul. 58-502, 1958-2 C.B. 271, *clarified by* Rev. Rul. 80-294, 1980-2 C.B. 187.

[450] Priv. Ltr. Rul. 8505047.

[451] Priv. Ltr. Rul. 8730060.

[452] Priv. Ltr. Rul. 8802079.

[453] Priv. Ltr. Rul. 9633044.

[454] Priv. Ltr. Rul. 201105043.

The certification of the accuracy and authenticity of export documents by a tax-exempt chamber of commerce,[455] for the purpose of providing an independent verification of the origin of exported goods, was ruled to be a related business because the activity "stimulates international commerce by facilitating the export of goods and, thus, promotes and stimulates business conditions in the community generally."[456]

(f) Labor and Agricultural Organizations

One of the principal issues in the unrelated income context for tax-exempt labor unions[457] is the taxation of revenue (dues) derived from associate members (sometimes termed limited benefit members) who joined the organization solely to be able to participate in the organization's health insurance plans. The evolving view is that this dues revenue is taxable.[458] When this issue was initially litigated, the government lost, basically on the ground that the courts lacked the authority to define the bona fide membership of exempt labor unions.[459] The prevailing view, however, is that the same rules that apply with respect to associations[460] apply in the case of labor organizations.

In other applications of the unrelated income rules to tax-exempt labor organizations, the IRS found to be taxable the income derived by an exempt labor organization from the operation of semiweekly bingo games[461] and from the performance of accounting and tax services for some of its members.[462]

Tax-exempt agricultural organizations are likewise subject to the tax on unrelated business income. As an illustration, the IRS ruled that the following is taxable: income received by an exempt agricultural organization from the sale of supplies and equipment to members,[463] commissions from the sale of members' cattle,[464] income from the sale of supplies to seedsmen,[465] and income from the operation of club facilities for its members and their guests.[466]

---

[455] See § 14.3.

[456] Rev. Rul. 81-27, 1981-1 C.B. 357.

[457] See § 16.1.

[458] American Postal Workers Union, AFL-CIO v. United States, 925 F.2d 480 (D.C. Cir. 1991); Nat'l Ass'n of Postal Supervisors v. United States, 90-2 U.S.T.C. ¶ 50,445 (Ct. Cl. 1990), aff'd, 944 F. 2d 859 (Fed. Cir. 1991).

[459] American Postal Workers Union, AFL-CIO, v. United States, 90-1 U.S.T.C. ¶ 50,013 (D.D.C. 1989), rev'd, 925 F.2d 480 (D.C. Cir. 1991).

[460] See § 25.2(l).

[461] Rev. Rul. 59-330, 1959-2 C.B. 153. Cf. § 25.2(h).

[462] Rev. Rul. 62-191, 1962-2 C.B. 146.

[463] Rev. Rul. 57-466, 1957-2 C.B. 311.

[464] Rev. Rul. 69-51, 1969-1 C.B. 159.

[465] Priv. Ltr. Rul. 8429010.

[466] Rev. Rul. 60-86, 1960-1 C.B. 198. An exclusion from the unrelated business income tax is available for income received by an exempt organization used to establish, maintain, or operate a retirement home, hospital, or similar facility for the exclusive use and benefit of the aged and infirm members of the organization, where the income (1) is derived from agricultural pursuits and conducted on grounds contiguous to the facility and (2) does not provide more than 75 percent of the cost of maintaining and operating the facility (pre-1976 IRC § 512(b)(4), which, although removed from the Code as a "deadwood" provision of the Tax Reform Act of 1976, remains preserved in the law).

(g) Credit Unions

In the context of the ongoing battle between commercial financial institutions and tax-exempt credit unions over the appropriate scope of services of the latter,[467] the IRS ruled that various insurance products and other financial services provided by exempt credit unions to the public constitute unrelated businesses.[468] Nonetheless, the government's position has been rejected by a court on two occasions.[469] However, the IRS remained, for a while, wedded to its position in this regard.[470]

Subsequently, however, the IRS revised its position.[471] Pursuant to the new policy, income from the following activities is being treated by the IRS as state credit unions' related business income: sale of checks, fees from check printing companies, debit and credit card programs' interchange fees, interest from credit card loans, and sale of collateral protection insurance. Nor will income from sales of the following products to members produce unrelated business income: credit life and credit disability insurance, and gap automobile insurance. Income from sales of these products to nonmembers, however, will be treated as unrelated income.

Income from the marketing of the following insurance products is considered by the IRS to be unrelated business income: automobile warranties, dental insurance, cancer insurance, accidental death and dismemberment insurance, life insurance, and health insurance. Also, ATM per-transaction fees from nonmembers are regarded as unrelated income. Royalty arrangements, however, may entail nontaxable income.

(h) Advertising

Generally, the net income derived by a tax-exempt organization from the sale of advertising is taxable as unrelated business income.[472]

(i) Concept of Advertising. Despite the extensive body of regulatory and case law in this area concerning when and how advertising revenue may be taxed, there is little law as to what constitutes *advertising*. In one instance, a court considered the publication of "business listings," consisting of "slogans, logos, trademarks, and other information which is similar, if not identical in content, composition and message to the listings found in other professional journals, newspapers, and the 'yellow pages' of telephone directories," and found them

---

[467] See § 19.7.

[468] E.g., Tech. Adv. Mem. 200709072.

[469] Bellco Credit Union v. United States, 2010-1 U.S.T.C. ¶ 50,343 (D. Col. 2010); Community First Credit Union v. United States, 2009-2 U.S.T.C. ¶ 50,496 (E.D. Wis. 2009).

[470] E.g., Tech. Adv. Mem. 200931064.

[471] Memorandum from Director, Exempt Organizations Division, dated March 24, 2014.

[472] IRC § 513(c); Reg. § 1.512(a)-1(f)(1). The IRS concluded that an association did not receive any unrelated business income from a newspaper advertising program because the association did not conduct the activity and there was no basis for attribution of the advertising activities of its members (Tech. Adv. Mem. 200102051).

to qualify as advertising.[473] The IRS ruled that the sale by an exempt organization of periodical and banner advertising on its website constituted an unrelated business.[474]

(ii) General Rules. Examples of application of these rules include taxation of the income of a tax-exempt organization derived from the sale of conventional advertising in its monthly journal,[475] in an annual yearbook,[476] and in concert programs.[477] Advertising income may not be taxable, however, if the economic activity is not regularly carried on[478] or if the volunteer exception is available.[479]

Under the rules defining a *trade or business*,[480] income from the sale of advertising in periodicals of tax-exempt organizations (even where the periodicals are related to the exempt purpose of the organization) and other types of communications generally constitutes unrelated business income, taxable to the extent that it exceeds the expenses directly related to the advertising. If, however, the editorial aspect of the periodical is carried on at a loss, the editorial loss may be offset against the advertising income from the periodical. Thus, there will be no taxable unrelated trade or business income because of advertising where the periodical as a whole is published at a loss. This rule embodies a preexisting regulation that was promulgated in an effort to carve out (and tax) income from advertising and other activities in competition with taxpaying businesses, even though the advertising may appear in a periodical related to the educational or other exempt purpose of the organization.[481]

Income attributable to a periodical of a tax-exempt organization basically is regarded as circulation income or (if any) gross advertising income.[482] *Circulation income* is the income attributable to the production, distribution, or circulation of a periodical (other than gross advertising income), including amounts realized from the sale of the readership content of the periodical. *Gross advertising income* is the amount derived from the unrelated advertising activities of an exempt organization periodical.[483]

Likewise, the costs attributable to a tax-exempt organization periodical are characterized as readership costs and direct advertising costs. A reasonable

---

[473] Fraternal Order of Police, Illinois State Troopers Lodge No. 41 v. Comm'r, 87 T.C. 747, 754 (1986), *aff'd*, 833 F.2d 717 (7th Cir. 1987).

[474] Priv. Ltr. Rul. 200303062.

[475] E.g., Florida Trucking Ass'n, Inc. v. Comm'r, 87 T.C. 1039 (1986); Rev. Rul. 74-38, 1974-1 C.B. 144, *clarified by* Rev. Rul. 76-93, 1976-1 C.B. 170.

[476] E.g., State Police Ass'n of Massachusetts v. Comm'r, 97-2 U.S.T.C. ¶ 50,627 (1st Cir. 1997); Rev. Rul. 73-424, 1973-2 C.B. 190.

[477] Rev. Rul. 75-200, 1975-1 C.B. 163.

[478] See § 24.3.

[479] E.g., Rev. Rul. 75-201, 1975-1 C.B. 164. See § 25.2(a).

[480] See § 24.2.

[481] Reg. § 1.513-1(b). The IRS held that a website is a periodical for purposes of these rules (Priv. Ltr. Rul. 201405029).

[482] Reg. § 1.512(a)-1(f)(3)(i).

[483] Reg. § 1.512(a)-1(f)(3)(ii), (iii).

allocation may be made between cost items attributable to an exempt organization periodical and to its other activities (such as salaries, occupancy costs, and depreciation). *Readership costs* are, therefore, the cost items directly connected with the production and distribution of the readership content of the periodical, other than the items properly allocable to direct advertising costs. *Direct advertising costs* include items that are directly connected with the sale and publication of advertising (such as agency commissions and other selling costs, artwork, and copy preparation), the portion of mechanical and distribution costs attributable to advertising lineage, and other elements of readership costs properly allocable to an advertising activity.[484]

As noted, a tax-exempt organization (assuming it is subject to the unrelated business income rules) is not taxable on its advertising income where its direct advertising costs equal such (gross) income. Even if gross advertising income exceeds direct advertising costs, costs attributable to the readership content of the periodical qualify as costs deductible in computing (unrelated) income from the advertising activity, to the extent that the costs exceed the income attributable to the readership content.[485] If the circulation income of the periodical exceeds its readership costs, any unrelated business taxable income attributable to the periodical is the excess of gross advertising income over direct advertising costs.

Another set of rules requires allocation of membership dues to circulation income where the right to receive a periodical is associated with membership status in the tax-exempt organization for which dues, fees, or other charges are received.[486] Three ways are used to determine the portion of membership dues that constitutes a part of circulation income (*allocable membership receipts*).[487]

A court held that this *right to receive* a tax-exempt membership organization's periodical must be a legal right.[488] The court found that an organization's members had a right to receive a magazine, based on language in the organization's bylaws

---

[484] Reg. § 1.512(a)-1(f)(6). Once a reasonable method of allocation is adopted, it must be used consistently (Reg. § 1.512(a)-1(f)(6)(i)). One court held that the application of a ratio used in previous years for this purpose is not a "method"; rather, it is the output of a method and cannot be automatically applied each year (Nat'l Ass'n of Life Underwriters, Inc. v. Comm'r, 94-2 U.S.T.C. ¶ 50,412 (D.C. Cir. 1994), *rev'g* 64 T.C.M. 379 (1992)).

[485] Reg. § 1.512(a)-1(f)(2)(ii), (d)(2).

[486] Reg. § 1.512(a)-1(f)(4). The IRS initially took the position that the requirement that membership receipts must be allocated on a pro rata basis to circulation income of a tax-exempt organization's periodical (Reg. § 1.512(a)-1(f)(4)(iii)) requires that the "cost of other exempt activities of the organization" must be offset by the income produced by the activities (the "net cost" rule) (Gen. Couns. Mem. 38104), but subsequently concluded that the gross cost of the other exempt activities must be used in computing the denominator of the formula (Gen. Couns. Mems. 38205, 38168).

[487] There has been considerable litigation in this context. E.g., North Carolina Citizens for Business & Indus. v. United States, 89-2 U.S.T.C. ¶ 9507 (Cl. Ct. 1989); American Medical Ass'n v. United States, 887 F.2d 760 (7th Cir. 1989), *aff'g and rev'g* 608 F. Supp. 1085 (N.D. Ill. 1987), 668 F. Supp. 1101 (N.D. Ill. 1987), 668 F. Supp. 358 (N.D. Ill. 1988), 691 F. Supp. 1170 (N.D. Ill. 1988); American Hosp. Ass'n v. United States, 654 F. Supp. 1152 (N.D. Ill. 1987); American Bar Ass'n v. United States, 84-1 U.S.T.C. ¶ 9179 (N.D. Ill. 1984)

[488] Nat'l Education Ass'n of the United States v. Comm'r, 137 T.C. 100 (2011). That is, the court wrote, this phraseology does not mean a "non-enforceable just or moral claim," adding that the regulation is not to be read "as conferring on the tax collector and the courts the responsibility of adjudicating justice and morality in the sphere of membership periodicals" (*id.* at 116).

and standing rules, the lengthy production schedule, the contracts with advertisers, language in the postal regulations, and provisions in its affiliates' enrollment forms.

These rules become more intricate where a tax-exempt organization publishes more than one periodical for the production of income. (A periodical is published *for the production of income* if the organization generally receives gross advertising income from the periodical equal to at least 25 percent of its readership costs and the periodical activity is engaged in for profit.) In this case, the organization may treat the gross income from all (but not just some) of the periodicals and the deductible items directly connected with the periodicals on a consolidated basis in determining the amount of unrelated business taxable income derived from the sale of advertising.[489]

It is the position of the IRS, as supported by the U.S. Tax Court, that the specific rules concerning the computation of net unrelated income derived from advertising are inapplicable in a case where the "issue of whether the . . . [organization's] publication of the readership content of the magazines is an exempt activity has not been decided, stipulated to, or presented for decision" and where the IRS "has not sought to apply such regulations, maintaining that they cannot be applied due to the . . . [organization's] failure to produce credible evidence of its advertising and publishing expenses."[490]

(iii) Concept of Related Advertising. It is possible for advertising to be a related business. In the principal case on the point, a tax-exempt medical organization was found to be engaging in an unrelated business by selling advertising in its scholarly journal, with the trial court rejecting the argument that the primary purpose of the advertising was educational.[491] This court, however, set forth standards as to when journal advertising might be an exempt function, such as advertising that comprehensively surveys a particular field or otherwise makes a systematic presentation on an appropriate subject. On appeal, it was held that the content of the advertising was substantially related to the organization's exempt purpose, in that the advertisements were confined to those directly relevant to the practice of medicine, only appeared in groups, were presented by subject matter, and were indexed by advertisers.[492]

This case moved to the Supreme Court, which concluded that the standard is whether the conduct of the tax-exempt organization in selling and publishing advertising is demonstrative of a related function, rather than a determination as to whether the advertising is inherently educational.[493] The test, wrote the Court, is whether the exempt organization uses the advertising to "provide its readers a comprehensive or systematic presentation of any aspect of the goods or services

---

[489] IRC § 446(e); Reg. § 1.446-1(e).

[490] CORE Special Purpose Fund v. Comm'r, 49 T.C.M. 626, 630 (1985). Notwithstanding the differences in the manner in which tax-exempt social clubs are treated for purposes of unrelated taxation (see § 25.4(c)), the rules concerning the taxation of advertising revenue are applicable to them (Chicago Metropolitan Ski Council v. Comm'r, 104 T.C. 341 (1995)).

[491] American College of Physicians v. United States, 83-2 U.S.T.C. ¶ 9652 (Ct. Cl. 1983).

[492] American College of Physicians v. United States, 743 F.2d 1570 (Fed. Cir. 1984).

[493] United States v. American College of Physicians, 475 U.S. 834 (1986).

publicized"; as the Court stated the matter, an exempt organization can "control its publication of advertisements in such a way as to reflect an intention to contribute importantly to its . . . [exempt] functions."[494] This can be done, said the Court, by "coordinating the content of the advertisements with the editorial content of the issue, or by publishing only advertisements reflecting new developments."[495]

The IRS ruled that a tax-exempt business league that sold a membership directory only to its members was not engaged in an unrelated business, inasmuch as the directory contributed importantly to the achievement of the organization's exempt purposes by facilitating communication among its members and encouraging the exchange of ideas and expertise.[496] In another case, a court held that an exempt organization's advertising, although the subject matter of some of it was related to exempt purposes, was unrelated business because the primary purpose of the advertising was the raising of revenue and thus commercial.[497] The IRS ruled that proceeds from the sale of advertising in the program published in promotion of a postseason all-star college football game were not unrelated income.[498]

(i) Fundraising

Fundraising practices of charitable organizations and the unrelated business rules have long had a precarious relationship. For this purpose, the term *fundraising* means the solicitation of contributions, grants, and other forms of financial support, usually by charitable organizations.[499] Fundraising activities are almost always distinct from program activities, and can be *businesses*.[500]

(i) Fundraising as Unrelated Business. The type of fundraising undertaking that is most likely to be considered a business is the *special event*. These events include functions such as auctions, dinners, sports tournaments, dances, theater events, fairs, car washes, and bake sales.[501] Sometimes a court applies the statutory definition of the term *business*[502] in concluding that the event is an unrelated business; on other occasions, a court will utilize other criteria—such as competition or commerciality—to find that the event is or is not an unrelated business.[503]

---

[494] *Id.* at 849.

[495] *Id.* at 849–50.

[496] Rev. Rul. 79-370, 1979-2 C.B. 238.

[497] Minnesota Holstein-Friesian Breeders Ass'n v. Comm'r, 64 T.C.M. 1319 (1992).

[498] Priv. Ltr. Rul. 7948113.

[499] The federal tax law does not generally define the term *fundraising*. The tax regulations promulgated in connection with the *expenditure test* (see § 22.3(d)(iii), text accompanied by note 98), however, provide that the term embraces three practices: (1) the solicitation of dues or contributions from members of the organization, from persons whose dues are in arrears, or from the general public; (2) the solicitation of gifts from businesses or gifts or grants from other organizations, including charitable entities; or (3) the solicitation of grants from a governmental unit or any agency or instrumentality of the unit (Reg. § 56.4911-4(f)(1)).

[500] See § 24.2.

[501] See, e.g., Instructions for Form 990 (2023) at 41.

[502] See § 24.2(a).

[503] See § 24.2(c), (d).

An early example of a fundraising event cast as an unrelated business was the conduct, three evenings each week, of bingo games and related concessions by a religious organization.[504] Subsequently, courts ruled that the conduct of lotteries by a charitable organization was an unrelated business;[505] that the offering of insurance, travel, and discount plans was not an exempt function;[506] that a real estate purchase-and-sale program was an unrelated business;[507] and that the distribution by a veterans' organization of greeting cards to its members was an unrelated business.[508] The Supreme Court held that income received by a charitable organization, as the result of assignments to it of dividends paid in connection with insurance coverage purchased by members of a related association at group rates, was taxable as unrelated business income.[509]

The IRS ruled that a fundraising event conducted by a tax-exempt alumni association, held every weekend for the benefit of a public college, is an unrelated business. The IRS rejected the association's contentions that the event is a substantially related activity because of the potential for student recruitment, generating donors, and endearing the college's alumni to that institution.[510]

(ii) Affinity Card Programs. A tax-exempt organization may be paid a portion of the revenue derived from the marketing of credit and debit cards to its members or other supports. With the IRS of the view that affinity card revenue cannot be considered exempt royalty income,[511] the matter was taken to the U.S.

---

[504] Priv. Ltr. Rul. 7946001. This organization was unable to utilize the exception from unrelated business income taxation accorded to the conduct of certain bingo games (see § 25.2(h)) because the games were, at that time, illegal under state law.

A court held that an organization that conducted bingo games as its sole activity and devoted its net profits to charitable purposes did not qualify for tax exemption (P.L.L. Scholarship Fund v. Comm'r, 82 T.C. 196 (1984); Piety, Inc. v. Comm'r, 82 T.C. 193 (1984)). Yet, the IRS wrote that an organization that conducts bingo games may be exempt as a charitable entity "if it uses the proceeds from bingo to conduct a charitable program, commensurate in scope with its financial resources, of making grants to other charitable organizations" (Priv. Ltr. Rul. 201103057).

[505] United States v. Auxiliary to the Knights of St. Peter Claver, Charities of the Ladies Court No. 97, 92-1 U.S.T.C. ¶ 50,176 (S.D. Ind. 1992).

[506] U.S. CB Radio Ass'n, No. 1, Inc. v. Comm'r, 42 T.C.M. 1441 (1981).

[507] Parklane Residential School, Inc. v. Comm'r, 45 T.C.M. 988 (1983).

[508] Veterans of Foreign Wars, Dep't of Mich. v. Comm'r, 89 T.C. 7 (1987). The IRS has agreed with this approach (e.g., Priv. Ltr. Ruls. 8203134, 8232011). Cf. Veterans of Foreign Wars of the United States, Dep't of Mo., Inc. v. United States, 85-2 U.S.T.C. ¶ 9605 (W.D. Mo. 1984). A greeting card program may not, however, rise to the level of a business (e.g., Disabled American Veterans v. United States, 650 F.2d 1179 (Ct. Cl. 1981)).

An exception from the definition of the term business is available in the case of the mailing of low-cost articles in connection with the solicitation of charitable contributions (see § 25.2(j)). This exception was applied to enable a tax-exempt school to send packages of greeting cards as inducements to prospective donors (premiums) without unrelated business income taxation (Hope School v. United States, 612 F.2d 298 (7th Cir. 1980)).

[509] United States v. American Bar Endowment, 447 U.S. 105 (1986). Revisions of this program led the IRS to conclude that it was no longer an unrelated business (Priv. Ltr. Rul. 8725056).

[510] Tech. Adv. Mem. 201544025. This case was taken to court, then settled (College of the Desert Alumni Ass'n, Inc. v. Comm'r, petition filed with the U.S. Tax Court on Feb. 8, 2017).

[511] Gen. Couns. Mem. 39727; Priv. Ltr. Rul. 8823109, *revoking* Priv. Ltr. Rul. 8747066. As to the mailing list approach, the IRS determined that the statutory exception (see § 25.2(k)) was not available because the lists were provided to noncharitable exempt organizations.

Tax Court, which held that this type of revenue can be structured as a royalty.[512] An appeal resulted in a revised definition of the term *royalty*;[513] on remand, the Tax Court again concluded that the organization's affinity card revenue was excludable as royalty income.[514]

(iii) Sales of Mailing Lists. The IRS held that the regular sales of membership mailing lists by a tax-exempt educational organization to colleges and business firms for the production of income was an unrelated business.[515] By contrast, the IRS ruled that the exchange of mailing lists by an exempt organization with similar exempt organizations does not give rise to unrelated business income (namely, barter income of an amount equal to the value of the lists received).[516] In this instance, the IRS considered the exchange to be substantially related to organization's exempt purposes as a generally accepted way of obtaining names of potential donors rather than as a way to generate income. However, where an exempt organization exchanges its mailing list to produce income, it is the position of the IRS that the transaction is economically the same as a rental and thus is an unrelated business.[517]

(iv) Application of Exceptions. Thus, many fundraising endeavors of tax-exempt organizations are businesses that are regularly carried on and are not related practices. Yet, they often escape taxation because of one or more exceptions.

The exception that is most frequently utilized to shelter fundraising activities from taxation is the one for business activities that are not regularly carried on.[518] The typical special event, for example, is usually not regularly carried on,[519] although on occasion the inclusion of preparatory time will convert the activity into a taxable unrelated business.[520] It is for this reason that many special-event fundraising activities, such as dances, auctions, tournaments, car washes, and bake sales do not give rise to unrelated business income.[521]

The IRS ruled, for example, that the net proceeds resulting from the annual conduct by a charitable organization of a charity ball and a golf tournament were not taxable because the events were not regularly carried on.[522] In one case, a court concluded that the annual fundraising activity of a tax-exempt charitable organization, consisting of the presentation and sponsoring of a professional vaudeville

---

[512] Sierra Club, Inc. v. Comm'r, 103 T.C. 307 (1994). Also, Mississippi State Univ. Alumni, Inc. v. Comm'r, 74 T.C.M. 458 (1997); Oregon State Univ. Alumni Ass'n, Inc. v. Comm'r, 71 T.C.M. 1935 (1996) *aff'd*, 99-2 U.S.T.C. ¶ 50,879 (9th Cir. 1999); Alumni Ass'n of the Univ. of Oregon, Inc. v. Comm'r, 71 T.C.M. 2093 (1996), *aff'd*, 99-2 U.S.T.C. ¶ 50,879 (9th Cir. 1999).

[513] Sierra Club, Inc. v. Comm'r, 86 F.3d 1526 (9th Cir. 1996).

[514] Sierra Club, Inc. v. Comm'r, 77 T.C.M. 1569 (1999).

[515] Rev. Rul. 72-431, 1972-2 C.B. 281.

[516] Priv. Ltr. Rul. 8127019.

[517] Priv. Ltr. Rul. 8216009.

[518] See § 24.3. A charitable organization, however, may be found to be engaged in an unrelated business for conducting this type of a fundraising event where it is done for the benefit of another charity (Rev. Rul. 75-201, 1975-1 C.B. 164).

[519] E.g., Priv. Ltr. Rul. 200128059 (concerning an annual charity ball and annual golf tournament).

[520] See § 24.3(c).

[521] E.g., Orange Cnty. Builders Ass'n, Inc. v. United States, 65-2 U.S.T.C. ¶ 9679 (S.D. Ca. 1965).

[522] Priv. Ltr. Rul. 200128059.

show, conducted one weekend per year, was a business that was not regularly carried on.[523]

Conventional fundraising—the solicitation and collection of gifts and grants—however, is usually regularly carried on, yet there have not been any assertions that these activities are taxable, even though they may be businesses and are not related to exempt purposes.

Other exceptions may be available in the fundraising setting. For example, a business, albeit regularly carried on, in which substantially all of the work is performed for the organization by volunteers is not taxable.[524] The same is the case for the sale of merchandise substantially all of which has been received by the organization as gifts.[525] Activities carried on primarily for the convenience of the organization's members, students, patients, officers, or employees are not taxable.[526] The receipts from certain gambling activities (bingo games) are exempted from unrelated business income taxation.[527]

(v) Tax Planning Consulting.   It is common for charitable organizations that engage in fundraising efforts to provide financial and tax planning information to prospective donors. This may entail modest amounts of information, such as direction as to valuation of property or the extent of the charitable deduction. In other settings, by contrast, the financial and tax information can be substantial and complex. This is particularly the case with respect to planned giving, where charities are directly involved in charitable gift planning and preparation of documents, such as charitable remainder trusts, other trust arrangements, and wills.

Three court opinions support the notion that undue tax planning consulting can amount to a private benefit imperiling charitable organizations' tax-exempt status.[528]

In the first of these cases, a court held that an organization could not qualify for tax exemption as a charitable entity because its tax planning services for wealthy individuals were private benefit, in that this activity, "albeit an exempt purpose furthering . . . fundraising efforts, has a nonexempt purpose of offering advice to individuals on tax matters that reduces an individual's personal and estate tax liabilities."[529] In the second case, the court held that a religious organization could not be exempt because it engaged in the substantial nonexempt activity of counseling individuals on the purported tax benefits of becoming ministers.[530] This court thereafter held that an organization whose membership was "religious

---

[523] Suffolk Cnty. Patrolmen's Benevolent Ass'n, Inc. v. Comm'r, 77 T.C. 1314 (1981).

[524] See § 25.2(a).

[525] See § 25.2(c).

[526] See § 25.2(b).

[527] See § 25.2(h).

[528] See § 20.13.

[529] Christian Stewardship Assistance, Inc. v. Comm'r, 70 T.C. 1037, 1041 (1978).

[530] Ecclesiastical Order of the Ism of Am, Inc. v. Comm'r, 80 T.C. 833 (1983), aff'd, 740 F.2d 967 (6th Cir. 1984), cert. denied, 471 U.S. 1015 (1985). The court attempted to mitigate its holding by writing that "[w]e are not holding today that any group which discusses the tax consequences of donations to and/or expenditures of its organization is in danger of losing or not acquiring tax-exempt status" (id., 80 T.C. at 842), which was the essence of its holding in the prior case.

missions" was not entitled to exempt status because it engaged in the substantial nonexempt activity of providing financial and tax advice.[531]

(j) Travel Tour Activities

Whether travel tour activities conducted by an exempt organization are substantially related to an exempt purpose is determined by an analysis of all of the relevant facts and circumstances, including how a travel tour is developed, promoted, and operated.[532]

This matter of travel opportunities as unrelated business started in the higher education context, in connection with tours offered by colleges, universities, and alumni and alumnae associations. In an unpublished technical advice memorandum issued in 1977, the IRS ruled that an international travel tour program conducted by an alumni association was an unrelated business; the agency cited the absence of any "formal educational program" and the lack of any plan for "contacting and meeting with alumni in the countries visited."[533] Tours that feature organized study, lectures, reports, library access, and reading lists may be considered educational in nature.[534] Tours that are "not significantly different from commercially sponsored" tours are usually unrelated businesses, however, as are extension (or add-on) tours.[535]

The balance of the law, as stated in regulations, on this point must be extracted from examples. An absence of "scheduled instruction or curriculum related to the destination being visited"[536] can lead to a finding of an unrelated business. Thus, for example, it is not a related business for a tax-exempt university alumni association to operate a tour program for its members and guests, where a faculty member is a guest on the tour and participants are encouraged to continue their "lifelong learning" by joining a tour.[537] Conversely, a tour conducted by teachers and directed to students enrolled in degree programs at educational institutions can be a related business, particularly where five or six hours per day are devoted to organized study, preparation of reports, lectures, instruction, and recitation by the students, and where a library of material is available, examinations are given at the end of the tour, and academic credit is offered for participation in the tour.[538]

A tax-exempt membership organization can exist to foster cultural unity and educate Americans about their country of origin. Tours of this organization that

---

[531] Nat'l Ass'n of Am. Churches v. Comm'r, 82 T.C. 18 (1984).

[532] Reg. § 1.513-7(a).

[533] This technical advice memorandum is the basis of Rev. Rul. 78-43, 1978-1 C.B. 164. The IRS revoked the tax-exempt status of a charitable organization because of the extent of its conduct of golf and tennis tours; the organization contended the tours were in furtherance of exempt purposes (Tech. Adv. Mem. 9540002).

The IRS held that the travel expenses incurred by an alumnus in participating in a university's continuing education program in foreign countries were not deductible as business expenses because they were personal outlays (Rev. Rul. 84-55, 1984-1 C.B. 29). Cf. IRC § 170(j).

[534] Rev. Rul. 70-534, 1970-2 C.B. 113.

[535] Tech. Adv. Mem. 9702004.

[536] Reg. § 1.513-7(b), Example (1).

[537] Id.

[538] Reg. § 1.513-7(b), Example (2).

are designed to "immerse participants in [the country's] history, culture and language" may be related businesses, particularly where "[s]ubstantially all of the daily itinerary" is devoted to instruction and visits to places of historical significance. If the trips, however, consist of optional tours and destinations of principally recreational interest and lack instruction or curriculum, they will likely be unrelated businesses.[539]

A tour where the participants assist in data collection to facilitate scientific research can qualify as a related business.[540] An archaeological expedition with a significant educational component can constitute a related business.[541] A tour enabling participants to attend plays and concerts will be an unrelated business, where the emphasis is on social and recreational activities rather than a "coordinated educational program."[542]

Advocacy travel can qualify as related business. For example, travel tours for a tax-exempt organization's members to Washington, D.C., where the participants spend substantially all of their time over several days attending meetings with legislators and government officials, and receiving briefings on policy developments related to the issue that is the organization's focus, are related businesses.[543] This is the case even though the participants have some time in the evenings to engage in social and recreational activities.

(k) Provision of Services

In general, net income from the provision of services by a tax-exempt organization to another organization, including another exempt organization, is unrelated business income.[544] This is because it is not automatically an exempt function for one exempt organization to provide services to another, even where both organizations have the same category of exempt status. For example, the IRS ruled that the provision of administrative services by an exempt association to an exempt voluntary employees' beneficiary association, where the latter entity provided a health and welfare benefit plan for the former entity's members' employees, was an unrelated business.[545] Likewise, the provision of management services by an exempt association to a charitable organization it founded was ruled by the IRS to be an unrelated business.[546] Indeed, the provision of management services by a nonprofit organization to unaffiliated charitable organizations led to the revocation of the organization's exemption as a charitable entity.[547]

---

[539] Reg. § 1.513-7(b), Example (4).

[540] Reg. § 1.513-7(b), Example (5).

[541] Reg. § 1.513-7(b), Example (6).

[542] Reg. § 1.513-7(b), Example (7).

[543] Reg. § 1.513-7(b), Example (3).

[544] E.g., Rev. Rul. 72-369, 1972-2 C.B. 245, which held that the provision of managerial and consulting services by an entity that would otherwise qualify under IRC § 501(c)(3) to other IRC § 501(c)(3) organizations on a regular basis for a fee is a business ordinarily undertaken for profit and that provision of such services at cost is insufficient to demonstrate the requisite donative element for exemption. See § 7.13(a), text accompanied by note 455.

[545] Tech. Adv. Mem. 9550001.

[546] Tech. Adv. Mem. 9811001.

[547] Tech. Adv. Mem. 9822004.

There are two exceptions to this general rule. One is that, under certain circumstances, it can be a related business for a tax-exempt organization to provide services of this nature to another exempt entity.[548] As an illustration, an exempt business association with an aggressive litigation strategy placed the litigation function in a separate exempt organization because of a substantial risk of counterclaims and other retaliatory actions against the association and its members; the IRS concluded that the provision by the association of management and administrative services to the other exempt organization was in furtherance of the association's exempt purposes.[549] Likewise, the IRS ruled that a national charitable organization engaged in related business activities when it provided certain coordination services for its chapters in connection with a new program it was implementing.[550] Additionally, an exempt organization that was an arm of an association of public school boards that administered the association's cash/risk management funds was found to be engaged in the charitable activity of lessening the burdens of government.[551] Similarly, the IRS ruled that charitable purposes were being served when a community foundation[552] sold grantmaking services to charitable organizations in its community.[553]

Also, the provision of professional, managerial, and administrative services among a group of interrelated health care organizations, directly or by means of a partnership, was ruled to be a bundle of related businesses.[554] Similarly, the lease and management of a computer system to a partnership by a supporting organization of a university's medical center, which system was used for billing, collection, and record keeping of the partners, was found to be a related business because the partners were physicians on the faculty of the university's medical school and teaching hospital.[555] Further, the IRS ruled that a graduate educational institution was engaged in a related business when it provided "central services" to a group of affiliated colleges (such as campus security, a central steam plant, accounting services, and a risk and property insurance program).[556] Other IRS rulings are issued from time to time on this point.[557]

The other exception is where the tax-exempt organizations are related entities, usually as parent and subsidiary. In the health care context, for example, the IRS has a ruling policy that the provision of services by and to related entities is not an unrelated business. This policy is articulated in rulings concerning the tax consequences of creation of a health care delivery system by means of a joint operating agreement. The arrangement entails what the IRS terms the provision

---

[548] E.g., Priv. Ltr. Rul. 9752023.

[549] Tech. Adv. Mem 9608003.

[550] Priv. Ltr. Rul. 9641011.

[551] Tech. Adv. Mem. 9711002.

[552] See § 12.3(b)(iii).

[553] Priv. Ltr. Rul. 200832027. Likewise, the IRS approved an arrangement by which a private operating foundation sells "technical assistance services" to "social sector organizations" (Priv. Ltr. Rul. 201701002).

[554] Priv. Ltr. Rul. 9839039.

[555] Tech. Adv. Mem. 9847002.

[556] Priv. Ltr. Rul. 9849027.

[557] E.g., Priv. Ltr. Rul. 199910060.

of *corporate services* by and among exempt organizations (in the case of this type of system, several hospitals and a parent supporting organization). The IRS stated that, if the participating exempt organizations are in a parent-and-subsidiary relationship, corporate services provided between them that are necessary to the accomplishment of their exempt purposes are treated as other than an unrelated business, and the financial arrangements between them are viewed as *merely a matter of accounting*.[558] Indeed, in these rulings, the IRS extended the matter-of-accounting rationale to relationships that are analogous to parent-subsidiary arrangements.

The first time this parent-subsidiary rationale was used outside the health care setting was in connection with a typical situation where a tax-exempt social welfare organization provided corporate services to its related foundation.[559] This arrangement was held not to generate unrelated business income, because of the "close structural relationship" between the two organizations. The IRS subsequently ruled on this point.[560]

As to arrangements where the relationship is analogous to that of parent and subsidiary, the first illustration was provided in the case of vertically, horizontally, and geographically integrated charitable health care systems, utilizing two supporting organizations, where the IRS ruled that the affiliation agreements involved relationships analogous to that of parent and subsidiary.[561] A subsequent case concerned two charitable organizations that managed health care facilities; they entered into a management agreement with a third such organization.[562]

Another instance, involving the leasing of facilities by a tax-exempt hospital to another exempt hospital, illustrated this approach. The IRS ruled that the leasing activity was an exempt function because of the direct physical connection and close professional affiliation of the institutions.[563] As to the latter factor, however, the lessor and lessee hospitals were closely associated with an exempt medical school; thus the IRS could have ruled that the two hospitals were in a relationship analogous to that of parent and subsidiary.

(l) Sales of Merchandise

Generally, the sale of merchandise to the public is a commercial enterprise and thus, from the standpoint of the law of tax-exempt organizations, usually is an unrelated business.[564] On occasion, nonetheless, sales of merchandise can be related activities, such as in the museum and fundraising contexts.[565] The facts and circumstances of each case will determine whether merchandise sales are a related or unrelated business.

---

[558] E.g., Priv. Ltr. Rul. 9651047.
[559] Priv. Ltr. Rul. 200022056.
[560] E.g., Priv. Ltr. Rul. 200037050.
[561] Priv. Ltr. Rul. 200101034.
[562] Priv. Ltr. Rul. 200108045.
[563] Priv. Ltr. Rul. 200314031.
[564] See § 4.9.
[565] See §§ 24.5(c), 24.5(i)(iv).

In one instance, a public charity had as its tax-exempt purpose the eradication of breast cancer by funding research, educating the public, and sponsoring screening and treatment programs. The IRS ruled that the sale of merchandise, bearing a breast cancer awareness symbol, by the organization and its affiliates is a related activity because it encourages early detection of the disease and thus the saving of lives.[566]

By contrast, in connection with a tax-exempt organization operating several community centers in furtherance of religious, charitable, and educational purposes, the IRS ruled (without analysis) that the sale of T-shirts, baseball caps, bottled water, and towels to the patrons of the centers is unrelated business income.[567] Similarly, the IRS determined that an exempt conservation and preservation organization, selling a product by means of its online store, by print catalog, and at various retail outlets, with almost no provision of educational information, was engaging in an unrelated business.[568]

(m) Share-Crop Leasing

The subject of the tax treatment accorded share-crop revenue received by tax-exempt organizations is informed by two bodies of law: the existence or non-existence of a general partnership or joint venture for tax purposes[569] and interpretation of the passive rent rules.[570]

A share-crop lease arrangement may involve land that is owned by a tax-exempt organization and leased by the organization to a farmer. Under the terms of the lease, the tenant is exclusively responsible for managing and operating the farm property. The tenant is also required to prepare a farm operating plan, including a schedule of crops to be grown on the land, seeding or planting rates, chemicals and fertilizers to be used, conservation practices and tillage plans, livestock breeding and market schedules, nutrition and feeding schedules, and harvesting and storage plans. After the operating plan is complete, the tenant is usually required to submit the plan to the exempt organization for review.

The tax-exempt organization is generally responsible for all of the costs associated with the land and fixed improvements, including the costs of wells and pumps, irrigation equipment, and initially required limestone and rock phosphates. In ascertaining whether amounts received by a tax-exempt organization pursuant to a share-crop lease constitute excludable rent, the first determination is whether the arrangement is a true lease or amounts to a joint venture. Secondly, there must be a decision as to whether the exclusion for rental income applies.

In the first court case on this point, it was concluded that the tax-exempt organization's income was "true rent" within the scope of the rental exclusion[571] and that the relationship between the parties was not a joint venture or partnership;

---

[566] Priv. Ltr. Rul. 200722028.
[567] Priv. Ltr. Rul. 201128027.
[568] Tech. Adv. Mem. 201633032.
[569] See Chapter 31.
[570] See § 25.1(h).
[571] IRC § 512(b)(3)(A)(i), (B)(ii). See § 25.1(h).

thus the income was not taxable as unrelated business income.[572] Other courts reached the same conclusion.[573]

(n) Retirement Plan Reversions

A tax-exempt organization may maintain a qualified pension or other retirement plan to provide retirement benefits to its employees. Generally, the assets of the plan must be used exclusively for the employees and their beneficiaries,[574] and the contributions of an employer to a qualified plan are deductible in the year in which the contributions are paid.[575] This type of plan may be terminated; in that instance, all benefits accrued to the date of termination must become completely vested and nonforfeitable, and plan benefits must be distributed to the participants in the plan, or annuities providing for the payment of comparable benefits must be purchased and distributed to the participants. Where the plan is terminated and assets remain after the satisfaction of all liabilities to plan participants and other beneficiaries, and if the excess of assets is attributable to actuarial error, the employer is permitted to recover the excess assets.[576] Generally, this excess must be included in the gross income of the employer.

Where the employer organization is a tax-exempt organization that is subject to the rule that all income other than exempt function income is taxable as unrelated business income,[577] such as a social club,[578] generally the amount of the reversion is includable in the organization's unrelated business income because it is not exempt function income.[579]

In other instances, however, this type of income may be excluded from taxation by reason of the *tax benefit rule*. Under the exclusionary portion of this rule, gross income does not include income attributable to the recovery during a tax year of any amount deducted in any prior tax year to the extent that amount did not reduce the amount of income tax involved.[580] By contrast, under the inclusionary aspect of this rule, where the amount previously deducted from gross income generates a tax benefit and is then recaptured in a subsequent year, the recaptured amount is includable in gross income in the year of the recapture.[581] Consequently, to the extent that this type of tax-exempt organization deducted contributions to a defined benefit plan in determining its taxable nonexempt function income, the inclusionary aspect of the tax benefit rule is applicable.[582]

---

[572] Harlan E. Moore Charitable Trust v. United States, 812 F. Supp. 130, 135 (C.D. Ill. 1993), *aff'd*, 9 F.3d 623 (7th Cir. 1993).

[573] Indep. Order of Odd Fellows Grand Lodge of Iowa v. United States, 93-2 U.S.T.C. ¶ 50,448 (S.D. Iowa 1993); Trust U/W Emily Oblinger v. Comm'r, 100 T.C. 114 (1993); White's Iowa Manual Labor Inst. v. Comm'r, 66 T.C.M. 389 (1993).

[574] IRC § 401(a)(2).

[575] IRC § 401(a)(1)(A).

[576] Reg. § 1.401-2(b)(1).

[577] See § 25.4(c).

[578] See Chapter 15.

[579] Gen. Couns. Mem. 39717.

[580] IRC § 111(a).

[581] IRC § 61; Rev. Rul. 68-104, 1968-1 C.B. 361; Gen. Couns. Mem. 39744.

[582] Gen. Couns. Mem. 39717.

Where the employer organization is a tax-exempt organization that is not subject to this rule concerning taxation of nonexempt function income, the tax consequences of a reversion of plan assets are different. Because (1) the operation of the plan is not a business but rather an administrative function that is part of the overall operations of the exempt organization and (2) the funds that revert on termination of the plan are a one-time source of income rather than income from an activity that is regularly carried on,[583] the reverted funds are generally not taxable as unrelated business income.[584] Thus, for example, the IRS ruled that the reversion of assets from a defined benefit pension plan to a tax-exempt charitable organization employer, as part of termination of the plan, would not give rise to unrelated business income.[585]

(o) Internet Communications

Although tax-exempt organizations obviously use the Internet to conduct related and unrelated business, little law specific to the subject has developed. It is clear, however, that the federal tax law does not provide unique treatment to transactions or activities of exempt organizations merely because the Internet is the medium. The IRS saliently observed that utilization of the Internet to "accomplish a particular task does not change the way the tax laws apply to that task."[586] The IRS added that "[a]dvertising is still advertising and fundraising is still fundraising."[587] Overall, unrelated business conducted by means of the Internet is still unrelated business.

The IRS has issued a few pronouncements in this field, such as a ruling that creation by a for-profit corporation of a website on which to conduct business is an expansion of the corporation's business rather than an acquisition of a new or different business.[588] The agency held that a public charity may conduct a portion of its health care provider services on a website.[589] The IRS ruled that certain website listings and links by a tax-exempt organization are not businesses, that they do not cause licensing royalties to be taxable, and that a website link to a corporate sponsor is not advertising.[590] The IRS held that activities conducted on the premises of an exempt business league's trade shows and on a special section of the organization's website that allows its members and the public to access the same information that is available at the physical shows constituted qualified convention and trade show activity.[591] However, this type of Internet activity is ineligible for the trade show exception if it does not coincide with or otherwise augment or enhance an exempt organization's convention or trade show.[592]

---

[583] See § 24.3.

[584] Gen. Couns. Mem. 39806.

[585] Priv. Ltr. Rul. 200131034.

[586] "Tax-Exempt Organizations and World Wide Web Fundraising and Advertising on the Internet," Topic I, IRS Exempt Organizations Continuing Professional Education Text for FY 2000.

[587] Id.

[588] Rev. Rul. 2003-38, 2003-1 C.B. 811.

[589] Priv. Ltr. Rul. 200307094.

[590] Priv. Ltr. Rul. 200303062.

[591] Rev. Rul. 2004-112, 2004-2 C.B. 985. See § 25.2(f).

[592] Id.

A significant issue in this context is the matter of tax-exempt organizations' website hypertext links to related or recommended sites. These exchanges may be treated by the IRS the same way as mailing list exchanges.[593] Compensation for a linkage may be unrelated business income. (An absence of compensation may entail private inurement, private benefit, or an excess benefit transaction.)[594]

Also involved are corporate sponsorships, inasmuch as some tax-exempt organizations seek corporate support to underwrite the production of all or a portion of the organization's website. These relationships may be short-term or continue on a long-term basis. The financial support may be acknowledged by means of display of a corporate logo, notation of the sponsor's Web address and/or 800 number, a "moving banner" (a graphic advertisement, usually a moving image, measured in pixels), or a link. The issue is whether the support is a qualified sponsorship payment (in which case the revenue is not taxable)[595] or is advertising income (which generally is taxable as unrelated business income).[596] Use of a link in an acknowledgment may change the character of a corporation's payment, converting it from nontaxable sponsorship to taxable advertising income.[597]

Another problem relates to the rule that qualified sponsorship payments do not include payments that entitle the sponsors to acknowledgments in regularly scheduled printed material published by or on behalf of the tax-exempt organization.[598] Here the issue is the characterization of website materials. Most of the material made available on exempt organizations' websites is prepared in a manner that is distinguishable from the methodology used in the preparation of periodicals.

Online storefronts, replete with virtual shopping carts, on tax-exempt organizations' websites may be subject to the same analysis the IRS applies in the context of museum gift shop sales.[599] Still other aspects of this subject include the tax treatment of online auctions, and affiliate and other co-venture programs with merchants (including booksellers). (A principal issue is whether any resulting income is a tax-excludable royalty.)[600]

(p) Debt Management Plan Services

Debt management plan services are regarded as unrelated trade or business when conducted by an organization that is not a credit counseling organization.[601] With respect to the provision of debt management plan services by a credit counseling organization, in order for the income from these services to not be unrelated business income, the debt management plan service with respect to such income must contribute importantly to the accomplishment of credit

---

[593] See § 24.5(i)(iii).
[594] See Chapters 20, 21.
[595] See § 24.6.
[596] See § 24.5(h).
[597] See § 24.6, text accompanied by *infra* note 634.
[598] *Id.*, text accompanied by *infra* notes 636-639.
[599] See § 24.5(c).
[600] See § 25.1(g).
[601] IRC § 513(j). See § 7.3(b).

counseling services and must not be conducted on a larger scale than reasonably necessary for the accomplishment of the services.[602]

(q) Other Organizations' Exempt Functions

An activity that is a related business when conducted by one type of tax-exempt organization may be an unrelated business when conducted by another type of exempt organization. For example, the IRS ruled that a certification program conducted by an exempt educational and scientific organization was an unrelated business, because it primarily advanced the interests of individuals in a particular profession and only incidentally served the interests of the public.[603] The activity was said to be appropriate when conducted by an exempt business league[604] but an activity promoting nonexempt purposes when conducted by a charitable organization.[605]

§ 24.6 CORPORATE SPONSORSHIPS

A payment made by a corporation to sponsor an event or activity of a tax-exempt organization may be a contribution or may be taxable as unrelated business income. Sponsorship payments received by exempt organizations that are *qualified* are not subject to unrelated business income taxation.[606]

This is a safe-harbor rule. Therefore, a corporate sponsorship payment that is not a qualified one is not necessarily taxable. Rather, the tax treatment of it is evaluated under the unrelated business rules generally. Thus, the transaction is evaluated as to whether it is a business,[607] whether it is regularly carried on,[608] whether it is subject to an exception for income or activities,[609] and the like.

A *qualified sponsorship payment* is a payment that a person who is engaged in a trade or business makes to a tax-exempt organization, with respect to which there is no arrangement or expectation that the person will receive a substantial return benefit from the exempt organization.[610] It is irrelevant whether the sponsored activity is related or unrelated to the recipient tax-exempt organization's exempt purpose. It is also irrelevant whether the sponsored activity is temporary or permanent. The word *payment* means the payment of money, transfer of property, or performance of services.[611]

---

[602] Staff of Joint Comm. on Tax'n, Technical Explanation of H.R. 4, the "Pension Protection Act of 2006," as Passed by the House on July 28, 2006, and as Considered by the Senate on August 3, 2006 319 (Comm. Print JCX-38-06).

[603] Priv. Ltr. Rul. 200439043.

[604] See § 14.1(g).

[605] See, e.g., §§ 7.8(a), 8.6.

[606] IRC § 513(i)(1); Reg. § 1.513-4(a).

[607] See § 24.2.

[608] See § 24.3.

[609] See §§ 25.1, 25.2.

[610] IRC § 513(i)(2)(A); Reg. § 1.513-4(c)(1).

[611] Reg. § 1.513-4(c)(1).

A *substantial return benefit* is a benefit other than certain uses or acknowledgments and other than certain disregarded benefits.[612] Benefits are disregarded if the aggregate fair market value of all the benefits provided to the payor or persons designated by the payor in connection with the payment during the organization's tax year is not more than 2 percent of the amount of the payment.[613] If the aggregate fair market value of the benefits exceeds 2 percent of the amount of the payment, then (unless it is a shielded use or acknowledgment) the entire fair market value of the benefits is a substantial return benefit.[614]

Benefits provided to the payor or a designated person may include advertising; an exclusive provider arrangement; goods, facilities, services, or other privileges; and/or exclusive or nonexclusive rights to use an intangible asset (such as a trademark, patent, logo, or designation) of the exempt organization.[615]

A substantial return benefit does not include the use or acknowledgment of the name, logo, or product lines of the payor's trade or business in connection with the activities of the exempt organization. While a use or acknowledgment does not include advertising, it may include an exclusive sponsorship arrangement; logos and slogans that do not contain qualitative or comparative descriptions of the payor's products, services, facilities, or company; a list of the payor's locations, telephone numbers, or Internet address; value-neutral descriptions, including displays or visual depictions, of the payor's product line or services; and/or reference to the payor's brand or trade names and product or service listings.[616]

The term *advertising* means any message or other programming material that is broadcast or otherwise transmitted, published, displayed, or distributed, and that promotes or markets any trade or business, or any service, facility, or product.[617] The term includes messages containing qualitative or comparative language, price information or other indications of savings or value, an endorsement, or an inducement to purchase, sell, or use any company, service, facility, or product.[618] A single message that contains both advertising and an acknowledgment is advertising.[619]

An arrangement that acknowledges the payor as the exclusive sponsor of a tax-exempt organization's activity, or the exclusive sponsor representing a particular trade, business, or industry, generally does not, by itself, result in a substantial return benefit.[620] For example, if in exchange for a payment, an exempt organization announces that its event is sponsored exclusively by the payor (and does not provide any advertising or other substantial return benefit to the payor), the payor has not received a substantial return benefit. An arrangement that limits the sale, distribution, availability, or use of competing products, services, or facilities in

[612] Reg. § 1.513-4(c)(2)(i).
[613] Reg. § 1.513-4(c)(2)(ii).
[614] Id.
[615] Reg. § 1.513-4(c)(2)(iii).
[616] Reg. § 1.513-4(c)(2)(iv).
[617] Reg. § 1.513-4(c)(2)(v).
[618] IRC § 513(i)(2)(A).
[619] Id.
[620] Reg. § 1.513-4(c)(2)(vi)(A).

connection with an exempt organization's activity generally results in a substantial return benefit.[621]

To the extent that a portion of a payment would (if made as a separate payment) be a qualified sponsorship payment, that portion of the payment and the other portion of the payment are treated as separate payments.[622] Thus, if there is an arrangement or expectation that the payor will receive a substantial return benefit with respect to any payment, then only the portion, if any, of the payment that exceeds the fair market value of the substantial return benefit is a qualified sponsorship payment.[623] If the exempt organization, however, does not establish that the payment exceeds the fair market value of a substantial return benefit, then no portion of the payment constitutes a qualified sponsorship payment.[624]

The *fair market value* of a substantial return benefit provided as part of a sponsorship arrangement is the price at which the benefit would be provided between a willing recipient and a willing provider of the benefit, neither being under any compulsion to enter into the arrangement and both having reasonable knowledge of relevant facts, and without regard to any other aspect of the sponsorship arrangement.[625]

In general, the fair market value of a substantial return benefit is determined when the benefit is provided. If the parties enter into a binding, written sponsorship contract, however, the fair market value of any substantial return benefit provided pursuant to that contract is determined on the date the parties enter into the sponsorship contract. If the parties make a material change to a sponsorship contract, it is treated as a new sponsorship contract as of the date the material change is effective. A *material change* includes an extension or renewal of the contract, or a more-than-incidental change to any amount payable (or other consideration) pursuant to the contract.[626]

The existence of a written sponsorship agreement does not, in itself, cause a payment to fail to be a qualified sponsorship payment. The terms of the agreement, not its existence or degree of detail, are relevant to the determination of whether a payment is a qualified sponsorship payment. Similarly, the terms of the agreement and not the title or responsibilities of the individuals negotiating the agreement determine whether a payment, or a portion of a payment, made pursuant to the agreement is a qualified sponsorship payment.[627]

The term *qualified sponsorship payment* does not include any payment whose amount is contingent, by contract or otherwise, on the level of attendance at one or more events, broadcast ratings, or other factors indicating the degree of public exposure to the sponsored activity. The fact that a payment is contingent on sponsored events or activities actually being conducted does not, by itself, cause the payment to fail to be a qualified sponsorship payment.[628]

---

[621] Reg. § 1.513-4(c)(2)(vi)(B).
[622] IRC § 513(i)(3).
[623] Reg. § 1.513-4(d)(1).
[624] *Id.*
[625] Reg. § 1.513-4(d)(1)(ii).
[626] Reg. § 1.513-4(d)(1)(iii).
[627] Reg. § 1.513-4(e)(1).
[628] IRC § 513(i)(2)(B)(i); Reg. § 1.513-4(e)(2).

Qualified sponsorship payments in the form of money or property—but not services—are contributions received by the tax-exempt organization involved. For organizations that are required to or need to compute public support,[629] these payments are contributions for that purpose.[630] The fact that a payment to an exempt organization constitutes a qualified sponsorship payment that is treated as a contribution to the payee organization does not determine whether the payment is deductible by the payor.[631] The payment may be deductible as a charitable contribution[632] or as a business expense.[633]

The tax regulations address the matter of the import of website links by means of two examples. The essence of these examples is that the mere existence of a link from the sponsored tax-exempt organization to the corporate sponsor does not cause a payment to fail to be a qualified sponsorship payment, but material on the linked site can cause the payment to entail a substantial return benefit.[634]

This safe-harbor rule does not apply to payments made in connection with qualified convention and trade show activities.[635] It also does not apply to income derived from the sale of an acknowledgment or advertising in the periodical of a tax-exempt organization.[636] The term *periodical* means regularly scheduled and printed material published by or on behalf of an exempt organization that is not related to and primarily distributed in connection with a specific event conducted by the exempt organization.[637] Separate rules govern the sale of advertising in exempt organization periodicals.[638] For purposes of the corporate sponsorship rules, at least, the phrase *printed material* includes material that is published electronically.[639]

§ 24.7   DEEMED UNRELATED BUSINESS INCOME

In four instances, tax-exempt organizations must take forms of income into account as unrelated income because the income is deemed to be unrelated business income, in whole or in part, by statute. These instances are (1) certain amounts of income derived from partnerships and other joint ventures,[640] (2) forms of debt-financed income (with exceptions),[641] (3) certain amounts received by controlling

---

[629] See § 12.3(b).

[630] Reg. § 1.513-4(e)(3).

[631] *Id.*

[632] IRC § 170.

[633] IRC § 162.

[634] Reg. § 1.513-4(f), Examples (11), (12). The IRS ruled that, at least in the context of the case, an exempt organization's website link to a corporate sponsor is an acknowledgment rather than advertising (Priv. Ltr. Rul. 200303062).

[635] IRC § 513(i)(2)(B)(ii)(II); Reg. § 1.513-4(b). See § 25.2(f).

[636] IRC § 513(i)(2)(B)(ii)(I); Reg. § 1.513-4(b).

[637] *Id.*

[638] See § 24.5(h).

[639] Reg. § 1.513-4(b). The IRS ruled that an educational organization's website satisfied the definition of the term *periodical*; thus, the organization was able to utilize the unrelated business income tax cost allocation rules (Priv. Ltr. Rul. 201405029).

[640] See § 24.8.

[641] See § 24.10.

organizations from controlled organizations,[642] and (4) income from insurance activities conducted by offshore captives of tax-exempt organizations.[643]

§ 24.8 PARTNERSHIP RULES

If a trade or business regularly carried on by a partnership, of which a tax-exempt organization is a member, is an unrelated trade or business with respect to the organization, in computing its unrelated business taxable income the organization must include its share (whether or not distributed and subject to certain modifications)[644] of the gross income of the partnership from the unrelated trade or business and its share of the partnership deductions directly connected with the gross income.[645] This rule (known as a *look-through rule*) applies irrespective of whether the tax-exempt organization is a general or limited partner.[646] The courts reject the thought that income derived by an exempt organization from a limited partnership interest is, for that reason alone, not taxable because a limited partnership interest is a passive investment by which the organization lacks any ability to actively engage in the management, operation, or control of the partnership.[647]

An illustration of this rule was provided when the IRS ruled that income from utility services, to be provided in the context of the provision of telecommunications services, will be rental income to exempt organizations that is excluded from unrelated business income taxation;[648] this income will flow to the exempt organizations from partnerships and limited liability companies.[649]

The look-through rule also applies when a partnership of which a tax-exempt organization is a member engages in activities that are related to the exempt purposes of the exempt organization. In this situation, any income generated by the related business is not subject to taxation as unrelated business income.[650]

§ 24.9 COMMERCIAL-TYPE INSURANCE

The provision of commercial-type insurance by a tax-exempt charitable organization[651] or social welfare organization,[652] where the activity is not sufficiently extensive to warrant denial or revocation of exempt status, is treated as the conduct of

---

[642] See §§ 25.1(k), 29.7, 30.6.

[643] See § 25.1(n)(i).

[644] See § 25.1.

[645] IRC § 512(c)(1), Reg. § 1.512(c)-1.

[646] Rev. Rul. 79-222, 1979-2 C.B. 236; Service Bolt & Nut Co. Profit Sharing Trust v. Comm'r, 78 T.C. 812 (1982).

[647] Service Bolt & Nut Co. Profit Sharing Trust v. Comm'r, 724 F.2d 519 (6th Cir. 1983), *aff'g* 78 T.C. 812 (1982).

[648] See § 25.1(h).

[649] Priv. Ltr. Rul. 200147058.

[650] E.g., Priv. Ltr. Rul. 9839039.

[651] See Part Three.

[652] See Chapter 13.

unrelated business.[653] The income from this activity is taxed in accordance with the rules pertaining to taxable insurance companies.[654] The term *commercial-type insurance* generally is any insurance of a type provided by commercial insurance companies.[655] This term does not, however, include conventional charitable gift annuities.[656]

§ 24.10 UNRELATED DEBT-FINANCED INCOME

The unrelated debt-financed income rules cause certain forms of income received by tax-exempt organizations, which would otherwise be exempt from taxation, to be subject to the unrelated business income tax.

(a) General Principles

In computing a tax-exempt organization's unrelated business taxable income, there must be included with respect to each debt-financed property that is unrelated to the organization's exempt function—as an item of gross income derived from an unrelated trade or business—an amount of income from the property, subject to tax in the proportion in which the property is financed by the debt.[657] Basically, deductions are allowed with respect to each debt-financed property in the same proportion.[658] The allowable deductions are those that are directly connected with the debt-financed property or its income, although any depreciation may only be computed on the straight-line method.[659] As the mortgage is paid, the percentage taken into account usually diminishes. Capital gains on the sale of unrelated debt-financed property are also taxed in the same proportions.[660]

(b) Debt-Financed Property

The term *debt-financed property* means, with certain exceptions, all property (for example, rental real estate, tangible personalty, and corporate stock) that is held to produce income (for example, rents, royalties, interest, and dividends) and with respect to which there is an acquisition indebtedness[661] at any time during the tax year (or during the preceding 12 months, if the property is disposed of during the year).[662]

Excepted from the term *debt-financed property* is (1) property where substantially all (at least 85 percent) of its use is substantially related (aside from the need of the tax-exempt organization for income or funds) to the exercise or performance

---

[653] IRC § 501(m)(2)(A).
[654] IRC § 501(m)(2)(B); IRC Subchapter L.
[655] See § 28.13(b).
[656] IRC § 501(m)(3)(E), (5). See § 24.10(c), text accompanied by *infra* note 688.
[657] IRC §§ 514(a)(1), 512(b)(4).
[658] IRC § 514(a)(2).
[659] IRC § 514(a)(3).
[660] Reg. § 1.514(a)-1.
[661] See § 24.10(c).
[662] IRC § 514(b)(1).

by the organization of its exempt purpose or, if less than substantially all of its use is related, to the extent that its use is substantially related to the organization's exempt purpose;[663] (2) property to the extent that its income is already subject to tax as income from the conduct of an unrelated trade or business;[664] (3) property to the extent that the income is derived from research activities and therefore excluded from unrelated business taxable income;[665] and (4) property to the extent that its use is in a trade or business exempted from tax because substantially all the work is performed without compensation, the business is carried on primarily for the convenience of members, students, patients, officers, or employees, or the business is the selling of merchandise, substantially all of which was received as gifts or contributions.[666]

Likewise, the IRS ruled that rental income derived by a public charity from debt-financed property was not unrelated debt-financed income because the property was an "innovation and incubator center," designed to create employment opportunities and increase higher education in technology, that was operated in furtherance of charitable purposes.[667] Similarly, the agency held that rental income derived by a public charity (which operated a continuing care retirement community) from debt-financed property leased (by means of a limited liability company that is a disregarded entity)[668] to a tax-exempt hospital, which will use it for an outpatient medical clinic to serve the residents of the community, was not unrelated debt-financed income because the leasing function was a charitable undertaking.[669] Further, the IRS held that rental income to be derived by a public charity that assists individuals with disabilities from the leasing of a portion of a tax-exempt bond-financed building to another public charity with similar purposes was not unrelated debt-financed income because the rental activity was in furtherance of the lessor's charitable purposes.[670]

Property owned by a tax-exempt organization and used by a related exempt organization or by an exempt organization related to the related exempt organization is not treated as debt-financed property to the extent the property is used by either organization in furtherance of its tax-exempt purpose.[671] In one instance, the IRS held that a charitable organization may acquire a building, use a portion of it, and lease the other portion to a related charitable organization and a related

---

[663] IRC § 514(b)(1)(A). The IRS ruled that proceeds to be received by a private foundation from loans will not constitute income from debt-financed property when the funds will be distributed, as grants, by the foundation to public charities (Priv. Ltr. Rul. 200432026). The IRS also ruled that, inasmuch as the operation of community centers, financed by means of construction bonds, is in furtherance of charitable purposes, the centers are not debt-financed property, so that income from these operations, including rental income, will not be unrelated business income (Priv. Ltr. Rul. 201131029).

[664] IRC § 514(b)(1)(B). This rule does not apply in the case of income excluded under IRC § 512(b)(5) (principally, capital gain). See § 25.1(j).

[665] IRC § 514(b)(1)(C). See § 25.1(l).

[666] IRC § 514(b)(1)(D). See § 25.2(a)–(c).

[667] Priv. Ltr. Rul. 200537038. The charitable purposes were lessening the burdens of government (see § 7.7) and providing economic development to an underprivileged area (see § 7.16(e)).

[668] See § 4.1(b)(ii).

[669] Priv. Ltr. Rul. 200538027.

[670] Priv. Ltr. Rul. 200843036.

[671] Reg. § 1.514(b)-1(c)(2)(i).

business league for their offices and activities, and that the building will not be treated as debt-financed property.[672]

The *neighborhood land rule* provides an exemption from the debt-financed property rules for interim income from neighborhood real property acquired for a tax-exempt purpose. The tax on unrelated debt-financed income does not apply to income from real property, located in the neighborhood of other property owned by the tax-exempt organization, which it plans to devote to exempt uses within 10 years of the time of acquisition.[673] The exemption applies with respect to any structure on the land when acquired by the organization, and to the land occupied by the structure, only if (and so long as) the intended future use of the land in the manner covered by the neighborhood land rule requires that the structure be demolished or removed in order to use the land in such manner.[674] This rule applies after the first five years of the 10-year period only if the exempt organization satisfies the IRS that future use of the acquired land in furtherance of its exempt purposes before the expiration of the period is reasonably certain;[675] this process is to be initiated by filing a ruling request at least 90 days before the end of the fifth year.[676] A more generous 15-year rule is established for churches; also, it is not required that the property be in the neighborhood of the church.[677]

If debt-financed property is sold or otherwise disposed of, a percentage of the total gain or loss derived from the disposition is included in the computation of unrelated business taxable income.[678] The IRS recognizes, however, that the unrelated debt-financed income rules do not render taxable a transaction that would not be taxable by virtue of a nonrecognition provision of the federal tax law if it were carried out by an entity that is not tax-exempt.[679]

(c)   Acquisition Indebtedness

Income-producing property is considered to be unrelated debt-financed property (making income from it, less deductions, taxable) only where there is an acquisition indebtedness attributable to it. *Acquisition indebtedness*, with respect to debt-financed property, means the unpaid amount of the indebtedness incurred by the tax-exempt organization in acquiring or improving the property, the indebtedness

---

[672] Priv. Ltr. Rul. 7833055.

[673] IRC § 514(b)(3)(A)–(C). Where a tax-exempt organization did not own the original site property in the neighborhood, since the property was owned by a supporting organization (see § 12.3(c)) with respect to the organization, the IRS concluded that the neighborhood land rule nonetheless applied because of the supported organization's "interrelated nature" with the property by means of the supporting organization (Priv. Ltr. Rul. 9603019).

[674] IRC § 514(b)(3)(C)(i); Reg. § 1.514(b)-1(d)(3)(i). The rule does not apply to exempt any structures erected on the land after the acquisition of the land (IRC § 514(b)(3)(C)(ii)), or to any property subject to a lease that is a business lease (IRC § 514(b)(3)(C)(iii); Reg. § 1.514(b)-1(d)(3)(iii)). As to the definition of business lease, see Reg. § 1.514(f)-1.

[675] IRC § 514(b)(3)(A).

[676] Reg. § 1.514(b)-1(d)(1)(iii). Where the IRS was satisfied with the plans an organization submitted for the future use of the property, but the organization failed to timely seek this ruling, The IRS granted administrative relief (Reg. § 301.9100-1(a)) by extending the filing period (Priv. Ltr. Rul. 9603019).

[677] IRC § 514(b)(3)(E). In general, Reg. § 1.514(b)-1.

[678] Reg. § 1.514(a)-1(a)(1)(v).

[679] Rev. Rul. 77-71, 1977-1 C.B. 156.

incurred before any acquisition or improvement of the property if the indebtedness would not have been incurred but for the acquisition or improvement, and the indebtedness incurred after the acquisition or improvement of the property if the indebtedness would not have been incurred but for the acquisition or improvement and the incurring of the indebtedness was reasonably foreseeable at the time of the acquisition or improvement.[680]

If property is acquired by a tax-exempt organization subject to a mortgage or other similar lien, the indebtedness thereby secured is considered an acquisition indebtedness incurred by the organization when the property is acquired, even though the organization did not assume or agree to pay the indebtedness.[681] Some relief is provided, however, with respect to mortgaged property acquired as a result of a bequest or devise. That is, the indebtedness secured by this type of mortgage is not treated as acquisition indebtedness during the 10-year period following the date of acquisition.[682] A similar rule applies to mortgaged property received by gift, where the mortgage was placed on the property more than five years before the gift and the property was held by the donor more than five years before the gift.[683] These two exceptions are not available if, in order to acquire the equity in the property by bequest, devise, or gift, the organization assumes and agrees to pay the indebtedness secured by the mortgage, or if the organization makes any payment for the equity in the property owned by the decedent or the donor.[684]

Other exceptions from the scope of acquisition indebtedness are the following:

- The term *acquisition indebtedness* does not include indebtedness that was incurred in circumstances where incurrence of the debt was inherent in the performance of a tax-exempt function of an organization or otherwise in advancement of the organization's exempt purpose,[685] such as the indebtedness incurred by an exempt credit union[686] in accepting deposits from its members. It has been held, however, that the purchase of securities on margin and with borrowed funds is not inherent in (meaning essential to) the

---

[680] IRC § 514(c)(1). The word *indebtedness* is not defined in this setting. In other contexts (e.g., the deduction for interest paid on indebtedness (IRC § 163(a)), courts have held that indebtedness is an unconditional and legally enforceable obligation for the payment of money (e.g., Autenreith v. Comm'r, 115 F.2d 856 (3d Cir. 1940); Kovtun v. Comm'r, 54 T.C. 331 (1970), *aff'd per curiam*, 448 F.2d 1268 (9th Cir. 1971)). The IRS uses this definition in connection with the unrelated debt-financed income rules, supplementing it by also borrowing from the law concerning the bad debt deduction (IRC § 166), which provides that a debt must be a fixed or determinable sum of money (Reg. § 1.166-1(c)) (e.g., Priv. Ltr. Rul. 201740002).

[681] IRC § 514(c)(2)(A).

[682] IRC § 514(c)(2)(B). This rule was applied by the IRS in connection with a distribution of a trust's interest in a limited liability company, which included debt-financed property, to a private foundation after the death of an individual, with the distribution treated as a devise from the individual (Priv. Ltr. Rul. 201849009).

[683] IRC § 514(c)(2)(B).

[684] *Id.*

[685] IRC § 514(c)(4). Leasing of its premises by a tax-exempt hospital to a state university as part of the state's reorganization of its health care system was held to be an activity in furtherance of charitable purposes, so that the debt-financed property being leased will not generate unrelated business income (Priv. Ltr. Rul. 201702002).

[686] See § 19.7.

performance or exercise of a credit union's exempt purposes or function, so that a portion of the resulting income is taxable as debt-financed income.[687]

- The term does not include an obligation to pay an annuity that (1) is the sole consideration issued in exchange for property if, at the time of the exchange, the value of the annuity is less than 90 percent of the value of the property received in the exchange; (2) is payable over the life of one individual who is living at the time the annuity is issued, or over the lives of two individuals living at that time; and (3) is payable under a contract that does not guarantee a minimum amount of payments or specify a maximum amount of payments and does not provide for any adjustment of the amount of the annuity payments by reference to the income received from the transferred property or any other property.[688]

- The term does not include an obligation to finance the purchase, rehabilitation, or construction of housing for low- and moderate-income persons to the extent that it is insured by the Federal Housing Administration.[689]

- The term does not include indebtedness incurred by certain small business investment companies if the indebtedness is evidenced by a certain type of debenture.[690]

- The term does not include a tax-exempt organization's obligation to return collateral security pursuant to a securities lending arrangement, thereby making it clear that, in ordinary circumstances, payments on securities loans are not debt-financed income.[691]

For these purposes, the term *acquisition indebtedness* generally does not include indebtedness incurred by a qualified organization in acquiring or improving any real property.[692] A *qualified organization* is an operating educational institution,[693] any affiliated support organization,[694] and a tax-exempt multiparent title-holding organization,[695] as well as any trust that constitutes a pension trust.[696] Nonetheless,

---

[687] Alabama Central Credit Union v. United States, 646 F. Supp. 1199 (N.D. Ala. 1986).

[688] IRC § 514(c)(5).

[689] IRC § 514(c)(6)(A)(i). In general, Reg. § 1.514(c)-1.

[690] IRC § 514(c)(6)(A)(ii), (B).

[691] IRC § 514(c)(8). See § 25.1(d). Although, in a net profit interest/royalty arrangement (see § 25.1(g)), the corporation will acquire its working interest in the oil and gas properties with borrowed funds, this debt financing was held by the IRS to not amount to acquisition indebtedness with respect to the net profits interest of the foundation (Priv. Ltr. Rul. 201142026).

[692] IRC § 514(c)(9)(A). This exception does not apply if the qualified organization leases the property back to the seller (IRC § 514(c)(9)(B)(iii); e.g., Priv. Ltr. Rul. 9031052).

[693] That is, one described in IRC § 170(b)(1)(A)(ii). See § 12.3(a). An organization whose primary purpose was management of portions of a health care system's significant investment portfolio was ruled to not be a qualified organization; its formal educational activities represented only 13 percent of its expenses and 6 percent of its revenues (Tech. Adv. Mem. 201407024). See § 8.3(a), text accompanied by notes 46–54.

[694] That is, one described in IRC § 509(a)(3). See § 12.3(c).

[695] That is, one described in IRC § 501(c)(25). See § 19.2(b).

[696] That is, one described in IRC § 401. The definition of *qualified organization* is the subject of IRC § 514(c)(9)(C).

in computing the unrelated income of a shareholder or beneficiary of a disqualified holder (namely, a multiparent title-holding organization)[697] of an interest in a multiparent title-holding entity attributable to the interest, the holder's pro rata share of the items of income that are treated as gross income derived from an unrelated business (without regard to the exception for debt-financed property) is taken into account as gross income of the disqualified holder derived from an unrelated business; the holder's pro rata share of deductions is likewise taken into account.[698]

Thus, under this exception, income from investments in real property is not treated as income from debt-financed property and therefore as unrelated business income. Mortgages are not considered real property for purposes of this exception.[699] Thus, a supporting organization with respect to an exempt university was able to acquire, in a partial debt financing and by means of a single-member limited liability company, a commercial retail center, without having the tenants' rents be taxable.[700]

The intent of these rules is to treat an otherwise tax-exempt organization in the same manner as an ordinary business enterprise to the extent that the exempt organization purchases property through the use of borrowed funds.[701] The IRS recalled this intent in passing on the tax status of indebtedness owed to an exempt labor union by its wholly owned subsidiary title-holding company resulting from a loan to pay debts incurred to acquire two income-producing office buildings. The IRS ruled that this *interorganizational indebtedness* was not an acquisition indebtedness because the "very nature of the title-holding company as well as the parent-subsidiary relationship show this indebtedness to be merely a matter of accounting between the organizations rather than an indebtedness as contemplated by" these rules.[702]

The income of a tax-exempt organization that is attributable to a short sale of publicly traded stock through a broker is not unrelated debt-financed income and thus is not taxable as unrelated business income.[703] This is because, although a short sale creates an obligation, it does not create an indebtedness for tax purposes[704]

---

[697] IRC § 514(c)(9)(F)(iii). An entity that is this type of shareholder or beneficiary, however, is not a disqualified holder if it otherwise constitutes a qualified organization by reason of being an educational institution, a supporting organization of an educational institution, or a pension trust (*id.*).

[698] IRC § 514(c)(9)(F)(i), (ii). The purpose of this rule is to prevent the benefits of this exception from flowing through the title-holding company to its shareholders or beneficiaries unless those organizations themselves are qualified organizations. Regulations were proposed with respect to allocations of items by partnerships that have debt-financed property and have one or more (but not all) qualified tax-exempt organization partners (Prop. Reg. § 1.514(c)-2, 81 Fed. Reg. 84518 (2016)); this proposal would amend existing regulations to facilitate compliance, regarding certain allocations resulting from specified common business practices, with the statutory law (the *fractions rule*).

[699] IRC § 514(c)(9)(B), last sentence.

[700] Priv. Ltr. Rul. 201444013.

[701] H.R. Rep. No. 91-413, at 46 (1969).

[702] Rev. Rul. 77-72, 1977-1 C.B. 157. This rationale was also applied to avoid the prospect of unrelated business income taxation resulting from use of joint operating agreements in the health care context (see § 24.5(k)).

[703] Rev. Rul. 95-8, 1995-1 C.B. 107. The same is true with respect to income from commodity futures contract, which are not considered a form of indebtedness (e.g., Priv. Ltr. Rul. 8044023).

[704] Deputy v. du Pont, 308 U.S. 488 (1940).

and thus there is no acquisition indebtedness.[705] This position of the IRS is not intended to cause any inference with respect to a borrowing of property other than publicly traded stock sold short through a broker. Securities purchased on margin by a tax-exempt organization constitute debt-financed property, which generates unrelated business income.[706]

(d) Exempt Function Borrowing

Tax-exempt organizations holding investment assets may nonetheless need to borrow money to fund their exempt functions. Borrowing in lieu of asset liquidation may be preferable because liquidation of investments may be disadvantageous or even impossible in the face of difficult economic conditions, illiquidity, contractual provisions, or other circumstances.[707]

Although existing law is not clear on the point, it appears that debt incurred to sustain exempt organization programs is not acquisition indebtedness. This position is reflected in the legislative history of the unrelated debt-financed income law.[708] The IRS privately ruled that borrowing by a title-holding company to make an exempt function rental payment was not acquisition indebtedness.[709] The IRS also ruled that borrowing by an exempt investment fund was incurred for the entity's "convenience" in administering its exempt functions and likewise was not acquisition indebtedness.[710]

It has been argued that, in determining whether a borrowing constitutes an acquisition indebtedness, an exempt organization should be allowed, as a general rule, to trace use of the proceeds of the debt to the asset acquired or expense paid with the proceeds; if the proceeds are used for an exempt purpose, the borrowing would not, in accordance with this argument, be treated as acquisition indebtedness with respect to any investment assets the organization may contemporaneously own or acquire.[711] If an organization is attempting to circumvent the unrelated debt-financed property law, the *but for* and *reasonably foreseeable* tests could be used to override the tracing approach. The IRS, however, has informally expressed concern that a borrowing to fund exempt activities is acquisition indebtedness attributable to investment assets when the debt, albeit motivated by the needs of the organization's exempt programs, is incurred contemporaneously with the purchase of investment assets.

---

[705] E.g., Priv. Ltr. Rul. 201418061.

[706] E.g., Henry E. & Nancy Horton Bartels Trust for the Benefit of the Univ. of New Haven v. United States, 209 F.3d 147 (2d Cir. 2000), *cert. denied*, 531 U.S. 978 (2000). Also, Henry E. & Nancy Horton Bartels Trust for the Benefit of Cornell Univ. v. United States, 2009-2 U.S.T.C. ¶ 50,475 (U.S. Ct. Fed. Cl. 2009, *aff'd*, 617 F. 3d 1357 (Fed. Cir. 2010)).

[707] Financial climates of this nature occurred during the so-called Great Recession (2008–2009) and the years of the COVID-19 pandemic (2020–2022).

[708] For example, it is there stated that a church, having a portfolio of investments and no debt, that incurs debt to construct a seminary, has borrowed money with the debt not considered acquisition indebtedness with respect to the investment portfolio (Staff of Joint Comm. on Tax'n, 91st Cong., General Explanation of the Tax Reform Act of 1969 63 (Comm. Print 1970)).

[709] Priv. Ltr. Rul. 7841005.

[710] Priv. Ltr. Rul. 200010061.

[711] E.g., New York State Bar Association Tax Section, "Report on Section 514: Debt-Financed Income Subject to UBIT" (Aug. 12, 2020) at 22.

(e) Administrative Needs Borrowing

Likewise, short-term borrowing to meet administrative needs of tax-exempt organizations may not be acquisition indebtedness. IRS private letter rulings indicate that borrowing by exempt entities that occurs as part of ordinary and routine activities undertaken in the administration of investment properties does not give rise to acquisition indebtedness. For example, an exempt investment fund with participants confined to exempt entities proposed to establish a short-term credit facility with a bank in order to ensure its ability to pay redemption proceeds on a timely basis in the infrequent circumstance that its cash reserve was depleted. The IRS ruled that this "transitory indebtedness" amounted to "temporary payment obligations" that were incurred for the organization's convenience in administering the fund's exempt function and to minimize adverse effects stemming from settlement delays.[712] Similarly, the IRS ruled that loans pursuant to a line of credit to an exempt organization, for short-term purposes, would not constitute acquisition indebtedness, noting that the loan proceeds would not be used to acquire or improve investment property.[713] Like rulings have been issued in the pension fund context.[714] There is, however, no exemption from the debt-financed property rules for short-term borrowings as such.

This ruling position of the IRS is based in part on a revenue ruling concerning application of the unrelated business rules to securities lending programs engaged in by tax-exempt organizations.[715] Under the facts of that ruling, an exempt organization transferred, for temporary periods, securities from its investment portfolio to a brokerage house to enable the brokerage firm to cover short sales. As part of its compensation for the securities lending, the organization received cash equal to the value of the securities as collateral, which it had the right to invest and retain the income therefrom. This ruling holds that the securities-lending program does not give rise to unrelated business income because "Congress did not intend for ordinary and routine investment activities [of an exempt organization] in connection with its securities portfolio to be treated as the conduct of a trade or business."[716] In addition, this ruling states that the organization would not have debt-financed income as a result of the lending program because the organization had not "incurred indebtedness for the purpose of making additional investments," although it had clearly incurred debt because it had the right in the interim to invest and retain the income from the cash received as "collateral" and the ultimate obligation to repay the money.[717]

---

[712] Priv. Ltr. Rul. 200010061.

[713] Priv. Ltr. Rul. 200320027.

[714] E.g., Priv. Ltr. Ruls. 8721107, 9644063.

[715] Rev. Rul. 78-88, 1978-1 C.B. 163. See § 25.1(d).

[716] Rev. Rul. 78-88, 1978-1 C.B. 163. This statement, although accurate at the time, appears quaint considering the enactment of the bucketing rule (see § 25.5) and the ever-changing reality of what constitutes "ordinary and routine" investment activities of an exempt organization.

[717] Rev. Rul. 78-88, 1978-1 C.B. 163.

CHAPTER TWENTY-FIVE

Unrelated Business: Modifications, Exceptions, Special Rules, and Taxation

The federal tax law is replete with exceptions, exceptions to exceptions, and exceptions to exceptions to exceptions. Nowhere in the law of tax-exempt organizations is this fact more manifested than in the unrelated business rules. The general rules, the subject of the previous chapter, are colorfully complemented by a host of exceptions, some denominated as such and some dressed up in other terminology, namely, *modifications* and *special rules*.

§ 25.1 MODIFICATIONS

Pursuant to the general rules, an activity may constitute an unrelated business that is regularly carried on,[1] yet the income generated by the activity may escape federal taxation as unrelated business income pursuant to one or more statutory exceptions. Some of these exceptions are formally denominated as such.[2] Other exceptions are labeled *modifications*;[3] they are applied in computing unrelated business income. Various deductions and losses are also taken into account in this regard.

(a) Passive Income in General

The unrelated business rules were enacted to ameliorate the effects of competition between tax-exempt organizations and for-profit businesses by taxing the net income derived by exempt organizations from unrelated business activities.[4] The principle underlying this statutory scheme is that the business endeavors of exempt entities must be *active* ones for competitive activity to result. Correspondingly, income obtained by an exempt organization in a passive manner generally is income that is not acquired as the result of competitive undertakings; consequently, most forms of passive income received by exempt organizations are not taxed as unrelated business income.[5]

The legislative history of these provisions indicates that Congress believed that passive income received by tax-exempt organizations should not be taxed as unrelated business income "where it is used for exempt purposes because investments producing incomes of these types have long been recognized as proper for educational and charitable organizations."[6] Forms of passive income incurred by exempt organizations that may not be strictly within the technical meaning of one of the specific terms referenced in the passive income rules may nonetheless be outside the framework of unrelated business income taxation.[7]

(b) Dividends

Dividends paid to tax-exempt organizations generally are not taxable as unrelated business income.[8] Basically, a *dividend* is an amount of income allotted to

---

[1] See §§ 24.2–24.4.

[2] See § 25.2.

[3] IRC § 512(b).

[4] See § 24.1.

[5] Two significant exceptions to this rule pertain to certain income from unrelated debt-financed property (see § 24.10) and certain income from controlled subsidiaries (see §§ 29.7, 30.6).

[6] H.R. Rep. No. 81-2319, at 38 (1950). Also, S. Rep. No. 81-2375, at 30–31 (1950).

[7] H.R. Rep. No, 81-2319, at 36–38 (1950); S. Rep. No. 81-2375, at 27-28, 30–31 (1950).

[8] IRC § 512(b)(1).

each of one or more persons who are entitled (by reason of their capital contributions) to share in the net profits generated by a business undertaking, usually a corporation; it is a payment to shareholders (stockholders) out of the payor's net profits.[9]

It has been, for some time, conventional wisdom that income received by a tax-exempt organization from a controlled foreign corporation is not taxable as unrelated business income because the income is considered a nontaxable dividend. This is a fundamental concept underlying use of blocker corporations.[10] The statutory law that is indirectly on point pertains to controlled foreign corporations;[11] the thought has been that this *included* income is to be treated as a dividend.[12]

When Congress enacted the rule that, where a controlled foreign corporation is insuring third-party risks, the income from that activity is subject to tax as unrelated business income, it inserted language in the legislative history to the effect that, generally, this type of included income is dividend income and not unrelated business income.[13]

(c) Interest

Interest paid to a tax-exempt organization generally is not taxable as unrelated business income.[14] Basically, *interest* is an amount of income constituting compensation that one person pays to another for the use of money.[15]

(d) Securities Lending Income

Qualified payments with respect to loans of securities are generally excluded from unrelated business income taxation.[16] This exclusion is available for the lending of securities to a broker and the return of identical securities.[17] For this nontaxation treatment to apply, the security loans must be fully collateralized and be terminable on five business days' notice by the lending organization. Further, an agreement between the parties must provide for reasonable procedures to implement the obligation of the borrower to furnish collateral to the lender with a fair market value on each business day the loan is outstanding in an amount at least equal to the fair market value of the security at the close of business on the preceding day.[18]

---

[9] E.g., Watson v. Comm'r, 19 T.C.M. 1409 (1960).

[10] E.g., Priv. Ltr. Rul. 201430017.

[11] IRC §§ 951–956.

[12] A court, however, held that payments to controlled foreign corporations were not dividends because these types of payments require a distribution by a corporation and receipt by one or more shareholders (Rodriguez v. Comm'r, 772 F.3d 306 (5th Cir. 2013)).

[13] See § 25.1(n)(i).

[14] IRC § 512(b)(1).

[15] E.g., Deputy v. duPont, 308 U.S. 488 (1940).

[16] IRC § 512(b)(1).

[17] IRC § 512(a)(5).

[18] *Id.*

(e) Loan Commitment Fees

Amounts received or accrued by tax-exempt organizations as consideration for entering into agreements to make loans are excluded from unrelated business income taxation.[19]

(f) Annuities

Income received by a tax-exempt organization as an annuity generally is not taxable as unrelated business income.[20] Basically, an *annuity* is an amount of money, fixed by contract between the annuitor and the annuitant, that is paid annually in one sum, or otherwise during the course of a year in installments (such as semiannually or quarterly).

(g) Royalties

Generally, a royalty paid to a tax-exempt organization is excludable from unrelated income taxation.[21] Basically, a *royalty* is a payment for the use of a valuable intangible right, such as a trademark, trade name, service mark, logo, or copyright, regardless of whether payment is based on the use made of such property; royalties also include the right to a share of production reserved to the owner of the property for permitting another to work mines and quarries or to drill for oil or gas.[22] Royalties have also been characterized as payments that constitute passive income, such as the compensation paid by a licensee to the licensor for the use of the licensor's patented invention.[23]

One of the issues in this area is the extent to which a tax-exempt organization can be involved in the enterprise that generates the revenue, such as through the provision of services. In the principal opinion on the point, a federal appellate court wrote that a payment cannot constitute a royalty for these purposes to the extent it represents "compensation for services [other than insubstantial ones] rendered by the owner of the property."[24] If the exempt organization's services in this context are more than incidental, the IRS may view the relationship between the parties as that of partners or joint venturers, thus defeating the exception.[25]

A court relied heavily on the foregoing definition of *royalties* in concluding that a tax-exempt organization is liable for the unrelated business income tax on

---

[19] IRC § 512(b)(1).

[20] IRC § 512(b)(1).

[21] IRC § 512(b)(2).

[22] E.g., Fraternal Order of Police Ill. State Troopers Lodge No. 41 v. Comm'r, 833 F.2d 717, 723 (7th Cir. 1987).

[23] Disabled Am. Veterans v. United States, 650 F.2d 1178, 1189 (Ct. Cl. 1981). In an instance of a tax-exempt organization with an agreement with an unrelated for-profit corporation, engaged in the business of oil and gas production, pursuant to which the corporation acquires the working interest in oil and gas properties, and carves out and sells to the organization a net profit interest in the properties, where the organization is not responsible or liable for the operating costs or liabilities attributable to the corporation's developing, exploring, equipping, owning, operating, and/or maintaining the oil and gas properties, or for storing, handling, treating, or marketing the oil and gas, the IRS ruled that this income from its investment will constitute an excludable royalty (Priv. Ltr. Rul. 201142026).

[24] Sierra Club, Inc. v. Comm'r, 86 F.3d 1526, 1532 (9th Cir. 1996). Also, Rev. Rul. 81-178, 1981-2 C.B. 135.

[25] E.g., Tech. Adv. Mem. 9509002.

payments it received from vendors for its services, rejecting the argument that the revenue constituted royalties.[26] The court noted that agreements with these vendors do not license them to use the exempt organization's intangible property or obligate it to make intangible property available to them. The payments were held to be for services rendered, with the exempt organization "exploit[ing] its own reputation with its members by endorsing [one of the vendors] and inducing its members to patronize that company."[27]

Mineral royalties, whether measured by production or by gross or taxable income from the mineral property, are excludable in computing unrelated business taxable income. Where, however, a tax-exempt organization owns a working interest in a mineral property and is not relieved of its share of the development costs by the terms of any agreement with an operator, income received is not excludable from unrelated income taxation.[28] The holder of a mineral interest is not liable for the expenses of development (or operations) for these purposes where the holder's interest is a net profit interest not subject to expenses that exceed gross profits. Thus, a tax-exempt university was ruled to have excludable royalty interests, where the interests it held in various oil- and gas-producing properties were based on the gross profits from the properties reduced by all expenses of development and operations.[29]

The IRS ruled that patent development and management service fees deducted from royalties collected from licensees by a tax-exempt charitable organization for distribution to the beneficial owners of the patents were not within this exception for royalties; the IRS said that "although the amounts paid to the [exempt] organization are derived from royalties, they do not retain the character of royalties in the organization's hands" for these purposes.[30] However, the IRS decided that income derived by an exempt organization from the sale of advertising in publications produced by an independent firm was properly characterized as royalty income.[31] Likewise, the IRS determined that amounts received from licensees by an exempt organization, which was the legal and beneficial owner of patents assigned to it by inventors for specified percentages of future royalties, constituted excludable royalty income.[32] A federal court of appeals held that income consisting of 100 percent of the net profits in certain oil properties, received by an exempt organization from two corporations controlled by it, constituted income from overriding royalties and thus was excluded from taxation.[33]

---

[26] New Jersey Council of Teaching Hospitals v. Comm'r, 149 T.C. 466 (2017).

[27] Id. at 477. In a similar case, the IRS ruled that operation of an online job placement service by a public charity constituted an unrelated business and that the resulting income did not qualify as a royalty (Tech. Adv. Mem. 202039018).

[28] Reg. § 1.512(b)-1(b).

[29] Priv. Ltr. Rul. 7741004.

[30] Rev. Rul. 73-193, 1973-1 C.B. 262.

[31] Priv. Ltr. Rul. 7926003.

[32] Rev. Rul. 76-297, 1976-2 C.B. 178. Also, J. E. & L. E. Mabee Found., Inc. v. United States, 533 F.2d 521 (10th Cir. 1976), aff'g 389 F. Supp. 673 (N.D. Okla. 1975).

[33] United States v. Robert A. Welch Found., 334 F.2d 774 (5th Cir. 1964), aff'g 228 F. Supp. 881 (S.D. Tex. 1963). The IRS refused to follow this decision, as stated in Rev. Rul. 69-162, 1969-1 C.B. 158.

(h) Rent

Another exclusion from unrelated business income taxation is available with respect to certain rents.[34] The principal exclusion is for rents from real property.[35] *Rent* is a form of income that is paid for the occupation or similar use of property.

(i) General Rules. The exclusion from unrelated business taxable income for rent is not unlimited, inasmuch as not all income labeled *rent* qualifies for the exclusion. Where a tax-exempt organization conducts activities that constitute an activity carried on for trade or business, even though the activities involve the leasing of real estate, the exclusion will not be available.[36] Payments for the use or occupancy of entire private residences or living quarters in duplex or multiple housing units, or of offices in an office building and the like, are generally treated as rent from real property.[37] For example, an exempt organization may own a building and lease space in it, and the income from this activity will constitute excludable rent even where the organization performs normal maintenance services, such as the furnishing of heat, air-conditioning, and light; the cleaning of public entrances, exits, stairways, and lobbies; and the collection of trash. Where, however, the organization undertakes functions beyond these maintenance services, such as services rendered primarily for the convenience of the occupants (for example, the supplying of cleaning services), the payments will not be considered as being from a passive source but instead from an unrelated trade or business (assuming that the activity is regularly carried on and is not substantially related to the organization's tax-exempt purposes).[38]

The exclusion for rent also does not encompass income from payments for the use or occupancy of rooms and other space where services are also rendered to the occupant, such as for the use or occupancy of rooms or other quarters in hotels, boarding houses, or apartment houses furnishing hotel services, or in tourist camps or tourist homes, motor courts, or motels, or for the use or occupancy of space in parking lots,[39] warehouses, or storage garages.[40] For example, the IRS ruled that revenue paid by vendors at an event sponsored by a tax-exempt organization was not rent, largely because of the extensive services provided to the vendors that were said to go "far beyond" services "usually rendered for occupancy only."[41]

---

[34] IRC § 512(b)(3).

[35] IRC § 512(b)(3)(A)(i).

[36] In general, the rental of real estate constitutes the carrying on of a trade or business (e.g., Hazard v. Comm'r, 7 T.C. 372 (1946)).

[37] Reg. § 1.512(b)-1(c)(5).

[38] *Id.* For example, the IRS ruled that payments from tenants received by a company, in which a charity had an expectancy and thus indirectly received the payments, were rent from real property excluded from unrelated business income because the services provided to the tenants were limited to necessary and customary maintenance and utility services (except to the extent attributable to debt-financed property (see § 24.10)) (Priv. Ltr. Rul. 201849009).

[39] E.g., Ocean Pines Ass'n, Inc. v. Comm'r, 135 T.C. 276 (2010), *aff'd*, 672 F.3d 284 (4th Cir. 2012).

[40] Reg. § 1.512(b)-1(c)(5). For example, the IRS held that the storage by a tax-exempt organization of trailers, campers, motor homes, boats, and cars for several months annually is a business, with the activity being "no different than a mini-storage business operating on a for-profit basis" (Tech. Adv. Mem. 9822006). In this context, the income yielded from a storage operation is not rent (Tech. Adv. Mem. 9901002).

[41] Tech. Adv. Mem. 201544025. See § 24.5(i)(i), note 510.

By contrast, revenue from the operation of parking garages was ruled by the IRS to constitute excludable rent, where the services rendered (by a real estate investment trust) were confined to those customarily furnished in connection with the rental of that type of space and an independent contractor would provide any other "unique" services.[42]

The contractual relationship between the parties from which the ostensible rental income is derived must be that as reflected in a *lease*, rather than a *license*, for the exclusion for rental income to be available. A lease "confers upon a tenant exclusive possession of the subject premises as against all the world, including the owner."[43] The difference is the conferring of a privilege to occupy the owner's property for a particular use, rather than general possession of the premises. Thus, a tax-exempt organization that conferred to an advertising agency the permission to maintain signs and other advertisements on the wall space in the organization's premises was held to be receiving income from a license arrangement, rather than a rental one, so that the exclusion for rental income was not available.[44]

The exclusion from unrelated business taxable income for rents of personal property leased with real property is limited to instances where the rent attributable to the personalty is incidental (no more than 10 percent).[45] Moreover, the exclusion is not available where more than 50 percent of the total rent is attributable to the personalty leased.[46] Thus, where the rent attributable to personalty is between 10 percent and 50 percent of the total, only the exclusion with respect to personalty is lost.[47]

Notwithstanding these general rules, the exclusion for rent does not apply if the determination of the amount of the rent depends in whole or in part on the income or profits derived by any person from the property leased (other than an amount based on a fixed percentage or percentages of receipts or sales).[48] Under this rule, an amount will not qualify as rents from real property if, considering the lease and all of the surrounding circumstances, the arrangement does not conform with normal business practice and is in reality a means of basing the rent on income or profits.[49] This rule is intended to prevent avoidance of the unrelated business income tax where a profit-sharing arrangement would, in effect, make the lessor an active participant in the operation of the property.

(ii) Related Rental Activities. On occasion, rental income is derived by a tax-exempt organization from the operation of a related business, so the revenue is nontaxable for that reason.[50] In one instance, a public charity with a training

---

[42] Priv. Ltr. Rul. 202013006.

[43] Union Travel Associates, Inc. v. Int'l Associates, Inc., 401 A.2d 105 (D.C. Ct. App. 1979).

[44] Priv. Ltr. Rul. 9740032.

[45] IRC § 512(b)(3)(A)(ii).

[46] IRC § 512(b)(3)(B)(i).

[47] Reg. § 1.512(b)-1(c)(2).

[48] IRC § 512(b)(3)(B)(ii); Reg. § 1.512(b)-1(c)(2)(iii)(b). The rules in Reg. §§ 1.856-4(b)(3), (b)(6) (other than (b)(6)(ii) (which are part of the rules pertaining to real estate investment trusts) apply in determining whether rents depend in whole or in part on the income or profits (*id.*).

[49] Reg. § 1.856-4(b)(3).

[50] E.g., Museum of Flight Found. v. United States, 63 F. Supp. 2d 1257 (W.D. Wash. 1999), which held that the income a tax-exempt museum received from the lease of a historic test airplane to the airplane's

program shared office space with an exempt association that owned the building, in part because the tenants of the association provided volunteer teaching faculty to the charitable organization; the charity accorded the association the right to allow the tenants use of its research equipment in exchange for maintenance of the equipment; the IRS held that the value of the maintenance services constituted non-taxable phantom rent.[51] Similarly, the agency ruled that an exempt hospital may lease facilities to another exempt hospital, with the leasing activity constituting an exempt function, because of a direct physical connection and close professional affiliation of the institutions.[52] Likewise, the IRS ruled that a charitable organization owning and operating nursing homes could lease, as a related business, a skilled nursing facility to another charitable organization that owned and operated nursing homes.[53] Moreover, the IRS held that a public charity operating a continuing care retirement community may lease, as a charitable undertaking, a building to an exempt hospital, which will use it as an outpatient medical clinic to serve the residents of this retirement community.[54] Also, the leasing of a medical office building by a partnership involving a supporting organization[55] was ruled by the IRS to be related to the organization's exempt purpose.[56] The IRS ruled that leasing of its premises by an exempt hospital to a state university as part of the state's reorganization of its health care system was an activity in furtherance of charitable purposes.[57]

(i) Other Investment Income

The IRS ruled that the interest earned by a tax-exempt organization pursuant to *interest rate swap agreements* is not taxable as unrelated business income.[58] The anticipated result of the interest rate swap is to provide the tax-exempt organization with interest payments that are preferable, from its investment standpoint, to those provided for in a floating rate note.

In addition to the foregoing forms of investment income, income from notional principal contracts,[59] and other substantially similar income from ordinary and routine investments to the extent determined by the IRS, is excluded in computing unrelated business taxable income.[60] This exclusion embraces interest rate and currency swaps, as well as equity and commodity swaps.[61]

---

manufacturer was not unrelated business income because the lease "significantly advanced the [m]useum's mission to restore and display historic aircraft" (*id.* at 1260).

[51] Priv. Ltr. Rul. 9615045.
[52] Priv. Ltr. Rul. 200314031.
[53] Priv. Ltr. Rul. 200404057.
[54] Priv. Ltr. Rul. 200538027.
[55] See § 12.3(c).
[56] Priv. Ltr. Rul. 200717019.
[57] Priv. Ltr. Rul. 201702002.
[58] Priv. Ltr. Rul. 9042038.
[59] Reg. § 1.863-7.
[60] Reg. § 1.512(b)-1(a)(3).
[61] T.D. 8423 (57 Fed. Reg. 33442 (1992)).

(j)   Capital Gains

Excluded from unrelated business income taxation generally are gains from the sale, exchange, or other disposition of capital gain property.[62] This exclusion for capital gains does not extend to dispositions of inventory or property held primarily for sale to customers in the ordinary course of a business.[63] The U.S. Tax Court and the IRS apply multiple factors in determining whether property is being sold in the ordinary course of business: (1) the purpose for which the property was acquired; (2) the cost of it; (3) the activities of the owner in the improvement and disposition of the property; (4) the extent of improvements made to the property; (5) the proximity of the sale to the purchase; (6) the purpose for which the property was held; (7) prevailing market conditions; and (8) the frequency, continuity, and size of the sales.[64] For example, the IRS ruled that the gain from the sale by tax-exempt organizations of leased fee interests in condominium apartments to lessees was not taxable because of the exclusion for capital gain.[65] Likewise, the IRS ruled that the sale by a charitable organization of its entire interest in an apartment building would generate excludable capital gain, with the agency emphasizing that the organization did not play any role in the sale or marketing of individual condominium units.[66] Conversely, the improvement and frequent sale of land by an exempt organization was held to be an unrelated business.[67]

Nonetheless, there is an exception from this second limitation[68] that excludes gains and losses from the sale, exchange, or other disposition of certain real property and mortgages acquired from financial institutions that are in conservatorship or receivership.[69] Only real property and mortgages owned by a financial institution (or held by the financial institution as security for a loan) at the time when the institution entered conservatorship or receivership are eligible for the exception.

(k)   Income from Controlled Entities

In the case of income flows from controlled entities to controlling organizations, certain forms of passive income otherwise excluded from unrelated business income taxation are treated as unrelated income.[70] These rules apply where the controlled subsidiary is a tax-exempt organization[71] or a taxable entity.[72]

---

[62] IRC § 512(b)(5).

[63] IRC § 512(b)(5)(A), (B); Reg. § 1.512(b)-1(d). In this context, *primarily* means "of first importance" or "principally" (Malat v. Riddell, 383 U.S. 569 (1966)).

[64] Adam v. Comm'r, 60 T.C. 996 (1973); e.g., Priv. Ltr. Rul. 9619069. See § 24.2(h).

[65] E.g., Priv. Ltr. Rul. 9629030.

[66] Priv. Ltr. Rul. 200246032.

[67] Priv. Ltr. Rul. 200119061.

[68] IRC § 512(b)(5)(B).

[69] IRC § 512(b)(16).

[70] IRC § 512(b)(13). As to the matter of controlled entities and controlling organizations, see § 30.6.

[71] See § 29.7.

[72] See § 30.6.

(l) Research Income

Income derived from research[73] for government is excluded from unrelated business income taxation, as is income derived from research for anyone in the case of a tax-exempt college, university, or hospital, and of "fundamental research" units.[74] According to the legislative history, the term *research* includes "not only fundamental research but also applied research such as testing and experimental construction and production."[75] With respect to the separate exclusion for college, university, or hospital research, "funds received for research by other institutions [do not] necessarily represent unrelated business income," such as a grant by a corporation to a foundation to finance scientific research if the results of the research are to be made freely available to the public.[76] Without defining the term *research*, the IRS was content to find applicability of this rule because the studies were not "merely quality control programs or ordinary testing for certification purposes, as a final procedural step before marketing."[77]

In employing the term *research* in this context, the IRS generally looks to the body of law defining the term in relation to what is considered tax-exempt scientific research.[78] Thus, the issue is usually whether the activity is being carried on in connection with commercial or industrial operations; if it is, it will almost assuredly be regarded by the IRS as an unrelated trade or business.[79] In one instance, the IRS found applicability of the exclusion because the studies undertaken by an exempt medical college in the testing of pharmaceutical products under contracts with the manufacturers were held to be more than ordinary testing.[80] In another instance, the exclusion was held to be applicable to contract work done by an exempt educational institution for the federal government in the field of rocketry.[81]

(m) Electric Companies' Member Income

In the case of a tax-exempt mutual or cooperative electric company,[82] there is an exclusion from unrelated business income taxation for income that is treated as member income.[83]

(n) Foreign Source Income

(i) General Rules. A look-through rule characterizes certain foreign source income—namely, income from insurance activities conducted by offshore

---

[73] The concept of scientific research is the subject of § 9.2.
[74] IRC § 512(b)(7)–(9). See Reg. § 1.512(b)-1(f). Also, Rev. Rul. 54-73, 1954-1 C.B. 160; IIT Research Inst. v. United States, 9 Cl. Ct. 13 (1985).
[75] H.R. Rep. No. 81-2319, at 37 (1950).
[76] S. Rep. No. 81-2375, at 30 (1950).
[77] Priv. Ltr. Rul. 7936006.
[78] Rev. Rul. 76-296, 1976-2 C.B. 141.
[79] Rev. Rul. 68-373, 1968-2 C.B. 206.
[80] Priv. Ltr. Rul. 7936006.
[81] Priv. Ltr. Rul. 7924009.
[82] See § 19.5(b).
[83] IRC §§ 501(c)(12)(H), 512(b)(18).

captives of tax-exempt organizations—as unrelated business income.[84] Generally, U.S. shareholders of controlled foreign corporations must include in income their shares of the foreign entities' income, including certain insurance income.[85] The IRS, before creation of this statutory rule, treated these income inclusions as dividends, with the consequence that the income received by exempt organizations was excludable from tax.[86] This look-through rule, however, overrides the former treatment of this type of income as dividends.

This rule does not apply to amounts that are attributable to insurance of risks of the tax-exempt organization itself, certain of its exempt affiliates, or an officer or director of, or an individual who (directly or indirectly) performs services for, the exempt organization (or certain exempt affiliates), provided that the insurance primarily covers risks associated with the individual's performance of services in connection with the exempt organization (or exempt affiliates).[87]

The notion that income derived by tax-exempt organizations from controlled foreign corporations[88] is generally treated as dividend income has a curious provenance. That has been the ruling policy of the IRS since at least 1988.[89] In the context of enactment of the insurance rule in 1996, the House Committee on Ways and Means reviewed this ruling policy and pronounced it correct.[90] The Committee stated that "income exclusions under Subpart F have been characterized as dividends for unrelated business income tax purposes."[91] The IRS ruling policy has continued to follow its general approach.[92]

Case law, however, is contrary to the general position taken by the IRS in its private letter rulings and the assumption as to the state of the law found in the Ways and Means Committee report. Two courts have held that Subpart F inclusions do not constitute (1) actual dividends because such dividends require a distribution by the corporation and receipt by the shareholder, and a change of ownership of something of value, neither of which occurred in the facts of the case,[93] and (2) deemed dividends because, when Congress decides to deem a

---

[84] IRC § 512(b)(17)(A). The reason for this focus on insurance activities and income was to bring parity in connection with the unrelated business rules pertaining to U.S.-derived income from commercial-type insurance activities (see § 24.9).

[85] IRC §§ 951(a)(1)(A), 953.

[86] See § 25.1(b).

[87] IRC § 512(b)(17)(B).

[88] This type of income, being the subject of IRC §§ 951–956, which is Subpart F of the Internal Revenue Code, is sometimes referred to as *Subpart F inclusions*.

[89] Priv. Ltr. Rul. 8819034. Following that ruling and before enactment of the insurance rule (*supra* note 87), the IRS issued six comparable rulings (Priv. Ltr. Ruls. 9407007, 9027051, 9024086, 9024026, 8922047, and 8836037). Nonetheless, the IRS issued one ruling holding that Subpart F inclusions are treated as if the underlying income was realized directly by the U.S. shareholder (a tax-exempt organization) for purposes of computing unrelated business income (Priv. Ltr. Rul. 9043039); this ruling does not explain its departure from the general IRS ruling policy. Of course, one of the foregoing six rulings was issued after this rogue ruling.

[90] H.R. Rep. No. 104-586, at 136 (1966).

[91] *Id.* at 136. The Committee also wrote that the ruling imposing a look-through rule (see text accompanied by *supra* note 84) was "incorrect" (*id.* at 401 n.14).

[92] Priv. Ltr. Ruls. 201430017, 201043041, 200623069, 200251016–200251018.

[93] Rodriguez v. Comm'r, 772 F.3d 306 (5th Cir. 2013), *aff'g* 137 T.C. 174 (2011). These courts relied, in connection with this portion of the analysis, on the statutory definition of the term *dividend* in IRC §§ 1(h)(11)(B)(i), 316(a).

payment a dividend, it states as much in the Internal Revenue Code, which was not done in the law pertaining to this case.[94]

It may be that Subpart F inclusions can be considered one or more forms of passive income that are excludible from unrelated business income taxation, without reliance on specific characterization as a dividend.[95] Also, controlled foreign corporations can make payments that qualify as dividends under the explicit statutory rules.

(ii) Global Intangible Low-Taxed Income. For any tax year in which a U.S. person is a shareholder of a controlled foreign corporation, such shareholder must include in gross income the shareholder's global intangible low-taxed income for the tax year.[96] This category of income is any excess of the shareholder's net controlled foreign corporation tested income for the year, over the shareholder's net deemed tangible income return for the year.[97]

The Treasury Department and the IRS determined that an inclusion of GILTI should be treated in the same manner as an inclusion of subpart F income.[98] Accordingly, an inclusion of GILTI is treated as a dividend.[99]

(o) Brownfield Sites Gain

An exclusion from unrelated business taxable income is available for gain or loss from the sale or exchange of certain brownfield properties by a tax-exempt organization, whether the properties are held directly or indirectly through a partnership.[100] For property to qualify for the exclusion, the property must be acquired during the period beginning January 1, 2005, and ending December 31, 2009, although the property may be disposed of after that date. Certain certification requirements must be met. Also, the exempt organization or the partnership of which it is a partner must expend a minimum amount on remediation expenses, which may be determined by averaging expenses across multiple qualifying brownfield properties for a period of as many as eight years.[101]

(p) Religious Order Rule

The unrelated business income tax does not apply to a trade or business conducted by a tax-exempt or educational institution maintained by a religious order,[102] even

---

[94] The appellate court cited the "myriad [IRC] provisions specifically stating that certain income is to be treated as if it were a dividend." The court added, if all Subpart F inclusions "constituted qualified dividends, the statutory provisions specifically designating certain inclusions as dividends would amount to surplusage," which is contrary to the rules of statutory construction.

[95] See § 25.1(a), text accompanied by *supra* note 7.

[96] IRC § 951A(a), enacted by the Tax Cuts and Jobs Act (Pub. L. No. 115-97, § 14201, 131 Stat. 2054, 2208–12 (2017)).

[97] IRC § 951A(b).

[98] Notice 2018-67, 2018-36 I.R.B. 409 § 10.

[99] *Id.* See § 25.1(b).

[100] IRC § 512(b)(19). A *brownfield property* is a parcel of real property where there is a presence of a hazardous substance, pollutant, or contaminant that is complicating the expansion, redevelopment, or use of the property (IRC § 512(b)(19)(C)).

[101] IRC § 512(b)(19).

[102] That is, an institution described in IRC § 170(b)(1)(A)(ii). See § 12.3(a).

if the business is an unrelated one, if (1) the business consists of the provision of services under a license issued by a federal regulatory agency; (2) less than 10 percent of its net income is used for unrelated activities; and (3) the business has been operated by the order or educational institution since before May 27, 1969.[103]

§ 25.2 EXCEPTIONS

In addition to the exceptions provided in the rules concerning modifications,[104] various other exceptions from unrelated business income taxation are available.

(a) Volunteer-Conducted Businesses

Exempt from the scope of taxable unrelated trade or business is a business in which substantially all of the work in carrying on the business is performed for the tax-exempt organization without compensation.[105] An example of applicability of this exception is an exempt orphanage operating a secondhand clothing store and selling to the public, where substantially all of the work in operating the store is performed by volunteers.[106] Another illustration of this rule is the production and sale of phonograph records by a medical society, where the services of the performers were provided without compensation.[107] Still another illustration of this exception concerned a trade association that sold advertising in a commercial, unrelated manner, but avoided unrelated income taxation of the activity because the work involved was provided solely by volunteers.[108]

A court ruled that this exemption was defeated in part because free drinks provided to the collectors and cashiers in connection with the conduct of a bingo game by a tax-exempt organization were considered "liquid compensation."[109] This position was, however, rejected on appeal.[110] This court subsequently held that this exception was not available, in the case of an exempt organization that regularly carried on gambling activities, because the dealers and other individuals received tips from patrons of the games.[111] In another case, this court found that an exempt religious order that operated a farm was not taxable on the income derived from the farming operations because the farm was maintained by the uncompensated labor of the members of the order.[112]

---

[103] IRC § 512(b)(15); Reg. § 1.512(b)-1(j)(1)(i)–(iii).

[104] See § 25.1.

[105] IRC § 513(a)(1).

[106] S. Rep. No. 81-2375, at 108 (1950).

[107] Greene Cnty. Med. Soc'y Found. V. United States, 345 F. Supp. 900 (W.D. Mo. 1972).

[108] Priv. Ltr. Rul. 9302023.

[109] Waco Lodge No. 166, Benevolent & Protective Order of Elks v. Comm'r, 42 T.C.M. 1202 (1981).

[110] 696 F.2d 372 (5th Cir. 1983).

[111] Executive Network Club, Inc. v. Comm'r, 69 T.C.M. 1680 (1995).

[112] St. Joseph Farms of Ind. Bros. of the Congregation of Holy Cross, Southwest Province, Inc. v. Comm'r, 85 T.C. 9 (1985), *appeal dismissed* (7th Cir. 1986). Cf. Shiloh Youth Revival Centers v. Comm'r, 88 T.C. 565 (1987).

The matter of *substantiality* does not arise, of course, where all of the work in conducting the business is performed without compensation.[113] Where there are one or more compensated persons (whether as employees or independent contractors), substantiality is generally assessed in terms of hours expended. Although the term *substantially all* is not defined in this setting, it is defined in other contexts to mean at least 85 percent; the IRS follows that rule when applying the volunteer exception.[114]

The volunteer exception was held by a court to be unavailable where 77 percent of the services were provided to an exempt organization without compensation.[115] By contrast, another court ruled that the exception was available where the volunteer services amounted to 94 percent of total hours worked.[116] The IRS has ruled that the exception is available where the percentage of volunteer labor was 87 percent,[117] 91 percent,[118] and 97 percent.[119]

This exception references receipt of compensation. Thus, individuals who do not receive any economic benefits in exchange for their services to an exempt organization are uncompensated workers (volunteers).[120] Mere reimbursement of expenses incurred by volunteers is not compensation.[121] Economic benefits, however, can be considered compensation, even if not formally cast as a salary or fee for service,[122] unless they are incidental.[123] In some circumstances, nonmonetary benefits can amount to compensation.[124]

Payments by third parties can constitute the requisite compensation, where the tax-exempt organization involved transferred funds to the third party. For example, where security guards were present at and integral to bingo operations conducted by an exempt organization,[125] the compensation of the guards by a company through a contract with the exempt organization was held to be the type of compensation that defeated the exception for volunteer-conducted businesses.[126]

---

[113] E.g., Rev. Rul. 74-361, 1974-2 C.B. 159.

[114] E.g., Tech. Adv. Mem. 8433010.

[115] Waco Lodge No. 166, Benevolent & Protective Order of Elks v. Comm'r, 42 T.C.M. 1202 (1981), *rev'd*, 696 F.2d 372 (5th Cir. 1983).

[116] St. Joseph Farms of Ind. Bros. of the Congregation of Holy Cross, Southwest Province, Inc. v. Comm'r, 85 T.C. 9 (1985), *appeal dismissed* (7th Cir. 1986).

[117] Priv. Ltr. Rul. 7806039.

[118] Priv. Ltr. Rul. 9544029.

[119] Tech. Adv. Mem. 8040014.

[120] E.g., Tech. Adv. Mem. 8211002.

[121] E.g., Greene Cnty. Med. Soc'y Found. V. United States, 345 F. Supp. 900 (W.D. Mo. 1972).

[122] E.g., Executive Network Club, Inc. v. Comm'r, 69 T.C.M. 1680 (1995).

[123] E.g., Waco Lodge No. 166, Benevolent & Protective Order of Elks v. Comm'r, 696 F.2d 372, 375 (5th Cir. 1983) (free drinks were considered a "trifling inducement").

[124] E.g., Shiloh Youth Revival Centers v. Comm'r, 88 T.C. 565 (1987). On occasion, the essence of this exception is used to determine the basis for tax exemption (e.g., South Community Ass'n v. Comm'r, 90 T.C.M. 568 (2005)) (where an organization, which engaged in gaming operations to raise funds for charitable purposes, had its exempt status revoked because those who worked the operations were not volunteers).

[125] These bingo operations were not exempted from the definition of unrelated business (see § 25.2(h)).

[126] South Community Ass'n v. Comm'r, 90 T.C.M. 568 (2005). This case also illustrates the point that, for purposes of analyzing the availability of this exception, the individuals compensated may be independent contractors rather than employees.

Likewise, workers who conducted activities in a building rented by an exempt organization were held to be compensated by the organization where the rental payments included payments for "all labor for the supervision and handling of [each activity] upon the premises."[127]

This exclusion from unrelated business income for volunteer labor is only available when the activity performed by volunteers is a material income-producing factor in carrying on the activity.[128] The IRS held that finding a lessee for certain heavy machinery, renegotiating a lease, and processing rental payments, all by volunteers, was not a material income-producing factor in the business carried on by a tax-exempt organization, so this exception did not apply.[129] Similarly, the IRS ruled that services provided by volunteers, in connection with the conduct by an exempt organization of a storage business, consisting of moving items in and out of buildings and security, were "minimal" and constituted the provision of a "few more services," resulting in the unavailability of the exception.[130]

(b) Convenience Businesses

Excluded from unrelated income taxation, in the case of a tax-exempt charitable organization or a state college or university, is a business that is carried on by the organization primarily for the convenience of its members, students, patients, officers, or employees.[131] An example of this exception is a laundry operated by an exempt college for the purpose of laundering dormitory linens and the clothing of students.[132] As another illustration, the provision by an exempt hospital of mobile services to its patients by means of specially designed vans was ruled to be a convenience business.[133]

A court expanded this concept by holding that physicians on the staff of a teaching hospital were "members" of the hospital, in that the term "refers to any group of persons who are closely associated with the entity involved and who are necessary to the achievement of the organization's purposes."[134] The IRS disagrees with this opinion, however, taking the position that the "hospital's staff physicians are neither 'members' nor 'employees' of the hospital in their capacities as private practitioners of medicine."[135]

A court rejected the contention that fees for promotional services received by a tax-exempt organization from vendors were exempt from unrelated business income taxation on the basis of the convenience exception involving the organization's members.[136] The court concluded that (1) by helping its members save time

---

[127] Piety, Inc. v. Comm'r, 82 T.C. 193, 194 (1984).
[128] H.R. Rep. No. 81-2319 (1950); S. Rep. No. 81-2375 (1950).
[129] Rev. Rul. 78-144, 1978-1 C.B. 168.
[130] Tech. Adv. Mem. 9822006.
[131] IRC § 513(a)(2). Also, Rev. Rul. 81-19, 1981-1 C.B. 354; Rev. Rul. 69-268, 1969-1 C.B. 160; Rev. Rul. 55-676, 1955-2 C.B. 266. Cf. Carle Found. V. United States, 611 F.2d 1192 (7th Cir. 1979), *cert. denied*, 449 U.S. 824 (1980).
[132] Reg. § 1.513-2(b); S. Rep. No. 81-2375, at 108 (1950).
[133] Priv. Ltr. Rul. 9841049.
[134] St. Luke's Hosp. of Kansas City v. United States, 494 F. Supp. 85, 92 (W.D. Mo. 1980).
[135] Rev. Rul. 85-109, 1985-2 C.B. 165.
[136] New Jersey Council of Teaching Hospitals v. Comm'r, 149 T.C. 466 (2017).

or money by directing them to low-cost or high-quality vendors, the organization was not serving the convenience of its members in their capacity as members; (2) the organization did not establish that its activity "benefitted its members in any meaningful way"; (3) even if the organization's business activity saved its members money, "there is no legal support for the notion that saving money, without more, is enough to qualify for" the convenience exception; and (4) even if the organization's business activity "were thought to provide a convenience to its members by saving them time or money," the organization "has not shown that it conducted this activity *primarily* for the convenience of its members."[137] "[I]t seems clear," the court stated, that the organization's "primary purpose for engaging in these activities was to raise revenue for itself."[138]

Read literally, this exception pertains only to the classes of individuals who have the requisite relationship directly with the exempt organization; for example, it applies with respect to services carried on by an exempt hospital for the convenience of *its* patients. The IRS ruled, however, that the doctrine was available when an exempt organization's activities were for the convenience of patients of another, albeit related, exempt entity.[139] At the same time, the IRS refused to extend the doctrine to embrace spouses and children of a university's students.[140]

(c) Sales of Gift Items

Unrelated trade or business does not include a business, conducted by a tax-exempt organization, that constitutes the selling of merchandise, substantially all of which has been received by the organization by means of contributions.[141] This exception is available for thrift shops that sell donated clothes, books, furniture, and similar items (merchandise) to the general public.[142]

Despite its origin, however, this exception is not confined to businesses that are thrift shops, either independent stores or thrift shops operated by tax-exempt organizations such as schools. For example, the IRS ruled that an exempt organization could solicit contributions of home heating oil from individuals who had converted to gas heat, extract the oil from fuel tanks, and sell it to the public, and not be involved in an unrelated business by reason of this exception.[143] Likewise, the IRS held that a charitable organization may maintain a property donation program, where contributed vehicles and other properties are sold to generate funds, with the program not considered an unrelated business by virtue of this exception.[144]

This exception was overlooked, however, in a case where a tax-exempt charitable organization, in the words of a court, "operated a business that facilitated the donation of timeshares."[145] The federal government took the position that this charitable organization operated a "bogus tax scheme," asserting that the charity

[137] *Id*. at 481–83.
[138] *Id*. at 484.
[139] Priv. Ltr. Rul. 9535023.
[140] Tech. Adv. Mem. 9645004.
[141] IRC § 513(a)(3).
[142] Reg. § 1.513-1(e), last sentence; Rev. Rul. 71-581, 1971-2 C.B. 236.
[143] Priv. Ltr. Rul. 8116095.
[144] Priv. Ltr. Rul. 200230005.
[145] Tarpey v. United States, 123 A.F.T.R. 2d 2019-1138 (D. Mont. 2019), *aff'd*, 78 F.4th 1119 (9th Cir. 2023).

"acted merely as a conduit to hold title briefly to timeshares before being sold for a fraction of the appraised amount." The appraisers overstated the value of the timeshares; the charity "falsely told customers that they could deduct the full appraised amount of the timeshares." The government obtained a permanent injunction, closing the charity. False information may have been disseminated and values overstated, but the underlying "business" in this case appears to be protected under this merchandise-sales exception.

In a private letter ruling preceding this litigation, the IRS also failed to apply this exception, instead turning the sales-of-gift-items rule inside out. The IRS ruled that the primary purpose of the organization was "attracting customers who would otherwise have gone elsewhere to sell their timeshares."[146] The IRS also found that the organization was "principally operating to serve the business needs" of the companies the charity hired to conduct real estate closings, deed transfers, and appraisals, concluding that the organization was "conducting itself as a commercial-profit-making enterprise."

As noted, for this exception to apply, substantially all of the merchandise involved must have been contributed. In one instance, the IRS held that the exception was available where less than 5 percent of total sales was of purchased items.[147] Generally, however, the IRS defines *substantially all* to require that at least 85 percent of the items sold are donated items. For this exception to be utilized, however, the tax-exempt organization itself must be in the requisite business; it is not enough to have the business owned and operated by an independent contractor who merely uses an exempt organization's name and pays over certain receipts to the exempt organization.[148]

(d) Businesses of Employees' Associations

Excluded from unrelated business income taxation is a business, in the case of a tax-exempt local association of employees[149] organized before May 27, 1969, that is the selling by the organization of items of work-related clothing and equipment and items normally sold through vending machines, through food-dispensing facilities, or by snack bars, for the convenience of its members at their usual places of employment.[150] The IRS ruled that this type of association may change its form from unincorporated entity to a corporation without losing its grandfathered status.[151]

(e) Entertainment Activities

Another exception from unrelated business income taxation is applicable with respect to the conduct of entertainment at fairs and expositions.[152] This rule applies

---

[146] Priv. Ltr. Rul. 201734009.

[147] Priv. Ltr. Rul. 8122007.

[148] Tech. Adv. Mem. 8041007. Likewise, when the thrift stores were in a separate corporation, their operation was not imputed to a related tax-exempt organization for purposes of this exception (Disabled American Veterans Service Found., Inc. v. Comm'r, 29 T.C.M. 202 (1970)).

[149] IRC § 501(c)(4). See § 19.3.

[150] IRC § 513(a)(2).

[151] Priv. Ltr. Rul. 9442013.

[152] IRC § 513(d)(1), (2).

to charitable, social welfare, labor, agricultural, and horticultural organizations[153] that regularly conduct, as a substantial tax-exempt purpose, an agricultural and/ or educational fair or exposition.[154] This exemption from the unrelated income tax overrides an IRS pronouncement.[155]

The term *unrelated trade or business* does not include qualified *public entertainment activities* of an eligible organization.[156] This term is defined to mean any "entertainment or recreational activity of a kind traditionally conducted at fairs or expositions promoting agricultural and educational purposes, including, but not limited to, any activity one of the purposes of which is to attract the public to fairs or expositions or to promote the breeding of animals or the development of products or equipment."[157]

Unrelated income taxation is not to occur with respect to the operation of a *qualified public entertainment activity* that meets one of the following conditions: The public entertainment activity is conducted (1) in conjunction with an international, national, state, regional, or local fair or exposition; (2) in accordance with state law that permits that activity to be conducted solely by an eligible type of tax-exempt organization or by a governmental entity; or (3) in accordance with state law that permits that activity to be conducted under license for not more than 20 days in any year and that permits the organization to pay a lower percentage of the revenue from this activity than the state requires from other organizations.[158]

(f) Trade Shows

Activities that promote demand for industry products and services, like advertising and other promotional activities, generally constitute businesses if carried on for the production of income. The federal tax law provides what the IRS termed a "narrow exception" in this context[159] for certain tax-exempt organizations that conduct industry-promotion activities in connection with a convention, annual meeting, or trade show.

This exception with respect to trade show activities[160] is available for qualifying organizations, namely, tax-exempt labor, agricultural, and horticultural organizations, business leagues,[161] and charitable and social welfare organizations[162] that regularly conduct, as a substantial exempt purpose, shows that stimulate interest in and demand for the products of a particular industry or segment of industry or that educate persons in attendance regarding new developments or products or services related to the exempt activities of the organization.[163]

---

[153] IRC § 501(c)(3), (4), or (5). See Chapters 6–11, 13, 16.
[154] IRC § 513(d)(2)(C).
[155] Rev. Rul. 68-505, 1968-2 C.B. 248.
[156] IRC § 513(d)(1).
[157] IRC § 513(d)(2)(A).
[158] IRC § 513(d)(2)(B).
[159] Rev. Rul. 2004-112, 2004-2 C.B. 985.
[160] IRC § 513(d)(1), (3).
[161] IRC § 501(c)(5), (6). See Chapters 14, 16.
[162] IRC § 501(c)(3), (4). See Chapters 6–11, 13, respectively.
[163] IRC § 513(d)(3).

Under these rules, the term *unrelated trade or business* does not include qualified convention and trade show activities of an eligible organization.[164] The term
qualified convention and trade show activities is defined to mean any "activity of a
kind traditionally conducted at conventions, annual meetings, or trade shows,
including but not limited to, any activity one of the purposes of which is to attract
persons in an industry generally (without regard to membership in the sponsoring organization) as well as members of the public to the show for the purpose
of displaying industry products or services, or to educate persons engaged in the
industry in the development of new products and services or new rules and regulations affecting the industry."[165] This term thus refers to a "specific event at which
individuals representing a particular industry and members of the general public
gather in person at one location during a certain period of time."[166]

A *qualified convention and trade show activity* is a convention and trade show
activity that is (1) carried on by a qualifying organization; (2) conducted in conjunction with an international, national, state, regional, or local convention, annual
meeting, or show; (3) sponsored by a qualifying organization that has as one of its
purposes in sponsoring the activity the promotion and stimulation of interest in
and demand for the products and services of the industry involved in general or
the education of persons in attendance regarding new developments or products
and services related to the exempt activities of the organization; and (4) designed
to achieve this purpose through the character of the exhibits and the extent of the
industry products displayed.[167]

The income that is excluded from taxation by these rules is derived from the
rental of display space to exhibitors. This is the case even though the exhibitors
who rent the space are permitted to sell or solicit orders, as long as the show is a
qualified trade show or a qualified convention and trade show.[168] This exclusion is
also available with respect to a "supplier's exhibit" that is conducted by a qualifying organization in conjunction with a qualified convention or trade show.[169] This
exclusion is not available, however, to a stand-alone suppliers' exhibit that is not
a qualified convention or trade show.[170] Nonetheless, income from a suppliers'
exhibit is not taxable where the displays are educational in nature and are displays
at which soliciting and selling are prohibited.[171]

There is, moreover, an aspect of this issue that may resolve the tax issue for
many tax-exempt organizations not expressly covered by these rules. This relates
to the fact that an unrelated business must be *regularly carried on* before the revenue

---

[164] IRC § 513(d)(1).

[165] IRC § 513(d)(3)(A); Reg. § 1.513-3(c)(4).

[166] Rev. Rul. 2004-112, 2004-2 C.B. 985.

[167] IRC § 513(d)(3)(B). E.g., Orange Cnty. Agric. Soc'y, Inc. v. Comm'r, 893 F.2d 529 (2d Cir. 1990), *aff'g*
55 T.C.M. 1602 (1988); Ohio Cnty. & Indep. Agric. Soc'y Delaware Cnty. Fair v. Comm'r, 43 T.C.M.
1126 (1982).

[168] Reg. § 1.513-3(d)(1).

[169] Reg. § 1.513-3(c), Example (2). A *supplier's exhibit* is one in which the exhibitor displays goods or services that are supplied to, rather than by, the members of the qualifying organization in the conduct of
the members' own trade or business (Reg. § 1.513-3(d)(2)).

[170] Reg. § 1.513-3(e), Example (4).

[171] Rev. Rul. 75-516, 1975-2 C.B. 220.

from the business can be taxed as unrelated income.[172] Thus, the net income derived by an exempt organization (irrespective of the statutory basis for its tax exemption) from the conduct of a trade show would not be taxable as unrelated income if the trade show is not regularly carried on. A court case gives support to the premise that the conduct of a typical trade show is not an activity that is regularly carried on.[173]

A tax-exempt organization may sponsor and perform educational and supporting services for a trade show (such as use of its name, promotion of attendance, planning of exhibits and demonstrations, and provision of lectures for the exhibits and demonstrations) without having the compensation for its efforts taxed as unrelated income, as long as the trade show is not a sales facility.[174] The IRS ruled that the convention and trade show activities qualified for this exception, and that the fact that this sponsorship of and participation in "commercial trade shows" with a for-profit entity did not change their nature as qualified activities.[175]

The IRS issued guidance as to when Internet activities conducted by qualifying organizations (or at least exempt business leagues) fall within this exception for qualified convention and trade show activity.[176]

(g) Hospital Services

An exception from unrelated business income taxation is applicable with respect to the performance of certain services for small hospitals. It generally is the position of the IRS that income that a tax-exempt hospital derives from provision of services to other exempt hospitals constitutes unrelated business income to the hospital that is the provider of the services, on the theory that the providing of services to other hospitals is not an activity that is substantially related to the exempt purpose of the provider hospital.[177] Congress acted to reverse this rule in the case of small hospitals.

This special rule[178] applies where a tax-exempt hospital[179] provides services only to other exempt hospitals, as long as each of the recipient hospitals has facilities to serve no more than 100 inpatients and the services would be consistent with the recipient hospitals' exempt purposes if performed by them on their own behalf. The services that qualify for this special rule are confined to data processing, purchasing (including the purchasing of insurance on a group basis), warehousing, billing and collection (including the purchase of patron accounts receivable on a recourse basis), food, clinical, industrial engineering, laboratory, printing, communications, record center, and personnel (including selection, testing, training, and education of personnel) services.[180]

---

[172] See § 24.3.
[173] Suffolk Cnty. Patrolmen's Benevolent Ass'n, Inc. v. Comm'r, 77 T.C. 1314 (1982).
[174] Rev. Rul. 78-240, 1978-1 C.B. 170.
[175] Priv. Ltr. Rul. 200713024.
[176] See § 24.5(o), text accompanied by notes 591–592.
[177] Rev. Rul. 69-633, 1969-2 C.B. 121. See § 24.5(k).
[178] IRC § 513(e).
[179] IRC § 170(b)(1)(A)(iii). See §§ 7.6(a), 12.3(a).
[180] IRC § 501(e)(1)(A). See § 11.4.

(h) Bingo Game Income

Bingo game income realized by most tax-exempt organizations is not subject to unrelated business income taxation.[181] This exclusion applies where the bingo game[182] is not conducted on a commercial basis and where the games do not violate state or local laws.[183]

It is the view of the IRS that this exception applies only to gambling activities in which all wagers are placed, all winners are determined, and all prizes are distributed in the presence of the players of the game, so that the conduct of a "pull-tab operation" is not embraced by the exception.[184] Consequently, the IRS held that the game of standard flash does not qualify as a bingo game for this purpose because it fails to meet the requirement that the winners be determined in the presence of all individuals placing wagers in the games.[185] This view was also reflected in a court opinion holding that proceeds attributable to an organization's "instant bingo" activities were not protected by the exception because individuals could play and win in isolation.[186]

By virtue of the way the organizations are taxed, the bingo game exception is not applicable to social clubs, voluntary employees' beneficiary associations, political organizations, and homeowners' associations.[187]

(i) Pole Rentals

In the case of a mutual or cooperative telephone or electric company,[188] the term *unrelated trade or business* does not include engaging in qualified utility pole rentals.[189]

(j) Low-Cost Articles

Another exception from unrelated business income taxation is available only to tax-exempt organizations eligible to receive tax-deductible charitable contributions,[190] for activities relating to certain distributions of *low-cost articles* incidental to the solicitation of charitable contributions.[191] While this statutory provision is generally reflective of a similar rule stated in the income tax regulations,[192] there is one important refinement, which is that the term *low-cost article* is defined as

---

[181] IRC § 513(f).

[182] IRC § 513(f)(2)(A).

[183] H.R. Rep. No. 95-1608 (1978).

[184] Tech. Adv. Mem. 8602001.

[185] Tech. Adv. Mem. 202002010. The IRS also ruled that this game cannot be bifurcated so that part of it qualifies as a bingo game.

[186] Julius M. Israel Lodge of B'nai B'rith No. 2113 v. Comm'r, 70 T.C.M. 673 (1995), aff'd, 98 F.3d 190 (5th Cir. 1996). Also, Variety Club Tent No. 6 Charities, Inc. v. Comm'r, 74 T.C.M. 1485 (1997); Tech. Adv. Mem. 199924057.

[187] See Chapter 15, § 18.3, Chapter 17, and § 19.14, respectively.

[188] See § 19.5(b).

[189] IRC § 513(g).

[190] That is, an organization described in IRC § 501, where it qualifies as a charitable donee under IRC § 170(c)(2) or § 170(c)(3) (namely, as a charitable or veterans' organization).

[191] IRC § 513(h)(1)(A).

[192] Reg. § 1.513-1(b).

any article (or aggregate of articles distributed to a single distributee in a year) that has a cost not in excess of $5 (adjusted for inflation)[193] to the organization that distributes the item or on behalf of which the item is distributed.[194] These rules also require that the distribution of the items be unsolicited and be accompanied by a statement that the distributee may retain the low-cost article irrespective of whether a charitable contribution is made.[195]

(k) Mailing Lists

Another exception from unrelated business income taxation available to the category of tax-exempt organizations eligible for the low-cost articles exception[196] is applicable to the exchanging or renting of membership or donor mailing lists with or to another of these exempt organizations.[197]

Absent this exception, however, the rental or exchange of a mailing list by a tax-exempt organization, when regularly carried on, is considered by the IRS to be an unrelated business. This is not a problem from an economic standpoint when the activity involves a list rental,[198] in that taxes can be paid from the resulting net income. When the activity is a list exchange, however, there is no income from the transaction available to pay the tax; it is nonetheless the view of the IRS that these exchanges are unrelated businesses.[199] In calculating the amount of "income" of this nature, the IRS advised that the method to use should be in accordance with the rules concerning facilities used for related and unrelated purposes; thus, expenses and deductions are to be allocated between the two uses on a reasonable basis.[200]

If properly structured, however, a mailing list rental or exchange program involving a noncharitable tax-exempt organization can avoid unrelated business income taxation by reason of treatment of the income as an excludable royalty.[201]

(l) Associate Member Dues

If a tax-exempt agricultural or horticultural organization[202] requires annual dues not exceeding $100 (indexed for inflation)[203] to be paid in order to be a member of the organization, no portion of the dues may be considered unrelated business income because of any benefits or privileges to which these members are entitled.[204]

---

[193] IRC § 513(h)(2)(C). The IRS calculated that the low-cost article threshold for tax years beginning in 2025 is $13.60 (Rev. Proc. 2024-40, 2024-45 I.R.B. 1100 § 3.34(1)).

[194] IRC § 513(h)(2).

[195] IRC § 513(h)(3).

[196] See § 25.2(j).

[197] IRC § 513(h)(1)(B).

[198] Rev. Rul. 72-431, 1972-2 C.B. 281.

[199] Tech. Adv. Mem. 9502009.

[200] See § 24.4(d).

[201] So held in Sierra Club, Inc. v. Comm'r, 86 F.3d 1526 (9th Cir. 1996). See § 25.1(g).

[202] See §§ 16.2, 16.3.

[203] IRC § 512(d)(2). For tax years beginning in 2025, this threshold is $207 (Rev. Proc. 2024-40, 2024-45 I.R.B. 1100 § 3.33).

[204] IRC § 512(d)(1).

The term *dues* is defined as any "payment required to be made in order to be recognized by the organization as a member of the organization."[205] If a person makes a single payment that entitles the person to be recognized as a member of the organization for more than 12 months, the payment can be prorated for the purposes of applying the $100 cap.[206]

§ 25.3 SMALL BUSINESS CORPORATION RULES

A charitable tax-exempt organization[207] may be a shareholder in an *S corporation*, which is a corporation that is treated for federal income tax purposes as a partnership.[208] The authorization to own this type of a security is a revision of prior law.[209]

This type of interest is an interest in an unrelated business.[210] Items of income, loss, or deduction of an S corporation flow through to eligible tax-exempt organization shareholders as unrelated business income, regardless of whether they would otherwise be excluded under a modification.[211] Gain or loss on the disposition of stock in an S corporation also results in unrelated business income.[212]

§ 25.4 SPECIAL RULES

(a) Foreign Organizations

Federal tax law provides a definition of *unrelated business taxable income* specifically applicable to foreign organizations that are subject to the tax on unrelated income.[213] Basically, foreign organizations are taxed on their unrelated business taxable income that is *effectively connected* with the conduct of a trade or business within the United States and on unrelated business taxable income derived from sources within the United States that is not effectively connected income.

(b) Veterans' Organizations

In the case of certain veterans' organizations,[214] the term *unrelated business taxable income* does not include any amount attributable to payments for life, sick, accident, or health insurance with respect to members of the organizations or their dependents that is set aside for the purpose of providing for the payment of insurance benefits or for a charitable purpose.[215]

---

[205] IRC § 512(d)(3).

[206] H.R. Rep. No. 104-737, at 14 (1996).

[207] That is, an organization described in IRC § 501(c)(3) and exempt by reason of IRC § 501(a).

[208] IRC §§ 1361–1363.

[209] IRC § 1361(c)(6). Also, an employee plan described in IRC § 401(a) and exempt by reason of IRC § 501(a) can own stock in an S corporation.

[210] IRC § 512(e)(1)(A).

[211] IRC § 512(e)(1)(B)(i). This rule does not apply to employer securities (IRC § 409(l)) held by an employee stock ownership plan (IRC § 4975(e)(7)) (IRC § 512(e)(3); e.g., Priv. Ltr. Rul. 200029055).

[212] IRC § 512(e)(1)(B)(ii).

[213] IRC § 512(a)(2).

[214] See § 19.11.

[215] IRC § 512(a)(4).

(c) Social Clubs, VEBAs, and SUB Trusts

Special rules are applicable to social clubs,[216] voluntary employees' beneficiary associations,[217] and supplemental unemployment benefit trusts.[218] These rules[219] apply the unrelated business income tax to all of these organizations' net income other than so-called *exempt function income.*[220] For example, an exempt VEBA was required to pay the unrelated business income tax on revenue allocable to temporary excess office space, notwithstanding the court's belief that the space was acquired, in the exercise of sound business judgment, in anticipation of growth of the organization.[221]

Exempt function income is of two types: gross income from amounts (such as dues or fees) paid by members of the organization as consideration for the provision of goods, facilities, or services in furtherance of tax-exempt purposes, and income that is set aside for a charitable[222] purpose or (other than in the case of a social club) to provide for the payment of life, sick, accident, or other benefits, subject to certain account limits.[223] For example, with respect to tax-exempt voluntary employees' beneficiary associations, investment income, employer contributions, and other income received by a voluntary employees' beneficiary association set aside to pay plan benefits are exempt function income.[224] The IRS ruled that a voluntary employees' beneficiary association may, for the purposes of determining exempt function income, include in its applicable account limit, with respect to

---

[216] IRC § 501(c)(7) (see Chapter 15).

[217] IRC § 501(c)(9) (see § 18.3).

[218] IRC § 501(c)(17) (see § 18.4).

[219] IRC § 512(a)(3).

[220] IRC § 512(a)(3)(B). Interest on obligations of a state (see IRC § 103(a)) received by a tax-exempt social club is not included in gross income for purposes of IRC § 512(a)(3) (Rev. Rul. 76-337, 1976-2 C.B. 177). An exempt social club may, in computing its unrelated business taxable income, claim the tax credit for the portion of employer Social Security taxes paid with respect to employee tips (IRC § 45B) received from members and nonmembers (Rev. Rul. 2003-64, 2003-1 C.B. 1036).

[221] Uniformed Servs. Benefit Ass'n v. United States, 727 F. Supp. 533 (W.D. Mo. 1990).

[222] IRC § 170(c)(4).

[223] IRC § 512(a)(3)(E). As to the applicable account limit, see text accompanied by *infra* notes 230–231. For the purposes of the rule that makes this set-aside limitation inapplicable to an organization that receives substantially all of its contributions from tax-exempt employers (IRC § 512(a)(3)(E)(iii)), the term *substantially all* means at least 85 percent (INFO 2003-0225).

The IRS held that funds of a tax-exempt voluntary employees' beneficiary association providing postretirement medical benefits may be aggregated by a sponsoring employer with funds of the association providing postretirement life benefits for the purpose of computing the unrelated business income of the funds (Tech. Adv. Mem. 201225019).

The IRS also held that a nonvoluntary employees' beneficiary association fund that also qualifies as a welfare benefit fund (IRC § 419(e)(1)), maintained by the employer to provide retiree death benefits, may be aggregated with the association's funds in computing unrelated business income (IRC §§ 419A(g) (deemed unrelated business income) and 512(a)(3)); this is the case notwithstanding that the nonvoluntary employees' beneficiary association fund contains a reserve. These funds may be aggregated under certain circumstances (IRC § 419A(h)(1)(B)). The IRS stated: "Since section 512(a)(3)(E)(ii)(I) provides that the set aside limitation in section 512(a)(3)(E)(i) does not apply to income attributable to an existing reserve, the income of [the non-VEBA account] is not generally subject to [the unrelated business income tax]. Therefore, it is consistent with the purpose of section 512 to aggregate [this account], which has an existing reserve, with the VEBAs, which do not have existing reserves."

[224] IRC § 513(a)(3)(B)(ii); e.g., Priv. Ltr. Rul. 201512006.

medical benefits provided through its plan, a reserve, and, as to its set-aside, the applicable account limit may include medical insurance premiums.[225]

In one instance, a voluntary employees' beneficiary association, providing benefits to a tax-exempt business league[226] and its members that received demutualization proceeds from an insurance company (not a form of exempt function revenue) avoided unrelated business income taxation of the proceeds by setting them aside for charitable purposes, in the form of transfer to a supporting organization[227] that carries out the charitable and educational purposes of the business league.[228] In another instance, a voluntary employees' beneficiary association prevented taxation of demutualization proceeds by setting the amounts aside for the provision of permissible welfare benefits.[229]

As noted, in determining the unrelated business taxable income of a voluntary employees' beneficiary association, a limit is imposed on the amount that can be treated as exempt function income because it is set aside;[230] it is an amount that does not exceed certain account limits.[231] The U.S. Court of Federal Claims held that this limitation on exempt function income cannot be avoided by allocating investment income to the payment of welfare benefits during the year involved (that is, by spending rather than accumulating);[232] this decision was affirmed by the U.S. Court of Appeals for the Federal Circuit.[233] The U.S. Court of Federal Claims subsequently issued an identical decision.[234] The U.S. Court of Appeals for the Sixth Circuit, however, earlier held that the limitation is applicable only to income actually accumulated during the course of a voluntary employees' beneficiary association's tax year.[235] Subsequently issued tax regulations follow the Sixth Circuit approach in provides guidance as to how voluntary employees' beneficiary associations must calculate their unrelated business taxable income.[236]

(d)   Title-Holding Companies

It was the position of the IRS that a title-holding company[237] must lose its tax-exempt status if it generates any amount of certain types of unrelated business taxable income.[238] The federal tax law was amended in 1993, however, to permit an

---

[225] Priv. Ltr. Rul. 201844005.

[226] See Chapter 14.

[227] See § 12.3(c).

[228] Priv. Ltr. Rul. 200223068.

[229] Priv. Ltr. Rul. 200011063.

[230] IRC § 512(a)(3)(E)(i).

[231] IRC § 419A(c).

[232] CNG Transmission Management VEBA v. United States, 84 Fed. Cl. 327 (Ct. Fed. Cl. 2008).

[233] CNG Transmission Management VEBA v. United States, 588 F.3d 1376 (Fed. Cir. 2009).

[234] Northrop Corp. Employee Ins. Benefit Plans Master Trust v. United States, 2011-2 U.S.T.C. ¶ 50,396 (Ct. Fed. Cl. 2011), aff'd, 2012-2 U.S.T.C. ¶ 50,396 (Fed. Cir. 2012), cert. denied, 133 S. Ct. 756 (2012).

[235] Sherwin-Williams Co. Employee Health Plan Trust v. Comm'r, 330 F.3d 449 (6th Cir. 2003), rev'g 115 T.C. 440 (2001), nonacq. AOD 2005-02, 2005-35 I.R.B. 422.

[236] Reg. § 1.512(a)-5. This regulation follows the CNG Transmission (supra notes 232 and 233) and Northrop (supra note 234) approaches and rejects the Sherwin-Williams (supra note 235) approach (84 Fed. Reg. 67370, 67372 (2019)).

[237] See § 19.2.

[238] IRS Notice 88-121, 1988-2 C.B. 457. Also, Reg. § 1.501(c)(2)-1(a).

exempt title-holding company to receive unrelated business taxable income (that would otherwise disqualify the company for tax exemption) in an amount up to 10 percent of its gross income for the tax year, provided that the unrelated business taxable income is incidentally derived from the holding of real property.[239] For example, income generated from fees for parking or from the operation of vending machines located on real property owned by a title-holding company generally qualifies for the 10 percent *de minimis* rule, but income derived from an activity that is not incidental to the holding of real property (such as manufacturing) does not qualify.[240] Permissible unrelated business income is nonetheless subject to taxation.

Also, a tax-exempt title-holding company will not lose its tax exemption if unrelated business taxable income that is incidentally derived from the holding of real property exceeds the 10 percent limitation, where the organization establishes to the satisfaction of the IRS that the receipt of unrelated business taxable income in excess of the 10 percent limitation was "inadvertent and reasonable steps are being taken to correct the circumstances giving rise to such income."[241]

A tax-exempt organization and a single-parent title-holding corporation[242] may file a consolidated annual information return for a tax year. When this is done, and where the title-holding corporation pays any amount of its net income over the year to the exempt organization (or would have paid the amount but for the fact that the expenses of collecting the income exceeded its income), the corporation is treated as if it was organized and operated for the same purpose(s) as the other exempt organization (in addition to its title-holding purpose).[243] The effect of this rule is to exclude from any unrelated income taxation the income received by the exempt parent organization from the title-holding corporation.

§ 25.5 "BUCKETING" RULE

(a) Statutory Law

Where a tax-exempt organization has two or more unrelated businesses, unrelated business taxable income must first be computed separately with respect to each business.[244] The organization's unrelated business taxable income for a year is the sum of the amounts (not less than zero) computed for each separate unrelated business, less the specific deduction.[245] A net operating loss deduction[246] is allowed only with respect to a business from which the loss arose.

---

[239] IRC § 501(c)(2), last sentence; IRC § 501(c)(25)(G)(i).

[240] H.R. Rep. No. 103-111, at 618 (1993). The IRS revoked the tax-exempt status of a title holding company that provided bar and beverage sales and service for private functions, concluding that these activities were not incidental to the organization's rental activities (Priv. Ltr. Rul. 202221008).

[241] IRC § 501(c)(2), last sentence; IRC § 501(c)(25)(G)(ii).

[242] See § 19.2(a).

[243] IRC § 511(c).

[244] IRC § 512(a)(6), added by the Tax Cuts and Jobs Act (Pub. L. No. 115-97, § 13702(a), 131 Stat. 2054, 2168 (2017)). This computation does not use the specific deduction (see § 25.7(c)). This law, also termed the "silo" rule, generally is effective for tax years beginning after 2017 (Tax Cuts and Jobs Act, *supra*, at § 13702(b)).

[245] See § 25.7(c).

[246] See § 25.7(d).

The result of this body of law is that a deduction from one unrelated business for a tax year may not be used by a tax-exempt organization to offset income from another unrelated business for the same tax year. This law generally does not, however, prevent an exempt organization from using a deduction from one tax year to offset income from the same unrelated business in another tax year, where appropriate.

Congress, in fashioning the bucketing rule, did not provide criteria for determining when an exempt organization has more than one unrelated business or how to identify separate unrelated businesses for the purposes of calculating unrelated business taxable income.

(b)   Regulations

As noted, the bucketing rule requires an exempt organization with more than one unrelated business to compute its unrelated business taxable income separately with respect to each unrelated business.[247]

Organizations determine whether they regularly carry on one or more unrelated trades or businesses by applying four sections of the federal tax code.[248] An organization identifies its separate unrelated businesses by using the rules in the bucketing rule regulations.[249] An organization that changes the identification of a separate unrelated business must report the change in the tax year of the change in accordance with forms and instructions.[250]

(i) Separate Unrelated Businesses in General.   Generally, an organization identifies each of its separate unrelated businesses using the first two digits of the North American Industry Classification System (NAICS) code that most accurately describes the unrelated business.[251] In the case of goods sold both online and in stores, the separate unrelated business is identified by the goods sold in stores.[252]

The NAICS two-digit code must identify the unrelated business in which the exempt organization engages, directly or indirectly, and not activities the conduct of which is substantially related to the exercise or performance by the organization of its exempt purpose or function.[253] These codes must be reported only once.[254]

An exempt organization must allocate deductions between or among separate unrelated businesses using an existing method.[255]

(ii) Investment Activities.   Most forms of passive income, such as dividends, interest, annuities, rents, royalties, and capital gains, are excluded from unrelated

---

[247] Reg. § 1.512(a)-6(a)(1).

[248] IRC §§ 511-514.

[249] Reg. § 1.512(a)-6(a)(2).

[250] Reg. § 1.512(a)-6(a)(3).

[251] Reg. § 1.512(a)-6(b)(1).

[252] *Id.*

[253] Reg. § 1.512(a)-6(b)(2).

[254] Reg. § 1.512(a)-6(b)(3).

[255] Reg. § 1.512(a)-6(f). This method is the subject of Reg. § 1.512(a)-1(c). The IRS is in the process of modifying the regulations as they pertain to the allocation of deductions (Department of the Treasury, 2024–2025 Priority Guidance Plan (Oct. 3, 2024)).

business income taxation.[256] Inclusions of subpart F income[257] and inclusions of global intangible low-taxed income[258] are treated in the same manner as dividends.[259] In the preamble accompanying these regulations, however, the Treasury Department and the IRS noted that whether an activity produces passive rental income depends, in part, on whether other services are provided by the exempt organization in connection with the ostensible rental activity.[260]

Investment activities that generate (or potentially generate) unrelated business income are subject to one of two sets of rules.[261] Certain investment activities are collectively regarded as one separate business for the purposes of the bucketing rule. Other investment activities must be treated as separate businesses and identified using the applicable NAICS two-digit code for each business. A tax-exempt organization's investment activities that collectively may be treated as a single business are its qualifying partnerships interests, qualifying S corporation interests, and debt-financed property or properties.[262]

(iii) Qualifying Partnership Interests. An interest in a general partnership is not a qualifying partnership interest (QPI).[263] An interest in a limited partnership is a QPI if the tax-exempt organization holds, directly or indirectly, an interest in the partnership where that interest meets a de minimis test or a participation test.[264] Pursuant to a look-through rule, if an exempt organization holds a direct interest in a limited partnership but that interest is not a QPI, a partnership in which the organization holds an indirect interest, through the directly held partnership interest, may be a QPI if the indirectly held interest meets the *de minimis* test or the participation test.[265]

An organization that has a limited partnership interest meeting the previously noted requirements concerning direct and indirect interests in a tax year may designate that partnership interest as a QPI by including its share of partnership gross income (and directly connected deductions) with the gross income (and such deductions) from its other investment activities in accordance with forms and instructions.[266]

A limited partnership interest will qualify as a QPI under the *de minimis test* if it holds, directly or indirectly, no more than 2 percent of the profits interest and no more than 2 percent of the capital interest of the partnership during the organization's tax year with which or in which the partnership's tax year ends.[267]

---

[256] IRC § 512(b)(1)-(3), (5). See § 25.1(a)-(k).

[257] IRC § 951(a)(1)(A); see § 25.1(n)(i).

[258] IRC § 951A(a); see § 25.1(n)(ii).

[259] Reg. § 1.512(b)-1(a)(1).

[260] T.D. 9933, 85 Fed. Reg. 77952, 77954 (2020). To the extent that other services are provided, income from the use of space may cease to be excludible rent from real property and instead take on the character of the unrelated business services being provided (*id.*; Reg. § 1.512(b)-1(c)(5); see § 25.1(h)).

[261] Reg. § 1.512(a)-6(c)(1).

[262] *Id.* As to debt-financed property, see § 24.10. Special rules apply when determining the unrelated business income from the investment activities of voluntary employees' beneficiary associations, and supplemental unemployment benefits trusts (Reg. § 1.512(a)-6(c)(7); see § 25.4(c)).

[263] Reg. § 1.512(a)-6(c)(8)(ii).

[264] Reg. § 1.512(a)-6(c)(2)(i). These QPI rules do not apply to social clubs (Reg. § 1.512(a)-6(c)(8)(i)).

[265] Reg. § 1.512(a)-6(c)(2)(ii).

[266] Reg. § 1.512(a)-6(c)(2)(iii).

[267] Reg. § 1.512(a)-6(c)(3).

A limited partnership interest will qualify as a QPI under the *participation test* if the tax-exempt organization holds, directly or indirectly, no more than 20 percent of the capital interest in the partnership during the organization's tax year with which or in which the partnership's tax year ends and the organization does not significantly participate in the partnership.[268] In determining an organization's percentage interest in a partnership for this purpose, the interests of a supporting organization, other than a Type III supporting organization that is not a parent of its supported organization,[269] or of a controlled entity,[270] in the same partnership is taken into account.[271]

An exempt organization is considered to *significantly participate* in a partnership if (1) the organization, by itself, may require the partnership to perform, or may prevent the partnership from performing (other than through a unanimous voting requirement or through minority consent rights), any act that significantly affects the operations of the partnership; (2) any of the organization's officers, directors, trustees, or employees have rights to participate in the management of the partnership at any time; (3) any of the organization's officers, directors, trustees, or employees have rights to conduct the partnership's business at any time; or (4) the organization, by itself, has the power to appoint or remove any of the partnership's officers or employees or a majority of directors.[272]

For the purposes of the *de minimis* test, an organization's profits interest in a limited partnership is determined in the same manner as its distributive share of partnership taxable income.[273] For the purposes of the *de minimis* test and the participation test, in the absence of a provision of the partnership agreement, an organization's capital interest in a partnership is determined on the basis of its interest in the assets of the partnership that would be distributed to it on its withdrawal from the partnership or on liquidation of the partnership, whichever is greater.[274]

For the purposes of both tests, an exempt organization must determine its percentage interest by taking the average of its percentage interest at the beginning and the end of the partnership's taxable year (or, if held for less than a year, the percentage interest held at the beginning and end of the period of ownership within the partnership's taxable year).[275] When determining the exempt organization's average percentage interest in a partnership for the purposes of these tests, an organization may rely on the Schedule K-1 (Form 1065) it receives from the partnership if the form lists the organization's percentage profits interest or its percentage capital interest, or both, at the beginning and end of the year. An organization may not rely on the schedule, however, to the extent that any information about the organization's percentage interest is not specifically provided.[276]

---

[268] Reg. § 1.512(a)-6(c)(4)(i).
[269] See § 12.3(c).
[270] See §§ 29.7, 30.6.
[271] Reg. § 1.512(a)-6(c)(4)(ii).
[272] Reg. § 1.512(a)-6(c)(4)(iii).
[273] Reg. § 1.512(a)-6(c)(5)(i).
[274] Reg. § 1.512(a)-6(c)(5)(ii).
[275] Reg. § 1.512(a)-6(c)(5)(iii).
[276] Reg. § 1.512(a)-6(c)(5)(iv).

A limited partnership interest that fails to meet the *de minimis* test or the participation test because of an increase in percentage interest in the organization's current tax year may be treated, for the tax year of the change, as meeting the requirements of the test it met in the prior tax year under certain circumstances.[277]

(iv) Qualifying S Corporation Interests. Where a tax-exempt organization owns stock in an S corporation, the interest is treated as an interest in a separate unrelated business for purposes of the bucketing rule, unless it meets the definition of a *qualifying S corporation interest.*[278] Rules similar to those that apply to determine whether a partnership interest is a QPI apply for purposes of determining whether an S corporation interest is a qualified interest eligible to be aggregated with other qualified investment activities for purposes of the bucketing rule.[279] An organization may rely on the Schedule K-1 (Form 1120-S) (or its successor) it receives from the S corporation only if the form lists information sufficient to determine the organization's percentage of stock ownership for the year.[280] An organization may not, however, rely on such a schedule for stock ownership purposes if it reports "zero" as the organization's number of shares of stock in either the beginning or the end of the S corporation's taxable year.[281]

(v) Controlled Entities. If a tax-exempt organization controls another entity,[282] all specified payments[283] received by the controlling organization from the controlled entity are treated as gross income from a separate unrelated business for purposes of the bucketing rule.[284] If a controlling organization receives specified payments from two controlled entities, the payments from each controlled entity are treated as separate unrelated businesses.[285]

All amounts included in unrelated business taxable income from controlled foreign corporations[286] are treated as income from a separate unrelated business for purposes of the bucketing rule.[287]

(vi) Total UBTI. The total unrelated business taxable income of an exempt organization with more than one unrelated business is the sum of the unrelated business taxable income computed with respect to each unrelated business, less a charitable contribution deduction,[288] a net operating loss deduction[289] for losses arising in tax years beginning before January 1, 2018, and the specific deduction.[290]

---

[277] Reg. § 1.512(a)-6(c)(6).
[278] Reg. § 1.512(a)-6(e).
[279] Reg. § 1.512(a)-6(e)(2).
[280] *Id.*
[281] *Id.*
[282] IRC § 512(b)(13)(D); see § 30.6(b).
[283] IRC § 512(b)(13)(C); see § 30.6(b).
[284] Reg. § 1.512(a)-6(d)(1).
[285] *Id.*
[286] See § 25.1(n)(i).
[287] Reg. § 1.512(a)-6(d)(2).
[288] See § 25.7(b).
[289] See § 25.7(d).
[290] Reg. § 1.512(a)-6(g)(1). The specific deduction is the subject of § 25.7(c).

(c) Medical Marijuana Dispensary Cases

Much discussion has ensued, in the aftermath of enactment of the bucketing rule, about the absence of law that tax-exempt organizations may use in ascertaining whether they have more than one unrelated business. Certainly, as noted, nothing in the statute addresses the topic, and the bucketing regulations leave the determination of what constitutes a separate trade or business in the hands of the tax-exempt organization.

There is case law, nonetheless, that can be of assistance in this context. This body of law has arisen in connection with the federal tax law treatment of the expenses incurred by marijuana dispensaries. Marijuana, of course, is a controlled substance under federal law, and its manufacture and distribution are thus forbidden at that law level.[291] Some states, however, have adopted laws allowing for the cultivation, sale, and use of marijuana for personal medicinal purposes. The tensions between these two bodies of law are manifold, two being that a business that "consists of trafficking in controlled substances" may not deduct (under federal law) any business expenses[292] and thus cannot capitalize costs.[293] This state of the federal tax law has incentivized these companies to assert that they are operating one or more businesses of a type other than dispensation of marijuana and required courts (so far, only the U.S. Tax Court) to rule on that assertion.

As an example, the Tax Court held that one of these companies operated two separate businesses—one involving the sale of marijuana and one that provides caregiving services.[294] This decision enabled the company to deduct the expenses allocable to the caregiving business. In two subsequent cases, the court found that a marijuana dispensary was engaged in a single business.[295]

In a case decided near the close of 2018, the Tax Court considered a company's contention that it was engaging in four discrete businesses: sales of marijuana and products containing it, sales of products without marijuana, therapeutic services, and brand development. The court, however, held that this entity is engaged in merely one business: trafficking in a controlled substance.[296] Thus, the company cannot, pursuant to this holding, deduct any of its expenses.

In this 2018 opinion, the Tax Court enunciated principles that are useful in the exempt organizations unrelated business setting. The court first noted that an "activity is a trade or business if the taxpayer does it continuously and regularly with the intent of making a profit."[297] Then, it provided four basic guidelines: (1) an organization can operate more than one business; (2) multiple activities can amount to a single business; (3) whether two activities are two businesses or only one is a question of fact; and (4) the court primarily considers, in ascertaining the number of an organization's businesses, the degree of organizational and economic interrelationship of various undertakings, the business purpose that is (or might be)

---

[291] 21 U.S.C. §§ 812, 841(a).

[292] IRC § 280E.

[293] IRC § 263A(a)(2).

[294] Californians Helping to Alleviate Med. Problems, Inc. v. Comm'r, 128 T.C. 173 (2007).

[295] Canna Care, Inc. v. Comm'r, 110 T.C.M. 408 (2015), aff'd, 694 Fed. Appx. 570 (9th Cir. 2017); Olive v. Comm'r, 139 T.C. 19 (2012), aff'd, 792 F.3d 1146 (9th Cir. 2015).

[296] Patients Mut. Assistance Collective Corp. v. Comm'r, 151 T.C. 176 (2018).

[297] Id. at 198.

served by carrying on the various undertakings separately or together, and the similarity of the various undertakings.

Factors in the cases were elements such as different employees for different functions, substantial differences in services, the bundling of services, the fact that some activities were incidental to others, the income amounts associated with each activity, and use of one entity, management, capital structure, and facilities. In this case, the court noted that the organization's marijuana and marijuana products sales accounted for 99.5 percent of its revenue. Its other activities were "neither economically separate nor substantially different."[298]

Thus, while the nonprofit community and the Treasury Department are now struggling to understand and implement the bucketing rule, the U.S. Tax Court has been working on and developing these concepts since 2007.

§ 25.6 TAX STRUCTURE

The federal tax law imposes a tax on unrelated business taxable income.[299] The unrelated business income tax rate payable by most tax-exempt organizations is the corporate rate.[300] Some organizations, such as trusts, are subject to the individual income rates.[301]

The tax law, prior to 2018, featured a three-bracket structure for corporations. The unrelated business tax rate for corporations was the highest rate, at 35 percent. The tax rate for corporations has been lowered to a single rate of 21 percent,[302] causing the corporate tax rate for unrelated business taxable income to be 21 percent.[303]

This tax structure is inapplicable to the taxation of insurance companies,[304] which is the tax law paradigm that is used to tax organizations that cannot qualify as charitable organizations or social welfare organizations because a substantial part of their activities consists of the provision of commercial-type insurance.[305]

Tax-exempt organizations must make quarterly estimated payments of the tax on unrelated business income, under the same rules that require quarterly estimated payments of corporate income taxes.[306] Revenue and expenses associated with unrelated business activity are reported to the IRS on a tax return (Form 990-T).[307]

§ 25.7 DEDUCTION RULES

Generally, the term *unrelated business taxable income* means the gross income derived by a tax-exempt organization from an unrelated trade or business,

---

[298] *Id.* at 204. Likewise, Alternative Health Care Advocates v. Comm'r, 151 T.C. 225 (2018).

[299] IRC §§ 511(a), 512(a)(1). Also, IRC § 12(1).

[300] IRC § 11.

[301] IRC § 1(e).

[302] IRC § 11(b). This rate reduction, effective for tax years beginning after 2017, was enacted as part of the Tax Cuts and Jobs Act (Pub. L. No. 115-97, § 13001(a), 131 Stat. 2054, 2096 (2017)).

[303] IRC § 511(a)(1), (2)(A).

[304] IRC § 11(c)(2). See IRC § 801 *et seq.* (IRC Subchapter L).

[305] IRC § 501(m)(2)(B). See § 28.13(b).

[306] IRC § 6655(g)(3).

[307] IRC § 6012(a)(2), 6012(a)(4).

regularly carried on by the organization, less business deductions that are directly connected with the carrying on of the trade or business.[308] For the purposes of computing unrelated business taxable income, both gross income and business deductions are computed with certain modifications.[309] In the case of an exempt organization with more than one unrelated trade or business, unrelated business taxable income is calculated separately with respect to each trade or business.[310]

(a)   General Rules

Generally, to be *directly connected with* the conduct of an unrelated business, an item of deduction must have a proximate and primary relationship to the carrying on of that business. Expenses, depreciation, and similar items attributable solely to the conduct of unrelated business are proximately and primarily related to that business and therefore qualify for deduction to the extent that they meet the requirements of relevant provisions of the federal income tax law.[311] A loss incurred in the conduct of an unrelated activity may be offset against the net gain occasioned by the conduct of another unrelated activity only where the loss activity is conducted with a profit objective.[312]

Where facilities and/or personnel are used both to carry on tax-exempt activities and to conduct unrelated trade or business, the expenses, depreciation, and similar items attributable to the facilities and/or personnel, such as overhead or items of salary, must be allocated between the two uses on a reasonable basis.[313] An organization must also use this method of allocation, that is, a reasonable basis, when allocating deductions between two or more separate unrelated trades or businesses.[314] Despite the statutory rule that an expense must be directly connected with an unrelated business, the regulations merely state that the portion of the expense allocated to the unrelated business activity is, where the allocation is on a reasonable basis, proximately and primarily related to the business activity.[315] Once an item is proximately and primarily related to a business undertaking, it is allowable as a deduction in computing unrelated business income in the manner and to the extent permitted by federal income tax law generally.[316]

The preamble to the final "bucketing" regulations[317] reflects the IRS's view that an unadjusted gross-to-gross method for allocation of expenses, which fails to equalize price differences between related activities and unrelated trade or business activities, is not a reasonable method of allocation. The preamble states that,

---

[308] IRC § 512(a)(1).

[309] See § 25.1.

[310] Reg. §§ 1.512(a)-1(a), -6. See § 25.5.

[311] E.g., IRC §§ 162, 167. Reg. § 1.512(a)-1(b). For example, salaries of personnel employed full time in carrying on unrelated business activities are directly connected with the conduct of that activity and are deductible in computing unrelated business taxable income if they otherwise qualify for deduction under the business deduction rules (*id.*).

[312] E.g., West Va. State Med. Ass'n v. Comm'r, 91 T.C. 651 (1988), *aff'd*, 882 F.2d 123 (4th Cir. 1989), *cert. denied*, 493 U.S. 1044 (1990).

[313] Reg. § 1.512(a)-1(c).

[314] Reg. §§ 1.512(a)-1(c), -6(f).

[315] Reg. § 1.512(a)-1(c).

[316] *Id.*

[317] See § 25.5(b).

although the IRS will challenge this method of allocation, the IRS will refrain from litigating the reasonableness of other allocation methods pending the publication of further guidance. This issue is under further consideration by the Treasury Department and the IRS, and they expect to publish separate proposed regulations amending the existing regulations applicable to expense allocations.[318]

Gross income may be derived from an unrelated trade or business that exploits a tax-exempt function. Generally, in these situations, expenses, depreciation, and similar items attributable to the conduct of the tax-exempt function are not deductible in computing unrelated business taxable income. Since the items are incident to a function of the type that is the chief purpose of the organization to conduct, they do not possess a proximate and primary relationship to the unrelated trade or business. Therefore, they do not qualify as being directly connected with that business.[319]

A tax-exempt organization will be denied business expense deductions in computing its unrelated business taxable income if it cannot adequately substantiate that the expenses were incurred or that they were directly connected with the unrelated activity. In one instance, an organization derived unrelated business income from the sale of advertising space in two magazines and incurred expenses in connection with solicitation of the advertising and publication of the magazines. A court basically upheld the position of the IRS, which disallowed all of the claimed deductions (other than those for certain printing expenses) because the organization failed to establish the existence or relevance of the expenses.[320]

(b) Charitable Deduction

Tax-exempt organizations[321] are allowed, in computing their unrelated business taxable income (if any), a federal income tax charitable contribution deduction.[322] This deduction is allowable irrespective of whether the contribution is directly connected with the carrying on of the trade or business. This deduction may not exceed 10 percent of the organization's unrelated business taxable income computed without regard to the deduction.[323]

Trusts[324] are allowed a charitable contribution deduction;[325] the amount that is deductible is basically the same as that allowable pursuant to the rules applicable to charitable gifts by individuals.[326] Again, a deductible charitable gift from a trust need not be directly connected to the conduct of an unrelated business.

---

[318] T.D. 9933, 85 Fed. Reg. 77952, 77956–57 (2020).

[319] Reg. § 1.512(a)-1(d).

[320] CORE Special Purpose Fund v. Comm'r, 49 T.C.M. 626 (1985).

[321] That is, entities described in IRC § 511(a). See § 24.1, text accompanied by notes 21–22.

[322] IRC § 512(b)(10); Reg. § 1.512(b)-1(g)(1). This deduction is provided by IRC § 170.

[323] IRC § 512(b)(10); Reg. § 1.512(b)-1(g)(1) (which has not been revised to reflect the increase in this percentage limitation, in 1982, from 5 to 10 percent). E.g., Indep. Ins. Agents of Huntsville, Inc. v. Comm'r, 63 T.C.M. 2468 (1992), aff'd, 998 F.2d 898 (11th Cir. 1993) (percentage limitation was applied with respect to the related business income of a business league).

[324] That is, trusts described in IRC § 511(b)(2).

[325] IRC § 512(b)(11); Reg. § 1.512(b)-1(g)(2).

[326] In applying the percentage limitations, the contribution base is determined by reference to the organization's unrelated business taxable income (computed with the charitable deduction), rather than by reference to adjusted gross income.

Qualification for either of these charitable contribution deductions requires that the payments be made to another organization; that is, the funds may not be used by the organization in administration of its own charitable programs. For example, a tax-exempt university that operates an unrelated business is allowed this charitable deduction for contributions to another exempt university for educational purposes but is not allowed the deduction for amounts expended in administering its own educational program.[327]

(c) Specific Deduction

In computing unrelated business taxable income, a specific deduction of $1,000 is available.[328] The total unrelated business taxable income of an exempt organization with more than one unrelated trade or business is the sum of the unrelated business taxable income computed with respect to each unrelated business, less the specific deduction.[329] This deduction, however, is not allowed in computing net operating losses.[330] A diocese, province of a religious order, or convention or association of churches is allowed, with respect to each parish, individual church, district, or other local unit, a specific deduction equal to the lower of $1,000 or the gross income derived from an unrelated business regularly carried on by such an entity.[331] This deduction is intended to eliminate imposition of the unrelated income tax in cases in which exaction of the tax would involve excessive costs of collection in relation to any payments received by the government.[332]

As to this local unit rule, however, a diocese, province of a religious order, or convention or association of churches is not entitled to a specific deduction for a local unit that, for a tax year, files a separate return. In that instance, the local unit may claim a specific deduction equal to the lower of $1,000 or the gross income derived from any unrelated trade or business that it regularly conducts.[333]

(d) Net Operating Losses

The net operating loss deduction[334] is allowed in computing unrelated business taxable income.[335] The net operating loss carryback or carryover (from a tax year for which the exempt organization is subject to the unrelated business income tax) is determined under the net operating loss deduction rules without taking into account any amount of income or deduction that is not included under the unrelated business income tax rules in computing unrelated business taxable income. For example, a loss attributable to an unrelated trade or business is not to be diminished by reason of the receipt of dividend income.[336]

---

[327] Reg. § 1.512(b)-1(g)(3).
[328] IRC § 512(b)(12); Reg. § 1.512(b)-1(h)(1).
[329] Reg. § 1.512(a)-6(g)(1).
[330] Id. See § 25.7(d).
[331] IRC § 512(b)(12); Reg. § 1.512(b)-1(h)(2).
[332] H.R. Rep. No. 81-2319, at 37 (1950); S. Rep. No. 81-2375, at 30 (1950).
[333] Reg. § 1.512(b)-1(h)(2)(i).
[334] IRC § 172.
[335] IRC § 512(b)(6); Reg. § 1.512(b)-1(e)(1).
[336] Reg. § 1.512(b)-1(e)(1).

MODIFICATIONS, EXCEPTIONS, SPECIAL RULES, AND TAXATION

For the purpose of computing the net operating loss deduction, any prior tax year for which a tax-exempt organization was not subject to the unrelated business income tax may not be taken into account. Thus, if the organization was not subject to this tax for a preceding tax year, the net operating loss is not a carryback to such preceding tax year, and the net operating loss carryover to succeeding tax years is not reduced by the taxable income for such preceding tax year.[337]

A net operating loss carryback or carryover is allowed only from a tax year for which the exempt organization is subject to the unrelated business income tax rules.[338] In determining the span of years for which a net operating loss may be carried for the purposes of the net operating loss deduction rules, tax years in which an exempt organization was not subject to the unrelated business income tax regime may be taken into account.[339]

For tax years beginning after December 31, 2017, an exempt organization with more than one unrelated business determines the net operating loss deduction separately with respect to each of its unrelated businesses.[340] The regulations explain coordination of pre-2018 and post-2017 net operating losses,[341] the treatment of net operating losses on dispositions of separate unrelated businesses,[342] and the treatment of net operating losses when identification of a separate unrelated business changes.[343]

Changes to the net operating loss rules made in 2017, however, make application of this law daunting. Prior to these law changes, net operating losses for corporate taxpayers were generally eligible for a two-year carryback and a 20-year carryforward, and these carryovers and carrybacks could fully offset the taxable income of taxpayers.

This law was revised in 2017 by (1) eliminating the option for most taxpayers to carry back a net operating loss, (2) providing that most taxpayers can only carry net operating losses arising in tax years ending after 2017 to a subsequent year (albeit indefinitely), and (3) placing a limitation on net operating loss deductions for post-2017 losses by means of a rule that these deductions cannot exceed 80 percent of taxable income (determined without any net operating loss deduction) in tax years beginning after 2017.[344]

This body of law was altered again, in 2020, to help improve businesses' cash flow in the face of the COVID-19 pandemic.[345] The principal changes made at that time are a five-year carryback for losses incurred in 2018, 2019, or 2020, and suspension of the 80 percent limitation for tax years beginning before January 1, 2021.[346]

[337] Reg. § 1.512(b)-1(e)(2).
[338] Reg. § 1.512(b)-1(e)(3).
[339] Reg. § 1.512(b)-1(e)(4).
[340] Reg. § 1.512(a)-6(h)(1).
[341] Reg. § 1.512(a)-6(h)(2).
[342] Reg. § 1.512(a)-6(h)(3).
[343] Reg. § 1.512(a)-6(h)(4).
[344] IRC § 172(a)(2), as amended by the Tax Cuts and Jobs Act (Pub. L. No. 115-97, § 13302, 131 Stat. 2054, 2121–23 (2017)).
[345] CARES Act, Pub. L. No. 116-136, § 2303, 134 Stat. 281, 352–54 (2020).
[346] IRC §§ 172(b)(1)(D)(i)(I), 172(a)(1). Proposed regulations will address how changes made to the net operating loss rules by the CARES Act, *supra* note 345, apply for purposes of the bucketing rule.

CHAPTER TWENTY-SIX

Exemption Recognition and Notice Processes

Every element of gross income received by a person, including a corporation or trust, is potentially subject to the federal income tax.[1] The presumption is that all income is taxable; income, to not be taxable, must be exempt by virtue of an express tax law provision. Examples of this are the provisions for tax-exempt organizations.

An organization is not exempt from the federal income tax merely because it is organized and operated as a *nonprofit* entity.[2] Tax exemption[3] is achieved only where the organization satisfies the requirements of a particular provision in the Internal Revenue Code.[4] That is, whether an organization is entitled to exemption, on an initial or ongoing basis, is a matter of statutory law. It is Congress that, by statute, defines the categories of organizations that are eligible for federal income tax exemption;[5] it is Congress that determines whether a type of tax exemption should be continued.[6]

§ 26.1 RECOGNITION APPLICATION PROCEDURE

The IRS annually promulgates procedures by which a determination letter may be issued to an organization in response to the filing of an application for recognition[7] of exemption of tax-exempt status.[8]

---

[1] IRC § 61(a).

[2] See § 1.1.

[3] IRC § 501(a).

[4] IRC §§ 501(c), 521, or 526–529A; Reg. § 1.501(a)-1(a)(1).

[5] E.g., HCSC-Laundry v. United States, 450 U.S. 1 (1981) (where the Supreme Court held that Congress had the authority to exclude nonprofit laundry organizations from the scope of the tax exemption accorded to cooperative hospital service organizations (see § 11.4)).

[6] E.g., Maryland Sav.-Share Ins. Corp. v. United States, 400 U.S. 4 (1970) (where the Supreme Court held that Congress did not exceed its power to tax nor violate the Fifth Amendment to the Constitution in denying tax-exempt status to nonprofit insurers of deposits in savings banks and similar entities where the insurers were organized after September 1, 1957 (see § 19.8)). Likewise, for example, IRC § 501(c) (18) (see § 18.7) is applicable only to trusts created before June 25, 1959; IRC § 501(c)(27)(A) (see § 19.16) is applicable only to entities established before June 1, 1996, and IRC § 501(c)(23) (see § 19.11(b)) is available only to an organization organized before 1880.

[7] See § 3.2.

[8] These procedures are updated annually; the version in effect for 2024 is the subject of Rev. Proc. 2024-5, 2024-1 I.R.B. 262. The procedures apply to organizations seeking, by means of a determination letter (see text accompanied by and the contents of *infra* note 14), recognition of exemption from federal income tax under IRC §§ 501 and 521, other than pension, profit-sharing, stock bonus, annuity, and employee stock ownership plans, which are currently the subject of Rev. Proc. 2024-4, 2024-1 I.R.B. 160. These procedures also apply to revocation or modification of determination letters. Rev. Proc. 2024-5, *supra*, § 1, first paragraph.

The information that must be in applications for recognition of exemption filed by certain religious and apostolic organizations (see § 10.8) is the subject of Rev. Proc. 72-5, 1972-1 C.B. 709, as supplemented by Rev. Proc. 2024-5, *supra*. Rev. Proc. 80-27, 1980-1 C.B. 677, sets forth procedures pursuant to which tax exemption may be recognized on a group basis (see § 26.11).

Occasionally, the IRS announces a process for expediting applications for recognition of exemption for charitable organizations in aid of entities that are quickly formed to solicit contributions and conduct programs in response to an emergency.

(a) Introduction

These procedures pertain to the issuance of determination letters on issues under the jurisdiction of the IRS's Director, Exempt Organizations Rulings and Agreements.[9]

EO Determinations is the office in EO Rulings and Agreements that is primarily responsible for processing requests for determination letters.[10] A *determination letter* is a written statement issued by EO Determinations or the Independent Office of Appeals[11] in response to a request for the IRS's ruling on a the initial qualification for tax-exempt status of eligible organizations,[12] public charity/private foundation status,[13] or other determination under the jurisdiction of the Director, EO Rulings and Agreements.[14]

The IRS may decline to issue a determination letter "when appropriate in the interest of sound tax administration or on other grounds whenever warranted by the facts or circumstances of a particular case."[15] Also, the IRS will not issue a determination letter in response to a request if (1) the request involves an issue under the jurisdiction of the Associate Chief Counsel;[16] (2) the same issue involving the same taxpayer or a related taxpayer is pending in a case in litigation or before the Independent Office of Appeals; (3) the determination letter is requested by an industry, trade association, or similar group on behalf of individual taxpayers within the group; (4) the determination letter is requested by a labor, agricultural, or horticultural organization, or an organization the purpose of which is improvement of business conditions within one or more lines of business, relating to an activity involving controlled substances which is prohibited by federal law regardless of its legality under state law; (5) the request is based on alternative plans of proposed transactions or on hypothetical situations; (6) an organization

---

[9] EO Rulings and Agreements is the office in the EO Division that is primarily responsible for "up-front, customer-initiated activities" such as determination letter requests, taxpayer assistance, and assistance to other EO offices. This office includes the offices of EO Determinations and EO Determinations Quality Assurance. Rev. Proc. 2024-5, 2024-1 I.R.B. 262 § 1.01(2).

[10] *Id.* § 1.01(3).

[11] The term *Independent Office of Appeals* means any office under the direction and control of the Chief of Appeals. Rev. Proc. 2024-5, 2024-1 I.R.B. 262 § 1.01(4). The purpose of the Independent Office of Appeals is to resolve tax controversies, without litigation, on a "fair and impartial" basis. As its name indicates, I Independent Office of Appeals is independent of EO Rulings and Agreements (*id.*).

[12] This includes reinstatement of organizations that have had exempt status automatically revoked (see § 28.4) and subordinate organizations included in a group exemption letter (see § 26.11) that have been automatically revoked.

[13] See §§ 12.1(a), 12.3.

[14] Rev. Proc. 2024-5, 2024-1 I.R.B. 262 § 1.01(5). The term *determination letter* includes a written statement issued by EO Determinations or the Independent Office of Appeals based on advice secured from the Office of Associate Chief Counsel (Employee Benefits, Exempt Organizations, and Employment Taxes) pursuant to the procedures in Rev. Proc. 2024-2, 2024-1 I.R.B. 119. A determination letter "applies the principles and precedents previously announced to a specific set of facts" (*id.*). For a discussion of determination letter requests other than those related to an organization's initial qualification for tax-exempt status, see § 28.1(c), (d).

[15] Rev. Proc. 2024-5, 2024-1 I.R.B. 262 § 3.02.

[16] See Rev. Proc. 2024-1, 2024-1 I.R.B. 1.

currently recognized as exempt seeks a new determination letter confirming that the organization is still recognized under the same exemption category under current facts; (7) an organization seeks a determination of public charity/private foundation status that is identical to its current foundation status as determined by EO Determinations; (8) an organization currently recognized as exempt (other than a government entity) requests a determination to relinquish its exempt status; (9) a domestic organization currently recognized as exempt seeks a new determination letter but is not required to reapply because it has changed its form or state of organization in accordance with published IRS procedures; and (10) an organization applies for a group exemption letter.[17]

EO Determinations generally issues determination letters only if the question presented is answered by a statute, tax treaty, regulation, court opinion, or guidance published in the *Internal Revenue Bulletin*. At any time during the course of consideration by EO Determinations, if EO Determinations or the organization believes that its case involves an issue as to which precedent has not been published or there has been nonuniformity in the IRS's handling of certain cases, EO Determinations may decide to seek, or the organization may request, that EO Determinations seek, technical advice from the Office of Associate Chief Counsel with subject matter jurisdiction over the issue.[18]

A determination letter is issued solely on the basis of the facts, attestations, and representations in the administrative record. Any oral representation of additional facts, or modification of facts, as represented or alleged in the request, must be reduced to writing and signed by the taxpayer under a penalty-of-perjury statement. The failure to disclose a material fact or misrepresentation of a material fact on a request that includes an incorrect representation or attestation may adversely affect the reliance that would otherwise be obtained through issuance by the IRS of a favorable determination letter.[19]

---

[17] Rev. Proc. 2024-5, 2024-1 I.R.B. 262 § 3.02. As to a domestic organization changing its form or state of organization, see § 28.1(b); as to procedures relating to group exemption letter applications, see § 26.11.

In some circumstances, an organization may seek a letter ruling from the Office of Associate Chief Counsel (EEE) on a specific legal issue, such as whether a new activity of an organization furthers an exempt purpose (see Rev. Proc. 2024-1, 2024-1 I.R.B. 1; Rev. Proc. 2024-3, 2024-1 I.R.B. 143 § 3.01(77)). The Office of Associate Chief Counsel (EEE) will not, however, issue a ruling on whether an exempt organization continues to be exempt as an organization described in IRC §§ 501(c) or (d), including, for example, whether changes in an organization's activities or operations will affect or jeopardize the organization's exempt status, or its status as a public charity (Rev. Proc. 2024-3, 2024-1 I.R.B. 143 § 3.01(77), (80)). Thus, where a letter ruling is sought on the impact of a change in activities on exempt status, care is advised when fashioning the precise question on which the ruling is sought.

[18] Rev. Proc. 2024-5, 2024-1 I.R.B. 262 § 3.03. The procedures for seeking technical advice are the subject of Rev. Proc. 2024-2, 2024-1 I.R.B. 119.

[19] Rev. Proc. 2024-5, 2024-1 I.R.B. 262 § 3.05. As an illustration, an organization filed an application for recognition of exemption; it received a favorable determination letter as to exempt and supporting organization (see § 12.3(c)) status. This application, however, failed to disclose that the supporting organization was created as part of a "comprehensive master financial plan," which the IRS regarded as an inappropriate tax shelter. The IRS revoked the exemption on the grounds of private inurement and private benefit (see Chapter 20), and use of the organization for tax avoidance purposes, with the revocation made retroactive (see § 27.3) to the date of its formation (Priv. Ltr. Rul. 201004046).

Notice requirements are applicable with respect to entities seeking to be tax-exempt social welfare organizations,[20] certain political organizations,[21] and ABLE programs.[22]

(b)   General Procedures

An organization seeking recognition of tax-exempt status is required to submit the appropriate completed application form or the appropriate completed letter request.[23] An organization seeking recognition of exemption as a charitable entity generally must submit electronically, at www.pay.gov, a completed application on Form 1023.[24] Alternatively, an eligible organization may seek recognition of exemption as a charity by electronically submitting a completed streamlined application on Form 1023-EZ.[25] Most other applicant organizations[26] file Form 1024, which also must be filed electronically.[27] Social welfare organizations[28] electronically file Form 1024-A.[29] Homeowners' associations[30] file Form 1120-H.[31] Farmers' cooperative organizations[32] file Form 1028.[33] Other applicant organizations submit an exemption recognition request by letter.[34]

As noted, all applications for recognition of exemption on Form 1023, 1023-EZ, 1024, and 1024-A are now required to be filed electronically. This move to electronic

[20] See Chapter 13. This notice requirement is the subject of § 26.13.

[21] See Chapter 17. This notice requirement is the subject of § 26.14.

[22] See § 19.20. This notice requirement is the subject of § 26.9.

[23] Rev. Proc. 2024-5, 2024-1 I.R.B. 262 § 6.03.

[24] Rev. Proc. 2024-5, 2024-1 I.R.B. 262 § 4.02(1). See Part Three. This rule also includes organizations seeking recognition of exemption as a cooperative hospital service organization (see § 11.4), cooperative educational service organization (see § 11.5), child care organization (see § 8.8), charitable risk pool (see § 11.6), credit counseling entity (see § 7.3), and an organization providing one or more hospital facilities (see § 7.6(b)).

[25] Rev. Proc. 2024-5, 2024-1 I.R.B. 262 § 4.02(2). As to organization eligible to file Form 1023-EZ, see § 26.1(f).

[26] This rule applies to organizations seeking recognition of exemption as a single- or multiple-member title-holding company (see § 19.2), labor, agricultural, or horticultural organization (see Chapter 16), business league or similar organization (see Chapter 14), social club (see Chapter 15), fraternal beneficiary society (see § 19.4(a)), voluntary employees' beneficiary association (see § 18.3), domestic fraternal society (see § 19.4(b)), teachers' retirement fund association (see § 18.7), benevolent or mutual organization (see § 19.5), cemetery company (see § 19.6), credit union (see § 19.7), insurance company (see § 19.9), crop operations finance corporation (§ 19.10), supplemental unemployment benefit trust (see § 18.4), pre-1959 trust (see § 18.7), veterans' organization (see § 19.11(a)), black lung benefits trust (see § 18.5), multiemployer pension plan trust (see § 18.7), high-risk individuals' health care coverage organization (see § 19.15), workers' compensation reinsurance organization (see § 19.16), qualified health insurance issuer (see § 19.18), or religious or apostolic organization (see § 10.8) (Rev. Proc. 2024-5, 2024-1 I.R.B. 262 § 4.02(3)).

[27] Rev. Proc. 2024-5, 2024-1 I.R.B. 262 § 4.02(3).

[28] See Chapter 13.

[29] Rev. Proc. 2024-5, 2024-1 I.R.B. 262 § 4.02(4).

[30] See § 19.14.

[31] Form 1120-H must be filed annually to take advantage of the tax benefits provided by IRC § 528 (see § 19.14).

[32] See § 19.12.

[33] Rev. Proc. 2024-5, 2024-1 I.R.B. 262 § 4.02(5).

[34] Id. §§ 4.02(7), 5.

filing has occasioned modification of the application, in part by embedding narrative responses to questions in the application itself, and by eliminating the need (and opportunity) for exhibits and copies of documents. Revisions have been made to the flow of the application, with many sets of questions reworked, expanded, or both.

(i) Required Information. A determination letter recognizing tax-exempt status will be issued by the IRS to an organization if its application for recognition of exemption and supporting documents establish that it meets the requirements of the category of exemption that it claimed.[35]

Tax exemption of an organization may be recognized by the IRS in advance of the organization's operations (other than instances of submission of the streamlined application)[36] if the proposed activities are described in sufficient detail to permit a conclusion that the organization will clearly meet the pertinent federal tax law requirements.[37] A mere restatement of exempt purposes or a statement that proposed activities will be in furtherance of exempt purposes does not satisfy this requirement.[38] An applicant organization must fully describe all of the activities in which it expects to engage, including the standards, criteria, procedures, or other means adopted or planned for carrying out the activities, the anticipated sources of receipts, and the nature of contemplated expenditures.[39] Where an organization cannot demonstrate to the satisfaction of the IRS that it qualifies for the tax exemption being sought, the IRS generally will issue a proposed adverse determination letter.[40]

The tax regulations in essence require that an applicant organization describe its character, purposes, and methods of operation.[41] They require that an application for recognition of exemption be properly prepared.[42]

The courts also reflect the view that an organization seeking a determination letter or ruling as to recognition of its tax-exempt status has the burden of proving that it satisfies all of the requirements of the particular tax exemption category.[43] The IRS may deny an application for recognition of exemption for failure on the part of the applicant organization to establish compliance with one or more of the statutory requirements for exemption; in the case of an organization seeking qualification as a charitable entity, compliance with the private benefit doctrine[44] is also required.[45]

---

[35] *Id.* § 6.07(1).

[36] Form 1023-EZ. See § 26.1(f).

[37] Rev. Proc. 2024-5, 2024-1 I.R.B. 262 § 6.07(2)(a).

[38] *Id.* § 6.07(2)(a)(i).

[39] *Id.* § 6.07(2)(a)(ii).

[40] *Id.* § 6.07(2)(a)(iii).

[41] Reg. § 1.501(a)-1(a)(2).

[42] Reg. § 1.508-1(a)(2)(i) (at least in the case of organizations seeking to qualify for tax exemption by reason of IRC § 501(c)(3)).

[43] E.g., Harding Hosp., Inc. v. United States, 505 F.2d 1068 (6th Cir. 1974); Kenner v. Comm'r, 318 F.2d 632 (7th Cir. 1963); Cleveland Chiropractic College v. Comm'r, 312 F.2d 203 (8th Cir. 1963); Church of Spiritual Technology v. United States, 92-1 U.S.T.C. ¶ 50,305 (Fed. Cl. 1992); Nelson v. Comm'r, 30 T.C. 1151 (1958).

[44] See § 20.13.

[45] Reg. § 1.501(c)(3)-1(f)(1).

The IRS, generally supported by the courts, usually will refuse to recognize an organization's tax-exempt status unless the entity tenders sufficient information regarding its operations and finances. For example, an organization applied for recognition of exemption, stating its "long-range plan" to form a school; it was unable to substantively respond to any of the requests from the IRS for additional information. The IRS refused to recognize the organization as an exempt entity; a court agreed, holding that the organization "failed to supply such information as would enable a conclusion that when operational, if ever, . . . [the organization] will conduct all of its activities in a manner which will accomplish its exempt purposes."[46] The court chided the entity for having only "vague generalizations" of its ostensibly planned activities and strongly suggested that the organization had "no plan to operate a school in the foreseeable future."[47]

Likewise, a court concluded that an organization failed to meet its burden of proof as to its eligibility for exemption because it did not provide a "meaningful explanation" of its activities to the IRS.[48] In another instance, a court concluded that an organization's failure to respond "completely or candidly" to many of the inquiries of the IRS precluded it from receiving a determination as to its exempt status.[49]

The IRS refuses to grant recognition of tax exemption when the application, in the agency's view, provides "only general information," lacks "sufficient detail," does not "fully describe" the organization's programs and other activities, and otherwise is "vague."[50] Matters can further decline when the information submitted to the IRS in response to follow-up queries is "contradictory."[51] Likewise, where an organization provided "implausible information as well as documents that appear to be inauthentic," the IRS declined to recognize the organization as exempt.[52]

In one instance, the IRS did not recognize exempt status in connection with an organization that did not provide acceptable financial information; indeed, the agency asserted that the organization's budget estimates "do not appear to be grounded in reality."[53] In another instance, the IRS had this to say about the contents of an application: "The description you have provided of your activities is persistently incoherent, full of gaps and omissions, and lacking in necessary explanatory matter, frustrating all attempts to attain an understanding of them

---

[46] Pius XII Academy, Inc. v. Comm'r, 43 T.C.M. 634, 636 (1982).

[47] Id. Also, Peoples Prize v. Comm'r, 87 T.C.M. 813 (2004); Ohio Disability Ass'n v. Comm'r, 98 T.C.M. 462 (2009).

[48] Public Indus., Inc. v. Comm'r, 61 T.C.M. 1626, 1629 (1991).

[49] Nat'l Ass'n of Am. Churches v. Comm'r, 82 T.C. 18, 32 (1984). Also, United Libertarian Fellowship, Inc. v. Comm'r, 65 T.C.M. 2178 (1993); Church of Nature in Man v. Comm'r, 49 T.C.M. 1393 (1985); LaVerdad v. Comm'r, 82 T.C. 215 (1984); Basic Unit Ministry of Alma Karl Schurig v. United States, 511 F. Supp. 166 (D.D.C. 1981).

[50] E.g., Priv. Ltr. Rul. 200536021.

[51] E.g., Priv. Ltr. Rul. 200851033.

[52] Priv. Ltr. Rul. 202218025.

[53] Priv. Ltr. Rul. 200535029. Moreover, the IRS went so far as to observe, in response to the organization's plans to construct and operate a rehabilitation facility, that it was "not convinced that your community needs the facility that you propose to build." (The IRS has the authority to determine whether an activity is an exempt function; it does not have the authority to judge whether the activity is necessary.)

sufficient to support a determination that you are operated exclusively for exempt purposes."[54]

An organization is considered by the IRS to have made the required "threshold showing," however, where it answered all of the questions the IRS.[55] In another instance, a court observed that, although the law "requires that the organization establish reasonable standards and criteria for its operation as an exempt organization," the standard does not necessitate "some sort of metaphysical proof of future events."[56]

Irrespective of the content of an application for recognition of exemption, the IRS is likely to visit the applicant's website in search of additional (or, worse, inconsistent or contradictory) information.[57] Also, the IRS is beginning to locate statements made in social media that may have a bearing on an organization's eligibility for exemption.[58]

When the representatives of a would-be tax-exempt organization fail to submit its books and records to the IRS, an inference arises that the facts involved would denigrate the organization's cause.[59] (At the same time, it has been held that the refusal by an organization to turn records over to the IRS, in response to a summons, does not give the IRS the authority to summarily revoke the organization's exempt status.)[60] As one court stated the matter, in "order to gain [charitable] status, a taxpayer must openly and candidly disclose all facts bearing upon the organization, its operations, and its finances so that the [c]ourt may be assured that it is not sanctioning an abuse of the revenue laws by granting a claimed exemption."[61]

The IRS, from time to time, issues adverse rulings to organizations that did not provide sufficient information to the agency on their applications for recognition of exemption.[62]

(ii) Other Procedural Elements. The IRS will not accept for processing a request for a determination letter that is substantially incomplete.[63]

An application (other than the streamlined one)[64] that is missing any item of information required of a completed application[65] is considered by the IRS to be

---

[54] Priv. Ltr. Rul. 201931011.
[55] E.g., Church of the Visible Intelligence That Governs the Universe v. United States, 83-2 U.S.T.C. ¶ 9726 (Ct. Cl. 1983).
[56] American Science Found. v. Comm'r, 52 T.C.M. 1049, 1051 (1986).
[57] E.g., Priv. Ltr. Rul. 200815035.
[58] E.g., Priv. Ltr. Rul. 201417017.
[59] E.g., New Concordia Bible Church v. Comm'r, 49 T.C.M. 176 (1984) (*appeal dismissed*, 9th Cir. (1985)). Also, Chief Steward of the Ecumenical Temples & the Worldwide Peace Movement & His Successors v. Comm'r, 49 T.C.M. 640 (1985); Basic Bible Church of Am., Auxiliary Chapter 11004 v. Comm'r, 46 T.C.M. 223 (1983); McElhannon v. Comm'r, 44 T.C.M. 1392 (1982); Bubbling Well Church of Universal Love, Inc. v. Comm'r, 74 T.C. 531 (1980), *aff'd*, 670 F.2d 104 (9th Cir. 1981); Founding Church of Scientology v. United States, 412 F.2d 1197 (Ct. Cl. 1969), *cert. denied*, 397 U.S. 1009 (1970); Parker v. Comm'r, 365 F.2d 792 (8th Cir. 1966), *cert. denied*, 385 U.S. 1026 (1967).
[60] Church of World Peace, Inc. v. Internal Revenue Serv., 715 F.2d 492 (10th Cir. 1983).
[61] Nationalist Found. v. Comm'r, 80 T.C.M. 507, 510 (2000).
[62] E.g., Priv. Ltr. Rul. 200904026.
[63] Rev. Proc. 2024-5, 2024-1 I.R.B. 262 § 4.10.
[64] Form 1023-EZ. See § 26.1(f).
[65] See § 26.1(c).

substantially incomplete and will not be accepted for processing.[66] A similar rule applies in connection with the streamlined application.[67]

An organization will be notified if its request is not accepted for processing; any user fee that was paid with the request will be returned or refunded. An organization may thereafter submit a new request, including the missing information, with a new user fee.[68]

Even though an application is complete, the IRS may request additional information before issuing a determination letter. Failure to respond to a request for additional information may result in closure of the application without a determination letter being issued and without a refund of the user fee. If the failure to respond to a request for additional information results in the IRS issuing a proposed adverse determination letter to the organization, the proposed adverse determination letter will inform the organization of its opportunity to protest/appeal the decision.[69]

A determination letter recognizing tax exemption of an organization is generally effective as of the date of formation of the organization if (1) its purposes and activities prior to the date of the determination letter have been consistent with the requirements for exemption and (2) it filed its application for recognition of exemption within 27 months from the end of the month in which it was organized.[70]

If the IRS requires the organization to alter its activities or make substantive amendments to its enabling instrument, the tax exemption will be effective as of the date specified in the determination letter. If the IRS requires the organization to make a nonsubstantive amendment, exemption will ordinarily be recognized as of the date of formation.[71]

An organization that otherwise meets the requirements for tax-exempt status and issuance of a determination letter that does not meet the requirements for recognition from the date of formation will be recognized from the postmark or electronic submission date of its application, as applicable.[72]

Applications for recognition of exemption are normally processed in the order of receipt by the IRS. Expedited handling of an application (other than a streamlined one),[73] however, may be approved where a request is made in writing and contains a "compelling reason" why the application should be processed ahead of others. On approval of a request for expedited processing, an application will be considered out of its normal order; however, this rule does not mean that the application will be immediately approved or denied.[74]

---

[66] Rev. Proc. 2024-5, 2024-1 I.R.B. 262 § 4.10(1).

[67] Id. § 4.10(2).

[68] Id. § 4.10(3).

[69] Id. § 6.07(3).

[70] Id. § 6.08(1). As to the 27-month rule, see § 26.2(a).

[71] Id. § 6.08(5). Examples of nonsubstantive amendments include correction of a clerical error in the enabling instrument or the addition of a dissolution clause where the activities of the organization prior to the determination letter are consistent with the requirements for tax-exempt status (id.).

[72] Id. § 6.08(2).

[73] Form 1023-EZ. See § 26.1(f).

[74] Rev. Proc. 2024-5, 2024-1 I.R.B. 262 § 4.09.

Circumstances generally warranting expedited processing include (1) a grant to the applicant is pending and failure to secure the grant (because of absence of recognition of exemption) may have an adverse impact on the organization's ability to continue operations; (2) the purpose of the newly created organization is to provide disaster relief to victims of emergencies; and (3) undue delays in issuing a determination letter or ruling were caused by IRS error.[75]

(iii) Preparation of Application. The proper preparation of an application for recognition of tax exemption involves far more than merely responding to the questions on a government form. It is a process not unlike the preparation of a prospectus for a business in conformity with securities law requirements. Every statement made in the application should be carefully considered. Some of the questions may force the applicant organization to focus on matters that good management practices should cause it to consider, even in the absence of the application requirements.

The prime objective must be accuracy; it is essential that all material facts be correctly and fully disclosed. Of course, the determination of which facts are material and the marshaling of these facts require judgment. Also, the way the answers are phrased can be extremely significant; in this regard, the exercise can be more one of art than of science. The preparer or reviewer of the application should be able to anticipate the concerns that the contents of the application may cause the IRS and to see that the application is properly prepared, while simultaneously minimizing the likelihood of conflict with the IRS. Organizations that are entitled to tax-exempt status have been denied recognition of exemption by the IRS, or at least have caused the process of gaining the recognition to be more protracted, because of unartful phraseologies in the application that motivated the agency to muster a case that the organization did not qualify for exemption. Therefore, the application for recognition of exemption should be regarded as an important legal document and be prepared accordingly. The fact that the application is available for public inspection only underscores the need for the thoughtful preparation of it.

(c) Completed Application

A completed application for recognition of tax exemption (other than the streamlined application) is one that (1) is signed electronically by an authorized individual under penalties of perjury; (2) includes the organization's correct employer identification number; (3) includes (where the applicant is not a charitable entity or a social welfare organization) a statement of receipts and expenditures, and a balance sheet, for the current year and three preceding years (or, if a shorter period of time, the years the entity has been in existence);[76] (4) includes a detailed narrative statement of proposed program and fundraising activities (the latter if

---

[75] *Id.* § 4.09(1).

[76] If the organization has not commenced operations or has not completed one accounting period, a proposed budget for two complete accounting periods and a current statement of assets and liabilities may be submitted. In the case of a charitable entity or a social welfare organization, the financial information required to be submitted is identified on Form 1023 or Form 1024-A and the instructions thereto, respectively.

a charitable organization) and a narrative description of anticipated receipts and contemplated expenditures; (5) includes a copy of the entity's articles of organization, signed by a principal officer or accompanied by a written declaration signed by an authorized individual certifying that the document is a complete and accurate copy of the original or otherwise meets the requirement that it be a *conformed* copy;[77] (6) includes, if the organizing document is a set of articles of incorporation, evidence that it was filed with and approved by an appropriate state official or includes a copy of the articles accompanied by a written declaration signed by an authorized individual that the copy is a complete and accurate copy of the original document that was approved by the state, and stating the date of filing with the state; (7) includes, if the organization has adopted bylaws, a current copy of that document, which need not be signed if submitted as an attachment to the application; and (8) is accompanied by the correct user fee.[78]

A streamlined (Form 1023-EZ) application submitted (online) by an eligible organization[79] is complete if it (1) includes responses for each required line item, including an accurate date of organization and an attestation that it has completed the eligibility worksheet and has read the accompanying instructions and understands the requirements for exemption as expressed in the instructions; (3) includes the organization's correct employer identification number; (4) is electronically signed, under penalties of perjury, by an authorized individual; and (5) is accompanied by the correct user fee.[80] A streamlined application will not be considered complete if the organization's name and employer identification number do not match the records in the IRS's Business Master File. Additionally, a streamlined application submitted by an organization that is not an eligible one is not a complete application.[81]

(d) User Fees

Congress enacted a program of user fees, payable to the IRS, for requests for rulings, information letters, determination letters, and similar requests.[82] Submission of an application for recognition of exemption must be accompanied by the correct user fee.[83]

Under the IRS's user fee schedule,[84] the fee for the processing of an application for recognition of tax exemption in general is $600. The user fee for submission of the streamlined application is $275. The fee for group exemption letters[85]

---

[77] Rev. Proc. 68-14, 1968-1 C.B. 768.

[78] Rev. Proc. 2024-5, 2024-1 I.R.B. 262 § 6.06(1). As to user fees, see § 26.1(d).

[79] See § 26.1(f).

[80] Rev. Proc. 2024-5, 2024-1 I.R.B. 262 § 6.06(2).

[81] *Id.*

[82] The user fee regime is authorized by IRC § 7528. See Rev. Proc. 2024-5, 2024-1 I.R.B. 262 § 14.01.

[83] *Id.* §§ 4.07, 14.02. User fees for Form 1023, Form 1023-EZ, Form 1024, or Form 1024-A must be paid through www.pay.gov when the form is submitted. For other applications for recognition of exemption (not filed electronically), an organization must attach a completed Form 8718 (User Fee for Exempt Organization Determination Letter Request) to its application (*id.* §§ 6.04, 14.07).

[84] *Id.*, Appendix A.

[85] However, the IRS is not accepting any requests for group exemption letters until publication of final guidance on the subject in the Internal Revenue Bulletin (*id.* § 3.02(11)). See § 26.11.

is $3,500 (which is in addition to the initial application fees a central organization must pay if it submits an initial application for recognition of exemption with its request for a group exemption letter).

There is no user fee for seeking an *affirmation letter*, confirming an organization's tax-exempt status, or replacing a lost tax-exempt status letter and/or reflecting name and address changes.[86]

(e) Penalties for Perjury

The individual who signs an application for recognition of tax-exempt status does so under penalty of perjury, stating that to the best of the individual's knowledge it is true, correct, and complete.[87] The IRS can revoke or amend an organization's exempt status if the agency determines that the organization omitted or misstated a material fact in its application or operates in a manner materially different from that originally represented in the application. If the changed or expanded activities, which were not reported, further the organization's exempt purposes or are unrelated but insubstantial, the IRS probably will not take any action against the entity.[88]

Because of the "penalty of perjury" statement, the IRS could impose a penalty for the commission of a felony if a representation was made willfully under the belief that it was untrue and incorrect as to every material manner.[89] The organization and its officers may be fined up to $100,000 ($500,000 in the case of a corporation) or imprisoned for up to three years, or both. A lesser violation (a misdemeanor) that does not require penalties of perjury may involve a penalty if the organization or one or more of its officers willfully delivered the organization's application knowing it contained information that was false as to any material matter.[90] The organization and its officers may be fined up to $10,000 ($50,000 in the case of a corporation) or imprisoned not more than one year, or both.

In general, federal law imposes penalties for making false statements, making false claims, and otherwise committing perjury.

(f) Streamlined Application

Eligible organizations may use a streamlined application—Form 1023-EZ—to apply for recognition of tax-exempt status as a charitable entity. The application requests basic information about the applicant and its organizational structure, check-the-box responses to questions about the organization's activities, and an indication as to public charity or private foundation status. The IRS may request additional information before accepting this application.

Expedited consideration of the application is not available.[91]

The streamlined application is available, with many exceptions, to organizations with gross receipts of no more than $50,000 and assets of no more than

---

[86] Rev. Proc. 2024-5, 2024-1 I.R.B. 262 §§ 3.01(2), 15.03. Instructions for obtaining an affirmation letter also may be found at https://www.irs.gov/charities-non-profits/exempt-organizations-affirmation-letters.

[87] Rev. Proc. 2024-5, 2024-1 I.R.B. 262 § 4.06.

[88] E.g. Tech. Adv. Mem. 9835003.

[89] IRC § 7206.

[90] IRC § 7207.

[91] Rev. Proc. 2024-5, 2024-1 I.R.B. 262 § 4.09(2).

$250,000 (and thus Form 990-N submitters). The $50,000 rule applies with respect to projected annual gross receipts in the current tax year or the next two years, or annual gross receipts that have exceeded $50,000 in any of the past three years.[92] An eligibility worksheet must be completed in connection with this application, which must be filed electronically.

This application may not be filed by (in addition to entities over the aforementioned thresholds) organizations formed under the laws of a foreign country; organizations that do not have a mailing address in the United States; organizations that are terrorist organizations, or are successors to or controlled by a terrorist entity suspended from tax exemption;[93] organizations that are not corporations, unincorporated associations, or trusts; organizations that are for-profit entities or are successors to a for-profit entity; organizations that were previously revoked or that are successors to a previously revoked organization (other than an organization that was revoked for failure to file or submit a Form 990 series return or notice for three consecutive years);[94] churches, conventions of churches, or associations of churches;[95] schools, colleges, or universities;[96] hospitals or medical research organizations;[97] cooperative hospital service organizations;[98] cooperative educational service organizations;[99] qualified charitable risk pools;[100] supporting organizations;[101] organizations that have as a substantial purpose the provision of assistance to individuals through credit counseling activities, such as budgeting, personal finance, financial literacy, mortgage foreclosure assistance, or other consumer credit areas;[102] organizations that invest, or intend to invest, 5 percent or more of their total assets in securities or funds that are not publicly traded; organizations that participate, or intend to participate, in partnerships (or entities treated as partnerships) in which they share profits and losses with partners other than exempt charitable organizations; organizations that sell, or intend to sell, carbon credits or carbon offsets; health maintenance organizations;[103] accountable care organizations (ACOs) or organizations that engage in, or intend to engage in, ACO activities (such as participation in the Medicare Shared Savings Program);[104] organizations that maintain, or intend to maintain, one or more donor-advised funds;[105] organizations that are organized and operated exclusively for testing for public safety and that are requesting public charity classification;[106] private

---

[92] Rev. Proc. 2024-5, 2024-1 I.R.B. 262 §§ 4.02(2), 6.05(1).
[93] See § 26.12.
[94] See § 28.4.
[95] See §§ 10.3, 10.4.
[96] See § 8.3(a).
[97] See §§ 7.6(a), (b), (d).
[98] See § 11.4.
[99] See § 11.5.
[100] See § 11.6.
[101] See § 12.3(c).
[102] See § 7.3.
[103] See § 7.6(f).
[104] See § 7.6(m).
[105] See § 12.5.
[106] See § 12.3(d).

operating foundations;[107] organizations that are applying for retroactive reinstatement of exemption after being automatically revoked;[108] agricultural research organizations;[109] and organizations that are currently or were previously exempt as an entity other than a charitable one.[110]

(g) Withdrawal of Request

A request for a determination letter may be withdrawn at any time before the letter is issued by the IRS. An authorized representative of the organization must make this request in writing in accordance with the instructions for the form on which the request for a determination letter was submitted, if applicable. For these purposes, the issuance of a determination letter includes a proposed adverse determination letter.[111]

When a request for a determination letter is withdrawn, the IRS will retain the application, Form 8940, or letter request and all supporting documents. The IRS may consider the information submitted in connection with the withdrawn request in a subsequent examination of the organization or in connection with an application subsequently submitted by the organization. Generally, the user fee[112] will not be refunded if a request is withdrawn.[113]

The withdrawal of an application for recognition of exemption is not a failure to make a determination or an exhaustion of administrative remedies for purposes of the declaratory judgment rules.[114]

(h) Reliance on Determination Letters

An organization may ordinarily rely on a favorable determination letter issued by the IRS, irrespective of the format of the request submitted in pursuit of the letter.[115] A person may not, however, rely on, use, or cite as precedent a determination letter issued to another person.[116]

A determination letter may not be relied on by the organization submitting the request if there is a material change in facts. For a determination letter as to tax-exempt status, a *material change* includes a change in the character, the purpose, or the method of operation of the organization that is inconsistent with the organization's tax-exempt status.[117] A change in an organization's form may result in a material change that would affect the organization's ability to rely on its determination letter.[118]

---

[107] See § 12.1(b).

[108] See § 28.4.

[109] See §§ 7.16(f), § 12.3(a).

[110] Rev. Proc. 2024-5, 2024-1 I.R.B. 262 § 6.05(2).

[111] *Id.* § 8.01.

[112] See § 26.1(d).

[113] Rev. Proc. 2024-5, 2024-1 I.R.B. 262 § 8.01.

[114] *Id.* § 8.02. See § 27.5(c)(ii).

[115] Rev. Proc. 2024-5, 2024-1 I.R.B. 262 § 11.01.

[116] IRC § 6110(k)(3); Rev. Proc. 2024-5, 2024-1 I.R.B. 262 § 11.02(1).

[117] Reg. §§ 1.501(a)-1(a)(2), 601.201(n)(3)(ii); Rev. Proc. 2024-5, 2024-1 I.R.B. 262 § 11.02(2).

[118] See § 28.1(b).

A determination letter issued to an organization that submitted a request in accordance with the applicable requirements may not be relied on by the organization if it was based on any omission or inaccurate material information submitted by the organization. *Inaccurate material information* includes an incorrect representation or attestation as to the organization's organizational documents, the organization's exempt purpose, the organization's conduct of prohibited and restricted activities, or the organization's eligibility to file the streamlined application.[119]

A change in law also may affect this form of reliance.[120] A change in law includes the enactment of legislation, a decision of the Supreme Court of the United States, the issuance of temporary or final regulations, and the issuance of a revenue ruling, revenue procedure, or other statement published in the Internal Revenue Bulletin.[121]

(i)   Post-Determination Review

Determination letters may be reviewed by the EO Determinations Quality Assurance function to ensure uniform application of the statutes, tax treaties, regulations, court opinions, or guidance published in the *Internal Revenue Bulletin*.[122] If a post-determination review based on the information contained in the existing application file concludes that a determination letter issued by EO Determinations was issued in error, the matter will be referred to EO Examinations for consideration.[123]

§ 26.2   REQUIREMENTS FOR CHARITABLE ORGANIZATIONS

Special requirements in this regard apply with respect to charitable organizations[124] that desire to be tax-exempt under federal law.

(a)   General Rules

An organization that desires to be tax-exempt as a charitable organization generally must obtain a determination letter or a ruling from the IRS to that effect.[125] An organization that desires recognition as an exempt charitable organization as of the date of its formation generally must notify the IRS that it is applying for recognition of exemption on that basis. Thus, where the IRS recognizes the tax exemption of an organization that made a timely filing of the notice—that is, within 27 months from the end of the month in which the organization was organized— the exemption is effective as of the date the organization was created.[126] (The requisite notice is given by the timely filing with the IRS of a properly completed and

---

[119] Rev. Proc. 2024-5, 2024-1 I.R.B. 262 § 11.02(3).
[120] *Id.* § 11.02(4).
[121] *Id.* § 12.01.
[122] *Id.* § 11.03(1).
[123] *Id.* § 11.03(2).
[124] That is, entities described in IRC § 501(c)(3) and tax-exempt by reason of IRC § 501(a). See Part Three.
[125] IRC § 508(a).
[126] Rev. Proc. 2024-5, 2024-1 I.R.B. 262 § 6.08(1), (3).

executed application for recognition of tax exemption.)[127] Otherwise, the recognition of tax exemption as a charitable organization by the IRS generally is effective only on a prospective basis.[128]

An organization is considered *organized* on the date it became a charitable entity.[129] In determining the date on which a corporation is organized for purposes of this exemption recognition process, the IRS looks to the date the entity came into existence under the law of the state in which it was incorporated, which usually is the date its articles of incorporation were filed in the appropriate state office.[130] This date is not the date the organizational meeting was held, bylaws adopted, or actual operations began.

In general, if any return, claim, statement, or other document is required by law to be filed before a specified date and the document is delivered by mail after that date to the agency, officer, or office with which the document is required to be filed, it is deemed to have been filed on or before that specified date if the postmark stamped on the envelope or other cover in which the document was mailed was dated on or before the date prescribed for filing.[131] In application of this standard, the date of notice for purposes of the threshold notice rule is the date of the postmark stamped on the cover in which the application for recognition of tax exemption was mailed; in the absence of a postmark, the date of notice is the date the application was stamped as received by the IRS.[132]

An organization's eligibility to receive deductible charitable contributions also is governed by these rules. Thus, where a charitable organization timely files the application for recognition of tax exemption, and the determination letter or ruling ultimately is favorable, the ability to receive deductible charitable gifts is effective as of the date the organization was formed.

An organization that qualifies for tax exemption as a charitable organization but files for recognition of exemption after the threshold notice period can be tax-exempt as a social welfare organization[133] for the period commencing on the date of its inception to the date tax exemption as a charitable organization becomes effective.[134] Contributions to social welfare organizations, however, are generally not deductible as charitable gifts,[135] so this approach is of little utility to charitable organizations that rely significantly on contributions.

Under certain circumstances, the IRS will grant relief from application of the 27-month rule.[136] For the IRS to grant this relief, an organization must explain why

---

[127] See § 26.1(b).

[128] IRC §§ 508(a)(2), 508(d)(2)(B); Reg. § 1.508-2. The statute does not fix the time for giving this notice, but rather leaves it to the IRS's discretion to set through regulations. The regulations state this rule in terms of a 15-month filing period (Reg. § 1.508-1(a)(2)(i)), with an automatic 12-month extension of time for this filing (Reg. § 301.9100-2(a)(2)(iv)), thereby converting it to a 27-month period.

[129] Reg. § 1.508-1(a)(2)(iii).

[130] Rev. Rul. 75-290, 1975-2 C.B. 215.

[131] IRC § 7502(a)(1).

[132] Rev. Rul. 77-114, 1977-1 C.B. 152.

[133] See Chapter 13.

[134] Rev. Rul. 80-108, 1980-1 C.B. 119. This is because social welfare organizations generally are not required to apply for recognition of tax-exempt status (see § 26.4). See, however, §§ 26.13.

[135] E.g., Smith v. Comm'r, 51 T.C.M. 1114 (1986).

[136] Rev. Proc. 2024-5, 2024-1 I.R.B. 262 § 6.08(3); Reg. § 301.9100-3.

it did not file its application within 27 months of formation, how it acted reasonably and in good faith, and how granting an earlier effective date will not prejudice the interests of the government.[137] The IRS will consider the following factors in this regard: the effect the granting of an extension to file would have on the organization's aggregate tax liability (compared to what it would be without the extension); how the organization discovered its failure to file; whether the organization filed its application before the IRS discovered its failure to file; whether the organization failed to file because of intervening events beyond its control; whether the organization exercised reasonable diligence, but was not aware of the filing requirements (with the complexity of the organization's filing and its experience in these matters taken into consideration); whether the organization reasonably relied on written advice from the IRS; and whether the organization reasonably relied on the advice of a qualified tax professional who failed to file or advise it to file an application.[138]

This relief does not apply to an organization that is not required to apply for recognition of exemption to be tax-exempt,[139] and the IRS will not consider a request for relief from such an organization.[140] The IRS also will not grant this relief if either (1) granting the request for relief would result in the organization's tax-exempt status being automatically revoked for failure to file returns for three consecutive years,[141] or (2) the period of limitations on assessment[142] for any taxable year for which the organization claims tax-exempt status has expired prior to the date of application.[143]

(b) Exceptions

This requirement of filing an application for recognition of exemption is not applicable to (1) churches, interchurch organizations of local units of a church, conventions or associations of churches, and integrated auxiliaries of churches;[144] (2) charitable organizations the gross receipts of which in each tax year are normally not more than $5,000 (as long as they are not private foundations[145] or supporting organizations);[146,147] and (3) subordinate organizations covered by a group exemption where the central organization has submitted to the IRS the requisite notice covering the subordinates.[148]

---

[137] Reg. § 301.9100-3. An organization provides this explanation on Form 1023, Schedule E.

[138] Reg. § 301.9100-3(b); Also, Instructions for Form 1023 (Jan. 2020).

[139] See § 26.2(b).

[140] Rev. Proc. 2024-5, 2024-1 I.R.B. 262 § 6.08(4). The IRS Office of Chief Counsel surveyed the various bases for denial of this relief in the case of self-declarers (see § 26.10) and organizations failing to file Forms 990 since their formation (Chief Couns. Adv. Mem. 20205201F).

[141] IRC § 6033(j). See § 28.4.

[142] IRC § 6501(a). See § 27.4.

[143] Rev. Proc. 2024-5, 2024-1 I.R.B. 262 § 6.08(3).

[144] IRC § 508(c)(1), (2); Reg. § 1.508-1(a)(3)(i)(A). Also, Gen. Couns. Mems. 36078, 37458. See §§ 10.3–10.5.

[145] See § 12.1(a).

[146] See § 12.3(c).

[147] IRC § 508(c)(1).

[148] See § 26.11.

The IRS is authorized to exempt from the notice requirement educational institutions[149] and any other class of organizations as to which compliance with the requirement is not necessary to the efficient administration of the tax law rules pertaining to private foundations.[150]

(c) Limited Liability Companies

A charitable organization can be the sole member of a limited liability company, or two or more charitable organizations can be members of an LLC. In the case of the single-member LLC, the LLC is a disregarded entity for federal tax purposes, and thus its activities are treated as the activities of the member.[151] In this instance, then, the single-member LLC is not required to file an application for recognition of tax exemption.[152] When, however, there is a multiple-member LLC whose the members are charitable organizations, the LLC can qualify as a charitable organization[153] and thus is subject to the exemption recognition process.

§ 26.3 NONPRIVATE FOUNDATION STATUS

In general, every charitable organization is presumed to be a private foundation; usually the presumption can be rebutted.[154]

(a) Notice Requirement

The rebuttal process entails the filing of the requisite notice with the IRS;[155] this is done as part of the application for recognition of tax exemption.[156] Thus, procedurally, a charitable organization endeavoring to be a public charity[157] must successfully rebut this presumption. The time for the giving of this notice is, by IRS rule, the same as for the notice requirement with respect to tax exemption.[158] The public charity status of a tax-exempt charitable organization will be included in the organization's determination letter as to exempt status.[159]

---

[149] IRC § 508(c)(3)(A). These are entities described in IRC § 170(b)(1)(A)(ii). See § 8.3(a).

[150] IRC § 508(c)(2)(B).

[151] In general, see § 4.1(b).

[152] E.g., Priv. Ltr. Rul. 200134025.

[153] See § 4.3(e).

[154] IRC § 508(b). See § 12.1.

[155] IRC § 508(a).

[156] Rev. Proc. 2024-5, 2024-1 I.R.B. 262 § 7.03; Form 1023 (Jan. 2020), Part VII.

[157] See § 12.3.

[158] Reg. § 1.508-1(a)(2). An exception to the standard 27-month timing for filing this notice (see § 26.2(a)) applies in the case of an organization that initially qualifies for the $5,000 gross receipts exception to the notice requirement (Reg. § 1.508-1(a)(3)(i)(b); see text accompanied by *supra* note 147). For purposes of this exception, an organization must file the required notice by filing Form 1023 within 90 days after the end of the first taxable year in which it does not qualify for the exception (Reg. § 1.508-1(a)(3)(ii); e.g., Priv. Ltr. Rul. 200742024).

[159] Rev. Proc. 2024-5, 2024-1 I.R.B. 262 § 7.03.

The requirement of notification to the IRS as to nonprivate foundation status does not apply to churches, conventions or associations of churches, and integrated auxiliaries of churches.[160]

The law is vague as to the time when a notice of nonprivate foundation status must be filed to be effective. As noted, a charitable organization that is not a private foundation is able to rebut the presumption that it is a foundation by showing that it is a public charity. An organization that failed to timely file a notice may nonetheless establish its public charity status by submitting a request to the IRS for a determination as to that status.[161]

In one instance, a charitable organization (not exempt from the notice requirement) did not apply for recognition of tax exemption until after expiration of the threshold notice rule. Tax exemption of this organization was ultimately approved; it was a private foundation. Inasmuch as the organization could be treated as a charitable organization only as of the date the application was filed, however, it could not be classified as a private foundation until that date.[162] The same result obtains with respect to an organization's public charity status.[163] When an applicant organization withdraws its application for recognition of exemption in the face of issuance of an adverse determination, it also cancels its notification to the IRS that it is seeking public charity status, so the threshold notice rule period continues to run.[164]

(b)   Rules for New Publicly Supported Charities

Special rules are applicable to newly created charitable organizations seeking classification as publicly supported entities.[165] An organization will be classified as a publicly supported charity if, as part of the process for seeking recognition of tax exemption, it can show that (in addition to qualification for tax exemption) it can reasonably be expected to be publicly supported during its first five years of existence.[166] The organization has public charity status for this five-year period irrespective of the amount of public support it receives.

Beginning with the organization's sixth year, it must establish (if it can) that it meets the applicable public support test by showing that it is publicly supported.[167] The organization will not owe a private foundation investment income tax[168] or private foundation termination tax[169] with respect to its first five years. Beginning

---

[160] IRC § 508(c)(1)(A).

[161] Rev. Rul. 73-504, 1973-2 C.B. 190.

[162] Rev. Rul. 77-207, 1977-1 C.B. 152.

[163] Rev. Rul. 80-113, 1980-1 C.B. 58; Rev. Rul. 77-208, 1977-1 C.B. 153.

[164] Rev. Rul. 90-100, 1990-2 C.B. 156.

[165] See § 12.3(b)(i), (iv).

[166] Reg. §§ 1.170A-9(f)(4)(v), 1.509(a)-3(d)(1).

[167] Reg. §§ 1.170A-9(f)(4)(vi), 1.509(a)-3(d)(1). Compliance with a public support test is evidenced on Form 990, Schedule A.

[168] See § 12.4(f). See *Private Foundations*, Chapter 10.

[169] See IRC § 507. See *Private Foundations* § 13.7.

with the organization's sixth year, for every year when it cannot establish that it is a public charity, it will be liable for the private foundation taxes.[170]

§ 26.4 REQUIREMENTS FOR SOCIAL WELFARE ORGANIZATIONS

An organization operating as a social welfare organization may, but is not required to, file with the IRS for recognition of tax-exempt status.[171] If it chooses to do so, it must do so electronically using Form 1024-A.[172] The filing of Form 1024-A does not satisfy the separate requirement for an organization to notify the IRS of its intent to operate as a social welfare organization.[173]

§ 26.5 REQUIREMENTS FOR CERTAIN CREDIT COUNSELING ORGANIZATIONS

A social welfare organization that has the provision of credit counseling services[174] as a substantial purpose must obtain a determination letter or ruling from the IRS to be tax-exempt.[175] Presumably, the 27-month rule[176] applies in this context.[177]

§ 26.6 REQUIREMENTS FOR CERTAIN EMPLOYEE BENEFIT ORGANIZATIONS

An organization that desires status as a tax-exempt *employee benefit organization*[178] as of the date of its establishment must apply for recognition of tax exemption on that basis.[179] The 27-month rule[180] is applicable in this context.[181] Thus, where the

---

[170] Under prior law, where an incorporated charitable organization is claiming qualification as a publicly supported entity, it is the successor to an unincorporated charitable organization, and incorporation is the only significant change in the facts, the public support data for the unincorporated entity may be tacked to the public support data for the incorporated entity for purposes of ascertaining whether the corporation qualifies as a publicly supported charity (Rev. Rul. 73-422, 1973-2 C.B. 70). Presumably, this concept applies in connection with these rules.

[171] Rev. Proc. 2024-5, 2024-1 I.R.B. 262 § 4.02(4).

[172] *Id.*

[173] See § 26.13.

[174] See § 7.3(b).

[175] IRC § 501(q)(3).

[176] See § 26.2(a).

[177] This notice is given by submitting a properly completed and executed Form 1024-A (see § 26.4) to the IRS (Rev. Proc. 2024-5, 2024-1 I.R.B. 262 § 4.02(4)).

[178] That is, one described in IRC § 501(c)(9) (a voluntary employees' beneficiary association—see § 18.3) or IRC § 501(c)(17) (a supplemental unemployment compensation benefit trust—see § 18.4).

[179] IRC § 505(c)(1); Rev. Proc. 2024-5, 2024-1 I.R.B. 262 § 4.02(3). This application is made using Form 1024 (*id.*).

[180] See § 26.2(a).

[181] Rev. Proc. 2024-5, 2024-1 I.R.B. 262 § 6.08(3).

application is timely filed, the organization's tax exemption will be recognized retroactively to the date the organization was organized.[182] If the application is not timely filed, the IRS may exercise its discretion to recognize and treat the organization as tax-exempt effective as of a date earlier than the date of application, if the requirements for this discretionary relief are met.[183]

§ 26.7   REQUIREMENTS FOR CERTAIN PREPAID TUITION PLANS

A *prepaid tuition plan* operated by a qualified private educational institution[184] must receive a determination letter or ruling from the IRS that it meets the requirements for tax exemption.[185]

§ 26.8   REQUIREMENTS FOR CERTAIN HEALTH INSURANCE ISSUERS

An organization seeking status as a tax-exempt *qualified nonprofit health insurance issuer*[186] must obtain a determination letter or ruling from the IRS by electronically filing Form 1024.[187] An organization seeking status as a QNHII also must upload with its completed Form 1024 a copy of both the Notice of Award issued by Centers for Medicare and Medicaid Services (CMS) and the fully executed Loan Agreement with CMS.[188] The issuer's application must also include representations that it is in compliance with the private inurement, substantial legislative activities, and political campaign activities prohibitions.[189] A determination letter or ruling recognizing exemption in this context is usually effective as of the later of the date of formation of the issuer or March 23, 2010.[190] If, however, the issuer does not submit a substantially completed letter application within 15 months of the date of its loan agreement with the CMS, it will not qualify for exempt status before the postmark date of the letter application unless the IRS grants relief from this 15-month rule.[191]

---

[182] *Id.*; Reg. § 1.505(c)-1T.
[183] Rev. Proc. 2024-5, 2024-1 I.R.B. 262 § 6.08(3). See text accompanied by *supra* notes 136–138.
[184] See § 19.19(b).
[185] IRC § 529(b)(1). E.g., Priv. Ltr. Rul. 200311034.
[186] IRC § 501(c)(29). See § 19.18.
[187] Rev. Proc. 2024-5, 2024-1 I.R.B. 262 § 4.01(3).
[188] Instructions for Form 1024 (Jan. 2022), Part III, line 1.
[189] *Id.* See § 19.18.
[190] Reg. § 1.501(c)(29)-1(b); Rev. Proc. 2024-5, 2024-1 I.R.B. 262 § 2.02(3); Rev. Proc. 2015-17, 2015-7 I.R.B. 599 § 5.
[191] Rev. Proc. 2024-5, 2024-1 I.R.B. 262 § 6.08(3); Rev. Proc. 2015-17, 2015-7 I.R.B. 599 § 5. The IRS's requirements for granting relief from this 15-month rule are the same as those that apply for granting relief from the 27-month rule (Rev. Proc. 2024-5, *supra* § 6.08(3); see § 26.2(a)).

§ 26.9 REQUIREMENT FOR ABLE PROGRAMS

A qualified ABLE program is required to submit a notice to the IRS on the establishment of an ABLE account. This notice must contain the name and state of residence of the designated beneficiary and other information as the IRS may require.[192]

§ 26.10 RULES FOR OTHER CATEGORIES OF ORGANIZATIONS

Consequently, to be tax-exempt, organizations other than those previously noted[193] are not required to file with the IRS for recognition of exemption.[194] They are tax-exempt, assuming they qualify, by operation of law. The IRS refers to organizations that do not seek recognition of exemption (when they are not required to) as *self-declarers.*

These organizations may, however, voluntarily seek recognition of tax-exempt status.[195] When they so file, they must follow the standard procedures for requesting determination letters.[196]

Another assumption must be factored into this analysis: the filing of annual information returns and/or the submission of e-postcards. (An organization that is not required to file for recognition of exemption is nonetheless usually required to make these annual filings and/or submissions.)[197] Organizations that have not filed an application and that are required to annually file with and/or notify the IRS, but do not do so for three consecutive years, cannot be tax-exempt without thereafter seeking recognition of exemption.[198]

The IRS permits recognition of exemption in these circumstances from the date of formation only if the organization has always met the requirements for the tax exemption involved, has not failed to file or submit annual returns or notices for three consecutive years, and has applied within 27 months from the end of the month in which it was organized.[199]

§ 26.11 GROUP EXEMPTION RULES

An organization (such as a chapter, local, post, or unit) that is affiliated with and is subject to the general supervision or control of a central organization (usually, a state, regional, or national organization) may be recognized as a tax-exempt organization solely by reason of its relationship with the parent organization. Tax-exempt status acquired in this manner is referred to as tax exemption on a *group*

---

[192] IRC § 529A(d)(3). See § 19.20.
[193] That is, the categories of organizations referenced in §§ 26.2, 26.5–26.8.
[194] See § 3.2.
[195] Most of these categories of entities file Form 1024 as their application.
[196] Currently, Rev. Proc. 2024-5, 2024-1 I.R.B. 262 233.
[197] See §§ 28.2(c), 28.3.
[198] See § 28.4.
[199] This 27-month rule is imported from the application rules applicable in the IRC § 501(c)(3) context (see § 26.2(a)). Rev. Proc. 2024-5, 2024-1 I.R.B. 262 § 6.08(1).

basis. The advantage of the group exemption is that each of the organizations covered by a group exemption letter—termed *subordinate* organizations[200]—is relieved from filing its own application for recognition of tax exemption.

(a)   Existing Procedures

The existing procedures by which a group exemption may be recognized by the IRS[201] contemplate that the parent organization will function as an agent of the IRS, requiring that the parent organization responsibly and independently evaluate the tax-exempt status of its subordinate organizations from the standpoint of the organizational and operational tests applicable to them.[202] A parent organization is required to annually file with the IRS a list of its qualifying tax-exempt subordinate organizations; this listing amounts to an attestation by the central organization that the subordinate organizations qualify as tax-exempt organizations so that the IRS need not carry out an independent evaluation as to the tax-exempt status of the organizations. Therefore, it is essential that the central organization, in performing this agency function, exercise responsibility in evaluating the tax status of its subordinates.[203]

Assuming that the general requirements for recognition of tax-exempt status[204] are satisfied, a group exemption letter will be issued to a central organization where the foregoing requirements as to subordinate organizations are met, the exemption to be recognized is under the general exemption rules,[205] and each of the subordinate organizations has an organizing document (although they do not have to be incorporated). Neither private foundations nor organizations organized and operated in a foreign country may be included in a group exemption letter.

Thus, a central organization applying for a group exemption must first obtain recognition of its own tax-exempt status. Then it must establish that all of the subordinate organizations to be included in the group exemption letter are (1) affiliated with it, (2) subject to its general supervision or control, (3) exempt under the same paragraph of the general exemption rules (although not necessarily the section under which the central organization is tax-exempt), (4) not private foundations or foreign organizations, (5) on the same accounting period as the central organization if they are to be included in group returns, and (6) formed within the 27-month period prior to the date of submission of the group exemption application (assuming

---

[200] This is an unfortunate choice of terminology, in that many organizations and those who manage them do not care to be regarded as *subordinates*; a preferable term would be *affiliates*.

[201] Rev. Proc. 80-27, 1980-1 C.B. 677. Also Reg. § 601.201(n)(7). The IRS has proposed updated procedures (see § 26.11(c)) under which recognition of exemption may be obtained on a group basis for subordinate organizations affiliated with and under the general supervision or control of a central organization, which, once finalized, will supersede this four-decades-old guidance (Notice 2020-36, 2020-21 I.R.B. 840). Until the new procedures are finalized, Rev. Proc. 80-27 continues to apply, but the IRS will not accept any requests for group exemption letters starting (*id.*; Rev. Proc. 2024-5, 2024-1 I.R.B. 262 § 3.02(11)).

[202] See §§ 4.3, 4.5.

[203] There is no law that addresses the matter of the process by which a central organization initially determines the qualification of entities for its group exemption and thereafter continues this determination.

[204] See §§ 26.1–26.2.

[205] IRC § 501(c). Thus, the group exemption procedures are unavailable to organizations described in IRC §§ 521 (see § 19.12), 526 (see § 19.13), 527 (see Chapter 17), 528 (see § 19.14), and 529 (see § 19.19).

this is the case, these entities are claiming charitable status, and are subject to the requirements for application for recognition of tax exemption).[206],[207] For example, with respect to the third requirement, a central organization may be tax-exempt as a charitable entity with all of the subordinates thereof exempt as social welfare organizations. Concerning the sixth requirement, the procedures state that if one or more of the subordinates have not been organized within the 27-month period, the group exemption letter will be issued only if all the subordinates agree to be recognized as tax-exempt from the date of the application rather than the date of their creation. Subordinate charitable organizations are exempt from the notice requirements generally applicable to charitable organizations.[208]

A central organization may be involved in more than one group exemption arrangement, such as a charitable parent organization having both charitable and social welfare/civic organization subordinates. Also, a central organization may be a subordinate organization with respect to another central organization, such as a state organization that has subordinate units and is itself affiliated with a national organization.[209]

An instrumentality or agency of a political subdivision that exercises control or supervision over other organizations similar in purposes and operations, each of which may qualify for tax exemption under the same category of exempt organizations, may obtain a group exemption letter covering the organizations in the same manner as a central organization.[210] Under this approach, the group exemption for organizations such as federal credit unions, state-chartered credit unions, and federal land bank associations may be established.[211]

A central organization must submit to the IRS, in addition to certain information about itself, the following information on behalf of its group exemption subordinates: (1) a letter signed by a principal officer of the central organization setting forth or including as attachments (a) information verifying the existence of the foregoing six relationships and requirements, (b) a detailed description of the principal purposes and activities of the subordinates, including financial information, (c) a sample copy of a uniform or representative governing instrument adopted by the subordinates, (d) an affirmation that, to the best of the officer's knowledge, the subordinates are operating in accordance with the stated purposes, (e) a statement that each subordinate to be included within the group exemption has furnished the requisite written authorization, (f) a list of subordinates to be included in the group exemption to which the IRS has issued an outstanding ruling or determination letter relating to tax exemption, and (g), if relevant, an affirmation that no subordinate organization is a private foundation; and (2) a list of the names, addresses, and employer identification numbers of subordinates to be included in the group exemption (or, in lieu thereof, a satisfactory directory of subordinates).[212] Certain additional information is required if a subordinate is claiming tax-exempt

---

[206] See § 26.2.
[207] Rev. Proc. 80-27, 1980-1 C.B. 677 § 4.
[208] Reg. § 1.508-1(a)(3)(i) (c); Rev. Rul. 90-100, 1990-2 C.B. 156.
[209] Rev. Proc. 80-27, 1980-1 C.B. 677 § 3.03.
[210] Id. § 8.
[211] See § 19.7.
[212] Rev. Proc. 80-27, 1980-1 C.B. 677 § 5.

status as a school. In the only court decision involving the group exemption rules, the U.S. Tax Court upheld the requirement that detailed information concerning the activities and finances of subordinates be submitted to the IRS, in holding that an organization is not eligible for classification as a central organization because the requisite information was not provided.[213]

Once a group exemption letter is issued, certain information must be submitted annually by the central organization (at least 90 days before the close of its annual accounting period) to the IRS to maintain the letter. This information consists of (1) information regarding any changes in the purposes, character, or method of operation of the subordinates; (2) lists of (a) subordinates that have changed their names or addresses during the year, (b) subordinates no longer to be included in the group exemption letter (for whatever reason), and (c) subordinates to be added to the group exemption letter (for whatever reason); and (3) the information summarized in the foregoing paragraph (items (1)(a)–(g)) with respect to subordinates to be added to the group exemption letter.[214]

There are two ways in which a group exemption letter may be terminated. When a termination occurs, the tax-exempt status of the subordinate organizations is no longer recognized by the IRS, thereby requiring (where continuing recognition of tax-exempt status is required or desired) each subordinate to file an application for recognition of tax exemption, the central organization to file for a new group exemption letter, or the subordinates (or a portion of them) to become tax-exempt by reason of their status with respect to another qualifying central organization. Termination of a group exemption letter will be occasioned where (1) the central organization dissolves or otherwise ceases to exist, or (2) the central organization fails to qualify for tax exemption, to submit the information required to obtain the letter, to file the annual information return, or to otherwise comply with the reporting requirements.[215]

If the IRS revokes the tax-exempt status of a central organization, the group exemption letter involved is also revoked, thereby simultaneously revoking the tax-exempt status of all the subordinates. To regain recognition of tax exemption in this instance, or in the case of its withdrawal from the group exemption, a subordinate organization must file an application for recognition of exemption or become a member of another tax-exempt group. As of the date an organization is no longer in a group, the 27-month notice period begins to run,[216] so that an organization desiring to maintain tax exemption on an ongoing basis must file the application within that period or timely join another group.[217]

Where a subordinate organization has an outstanding ruling of tax exemption and becomes included in a group exemption letter, the prior exemption letter is superseded. The central organization, in this circumstance, is obligated to notify the affected subordinate organization(s) of this supersession.

---

[213] Nat'l Ass'n of Am. Churches v. Comm'r, 82 T.C. 18 (1984).
[214] Rev. Proc. 80-27, 1980-1 C.B. 677 § 6. Group exemption reports are filed with the IRS Service Center in Ogden, Utah (Rev. Proc. 96-40, 1996-2 C.B. 301).
[215] IRC §§ 6001, 6033. Loss of tax exemption by some members of the group does not adversely affect the group exemption ruling as it pertains to the other members in the group (Tech. Adv. Mem. 9711004).
[216] See § 26.2(a).
[217] Rev. Rul. 90-100, 1990-2 C.B. 156.

Where the subordinates are charitable organizations, their publicly supported charity status must be considered, inasmuch as, as noted, they may not be private foundations and qualify under the group exemption rules.[218]

(b)   Advantages and Disadvantages of Group Exemption

The group exemption generally is favorable for clusters of nonprofit organizations that are affiliated. This approach to tax exemption obviates the need for each entity in the group to file a separate application for recognition of tax exemption, and this can result in savings of time, effort, and expenses—for the organizations and for the IRS. It is, then, a streamlined approach to the establishment of tax-exempt status for related organizations.

There are, however, disadvantages to a tax-exempt status based on the group exemption. One is that the members of the group do not individually possess determination letters as to their tax exemption. This can pose difficulties for donors and grantors,[219] as well as problems for the organization in securing state tax exemptions. Second, there is no separate assessment of these organizations' publicly supported status.[220] Third, if a member of the group is found liable for damages, the existence of the group exemption may be used in an effort to assert "ascending" liability on the part of the central organization.

(c)   Proposed Revised Procedures

The IRS, in mid-2020, issued a proposed revenue procedure setting forth updated group exemption procedures.[221] This proposal includes new procedures a central organization will be required to follow to maintain a group exemption. In understatements, the IRS recognized in the preamble accompanying this proposal that the proposal would make "substantial changes" to the existing procedures and "may" impose "additional administrative burden[s]" on central organizations. Although as a technical matter the existing revenue procedure concerning group rulings continues to apply,[222] the IRS has stopped accepting requests for group exemption letters and will not accept any new ones until the proposed revenue procedure is finalized.[223]

---

[218] The IRS has the authority to modify the tax-exempt status of subordinate organizations and will do so where the subordinates satisfy the applicable criteria for exemption. Cf. Priv. Ltr. Rul. 201123041 (where the IRS declined to convert the exempt status of subordinates in a group exemption from IRC § 501(c)(4) status to IRC § 501(c)(3) status).

[219] A donor of a major gift may want the security of a determination letter so as to have the requisite basis for relying on the organization's representation that it is a charitable entity. A private foundation grantor may desire similar assurance to be certain that the grant constitutes a qualifying distribution (see § 12.4(b)), is not an expenditure responsibility grant (see § 12.4(e)), or is not otherwise a taxable expenditure (*id.*).

[220] For example, private foundations rarely make grants to other private foundations, and a private foundation grantor usually wants meaningful assurance that the grantee is a public or publicly supported charity.

[221] Notice 2020-36, 2020-21 I.R.B. 840.

[222] See § 26.11(a).

[223] Rev. Proc. 2024-5, 2024-1 I.R.B. 262 § 3.02(11).

(i) General Rules.   The proposed revenue procedure would require that a central organization have at least five subordinate organizations to obtain a group exemption and have at least one subordinate to maintain the group exemption thereafter.[224] A central organization would be able to maintain only one group exemption.[225]

A central organization would be required to establish that each subordinate organization to be included in the group exemption is affiliated with the central organization and is subject to its general supervision or control.[226]

The term *affiliation* is not defined as such. Rather, the concept of affiliation with a central organization would be demonstrated by the entirety of the information required to be submitted by the central organization about its subordinates.[227] This information would consist of (1) information verifying that each subordinate is affiliated with, and subject to, the central organization's general supervision or control; (2) a representation that all of the subordinates are described in the same paragraph of IRC § 501(c) as the central organization (with a different rule for central organizations that are an instrumentality or an agency of a political subdivision); (3) if the subordinates are, or will be, described in IRC § 501(c)(3), their public charity status; (4) a representation that none of the subordinates is organized in a foreign country; (5) if the subordinates are, or will be, described in IRC § 501(c)(3), a representation that none of them is classified as a private foundation[228] or a Type III supporting organization;[229] (6) a summary of the subordinates' purposes and activities, including their revenue and expenditures; (7) a representation that the primary purpose of all the subordinates (other than those described in IRC § 501(c)(3)) is described by the same National Taxonomy of Exempt Entities code; (8) a statement that each subordinate has furnished the requisite written authorization to the central organization; (9) a statement confirming that all subordinates were organized within 27 months of the postmark date of the group exemption letter request (with exceptions); and (10) if applicable, a statement that any subordinates on behalf of which the central organization will file group returns are on the same accounting period as the central organization.[230]

A subordinate organization would be subject to the central organization's *general supervision* if the central organization (1) annually obtains, reviews, and retains information on the subordinate's finances, activities, and compliance with the annual filing requirements and (2) transmits written information, or otherwise educates, the subordinate about the requirements to maintain its tax-exempt status.[231]

A subordinate organization would be subject to the central organization's *control* if (1) the central organization appoints a majority of the subordinate's trustees, directors, or officers, or (2) a majority of the subordinate's trustees, directors, or officers are trustees, directors, or officers of the central organization.[232]

---

[224] Proposed Revenue Procedure § 3.01(2) (Notice 2020-36, 2020-21 I.R.B. 840).
[225] *Id.* § 3.01(3).
[226] *Id.* § 3.02(1).
[227] *Id.* § 3.02(2).
[228] See § 12.1(a).
[229] See § 12.3(c).
[230] Proposed Revenue Procedure § 5.03 (Notice 2020-36, 2020-21 I.R.B. 840).
[231] *Id.* § 3.02(3).
[232] *Id.* § 3.02(4).

(ii) Subordinate Organizations. All subordinate organizations initially included in or added to a group exemption would generally have to meet four requirements.[233] One of these requirements is a set of matching requirements. All subordinates initially included in or added to a group exemption would have to be described in the same paragraph of IRC § 501(c). If the central organization is described in IRC § 501(c), all subordinates initially included in or added to a group exemption would have to be described in the same paragraph of IRC § 501(c) as the central organization. Rules would apply in connection with central organizations not described in IRC § 501(c).[234]

Another requirement pertains to public charity status. All subordinates described in IRC § 501(c)(3) that are initially included in or added to a group exemption would have to be classified as public charities under the same paragraph of IRC § 509(a).[235] Subordinates classified as public charities under IRC § 509(a)(1) would not be required to be classified under the same paragraph of IRC § 170(b)(1)(A).[236] Subordinates classified as publicly supported organizations either under IRC § 170(b)(1)(A)(vi)[237] or 509(a)(2)[238] would be considered, for these purposes, to be classified under the same paragraph of IRC § 509(a). Subordinates described in IRC § 501(c)(3) would not be required to be classified under the same paragraph of IRC § 509(a) as the central organization.[239]

A third requirement would be that the primary purpose of all the subordinates described in IRC § 501(c) (other than IRC § 501(c)(3)) initially included in, or added to, a group exemption must be described in the same NTEE code.[240]

A fourth requirement concerns governing instruments. All subordinates would have to adopt a uniform governing instrument; representative instruments would not be acceptable. If, however, a group exemption includes subordinates that are charitable entities with different purposes, the governing instrument describing each distinct charitable, educational, scientific, and like purpose would have to be a uniform governing instrument.[241]

The following types of organizations would not be eligible to be subordinates: (1) entities that are organized in a foreign country, (2) private foundations, (3) a Type III supporting organization, (4) qualified nonprofit health insurance issuers,[242] and (5) organizations that have had their tax exemption automatically revoked[243] and have not had their exemption reinstated after filing an application for reinstatement.[244]

---

[233] *Id.* § 3.03(2).
[234] *Id.* § 3.03(2)(a).
[235] See § 12.3.
[236] See § 12.3(a), (b).
[237] See § 12.3(b)(i).
[238] See § 12.3(b)(iv).
[239] Proposed Revenue Procedure § 3.03(2)(b) (Notice 2020-36, 2020-21 I.R.B. 840).
[240] *Id.* § 3.03(2)(c).
[241] *Id.* § 3.03(2)(d).
[242] See § 19.18.
[243] See § 28.4.
[244] Proposed Revenue Procedure § 3.04 (Notice 2020-36, 2020-21 I.R.B. 840).

A subordinate organization would be required to authorize the central organization, in writing, to include the subordinate in the request for the group exemption or add the subordinate to an existing group exemption.[245] This authorization would have to acknowledge that the central organization may remove the subordinate from the group exemption if the subordinate fails to comply with the group exemption requirements.[246] The central organization would be required to retain these authorizations.[247]

(iii) Requesting Group Exemption Letter. Once this proposed revenue procedure is finalized, tax-exempt organizations may submit requests for classification as central organizations.[248] A request that is missing any item of required information would not be accepted by the IRS.[249] The IRS would have the authority to decline to issue a group exemption letter where the activities described in the request involve complex facts and circumstances that, in the interest of sound tax administration, are more appropriate for determination on an organization-by-organization basis.[250]

The information about the subordinates that the central organization must submit to the IRS would be those items required by reason of the affiliation requirement.[251] Also, the central organization would be required to provide (1) a sample copy of the uniform governing instrument (or, if the subordinates are charitable entities and have different purposes, sample copies of the uniform instrument describing each distinct purpose); (2) a list of the names, mailing addresses, identification numbers, and dates of formation of the subordinates; and (3) if applicable, a list of subordinates to which the IRS has issued determination letters.[252] The central organization may be required to submit information establishing that its subordinates meet additional requirements, such as in the case of private schools, charitable hospitals, and social welfare organizations.[253]

(iv) Maintenance of Group Exemption. A central organization would be required to submit certain information to the IRS annually at least 30 days before the close of its annual accounting period, including information as to any changes in subordinates' purposes or activities and certain information concerning subordinates being added to the group exemption.[254] A central organization that is a church or convention or association of churches[255] may, but is not required to, submit this information.[256]

---

[245] *Id.* § 3.05(1).

[246] *Id.* § 3.05(2).

[247] *Id.* § 3.05(3).

[248] *Id.* § 4.01.

[249] *Id.* § 4.02.

[250] *Id.* § 4.03.

[251] *Id.* § 5.03(1). See text accompanied by *supra* notes 227–230.

[252] Proposed Revenue Procedure § 5.03(2) (Notice 2020-36, 2020-21 I.R.B. 840).

[253] *Id.* § 5.03(3).

[254] *Id.* §§ 6.01–6.04.

[255] See §§ 10.3, 10.4.

[256] Proposed Revenue Procedure § 6.05 (Notice 2020-36, 2020-21 I.R.B. 840).

(v) Preexisting Arrangements. This proposed revenue procedure would apply with respect to group exemption letters requested and issued after its effective date.[257]

Generally, the proposed revenue procedure would apply to existing group exemptions.[258] The following elements of the revenue procedure, however, would apply to existing group exemptions one year after the date the final revenue procedure is published by the IRS: the requirement that a central organization have at least one subordinate to maintain a group exemption and the rule that a central organization may hold only one group exemption letter.[259] If a central organization has an existing group exemption letter but does not have at least one subordinate, the central organization, during this transition period, would be required to add at least one subordinate.[260] During the transition period, a central organization that maintains more than one existing group exemption letter would be required to terminate all but one of them.[261]

The proposed revenue procedure would apply to new subordinate organizations.[262] The first time after the effective date of the proposed revenue procedure a central organization adds a subordinate to any existing group exemption, the central organization would be required to provide to the IRS the required information about the new subordinate.[263] On the second and any subsequent addition of subordinates, the central organization would need to provide only the information required when adding subordinates to a group exemption.[264]

The following elements of this proposed revenue procedure would not apply to existing subordinates: (1) the definition and description of the applicability of the terms *general supervision* and *control*;[265] (2) the requirements pertaining to matching,[266] public charity classification,[267] similar purpose,[268] and uniform governing instruments;[269] (3) the exclusion of Type III supporting organizations as subordinates;[270] and (4) the requirement in the authorization rule[271] for removal of recalcitrant subordinates.[272]

Existing subordinate organizations (1) would have to be described in the same paragraph of IRC § 501(c), although not the same paragraph as the central

---

[257] *Id.* § 14.01.

[258] *Id.* § 14.02(1).

[259] *Id.* § 14.02(2)(a).

[260] *Id.* § 14.02(2)(b).

[261] *Id.* § 14.02(2)(c).

[262] *Id.* § 14.02(3)(a).

[263] *Id.* § 14.02(3)(b). See text accompanied by *supra* notes 227–230.

[264] Proposed Revenue Procedure § 14.02(3)(b) (Notice 2020-36, 2020-21 I.R.B. 840). See text accompanied by *supra* note 254.

[265] See text accompanied by *supra* notes 231–232.

[266] See text accompanied by *supra* note 234.

[267] See text accompanied by *supra* notes 235–239.

[268] See text accompanied by *supra* note 240.

[269] See text accompanied by *supra* note 241.

[270] See text accompanied by *supra* note 244.

[271] See text accompanied by *supra* note 245.

[272] See text accompanied by *supra* note 246. Proposed Revenue Procedure § 14.02(4)(b) (Notice 2020-36, 2020-21 I.R.B. 840).

organization; (2) if described in IRC § 501(c)(3), may be classified in any paragraph of IRC § 509(a); (3) may have different primary purposes; and (4) may have unique governing instruments.[273] If an existing group exemption includes subordinates that are described in different paragraphs of IRC § 501(c), the central organization, during the transition period, would be required to remove the subordinates described in the paragraph of IRC § 501(c) that is different from the paragraph in which the central organization stated that the subordinates would be described in its group exemption letter request.[274]

(vi) Other Rules.   This proposed revenue procedure also addresses terminations of group exemption letters;[275] the effect of nonacceptance, nonissuance, termination, or removals;[276] the effective date of group exemptions;[277] the interrelationship with the declaratory judgment rules;[278] the reliance rules;[279] and the disclosure rules.[280]

§ 26.12   TERRORISM-RELATED SUSPENSION OF TAX EXEMPTION

The tax-exempt status of an organization that has been designated as supporting or engaging in terrorist activity or supporting terrorism is suspended. Contributions made to an organization during the period of suspension of exemption are not deductible for federal tax purposes.[281]

Specifically, federal income tax exemption, and the eligibility of an organization to apply for recognition of exemption,[282] must be suspended for a particular period if it is a terrorist organization.[283] Contributions to such an organization are not deductible during the period for income, estate, and gift tax purposes.[284]

An organization is a *terrorist organization* if it is designated or otherwise individually identified (1) under provisions of the Immigration and Nationality Act[285] as a terrorist organization or foreign terrorist organization, (2) in or pursuant to an executive order that is related to terrorism and issued under the authority of the International Emergency Economic Powers Act or the United Nations Participation Act of 1945 for the purpose of imposing on such organization an economic or other sanction, or (3) in or pursuant to an executive order issued under the authority of any federal law, if the organization is designated or otherwise individually identified in or pursuant to the executive order as supporting or engaging

[273] *Id.* § 14.02(4)(c).
[274] *Id.* § 14.02(4)(d).
[275] *Id.* § 8.
[276] *Id.* § 9.
[277] *Id.* § 10.
[278] *Id.* § 11. See § 27.5(c).
[279] Proposed Revenue Procedure § 12 (Notice 2020-36, 2020-21 I.R.B. 840).
[280] *Id.* § 13. See § 28.10.
[281] IRC § 501(p).
[282] Rev. Proc. 2024-5, 2024-1 I.R.B. 262 § 6.02. See §§ 26.1, 26.2.
[283] IRC § 501(p)(1).
[284] IRC § 501(p)(4).
[285] That is, § 212(a)(3)(B)(vi)(II) or 219 of that act (8 U.S.C. §§ 1182(a)(3)(B)(vi)(II), 1189).

in terrorist activity[286] or supporting terrorism,[287] and the executive order refers to this federal tax law.[288]

The period of suspension of tax exemption begins on the date of the first publication by the IRS of a designation or identification with respect to the organization and ends on the first date that all designations and identifications with respect to the organization are rescinded pursuant to the applicable law or executive order.[289]

A person may not challenge a suspension of tax exemption, a designation or identification of an entity as a terrorist organization, the period of a suspension, or a denial of a charitable deduction in this context in an administrative or judicial proceeding.[290] This law provides for a refund or credit of income tax (if necessary) in the case of an erroneous designation or identification of an entity as a terrorist organization.[291]

Likewise, organizations can be denied recognition of tax exemption if the federal government suspects they are terrorist organizations.[292]

§ 26.13 NOTICE REQUIREMENTS FOR SOCIAL WELFARE ORGANIZATIONS

An organization qualifying as a tax-exempt exempt social welfare organization[293] must provide to the IRS notice of its formation and intent to operate as this type of organization no later than 60 days following establishment of the organization.[294] This notice must include the name, address, and taxpayer identification number of the organization; the date on which, and the state under the laws of which, the organization was organized; and a statement of the purposes of the organization.[295] The IRS may extend this period for reasonable cause.[296] Within 60 days of receipt of this notice, the IRS must issue acknowledgement of it to the organization.[297] The notice and acknowledgement are subject to the disclosure requirements.[298]

An organization that fails to file this notice in a timely manner is subject to a penalty equal to $20 for each day during which the failure occurs, up to a

---

[286] As defined in the Immigration and Nationality Act § 212(a)(3)(B) (8 U.S.C. §§ 1182(a)(3)(B)).

[287] As defined in the Foreign Relations Authorization Act, Fiscal Years 1988 and 1989 § 140(d)(2) (Pub. Law. No. 100-204, 101 Stat. 1331, 1349).

[288] IRC § 501(p)(2).

[289] IRC § 501(p)(3).

[290] IRC § 501(p)(5). This rule overrides provisions of law such as the exempt organizations declaratory judgment rules (see § 27.5(c)).

[291] IRC § 501(p)(6).

[292] E.g., Priv. Ltr. Rul. 201712014.

[293] See Chapter 13.

[294] IRC § 506(a); Reg. § 1.506-1(a)(1).

[295] IRC § 506(b); Reg. § 1.506-1(a)(2). This notice is given by electronically filing Form 8976 on www.irs. gov (Rev. Proc. 2024-5, 2024-1 I.R.B. 262 § 2.03(3)). A user fee, currently $50, is imposed for the filing of this notice (IRC § 506(e)).

[296] IRC § 506(d); Reg. § 1.506-1(a)(4).

[297] IRC § 506(c); Reg. § 1.506-1(d).

[298] See §§ 28.9(a)(ii), 28.10.

maximum of $5,000.[299] In the event this penalty is imposed, the IRS may make a written demand on the organization specifying a date by which the notice must be provided. If any person fails to comply with the demand on or before the specified date, a penalty of $20 is to be imposed for each day the failure continues, up to a maximum of $5,000.[300]

With its first annual information return filed after the filing of this notice, the organization must provide such information as the IRS may require in support of its qualification as a tax-exempt social welfare organization.[301]

Submission of this notification does not constitute a request by an organization for a determination by the IRS that the organization qualifies for exemption as a social welfare organization.[302] An organization that desires IRS recognition of its qualification as a tax-exempt social welfare organization must file a request for a determination, together with the requisite user fee, with the IRS.[303]

§ 26.14   NOTICE REQUIREMENTS FOR POLITICAL ORGANIZATIONS

Generally, for an organization to be treated as a tax-exempt political organization,[304] it must give notice to the IRS of its existence.[305] This notice must be transmitted no later than 24 hours after the date on which the organization is established.[306] The notice must be submitted electronically. If this notice is given after the 24-hour period, the exemption treatment is only prospective, although the IRS has the authority to waive any tax resulting from a failure to comply with the notice requirements on a showing that the failure was due to reasonable cause and not due to willful neglect.[307]

This notice must contain the following: the name and address of the organization and its electronic mailing address; the purpose of the organization; the names and addresses of its officers, highly compensated employees, contact person, custodian of records, and members of its board of directors; the name and address of, and relationship to, any related entities; and such other information as the IRS may require. Any material change in the information provided in the initial notice must be reported to the IRS within 30 days of the change.

The phrase *highly compensated employees*, for this purpose, means the five employees (other than officers or directors) who are expected to have the highest

---

[299] IRC § 6652(c)(4)(A).

[300] IRC § 6652(c)(4)(B). This penalty and the one referenced in the text accompanied by *supra* note 299 may not be imposed if there is a showing of reasonable cause (IRC § 6652(c)(5)).

[301] IRC § 6033(f)(2).

[302] Reg. § 1.506-1(e).

[303] IRC § 506(f); Reg. § 1.506-1(e). See § 26.4.

[304] These organizations are the subject of Chapter 17.

[305] IRC § 527(i). This notice is given by electronically filing Form 8871 on www.irs.gov (Rev. Proc. 2024-5, 2024-1 I.R.B. 262 § 2.03(2)).

[306] Some of the provisions of this law, however, were struck down as violative of the First and Tenth Amendments to the U.S. Constitution (Nat'l Federation of Republican Assemblies v. United States, 263 F. Supp. 2d 1372 (S.D. Ala. 2003). Revisions to this body of law were subsequently enacted (Pub. L. 107-276, 107th Cong., 2d Sess. (2002)).

[307] IRC § 527(l).

annual compensation over $50,000. The term *compensation* includes cash and non-cash amounts, whether paid currently or deferred, for the 12-month period that began with the date the organization was formed.

An entity is a *related entity* under two circumstances: (1) the organization and that entity have significant common purposes and substantial common membership or substantial common direction or control, whether directly or indirectly, or (2) either the organization or that entity owns, directly or through one or more entities, at least a 50 percent capital or profits interest in the other.[308]

Where an organization fails to submit the requisite notice on a timely basis, it is taxable (unless the IRS waives the tax(es) or the entity is otherwise exempt, such as by reason of qualifying as a social welfare organization).[309] The taxable income of the organization is computed by taking into account any exempt function income and any directly related deductions.

This notice requirement does not apply in the case of a political organization that reasonably anticipates that it will not have gross receipts of $25,000 or more for any year.[310] The requirement also does not apply to an entity required to report under the Federal Election Campaign Act[311] as a political committee. Further, the requirement is not applicable to any other type of tax-exempt organization that is nonetheless subject to the political campaign activities tax.[312] (This latter exception is basically for social welfare and labor organizations, and for associations.)[313] This notice requirement applies, however, to state or local political organizations that are not committees of candidates or of political parties.[314]

§ 26.15 INTEGRAL PART DOCTRINE

The *integral part doctrine* is a basis in law for the acquisition of tax-exempt status, by means of recognition of that status by the IRS or otherwise. There are two variants of this doctrine. One concerns an organization that obtained tax exemption because of its relationship with one or more tax-exempt entities. This type of organization is, in law, a separate entity, with tax exemption a function of the affiliation. The other application of the doctrine pertains to tax-exempt organizations that have component entities that, while appearing to be separate organizations, are not, in law, separate but are instead *integral parts* of the larger organization. These component entities are in the nature of divisions of a tax-exempt organization.

---

[308] IRC § 168(h)(4).

[309] See Chapter 13.

[310] This $25,000 filing threshold is not the same as for other tax-exempt organizations, which is based on the concept of receipts *normally* received (see § 26.2(b)). The form must be filed unless the political organization reasonably expects annual gross receipts to *always* be less than $25,000 in each tax year.

[311] 2 U.S.C. § 431 *et seq.*

[312] IRC § 527(f)(1). See § 17.5.

[313] See Chapters 13 and 14, and § 16.1.

[314] The IRS issued guidance, in a question-and-answer format, concerning the state of the law as to the notice-of-status requirement subsequent to the 2002 revision (Rev. Rul. 2003-49, 2003-2 C.B. 903).

(a)   Affiliated Organizations

As noted, in general, the entitlement of a nonprofit organization to tax-exempt status is derived solely from the entity's own characteristics.[315] There is, however, an exception to this general rule, which is one of two aspects of the integral part doctrine. This facet of the doctrine, applied largely with respect to tax exemption as a charitable organization, enables an organization that functions as an integral part of the exempt activities of a related entity or entities to derive tax exemption by reason of the relationship with its affiliate or affiliates. Tax exemption of this nature is also known as a *derivative* or *vicarious* exemption.

The genesis of this element of the doctrine is language in the federal tax regulations on the subject of feeder organizations.[316] There it is stated that, as an exception to these rules, a "subsidiary" of a tax-exempt organization can be exempt "on the ground that its activities are an integral part of the activities of the parent organization."[317] As an illustration, the regulations describe a "subsidiary organization that is operated for the sole purpose of furnishing electric power used by its parent, a tax-exempt organization, in carrying out its educational activities."[318] These regulations also state that an entity seeking tax exemption as an integral part of another entity cannot primarily be engaged in an activity that would generate more than insubstantial unrelated business income for the other entity.[319]

The traditional view of achievement of tax exemption by affiliation with a charitable entity is that the integral part doctrine applies where the activities of the organization whose tax status is being evaluated are carried on under the supervision or control of an exempt organization and could be carried on by the exempt parent organization without materially constituting an unrelated trade or business.[320] Interpretations along this line from the IRS include tax exemption for a trust existing solely as a repository of funds set aside by a nonprofit hospital for the payment of malpractice claims against the hospital and as the payor of those claims,[321] a corporation that published and sold law journals as an adjunct to a tax-exempt law school,[322] and a bookstore used almost exclusively by the faculty and students of a university with which it was associated.[323] This explication of the doctrine is also found in court opinions. For example, one court ruled that a corporation operating a bookstore and restaurant that sold college texts was wholly owned by a tax-exempt college, used college facilities without charge, served mostly faculty and students, and devoted its earnings to educational purposes

---

[315] See § 26.1.

[316] See § 28.14.

[317] Reg. § 502-1(b). Also, Gen. Couns. Mem. 39830.

[318] Reg. § 1.502-1(b).

[319] *Id.*

[320] E.g., Geisinger Health Plan v. Comm'r, 100 T.C. 394, 402 (1993), *aff'd*, 30 F.3d 494 (3d Cir. 1994).

[321] Rev. Rul. 78-41, 1978-1 C.B. 148.

[322] Rev. Rul. 63-235, 1963-2 C.B. 210.

[323] Rev. Rul. 58-194, 1958-1 C.B. 240.

was tax-exempt because it "obviously bears a close and intimate relationship to the functioning of the [c]ollege itself."[324]

Nonetheless, a court decided that the law is not clear as to "whether there are any other necessary qualifications" surrounding the doctrine.[325] Indeed, the court also concluded that there is one additional criterion—and, "[d]istilling . . . [this body of law] into a general rule," wrote that a "subsidiary that is not entitled to exempt status on its own may only receive such status as an integral part of its . . . [charitable] parent if (i) it is not carrying on a trade or business that would be an unrelated trade or business (that is, unrelated to exempt activities) if regularly carried on by the parent, and (ii) its relationship to its parent somehow enhances the subsidiary's own exempt character to the point that, when the boost provided by the parent is added to the contribution made by the subsidiary itself, the subsidiary would be entitled to . . . [exempt, charitable] status"[326] Applying this *boost principle*, the court held that a health maintenance organization could not qualify for tax exemption on the ground that it was an integral part of a hospital system, because the plan did not receive any boost from its association with the system.[327]

There are other instances where this variant of the integral part doctrine has been applied that escaped the analysis of the boost principle court. One is the determination by the IRS that a vending machine management organization was an integral part of a tax-exempt university.[328] Another is an IRS ruling that an organization formed and controlled by a tax-exempt conference of churches, which borrowed funds from individuals and made mortgage loans at less than the commercial rate of interest to affiliated churches to finance the construction of church buildings, qualified as an integral part of the parent organization.[329] A court subsequently held, without reference to the boost principle, that two organizations did not qualify for tax exemption on the basis of the integral part doctrine; indeed, the entities were dismissed as "appendages rather than integral parts" and "superfluous corporate shells that make no cognizable contribution" to the

---

[324] Squire v. Students Book Corp., 191 F.2d 1018, 1020 (9th Cir. 1951). Also, Univ. of Md. Physicians, P.A., v. Comm'r, 41 T.C.M. 732 (1981); Univ. of Mass. Med. School Group Practice v. Comm'r, 74 T.C. 1299 (1980); B.H.W. Anesthesia Found., Inc. v. Comm'r, 72 T.C. 681 (1979); B.S.W. Group, Inc. v. Comm'r, 70 T.C. 352 (1978); Brundage v. Comm'r, 54 T.C. 1468 (1970).

[325] Geisinger Health Plan v. Comm'r, 30 F.3d 494 (3d Cir. 1994).

[326] *Id.* at 501.

[327] The court concluded that the association of the health maintenance organization with the other entities in the hospital system "does nothing to increase the portion of the community for which . . . [the plan] promotes health—it serves no more people as a part of the [s]ystem than it would serve otherwise. It may contribute to the [s]ystem by providing more patients than the [s]ystem might otherwise have served, thus arguably allowing the [s]ystem to promote health among a broader segment of the community than could be served without it, but its provision of patients to the [s]ystem does not enhance its own promotion of health; the patients it provides—its subscribers—are the same patients it serves without its association with the [s]ystem. To the extent it promotes health among non- . . . [plan]-subscriber patients of the [s]ystem, it does so only because . . . [plan] subscribers' payments to the [s]ystem help finance the provision of health care to others" (*id.* at 502).

This appellate court earlier held that this health maintenance organization could not qualify as a charitable entity on its own merits (Geisinger Health Plan v. Comm'r, 985 F.2d 1210 (3d Cir. 1993) (see § 7.6(f)).

[328] Rev. Rul. 81-19, 1981-1 C.B. 353.

[329] Rev. Rul. 75-282, 1975-2 C.B. 201.

exempt organizations' purposes.[330] This court thereafter concluded that a health maintenance organization could not be considered an integral part of a health system because its enrollees received nearly 80 percent of their physician services from physicians with no direct link to any of the organization's tax-exempt affiliates; the boost principle was not considered.[331]

(b)   Divisions

An organization may be viewed as a composite of integrated components—being "composed of constituent parts making a whole."[332] In comparable instances, the law regards an item of property as an integral part of a larger property or process, such as bottles and cartons being an integral part of manufactured beer for purpose of state use tax exemptions[333] and executed contracts being an integral part of a baseball team for purposes of defining the team's "raw materials."[334] The fragmentation rule utilized in the unrelated business setting is predicated on this view of an organization.[335]

A tax-exempt organization may have component entities that are not separate organizations (although they may appear to be) and thus are "exempt" from tax because of the tax exemption of the host organization. For example, an exempt university may have scholarship funds, an exempt hospital may have research funds, and an exempt charitable organization may have one or more endowment funds; these funds may have separate names and be recipients of contributions made in those names. By analogy to the terminology in the for-profit setting, these component entities are akin to divisions (as is the case with the schools of a university or the departments of a hospital).[336] Thus, a youth club, operated as a program within a state university system, engaging in educational activities was ruled by the IRS to properly be the subject of earmarked (and deductible) charitable contributions.[337] The principal distinction from a tax standpoint is that the entity that is an integral part of a tax-exempt organization as a division is itself tax-exempt solely by virtue of the exemption of the host organization, while the tax exemption of a subsidiary must be obtained (if it can) by reason of the other definition of the integral part doctrine or on the merits of its own characteristics.[338]

It has been held that a principal element leading to a finding that one organization functions as an integral part of another organization is the fact that the

---

[330] Univ. Med. Resident Servs., P.C. v. Comm'r, 71 T.C.M. 3130, 3131–35 (1996).

[331] IHC Health Plans, Inc. v. Comm'r, 82 T.C.M. 593 (2001).

[332] Application of Larson, 340 F.2d 965, 967 (U.S. Ct. Cust. Pat. Appl. 1965).

[333] Zoller Brewing Co. v. State Tax Comm'r, 5 N.W.2d 643 (Iowa 1942).

[334] Hollywood Baseball Ass'n v. Comm'r, 423 F.2d 494 (9th Cir. 1970), *cert. denied*, 400 U.S. 848 (1970).

[335] See § 24.2(f).

[336] By contrast, the organizations that are tax-exempt by reason of the other application of the integral part doctrine (see § 26.15(a)) or the group exemption procedures (see § 26.11) are comparable to a for-profit organization's subsidiaries. A somewhat similar body of federal tax law is that concerning the supporting organization (see § 12.3(c)).

[337] Priv. Ltr. Rul. 201415009.

[338] The *division* aspect of the doctrine assumes that the attributes of this type of component entity do not cause it to be considered a separate organization; for example, one nonprofit corporation cannot be a division of another nonprofit corporation (although it can be an integral part of one).

function of the integrated organization is "essential" to the operation of the larger organization, and is an "ordinary and proper" function of the larger organization.[339] While this may be the case in general, in the tax-exempt organizations context it is largely an irrelevant criterion, inasmuch as the decision as to whether to establish the would-be integrated organization will nearly always be that of the larger organization.

Thus, the use of the integral part doctrine can be an efficient manner in which to acquire tax exemption for an organization, being a considerably speedier approach than the conventional exemption application process and even more rapid than the group exemption approach.[340]

§ 26.16 FORFEITURE OF TAX EXEMPTION

In general, there is no procedure for voluntarily forfeiting tax exemption, once the IRS has recognized the exempt status of an organization.[341] That is, other than by violating an element of the law of tax-exempt organizations, there is no general mechanism in the law for shedding exempt status. Thus, for example, a charitable organization could abandon its exempt status by violating the organizational test, such as by amending its organizational document to remove the dissolution clause.[342] Likewise, an exempt charitable organization could lose its exemption by violating the private inurement doctrine[343] or the private benefit doctrine,[344] engaging in excessive lobbying activities,[345] participating or intervening in a political campaign,[346] or undertaking substantial commercial activities.[347] Other categories of exempt organizations could effect forfeiture of

---

[339] E.g., Schwarz v. United States, 284 F. Supp. 792, 797 (U.S. Customs Ct. 1968); also, Matczak v. Secretary of Health, Educ. & Welfare, 299 F. Supp. 409 (E.D.N.Y. 1969).

[340] One of the issues involving the integral part doctrine is whether the many unincorporated congregations established by the Universal Life Church are tax-exempt by reason of the church's tax-exempt status (see § 10.2(c)). To date, the U.S. Tax Court (the only court to consider the issue) has held that the congregations cannot partake of the church's tax exemption (Stephenson v. Comm'r, 79 T.C. 995 (1982), aff'd, 748 F.2d 331 (6th Cir. 1984); Murphy v. Comm'r, 45 T.C.M. 621 (1983); Riemers v. Comm'r, 42 T.C.M. 838 (1981)).

[341] The IRS will not issue a determination letter in response to a request from an organization currently recognized as exempt (other than a government entity) to relinquish its tax-exempt status (Rev. Proc. 2024-5, 2024-1 I.R.B. 262 § 3.02(9)). In Priv. Ltr. Rul. 9141050, the IRS informed an organization requesting termination of its tax-exempt status that the IRS lacked the authority to terminate the exemption, adding that because it had filed an application for recognition of exemption, "you surrendered yourself to the rules and regulations governing tax exempt organizations."

[342] See § 4.3(b). There may, however, be some state law complexities in doing this.

[343] See Chapter 20.

[344] See § 20.13.

[345] See Chapter 22.

[346] See Chapter 23.

[347] See § 4.9. Again, there may be state law barriers to one or more of these undertakings. Also, even if the forfeiture of tax exemption is successful, there may be excise taxation, such as for impermissible expenditures for lobbying (see §§ 22.3(d)(iii), 22.4) or for expenditures for political campaign activity (see § 23.3).

their exemptions by transgressing one or more of the applicable operational requirements.[348]

Where an exempt organization engages in activities inconsistent with its exempt status, however, the IRS may not accept the organization's own determination that it no longer qualifies for exempt status. In one instance, a social club received most of its income from nonmember sources, thereby failing the gross receipts test.[349] Recognizing that it no longer qualified for exemption, it began filing corporate tax returns. The IRS rejected these tax returns, however, and informed the club that it was required to continue filing Forms 990 as a tax-exempt organization. The situation was rectified only when the IRS subsequently revoked the club's exempt status.[350]

The IRS ruled that a tax-exempt cooperative[351] may "surrender" its exemption (to enable it to seek financing otherwise unavailable) and operate as a taxable entity simply by filing a final return.[352] The IRS wrote that an organization "that no longer wants to be exempt under section 501(a) of the Code will need to file a final return," and, "[o]nce the final return is filed, the organization will no longer be described under section 501(a)."[353] This view is obviously in conflict with the IRS's prior position.[354] The return rule is triggered only when an exempt organization liquidates, dissolves, terminates, or substantially contracts; it is not a pathway to forfeiture of exemption.[355] This latter ruling does not indicate whether the cooperative filed an application for recognition of exemption and received a determination letter or ruling. This ruling may be unique to exempt cooperatives (which can annually drift in and out of exempt status),[356] represent a change in IRS policy, or be erroneous.

The IRS will, however, issue a determination letter to a dual-status governmental entity [357] that requests to voluntarily terminate its status as a charitable organization.[358] Organizations have this dual status because it was needed (years ago) to participate in qualified retirement plans, is needed in support of issuance

---

[348] The IRS developed an online search tool that allows users to check on the federal tax law status of exempt organizations; it is called Tax Exempt Organizations Search. Searches may be made of organizations that are eligible to receive tax-deductible charitable contributions, organizations that have had their exempt status automatically revoked for lack of filings or submissions (see § 28.4), and organizations that have electronically submitted an annual notice (see § 28.3).

[349] See § 15.2.

[350] Priv. Ltr. Rul. 202150024.

[351] See § 19.5(b).

[352] This return is the subject of IRC § 6043(b).

[353] Priv. Ltr. Rul. 201123035.

[354] See text accompanied by *supra* note 341.

[355] Where an organization disposes of all of its assets and ceases to conduct exempt activities but does not file articles of dissolution with the state in which it is formed, the IRS has taken the position that "the only way to terminate an organization's tax-exempt status with the IRS is for the IRS to propose the revocation of that status" (Priv. Ltr. Rul. 202149024).

[356] Rev. Rul. 65-99, 1965-1 C.B. 242.

[357] A dual-status governmental entity is an entity that is tax-exempt by reason of its governmental status (see § 19.22) that has also been recognized by the IRS as an organization that is exempt by reason of IRC § 501(a) because it is described in IRC § 501(c)(3).

[358] Rev. Proc. 2024-5, 2024-1 I.R.B. 262 § 3.01(12).

of certain types of bonds, or was thought to be needed to make it clear to potential donors that contributions to them are deductible. In some instances, however, the tax exemption of a governmental institution as a charitable entity causes regulatory burdens that would be inapplicable if the institution were exempt solely as a governmental entity. For example, a dual-status hospital must comply with a variety of federal tax law requirements[359] that do not apply to a hospital that is exempt solely as a governmental organization. To secure a determination letter involving this type of relinquishment of exemption, the entity must submit documentation as to its governmental status.[360]

§ 26.17 CONSTITUTIONAL LAW ASPECTS OF PROCESS

As is the case with all federal government procedures, the process by which a nonprofit organization seeks recognition of tax-exempt status is required to comport with constitutional law principles. In general, the principles usually implicated in this context are free speech, equal protection, and due process. For example, the notion that the IRS can determine whether an undertaking is *educational* is fraught with the potential for violation of free speech principles.[361]

Constitutional law principles may arise is more discrete areas. As illustrations, constitutional law questions can arise in connection with the operations of churches and other religious organizations[362] and entities such as associations, clubs, and fraternal groups.[363]

Considerable litigation resulted from allegations that employees of the IRS acted in a discriminatory fashion, on the basis of organizations' political stances, in processing applications for recognition of exemption. This litigation was based on assertions that the IRS used inappropriate criteria in this regard, with an appellate court referencing an "unequal treatment" of "victim" applicant organizations by the IRS, the agency's "unconstitutional acts," and the IRS's "discriminatory processing" of applications.[364]

Following this appellate court decision, on remand, the district court signed a consent order, containing a declaratory judgment stating that (1) "it is wrong to apply the United States tax laws ... to any tax-exempt application or entity based solely on such entity's name, any lawful positions it espouses on any issues, or its

---

[359] See § 7.6(b).

[360] That is, the entity must prove that it has a basis for exemption other than pursuant to IRC § 501(a). A request for this type of determination letter request is made by filing Form 8940. See § 28.1(d)).

[361] See § 8.2.

[362] See § 10.1.

[363] See § 4.8.

[364] True the Vote, Inc. v. Internal Revenue Serv., 831 F.3d 551, 559 (D.C. Cir. 2016), *cert. denied*, 137 S. Ct. 1068 (2017). Similarly, United States v. NorCal Tea Party Patriots, 817 F.3d 953 (6th Cir. 2016). Settlement of the *NorCal Tea Party Patriots* case was approved on August 8, 2018, with the court distributing one-half of a $3.5 million settlement fund to over 400 organizations (NorCal Tea Party Patriots v. Internal Revenue Service, Case No. 1:13cv341 (S.D. Ohio 2018)); the court quoted an earlier decision, which stated that "[a]mong the most serious allegations a federal court can address are that an Executive agency has targeted citizens for mistreatment based on their political views" (NorCal Tea Party, *supra*, 817 F.3d at 955).

associations or perceived associations with a particular political movement, position or viewpoint"; (2) "any action or inaction taken by the IRS must be applied evenhandedly and not based solely on a tax-exempt applicant or entity's name, political viewpoint, or associations or perceived associations with a political movement, position, or viewpoint"; and (3) "discrimination on the basis of political viewpoint in administering the United States tax code violates fundamental First Amendment rights."[365]

Therefore, this court ordered payment of lawyers' fees to the organization. Moreover, the court ruled that the IRS's pre-litigation conduct rose to a level of "bad faith sufficient to justify" an award of fees above the Equal Access to Justice Act's cap on fees.[366] The court found that the IRS defendants "were confronted with a clear judicially imposed duty not to engage in viewpoint discrimination as required by the First Amendment."[367] The organization was held entitled to an award of lawyers' fees calculated at prevailing market rates pursuant to this "bad faith enhancement."[368]

Similarly, a nonprofit organization asserted that the Obama administration had a special policy pertaining to applicant organizations that are concerned with Israel and have policies inconsistent with that of the administration; a lawsuit was filed, asserting that this policy constitutes viewpoint discrimination in violation of the First Amendment, with the court seeming to agree.[369]

---

[365] This portion of the consent order is quoted in True the Vote, Inc. v. Internal Revenue Serv., 123 A.F.T.R. 2d 2019-2024 (D.D.C. 2019).

[366] Id.

[367] Id.

[368] Id. The court subsequently awarded attorneys' fees of $788,539.30 to the organization (True the Vote, Inc. v. Internal Revenue Serv., 132 A.F.T.R. 2d 2023-5666 (D.D.C. 2023)).

[369] Z Street, Inc. v. Koskinen, 44 F. Supp. 3d 48 (D.D.C. 2014). This decision was affirmed, with the appellate court stating that the appellee was not seeking to "restrain the assessment or collection of a tax, but rather to obtain relief from unconstitutional delay, the effects of which it is now suffering" (Z Street v. Koskinen, 791 F.3d 24, 32 (D.C. Cir. 2015)). Subsequently, in 2016, the IRS recognized Z Street's tax-exempt status.

CHAPTER TWENTY-SEVEN

Administrative and Litigation Procedures

A nonprofit organization may become adverse to the IRS, such as where its application for recognition of exemption is denied, its tax exemption is being revoked, or it is the subject of an IRS examination.

§ 27.1 ADMINISTRATIVE PROCEDURES WHERE RECOGNITION DENIED

The filing of an application for recognition of tax exemption with the IRS[1] may lead to denial of the requested recognition, resulting in an adverse determination letter. The procedures in this regard differ, depending on whether the adverse determination letter involves an issue that may receive consideration by the Independent Office of Appeals.[2]

(a) Requests Receiving IRS Appeals Consideration

The following types of determination letter requests will provide an organization with an opportunity to protest/appeal a proposed adverse determination: (1) the initial qualification of the organization as a tax-exempt entity,[3] (2) the initial qualification of the organization as a charitable entity,[4] (3) the classification or reclassification of the organization as a public charity or a private foundation, including classification or reclassification of a non-exempt charitable trust as a supporting organization,[5] or (4) the classification of the organization as a private operating foundation.[6]

If EO Determinations[7] concludes that the organization does not satisfy the requirements for a favorable determination letter and the letter is a type for which an opportunity for protest/appear is available, the IRS will issue a proposed adverse determination letter. This letter will include a detailed discussion of the basis for the IRS's conclusion and advise the organization of its opportunity to protest/appeal the decision and request a conference.[8]

To protest/appeal a proposed adverse determination letter, the organization must submit a statement of the facts, law, and arguments in support of its position within 30 days from the date of the proposed adverse determination letter. The organization must also state whether it wishes conference with the Independent Office of Appeals.[9] If an organization does not timely submit a protest/appeal, a final adverse determination letter will be issued to the organization. This letter

---

[1] See § 26.1.

[2] Rev. Proc. 2024-5, 2024-1 I.R.B. 262 § 9.01.

[3] That is, an organization exempt from tax by reason of IRC § 501(a) or 521.

[4] That is, an organization described in IRC § 170(c)(2).

[5] See § 12.3(c).

[6] See § 12.1(b). As to *supra* notes 3–6, Rev. Proc. 2024-5, 2024-1 I.R.B. 262 § 9.02. IRS procedures previously provided that an organization could not administratively appeal an adverse determination letter issued that was based on technical advice. The IRS changed these procedures in 2014 to allow organizations to appeal an adverse determination based on technical advice if it fell within one of the four types of determinations described in the text accompanied by *supra* notes 3–6. As part of the Protecting Americans from Tax Hikes Act of 2015 (Pub. L. No. 114-113, div. Q, tit. IV, § 404, 129 Stat. 2242, 3118), Congress enacted IRC § 7123(c), which effectively codified this change by requiring the IRS to provide procedures under which an organization may request an administrative appeal of these four types of adverse determinations (Staff of Joint Comm. on Tax'n, 114th Cong., General Explanation of Tax Legislation Enacted in 2015 324–25 (Comm. Print 2016)).

[7] See § 26.1(a).

[8] Rev. Proc. 2024-5, 2024-1 I.R.B. 262 § 9.03.

[9] *Id.* § 9.04.

will provide information about the disclosure of the proposed and final adverse letters.[10]

If an organization submits a protest/appeal of a proposed adverse determination letter that is one of the foregoing four types, EO Determinations will review the protest. If it determines that the organization meets the requirements for approval of its request, it will issue a favorable determination letter. If, however, EO Determinations maintains its adverse position after reviewing the protest, it will forward the case file to Appeals. If new information is raised in the protest, EO Determinations will follow the procedure described below,[11] which may require issuance of a new proposed denial, prior to sending the case to Appeals.[12]

The Independent Office of Appeals will consider the organization's protest/appeal submitted in response to a proposed adverse determination letter. If the Independent Office of Appeals agrees with the proposed adverse determination, it will issue a final adverse determination or, if a conference was requested, contact the organization to schedule the conference. At the end of the conference process, which may entail submission of additional information, the Independent Office of Appeals will generally issue a final adverse determination letter or a favorable determination letter. If the Independent Office of Appeals believes that a tax exemption or public charity issue is not covered by published precedent or that there is nonuniformity, the Independent Office of Appeals must request technical advice from the Office of Associate Chief Counsel (Employee Benefits, Exempt Organizations, and Employment Taxes).[13]

If the organization submits new information as part of a protest or during Appeals consideration, the matter may be returned to EO Determinations for further consideration. As a result of its review of the new information, EO Determinations may issue a favorable determination letter, rebuttal letter, or new proposed adverse determination letter. If a rebuttal letter is issued, EO Determinations will forward the case to the Independent Office of Appeals. If a new proposed adverse determination letter is issued, the organization must submit a protest/appeal of the new proposed adverse determination letter in order to have the Independent Office of Appeals consider the issue.[14]

An organization may withdraw its protest/appeal before the IRS issues a final adverse determination letter. On receipt of a withdrawal request, the IRS will complete processing of the case in the same manner as if an appeal or protest had not been received. An organization that withdraws a protest/appeal is not considered to have exhausted its administrative remedies for declaratory judgment purposes.[15]

The opportunity to appeal a proposed adverse determination letter and the conference rights are inapplicable to matters where delay would be "prejudicial to the interests" of the IRS, such as in cases involving fraud, jeopardy, or imminence

---

[10] Id. §§ 9.05, 13.04.
[11] See text accompanied by *infra* note 14.
[12] Rev. Proc. 2024-5, 2024-1 I.R.B. 262 § 9.06.
[13] Id. § 9.07. As to the matter of technical advice, see Rev. Proc. 2024-2, 2024-1 I.R.B. 119.
[14] Rev. Proc. 2024-5, 2024-1 I.R.B. 262 § 9.08.
[15] Id. § 9.09. The declaratory judgment procedure rules are the subject of § 27.5(c).

of expiration of the statute of limitations, or where immediate action is necessary to protect the interests of the federal government.[16]

(b)   Matters Not Receiving IRS Appeals Consideration

If EO Determinations concludes that an organization does not meet the requirements for a favorable determination on an issue that is not one of the four types referenced earlier,[17] the IRS generally will advise the organization of its adverse position and afford the organization the opportunity to submit additional information or withdraw the request before issuing an adverse determination letter, which is to include a detailed discussion of the basis for the IRS's conclusion. The organization is precluded from protesting/appealing this adverse determination letter.[18]

§ 27.2 REVOCATION OR MODIFICATION OF TAX-EXEMPT STATUS: ADMINISTRATIVE PROCEDURES

A determination letter recognizing tax exemption may be revoked or modified by a notice sent to the organization involved, enactment of legislation, ratification of a tax treaty, a decision of the U.S. Supreme Court, or issuance of temporary or final regulations; it may also be revoked or modified by issuance of a revenue ruling, revenue procedure, or other statement published in the *Internal Revenue Bulletin*, or automatically for failure to file a required annual information return or submit a notice for three consecutive years.[19] If an organization no longer qualifies under the legal category pursuant to which it originally applied for recognition of tax-exempt status, the determination letter will be revoked rather than modified.[20]

In the case of a revocation or modification of a determination letter, the appeal and conference procedures generally are the same as those followed in connection with proposed denials of recognition of exemption. Consideration by the Independent Office of Appeals is not available, however, where an organization's exemption is revoked automatically for failure to file an annual return or notice for three consecutive years.[21]

Once the IRS has acted to revoke recognition of the tax exemption of an organization, it may expect the entity to begin paying income taxes with respect to

---

[16] Rev. Proc. 2024-5, 2024-1 I.R.B. 262 § 9.10.

[17] See text accompanied by *supra* notes 3–6. Examples of other issues not included in these four types of determinations are advance approval that a grant is an unusual grant, exemption from annual information return filing requirements, and advance approval of private foundation scholarship procedures (see § 28.1(d)).

[18] Rev. Proc. 2024-5, 2024-1 I.R.B. 262 § 9.11.

[19] *Id.* § 12.01. As to automatic revocation of tax-exempt status for failure to file a required return or notice for three years, see § 28.4.

[20] Rev. Proc. 2024-5, 2024-1 I.R.B. 262 § 12.01.

[21] *Id.* § 12.02.

tax years as to which a statute of limitations has not run.[22] Should the organization not do so, however, the IRS may be expected to commence proceedings to assess and collect the tax due. This activity is begun by the mailing to the organization of a statutory notice of deficiency. The IRS is authorized to do so following a determination that there is a tax deficiency.[23] Because there cannot be general income tax liability for an exempt organization, however, the statutory notice of deficiency must be preceded by a valid letter of revocation for the government to collect the tax. To be valid, the IRS must at least generally apprise the organization of the basis for the revocation.

The revocation itself must be in conformity with all requirements of law, because if, for example, the grounds upon which the revocation is based were erroneous, the revocation is not proper.[24] Likewise, if the letter of revocation was prompted by political or similar considerations that demonstrate lack of objectivity by the IRS, the revocation becomes null and void.[25] Thus, a letter of revocation can be shown to be void *ab initio* because of the considerations governing its issuance. Also, subsequent actions by the IRS indicating a continuing recognition of exempt status can operate to make a prior revocation of recognition nugatory. In either event, the letter of revocation is not valid, so that the exemption has not been properly revoked; meaning that any notice of deficiency based upon the letter of revocation is of no force and effect.[26]

Other procedures have been promulgated for appeals from the attempted imposition of certain taxes on most tax-exempt organizations and on certain individuals under the private foundation rules. These taxes are the excise taxes imposed by the federal tax law pertaining to private foundations,[27] the unrelated business income tax,[28] the private foundation termination tax,[29] the political activities tax,[30] and the tax[31] on charitable and split-interest trusts.[32]

---

[22] See, e.g., §§ 27.3 (concerning the tax consequences of retroactive revocation of tax-exempt status of public charities) and § 27.4 (concerning statute of limitations matters). Usually, when an organization's exemption is revoked, it becomes a taxable nonprofit organization, liable for the regular federal income tax imposed on corporations. When the tax exemption of a social club (see Chapter 15) was revoked, however, the issue arose as to whether the club should be treated as a personal holding company. One of the tests for a personal holding company is that, at any time during the last half of the tax year, more than 50 percent in value of its stock is owned by or for no more than five individuals (IRC § 542(a)). The IRS treated the club's members as shareholders for this purpose, found that the stock ownership test was met, and held that the club, as a nonexempt entity, was a personal holding company (Tech. Adv. Mem. 9728004). The result was that the club became liable not only for the regular corporate income tax, but also for a tax of 39.6 percent of the club's undistributed personal holding company income.

[23] IRC § 6212.

[24] A. Duda & Sons Coop. Ass'n v. United States, 504 F.2d 970, 975 (5th Cir. 1974).

[25] Center on Corporate Responsibility, Inc. v. Schultz, 368 F. Supp. 863, 871–73 (D.D.C. 1973).

[26] Cf. Church of Scientology of Calif. v. Comm'r, 83 T.C. 381 (1984), *aff'd*, 823 F.2d 1310 (9th Cir. 1987).

[27] See § 12.4.

[28] See Chapters 24, 25.

[29] See § 12.4.

[30] See § 23.4.

[31] IRC § 641.

[32] IRC § 4947.

§ 27.3 RETROACTIVE REVOCATION OF TAX-EXEMPT STATUS

(a) Administrative Procedures

The IRS has the authority to retroactively revoke a determination letter as to an organization's tax-exempt status.[33] An exemption determination letter may be retroactively revoked or modified if there has been a change in the applicable law, the organization omitted or misstated material information, or operated in a manner materially different from that originally represented.[34]

Where there is a material change in the character, the purpose, or the method of operation of the organization (a *material change in facts*) inconsistent with the conclusion of a determination letter, revocation or modification will ordinarily take effect as of the date of the change.[35] For example, an organization that was recognized as an exempt charitable entity in 1947, and engaged in private inurement transactions[36] the next year, had its exemption revoked in 1954, with the revocation retroactive to 1948.[37] Where the organization omitted or misstated material information in a request, revocation or modification will be effective as of the effective date of the determination letter issued in response to the request.[38]

Revocation of tax exemption may be retroactive to the date of the organization's inception. Thus, the exempt status of a supporting organization[39] was so revoked where several loans, made on terms that an independent lender would not agree to, were made to the donor, and grants to the supported organization were made, accompanied by the donor's "wish" to use funds for her private purposes, to which the supported organization always acceded.[40] Likewise, such a revocation occurred where the individuals who formed the organization agreed with the IRS that the arrangement constituted an "abusive trust" and a "sham."[41] Similarly, the exempt status of a supporting organization was so revoked due to material misstatements in the application for recognition of exemption, tax avoidance, and prohibited transactions, such as noncollateralized, interest-only loans to donors, and use of grant funds to pay the tuition of the donors' children and to satisfy their tithing obligations.[42]

---

[33] IRC § 7805(b)(8); Reg. § 301.7805-1(b). The U.S. Tax Court declared that "[r]etroactive revocation [of tax exemption] is not just a slap on the wrist; it has real tax consequences" (Creditguard of America, Inc. v. Comm'r, 149 T.C. 370 (2017)).

[34] Reg. § 601.201(n)(6)(i); Rev. Proc. 2024-5, 2024-1 I.R.B. 262 § 12.03. In the case of a supplemental unemployment benefit trust (see § 18.4) or a veterans' organization (see § 19.11(a)), an exemption determination letter also may be retroactively revoked or modified if the organization engaged in a prohibited transaction (as defined in IRC § 503) for the purpose of diverting a substantial part of an organization's corpus or income from its exempt purpose (Reg. § 601.201(n)(6)(vii); Rev. Proc. 2024-5, 2024-1 I.R.B. 262 § 12.03(4)).

[35] Rev. Proc. 2024-5, 2024-1 I.R.B. 262 §§ 11.02(2), 12.05(2). Also, Rev. Rul. 58-617, 1958-2 C.B. 260.

[36] See Chapter 20.

[37] Stevens Bros. Found., Inc. v. Comm'r, 324 F.2d 633 (8th Cir. 1963), *cert. denied*, 376 U.S. 969 (1964).

[38] Rev. Proc. 2024-5, 2024-1 I.R.B. 262 § 12.05(1).

[39] See § 12.3(c).

[40] Priv. Ltr. Rul. 200752043.

[41] Priv. Ltr. Rul. 200810025.

[42] Priv. Ltr. Rul. 200844022. In one of these instances, having found that an organization omitted or misstated material facts and has been operating in a manner materially different from that originally represented, thus justifying retroactive revocation of exemption, the IRS observed that the organization "has not turned square corners in dealing with the Federal government" (Priv. Ltr. Rul. 201543019).

A fourth way in which an exemption ruling may be retroactively revoked arises when there is a change in or clarification of the pertinent law, and the tax-exempt organization was provided formal notice of the change. For example, a farmers' cooperative[43] whose exemption was recognized in 1958 had its exemption revoked in 1978; the revocation was effective as of 1974, because the organization was accorded notice of a law change (by publication of a revenue ruling) in 1973.[44]

In another of these instances, an organization was recognized as a tax-exempt school[45] in 1959. In 1970, when the IRS's rules prohibiting exempt schools from maintaining racially discriminatory policies were introduced,[46] the agency notified the school of its concern that the school was engaging in racially discriminatory practices. The IRS commenced the process of revoking the school's exemption in 1976; this culminated in loss of the organization's exemption by court order. When the IRS endeavored to revoke the school's exempt status effective as of 1959, the court upheld retroactive revocation of this exemption but only as of 1970, the year the agency expressly provided the organization with notice of the law change.[47] In a comparable case, an educational organization was recognized by the IRS as an exempt entity in 1961 and had its exemption revoked in 1977 for funding racially discriminatory schools; the revocation was made effective as of 1974, with notice having been given by the agency in 1972.[48]

Thus, the IRS has the discretion as to whether to revoke an organization's tax-exempt status prospectively or retroactively. This discretion is broad, reviewable by the courts only for its abuse.[49] For example, an organization that was recognized in 1936 as an exempt religious organization engaging in missionary activities faced revocation of exemption in 1976 on the ground that these activities had ceased in 1963 and were replaced by commercial publishing operations; a court concluded that the IRS did not abuse its discretion in revoking this exemption, retroactive to 1963.[50] In another case, a religious publishing company was recognized as exempt in 1939; in 1980, the IRS proposed retroactive revocation of the exemption to 1969 on the ground that the organization started operating in a commercial manner[51] in that year. A court agreed with the IRS as to revocation of exemption but held that the agency abused its discretion in making the revocation effective as of 1969, ruling that retroactivity of the exemption should occur as of 1975.[52]

---

[43] See § 19.12.

[44] West Central Coop. v. United States, 758 F.2d 1269 (8th Cir. 1985).

[45] See § 8.3(a).

[46] See § 6.2(b)(ii).

[47] Prince Edward School Found. v. United States, 478 F. Supp. 107 (D.D.C. 1979), *aff'd without published opinion* (D.C. Cir. 1980), *cert. denied*, 450 U.S. 944 (1981).

[48] Virginia Educ. Fund v. Comm'r, 85 T.C. 743 (1985), *aff'd*, 799 F.2d 903 (4th Cir. 1986). Thereafter, an estate tax charitable contribution deduction was denied for a gift to this organization (Estate of Clopton v. Comm'r, 93 T.C. 275 (1989)).

[49] Automobile Club of Mich. v. Comm'r, 353 U.S. 180 (1957). Also, Dixon v. United States, 381 U.S. 68 (1965).

[50] Incorporated Trustees of Gospel Worker Soc'y v. United States, 510 F. Supp. 374 (D.D.C. 1981), *aff'd*, 672 F.2d 894 (D.C. Cir. 1981), *cert. denied*, 456 U.S. 944 (1982).

[51] See § 4.9.

[52] Presbyterian & Reformed Publishing Co. v. Comm'r, 79 T.C. 1070 (1982). An appellate court concluded that this organization was engaged in exempt activities, however, thereby voiding this revocation of exempt status (743 F.2d 148 (3d Cir. 1984)).

In other cases on the point, a court upheld revocation in 2010 of exemption recognized in 2000, retroactive to 2000;[53] a court upheld revocation in 1982 of tax exemption recognized in 1979, retroactive to 1978;[54] a court upheld revocation in 1990 of exemption recognized in 1969, retroactive to 1984;[55] a court upheld revocation in 1952 of exemption recognized in 1946, retroactive to 1946;[56] and a court upheld revocation in 1956 of exemption recognized in 1948, retroactive to 1948.[57] The IRS, from time to time, issues technical advice memoranda reflecting revocations of this nature.[58]

In one of two principal cases the IRS lost in this regard, the "bounds of permissible discretion were exceeded" by the IRS when the agency attempted to retroactively revoke, in 1951, recognition of tax exemption it had issued in 1945.[59] The facts had not changed during the period involved, the organization adequately disclosed on its annual information returns the facts that prompted the attempted revocation of exemption, there were no misrepresentations of fact or fraud, and the proposed assessment of tax was "so large as to wipe [the organization] out of existence."[60] The court stated that it "realize[d] that the Commissioner may change his mind when he believes he has made a mistake in a matter of fact or law."[61] This court continued: "But it is quite a different matter to say that having once changed his mind the Commissioner may arbitrarily and without limit have the effect of that change go back over previous years during which the taxpayer operated under the previous ruling." The court refused to sustain this proposed "harsh result,"[62] thereby precluding this retroactive revocation of exemption.

In the second case, a court ruled that the IRS abused its discretion in retroactively revoking the tax-exempt status of an organization that, over the years, engaged in activities that were materially similar to those stated in its application for recognition of exemption.[63] The IRS, in 2002, attempted to revoke the exempt status of the organization, formed in 1985, for its years 1997–1999. The court found that this organization did not omit or misstate a material fact or operate in a manner materially different in the three years at issue from that originally represented. Thus, the court concluded that, once the IRS made its determination as to this entity's

---

[53] Partners In Charity, Inc. v. Comm'r, 141 T.C. 151 (2013).

[54] Freedom Church of Revelation v. United States, 588 F. Supp. 693 (D.D.C. 1984).

[55] United Cancer Council, Inc. v. Comm'r, 109 T.C. 326 (1997), rev'd and remanded, 165 F.3d 1173 (7th Cir. 1999).

[56] Birmingham Business College, Inc. v. Comm'r, 276 F.2d 476 (5th Cir. 1960), aff'g, modifying and remanding 17 T.C.M. 816 (1958) (revocation due to material misrepresentations in the organization's application for recognition of exemption). Likewise, Variety Club Tent No. 6 Charities, Inc. v. Comm'r, 74 T.C.M. 1485 (1997).

[57] Cleveland Chiropractic College v. Comm'r, 312 F.2d 203 (8th Cir. 1963), aff'g 21 T.C.M. 1 (1962) (consistent private inurement throughout the period).

[58] E.g., Tech. Adv. Mem. 201318034.

[59] Lesavoy Found. v. Comm'r, 238 F.2d 589, 594 (3d Cir. 1956), rev'g 25 T.C. 924 (1956).

[60] Id., 238 F.2d at 594.

[61] Id. at 591.

[62] Id. at 594.

[63] Democratic Leadership Council, Inc. v. United States, 542 F. Supp. 2d 63 (D.D.C. 2008).

exemption, the agency was bound to follow it (without retroactivity) as long as the organization continued to operate in the manner originally propounded to the IRS.

An organization may seek relief from retroactive revocation or modification of a determination letter.[64] A request for relief must be submitted, in writing, to the IRS agent or specialist assigned to the case. An organization's request to limit the retroactive effect of the revocation or modification of the determination letter must state the relief being sought, explain the reasons and arguments in support of the relief sought, and include any documents relevant to the request.[65]

Where the IRS erroneously grants tax-exempt status to an organization that does not in fact meet the requirements for that status, and there has been no change in the applicable law and the organization did not omit or misstate any material information in its application for exemption, the IRS is likely to grant this relief.[66]

If the request for this relief is denied, the organization will be notified in writing of the denial.[67] If a determination letter was issued in error or is no longer in accord with the IRS's position, and this relief is granted, ordinarily the revocation or modification of the letter will be effective not earlier than the date on which the IRS modifies or revokes the original determination letter.[68]

In one instance where the IRS retroactively revoked a charitable organization's exempt status, it contended that, as a taxable entity, the organization must "relinquish all assets" and transfer them to an "eligible" charitable entity.[69] While, as a state law matter, this may be required by a dissolution clause in the organization's formation document, the IRS does not have the authority to compel such a result merely because an organization loses its exempt status and becomes taxable.[70]

(b)   Consequences of Retroactive Revocation of Exempt Status

Numerous federal tax consequences can flow from the revocation of the tax-exempt status of an organization that is not a private foundation where the revocation is retroactive.[71] As noted,[72] revocation of the exemption of an organization is made retroactive if the organization omitted or misstated a material fact in seeking recognition of exemption or operated in a manner materially different from that originally represented. Where revocation is retroactive, charitable contribution

---

[64] IRC § 7805(b)(8).

[65] Rev. Proc. 2024-5, 2024-1 I.R.B. 262 § 12.04(1).

[66] E.g., Priv. Ltr. Rul. 202221008. The doctrine of equitable estoppel, however, does not prevent the IRS from retroactively revoking exempt status to correct a mistake of law (Korean-American Senior Mut. Ass'n, Inc. v. Comm'r, T.C. Memo. 2020-129).

[67] Rev. Proc. 2024-5, 2024-1 I.R.B. 262 § 12.04(2).

[68] *Id.* § 12.05(3).

[69] Priv. Ltr. Rul. 202240026.

[70] See § 32.6(b).

[71] Many of these considerations are also applicable with respect to private foundations. In those situations, however, rules pertaining to the termination of private foundation status may be applicable, including the imposition of a termination tax (IRC § 507; see *Private Foundations* § 13.7).

[72] See § 27.3(a).

deductions generally are protected until public announcement of the revocation of charitable donee status; however, the IRS may disallow a contribution deduction where the donor knew of actual or imminent revocation or was responsible for or aware of the activities that gave rise to the revocation.[73]

Generally, a public charity that has its tax-exempt status retroactively revoked will be treated as a corporation for tax purposes.[74] Some organizations, however, are established as charitable trusts. In addition, the corporate form may be disregarded and the tax liabilities passed through to another entity where the revoked corporation is in substance a sham that should be disregarded as the "alter ego" of a controlling individual or group,[75] or where the corporation is functioning as an agent with respect to contributed funds.[76]

(i) Tax Treatment: Corporations. When a tax-exempt organization loses its exempt status, it becomes a taxable entity, generally in accordance with the federal tax law applicable with respect to for-profit organizations.

When a revoked charitable organization is engaged in tax-exempt activities, in nonprofit, nonexempt (for example, political) activities, and/or in for-profit activities, the tax outcome is dependent on whether the income is business income, investment income, or contribution income.

As to income from a related or unrelated business, a revoked organization would have gross income to the extent of receipts from trade or business activity, offset by deductions for related expenses.[77] Investment income, net of related expenses, would be taxable, including passive income that generally is excluded from taxation when received by a tax-exempt organization.[78]

The law on this point is more complicated where the receipts are voluntary contributions intended, by the donor or donors, to further the organization's stated tax-exempt purposes.

Generally, donated funds and the value of donated property are not considered items of income to the recipient organization.[79] For this purpose, a gift is a payment where the donor does not receive something of equivalent value in return. Thus, the U.S. Supreme Court wrote that a "payment of money [or transfer of property] generally cannot constitute a charitable contribution if the contributor expects a substantial benefit in return."[80] Essentially, the same rule was subsequently articulated by the Court, when it ruled that an exchange having an "inherently reciprocal nature" is not a gift and thus cannot be a charitable gift, where the recipient is a charity.[81] An earlier Supreme Court opinion stated that a

---

[73] Rev. Proc. 2018-32, 2018-23 I.R.B. 739 § 4.04. In the context of declaratory judgment litigation, contributions not exceeding $1,000 are deductible after notice of revocation and during the pendency of the litigation (see § 27.5(c)(iii)).

[74] IRC § 7701(a)(3).

[75] Generally, however, the corporate form is respected. See § 30.2.

[76] E.g., Comm'r v. Bollinger, 485 U.S. 340 (1988); National Carbide Corp. v. Comm'r, 336 U.S. 422 (1949).

[77] See § 25.7.

[78] See § 25.1(a).

[79] IRC § 102.

[80] United States v. American Bar Endowment, 477 U.S. 105, 116–17 (1986).

[81] Hernandez v. Comm'r, 490 U.S. 680, 692 (1989).

gift proceeds from a "detached and disinterested generosity" and is "out of affection, respect, admiration, charity or like impulses."[82]

Therefore, while an authentic gift to an organization is not income,[83] the IRS may contend that the payments are in fact gross income, such as where contributions are considered income to individuals associated with an organization rather than gifts to the organization,[84] or where the "contributions" are considered payments in exchange for a quid pro quo.[85] Another contention may be that the "contributions" are items of unrelated business income.[86]

It is the position of the IRS that contributions given in good faith are generally excludable by a revoked tax-exempt organization, as long as the organization also acted in good faith in soliciting the contributions.[87] It is also the view of the IRS that the intent of the donor is not determinative of the gift issue in instances of misrepresentation or fraud where "it is clear that from the outset an organization intentionally misrepresented in its solicitations that it was validly tax-exempt and would use all the donations for exempt purposes."[88] By contrast, it has been held that excludable gift treatment is not appropriate where the recipient organization, "misrepresenting itself to be a tax-exempt charity, seeks and obtains donations which it plans to, and does, use in carrying on business activities for profit and thereby enriches itself."[89] Thus, where the "misrepresentation exception" is applicable, contributions to the revoked exempt organization are not excludable gifts but are items of gross income. This exception will apply where the fraudulent acts and intentions are attributable to the organization,[90] as opposed to actions by individuals in their separate capacities.[91]

The determination as to this type of corporate-level responsibility is a matter of fact. Nonetheless, it is the view of the IRS's lawyers that "misrepresentation by an organization should be presumed to exist when the facts show that an organization soliciting contributions was engaged in a pattern of activities inconsistent with the basis for its exemption."[92] It is also their view that contributions are taxable pursuant to the misrepresentation exception when the organization's exemption is revoked for engaging in nonprofit, nonexempt (for example, political) activities, inasmuch as this type of activity does not "benefit" the organization.[93] Under

---

[82] Comm'r v. Duberstein, 363 U.S. 278, 285–86 (1960). See *Charitable Giving* § 2.1(a).

[83] E.g., Bail Fund of the Civil Rights Congress of N.Y. v. Comm'r, 26 T.C. 482 (1956).

[84] E.g., Webber v. Comm'r, 21 T.C. 742 (1954), *aff'd*, 219 F.2d 834 (10th Cir. 1955).

[85] E.g., Found. For Divine Meditation, Inc. v. Comm'r, 24 T.C.M. 411 (1965); Publishers New Press, Inc. v. Comm'r, 42 T.C. 396 (1964); Teleservice Co. of Wyoming Valley v. Comm'r, 27 TC. 722 (1957), *aff'd*, 254 F.2d 105 (3d Cir. 1958).

[86] E.g., Veterans of Foreign Wars, Dep't of Mich. v. Comm'r, 89 T.C. 7 (1987), *appeal dismissed*, (6th Cir. 1988).

[87] Gen. Couns. Mem. 39813.

[88] *Id.*

[89] Synanon Church v. Comm'r, 57 T.C.M. 602, 628 (1989). Also, Altman v. Comm'r, 475 F.2d 876 (2d Cir. 1973); Peters v. Comm'r, 51 T.C. 226 (1968); Zips v. Comm'r, 38 T.C. 620 (1962), *appeal dismissed* (5th Cir. 1963).

[90] E.g., Asphalt Indus., Inc. v. Comm'r, 384 F.2d 229 (3d Cir. 1967).

[91] E.g., Sherin v. Comm'r, 13 T.C. 221 (1949).

[92] Gen. Couns. Mem. 39813.

[93] *Id.*

these views, however, the misrepresentation rationale does not extend to situations where contributions initially obtained through "sincere representations" are diverted to noncharitable uses.[94]

Some "contributions" will not be regarded as gifts but as contributions to the capital of the corporation involved.[95] Contributions to capital, whether by a shareholder or by a nonshareholder, are not includable in the recipient's gross income.[96] It is unlikely, however, that contributions to a revoked exempt organization would qualify as contributions to capital. Should a contribution potentially so qualify, the contribution would usually be by a "nonshareholder"; even then, the contribution probably would not be a contribution to capital, if only because the contribution would not have become a permanent part of the recipient's working capital structure.[97]

If contributions are included in the gross income of a revoked organization, the organization's tax would depend on its ability to offset expenditures against that income. Where the expenditures (including an allocable portion of fundraising costs) were for exempt purposes, a deduction will be allowed to the extent of income from the related activity.[98] Charitable expenditures that are attributable to income from other sources (such as business or investment income) would be subject to other income tax restrictions.[99] If the expenditures represent reasonable compensation for services, the expenditures would be deductible; however, amounts in excess of reasonable compensation for services, or otherwise found not to have been intended as compensation for services, would not be deductible.[100] Amounts for expenditures by public charities that are specifically disallowed by federal tax law (such as political campaign expenses[101] or substantial lobbying expenses)[102] would not be deductible. Most expenditures for illegal activities could not be offset against contribution income.

In addition to income tax consequences, there may be excise tax consequences when the tax-exempt status of a public charity is retroactively revoked. For example, where the exempt status is revoked due to excessive lobbying, an excise tax is

---

[94] *Id.* An alternative approach that would bypass the IRC § 102 issue rests on the principle that funds or assets received by persons acting under the control and for the benefit of others are not includable in the gross income of the initial recipients under the "conduit" doctrine. See §§ 29.2(c), 29.6.

[95] E.g., Veterans Found. v. Comm'r, 38 T.C. 66 (1962), *aff'd*, 317 F.2d 456 (10th Cir. 1963).

[96] IRC § 118.

[97] The characteristics of nonshareholder contributions to capital are analyzed in United States v. Chicago, Burlington & Quincy R.R., 412 U.S. 401 (1973). Another consequence of this classification is that a gift accords the donee the donor's basis in the property (carryover basis) (IRC § 1015), while a contribution to capital results in zero basis to the recipient (IRC § 362(c)). Also, generally, the basis of an asset acquired or held in periods during which the organization was exempt from income tax would be the original cost or other basis of the asset, reduced by depreciation (IRC § 1016(a)(3)(B); Reg. § 1.1016-4; Polish Am. Club, Inc. v. Comm'r, 33 T.C.M. 925, 931–32 (1974)). As to capital contributions in the context of the social club rules, see § 15.2.

[98] Gen. Couns. Mem. 39813.

[99] IRC § 162 (business expense deduction) and/or IRC § 170 (charitable contribution deduction).

[100] E.g., Kenner v. Comm'r, 33 T.C.M. 1239 (1974); Synanon Church v. Comm'r, 57 T.C.M. 602, 633–35 (1989).

[101] See Chapter 23.

[102] See Chapter 22.

applicable to the organization,[103] as is the case when the revocation occurs because the organization participated in political campaign activities.[104]

(ii) Tax Treatment: Individuals.   If a purported organization is no more than a sham or "alter ego" of an individual, on the retroactive revocation of the tax exemption of the "organization" there would not be any tax at the organizational level. Should this occur, all income (including charitable contributions) and expenditures would be attributed to the individual.[105] This result would also occur should the "organization" be considered merely a conduit in relation to an individual.[106]

Where an organization is a separate entity and a principal of the organization obtains dominion and control over its funds (other than as a borrower or agent), the individual is taxable on the payment (unless it is a return of capital). Likewise, payments made by the organization to others, where made for the benefit of an individual, would constitute constructive payments includable in the individual's income. For these rules to apply, however, the payment must confer benefit (usually financial in nature) to the individual rather than to the corporation;[107] these rules do not apply simply because an individual has control over an organization's income and expenditures in their capacity as a director, officer, or employee. Thus, a "principal of a revoked exempt organization would not realize income merely by virtue of having authorized, or acquiesced in, a diversion of funds to nonexempt purposes, in the absence of a financial or economic benefit."[108]

Usually this type of payment (direct or constructive) to an individual is regarded as ordinary income in the nature of compensation for services provided. It is possible, however, for the payment to be taxed as capital gain (where made in return for property furnished to the organization) or as a dividend.[109] Nonetheless, there is authority for the conclusion that, when controlling persons divert corporate funds to their personal use, the persons are taxable in full on the amount involved without regard to the technicalities of dividend treatment.[110]

Principals of an organization that had its tax exemption revoked may be liable for the organization's taxes and/or penalties, to the extent that they obtained assets of the organization and are liable as transferees.[111] Also, courts have occasionally disregarded the corporate form to collect a corporate liability from a

[103] IRC § 4912. See § 22.4.
[104] IRC § 4955. See § 23.3.
[105] E.g., Universal Church of Jesus Christ, Inc. v. Comm'r, 55 T.C.M. 144 (1988); Sly v. Comm'r, 56 T.C.M. 209 (1988).
[106] See text accompanied by *supra* note 94.
[107] E.g., Knott v. Comm'r, 67 T.C. 681 (1977); Rev. Rul. 79-9, 1979-1 C.B. 125.
[108] Gen. Couns. Mem. 39813.
[109] As to dividend treatment, see, e.g., Sly v. Comm'r, 56 T.C.M. 209 (1988); Kenner v. Comm'r, 33 T.C.M. 1239 (1974); Grant v. Comm'r, 18 T.C.M. 601 (1959). Also, Stevens Bros. Found v. Comm'r, 324 F.2d 633 (8th Cir. 1963), *cert. denied*, 376 U.S. 969 (1964).
[110] Truesdell v. Comm'r, 89 T.C. 1280 (1987). Cf. Benes v. Comm'r, 42 T.C. 358 (1964), *aff'd*, 355 F.2d 929 (6th Cir. 1966), *cert. denied*, 384 U.S. 961 (1966); Weir v. Comm'r, 283 F.2d 675 (6th Cir. 1960); Davis v. United States, 226 F.2d 331 (6th Cir. 1955). Also, DiZenzo v. Comm'r, 348 F.2d 122 (2d Cir. 1965); Leaf v. Comm'r, 33 T.C. 1093 (1960), *aff'd*, 295 F.2d 503 (6th Cir. 1961); Simon v. Comm'r, 248 F.2d 869 (8th Cir. 1957).
[111] IRC § 6901. E.g., Wade v. Comm'r, 16 T.C.M. 308 (1957).

controlling individual, under an "alter ego" theory, even though the corporate entity was considered viable for purposes of imposing a corporate-level tax.[112]

Aside from income tax consequences, an individual who is a manager of a public charity that has its tax-exempt status retroactively revoked can be liable for an excise tax where the organization lost its exemption because of substantial lobbying[113] or political campaign activities.[114]

§ 27.4 STATUTE OF LIMITATIONS MATTERS

As noted, when an organization's tax-exempt status is revoked or forfeited, the organization becomes subject to taxation.[115] This exposure to income tax is usually as of the effective date of the loss of exemption. An organization in this position is, of course, expected to start filing tax returns. The filing of a tax return starts the running of the applicable statute of limitations. For a tax assessment to be valid, it must take place within the applicable statutory period.

The statute of limitations for assessment of income tax generally expires three years after the taxpayer files its return.[116] There are, however, several exceptions to this general rule. A commonly utilized one is that the taxpayer and the government may agree to an extension of the tax assessment period.[117] In certain instances, there is no limitations period as to a tax assessment, such as where there is a filing of a false or fraudulent return, a willful attempt to evade tax, or a failure to file a return.[118] A six-year statute of limitations applies where a taxpayer's return omits from gross income an amount in excess of 25 percent of the amount of gross income stated in the return.[119]

Organizations, while tax-exempt, do not file tax returns but rather file information returns.[120] Thus, the federal tax law contains a provision governing the statute of limitations in instances of exempt organizations that are subsequently determined to be taxable.[121] This provision states that "[i]f a taxpayer determines in good faith that it is an exempt organization and files a return as such . . . and

---

[112] E.g., Wolfe v. United States, 798 F.2d 1241, *amended by* 806 F.2d 1410 (9th Cir. 1986), *cert. denied*, 482 U.S. 927 (1987); Harris v. United States, 764 F.2d 1126 (5th Cir. 1985).
[113] IRC § 4912. See § 22.4.
[114] IRC § 4955. See § 23.3. An IRS analysis of this aspect of the law stated that the Internal Revenue Code "does not provide clear-cut answers to many of these questions," in that the "statutory scheme is oriented toward normal, profit-making corporations" (Gen. Couns. Mem. 39813). This analysis concluded: "If the treatment of revoked organizations continues to pose a problem, a legislative solution may be appropriate" (*id.*).
[115] See, §§ 27.2, 27.3.
[116] IRC § 6501(a).
[117] IRC § 6501(c)(4).
[118] IRC § 6501(c)(1)-(3). As to the latter, the filing of an unsigned return (see IRC § 6062) is not the filing of a valid return for purposes of commencing the running of a statute of limitations (e.g., Lucas v. Pilliod Lumber Co., 281 U.S. 245 (1930)). An example of application of this rule in the exempt organizations context is in Chapman Glen Limited v. Comm'r, 140 T.C. 294 (2013).
[119] IRC § 6501(e).
[120] IRC § 6033. See § 28.2.
[121] IRC § 6501(g)(2).

if such taxpayer is thereafter held to be a taxable organization for the taxable year for which the return is filed, such return shall be deemed the return of the organization" for purposes of applying the statute of limitations for assessment of income tax.[122]

Essential to this element of the law, from an exempt organizations' standpoint, is the *good-faith requirement*. The U.S. Tax Court held that the standard is whether an organization had, at the time the return was filed, a "good faith belief under the organization's own reasonable view of the law (which may differ from the Commissioner's view) that it is exempt."[123] A similar finding was subsequently made by the court, despite omissions of information from and misleading statements in the organization's information returns, with the court observing that "some of the information which the returns failed to disclose was available to the Commissioner from other sources."[124]

The IRS office of general counsel has addressed this matter. In one instance, the requisite good faith was found because the organization appropriately relied on a court decision (in which the IRS initially acquiesced).[125] On another occasion, the agency lawyers urged that compliance with the requirement should be litigated, in part because, during the years at issue, the organization was using its income and assets for a nonexempt purpose.[126] In still another instance, the IRS conceded that most of the years at issue were likely barred by the statute of limitations because the organization involved relied on the advice of legal counsel.[127]

In connection with the six-year statute of limitations, the term *gross income* means the "total of the amounts received or accrued from the sale of goods or services."[128] Also, an "amount shall not be considered as omitted from gross income if information sufficient to apprise the Commissioner of the nature and amount of the item is disclosed in the return, including any schedule or statement attached to the return."[129]

§ 27.5   DENIAL OR REVOCATION OF TAX-EXEMPT STATUS: LITIGATION PROCEDURES

The IRS may revoke an organization's tax exemption, notwithstanding an earlier recognition of its exemption by IRS ruling or court order, where the organization

---

[122] The reason for enactment of this provision is discussed in California Thoroughbred Breeders Ass'n v. Comm'r, 47 T.C. 335 (1966). Earlier, it was held that the filing of an information return by a tax-exempt organization could not start the running of a statute of limitations for an exempt organization that was later found to be taxable because this type of return did not contain sufficient data from which the taxpayer's income and other taxes could be computed and assessed (Automobile Club of Mich. v. Comm'r, 20 T.C. 1033 (1953), aff'd, 230 F.2d 585 (6th Cir. 1956), aff'd, 353 U.S. 180 (1957)).

[123] Knollwood Memorial Gardens v. Comm'r, 46 T.C. 764, 792–93 (1966).

[124] Maynard Hosp., Inc. v. Comm'r, 52 T.C. 1006, 1033 (1969).

[125] Gen. Couns. Mem. 32287.

[126] Gen. Couns. Mem. 32583.

[127] Gen. Couns. Mem. 35719.

[128] Reg. § 301.6501(e)-1(a)(1)(ii).

[129] Id.

violates one or more of the requirements for the applicable exempt status. If the recognition of exemption was by court order, the IRS is not collaterally estopped from subsequently revoking the exemption where the ground for disqualification is different from that asserted in the prior court proceeding.[130]

The principle of procedural due process embodied in the Fifth Amendment to the U.S. Constitution does not require the IRS to initiate a judicial hearing on the qualification of an organization for tax-exempt status before revoking the organization's favorable determination letter. This point was addressed by the Supreme Court in 1974.[131] It was reaffirmed nearly 20 years later, when another court found that the Supreme Court's analysis was still the law, that the revocation did not infringe on the organization's exercise of First Amendment rights,[132] and that, even if the organization had a property interest in the IRS's prior recognition of its exempt status, the revocation was not a deprivation of property without procedural due process.[133]

(a) Anti-Injunction Act

The ancient principle that "the king can do no wrong" lives on in the doctrine of sovereign immunity, which states that a government cannot be sued without its consent. This doctrine is a fundamental concept in United States law. Thus, federal courts have jurisdiction over lawsuits against the departments and agencies of the United States (including, of course, the IRS) but only to the extent that sovereign immunity has been waived.[134] A waiver of the federal government's sovereign immunity must be "unequivocally expressed in statutory text and will not be implied."[135] The scope of any waiver must be strictly construed in favor of the government.[136] A plaintiff bears the burden of establishing subject matter jurisdiction and, consequently, must prove an "explicit waiver" of immunity.[137]

Facing revocation of tax-exempt status and having exhausted its administrative remedies, an organization's initial impulse may be to seek injunctive relief in the courts, to restrain the IRS from taking such action. The Anti-Injunction Act,[138] however, provides that, aside from minor exceptions, "no suit for the purpose of restraining the assessment or collection of any tax shall be maintained in any court

---

[130] Universal Life Church, Inc. v. United States, 86-1 U.S.T.C ¶ 9271 (Cl. Ct. 1986).

[131] Bob Jones Univ. v. Simon, 416 U.S. 725 (1974), aff'g 472 F.2d 903 (4th Cir. 1973), reh'g denied, 476 F.2d 259 (4th Cir. 1973).

[132] The basis of this argument was that the organization involved, a charitable (IRC § 501(c)(3)) entity, has a First Amendment (free speech) right to solicit charitable contributions. See Fundraising § 4.5.

[133] United Cancer Council, Inc. v. Comm'r, 100 T.C. 162 (1993). The church audit rules (see § 27.6(c)) require that a church tax examination take no more than two years to complete. A federal court of appeals held that the revocation of the exempt status of a church cannot be defended against on the ground that the IRS failed to complete its audit of the church within the requisite period (Music Square Church v. United States, 218 F.3d 1367 (Fed. Cir. 2000)).

[134] United States v. Mitchell, 463 U.S. 206 (1983).

[135] Lane v. Pena, 518 U.S. 187, 192 (1996).

[136] E.g., McCarty v. United States, 929 F.2d 1085 (5th Cir. 1991).

[137] E.g., Sweet Pea Marine, Ltd. v. APJ Marine, Inc., 411 F.3d 1242, 1248 n.2 (11th Cir. 2005).

[138] IRC § 7421(a). This statute is broadly construed (e.g., Hobson v. Fischbeck, 758 F.2d 579 (11th Cir. 1985)).

by any person."[139] This enactment aims to ensure "prompt collection [by the federal government] of . . . lawful revenue" by preventing taxpayers from inundating tax collectors with pre-enforcement lawsuits over "disputed sums."[140] Despite the explicitly inflexible language of the statute, the U.S. Supreme Court carved out a narrow exception, in that a pre-enforcement injunction against tax assessment or collection may be granted only if it is clear that under no circumstances could the government ultimately prevail and if equity jurisdiction otherwise exists (that is, a showing of irreparable injury, no adequate remedy at law, and advancement of the public interest).[141] Generally, loss of exempt status will not bring an organization within the ambit of this exception, under Supreme Court rulings[142] and other cases.[143] An exception may be available in this context, but success will require rather unusual factual circumstances.[144]

Thus, the Anti-Injunction Act, when applicable, divests federal courts of subject-matter jurisdiction. This provision is reflective of the fact that the federal courts are courts of limited jurisdiction. They possess "only that power authorized by Constitution and statute, which is not to be expanded by judicial decree."[145] Indeed, a federal court has an "independent obligation" to investigate the limits of its subject-matter jurisdiction.[146] This is the case even when the parties "either overlook or elect not to press" the issue[147] or attempt to consent to a court's jurisdiction.[148] A federal court's obligation to examine its subject-matter jurisdiction is triggered whenever that jurisdiction is "fairly in doubt."[149]

By its terms, the Anti-Injunction Act bars suits seeking to restrain the assessment or collection of a tax. Thus, the act forbids only pre-enforcement actions, that is, those brought before the IRS has assessed or collected an exaction. A taxpayer

---

[139] The Anti-Injunction Act was held to bar a lawsuit by a tax-exempt organization against the Commissioner of Internal Revenue and other representatives of the IRS for damages for initiating an allegedly political audit against the organization (Judicial Watch, Inc. v. Rossotti, 317 F.3d 401 (4th Cir. 2003)). Also, the Tax Exception to the Declaratory Judgment Act, 28 U.S.C. § 2201.

[140] Enochs v. Williams Packing & Navigation Co., 370 U.S. 1, 7–8 (1962).

[141] Id. at 1. E.g., Investment Annuity v. Blumenthal, 437 F. Supp. 1095 (D.D.C. 1977), 442 F. Supp. 681 (D.D.C. 1977), rev'd, 609 F.2d 1 (D.C. Cir. 1979); State of Minn., Spannaus v. United States, 525 F.2d 231 (8th Cir. 1975).

[142] Bob Jones Univ. v. Simon, 416 U.S. 725 (1974); "Americans United," Inc. v. Walters, 416 U.S. 752 (1974), rev'g 477 F.2d 1169 (D.C. Cir. 1973). Also, United States v. American Friends Serv. Comm., 419 U.S. 7 (1974); Cattle Feeders Tax Comm'n v. Shultz, 504 F.2d 462 (10th Cir. 1974); Vietnam Veterans Against the War, Inc. v. Voskuil, 389 F. Supp. 412 (E.D. Mo. 1974).

[143] E.g., Crenshaw Cnty. Private School Found. v. Connally, 474 F.2d 1185 (5th Cir. 1973); Judicial Watch, Inc. v. Rossotti, 223 F. Supp. 2d 698 (D. Md. 2002); Nat'l Council on the Facts of Overpopulation v. Caplin, 224 F. Supp. 313 (D.D.C. 1963); Israelite House of David v. Holden, 14 F.2d 701 (W.D. Mich. 1926).

[144] Center on Corporate Responsibility, Inc. v. Shultz, 368 F. Supp. 863 (D.D.C. 1973). In Founding Church of Scientology of Washington, D.C., Inc. v. Director, Federal Bureau of Investigation, 84-1 U.S.T.C. ¶ 9468 (D.D.C. 1984), the organization was permitted to seek an injunction against the IRS for allegedly engaging in illegal law-enforcement and information-gathering activities in violation of the organization's constitutional rights, inasmuch as the lawsuit was not related to tax assessment or collection.

[145] Kokkonen v. Guardian Life Ins. Co. of America, 511 U.S. 375, 377 (1994) (internal citation omitted).

[146] Arbaugh v. Y & H Corp., 546 U.S. 500, 514 (2006).

[147] Henderson v. Shinseki, 562 U.S. 428 (2011).

[148] E.g., Sosna v. Iowa, 419 U.S. 393 (1975).

[149] Ashcroft v. Iqbal, 556 U.S. 662 (2009).

can always pay an assessed tax, seek a refund from the IRS, and then bring a refund action in federal court.[150]

Application of the Anti-Injunction Act has many contours, but a rare one is whether the attempted restraint is of an assessment or a collection of a tax. Yet that issue came rushing to the forefront when a federal court of appeals, considering a challenge to the constitutionality of the health care reform legislation's individual health insurance mandate,[151] held, after another federal court of appeals upheld the constitutionality of the mandate[152] and a third one held the mandate to be unconstitutional,[153] that the challenge constitutes a pre-enforcement action seeking to restrain the assessment of a tax and thus that the Anti-Injunction Act "strips" the courts of jurisdiction over the matter.[154]

In reaching this conclusion, this appellate court embarked on an analysis of whether the individual mandate's enforcement penalty is, at least for purposes of the Anti-Injunction Act, a tax. In summary, a "tax, in the general understanding of the term," is an "exaction for the support of the government."[155] An exaction qualifies as a tax even when it raises "obviously negligible" revenue and furthers a revenue purpose "secondary" to the primary goal of regulation.[156] The term *tax* can embrace a wide variety of exactions.[157]

The Supreme Court stated that the Anti-Injunction Act uses the term *tax* in a broad sense, such as in holding that the statute bars pre-enforcement challenges to exactions that do not constitute taxes under the Constitution.[158] That is, the term in the Act encompasses penalties that function as mere "regulatory measure[s] beyond the taxing power of Congress."[159]

In this appellate court case concerning the mandate, the government asserted that the mandate law labels the imposed exaction a penalty, thus rendering the Anti-Injunction Act inapplicable.[160] This argument was rejected by the court, writing that the Supreme Court's jurisprudence on the point makes it seem "inconceivable that Congress would intend to exclude an exaction from the [Act] merely by describing it as a 'penalty'," adding that the Court has "repeatedly instructed that congressional labels have little bearing on whether an exaction qualifies as

---

[150] United States v. Clintwood Elkhorn Mining Co., 553 U.S. 1 (2008). See § 27.5(b).

[151] Patient Protection and Affordable Care Act § 1501.

[152] Thomas More Law Center v. Obama, 651 F.3d 529 (6th Cir. 2011).

[153] Florida v. Dep't of Health & Human Services, 648 F.3d 1235 (11th Cir. 2011).

[154] Liberty Univ., Inc. v. Geithner, 2011 WL 3962915 (4th Cir. 2011).

[155] United States v. Butler, 297 U.S. 1 (1936).

[156] United States v. Sanchez, 340 U.S. 42, 44 (1950). Also, Bob Jones Univ. v. Simon, 416 U.S. 725, 741 n.12 (1974).

[157] E.g., Trailer Marine Transportation Corp. v. Rivera Vasquez, 977 F.2d 1 (1st Cir. 1992).

[158] E.g., Bailey v. George, 259 U.S. 16 (1922); Bailey v. Drexel Furniture Co., 259 U.S. 20 (1922). That is, the term in the Act encompasses penalties that function as mere "regulatory measure[s] beyond the taxing power of Congress."

[159] Bob Jones Univ. v. Simon, 416 U.S. 725, 740 (1974). The Anti-Injunction Act was held to bar suits challenging "penalties imposed" for violating disclosure conditions of tax-exempt status (Mobile Republican Assembly v. United States, 353 F.3d 1357, 1362 n.5 (11th Cir. 2003)).

[160] This argument was accepted in Thomas More Law Center v. Obama, 651 F.3d 529 (6th Cir. 2011).

a 'tax' for statutory purposes."[161] The court concluded that the term *tax* "in the [Act] reaches any exaction assessed by the Secretary [IRS] pursuant to his authority under the Internal Revenue Code—even one that constitutes a 'penalty' for constitutional [law] purposes."[162]

Consequently, wrote this appellate court, "once we conclude that the term 'tax' in the [Act] does encompass a challenged exaction, we can go no further."[163] And: "This expansive language [in the Act] leaves no room for a court to carve out exceptions based on the policy ramifications of a particular pre-enforcement challenge."[164]

The U.S. Supreme Court resolved this matter, with a majority respecting the decision of Congress to label the mandate a penalty, rather than a tax.[165] The Court wrote that the Anti-Injunction Act and the Affordable Care Act "are creatures of Congress's own creation" and "[h]ow they relate to each other is up to Congress."[166] Thus, the Anti-Injunction Act was held to not apply in the context of this litigation.[167]

An important change in this aspect of the law occurred in mid-2021. Prior law basically held that, if a pre-enforcement suit would necessarily preclude the assessment or collection of a tax, the suit is barred by the Anti-Injunction Act (so that the taxpayer would have to pay the tax and sue for a refund). These cases essentially instructed courts to look to the *effect* of these lawsuits. One of the most striking aspects of a decision issued that year by the U.S. Supreme Court is that the Court changed the core analysis by requiring courts to focus on the *purpose* of the lawsuits.[168]

After deciding that the purpose of the taxpayer's complaint in this case was to contest the legality of the IRS notice, not the tax penalty that is part of the enforcement regime, the Court "refute[d] [the government's contention] that this is a tax action in disguise." First, the Court observed that the notice "imposes affirmative reporting obligations, inflicting costs separate and apart from the statutory tax penalty," characterizing the suit as an "attempt[] to get out from under the

---

[161] Liberty Univ., Inc. v. Geithner, 2011 WL 3962915 (4th Cir. 2011), citing Helwig v. United States, 188 U.S. 605, 613 (1903) (holding that "use of words" does not "change the nature and character of the enactment").

[162] Liberty Univ., Inc. v. Geithner, 2011 WL 3962915 (4th Cir. 2011).

[163] *Id.*

[164] The Supreme Court earlier stated that the courts must give the Anti-Injunction Act "literal force, without regard to the. . .nature of the pre-enforcement challenge" (Bob Jones Univ. v. Simon, 416 U.S. 725, 742 (1974)).

[165] Nat'l Fed'n of Indep. Business v. Sebelius, 567 U.S. 519 (2012).

[166] *Id.* at 2583.

[167] In general, see *Constitutional Law* § 8.13(b).

[168] CIC Servs., LLC v. Internal Revenue Serv., 593 U.S. 209 (2021). The purpose of this lawsuit was to challenge the lawfulness of a notice designating certain micro-captive insurance transactions as "listed" transactions. Subsequent to the Court's decision, a district court granted an injunction barring the IRS from enforcing the notice (CIC Servs., LLC v. Internal Revenue Serv., 128 A.F.T.R.2d 2021-5972 (E.D. Tenn. 2021)) and then invalidated the notice, which it also found to be arbitrary and capricious, for the IRS's failure to comply with notice-and-comment procedure requirements under the Administrative Procedure Act (CIC Servs., LLC v. Internal Revenue Serv., 129 A.F.T.R.2d 2022-1119 (E.D. Tenn. 2022)).

(non-tax) burdens of a (non-tax) reporting obligation." Second, the Court noted that the notice's "reporting rule and the statutory tax penalty are several steps removed from each other"—"[b]etween the upstream notice and the downstream tax, the river runs long." Third, the Court emphasized that "violation of the notice is punishable not only by a tax, but by separate criminal penalties," stating an "ordinary person" is not likely to risk criminal punishment, "[s]o the criminal penalties here practically necessitate a pre-enforcement, rather than a refund, suit—if there is to be a suit at all." Thus, this lawsuit, the Court concluded, "targets the upstream reporting mandate, not the downstream tax"—"[a]nd because that is the suit's aim, the Anti-Injunction Act imposes no bar."[169]

(b) Tax Deficiency and Refund Actions

An organization facing loss of tax-exempt status that has received a notice of deficiency from the IRS may petition the U.S. Tax Court for relief,[170] or may pay the tax and sue for a refund in federal district court or the U.S. Court of Federal Claims following expiration of the statutory six-month waiting period.[171] The organization, however, may well become defunct before any relief can be obtained in this fashion, particularly where the ability to attract charitable contributions is a factor, since denial of exempt status also means (where applicable) loss of advance assurance by the IRS of deductibility of contributions. The U.S. Supreme Court recognized the seriousness of this dilemma but concluded that "although the congressional restriction to post-enforcement review may place an organization claiming tax-exempt status in a precarious financial position, the problems presented do not rise to the level of constitutional infirmities, in light of the powerful governmental interests in protecting the administration of the tax system from premature judicial interference . . . and of the opportunities for review that are available."[172]

(c) Declaratory Judgment Rules

The Declaratory Judgment Act generally allows federal courts to enter declaratory judgments but excludes controversies "with respect to Federal taxes."[173] Thus,

---

[169] CIC Servs., LLC v. Internal Revenue Serv., 593 U.S. 209 (2021). A court subsequently contrasted the situation at issue in *CIC Services*, where the taxpayer sought relief from a regulation ex ante (before violation of any requirement or imposition of any tax or penalty, so the Anti-Injunction Act did not yet have a role to play) from a taxpayer's attempt to obtain ex post relief from a penalty (treated as a tax) after it had been imposed, "which is the prototypical posture of a case barred by the Anti-Injunction Act" (Summerour v. Internal Revenue Serv., 134 A.F.T.R. 2d 2024-5090 (D.D.C. 2024)).

[170] IRC §§ 6212, 6213. E.g., Golden Rule Church Ass'n v. Comm'r, 41 T.C. 719 (1964). The role and responsibilities of the Chief Counsel of the IRS in tax-exempt organization cases docketed in the U.S. Tax Court is the subject of Rev. Proc. 2016-22, 2016-15 I.R.B 577.

[171] IRC § 7422; 28 U.S.C. §§ 1346(x)(1), 1491. In the absence of the timely filing of a claim for refund (a jurisdictional prerequisite to this type of court action), this type of suit may not be maintained. Also, American Ass'n of Commodity Traders v. Department of the Treasury, 79-1 U.S.T.C. ¶ 9183 (D.N.H. 1978), aff'd, 598 F.2d 1233 (1st Cir. 1979).

[172] Bob Jones Univ. v. Simon, 416 U.S. 725, 747–48 (1974).

[173] 28 U.S.C. § 2201(a). This is sometimes referenced as the "tax exception" to the Declaratory Judgment Act.

federal courts generally[174] lack subject matter jurisdiction to issue declaratory relief in tax cases.[175] This law has been applied in the tax-exempt organizations context.[176]

However, federal tax law provides for declaratory judgments as to the initial or continuing qualification of an organization in five instances.[177] Jurisdiction over these cases is vested in the U.S. District Court for the District of Columbia, the U.S. Court of Federal Claims, and the U.S. Tax Court.[178]

This declaratory judgment procedure is designed to facilitate relatively prompt judicial review of five categories of tax-exempt organizations issues. This procedure is not, however, intended to supplant the preexisting avenues available for exempt organizations for judicial review. Jury trials are not available in these types of cases.[179]

(i) General Requirements.   These rules create a remedy in a case of "actual controversy" involving a determination by the IRS with respect to the initial qualification or continuing qualification of an entity as (1) a charitable organization for tax exemption purposes[180] and/or charitable contribution deduction purposes,[181] (2) a public charity,[182] (3) a private operating foundation,[183] (4) a farmers' cooperative[184] for tax exemption purposes, and (5) nearly any other type of tax-exempt

---

[174] See § 27.5(b).

[175] E.g., Branca v. United States, 312 F. App'x 160 (11th Cir. 2008).

[176] E.g., American Soc'y of Ass'n Executives v. Bentsen, 848 F. Supp. 245 (D.D.C. 1994) (holding that this law deprived the court of jurisdiction over a challenge of the constitutionality of the law denying the business expense deduction for portions of dues paid to tax-exempt associations that engage in lobbying (see § 22.6(b)); Alpine Fellowship Church of Love & Enlightenment v. United States, 87-1 U.S.T.C. ¶ 9203 (N.D. Cal. 1987)).

[177] IRC § 7428. E.g., Church of the New Testament v. United States, 783 F.2d 771 (9th Cir. 1986). Thus, the observation that it is "well settled that a declaratory judgment cannot be issued in a tax case" (Horne v. United States, 519 F.2d 51, 52 (5th Cir. 1975)) is an overstatement.

[178] IRC § 7428(a); Rev. Proc. 2024-5, 2024-1 I.R.B. 262 § 10.01. A lawsuit claiming an organization does not qualify for tax exemption was dismissed because the court involved was not one of these courts (Allen v. Beirich, 128 A.F.T.R. 2d 2021-5184 (4th Cir. 2021)). The U.S. Tax Court is the only one of these courts where this type of a declaratory judgment case can be pursued without the services of a lawyer; these *pro se* cases will be dismissed for that reason in the other two courts (e.g., Point of Wisdom No. 1 v. United States, 77 A.F.T.R. 2d 96-986 (D.D.C. 1996)).

[179] Synanon Church v. United States, 83-1 U.S.T.C. ¶ 9230 (D.D.C. 1983).

[180] That is, an organization described in IRC § 501(c)(3) and exempt from federal income taxation by reason of IRC § 501(a). See Part Three. Reasoning that the question as to whether a trust is a charitable trust within the meaning of IRC § 4947(a)(1) (see § 12.4(f)) is "inextricably related" to the issue of whether it is qualified under IRC § 501(c)(3), the Tax Court held that it has declaratory judgment jurisdiction to decide the IRC § 4947(a)(1) issue (Allen Eiry Trust v. Comm'r, 77 T.C. 1263 (1981)). In this case, however, the court declined to take jurisdiction over the question whether the trust is qualified to have its income exempt from tax under IRC § 115 (see § 19.22(b)). The court also declined jurisdiction in an instance where the organization was dissolved prior to the filing of the petition for declaratory relief, on the ground that there was not an actual controversy (Nat'l Republican Found. v. Comm'r, 55 T.C.M. 1395 (1988)). Likewise, where an audit by the IRS is undertaken and the organization's tax-exempt status is not altered, there is no actual controversy (Founding Church of Scientology of Washington, D.C., Inc. v. United States, 92-1 U.S.T.C. ¶ 50,302 (Cl. Ct. 1992)).

[181] IRC § 170(c)(2).

[182] IRC § 509(a). See § 12.3.

[183] IRC § 4942(j)(3). See § 12.1(b).

[184] IRC § 521. See § 19.12.

organization.[185] The remedy is available in the case of a failure by the IRS to make a determination as respects one or more of these issues.[186] The remedy is pursued in one of the three previously noted courts, which is authorized to "make a declaration" with respect to the issues.[187] A pleading may be filed under these rules "only by the organization the qualification or classification of which is at issue."[188]

A *determination* within the meaning of these rules[189] is a final decision by the IRS, by means of a determination letter, which holds that the organization is not tax-exempt, is a public charity under a status other than the one requested, is not a private operating foundation, or is a private foundation (a *final adverse determination*).[190] The term does not encompass an IRS ruling that a proposed transaction will jeopardize and organization's tax-exempt status, inasmuch as this type of ruling does not constitute a revocation of an organization's tax-exempt status, nor does it jeopardize the deductibility of contributions to it.[191] The same principle applies to an IRS ruling whether certain revenues constitute public support for purposes of the public support test.[192]

In the case of a church, a final report of an IRS agent (the 30-day letter) constitutes the requisite final determination.[193]

A determination can, in this context, include a proposed revocation of an organization's tax-exempt status or public charity classification. In one case, an exempt charitable organization received a letter in which the IRS proposed to

---

[185] IRC § 7428(a)(1).

[186] IRC § 7428(a)(2). Thus, the rulings and determination letters in cases subject to the declaratory judgment procedure of IRC § 7428 are those issued pursuant to the procedures currently stated in Rev. Proc. 2024-5, 2024-1 I.R.B. 262. The withdrawal of an application for recognition of tax exemption is not a failure to make a determination under IRC § 7428(a)(2) (*id*. § 10.04(2)).

[187] An action pursuant to these procedures may not, however, be brought with respect to a revocation of tax-exempt status, by operation of law, occasioned by a failure to file an annual information return and/or submit an e-postcard for three consecutive years (see § 28.4) (IRC § 7428(b)(4)).

[188] IRC § 7428(b)(1). Thus, for example, as regards an unincorporated organization that applied for recognition of tax exemption and subsequently (during the administrative process) incorporated, when the IRS denied exemption for the unincorporated entity, the corporation (being a separate legal entity) was held to lack standing to seek a declaratory judgment on the qualification as an exempt organization of the unincorporated organization (American New Covenant Church v. Comm'r, 74 T.C. 293 (1980)). By contrast, a surviving exempt corporation in a merger was held to be able to litigate, under these rules, the issue of exemption of the merged entity; the appellate court looked to state law to determine that the suit could be said to be maintained by "the organization" (Baptist Hosp., Inc. v. United States, 851 F.2d 1397 (Fed. Cir. 1988), *rev'g* 87-1 U.S.T.C. ¶ 9290 (Ct. Cl. 1987)). A director of an exempt organization lacks standing to bring an action pursuant to these rules (Fondel v. United States, 178 F.3d 1313 (Fed. Cir. 1999)). Likewise, an individual, who filed a lawsuit alleging that a tax-exempt organization misused its exempt status to their detriment, was held to not have standing to challenge the entity's exemption (Allen v. Beirich, 128 A.F.T.R. 2d 2021-5184 (4th Cir. 2021)).

[189] IRC § 7428(a)(1).

[190] Rev. Proc. 2024-5, 2024-1 I.R.B. 262 § 10.02. If the IRS declines to issue a determination letter to an organization seeking a determination, the organization may be able to pursue a declaratory judgment if it has exhausted its administrative remedies (*id*. § 10.03).

[191] New Community Senior Citizen Hous. Corp. v. Comm'r, 72 T.C. 372 (1979).

[192] Urantia Found. v. Comm'r, 77 T.C. 507 (1981), *aff'd*, 684 F.2d 521 (7th Cir. 1982).

[193] IRC § 7611(g). A court dismissed the complaint of an organization seeking a declaratory judgment that it was a church on the basis that it lacked jurisdiction; the organization did not file an application for recognition of tax-exempt status and therefore lacked an "official determination by the IRS" (Alearis, Inc. v. United States, 158 Fed. Cl. 64 (2022)).

revoke its public charity status; in response, it filed a written protest and thereafter filed a petition for a declaratory judgment. The court found that the proposed revocation was sufficient to create the requisite actual controversy and that the written protest constituted the requisite request for a determination.[194]

By contrast, where the administrative process is ongoing and where the IRS has merely threatened to issue a notice of proposed revocation, the courts will decline to assume declaratory judgment jurisdiction.[195] Emphasizing the requirement of an *actual controversy*, a court observed that "[w]e find no grounds for believing that Congress intended this [declaratory judgment] section to grant us plenary authority to supervise examinations of exempt organizations."[196] This determination was upheld, with the appellate court rejecting the claim of jurisdiction in that the IRS was "still only in the investigative stage and has not issued any ruling affecting . . . [the organization's] tax exempt status, directly or indirectly."[197]

In one instance, a court concluded that it had declaratory judgment jurisdiction over a case, where the IRS notified a tax-exempt organization that the agency was considering revocation of its exempt status, even though the complaint in the case was filed before the IRS issued its final adverse determination letter to the organization.[198]

When issuing a favorable determination letter recognizing an organization's tax-exempt status, the IRS may condition its ruling on the organization's agreement to not engage in a particular activity. A court held that this type of favorable final ruling does not constitute the requisite adverse determination.[199]

Although once the subject of some debate,[200] it is now accepted that the receipt of a favorable ruling on a non-private-foundation status that is a different and less advantageous status than the one sought by the organization qualifies as an adverse determination sufficient to meet the "actual controversy" requirement of the declaratory judgment procedures.[201]

Where an organization's corporate status has been suspended under state law, it will be unable to initiate or prosecute a declaratory judgment action.[202]

---

[194] J. David Gladstone Found. v. Comm'r, 77 T.C. 221 (1981).

[195] High Adventure Ministries, Inc. v. Comm'r, 80 T.C. 292 (1983).

[196] *Id.* at 302.

[197] 726 F.2d 555, 557 (9th Cir. 1984).

[198] Anclote Psychiatric Center, Inc. v. Comm'r, 95 T.C. 371 (1992).

[199] AHW Corp. v. Comm'r, 79 T.C. 390 (1982).

[200] In Found. of Human Understanding v. Comm'r, for example, the majority opinion found that the actual controversy requirement was met (88 T.C. 1341, 1355 (1987)); the dissent, however, stated that classification as a publicly supported charity under IRC § 170(b)(1)(A)(vi), instead of as a church, was insufficient to establish the actual controversy requirement of IRC § 7428 because the organization retained its non-private-foundation status notwithstanding the loss of its church status (88 T.C. at 1384).

[201] Found. of Human Understanding v. United States, 88 Fed. Cl. 203 (2009). Also, Friends of the Soc'y of Servants of God v. Comm'r, 75 T.C. 209, 217 (1980) (holding that the court had jurisdiction over the matter because the IRS's ruling was adverse in many respects, including imposing requirements on the organization that would not have been imposed on a church); CREATE, Inc. v. Comm'r, 634 F.2d 803 (5th Cir. 1981); Rev. Proc. 2024-5, 2024-1 I.R.B. 262 § 10.02(2).

[202] A private foundation's challenge to the IRS's revocation of its tax-exempt status was dismissed because its corporate powers and privileges were suspended at the time it filed its petition for a declaratory judgment (XC Found. v. Comm'r, T.C. Memo. 2023-3, *aff'd*, 133 A.F.T.R. 2d 2024-1678 (9th Cir. 20204)).

(ii) Exhaustion of Administrative Remedies. Prior to utilizing the declaratory judgment procedure, an organization must have exhausted all administrative remedies available to it within the IRS.[203]

For the first 270 days after a request for a determination is made, an organization is deemed to not have exhausted its administrative remedies, assuming a determination has not been made during that period.[204] After this 270-day period has elapsed, the organization may initiate an action for a declaratory judgment. An action may also be initiated if the IRS makes an adverse determination during this jurisdictional period. In either event, all actions under these rules must be initiated within 90 days after the date on which the final determination by the IRS is made.[205]

This 270-day period does not begin until the date a completed application for recognition of tax exemption is sent to the agency.[206] If the IRS requests additional information from an organization, the period beginning on the date the IRS requests additional information until the date the information is submitted to the IRS will not be counted for purposes of the 270-day period.[207]

Exhaustion of administrative remedies means taking, in a timely manner, all reasonable steps to secure a determination from the IRS, including (1) the filing of a completed application for recognition of exemption,[208] a group exemption request,[209] or a request for a determination of public charity/private foundation status;[210] (2) in appropriate circumstances, requesting relief[211] with respect to an extension of time for making an election or application for relief from tax;[212] (3) the timely submission of all additional information requested by the IRS necessary to perfect an application for recognition of exemption or request for determination of public charity or private foundation status; and (4) exhaustion of all appeals within the IRS.[213]

In the case of a church, the receipt of a final report of an IRS agent is deemed to constitute the exhaustion of administrative remedies.[214]

According to the IRS, an organization cannot be deemed to have exhausted its administrative remedies prior to the earlier of (1) the completion of the foregoing steps and the IRS's sending of a final determination letter by certified or

---

[203] IRC § 7428(b)(2).

[204] *Id.* The filing of an application for recognition of exemption is not a required administrative step for organizations claiming status as a church (see § 27.6(c)) (Universal Life Church, Inc. (Full Circle) v. Comm'r, 83 T.C. 292 (1984)).

[205] IRC § 7428(b)(3). E.g., Metropolitan Community Serv., Inc. v. Comm'r, 53 T.C.M. 810 (1987).

[206] Rev. Proc. 2024-5, 2024-1 I.R.B. 262 § 10.06(2). As to the requirements for an application to be considered *completed*, see § 26.1(c).

[207] Rev. Proc. 2024-5, 2024-1 I.R.B. 262 § 10.06(2).

[208] See § 26.1(c).

[209] See § 26.11.

[210] Rev. Proc. 2024-5, 2024-1 I.R.B. 262 § 7.04.

[211] Reg. § 301.9100-1.

[212] See Reg. § 301.9100-1.

[213] Rev. Proc. 2024-5, 2024-1 I.R.B. 262 § 10.05. In Sense of Self Soc'y v. United States, 79-2 U.S.T.C. ¶ 9673 (D.D.C. 1979), the court ruled that the organization failed to exhaust its administrative remedies because it did not respond to the IRS' "repeated" requests for information. Cf. Change-All Souls Hous. Corp. v. United States, 671 F.2d 463 (Ct. Cl. 1982).

[214] IRC § 7611(g).

registered mail, or (2) the expiration of the 270-day period in a case where the IRS has not issued a final determination letter and the organization has taken, in a timely manner, all reasonable steps to secure a determination letter.[215]

Further, the IRS stated that the foregoing steps "will not be considered completed until the Service has had a reasonable time to act on an appeal."[216] (As noted, nonetheless, once the statutory 270 days have elapsed, the action can be initiated, without regard to the pace of the IRS in relation to these steps.)

The refusal by an organization to turn records over to the IRS, during the pendency of a contest of an IRS summons, is not a failure to exhaust administrative remedies that could result in a loss of declaratory judgment rights.[217]

(iii) Deductibility of Contributions. To protect the financial status of an allegedly charitable organization during the litigation period, the law provides for circumstances under which contributions made to the organization during that period are deductible[218] even though the court ultimately decides against the organization.[219] Basically, this relief can be accorded only where the IRS is proposing to revoke, rather than initially deny, an organization's charitable status. The total deductions to any one organization from a single donor, to be so protected during this period, however, may not exceed $1,000.[220] (Where an organization ultimately prevails in a declaratory judgment case, this $1,000 limitation on deductibility becomes inapplicable, so that all gifts are fully deductible within the general limitations of the charitable deduction rules.)[221]

This benefit is not available to any individual who was responsible, in whole or in part, for the actions (or failures to act) on the part of the organization that were the basis for the revocation of tax-exempt status.[222]

(iv) Administrative Record. The U.S. Tax Court adopted procedural rules for actions filed under these rules.[223] The single most significant feature of these rules is the decision of the court to generally confine its role to review of the denial by the IRS of a request for a determination of tax exemption based solely on the facts contained in the administrative record, that is, not to conduct a trial *de novo*

---

[215] Rev. Proc. 2024-5, 2024-1 I.R.B. 262 § 10.06.

[216] *Id.* § 10.07. The U.S. District Court for the District of Columbia held that it lacks subject matter jurisdiction in these cases until the IRS makes an adverse determination or the 270-day period (commenced by the filing of a substantially completed application for recognition of exemption) has elapsed (New York Cnty. Health Servs. Review Org., Inc. v. Comm'r, 80-1 U.S.T.C. ¶ 9398 (D.D.C. 1980)).

[217] Church of World Peace, Inc. v. Internal Revenue Service, 715 F.2d 492 (10th Cir. 1983).

[218] IRC § 170(c)(2).

[219] IRC § 7428(c)(1).

[220] IRC § 7428(c)(2)(A).

[221] See *Charitable Giving*, Chapter 5.

[222] IRC 7428(c)(3). The IRS publishes, in the *Internal Revenue Bulletin*, the names of organizations that are challenging, under IRC § 7428, the revocation of their status as organizations entitled to receive deductible charitable contributions, so as to inform potential donors to these organizations of the protection, to the extent provided under IRC § 7428(c), for their contributions made during the litigation period (Ann. 85-169, 1985-48 I.R.B. 40).

[223] Rules of Practice and Procedure, U.S. Tax Court, Title XXI. For purposes of these rules, the *administrative record* "generally refers to all documents and materials received, developed, considered, or exchanged in connection with the administrative determination" (*id.*, Rule 210(b)(12)).

at which new evidence may be adduced.[224] (This approach does not apply where the exemption has been revoked.) Thus, in one case, the court refused to permit information orally furnished to IRS representatives during a conference at the administrative level to be introduced in evidence during the pendency of the case before it.[225] Likewise, it was held that the administrative record may consist only of material submitted by either the applicant organization or the IRS, so that materials submitted by third parties are inadmissible.[226] Similarly, the court is to base its decision only on theories advanced in the IRS notice or at trial, and not on arguments advanced anew by the IRS during the litigation.[227]

The U.S. District Court for the District of Columbia and the U.S. Court of Federal Claims generally follow the Tax Court's approach to processing these declaratory judgment cases.

An organization's fate before a court may well depend on the quality of the contents of the administrative record. The applicant organization, significantly, generally controls what comprises the administrative record. Even when the record includes responses to IRS inquiries, it is the organization that decides the phraseology of the answers and what, if anything, to attach as exhibits. It is, therefore, important that the administrative record be carefully constructed, particularly in instances where there is a reasonable likelihood that an initial determination case will be unsuccessful at the IRS level and thus ripen into a declaratory judgment case.

As an illustration, a court had before it the issue as to whether an organization that operated a mountain lodge as a retreat facility could qualify as a tax-exempt religious organization. The opinion in the case reflected the court's view that this type of organization can so qualify under appropriate circumstances, yet the organization involved lost the case primarily because the administrative record did not show that the recreational facilities were used for exempt purposes

---

[224] *Id.*, Rule 217(a). E.g., Nationalist Movement v. Comm'r, 64 T.C.M. 1479 (1992); Dr. Erol Bastug, Inc. v. Comm'r, 57 T.C.M. 562 (1989); Colorado State Chiropractic Soc'y, Inc. v. Comm'r, 56 T.C.M. 1018 (1989); Liberty Ministries Int'l v. Comm'r, 48 T.C.M. 105 (1984); Unitary Mission Church of Long Island v. Comm'r, 74 T.C. 507 (1980). The U.S. Tax Court is concerned about "fishing expeditions" in these situations (e.g., Wisconsin Psychiatric Servs. v. Comm'r, 76 T.C. 839, 846 (1981)). This court has allowed supplementation of the administrative record in a denial-of-exemption case (First Libertarian Church v. Comm'r, 74 T.C. 396 (1980)). The U.S. District Court for the District of Columbia, however, appears more willing to review facts beyond the administrative record (e.g., Freedom Church of Revelation v. United States, 588 F. Supp. 693 (D.D.C. 1984); Incorporated Trustees of the Gospel Worker Soc'y v. United States, 510 F. Supp. 374 (D.D.C. 1981), *aff'd*, 672 F.2d 894 (D.C. Cir. 1981), *cert. denied*, 456 U.S. 944 (1982); cf. Airlie Found., Inc. v. United States, 92-2 U.S.T.C. ¶ 50,462 (D.D.C. 1992)). Because the Tax Court will render a declaratory judgment in a nonrevocation case on the petition, the answer, and the administrative record, it has held that a motion for summary judgment in that court is "superfluous" and "pointless" (Pulpit Resource v. Comm'r, 70 T.C. 594, 602 (1978)).
[225] Houston Lawyer Referral Serv., Inc. v. Comm'r, 69 T.C. 570 (1978). Also, Church in Boston v. Comm'r, 71 T.C. 102 (1979).
[226] Church of Spiritual Technology v. United States, 90-1 U.S.T.C. ¶ 50,097 (Ct. Cl. 1989). A court ruled that transcripts from the criminal trials and the grand jury materials from the criminal case, involving the founder and executive director of an organization, were part of the administrative record in a subsequent case where the organization's ongoing tax-exempt status was at issue (Airlie Found., Inc. v. United States, 92-2 U.S.T.C. ¶ 50,462 (D.D.C. 1992)).
[227] Peoples Translation Service/Newsfront Int'l v. Comm'r, 72 T.C. 42 (1979); Goodspeed Scholarship Fund v. Comm'r, 70 T.C. 515 (1978); Schuster's Express, Inc. v. Comm'r, 66 T.C. 585 (1976), *aff'd*, 562 F.2d 39 (2d Cir. 1977).

or otherwise used only in an insubstantial manner.[228] By contrast, where the administrative record is able to show that an organization is advancing exempt purposes by means of a religious retreat, the courts will not deprive the organization of exemption, even where the retreats are held in an environment somewhat more comfortable than the wilderness.[229]

In one instance, the IRS refused to rule on a request for recognition of exemption, saying that the issue raised was under study. Once the 270-day administrative remedies period expired, the organization launched a lawsuit. Within 60 days after the complaint was filed, the Department of Justice made it known that the IRS was willing to issue a favorable ruling (thereby mooting the case). Thus, soon after instituting a declaratory judgment request, the organization came into possession of a favorable ruling, under circumstances where, if this form of relief were not available, the IRS probably would not have acted for some time or would have issued an unfavorable determination.[230]

(d)   Other Approaches

Other options may be available as to court jurisdiction for the organization confronted with revocation (or denial) of tax-exempt status. Where charitable contributions are involved, a "friendly donor" may bring an action contesting the legality of the IRS disallowance of the charitable deduction (which generally will involve the same issues) as those relating to exemption.[231] An organization may also sue for refund of Federal Unemployment Tax Act taxes,[232] certain excise taxes,[233] or wagering taxes.[234] While these avenues of review can take much more time than a declaratory judgment action, they offer the distinct advantage of enabling the organization to initiate the litigation in a federal court geographically proximate to it.

Conventional declaratory judgment suits[235] are of no avail in this setting, as the Declaratory Judgment Act expressly excludes controversies over federal taxes from its purview.[236]

---

[228] Schoger Found. v. Comm'r, 76 T.C. 380 (1981). The organization argued that the administrative record did not show that the recreational facilities were used in an insubstantial manner for exempt purposes, but this failed because the organization had the burden of showing that the determination of the IRS was incorrect. Cf. Alive Fellowship of Harmonious Living v. Comm'r, 47 T.C.M. 1134 (1984).

[229] Junaluska Assembly Hous., Inc. v. Comm'r, 86 T.C. 1114 (1986).

[230] Infant Formula Action Coalition v. United States (C.A. No. 79-0129, D.D.C.). Also, Fair Campaign Practices Comm., Inc. v. United States (C.A. No. 77-0830, D.D.C.).

[231] E.g., Teich v. Comm'r, 48 T.C. 963 (1967), aff'd, 407 F.2d 815 (7th Cir. 1969); Krohn v. United States, 246 F. Supp. 341 (D. Col. 1965); Kuper v. Comm'r, 332 F.2d 562 (3d Cir. 1964), cert. denied, 379 U.S. 902 (1964); Bolton v. Comm'r, 1 T.C. 717 (1943).

[232] IRC § 3306(c)(8).

[233] IRC § 4253(h).

[234] IRC § 4421. E.g., Rochester Liederkranz, Inc. v. United States, 456 F.2d 152 (2d Cir. 1972); Hessman v. Campbell, 134 F. Supp. 415 (S.D. Ind. 1955).

[235] 28 U.S.C. §§ 2201–2202.

[236] E.g., Ecclesiastical Order of the Ism of Am, Inc. v. Internal Revenue Service, 725 F.2d 398 (6th Cir. 1984); Mitchell v. Riddell, 401 F.2d 842 (9th Cir. 1968), cert. denied, 394 U.S. 456 (1969); In re Wingreen Co., 412 F.2d 1048 (5th Cir. 1969); Jolles Found., Inc. v. Moysey, 250 F.2d 1966 (2d Cir. 1957); Church of the New Testament v. United States, 85-1 U.S.T.C. ¶ 9227 (E.D. Col. 1984); Int'l Tel. & Tel. Corp. v. Alexander, 396 F. Supp. 1150 (D. Del. 1975); Kyron Found. v. Dunlop, 110 F. Supp. 428 (D.D.C. 1952).

One of the considerations in determining the nature of litigation in the tax-exempt organizations context is the likelihood of the award of reasonable litigation costs. This type of award can be made in the case of a civil proceeding brought by or against the federal government in connection with the determination, collection, or refund of any federal tax.[237] This award is accorded to the prevailing party that establishes that the position of the government in the proceeding "was not substantially justified" and has substantially prevailed with respect to the amount in controversy or the "most significant issue or set of issues presented."[238] An award is not available with respect to any declaratory judgment proceeding, however, other than a proceeding that involves the revocation of a determination that the organization is a charitable entity.[239]

Once an organization has secured a final determination from a court that it is tax-exempt, and if the material facts and law have not changed since court consideration, the IRS will, on request, issue a ruling or determination letter recognizing the exemption. If, however, the organization did not previously file an application for recognition of exempt status, the IRS will not issue the ruling or determination letter until the application is submitted.[240]

Absent relief administratively or in the courts, an organization facing loss of tax-exempt status has no choice but to accept the revocation, discontinue the disqualifying activity (if its activities are sufficiently separable), and reestablish its exemption,[241] or to spin the disqualifying activity off into a taxable subsidiary[242] or an auxiliary exempt organization[243] and reestablish its exemption. Or the organization may attempt an alternative to formal exempt status, such as by operating as a nonexempt cooperative.[244]

§ 27.6 IRS EXAMINATION PROCEDURES AND PRACTICES

Federal tax law includes procedures for IRS examinations of tax-exempt organizations; special rules apply in instances of church audits. The IRS has provided considerable detail as to its approach to examinations of exempt organizations in audit guidelines promulgated for examinations of hospitals, colleges, and universities.

(a) General IRS Exempt Organizations Audit Procedures and Practices

The IRS examines the activities and records of tax-exempt organizations. In general, the agency is authorized to ascertain the correctness of any return, make a return

---

[237] IRC § 7430(a).

[238] IRC § 7430(c)(2).

[239] IRC § 7430(b)(3).

[240] Rev. Proc. 80-28, 1980-1 C.B. 680.

[241] Compare Danz v. Comm'r, 18 T.C. 454 (1952), aff'd, 231 F.2d 673 (9th Cir. 1955), cert. denied, 352 U.S. 828 (1956), reh'g denied, 353 U.S. 951 (1957), with John Danz Charitable Trust v. Comm'r, 32 T.C. 469 (1959), aff'd, 284 F.2d 726 (9th Cir. 1960).

[242] American Inst. for Economic Research, Inc. v. United States, 302 F.2d 934 (Ct. Cl. 1962), cert. denied, 372 U.S. 976 (1963); Rev. Rul. 54-243, 1954-1 C.B. 92. See Chapter 30.

[243] Center on Corporate Responsibility, Inc. v. Shultz, 368 F. Supp. 863 (D.D.C. 1973). See Chapter 29.

[244] See § 3.4.

where none has been made, and determine the liability of any person for any internal revenue tax.[245] To this end, the IRS may examine any books, papers, records, or other data that may be relevant or material to its inquiry; summon persons liable for tax and/or having possession of pertinent records to appear before a representative of the agency, produce books and records, and give relevant testimony; and take testimony of persons under oath when relevant or material to an inquiry.[246]

(i) Case Preparation System   The IRS uses an inventory management system to create and control its tax-exempt organizations examinations cases. When examiners are assigned cases for review, they initially analyze the scope of the examination. This analysis includes checking the statute of limitations to verify that there is sufficient time to conduct a quality examination, conducting filing checks to determine whether the organization complies with federal tax and information return filing requirements, documenting the organizational requirements for exemption for the type of organization being examined, and performing additional internal and external research. The analysis also includes evaluating the issues that have been pre-identified during the return's selection process[247] and reviewing the return for any large, unusual, and/or questionable items.

Every IRS examinations case involves a focused examination, limited to the pre-identified issues and these items, unless a full-scope examination is warranted for reasons such as fraud or egregious noncompliance. The issues identified are set forth in an examination plan, along with examinations steps, timelines, and the method for conducting the examination (whether remotely or in person). The IRS views the examination plan as "nimble, agile and when warranted, adjusted throughout the examination"; thus, throughout an examination, examiners may expand or reduce its scope as deemed appropriate or necessary with their managers' concurrence.[248]

(ii) General Procedures.   An IRS examination is initiated and conducted in the field—that is, by a local IRS office. The initiation of this type of examination will be by mail. The agency will set the time and place of the examination, making efforts to be reasonable under the circumstances, balancing the convenience of the organization with the requirements of sound and efficient tax administration.[249] The examiners are specialists in the law of tax-exempt organizations. The Tax Exempt and Government Entities (TE/GE) Division in the IRS National Office[250] establishes the procedures and policies for the initiation and conduct of exempt organizations examinations. These examinations are coordinated in the IRS Exempt Organizations Examinations unit headquartered in Dallas, Texas.

Almost always, an IRS examination of a tax-exempt organization will focus on its documents and activities encompassed by one to three of the organization's years. In many instances (particularly where the exempt organization is a large

[245] IRC § 7602(a). "Congress has endowed the IRS with broad authority to conduct tax investigations" (United States v. El Paso Co., 682 F.2d 530, 544 (5th Cir. 1982)).

[246] *Id.*; Reg. § 301.7602-1(a).

[247] See § 27.6(b).

[248] Mem. TEGE-04-0622-0027 (Jun. 21, 2022).

[249] Reg. § 301.7605-1(a)(1).

[250] See § 2.2(a).

one and/or there are many issues involved in the inquiry), the IRS will set an initial conference (sometimes termed the *opening meeting*). Once that date is confirmed, the revenue agent(s) conducting the examination will begin the process of collecting documents and other information. The formal procedure is for the IRS to seek this information by submitting to the exempt organization one or more *information document requests*.[251]

The reasons for an IRS examination of a tax-exempt organization are manifold. The agency often focuses on particular categories of exempt organizations, such as health care institutions, colleges and universities, private foundations, and credit counseling and down payment assistance organizations. An examination may be initiated based on the size of the organization or the length of time that has elapsed since a prior audit. An examination may be undertaken following the filing of an information or tax return,[252] inasmuch as one of the functions of the IRS is to ascertain the correctness of returns.[253] Other reasons for the development of an examination include media reports, a state attorney general's inquiry, or other third-party reports of alleged wrongdoing.[254]

The records of a tax-exempt organization that must be produced in connection with an examination are likely to include all organizational documents (such as articles of organization, bylaws, resolutions, and minutes of board meetings), documents relating to tax status (such as the application for recognition of exemption and IRS rulings as to exempt and public charity status), financial statements, and newsletters and similar publications. The items that must be produced will depend in part on the type of examination being conducted; the examination may or may not encompass review of payroll records, retirement plan and deferred compensation matters, tax returns of associated individuals or affiliated entities, and the like. The exempt organization should produce documents and other information only in response to an information document request; in some instances, the exempt organization may be advised to produce information only in response to a summons.[255] The IRS is quite aggressive in revoking the exempt status of organizations that fail to respond to its requests for information.[256]

---

[251] IRS Form 4564.

[252] Reg. § 601.103(b).

[253] See text accompanied by *supra* note 245.

[254] As to this third reason for an examination, the IRS refers to these reports as containing *information items*, defined as information from an internal or external source concerning potential noncompliance with the tax law by an exempt organization.

[255] The authority of the IRS to issue summonses is one of the subjects of IRC § 7602. A discussion of enforcement proceedings in connection with IRS administrative summonses issued to exempt organizations is in United States v. Church of Scientology of Calif., 500 F.2d 818 (9th Cir. 1975). In general, the U.S. Supreme Court broadly construes the IRS summons power (e.g., United States v. LaSalle Nat'l Bank, 437 U.S. 298 (1978), *rev'g and remanding* 554 F.2d 302 (7th Cir. 1977)). The IRS may establish a prima facie case to enforce a summons if it shows the summons was issued for a legitimate purpose; the summoned data may be relevant to that purpose; the data is not already in the IRS's possession; and the IRS has followed the administrative steps for issuing and serving the summons (United States v. Powell, 379 U.S. 48, 57–58 (1964)).

A federal district court upheld and ordered enforced an IRS summons to a tax-exempt organization, issued in connection with an examination of the entity; the court rejected the organization's assertion that the summons was unenforceable because the audit was politically motivated (United States v. Judicial Watch, Inc., 266 F. Supp. 2d 1 (D.D.C. 2002), *aff'd*, 2004-1 U.S.T.C. ¶ 50,115 (D.C. Cir. 2004)).

[256] See § 28.17.

The IRS examiner reviews and verifies supporting documentation to develop the potential issues identified, researches the applicable tax law, and determines the extent of compliance in connection with the identified issues. The examiner documents the findings and conclusions in work papers stored in the case inventory management system. Once the issues are developed, the examiner communicates them to the organization and receives the organization's response. Thereafter, the examiner will issue a final report, finalize case file work papers, and close the case for the manager's review.[257]

If an examiner identifies indicators of fraud during an examination, and the group manager and a TE/GE Fraud Specialist agree that the indicators have fraud potential, the examiner is to work with a fraud technical advisor to create an action place for development of the potential fraud case. The examiner will proceed with the plan of action until acts of fraud are affirmatively established or a determination is made that fraud is no longer an issue. If fraud is substantiated, the case is to be closed by the examiner with civil fraud penalties or referred to the Criminal Investigation Division. If fraud does not exist, the examiner is to close the case in accordance with normal closing procedures.[258] The criminal investigation function is rarely used in tax-exempt organization cases.

The IRS has in the Internal Revenue Manual detailed *Tax-Exempt Organizations Examination Procedures* for the agency's examinations of tax-exempt organizations.[259] These procedures explain the processes for the pre-examination phase, various types of examinations, the examiner's responsibilities, use of closing agreements, the team examination program procedures, and more.

Prior to 2020, the Internal Revenue Manual also included information on audit guidelines and techniques for exempt organizations. After 2019, however, this information was removed from the Internal Revenue Manual, reserving it for procedural guidance. To retain this information, the IRS initially created Audit Technique Guides (ATGs), but in 2021 began publishing Technical Guides (TGs) and will continue publishing them until all the topics in the ATGs and other relevant tax-exempt status matters are covered in TGs. The TGs are intended, in part, to serve as a research aid and training tool for Exempt Organizations specialists conducting examinations,[260] and they recommend specific examination techniques. The ATGs and TGs currently published by the IRS are available on its website.[261]

(iii) Types of Examinations   There are several types of IRS examinations; there are formal and informal classifications of them. Common among these examinations are, as noted, *field examinations*, in which one or more IRS revenue agents review the books, records, and other documents and information of the organization under examination, at an IRS office or on the premises of the organization.[262]

---

[257] Treasury Inspector General for Tax Administration, "Obstacles Exist in Detecting Noncompliance of Tax-Exempt Organizations," Rep. No. 2021-10-013 (Feb. 17, 2021), App. II.

[258] *Id.*

[259] Internal Revenue Manual, Part 4, Chapter 4.75.

[260] Pub. 5729, *Exempt Organizations Technical Guide TG 0: Technical Guide Overview* (Dec. 2023).

[261] https://www.irs.gov/charities-non-profits/audit-technique-guides-atgs-and-technical-guides-tgs-for-exempt-organizations.

[262] Reg. § 601.105(b)(3).

In general, the primary objective of an exempt organization examination is to determine whether the organization is organized and operated in accordance with its exempt function. The examiner is also expected to determine the organization's liability for the unrelated business income tax, its liability for any excise taxes, whether it engaged in political activities that require filing of a return,[263] and whether it has properly filed annual information returns, other returns, and forms. The procedures require the examiner to establish the scope of the examination, outline when the examination will be limited in scope, state the documentation requirements imposed on the examiner, and summarize the examination techniques (such as interviews, tours of facilities, and review of books and records). The IRS Tax Exempt Quality Measurement System established quality standards applicable to exempt organizations examinations.

The IRS has an Office/Correspondence Examination Program pursuant to which exempt organizations examiners conduct the examination of returns by an office interview or by means of correspondence. An *office interview case* is one where the examiner requests review of records in an IRS office; this may entail an interview with a representative of the organization.[264] On occasion, the interview will occur elsewhere, such as in the office of the organization or its authorized representative. A *correspondence examination* involves an IRS request for information from an organization by letter, fax, or e-mail communication.[265] OCEP examinations generally are limited in scope, usually focusing on no more than three issues, conducted by lower-grade examiners. If warranted, a correspondence examination will be converted to an office or field examination.

For years, one of the mainstays of the IRS exempt organizations examination effort was the *coordinated examination program* (CEP), which focused not only on tax-exempt organizations but also on affiliated entities and arrangements (such as subsidiaries, partnerships, and other joint ventures) and collateral areas of the law (such as employment and exempt bond law). This program has been abandoned, however, and replaced by the *team examination program* (TEP). The CEP and TEP approaches share the same objective, however, which is to avoid a fragmenting of the examination process by using a multi-agent approach. The essential characteristics of this team approach that differentiate it from the coordinated examination approach are that the team examinations are utilized in connection with a wider array of exempt organizations, the number of revenue agents involved in each examination is smaller, and the revenue agents are less likely to establish audit offices at the exempt organizations.

A TEP case generally is one where the tax-exempt organization's annual information return reflects either total revenue or assets greater than $100 million (or, in the case of a private foundation, $500 million). Nonetheless, the IRS may initiate a team examination where the case would benefit (from the government's standpoint) from a team examination approach or where there is no annual information return filing requirement. There is a presumption that a team examination approach will be utilized in all cases meeting the TEP criteria.

---

[263] Form 1120-POL.
[264] Reg. § 601.105(b)(2).
[265] *Id.*

In a TEP case, the examination will proceed under the direction of a case manager. There will be one or more exempt organizations revenue agents, possibly coupled with the involvement of employee plans specialists, actuarial examiners, engineers, excise tax agents, international examiners, computer audit specialists, income tax revenue agents, and economists. These examinations are likely to last two to three years; a post-examination critique may lead to a cycling of the examination into following years. The procedures stipulate the planning that case managers, assisted by team coordinators, should engage in when starting a team examination; they also provide for the exempt organizations' involvement in the planning process. The procedures, of course, detail the flow of the examination.

(b)   IRS Exempt Organizations Examination Management

Within the TE/GE Division, the EO Examinations unit provides a centralized approach to compliance planning, examination selection and assignment, and planning and monitoring activities. (Technically, the IRS examines returns, not organizations.)

Within the Examinations unit, the Compliance Planning and Classification (CP&C) function is responsible for these centralization programs. This function has three groups: (1) Issue Identification and Special Review, which identifies and develops issues for examinations or compliance activities and criteria for examination selection; (2) Classification and Case Assignment, which reviews returns for examination;[266] and (3) Planning and Monitoring, which develops an annual work plan, detailing the number of examination starts, closures, and other measures, and monitors performance.

TE/GE's Compliance Governance Board oversees TE/GE's compliance program, including CP&C operations such as approving priority issue areas (i.e., compliance strategies). This board reviews program goals, considers metrics and reporting, and reviews performance of compliance strategies.[267]

TE/GE identifies exempt organization returns for examination from many sources and categorizes examinations into three groups:[268] data-driven approaches, referrals and other casework, and compliance strategies. All three of these portfolios rely on data, to some extent, to make decisions on selecting returns for examination.

The data-driven-approach portfolio uses analytical models and queries based on quantitative criteria (or *query sets*) to identify potential examinations.[269] Three

---

[266] IRS personnel in this regard are referred to as *classifiers*. *Classification* is the process of determining whether a return should be selected for compliance activities, what issues should be the primary focus of the compliance activity, and the type of compliance activity that should be conducted.

[267] This board has five TE/GE executives, along with counsel, who are voting members; there are three nonvoting members.

[268] The IRS refers to these groups as *portfolios*.

[269] Most of the text in this section is derived from U.S. Government Accountability Office, "Tax Exempt Organizations: IRS Increasingly Uses Data in Examination Selection, but Could Further Improve Selection Processes," Rep. No. GAO-20-454 (June 2020). The IRS was criticized for not fully implementing or documenting internal controls in its processes for analyzing data for examination selection. The GAO stated that (1) the IRS has not defined measurable objectives for using data to select returns for examination, (2) IRS's models have deficiencies affecting the validity and reliability of return scoring and selection, (3) the IRS did not consistently document the processing and use of data in decision-making on examination selection, and (4) the IRS does not regularly evaluate examination selection.

models are used to review exempt organization data from annual information returns for compliance. The models score returns for examination based on potential noncompliance; these models have 354 unique queries. A query reviews databases to identify responses on returns that may indicate noncompliance because they do not meet certain criteria or expected values, such as exceeding a dollar threshold. The models use a scoring system that applies weights, or points, to each query result to generate a score for a return. Biannually, each model is run using the latest data; the run generates a model score sheet, which is a ranked list of returns that score above a minimum threshold. A classifier uses the ranking to identify returns for potential examination, selecting returns in fulfillment of a "stocking plan," which identifies the number and type of returns to be examined in satisfaction of IRS work plan requirements.[270] Aside from the three models, the TE/GE Division uses other methods and data to identify and develop its compliance work.[271]

As to the referrals and other casework portfolios, returns are selected for examination (1) based on referrals (complaints) about exempt organization noncompliance submitted by third parties; (2) in connection with post-determination compliance queries with respect to organizations that filed Form 1023-EZ;[272] (3) in response to requests for tax refunds, adjustments of tax paid, or credits; and (4) as part of the training of examiners.

The compliance strategies portfolio concerns compliance issues that originated from a Compliance Issue Submission Portal for TE/GE Division staff. The strategies are approved by the Governance Board, which results in adding the compliance strategies to the IRS work plan. Returns are selected using sampling or other uses of data.

Once an examination is under way, an examiner may expand it to include an organization's returns for other tax years or other types of returns, such as employment tax returns. These additional examinations, which the IRS refers to as *pick-ups*, are counted by the IRS as separate examinations. Examiners must obtain manager approval to expand an examination.

Examiners are required to check that an exempt organization filed all returns that are required. If an examiner finds that a return was not filed by an organization and is unable to secure the return, the examiner has the authority to prepare a "dummy" return (termed a *substitute for return*), leading to an examination of the organization's activities, records, and documents.

The TE/GE Division also conducts *compliance contacts*, that is, nonexamination correspondence in the form of compliance checks and soft letters, in connection with some compliance issues. Compliance checks determine whether specific reporting or filing requirements have been met. A soft letter is used to notify an exempt organization of changes in the law of tax-exempt organizations or potential compliance issues.

---

[270] For example, the model is run against Form 990 series returns, leading to a ranked list of scored returns for examination consideration. A classifier reviews the list, makes eliminations, fills the stocking plan, and selects returns that are placed into data systems to await assignment. Managers then assign cases to examiners, who commence examinations.

[271] For example, this portfolio includes approaches that the division developed in partnership with the IRS's Research, Applied Analytics, and Statistics Division.

[272] See § 26.1(f).

Examinations have various outcomes, the most severe being revocation of the organization's tax-exempt status. Income, employment, and/or excise taxes may be assessed as a result of an examination.[273]

(c) Church Audits

Special statutory rules govern federal tax inquiries and churches.[274] For these purposes, a *church* includes any organization claiming to be a church or a convention or association of churches,[275] but the term does not include church-supported schools or other organizations that are incorporated separately from the church.[276]

An inquiry of a church's tax liabilities—a *church tax inquiry*—may be commenced by the IRS only where an appropriate high-level U.S. Treasury official[277] reasonably believes, based on facts and circumstances recorded in writing, that

---

[273] In the government's 2023 fiscal year, 2,464 exempt organization examinations were closed; 746 of these cases involved the data-driven portfolio approach, 1,497 originated with the referrals and other casework portfolio, and 221 involved the compliance strategies portfolio. Overall, 76% of closed examinations resulted in a tax change (change percentage) and 40% of the examinations were pick-ups from a related examination. Revocation of exempt status was proposed for 141 tax-exempt entities because of these examinations (Pub. 5329, *Fiscal Year 2023 Accomplishments Letter* (Jan. 2024).

[274] IRC § 7611. A court characterized these rules as follows: "The IRS has broad authority with respect to tax inquiries," although Congress "has scaled back these powers with respect to church tax inquiries"; also, this provision "provides certain procedural protections to insure that the IRS does not embark on an impermissibly intrusive inquiry into church affairs" (United States v. Church of Scientology of Boston, Inc., 739 F. Supp. 46, 47 (D. Mass. 1990), *aff'd*, 933 F.2d 1074 (1st Cir. 1991)).

These rules are inapplicable where the inquiry is directed at one or more church leaders personally, rather than the church (e.g., Rowe v. United States, 2018 WL 2234810 (E.D. La. 2018); St. German of Alaska E. Orthodox Catholic Church v. United States, 653 F. Supp. 1342 (S.D.N.Y. 1987), *aff'd*, 840 F.2d 1087 (2d Cir. 1988)). Cf. Assembly of Yahveh Beth Israel v. United States, 87-1 U.S.T.C. ¶ 9353 (D. Col. 1984).

[275] IRC § 7611(h)(1). See §§ 10.3, 10.4.

[276] H.R. Rep. No. 98-861, at 1102 (1984).

[277] That phrase is defined to mean the Secretary of the Treasury "or any delegate of the Secretary whose rank is no lower than that of a principal Internal Revenue officer for an internal revenue region" (IRC § 7611(h)(7)). Prior to its reorganization (see § 2.2(a)), the IRS identified the appropriate Regional Commissioner (or higher Treasury official) as this appropriate high-level official (Reg. § 301.7611-1, Q&A(1)). The Regional Commissioner positions, however, were abolished as part of the reorganization. The IRS thereafter designated the Director, Examinations, as that official. A federal district court ruled, in a summons enforcement proceeding, that, based principally on the constitutional law reasons for the church audit rules, the Director, Examinations, is too low in rank to qualify (and thus that the church tax inquiry was improperly commenced) (United States v. Living Word Christian Center, 2009-1 U.S.T.C. ¶ 50,199 (D. Minn. 2009)). The IRS thereafter, in 2009, proposed regulations that would denominate the Director, Exempt Organizations, as the appropriate high-level Treasury official (Prop. Reg. § 301-7611-1).

A court subsequently held that the EO Director holds too low a rank in the IRS bureaucracy to qualify as the official to initiate church tax audits, but that the Commissioner, TEGE is sufficiently high ranking within the meaning of IRC § 7611(h)(7) to initiate such an inquiry (United States v. Bible Study Time, Inc., 295 F. Supp. 3d 606 (D.S.C. 2018)). The Internal Revenue Manual (§ 25.5.8.3.2) was revised in 2020, in connection with the section concerning use of summonses; this revision states that the "designated official to approve a church tax inquiry under IRC [§] 7611(a) is the Commissioner, TEGE." It is not known at this time how this development will affect the designation of the Director, Exempt Organizations as the appropriate official under the existing regulation project. However, the IRS currently appears to be operating under this procedure by having the Commissioner, TEGE make the determination to commence a church tax inquiry (God's Storehouse Topeka Church v. United States, 131 A.F.T.R. 2d 2023-1177 (D. Kan. 2023); Priv. Ltr. Rul. 201921014).

the organization may not qualify for tax exemption as a church, may be carrying on an unrelated trade or business,[278] or may otherwise be engaged in nonexempt activities.[279]

The IRS may examine church records or religious activities—a *church tax examination*—only if, at least 15 days prior to the examination, the IRS provides written notice to the church and to the appropriate IRS regional counsel of the proposed examination.[280] This notice is in addition to the notice of commencement of a tax inquiry previously provided to the church. A *church tax examination* is any examination, for purposes of making a determination as described in the *church tax inquiry* definition, of church records at the request of the IRS or of the religious activities of any church.[281] For purposes of these rules, church records exclude records acquired from a third party pursuant to a summons.[282]

§ 27.7 COMPLIANCE CHECKS

An overlay to the IRS program of examinations of tax-exempt organizations is the agency's compliance check program, which focuses on specific compliance issues. The term *compliance check* has two meanings.

When the compliance check concept originated, it was manifested in IRS's inquiries into the operations of tax-exempt hospitals, institutions of higher education, and community foundations; the levels and types of compensation provided by exempt organizations; involvement by public charities in political campaign activities; compliance by applicable exempt organizations in annual information return reporting of any involvement in excess benefit transactions; tax-exempt bonds record-keeping compliance by exempt organizations; and a charitable spending initiative. These compliance checks were usually initiated by the mailing of questionnaires to appropriate exempt organizations. The IRS currently lacks the capacity to administer this type of program.

Today, a compliance is a review conducted by the IRS to determine whether an organization is adhering to record-keeping and information reporting requirements or whether its activities are consistent with its stated tax-exempt purpose. This approach does not entail an examination of the organization's books and records and does not directly relate to determining tax liability for any specific tax year(s). An exempt organization may refuse to participate in a compliance check without penalty; however, the IRS has the option of opening a formal

---

[278] See Chapters 24, 25.

[279] IRC §§ 7611(a)(1)(A), (2).

[280] IRC §§ 7611(b)(1), (2)(A).

[281] IRC § 7611(h)(3).

[282] IRC §§ 7609 and 7611(h)(4). Third-party summonses are governed by IRC § 7609, not IRC § 7611, even when the summons is issued in connection with a church tax inquiry (God's Storehouse Topeka Church v. United States, 133 A.F.T.R. 2d 2024-1333 (10th Cir. 2024) *aff'g* 131 A.F.T.R. 2d 2023-1177 (D. Kan. 2023); United States v. C.E. Hobbs Found. for Religious Training & Educ., Inc., 7 F.3d 169 (9th Cir. 1993); Bible Study Time, Inc. v. United States, 240 F. Supp. 3d 409 (D.S.C. 2017)). However, if the IRS issues a summons to a third party, the affected taxpayer is entitled to notice of the summons (subject to certain exceptions) and has a right to intervene and to move to quash the summons (IRC § 7609(a)).

examination regardless of whether the organization agrees to participate in a compliance check.[283]

§ 27.8   FAST-TRACK CASE SETTLEMENT PROGRAM

The IRS maintains a program enabling tax-exempt organizations with issues under examination by the TE/GE Division to use a fast-track settlement (FTS) process to expedite resolution of their cases.[284] This program is intended to allow exempt organizations that have unagreed issues in at least one open period under examination to work with the Division and the Independent Office of Appeals to resolve outstanding disputed issues while the case is still in the jurisdiction of the TE/GE Division. The Division and Appeals jointly administer this FTS process.

The procedures for using this FTS program are based on those the IRS developed to implement the Large and Mid-Size Business Division FTS dispute resolution program[285] and the Small Business/Self-Employed Taxpayer Division FTS dispute resolution program.[286] FTS is available for exemption, public charity/private foundation status, and certain other issues where the exempt organization has a written statement of its position and there is a "limited number" of factual and/or law issues. FTS is not available for a list of matters, including issues designated for litigation, correspondence examination cases, frivolous issues, and cases involving civil or criminal fraud.

An organization that is interested in participating in this FTS process, or that has questions about the program and its suitability for a particular case, may contact the TE/GE group manager of the agent conducting the audit for the period(s) under examination. The organization, examining agent, or group manager may initiate an application[287] to the FTS process. A notice of proposed adjustment[288] or a revenue agent report will be prepared by the examining agent. If a case is not accepted for inclusion in the program, the IRS will discuss other dispute resolution opportunities with the organization.

FTS employs various alternative dispute resolution techniques to promote agreement. An FTS Appeals official will serve as a neutral party. This official thus will not perform in a traditional Appeals role but rather will use dispute resolution techniques to facilitate settlement. An FTS session report will be developed to assist in planning, and reporting on developments during, the FTS session. This report will include a description of the issues, the amounts in dispute, conference dates, and a plan of action for the session. If the parties resolve any of the issues at the session, the parties and the Appeals official will sign the session report acknowledging acceptance of the terms of settlement for purposes of preparing computations. The TE/GE FTS process is confidential.

---

[283] Pub. 4386, *Compliance Checks: Examination, Audit or Compliance Check* (Apr. 2006). Also, FS-2008-14.
[284] Ann. 2012-34, 2012-36 I.R.B. 334.
[285] Rev. Proc. 2003-40, 2003-1 C.B. 1044.
[286] Ann. 2006-61, 2006-2 C.B. 390.
[287] Form 14017.
[288] Form 5701.

FTS may be initiated at any time after an issue has been fully developed but before issuance of a 30-day letter (or its equivalent). After starting as a two-year pilot program, the FTS program is now permanent, as the IRS determined that it supports the agency-wide initiative of reducing the time and cost of examination and case resolution.[289]

§ 27.9 IRS DISCLOSURE TO STATE OFFICIALS

In response to a written request by an appropriate state officer, the IRS may disclose (1) a refusal or notice of proposed refusal to recognize an organization as a charitable entity;[290] (2) a revocation or notice of proposed revocation of tax exemption of a charitable organization; (3) the issuance of a notice of deficiency or proposed notice of deficiency of certain taxes;[291] (4) the names, addresses, and taxpayer identification numbers of organizations that have applied for recognition of exemption as charitable organizations; and (5) returns and return information of organizations with respect to which information has been disclosed pursuant to the foregoing four categories of disclosure.[292] These returns and return information also may be open to inspection by an appropriate state officer.[293] Disclosure or inspection is permitted for the purpose of, and only to the extent necessary in, the administration of state laws regulating charitable organizations, such as laws regulating exempt status, charitable trusts, charitable solicitation, and fraud.[294]

On the written request by an appropriate state officer, the IRS may make available for inspection or disclosure returns and return information of any other type of tax-exempt organization.[295] These returns and return information are available for inspection or disclosure only for the purpose of, and to the extent necessary

---

[289] Ann. 2012-34, 2012-36 I.R.B. 334.

[290] That is, an organization described in IRC § 501(c)(3). See Part Three.

[291] That is, taxes imposed pursuant to IRC § 507, and IRC Chapter 41 or 42.

[292] IRC § 6104(c)(2); also, Rev. Proc. 2024-5, 2024-1 I.R.B. 262 §§ 13.06, 13.07. Under certain circumstances, the IRS on its own initiative may disclose the returns and return information of a charitable organization if the IRS determines that such information might constitute evidence of noncompliance with the laws under the jurisdiction of the appropriate state officer regulating charitable organizations (Reg. § 301.6104(c)-1(c)(2)).

[293] IRC § 6104(c)(2)(B). The terms "return" and "return information" are defined by IRC § 6103(b). State officials who receive returns or return information are subject to restrictions on redisclosure of such information (IRC § 6103(a)(2); Reg. § 301.6104(c)-1(g)), are required to establish and maintain certain safeguards to protect the confidentiality of such records as a condition for receiving such information (IRC § 6103(p)(4)), and are subject to civil and criminal penalties for the unauthorized disclosure of such information (IRC §§ 7213, 7213A, and 7431). A report by the Treasury Inspector General for Tax Administration found that both the IRS and state charity regulators are limited by their respective laws and procedures for coordinating with each other to identify tax-exempt organizations potentially engaging in illegal or other nonexempt activities (TIGTA, "Review of the IRS's Enforcement Program for Tax-Exempt Organizations That Participate in Illegal or Nonexempt Activities," Rep. No. 2022-10-064 (Sept. 29, 2022)). This report noted that, as of its publication date, no State Attorneys General Offices have formal disclosure agreements with the IRS (id.).

[294] IRC § 6104(c)(2)(C).

[295] IRC § 6104(c)(3). This rule does not extend, however, to organizations described in IRC § 501(c)(1) (see § 19.1).

in, the administration of state laws regulating the solicitation or administration of the charitable funds or charitable assets of those organizations.[296]

Any returns and return information disclosed may also be disclosed in civil administrative and civil judicial proceedings pertaining to the enforcement of state laws regulating the applicable tax-exempt organization.[297] Returns and return information may not be disclosed to the extent that the IRS determines that the disclosure would seriously impair federal tax administration.[298]

For these purposes, the term *appropriate state officer* means the state attorney general; the state tax officer; in the case of a tax-exempt charitable organization, any other state official charged with oversight of charitable organizations; and, in the case of another category of exempt organization, the head of the agency designated by the state attorney general who has the primary responsibility for overseeing the solicitation of funds for charitable purposes (in the case of exempt organizations generally).[299]

---

[296] IRC § 6104(c)(3).
[297] IRC § 6104(c)(4).
[298] IRC § 6104(c)(5).
[299] IRC § 6104(c)(6)(B); Reg. § 301.6104(c)-1(i)(1).

Operational Requirements

The federal tax law imposes a plethora of operational requirements on tax-exempt organizations, irrespective of whether they have received recognition of tax-exempt status from the IRS. For most exempt organizations, the principal responsibility is the filing of an annual information return with the IRS. Other reporting, disclosure, and record-keeping obligations are imposed on exempt organizations.

§ 28.1 CHANGES IN OPERATIONS OR FORM

Once an organization achieves tax-exempt status, that qualification can be maintained as long as the entity does not materially change its character, purposes, or methods of operation.[1] A change in an organization's form may have tax consequences.

(a) Changes in Operations

An organization's tax-exempt status remains in effect as long as there are no substantial—*material*—changes in the organization's character, purposes, or methods of operation.[2] An organization and its advisers have the burden of determining

---

[1] Reg. § 1.501(a)-1(a)(2). Also, Rev. Rul. 68-217, 1968-2 C.B. 260. The IRS may revoke a ruling letter that recognized an organization's tax exemption, without retroactive effect, pursuant to IRC § 7805(b), but in this case the organization would be subject to taxation on any unrelated business taxable income (see Chapters 24, 25) during the IRC § 7805(b) relief period (Rev. Rul. 78-289, 1978-2 C.B. 180). It is the view of the IRS that the principle of this 1978 ruling is applicable with respect to the political activities tax (see §§ 17.5, 17.6) (Gen. Couns. Mem. 39811).

[2] Reg. §§ 1.501(a)-1(a)(2), 601.201(n)(3)(ii).

whether a change of this nature is material or immaterial. These changes should be reported on the annual information return.[3]

A substantial change in an organization's character, purposes, or methods of operation may result in retroactive modification or revocation of the organization's tax-exempt status.[4] Indeed, a ruling or determination letter recognizing tax exemption may not be relied on if there is a material change, inconsistent with exemption, in the character, purpose, or method of operation of the organization.[5]

There is no sanction that is automatically levied by the IRS for failure to notify the agency of a change of facts, in relation to those stated on the application for recognition of tax exemption, concerning the operations of an exempt organization. This is the case even when the fact change is material. It may be that the change of facts involves a substantial expansion of exempt function activities, so that the exempt status of the entity is not imperiled. Even if new facts reveal nonexempt activities, exemption will not be disturbed if the fact change is insubstantial (although there may be unrelated business tax implications).[6] A misrepresentation of fact on the application for recognition of exemption will not necessarily have adverse consequences to the organization if the circumstances do not involve a violation of the law of tax-exempt organizations. As to the latter, for example, a charitable organization represented on its application that insiders with respect to it[7] were providing the organization facilities without charge, when in fact there was a rental arrangement; when the IRS discovered the truth, the agency did not revoke the exemption because it accepted the rent as being of fair value.[8]

(b) Changes in Form

A change in organizational form technically entails creation of a new legal entity, even though the organization's purposes, methods of operation, sources of support, and accounting method remain the same. For decades, it was the position of the IRS that often this change in form required the filing of an application for recognition of exemption for the successor entity.[9]

This is no longer the case; generally, a new application for recognition of exemption from a tax-exempt organization that changes its form or place of organization is not required.[10] This policy applies where (1) the restructuring organization is recognized as exempt and is in good standing in its state of formation; (2) the restructuring organization and the surviving organization (perhaps the same entity) must be domestic business entities that are classified as corporations; (3) the surviving organization continues to carry out the same purposes as the restructuring organization; and (4), in the case of charitable

---

[3] E.g., Form 990, Part III, lines 2 and 3.
[4] See § 27.3(a).
[5] See § 26.1(h).
[6] See Chapters 24, 25.
[7] See § 20.3.
[8] Tech. Adv. Mem. 9835003.
[9] Rev. Rul. 67-390, 1967-2 C.B. 179, *obsoleted by* Rev. Proc. 2018-15, 2018-9 I.R.B. 376.
[10] Rev. Proc. 2018-15, 2018-9 I.R.B. 379.

organizations, the articles of incorporation must continue to meet the organizational test,[11] including the requirement of a dissolution clause.[12] These rules are inapplicable to a restructuring in which (1) the restructuring organization is a disregarded entity,[13] limited liability company, partnership, or foreign business entity; or (2) the surviving organization obtains a new employer identification number. This change in policy also does not apply to a corporate restructuring in which the surviving organization seeks a determination that it is exempt under a category of exemption that is different from its prior determination.

When the IRS issues a determination letter recognizing the tax-exempt status of a corporation, generally the effective date is the date of incorporation or the date the entity became organized and operated for exempt purposes.[14] When prior to incorporation an organization was formed and operated in an exempt manner and its incorporation merely had the effect of changing the form of organization from that of an unincorporated organization to a corporation, however, the determination letter embraces the period during which the organization operated in an unincorporated status.[15]

It should not be assumed that the tax status of a predecessor entity will automatically be transmitted to a successor entity. For example, as noted, the policies and views of the IRS may change, and the IRS may deny recognition of tax exemption to an organization even though it granted recognition of exemption to a predecessor organization and the material facts did not differ.[16]

The law also imposes comparable requirements in other areas. Thus, an organization that remains in existence after terminating its private foundation status[17] must file a new application for recognition of exemption if it wishes to be treated as a charitable organization, since the IRS regards it as a newly created entity.[18] Similarly, a tax-exempt corporation formed to take over the operations of an exempt unincorporated association is regarded as a new organization for purposes of filing the Social Security tax waiver certificate.[19]

The continuity of existence of a charitable organization is of importance, notwithstanding a change in form. This is particularly the case where the organization has its nonprivate foundation status predicated on classification as a publicly supported organization, which classification contemplates a history of required financial support.[20] Where certain requirements are met, the IRS allows the financial history of the predecessor entity to be used in establishing a public support record for the successor entity.[21]

---

[11] See § 4.3.

[12] See § 4.3(b).

[13] See § 4.1(b).

[14] Rev. Rul. 54-134, 1954-1 C.B. 88.

[15] Id.

[16] E.g., MIB, Inc. v. Comm'r, 734 F.2d 71 (1st Cir. 1984); Nat'l Right to Work Legal Defense Educ. Found., Inc. v. United States, 487 F. Supp. 801 (E.D.N.C. 1979).

[17] See *Private Foundations*, Chapter 13.

[18] Rev. Rul. 74-490, 1974-2 C.B. 171.

[19] Rev. Rul. 77-159, 1977-1 C.B. 302. Also, Rev. Rul. 71-276, 1971-1 C.B. 289.

[20] See § 12.3(b).

[21] Rev. Rul. 73-422, 1973-2 C.B. 70.

If a tax-exempt organization converts to a taxable entity,[22] the termination of exempt status is ordinarily operative prospectively; retroactive loss of exemption would occur only if there had been a material misrepresentation of fact or material difference in actual operation.[23]

(c) Changes in Foundation or Public Charity Status

Because of changes in its activities or operations, an organization's current public charity status may differ from the public charity status referenced in its original determination letter. An organization is not required to obtain a new determination letter to qualify for a different public charity status. For IRS records to recognize a change in public charity status, however, an organization must obtain a new determination letter as to public charity status by filing Form 8940.[24]

If a tax-exempt charitable organization ceases to qualify as a public charity, it becomes a private foundation by operation of law.[25] Thereafter, if the organization again qualifies as a public charity for a 60-month period, the organization may terminate its private foundation status, by giving the appropriate notice to the IRS.[26]

A tax-exempt charitable organization that erroneously determined that it was a private foundation, such as by mistakenly classifying an item or items in its calculation of public support,[27] and wishes to correct the error may request a determination letter classifying it as a public charity by showing that it continuously satisfied the applicable public support test, or otherwise qualified as a public charity, during the relevant periods.[28]

A private foundation may qualify as a private operating foundation[29] without a determination letter from the IRS. The IRS, however, will not recognize private operating foundation status in its records without a determination letter from the IRS.[30] An organization claiming to be an exempt operating foundation[31] must obtain a determination letter from the IRS recognizing that status.[32]

---

[22] See § 32.6.

[23] E.g., Priv. Ltr. Rul. 8446047. See § 27.3(a).

[24] Rev. Proc. 2024-5, 2024-1 I.R.B. 262 § 7.04(1). As to filing Form 8940, see § 28.1(d).

[25] IRC § 508(b); Rev. Proc. 2024-5, 2024-1 I.R.B. 262 § 7.04(2). See § 12.1(a); *Private Foundations* §§ 1.2, 15.8. The organization indicates this change in status on the appropriate annual information return (Form 990-PF).

[26] Rev. Proc. 2024-5, 2024-1 I.R.B. 262 § 7.04(2). As to the required notice, see *Private Foundations* § 13.4. This notice is given by filing Form 8940 (see § 28.1(d)).

[27] See § 12.3(b).

[28] Rev. Proc. 2024-5, 2024-1 I.R.B. 262 § 7.04(3). This request is made by filing Form 8940 (see § 28.1(d)).

[29] See § 12.1(b); *Private Foundations* § 3.1.

[30] Rev. Proc. 2024-5, 2024-1 I.R.B. 262 § 7.04(4). A request for a determination letter recognizing private operating foundation status is made by filing Form 8940 (see § 28.1(d)).

[31] See § 12.1(c); *Private Foundations* § 3.2.

[32] Rev. Proc. 2024-5, 2024-1 I.R.B. 262 § 7.04(4). In other words, an organization in this position cannot be exempt from the tax on net investment income (see § 12.4(f); *Private Foundations*, Chapter 10) without a determination letter. A request for a determination letter recognizing exempt operating foundation status is made by filing Form 8940 (see § 28.1(d)).

The procedures for requesting updated determination letters do not, however, apply to changes to an organization's public charity or private foundation status resulting from an IRS examination.[33]

(d) Form 8940 Determination Letter Requests

Determination letter requests relating to certain changes in an organization's character or methods of operations must be made by filing Form 8940.[34] These requests must be electronically submitted on Form 8940 at www.pay.gov and include all required documentation and other required information, including the appropriate user fee.[35]

The following determination letter requests must be made by means of submission of Form 8940:[36] advance approval of certain private foundation and supporting organization set-asides;[37] advance approval of private foundation voter registration activities;[38] advance approval of private foundation procedures for certain grants to individuals;[39] exemption from annual information return filing requirements;[40] advance approval that a prospective grant or contribution is an unusual grant;[41] change in type, or initial determination of type, of a supporting organization (including whether it is a functionally integrated or nonfunctionally integrated Type III supporting organization);[42] reclassification of private foundation/public charity status, including a voluntary request from a public charity for private foundation status;[43] requests for an advance ruling on termination of private foundation status, giving notice of intent to terminate private foundation status without an advance ruling, or giving notice of the end of the 60-month period for termination of private foundation status by operating as a public charity;[44] requests by a government entity for voluntary termination of recognition of tax-exempt status as a charitable organization;[45] and requests by Canadian registered charities for inclusion in the IRS's *Tax Exempt Organization Search* database of organizations eligible to receive tax-deductible charitable contributions or a determination on their public charity classification.[46]

---

[33] Rev. Proc. 2024-5, 2024-1 I.R.B. 262 § 7.05(2).

[34] EO Determinations (see § 26.1, text accompanied by note 10) issues determination letters in response to requests submitted on Form 8940 (Rev. Proc. 2024-5, 2024-1 I.R.B. 262 § 4.02(6)). For determination letters in response to applications for initial qualification for tax-exempt status, see § 26.1.

[35] Rev. Proc. 2024-5, 2024-1 I.R.B. 262 §§ 4.02(6), 7.02.

[36] *Id.* § 4.02(6).

[37] See §§ 12.3(c), 12.4(b); *Private Foundations* § 6.4(g).

[38] See § 12.4(e); *Private Foundations* § 9.2(c).

[39] See § 12.4(e); *Private Foundations* § 9.3(d)–(f).

[40] See § 28.2(c).

[41] See § 12.3(b)(i), (iv); *Private Foundations* § 15.5(c).

[42] See § 12.3(c); *Private Foundations* §§ 15.6, 15.7(c), (d). This includes the initial classification or reclassification of a nonexempt charitable trust (IRC § 4947(a)(1); see *Private Foundations* § 3.6) as a supporting organization (Rev. Proc. 2024-5, 2024-1 I.R.B. 262 § 3.01(11)).

[43] See §§ 12.1, 12.3.

[44] See *Private Foundations* § 13.4.

[45] See § 26.16.

[46] See *Private Foundations* § 2.7(f).

User fees for determination letter requests submitted on Form 8940 currently range from $600 to $3,500.[47] No user fee is required for giving notice of intent to terminate private foundation status without an advance ruling request or for the requests made by Canadian registered charities previously described.[48] An organization may rely on an IRS determination letter issued in response to a request submitted on Form 8940 to the same extent and subject to the same limitations as an IRS determination letter as to initial qualification for tax-exempt status.[49]

§ 28.2 ANNUAL REPORTING RULES

Nearly every organization that is exempt from federal income taxation must file or submit an annual information return with the IRS.[50] This return generally is:

- Larger tax-exempt organizations—Form 990[51]

- Modest-sized tax-exempt organizations—Form 990-EZ[52]

- Small tax-exempt organizations—Form 990-N[53]

- Private foundations—Form 990-PF[54]

- Black lung benefit trusts—Form 990-BL[55]

Political organizations[56] also file tax returns on Form 1120-POL and homeowners' associations[57] file tax returns on Form 1120-H.

An organization's tax return filing obligation generally begins on formation; therefore, an organization whose exemption application is pending on the due date for filing the return must file a Form 990 series return.[58]

The annual information return must state a tax-exempt organization's items of gross income, disbursements, and other information; an exempt organization

---

[47] Rev. Proc. 2024-5, 2024-1 I.R.B. 262, App. A (Schedule of User Fees). As to the user fee regime generally, see § 26.1(d).

[48] Rev. Proc. 2024-5, 2024-1 I.R.B. 262, App. A.

[49] *Id.* § 11.01. See § 26.1(h).

[50] IRC § 6033(a)(1); Reg. § 1.6033-2(a)(1). This filing requirement applies to organizations that are tax-exempt by reason of IRC §§ 501(a) and 527. Thus, it is not applicable to those entities that are exempt pursuant to IRC §§ 521 (see § 19.12), 526 (see § 19.13), 528 (see § 19.14), or 529 (see § 19.19). In the fiscal year ending September 30, 2023, tax-exempt organizations filed 1,789,884 returns (Pub. 55-B, *IRS Data Book, 2023* (Apr. 2024) at 4 (Table 2)). These returns include Form 990 series returns, plus Forms 4720, 5227, and 8872 (*id.*).

[51] See § 28.2(a)(i).

[52] See § 28.2(a)(ii).

[53] See §§ 28.2(c), 28.3.

[54] See § 28.2(a)(iii). Form 990-PF is also generally filed by nonexempt charitable trusts (IRC § 4947(a)(1)) (IRC § 6033(d)). The filing requirements for charitable trusts (IRC § 4947) are the subject of Rev. Proc. 83-32, 1983-1 C.B. 723.

[55] See § 18.5.

[56] See Chapter 17; § 28.2(b)(vii).

[57] See § 19.14.

[58] Reg. § 1.6033-2(c); Instructions for Form 990-PF (2023), General Instruction A.

must keep appropriate records, render statements under oath, make other returns, and comply with other requirements, as the tax regulations, return instructions, and the return itself prescribe.[59] Generally, an exempt organization must file an annual information return irrespective of whether it is chartered by, or affiliated or associated with, any central, parent, or other organization.[60]

(a) Overview of Annual Information Returns

The annual information return filed with the IRS by the larger tax-exempt organizations—Form 990—is not merely akin to a tax return that principally requires the submission of financial information. There is also a substantial amount of other factual information, communicated by sentences and paragraphs, that is required to be provided. This annual return is often the document that is principally used by government officials, prospective contributors, representatives of the media, and others to evaluate the finances, operations, programs, and overall merit of an exempt organization. The return is also structured to influence and modify behaviors, particularly in connection with governance, and it introduced many new concepts in the law of tax-exempt organizations.

An annual information return must be on the basis of the established annual accounting period of the tax-exempt organization. If the organization lacks such a period, the return must be on the basis of the calendar year.[61]

(i) Form 990. Form 990 includes an 11-page core form. A one-page summary of the organization (Part I) is followed by a signature block (Part II) and nine other parts. This core return is accompanied by 16 schedules.

Part III of Form 990 enables the filing organization to describe its program service accomplishments. Part IV of the return is a checklist of required schedules. Part V pertains to a variety of activities and IRS filings. Part VI concerns governance, management, policies, and disclosure. Part VII focuses on compensation of insiders and independent contractors. Part VIII is a revenue statement. Part IX is a statement of expenses. Part X is a balance sheet. Part XI concerns financial statements.

Schedule A of Form 990 is used by charitable organizations to report their public charity status. Schedule B is used to report charitable contributions and grants.[62] Schedule C comprises questions concerning attempts to influence legislation and political campaign activities. Schedule D is used to report additional financial information. Schedule E is filed by organizations that operate tax-exempt private schools. The essence of Schedule F is the reporting of activities outside the United States. Schedule G largely concerns fundraising activities. Schedule H is filed by organizations that operate exempt hospitals. Schedule I is used to solicit information about the filing organization's domestic grant and other assistance programs. Schedule J is used to collect additional information

---

[59] IRC § 6033(a)(1); Reg. § 1.6033-2(a)(1), (i). The contents of the return for charitable organizations (entities described in IRC § 501(c)(3) and tax-exempt by reason of IRC § 501(a)) are stated in IRC § 6033(b); Reg. § 1.6033-2(a)(2). See § 28.2(b).

[60] Reg. § 1.6033-2(a)(1).

[61] Reg. § 1.6033-2(b).

[62] See § 28.10(i).

about compensatory arrangements. Schedule K is used to solicit information about tax-exempt bond issuers and use of the proceeds. Schedule L concerns excess benefit transactions and loans to and from interested persons. Schedule M pertains to noncash contributions. Schedule N pertains to liquidations, terminations, dissolutions, and significant dispositions of assets. Schedule R has as its principal purpose identification of disregarded entities and related exempt organizations. Schedule O is used by filing organizations to provide additional information.

Supporting organizations[63] are required to file either Form 990 or Form 990-EZ, depending on the level of gross receipts and asset value.[64] Sponsoring organizations with donor-advised funds,[65] organizations that operate one or more hospital facilities,[66] and controlling organizations[67] are required to file Form 990.[68]

(ii) Form 990-EZ.   To alleviate the annual reporting burden for modest-sized tax-exempt organizations, the IRS promulgated a less extensive annual information return. This is the two-page Form 990-EZ.

This return may be used by tax-exempt organizations that have gross receipts that are less than $200,000 and total assets that are less than $500,000 in value at the end of the reporting year.

An organization can use this annual information return in any year in which it meets the two criteria, even though it was and/or is required to file a Form 990 in other years. An exempt organization filing a Form 990-EZ may have to file one or more schedules that accompany Form 990.

(iii) Form 990-PF.   Private foundations[69] must file an annual information return.[70] This return, which is Form 990-PF, must be filed irrespective of a foundation's level of gross receipts or asset value.[71]

(iv) Filing Dates.   The annual information return (Form 990, Form 990-EZ, or Form 990-PF) is due on or before the 15th day of the fifth month following the close of the tax-exempt organization's tax year.[72] Thus, the return for a calendar-year exempt organization should be filed by May 15 of each year. One or more extensions may be obtained. These returns are required to be filed electronically.[73]

---

[63] See § 12.3(c).

[64] See § 28.2(a)(ii).

[65] See § 12.5.

[66] See § 7.6(a), (b).

[67] See § 30.6(b).

[68] IRC § 6033(l), (k), and (h), respectively. Two or more organizations exempt from taxation under IRC § 501, one or more of which is described in IRC § 501(c)(2) (see § 19.2(a)) and the other(s) of which derive income from IRC § 501(c)(2) organization(s), are eligible to file a consolidated return Form 990 (and/or Form 990-T) in lieu of separate returns (IRC § 1504(e)).

[69] See § 12.1.

[70] IRC § 6033(a)–(c).

[71] See *Private Foundations* § 12.1(a).

[72] IRC § 6072(e); Reg. § 1.6033-2(e). This due date is also applicable with respect to Form 4720 (the tax return by which certain excise taxes imposed on private foundations, public charities, and other persons are paid).

[73] See § 28.7.

At the time a private foundation files its annual return, a copy of the return must be sent to the attorney general of one or more states, including the state in which the foundation was created and in which the foundation's principal office is located.[74]

The filing date for an annual information return (Form 990, Form 990-EZ, or Form 990-PF) may fall due while the organization's application for recognition of tax-exempt status is pending with the IRS. In that instance, the organization should nonetheless file the information return (rather than a tax return) and check the box on the first page of the return indicating that the application is pending.[75]

(v) Penalties. Failure to timely file the appropriate annual information return, or failure to include any information required to be shown on the return (or failure to show the correct information) absent reasonable cause, can give rise to a $20-per-day penalty, payable by the organization, for each day the failure continues, with a maximum penalty for any one return not to exceed the lesser of $10,000 or 5 percent of the gross receipts of the organization for the year.[76] There is a much larger penalty on organizations having gross receipts in excess of $1 million for a year; in this circumstance, the per-day penalty is $100, and the maximum penalty is $50,000.[77] The penalty may apply if a return is submitted on paper instead of electronically.[78]

As noted, this daily delinquency penalty applies in two different situations: the failure to file a return in a timely manner and the failure to include any of the required information or show the correct information. In the first situation, the penalty applies where the return that is filed omits material information and therefore is so deficient that the submission is not considered to be a return. In the second situation, the penalty applies because although the return contains all the material information, it omits information required to be shown or furnishes incorrect information.[79] Because in the first situation an organization is not considered to have filed a return at all, the period of limitations on assessment and collection of tax does not begin to run[80] and a tax may be assessed, or a proceeding in court for the collection of tax may be begun without assessment, at any time.[81]

---

[74] Reg. § 1.6033-3(c).

[75] Reg. § 1.6033-2(c).

[76] IRC § 6652(c)(1)(A). Adjusted for inflation (IRC § 6652(c)(7)), the daily penalty is $25 and the maximum penalty under this section is $12,500 for returns required to be filed in 2025 (Rev. Proc. 2023-34, 2023-48 IRB 1287 § 3.54). In one instance, this penalty was applied where the exempt organization's president was found to be a "very sophisticated and intelligent professional," who had a practice of not filing returns until the IRS notified the organization that they were late (Child Adult Intervention Services, Inc. v. Comm'r, 103 T.C.M. 1494 (2012)).

[77] IRC § 6652(c)(1)(A), last sentence. Adjusted for inflation (IRC § 6652(c)(7)), the gross receipts threshold is $1,274,000, the daily penalty is $125, and the maximum penalty under this section is $63,500 for returns required to be filed in 2025 (Rev. Proc. 2023-34, 2023-48 IRB 1287 § 3.54).

[78] Reg. § 301.6033-4(b); see § 28.7.

[79] Gen. Couns. Mem. 39861.

[80] Rev. Rul. 77-162, 1977-1 C.B. 401.

[81] IRC § 6501(c)(3).

A penalty of $10 per day also may be imposed on any individual(s) responsible for the failure to file, absent reasonable cause,[82] where the return remains unfiled following demand for the return by the IRS; the maximum penalty on all individuals with respect to any one return may not exceed $5,000.[83]

None of the daily delinquency penalties is subject to the requirement that the initial determination of a penalty assessment be personally approved in writing by the immediate supervisor of the IRS employee making the determination, because the penalty is automatically calculated through electronic means.[84] Under proposed regulations, however, this penalty will no longer be considered automatically calculated through electronic means if an organization responds to a computer-generated notice proposing a penalty, challenges the penalty, and an IRS employee works the case.[85]

(vi) Assessments.   The IRS generally must assess any tax within three years of the due date of the return or the date on which the return involved is actually filed, whichever is later.[86] A six-year statute of limitations applies, however, if an excise tax return[87] "omits an amount of such tax properly includible thereon which exceeds 25 percent of the amount of such tax reported thereon"; this extended period does not apply, in the case of the private foundation and certain other taxes, where there is adequate disclosure in the return to the IRS.[88]

In one case, a private foundation timely filed its annual information return, reflecting certain salary payments to an officer; believing the payments to be reasonable, the foundation did not file a return showing any excise taxes due. A court held that, under these facts, only the annual information return was due, that adequate disclosure was made on that return, and that the six-year statute of limitations was inapplicable (thereby precluding the IRS from assessing the tax, because the deficiency notice was mailed more than three years after the organization's returns were filed).[89]

---

[82] In general, reliance on the advice of a competent tax adviser can constitute reasonable cause for a failure to file a return, for purposes of the IRC § 6651(a)(1) addition to tax (see § 28.8(b)), and the IRC § 6652(c)(1)(A) or § 6652(c)(1)(B) penalty (e.g., Waco Lodge No. 166, Benevolent & Protective Order of Elks v. Comm'r, 42 T.C.M. 1202 (1981), *aff'd in part and rev'd in part*, 696 F.2d 372 (5th Cir. 1983); Coldwater Seafood Corp. v. Comm'r, 69 T.C. 966 (1978); West Coast Ice Co. v. Comm'r, 49 T.C. 345 (1968)).

[83] IRC § 6652(c)(1)(B); Reg. § 301.6652-2. Adjusted for inflation (IRC § 6652(c)(7)), the maximum penalty under this section is $6,000 for returns required to be filed in 2025 (Rev. Proc. 2023-34, 2023-48 IRB 1287 § 3.54).

[84] IRC § 6751(b)(2)(B); Grace Found. v. Comm'r, 108 T.C.M. 513 (2014).

[85] Prop. Reg. § 301.6751(b)-1(a)(3)(vi). This is because where an organization's response challenges the validity of the penalty or the adjustments to which the penalty relates, and an examiner considers the response, any subsequent assessment of the penalty would not be based solely on the automatic calculation of the penalty by the computer program. Instead, it would be at least partially based on a decision by an IRS employee as to whether the penalty is appropriate (88 Fed. Reg. 21564, 21569 (2023)).

[86] IRC § 6501(a).

[87] E.g., Form 4720.

[88] IRC § 6501(e)(3).

[89] Cline v. Comm'r, 55 T.C.M. 540 (1988).

(vii) Change in Tax Year. The filing of an annual information return is also the opportunity for the changing of annual accounting periods by most tax-exempt organizations. Most exempt organizations desiring to change their annual accounting period (tax year) may effect the change by timely filing an annual information return with the IRS for the short period for which the return is required, indicating in the return that a change of accounting period is being made. If an organization is not required to file an annual information return or a tax return reflecting unrelated income, it is not necessary to otherwise notify the IRS that a change of accounting period is being made.[90]

If, however, an organization has previously changed its annual accounting period at any time within the 10 calendar years ending with the calendar year that includes the beginning of the short period resulting from the change of an annual accounting period, and if the organization had a filing requirement at any time during the 10-year period, it must file an application for a change in accounting period with the IRS.[91]

(b) Content of Annual Information Returns

(i) Financial Information. By means of annual information returns, tax-exempt organizations are required to report their gross income for the year. For this purpose, gross income generally includes tax-exempt income, other than contributions, grants, and similar amounts. The computation of gross income must be made by subtracting the cost of goods sold from all receipts.[92] Dues and assessments from members and affiliates must also be reported.[93]

Expenses incurred within the year attributable to gross income must be reported,[94] as must disbursements made within the year for tax-exempt purposes.[95] A balance sheet showing assets, liabilities, and net worth as of the beginning and end of the year is required.[96]

(ii) Contributions and Grants. Organizations must report the total of contributions, grants, and similar amounts received during the year. Charitable organizations[97] must report the names and addresses of persons that contributed, bequeathed, or devised $5,000 or more, in money or other property, during the year. Private foundations must disclose their substantial contributors.[98]

---

[90] Rev. Proc. 85-58, 1985-2 C.B. 740 § 3. This simplified procedure is inapplicable to farmers' cooperatives (see § 19.12), shipowners' protective associations (see § 19.13), political organizations (see Chapter 17), or homeowners' associations (see § 19.14). These entities change their annual accounting period by filing an application for change in accounting period (Form 1128) with the IRS National Office (Rev. Proc. 85-58, *supra* § 4.01).

[91] *Id.* § 3.03. The application is made on Form 1128.

[92] Reg. § 1.6033-2(a)(2)(ii)(A).

[93] Reg. § 1.6033-2(a)(2)(ii)(B).

[94] Reg. § 1.6033-2(a)(2)(ii)(C).

[95] Reg. § 1.6033-2(a)(2)(ii)(D).

[96] Reg. § 1.6033-2(a)(2)(ii)(E).

[97] That is, organizations described in IRC § 501(c)(3).

[98] Reg. § 1.6033-2(a)(2)(ii)(F). See § 12.2(a).

Donative publicly supported organizations are required to report donors of $5,000 or more only where the amount of the gift exceeds 2 percent of the total contributions received during the year.[99]

An organization (other than a private foundation) is required to report only the names and addresses of contributors of whom it has actual knowledge.[100] Separate and independent gifts made by a person in a year must be aggregated to determine whether contributions exceed the $5,000 threshold or the 2 percent threshold but only if the gifts are of at least $1,000.[101]

Tax-exempt social clubs[102] and fraternal organizations[103] that receive charitable contributions and bequests must attach a schedule with respect to all gifts that aggregate more than $1,000 from any one person showing the total amount of the contributions or bequests from each person, the purpose or purposes involved, and the use or uses to which the amount was put.[104]

(iii) Compensation.   Organizations must report the names and addresses of their trustees, directors, and officers (or persons having similar responsibilities or powers). Private foundations must report as to their foundation managers.[105] Organizations must further report the names and addresses and/or total numbers of key employees, highly compensated employees, and independent contractors.[106] A schedule showing the compensation and other payments made to these persons is required.[107]

(iv) Excise Taxes.   Private foundations liable for excise taxes must report the pertinent information required by Form 4720.[108] Charitable organizations must report the amounts of taxes imposed on them, or any organization manager, during the year in connection with excess expenditures to influence legislation,[109] certain disqualifying lobbying expenditures,[110] and political expenditures.[111] Charitable

---

[99] Reg. § 1.6033-2(a)(2)(iii)(A). See § 12.3(b)(i).

[100] Reg. § 1.6033-2(a)(2)(iii)(B). For example, an organization need not require an employer, who withholds contributions from the compensation of employees and pays over to the organization periodically the total amounts withheld, to specify the amounts paid over with respect to a particular employee; in this case, unless the organization has actual knowledge that a particular employee gave more than $5,000 (or in excess of the 2 percent limitation, if greater), the organization need report only the name and address of the employer, and the total amount paid over by the employer (*id.*).

[101] Reg. § 1.6033-2(a)(2)(iii)(C).

[102] See Chapter 15.

[103] See § 19.4.

[104] Reg. § 1.6033-2(a)(2)(iii)(D).

[105] See § 12.2(b); *Private Foundations* § 4.2.

[106] Reg. § 1.6033-2(a)(2)(ii)(G).

[107] Reg. § 1.6033-2(a)(2)(ii)(H).

[108] Reg. § 1.6033-2(a)(2)(ii)(J).

[109] See § 22.3(d)(iii).

[110] See § 22.4.

[111] See § 23.3. Reg. § 1.6033-2(a)(2)(ii)(K).

organizations, social welfare organizations,[112] and health insurance issuers[113] must similarly report with respect to excess benefit transactions taxes.[114]

Charitable organizations that have elected the expenditure test must report their lobbying expenditures, grass roots expenditures, exempt purpose expenditures, lobbying nontaxable amount, and grass roots nontaxable amount for the year.[115]

(v) Hospitals. Tax-exempt hospitals must provide (1) a copy of their audited financial statements or consolidated financial statements for the year; (2) a copy of their most recently adopted implementation strategy for each hospital facility or the URL of each webpage where it has made the strategy widely available on a website, along with their report documenting the related community health needs assessment (CHNA); (3) for each hospital facility, a description of the actions taken during the year to address the significant health needs identified through its most recently conducted CHNA or an explanation as to why actions were not taken; and (4) a statement of the amount of excise tax[116] imposed on the organization during the year.[117]

(vi) Private Foundations. A private foundation is required to attach to its annual information return a list of the states (1) to which it reports concerning its organization, assets, or activities, or (2) with which it has registered that it intends to be or is a charitable organization or a holder of property devoted to a charitable purpose.[118]

References to private foundations in this context encompass nonexempt charitable trusts[119] and nonexempt private foundations.[120]

(vii) Political Organizations. Political organizations that have gross receipts of at least $25,000 for a year, and qualified state or local political organizations[121] that have gross receipts of at least $100,000 for a year, generally must comply with the annual information return reporting requirements. In addition to those reporting requirements generally applicable to all exempt organizations, these organizations also must report the names and addresses of all persons that contributed, bequeathed, or devised at least $5,000 during the year.[122]

(viii) Controlling Organizations. A controlling organization must include on its annual information return information regarding any (1) interest, annuities, royalties, or rents received from each controlled entity; (2) loans made to a

---

[112] See Chapter 13.

[113] See § 19.18.

[114] See § 21.10. Reg. § 1.6033-2(a)(2)(ii)(L).

[115] Reg. § 1.6033-2(a)(2)(ii)(M). See § 22.3(d).

[116] Under IRC § 4959. See § 7.6(b)(ii).

[117] IRC § 6033(b)(15); Reg. § 1.6033-2(a)(2)(ii)(N).

[118] Reg. § 1.6033-2(a)(2)(iv).

[119] IRC § 4947(a)(1). See *Private Foundations* § 3.6.

[120] IRC § 6033(d). Reg. § 1.6033-2(a)(4). In this context, a "nonexempt private foundation" is a taxable organization (other than a nonexempt charitable trust) that is a private foundation (*id.*).

[121] IRC § 527(e)(5).

[122] IRC § 6033(g); Reg. § 1.6033-2(a)(5). See Chapter 17.

controlled entity; and (3) transfers of funds between the organization and a controlled entity.[123]

(ix) Sponsoring Organizations. Every sponsoring organization that maintains donor-advised funds must, on its annual information return, (1) list the total number of donor-advised funds it owned at the end of the tax year involved, (2) report the aggregate value of assets held in donor-advised funds at the end of the year, and (3) report the aggregate contributions to and grants made from the funds during the tax year.[124]

(x) Supporting Organizations. Every supporting organization must, on its annual information return, (1) list the supported organizations with respect to which the supporting organization provides support, (2) specify whether it meets the requirements for one of the three types of supporting organizations, and (3) certify that it is not controlled by disqualified persons with respect to it.[125]

(c) Exceptions to Reporting Requirements

This requirement of filing an annual information return does not apply to several categories of tax-exempt organizations.

Some of these exceptions are mandatory,[126] while others are at the discretion of the IRS.[127]

(i) Churches and Other Religious Organizations. Churches (including an interchurch organization of local units of a church), their integrated auxiliaries, and conventions or associations of churches do not have to file annual information returns.[128] The definitions given the terms *church, integrated auxiliary of a church,* and *convention or association of churches* are discussed elsewhere.[129]

Also, these reporting requirements do not apply to the exclusively religious activities of a religious order[130] and to a mission society (other than one that is a supporting organization)[131] sponsored by or affiliated with one or more churches or church denominations, more than one-half of the activities of which are conducted in or directed at persons in foreign countries.[132]

Other categories of church-related or religious organizations also are not required to file annual information returns. One of these types of entities is a tax-exempt charitable organization that is operated, supervised, or controlled by one or more churches, integrated auxiliaries, or conventions or associations

---

[123] IRC § 6033(h); Reg. § 1.6033-2(a)(6). See, e.g., § 30.6(b).

[124] Reg. § 1.6033-2(a)(7). See § 12.5.

[125] IRC § 6033(l); Reg. § 1.6033-2(a)(8). See § 12.3(c).

[126] IRC § 6033(a)(3)(A).

[127] IRC § 6033(a)(3)(B).

[128] IRC § 6033(a)(3)(A)(i); Reg. § 1.6033-2(g)(1)(i). Apostolic organizations (see § 10.8) do not file Form 990; instead, because they are treated as partnerships for tax purposes, they file the partnership return (Form 1065).

[129] See §§ 10.3–10.5.

[130] IRC § 6033(a)(3)(iii); Reg. § 1.6033-2(g)(1)(ii). See § 10.7.

[131] See § 12.3(c).

[132] Reg. § 1.6033-2(g)(1)(iv). See §§ 10.6, 28.2(c)(iii).

of churches, and: (1) is engaged exclusively in financing, funding the activities of, or managing the funds of (a) a church, integrated auxiliary, or convention or association of churches, or (b) a group of organizations substantially all of which are described in the foregoing three categories of entities, if substantially all of its assets are provided by, or held for the benefit of, such entities; or (2) maintains retirement insurance programs primarily for these categories of organizations and (a) more than 50 percent of the individuals covered by the programs are directly employed by these organizations, or (b) more than 50 percent of the assets are contributed by, or held for the benefit of, employees of these organizations. Another type of exempted entity is a tax-exempt charitable organization that is operated, supervised, or controlled by one or more religious orders and is engaged in financing, funding, or managing assets used for exclusively religious activities.[133]

(ii) Small Organizations. By statute, the requirement of filing an annual information return is inapplicable to certain organizations (other than private foundations) whose gross receipts[134] in each year are normally not more than $5,000.[135] This category of organizations[136] embraces (1) religious organizations;[137] (2) educational organizations;[138] (3) charitable organizations or organizations operated for the prevention of cruelty to children or animals,[139] if the organizations are supported by funds granted by the federal or a state government or are primarily supported by contributions from the public; (4) organizations operated, supervised, or controlled by or in connection with a religious organization; (5) certain fraternal beneficiary organizations;[140] and (6) corporations organized pursuant to an act of Congress if wholly owned by the United States or any agency or instrumentality of the United States, or are wholly owned subsidiaries of the United States.[141]

The IRS has the discretion to relieve other organizations (but not supporting organizations) of the requirement of filing annual information returns where

[133] Rev. Proc. 96-10, 1996-1 C.B. 577.

[134] The term *gross receipts* means total receipts without any reduction for costs or expenses, including costs of goods sold (Reg. § 1.6033-2(g)(4)). Thus, gross receipts include but are not limited to the gross amount received (1) as contributions, gifts, grants, and similar amounts, (2) as dues or assessments from members or affiliated organizations, (3) from sales or receipts from business activities (including unrelated business activities), (4) from asset sales, and (5) as investment income, such as interest, dividends, rents, and royalties (*id.*). For this purpose, insurance premiums collected by the local lodge of a tax-exempt fraternal beneficiary society from its members, maintained separately without use or benefit, and remitted to its parent organization that issued the insurance contracts, were ruled by the IRS to not be gross receipts of the local lodge (Rev. Rul. 73-364, 1973-2 C.B. 393).

[135] IRC § 6033(a)(3)(A)(ii).

[136] IRC § 6033(a)(3)(C). The IRS has exercised its discretionary authority (see text accompanied by *infra* note 142) to eliminate the $5,000 gross receipts threshold for certain organizations described in the second (see text accompanied by *infra* note 145), fourth (see text accompanied by *infra* note 152), and sixth categories (see text accompanied by *infra* notes 150–151), and to increase the threshold to $50,000 for organizations in the third category (see text accompanied by *infra* note 143).

[137] See Chapter 10.

[138] IRC § 170(b)(1)(A)(ii). See Chapter 8, § 12.3(a).

[139] IRC § 501(c)(3). See § 11.1.

[140] IRC § 501(c)(8). See § 19.4(a).

[141] IRC § 501(c)(1). See § 19.1. The IRS ruled that the National Credit Union Administration and the tax-exempt federal credit unions under its supervision are organizations described in IRC § 501(c)(1) and thus are not required to file annual information returns (Rev. Rul. 89-94, 1989-2 C.B. 233).

a filing of these returns by them is not necessary to the efficient administration of the internal revenue laws.[142] In the exercise of this discretionary authority, the IRS has relieved all tax-exempt organizations described in IRC § 501(c), other than private foundations and supporting organizations, with gross receipts not normally in excess of $50,000 from the requirement to file annual information returns.[143]

Nonetheless, these small organizations are required to electronically submit a Form 990-N e-postcard.[144]

(iii) Other Organizations.   Other organizations that are not required to file annual returns because the IRS has exercised its discretionary authority include: (1) an educational organization (below college level) that is qualified as a school, has a program of a general academic nature, and is affiliated with a church or operated by a religious order;[145] (2) mission societies sponsored by or affiliated with one or more churches or church denominations, more than one-half of the activities of which are conducted in, or directed at persons in, foreign countries;[146] (3) state institutions the income of which is excluded from gross income because the income is accruing to the state;[147] (4) an exempt foreign organization or an exempt U.S. possession organization (other than a private foundation) that normally does not annually receive more than $50,000 in gross receipts from sources in the United States[148] and that does not have any significant activity in the United States;[149] (5) certain government corporations;[150] (6) governmental units and affiliates of a governmental unit;[151] and (7) certain organizations operated, supervised, or controlled by one or more religious orders or churches, integrated auxiliaries, or conventions or associations of churches.[152]

A tax-exempt organization may request a determination that it is exempt from the requirement of filing an annual information return by submitting the request on Form 8940.[153]

(d)   Limited Liability Companies

A tax-exempt organization can be the sole member of a limited liability company, or two or more exempt organizations can be members of an LLC.[154] In the case of the single-member LLC, the LLC generally is treated as a disregarded entity

---

[142] IRC § 6033(a)(3)(B); Reg. § 1.6033-2(g)(6).

[143] Rev. Proc. 2011-15, 2011-3 I.R.B. 322 § 3.01.

[144] IRC § 6033(i); Reg. § 1.6033-2(g)(5); Rev. Proc. 2011-15, 2011-3 I.R.B. 322 § 3.03. See § 28.3.

[145] Reg. § 1.6033-2(g)(1)(vii). See § 8.3. Also, Rev. Rul. 78-316, 1978-2 C.B. 304. For this purpose, the rules as to *affiliation* are the same as those discussed in § 10.5.

[146] Reg. § 1.6033-2(g)(1)(iv).

[147] Reg. § 1.6033-2(g)(1)(v).

[148] IRC §§ 861-865; Reg. § 53.4948-1(b).

[149] Reg. § 1.6033-2(g)(1)(viii); Rev. Proc. 2011-15, 2011-3 I.R.B. 322 § 3.02. These organizations are required to electronically submit the e-postcard (IRC § 6033(i); Reg. § 1.6033-2(g)(5); Rev. Proc. 2011-15, *supra* § 3.03; see § 28.3).

[150] Reg. § 1.6033-2(g)(1)(vi). These government corporations are described in IRC § 501(c)(1).

[151] Rev. Proc. 95-48, 1995-2 C.B. 418.

[152] Rev. Proc. 96-10, 1996-1 C.B. 577. See § 28.2(c)(i).

[153] Rev. Proc. 2024-5, 2024-1 I.R.B. 262 § 4.02(6). See § 28.1(d).

[154] See §§ 4.1(b), 32.3, 32.4.

for federal tax purposes, and thus its activities are treated as the activities of the member.[155] In this instance, then, the single-member LLC is not required to file annual information returns; rather, the activities of the LLC are reported as activities of the exempt member.[156]

A single-member LLC may elect, however, to be treated as a separate entity,[157] or by seeking tax-exempt status by filing an application for recognition of tax-exempt status.[158] A single-member LLC that has been determined to be, or claims to be, tax-exempt is treated as having made an election to be classified as an association. Once the IRS determines a single-member LLC to be tax-exempt, it will not be treated as a disregarded entity unless and until the determination is revoked and the LLC files a new election to be treated as a disregarded entity. Likewise, if an LLC has claimed to be tax-exempt, but has not received an IRS determination to that effect, it will not be eligible to be treated as a disregarded entity until the claim is withdrawn or rejected and the LLC files an election to be treated as a disregarded entity.[159]

Additionally, where there is a multiple-member LLC whose members are exempt organizations, the LLC may be able to qualify as an exempt organization[160] and if so would be subject to the annual reporting requirements.

(e) Group Returns

A tax-exempt central organization[161] is generally required to file an annual information return. Also, it may annually file a *group return* or notice for two or more of its subordinate organizations. A group return may be filed where the subordinate organizations are affiliated with the central organization at the close of its annual accounting period, subject to the general supervision or control of the central organization, and exempt from taxation pursuant to the same federal tax law provision.[162]

The filing of a group return is in lieu of the filing of a separate return by each of the subordinate organizations included in the group return. Utilization of the group return option requires the subordinate entities to file with the central organization statements indicating their items of gross income, disbursements, and other required items.[163] A group return must contain a schedule identifying the subordinate organizations included in the return and a schedule identifying those that are not included.[164]

A group return must be prepared based on the annual accounting period of the central organization.[165]

---

[155] See §§ 4.1(b), 32.4.

[156] E.g., Priv. Ltr. Rul. 200134025.

[157] This election is made by filing Form 8832.

[158] See § 26.1.

[159] Reg § 301.7701-3(c)(1)(v)(A).

[160] See § 4.3(e).

[161] See § 26.11.

[162] Reg. § 1.6033-2(d)(1).

[163] Reg. § 1.6033-2(d)(2)(i).

[164] Reg. § 1.6033-2(d)(2)(ii).

[165] Reg. § 1.6033-2(d)(3). The IRS has published proposed revised group exemption procedures (see § 26.11(c)). The annual reporting requirements are the subject of § 7 of the proposed revenue procedure.

(f)   ABLE Program Reports

Each officer or employee having control of a qualified ABLE program or their designee is required to make reports regarding the program to the IRS and to designated beneficiaries with respect to contributions, distributions, the return of excess contributions, and such other matters as the IRS may require.[166]

§ 28.3   ANNUAL NOTICE REQUIREMENT (FORM 990-N) FOR SMALL ORGANIZATIONS

Tax-exempt organizations that are not required to file an annual information return because they have annual gross receipts that are normally less than $50,000[167] must, to remain exempt,[168] furnish the IRS, annually and in electronic form, a notice[169] containing the legal name of the organization, any name under which the organization operates or does business, the organization's mailing address and any Internet website address, the organization's taxpayer identification number, the name and address of a principal officer, and evidence of the organization's continuing basis for its exemption from the annual filing requirement.[170] Should the organization terminate its existence, notice of the termination must be provided to the IRS.[171]

A tax-exempt foreign organization or a U.S. possession organization is not required to file an annual information return if (1) it normally does not receive more than $50,000 in annual gross receipts from sources within the United States, and (2) it has no significant activity (including lobbying, political activity, and operation of a trade or business but excluding investment activity) in the United States.[172]

If an organization ceases to meet a condition in connection with these rules, it must file an annual information return for the year in which the cessation occurred and for all subsequent years in which it cannot meet the conditions.[173]

---

[166] IRC § 529A(d)(1). ABLE programs use Form 1099-QA, *Distributions from ABLE Accounts*, and Form 5498-QA, *ABLE Account Contribution Information*, to report relevant account information annually to designated beneficiaries and the IRS.

[167] Rev. Proc. 2011-15, 2011-3 I.R.B. 322 § 3.01. These are organizations exempt from federal income tax under IRC § 501(a) because they are described in IRC § 501(c) (other than a private foundation or a supporting organization) that normally have annual gross receipts of not more than $50,000 (see text accompanied by *supra* note 143).

[168] See § 28.4.

[169] Rev. Proc. 2011-15, 2011-3 I.R.B. 322 § 3.03.

[170] IRC § 6033(i)(1); Reg. § 1.6033-6. This notification requirement entails the submission of Form 990-N, also known as the e-postcard. In addition to applying to organizations described in *supra* note 167, this notice requirement also applies to certain other organizations exempted from filing by statute or through the exercise of the IRS's discretionary authority to do so (IRC § 6033(i); see § 28.2(c)(ii), (iii)). This notice requirement does not apply to political organizations (Rev. Proc. 2011-15, 2011-3 I.R.B. 322 § 1; see Chapter 17), but they are subject to other filing and reporting requirements (see §§ 28.2(b)(vii), 28.6).

[171] IRC § 6033(i)(2).

[172] Rev. Proc. 2011-15, 2011-3 I.R.B. 322 § 3.02.

[173] *Id.* § 3.04.

The annual gross receipts of an organization are considered to be normally not more than $50,000 if (1) in the case of an organization that has been in existence for no more than one year, the organization's gross receipts, including pledges, are $75,000 or less during its first tax year; (2) in the case of an organization that has been in existence for more than one year but less than three years, the organization's average annual gross receipts for its first two tax years are $60,000 or less; and (3) in the case of an organization that has been in existence for three years or more, the organization's average annual gross receipts for the immediately preceding three tax years, including the year for which the return is filed, are $50,000 or less.[174]

This notice is not a *return*; also, it is not *filed* but rather is *submitted*. One significance of these distinctions is that the daily delinquency penalty for failure to timely file a complete annual return[175] does not apply with respect to this notice.[176] Another significance is that the submission of this electronic notification does not start the running of the statute of limitations for assessment of tax. Moreover, because the requirement that the notice be submitted electronically is statutory, the IRS does not have the authority to allow submission of the notice in hard-copy form. The voluntary filing of an annual information return,[177] by contrast, starts the running of the limitations period and satisfies the annual electronic notice requirement, provided that the return is prepared in full.[178] If a small organization is a subordinate entity as part of a group exemption,[179] and its information is included in the central organization's group return, the small organization need not submit this notice.[180]

§ 28.4 AUTOMATIC REVOCATION FOR FAILURE TO FILE

An organization claiming tax-exempt status generally must file an annual information return,[181] or submit a notice in lieu thereof,[182] even if it has not yet received a determination letter recognizing its tax-exempt status.[183] If an exempt organization that is required to file an annual information return or submit a notice fails to do so for three consecutive years, the organization's exempt status is revoked by operation of law.[184] If an exempt organization fails to meet its filing obligation to the IRS for three consecutive years in instances where the organization is subject to the annual information return filing requirement in one or more years during a three-year period and also is subject to the notice requirement for one or

---

[174] *Id.* § 4.
[175] IRC § 6652(c)(1)(A). See § 28.2(a)(v).
[176] IRC § 6652(c)(1)(E).
[177] Either a Form 990 or a Form 990-EZ. See § 28.2(a)(i), (ii).
[178] Reg. § 1.6033-6(d).
[179] See § 26.11.
[180] Reg. § 1.6033-6(b)(1)(i).
[181] See § 28.2.
[182] See § 28.3.
[183] Rev. Proc. 2024-5, 2024-1 I.R.B. 262 § 6.05(3).
[184] IRC § 6033(j)(1)(B); Rev. Proc. 2024-5, 2024-1 I.R.B. 262 §§ 6.05(3), 12.01(6).

more years during the same three-year period, the organization's exempt status is revoked by operation of law.[185]

A revocation under this rules is effective from the date the IRS determined was the last day the organization could have timely filed or submitted the third required annual information return or notice. An organization may not challenge, pursuant to declaratory judgment procedures,[186] a revocation of tax exemption made pursuant to this rule.[187] The IRS publishes the names of organizations that have lost exempt status pursuant to this rule on its website.[188] An auto-revocation list does not appear in the Internal Revenue Bulletin.[189]

To again be recognized as tax-exempt, the organization must apply to the IRS for recognition of exemption irrespective of whether the organization was originally required to make an application for recognition of exemption in order to acquire exemption.[190] If, on application for recognition of exemption after a revocation under these rules, the organization demonstrates to the satisfaction of the IRS reasonable cause for failing to file the required notices or returns, the organization's exempt status may, in the discretion of the IRS, be reinstated retroactively to the date of revocation.[191] The IRS has published procedures for reinstatement of tax-exempt status of organizations that had their exemptions revoked by operation of law for failure to file or submit annual information returns or notices for three consecutive years.[192]

If a tax-exempt organization fails to file an annual information return or submit a notice for two consecutive years, the IRS is required to notify the organization of that fact and of the revocation that will occur under the three-year auto-revocation rule. This notice must include information about compliance with the filing or submission requirements.[193] This notification requirement is separate from, and not a condition precedent to, automatic revocation.[194] Presumably, however, the IRS's failure to satisfy this notification requirement would be a factor in establishing reasonable cause for reinstatement of an organization's tax-exempt status.[195]

§ 28.5 CHARITABLE ORGANIZATIONS LISTING RELIANCE RULES

For a contribution to be tax-deductible, the recipient of it must be a charitable organization[196] and so qualify at the time of the gift. Thus, it is the responsibility of an organization receiving contributions (and grants) to ensure that its character,

---

[185] Id.
[186] See § 27.5(c).
[187] IRC § 7428(b)(4).
[188] https://www.irs.gov/charities-non-profits/search-for-tax-exempt-organizations.
[189] E.g., Ann. 2011-35, 2011-25 I.R.B. 916.
[190] IRC § 6033(j)(2). See §§ 3.2, 26.1.
[191] IRC § 6033(j)(3).
[192] Rev. Proc. 2014-11, 2014-3 I.R.B. 411; Rev. Proc. 2024-5, 2024-1 I.R.B. 262 § 6.05(3).
[193] IRC § 6033(j)(1)(A).
[194] E.g., Field Att'y Advice 20221101F.
[195] See text accompanied by *supra* note 191.
[196] See Part Three.

purposes, activities, and method of operation satisfy the qualification requirements for charitable entities in order for contributors (and grantors) to have the
assurance that their contributions are deductible at the time they are made.[197]

(a) IRS's Searchable Databases

The IRS's *Tax Exempt Organization Search* database lists entities eligible to receive
deductible charitable contributions, lists entities that have had their exemption
automatically revoked for failure to file returns or notices, and contains the information reported in e-postcards (Form 990-N).[198] TEOS also includes images of
Form 990 series returns filed by tax-exempt organizations on or after January 1,
2018 (to the extent this information is available to the public) and images of favorable determination letters (but not application materials) issued by the IRS recognizing exemption on or after January 1, 2014.[199]

   The *Exempt Organizations Business Master File Extract* is another IRS database
that contains certain information concerning most categories of tax-exempt organizations. Among the data fields provided by the EO BMF Extract are indications
as to whether a charitable entity is a public charity or private foundation and the
types of supporting organizations. This database is generally updated monthly.[200]

(b) Charitable Status Reliance Rules

If an organization listed in or covered by TEOS or the EO BMF Extract ceases to
qualify as an entity as to which contributions are deductible and the IRS revokes
the organization's determination letter, contributors to the entity may generally
rely on the letter information provided in either database that contributions are
deductible until the date of a public announcement (such as in the *Internal Revenue
Bulletin*) stating that the organization no longer qualifies as a charitable entity.[201]

   If an organization listed in or covered by either of these databases ceases to
qualify as a charitable entity as a result of an automatic revocation of tax-exempt
status,[202] contributions made to the organization by persons unaware of the organization's change in status generally will be considered deductible if made on or
before the date its name is posted on the auto-revocation list.[203]

   The IRS has the authority to extend the period for which a contribution is
deductible under certain circumstances. One circumstance is where a legally enforceable obligation was made to an organization prior to the date of a public announcement or posting, and satisfaction of the obligation occurs on or after that date.[204]

   The IRS, however, is not precluded from disallowing a deduction for a contribution made after an organization ceases to qualify as a charitable entity and prior
to public announcement or posting of revocation if the contributor had knowledge

[197] Rev. Proc. 2018-32, 2018-23 I.R.B. 739 § 2.01.
[198] *Id.* § 3.01.
[199] *Id.*
[200] *Id.* § 3.04.
[201] *Id.* § 4.01.
[202] See § 28.4.
[203] Rev. Proc. 2018-32, 2018-23 I.R.B. 739 § 4.02.
[204] *Id.* § 4.03.

of revocation of the determination letter prior to the public announcement or posting, was aware that the revocation was imminent, or was in part responsible for,
or was aware of, the activities or deficiencies on the part of the organization that
gave rise to the loss of qualification.[205]

Contributors may rely on an organization's subsequent listing in TEOS or
the EO BMF Extract for contributions made after the date of the subsequent listing
even if the organization's tax-exempt status was previously revoked if the date the
organization is posted in TEOS or the EO BMF Extract is after the date of public
announcement of revocation of the organization's exempt status.[206] A similar reliance rule applies in connection with the auto-revocation process.[207]

(c) Safe Harbor Rules as to Public Charity Status

Rules similar to those concerning charitable status apply with regard to reliance on
these databases in connection with organization's public charity status.[208]

Grantors and contributors are not considered responsible for, or aware of,
an act that results in the loss of classification of publicly supported charity status
due to a change in financial support if the aggregate of grants or contributions
received from a grantor or contributor for the tax year of the recipient organization
in which the grant or contribution is received is 25 percent or less of the aggregate
support received by the organization for the four tax years immediately preceding
the tax year.[209]

This safe harbor is not available to a grantor or contributor who is in a position of authority with respect to the recipient organization (or who otherwise is
able to exercise control over the recipient organization), or to a person standing in
a relationship with respect to the person who is in a position of authority or control.[210] The safe harbor also is not applicable if the grantor or contributor has actual
knowledge of the loss of classification of public charity status or after the date of
public announcement that the organization ceases to qualify as a public charity.[211]

Private foundation grantors are not considered responsible for, or aware of,
an act that results in a recipient organization's loss of classification as a public charity due to a change in financial support if the recipient organization has received a
determination letter that it is a publicly supported charity and the organization is
not controlled, directly or indirectly, by the private foundation. This safe harbor is
inapplicable if the private foundation grantor has actual knowledge of the loss of
classification of public charity status or after the date of public announcement that
the organization ceases to qualify as a public charity.[212]

This guidance also includes a safe harbor set of rules with respect to unusual
grants.[213]

---

[205] *Id.* § 4.04.
[206] *Id.* § 4.05.
[207] *Id.* § 4.06.
[208] *Id.* § 5.01.
[209] *Id.* § 7.01(1)–(3).
[210] These relationships are the ones described in IRC § 4946(a)(1)(C)–(G). See § 12.2.
[211] *Id.* § 7.01(4), (5).
[212] *Id.* § 7.02.
[213] *Id.* § 7.03.

A remedy under declaratory judgment procedures is available, in part, for cases involving a determination by the IRS with respect to the continuing qualification of an organization as a charitable entity or a public charity.[214] This body of law nonetheless provides for the "validation of certain contributions" made during the pendency of a declaratory judgment proceeding; under this rule, the organization continues to be treated as an eligible charitable organization with respect to contributions from individuals (up to a maximum of $1,000 in the aggregate for the duration of the proceeding).[215] Statutory protection for these contributions, if declaratory judgment is sought on the revocation action, begins on the date of publication of the revocation and ends on the date on which a court decision becomes final or court judgment is entered that the organization is not a charitable entity. This reliance, however, is not extended to any individual who was responsible, in whole or in part, for the activities or failures to act on the part of the organization that were the basis for the revocation.[216]

§ 28.6 REPORTING BY POLITICAL ORGANIZATIONS

In addition to filing an annual information return,[217] a political organization,[218] other than one involved only in state or local electoral activities and subject to comparable state disclosure laws that accepts a contribution or makes an expenditure for an exempt (political) function during a year, must file quarterly reports with the IRS in the case of a year in which a federal election is held. Also, pre-election and postelection reports may be required. Otherwise, generally, the reports are due semiannually. A political organization has the option of filing these reports monthly. Whatever the choice, the organization must file on the same schedule basis for the entire calendar year.[219]

---

[214] IRC § 7428. See § 27.5(c). An action pursuant to these procedures may not, however, be brought with respect to a revocation of status caused by application of IRC § 6033(j) (see § 28.4).

[215] IRC § 7428(c).

[216] Rev. Proc. 2018-32, 2018-23 I.R.B. 739 § 9.

[217] See § 28.2(b)(vii).

[218] See Chapter 17.

[219] IRC § 527(j)(2). This return is Form 8872. These rules are summarized in Rev. Rul. 2000-44, 2000-2 C.B. 409. These rules were first enacted in 2000 (Pub. L. 106-230, 114 Stat. 477 (2000)). The exception for state and local political organizations and certain other changes in this aspect of the law were enacted in 2002 (Pub. L. 107-276, 107th Cong., 2d Sess. (2002); see § 26.14, note 314) and made retroactive to 2000. This law change followed a decision by a federal district court striking down as unconstitutional the requirements of the law that political organizations disclose their expenditures and that they disclose contributions associated with state and local elections (Nat'l Fed'n of Republican Assemblies v. United States, 218 F. Supp. 2d 1300 (S.D. Ala. 2002)). A federal court of appeals vacated a decision by a district court that IRC § 527(j) is unconstitutional (Mobile Republican Assembly v. United States, 353 F.3d 1357 (11th Cir. 2003)), *vacating and remanding* 148 F. Supp. 2d 1273 (S.D. Ala. 2001), the appellate court concluded that the action was barred by the Anti-Injunction Act (see § 27.5(a)). The IRS issued guidance, in a question-and-answer format, concerning the state of the law as to these periodic reporting requirements subsequent to the 2002 revision (Rev. Rul. 2003-49, 2003-2 C.B. 903).

(a) General Rules

This report must contain the following: the amount and date of each expenditure made to a person if the aggregate amount of expenditures to the person during the year is at least $200; the purpose of the contribution if it is at least $500; the name and address of the person (in the case of an individual, including the individual's occupation and employer); the name and address (including occupation and employer in the case of an individual) of all persons who contributed an aggregate amount of at least $200 to the organization during the year; and the amount of such contribution.[220]

This set of rules does not apply to a person required to report under the Federal Election Campaign Act as a political committee; a state or local committee of a political party or political committee of a state or local candidate; an organization that reasonably anticipates that it will not have gross receipts of $25,000 or more for any year; another type of tax-exempt organization that is subject to the political campaign activities tax; or independent expenditures (as that term is defined in the Federal Election Campaign Act).[221]

There are penalties for failure to comply with this reporting requirement (by filing late, insufficiently, or incorrectly). The penalty is 35 percent of the total amount of contributions and expenditures not properly reported.[222]

Political organizations are also required to file income tax returns.[223] This income tax return must be filed electronically if the political organization is required to file at least 10 returns of any type during the calendar year.[224] This electronic filing rule applies to Forms 1120-POL required to be filed for tax years ending on or after December 31, 2023.[225] An addition to tax[226] may also apply if Form 1120-POL is submitted on paper when required to be filed electronically.[227]

The IRS has the authority to waive all or any portion of an amount imposed for failure to make the requisite disclosures, on a showing that the failure was due to reasonable cause and was not due to willful neglect.[228] The IRS issued guidance providing the elements of a safe harbor for establishing that failure by a political organization to report certain contributor information satisfies this waiver regime.[229]

(b) Filing Dates

Political organizations that choose to file monthly generally must file their reports by the 20th day after the end of the month; the reports must be complete as of the

---

[220] IRC § 527(j)(3).

[221] IRC § 527(j)(5).

[222] IRC § 527(j)(1).

[223] IRC § 6012(a)(6). This return is Form 1120-POL.

[224] Reg. § 301.6012-2. A "return" for these purposes is a return of "any type," including information returns (for example, Forms W-2 and Forms 1099), income tax returns, employment tax returns, and excise tax returns (Reg. § 301.6012-2(d)(3)).

[225] Reg. § 301.6012-2(f).

[226] IRC § 6651(a)(1). See § 28.8(b).

[227] Reg. § 301.6012-2(c).

[228] IRC § 527(1).

[229] Rev. Proc. 2007-27, 2007-1 C.B. 887.

last day of the month. The year-end report, however, is due by January 31 of the following year.

If, however, the year is one in which a regularly scheduled election is to be held, the organization filing monthly does not file the reports regularly due on November and December (that is, the monthly reports for October and November). Instead, the organization must file a report 12 days before the general election (or 15 days before the general election if posted by registered or certified mail) that contains information through the 20th day before the general election. The organization must also file a report no more than 30 days after the general election that contains information through the 20th day after the election. Rather than a December monthly report, the year-end report is due by January 31 of the following year.

As noted previously, political organizations that choose to not file monthly must file semiannual reports in nonelection years. These reports are due on July 31 for the first half of the year and, for the second half of the year, on January 31 of the following year.

In an election year, these political organizations must file quarterly reports that are due on the 15th day after the last day of the quarter, except that the return for the final quarter is due on January 31 of the following year. These organizations must also file preelection reports with respect to any election for which they receive a contribution or make an expenditure. These reports are due 12 days before the election (15 days if posted by registered or certified mail) and must contain information through the 20th day before the election. These organizations must also file a post–general election report, due 30 days after the general election and containing information through the 20th day after the election.

§ 28.7 ELECTRONIC FILING RULES

Any tax-exempt organization required to file an annual information return, or an unrelated business income tax return,[230] is now required to file the return electronically.[231] The IRS is required to make electronically filed returns available to the public "as soon as practicable in a machine-readable format."[232]

The tax regulations governing the mandatory electronic filing of Form 990 series returns and Form 990-T do not provide for any waiver or exemption from the electronic filing requirements. In the IRS's view, provision for a waiver or exemption would be contrary to the plain language of the statute and its legislative history.[233]

---

[230] Form 990-T. See § 28.8(a).

[231] IRC § 6033(n), enacted as part of the Taxpayer First Act (Pub. L. No. 116-25, § 3101, 133 Stat. 981, 1015 (2019)).

[232] IRC § 6104(b). Transitional relief, for tax years ending before July 31, 2021, is provided for small organizations or other entities that the IRS determines will otherwise suffer "undue burden." For this purpose, a *small organization* is an organization the gross receipts of which for a tax year are less than $200,000 and the aggregate gross assets of which at the end of the tax year are less than $500,000. Similar transitional relief is provided as to electronic filing of Forms 990-T (Pub. L. No. 116-25, § 3101(d)(2), 133 Stat. 981, 1015–16 (2019)).

[233] T.D. 9972, 88 Fed. Reg. 11754, 11759 (2023).

However, the IRS has recognized that the Religious Freedom Restoration Act of 1993[234] may provide an exemption if using the technology required to file electronically conflicts with the filer's religious beliefs.[235] The IRS accepts returns directly from tax-exempt organizations or via a third-party preparer; however, an IRS-approved e-file provider must be used. Tax professionals who plan to file these returns electronically are required to submit an electronic IRS e-file application.[236]

Instructions regarding timely filing and correcting returns that are rejected during attempts to file electronically using the IRS electronic filing systems are found in IRS publications specific to each IRS electronic filing system.[237]

§ 28.8 UNRELATED BUSINESS INCOME TAX RETURNS

(a) Filing and Reporting Requirements

Revenue and expenses associated with unrelated business activity by a tax-exempt organization are reported to the IRS on Form 990-T.[238] This is a *tax return*, rather than an *information return*. Nonetheless, the public inspection and disclosure requirements applicable to annual information returns[239] are applicable to the unrelated business income tax returns filed by charitable organizations.[240]

A tax-exempt organization with unrelated business taxable income[241] must file a Form 990-T, in addition to Form 990 or Form 990-EZ (or, in the case of a private foundation, Form 990-PF). It is on this form that the source (or sources) of unrelated income is reported and any tax computed.[242] Form 990-T must be filed electronically for all tax years beginning after July 1, 2019.[243]

Tax-exempt organizations must report their unrelated trade or business income. These reporting obligations are less where the unrelated trade or business gross income is no more than $10,000.

Gross income from an unrelated trade or business must be reported, along with associated deductions.[244] In reflection of the bucketing rule,[245] an organization with more than one unrelated trade or business should complete and attach a separate schedule to report income and allowable deductions for each separate

---

[234] Pub. L. No. 103-141, 107 Stat. 1488.

[235] T.D. 9972, 88 Fed. Reg. 11754, 11759 (2023).

[236] Pub. 3112, *IRS e-file Application & Participation* (Nov. 2023), describes the application process, which must be completed online.

[237] Notice 2024-18, 2024-5 I.R.B. 625; e.g., IRS Pub. 4164, *Modernized e-File Guide for Software Developers and Transmitters*, and IRS Pub. 5717, *Information Returns Intake System (IRIS) Taxpayer Portal User Guide*.

[238] IRC §§ 6011, 6012(a)(2), (4); Reg. §§ 1.6012-2(e), 1.6012-3(a)(5), 1.6033-2(j).

[239] See §§ 28.9(a)(ii), 28.10.

[240] IRC § 6104(a), (b), (d)(1)(A)(ii). See §§ 28.9(a)(ii), 28.10.

[241] See Chapters 24, 25.

[242] Reg. § 1.6012(e).

[243] Reg. §§ 1.6012-2(e), 301.6011-10. See § 28.7.

[244] Form 990-T, Part I.

[245] See § 25.5.

unrelated trade or business[246] and report the sum of the income and deductions from all schedules on the face of the return.[247]

Additional reporting requirements pertain to rental income,[248] unrelated debt-financed income,[249] income (other than dividends) from controlled organizations,[250] investment income of certain organizations that must treat that type of income as unrelated business income,[251] exploited exempt activity income (other than advertising income),[252] and advertising income.[253]

(b) Additions to Tax and Penalties

An addition to tax is imposed for failure to timely file Form 990-T and Form 4720[254] tax returns, unless it is shown that the failure to file is due to reasonable cause and not to willful neglect. This addition to tax set at the rate of 5 percent per month, not exceeding 25 percent in the aggregate.[255] Another addition to tax is imposed for failure to pay an amount of tax shown on a return, on or before the payment date, unless it is shown that the failure is due to reasonable cause and not to willful neglect.[256] This addition to tax is set at the rate of 0.5 percent per month, not exceeding 25 percent in the aggregate.[257]

For purposes of these additions to tax, the term *willful neglect* means a "conscious, intentional failure or reckless indifference," and *reasonable cause* is equated with the exercise of "ordinary business care and prudence."[258] If a taxpayer exercised ordinary business care and prudence and was nevertheless unable to file a return within the prescribed time, then the delay is due to reasonable cause.[259] One court held that, for purposes of the failure to file penalty, when a "taxpayer selects a competent tax expert, supplies him with all necessary information, and requests him to prepare proper tax returns, . . . the taxpayer has done all that ordinary business care and prudence can reasonably demand."[260]

An accuracy-related penalty may also be imposed if an underpayment of tax is attributable to negligence or disregard of rules or regulations, or if there is a

---

[246] Form 990-T, Schedule A.
[247] Form 990-T, Part I.
[248] Form 990-T, Schedule A, Part IV. See § 25.1(h).
[249] Form 990-T, Schedule A, Part V. See § 24.10.
[250] Form 990-T, Schedule A, Part VI. See §§ 29.7, 30.6(b).
[251] Form 990-T, Schedule A, Part VII. See § 25.4(c). These organizations are social clubs (see Chapter 15), voluntary employees' beneficiary associations (see § 18.3), and supplemental unemployment benefit trusts (see § 18.4).
[252] Form 990-T, Schedule A, Part VIII. See § 24.4(e).
[253] Form 990-T, Schedule A, Part IX. See § 24.5(h).
[254] See § 21.14.
[255] IRC § 6651(a)(1). This addition to tax may also apply if Form 990-T is submitted on paper instead of electronically (Reg. § 301.6011-10(b)).
[256] IRC § 6651(a)(2).
[257] The requirement that the initial determination of a penalty assessment be personally approved in writing by the immediate supervisor of the IRS employee making the determination does not apply to these additions to tax (IRC § 6751(b)(2)(A); Prop. Reg. § 301.6751(b)-1(a)(2)(i)).
[258] United States v. Boyle, 469 U.S. 241 (1985).
[259] Reg. § 1.6651-1(c)(1).
[260] Haywood Lumber & Mining Co. v. Comm'r, 178 F.2d 769, 771 (2d Cir. 1950).

substantial understatement of income tax required to be shown on the return.[261] The penalty is equal to 20 percent of the amount of the understatement.[262] For purposes of this penalty, *negligence* includes any failure to make a reasonable attempt to comply with the tax laws, and disregard includes any careless, reckless, or intentional disregard.[263] A *substantial understatement* of tax occurs if the amount of the understatement exceeds the greater of 10 percent of the tax required to be shown on the return for the taxable year, or $5,000.[264] There is no stacking of accuracy-related penalty components; thus, if a portion of an underpayment of tax required to be shown on a return is attributable both to negligence and a substantial understatement of income tax, the maximum accuracy-related penalty is 20 percent of such portion.[265]

These accuracy-related penalties do not apply to any portion of an underpayment if it is shown that there was a reasonable cause for such portion and that the taxpayer acted in good faith with respect to such portion.[266] One court upheld the imposition of the accuracy-related penalty for negligence or disregard of rules and regulations on a social club where the club's return preparers were aware of case law holding that the income on which the club failed to pay tax was indeed taxable to the club. Additionally, there was no evidence that the return preparers had sufficient expertise to justify reliance, that they were provided with necessary and accurate information, or that the club relied in good faith on the return preparers' judgment. Thus, this court held that the returns were not prepared in good faith and the club did not have reasonable cause for the underpayments of unrelated business income tax.[267]

Another court, after finding a labor organization was liable for unrelated business income tax on its advertising income, went on to hold that the organization was not liable for negligence and substantial understatement penalties on this income. The court observed that the case involved "a complex and close question of law" and that the applicable law "was developing during the periods in issue." The court distinguished a case relied on by the organization but held that the case nevertheless provided the organization with substantial authority for not treating its income as subject to tax. Under the circumstances, the court determined that the organization reasonably relied on the case law and on the advice of its counsel that it was not required to file Form 990-T.[268]

§ 28.9 DOCUMENT DISCLOSURE OBLIGATIONS OF IRS

The IRS is subject to two bodies of federal law mandating public disclosure of certain types of documents. One of these bodies of law is part of the Internal Revenue Code; the other is the Freedom of Information Act (FOIA). A document

---

[261] IRC § 6662(a), (b)(1), (2).
[262] IRC § 6662(a).
[263] IRC § 6662(c).
[264] IRC § 6662(d)(1)(A).
[265] Treas. Reg. 1.6662-2(c).
[266] IRC § 6664(c)(1).
[267] Losantiville Country Club v. Comm'r, 114 T.C.M 198 (2017).
[268] State Police Ass'n of Massachusetts v. Comm'r, 72 T.C.M. 582 (1996).

mandated for disclosure by the tax law may nonetheless be sheltered from disclosure by the FOIA.

(a) Federal Tax Law Disclosure Requirements

Generally, the IRS is required by law to disclose the text of any document prepared by the agency, as well as the related file.

(i) General Rules. In general, the IRS is required to disclose the text of any of the agency's written determinations and any background file document relating to a written determination.[269] A *written determination* is an IRS ruling, determination letter, technical advice memorandum, or Chief Counsel advice memorandum.[270] The term *background file document* with respect to a written determination includes the request for the determination, any written material submitted in support of the request, and certain communications between the IRS and other persons.[271] Before making a written determination or background file document available to the public, the agency is required to delete (redact) various items, including certain identifying information (such as persons' names and addresses), information classified by executive order, trade secrets, and information whose disclosure would constitute an unwarranted invasion of personal privacy.[272]

Special rules apply in connection with the disclosure of Chief Counsel advice.[273] The term *Chief Counsel advice* means (1) written advice or instruction prepared by a "national office component" of the IRS's Office of Chief Counsel, (2) which is issued to field or service center employees of the IRS or regional or district employees of that Office, and (3) which conveys a legal interpretation of a revenue provision, an IRS or Office of Chief Counsel position or policy concerning a revenue provision, or a legal interpretation of state law, foreign law, or other federal law relating to the assessment or collection of any liability under a revenue provision.[274] Most of the redaction rules[275] do not apply in this context, but certain deletions of material may be made in accordance with the FOIA.[276]

The IRS may charge a fee for the duplication of written determinations and background file documents made available to the public or for the process of searching for and making redactions from these documents.[277] If the IRS assesses

---

[269] IRC § 6110(a). The U.S. Tax Court ruled that it lacked jurisdiction to order a properly issued determination letter "un-issued" and thus not disclosable, where the IRS agreed to withdraw the letter as part of a settlement of litigation (Anonymous v. Comm'r, 145 T.C.M. 246 (2015)).

[270] IRC § 6110(b)(1)(A).

[271] IRC § 6110(b)(2).

[272] IRC § 6110(c).

[273] IRC § 6110(i).

[274] IRC § 6110(i)(1)(A). A *revenue provision* includes federal tax statutes, regulations, revenue rulings, revenue procedures, and other published IRS guidance (IRC § 6110(i)(1)(B)).

The IRS failed in an attempt to withhold advice that was "informal" or prepared and disseminated within two hours (such as by e-mail) (Tax Analysts v. Internal Revenue Serv., 416 F. Supp. 2d 119 (D.D.C. 2006)), although the court also held that the information was protected by the Freedom of Information Act (see § 28.9(b)).

[275] See text accompanied by *supra* note 272.

[276] IRC § 6110(i)(3). See § 28.9(b).

[277] IRC § 6110(k)(1).

a fee in connection with the production of this information (including photocopying), the fee may be no more than the fee that would be assessed under the schedule promulgated pursuant to the FOIA.[278] A written determination or background file document may be furnished by the IRS without charge or at a reduced charge if the agency determines that practice is in the public interest.[279] In general, these written determinations may not be used or cited as precedent.[280]

This body of law does not, however, apply to all written determinations from the IRS. For example, closing agreements[281] and related background information are not disclosable.[282]

(ii) Exempt Organizations Documents. Applications for recognition of exemption and supporting materials filed by tax-exempt organizations and IRS determinations with respect to these applications must be disclosed by the agency.[283] At the request of the organization, information pertaining to trade secrets, patents, processes, style of work, or an apparatus may be withheld by the IRS if the disclosure would adversely affect the organization.[284] The IRS may also withhold from public inspection information contained in supporting papers where public disclosure would adversely affect the national defense.[285]

Also open to inspection under these rules are technical advice memoranda.[286] These applications and related materials may be inspected at IRS service centers or the IRS's National Office.[287] Further, a ruling issued by the National Office and

---

[278] Reg. §§ 301.6104(a)-6(d), 301.6104(b)-1(d); 5 U.S.C. § 552(a)(4)(A)(i).

[279] IRC § 6110(k)(1), last sentence.

[280] IRC § 6110(k)(3). Accordingly, no citations to written determinations of the IRS in this book should be used or cited as precedent.

[281] IRC § 7121.

[282] IRC § 6103(b)(2)(D). This rule assumes that this type of agreement does not contain information that is subject to disclosure under IRC § 6104 (see § 28.9(a)(ii)). That is, if a closing agreement is or contains information making it a supporting document to an exemption application (Reg. § 301.6104(a)-1(e)), disclosure of it, or one or more portions of it, may be required. These distinctions are the subject of a court opinion holding that a closing agreement between the IRS and a tax-exempt organization need not be disclosed by the IRS (Tax Analysts v. Internal Revenue Serv., 410 F.3d 715 (D.C. Cir. 2005)).

[283] IRC § 6104(a)(1)(A); Rev. Proc. 2024-5, 2024-1 I.R.B. 262 § 13.02(1). IRC § 6104 was characterized as an "exception to the exception from the general disclosure rules offered by FOIA Exemption 3 [see § 28.9(b)] and I.R.C. § 6103" (Tax Analysts v. Internal Revenue Serv., 214 F.3d 179, 181–83 (D.C. Cir. 2000)).

This disclosure requirement is confined to documents submitted in support of the application by the organization (Reg. § 301.6104(a)-1(e)). It does not apply to letters or other documents submitted by any other person, such as a member of Congress (Lehrfeld v. Richardson, 132 F.3d 1463 (D.C. Cir. 1998)). For this purpose, the term *tax-exempt organization* means an entity described in IRC § 501(c) (see § 1.2) or 501(d) (see § 10.8) that is exempt from tax under IRC § 501(a) (see § 3.1), or a political organization (see Chapter 17).

A different disclosure regime is applicable with respect to pension, profit-sharing, and like plans (IRC § 6104(a)(1)(B)). This rule requires disclosure of applications and written determinations regarding tax exemptions for the funds underlying these plans. This provision references "any applications" filed with the IRS, which encompasses those that result in a granting or a denial of exemption (and perhaps revocation of exemption).

[284] IRC § 6104(a)(1)(D); Reg. § 301.6104(a)-5.

[285] *Id.*

[286] Reg. § 601.201(n)(9).

[287] Reg. § 301.6104(a)-6(b).

underlying applications for recognition of exemption are available for inspection in the IRS Freedom of Information Reading Room in Washington, DC.[288]

These document availability rules are applicable to the notice that must be filed by political organizations[289] to establish their tax-exempt status[290] and to the reports they must file.[291] The IRS is required to make publicly available, at its offices and on the Internet, a list of all political organizations that file a notice with the IRS, and the name, address, electronic mailing address, custodian of records, and contact person for each of these organizations.[292] This information must be made available not later than five business days after the notice is received.

This general disclosure regime for tax-exempt organizations (pertaining to applications for recognition of exemption, supporting documents, technical advice memoranda, and determination letters) applies where the IRS has determined that the organization is exempt[293] and where there is a denial or revocation of exemption.[294]

Additionally, the IRS is required to make Forms 990, and Forms 990-T filed by charitable organizations,[295] available for public inspection.[296]

The IRS's *Tax Exempt Organization Search* database[297] is the primary source for publicly available data on electronically filed Form 990 series returns required to be disclosed by the IRS. It also allows the public to view determination letters, but not exemption application materials, issued since January 1, 2014. Returns and exemption application materials that are not available through this database may be requested by filing the correct form with the IRS.[298]

The excise tax return filed by private foundations[299] is available to the public.[300] This return as filed by a person other than a private foundation, such as in the intermediate sanctions, legislative activities, or political campaign activities context,[301] is, however, not disclosable. Therefore, if disclosure of this return

---

[288] Reg. § 301.6104(a)-6(a).

[289] See Chapter 17.

[290] See § 26.14.

[291] See § 28.6.

[292] IRC § 6104(a)(3).

[293] Reg. § 301.6104(a)-1(a), (b).

[294] Tax Analysts v. Internal Revenue Serv., 350 F.3d 100 (D.C. Cir. 2003), *rev'g* 215 F. Supp. 2d 192 (D.D.C. 2002). See Rev. Proc. 2024-5, 2024-1 I.R.B. 262 § 13.02.

[295] That is, an organization described in IRC § 501(c)(3), which includes a private foundation required to file Form 990-PF.

[296] IRC § 6104(b); Reg. § 301.6104(b)-1.

[297] https://www.irs.gov/charities-non-profits/tax-exempt-organization-search. See § 28.5(a).

[298] To request a copy of a Form 990 or 990-T that is not available through the *Tax Exempt Organization Search* database, Form 4506-A, *Request for Copy of Exempt or Political Organization IRS Form,* may be filed by fax or mail (but not by email). To request a copy of a determination letter issued before 2014, Form 4506-B, *Request for a Copy of Exempt Organization IRS Application or Letter,* may be submitted using the email feature on the form (but not by fax or mail). Form 4506-B may also be used to request a copy of an organization's Form 1023 application for recognition of tax-exempt status or an affirmation letter confirming the organization's current exempt status.

[299] Form 4720.

[300] Reg. § 1.6033-2(a)(2)(ii)(J).

[301] See § 21.14 (Form 4720, Schedule I), §§ 22.3(d)(iii), 22.4 (Form 4720, Schedules G, H), § 23.3 (Form 4720, Schedule F), respectively.

containing private foundation information filed by a person other than a private foundation is not desired, the person should file separately rather than jointly with the foundation, inasmuch as the joint filing is disclosable.[302]

(b)   Freedom of Information Act

The FOIA provides basic rules for disclosure of federal records;[303] this law is applicable to the IRS. Nonetheless, there are several exceptions to the FOIA. One of these exceptions is for documents specifically exempted by statute (known as *FOIA Exemption 3*).[304] As discussed, the basic rule in the federal tax law context requires disclosure by the IRS of documents pertaining to applications for recognition of tax-exempt status.[305] By contrast, federal tax law explicitly protects the confidentiality of such tax return information as closing agreements, as long as the return information is not subject to disclosure under the general rule.[306] In an opinion analyzing the intersection of these two federal tax law rules, a federal court of appeals held that a closing agreement between the IRS and a tax-exempt organization was shielded from disclosure by FOIA Exemption 3.[307]

Another exception in this setting incorporates the traditional attorney work product doctrine by exempting from the general rule of disclosure any documents "which would not be available by law to a party . . . in litigation with the agency" (known as *FOIA Exemption 5*).[308] The FOIA, however, does not provide complete protection for documents containing privileged material; the governmental agency must disclose any reasonably segregable nonexempt portions of a record unless they are "inextricably intertwined" with the exempt portions.[309] For example, IRS technical advice memoranda may be shielded from disclosure pursuant to this exception where they are documents prepared in anticipation of litigation or for trial (even if they contain a discussion of general applications of the

---

[302] T.D. 7785, 1981-2 C.B. 233.

[303] 5 U.S.C. § 552(a).

[304] 5 U.S.C. § 552(b)(3).

[305] IRC § 6104(a)(1)(A). See § 28.9(a)(ii).

[306] IRS § 6103(b)(2)(D). See § 28.9(a)(i). A federal appellate court concluded that the fact that IRC § 6103 is a statute "contemplated by FOIA Exemption 3 is beyond dispute" (Tax Analysts v. Internal Revenue Serv., 117 F.3d 607, 611 (D.C. Cir. 1997)).

[307] Tax Analysts v. Internal Revenue Serv. and Christian Broadcasting Network, Inc., 410 F.3d 715 (D.C. Cir. 2005).

[308] 5 U.S.C. § 552(b)(5). This is also known as the deliberative process privilege. This doctrine (first enunciated by the Supreme Court in Hickman v. Taylor, 329 U.S. 495 (1947)) protects documents prepared in "contemplation of litigation" and "provides a working attorney with a 'zone of privacy' within which to think, plan, weigh facts and evidence, candidly evaluate a client's case, and prepare legal theories" (Coastal States Gas Corp. v. Dep't of Energy, 617 F.2d 854, 864 (D.C. Cir. 1980)). This privilege does not, however, extend to every document prepared by a lawyer; protection is extended only where the document was prepared in anticipation of litigation (Jordan v. United States Dep't of Justice, 591 F.2d 753 (D.C. Cir. 1978)).

[309] Trans-Pacific Policing Agreement v. United States Customs Serv., 177 F.3d 1022 (D.C. Cir. 1999); Judicial Watch v. United States Dep't of Justice, 337 F. Supp. 2d 183 (D.D.C. 2004).

federal tax law).[310] The same is the case for IRS Field Service advice memoranda[311] and Chief Counsel advice memoranda.[312]

§ 28.10 DOCUMENT DISCLOSURE OBLIGATIONS OF EXEMPT ORGANIZATIONS

A tax-exempt organization[313] is generally required to make available for inspection and is required to disseminate copies of its application for recognition of exemption and its three most recent annual information returns.[314] There are exceptions from these document dissemination rules. This disclosure obligation also extends to notices and reports filed by political organizations.

(a) General Rules

In general, an organization, that has been issued a favorable determination letter as to recognition of exemption, is required to make available for inspection during regular business hours a copy of the application for recognition of exemption filed by the organization (if any),[315] and of the organization's three most recent annual information returns,[316] and to provide copies of these documents to those who properly request them.[317] If an application for recognition of exemption was filed, this disclosure obligation extends to the organization's exempt status application materials, which is defined as the application, any papers submitted in support of the application, and any letter or other document issued by the IRS with respect to the application.[318]

Organizations that are covered by a group exemption and do not file their own annual information returns,[319] and that receive a request for inspection, must make available for public inspection, or provide a copy of, (1) the application

---

[310] Tax Analysts v. Internal Revenue Serv., 152 F. Supp. 2d 1 (D.D.C. 2001), aff'd, 294 F.3d 71 (D.C. Cir. 2002).

[311] Tax Analysts v. Internal Revenue Serv., 117 F.3d 607 (D.C. Cir. 1997).

[312] Tax Analysts v. Internal Revenue Serv., 416 F. Supp. 2d 119 (D.D.C. 2006); Tax Analysts v. Internal Revenue Serv., 391 F. Supp. 2d 122 (D.D.C. 2005). An opinion by a federal district court provides an excellent survey of application of the FOIA where the requestor of government-held information is a tax-exempt organization (Sea Shepherd Conservation Soc'y v. Internal Revenue Serv., 89 F. Supp. 3d (D.D.C. 2015)).

[313] See supra note 283, third paragraph.

[314] IRC § 6104(d).

[315] See § 26.1.

[316] See § 28.2.

[317] IRC § 6104(d)(1), (2); Rev. Proc. 2024-5, 2024-1 I.R.B. 262 § 13.02(2). These requirements are inapplicable with respect to an application for recognition of exemption filed before July 15, 1987, unless the organization that filed it had a copy of it on that date (Reg. § 301.6104(d)-1(b)(3)(iii)(B)). An organization is required to disclose its application materials only where it is exempt under IRC § 501(a) (IRC § 6104(d)(1)); therefore, an organization is not required to disclose its application materials while its exemption application is pending or in a case where the IRS issues an adverse determination (T.D. 8818, 64 Fed. Reg. 17279, 17281 (1999)).

[318] IRC § 6104(d)(5).

[319] See § 26.11.

submitted by the central organization to obtain the group exemption letter and those documents that the central organization submitted to include the subordinate organization in the group exemption letter, and (2) the group return from the central organization (omitting any schedules relating solely to other organizations included in the group return). Alternatively, the requestor can request, from the central organization, inspection of the group return materials or group returns at the principal office of the parent organization.[320]

This disclosure regime also applies with respect to the annual returns filed by nonexempt private foundations and nonexempt charitable trusts,[321] and unrelated business income tax returns filed by charitable organizations.[322] Also subject to this disclosure are the notices and reports filed by political organizations,[323] and *notice materials*, which are defined as the notice, any papers submitted in support of the notice, and any letter or other document issued by the IRS with respect to the notice.[324]

Generally, an organization need not disclose the names and addresses of donors, except in the case of a private foundation or political organization.[325] Certain information, such as trade secrets, patents, processes, styles of work, and apparatuses, also can be withheld if the IRS withheld that information from public inspection when it issued the organization's determination letter.[326] However, because in general applications and supporting documentation are otherwise open to public inspection, organizations should ensure that they do not include unnecessary personal identifying information, such as bank account or Social Security numbers, that could result in identity theft or other adverse consequences.[327]

A tax-exempt organization must provide a copy without charge, other than a reasonable fee for reproduction and mailing costs, of all or any part of an application for recognition of exemption or return required to be made available for public inspection to any individual who makes a request for the copy in person or in writing.[328] Exact copies of the organization's annual information return must be

---

[320] Reg. § 301.6104(d)-1(f).

[321] IRC § 6104(d)(8).

[322] IRC § 6104(d)(1)(A)(ii). All charitable (IRC § 501(c)(3)) organizations that file Form 990-T are required to make the return public, even if the organization is not otherwise subject to the disclosure requirements, such as a church (see § 28.2(c)(i)). Also, state colleges and universities, and certain other entities, have tax exemption (technically, income exclusion) based on IRC § 115 (see § 19.22(b)); if that is the sole basis for exemption and the organization has reportable unrelated business income, the organization is not required to make its Forms 990-T public, whereas if the organization also has tax exemption based on IRC § 501(c)(3), Forms 990-T must be made publicly available.

Until existing regulations are revised, organizations may rely on Reg. §§ 301.6104(d)-1, -2, and -3 on how to comply with the disclosure rule for Forms 990-T, except as otherwise provided interim guidance published by the IRS (Notice 2007-45, 2007-1 C.B. 1320).

[323] Political organizations are the subject of Chapter 17, this notice is the subject of § 26.14, and these reports are the subject of § 28.6.

[324] IRC § 6104(d)(6).

[325] IRC § 6104(d)(3)(A).

[326] IRC § 6104(d)(3)(B); Rev. Proc. 2024-5, 2024-1 I.R.B. 262 § 13.02.

[327] Rev. Proc. 2024-5, 2024-1 I.R.B. 262 § 13.02(1).

[328] IRC § 6104(d)(1)(B); Reg. § 301.6104(d)-1(d).

provided (unless the previously noted exceptions to disclosure for donor information or trade secrets and the like apply).[329]

(b) Rules as to Inspection

A tax-exempt organization must make its application for recognition of exemption available for public inspection at its principal office and, if the organization regularly maintains one or more regional or district offices having three or more employees, at each of its regional and/or district offices.[330] Likewise, an exempt organization must make its recent annual information returns available for public inspection in the same offices.[331]

(c) Rules as to Copies

Generally, a tax-exempt organization must provide copies of the documents, in response to an in-person request, at its principal, regional, and/or district offices "immediately" on request. If the request is in writing, the exempt organization has 30 days in which to respond.[332]

In the case of an in-person request, when unusual circumstances exist so that fulfillment of the request on the same business day places an unreasonable burden on the exempt organization, the copies must be provided on the next business day following the day on which the unusual circumstances cease to exist or the fifth business day after the date of the request, whichever occurs first. *Unusual circumstances* include receipt of a volume of requests that exceeds the organization's daily capacity to make copies, requests received shortly before the end of regular business hours that require an extensive amount of copying, and requests received on a day when the organization's managerial staff capable of fulfilling the request is conducting special duties. *Special duties* are activities such as student registration or attendance at an off-site meeting or convention, rather than regular administrative duties.[333]

If a request for a document is made in writing, the tax-exempt organization must honor it if the request (1) is addressed to and delivered by U.S. mail, electronic mail, facsimile, or a private delivery service to a principal, regional, or district office of the organization, and (2) sets forth the address to which the copy of the document should be sent.[334]

A tax-exempt organization receiving a written request for a copy must mail the copy within 30 days from the date it receives the request. If, however, an exempt organization requires payment in advance, it is only required to provide the copy within 30 days from the date it receives payment. An exempt organization must fulfill a request for a copy of the organization's entire application or annual information return or any specific part or schedule of its application or return.[335]

---

[329] Reg. § 301.6104(d)-1(b)(4)(i).
[330] IRC § 6104(d)(1)(A)(ii); Reg. § 301.6104(d)-1(a).
[331] IRC § 6104(d)(1)(A)(i); Reg. § 301.6104(d)-1(a).
[332] IRC § 6104(d)(1), last sentence; Reg. § 301.6104(d)-1(d)(1)(i).
[333] Reg. § 301.6104(d)-1(d)(1)(ii).
[334] Reg. § 301.6104(d)-1(d)(2)(i).
[335] Reg. § 301.6104(d)-1(d)(2)(ii).

A tax-exempt organization may charge a reasonable fee for providing copies. The photocopying fee that may be charged by an exempt organization is not reasonable if it exceeds the comparable fee assessed by the IRS.[336] It can also include actual postage costs. The requestor may be required to pay the fee in advance.[337]

(d) Failure to Comply

If a tax-exempt organization denies an individual's request for inspection or a copy of an application or return and the person wishes to alert the IRS to the possible need for enforcement action, they may send a statement to the appropriate IRS district office, describing the reason why the individual believes the denial was in violation of these requirements.[338]

(e) Widely Available Exception

A tax-exempt organization is not required to comply with requests for copies of its application for recognition of exemption or an annual information return if the organization has made the document widely available.[339] The rules as to public inspection of the documents nonetheless continue to apply.

A tax-exempt organization can make its application or a return *widely available* by posting the document on a webpage that the organization establishes and maintains. It can also satisfy the exception if the document is posted as part of a database of similar documents of other exempt organizations on a webpage established and maintained by another entity.[340]

The document is considered widely available only if (1) the webpage by means of which it is available clearly informs readers that the document is available and provides instructions for downloading it; (2) the document is posted in a format that, when accessed, downloaded, viewed, and printed in hard copy, exactly reproduces the image of the application or return as it was filed with the IRS, except for any information permitted by statute to be withheld from public disclosure; and (3) any individual with access to the Internet can access, download, view, and print the document without special computer hardware or software required for that format, and can do so without payment of a fee to the exempt organization or to another entity maintaining the webpage.[341]

The organization maintaining the webpage must have procedures for ensuring the reliability and accuracy of the documents that it posts on the page. It must take reasonable precautions to prevent alteration, destruction, or accidental loss of the document when printed on its page. In the event a posted document is altered, destroyed, or lost, the organization must correct or replace the document.[342]

---

[336] See *supra* note 278.

[337] Reg. § 301.6104(d)-1(d)(3).

[338] Reg. § 301.6104(d)-1(g). Violation of this statute does not give rise to a private cause of action (e.g., Doan v. Vietnamese Buddhist Ass'n of Sacramento, 2019 WL 2763167 (E.D. Cal. 2019) and cases cited therein).

[339] IRC § 6104(d)(4); Reg. § 301.6104(d)-2(a).

[340] Reg. § 301.6104(d)-2(b)(2)(i).

[341] *Id.*

[342] Reg. § 301.6104(d)-2(b)(2)(iii).

(f) Harassment Campaign Exception

If the IRS determines that a tax-exempt organization is the subject of a harassment campaign and that compliance with the requests that are part of the campaign would not be in the public interest, the organization is not required to fulfill a request for a copy that it reasonably believes is part of the campaign.[343]

A group of requests for a tax-exempt organization's application or returns is indicative of a *harassment campaign* if the requests are part of a single coordinated effort to disrupt the operations of the organization, rather than to collect information about it. This is a facts-and-circumstances test.[344]

A tax-exempt organization may disregard any request for copies of all or part of any document beyond the first two received within any 30-day period or the first four received within any one-year period from the same individual or the same address, irrespective of whether the IRS has determined that the organization is subject to a harassment campaign.[345]

There is a procedure to follow for applying to the IRS for a determination that the organization is the subject of a harassment campaign. (There is no form.) As long as the organization files the application within 10 days after harassment is suspected, it may suspend compliance with respect to the request until it receives a response from the IRS.[346]

(g) Penalties

A person failing to allow inspection of an organization's annual information returns is subject to a penalty of $20 per day for each day the failure continues, absent reasonable cause, with a maximum penalty per return of $10,000.[347] A person failing to allow inspection of an organization's application for recognition of tax exemption must, absent reasonable cause, pay $20 per day for each day the failure continues, with no maximum.[348] A person who willfully fails to comply with these inspection requirements is subject to a penalty of $5,000 with respect to each return or application.[349]

---

[343] IRC § 6104(d)(4); Reg. § 301.6104(d)-3(a).

[344] Reg. § 301.6104(d)-3(b). In ruling that an organization was not the subject of a harassment campaign, the IRS wrote that a request for information "from one requestor cannot serve as a basis for a harassment campaign determination, regardless of the motivation of the person requesting the documents" (Priv. Ltr. Rul. 201123046).

[345] Reg. § 301.6104(d)-3(c).

[346] Reg. § 301.6104(d)-3(d), (e).

[347] IRC § 6652(c)(1)(C), (5). Adjusted for inflation (IRC § 6652(c)(7)), the daily penalty is $25, and the maximum penalty is $12,500 for returns required to be filed in 2025 (Rev. Proc. 2023-34, 2023-48 I.R.B. 1287 § 3.54).

[348] IRC § 6652(c)(1)(D), (5). Adjusted for inflation (IRC § 6652(c)(7)), the daily penalty is $25, for returns required to be filed in 2025 (Rev. Proc. 2023-34, 2023-48 I.R.B. 1287 § 3.54).

[349] IRC § 6685.

(h)   Political Organizations

These document availability rules are applicable to the annual information returns filed by political organizations,[350] the notice that they must file to establish their tax-exempt status[351] and the reports that they must file.[352]

(i)   Donor Information Disclosure

Federal tax statutory law outlines the requirements for annual information returns filed by tax-exempt organizations, including exceptions to the requirements.[353] The general elements to be reported are stated,[354] as are items to be reported by exempt charitable entities.[355] Annual information returns are required to contain "such other information for the purpose of carrying out the internal revenue laws as the [Treasury Department] may by forms or regulations prescribe."[356]

One of the elements to be generally reported is the total of the contributions, grants, and similar amounts received by tax-exempt organizations in the reporting year.[357] Exempt charitable organizations, however, must also report the names and addresses of their donors.[358]

The previous version of the tax regulations extended this requirement of disclosing the identity of donors to all tax-exempt organizations. This overreach was corrected by final regulations issued in 2020.[359]

As the Treasury Department and the IRS stated in the preamble to these final regulations, they "sought to balance the IRS's need for the information for tax administration purposes against the costs and risks associated with reporting of the information." [360] The preamble states that the IRS "does not need the names and addresses of substantial contributors to tax-exempt organizations not described in section 501(c)(3) to be reported annually on Schedule B of Form 990 or Form 990-EZ in order to administer the internal revenue laws." [361] The IRS, it is said, can obtain sufficient information from other elements of these returns[362] and can obtain donor information by examination.

---

[350] Rev. Rul. 2003-49, 2003-1 C.B. 903, Q&A 54. See § 28.2(b)(vii).

[351] See § 26.14.

[352] See § 28.6.

[353] IRC § 6033. See § 28.2.

[354] IRC § 6033(a); Reg. § 1.6033-2(a)(2)(ii).

[355] IRC § 6033(b).

[356] IRC § 6033(a)(1).

[357] Reg. § 1.6033-2(a)(2)(ii)(F).

[358] IRC § 6033(b)(5); Reg. § 1.6033-2(a)(2)(ii)(F). This disclosure is on Schedule B accompanying the annual information return. See § 28.2(a)(i).

[359] T.D. 9898, 85 Fed. Reg. 31962 (2020).

[360] Id.

[361] Id. at 31963. However, in addition to charitable organizations, political organizations (see Chapter 17) generally must continue to report the names and addresses of all persons that contributed, bequeathed, or devised $5,000 or more (in money or other property) during the taxable year (Reg. § 1.6033-2(a)(5); see § 28.2(b)(vii)).

[362] E.g., Form 990, Schedules J, L, and R.

It is also noted in the preamble that "reporting the names and addresses of substantial contributors on an annual basis poses a risk of inadvertent disclosure of information that is not open to public inspection."[363] These regulations are intended to reduce the risk of inadvertent disclosure of this information. The preamble takes notice of concerns that supporters of certain causes or organizations "face possible reprisals (such as harassment, threats of violence, or economic retribution) if their status as contributors is revealed publicly" and of "fear of exposure and fear of reprisal [that] may have a 'chilling effect', discouraging or deterring potential contributors from giving to certain tax-exempt organizations and reducing public participation in organizations benefiting social welfare."[364] Many commentators expressed their belief that this "chilling effect," in the language of the preamble, "implicates constitutional rights such as freedom of speech and freedom of association."[365]

In the preamble, the Treasury Department and the IRS stated that they "agree with certain commenters that limiting the general requirement to report names and addresses of substantial contributors will reduce costs with respect to federal tax compliance."[366] They determined "it is valuable to save tax-exempt organizations the administrative burdens of reporting and redacting" donor information.[367] Moreover, the "potential burden on the IRS associated with redacting Schedule B information is lessened when fewer organizations are required to report names and addresses on Schedule B."[368]

§ 28.11 INFORMATION OR SERVICES DISCLOSURE

A tax-exempt organization[369] must pay a penalty if it fails to disclose that information or services it is offering are available without charge from the federal government.

Specifically, this penalty may be imposed if (1) a tax-exempt organization offers to sell (or solicits money for) specific information or a routine service for any individual that could be readily obtained by the individual without charge (or for a nominal charge) from an agency of the federal government; (2) the exempt organization, when making the offer or solicitation, fails to make an "express

---

[363] 85 Fed. Reg. 31962, 31963 (2020).

[364] *Id.* at 31963–64.

[365] The U.S. Supreme Court found unconstitutional a state law requirement that organizations include an unredacted Schedule B for state law charitable registration reporting purposes. Americans for Prosperity Found. v. Bonta; Thomas More Law Center v. Bonta, 141 S. Ct. 2373 (2021). See *Fundraising* § 7.10(d).

[366] *Id.* at 31964.

[367] *Id.*

[368] *Id.* All tax-exempt organizations, however, must continue to maintain amounts received from and names and addresses of each substantial contributor in their books and records and make them available to the IRS on examination (*id.* at 31966).

[369] That is, an entity described in IRC §§ 501(c) or (d) and exempt from federal income tax under IRC § 501(a) or a political organization as defined in IRC § 527(e) (see Parts Three and Four).

statement (in a conspicuous and easily recognizable format)" that the information or service can be so obtained; and (3) the failure is due to "intentional disregard" of these requirements.[370]

This requirement applies only if the information to be provided involves the specific individual solicited. Thus, for example, the requirement applies with respect to obtaining the Social Security earnings record or the Social Security identification number of an individual solicited, while the requirement is inapplicable with respect to the furnishing of copies of newsletters issued by federal agencies or providing copies of or descriptive material on pending legislation. Also, this requirement is inapplicable to the provision of professional services (such as tax return preparation, grant application preparation, or medical services), as opposed to routine information retrieval services, to an individual even if they may be available from the federal government without charge or at a nominal charge.[371]

The penalty, which is applicable for each day on which the failure occurred, is the greater of $1,000 or 50 percent of the aggregate cost of the offers and solicitations that occurred on any day on which the failure occurred and with respect to which there was this type of failure.[372]

§ 28.12   FUNDRAISING DISCLOSURE

A provision of federal tax law pertains to fundraising by most tax-exempt organizations.[373] These rules, however, are not applicable with respect to exempt charitable organizations.[374]

This body of law is designed to prevent noncharitable organizations (principally, social welfare entities)[375] from engaging in public fundraising activities under circumstances where donors are likely to assume that the contributions are tax-deductible as charitable gifts, when in fact they are not.

Thus, under these rules, each *fundraising solicitation* by (or on behalf of) a noncharitable tax-exempt organization is required to "contain an express statement (in a conspicuous and easily recognizable format)" that gifts to it are not deductible as charitable contributions for federal income tax purposes.[376] A fundraising solicitation that is in conformity with rules promulgated by the IRS (concerning the format of the disclosure statement in instances of use of print media, telephone,

---

[370] IRC § 6711(a). IRS guidelines (Notice 88-120, 1988-2 C.B. 454) state that if materials and/or services are available from the federal government for less than $2.50 (including postage and handling costs), the materials are considered by the IRS as being available from the federal government at a nominal charge.

[371] Notice 88-120, 1988-2 C.B. 454.

[372] IRC § 6711(b).

[373] IRC § 6113.

[374] That is, this element of the legislation does not apply to organizations described in IRC § 501(c)(3) (see Part Three).

[375] See Chapter 13.

[376] IRC § 6113(a).

television, and radio), which include guidance in the form of "safe harbor" provisions, is deemed to satisfy the statutory requirements.[377]

Generally, this rule applies to any organization to which contributions are not deductible as charitable gifts and that (1) is tax-exempt,[378] (2) is a political organization,[379] (3) was either type of organization at any time during the five-year period ending on the date of the fundraising solicitation, or (4) is a successor to this type of an organization at any time during the five-year period.[380] This rule is inapplicable, however, to any organization that has annual gross receipts that are normally no more than $100,000. Also, where all of the parties being solicited are exempt organizations, a solicitation need not include the disclosure statement (inasmuch as these grantors do not utilize a charitable contribution deduction).[381]

Further exempt from this disclosure rule is the billing of those who advertise in an organization's publications, billings by social clubs for food and beverages, billing of attendees at a conference, billing for insurance premiums of an insurance program operated or sponsored by an organization, billing of members of a community association for mandatory payments for police and fire (and similar) protection, or billing for payments to a voluntary employees' beneficiary association, as well as similar payments to a trust for pension and/or health benefits.[382]

The IRS is accorded the authority to treat any group of two or more organizations as one organization for these purposes where "necessary or appropriate" to prevent the avoidance of these rules through the use of multiple organizations. The term *fundraising solicitation* means any solicitation of gifts made in written or printed form, or by television, radio, or telephone. An exclusion is provided for letters or calls not part of a "coordinated fundraising campaign soliciting more than 10 persons during the calendar year."[383]

Failure to satisfy this disclosure requirement can result in penalties.[384] The penalty is $1,000 per day (maximum of $10,000 per year), albeit with a reasonable cause exception. In the case of an "intentional disregard" of these rules, however, the penalty for the day on which the offense occurred is the greater of $1,000 or 50 percent of the aggregate cost of the solicitation that took place on that day and the $10,000 limitation would be inapplicable. For these purposes, the days involved are those on which the solicitation was telecast, broadcast, mailed, otherwise distributed, or telephoned.

---

[377] Notice 88-120, 1988-2 C.B. 454. In one instance, a political organization (see Chapter 17) that conducted fundraising by means of telemarketing and direct mail was found to be in violation of these rules; a notice of nondeductibility of contributions was not included in its telephone solicitations or pledge statements, and the print used in some of its written notices was too small (Priv. Ltr. Rul. 9315001).

[378] That is, is described in IRC § 501(c) (other than IRC § 501(c)(3)).

[379] That is, an organization described in IRC § 527. See Chapter 17.

[380] IRC § 6113(b). For this purpose, a fraternal organization (one described in IRC § 170(c)(4)) is treated as a charitable organization only with respect to solicitations for contributions that are to be used exclusively for purposes referred to in IRC § 170(c)(4) (IRC § 6113(b)(3)).

[381] Notice 88-120, 1988-2 C.B. 454.

[382] *Id.*

[383] IRC § 6113(c).

[384] IRC § 6710.

§ 28.13 INSURANCE ACTIVITIES

(a) General Rules

In general, and including the time prior to the effective date of the rules concerning commercial-type insurance,[385] nonprofit organizations that provide various types of insurance cannot qualify as charitable entities.[386] Indeed, in some instances, organizations of this nature were unable to qualify as exempt social welfare organizations.[387]

A federal appellate court held that an entity, organized by a church, providing property insurance only to church members was not exempt on the ground it advanced religion,[388] observing that it "does not give succor to souls; it sells insurance coverage."[389] The same fate befell a trust, affiliated with religious schools, that operated as an insurance company, extending insurance benefits in return for premiums.[390] Likewise, a health care sharing ministry was denied tax-exempt status where members paid a monthly fee to enroll and, in return, received benefits including access to telemedicine, discount services, health care navigation, and medical bill negotiation.[391]

A program activity of a church, such as a medical aid plan, involving a single congregation and funded with voluntary contributions taken at church services, can be a charitable undertaking.[392] In such a case, the church's doctrine considers all of its members to be needy and thus "deserving of one another's assistance, regardless of their own financial means."[393]

(b) Commercial-Type Insurance Rules

An otherwise tax-exempt charitable organization[394] or social welfare organization[395] will lose or be denied tax exemption if a substantial part of its activities consists of the provision of *commercial-type insurance*.[396] Otherwise, the activity of these exempt organizations providing commercial-type insurance is treated as the

---

[385] See §§ 24.9, 28.13(b).

[386] See Chapter 7.

[387] See Chapter 13.

[388] See § 7.10.

[389] Mutual Aid Ass'n of Church of the Brethren v. United States, 759 F.2d 792, 795 (10th Cir. 1985), *aff'g* 578 F. Supp. 451 (D. Kan. 1983).

[390] American Ass'n of Christian Schs. Voluntary Employees Beneficiary Ass'n Welfare Plan Trust v. United States, 850 F.2d 1510, 1513 (11th Cir. 1988), *aff'g* 663 F. Supp. 275 (M.D. Ala. 1987).

[391] Priv. Ltr. Rul. 202318021. This organization initially requested recognition of exemption as a church but was unsuccessful because did not have a form of worship, regularly scheduled religious services, an established place of worship, or an established congregation (*id.*; see § 10.3).

[392] E.g., Bethel Conservative Mennonite Church v. Comm'r, 746 F.2d 388 (7th Cir. 1984).

[393] *Id.* at 391.

[394] See Part Three.

[395] See Chapter 13 and § 19.3. As to the latter, see Priv. Ltr. Rul. 201321036.

[396] IRC § 501(m). The IRS has taken the position that if an organization described in IRC § 501(c)(4) loses its exempt status by operation of IRC § 501(m), then its supporting organization will cease to be excepted from private foundation status under IRC § 509(a) (Gen. Couns. Mem. 39718; see § 12.3(c)).

conduct of an unrelated trade or business,[397] and the income from it is taxed under the rules pertaining to taxable insurance companies.[398]

The term *commercial-type insurance* generally is any insurance of a type provided by commercial insurance companies.[399] For example, an organization was held to not qualify as a tax-exempt social welfare organization because its sole activity was the provision of certain benefits to students in a school who were injured in the course of school-related activities, in that the coverage was similar to contingent or excess insurance coverage.[400] This term does not include insurance provided at substantially below cost to a class of charitable recipients, incidental health insurance provided by a health maintenance organization of a kind customarily provided by these organizations,[401] property or casualty insurance provided (directly or through a qualified employer)[402] by a church or convention or association of churches for the church or convention or association of churches, and the provision of retirement or welfare benefits (or both) by a church or a convention or association of churches (directly or through a qualified organization)[403] for the employees of the church or convention or association of churches or the beneficiaries of these employees.[404] This rule is also inapplicable to income from an insurance activity conducted by a political subdivision of a government.[405]

The IRS endeavored to define the term *commercial-type insurance*, since the phrase is undefined in the statute. Following a review of tax cases defining the term *insurance*, the Chief Counsel's office concluded that the definition of commercial-type insurance "should include some form of risk-sharing and risk-distribution."[406] The IRS's lawyers also said that, despite the statutory exception for HMO insurance, "it is our opinion that in certain circumstances a health maintenance organization may be found to provide" commercial-type insurance.

Of course, for these rules to apply, the underlying activity must be the provision of *insurance* in the first instance. (The essence of the concept of insurance is that the risk of liability is shifted to at least one third party—the insurer—and that the risk is shared and distributed across a group of persons.)[407] For these purposes,

---

[397] See § 24.9.

[398] IRC Subchapter L.

[399] H.R. Rep. 99-841, at II-345 (1986).

[400] Gen. Couns. Mem. 39703.

[401] E.g., Priv. Ltr. Rul. 9246004.

[402] That is, an organization described in IRC § 414(e)(3)(B)(ii).

[403] That is, an organization described in IRC § 414(e)(3)(A) or § 414(e)(3)(B)(ii).

[404] IRC § 501(m)(3). The management, by supporting organizations (see § 12.3(c)), for a church of regulated investment companies to provide benefits for church employees was ruled by the IRS to not cause loss of tax-exempt status of the organizations by reason of IRC § 501(m) (Priv. Ltr. Rul. 9645007).

[405] Priv. Ltr. Rul. 8836038.

[406] Gen. Couns. Mem. 39828.

[407] E.g., Sears, Roebuck & Co. v. Comm'r, 96 T.C. 61 (1991); Harper Group v. Comm'r, 96 T.C. 45 (1991); Americo & Subsidiaries v. Comm'r, 96 T.C. 18 (1991); Humana, Inc. v. Comm'r, 88 T.C. 197 (1987), aff'd in part, rev'd in part, 881 F.2d 276 (6th Cir. 1989); Beech Aircraft Corp. v. United States, 797 F.2d 920 (10th Cir. 1986); Clougherty Packing Co. v. Comm'r, 84 T.C. 948 (1985), aff'd, 811 F.2d 1297 (9th Cir. 1987); Stearns-Roger Corp. v. United States, 774 F.2d 414 (10th Cir. 1985); Carnation Co. v. Comm'r, 71 T.C. 400 (1978), aff'd, 640 F.2d 1010 (9th Cir. 1981), cert. denied, 454 U.S. 965 (1981); Helvering v. LeGierse, 312 U.S. 531 (1941).

the issuance of annuity contracts is considered the provision of insurance.[408] These rules do not, however, apply to a charitable gift annuity, which is defined for this purpose as an annuity where a portion of the amount paid in connection with the issuance of the annuity is allowable as a charitable deduction for federal income or estate tax purposes, and the annuity is described in the special rule for annuities in the unrelated debt-financed income provisions[409] (determined as if any amount paid in cash in connection with the issuance were property).[410]

A court ruled that a nonprofit organization established to create and administer a group self-insurance pool for the benefit of tax-exempt social service para-transit providers, to provide the necessary financing for comprehensive automobile liability, risk management, and related services for pool members, did not qualify for exemption as a charitable organization because it provided commercial-type insurance.[411] This court subsequently held that three types of hospital membership funds cannot qualify as tax-exempt because they provided forms of commercial-type insurance.[412]

Another case finding commercial-type insurance concerned an organization that administers a group self-insurance risk pool for a membership of nearly 500 charitable organizations that operate to fund or provide health or human services.[413] Likewise, an association of tax-exempt secondary schools in a state, operated to pool risk and obtain insurance for its members, was held to not qualify for exemption as a charitable entity because it is providing commercial-type insurance to its members.[414] Not surprisingly, an organization established to form an insurance company to provide health care coverage for individuals in a state was denied recognition of exemption as a charitable entity.[415]

The foregoing body of case law, however, has been somewhat supplanted by statutory law providing tax-exempt status for charitable risk pools.[416]

As noted, these rules are inapplicable to the provision of insurance by a nonprofit organization at substantially below cost to a class of charitable recipients.[417] The courts emphasize a ruling by the IRS, issued in a different context, that the phrase *substantially below cost* entails a subsidy of at least 85 percent.[418]

Thus, in one case, while the court declined to "draw a bright line" defining that phrase, it rejected the proposition that a subsidy of about 35 percent

---

[408] IRC § 501(m)(4).

[409] IRC § 514(c)(5). See § 24.10.

[410] IRC §§ 501(m)(3)(E), (5). The IRS held that a supporting organization's global capitation agreements with unrelated insurance companies and individuals do not entail the provision of commercial-type insurance (and thus do not cause unrelated business income) (Priv. Ltr. Rul. 200044039).

[411] Paratransit Ins. Corp. v. Comm'r, 102 T.C. 745 (1994).

[412] Florida Hosp. Trust Fund v. Comm'r, 103 T.C. 140 (1994), *aff'd*, 71 F.3d 808 (11th Cir. 1996).

[413] Nonprofits' Ins. Alliance of Cal. v. United States, 94-2 USTC ¶ 50,593 (Ct. Fed. Cl. 1994).

[414] Florida Indep. Colleges & Universities Risk Management Ass'n v. United States, 850 F. Supp. 2d 125 (D.D.C. 2012).

[415] Priv. Ltr. Rul. 202015035.

[416] See § 11.6.

[417] IRC § 501(m)(3)(A).

[418] Rev. Rul. 71-529, 1971-2 C.B. 234.

qualified.[419] In another instance, this exception was ruled not applicable where member contributions for one year were in excess of 80 percent.[420]

(c) Charitable Split-Dollar Insurance Plans

Charitable split-dollar insurance plans,[421] whereby life insurance became the basis for a form of endowment-building investment vehicle for charitable organizations, is effectively outlawed by the federal tax law. That is, the federal tax law denies an income tax charitable contribution deduction for, and imposes excise tax penalties on, transfers associated with the use of these plans.[422]

Thus, there is no federal charitable contribution deduction for a transfer to or for the use of a charitable organization, if, in connection with the transfer, (1) the organization directly or indirectly pays, or has previously paid, any premium on any personal benefit contract with respect to the transferor, or (2) there is an understanding or expectation that any person will directly or indirectly pay any premium on this type of contract with respect to the transferor.[423] A *personal benefit contract* with respect to a transferor is any life insurance, annuity, or endowment contract if any direct or indirect beneficiary under the contract is the transferor, any member of the transferor's family, or any other person (other than a charitable organization) designated by the transferor.[424]

§ 28.14 FEEDER ORGANIZATIONS

Federal tax law provides that an "organization operated for the primary purpose of carrying on a trade or business for profit shall not be exempt from taxation under [IRC] section 501 on the ground that all of its profits are payable to one or more organizations exempt from taxation under section 501."[425] This type of nonexempt entity is a *feeder organization*, inasmuch as it is a business operation that "feeds" monies to one or more tax-exempt organizations. In determining the primary purpose of an organization, all pertinent circumstances are considered, including the size and extent of the trade or business and the size and extent of the activities of the exempt organization.[426] If an organization carries on a trade or

---

[419] Nonprofits' Ins. Alliance of Cal. v. United States, 94-2 U.S.T.C. ¶ 50,593 (Ct. Fed. Cl. 1994).

[420] Paratransit Ins. Corp. v. Comm'r, 102 T.C. 745 (1994). This body of law (IRC § 501(m)) was enacted (in 1986) for the purpose of depriving Blue Cross and Blue Shield organizations of their tax exemption (by reason of IRC § 501(c)(4) (see Chapter 13)) essentially because of their evolution as commercial entities. The federal tax law, however, provides a special deduction (that facilitates the accumulation of capital) and higher unearned premium reserve for these organizations (and comparable entities) that satisfy various criteria (IRC § 833). This latter body of law was amended in 2010 to provide that it does not apply to an organization unless the organization's percentage of total premium revenue expended on reimbursement for clinical services is not less than 85 percent (IRC § 833(c)(5)).

[421] See *Charitable Giving* § 15.6(a).

[422] IRC § 170(f)(10). See *Charitable Giving* § 15.6(b).

[423] IRC § 170(f)(10)(A).

[424] IRC § 170(f)(10)(B).

[425] IRC § 502(a).

[426] Reg. § 1.502-1(a).

business but not as a primary function, the organization may be exempt, although the income from the trade or business may be taxed as unrelated business taxable income.[427]

The impact of the feeder organization rules may be vividly seen in the case of the SICO Foundation, which was a nonstock corporation that engaged in the business of selling and distributing petroleum products.[428] Its net income was distributed to teachers' colleges for scholarship purposes. The SICO Foundation was in court in 1952 seeking tax-exempt status for tax years prior to 1951. Following the destination-of-income test, the court found the organization to be educational in nature and hence exempt.[429] But when its tax status for years 1951, 1952, and 1953 was litigated, the court held that enactment of the feeder organization rules in 1950[430] caused the organization to lose its exempt status.[431]

One vestige of the destination-of-income test remains, however. Under the rules defining the meaning of the term *gross income*,[432] the value of services is not includable in gross income when the services are rendered directly and gratuitously to a charitable organization.[433] Thus, a parimutuel racetrack corporation was able to distribute charity-day race proceeds to a charitable organization, which agreed to absorb any losses arising from the event and to assume all responsibility for the promotion, and not include any of the proceeds in its gross income for federal income tax purposes.[434] Where, by contrast, the racetrack corporation was the promoter of the charity-day racing event, rather than the agent of the charity, the proceeds from the event were taxable to the corporation.[435]

The distinctions at play in the feeder organization context are frequently difficult to discern initially. For example, the IRS accorded tax-exempt status to a nonprofit corporation controlled by a church, where the organization's function was to print and sell educational and religious material to the church's parochial system at a profit, with the profits returned to the system.[436] But an organization formed by a church to operate a commercial printing business (which generated a substantial profit) and to print religious materials for the church at cost (about 10 percent of its activities), where all net income was paid over to the church, was ruled a feeder organization and thus not exempt.[437] The distinguishing feature was the fact that an overwhelming percentage of the organization's activities in the latter instance was the provision of commercial services to entities other than the related tax-exempt organization.

---

[427] Reg. § 1.502-1(c). See Chapters 24, 25.

[428] SICO Found. v. United States, 295 F.2d 924 (Ct. Cl. 1961), *reh'g denied*, 297 F.2d 557 (Ct. Cl. 1962).

[429] SICO Co. v. United States, 102 F. Supp. 197 (Ct. Cl. 1952).

[430] 26 U.S.C. § 101.

[431] SICO Found. v. United States, 295 F.2d 924, 925 (Ct. Cl. 1961).

[432] IRC § 61(a).

[433] Reg. § 1.61-2(c).

[434] Rev. Rul. 77-121, 1977-1 C.B. 17.

[435] Rev. Rul. 72-542, 1972-2 C.B. 37. In this instance, however, the corporation received a business expense deduction under IRC § 162 or a charitable contribution deduction under IRC § 170 for the proceeds turned over to charity (Rev. Rul. 77-124, 1977-1 C.B. 39; Rev. Rul. 72-542, *supra*).

[436] Rev. Rul. 68-26, 1968-1 C.B. 272. Also, Pulpit Resource v. Comm'r, 70 T.C. 594 (1978).

[437] Rev. Rul. 73-164, 1973-1 C.B. 223.

The government's position is that where a subsidiary organization of a tax-exempt parent would itself be exempt, because its activities are an integral part of the activities of the parent, the tax-exempt status of the subsidiary will not be lost because the subsidiary derived a profit from its dealings with the parent.[438] For example, the income tax regulations contain an illustration of a subsidiary organization operated for the sole purpose of furnishing electric power used by the parent organization (an exempt educational institution) in carrying on its tax-exempt activities; thus, the subsidiary is itself a charitable entity.[439] Likewise, a graduate school providing a variety of services to a group of affiliated colleges was ruled not to be a feeder organization, inasmuch as it was controlled and supervised by the colleges, and the services were regarded as an integral part of the activities of the colleges.[440] Where a subsidiary of an exempt parent is operated for the primary purpose of carrying on a trade or business that would be an unrelated trade or business if regularly carried on by the parent, the subsidiary would not be exempt.[441] The regulations contain the example of a subsidiary of an exempt parent that is not exempt because it is operated primarily for the purpose of furnishing electric power to consumers other than the parent.

With the emphasis on determination of unrelated business taxable income, rather than deprivation of tax-exempt status, the IRS has retreated somewhat from vigorous assertion of the feeder organization rules.[442] Also, the courts have infrequently construed the feeder rules against the affected organizations.[443]

For purposes of these rules,[444] the term *trade or business* does not include (1) the derivation of most types of rents,[445] (2) any trade or business in which substantially all the work in carrying on the trade or business is performed for the organization without compensation,[446] or (3) any trade or business that consists of the selling of merchandise, substantially all of which has been received by the organization as gifts.[447] For example, a thrift shop may avoid feeder organization status because the work is performed by volunteers[448] or because the merchandise was received as gifts.[449]

---

[438] Reg. § 1.502-1(b). A technical parent-subsidiary relationship need not be present (Rev. Rul. 68-26, 1968-1 C.B. 272); the revenue flowing to the exempt organization is disregarded for tax purposes, because the "profits" are essentially regarded as a matter of accounting between the organizations.

[439] Id.

[440] Priv. Ltr. Rul. 9849027.

[441] Reg. § 1.502-1(b).

[442] E.g., Rev. Rul. 66-296, 1966-2 C.B. 215; Rev. Rul. 66-295, 1966-2 C.B. 207.

[443] Cases where IRC § 502 was not applied include Industrial Aid for the Blind v. Comm'r, 73 T.C. 96 (1979); Edward Orton, Jr. Ceramic Found. v. Comm'r, 56 T.C. 147 (1971); Duluth Clinic Found. v. United States, 67-1, U.S.T.C. ¶ 9926 (D. Minn. 1967); Bright Star Found. v. Campbell, 191 F. Supp. 845 (N.D. Tex. 1960). The feeder organization rule was applied in, e.g., Veterans Found. v. United States, 281 F.2d 912 (10th Cir. 1960); Disabled American Veterans Serv. Found., Inc. v. Comm'r, 29 T.C.M. 202 (1970).

[444] IRC § 502(b).

[445] See § 25.1(h).

[446] See § 25.2(a).

[447] See § 25.2(c).

[448] Rev. Rul. 80-106, 1980-1 C.B. 113.

[449] Rev. Rul. 71-581, 1971-2 C.B. 236. Universal Life Church, Inc. v. United States, 86-1 U.S.T.C. ¶ 9271 (Cl. Ct. 1986). A court concluded that an organization claiming to be a supporting organization (see § 12.3(c)) that passively rented commercial real estate and distributed its net revenue to a public charity was instead a (nonexempt) feeder organization (CRSO v. Comm'r, 128 T.C. 153 (2007)).

§ 28.15   TAX-EXEMPT ENTITY LEASING RULES

The federal income tax law contains a body of law concerning certain situations where tax-exempt organizations lease real and/or personal property in practices known as *tax-exempt entity leasing*. These rules have two purposes. One is to impose restrictions on the federal tax benefits of leasing property (including relationships evidenced by service contracts) to exempt organizations. The other is to place restrictions on the federal tax benefits available to investors in partnerships composed of taxable and exempt entities.

These rules are intended to remedy three perceived abuses. One concern was that lessors indirectly made investment tax incentives available to tax-exempt organizations through reduced rents. Another concern was that exempt organizations were being encouraged to enter into sale-leaseback transactions with taxpayers that resulted in substantial revenue losses to the federal government. The third perceived abuse was that partnerships that included exempt and taxable entities could allocate all tax losses to taxable entities, while exempt entities shared in profits and cash distributions.

The essence of the tax-exempt entity leasing rules is to cause investors to compute their depreciation deduction over a longer recovery period where the property is *tax-exempt use property*.[450]

§ 28.16   TAX-EXEMPT ORGANIZATIONS AND TAX SHELTERS

An excise tax is imposed on most tax-exempt entities and/or entity managers that participate in prohibited tax shelter transactions as accommodation parties. If a transaction is a prohibited tax shelter transaction at the time a tax-exempt entity becomes a party to the transaction, the entity must pay an excise tax for the tax year in which the entity became such a party and any subsequent tax year.[451] If a tax-exempt entity is a party to a subsequently listed transaction at any time during a tax year, the entity must pay an excise tax for the year.[452] If an entity manager of a tax-exempt entity approves the entity as (or otherwise causes the entity to be) a party to a prohibited tax shelter transaction at any time during the tax year and knows or has reason to know that the transaction is a prohibited tax shelter transaction, the manager must pay an excise tax for that tax year.[453]

For these purposes, a *prohibited tax shelter transaction* means a listed transaction or a prohibited reportable transaction.[454] A *listed transaction* is a transaction that is the same as or substantially similar to one of the types of transactions that the IRS has determined to be a tax avoidance transaction and identified by notice, regulation, or other form of published guidance as a listed transaction.[455] A *prohibited reportable transaction* means any confidential transaction or

---

[450] IRC § 168(h).
[451] IRC § 4965(a)(1)(A).
[452] IRC § 4965(a)(1)(B).
[453] IRC § 4965(a)(2).
[454] IRC § 4965(e)(1)(A).
[455] IRC §§ 4965(e)(1)(B), 6707A(c)(2); Reg. § 1.6011-4(b)(2).

any transaction with contractual protection that is a reportable transaction.[456] A *reportable transaction* is any transaction with respect to which information is required to be included with a return or statement because the IRS has determined under regulations that the transaction is of a type having a potential for tax avoidance or evasion.[457] A *confidential transaction* is a transaction that is offered to a taxpayer under conditions of confidentiality and for which the taxpayer has paid an advisor a minimum fee.[458] A *transaction with contractual protection* is a transaction for which the taxpayer or a related party has the right to a full or partial refund of fees if all or part of the intended tax consequences from the transaction are not sustained by the IRS.[459]

The term *tax-exempt entity*[460] includes an entity that is (1) described in one of the categories of conventional tax-exempt organizations,[461] (2) an apostolic organization,[462] (3) a charitable organization qualified to receive deductible contributions,[463] (4) an Indian tribal government,[464] (5) a prepaid tuition organization,[465] or (6) an ABLE program.[466]

A tax-exempt entity must file a *disclosure* of the entity's being a party to any prohibited tax shelter transaction and the identity of any other party to such transaction that is known by the tax-exempt entity.[467] If a tax-exempt entity fails to file this disclosure, a penalty of $100 applies for each day during which the failure continues, up to a maximum of $50,000 with respect to any one failure to disclose.[468] If the IRS makes a written demand on any entity subject to this failure to disclose penalty specifying a reasonable future date by which the disclosure is to be filed, an additional penalty of $100 applies for each day during which the failure continues, up to a maximum of $10,000 with respect to any one failure to disclose.[469]

The term *entity manager* means, in the case of tax-exempt entities in the first four of the foregoing categories, the person with authority or responsibility similar to that exercised by an officer, director, or trustee of an organization and, with respect to any act, the person having authority or responsibility with respect to the act.[470] In the case of a prepaid tuition organization, the term means the person who

---

[456] IRC § 4965(e)(1)(C).

[457] IRC § 6707A(c)(1).

[458] Reg. § 1.6011-4(b)(3).

[459] Reg. § 1.6011-4(b)(4).

[460] IRC § 4965(c).

[461] That is, is described in IRC § 501(c) and thus is tax-exempt by reason of IRC § 501(a). See, generally, Parts Three and Four.

[462] That is, an entity described in IRC § 501(d). See § 10.8.

[463] That is, an entity described in IRC § 170(c) (other than the United States). See *Charitable Giving* § 2.3(a).

[464] Within the meaning of IRC § 7701(a)(40).

[465] That is, an entity described in IRC § 529. See § 19.19.

[466] That is, an entity described in IRC § 529A. See § 19.20.

[467] IRC § 6033(a)(2).

[468] IRC § 6652(c)(3)(A). Adjusted for inflation, these amounts are $125 and $63,500, respectively, for disclosures required to be filed in 2025 (Rev. Proc. 2023-34, 2023-48 IRB 1287 § 3.54(3)).

[469] IRC § 6652(c)(3)(B). Adjusted for inflation, these amounts are $125 and $12,500, respectively, for disclosures required to be filed in 2025 (Rev. Proc. 2023-34, 2023-48 IRB 1287 § 3.54(3)).

[470] IRC § 4965(d)(1).

approves or otherwise causes the entity to be a party to the prohibited tax shelter transaction.[471]

The phrase *subsequently listed transaction* means a transaction to which a tax-exempt entity is a party and which is determined by the IRS to be a listed transaction at any time after the entity has become a party to the transaction. The term does not encompass a transaction that is a prohibited reportable transaction at the time the entity became a party to the transaction.[472]

As to the penalty, in the case of a tax-exempt entity, the general rule is that the amount of this excise tax is, with respect to any transaction for a tax year, an amount equal to the product of the corporate tax rate[473] and the greater of (1) the entity's net income with respect to the transaction for the tax year which (a) in the case of a prohibited tax shelter transaction (other than a subsequently listed transaction), is attributable to the transaction, or (b) in the case of a subsequently listed transaction, is attributable to the transaction and which is properly allocable to the period beginning on the later of the date the transaction is identified by guidance as a listed transaction by the IRS or the first day of the tax year, or (2) 75 percent of the proceeds received by the entity for the tax year which (a) in the case of a prohibited tax shelter transaction (other than a subsequently listed transaction), are attributable to the transaction, or (b) in the case of a subsequently listed transaction, are attributable to the transaction and which are properly allocable to the period beginning on the later of the date the transaction is identified by guidance as a listed transaction by the IRS or the first day of the tax year.[474]

In the case of a tax-exempt entity that knew, or had reason to know, that a transaction was a prohibited tax shelter transaction at the time the entity became a party to the transaction, the amount of the excise tax imposed with respect to a transaction for a tax year is the greater of (1) 100 percent of the entity's net income for the tax year that is attributable to the prohibited tax shelter transaction or (2) 75 percent of the proceeds received by the entity for the tax year that are attributable to the prohibited tax shelter transaction.[475]

In the case of an entity manager, the amount of the excise tax is $20,000 for each approval or other act causing participation in the tax shelter transaction.[476]

§ 28.17 RECORD-KEEPING REQUIREMENTS

Persons subject to tax must keep appropriate records, render appropriate statements, make timely returns, and otherwise comply with IRS rules and regulations. When the IRS deems it necessary, the agency may require a person, by notice or regulation, to make such returns, render such statements, or keep such records as it "deems sufficient to show whether or not such person is liable for tax."[477] This

---

[471] IRC § 4965(d)(2).
[472] IRC § 4965(e)(2).
[473] IRC § 11 (currently, 21 percent).
[474] IRC § 4965(b)(1)(A).
[475] IRC § 4965(b)(1)(B).
[476] IRC § 4965(b)(2).
[477] IRC § 6001.

law requires persons to keep permanent books of account or records as are sufficient to establish the amount of gross income, deductions, credits, or other matters required to be shown by the person in tax or information returns.[478]

Tax-exempt organizations are required to keep such permanent books of account or records as are sufficient to show specifically the items of gross income, receipts, and disbursements.[479] Exempt organizations must also keep such books and records as are required to substantiate the information needed to prepare and file their annual information returns.[480]

These records must be accurate.[481] No particular form is required for keeping the records.[482] The records must be kept at one or more "convenient and safe" locations that are accessible by the IRS and be available for inspection by the agency.[483]

A tax-exempt organization, whether or not it is required to file an annual information return, must provide such additional information as may be requested by the IRS to enable it to inquire further into the organization's exempt status and administer the provisions of tax law applicable to such organizations.[484]

The IRS frequently revokes the tax-exempt status of an organization for its failure to file information returns or to maintain or provide the requisite records or documentation.[485]

§ 28.18 INTERNATIONAL GRANTMAKING REQUIREMENTS

There is limited federal tax law on the subject of international charitable grantmaking and related activities by U.S.-based organizations.

(a) Charitable Organizations

A U.S.-based tax-exempt charitable organization may conduct part or all of its program activities in one or more foreign countries.[486] An exempt charitable organization generally may make grants to one or more other charitable entities; in nearly all instances, there is (in law) no geographic or similar limitation.[487] A charitable organization will not jeopardize its tax exemption by making a grant to a nonexempt entity, provided use of the grant is confined to charitable purposes, and the grantor retains discretion and control as to use of the funds and maintains

[478] Reg. § 1.6001-1(a).
[479] Reg. § 1.6001-1(c).
[480] Id.
[481] Reg. § 31.6001-1(a).
[482] Id.
[483] Reg. § 31-6001-1(e)(1). Similar record-keeping requirements relate to tax liability under IRC Chapters 41 (Reg. § 56.6001-1) and 42 (Reg. § 53.6001-1).
[484] Reg. §§ 1.6033-1(h)(2), 1.6033-2(i)(2); Rev. Rul. 59-95, 1959-1 C.B. 627.
[485] E.g., Priv. Ltr. Rul. 202414010.
[486] Rev. Rul. 71-460, 1971-2 C.B. 231.
[487] Rev. Rul. 67-149, 1967-1 C. B. 149. A Type III supporting organization, however, may not operate in support of any foreign charities (see § 12.3(c)).

adequate records.[488] Conversely, an organization that does not exercise adequate discretion and control over funds it has distributed to a foreign charity, and is merely a conduit for the grantee, is ineligible for tax exemption as a charitable entity.[489]

A tax-exempt charitable organization may make grants to individuals for charitable purposes, regardless of their geographical location, as long as sufficient records are maintained. This type of assistance includes disaster relief.[490]

Contributions to a tax-exempt charitable organization that transmits the funds to one or more foreign charitable organizations are deductible as charitable contributions for federal income tax purposes as long as the U.S. entity is not merely a conduit for the funds.[491]

(b) Private Foundations

Grants by a private foundation to individuals for travel, study, or similar purposes are not taxable expenditures if the grants were awarded on an objective and nondiscriminatory basis, made pursuant to an IRS-approved procedure, and the process includes sufficient record-keeping.[492] Grants by a private foundation to organizations that are not public charities[493] are subject to expenditure responsibility rules.[494] Private foundation grants to foreign organizations are not taxable expenditures if certain rules are followed and if the grantees are the equivalents of U.S. public charities.[495]

(c) Anti-Terrorist Financing Guidelines

The Treasury Department developed voluntary best practices for U.S.-based charitable organizations that engage in grantmaking and/or operations in foreign countries.[496] These guidelines recommend that charitable organizations maintain and make publicly available a current list of any branches, subsidiaries, and/or affiliates that receive resources or services from the charity.

---

[488] Rev. Rul. 68-489, 1968-2 C.B. 210. This revenue ruling continues to reflect the IRS's official interpretation of the rules that apply to public charities in the context of international grantmaking (IRS Info. Ltr. 2019-0007).

[489] The IRS declined to recognize the tax-exempt status of an organization that acted as a mere "channel" for a foreign organization, opining that the lack of discretion and control over funds granted to the foreign organization "preclude[s] exemption when there is no evidence that the funds are spent exclusively for exempt purposes" (Priv. Ltr. Rul. 201345031). See *Charitable Giving* § 16.3.

[490] Rev. Rul. 56-304, 1956-2 C.B. 306. See §§ 7.2(b), 7.18.

[491] Rev. Rul. 63-252, 1963-2 C.B. 101, *amplified by* Rev. Rul. 66-79, 1966-1 C.B. 48. Also, Chief Counsel Adv. Mem. 200504031.

[492] See § 12.4(e); *Private Foundations* § 9.3(d)–(f).

[493] See § 12.3.

[494] See § 12.4(e); *Private Foundations* § 9.7.

[495] See *Private Foundations* § 9.6(b).

[496] "U.S. Department of the Treasury Anti-Terrorist Financing Guidelines: Voluntary Best Practices for U.S.-Based Charities" (Nov. 2005).

CHAPTER TWENTY-NINE

Tax-Exempt Organizations and Exempt Subsidiaries

This chapter contains an analysis of the law concerning tax-exempt organizations and exempt subsidiaries; the following two chapters discuss the utilization of for-profit subsidiaries and partnerships and other joint ventures.

§ 29.1 SUBSIDIARIES BASICS

The reasons for the advent of combinations of tax-exempt organizations are varying and manifold. In the early years, the law mandated most of the structuring, such as the placement of lobbying activities by a charitable organization[1] into a separate organization, or the placement of property with a potential for incurring liability into a title-holding corporation.[2] Likewise, as discussed in the next chapter, the law frequently dictated the placement by an exempt organization of a substantial unrelated business in a for-profit subsidiary.

The basic concepts of restructuring and the potential for use of various operational forms offer great opportunities and flexibility for an exempt organization in the performance of its exempt functions and in the financing of its operations in the most legally efficacious and efficient manner. As an illustration of these points, an exempt fraternal beneficiary society[3] that conducted a variety of charitable

---

[1] That is, an organization described in IRC § 501(c)(3) and exempt from federal income taxation under IRC § 501(a).

[2] See § 19.2.

[3] See § 19.4(a).

activities deemed it appropriate to reorganize and establish five additional exempt organizations, namely, a title-holding company[4] and four public charities: a school,[5] a home for the aged,[6] a publicly supported charity,[7] and a supporting organization[8] for the three other charitable entities.[9]

The parent-subsidiary relationship where both entities are tax-exempt is established in a variety of ways. A common approach is use of overlapping boards of directors, such as where the board of the parent entity selects the board (or at least a majority of it) of the subsidiary entity, *ex officio* positions are used in composing a subsidiary's board, or there is a combination of these approaches.[10] Another way to structure the relationship is to cause the subsidiary to be a membership entity, with the parent entity the sole member; the member is empowered to select the board of the subsidiary.[11] A third approach, by far the least likely of the choices, is to create the subsidiary in a state that provides for stock-based nonprofit corporations, with the parent entity being the sole stockholder. The rules as to attribution of the activities of the subsidiary organization to the parent organization are applicable in this context.[12]

§ 29.2 CHARITABLE ORGANIZATIONS AS SUBSIDIARIES

A common development in the law of tax-exempt organizations is establishment by an exempt organization, which is not itself a charitable organization, of an auxiliary charitable organization for program operation and/or fundraising purposes.

(a) Introduction

The auxiliary charitable organization functions in tandem with the sponsoring (or parent) organization to achieve common objectives.[13] Frequently termed a

[4] See § 19.2(a).
[5] See § 12.3(a).
[6] See § 12.3(b)(iv).
[7] See § 12.3(b)(i).
[8] See § 12.3(c).
[9] Priv. Ltr. Rul. 9527043. For bifurcation to be successful, the same considerations that are discussed at § 30.2 apply: The entities must be separate, bona fide legal organizations and not operated so closely that the activities of one are considered the activities of the other (sham arrangements). A court case that the IRS lost could have had enormous adverse implications for these forms of restructuring had the IRS prevailed, in that the government asserted six forms of private benefit in the arrangement, including the payment of rent, use of common employees, overlapping boards of directors, and similarity of organizations' names (Bob Jones Univ. Museum & Gallery, Inc. v. Comm'r, 71 T.C.M. 3120 (1996)). In the case, a taxable nonprofit university spun off a tax-exempt educational museum to be operated on the university's campus.
[10] As an illustration, every director of a charitable subsidiary is appointed by, and may be removed by, the executive committee of an exempt fraternal beneficiary society (see § 19.4(a)) (Priv. Ltr. Rul. 201147035). Oddly, the IRS chastised an exempt social club (see Chapter 15) for controlling a charity (by means of identical directors and officers), stating (incorrectly) that the charitable entity needed to have an "independent" board (Priv. Ltr. Rul. 201146022).
[11] This is a common approach in the health care setting.
[12] See § 30.2.
[13] Historically, the IRS has been tolerant of the use by a tax-exempt organization of a related subsidiary organization (e.g., Rev. Rul. 58-143, 1958-1 C.B. 239 (revoked on another issue)).

related foundation, the related charitable organization is rarely a private foundation, due to its ability to qualify as a publicly supported organization or a supporting organization.[14]

These related foundations typically engage in activities such as seminars, educational publications, research, and granting of scholarships and awards. Commonly, the parent entities are tax-exempt social welfare organizations[15] or exempt business leagues.[16] Other exempt entities that may have charitable subsidiaries are exempt labor organizations,[17] social clubs,[18] and veterans' organizations.[19]

(b)   Subsidiaries of Domestic Charitable Organizations

The general reason for the establishment by a noncharitable organization (whether tax-exempt or taxable) of a charitable organization is to attract deductible charitable contributions and perhaps private foundation and other grants. Thus, it may appear that the establishment of a charitable organization by a charitable organization solely for fundraising purposes would be of little utility inasmuch as the qualifying gifts and grants could be made directly to the parent entity.

In some instances, however, the establishment of a separate fundraising entity by a charitable organization is warranted. Usually the objective in these circumstances is to concentrate the fundraising function in a single organization, essentially by creating a governing board and other support systems and resources that are present principally or solely to enhance fundraising. This enhancement can also occur by creating a governing body of which substantial contributors (and/or those that can lead to them) can be members and by giving the fundraising entity a name that is more conducive to fundraising than that of the parent. Further, the subsidiary may have a characteristic that the parent entity lacks, such as the ability to maintain a pooled income fund.[20]

Many of the federal tax considerations discussed previously likewise pertain to the auxiliary charitable organization of a charitable parent. Thus, for example, the auxiliary charitable organization can avoid private foundation classification by using one of the three approaches generally available.[21] In some situations, the charitable parent will be one of the tax-recognized institutions, such as a church, university, college, or hospital. Indeed, the auxiliary charitable organization serving a governmental college or university is expressly referenced in the federal

---

[14] See § 12.3(b), (c).

[15] See Chapter 13.

[16] See Chapter 14. In a peculiar ruling, the IRS revoked the tax exemption of a supporting organization with respect to an exempt business league because the supporting activities were considered to provide undue private benefit (see § 20.13) to the membership of the league (Priv. Ltr. Rul. 201338059).

[17] See § 16.1.

[18] See Chapter 15. In Priv. Ltr. Rul. 200532052, the IRS observed: "A section 501(c)(3) public charity may enter into financial transactions and other arrangements with related parties, including section 501(c)(7) organizations, provided that the public charity receives at least fair market value for the consideration it brings to the transaction, that the transaction is not unfair to the public charity, and that the transaction will not result in inurement or private benefit to any of the parties involved."

[19] See § 19.11(a).

[20] See *Charitable Giving*, Chapter 11.

[21] See Chapter 12.

tax law.[22] Likewise, the supporting organization rules generally contemplate a charitable parent and a charitable subsidiary.[23]

For the most part, however, the use of an auxiliary charitable organization by a charitable organization is done to enhance the nontax aspects of fundraising, by concentrating the fundraising function with a group that has fundraising as its principal, if not sole, responsibility.[24] Other uses include a function that the charitable organization parent could itself perform without jeopardizing its tax-exempt status, such as the maintenance by a hospital of a separate charitable fund from which to pay malpractice claims[25] or the maintenance by a college of an endowment fund in a separate charitable organization.[26]

(c) Subsidiaries of Foreign Charitable Organizations

A U.S. organization that otherwise qualifies as a charitable entity and that carries on part or all of its charitable activities in foreign countries is not precluded because of these activities from qualifying as a charitable organization.[27] For example, the charitable activity of "relief of the poor and distressed or of the underprivileged"[28] is nonetheless charitable where the beneficiaries of the assistance are outside the United States. Thus, the IRS ruled the following organizations were tax-exempt as a charitable group: an organization formed to help poor rural inhabitants of developing countries[29] and an organization created for the purpose of assisting underprivileged people in Latin America to improve their living conditions through educational and self-help programs.[30]

The foregoing distinctions are well illustrated by the tax treatment accorded the *friends organization*. This is an organization formed to solicit and receive contributions in the United States and to expend the funds on behalf of a charitable organization in another country. Its support may be provided in a variety of ways, including program or project grants, provision of equipment or materials, or scholarship or fellowship grants.

Charitable contributions made directly to an organization not created or organized in the United States, a state or territory, the District of Columbia, or a possession of the United States are not deductible.[31] Also, contributions to a U.S. charity that transmits the funds to a foreign charity are deductible only in certain limited circumstances.

An IRS ruling provided five illustrations of supporting domestic charities and the tax treatment to be given contributions to them.[32] One example involved

[22] See § 12.3(b)(v).

[23] See § 12.3(c).

[24] E.g., Priv. Ltr. Rul. 9019004.

[25] Rev. Rul. 78-41, 1978-1 C.B. 148.

[26] E.g., Priv. Ltr. Rul. 9242002.

[27] Rev. Rul. 71-460, 1971-2 C.B. 231.

[28] See §§ 7.1, 7.2.

[29] Rev. Rul. 68-117, 1968-1 C.B. 251.

[30] Rev. Rul. 68-165, 1968-1 C.B. 253. Also, Rev. Rul. 80-286, 1980-2 C.B. 179.

[31] IRC § 170(c)(2)(A); Rev. Rul. 63-252, 1963-2 C.B. 101. Also, Tobjy v. Comm'r, 51 T.C.M. 449 (1986); Erselcuk v. Comm'r, 30 T.C. 962 (1958); Welti v. Comm'r, 1 T.C. 905 (1943).

[32] Rev. Rul. 63-252, 1963-2 C.B. 101.

a mere conduit entity formed by a foreign organization. The second example involved a mere conduit entity formed by individuals in the United States. The third example involved a tax-exempt U.S. charitable organization that agrees to solicit and funnel contributions to a foreign organization. The fourth example involved a U.S. charitable organization that frequently makes grants to charities in a foreign country in furtherance of its exempt purposes, following review and approval of the uses to which the funds are to be put. The fifth example involved a U.S. charitable organization that formed a subsidiary organization in a foreign country to facilitate its tax-exempt operations there, with certain of its funds transmitted directly to the subsidiary.

This ruling stated a rationale of earmarking and of nominal as opposed to real donees and thus concluded that contributions to the U.S. entities in the first, second, and third examples were not deductible. Contributions to the U.S. organization described in the fourth example were deductible because there was no earmarking of contributions and "use of such contributions will be subject to control by the domestic organization."[33] Contributions to the U.S. organization described in the fifth example were deductible because the "foreign organization [was] merely an administrative arm of the domestic organization,"[34] with the domestic organization considered the "real recipient"[35] of the contributions.

These rules were amplified, with the IRS describing the necessary attributes of the friends organization (in essence, the entity in the fourth example of the earlier ruling).[36] Again, the IRS emphasized the earmarking problem,[37] stating that the "test in each case is whether the organization has full control of the donated funds, and discretion as to their use, so as to insure that they will be used to carry out its functions and purposes."[38] The point of this fourth example was subsequently illustrated.[39]

These rules concerning prohibited *earmarking* and *conduits* contemplate two separate organizations: the domestic (U.S.) entity and the foreign entity. Where, therefore, the domestic and foreign activities are housed in one entity (such as a corporation), and that entity qualifies as a domestic charitable organization, the rules do not apply, and the contributions to the organization are deductible as charitable gifts. Thus, a court held that a charitable entity organized under the law of a state and operating a private school in France was fully qualified as a recipient of deductible contributions from U.S. sources.[40] The organization did not have any employees, activities, or assets in the United States, and all expenditures were in France. These facts led the IRS to contend that the U.S. corporation was a mere "shell"

---

[33] *Id.*

[34] *Id.*

[35] *Id.*

[36] Rev. Rul. 66-79, 1966-1 C.B. 48.

[37] Citing Rev. Rul. 62-113, 1962-2 C.B. 10.

[38] Rev. Rul. 66-79, 1966-1 C.B. 48.

[39] Rev. Rul. 75-65, 1975-1 C.B. 79. Because an organization did not "review and approve the disbursements" and did not "maintain control and discretion over the use of the funds," the IRS concluded that it was a conduit entity; the funds did not flow through to a foreign charity, however, but flowed through to individuals (scholarship recipients) (Priv. Ltr. Rul. 200931059).

[40] Bilingual Montessori School of Paris, Inc. v. Comm'r, 75 T.C. 480 (1980).

and functioned solely to funnel contributions to a foreign organization (namely, the school). But the court refused to go much beyond the fact that the corporation was a valid legal entity[41] and that the charitable giving rules do not require a substantial operational nexus in the United States in order to qualify as an eligible recipient of deductible gifts.

Assuming, however, that the friends organization has been properly created and operated so as to qualify as a charitable entity for purposes of charitable giving and tax exemption, a determination must also be sought as to whether it is a private foundation.[42] This type of entity can qualify as a publicly supported organization if it can demonstrate sufficient support from the public.[43] Inasmuch as grants from substantial contributors often cannot be fully utilized in computing the public support fraction, however, a form of publicly supported charity status may not be available.

A "friends of" organization may be structured as a supporting organization.[44] These entities may not, however, be a Type III supporting organization.[45]

As to the charitable contribution deduction, however, the IRS ruled that contributions to a U.S. charity that solicits contributions for a specific project of a foreign charity are deductible only under certain circumstances. Contributions made directly to a foreign organization are not deductible.[46] Organizations formed in the United States for the purpose of raising funds and merely transmitting them as a conduit to a foreign charity are not eligible to attract deductible charitable contributions.[47] Conversely, where a domestic organization makes grants to a foreign charity out of its general fund following review and approval of the specific grant or where the foreign organization is merely an administrative arm of the domestic organization, contributions to the domestic charity are deductible.[48] The test is whether the domestic organization is the real recipient of the contributions, as it must be for the charitable contribution deduction to be allowed. The domestic organization must have full control over the donated funds and discretion as to their use.[49]

As a general rule, a contribution by a corporation to a charitable organization is deductible only if the gift is to be used within the United States or its possessions exclusively for permissible charitable purposes.[50] Where the recipient charitable organization is itself a corporation, however, this restriction is inapplicable.[51]

---

[41] IRC § 170(c)(2)(A).

[42] See Chapter 12.

[43] IRC §§ 170(b)(1)(A)(vi), 509(a)(1), and 509(a)(2).

[44] See § 12.3(c).

[45] See § 12.3(c), text accompanied by note 203.

[46] IRC § 170(c)(2)(A).

[47] Rev. Rul. 63-252, 1963-2 C.B. 101.

[48] Id.

[49] Rev. Rul. 75-434, 1975-2 C.B. 205; Rev. Rul. 66-79, 1966-1 C.B. 48. Also, Rev. Rul. 75-65, 1975-1 C.B. 79. A related issue is the availability of the estate tax deduction for charitable transfers to foreign governments or political subdivisions thereof, as discussed in Rev. Rul. 74-523, 1974-2 C.B. 304, and the cases cited therein.

[50] IRC § 170(c)(2), last sentence. This limitation does not apply with respect to contributions by individuals, nor to contributions from a small business corporation (an *S corporation*) (e.g., Priv. Ltr. Rul. 9703028).

[51] This results from the fact that IRC § 170(c)(2) opens with the phrase that a "corporation, trust, or community chest, fund, or foundation" may qualify as a charitable donee, while the restriction in the

Because of the U.S.–Canada tax treaty, the general rule that contributions to a foreign charity are not deductible does not apply in the case of certain contributions to Canadian charities.[52] For the contribution to be deductible, the Canadian organization must be one that, if it were a U.S. organization, would be eligible for deductible charitable contributions. In addition, the deduction may not exceed the charitable deduction allowable under Canadian law, computed as though the corporation's taxable income from Canadian sources was its aggregate income.

§ 29.3   TAX-EXEMPT SUBSIDIARIES OF CHARITABLE ORGANIZATIONS

There are, as discussed, circumstances where, in an in-tandem relationship between two tax-exempt organizations, the parent exempt organization is a noncharitable organization and the subsidiary is a charitable organization.[53] This arrangement can, however, be reversed.

Thus, another application of these precepts occurs where a charitable organization has a noncharitable, albeit tax-exempt, subsidiary. This will occur where a charitable organization, which is engaging in or planning to engage in an activity that may or would jeopardize its exempt status, spins off to or initiates that potentially disqualifying activity in a separate organization that qualifies under another category of exemption. For example, a charitable organization may be concerned about the extent of its legislative activities[54] and thus elect to operate them out of an exempt social welfare organization.[55] As another illustration, a charitable organization desiring to conduct a program of certification of individuals is well advised to house such an activity in a related exempt business league so as to maintain the charitable entity's exemption.[56]

Other functions that a charitable organization cannot properly pursue itself can be housed in a noncharitable exempt organization, such as a title-holding corporation or a business league.[57] For example, as to the use of a business league (although not as a subsidiary) by a charitable organization, the IRS ruled that a charitable entity could advance its charitable purpose of lessening the burdens of government[58] by purchasing an office building and leasing it to a business league for job creation and world trade purposes, where the business league would sublease the property to appropriate businesses.[59] This technique generally cannot work, however, in the context of political activities,[60] in that a charitable

---

last sentence of IRC § 170(c)(2) applies to a gift to a "trust, chest, fund, or foundation." E.g., Rev. Rul. 69-80, 1969-1 C.B. 65.

[52] Rev. Proc. 59-31, 1959-2 C.B. 949.

[53] See § 29.2.

[54] See Chapter 22.

[55] See Chapter 13.

[56] See § 7.8, text accompanied by notes 340–344; § 14.1(g). Cf. § 24.5(q).

[57] See § 19.2, Chapter 14, respectively.

[58] See § 7.7.

[59] Priv. Ltr. Rul. 9246032.

[60] See Chapter 23.

organization usually cannot properly establish a related political action commit-tee.[61] Similarly, the IRS ruled that a public charity, to provide broader services to its members and more vigorously engage in legislative activities, may form a related business league.[62] Indeed, when the grants are properly restricted, the charitable organization may make grants to the noncharitable tax-exempt organization.[63]

The use by a charitable organization of entities such as charitable remain-der trusts and pooled income funds[64] can also be viewed as illustrative of this technique.

Thus, the use by a charitable organization of noncharitable tax-exempt sub-sidiaries is still another application of the concept of bifurcation in the exempt organizations setting. When coupled with other combinations of exempt organi-zations, as well as with the use of taxable subsidiaries by exempt organizations,[65] there are many occasions and opportunities warranting the splitting of functions of exempt organizations and the housing of them in separate entities.

§ 29.4 OTHER COMBINATIONS OF TAX-EXEMPT ORGANIZATIONS

There are combinations of tax-exempt organizations where none of the entities involved are charitable ones. The most common of these arrangements entails the use of political action committees, title-holding corporations, and employee ben-efit funds.

As discussed, several types of tax-exempt organizations utilize politi-cal action committees.[66] The usual users of these entities are business leagues[67] and labor organizations;[68] occasionally, social welfare organizations[69] and other exempt organizations will have occasion to create and operate a related political organization.

---

[61] See Chapter 17. An illustration as to how close to the edge a charitable organization can go in this regard was provided in the case of a public charity that was permitted by the IRS to administer a pay-roll deduction plan to collect political contributions from its employees and remit the contributions to unions representing its employees for transfer to union-sponsored political action committees (Priv. Ltr. Rul. 200151060). Nonetheless, a payroll-deduction plan administered by a charitable organization in support of a political action committee was determined by the IRS to be a violation of the political campaign restraint (Tech. Adv. Mem. 200446033). Subsequently, however, the IRS ruled that a pub-lic charity may form and control a tax-exempt social welfare organization, which in turn forms and maintains a political action committee, and may maintain a payroll deduction plan for its employees for contributions to political action committees, without the activity of the political action committee being attributed to it and without operation of the plan constituting participation in political campaign activity, inasmuch as the recipients of the political contributions are selected solely by the employees (Priv. Ltr. Rul. 201127013).

[62] Priv. Ltr. Rul. 200041034.

[63] E.g., Priv. Ltr. Rul. 200234071.

[64] See *Charitable Giving*, Chapters 10, 11.

[65] See Chapter 30.

[66] See § 17.1(a).

[67] See Chapter 14.

[68] See § 16.1.

[69] See Chapter 13.

Any type of tax-exempt organization can have a related title-holding corporation. The usual model is a parent exempt organization and a title-holding entity.[70] Unrelated exempt organizations can, however, share a title-holding corporation.[71]

Various employee benefit funds are themselves tax-exempt organizations[72] and can be related to other exempt organizations. This includes pension and retirement funds in general, and voluntary employees' beneficiary associations.[73]

Still other combinations of tax-exempt organizations entail groupings that go far beyond bifurcation, involving perhaps tens of these entities. This is most common in the health care field, where contemporary systems of health care providers and related entities can involve a multitude of exempt organizations.[74] These systems may involve partnerships and/or other forms of joint ventures;[75] or they may be created by means of joint operating agreements;[76] or they may entail less formal relationships, cast perhaps as affiliations;[77] often, these clusters of entities are orchestrated by one or more supporting organizations.[78] Collectives of this nature are also arising outside the health care field, principally in the realm of education.[79]

§ 29.5 POTENTIAL OF ATTRIBUTION

When two tax-exempt organizations, with differing categories of exemption, affiliate or otherwise operate in tandem, the activities of one entity can be attributed, for federal tax purposes, to the other entity, usually with adverse tax law consequences.[80] While this attribution issue can arise in connection with any combination of exempt organizations, the relationships that tend to raise the issue are those involving public charities and social welfare organizations[81] or public charities and business leagues.[82]

For example, the IRS denied an organization recognition of tax exemption as a charitable entity in part because its activities were unduly integrated with an affiliated social welfare entity; the IRS faulted the applicant organization for being controlled by the social welfare organization, sharing employees and equipment, and having similar names.[83] By contrast, where a public charity and a social welfare organization

---

[70] See § 19.2(a).

[71] See § 19.2(b).

[72] See Chapter 18.

[73] See § 18.3. There can be combinations of entities where some are tax-exempt and some are taxable. This includes the use of for-profit subsidiaries (see Chapter 30) and partnerships (see Chapter 31). Related to a for-profit organization can be a political action committee, a private foundation, and/or one or more employee benefit funds.

[74] E.g., Priv. Ltr. Rul. 9840049. In general, see *Healthcare Organizations*, Chapter 20.

[75] See Chapter 31.

[76] See § 24.5(k).

[77] E.g., Priv. Ltr. Rul. 9809054.

[78] See § 12.3(c). *Private Foundations*, § 15.6.

[79] E.g., Priv. Ltr. Rul. 9840051.

[80] The elements of fact that are taken into account in this regard are summarized in § 30.2.

[81] See Chapter 13.

[82] See Chapter 14.

[83] Priv. Ltr. Rul. 201408030.

will "operate independently of each other and administer its own affairs separately," operation of a political action committee[84] by the social welfare organization was not considered by the IRS to be political campaign activity[85] by the charity.[86]

§ 29.6 CONTRIBUTIONS AND OTHER PAYMENTS

As a consequence of these in-tandem arrangements, it is not uncommon for a payment by a third party to be made to one organization, with some or all of the payment directed to another organization. The tax treatment accorded to some or all of the payment (such as deductibility as a charitable contribution) can depend on whether the payment is deemed made to the initial payee or whether it or a portion of it is deemed made to another, sometimes related, organization that is the transferee of the initial payee. In many of these instances, the initial payee organization is regarded as the agent of the organization that is the ultimate recipient of the payment, so that the payor is considered, for tax purposes, to have made the payment directly to the ultimate transferee, notwithstanding the flow of the payment through one or more intermediate organizations (conduit entities).[87]

For example, a contribution to a tax-exempt organization is deductible as a charitable gift where the recipient is a qualified donee.[88] Yet the recipient entity may not inherently be a qualified donee but be considered so by operation of law. Thus, a contribution to a single-member limited liability company that is a disregarded entity,[89] that was created or organized in or under the law of the United States, a U.S. possession, a state, or the District of Columbia, and that is wholly owned and controlled by a U.S. charity is considered a deductible contribution having been donated to a branch or division of the charity; the charity is, for law purposes, the donee.[90] Consistent with that rationale, the IRS stated that a private foundation may make a grant for charitable purposes to a disregarded limited liability company, where the member is an unrelated public charity, and properly treat the transfer as a qualifying distribution, without the need to exercise expenditure responsibility.[91]

Contributions to a tax-exempt social club[92] were held to be deductible, where the club functioned as an authorized agent for one or more charitable organizations, enabling the members of the club, when purchasing tickets for a social event, to direct that the amount of their total payment in excess of the price of the tickets be transferred to charitable organizations, and deduct, as charitable gifts, that portion of the payment to the club that was paid over to the charitable organizations.[93]

---

[84] See Chapter 17.
[85] See Chapter 23.
[86] Priv. Ltr. Rul. 201127013.
[87] Cf. § 29.2(c).
[88] IRC § 170(c).
[89] See § 4.1(b)(ii).
[90] Notice 2012-52, 2012-35 I.R.B. 317.
[91] INFO 2010-0052. See § 12.4(b), (e).
[92] See Chapter 15.
[93] Rev. Rul. 55-192, 1955-1 C.B. 294.

In this type of instance, the initial payee organization is considered the mere conduit of some or all of the payments, and thus the federal tax consequences of the payment are determined as if the payment (or a portion of it) were made directly to the ultimate recipient.

Likewise, charitable gift deductibility treatment was accorded to additional amounts paid by customers of a utility company, when paying their bills to the company, where the additional amounts were earmarked for a tax-exempt charitable organization that assisted individuals with emergency energy-related needs.[94] Again, the utility company was considered the agent of the charitable organization; the company did not exercise any control over the funds and segregated them from its own funds. In a similar instance, contributions paid to an exempt title-holding company[95] for purposes of maintaining and operating a historic property were once ruled by the IRS to be deductible as charitable gifts, where the gifts were segregated from the company's funds and otherwise clearly devoted to charitable ends.[96] In this instance, however, the ruling was withdrawn,[97] although the effect of the withdrawal was not retroactive.[98] Similarly, the IRS ruled that an exempt charitable organization may maintain a property donation program, with the contributions of property qualifying for a contribution deduction, where the transfers are to a for-profit fundraising entity, in that the entity was functioning as an agent of the charity.[99]

Similarly, a contribution to a charitable entity is not deductible as a charitable gift where the ultimate recipient is not a qualified donee. For example, a contribution to a tax-exempt university for the general use of an exempt fraternity or sorority on its campus is not deductible, in that the recipient of the funds is a social club. By contrast, a contribution of this nature would be deductible if the use of the funds is confined to charitable or educational purposes.[100] Thus, where an exempt university owns the property and leases it to fraternities and sororities as part of its overall program of provision of student housing, contributions to the university for fraternity or sorority housing are deductible.[101]

Another variant of these principles is the rule that amounts paid to a tax-exempt organization for transfer to a political action committee do not, when promptly and directly transferred, constitute political campaign expenditures by the exempt organization.[102] A transfer is considered *promptly* and *directly* made if (1) the procedures followed by the organization satisfy the requirements of applicable federal and state campaign laws; (2) the organization maintains adequate records to demonstrate that the amounts transferred do in fact consist of political contributions

---

[94] Rev. Rul. 85-184, 1985-2 C.B. 84.
[95] See § 19.2(a).
[96] Priv. Ltr. Rul. 8705041.
[97] Priv. Ltr. Rul. 8826012.
[98] Priv. Ltr. Rul. 8836040.
[99] Priv. Ltr. Rul. 200230005. Cf. Kaplan v. Comm'r, 43 T.C. 663 (1965) (concerning a property donation program operated by a for-profit corporation on behalf of a tax-exempt hospital, although the issue of agency was not raised).
[100] Rev. Rul. 60-367, 1960-2 C.B. 73.
[101] E.g., Priv. Ltr. Rul. 9733015.
[102] See § 17.7. E.g., Priv. Ltr. Rul. 7903079.

or dues, rather than investment income; and (3) the political contributions or dues transferred were not used to earn investment income for the payor organization.[103]

Consequently, a payment to an organization (whether or not tax-exempt) can be treated, for federal tax purposes, as a payment to another organization (whether or not exempt) where the initial payee is the agent of the ultimate transferee, the funds are clearly earmarked by the payor for the ultimate payee, and the funds are not subject to the control of (for example, invested for the benefit of) the initial payee.[104]

§ 29.7 REVENUE FROM TAX-EXEMPT SUBSIDIARY

Certain types of income, even though they are passive in nature,[105] are taxable as unrelated business income when paid from a tax-exempt subsidiary. The rules in this regard, which are primarily directed at the tax treatment of revenue from a for-profit subsidiary,[106] can cause payments of interest, annuities, royalties, and/or rents from a controlled exempt organization to the controlling exempt organization to be regarded as unrelated business income.[107]

Pursuant to these rules, the percentage threshold for determining control is a more-than-50-percent standard. Where the parent and subsidiary organizations are both tax-exempt, therefore, the analysis as to the existence of control will almost certainly focus on the composition of the two organizations' governing boards or a membership structure. Constructive ownership rules[108] may be applicable in this context.

The types of income that are potentially taxable under these rules are collectively termed *specified payments*.[109] A specified payment must be treated as unrelated business income to the extent the payment reduced the net unrelated income of the controlled entity or increased any net unrelated loss of the controlled entity.[110] In instances where the controlled entity is a tax-exempt organization, the phrase *net unrelated income* means the amount of the unrelated business taxable income of the controlled entity.[111] The term *net unrelated loss* means the net operating loss adjusted under rules similar to those pertaining to net unrelated income.[112]

---

[103] Reg. § 1.527-6(e).

[104] Thus, an association of banks that made contributions to charitable organizations on behalf of its members was found to be merely a "disbursing agent" for the banks, so that the member banks received charitable contribution deductions for the gifts (First Nat'l Bank of Omaha v. Comm'r, 17 B.T.A. 1358 (1929), *aff'd* 49 F.2d 70 (8th Cir. 1931)).

[105] See, e.g., § 25.1(a).

[106] See § 30.6.

[107] IRC § 512(b)(13).

[108] IRC § 318.

[109] IRC § 512(b)(13)(C).

[110] IRC § 512(b)(13)(A). A special rule applies whereby certain types of revenue paid from a subsidiary to a controlling tax-exempt organization are not treated as forms of unrelated business income if they are made pursuant to a binding written contract in effect on August 17, 2006, and other criteria are satisfied (see § 30.6(c)).

[111] IRC § 512(b)(13)(B)(i)(II).

[112] IRC § 512(b)(13)(B)(ii).

CHAPTER THIRTY

Tax-Exempt Organizations and For-Profit Subsidiaries

It is common, if not sometimes essential, for a tax-exempt organization to utilize a for-profit subsidiary, usually to house one or more unrelated business activities[1] that are too extensive to be operated within the organization without jeopardizing or losing the parent entity's exempt status.

There are at least five other reasons for use of this technique: situations where the management of a tax-exempt organization (1) does not want to report the receipt of unrelated business income and so shifts the generation of it to a separate subsidiary, (2) wants to insulate the assets of the parent exempt organization from potential liability, (3) desires expansion of the sources of revenue or capital, (4) wishes to use a subsidiary in a partnership, and/or (5) simply is enamored with the idea of utilization of a for-profit subsidiary.[2] For example, in illustration of the third of these five reasons, a tax-exempt educational organization licensed to and otherwise utilized a for-profit subsidiary to maximize, for membership and business purposes, the operation of its website;[3] a scientific research institution developed an IRS-approved arrangement to further technology transfer by means of a supporting organization and a for-profit subsidiary;[4] and an organization that operated a multiservice geriatric center was allowed by the IRS to market

---

[1] See Chapters 24, 25.
[2] In general, Sanders, *Joint Ventures Involving Tax-Exempt Organizations, Fourth Edition* (John Wiley & Sons, 2013), § 6.3(a), (e).
[3] Priv. Ltr. Rul. 200225046.
[4] Priv. Ltr. Rul. 200326035.

its software, developed for tracking services to the elderly, by means of a taxable subsidiary.[5]

An unrelated business may be operated as an activity within a tax-exempt organization, as long as the primary purpose of the organization is the carrying out of one or more exempt functions or the commensurate test is satisfied.[6] With one exception, there is no fixed percentage of unrelated activity that may be engaged in by an exempt organization.[7]

Therefore, if a tax-exempt organization engages in one or more unrelated activities where the activities are substantial in relation to exempt activities, the use of a for-profit subsidiary is necessary if exemption is to be retained.[8] Indeed, tax exemption cannot be maintained as a matter of law if there is a substantial nonexempt activity or set of activities.[9] An organization can lose its exempt status for a period of time because of extensive unrelated activities, before transfer of unrelated operations to a for-profit subsidiary.[10]

§ 30.1 FOR-PROFIT SUBSIDIARIES IN GENERAL

There are several matters concerning structure that should be taken into account when contemplating the use by a tax-exempt organization of a for-profit subsidiary. They include choice of form and the control mechanism.

(a) Establishing For-Profit Subsidiaries

The law is clear that a tax-exempt organization can have one or more exempt (or at least nonprofit) subsidiaries and/or one or more for-profit subsidiaries.[11] Thus, the IRS observed that an exempt organization can "organize, capitalize and own, provide services and assets (real and personal, tangible and intangible) to a taxable entity without violating the requirements for [tax] exemption, regardless of whether the taxable entity is wholly or partially owned."[12] Indeed, the agency acknowledged that the "number of subsidiaries or related entities an exempt organization can create for the purpose of conducting business activities is not set."[13] With respect to for-profit subsidiaries, the exempt parent organization can own some or all of the equity (usually stock) of the for-profit subsidiary (unless the

---

[5] Priv. Ltr. Rul. 200425050, reissued as Priv. Ltr. Rul. 200444044.

[6] Reg. § 1.501(c)(3)-1(e)(1). Also, Reg. § 1.501(c)(3)-1(c)(1). The commensurate test is the subject of § 4.7.

[7] The one exception is a 10 percent limit on the unrelated business activities of title-holding companies (see § 19.2).

[8] In Orange Cnty. Agric. Soc'y, Inc. v. Comm'r, 893 F.2d 529 (2d Cir. 1990), the court discussed the fact that the operation of a substantial unrelated business by a tax-exempt organization is likely to result in loss of the organization's exemption.

[9] Better Business Bur. of Washington, D.C. v. United States, 326 U.S. 279 (1945).

[10] E.g., Tech. Adv. Mem. 200203069.

[11] E.g., Priv. Ltr. Rul. 9016072 (where a tax-exempt organization owned a for-profit subsidiary, and that subsidiary in turn owned a network of for-profit subsidiaries).

[12] Priv. Ltr. Rul. 199938041.

[13] Priv. Ltr. Rul. 8304112.

parent is a private foundation, in which case special rules apply).[14],[15] For example, a public charity created a for-profit management corporation to provide services to it and two other exempt organizations, and provided it operating funds in exchange for 100 percent of the subsidiary's stock.[16] Likewise, an exempt cemetery association established a for-profit subsidiary (to do what it cannot directly do, which is operate a funeral home), owning 100 percent of its stock, obtained in exchange for money and a nonexclusive license to use the parent's name and address.[17]

The IRS from time to time issues private letter rulings concerning the use of for-profit subsidiaries by tax-exempt organizations.[18]

(b) Choice of Form

Just as in forming a tax-exempt organization, consideration should be given to organizational form when establishing a for-profit subsidiary. Most will be corporations, inasmuch as a corporation is the most common of the business forms, provides a shield against liability for management and the exempt parent, and enables the exempt parent to own the subsidiary by holding all or at least a majority of its stock.[19]

Some taxable businesses are organized as sole proprietorships; however, this approach is of no avail in the tax-exempt organization context, since the business activity conducted as a sole proprietorship is an undertaking conducted directly by the exempt organization and thus does not lead to the desired goal of having the related activity in a separate entity.

Some taxable businesses are structured as partnerships; however, the participation by a tax-exempt organization in a partnership can involve unique legal complications.[20] Another alternative is use of a limited liability company for this purpose.[21] This aspect of the law is evolving and offers interesting opportunities for tax-exempt organizations.[22]

In some instances, an activity of a tax-exempt organization can be placed in a taxable nonprofit organization.[23] This approach is a product of the distinction between a nonprofit organization and a tax-exempt organization.[24] The former is a

---

[14] See § 12.4(c).

[15] The extent of stock ownership may determine whether income from a subsidiary to a tax-exempt parent is taxable (see § 30.6). A transfer without consideration from a taxable corporation to a charitable organization that is its sole stockholder is considered a dividend rather than a charitable contribution (Rev. Rul. 68-296, 1968-1 C.B. 105).

[16] Priv. Ltr. Rul. 9308047.

[17] Priv. Ltr. Rul. 201409009.

[18] E.g., Priv. Ltr. Rul. 8706012.

[19] Often, the corporation form selected will be that of the regular business corporation (*C corporation* (IRC § 1361(a)(2)), inasmuch as a C corporation is not a flow-through entity (see § 31.1(a)). Charitable organizations may be shareholders in small business corporations (*S corporations*) (IRC § 1361(a)(1)) (IRC § 1361(b)(1)(B), (c)(6)), which are a type of flow-through entity. The applicability of the unrelated business income rules in this context is the subject of § 25.3.

[20] See Chapter 31.

[21] E.g., Priv. Ltr. Rul. 9637050.

[22] See §§ 32.3, 32.4.

[23] Still another approach is use of a tax-exempt subsidiary, such as a supporting organization (see § 12.3(c)), a title-holding company (see § 19.2), a lobbying arm of a charitable organization (see § 22.5), a political organization (see Chapter 17), and fundraising vehicles for foreign charitable organizations (see § 29.2(c)).

[24] See §§ 1.1, 1.2.

state law concept; the latter essentially is a federal tax law concept. Assuming state law permits (in that an activity may be *unrelated* to the parent's exempt functions, yet still be a *nonprofit* one), a business activity may be placed in a nonprofit, albeit taxable, corporation.[25] There may be some advantage (such as public relations) to this approach.[26]

(c) Control Element

Presumably, a tax-exempt organization will, when forming a taxable subsidiary, intend to maintain control over the subsidiary.

Where the taxable subsidiary is structured as a business corporation, the tax-exempt organization parent can own the entity and ultimately control it simply by owning the stock (received in exchange for the capital contributed). The exempt organization parent as the stockholder can thereafter select the board of directors of the subsidiary corporation and, if desired, its officers.

If the taxable subsidiary is structured as a nonprofit corporation, three choices are available. The tax-exempt organization parent can control the subsidiary by means of interlocking directorates. Alternatively, the subsidiary can be a membership corporation, with the parent entity the sole member. In the third and least utilized approach, the entity can be structured as a nonprofit organization that can issue stock, in which instance the exempt organization parent would control the subsidiary by holding its stock. If the latter course is chosen and if the nonprofit subsidiary is to be headquartered in a (foreign) state where stock-based nonprofit organizations are not authorized, the subsidiary can be incorporated in a state that allows nonprofit organizations to issue stock and thereafter be qualified to do business in the home (domestic) state.

§ 30.2 POTENTIAL OF ATTRIBUTION TO PARENT

For federal income tax purposes, a parent corporation and its subsidiary are respected as separate entities as long as the purposes for which the subsidiary is formed are reflected in authentic business activities.[27] That is, where an organization is established with the bona fide intention that it will have some real and substantial business function, its existence will generally not be disregarded for tax purposes.[28]

By contrast, where the parent organization so controls the affairs of the subsidiary that it is merely an extension of the parent, the subsidiary may not be regarded as a separate entity.[29] In an extreme situation (such as where the parent

---

[25] Of course, in this situation, the subsidiary, then, is not a for-profit one.

[26] Occasionally, the reverse of this approach is utilized.

[27] E.g., Comm'r v. Bollinger, 485 U.S. 340 (1988); Nat'l Carbide Corp. v. Comm'r, 336 U.S. 422 (1949); Moline Properties, Inc. v. Comm'r, 319 U.S. 436 (1943); Britt v. United States, 431 F.2d 227 (5th Cir. 1970). Also, Sly v. Comm'r, 56 T.C.M. 209 (1988); Universal Church of Jesus Christ, Inc. v. Comm'r, 55 T.C.M. 143 (1988).

[28] Britt v. United States, 431 F.2d 227 (5th Cir. 1970).

[29] E.g., Krivo Industrial Supply Co. v. Nat'l Distillers & Chemical Corp., 483 F.2d 1098 (5th Cir. 1973); Orange Cnty. Agric. Soc'y, Inc. v. Comm'r, 55 T.C.M. 1602 (1988), *aff'd*, 893 F.2d 529 (2d Cir. 1990).

is directly involved in the day-to-day management of the subsidiary), the establishment and operation of an ostensibly separate subsidiary may be regarded as a sham perpetrated by the parent and thus ignored for tax purposes; with this outcome, the tax consequences are the same as if the two "entities" were one.[30] Where there are inappropriate in-tandem operations, the IRS sees a form of impermissible private benefit[31] inherent in this type of "functional interrelationship."[32] Thus, an organization was denied recognition as a charitable entity in part because its operations and those of its for-profit subsidiary were "indistinguishably entangle[d]."[33]

The IRS distilled the law on the point as follows: "The activities of a separately incorporated subsidiary cannot ordinarily be attributed to its parent organization unless the facts provide clear and convincing evidence that the subsidiary is in reality an arm, agent or integral part of the parent."[34] In that instance, the IRS offered a most munificent application of this aspect of the law, concluding that the activities of a for-profit subsidiary were not to be attributed to the tax-exempt organization that was its parent, notwithstanding extensive and ongoing in-tandem administrative and programmatic functions. That is, the agency observed that the two entities would "maintain a close working relationship," they would be "sharing investment leads," they would coinvest in companies, the subsidiary would rent office space from the exempt parent, the subsidiary would purchase administrative and professional services from the parent, and the subsidiary would reimburse its parent for the services of some of the parent's employees. The IRS subsequently ruled that payments to its subsidiary by a tax-exempt organization for services rendered did not cause attribution[35] and reiterated that an employee-leasing arrangement between a tax-exempt parent and its subsidiary will not trigger attribution.[36]

A determination as to whether one organization is involved in the day-to-day management of another is based entirely on a facts-and-circumstances analysis.

---

[30] Gen. Couns. Mem. 39598. In a similar set of circumstances, courts are finding nonprofit organizations to be the alter ego of the debtor, with the result that the assets of the organization are made available to IRS levies (see the cases collected in § 4.1, note 22).In the reverse situation, where a for-profit entity controls a tax-exempt organization (such as by day-to-day management of it), the exemption of the controlled entity may be jeopardized (see, for example, United Cancer Council, Inc. v. Comm'r, 109 T.C. 326 (1997), rev'd and remanded, 165 F.3d 1173 (7th Cir. 1999)). Thus, the IRS ruled that a hospital's exemption must be revoked where it transferred excessive control over its operations to a for-profit management company, thereby ceding "complete control" of itself to the company and maintaining merely an "advisory role" (Priv. Ltr. Rul. 201744019). This may be contrasted with an IRS ruling approving of an arrangement with a management company and an exempt hospital where the hospital's board of trustees "will maintain only a minimum degree of direction and control over the operation of the hospital" (Priv. Ltr. Rul. 9715031).

[31] See § 20.13.

[32] E.g., Priv. Ltr. Rul. 201216040.

[33] Priv. Ltr. Rul. 201918019. On occasion, although not necessarily involving subsidiaries, the IRS will reach the same conclusion, albeit invoking the private benefit doctrine (see § 20.13), as was the case where the activities of a nonprofit organization and a for-profit company, operating in tandem, were held to be "so interrelated" that it was "difficult" for the IRS to "clearly distinguish" between the two entities, causing the nonprofit entity to fail to be recognized as tax-exempt (Priv. Ltr. Rul. 202041007).

[34] Priv. Ltr. Rul. 200132040.

[35] Priv. Ltr. Rul. 200149043.

[36] Priv. Ltr. Rul. 200405016.

The principal factor in this regard is any overlap of officers[37] and/or employees. Other factors include the similarity of activities, location, and identity of the names of the entities. In one instance, in concluding there was no day-to-day management by three exempt organizations of their for-profit subsidiary, the IRS observed that the subsidiary will have separate directors and employees, with an overlap of one officer.[38] In another, the IRS approved use of a blocker corporation to enable a charitable remainder trust to convert otherwise taxable income into nontaxable dividends,[39] respecting the corporation as a separate legal entity.[40] Likewise, the IRS respected the separateness of two subsidiaries, offering health insurance products, of an exempt health maintenance organization, noting that they are engaging in a line of business distinct from that of the parent and have materially different governance structures.[41]

Thus, the IRS is highly unlikely to attribute the activities of a for-profit subsidiary of a tax-exempt organization to the parent entity, by reason of the foregoing elements of law. The use of for-profit subsidiaries in the contemporary exempt organizations setting has become too customary for this form of attribution to occur, absent the most egregious of facts.[42] Yet the IRS revoked an organization's tax-exempt status on the ground of attribution, where the organization controlled the affairs of its wholly owned subsidiary to the point that it was considered a mere instrumentality of the parent entity.[43] Similarly, the IRS, finding "little meaningful separation" between the commercial activities of a wholly owned for-profit subsidiary and its nonprofit parent, denied recognition of exempt status to the parent entity.[44] Likewise, denial of recognition of exemption occurred in part because the IRS concluded that there "does not appear to be a clear separation" between a for-profit business and the nonprofit organization.[45] As still another illustration of this point, the operation of a political action committee by a for-profit subsidiary of a public charity was attributed by the IRS to the charity itself; there was a resources-sharing arrangement between the parties, with the subsidiary lacking employees, office space, equipment, and the like.[46]

An organization was denied recognition of exemption as a charitable entity in part because it was found by the IRS to be "virtually indistinguishable" from a for-profit company; the two entities were said to be marketing the same program, have similar names, and share a website.[47] By contrast, an exempt university that

---

[37] E.g., Asmark Institute, Inc. v. Comm'r, 101 T.C.M. 1067 (2011), aff'd, 486 Fed. Appx. 655 (6th Cir. 2012).

[38] Priv. Ltr. Rul. 200602039.

[39] See § 25.1(b).

[40] Priv. Ltr. Rul. 201043041.

[41] Priv. Ltr. Rul. 201406019.

[42] This does not mean that revenue from a for-profit subsidiary to an exempt parent is not taxable; in fact, just the opposite is often the case (see § 30.6).

[43] Priv. Ltr. Rul. 2008050. In this ruling, the IRS did not explain the factors that led to this conclusion. In any event, the test is not *control* (which is obviously always present when the subsidiary is wholly owned) but is *day-to-day management*.

[44] Priv. Ltr. Rul. 201044016.

[45] Priv. Ltr. Rul. 201115026.

[46] Priv. Ltr. Rul. 202005020.

[47] Priv. Ltr. Rul. 201714031.

formed a for-profit subsidiary to conduct online educational programs for adults received a ruling from the IRS holding that the subsidiary was a separate legal entity with its own "activities and management," having a "real and substantial business purpose," so that its operations were not attributed to its parent.[48]

§ 30.3 FINANCIAL CONSIDERATIONS

Financial considerations relating to the establishment and maintenance of a for-profit subsidiary by a tax-exempt organization include the capitalization of the subsidiary, the compensation of employees of either or both entities, and the sharing of resources.

(a) Capitalization

A tax-exempt organization can invest a portion of its assets and engage in a certain level of unrelated business activities. At the same time, the governing board of an exempt organization must act in conformity with basic fiduciary responsibilities, and the organization cannot (without jeopardizing its exemption) contravene the prohibitions on private inurement and private benefit.[49]

IRS private letter rulings suggest that only a small percentage of a tax-exempt organization's resources ought to be transferred to controlled for-profit subsidiaries.[50] These percentages approved by the IRS are usually low and, in any event, probably pertain only to cash.[51] (Many IRS rulings in this area do not state the amount of capital involved.)[52] In some cases, a specific asset may—indeed, perhaps must—be best utilized in an unrelated activity, even though its value represents a meaningful portion of the organization's total resources.[53] Also, the exempt parent may want to make subsequent advances or loans to the subsidiary.

The best guiding standard in this regard is that of the prudent investor. In capitalizing a subsidiary, a tax-exempt organization should only part with an amount of resources that is reasonable under the circumstances and that can be rationalized in relation to amounts devoted to programs and invested in other fashions. Relevant to all of this is the projected return on the investment, in terms of income and capital appreciation. If a contribution to a subsidiary's capital seems unwise, the putative parent should consider a loan (albeit one bearing a fair rate of interest and accompanied by adequate security).[54]

[48] Priv. Ltr. Rul. 201503018.
[49] See § 5.3, Chapter 20.
[50] E.g., Priv. Ltr. Rul. 8505044.
[51] In one instance, the IRS specifically ruled that a tax-exempt charitable organization may transfer funds to its for-profit subsidiary (Priv. Ltr. Rul. 201438032).
[52] E.g., Priv. Ltr. Rul. 9305026.
[53] In one instance, the IRS characterized the amount of capital transferred as "substantial"; the exempt parent was not a charitable entity but rather a tax-exempt social welfare organization (see Chapter 13) (Priv. Ltr. Rul. 9245031).
[54] Payments by a tax-exempt organization to its subsidiary for services provided, with the payments from revenues generated by the services, are likely to be considered by the IRS to be compensation for services rather than contributions to capital (Priv. Ltr. Rul. 200227007).

In all instances, it is preferable that the operation of the subsidiary further (if only by providing funds for) the exempt purposes of the parent.[55] Certainly, circumstances where exempt purposes are thwarted by reason of operation of a for-profit subsidiary are to be avoided.

(b) Compensation

The structure of a tax-exempt parent and a taxable subsidiary may generate questions and issues as to compensation of employees.

The compensation of the employees of the taxable subsidiary is subject to an overarching requirement that the amount paid may not exceed a reasonable salary or wage.[56] The compensation of the employees of the parent tax-exempt organization is subject to a like limitation, by reason of the private inurement, private benefit, and/or excess benefit transaction doctrines.[57] An individual may be an employee of both the parent and subsidiary organizations; in that circumstance, a reasonable allocation of compensation between the entities is required.[58] Also, an exempt organization may be required to report, on its annual information return, compensation paid by related organizations; amounts paid by a common paymaster for services performed for the organization are to be reported as if paid directly by the organization.[59] The employees of a for-profit subsidiary of a parent exempt organization may be included in one or more employee benefit plans of the parent, without endangering the exempt status of the parent, as long as the costs of the plan are allocated among the two groups of employees on a per-capita basis.[60]

The employees of the tax-exempt parent could participate in deferred compensation plans[61] or perhaps tax-sheltered annuity programs.[62] Deferred salary plans may also be used by the subsidiary, as may qualified pension plans. Both the parent and the subsidiary may sponsor cash or deferred arrangements.[63]

Use of a taxable subsidiary may facilitate the offering of stock options to employees, to enable them to share in the growth of the corporation. The subsidiary similarly may offer an employee stock ownership plan, which is a plan that invests in the stock of the sponsoring company.[64] The subsidiary may issue unqualified options to buy stock or qualified incentive stock options.[65]

---

[55] E.g., Priv. Ltr. Rul. 8709051.

[56] IRC § 162.

[57] See Chapters 20, 21.

[58] One of the burgeoning issues in this regard is potential misuses of for-profit subsidiaries, such as by unduly shifting expenses to them, excess and/or additional compensation paid by them, and lack of disclosure of the relationship; sometimes there are also conflict-of-interest issues.

[59] E.g., Form 990, Part VII, Section A, line 1a, column (E); Schedule J, Part 1, lines 5–6, and Part II, row (ii). See 3(f), (q).

[60] E.g., Priv. Ltr. Rul. 9242039.

[61] IRC § 457.

[62] IRC § 403(b).

[63] IRC § 401(k).

[64] IRC § 4975(e)(7).

[65] E.g., Priv. Ltr. Rul. 9242038.

(c)   Sharing of Resources

Generally, a tax-exempt organization and its for-profit subsidiary may share resources without adverse consequences to the exempt entity, as a matter of the law of tax-exempt organizations. That is, the two organizations may share office facilities, equipment, supplies, and the like. Particularly where the exempt entity is a charitable one, however, all relevant costs must be allocated on the basis of actual use, and each organization must pay fair market value for the resources used.[66]

It is generally preferable for the tax-exempt organization to reimburse the for-profit entity for the exempt organization's use of resources to avoid even a perception that the funds of an exempt organization are being used to subsidize a for-profit organization. Nonetheless, this approach often is impractical where the exempt organization is the parent entity.[67]

§ 30.4   ASSET ACCUMULATIONS

The IRS evidenced concern about the undue accumulation of assets in a for-profit subsidiary of a tax-exempt organization. The issue is whether this type of an accumulation is evidence of a substantial nonexempt purpose.[68]

The agency's lawyers wrote that, in cases involving exempt organizations, entities "bear a very heavy burden" to demonstrate, by "contemporaneous and clear evidence," that they have plans to use the substantial assets in a subsidiary for exempt purposes.[69]

The IRS is particularly concerned about asset accumulations in a subsidiary when the tax-exempt organization is a closely controlled entity. The IRS admonished the bar that "counsel to closely held [that is, controlled] organizations should take care to ensure that for-profit subsidiaries are not being used to divert exempt organization financial assets, resources, and income to the founding families and other insiders."

§ 30.5   SUBSIDIARIES IN PARTNERSHIPS

There is a dimension to the use of a taxable subsidiary by a tax-exempt organization parent that is alluded to in the discussion of exempt organizations in partnerships.[70] This is the attempt by a charitable organization to avoid endangering its exempt status because of involvement in a partnership as a general partner by causing a taxable subsidiary to be the general partner in its stead.[71]

---

[66] E.g., Priv. Ltr. Rul. 9308047.

[67] The IRS approved of a restructuring of an exempt organization whereby the organization transferred a variety of activities to for-profit subsidiaries to enable the organization to increase the value of the subsidiaries, attract investment capital, and attract and retain employees by means of an equity-based compensation system (Priv. Ltr. Rul. 201125043).

[68] In general, see § 4.4.

[69] Tech. Adv. Mem. 200437040.

[70] See Chapter 31.

[71] E.g., Gen. Couns. Mem. 39598. One area of the federal tax law concerning tax-exempt organizations where the use of a for-profit subsidiary in a partnership, instead of an exempt organization, generally

This can be an effective stratagem as long as all of the requirements of the law as to the bona fides of the subsidiary are satisfied, including the requirement that the subsidiary be an authentic business entity. As discussed,[72] however, if the tax-exempt organization parent is intimately involved in the day-to-day management of the subsidiary, the IRS may impute the activities of the subsidiary to the parent, thereby endangering the exempt status of the parent by treating it as if it were directly involved as a general partner of the limited partnership.[73]

An illustration of this use of a partnership was presented in an IRS ruling.[74] A tax-exempt hospital wanted to expand its provision of medical rehabilitation services; a for-profit corporation that managed the rehabilitation program at the hospital was a subsidiary of the nation's largest independent provider of comprehensive rehabilitation services. The hospital, through this subsidiary, sought a joint venture with its for-profit parent to utilize its expertise and methodologies and to operate the rehabilitation facility as a venture so that the expansion would not jeopardize the institution's role as a community hospital. The joint venture was structured so that it was between the hospital and a system of which it was a component, and a wholly owned for-profit subsidiary of the for-profit parent entity and its subsidiary. The IRS ruled favorably in the case, concluding that the hospital's participation in the venture was consistent with its purposes of promoting health.[75]

§ 30.6 REVENUE FROM FOR-PROFIT SUBSIDIARY

Most tax-exempt organizations assume that an unrelated business will serve as a source of revenue. Thus, development within, or shifting of unrelated business to, a taxable subsidiary of an exempt organization should be done in such a way as to not preclude or inhibit the flow of income from the subsidiary to the parent. At the same time, the parent exempt organization needs to be cognizant of the federal income tax consequences of this income flow.

(a) Income Flows to Parent

The staff and other resources of an affiliated business may be those of the tax-exempt organization parent. Thus, the headquarters of the taxable subsidiary is likely to be the same as its exempt parent. This means that the taxable subsidiary may have to reimburse the exempt organization parent for the subsidiary's occupancy costs, share of employees' time, and use of the parent's equipment and supplies. Therefore, one way for money to flow from a subsidiary to an exempt parent is as this form of reimbursement, which may include an element of rent.

will not alter the tax outcome is the set of rules pertaining to tax-exempt entity leasing (see § 28.15). On occasion, some or all of these results can be accomplished by the use of a tax-exempt subsidiary (e.g., Priv. Ltr. Rul. 8638131).

[72] See § 30.2.

[73] In one instance, the IRS, without explanation, expressly ignored a tax-exempt organization's use of a for-profit subsidiary as the general partner in a partnership, reviewing the facts as if the exempt organization were directly involved in the partnership (Tech. Adv. Mem. 8939002).

[74] Priv. Ltr. Rul. 9352030.

[75] In general, see § 7.6.

Another type of relationship between a tax-exempt organization parent and a taxable subsidiary is that of lender and borrower. That is, in addition to funding its subsidiary by means of one or more capital contributions (resulting in a holding of equity by the parent), the parent may find it appropriate to lend money to its subsidiary. Inasmuch as a no-interest loan to a for-profit subsidiary by a tax-exempt organization parent may endanger the exempt status of the parent and trigger problems under the below-market interest rules,[76] it would be prudent for this type of loan to bear a fair market rate of interest. Therefore, another way for money to flow from the subsidiary to the parent is in the form of interest.

The business activities of a for-profit subsidiary of a tax-exempt organization may be to market and sell a product or service. When done in conformity with its tax-exempt status, the parent can license the use of its name, logo, acronym, and/or some other feature that would enhance the sale of the product or service provided by the subsidiary. For this license, the subsidiary would pay to the parent a royalty—another way of transferring money from a for-profit subsidiary to a tax-exempt parent.

A conventional way of transferring money from a corporation to its stockholders is for the corporation to distribute its earnings and profits to them. These distributions are dividends and represent yet another way in which a taxable subsidiary can transfer money to its tax-exempt parent.[77]

(b)   Tax Treatment of Income from Subsidiary

Certain types of income generally are exempt from taxation as unrelated income—principally the various forms of passive income.[78] Were it not for a special rule of federal tax law, a tax-exempt organization could have it both ways: avoid taxation of the exempt organization on unrelated income by housing the activity in a subsidiary and thereafter receive passive, nontaxable income from the subsidiary.

Congress, however, was mindful of this potential double benefit and thus legislated a rule that is an exception to the general body of law that exempts passive income from taxation: Otherwise, passive nontaxable income that is derived by a tax-exempt organization from a controlled taxable subsidiary is generally treated as unrelated income. Thus, when an exempt organization parent receives interest, annuities, royalties, and/or rent from a controlled taxable subsidiary, those revenues must generally be regarded as unrelated business income taxable to the parent.[79]

There is no tax deduction, however, for the payment of dividends. Consequently, when a for-profit subsidiary pays a dividend to its tax-exempt organization parent, the dividend payments are not deductible by the subsidiary. Therefore, Congress determined that it would not be appropriate to tax revenue to an exempt organization parent where it is not deductible by the taxable subsidiary.[80]

---

[76] IRC § 7872.

[77] These interrelationships should be carefully considered, however, because of the attribution rules (see § 30.2).

[78] See, e.g., § 25.1(a).

[79] IRC § 512(b)(13). As a result of the special unrelated business income tax rules applicable to social clubs, voluntary employees' beneficiary associations, and supplemental unemployment benefit trusts (IRC § 513(a)(3); see § 25.4(c)), however, IRC § 512(b)(13) is inapplicable to those entities (e.g., Priv. Ltr. Rul. 8832084).

[80] See § 25.1(b).

Thus, payments of interest, annuities, royalties, and/or rents (but not dividends) by a controlled organization to a tax-exempt, controlling organization can be taxable as unrelated income, notwithstanding the fact that these forms of income are generally otherwise nontaxable as passive income.[81] The purpose of this provision is to prevent an exempt organization from housing an unrelated activity in a separate but controlled organization and receiving nontaxable income by reason of the passive income rules (for example, by renting unrelated income property to a subsidiary).[82]

Under these rules, the percentage threshold for determining control is a more-than-50-percent standard. Thus, in the case of a corporation, *control* means ownership by vote or value of more than 50 percent of the stock in the corporation.[83] In the case of a partnership, control is ownership of more than 50 percent of the profits interest or capital interests in the partnership.[84] In an instance of a trust or any other case, control is measured in terms of more than 50 percent of the beneficial interests in the entity.[85]

Constructive ownership rules, which were in existence when this body of law was enacted, were grafted onto this area for purposes of determining ownership of stock in a corporation.[86] Similar principles apply for purposes of determining ownership of interests in any other entity.[87] For example, if 50 percent or more in value of the stock in a corporation is owned, directly or indirectly, by or for any person, that person is considered to be the owner of the stock owned directly or indirectly, by or for the corporation, in the proportion that the value of the stock the person so owns bears to the value of all of the stock in the corporation.[88] Likewise, if 50 percent or more in value of the stock in a corporation is owned, directly or indirectly, by or for any person, the corporation is considered as owning the stock owned, directly or indirectly, by or for that person.[89] Attribution rules apply with respect to stock owned by members of a family, partnerships, estates, and trusts.[90] Thus, when a controlling organization receives, directly or indirectly, a specified payment from a controlled entity (whether or not tax-exempt), the controlling entity may have to treat that payment as income from an unrelated business.[91] The term *specified payment* means interest, annuity, royalties, or rent.[92]

---

[81] IRC § 512(b)(13); Reg. § 1.512(b)-1(1). Also, J.E. & L.E. Mabee Found., Inc. v. United States, 533 F.2d 521 (10th Cir. 1976); United States v. Robert A. Welch Found., 334 F.2d 774 (5th Cir. 1964); Campbell v. Carter Found. Prod. Co., 322 F.2d 827 (5th Cir. 1963), *aff'g in part* 61-2 U.S.T.C. ¶ 9630 (N.D. Tex. 1961).

[82] S. Rep. No. 91-552, at 73 (1969); Crosby Valve & Gage Co. v. Comm'r, 380 F.2d 146 (1st Cir. 1967).

[83] IRC § 512(b)(13)(D)(i)(I).

[84] IRC § 512(b)(13)(D)(i)(II).

[85] IRC § 512(b)(13)(D)(i)(III).

[86] IRC §§ 512(b)(13)(D)(ii), 318. Applying these rules, the IRS held that a tax-exempt hospital that constructively owns several professional medical corporations received unrelated business income from them (Priv. Ltr. Rul. 200716034).

[87] IRC § 512(b)(13)(D)(ii).

[88] IRC § 318(a)(2)(C).

[89] IRC § 318(a)(3)(C).

[90] IRC § 318(a)(1), (2)(A), (B), and (3)(A), (B).

[91] IRC § 512(b)(13)(A). Examples of indirect payments appear in J.E. & L.E. Mabee Found., Inc. v. United States, 533 F. 2d 521 (10th Cir. 1976), and Gen. Couns. Mem. 38878.

[92] IRC § 512(b)(13)(C). The term does not include capital gain, enabling a controlling organization to sell appreciated property to a controlled entity without generating unrelated business income. Cf. IRC § 4940(c).

A specified payment must be treated as unrelated business income to the extent that the payment reduced the net unrelated income of the controlled entity or increased any net unrelated loss of the controlled entity.[93] The controlling organization may deduct expenses that are directly connected with amounts that are treated as unrelated business income under this rule.[94]

In the case of a controlled entity that is not tax-exempt, the phrase *net unrelated income* means the portion of the entity's taxable income that would be unrelated business taxable income if the entity were exempt and had the same exempt purposes as the controlling organization.[95] Stated in the reverse, income received by a taxable subsidiary that would be excludable from unrelated business income taxation, either because it is income that would be related business income if received directly by the exempt organization parent or because it is income that would be excluded from such taxation by the modification rules[96] if received directly by the exempt parent, is not net unrelated income. For example, in a situation where three exempt organizations shared a for-profit subsidiary, the IRS ruled that royalties to be received by the subsidiary from the sale and sublicensing of its parents' intellectual property, rent to be received by the subsidiary from the subleasing of its parents' real property, capital gain to be received on sales of its stock, and income received by the subsidiary from activities that are substantially related to the exempt purposes of its parents would be excluded from the computation of the subsidiary's unrelated business taxable income if the subsidiary were exempt and had the same exempt purposes as its exempt controlling organizations.[97]

(c)   Special Rule

Notwithstanding the foregoing, a special rule applies with respect to certain payments to tax-exempt controlling organizations.[98] Pursuant to this rule, the general law, which causes interest, rent, annuity, or royalty payments made by a controlled entity to the controlling tax-exempt organization to be included in the latter organization's unrelated business income to the extent the payment reduces the net unrelated income (or increases any net unrelated loss) of the controlled entity, applies only to the portion of payments received or accrued in a tax year that exceeds the amount of the payment that would have been paid or accrued if the payment had been determined under the rules concerning the allocation of tax items among taxpayers.[99] This special rule applies, however, only with respect to payments made pursuant to a binding written contract in effect on August 17, 2006, or a contract that is a renewal under terms substantially similar to those of a contract in effect on that date.[100] Thus, if one of these four types of payments by a subsidiary to an exempt parent exceeds fair market value, the excess amount of the payment is

---

[93] IRC § 512(b)(13)(A).
[94] *Id.*
[95] IRC § 512(b)(13)(B)(i)(I).
[96] See § 25.1.
[97] Priv. Ltr. Rul. 200602039.
[98] IRC § 512(b)(13)(E).
[99] IRC § 482.
[100] IRC § 512(b)(13)(E)(iii).

included in the parent's unrelated business income (unless it may be characterized as a contribution), to the extent that the excess reduced the net unrelated income (or increased any net unrelated loss) of the controlled entity.

A 20 percent penalty is imposed on the larger of the excess determined without regard to any amendment or supplement to a return of tax or the excess determined with regard to all such amendments and supplements.[101] A tax-exempt organization that receives interest, rent, annuity, and/or royalty payments from a controlled entity must report the payments on its annual information return, as well as any loans made to a controlled entity and any transfers between such an organization and a controlled entity.[102]

§ 30.7 LIQUIDATIONS

The federal tax law causes recognition of gain or loss by a for-profit corporation in an instance of a liquidating distribution of its assets (as if the corporation had sold the assets to the distributee at fair market value) and in the event of liquidating sales. There is an exception for liquidating transfers within an affiliated group (which is regarded as a single economic unit), so that the basis in the property is carried over from the distributor to the distributee in lieu of recognition of gain or loss.

This nonrecognition exception is modified for eligible liquidations in which an 80 percent corporate shareholder receives property with a carryover basis, to provide for nonrecognition of gain or loss with respect to any property actually distributed to that shareholder. Nonetheless, this nonrecognition rule under the exception for 80 percent corporate shareholders is generally not available where the shareholder is a tax-exempt organization. That is, any gain or loss generally must be recognized by the subsidiary on the distribution of its assets in liquidation as if the assets were sold to the exempt parent at their fair market value.[103] (Gain or loss is not recognized by the parent entity on its receipt of the subsidiary's assets pursuant to the liquidation.)[104] This nonrecognition treatment is available in the exempt organizations context, however, where the property distributed is used by the exempt organization in an unrelated business immediately after the distribution. If the property subsequently ceases to be used in an unrelated business, the exempt organization will be taxed on the gain at that time.[105]

In another instance, one of the functions of a tax-exempt charitable entity was the publication and circulation of religious materials. This organization had a

---

[101] IRC § 512(b)(13)(E)(ii).

[102] IRC § 6033(h).

[103] IRC § 337(b)(2)(A).

[104] IRC § 332(a).

[105] IRC § 337(b)(2)(B)(ii). Cf. Centre for Int'l Understanding v. Comm'r, 62 T.C.M. 629 (1991) (applying the liquidation rules of IRC § 337(c)(2)(A)). Regulations were issued in final form, under authority of IRC § 337(d), concerning the liquidation of for-profit entities into tax-exempt organizations, when the relationship is not that of parent and subsidiary. The rules in this regard are essentially the same as those that apply to liquidations of subsidiaries, although they also apply when a for-profit corporation converts to an exempt entity (see § 32.7).

for-profit subsidiary that engaged in both exempt and commercial printing activities. Once it decided to discontinue the commercial printing operations, the exempt parent proposed to liquidate the subsidiary and distribute its assets to the parent organization. The IRS ruled that any gain or loss must be recognized by the subsidiary on the distribution of its assets in liquidation (as if they were sold to the exempt parent at fair market value) to the extent that the assets were to be used in related business activities.[106]

These rules as to liquidations may be contrasted with the rules as to tax-free distributions of securities (spin-offs) of controlled operations,[107] where one of the requirements is that the transaction not be used principally as a device for distribution of the earnings and profits of the distributing corporation and/or the controlled corporation.[108] In one instance, a for-profit corporation, wholly owned by a supporting organization,[109] distributed all of the stock of nine subsidiaries (an affiliated group) to the supporting organization, which subsequently transferred the stock to another supporting organization; both supporting organizations operated to benefit the same supported organization. The reason for this transfer was to enhance the success of the various for-profit businesses by eliminating control and management inefficiencies caused by the prior structure; the IRS ruled[110] that no gain or loss was recognized when the stock was distributed.[111]

---

[106] Priv. Ltr. Rul. 9645017. This ruling expressly addressed the point that, to the extent the assets were to be used by the parent in unrelated activities, any gain would not be recognized during the pendency of that type of use (IRC § 337(b)(2)(B)(ii)).

[107] IRC § 355.

[108] IRC § 355(a)(1)(B).

[109] See § 12.3(c)

[110] Priv. Ltr. Rul. 200435005.

[111] IRC § 355(c). An organization that was tax-exempt (IRC § 501(a)) during any of its last five tax years preceding its liquidation, dissolution, termination, or substantial contraction may be required to disclose the development to the IRS (IRC § 6043(b)).

Tax-Exempt Organizations and Joint Ventures

One of the most important developments involving tax-exempt organizations in the modern era is the use of related organizations. This phenomenon is reflected, for example, in the use of subsidiaries and single-member limited liability companies by exempt organizations.[1] What is striking, nonetheless, is the contemporary willingness—and, in some instances, necessity—of many exempt organizations to simultaneously use different forms of related entities, be they for-profit or non-profit, trust or corporation, taxable or nontaxable. This includes participation by exempt organizations in joint ventures.

§ 31.1 PARTNERSHIPS AND JOINT VENTURES BASICS

The concept of a joint venture encompasses partnerships; a partnership, however, is a form of business entity formally recognized in the law as a discrete legal entity, as is a corporation, trust, or LLC, while the term *joint venture* can be applied to more informal (and, in some instances, unintended) arrangements.

(a) Partnerships

A partnership is usually evidenced by a partnership agreement, executed between persons who are the partners; the persons may be individuals, corporations, tax-exempt organizations, and/or other partnerships. Each partner owns one or more interests, called units, in the partnership.

The term *partnership* is defined in the federal tax law to include a "syndicate, group, pool, joint venture, or other unincorporated organization, through or by

[1] See Chapters 29 and 30, § 32.4.

means of which any business, financial operation, or venture is carried on, and which is not. . .a trust or estate or a corporation."[2] This term is broadly applied. For example, co-owners of income-producing real estate who operate the property (either directly or through an agent of one or more of them) for their joint profit are operating a partnership.[3]

A partnership usually entails a profit motive. Thus, a court defined a partnership as a "contract of two or more persons to place their money, efforts, labor, and skill, or some or all of them, in lawful commerce or business, and to divide the profit and bear the loss in definite proportions."[4]

Partners are of two types: general and limited. The types are delineated principally by their role in the venture (active or passive) and the extent of the partners' liability for the acts of the partnership. Generally, liability for the consequences of a partnership's operations rests with the general partner or partners, while the exposure to liability for the functions of the partnership for the limited partners is confined to the amount of the limited partner's contribution to the partnership. A general partner is liable for satisfaction of the ongoing obligations of the partnership and can be called on to make additional contributions of capital to it. Every partnership must have at least one general partner. Sometimes where there is more than one general partner, one of them is designated the managing general partner.

Many partnerships have only general partners, who contribute cash, property, and/or services. This type of partnership is termed a *general partnership*. The interests of the general partners may or may not be equal. In this type of partnership, which is essentially akin to a joint venture,[5] generally all of the partners are equally liable for satisfaction of the obligations of the partnership and can be called on to make additional capital contributions to the entity.

Some partnerships, however, need or want to attract capital from sources other than the general partners. This capital can come from investors, who are termed *limited partners*. Their interest in the partnership is, as noted, limited in the sense that their liability is limited. The liability of a limited partner is confined to the amount of the capital contribution—the investment. The limited partners are in the venture to obtain a return on their investment and perhaps to procure some tax advantages. A partnership with both general and limited partners is termed a *limited partnership*.

The partnership is the entity that acquires the property, develops it (if necessary), and sometimes continues to operate and maintain the property. Where a tax-exempt organization is the general partner, it is not the owner of the property (the partnership is), but nonetheless it can have many of the incidents of ownership, such as participation in the cash flow generated by the property, a preferential leasing arrangement, and/or the general perception by the outside world that the property is owned by the exempt organization. The exempt organization may lease space in property owned by the partnership. The exempt entity may have an option to purchase the property from the partnership after the passage of a stated period of time.

---

[2] IRC § 7701(a)(2).

[3] Rev. Rul. 54-369, 1954-2 C.B. 364; Rev. Rul. 54-170, 1954-1 C.B. 213.

[4] Whiteford v. United States, 61-1 U.S.T.C. ¶ 9301, at 79,762 (D. Kan. 1960). Also, Luna v. Comm'r, 42 T.C. 1067 (1964). A partnership was not found in the facts of White v. Comm'r, T.C. Memo. 2018-102.

[5] See § 31.1(b).

Partnerships do not pay taxes—and, in this sense, are themselves tax-exempt organizations.[6] They are conduits—technically, flow-through entities—of net revenue to the partners, who bear the responsibility for paying tax on their net income. Partnerships are also conduits of the tax advantages of the ownership of property, and thus can pass through preference items, such as depreciation and interest deductions.[7]

If an entity fails to qualify under the federal tax laws as a partnership, it will be treated as an *association*, which means it will be taxed as a corporation. When that occurs, as a general rule the entity will have to pay taxes, and the ability to pass through tax advantages to the equity owners is lost.[8]

In many instances, it is clear that the parties in an arrangement intend to create and operate a partnership. In some cases, however, the law will treat an arrangement as a general partnership (or other joint venture) for tax purposes, even though the parties involved intended (or insist they intended) that their relationship is something else (such as landlord and tenant or payor and payee of royalties). The issue often arises in the unrelated business context, where a tax-exempt organization is asserting that certain income is passive in nature (most frequently, rent or royalty income) and the IRS is contending that the income was derived from active participation in a partnership (or joint venture).[9]

Federal tax law is inconsistent in stating the criteria for ascertaining whether a partnership is to be found as a matter of law. The U.S. Supreme Court stated: "When the existence of an alleged partnership arrangement is challenged by outsiders, the question arises whether the partners really and truly intended to join together for the purpose of carrying on business and sharing in the profits or losses or both."[10] The Court added that the parties' "intention is a question of fact, to be determined from testimony disclosed by their 'agreement considered as a whole, and by their conduct in execution of its provisions.'"[11] In one instance, a court examined state law and concluded that the most important element in determining whether a landlord-tenant relationship or joint venture agreement exists is the intention of the parties.[12]

Conversely, another court declared that it is "well settled that neither local law nor the expressed intent of the parties is conclusive as to the existence or non-existence of a partnership or joint venture for federal tax purposes."[13] The court

---

[6] See § 1.2.

[7] See § 24.8.

[8] Moreover, the partnership must have effective ownership of the property for these deductions to be available, rather than have the ownership be by the exempt organization/general partner (e.g., Smith v. Comm'r, 50 T.C.M. 1444 (1985)).

[9] See, e.g., §§ 25.1(g), 31.1(c).

[10] Comm'r v. Tower, 327 U.S. 280, 286–87 (1946).

[11] *Id.* at 287 (citations omitted). These principles are equally applicable in determining the existence of a joint venture (e.g., Estate of Smith v. Comm'r, 313 F.2d 724 (8th Cir. 1963), *aff'g in part, rev'g in part, and remanding* 33 T.C. 465 (1959); Luna v. Comm'r, 42 T.C. 1067 (1964); Beck Chemical Equip. Corp. v. Comm'r, 27 T.C. 840 (1957)).

[12] Harlan E. Moore Charitable Trust v. United States, 812 F. Supp. 130, 132 (C.D. Ill. 1993), *aff'd*, 9 F.3d 623 (7th Cir. 1993).

[13] Trust U/W Emily Oblinger v. Comm'r, 100 T.C. 114 (1993). The court cited several court opinions as authority for this proposition, relying principally on Haley v. Comm'r, 203 F.2d 815 (5th Cir. 1953), *rev'g and remanding* 16 T.C. 1509 (1951).

stated that the standard to follow is "whether, considering all the facts—the agreement, the conduct of the parties in execution of its provisions, their statements, the testimony of disinterested persons, the relationship of the parties, their respective abilities and capital contributions, the actual control of income and the purposes for which it is used, and any other facts throwing light on their true intent—the parties in good faith and acting with a business purpose intended to join together in the present conduct of the enterprise."[14]

This dichotomy was illustrated by a case involving a tax-exempt charitable organization and its tenant-farmer; the issue was whether the relationship was landlord-tenant, partnership, or other joint venture.[15] The question before the court was whether the rent, equaling 50 percent of the crops and produce grown on the farm, constituted rent that was excludable from taxation as unrelated business income.[16] The court looked to state law to ascertain the meaning to be given the term *rent*. The court concluded that the contracts as a whole clearly reflected the intention of the parties to create a landlord-tenant relationship, rather than a partnership.

As a general rule, a partnership is a useful and beneficial way for one or more individuals or organizations to acquire, finance, own, and/or operate property. There can be problems with this approach, however, in the tax-exempt organizations context.[17]

(b) Joint Ventures

A tax-exempt organization may enter into a joint venture with a for-profit organization without adversely affecting its exempt status, as long as doing so furthers exempt purposes and the joint venture agreement does not prevent it from acting exclusively to further those purposes.[18] A joint venture does not present the private inurement problems that the IRS associates with participation by charitable organizations as general partners in limited partnerships. By contrast, an involvement in a joint venture by an exempt organization would lead to loss (or denial) of exemption if the primary purpose of the exempt organization is to participate in the venture and if the function of the venture is unrelated to the exempt purposes of the exempt organization. Nearly all the federal law concerning exempt organizations in joint ventures concerns the involvement of public charities; nonetheless, this body of law can be applicable to other types of exempt entities, particularly those that are subject to the private inurement doctrine.[19]

---

[14] Trust U/W Emily Oblinger v. Comm'r, 100 T.C. 114, 118 (1993), citing Comm'r v. Culbertson, 337 U.S. 733, 742 (1949). Also, Luna v. Comm'r, 42 T.C. 1067, 1077–78 (1964).

[15] United States v. Myra Found, 382 F.2d 107 (8th Cir. 1967).

[16] This case was decided before enactment of the rule disallowing the exclusion of rents based on certain profit-sharing arrangements (see § 25.1(h)(i), text accompanied by notes 48–49).

[17] The foregoing is, by necessity, an overview of the law of partnerships. For a comprehensive analysis of these entities (from a tax-exempt organizations perspective), see Sanders, *Joint Ventures Involving Tax-Exempt Organizations, Fourth Edition* (John Wiley & Sons, 2014) (*Joint Ventures*), particularly Chapters 1, 3, and 4.

[18] E.g., Plumstead Theatre Soc'y, Inc. v. Comm'r, 74 T.C. 1324 (1980), *aff'd* 675 F.2d 244 (9th Cir. 1982).

[19] The private inurement doctrine is the subject of Chapter 20. For example, the IRS applied the joint venture rules in a situation concerning the involvement of an exempt business league (see Chapter 14),

A court defined a *joint venture* as an association of two or more persons with intent to carry out a single business venture for joint profit, for which purpose they combine their efforts, property, money, skill, and knowledge, but they do so without creating a formal partnership, trust, or corporation.[20] Thus, two or more entities (including tax-exempt organizations) may operate a business enterprise as a joint venture.[21]

Generally, when a tax-exempt organization acquires an interest in a joint venture (such as by transfer of funds), the event is not a taxable one, because the action is a one-time activity and thus is not a business that is regularly carried on.[22] That is, the exempt organization is not likely to be characterized as being in the business of establishing or investing in partnerships.[23]

Where the purpose of the joint venture is investment, the joint venture will be looked through to determine the nature of the revenue being received by the tax-exempt organization. It is rare that the investment income will be exempt function revenue. Usually the income is passive investment income and thus is not taxed.[24] But if the participation in the joint venture is the principal activity of the exempt organization and the purpose of the venture is not an exempt one for the organization, it will, as observed, lose (or be denied) exempt status by reason of participation in the venture. By contrast, where an exempt organization participates in a joint venture with one or more other exempt organizations in furtherance of exempt purposes, the exempt activities of the venture are attributed to the venturers and their exemption is not jeopardized by reason of their involvement in the venture.[25]

A tax-exempt organization may become involved in a joint venture with a for-profit organization in advancement of an exempt purpose. Again, the look-through principle applies, with the revenue derived by the exempt organization from the venture characterized as related revenue. For example, an exempt charitable organization participating as a general partner in a venture with a for-profit entity to own and operate an ambulatory surgical center was determined by the IRS to be engaging in a related activity.[26] Likewise, the IRS ruled that a joint venture between a charitable organization and a for-profit one, for the purpose of organizing and operating a free-standing alcoholism/substance abuse treatment center, would not jeopardize the exempt status of the charitable organization.[27] Still another illustration is an IRS ruling that an exempt hospital may, without endangering its exempt status, participate with a for-profit organization for the purpose

---

by means of a holding company, in a limited liability company with a for-profit corporation (Priv. Ltr. Rul. 200528029).

[20] Whiteford v. United States, 61-1 U.S.T.C. ¶ 9301 (D. Kan. 1960).

[21] Stevens Bros. Found., Inc. v. Comm'r, 324 F.2d 633 (8th Cir. 1963).

[22] See § 24.3.

[23] E.g., Priv. Ltr. Rul. 8818008.

[24] See § 25.1(a).

[25] E.g., Priv. Ltr. Rul. 200902013 (where two tax-exempt hospitals operated a network of six freestanding family health care clinics in medically underserved areas of their community). In this instance, the joint venture was converted to a formal partnership (see § 31.1(a)).

[26] Priv. Ltr. Rul. 8817039.

[27] Priv. Ltr. Rul. 8521055.

of providing magnetic resonance imaging services in an underserved community.[28] Other IRS private letter rulings provide examples of joint ventures that did not adversely affect the exempt status of the exempt organization involved.[29]

A joint venture of this nature may be structured as an LLC.[30] For example, a tax-exempt community-based health care system and a group of physicians formed an LLC to own and operate an ambulatory surgical center.[31] Likewise, an exempt hospital and physicians formed an LLC for the purpose of operating a cardiac catheterization laboratory.[32] Similarly, a public charity established a limited liability company, to finance small businesses for the benefit of low-income populations, to enable it to issue equity interests to investors.[33]

The IRS is concerned, nonetheless, about situations where the involvement of a tax-exempt organization in a joint venture gives rise, or may give rise, to private inurement.[34] For example, it is the view of the IRS, as noted, that an exempt hospital endangered its exemption because of its involvement in a joint venture with members of its medical staff, where the hospital sold to the joint venture the net revenue stream of a hospital department for a stated period of time.[35] In this situation and others that are similar, the application of the private inurement doctrine is triggered by the inherent structure of the joint venture and not by whether the compensation is reasonable.[36]

(c) Law-Imposed Joint Ventures

In some instances, the IRS will characterize an arrangement between parties as a joint venture for tax purposes.[37] That is, the agency may attempt to overlay the joint venture structure on a set of facts, irrespective of the intent of the participants. This can occur, for example, as an alternative to an assertion that a tax-exempt organization is directly engaged in an unrelated business.[38] As an illustration, in a case in which a court held that an exempt labor union[39] was not engaged in an unrelated business when it collected per capita taxes from its affiliated unions, the IRS retorted with the (unsuccessful) contention that the revenue should nonetheless be taxed because the unions were involved in a "joint enterprise."[40] Another example of this point was provided when, having lost the argument that a form

---

[28] Priv. Ltr. Rul. 8833038.

[29] E.g., Priv. Ltr. Rul. 8621059. Currently, the IRS is not issuing private letter rulings on whether a joint venture between a tax-exempt organization and a for-profit organization affects an organization's exempt status, furthers an exempt purpose, or results in unrelated business income (Rev. Proc. 2024-3, 2024-1 I.R.B. 143 § 3.01(78)).

[30] See §§ 32.3, 32.4.

[31] Priv. Ltr. Rul. 200118054.

[32] Priv. Ltr. Rul. 200304041.

[33] Priv. Ltr. Rul. 200351033.

[34] See Chapter 20.

[35] Gen. Couns. Mem. 39862.

[36] See § 20.7.

[37] See text accompanied by *supra* notes 9–14.

[38] See Chapters 24, 25.

[39] See § 16.1.

[40] Laborer's Int'l Union of North America v. Comm'r, 82 T.C.M. 158, 160 (2001).

of gambling—"tip jars" placed by an exempt organization in taverns so that the patrons could purchase tip-jar tickets to provide revenue to the organization—was not an unrelated business, the IRS's (unsuccessful) riposte was that the exempt organization and the taverns were engaged in a joint venture, with the activities of the employees of the taverns imputed to the exempt organization.[41] Indeed, the IRS has revoked the tax-exempt status of several cemetery companies[42] because of entry into management agreements that, in the view of the agency, caused private inurement[43] by reason of what were, in substance, joint ventures.[44]

As another example of a law-imposed joint venture, the IRS denied recognition of tax exemption to an organization seeking to be classified as an educational organization, in part because it was held to be primarily operated for the nonexempt purpose of commercially selling financial planning and consulting services. All of the organization's founding and controlling board members were involved in forms of financial planning in their businesses or professions; they conducted seminars and marketed their services in the name of the organization. Finding "inherent conflicts of interest," the IRS ruled that the organization was involved in a joint venture with its directors for the purpose of promoting and selling financial planning and similar services.[45]

§ 31.2   PUBLIC CHARITIES AS GENERAL PARTNERS

The IRS is not enamored with the involvement of tax-exempt organizations (particularly charitable ones) in partnerships, other than as limited partners in a prudent investment vehicle. To date, the controversy has centered on exempt charitable organizations in partnerships, although some or all of the principles of law being developed apply to other types of exempt organizations, particularly social welfare organizations and business leagues.[46]

Originally, the IRS was of the view that involvement by a charitable organization in a limited partnership as general partner was the basis for automatic revocation of tax exemption, irrespective of the purpose of the partnership. This view, predicated on the private inurement doctrine, is known as the *per se* rule.[47]

The concern of the IRS is that substantial benefits may be provided to the for-profit participants in a partnership (usually the limited partners) with a tax-exempt organization where the exempt organization is a general partner. This uneasiness in the agency has its origins in arrangements involving exempt hospitals and physicians, such as a limited partnership formed to build and manage a medical office

---

[41] Vigilant Hose Co. of Emmitsburg v. United States, 2001-2 U.S.T.C. ¶ 50,458 (D. Md. 2001).

[42] See § 19.6.

[43] See Chapter 20.

[44] E.g., Ex. Den. and Rev. Ltr. 20044018E.

[45] Priv. Ltr. Rul. 200622055.

[46] See Chapters 13, 14.

[47] The IRS created the private inurement *per se* doctrine in the health care context as a basis for revocation of hospitals' tax-exempt status using a joint venture theory (see § 20.76). The IRS revoked the exemption of hospitals for engaging in private inurement transactions (e.g., Priv. Ltr. Rul. 9130002). In general, Chapter 20 and *Healthcare Organizations*, Chapters 4, 22.

building, with a hospital as the general partner and investing physicians as limited partners.[48] Where these substantial benefits are present, the IRS usually will not be hesitant to deploy the doctrines of private inurement, excess benefit transaction, and/or private benefit.[49] Yet the law, in general, is now clear that an exempt charitable organization may participate as a general partner in a partnership without adversely affecting its exempt status.[50]

It is the position of the IRS that a tax-exempt charitable organization will lose or be denied exemption if it participates as the, or a, general partner in a limited partnership, unless the principal purpose of the partnership is to further charitable purposes.[51] Even where the partnership can so qualify, the exemption is not available if the charitable organization/general partner is not adequately insulated from the day-to-day management responsibilities of the partnership and/or if the limited partners are to receive an undue economic return. The IRS recognizes that a charitable organization can be operated exclusively for exempt purposes and simultaneously be a general partner and satisfy its fiduciary responsibilities with respect to the other partners.[52]

Confusion as to the ability of tax-exempt charitable organizations to participate as general partners in limited partnerships was added when a court held, without recognition, let alone discussion, of the considerable body of law developed on the point, that an organization did not qualify as an exempt entity where it was a co–general partner in limited partnerships, where the other general partner was a for-profit corporation and the limited partners were individuals, and where the purpose of the partnerships was to operate low-income housing projects.[53]

The IRS's current position as to whether a charitable organization will have its tax-exempt status revoked (or recognition denied) if it functions as a general partner in a limited partnership is the subject of a three-part test,[54] which is the successor to the *per se* rule.

Under this three-part test, the IRS first looks to determine whether the charitable organization/general partner is serving a charitable purpose by means of the partnership. If the partnership is advancing a charitable purpose, the IRS applies the remainder of the test. Should the partnership fail to adhere to the charitability standard, however, the charitable organization/general partner will be deprived of its tax-exempt status.

---

[48] The history of the position of the IRS in these regards is detailed in *Joint Ventures*, at § 4.2.

[49] The IRS is not averse to using its authority in this context. In general, Chapters 20 and 21.

[50] On one occasion, the IRS ruled that the tax-exempt status of a charitable organization should not be revoked; the issue was its participation as a general partner in seven limited partnerships (Priv. Ltr. Rul. 8938001). On another occasion, the IRS held that a hospital organization continued to qualify as an exempt charitable entity, notwithstanding its function as the sole partner of a limited partnership, where some of the limited partnership interests were held by related individuals (Tech. Adv. Mem. 200151045).

[51] Gen. Couns. Mem. 39005.

[52] Gen. Couns. Mem. 39546.

[53] Housing Pioneers, Inc. v. Comm'r, 65 T.C.M. 2191, 2196 (1993). This opinion was affirmed but on the ground that the organization failed to show that for purposes of the low-income housing tax credit (IRC § 42(h)(5)(B)) it was a qualified nonprofit organization (95-1 U.S.T.C. ¶ 50,126 (9th Cir. 1995)).

[54] This was articulated in Gen. Couns. Mem. 39005.

The balance of the test is designed to ascertain whether the charity's role as general partner inhibits its charitable purposes. Here, the IRS looks to means by which the organization may, under the particular facts and circumstances, be insulated from the day-to-day responsibilities as general partner and whether the limited partners are not receiving an undue economic benefit from the partnership. It remains the view of the IRS that there is an inherent tension between the ability of a charitable organization to function exclusively in furtherance of its exempt functions and the obligation of a general partner to operate the partnership for the economic benefit of the limited partners. This tension is the same perceived phenomenon that the IRS, when applying its *per se* rule, chose to characterize as a "conflict of interest."

An instance of application of this test appeared in an IRS private letter ruling made public in 1985.[55] In that case, a charitable organization became a general partner in a real estate limited partnership that leased all of the space in the property to the organization and a related charitable organization. The IRS applied the first part of the test and found that the partnership was serving exempt ends because both tenants were charitable organizations. (The IRS general counsel memorandum underlying this ruling[56] noted that, if the lessee organization that was not the general partner had not been a charitable entity, the general partner would have forfeited its tax exemption.) On application of the rest of the test, the IRS found that the general partner was adequately insulated from the day-to-day management responsibilities of the partnership and that the limited partners' economic return was reasonable.

Today, it is common for exempt organization to endeavor to avoid endangering their exempt status because of involvement in a partnership as a general partner by causing a taxable subsidiary to be the general partner in its stead.[57]

§ 31.3 WHOLE-ENTITY JOINT VENTURES

Developments in the health care field have generated significant implications for public charities and perhaps other types of tax-exempt organizations that are in, or are contemplating participation in, a joint venture. This matter concerns the *whole-hospital joint venture* or, generically, the *whole-entity joint venture*.

(a) Overview of Law

The whole-entity joint venture is different from a conventional joint venture. With this approach, the tax-exempt entity transfers the entirety of its assets to the joint venture, with the for-profit organization perhaps assuming control over the assets and managing the day-to-day operations of the venture. For example, ownership of one or more hospitals might be transferred. The exempt health care organization does not directly engage in health care activities; it receives income and other distributions attributable to its ownership interest in the venture. There usually is

---

[55] Priv. Ltr. Rul. 8541108.
[56] Gen. Couns. Mem. 39444.
[57] See § 30.5.

a board of directors of this joint venture. Technically, the venture is a partnership[58] or a limited liability company.[59]

A whole-hospital joint venture can lead to access to managed care contracts, greater efficiency of operations, and additional funding of charitable programs. From the standpoint of the for-profit entity, the venture provides a means to "acquire" a hospital without having to engage in an outright purchase of the institution.

Thus, the fundamental distinction between joint ventures in general and whole-hospital joint ventures—one that may determine whether the tax-exempt organization is able to obtain or maintain exemption—is that, in instances of the former, the exempt entity continues to engage in health care functions while, in the latter case, the entity is an owner of the venture that itself controls the assets and operates the programs underlying the health care activity. This raises the question as to whether participation in a whole-entity joint venture would cause the hospital or other health care organization to lose or be denied exempt status. Other issues are the imposition of the intermediate sanctions penalties[60] and/or the likelihood that income from the venture is unrelated business income to the exempt hospital.[61] Further complicating this area of the law is the impact of any new rules on entities outside the health care field, such as on exempt organizations that are managed by for-profit companies,[62] as well as on nuances concerning the future viability of these ventures.

(b) IRS Guidance

The IRS, in stating its position with respect to whole-hospital joint ventures, sketched two situations in which involvement by a tax-exempt hospital in one of these ventures does or does not jeopardize the hospital's exempt status.[63]

Two more of these rules are central to the findings by the IRS in this guidance: (1) A tax-exempt charitable organization may enter into a management contract with a private party, according that party authority to conduct activities on behalf of the organization and to direct use of the organization's assets, as long as the charity retains ultimate authority over the activities being managed and the assets, and the terms and conditions of the contract are reasonable; and (2) if a private party is allowed to control or use the nonprofit organization's activities or assets for the benefit of that party and the benefit is not merely incidental, the organization will not qualify for or will be deprived of tax exemption.

The IRS's position with respect to whole-hospital joint ventures was basically adopted wholesale when the issue was first litigated.[64] The court concluded that the tax-exempt health care entity involved in the venture (a surgical center) "ceded effective control" over its sole activity to for-profit parties that had an independent

---

[58] See § 31.1(a).

[59] See §§ 32.3, 32.4.

[60] See Chapter 21.

[61] See Chapters 24, 25.

[62] This utilization of management companies is quite common and appropriate (see, e.g., Priv. Ltr. Rul. 9715031). Cf. Priv. Ltr. Rul. 9709014.

[63] Rev. Rul. 98-15, 1998-1 C.B. 718. In general, *Joint Ventures* § 4.2(e).

[64] Redlands Surgical Servs. v. Comm'r, 113 T.C. 47 (1999), *aff'd*, 242 F.3d 904 (9th Cir. 2001).

economic interest in the same property.[65] The documents made it clear that the partnership lacked any obligation to place charitable purposes ahead of profit-making objectives. Significant private benefits were found to be conferred by the charitable entity on private parties, to the extent that the organization was no longer exempt because it failed both the primary purpose test and the operational test.

In the other case on the point, the government did not prevail.[66] This court concluded that there were "exceptional protections" in place to preclude the venture from being operated to serve private interests. For example, the venture agreement required that hospitals owned by the venture operate in accord with the community benefit standard, with the tax-exempt entity unilaterally able to dissolve the venture if that was not done. Other facts, such as enabling the charitable entity to appoint the chair of the venture's governing board and unilaterally remove its chief executive officer, led the court to conclude that "these provisions clearly protect the non-profit, charitable pursuits [of the exempt organization] as well as any community board could."[67]

§ 31.4 ANCILLARY JOINT VENTURES

The law as to tax-exempt organizations and joint ventures has evolved to the point where there are essentially three types of these ventures. In one, the entirety of the exempt organization is in the venture.[68] In another, the primary operations of the exempt organization are in the venture. In the third approach, concerning the *ancillary joint venture*, something less than primary operations of the exempt organization is in the venture.

The aggregate principle and the control test presumably are applicable in connection with the first two types of these ventures. Certainly the operational test[69] is. In the ancillary joint venture setting, however, the context is different. The IRS is of the view that the aggregate principle applies when determining if there is unrelated business.[70] When the involvement in a venture is a small portion of the exempt organization's overall activities, however, the operational test is not implicated (assuming the organization continues to be operated primarily for exempt purposes).[71]

Assuming that the tax-exempt organization (to date, only a public charity) must retain control of its assets in connection with entire and primary involvement in a joint venture, the question remains as to whether control is needed in the ancillary joint venture setting. In its first ruling on the point, the IRS took the position

---

[65] Redlands Surgical Servs. v. Comm'r, 113 T.C. 47, 78 (1999).

[66] St. David's Health Care System, Inc. v. United States, 2002-1 U.S.T.C. ¶ 50,452 (W.D. Tex. 2002).

[67] *Id.* at 84,253. An appellate court vacated the district court's summary decision and remanded it for trial (St. David's Health Care System, Inc. v. United States, 349 F.3d 232 (5th Cir. 2003)), with the trial (by jury) leading to the conclusion that the system was entitled to retain its tax-exempt status (No. 101CV-046 (W.D. Tex., Mar. 4, 2004)).

[68] See § 31.3.

[69] See § 4.5.

[70] Priv. Ltr. Rul. 200118054.

[71] See § 4.4.

that control was necessary in that context for a charitable organization to retain its exempt status.[72] Similarly, the IRS ruled that a public charity could enter into an ancillary joint venture with for-profit corporations for the purpose of financing small businesses for the benefit of low-income individuals without jeopardizing its tax-exempt status or incurring unrelated business income.[73] The agency observed that the venture (structured as a limited liability company) would be operated in conformity with its whole-entity joint-venture principles.

The IRS, in 2004, issued formal guidance as to the tax consequences of public charities' involvement in ancillary joint ventures, ruling that a public charity in this type of arrangement with a for-profit entity will not lose its tax-exempt status if the involvement is an insubstantial part of its total operations, and that it will not be subject to unrelated business income taxation if the charity retains control over the partnership arrangement and operations that constitute one or more related businesses.[74]

This ruling did not resolve all the federal tax issues as to public charities in ancillary joint ventures. It did demonstrate that the IRS agrees that an exempt organization in a joint venture can retain control over venture activities in ways other than by means of the composition of the governing board of the joint venture vehicle.[75] Inasmuch as the involvement of the university in the LLC was insubstantial, there could not be an issue as to the presence of undue private benefit.[76] Likewise, because the activities of the LLC were deemed to be inherently educational, the income flowing to the university could not, under the general flow-through rules, be unrelated business income.

The question remains, however, as to the tax consequences when the primary operations of the exempt organization are in the venture (the second type of joint venture referenced earlier). Even if the activity in the venture is related, if the public charity cedes its authority to the for-profit co-venturer, exempt status would seem to be an issue because of application of the private benefit doctrine.

§ 31.5 LOW-INCOME HOUSING VENTURES

The IRS provided criteria for the agency's use in processing applications for recognition of exemption[77] filed by organizations that propose to further their purposes by participating, as a general partner, in a low-income housing tax credit[78] limited

---

[72] Priv. Ltr. Rul. 200118054 (concerning a venture to operate an ambulatory surgery center, involving a public charity and a group of physicians).

[73] Priv. Ltr. Rul. 200351033.

[74] Rev. Rul. 2004-51, 2004-1 C.B. 974. Currently, the IRS is not issuing private letter rulings on whether a joint venture between a tax-exempt organization and a for-profit organization affects an organization's exempt status, furthers an exempt purpose, or results in unrelated business income (Rev. Proc. 2024-3, 2024-1 I.R.B. 143 § 3.01(78)).

[75] The IRS ruled that a tax-exempt hospital may participate in a joint venture in furtherance of its health care purposes and thus without loss of exemption, because the partnership and management agreements involved provided that charitable purposes overrode other purposes (Priv. Ltr. Rul. 200436022).

[76] See § 20.13(b).

[77] See §§ 26.1, 26.2.

[78] IRC § 42.

partnership.[79] This guidance pertains to tax-exempt charitable and social welfare organizations.[80] The applicant must explain how it will accomplish its charitable purposes, as an organization that provides low-income housing, consistent with the safe harbor of the facts-and-circumstances test set forth by the IRS.[81]

§ 31.6 INFORMATION REPORTING

If a partnership in which a tax-exempt organization is a partner regularly carries on a trade or business that would constitute an unrelated trade or business if directly carried on by the exempt organization, the organization generally must include its share of the partnership's income and deductions from the business in determining its unrelated income tax liability.[82]

A partnership generally must furnish to each partner a statement reflecting the information about the partnership required to be shown on the partner's tax return or information return.[83] The statement must set forth the partner's distributive share of the partnership income, gain, loss, deduction, or credit required to be shown on the partner's return, along with any additional information as provided by IRS forms or instructions that may be required to apply particular provisions of the federal tax law to the partner with respect to items related to the partnership.[84]

Partnerships of tax-exempt organizations, including those wholly comprising exempt organizations, must annually file federal information returns.[85]

---

[79] Memorandum to the Manager, EO Determinations, from the Acting Director, EO Rulings and Agreements, dated April 25, 2006.

[80] See § 7.4, Chapter 13, respectively.

[81] Rev. Proc. 96-32, 1996-1 C.B. 717.

[82] See § 24.8.

[83] IRC § 6031(b).

[84] Temp. Reg. § 1.6031(b)-1T.

[85] IRC § 6031. This return is Form 1065. E.g., Priv. Ltr. Rul. 8925092. In determining the tax year (the current year) of a partnership (IRC § 706(b)), a partner that is tax-exempt (IRC § 501(a)) is disregarded if the partner was not subject to tax on any income attributable to its investment in the partnership during the partnership's tax year immediately preceding the current year (Reg. § 1.706-1(b)(5)).

Tax-Exempt Organizations: Other Operations and Restructuring

The establishment of tax-exempt organizations, and interrelationships between exempt and other organizations, entails a variety of organizational and operational considerations.

§ 32.1 MERGERS

Notwithstanding the variety of in-tandem arrangements involving tax-exempt organizations, occasionally two or more of these organizations are merged. Likewise, on occasion, two or more unrelated exempt organizations merge. With one exception, there is not any statutory law on the point.[1]

When a merger of this nature occurs, often the organizations involved have the same tax-exempt status. Usually the two organizations in this type of a merger are public charitable organizations.[2] The rationale for these mergers varies. In one instance, the merger served to change the state of incorporation.[3] In another, the merger was intended to reduce the administrative burdens of operating two or

---

[1] This exception pertains to the special termination rules that apply with respect to the mergers of private foundations (see *Private Foundations* § 13.5).

[2] That is, public institutions, publicly supported charitable organizations, or supporting organizations (see Chapter 12).

[3] Priv. Ltr. Rul. 9309037.

more organizations.[4] In still another, the merger was undertaken to eliminate what had become a superfluous organization.[5] In one instance, a supporting organization for a boys' school and a supporting organization for a girls' school merged to form one supporting organization following a merger of the two schools.[6] As another illustration, an organization operating independent living housing for the elderly merged into a publicly supported organization, followed by a consolidation with a home for the elderly, all for the purpose of promoting efficient management, facilitating long-term planning, and enhancing philanthropy for the neediest elderly.[7]

Likewise, efficiencies were achieved when five business leagues[8] were consolidated into one.[9] Similarly, two exempt health care providers merged, with the objective of enhancing efficiency in the delivery of health care services and reducing fundraising costs.[10] In addition, three cancer treatment and cancer research facilities merged so as to improve the provision of cancer treatment to patients, improve the efficacy of medical research, and achieve operational economies of scale.[11] Also, three chambers of commerce merged.[12] In another instance, three public charities with similar programs merged so as to provide services in a more efficient and comprehensive manner; two of the organizations are reflected in operating divisions of the surviving entity and in two advisory boards.[13] In another instance, two public charities (one the sole member of the other) merged, to simplify their governance structure and reduce administrative expenses.[14]

Occasionally both of the merging organizations will be tax-exempt organizations, but under differing categories. For example, a lobbying organization[15] related to a public charitable organization may merge into the public charity, or a foundation related to a trade or professional organization[16] may merge into the association.[17] In examples of this type of merger, a single-parent title-holding corporation[18] merged into a publicly supported charity[19] and two multiple-parent title-holding companies[20] merged.[21]

---

[4] E.g., Priv. Ltr. Rul. 9314059.
[5] Priv. Ltr. Rul. 9303030 (a supporting organization (see § 12.3(c)) merged into a supported organization).
[6] Priv. Ltr. Rul. 9317054.
[7] Priv. Ltr. Rul. 199914051.
[8] That is, organizations described in IRC § 501(c)(6) (see Chapter 14).
[9] Priv. Ltr. Rul. 199916053.
[10] Priv. Ltr. Rul. 200030028.
[11] Priv. Ltr. Rul. 200348029.
[12] Priv. Ltr. Rul. 200425052.
[13] Priv. Ltr. Rul. 200541042.
[14] Priv. Ltr. Rul. 200843040.
[15] That is, an organization described in IRC § 501(c)(4) (see Chapter 13).
[16] That is, an organization described in IRC § 501(c)(6) (see Chapter 14).
[17] E.g., Priv. Ltr. Rul. 200234071.
[18] That is, an organization described in IRC § 501(c)(2) (see § 19.2(a)).
[19] Priv. Ltr. Rul. 9840053.
[20] That is, organizations described in IRC § 501(c)(25) (see § 19.2(b)).
[21] Priv. Ltr. Rul. 9840054.

These mergers usually do not adversely affect the tax-exempt status or the public charity status of the surviving organization or cause any unrelated business income.[22] Occasionally, however, a merger can trigger a revocation of tax exemption of the surviving entity, such as where a charitable and educational organization merged into an organization primarily maintaining a program of certification of individuals.[23]

An infrequent occurrence will be a merger of a for-profit organization into a tax-exempt organization. This can be done without endangering the exempt status of the surviving organization, and generally without causing unrelated business income for the exempt organization.[24] In one instance, a taxable corporation was merged into an exempt social welfare organization.[25] The activities of the corporation were consistent with the exempt organization's purposes.[26] The exempt organization issued "special notes" to the shareholders of the for-profit corporation in exchange for their stock. Again, the rationale for the merger was that the combination would reduce duplicative operations and expenses. In another case, the IRS approved a merger of a tax-exempt hospital and a for-profit medical practice clinic; this integration of operations was undertaken to enhance the quality of services provided and eliminate duplication of services.[27]

In still another instance, the IRS approved a consolidation of industry regulatory functions between two affiliated business leagues[28] and a nonprofit (nonexempt) corporate subsidiary of a publicly traded company; the effect of the transaction was said by the agency to produce benefits for the industry and the public that relies on these business leagues to ensure fairness in the industry.[29]

§ 32.2 REORGANIZATIONS

Occasionally a tax-exempt organization will reorganize its operations by adding entities (exempt and/or nonexempt) to its overall operational structure. The reasons for this are manifold, such as greater efficiency of operations, expansion of operations, separation of assets to limit liability, the need for utilization of different categories of exempt entities, enhancement of financial return, and/or tax law considerations. Supporting organizations[30] can be prevalent in this regard.

---

[22] E.g., Priv. Ltr. Ruls. 9738055, 9738056 (hospitals (see § 7.6(a)) merging into unrelated supporting organizations (see § 12.3(c)); Priv. Ltr. Rul. 9522022 (merger of two supplemental unemployment benefit trusts (see § 18.4)); Priv. Ltr. Rul. 9530008 (merger of a supporting organization into a private foundation (see § 12.1(a))); Priv. Ltr. Rul. 9530036 (merger of two trade associations (see Chapter 14)); Priv. Ltr. Rul. 9533015 (merger of a social club into a public charity (see Chapter 15)); Priv. Ltr. Rul. 9548019, as modified by Priv. Ltr. Rul. 9551009 (merger of two supporting organizations, followed by transfer to the survivor entity of the assets of a private foundation and 14 charitable trusts).

[23] Priv. Ltr. Rul. 201906010. See § 7.8, text accompanied by notes 340–344.

[24] See, however, § 30.7 (discussion of liquidations of for-profit subsidiaries into tax-exempt parents).

[25] See Chapter 13.

[26] Priv. Ltr. Rul. 9346015.

[27] Priv. Ltr. Rul. 200305032.

[28] That is, organizations described in IRC § 501(c)(6) (see Chapter 14).

[29] Priv. Ltr. Rul. 200723029.

[30] See § 12.3(c). Also, *Private Foundations* § 15.6.

For example, a public charity decided to dissolve into a new public charity to enhance operations; an exempt business league[31] and an exempt labor union[32] were also established.[33] Also, a U.S.-based public charity, with affiliated organizations under a group exemption, expanded its operations internationally by creating another public charity, with its set of worldwide program affiliates.[34] Likewise, an exempt organization transferred a variety of its activities to for-profit subsidiaries, to enable the organization to increase the value of its subsidiaries, attract investment capital, and attract and retain employees by means of an equity-based compensation system.[35] Further, the IRS approved the use of a blocker corporation by a charitable remainder trust to enable it to convert otherwise taxable income into nontaxable dividends.[36] Of course, some of these reasons for reorganizing are not inherently in furtherance of exempt purposes; thus, an organization failed to qualify as an exempt social welfare organization because the IRS concluded that its sole function was to protect against other exempt organizations' liability and not to engage in the promotion of social welfare for the benefit of a community.[37]

Restructuring is prevalent in the health care context, where hospital reorganizations are occurring for a variety of reasons, including facilitation of compliance with government reporting requirements, separation of assets to limit liability, enhancement of the ability to expand facilities, and development of a more flexible framework within which to conduct and expand management functions. Thus, many institutions perceived as hospitals today are actually an aggregation of organizations, including one or more entities that are formally qualified as tax-exempt hospitals,[38] one or more other types of charitable entities (including, perhaps, a related foundation used for development purposes),[39] and one or more for-profit entities. These entities are coordinated as a multientity health care system, which itself is an exempt charitable entity, and are managed by a parent organization that is also a charitable entity. The hospital entity (or entities) remains in being but with its oversight functions transferred to the parent and the services it performs for other organizations in the system transferred to an organization that provides centralized management and other support services for the system. The management entity, controlled by the parent, provides a variety of services, such as investment management, shared service arrangements, and the provision of data processing services. The management entity of a hospital system (or similar collection of institutions) can qualify as a supporting organization, with the nexus to the other organizations in the system based on any of the relationships available to supporting organizations.[40] Other reorganizations of exempt hospitals and similar entities are occurring without the use of a supporting organization.[41]

[31] See Chapter 14.
[32] See § 16.1.
[33] Priv. Ltr. Rul. 201217022.
[34] Priv. Ltr. Rul. 201219024.
[35] Priv. Ltr. Rul. 201125043.
[36] Priv. Ltr. Rul. 201043041.
[37] Priv. Ltr. Rul. 201219030.
[38] See § 7.6.
[39] See *Healthcare Organizations*, Chapter 14.
[40] E.g., Priv. Ltr. Rul. 200316043.
[41] E.g., Priv. Ltr. Rul. 199952088.

§ 32.3   MULTIPLE-MEMBER LIMITED LIABILITY COMPANIES

In the tax-exempt organizations setting, there are two models for the multiple-member LLC (MMLLC): The MMLLC has a mix of exempt and nonexempt members, or all of the members of the MMLLC are exempt entities. With either approach, an MMLLC can be engaged in exempt activities. Thus, exempt organizations can utilize an LLC for the performance of exempt functions; these functions are in a separate entity (thereby affording the protection of limited liability), that entity is not subject to federal income tax, and income that flows from the LLC to the exempt member organizations is not taxable, by reason of the partnership look-through rule.[42]

Illustrations of the first of these approaches are the whole entity and ancillary joint ventures.[43] For example, an exempt health care system and a group of physicians formed an LLC for the purpose of owning and operating an ambulatory surgery center.[44] In another example, an exempt hospital owned and operated six cardiac catheterization laboratories, with these facilities in the hospital's building; the hospital developed a seventh cardiac catheterization laboratory as an outpatient facility by means of an LLC consisting of a supporting organization[45] and physicians having staff privileges at the institution.[46]

Illustrations of the second of these models include these: (1) Tax-exempt health care organizations in the United States utilized an LLC to partner with public hospitals in another country to establish and operate a charitable hospital in that country;[47] (2) an exempt institution of higher education operating two neonatal intensive care units and an exempt hospital operating one of these units established an LLC to administer the hospital's facility and a new neonatal intensive care unit;[48] (3) an exempt organization providing support services to a health care provider and an exempt long-term health care facility formed and operated an LLC to provide rehabilitation services in a community;[49] (4) two public charities operating a medical center formed an LLC to operate an outpatient ambulatory surgery center;[50] (5) a single qualified tuition plan[51] was established for use by private colleges and universities throughout the United States as members of an LLC;[52] and (6) public charities used an LLC to acquire land and develop a center of technology, research, and entrepreneurial expertise.[53]

As an example of a "quasi-merger," three associations[54] having comparable (but not identical) exempt purposes and members with congruent interests

[42] See § 24.8.
[43] See §§ 31.3, 31.4.
[44] Priv. Ltr. Rul. 200118054.
[45] See § 12.3(c).
[46] Priv. Ltr. Rul. 200304041.
[47] Priv. Ltr. Rul. 9839039.
[48] Priv. Ltr. Rul. 200044040.
[49] Priv. Ltr. Rul. 200102052.
[50] Priv. Ltr. Rul. 200117043.
[51] See § 19.19(b).
[52] Priv. Ltr. Rul. 200311034.
[53] Priv. Ltr. Rul. 200411044.
[54] See Chapter 14.

conducted separate trade shows annually for years.[55] To reduce the administrative costs of the shows, and in the face of complaints from members of the industry about attendance at three trade shows each year but the unwillingness of these associations to merge, the associations transferred the trade show functions to an LLC, which then conducted a single (blended) annual trade show.[56]

§ 32.4 SINGLE-MEMBER LIMITED LIABILITY COMPANIES

The single-member LLC (SMLLC), where the member is a tax-exempt organization, can be a form of exempt subsidiary organization, in that the LLC is a separate legal entity, it is exempt from federal income taxes, it is wholly owned by the exempt member, and it can perform exempt functions.

Generally, SMLLCs are disregarded for federal income tax purposes. A disregarded LLC is considered a branch or a division of its member owner.[57] Thus, although an SMLLC is a separate legal entity for most purposes, it is treated as a component of its owner for federal income tax purposes, and in that sense is not literally a subsidiary of the member. In one instance, the IRS wrote that, when the sole member of an LLC is a tax-exempt organization, the function of the LLC is treated as an "activity" of the exempt organization.[58]

The exempt owner of an SMLLC treats the operations and finances of the LLC as its own for purposes of the annual information return filing requirements.[59]

Usually the SMLLC is deliberately created with the tax law feature of being disregarded. It is possible, however, for an MMLLC[60] to be treated for federal tax law purposes as an SMLLC. For example, the IRS ruled that an LLC with two members was nonetheless a disregarded entity, because one of the members did not have an economic interest in the LLC and thus failed to qualify as a member of the LLC for tax law purposes.[61]

Tax-exempt organizations are making creative use of disregarded SMLLCs, as the following illustrates: (1) a public charity established a SMLLC to address the needs for affordable parking in a city, with the IRS ruling that the charity, by means of the LLC, was lessening the burdens of government;[62] (2) a charitable organization utilized SMLLCs to hold contributed properties having potential legal liability, thereby protecting both the donee and the other properties;[63] (3) an exempt museum used a SMLLC to own and operate a racetrack and a campground;[64] (4) a public charity operating a student housing program for

---

[55] See § 25.2(f).
[56] Priv. Ltr. Rul. 200333031.
[57] See § 4.1(b).
[58] Priv. Ltr. Rul. 200134025.
[59] In general, see § 28.2(c).
[60] See § 32.3.
[61] Priv. Ltr. Rul. 200201024.
[62] Priv. Ltr. Rul. 200124022. See § 7.7.
[63] Priv. Ltr. Rul. 200134025.
[64] Priv. Ltr. Rul. 200202077.

the benefit of an exempt college undertook its projects by means of a SMLLC;[65] (5) a public charity established an SMLLC to finance small businesses for the benefit of low-income populations to enable it to issue equity interests to investors;[66] (6) a private foundation created an SMLLC for the purpose of funding and managing a school of an exempt college;[67] (7) a charitable hospital used an SMLLC to participate in a joint venture operated in furtherance of the hospital's health care purposes;[68] (8) an exempt association, concerned about legal liability, operated its trade shows in an SMLLC;[69] (9) a public charity conducted an activity, previously undertaken in a wholly owned for-profit subsidiary, in an SMLLC;[70] (10) an exempt labor union operated a pharmacy program for the benefit of its members by means of an SMLLC;[71] (11) a supporting organization affiliated with a university used an SMLLC to acquire and hold debt-financed rental real property, with the supporting organization obtaining a special tax exemption from the unrelated debt-financed income rules;[72] and (12) an exempt health care system used an SMLLC to extend to employees of a business housed in the LLC the benefits of an employee benefit plan.[73]

§ 32.5 CHOICE OF ENTITY CONSIDERATIONS

Tax-exempt organizations have a variety of entity forms from which to select, whether they be the form of entity for the organization itself,[74] a form of entity for a related organization,[75] or a form of entity in which it participates as a stockholder or member.[76] From a tax law perspective, the two principal issues to consider are the impact on exempt status and the potential for generation of unrelated business income.[77]

A key pivotal point is whether the federal tax law treats the organization as a separate legal entity for tax purposes (such as a corporation or trust) or as

---

[65] Priv. Ltr. Rul. 200249014.

[66] Priv. Ltr. Rul. 200351033.

[67] Priv. Ltr. Rul. 200431018.

[68] Priv. Ltr. Rul. 200436022. See §§ 31.3, 31.4.

[69] Priv. Ltr. Rul. 200510030. See § 25.2(f). The IRS subsequently ruled that a public charity operating a mobile home park, by means of an SMLLC, was engaged in charitable activities because it was providing affordable housing to the poor and/or distressed (see § 7.4) (Priv. Ltr. Rul. 200642009).

[70] Priv. Ltr. Rul. 200723030.

[71] Priv. Ltr. Rul. 201222043.

[72] Priv. Ltr. Rul. 200134025.

[73] Priv. Ltr. Rul. 200341023. Uses of SMLLCs in the exempt organizations context are illustrated by two other developments: The IRS stated that a private foundation may make a grant directly to a SMLLC and treat that transfer as a qualifying distribution (see § 12.4(b)) where the sole member of the LLC is a U.S. public charity (INFO-2010-0052) and that a donor may make a deductible charitable contribution directly to an SMLLC where the sole member of the LLC is a U.S. charity (Notice 2012-52, 2012-35 I.R.B. 317).

[74] See § 4.1.

[75] See Chapters 29, 30.

[76] See, e.g., §§ 32.3, 32.4.

[77] As to the latter, see Chapters 24, 25.

a flow-through entity (such as a partnership or limited liability company). This is a consideration particularly when the exempt organization is a member of a flow-through entity. If the flow-through entity is engaged in one or more nonexempt functions, the share of the revenue paid or attributed to the exempt organization will be unrelated business income.[78] Likewise, if the flow-through entity is engaged in one or more exempt functions, the exempt organization's share of the revenue will be exempt function income. Tax-exempt status may be imperiled if the flow-through entity is engaged in one or more nonexempt functions and the operations of the entity are deemed to be a substantial portion of the exempt organization's activities.[79]

§ 32.6 CONVERSION FROM EXEMPT TO NONEXEMPT STATUS

As has been discussed throughout, organizations can be nonprofit, tax-exempt entities or for-profit entities. On occasion, an entity of one type is desirous of converting to an entity of the other type. While both can be accomplished, the federal and state law on the point is scant.[80]

The state law on the subject concerns form and procedure. Most states have separate nonprofit corporation acts and business (for-profit) corporation acts; mergers from one to the other are not always permissible. Thus, a change in form is often required, entailing liquidations and reformations. The federal tax law on the subject focuses primarily on the need for new determinations as to tax status and disclosure of certain facts as part of any new application for recognition of exempt status.[81]

A tax-exempt organization may decide to shed that status and convert to a for-profit entity. (There is no prohibition in law as to doing that.) For example, a public charity may determine that the rules for maintaining exempt status as a charitable entity are too onerous, or those involved in its operations may wish to partake of its profits; operation as a for-profit entity may thus be more attractive.

(a) State Law

Nearly every tax-exempt organization is a creature of the law of a state or the District of Columbia. (In a rare instance, an exempt organization is established by a specific state statute or, even less frequently, is created by federal law.) These organizations almost always are shaped as one of three types of entity: nonprofit corporation, unincorporated association, or trust.[82]

---

[78] This is automatically the case where an exempt organization has an interest in an S corporation (see § 25.3).

[79] See § 4.5(c).

[80] The law on this subject is most pronounced when it involves the termination of a charitable organization's status as a private foundation (IRC § 507; see *Private Foundations*, Chapter 13). This is a separate body of law that is uniquely applicable to private foundations; the observations in this chapter as to charitable organizations assume that they are not private foundations.

[81] The process for obtaining a determination or ruling as to recognition by the IRS of tax-exempt status is the subject of § 26.1.

[82] See § 4.1(a).

Of these three categories, the unincorporated association is the least likely option for a nonprofit entity. The articles of organization of this type of organization are termed a *constitution*. It will undoubtedly have bylaws and otherwise function much like a corporation.

Some organizations are formed as trusts. The articles of organization of this type of entity are a *declaration of trust* or a *trust agreement*. Trusts, particularly charitable ones, are uniquely treated under state law; this treatment will vary from state to state.

The form that a tax-exempt entity most typically assumes is that of the nonprofit corporation. (The balance of this chapter is predicated on the assumption that the nonprofit and for-profit entities involved are corporations.) The corporate form is advantageous because the law as to its formation and operation is usually quite clear, and because it can provide a shield against personal liability for those individuals who are its directors and officers.[83]

As noted, nearly every state has a nonprofit corporation act and a for-profit corporation act. These are separate statutes; the extent of any interplay between them is a matter of state law, which can vary from state to state. For example, it may not be possible for a nonprofit corporation in a particular state to amend its *articles of incorporation* so as to become a for-profit corporation under the law of that state. This is because of the fundamental difference between the two types of corporations.[84]

Likewise, the issue of whether a nonprofit corporation can merge into a for-profit corporation, particularly where the survivor of the merger is the for-profit entity, can be problematic. In any event, the transformation of a tax-exempt charitable organization can easily attract the attention of a state's attorney general.

Suppose a tax-exempt charitable entity, organized as a nonprofit corporation, is desirous of becoming a for-profit organization, organized as a for-profit corporation. Theoretically, the easiest way to accomplish this is to amend the corporate documents and convert to the for-profit form. As noted, however, state law may not allow for this transformation, and it raises great problems under the federal tax law.[85]

Another approach would be to create a for-profit corporation and then merge the nonprofit corporation into it. Again, state law may preclude the merger of a nonprofit and a for-profit organization.

A third approach would be to create the for-profit corporation, liquidate the nonprofit corporation, and transfer the remaining assets and income of the nonprofit corporation to the for-profit corporation. As discussed next, however, this type of transfer must, for federal tax reasons, entail a sale or exchange of the assets for fair market value.

(b) Federal Tax Law

Generally, tax-exempt organizations cannot blithely abandon their exempt status and continue operations as a taxable nonprofit entity.[86] Organizations, primarily

[83] See § 5.4.
[84] An IRS private letter ruling, however, reflects a factual situation in which a state's law apparently permits a nonexempt nonprofit corporation to convert to a stock-based for-profit corporation (Priv. Ltr. Rul. 9545014).
[85] See § 32.6(b).
[86] See § 26.14.

charitable ones, with a dissolution clause requirement,[87] for example, are required to preserve their assets and income streams for exempt purposes. Absent such a requirement, the IRS may find private inurement or like exempt organizations law violation if assets are transferred for nonexempt purposes.[88]

Dissolution restrictions aside, generally, for a nonprofit organization to shed its tax exemption, one approach would entail violation of the applicable organizational and/or operational test.[89] For example, a public charity could voluntarily lose its exempt status by repealing its dissolution clause, or authorizing or engaging in substantial nonexempt activities, excessive legislative activities, or political campaign activities.[90] Another approach would be to refrain from filing annual information returns for three consecutive years.[91] (Law violations such as these, however, may trigger undesirable federal and/or state law enforcement reactions and/or harmful publicity.)

A tax-exempt organization may sell or lease its assets to an existing or successor entity (with receipt of fair value required), but this approach leaves the organization in existence (albeit without funds). This may cause the entity to lose its exemption due to inactivity.[92]

§ 32.7 CONVERSION FROM NONEXEMPT TO EXEMPT STATUS

A for-profit organization may decide to convert to a tax-exempt organization. (Like the reverse, there is no prohibition in law as to doing so.)

(a) State Law

Nearly every for-profit organization is subject to the law of a state or the District of Columbia. These organizations are usually organized as corporations. (Again, the balance of this chapter is predicated on the assumption that the nonprofit and for-profit entities involved are corporations.)

Nearly every state has a nonprofit corporation act and a for-profit corporation act. These are separate statutes; the extent of any interplay between them is a matter of state law, which can vary from state to state. For example, it may not be possible for a for-profit corporation in a particular state to amend its articles of incorporation so as to become a nonprofit corporation under the law of that state. Likewise, it can be problematic as to whether a for-profit corporation can merge into a nonprofit corporation.[93]

---

[87] See § 4.3(b).

[88] E.g., Priv. Ltr. Rul. 201622033, where an association was said to engage in a private inurement transaction (see Chapter 20) if it dissolved and transferred its assets to its members. In one instance, the IRS revoked the exempt status of a charitable organization that distributed its assets to a for-profit entity owned by one of its officers; surprisingly, the IRS made no mention of this transfer giving rise to an excess benefit transaction (see § 21.4(a)) (Priv. Ltr. Rul. 202417023).

[89] See §§ 4.3, 4.5.

[90] See Chapters 22, 23.

[91] See § 28.5.

[92] See 4.5(a), text accompanied by note 192.

[93] See § 32.1.

Suppose a hospital, organized as a for-profit corporation, is desirous of becoming a tax-exempt organization, organized as a charitable entity. As is the case when the conversion is to be the reverse, theoretically, the easiest way to accomplish this is to amend the corporate documents and convert to the nonprofit form. As noted, however, state law may not allow for this type of transformation.

Another approach would be to create a nonprofit corporation and then merge the for-profit corporation into it. Again, state law may preclude the merger of a nonprofit and a for-profit organization.

A third approach would be to create the nonprofit corporation, transfer the assets and income of the for-profit corporation to the nonprofit corporation, and dissolve the for-profit corporation. Presumably, there would not be a state law prohibition as to this type of transaction.

(b)   Federal Tax Law

The federal tax law does not prohibit a for-profit organization or an otherwise nonexempt entity from "converting" to a tax-exempt organization. Yet, current IRS ruling policy is quite hostile to these types of conversions. For example, the IRS ruled that it was a violation of the private benefit doctrine[94] for a nonprofit organization to continue the operations of a for-profit business, that it was a violation of the private inurement doctrine[95] for the successor entity to solicit contributions and grants, and that it was a violation of the commerciality doctrine[96] for the successor entity to market its services and charge fees.[97]

In one instance, an organization providing charitable and educational services was initially successful in "converting" from a for-profit company to a public charity. Yet, on examination, the IRS (incorrectly) revoked the organization's tax exemption because the boards of directors of the two organizations remained the same, as did two compensated individuals who effectively controlled the entities' operations.[98]

As a matter of law, an organization that qualifies for tax-exempt status does so even if it is a successor to a nonexempt organization. It is common, for example, for a for-profit hospital to convert to a nonprofit exempt one;[99] likewise, a for-profit

---

[94] See § 20.13.

[95] See Chapter 20.

[96] See § 4.9.

[97] Priv. Ltr. Rul. 201540019. The IRS is aided in this regard by a Tax Court decision holding that an entity is ineligible for tax exemption if its activities amount to the same operations as those conducted by its for-profit predecessor (Asmark Institute, Inc., 101 T.C.M. 1067 (2011), aff'd, 486 Fed. Appx. 566 (6th Cir. 2012)). An IRS ruling of this nature is correct, however, where the nonprofit entity continues to carry on nonexempt functions (e.g., Priv. Ltr. Rul. 201540016).

[98] Priv. Ltr. Rul. 201902032. An organization's management's intentions may change, shifting from a nonprofit (e.g., charitable) objective to a for-profit one. E.g., WP Realty, Ltd. P'ship v. Comm'r, 118 T.C.M. 248 (2019), which allowed an organization to deduct its business expenses because it had a profit motive (IRC § 183), thus validating the notion that a switch in position as to intent is permissible, with the successor entity evaluated based on its actual operations, not its management's original intent. This court, however, subsequently issued a decision, in the successor entity context, that is completely contrary to this notion (New World Infrastructure Org. v. Comm'r, 122 T.C.M. 88 (2021)), incorrectly invoking the private inurement doctrine (see § 20.6(n)).

[99] Rev. Rul. 76-91, 1976-1 C.B. 149.

school may convert to an exempt one.[100] When this is done by sale of assets by the nonexempt entity to an exempt successor, a key issue is likely to be the fairness of the price paid for the assets.[101]

Despite its ruling policy, the IRS, in the application for recognition of tax-exempt status as a charitable organization, incongruously established an inventory of the items of information it must have concerning the predecessor and successor organizations in order to issue a favorable ruling or determination letter to the nonprofit organization.[102] (This body of information is in addition to the information requested of all nonprofit organization applicants.) The form presupposes that the applicant nonprofit organization is an entity separate from the predecessor for-profit organization.[103]

The specific items of information a successor nonprofit organization must provide the IRS as part of the exemption recognition process are: (1) the name, address, and employer identification number of the predecessor organization; (2) a description of the activities of the predecessor organization; (3) a list of the owners, partners, principal stockholders, officers, and governing board members of the predecessor organization, including their names, addresses, and (if for-profit) share/interest in the predecessor organization; (4) if the predecessor entity is a for-profit organization, an explanation of the relationship with the predecessor organization that resulted in the creation of the successor organization and why the successor organization took over the activities or assets of a for-profit organization or converted from for-profit to nonprofit status; (5) otherwise, an explanation of the successor organization's relationship with the other organization that resulted in its creation and why the successor organization took over the activities or assets of the other organization; (6) a description of any ongoing working relationship with any of the persons referenced in the third element or with any for-profit organization in which these persons own more than a 35 percent interest; (7) an explanation as to whether any assets were transferred, either by gift or sale, from the predecessor entity to the successor entity;[104] (8) a statement as to any

---

[100] Rev. Rul. 76-441, 1976-2 C.B. 147. The conversion of for-profit colleges and universities where the successor entity is a nonprofit, tax-exempt institution has received considerable attention in recent years. The U.S. Government Accountability Office issued a report analyzing what the GAO terms "for-profit college conversions" and the potential risk of "improper benefits" to insiders from such conversions (GAO, "Higher Education: IRS and Education Could Better Address Risks Associated with Some For-Profit College Conversions," Rep. No. GAO-21-89 (Dec. 2020)). Also, in 2021, the House Committee on Education and Labor held a hearing on the topic of "For-Profit College Conversions: Examining Ways to Improve Accountability and Prevent Fraud." The GAO subsequently published the testimony from a GAO representative at this hearing (GAO, "Higher Education: IRS and Education Could Better Address Risks Associated with For-Profit College Conversions," Rep. No. GAO-21-500T (Apr. 20, 2021)).

[101] Rev. Rul. 76-91, 1976-1 C.B. 149.

[102] See § 26.1.

[103] For this purpose, a *for-profit* organization includes any organization in which a person may have a proprietary or partnership interest, hold corporate stock, or otherwise exercise an ownership interest (Instructions for Form 1023 (Jan. 2020), Schedule G). The organization need not have operated for the purpose of making a profit (*id.*).

[104] If there was such a transfer, a list of the assets must be provided, including an indication of the value of each asset, an explanation as to how the value was determined (with attachment of any appraisal(s)), an explanation as to whether the transfer was by gift or sale (or combination thereof), and a description of any restrictions placed on use or sale of the assets.

debts or liabilities transferred from the predecessor for-profit organization to the successor organization;[105] and (9) a statement as to whether the successor organization is leasing or renting any property or equipment to or from the predecessor organization, or any of the persons referenced in the third element, or any for-profit organization in which these persons own more than a 35 percent interest.[106]

Likewise, if a for-profit organization is endeavoring to convert to a nonprofit organization and be a tax-exempt social welfare organization[107] or a business league,[108] and is requesting a determination from the IRS as to recognition of tax-exempt status, it must reveal as part of the exemption application the name of the predecessor organization, the period during which it was in existence, and the reasons for its termination, as well as submit copies of all documents by which any transfer of assets was effected.[109]

If a for-profit organization sells assets to a nonprofit organization, the seller would be liable for taxes on any gain, just as would be the case were any other purchaser involved. There are special rules in this regard in the case of liquidations.[110]

If assets and/or income are contributed to a tax-exempt charitable organization by a for-profit organization, a charitable contribution deduction would likely result. This deduction may be limited by one or more factors, such as the percentage limitation on annual corporate charitable deductions[111] and the restrictions on the deductibility of gifts of inventory by businesses.[112]

(c) Gain or Loss Recognition

A conversion of a for-profit corporation into a tax-exempt one can cause recognition of gain or loss by the converting corporation. This type of transaction is treated essentially the same as a liquidation of the corporation when the assets transferred are all or substantially all of the assets of the corporation. That is, the corporation must recognize gain or loss as if the assets transferred had been sold at their fair market values.[113]

In general, a taxable corporation's change in status (conversion) to a tax-exempt organization is treated as if it had transferred all of its assets to the exempt organization immediately before the change in status became effective.[114] This rule does not

---

[105] If there was such a transfer, a list of the debts or liabilities must be provided, indicating the amount of each, how the amount was determined, and the name of the person to whom the debt or liability is owed.

[106] If there is such a rental or lease arrangement, the successor organization is required to describe it, including an explanation as to how the lease or rental value was determined.

[107] See Chapter 13.

[108] See Chapter 14.

[109] Form 1024-A (Jan. 2021), Part III, question 5; Form 1024 (Jan. 2022), Part III, question 4. In one instance, the IRS denied recognition of social welfare status to an organization that conducted a pharmacy benefit program for its members (a substantial nonexempt purpose (see § 13.1(b)), where it purchased the assets of, and continued to license (for a fee) proprietary methods and products developed by, a for-profit predecessor (Priv. Ltr. Rul. 202331004).

[110] See § 30.7.

[111] IRC § 170(b)(2). E.g., Priv. Ltr. Rul. 9703028.

[112] IRC § 170(e)(3).

[113] See § 30.7.

[114] Reg. § 1.337(d)-4(a)(2).

apply, however, to (1) a corporation previously exempt[115] that regains its exempt status within three years from the later of a final adverse adjudication on the corporation's exempt status or the filing of a federal income tax return; (2) a corporation previously exempt or that applied for but did not receive recognition of exemption[116] before January 15, 1997, if the corporation is exempt within three years from January 28, 1999;[117] (3) a newly formed corporation that is exempt (other than as a social club)[118] within three tax years from the end of the year in which it was formed; (4) a newly formed corporation that is exempt as a social club within seven years from the end of the tax year in which it was formed; (5) a corporation previously exempt as a mutual or cooperative organization[119] that lost its exemption solely because it failed the 85-percent-member-income requirement and then regained exempt status, as long as in each intervening year it met all of the requirements for this exemption except for the income requirement; and (6) a corporation previously taxable that becomes an exempt property or casualty insurance company,[120] where it is the subject of a court-supervised rehabilitation, conservatorship, liquidation, or similar state proceeding affecting premium income.[121]

If, during the first tax year following the transfer of an asset or the corporation's change to tax-exempt status, the asset is used by the exempt organization partly or wholly in an unrelated activity, the taxable corporation must recognize a pro rata amount of gain or loss. The corporation may rely on a written representation from the exempt organization estimating the percentage of the asset's anticipated use in an unrelated activity for that year, using a reasonable method of allocation, unless the corporation has reason to believe that the exempt organization's representation is not made in good faith.[122]

If, for any tax year, the percentage of an asset's use in the unrelated activity later decreases from the estimate used in computing gain or loss when the asset was transferred, the tax-exempt organization must recognize the part of the deferred gain or loss in an amount that is proportionate to the decrease in use in the unrelated activity, and the gain or loss recognized must be subject to unrelated business income taxation.[123]

---

[115] These references to tax exemption are to exemption by reason of IRC § 501(a).

[116] See § 3.2.

[117] Apparently in application of this rule, the IRS held that a stock-based organization that was formed prior to enactment of the Internal Revenue Code and that for decades filed tax returns was able to qualify for tax exemption as a social club on a retroactive basis, as long as the organization qualified for exemption as of a date prior to January 28, 1999 (Priv. Ltr. Rul. 200333008).

[118] See Chapter 15.

[119] See § 19.5.

[120] See § 19.9.

[121] Reg. § 1.337(d)-4(a)(3). In a case involving the second of these exceptions, the IRS required as a condition of the ruling that the organization file an application for recognition of exemption, even though the regulations state that the filing of the application is not required to obtain the exemption if the applicant is not otherwise required to file, which was the case with this organization (Priv. Ltr. Rul. 200217044). In a case involving the fifth of these exceptions, the IRS ruled that, where a previously tax-exempt cooperative became exempt again following a merger with its for-profit subsidiary, the transaction qualified for the exception (Priv. Ltr. Rul. 200303051).

[122] Reg. § 1.337(d)-4(b)(1)(i).

[123] Reg. § 1.337(d)-4(b)(1)(ii).

The tax-exempt organization must use the same reasonable method of allocation for determining the percentage of an asset's use in an unrelated activity as it uses for other tax purposes (such as determining the amount of depreciation deductions). Also, the exempt organization must use this reasonable method of allocation for each year that it holds the asset(s).[124]

Notwithstanding the foregoing, there can be continuing deferral of recognition of gain or loss to the extent that the tax-exempt organization disposes of assets in a transaction that qualifies for nonrecognition of gain or loss,[125] but only to the extent that the replacement is used in an unrelated activity.[126]

If the transferor entity is a subchapter S corporation, the gains and losses recognized on the deemed sale of the items of property are not taxable to it. Rather, each shareholder of the S corporation must take into account its distributive share of the gains and losses to be recognized and make the appropriate adjustments to the basis in the stock. If the transfer entails a bargain sale,[127] resulting in a charitable contribution deduction, each shareholder likewise takes into account their distributive share of that deduction.[128]

For these purposes, a *tax-exempt organization* is (1) an entity that is exempt from tax other than as a homeowners' association or a political organization;[129] (2) a charitable remainder trust;[130] (3) a governmental entity;[131] (4) an Indian tribal government or corporation;[132] (5) an international organization; (6) an entity whose income is excluded from taxation by reason of being a political subdivision or the like;[133] and (7) an entity that is not taxable "for reasons substantially similar" to those applicable to an entity in these previous categories, unless it is otherwise excluded from this law by statute or IRS action.[134]

§ 32.8 CONVERSION FROM ONE EXEMPT STATUS TO ANOTHER

A change in the federal tax law expanded declaratory judgment rights to nearly all categories of tax-exempt organizations.[135] This expansion of declaratory judgment rights applied retroactively to final adverse determination letters issued on or after December 18, 2015. This law revision prompted the IRS to issue revised procedures as to modifications of exempt status.[136]

---

[124] Reg. § 1.337(d)-4(b)(1)(iv).

[125] IRC § 1031 or 1033 (concerning certain property exchanges or conversions).

[126] Reg. § 1.337(d)-4(b)(1)(iii).

[127] See *Charitable Giving* § 7.18.

[128] E.g., Priv. Ltr. Rul. 200402003.

[129] IRC § 501(a) (listed in IRC § 501(c)) or 529. Homeowners' associations are the subject of § 19.14; political organizations are the subject of Chapter 17.

[130] See § 19.24. See *Charitable Giving*, Chapter 10.

[131] See § 19.22.

[132] See § 19.23.

[133] See § 19.22.

[134] Reg. § 1.337(d)-4(c)(2).

[135] See § 27.5(c).

[136] Mem. TEGE-04-0216-0003.

The IRS guidance is predicated on the fact that this law revision generally mandates that all revocations of exempt status are to be treated in the same manner. Pursuant to this approach, the IRS will revoke—or treat as a revocation for declaratory judgment purposes—the status of any organization that "no longer qualifies" under the Internal Revenue Code provision for which tax exemption was recognized or self-declared. A revoked organization may apply or reapply for recognition of exemption under a different Code section. A conversion of an organization's exempt status is thus regarded as commencing with a *deemed revocation*.

This revised approach apparently does not contemplate situations where an exempt organization continues to qualify for the exemption classification it has but nonetheless wants to switch to another category of exemption. As a practical matter, an effort to cause the IRS to change the classification of a noncharitable nonprofit organization (for example, a trade association) to a charitable classification is likely to be fruitless.[137] The more effective way to proceed in this regard is to pursue the desired tax exemption by means of a new, controlled entity.[138]

---

[137] E.g., Priv. Ltr. Rul. 202017035, where a tax-exempt business league (see Chapter 14) that conducts some charitable and educational activities failed in its effort to be reclassified as an exempt charitable entity. By contrast, there are published procedures whereby the IRS recognizes changes to or from private foundation status or among different classifications of public charities (see § 28.1(c)).

[138] See Chapter 29.

Index

INDEX